Used Tractor Price Guide

2000 Edition

Edited by Mike Hall

Intertec Publishing

P.O. Box 12901, Overland Park, KS 66282-2901

This book can be recycled. Please remove cover.

CONTENTS

The following books and guides are published by Intertec Publishing.

CLYMER SHOP MANUALS

Boat Motors and Drives
Motorcycles and ATVs
Snowmobiles
Personal Watercraft

ABOS/INTERTEC/CLYMER BLUE BOOKS AND TRADE-IN GUIDES

Recreational Vehicles
Outdoor Power Equipment
Agricultural Tractors
Lawn and Garden Tractors
Motorcycles and ATVs
Snowmobiles and Personal Watercraft
Boats and Motors

AIRCRAFT BLUEBOOK-PRICE DIGEST

Airplanes
Helicopters

AC-U-KWIK DIRECTORIES

The Corporate Pilot's Airport/FBO Directory
International Manager's Edition
Jet Book

I&T SHOP SERVICE MANUALS

Tractors

HOW TO USE THIS GUIDE

The Approx. Retail Price New column is the manufacturer's suggested retail price new for tractors with standard equipment, excluding shipping charges or options.

The "FAIR," "GOOD" and "PREMIUM" value columns are averaged selling prices of tractors in saleable condition, less repairs. Cost of any needed repairs should be considered when making appraisal. Prices quoted are approximate and represent an average. Local conditions can alter these estimates. When using this guide take into consideration two important variables: (1) The condition of the tractor; (2) The popularity of certain sizes and brands in your area.

Certain regions of the country support higher prices on certain brands than do other regions. The used values contained in this book were compiled from auction selling prices, tractor dealer asking and selling prices, as well as from classified advertisings in newspapers and magazines. The prices are to be considered averages, and as noted above, your own experience may be different.

Tractor Serial Numbers are listed in this book as they are supplied by the manufacturers. Where to locate the serial number on the tractor is also listed for most models.

A beginning serial number is given for each year that a tractor is produced. The actual year that the tractor was manufactured can be determined by comparing the tractor's serial number to the serial numbers given for your particular model number.

For Example: An International Harvester Model 1086 with a serial number of 35821. The tractor's serial number falls between the 1979 beginning serial number 34731 and the 1980 beginning serial number 42186, thus the tractor was manufactured during the year of 1979.

This publication is issued for guidance purposes only and should be used accordingly since the local demand for certain equipment, prices, costs and other conditions which affect the resale value vary in different regions of the country.

The publisher has used reasonable care in compiling this price guide. However, neither the publisher nor any of its representatives shall be liable for damages of any description whether incidental or consequential or otherwise, including loss of profits or other business damages occasioned by the use of this price guide, and in no event shall the liability of the publisher exceed the price paid for this guide.

CONDITION CLASSIFICATIONS

Condition	Description
Premium	Excellent condition – little evidence of wear, good running condition wih low hours of use. Size, type of equipment in demand.
Good	Clean, attractive condition – properly maintained and mechanically sound with average hours of use. May need minor cosmetic and/or mechanical repairs.
Fair	Below average condition – areas worn and faded even after cleanup. Scratches and chips in paint evident. Some mechanical repairs needed, parts missing or broken. Significant tire wear indicating high hours and severe usage.

EXPLANATION OF COLUMN HEADINGS, DEFINITIONS AND ABBREVIATIONS

Model . . . . Most commonly used model designation, name or number

Approx. Retail Price New . . . . Manufacturer's suggested retail price of tractor

Estimated Average Value . . . . Averaged used selling prices of tractors, less repairs

Engine Make . . . . AC-Allis Chalmers, CD-Consolidated Diesel, Cat-Caterpillar, DD-Detroit Diesel, IH-International Harvester, JD-John Deere, MM-Mineapolis Moline

Engine No. Cyls. Number of cylinders, T-Turbocharged, I-Intercooled, A-Aftercooled

Displ. Cu.-In. . . . . Piston displacement in cubic inches, D-Diesel, G-Gasoline, LP-Liquid Petroleum Gas

No. Speeds . . . . Number of transmission speeds, F-Forward, R-Reverse

PTO H.P. . . . . Horsepower from test or manufacturer's rating

Approx. Shipping Wt.-Lbs. . . . . Weight as shipped from factory

Cab . . . . No-None, C-Cab included in price, CH-Cab with heater, CHA-Cab with heater and air conditioner

Table of Contents

AGCO-Allis

Model	Approx. Retail Price New	Estimated Average Value Less Repairs: Fair	Good	Premium	Engine: Make	No. Cyls.	Displ. Cu.-In.	No. Speeds	P.T.O. H.P.	Approx. Shipping Wt.-Lbs.	Cab
1992											
4650	16355.00	9160.00	10470.00	11100.00	SLH	3	190D	16F-4R	40.37	4475	No
4650 4WD	21512.00	12050.00	13770.00	14600.00	SLH	3	190D	16F-4R	40.37	5070	No
4660	19203.00	10750.00	12290.00	13030.00	SLH	3	190D	16F-4R	52.17	4762	No
4660 4WD	25158.00	14090.00	16100.00	17070.00	SLH	3	190D	16F-4R	52.17	5203	No
5670	22718.00	13630.00	15450.00	16380.00	SLH	4	244D	24F-12R	63.13	5379	No
5670 4WD	27885.00	16730.00	18960.00	20100.00	SLH	4	244D	24F-12R	63.13	6096	No
5680	26354.00	14760.00	16870.00	17880.00	SLH	4	244D	24F-12R	72.70	5997	No
5680 4WD	32200.00	18030.00	20610.00	21850.00	SLH	4	244D	24F-12R	72.70	6658	No
6670	31756.00	17360.00	19840.00	21030.00	SLH	4	244D	24F-12R	63.13	5997	C,H,A
6670 4WD	36173.00	20040.00	22900.00	24270.00	SLH	4	244D	24F-12R	63.13	6658	C,H,A
6680	33180.00	18480.00	21120.00	22390.00	SLH	4	244D	24F-12R	72.70	6724	C,H,A
6680 4WD	38610.00	21280.00	24320.00	25780.00	SLH	4	244D	24F-12R	72.70	7385	C,H,A
6690	28900.00	16800.00	19040.00	20180.00	SLH	4T	244D	24F-12R	80.85	6173	No
6690 4WD	35114.00	20800.00	23570.00	24980.00	SLH	4T	244D	24F-12R	80.85	6779	No
6690 4WD w/Cab	41496.00	24600.00	27880.00	29550.00	SLH	4T	244D	24F-12R	80.85	7385	C,H,A
6690 w/Cab	35487.00	21000.00	23800.00	25230.00	SLH	4T	244D	24F-12R	80.85	6724	C,H,A
7600	31265.00	17360.00	19840.00	21030.00	SLH	5	317D	24F-12R	89.23	8179	No
7600 4WD	37615.00	20160.00	23040.00	24420.00	SLH	5	317D	24F-12R	89.23	9502	No
7600 4WD w/Cab	44524.00	23800.00	27200.00	28830.00	SLH	5	317D	24F-12R	89.23	9833	C,H,A
7600 w/Cab	37840.00	20630.00	23570.00	24980.00	SLH	5	317D	24F-12R	89.23	8686	C,H,A
8610	47968.00	22320.00	26040.00	27340.00	SLH	6	366D	36F-36R	103.12	9670	C,H,A
8610 4WD	54426.00	25650.00	29930.00	31430.00	SLH	6	366D	36F-36R	103.12	10870	C,H,A
8630	54708.00	25580.00	29850.00	31340.00	SLH	6T	366D	36F-36R	119.6	10159	C,H,A
8630 4WD	61570.00	28940.00	33770.00	35460.00	SLH	6T	366D	36F-36R	119.6	11100	C,H,A
9130	58628.00	25170.00	29170.00	31500.00	Deutz	6TI	374D	18F-6R	135.0	12300	C,H,A
9130 4WD	68371.00	29520.00	34220.00	36960.00	Deutz	6TI	374D	18F-6R	135.0	13600	C,H,A
9150	61174.00	26400.00	30600.00	33050.00	Deutz	6TI	374D	18F-6R	150.0	13520	C,H,A
9150 4WD	71945.00	30800.00	35700.00	38560.00	Deutz	6TI	374D	18F-6R	150.0	14880	C,H,A
9170	64719.00	27720.00	32130.00	34700.00	Deutz	6T	584D	18F-6R	172.0	15640	C,H,A
9170 4WD	79205.00	34320.00	39780.00	42960.00	Deutz	6T	584D	18F-6R	172.0	16040	C,H,A
9190 4WD	84756.00	36520.00	42330.00	45720.00	Deutz	6T	584D	18F-6R	193.0	16600	C,H,A
1993											
4650	16845.00	9770.00	10950.00	11610.00	SLH	3	190D	16F-4R	40.37	4475	No
4650 4WD	22157.00	12850.00	14400.00	15260.00	SLH	3	190D	16F-4R	40.37	5070	No
4660	19779.00	11470.00	12860.00	13630.00	SLH	3	190D	16F-4R	52.17	4762	No
4660 4WD	25912.00	15030.00	16840.00	17850.00	SLH	3	190D	16F-4R	52.17	5203	No
5670	23399.00	14510.00	16150.00	17120.00	SLH	4	244D	24F-12R	63.13	5379	No
5670 4WD	28721.00	17810.00	19820.00	21010.00	SLH	4	244D	24F-12R	63.13	6096	No
5680	27144.00	15740.00	17640.00	18700.00	SLH	4	244D	24F-12R	72.70	5997	No
5680 4WD	33166.00	19240.00	21560.00	22850.00	SLH	4	244D	24F-12R	72.70	6658	No
6670	32708.00	18560.00	20800.00	22050.00	SLH	4	244D	24F-12R	63.13	5997	C,H,A
6670 4WD	37258.00	21460.00	24050.00	25490.00	SLH	4	244D	24F-12R	63.13	6658	C,H,A
6680	34175.00	19720.00	22100.00	23430.00	SLH	4	244D	24F-12R	72.70	6724	C,H,A
6680 4WD	39768.00	22620.00	25350.00	26870.00	SLH	4	244D	24F-12R	72.70	7385	C,H,A
6690	29767.00	17980.00	20010.00	21210.00	SLH	4T	244D	24F-12R	80.85	6173	No
6690 4WD	36167.00	22010.00	24500.00	25970.00	SLH	4T	244D	24F-12R	80.85	6779	No
6690 4WD w/Cab	42740.00	26040.00	28980.00	30720.00	SLH	4T	244D	24F-12R	80.85	7385	C,H,A
6690 w/Cab	36551.00	22320.00	24840.00	26330.00	SLH	4T	244D	24F-12R	80.85	6724	C,H,A
7600	32202.00	18100.00	20280.00	21500.00	SLH	5	317D	24F-12R	89.23	8179	No
7600 4WD	38743.00	21750.00	24380.00	25840.00	SLH	5	317D	24F-12R	89.23	9502	No
7600 4WD w/Cab	45859.00	25400.00	28470.00	30180.00	SLH	5	317D	24F-12R	89.23	9833	C,H,A
7600 w/Cab	38975.00	21980.00	24640.00	26120.00	SLH	5	317D	24F-12R	89.23	8686	C,H,A
7630 4WD	54718.00	27000.00	31320.00	32890.00	SLH	6	380D	24F-12R	115.02	11398	C,H,A
7650 4WD	58716.00	28750.00	33350.00	35020.00	SLH	6T	380D	24F-12R	128.38	12566	C,H,A
8610	49407.00	24000.00	27840.00	29230.00	SLH	6	366D	36F-36R	103.12	9670	C,H,A
8610 4WD	56058.00	27530.00	31930.00	33530.00	SLH	6	366D	36F-36R	103.12	10870	C,H,A
8630	56349.00	27750.00	32190.00	33800.00	SLH	6T	366D	36F-36R	119.6	10159	C,H,A
8630 4WD	63417.00	31200.00	36190.00	38000.00	SLH	6T	366D	36F-36R	119.6	11100	C,H,A
9130	60386.00	27140.00	31860.00	34090.00	Deutz	6TI	374D	18F-6R	135.0	12300	C,H,A
9130 4WD	70422.00	31740.00	37260.00	39870.00	Deutz	6TI	374D	18F-6R	135.0	13600	C,H,A
9150	63009.00	28290.00	33210.00	35540.00	Deutz	6TI	374D	18F-6R	150.0	13520	C,H,A
9150 4WD	74103.00	33580.00	39420.00	42180.00	Deutz	6TI	374D	18F-6R	150.0	14880	C,H,A
9170	66660.00	30040.00	35260.00	37730.00	Deutz	6T	584D	18F-6R	172.0	15640	C,H,A
9170 4WD	81581.00	36800.00	43200.00	46220.00	Deutz	6T	584D	18F-6R	172.0	16040	C,H,A
9190 4WD	87298.00	39330.00	46170.00	49400.00	Deutz	6T	584D	18F-6R	193.0	16600	C,H,A
9630	67463.00	33000.00	38280.00	40190.00	Deutz	6TI	374D	18F-9R	135.0	15200	C,H,A
9630 4WD	77779.00	38000.00	44080.00	46280.00	Deutz	6TI	374D	18F-9R	135.0	16500	C,H,A
9650	71595.00	34500.00	40020.00	42020.00	Deutz	6TI	374D	18F-9R	155.0	15200	C,H,A
9650 4WD	82566.00	40200.00	46630.00	48960.00	Deutz	6TI	374D	18F-9R	155.0	16500	C,H,A
9670	78497.00	38250.00	44370.00	46590.00	Deutz	6T	584D	18F-9R	175.0	16770	C,H,A
9670 4WD	91504.00	44250.00	51330.00	53900.00	Deutz	6T	584D	18F-9R	175.0	18400	C,H,A
9690 4WD	99153.00	48300.00	56030.00	58830.00	Deutz	6T	584D	18F-9R	195.0	18500	C,H,A
1994											
4650	17399.00	10610.00	11660.00	12240.00	SLH	3	190D	16F-4R	40.37	4475	No
4650 4WD	22885.00	13960.00	15330.00	16100.00	SLH	3	190D	16F-4R	40.37	5070	No
4660	20429.00	12460.00	13690.00	14380.00	SLH	3	190D	16F-4R	52.17	4762	No
4660 4WD	26482.00	16150.00	17740.00	18630.00	SLH	3	190D	16F-4R	52.17	5203	No
5670	24168.00	15810.00	17290.00	18160.00	SLH	4	244D	24F-12R	63.13	5379	No
5670 4WD	29665.00	18990.00	20770.00	21810.00	SLH	4	244D	24F-12R	63.13	6096	No

AGCO-Allis (Cont.)

1994 (Cont.)

Model	Approx. Retail Price New	Estimated Average Value Less Repairs: Fair	Good	Premium	Engine: Make	No. Cyls.	Displ. Cu.-In.	No. Speeds	P.T.O. H.P.	Approx. Shipping Wt.-Lbs.	Cab
5680	28036.00	**17100.00**	**18780.00**	**19720.00**	SLH	4	244D	24F-12R	72.70	5997	No
5680 4WD	34101.00	**20800.00**	**22850.00**	**23990.00**	SLH	4	244D	16F-16R	72.70	6658	No
6670	33783.00	**20130.00**	**22110.00**	**23220.00**	SLH	4	244D	24F-12R	63.13	5997	C,H,A
6670 4WD	38482.00	**23180.00**	**25460.00**	**26730.00**	SLH	4	244D	24F-12R	63.13	6658	C,H,A
6680	35298.00	**21350.00**	**23450.00**	**24620.00**	SLH	4	244D	24F-12R	72.70	6724	C,H,A
6680 4WD	41074.00	**24770.00**	**27200.00**	**28560.00**	SLH	4	244D	24F-12R	72.70	7385	C,H,A
6690	30744.00	**19200.00**	**21000.00**	**22050.00**	SLH	4T	244D	24F-12R	80.85	6173	No
6690 4WD	37355.00	**23680.00**	**25900.00**	**27200.00**	SLH	4T	244D	24F-12R	80.85	6779	No
6690 4WD w/Cab	44145.00	**27970.00**	**30590.00**	**32120.00**	SLH	4T	244D	24F-12R	80.85	7385	C,H,A
6690 w/Cab	37752.00	**23680.00**	**25900.00**	**27200.00**	SLH	4T	244D	24F-12R	80.85	6724	C,H,A
7600 4WD	40016.00	**23790.00**	**26130.00**	**27440.00**	SLH	5	317D	24F-12R	89.23	9502	No
7600 4WD w/Cab	47366.00	**27630.00**	**30350.00**	**31870.00**	SLH	5	317D	24F-12R	89.23	9833	C,H,A
7600 w/Cab	40255.00	**23910.00**	**26260.00**	**27570.00**	SLH	5	317D	24F-12R	89.23	8686	C,H,A
7630 4WD	56411.00	**29680.00**	**33600.00**	**35280.00**	SLH	6	380D	24F-12R	115.02	11398	C,H,A
7650 4WD	60532.00	**31800.00**	**36000.00**	**37800.00**	SLH	6T	380D	24F-12R	128.38	12566	C,H,A
8610	51030.00	**26500.00**	**30000.00**	**31500.00**	SLH	6	366D	36F-36R	103.12	9670	C,H,A
8610 4WD	57900.00	**30000.00**	**33960.00**	**35660.00**	SLH	6	366D	36F-36R	103.12	10870	C,H,A
8630	58200.00	**30210.00**	**34200.00**	**35910.00**	SLH	6T	366D	36F-36R	119.6	10159	C,H,A
8630 4WD	65500.00	**33920.00**	**38400.00**	**40320.00**	SLH	6T	366D	36F-36R	119.6	11100	C,H,A
9435	64845.00	**38740.00**	**42550.00**	**44680.00**	DD	6T	466D	32F-32R	135.0	14600	C,H,A
9435 4WD	75480.00	**45140.00**	**49580.00**	**52060.00**	DD	6T	466D	32F-32R	135.0	15700	C,H,A
9455	69105.00	**42150.00**	**46300.00**	**48620.00**	DD	6T	466D	32F-32R	155.0	14600	C,H,A
9455 4WD	80390.00	**49040.00**	**53860.00**	**56550.00**	DD	6T	466D	32F-32R	155.0	15700	C,H,A
9630	69550.00	**36860.00**	**41730.00**	**43820.00**	Deutz	6TI	374D	18F-9R	135.0	15200	C,H,A
9630 4WD	80185.00	**41870.00**	**47400.00**	**49770.00**	Deutz	6TI	374D	18F-9R	135.0	16500	C,H,A
9635	69550.00	**42430.00**	**46600.00**	**48930.00**	DD	6T	466D	18F-9R	135.0	15350	C,H,A
9635 4WD	80185.00	**48910.00**	**53720.00**	**56410.00**	DD	6T	466D	18F-9R	135.0	16550	C,H,A
9650	73810.00	**38690.00**	**43800.00**	**45990.00**	Deutz	6TI	374D	18F-9R	155.0	15200	C,H,A
9650 4WD	85120.00	**44520.00**	**50400.00**	**52920.00**	Deutz	6TI	374D	18F-9R	155.0	16500	C,H,A
9655	73810.00	**45020.00**	**49450.00**	**51920.00**	DD	6T	466D	18F-9R	155.0	15350	C,H,A
9655 4WD	85120.00	**51920.00**	**57030.00**	**59880.00**	DD	6T	466D	18F-9R	155.0	16550	C,H,A
9670	80925.00	**42890.00**	**48560.00**	**50990.00**	SLH	6T	584D	18F-9R	175.0	16770	C,H,A
9670 4WD	94335.00	**47700.00**	**54000.00**	**56700.00**	SLH	6T	584D	18F-9R	175.0	18400	C,H,A
9675	80925.00	**48800.00**	**53600.00**	**56280.00**	DD	6T	530D	18F-9R	175.0	16300	C,H,A
9675 4WD	94335.00	**56910.00**	**62510.00**	**65640.00**	DD	6T	530D	18F-9R	175.0	17850	C,H,A
9690 4WD	102220.00	**51940.00**	**58800.00**	**61740.00**	Deutz	6T	584D	18F-9R	195.0	18500	C,H,A
9695 4WD	102220.00	**60510.00**	**66460.00**	**69780.00**	DD	6T	530D	18F-9R	195.0	17950	C,H,A
9815 4WD	115095.00	**67710.00**	**74370.00**	**78090.00**	DD	6TI	530D	18F-9R	215.0	17600	C,H,A

1995

Model	Approx. Retail Price New	Estimated Average Value Less Repairs: Fair	Good	Premium	Engine: Make	No. Cyls.	Displ. Cu.-In.	No. Speeds	P.T.O. H.P.	Approx. Shipping Wt.-Lbs.	Cab
4650	17503.00	**11200.00**	**12250.00**	**12860.00**	SLH	3	190D	16F-4R	40.37	4475	No
4650 4WD	23183.00	**14840.00**	**16230.00**	**17040.00**	SLH	3	190D	16F-4R	40.37	5070	No
4660	20654.00	**13220.00**	**14460.00**	**15180.00**	SLH	3	190D	16F-4R	52.17	4762	No
4660 4WD	26945.00	**17250.00**	**18860.00**	**19800.00**	SLH	3	190D	16F-4R	52.17	5203	No
5650	18572.00	**12260.00**	**13560.00**	**14240.00**	SLH	3	183D	12F-12R	45		No
5650 4WD	24156.00	**15940.00**	**17630.00**	**18510.00**	SLH	3	183D	12F-12R	45		No
5660	21818.00	**13960.00**	**15270.00**	**16030.00**	SLH	3	183D	12F-12R	55		No
5660 4WD	26884.00	**17210.00**	**18820.00**	**19760.00**	SLH	3	183D	12F-12R	55		No
5670	25014.00	**16510.00**	**18260.00**	**19170.00**	SLH	4	244D	24F-12R	63.13	5379	No
5670 4WD	30703.00	**20260.00**	**22410.00**	**23530.00**	SLH	4	244D	24F-12R	63.13	6096	No
5680	29017.00	**18570.00**	**20310.00**	**21330.00**	SLH	4	244D	24F-12R	72.70	5997	No
5680 4WD	35455.00	**22690.00**	**24820.00**	**26060.00**	SLH	4	244D	24F-12R	72.70	6658	No
6670	34965.00	**21760.00**	**23800.00**	**24990.00**	SLH	4	244D	24F-12R	63.13	5997	C,H,A
6670 4WD	39829.00	**24960.00**	**27300.00**	**28670.00**	SLH	4	244D	24F-12R	63.13	6658	C,H,A
6680	36533.00	**23040.00**	**25200.00**	**26460.00**	SLH	4	244D	24F-12R	72.70	6724	C,H,A
6680 4WD	42512.00	**26880.00**	**29400.00**	**30870.00**	SLH	4	244D	24F-12R	72.70	7385	C,H,A
6690	31820.00	**20460.00**	**22630.00**	**23760.00**	SLH	4T	244D	24F-12R	80.85	6173	No
6690 4WD	38662.00	**25080.00**	**27740.00**	**29130.00**	SLH	4T	244D	24F-12R	80.85	6779	No
6690 4WD w/Cab	45690.00	**29700.00**	**32850.00**	**34490.00**	SLH	4T	244D	24F-12R	80.85	7385	C,H,A
6690 w/Cab	39073.00	**25410.00**	**28110.00**	**29520.00**	SLH	4T	244D	24F-12R	80.85	6724	C,H,A
7600	34424.00	**21760.00**	**23800.00**	**24990.00**	SLH	5	317D	24F-12R	89.23	8179	No
7600 4WD	41417.00	**25600.00**	**28000.00**	**29400.00**	SLH	5	317D	24F-12R	89.23	9502	No
7600 4WD w/Cab	49024.00	**30720.00**	**33600.00**	**35280.00**	SLH	5	317D	24F-12R	89.23	9833	C,H,A
7600 w/Cab	41664.00	**25980.00**	**28420.00**	**29840.00**	SLH	5	317D	24F-12R	89.23	8686	C,H,A
7630 4WD	58385.00	**31920.00**	**35910.00**	**37350.00**	SLH	6	380D	24F-12R	115.02	11398	C,H,A
7650 4WD	62651.00	**34160.00**	**38430.00**	**39970.00**	SLH	6T	380D	24F-12R	128.38	12566	C,H,A
8610	52816.00	**28560.00**	**32130.00**	**33420.00**	SLH	6	366D	36F-36R	103.12	9670	C,H,A
8610 4WD	61231.00	**33600.00**	**37800.00**	**39310.00**	SLH	6	366D	36F-36R	103.12	10870	C,H,A
8630	60237.00	**32480.00**	**36540.00**	**38000.00**	SLH	6T	366D	36F-36R	119.6	10159	C,H,A
8630 4WD	67793.00	**36680.00**	**41270.00**	**42920.00**	SLH	6T	366D	36F-36R	119.6	11100	C,H,A
9435	68545.00	**36960.00**	**41580.00**	**43240.00**	DD	6T	466D	32F-32R	135.0	14600	C,H,A
9435 4WD	77290.00	**42000.00**	**47250.00**	**49140.00**	DD	6T	466D	32F-32R	135.0	15700	C,H,A
9455	71848.00	**44800.00**	**49000.00**	**51450.00**	DD	6T	466D	32F-32R	155.0	14600	C,H,A
9455 4WD	82315.00	**51390.00**	**56210.00**	**59020.00**	DD	6T	466D	32F-32R	155.0	15700	C,H,A
9630	73765.00	**40100.00**	**45110.00**	**46910.00**	Deutz	6TI	374D	18F-9R	135.0	15200	C,H,A
9630 4WD	84876.00	**46480.00**	**52290.00**	**54380.00**	Deutz	6TI	374D	18F-9R	135.0	16500	C,H,A
9635	73435.00	**46720.00**	**51100.00**	**53660.00**	DD	6T	466D	18F-9R	135.0	15350	C,H,A
9635 4WD	84506.00	**53440.00**	**58450.00**	**61370.00**	DD	6T	466D	18F-9R	135.0	16550	C,H,A
9650	78215.00	**42670.00**	**48010.00**	**49930.00**	Deutz	6TI	374D	18F-9R	155.0	15200	C,H,A
9650 4WD	90016.00	**49280.00**	**55440.00**	**57660.00**	Deutz	6TI	374D	18F-9R	155.0	16500	C,H,A
9655	77865.00	**49280.00**	**53900.00**	**56600.00**	DD	6T	466D	18F-9R	155.0	15350	C,H,A
9655 4WD	88836.00	**56320.00**	**61600.00**	**64680.00**	DD	6T	466D	18F-9R	155.0	16550	C,H,A
9670	87015.00	**48160.00**	**54180.00**	**56350.00**	Deutz	6T	584D	18F-9R	175.0	16770	C,H,A
9670 4WD	99206.00	**53870.00**	**60610.00**	**63030.00**	Deutz	6T	584D	18F-9R	175.0	18400	C,H,A

AGCO-Allis (Cont.)

1995 (Cont.)

Model	Approx. Retail Price New	Estimated Average Value Less Repairs Fair	Good	Premium	Engine Make	No. Cyls.	Displ. Cu.-In.	No. Speeds	P.T.O. H.P.	Approx. Shipping Wt.-Lbs.	Cab
9675	85845.00	**54400.00**	**59500.00**	**62480.00**	DD	6T	530D	18F-9R	175.0	16300	C,H,A
9675 4WD	97886.00	**61120.00**	**66850.00**	**70190.00**	DD	6T	530D	18F-9R	175.0	17850	C,H,A
9690 4WD	107406.00	**57340.00**	**64510.00**	**67090.00**	Deutz	6T	584D	18F-9R	195.0	18500	C,H,A
9695 4WD	105966.00	**65920.00**	**72100.00**	**75710.00**	DD	6T	530D	18F-9R	195.0	17950	C,H,A
9815 4WD	115244.00	**71840.00**	**78580.00**	**82510.00**	DD	6TI	530D	18F-9R	215.0	17600	C,H,A

1996

Model	Approx. Retail Price New	Fair	Good	Premium	Make	No. Cyls.	Displ. Cu.-In.	No. Speeds	P.T.O. H.P.	Approx. Shipping Wt.-Lbs.	Cab
4650	18290.00	**12250.00**	**13350.00**	**13880.00**	SLH	3	190D	16F-4R	40.37	4475	No
4650 4WD	24225.00	**16230.00**	**17680.00**	**18390.00**	SLH	3	190D	16F-4R	40.37	5070	No
4660	21585.00	**14460.00**	**15760.00**	**16390.00**	SLH	3	190D	16F-4R	52.17	4762	No
4660 4WD	28160.00	**18870.00**	**20560.00**	**21380.00**	SLH	3	190D	16F-4R	52.17	5203	No
5650	19410.00	**13590.00**	**14750.00**	**15340.00**	SLH	3	183D	12F-12R	47.8		No
5650 4WD	25245.00	**17670.00**	**19190.00**	**19960.00**	SLH	3	183D	12F-12R	47.8		No
5660	22800.00	**15280.00**	**16640.00**	**17310.00**	SLH	3	183D	12F-12R	56.9		No
5660 4WD	28095.00	**18820.00**	**20510.00**	**21330.00**	SLH	3	183D	12F-12R	56.9		No
5670	26140.00	**18300.00**	**19870.00**	**20670.00**	SLH	4	244D	24F-12R	63.13	5379	No
5670 4WD	32085.00	**22460.00**	**24390.00**	**25370.00**	SLH	4	244D	24F-12R	63.13	6096	No
5680	30325.00	**20320.00**	**22140.00**	**23030.00**	SLH	4	244D	24F-12R	72.70	5997	No
5680 4WD	37050.00	**24820.00**	**27050.00**	**28130.00**	SLH	4	244D	24F-12R	72.70	6658	No
6670	36540.00	**24120.00**	**26280.00**	**27330.00**	SLH	4	244D	24F-12R	63.13	5997	C,H,A
6670 4WD	41620.00	**27470.00**	**29930.00**	**31130.00**	SLH	4	244D	24F-12R	63.13	6658	C,H,A
6680	38175.00	**25260.00**	**27520.00**	**28620.00**	SLH	4	244D	24F-12R	72.70	6724	C,H,A
6680 4WD	44425.00	**29480.00**	**32120.00**	**33410.00**	SLH	4	244D	24F-12R	72.70	7385	C,H,A
6690	33250.00	**22820.00**	**24780.00**	**25770.00**	SLH	4T	244D	24F-12R	80.85	6173	No
6690 4WD	40400.00	**27930.00**	**30320.00**	**31530.00**	SLH	4T	244D	24F-12R	80.85	6779	No
6690 4WD w/Cab	47745.00	**32900.00**	**35720.00**	**37150.00**	SLH	4T	244D	24F-12R	80.85	7385	C,H,A
6690 w/Cab	40830.00	**28000.00**	**30400.00**	**31620.00**	SLH	4T	244D	24F-12R	80.85	6724	C,H,A
7600	35975.00	**23450.00**	**25550.00**	**26570.00**	SLH	5	317D	24F-12R	89.23	8179	No
7600 4WD	43280.00	**28610.00**	**31170.00**	**32420.00**	SLH	5	317D	24F-12R	89.23	9502	No
7600 4WD w/Cab	51230.00	**32630.00**	**35550.00**	**36970.00**	SLH	5	317D	24F-12R	89.23	9833	C,H,A
7600 w/Cab	43540.00	**28810.00**	**31390.00**	**32650.00**	SLH	5	317D	24F-12R	89.23	8686	C,H,A
8360 AGCOSTAR	118410.00	**63720.00**	**71280.00**	**74840.00**	Cummins	6TA	855D	18F-2R	360*		C,H,A
8425 AGCOSTAR	144575.00	**73460.00**	**82170.00**	**86280.00**	Cummins	6TA	855D	18F-2R	425*		C,H,A
8425 AGCOSTAR	146935.00	**74870.00**	**83750.00**	**87940.00**	DD	6TA	774D	18F-2R	425*		C,H,A
8610	55195.00	**32940.00**	**36180.00**	**37630.00**	SLH	6	366D	36F-36R	103.12	9670	C,H,A
8610 4WD	63985.00	**38130.00**	**41880.00**	**43560.00**	SLH	6	366D	36F-36R	103.12	10870	C,H,A
8630	62950.00	**37640.00**	**41340.00**	**42990.00**	SLH	6T	366D	36F-36R	119.6	10159	C,H,A
8630 4WD	72705.00	**43550.00**	**47840.00**	**49750.00**	SLH	6T	366D	36F-36R	119.6	11100	C,H,A
9435	69235.00	**41790.00**	**45900.00**	**47740.00**	DD	6T	466D	32F-32R	135.69	14600	C,H,A
9435 4WD	79290.00	**47580.00**	**52260.00**	**54350.00**	DD	6T	466D	32F-32R	135.69	15700	C,H,A
9455	73670.00	**48580.00**	**52930.00**	**55050.00**	DD	6T	466D	32F-32R	155.56	14600	C,H,A
9455 4WD	84360.00	**55950.00**	**60960.00**	**63400.00**	DD	6T	466D	32F-32R	155.56	15700	C,H,A
9635	74565.00	**45140.00**	**49580.00**	**51560.00**	DD	6T	466D	18F-9R	135.5	15350	C,H,A
9635 4WD	87080.00	**52460.00**	**57620.00**	**59930.00**	DD	6T	466D	18F-9R	135.5	16550	C,H,A
9655	80235.00	**52930.00**	**57670.00**	**59980.00**	DD	6T	466D	18F-9R	155.66	15350	C,H,A
9655 4WD	90275.00	**58960.00**	**64240.00**	**66810.00**	DD	6T	466D	18F-9R	155.66	16550	C,H,A
9675	88165.00	**57620.00**	**62780.00**	**65290.00**	DD	6T	530D	18F-9R	176.44	16300	C,H,A
9675 4WD	101765.00	**66330.00**	**72270.00**	**75160.00**	DD	6T	530D	18F-9R	176.44	17850	C,H,A
9695 4WD	108975.00	**69010.00**	**75190.00**	**78200.00**	DD	6T	530D	18F-9R	196.57	17950	C,H,A
9815 4WD	118505.00	**77390.00**	**84320.00**	**87690.00**	DD	6TI	530D	18F-9R	215.0	17600	C,H,A

* Engine horsepower

1997

Model	Approx. Retail Price New	Fair	Good	Premium	Make	No. Cyls.	Displ. Cu.-In.	No. Speeds	P.T.O. H.P.	Approx. Shipping Wt.-Lbs.	Cab
4650	18730.00	**13490.00**	**14420.00**	**15000.00**	SLH	3	190D	12F-3R	40.37	4475	No
4650 4WD	24890.00	**17920.00**	**19170.00**	**19940.00**	SLH	3	190D	12F-3R	40.37	5070	No
4660	22170.00	**15960.00**	**17070.00**	**17750.00**	SLH	3	190D	12F-3R	52.17	4762	No
4660 4WD	28945.00	**20840.00**	**22290.00**	**23180.00**	SLH	3	190D	12F-3R	52.17	5203	No
5650	20650.00	**15490.00**	**16520.00**	**17180.00**	SLH	3	183D	12F-12R	47.8		No
5650 4WD	26685.00	**20010.00**	**21350.00**	**22200.00**	SLH	3	183D	12F-12R	47.8		No
5660	24155.00	**17390.00**	**18600.00**	**19340.00**	SLH	3	183D	12F-12R	56.9		No
5660 4WD	29635.00	**21340.00**	**22820.00**	**23730.00**	SLH	3	183D	12F-12R	56.9		No
5670	27665.00	**20750.00**	**22130.00**	**23020.00**	SLH	4	244D	24F-12R	63.13	5379	No
5670 4WD	33820.00	**25370.00**	**27060.00**	**28140.00**	SLH	4	244D	24F-12R	63.13	6096	No
5680	31995.00	**23040.00**	**24640.00**	**25630.00**	SLH	4	244D	24F-12R	72.70	5997	No
5680 4WD	38955.00	**28050.00**	**30000.00**	**31200.00**	SLH	4	244D	24F-12R	72.70	6658	No
6670	37820.00	**26640.00**	**28490.00**	**29630.00**	SLH	4	244D	24F-12R	63.13	5997	C,H,A
6670 4WD	43075.00	**30240.00**	**32340.00**	**33630.00**	SLH	4	244D	24F-12R	63.13	6658	C,H,A
6680	39510.00	**27720.00**	**29650.00**	**30840.00**	SLH	4	244D	24F-12R	72.70	6724	C,H,A
6680 4WD	45980.00	**31680.00**	**33880.00**	**35240.00**	SLH	4	244D	24F-12R	72.70	7385	C,H,A
6690	34415.00	**25500.00**	**27200.00**	**28290.00**	SLH	4T	244D	24F-12R	80.85	6173	No
6690 4WD	41815.00	**30750.00**	**32800.00**	**34110.00**	SLH	4T	244D	24F-12R	80.85	6779	No
6690 4WD w/Cab	49415.00	**36380.00**	**38800.00**	**40350.00**	SLH	4T	244D	24F-12R	80.85	7385	C,H,A
6690 w/Cab	42260.00	**30900.00**	**32960.00**	**34280.00**	SLH	4T	244D	24F-12R	80.85	6724	C,H,A
7600	35975.00	**25200.00**	**26950.00**	**28030.00**	SLH	5	317D	24F-12R	89.23	8179	No
7600 4WD	43280.00	**30380.00**	**32490.00**	**33790.00**	SLH	5	317D	24F-12R	89.23	9502	No
7600 4WD w/Cab	51230.00	**34780.00**	**37190.00**	**38680.00**	SLH	5	317D	24F-12R	89.23	9833	C,H,A
7600 w/Cab	43540.00	**31350.00**	**33530.00**	**34870.00**	SLH	5	317D	24F-12R	89.23	8686	C,H,A
8360 AGCOSTAR	119590.00	**70850.00**	**77390.00**	**80490.00**	Cummins	6TA	855D	18F-2R	360*		C,H,A
8425 AGCOSTAR	145296.00	**81450.00**	**88960.00**	**92520.00**	Cummins	6TA	855D	18F-2R	425*		C,H,A
8425 AGCOSTAR	147726.00	**85870.00**	**93790.00**	**97540.00**	DD	6TA	774D	18F-2R	425*		C,H,A
8610	57125.00	**37520.00**	**40880.00**	**42520.00**	SLH	6	366D	36F-36R	103.12	9670	C,H,A
8610 4WD	64815.00	**42210.00**	**45990.00**	**47830.00**	SLH	6	366D	36F-36R	103.12	10870	C,H,A
8630	65155.00	**46150.00**	**49360.00**	**51330.00**	SLH	6T	366D	36F-36R	119.6	10159	C,H,A
8630 4WD	73325.00	**51340.00**	**54900.00**	**57100.00**	SLH	6T	366D	36F-36R	119.6	11100	C,H,A

AGCO-Allis (Cont.)

1997 (Cont.)

Model	Approx. Retail Price New	Estimated Average Value Less Repairs Fair	Good	Premium	Engine Make	No. Cyls.	Displ. Cu.-In.	No. Speeds	P.T.O. H.P.	Approx. Shipping Wt.-Lbs.	Cab
9435	71533.00	**46900.00**	**51100.00**	**53140.00**	DD	6T	466D	32F-32R	135.69	14600	C,H,A
9435 4WD	82090.00	**54270.00**	**59130.00**	**61500.00**	DD	6T	466D	32F-32R	135.69	15700	C,H,A
9455	76121.00	**54810.00**	**58610.00**	**60950.00**	DD	6T	466D	32F-32R	155.56	14600	C,H,A
9455 4WD	87314.00	**62280.00**	**66610.00**	**69270.00**	DD	6T	466D	32F-32R	155.56	15700	C,H,A
9635	75405.00	**53640.00**	**57370.00**	**59670.00**	DD	6T	466D	18F-9R	135.5	15350	C,H,A
9635 4WD	88737.00	**63000.00**	**67380.00**	**70080.00**	DD	6T	466D	18F-9R	135.5	16550	C,H,A
9655	83542.00	**59760.00**	**63910.00**	**66470.00**	DD	6T	466D	18F-9R	155.66	15350	C,H,A
9655 4WD	93993.00	**66600.00**	**71230.00**	**74080.00**	DD	6T	466D	18F-9R	155.66	16550	C,H,A
9675	93363.00	**66240.00**	**70840.00**	**73670.00**	DD	6T	530D	18F-9R	176.44	16300	C,H,A
9675 4WD	105960.00	**73440.00**	**78540.00**	**81680.00**	DD	6T	530D	18F-9R	176.44	17850	C,H,A
9695 4WD	115730.00	**80640.00**	**86240.00**	**89690.00**	DD	6T	530D	18F-9R	196.57	17950	C,H,A
9815 4WD	126025.00	**88560.00**	**94710.00**	**98500.00**	DD	6TI	530D	18F-9R	215.0	17600	C,H,A

* Engine horsepower

1998

Model	Approx. Retail Price New	Estimated Average Value Less Repairs Fair	Good	Premium	Engine Make	No. Cyls.	Displ. Cu.-In.	No. Speeds	P.T.O. H.P.	Approx. Shipping Wt.-Lbs.	Cab
4650	18730.00	**14610.00**	**15360.00**	**15820.00**	SLH	3	190D	12F-3R	40.37	4475	No
4650 4WD	24890.00	**19410.00**	**20410.00**	**21020.00**	SLH	3	190D	12F-3R	40.37	5070	No
4660	22170.00	**17290.00**	**18180.00**	**18730.00**	SLH	3	190D	12F-3R	52.17	4762	No
4660 4WD	28945.00	**22580.00**	**23740.00**	**24450.00**	SLH	3	190D	12F-3R	52.17	5203	No
5650	21270.00	**16800.00**	**17870.00**	**18410.00**	SLH	3	183D	12F-12R	47.8		No
5650 4WD	27485.00	**21710.00**	**23090.00**	**23780.00**	SLH	3	183D	12F-12R	47.8		No
5660	24880.00	**19410.00**	**20400.00**	**21010.00**	SLH	3	183D	12F-12R	56.9		No
5660 4WD	30525.00	**23810.00**	**25030.00**	**25780.00**	SLH	3	183D	12F-12R	56.9		No
5670	28495.00	**22510.00**	**23940.00**	**24660.00**	SLH	4	244D	24F-12R	63.13	5379	No
5670 4WD	34835.00	**27520.00**	**29260.00**	**30140.00**	SLH	4	244D	24F-12R	63.13	6096	No
5680	31995.00	**24960.00**	**26240.00**	**27030.00**	SLH	4	244D	24F-12R	72.70	5997	No
5680 4WD	38955.00	**30390.00**	**31940.00**	**32900.00**	SLH	4	244D	24F-12R	72.70	6658	No
6670	40295.00	**22850.00**	**24030.00**	**24750.00**	SLH	4	244D	24F-12R	63.13	5997	C,H,A
6670 4WD	45705.00	**35100.00**	**36900.00**	**38010.00**	SLH	4	244D	24F-12R	63.13	6658	C,H,A
6680	40850.00	**31080.00**	**32680.00**	**33660.00**	SLH	4	244D	24F-12R	72.70	6724	C,H,A
6680 4WD	47320.00	**36110.00**	**37970.00**	**39110.00**	SLH	4	244D	24F-12R	72.70	7385	C,H,A
6690	35755.00	**27650.00**	**29400.00**	**30280.00**	SLH	4T	244D	24F-12R	80.85	6173	No
6690 4WD	43155.00	**33260.00**	**35360.00**	**36420.00**	SLH	4T	244D	24F-12R	80.85	6779	No
6690 4WD w/Cab	50755.00	**39260.00**	**41750.00**	**43000.00**	SLH	4T	244D	24F-12R	80.85	7385	C,H,A
6690 w/Cab	43600.00	**33580.00**	**35700.00**	**36770.00**	SLH	4T	244D	24F-12R	80.85	6724	C,H,A
7600	35975.00	**27300.00**	**28700.00**	**29560.00**	SLH	5	317D	24F-12R	89.23	8179	No
7600 4WD	43280.00	**32920.00**	**34600.00**	**35640.00**	SLH	5	317D	24F-12R	89.23	9502	No
7600 4WD w/Cab	51230.00	**37440.00**	**39360.00**	**40540.00**	SLH	5	317D	24F-12R	89.23	9833	C,H,A
7600 w/Cab	43540.00	**33540.00**	**35260.00**	**36320.00**	SLH	5	317D	24F-12R	89.23	8686	C,H,A
8360 AGCOSTAR	135040.00	**90000.00**	**96250.00**	**99140.00**	Cummins	6TA	855D	18F-2R	360*		C,H,A
8425 AGCOSTAR	155710.00	**97700.00**	**104490.00**	**107630.00**	Cummins	6TA	855D	18F-2R	425*		C,H,A
8610	57125.00	**41530.00**	**44340.00**	**45670.00**	SLH	6	366D	36F-36R	103.12	9670	C,H,A
8610 4WD	66275.00	**48100.00**	**51350.00**	**52890.00**	SLH	6	366D	36F-36R	103.12	10870	C,H,A
8630	65155.00	**50000.00**	**52560.00**	**54140.00**	SLH	6T	366D	36F-36R	119.6	10159	C,H,A
8630 4WD	75250.00	**57720.00**	**60680.00**	**62500.00**	SLH	6T	366D	36F-36R	119.6	11100	C,H,A
8745	36170.00	**27380.00**	**28780.00**	**29640.00**	Own	4T	268D	12F-12R	70.0		No
8745 4WD	42565.00	**32370.00**	**34030.00**	**35050.00**	Own	4T	268D	12F-12R	70.0		No
8745 4WD w/Cab	50070.00	**38220.00**	**40180.00**	**41390.00**	Own	4T	268D	12F-12R	70.0		C,H,A
8745 w/Cab	43675.00	**33290.00**	**34990.00**	**36040.00**	Own	4T	268D	12F-12R	70.0		C,H,A
8765	38675.00	**29390.00**	**30890.00**	**31820.00**	Own	4T	268D	12F-12R	85.0		No
8765 4WD	46405.00	**35410.00**	**37230.00**	**38350.00**	Own	4T	268D	12F-12R	85.0		No
8765 4WD w/Cab	54305.00	**41570.00**	**43710.00**	**45020.00**	Own	4T	268D	12F-12R	85.0		C,H,A
8765 w/Cab	46575.00	**35530.00**	**37360.00**	**38480.00**	Own	4T	268D	12F-12R	85.0		C,H,A
8775	43850.00	**33380.00**	**35100.00**	**36150.00**	Own	6	402D	32F-32R	95.0		No
8775 4WD	51280.00	**39160.00**	**41160.00**	**42400.00**	Own	6	402D	32F-32R	95.0		No
8775 4WD w/Cab	63635.00	**48360.00**	**50840.00**	**52370.00**	Own	6	402D	32F-32R	95.0		C,H,A
8775 w/Cab	55917.00	**42900.00**	**45100.00**	**46450.00**	Own	6	402D	32F-32R	95.0		C,H,A
8785	52478.00	**40170.00**	**42230.00**	**43500.00**	Own	6T	402D	32F-32R	110.0		No
8785 4WD	62332.00	**47810.00**	**50270.00**	**51780.00**	Own	6T	402D	32F-32R	110.0		No
8785 4WD w/Cab	74686.00	**57410.00**	**60350.00**	**62160.00**	Own	6T	402D	32F-32R	110.0		C,H,A
8785 w/Cab	64550.00	**49530.00**	**52070.00**	**53630.00**	Own	6T	402D	32F-32R	110.0		C,H,A
9435	73555.00	**55380.00**	**58220.00**	**59970.00**	DD	6T	466D	32F-32R	135.69	14600	C,H,A
9435 4WD	83930.00	**62400.00**	**65600.00**	**67570.00**	DD	6T	466D	32F-32R	135.69	15700	C,H,A
9455	78142.00	**58110.00**	**61090.00**	**62920.00**	DD	6T	466D	32F-32R	155.56	14600	C,H,A
9455 4WD	89155.00	**66690.00**	**70110.00**	**72210.00**	DD	6T	466D	32F-32R	155.56	15700	C,H,A
9635	79065.00	**56240.00**	**60040.00**	**61840.00**	DD	6T	466D	18F-9R	135.5	15350	C,H,A
9635 4WD	90575.00	**64070.00**	**68390.00**	**70440.00**	DD	6T	466D	18F-9R	135.5	16550	C,H,A
9655	83765.00	**62400.00**	**65600.00**	**67570.00**	DD	6T	466D	18F-9R	155.66	15350	C,H,A
9655 4WD	95227.00	**71930.00**	**75620.00**	**77890.00**	DD	6T	466D	18F-9R	155.66	16550	C,H,A
9675	94192.00	**71130.00**	**74780.00**	**77020.00**	DD	6T	530D	18F-9R	176.44	16300	C,H,A
9675 4WD	105780.00	**79390.00**	**83460.00**	**85960.00**	DD	6T	530D	18F-9R	176.44	17850	C,H,A
9695 4WD	115730.00	**78570.00**	**82600.00**	**85080.00**	DD	6T	530D	18F-9R	196.57	17950	C,H,A
9735	78886.00	**59280.00**	**62320.00**	**64190.00**	Own	6T	402D	32F-32R	125.0		C,H,A
9735 4WD	91270.00	**68850.00**	**72380.00**	**74550.00**	Own	6T	402D	32F-32R	125.0		C,H,A
9745	85090.00	**64030.00**	**67310.00**	**69330.00**	Own	6T	402D	32F-32R	145.0		C,H,A
9745 4WD	97000.00	**72540.00**	**76260.00**	**78550.00**	Own	6T	402D	32F-32R	145.0		C,H,A
9815 4WD	126025.00	**95940.00**	**100860.00**	**103890.00**	DD	6TI	530D	18F-9R	215.0	17600	C,H,A

* Engine horsepower

1999

Model	Approx. Retail Price New	Estimated Average Value Less Repairs Fair	Good	Premium	Engine Make	No. Cyls.	Displ. Cu.-In.	No. Speeds	P.T.O. H.P.	Approx. Shipping Wt.-Lbs.	Cab
5650	22615.00	**19220.00**	**20130.00**	**20530.00**	SLH	3	183D	12F-12R	47.8		No
5650 4WD	29015.00	**24660.00**	**25820.00**	**26340.00**	SLH	3	183D	12F-12R	47.8		No
5660	26330.00	**22120.00**	**23170.00**	**23630.00**	SLH	3	183D	12F-12R	56.9		No
5660 4WD	32145.00	**27000.00**	**28290.00**	**28860.00**	SLH	3	183D	12F-12R	56.9		No

AGCO-Allis (Cont.)

1999 (Cont.)

Model	Approx. Retail Price New	Fair	Good	Premium	Make	No. Cyls.	Displ. Cu.-In.	No. Speeds	P.T.O. H.P.	Approx. Shipping Wt.-Lbs.	Cab
5670	30055.00	25550.00	26750.00	27290.00	SLH	4	244D	24F-12R	63.13	5379	No
5670 4WD	36585.00	31100.00	32560.00	33210.00	SLH	4	244D	24F-12R	63.13	6096	No
6670	42170.00	35420.00	37110.00	37850.00	SLH	4	244D	24F-12R	63.13	5997	C,H,A
6670 4WD	47740.00	40100.00	42010.00	42850.00	SLH	4	244D	24F-12R	63.13	6658	C,H,A
8360 AGCOSTAR	134411.00	102010.00	106980.00	109120.00	Cummins	6TA	855D	18F-2R	360*		C,H,A
8425 AGCOSTAR	155910.00	118900.00	124700.00	127190.00	Cummins	6TA	855D	18F-2R	425*		C,H,A
8745	38820.00	31920.00	33440.00	34110.00	Own	4T	268D	12F-12R	70.0		No
8745 4WD	45500.00	37800.00	39600.00	40390.00	Own	4T	268D	12F-12R	70.0		No
8745 4WD w/Cab	52850.00	43680.00	45760.00	46680.00	Own	4T	268D	12F-12R	70.0		C,H,A
8745 w/Cab	46170.00	38220.00	40040.00	40840.00	Own	4T	268D	12F-12R	70.0		C,H,A
8765	41560.00	34440.00	36080.00	36800.00	Own	4T	268D	12F-12R	85.0		No
8765 4WD	49730.00	41160.00	43120.00	43980.00	Own	4T	268D	12F-12R	85.0		No
8765 4WD w/Cab	57490.00	47880.00	50160.00	51160.00	Own	4T	268D	12F-12R	85.0		C,H,A
8765 w/Cab	49315.00	40740.00	42680.00	43530.00	Own	4T	268D	12F-12R	85.0		C,H,A
8775	46870.00	38640.00	40480.00	41290.00	Own	6	402D	32F-32R	95.0		No
8775 4WD	54115.00	44940.00	47080.00	48020.00	Own	6	402D	32F-32R	95.0		No
8775 4WD w/Cab	67025.00	55440.00	58080.00	59240.00	Own	6	402D	32F-32R	95.0		C,H,A
8775 w/Cab	58965.00	48720.00	51040.00	52060.00	Own	6	402D	32F-32R	95.0		C,H,A
8785	53367.00	44100.00	46200.00	47120.00	Own	6T	402D	32F-32R	110.0		No
8785 4WD	65552.00	53760.00	56320.00	57450.00	Own	6T	402D	32F-32R	110.0		No
8785 4WD w/Cab	78462.00	64680.00	67760.00	69120.00	Own	6T	402D	32F-32R	110.0		C,H,A
8785 w/Cab	67977.00	55440.00	58080.00	59240.00	Own	6T	402D	32F-32R	110.0		C,H,A
9435	74235.00	61490.00	64420.00	65710.00	DD	6T	466D	32F-32R	135.69	14600	C,H,A
9435 4WD	84615.00	70140.00	73480.00	74950.00	DD	6T	466D	32F-32R	135.69	15700	C,H,A
9455	78650.00	65100.00	68200.00	69560.00	DD	6T	466D	32F-32R	155.56	14600	C,H,A
9455 4WD	88160.00	73080.00	76560.00	78090.00	DD	6T	466D	32F-32R	155.56	15700	C,H,A
9635	79750.00	64740.00	67860.00	69900.00	DD	6T	466D	18F-9R	135.5	15350	C,H,A
9635 4WD	91420.00	75120.00	78740.00	81100.00	DD	6T	466D	18F-9R	135.5	16550	C,H,A
9655	84936.00	70560.00	73920.00	75400.00	DD	6T	466D	18F-9R	155.66	15350	C,H,A
9655 4WD	96500.00	79800.00	83600.00	85270.00	DD	6T	466D	18F-9R	155.66	16550	C,H,A
9675	98095.00	80640.00	84480.00	86170.00	DD	6T	530D	18F-9R	176.44	16300	C,H,A
9675 4WD	108406.00	88200.00	92400.00	94250.00	DD	6T	530D	18F-9R	176.44	17850	C,H,A
9695 4WD	116346.00	94920.00	99440.00	101430.00	DD	6T	530D	18F-9R	196.57	17950	C,H,A
9735	78225.00	64850.00	67940.00	69300.00	Own	6T	402D	32F-32R	125.0		C,H,A
9735	83670.00	68880.00	72160.00	73600.00	Own	6T	402D	18F-6R	125.0		C,H,A
9735 4WD	90110.00	74840.00	78410.00	79980.00	Own	6T	402D	32F-32R	125.0		C,H,A
9735 4WD	97180.00	80720.00	84570.00	86260.00	Own	6T	402D	18F-6R	125.0		C,H,A
9745	82960.00	68880.00	72160.00	73600.00	Own	6T	402D	32F-32R	145.0		C,H,A
9745	89590.00	73920.00	77440.00	78990.00	Own	6T	402D	18F-6R	145.0		C,H,A
9745 4WD	95480.00	78960.00	82720.00	84370.00	Own	6T	402D	32F-32R	145.0		C,H,A
9745 4WD	102870.00	83890.00	87890.00	89650.00	Own	6T	402D	18F-6R	145.0		C,H,A
9755 4WD	107300.00	87610.00	91780.00	93620.00	Own	6T	530D	18F-6R	160.0		C,H,A
9765 4WD	115950.00	94880.00	99400.00	101390.00	Own	6T	530D	18F-6R	180.0		C,H,A
9775 4WD	127305.00	103570.00	108500.00	110670.00	Own	6TI	530D	18F-6R	200.0		C,H,A
9785 4WD	142375.00	116240.00	121770.00	124210.00	Own	6TI	530D	18F-6R	225.0		C,H,A
9815 4WD	126660.00	103320.00	108240.00	110410.00	DD	6TI	530D	18F-9R	215.0	17600	C,H,A

* Engine horsepower

Allis-Chalmers

1939

Model	Approx. Retail Price New	Fair	Good	Premium	Make	No. Cyls.	Displ. Cu.-In.	No. Speeds	P.T.O. H.P.	Approx. Shipping Wt.-Lbs.	Cab
A	......	510.00	1170.00	1450.00	AC	4	510G	3F-1R	27	4275	No
B	......	570.00	1310.00	1620.00	AC	4	125G	3F-1R	23	2130	No
RC	......	560.00	1280.00	1590.00	AC	4	125G	4F-1R	18	2595	No
U	......	420.00	970.00	1200.00	AC	6	301D	4F-1R	22	5130	No
UC	......	470.00	1070.00	1330.00	AC	4	301D	4F-1R	30	5710	No
WC	......	440.00	1000.00	1240.00	AC	4	201D	4F-1R	22	3325	No
WF	......	480.00	1100.00	1360.00	AC	4	201G	4F-1R	22	3270	No

1940

Model	Approx. Retail Price New	Fair	Good	Premium	Make	No. Cyls.	Displ. Cu.-In.	No. Speeds	P.T.O. H.P.	Approx. Shipping Wt.-Lbs.	Cab
A	......	530.00	1210.00	1500.00	AC	4	510G	3F-1R	27	4275	No
B	......	590.00	1350.00	1670.00	AC	4	125G	3F-1R	23	2130	No
C	......	550.00	1260.00	1560.00	AC	4	125G	3F-1R	17	3025	No
RC	......	570.00	1310.00	1620.00	AC	4	125G	4F-1R	18	2595	No
U	......	440.00	1000.00	1240.00	AC	6	301D	4F-1R	22	5130	No
UC	......	480.00	1100.00	1360.00	AC	4	301D	4F-1R	30	5710	No
WC	......	450.00	1040.00	1290.00	AC	4	201D	4F-1R	22	3325	No
WF	......	500.00	1140.00	1410.00	AC	4	201G	4F-1R	22	3270	No

1941

Model	Approx. Retail Price New	Fair	Good	Premium	Make	No. Cyls.	Displ. Cu.-In.	No. Speeds	P.T.O. H.P.	Approx. Shipping Wt.-Lbs.	Cab
A	......	540.00	1240.00	1540.00	AC	4	510G	3F-1R	27	4275	No
B	......	600.00	1380.00	1710.00	AC	4	125G	3F-1R	23	2130	No
C	......	560.00	1290.00	1600.00	AC	4	125G	3F-1R	17	3025	No
RC	......	580.00	1340.00	1660.00	AC	4	125G	4F-1R	18	2595	No
U	......	450.00	1040.00	1290.00	AC	6	301D	4F-1R	22	5130	No
UC	......	510.00	1170.00	1450.00	AC	4	301D	4F-1R	30	5710	No
WC	......	480.00	1100.00	1360.00	AC	4	201D	4F-1R	22	3325	No
WF	......	530.00	1210.00	1500.00	AC	4	201G	4F-1R	22	3270	No

1942

Model	Approx. Retail Price New	Fair	Good	Premium	Make	No. Cyls.	Displ. Cu.-In.	No. Speeds	P.T.O. H.P.	Approx. Shipping Wt.-Lbs.	Cab
A	......	570.00	1310.00	1620.00	AC	4	510G	3F-1R	27	4275	No
B	......	620.00	1420.00	1760.00	AC	4	125G	3F-1R	23	2130	No
C	......	590.00	1350.00	1670.00	AC	4	125G	3F-1R	17	3025	No

Allis-Chalmers (Cont.)

Model	Approx. Retail Price New	Estimated Average Value Less Repairs Fair	Good	Premium	Engine Make	No. Cyls.	Displ. Cu.-In.	No. Speeds	P.T.O. H.P.	Approx. Shipping Wt.-Lbs.	Cab
1942 (Cont.)											
U	......	470.00	1070.00	1330.00	AC	6	301D	4F-1R	22	5130	No
WC	......	500.00	1140.00	1410.00	AC	4	201D	4F-1R	22	3325	No
WF	......	540.00	1240.00	1540.00	AC	4	201G	4F-1R	22	3270	No
1943											
B	......	650.00	1450.00	1800.00	AC	4	125G	3F-1R	23	2130	No
C	......	620.00	1380.00	1710.00	AC	4	125G	3F-1R	17	3025	No
U	......	500.00	1100.00	1360.00	AC	6	301D	4F-1R	22	5130	No
WC	......	530.00	1170.00	1450.00	AC	4	201D	4F-1R	22	3325	No
WF	......	570.00	1270.00	1580.00	AC	4	201G	4F-1R	22	3270	No
1944											
B	......	690.00	1490.00	1850.00	AC	4	125G	3F-1R	23	2130	No
C	......	670.00	1450.00	1800.00	AC	4	125G	3F-1R	17	3025	No
U	......	530.00	1140.00	1410.00	AC	6	301D	4F-1R	22	5130	No
WC	......	560.00	1210.00	1500.00	AC	4	201D	4F-1R	22	3325	No
WF	......	610.00	1310.00	1620.00	AC	4	201G	4F-1R	22	3270	No
1945											
B	......	740.00	1530.00	1900.00	AC	4	125G	3F-1R	23	2130	No
C	......	730.00	1510.00	1870.00	AC	4	125G	3F-1R	17	3025	No
U	......	560.00	1160.00	1440.00	AC	6	301D	4F-1R	22	5130	No
WC	......	590.00	1220.00	1510.00	AC	4	201D	4F-1R	22	3325	No
WF	......	660.00	1360.00	1690.00	AC	4	201G	4F-1R	22	3270	No
1946											
B	......	790.00	1580.00	1960.00	AC	4	125G	3F-1R	23	2130	No
C	......	800.00	1600.00	1980.00	AC	4	125G	3F-1R	17	3025	No
U	......	610.00	1220.00	1510.00	AC	6	301D	4F-1R	22	5130	No
WC	......	650.00	1290.00	1600.00	AC	4	201D	4F-1R	22	3325	No
WF	......	710.00	1430.00	1770.00	AC	4	201G	4F-1R	22	3270	No
1947											
B	......	840.00	1630.00	2020.00	AC	4	125G	3F-1R	23	2130	No
C	......	860.00	1670.00	2070.00	AC	4	125G	3F-1R	17	3025	No
U	......	670.00	1290.00	1600.00	AC	6	301D	4F-1R	22	5130	No
WC	......	680.00	1330.00	1650.00	AC	4	201D	4F-1R	22	3325	No
WF	......	750.00	1460.00	1810.00	AC	4	201G	4F-1R	22	3270	No
1948											
B	......	900.00	1700.00	2110.00	AC	4	125G	3F-1R	23	2130	No
C	......	920.00	1730.00	2150.00	AC	4	125G	3F-1R	17	3025	No
G	......	830.00	1560.00	1930.00	Continental	4	62G	3F-1R	10	1550	No
U	......	720.00	1360.00	1690.00	AC	6	301D	4F-1R	22	5130	No
WC	......	740.00	1400.00	1740.00	AC	4	201D	4F-1R	22	3325	No
WD	......	860.00	1630.00	2020.00	AC	4	201G	4F-1R	36	4050	No
WF	......	800.00	1510.00	1870.00	AC	4	201G	4F-1R	22	3270	No
1949											
B	......	950.00	1740.00	2160.00	AC	4	125G	3F-1R	23	2130	No
C	......	960.00	1770.00	2200.00	AC	4	125G	3F-1R	17	3025	No
G	......	890.00	1630.00	2020.00	Continental	4	62G	3F-1R	10	1550	No
U	......	780.00	1430.00	1770.00	AC	6	301D	4F-1R	22	5130	No
WD	......	940.00	1720.00	2130.00	AC	4	201G	4F-1R	36	4050	No
WF	......	850.00	1560.00	1930.00	AC	4	201G	4F-1R	22	3270	No
1950											
B	......	990.00	1770.00	2200.00	AC	4	125G	3F-1R	23	2130	No
C	......	1020.00	1820.00	2260.00	AC	4	125G	3F-1R	17	3025	No
CA	......	1060.00	1900.00	2360.00	AC	4	125G	4F-1R	27	2850	No
G	......	980.00	1750.00	2170.00	Continental	4	62G	3F-1R	10	1550	No
U	......	840.00	1500.00	1860.00	AC	6	301D	4F-1R	22	5130	No
WD	......	1000.00	1790.00	2220.00	AC	4	201G	4F-1R	36	4050	No
WF	......	900.00	1620.00	2010.00	AC	4	201G	4F-1R	22	3270	No
1951											
B	......	1060.00	1850.00	2290.00	AC	4	125G	3F-1R	23	2130	No
CA	......	1140.00	1980.00	2460.00	AC	4	125G	4F-1R	27	2850	No
G	......	1040.00	1820.00	2260.00	Continental	4	62G	3F-1R	10	1550	No
U	......	940.00	1630.00	2020.00	AC	6	301D	4F-1R	22	5130	No
WD	......	1030.00	1800.00	2230.00	AC	4	201G	4F-1R	36	4050	No
WF	......	960.00	1670.00	2070.00	AC	4	201G	4F-1R	22	3270	No
1952											
B	......	1130.00	1920.00	2380.00	AC	4	125G	3F-1R	23	2130	No
CA	......	1190.00	2020.00	2510.00	AC	4	125G	4F-1R	27	2850	No
G	......	1090.00	1850.00	2290.00	Continental	4	62G	3F-1R	10	1550	No
WD	......	1230.00	2090.00	2590.00	AC	4	201G	4F-1R	36	4050	No
1953											
B	......	1190.00	1980.00	2460.00	AC	4	125G	3F-1R	23	2130	No
CA	......	1260.00	2090.00	2590.00	AC	4	125G	4F-1R	27	2850	No
G	......	1150.00	1900.00	2360.00	Continental	4	62G	3F-1R	10	1550	No
WD	......	1300.00	2160.00	2680.00	AC	4	201G	4F-1R	36	4050	No

Allis-Chalmers (Cont.)

Model	Approx. Retail Price New	Estimated Average Value Less Repairs: Fair	Good	Premium	Engine: Make	No. Cyls.	Displ. Cu.-In.	No. Speeds	P.T.O. H.P.	Approx. Shipping Wt.-Lbs.	Cab
1953 (Cont.)											
WD-45	......	1320.00	2190.00	2720.00	AC	4	226G	4F-1R	45	4470	No
WD-45	......	1360.00	2260.00	2800.00	AC	4	230D	4F-1R	45	4730	No
1954											
B	......	1280.00	2070.00	2570.00	AC	4	125G	3F-1R	23	2130	No
CA	......	1340.00	2180.00	2700.00	AC	4	125G	4F-1R	27	2850	No
G	......	1240.00	2000.00	2480.00	Continental	4	62G	3F-1R	10	1550	No
WD-45	......	1390.00	2250.00	2790.00	AC	4	226G	4F-1R	45	4470	No
WD-45	......	1440.00	2330.00	2890.00	AC	4	230D	4F-1R	45	4730	No
1955											
B	......	1350.00	2130.00	2640.00	AC	4	125G	3F-1R	23	2130	No
CA	......	1450.00	2290.00	2840.00	AC	4	125G	4F-1R	27	2850	No
G	......	1360.00	2150.00	2670.00	Continental	4	62G	3F-1R	10	1550	No
WD-45	......	1490.00	2360.00	2930.00	AC	4	226G	4F-1R	45	4470	No
WD-45	......	1550.00	2450.00	3040.00	AC	4	230D	4F-1R	45	4730	No
1956											
B	......	1430.00	2210.00	2740.00	AC	4	125G	3F-1R	23	2130	No
CA	......	1540.00	2380.00	2950.00	AC	4	125G	4F-1R	27	2850	No
WD-45	......	1580.00	2450.00	3040.00	AC	4	226G	4F-1R	45	4470	No
WD-45	......	1670.00	2580.00	3200.00	AC	4	230D	4F-1R	45	4730	No
1957											
B	......	1510.00	2280.00	2830.00	AC	4	125G	3F-1R	23	2130	No
CA	......	1650.00	2490.00	3090.00	AC	4	125G	4F-1R	27	2850	No
D-14	......	1550.00	2830.00	3450.00	AC	4	149G	8F-2R	36	4140	No
D-17	......	1740.00	3180.00	3880.00	AC	4	226G	8F-2R	54	5240	No
D-17	......	1820.00	3330.00	4060.00	AC	4	262D	8F-2R	53	5570	No
D-17 III	......	1960.00	3580.00	4370.00	AC	4	226G	8F-2R	54	5500	No
D-17 III	......	2100.00	3840.00	4690.00	AC	6	262D	8F-2R	53	5785	No
D17 IV	......	1940.00	3560.00	4340.00	AC	4	226G	8F-2R	54	4650	No
D17 IV	......	2150.00	3940.00	4810.00	AC	6	262D	8F-2R	53	5390	No
WD-45	......	1710.00	2580.00	3200.00	AC	4	226G	4F-1R	45	4470	No
WD-45	......	1760.00	2650.00	3290.00	AC	4	230D	4F-1R	45	4730	No
1958											
D-14	......	1590.00	2920.00	3560.00	AC	4	149G	8F-2R	36	4140	No
D-17	......	1770.00	3230.00	3940.00	AC	4	226G	8F-2R	54	5240	No
D-17	......	1860.00	3390.00	4140.00	AC	6	262D	8F-2R	53	5570	No
D-17 III	......	2000.00	3650.00	4450.00	AC	4	226G	8F-2R	54	5500	No
D-17 III	......	2140.00	3900.00	4760.00	AC	6	262D	8F-2R	53	5785	No
D17 IV	......	1990.00	3630.00	4430.00	AC	4	226G	8F-2R	54	4650	No
D17 IV	......	2210.00	4030.00	4920.00	AC	6	262D	8F-2R	53	5390	No
1959											
D-10	......	1420.00	2590.00	3160.00	AC	4	139G	4F-1R	29	3370	No
D-12	......	1520.00	2780.00	3390.00	AC	4	139G	4F-1R	29	3420	No
D-14	......	1630.00	2980.00	3640.00	AC	4	149G	8F-2R	36	4140	No
D-17	......	1800.00	3300.00	4030.00	AC	4	226G	8F-2R	54	5240	No
D-17	......	1900.00	3470.00	4230.00	AC	6	262D	8F-2R	53	5570	No
D-17 III	......	2040.00	3730.00	4550.00	AC	4	226G	8F-2R	54	5500	No
D-17 III	......	2190.00	4010.00	4890.00	AC	6	262D	8F-2R	53	5785	No
D17 IV	......	2030.00	3710.00	4530.00	AC	4	226G	8F-2R	54	4650	No
D17 IV	......	2240.00	4100.00	5000.00	AC	6	262D	8F-2R	53	5390	No
1960											
D-10	......	1490.00	2660.00	3250.00	AC	4	139G	4F-1R	29	3370	No
D-12	......	1600.00	2850.00	3480.00	AC	4	139G	4F-1R	29	3420	No
D-14	......	1710.00	3040.00	3710.00	AC	4	149G	8F-2R	36	4140	No
D-15	......	1750.00	3100.00	3780.00	AC	4	149G	8F-2R	40	4270	No
D-17	......	1880.00	3350.00	4090.00	AC	4	226G	8F-2R	54	5240	No
D-17	......	2010.00	3570.00	4360.00	AC	6	262D	8F-2R	53	5570	No
D-17 III	......	2130.00	3790.00	4620.00	AC	4	226G	8F-2R	54	5500	No
D-17 III	......	2280.00	4050.00	4940.00	AC	6	262D	8F-2R	53	5785	No
D17 IV	......	2180.00	3870.00	4720.00	AC	4	226G	8F-2R	54	4650	No
D17 IV	......	2350.00	4180.00	5100.00	AC	6	262D	8F-2R	53	5390	No
1961											
D-10	......	1570.00	2720.00	3320.00	AC	4	139G	4F-1R	29	3370	No
D-12	......	1680.00	2910.00	3550.00	AC	4	139G	4F-1R	29	3420	No
D-15	......	1810.00	3140.00	3830.00	AC	4	149G	8F-2R	40	4270	No
D-17	......	2020.00	3490.00	4260.00	AC	4	226G	8F-2R	54	5240	No
D-17	......	2130.00	3680.00	4490.00	AC	6	262D	8F-2R	53	5570	No
D-17 III	......	2240.00	3870.00	4720.00	AC	4	226G	8F-2R	54	5500	No
D-17 III	......	2360.00	4080.00	4980.00	AC	6	262D	8F-2R	53	5785	No
D17 IV	......	2400.00	4150.00	5060.00	AC	4	226G	8F-2R	54	4650	No
D17 IV	......	2510.00	4340.00	5300.00	AC	6	262D	8F-2R	53	5390	No
D-19	......	2410.00	4160.00	5080.00	AC	6	262G	8F-2R	72	6475	No
D-19	......	2660.00	4610.00	5620.00	AC	6	262D	8F-2R	67	6570	No
1962											
D-10	......	1650.00	2780.00	3390.00	AC	4	139G	4F-1R	29	3370	No
D-12	......	1770.00	2980.00	3640.00	AC	4	139G	4F-1R	29	3420	No

Allis-Chalmers (Cont.)

Model	Approx. Retail Price New	Estimated Average Value Less Repairs Fair	Good	Premium	Engine Make	No. Cyls.	Displ. Cu.-In.	No. Speeds	P.T.O. H.P.	Approx. Shipping Wt.-Lbs.	Cab
			1962 (Cont.)								
D-15	......	1920.00	3240.00	3950.00	AC	4	149G	8F-2R	40	4270	No
D-17	......	2100.00	3540.00	4320.00	AC	4	226G	8F-2R	54	5240	No
D-17	......	2220.00	3730.00	4550.00	AC	6	262D	8F-2R	53	5570	No
D-17 III	......	2330.00	3920.00	4780.00	AC	4	226G	8F-2R	54	5500	No
D-17 III	......	2470.00	4160.00	5080.00	AC	6	262D	8F-2R	53	5785	No
D17 IV	......	2530.00	4260.00	5200.00	AC	4	226G	8F-2R	54	4650	No
D17 IV	......	2630.00	4430.00	5410.00	AC	6	262D	8F-2R	53	5390	No
D-19	......	2610.00	4390.00	5360.00	AC	6	262G	8F-2R	72	6475	No
D-19	......	2770.00	4670.00	5700.00	AC	6	262D	8F-2R	67	6570	No
			1963								
D-10	2075.00	1730.00	2840.00	3470.00	AC	4	149G	4F-1R	30	2800	No
D-12	2276.00	1850.00	3030.00	3700.00	AC	4	149G	4F-1R	30	2850	No
D-15	3485.00	2000.00	3280.00	4000.00	AC	4	149G	8F-2R	46	4270	No
D-15	4245.00	2190.00	3600.00	4390.00	AC	4	175D	8F-2R	44	4270	No
D-17	4414.00	2310.00	3800.00	4640.00	AC	4	226G	8F-2R	54	5240	No
D-17	5309.00	2540.00	4170.00	5090.00	AC	6	262D	8F-2R	53	5570	No
D-19	5303.00	2740.00	4490.00	5480.00	AC	6	262G	8F-2R	72	6475	No
D-19	6078.00	2910.00	4780.00	5830.00	AC	6	262D	8F-2R	67	6570	No
D-21	7995.00	2950.00	4850.00	5920.00	AC	6	426D	8F-2R	156	9610	No
			1964								
D-10	2630.00	1820.00	2910.00	3550.00	AC	4	139G	4F-1R	29	3370	No
D-12	2720.00	1930.00	3090.00	3770.00	AC	4	139G	4F-1R	29	3420	No
D-15	3600.00	2080.00	3330.00	4060.00	AC	4	149G	8F-2R	46	4270	No
D-15	4200.00	2280.00	3650.00	4450.00	AC	4	149G	8F-2R	44	4270	No
D-17	4772.00	2400.00	3840.00	4690.00	AC	4	226G	8F-2R	54	5240	No
D-17	5667.00	2640.00	4220.00	5150.00	AC	6	262D	8F-2R	53	5570	No
D-21	7995.00	3080.00	4930.00	6020.00	AC	6	426D	8F-2R	156	9610	No
190	4905.00	2820.00	4510.00	5500.00	AC	6	265G	8F-2R	75.3	7040	No
190	5600.00	2990.00	4780.00	5830.00	AC	6	301D	8F-2R	77.2	7840	No
			1965								
D-10	2630.00	1890.00	2940.00	3590.00	AC	4	139G	4F-1R	29	3370	No
D-12	2720.00	2010.00	3140.00	3830.00	AC	4	139G	4F-1R	29	3420	No
D-15	3750.00	2180.00	3400.00	4150.00	AC	4	149G	8F-2R	46	4270	No
D-15	4350.00	2380.00	3710.00	4530.00	AC	4	175D	8F-2R	44	4270	No
D-17	4772.00	2530.00	3950.00	4820.00	AC	4	226G	8F-2R	54	5240	No
D-17	5667.00	2740.00	4270.00	5210.00	AC	6	262D	8F-2R	53	5570	No
D-21 II	8766.00	3200.00	4990.00	6090.00	AC	6T	426D	8F-2R	127.7	9610	No
190	5000.00	2940.00	4590.00	5600.00	AC	6	265G	8F-2R	75.3	7040	No
190	5700.00	3120.00	4880.00	5950.00	AC	6	301D	8F-2R	77.2	7840	No
190XT	5455.00	2870.00	4490.00	5480.00	AC	6	301G	8F-2R	90	7800	No
190XT	6150.00	3010.00	4700.00	5730.00	AC	6T	301D	8F-2R	93.6	9100	No
			1966								
D-10	2980.00	1970.00	3010.00	3670.00	AC	4	139G	4F-1R	29	3370	No
D-12	3070.00	2100.00	3200.00	3900.00	AC	4	139G	4F-1R	29	3420	No
D-15	4050.00	2290.00	3490.00	4260.00	AC	4	149G	8F-2R	46	4270	No
D-15	4635.00	2480.00	3780.00	4610.00	AC	4	175D	8F-2R	44	4270	No
D-17	4772.00	2630.00	4000.00	4880.00	AC	4	226G	8F-2R	54	5240	No
D-17	5667.00	2860.00	4350.00	5310.00	AC	6	262D	8F-2R	53	5570	No
D-21 II	8766.00	3280.00	5010.00	6110.00	AC	6T	426D	8F-2R	127.7	9610	No
190	5881.00	2950.00	4490.00	5480.00	AC	6	265G	8F-2R	75.3	7040	No
190	6671.00	3090.00	4710.00	5750.00	AC	6	301D	8F-2R	77.2	7840	No
190XT	6331.00	2960.00	4510.00	5500.00	AC	6	301G	8F-2R	90	7800	No
190XT	7121.00	3050.00	4640.00	5660.00	AC	6T	301D	8F-2R	93.6	9100	No
			1967								
D-10	3165.00	2080.00	3100.00	3780.00	AC	4	139G	4F-1R	29	3370	No
D-12	3260.00	2220.00	3300.00	4030.00	AC	4	149G	4F-1R	29	3420	No
D-15	4432.00	2380.00	3550.00	4330.00	AC	4	149G	8F-2R	46	4270	No
D-15	5035.00	2600.00	3860.00	4710.00	AC	4	175D	8F-2R	44	4270	No
D-17	5193.00	2750.00	4090.00	4990.00	AC	4	226G	8F-2R	54	5240	No
D-17	5975.00	3000.00	4460.00	5440.00	AC	6	262D	8F-2R	53	5570	No
D-21	9348.00	3440.00	5120.00	6250.00	AC	6	426D	8F-2R	156	9610	No
190	6051.00	3150.00	4690.00	5720.00	AC	6	265G	8F-2R	75.3	7040	No
190	6841.00	3260.00	4850.00	5920.00	AC	6	301D	8F-2R	77.2	7840	No
190XT	6624.00	3140.00	4670.00	5700.00	AC	6	301G	8F-2R	90	7800	No
190XT	7414.00	3210.00	4770.00	5820.00	AC	6T	301D	8F-2R	93.6	9100	No
			1968								
D-21	9785.00	3670.00	5340.00	6520.00	AC	6	426D	8F-2R	156	9610	No
170	5130.00	3200.00	4650.00	5670.00	AC	4	226G	8F-2R	54.1	5545	No
170	5655.00	3390.00	4930.00	6020.00	Perkins	4	236D	8F-2R	54.0	5775	No
180	6200.00	3510.00	5100.00	6220.00	Perkins	6	301D	8F-2R	64.0	6330	No
190	6356.00	3280.00	4770.00	5820.00	AC	6	265G	8F-2R	75.3	7040	No
190	7154.00	3420.00	4980.00	6080.00	AC	6	301D	8F-2R	77.2	7840	No
190XT	6960.00	3210.00	4670.00	5700.00	AC	6	301G	8F-2R	90	7800	No
190XT	7757.00	3370.00	4900.00	5980.00	AC	6T	301D	8F-2R	93.6	9100	No
			1969								
D-21	10385.00	3850.00	5480.00	6690.00	AC	6	426D	8F-2R	156	9610	No
170	5390.00	3370.00	4790.00	5840.00	AC	4	226G	8F-2R	54.1	5545	No

Allis-Chalmers (Cont.)

Model	Approx. Retail Price New	Fair	Good	Premium	Make	Engine No. Cyls.	Engine Displ. Cu.-In.	No. Speeds	P.T.O. H.P.	Approx. Shipping Wt.-Lbs.	Cab
1969 (Cont.)											
170	5942.00	**3540.00**	**5040.00**	**6150.00**	Perkins	4	236D	8F-2R	54.0	5775	No
180	6300.00	**3690.00**	**5250.00**	**6410.00**	AC	6	265G	8F-2R	65.1	6245	No
180	6891.00	**3800.00**	**5410.00**	**6600.00**	Perkins	6	301D	8F-2R	64.0	6330	No
190	6941.00	**3510.00**	**4990.00**	**6090.00**	AC	6	265G	8F-2R	75.3	7040	No
190	7740.00	**3740.00**	**5310.00**	**6480.00**	AC	6	301D	8F-2R	77.2	7840	No
190XT	7530.00	**3390.00**	**4820.00**	**5880.00**	AC	6	301G	8F-2R	90	7800	No
190XT	8390.00	**3570.00**	**5080.00**	**6200.00**	AC	6T	301D	8F-2R	93.6	9100	No
1970											
160	4645.00	**3170.00**	**4420.00**	**5390.00**	Perkins	3	153D	10F-2R	40.36	4505	No
170	5513.00	**3500.00**	**4860.00**	**5930.00**	AC	4	226G	8F-2R	54.12	5545	No
170	6719.00	**3630.00**	**5060.00**	**6170.00**	Perkins	4	236D	8F-2R	54.04	5775	No
175	7169.00	**3730.00**	**5180.00**	**6320.00**	Perkins	4	236D	8F-2R	62.47	5800	No
180	7002.00	**3820.00**	**5310.00**	**6480.00**	AC	6	301D	8F-2R	64.01	6335	No
180	7200.00	**3930.00**	**5470.00**	**6670.00**	AC	6	265G	8F-2R	65.16	6245	No
185	7842.00	**3980.00**	**5540.00**	**6760.00**	AC	6	301D	8F-2R	74.87	6535	No
190	7787.00	**4030.00**	**5610.00**	**6840.00**	AC	6	301D	8F-2R	77.20	7279	No
190XT	7577.00	**3530.00**	**4910.00**	**5990.00**	AC	6	301G	8F-2R	89.53	7545	No
190XT	8437.00	**3720.00**	**5170.00**	**6310.00**	AC	6T	301D	8F-2R	93.63	7738	No
210	9600.00	**3990.00**	**4830.00**	**5460.00**	AC	6T	426D	8F-2R	122.74	11650	C
220	11880.00	**4510.00**	**5470.00**	**6180.00**	AC	6T	426D	8F-2R	135.95	11985	C
1971											
160	4645.00	**3340.00**	**4540.00**	**5540.00**	Perkins	3	153D	10F-2R	40.36	4505	No
170	6167.00	**3700.00**	**5040.00**	**6150.00**	AC	4	226G	8F-2R	54.12	5545	No
170	6719.00	**3900.00**	**5310.00**	**6480.00**	Perkins	4	236D	8F-2R	54.00	5775	No
175	7455.00	**3970.00**	**5410.00**	**6600.00**	Perkins	4	236D	8F-2R	62.47	5800	No
180	7300.00	**4010.00**	**5460.00**	**6660.00**	AC	6	265G	8F-2R	65.16	6245	No
180	7422.00	**4110.00**	**5590.00**	**6820.00**	AC	6	301D	8F-2R	64.01	6335	No
185	7928.00	**4170.00**	**5680.00**	**6930.00**	AC	6	301D	8F-2R	74.87	6535	No
190	8255.00	**4230.00**	**5760.00**	**7030.00**	AC	6	301D	8F-2R	77.20	7279	No
190XT	8050.00	**3950.00**	**5380.00**	**6560.00**	AC	6	301G	8F-2R	89.53	7545	No
190XT	8700.00	**4140.00**	**5630.00**	**6870.00**	AC	6T	301D	8F-2R	93.63	7738	No
210	9950.00	**4490.00**	**5410.00**	**6110.00**	AC	6T	426D	8F-2R	122.74	11650	C
220	12500.00	**4880.00**	**5880.00**	**6640.00**	AC	6T	426D	8F-2R	135.95	11985	C
1972											
160	4807.00	**3650.00**	**4870.00**	**5890.00**	Perkins	3	153D	10F-2R	40.36	4505	No
170	6409.00	**3890.00**	**5180.00**	**6270.00**	AC	4	226G	8F-2R	54.12	5545	No
170	6904.00	**4080.00**	**5440.00**	**6580.00**	Perkins	4	236D	8F-2R	54.04	5775	No
175	7455.00	**4350.00**	**5800.00**	**7020.00**	Perkins	4	248D	8F-2R	62.00	5800	No
180	7500.00	**4400.00**	**5860.00**	**7090.00**	AC	6	265G	8F-2R	65.16	6245	No
180	7608.00	**4500.00**	**6000.00**	**7260.00**	AC	6	301D	8F-2R	64.01	6335	No
185	8115.00	**4620.00**	**6150.00**	**7440.00**	AC	6	301D	8F-2R	74.87	6535	No
190	8500.00	**4800.00**	**6400.00**	**7740.00**	AC	6	301D	8F-2R	77.20	7279	No
200	9455.00	**4560.00**	**5470.00**	**6180.00**	AC	6T	301D	8F-2R	93.00	10000	No
210	10200.00	**4800.00**	**5760.00**	**6510.00**	AC	6T	426D	8F-2R	122.74	11650	C
220	12950.00	**5080.00**	**6100.00**	**6890.00**	AC	6T	426D	8F-2R	135.95	11985	C
1973											
160	6018.00	**3990.00**	**5220.00**	**6260.00**	Perkins	3	153D	10F-2R	40.36	4505	No
170	6540.00	**4140.00**	**5410.00**	**6490.00**	AC	4	226G	8F-2R	54.12	5545	No
170	7387.00	**4450.00**	**5820.00**	**6980.00**	Perkins	4	236D	8F-2R	54.04	5775	No
175	7950.00	**4560.00**	**5950.00**	**7140.00**	AC	4	226G	8F-2R	60.88	5550	No
175	8065.00	**4690.00**	**6120.00**	**7340.00**	Perkins	4	248D	8F-2R	62.00	5800	No
180	7600.00	**4750.00**	**6210.00**	**7450.00**	AC	6	265G	8F-2R	65.16	6245	No
180	8875.00	**4890.00**	**6380.00**	**7660.00**	AC	6	301D	8F-2R	64.01	6335	No
185	9219.00	**5100.00**	**6660.00**	**7990.00**	AC	6	301D	8F-2R	74.87	6535	No
190	9310.00	**5300.00**	**6920.00**	**8300.00**	AC	6	301D	8F-2R	77.20	7279	No
200	10586.00	**5000.00**	**5980.00**	**6760.00**	AC	6T	301D	8F-2R	93.00	10000	No
210	11642.00	**5180.00**	**6200.00**	**7010.00**	AC	6T	426D	8F-2R	122.74	11650	C
220	13000.00	**5330.00**	**6370.00**	**7200.00**	AC	6T	426D	8F-2R	135.95	11985	C
7030	13164.00	**2240.00**	**3420.00**	**3830.00**	AC	6T	426D	20F-4R	130.98	12430	C
7050	15543.00	**2640.00**	**4040.00**	**4530.00**	AC	6TI	426D	20F-4R	156.49	14525	C
1974											
160	6018.00	**4260.00**	**5450.00**	**6490.00**	Perkins	3	153D	10F-2R	40.36	4505	No
175	9250.00	**4450.00**	**5700.00**	**6780.00**	AC	4	226G	8F-2R	60.88	5550	No
175	9845.00	**4620.00**	**5920.00**	**7050.00**	Perkins	4	248D	8F-2R	62.00	5800	No
185	11465.00	**5500.00**	**7040.00**	**8380.00**	AC	6	301D	8F-2R	74.84	6535	No
200	13583.00	**5710.00**	**6790.00**	**7610.00**	AC	6T	301D	8F-2R	93.00	10000	No
7030	17035.00	**4940.00**	**6640.00**	**7440.00**	AC	6T	426D	20F-4R	130.98	12430	C,H,A
7050	19550.00	**5370.00**	**7220.00**	**8090.00**	AC	6TI	426D	20F-4R	156.49	14525	C,H,A
1975											
175	9530.00	**4860.00**	**6100.00**	**7200.00**	AC	4	226G	8F-2R	60.88	5550	No
175	10140.00	**5050.00**	**6340.00**	**7480.00**	Perkins	4	248D	8F-2R	62.00	5800	No
185	11925.00	**6080.00**	**7630.00**	**9000.00**	AC	6	301D	8F-2R	74.87	6535	No
200	14125.00	**6070.00**	**7200.00**	**8060.00**	AC	6T	301D	8F-2R	93.00	10000	C
6040	6934.00	**2980.00**	**3540.00**	**3970.00**	Perkins	3	153D	10F-2R	40.00	4505	No
7000 PS	17402.00	**5220.00**	**6790.00**	**7540.00**	AC	6T	301D	12F-3R	106.44	9550	No
7040 PD	21565.00	**6150.00**	**8000.00**	**8880.00**	AC	6T	426D	20F-4R	136.49	11620	C,H
7040 PS	23925.00	**6750.00**	**8780.00**	**9750.00**	AC	6T	426D	12F-2R	136.30	11595	C,H
7060 PD	24416.00	**4640.00**	**6840.00**	**7660.00**	AC	6TI	426D	20F-4R	161.51	12229	C,H,A

Allis-Chalmers (Cont.)

1975 (Cont.)

Model	Approx. Retail Price New	Fair	Good	Premium	Engine Make	Engine No. Cyls.	Engine Displ. Cu.-In.	No. Speeds	P.T.O. H.P.	Approx. Shipping Wt.-Lbs.	Cab
7060 PS	25111.00	4770.00	7030.00	7870.00	AC	6TI	426D	12F-2R	161.42	12299	C,H,A
7080 PD	28846.00	5320.00	7840.00	8780.00	AC	6TI	426D	20F-4R	181.51	13489	C,H,A

PD--Power Director PS--Power Shift

1976

Model	Approx. Retail Price New	Fair	Good	Premium	Engine Make	Engine No. Cyls.	Engine Displ. Cu.-In.	No. Speeds	P.T.O. H.P.	Approx. Shipping Wt.-Lbs.	Cab
175	10280.00	5240.00	6580.00	7700.00	AC	4	226G	8F-2R	60.88	5550	No
175	10865.00	6120.00	7680.00	8990.00	Perkins	4	248D	8F-2R	62.00	5800	No
185	12715.00	6380.00	8000.00	9360.00	AC	6	301D	8F-2R	74.87	6535	No
5040	5810.00	2770.00	3280.00	3670.00	UTB	3	143D	6F-2R	40.00	3980	No
5040	6098.00	3080.00	3640.00	4080.00	UTB	3	143D	9F-3R	40.05	4060	No
7000 PS	19460.00	5700.00	7360.00	8170.00	AC	6T	301D	12F-3R	106.44	9550	No
7040 PD	23140.00	6820.00	8800.00	9770.00	AC	6T	426D	20F-4R	136.49	11620	C,H
7040 PS	25500.00	7440.00	9600.00	10660.00	AC	6T	426D	12F-2R	136.30	11595	C,H
7060 PD	25920.00	5180.00	7520.00	8420.00	AC	6TI	426D	20F-4R	161.51	12229	C,H,A
7060 PS	26920.00	5380.00	7810.00	8750.00	AC	6TI	426D	12F-2R	161.42	12299	C,H,A
7080 PD	31200.00	6000.00	8700.00	9740.00	AC	6TI	426D	20F-4R	181.51	13489	C,H,A
7580 4WD	38599.00	7220.00	10470.00	11730.00	AC	6TI	426D	20F-4R	186.35	20775	C,H,A

PD--Power Director PS--Power Shift

1977

Model	Approx. Retail Price New	Fair	Good	Premium	Engine Make	Engine No. Cyls.	Engine Displ. Cu.-In.	No. Speeds	P.T.O. H.P.	Approx. Shipping Wt.-Lbs.	Cab
175	12157.00	6200.00	7780.00	9030.00	Perkins	4	248D	8F-2R	62.00	5800	No
185	14370.00	7330.00	9200.00	10670.00	AC	6	301D	8F-2R	74.87	6535	No
5020	4520.00	2830.00	3550.00	4120.00	Toyosha	2	77D	8F-2R	21.79	1850	No
5040	6344.00	3170.00	3740.00	4150.00	UTB	3	143D	6F-2R	40.00	3980	No
5040	6632.00	3350.00	3950.00	4390.00	UTB	3	143D	9F-3R	40.05	4060	No
5050	9778.00	4400.00	5180.00	5750.00	Fiat	3	168D	8F-2R	51.00	4150	No
5050	10378.00	4670.00	5500.00	6110.00	Fiat	3	168D	12F-3R	51.46	4300	No
5050 4WD	12073.00	5430.00	6400.00	7100.00	Fiat	3	168D	8F-2R	51.00	4740	No
5050 4WD	12673.00	5700.00	6720.00	7460.00	Fiat	3	168D	12F-3R	51.00	4820	No
7000 PS	20684.00	6400.00	8200.00	9100.00	AC	6T	301D	12F-3R	106.44	9550	No
7040 PD	24550.00	7200.00	9230.00	10250.00	AC	6T	426D	20F-4R	136.49	11620	C,H
7040 PS	25880.00	7520.00	9640.00	10700.00	AC	6T	426D	12F-2R	136.30	11595	C,H
7060 PD	27506.00	5670.00	8100.00	9070.00	AC	6TI	426D	20F-4R	161.51	12229	C,H,A
7060 PS	28536.00	5990.00	8550.00	9580.00	AC	6TI	426D	12F-2R	161.42	12299	C,H,A
7080	33261.00	6510.00	9300.00	10420.00	AC	6TI	426D	20F-4R	181.51	13489	C,H,A
7580 4WD	40143.00	7380.00	10540.00	11810.00	AC	6TI	426D	20F-4R	186.35	20775	C,H,A

PD--Power Director PS--Power Shift

1978

Model	Approx. Retail Price New	Fair	Good	Premium	Engine Make	Engine No. Cyls.	Engine Displ. Cu.-In.	No. Speeds	P.T.O. H.P.	Approx. Shipping Wt.-Lbs.	Cab
175	13164.00	6220.00	7810.00	8980.00	Perkins	4	248D	8F-2R	62.00	5800	No
185	15362.00	6890.00	8640.00	9940.00	AC	6	301D	8F-2R	74.87	6535	No
5020	4850.00	2980.00	3740.00	4300.00	Toyosha	2	77D	8F-2R	21.79	1850	No
5040	6900.00	3400.00	4000.00	4400.00	UTB	3	143D	9F-3R	40.05	4060	No
5050	11784.00	5420.00	6360.00	7000.00	Fiat	3	168D	12F-3R	51.46	4300	No
5050 4WD	15044.00	6920.00	8120.00	8930.00	Fiat	3	168D	12F-3R	51.00	4820	No
7000 PS	24404.00	7590.00	9660.00	10630.00	AC	6T	301D	12F-3R	106.44	9550	C,H
7020 PD	27325.00	8350.00	10630.00	11690.00	AC	6TI	301D	20F-4R	123.85	11570	C,H
7020 PS	28708.00	8810.00	11210.00	12330.00	AC	6TI	301D	12F-2R	123.79	11770	C,H
7045 PD	30213.00	9240.00	11760.00	12940.00	AC	6T	426D	20F-4R	146.18	11700	C,H
7045 PS	31359.00	9570.00	12180.00	13400.00	AC	6T	426D	12F-2R	146.88	12065	C,H
7060 PD	33118.00	6820.00	9610.00	10760.00	AC	6TI	426D	20F-4R	161.51	12229	C,H,A
7060 PS	34270.00	7040.00	9920.00	11110.00	AC	6TI	426D	12F-2R	161.42	12299	C,H,A
7080	38010.00	7790.00	10970.00	12290.00	AC	6TI	426D	20F-4R	181.51	13489	C,H,A
7580 4WD	45622.00	8910.00	12560.00	14070.00	AC	6TI	426D	20F-4R	186.35	20775	C,H,A
8550 4WD	58650.00	9470.00	13350.00	14950.00	AC	6T	731D	20F-4R	253.88	26400	C,H,A

PD--Power Director PS--Power Shift

1979

Model	Approx. Retail Price New	Fair	Good	Premium	Engine Make	Engine No. Cyls.	Engine Displ. Cu.-In.	No. Speeds	P.T.O. H.P.	Approx. Shipping Wt.-Lbs.	Cab
175	14700.00	6500.00	7880.00	8980.00	Perkins	4	248D	8F-2R	62.00	5800	No
185	17132.00	7330.00	8880.00	10120.00	AC	6	301D	8F-2R	74.87	6535	No
5020	5760.00	3520.00	4260.00	4860.00	Toyosha	2	77D	12F-3R	21.79	1850	No
5020 4WD	6395.00	3800.00	4600.00	5240.00	Toyosha	2	77D	12F-3R	21.00	1960	No
5030	6395.00	3850.00	4660.00	5310.00	Toyosha	2	90D	12F-3R	26.42	2280	No
5040	8450.00	4210.00	4920.00	5360.00	UTB	3	143D	12F-3R	40.00	4060	No
5050	13290.00	6250.00	7310.00	7970.00	Fiat	3	168D	12F-3R	51.46	4300	No
5050 4WD	16965.00	7970.00	9330.00	10170.00	Fiat	3	168D	12F-3R	51.00	4820	No
7000 PS	24860.00	7750.00	9800.00	10680.00	AC	6T	301D	12F-3R	106.44	9550	C,H
7020 PD	31186.00	9210.00	11650.00	12700.00	AC	6TI	301D	20F-4R	123.85	11570	C,H
7020 PS	32732.00	9760.00	12340.00	13450.00	AC	6TI	301D	12F-2R	123.79	11770	C,H
7045 PD	33810.00	10030.00	12690.00	13830.00	AC	6T	426D	20F-4R	146.18	11700	C,H
7045 PS	35090.00	10540.00	13330.00	14530.00	AC	6T	426D	12F-2R	146.88	12065	C,H
7060 PD	36460.00	7590.00	10560.00	11830.00	AC	6TI	426D	20F-4R	161.51	12229	C,H,A
7060 PS	37730.00	7820.00	10880.00	12190.00	AC	6TI	426D	12F-2R	161.42	12299	C,H,A
7080 PD	41690.00	8300.00	11550.00	12940.00	AC	6TI	426D	20F-4R	181.51	13489	C,H,A
7580 4WD	50680.00	10510.00	14620.00	16370.00	AC	6TI	426D	20F-4R	186.35	20775	C,H,A
8550 4WD	65275.00	10410.00	14490.00	16230.00	AC	6T	731D	20F-4R	253.88	26400	C,H,A

PD--Power Director PS--Power Shift

1980

Model	Approx. Retail Price New	Fair	Good	Premium	Engine Make	Engine No. Cyls.	Engine Displ. Cu.-In.	No. Speeds	P.T.O. H.P.	Approx. Shipping Wt.-Lbs.	Cab
175	15894.00	6890.00	8060.00	9110.00	Perkins	4	248D	8F-2R	62.47	5800	No
185	18341.00	7950.00	9300.00	10510.00	AC	6	301D	8F-2R	74.87	6535	No
5020	6655.00	3760.00	4400.00	4970.00	Toyosha	2	77D	12F-3R	21.79	1850	No
5020 4WD	6895.00	4030.00	4710.00	5320.00	Toyosha	2	77D	12F-3R	21.00	1960	No
5030	7446.00	3950.00	4620.00	5220.00	Toyosha	2	90D	12F-3R	26.42	2280	No

Allis-Chalmers (Cont.)

1980 (Cont.)

Model	Approx. Retail Price New	Estimated Average Value Less Repairs: Fair	Good	Premium	Engine Make	No. Cyls.	Displ. Cu.-In.	No. Speeds	P.T.O. H.P.	Approx. Shipping Wt.-Lbs.	Cab
5040	8450.00	4300.00	5010.00	5410.00	UTB	3	143D	12F-3R	40.00	4060	No
5050	14087.00	6760.00	7890.00	8520.00	Fiat	3	168D	12F-3R	51.46	4300	No
5050 4WD	17983.00	8630.00	10070.00	10880.00	Fiat	3	168D	12F-3R	51.00	4820	No
6060	16200.00	6540.00	7900.00	8530.00	AC	4T	200D	8F-2R	63.83	5700	No
6060 4WD	20400.00	8340.00	10090.00	10900.00	AC	4T	200D	8F-2R	63.00	6500	No
6080	20750.00	8490.00	10270.00	11090.00	AC	4TI	200D	12F-3R	83.66	6920	No
7010 PD	29230.00	9630.00	12100.00	13190.00	AC	6T	301D	16F-4R	106.00	10260	C,H
7010 PD	31234.00	10220.00	12850.00	14010.00	AC	6T	301D	20F-4R	106.53	10264	C,H
7010 PS	32908.00	10780.00	13550.00	14770.00	AC	6T	301D	12F-2R	106.72	10375	C,H
7020 PD	34832.00	11410.00	14340.00	15630.00	AC	6TI	301D	20F-4R	123.85	11570	C,H
7020 PS	36559.00	12080.00	15180.00	16550.00	AC	6TI	301D	12F-2R	123.79	11770	C,H
7045 PD	38317.00	12250.00	15400.00	16790.00	AC	6T	426D	20F-4R	146.18	11700	C,H
7045 PS	39768.00	12600.00	15840.00	17270.00	AC	6T	426D	12F-2R	146.88	12065	C,H
7060 PD	41122.00	9380.00	12900.00	14450.00	AC	6TI	426D	20F-4R	161.51	12229	C,H,A
7060 PS	42554.00	9720.00	13370.00	14970.00	AC	6TI	426D	12F-2R	161.42	12299	C,H,A
7080	47523.00	10440.00	14360.00	16080.00	AC	6TI	426D	20F-4R	181.51	13489	C,H,A
7580 4WD	56605.00	12120.00	16670.00	18670.00	AC	6TI	426D	20F-4R	186.35	20775	C,H,A
8550 4WD	79659.00	12240.00	16830.00	18850.00	AC	6T	731D	20F-4R	253.88	26400	C,H,A

PD--Power Director PS--Power Shift

1981

Model	Approx. Retail Price New	Estimated Average Value Less Repairs: Fair	Good	Premium	Engine Make	No. Cyls.	Displ. Cu.-In.	No. Speeds	P.T.O. H.P.	Approx. Shipping Wt.-Lbs.	Cab
185	18891.00	8640.00	10080.00	11290.00	AC	6	301D	8F-2R	78.87	6535	No
5020	6855.00	4240.00	4950.00	5540.00	Toyosha	2	77D	12F-3R	21.79	1850	No
5020 4WD	7599.00	4590.00	5360.00	6000.00	Toyosha	2	77D	12F-3R	21.00	1960	No
5030	7669.00	4690.00	5470.00	6130.00	Toyosha	2	90D	12F-3R	26.42	2280	No
5045	12560.00	5530.00	6660.00	7190.00	Fiat	3	158D	12F-3R	44.00	4080	No
5050	16131.00	7100.00	8550.00	9230.00	Fiat	3	168D	12F-3R	51.46	4300	No
5050 4WD	20027.00	8810.00	10610.00	11460.00	Fiat	3	168D	12F-3R	51.00	4820	No
6060	18362.00	7080.00	8530.00	9210.00	AC	4T	200D	8F-2R	63.83	5700	No
6060 4WD	22936.00	8890.00	10710.00	11570.00	AC	4T	200D	8F-2R	63.00	6500	No
6080	23059.00	9240.00	11130.00	12020.00	AC	4TI	200D	12F-3R	83.66	6920	No
6080 4WD	27851.00	11220.00	13520.00	14600.00	AC	4TI	200D	12F-3R	83.00	7600	No
7010 HC PD	41632.00	9410.00	12800.00	14340.00	AC	6T	301D	20F-4R	106.00	11264	C,H
7010 HC PS	43507.00	9880.00	13430.00	15040.00	AC	6T	301D	12F-2R	106.00	11375	C,H
7010 PD	35311.00	11880.00	14850.00	16190.00	AC	6T	301D	20F-4R	106.53	10264	C,H
7010 PS	37186.00	12600.00	15750.00	17170.00	AC	6T	301D	12F-2R	106.72	10375	C,H
7020 HC PD	45564.00	9890.00	13450.00	15060.00	AC	6TI	301D	20F-4R	123.00	12570	C,H
7020 HC PS	47438.00	10360.00	14090.00	15780.00	AC	6TI	301D	12F-2R	123.00	12770	C,H
7020 PD	39378.00	8750.00	11900.00	13330.00	AC	6TI	301D	20F-4R	123.85	11570	C,H
7020 PS	41252.00	9430.00	12820.00	14360.00	AC	6TI	301D	12F-2R	123.79	11770	C,H
7045 HC PD	49736.00	9180.00	12490.00	13990.00	AC	6T	426D	20F-4R	146.00	12700	C,H
7045 HC PS	51343.00	9590.00	13040.00	14610.00	AC	6T	426D	12F-2R	146.00	13065	C,H
7045 PD	43328.00	9800.00	13330.00	14930.00	AC	6T	426D	20F-4R	146.18	11700	C,H
7045 PS	44935.00	10500.00	14280.00	15990.00	AC	6T	426D	12F-2R	146.88	12065	C,H
7060 HC PD	54092.00	12520.00	17030.00	19070.00	AC	6TI	426D	20F-4R	161.00	13229	C,H,A
7060 HC PS	55696.00	12920.00	17580.00	19690.00	AC	6TI	426D	12F-2R	161.00	13299	C,H,A
7060 PD	47092.00	10500.00	14280.00	15990.00	AC	6TI	426D	20F-4R	161.51	12229	C,H,A
7060 PS	48696.00	11150.00	15160.00	16980.00	AC	6TI	426D	12F-2R	161.42	12299	C,H,A
7080	54561.00	12130.00	16490.00	18470.00	AC	6TI	426D	20F-4R	181.51	13484	C,H,A
7580 4WD	63084.00	12750.00	17340.00	19420.00	AC	6TI	426D	20F-4R	186.35	20775	C,H,A
7580 4WD w/3 Pt.	67179.00	13750.00	18700.00	20940.00	AC	6TI	426D	20F-4R	186.35	21775	C,H,A
8550 4WD	79659.00	13250.00	18020.00	20180.00	AC	6T	731D	20F-4R	253.88	26400	C,H,A
8550 4WD w/3 Pt.	84552.00	14250.00	19380.00	21710.00	AC	6T	731D	20F-4R	253.88	27400	C,H,A

PD--Power Director PS--Power Shift HC--High Clearance

1982

Model	Approx. Retail Price New	Estimated Average Value Less Repairs: Fair	Good	Premium	Engine Make	No. Cyls.	Displ. Cu.-In.	No. Speeds	P.T.O. H.P.	Approx. Shipping Wt.-Lbs.	Cab
4W-220 4WD	70220.00	13050.00	17570.00	19680.00	AC	6TI	426D	20F-4R	180.00	21475	C,H,A
4W-220 4WD w/3 Pt.	74427.00	14040.00	18900.00	21170.00	AC	6TI	426D	20F-4R	180.00	22475	C,H,A
4W-305 4WD	87455.00	14940.00	20110.00	22520.00	AC	6T	731D	20F-4R	250.00	27100	C,H,A
4W-305 4WD w/3 Pt.	92500.00	16120.00	21700.00	24300.00	AC	6T	731D	20F-4R	250.00	28100	C,H,A
5015	6149.00	3930.00	4580.00	5130.00	Toyosha	3	61D	9F-3R	15.00	1278	No
5015 4WD	6799.00	4240.00	4930.00	5520.00	Toyosha	3	61D	9F-3R	15.00	1448	No
5020	7560.00	4710.00	5480.00	6140.00	Toyosha	2	77D	12F-3R	21.79	1850	No
5020 4WD	8380.00	5160.00	6000.00	6720.00	Toyosha	2	77D	12F-3R	21.00	1960	No
5030	8395.00	5120.00	5950.00	6660.00	Toyosha	2	90D	12F-3R	26.42	2280	No
5045	12558.00	6280.00	7280.00	7860.00	Fiat	3	158D	8F-2R	44.00	4000	No
5050	16358.00	8180.00	9490.00	10250.00	Fiat	3	168D	12F-3R	51.46	4300	No
5050 4WD	20275.00	10140.00	11760.00	12700.00	Fiat	3	168D	12F-3R	51.00	4820	No
6060	20037.00	8100.00	9720.00	10500.00	AC	4T	200D	8F-2R	63.83	5700	No
6060 4WD	24840.00	10080.00	12100.00	13070.00	AC	4T	200D	8F-2R	63.00	6500	No
6080	30338.00	12650.00	15170.00	16380.00	AC	4TI	200D	12F-3R	83.66	6920	C,H
6080 4WD	35815.00	14940.00	17930.00	19360.00	AC	4TI	200D	12F-3R	83.00	7600	C,H
6140	12925.00	5820.00	6980.00	7540.00	Toyosha	3	142D	10F-2R	41.08	4000	No
6140 4WD	16275.00	7320.00	8790.00	9490.00	Toyosha	3	142D	10F-2R	40.00	4000	No
8010 PD	40096.00	9620.00	12950.00	14500.00	AC	6T	301D	20F-4R	109.00	10820	C,H,A
8010 PD 4WD	46696.00	10920.00	14700.00	16460.00	AC	6T	301D	20F-4R	109.00	12820	C,H,A
8010 PS	41326.00	9880.00	13300.00	14900.00	AC	6T	301D	12F-2R	109.55	10950	C,H,A
8010 PS 4WD	48226.00	11440.00	15400.00	17250.00	AC	6T	301D	12F-2R	109.00	12950	C,H,A
8030 PD	44676.00	12740.00	17150.00	19210.00	AC	6T	426D	20F-4R	134.00	11450	C,H,A
8030 PD 4WD	51576.00	12090.00	16280.00	18230.00	AC	6T	426D	20F-4R	134.00	13450	C,H,A
8030 PS	46256.00	10710.00	14420.00	16150.00	AC	6T	426D	12F-2R	134.42	11700	C,H,A
8030 PS 4WD	53156.00	12250.00	16490.00	18470.00	AC	6T	426D	12F-2R	134.00	13700	C,H,A
8050 PD	49415.00	11280.00	15190.00	17010.00	AC	6TI	426D	20F-4R	155.00	11530	C,H,A
8050 PD 4WD	56315.00	13000.00	17500.00	19600.00	AC	6TI	426D	20F-4R	155.00	13530	C,H,A

Allis-Chalmers (Cont.)

1982 (Cont.)

Model	Approx. Retail Price New	Fair	Good	Premium	Make	No. Cyls.	Displ. Cu.-In.	No. Speeds	P.T.O. H.P.	Approx. Shipping Wt.-Lbs.	Cab
8050 PS	51065.00	**12010.00**	**16170.00**	**18110.00**	AC	6TI	426D	12F-2R	155.15	11600	C,H,A
8050 PS 4WD	57965.00	**13360.00**	**17990.00**	**20150.00**	AC	6TI	426D	12F-2R	155.00	13600	C,H,A
8070 PD	51890.00	**11830.00**	**15930.00**	**17840.00**	AC	6TI	426D	20F-4R	171.00	12220	C,H,A
8070 PS	53540.00	**12220.00**	**16450.00**	**18420.00**	AC	6TI	426D	12F-2R	171.44	12400	C,H,A

PD--Power Director PS--Power Shift

1983

Model	Approx. Retail Price New	Fair	Good	Premium	Make	No. Cyls.	Displ. Cu.-In.	No. Speeds	P.T.O. H.P.	Approx. Shipping Wt.-Lbs.	Cab
4W-220 4WD	70220.00	**13560.00**	**18080.00**	**20250.00**	AC	6TI	426D	20F-4R	180.00	21475	C,H,A
4W-220 4WD w/3 Pt.	74427.00	**14700.00**	**19590.00**	**21940.00**	AC	6TI	426D	20F-4R	180.00	22475	C,H,A
4W-305 4WD	88195.00	**15710.00**	**20950.00**	**23460.00**	AC	6T	731D	20F-4R	250.00	27100	C,H,A
4W-305 4WD w/3 Pt.	93240.00	**17080.00**	**22770.00**	**25500.00**	AC	6T	731D	20F-4R	250.00	28100	C,H,A
5015	6424.00	**4160.00**	**4830.00**	**5410.00**	Toyosha	3	61D	9F-3R	15.00	1278	No
5015 4WD	7024.00	**4490.00**	**5220.00**	**5850.00**	Toyosha	3	61D	9F-3R	15.00	1448	No
5020	8075.00	**5080.00**	**5900.00**	**6610.00**	Toyosha	2	77D	12F-3R	21.79	1850	No
5020 4WD	8895.00	**5540.00**	**6430.00**	**7200.00**	Toyosha	2	77D	12F-3R	21.00	1960	No
5030	8910.00	**5550.00**	**6440.00**	**7210.00**	Toyosha	2	90D	12F-3R	26.42	2280	No
5050	16358.00	**7530.00**	**9000.00**	**9720.00**	Fiat	3	168D	12F-3R	51.46	4300	No
5050 4WD	20275.00	**9330.00**	**11150.00**	**12040.00**	Fiat	3	168D	12F-3R	51.00	4820	No
6060	21039.00	**8740.00**	**10450.00**	**11290.00**	AC	4T	200D	8F-2R	63.83	5700	No
6060 4WD	25842.00	**10760.00**	**12870.00**	**13900.00**	AC	4T	200D	8F-2R	63.00	6500	No
6060 4WD w/Cab	30822.00	**13060.00**	**15620.00**	**16870.00**	AC	4T	200D	8F-2R	63.00	7650	C,H,A
6060 w/Cab	26019.00	**11040.00**	**13200.00**	**14260.00**	AC	4T	200D	8F-2R	63.83	6850	C,H,A
6080	26980.00	**11320.00**	**13530.00**	**14610.00**	AC	4TI	200D	12F-3R	83.66	6920	No
6080 4WD	32457.00	**13960.00**	**16690.00**	**18030.00**	AC	4TI	200D	12F-3R	83.00	7600	No
6080 4WD w/Cab	37857.00	**16330.00**	**19530.00**	**21090.00**	AC	4TI	200D	12F-3R	83.00	8750	C,H,A
6080 w/Cab	32380.00	**13940.00**	**16670.00**	**18000.00**	AC	4TI	200D	12F-3R	83.66	8070	C,H,A
6140	13570.00	**6240.00**	**7460.00**	**8060.00**	Toyosha	3	142D	10F-2R	41.08	4000	No
6140 4WD	16820.00	**7740.00**	**9250.00**	**9990.00**	Toyosha	3	142D	10F-2R	41.00	4400	No
8010 PD	41788.00	**10720.00**	**14290.00**	**16010.00**	AC	6T	301D	20F-4R	109.00	10820	C,H,A
8010 PD 4WD	49465.00	**12420.00**	**16560.00**	**18550.00**	AC	6T	301D	20F-4R	109.00	12820	C,H,A
8010 PS	43300.00	**10880.00**	**14510.00**	**16250.00**	AC	6T	301D	12F-2R	109.55	10950	C,H,A
8010 PS 4WD	50977.00	**18050.00**	**22330.00**	**24120.00**	AC	6T	301D	12F-2R	109.00	12950	C,H,A
8030 PD	46908.00	**11390.00**	**15190.00**	**17010.00**	AC	6T	426D	20F-4R	134.00	11450	C,H,A
8030 PD 4WD	53818.00	**13420.00**	**17890.00**	**20040.00**	AC	6T	426D	20F-4R	134.00	13450	C,H,A
8030 PS	48470.00	**11880.00**	**15840.00**	**17740.00**	AC	6T	426D	12F-2R	134.42	11700	C,H,A
8030 PS 4WD	55370.00	**12960.00**	**17280.00**	**19350.00**	AC	6T	426D	12F-2R	134.00	13700	C,H,A
8050 PD	51885.00	**12420.00**	**16560.00**	**18550.00**	AC	6TI	426D	20F-4R	155.00	11530	C,H,A
8050 PD 4WD	58785.00	**13500.00**	**18000.00**	**20160.00**	AC	6TI	426D	20F-4R	155.00	13530	C,H,A
8050 PS	53535.00	**12690.00**	**16920.00**	**18950.00**	AC	6TI	426D	12F-2R	155.15	11600	C,H,A
8050 PS 4WD	60435.00	**14040.00**	**18720.00**	**20970.00**	AC	6TI	426D	12F-2R	155.00	13600	C,H,A
8070 PD	53600.00	**12850.00**	**17140.00**	**19200.00**	AC	6TI	426D	20F-4R	171.00	12220	C,H,A
8070 PS	55250.00	**12960.00**	**17280.00**	**19350.00**	AC	6TI	426D	12F-2R	171.44	12400	C,H,A

PD--Power Director PS--Power Shift

1984

Model	Approx. Retail Price New	Fair	Good	Premium	Make	No. Cyls.	Displ. Cu.-In.	No. Speeds	P.T.O. H.P.	Approx. Shipping Wt.-Lbs.	Cab
4W-220 4WD	71625.00	**14280.00**	**18870.00**	**21130.00**	AC	6TI	426D	20F-4R	180.00	21475	C,H,A
4W-220 4WD w/3 Pt.	75916.00	**15400.00**	**20350.00**	**22790.00**	AC	6TI	426D	20F-4R	180.00	22475	C,H,A
4W-305 4WD	90080.00	**16800.00**	**22200.00**	**24860.00**	AC	6T	731D	20F-4R	250.00	27100	C,H,A
4W-305 4WD w/3 Pt.	95877.00	**18200.00**	**24050.00**	**26940.00**	AC	6T	731D	20F-4R	250.00	28100	C,H,A
5015	6424.00	**4230.00**	**4900.00**	**5490.00**	Toyosha	3	61D	9F-3R	15.00	1278	No
5015 4WD	7024.00	**4570.00**	**5300.00**	**5940.00**	Toyosha	3	61D	9F-3R	15.00	1448	No
5020	8075.00	**5170.00**	**5990.00**	**6710.00**	Toyosha	2	77D	12F-3R	21.79	1850	No
5020 4WD	8895.00	**5640.00**	**6530.00**	**7310.00**	Toyosha	2	77D	12F-3R	21.00	1960	No
5030	8910.00	**5650.00**	**6540.00**	**7330.00**	Toyosha	2	90D	12F-3R	26.42	2280	No
5050	16675.00	**7840.00**	**9340.00**	**10090.00**	Fiat	3	168D	8F-2R	51.00	4280	No
5050 4WD	19667.00	**9240.00**	**11010.00**	**11890.00**	Fiat	3	168D	8F-2R	51.46	4780	No
5050 4WD	20275.00	**9530.00**	**11350.00**	**12260.00**	Fiat	3	168D	12F-3R	51.00	4820	No
6060	21460.00	**9150.00**	**10900.00**	**11770.00**	AC	4T	200D	8F-2R	63.83	5700	No
6060 4WD	25842.00	**11020.00**	**13130.00**	**14180.00**	AC	4T	200D	8F-2R	63.00	6500	No
6060 4WD w/Cab	30822.00	**13300.00**	**15850.00**	**17120.00**	AC	4T	200D	8F-2R	63.00	7650	C,H,A
6060 w/Cab	26019.00	**11280.00**	**13440.00**	**14520.00**	AC	4T	200D	8F-2R	63.83	6850	C,H,A
6080	27520.00	**11840.00**	**14110.00**	**15240.00**	AC	4TI	200D	12F-3R	83.66	7170	No
6080 4WD	33000.00	**14100.00**	**16800.00**	**18140.00**	AC	4TI	200D	12F-3R	83.00	7600	No
6080 4WD w/Cab	38410.00	**16920.00**	**20160.00**	**21770.00**	AC	4TI	200D	12F-3R	83.00	8750	C,H,A
6080 w/Cab	32920.00	**14240.00**	**16970.00**	**18330.00**	AC	4TI	200D	12F-3R	83.66	8070	C,H,A
6140	14460.00	**6800.00**	**8100.00**	**8750.00**	Toyosha	3	142D	10F-2R	41.08	4228	No
6140 4WD	17440.00	**8200.00**	**9770.00**	**10550.00**	Toyosha	3	142D	10F-2R	41.00	4628	No
8010 PD	42626.00	**11200.00**	**14800.00**	**16580.00**	AC	6T	301D	20F-4R	109.00	11857	C,H,A
8010 PD 4WD	49526.00	**12880.00**	**17020.00**	**19060.00**	AC	6T	301D	20F-4R	109.00	13457	C,H,A
8010 PS	44130.00	**11760.00**	**15540.00**	**17410.00**	AC	6T	301D	12F-2R	109.55	12000	C,H,A
8010 PS 4WD	51030.00	**13440.00**	**17760.00**	**19890.00**	AC	6T	301D	12F-2R	109.00	13600	C,H,A
8030 PD	47846.00	**12540.00**	**16580.00**	**18570.00**	AC	6T	426D	20F-4R	134.00	12457	C,H,A
8030 PD 4WD	54746.00	**14340.00**	**18940.00**	**21210.00**	AC	6T	426D	20F-4R	134.00	14057	C,H,A
8030 PS	49400.00	**12990.00**	**17170.00**	**19230.00**	AC	6T	426D	12F-2R	134.42	12600	C,H,A
8030 PS 4WD	56300.00	**14560.00**	**19240.00**	**21550.00**	AC	6T	426D	12F-2R	134.00	14200	C,H,A
8050 PD	52925.00	**13440.00**	**17760.00**	**19890.00**	AC	6TI	426D	20F-4R	155.00	12750	C,H,A
8050 PD 4WD	59825.00	**15120.00**	**19980.00**	**22380.00**	AC	6TI	426D	20F-4R	155.00	14350	C,H,A
8050 PS	54525.00	**13720.00**	**18130.00**	**20310.00**	AC	6TI	426D	12F-2R	155.15	12900	C,H,A
8050 PS 4WD	61475.00	**15400.00**	**20350.00**	**22790.00**	AC	6TI	426D	12F-2R	155.00	14500	C,H,A
8070 PD	54675.00	**13610.00**	**17980.00**	**20140.00**	AC	6TI	426D	20F-4R	171.00	13750	C,H,A
8070 PD 4WD	61575.00	**14840.00**	**19610.00**	**21960.00**	AC	6TI	426D	20F-4R	171.00	15350	C,H,A
8070 PS	56325.00	**13800.00**	**18240.00**	**20430.00**	AC	6TI	426D	12F-2R	171.44	13900	C,H,A
8070 PS 4WD	63225.00	**15400.00**	**20350.00**	**22790.00**	AC	6TI	426D	12F-2R	171.00	15500	C,H,A

HC--High Clearance PD--Power Director PS--Power Shift

Allis-Chalmers (Cont.)

Model	Approx. Retail Price New	Estimated Average Value Less Repairs: Fair	Good	Premium	Engine: Make	No. Cyls.	Displ. Cu.-In.	No. Speeds	P.T.O. H.P.	Approx. Shipping Wt.-Lbs.	Cab
1985											
4W-220 4WD	74490.00	16200.00	20520.00	22780.00	AC	6TI	426D	20F-4R	180.00	18064	C,H,A
4W-220 4WD w/3 Pt.	78781.00	17400.00	22040.00	24460.00	AC	6TI	426D	20F-4R	180.00	22475	C,H,A
4W-305 4WD	93685.00	18900.00	23940.00	26570.00	AC	6T	731D	20F-4R	250.00	27100	C,H,A
4W-305 4WD w/3 Pt.	98526.00	20400.00	25840.00	28680.00	AC	6T	731D	20F-4R	250.00	28100	C,H,A
5015	6550.00	4380.00	5060.00	5620.00	Toyosha	3	61D	9F-3R	15.00	1278	No
5015 4WD	7150.00	4730.00	5460.00	6060.00	Toyosha	3	61D	9F-3R	15.00	1448	No
5020	8280.00	5380.00	6220.00	6900.00	Toyosha	2	77D	12F-3R	21.79	1850	No
5020 4WD	9200.00	5920.00	6830.00	7580.00	Toyosha	2	77D	12F-3R	21.00	1960	No
5030	9230.00	5950.00	6870.00	7630.00	Toyosha	2	90D	12F-3R	26.42	2280	No
6070	24225.00	10670.00	12670.00	13680.00	AC	4T	200D	12F-3R	70.78	5900	No
6070 4WD	29225.00	12960.00	15390.00	16620.00	AC	4T	200D	12F-3R	70.00	6700	No
6070 4WD w/Cab	34665.00	15650.00	18580.00	20070.00	AC	4T	200D	12F-3R	70.00	7800	C,H,A
6070 w/Cab	29665.00	13250.00	15730.00	16990.00	AC	4T	200D	12F-3R	70.78	7050	C,H,A
6080	28625.00	12780.00	15180.00	16390.00	AC	4TI	200D	12F-3R	83.66	7170	No
6080 4WD	34100.00	15410.00	18300.00	19760.00	AC	4TI	200D	12F-3R	83.00	7600	No
6080 4WD w/Cab	38975.00	17470.00	20750.00	22410.00	AC	4TI	200D	12F-3R	83.00	8750	C,H,A
6080 w/Cab	33500.00	14880.00	17670.00	19080.00	AC	4TI	200D	12F-3R	83.66	8070	C,H,A
6140	15895.00	7630.00	9060.00	9790.00	Toyosha	3	142D	10F-2R	41.08	4228	No
6140 4WD	19545.00	9380.00	11140.00	12030.00	Toyosha	3	142D	10F-2R	41.00	4628	No
8010 PD	44835.00	12300.00	15580.00	17290.00	AC	6T	301D	20F-4R	109.00	11850	C,H,A
8010 PD 4WD	52485.00	14700.00	18620.00	20670.00	AC	6T	301D	20F-4R	109.00	13450	C,H,A
8010 PS	46320.00	12900.00	16340.00	18140.00	AC	6T	301D	12F-2R	109.55	12000	C,H,A
8010 PS 4WD	53970.00	15150.00	19190.00	21300.00	AC	6T	301D	12F-2R	109.00	13600	C,H,A
8030 PD	50875.00	14250.00	18050.00	20040.00	AC	6T	426D	20F-4R	134.00	12457	C,H,A
8030 PD 4WD	58225.00	16200.00	20520.00	22780.00	AC	6T	426D	20F-4R	134.00	14057	C,H,A
8030 PS	52410.00	14100.00	17860.00	19830.00	AC	6T	426D	12F-2R	134.42	12600	C,H,A
8030 PS 4WD	60060.00	16500.00	20900.00	23200.00	AC	6T	426D	12F-2R	134.00	14200	C,H,A
8050 PD	56710.00	15510.00	19650.00	21810.00	AC	6TI	426D	20F-4R	155.00	12750	C,H,A
8050 PD 4WD	64360.00	17100.00	21660.00	24040.00	AC	6TI	426D	20F-4R	155.00	14350	C,H,A
8050 PS	58360.00	15710.00	19900.00	22090.00	AC	6TI	426D	12F-3R	155.15	12900	C,H,A
8050 PS 4WD	66010.00	17700.00	22420.00	24890.00	AC	6TI	426D	12F-3R	155.00	14500	C,H,A
8070 PD	58580.00	15600.00	19760.00	21930.00	AC	6TI	426D	20F-4R	171.00	13750	C,H,A
8070 PD 4WD	66230.00	16860.00	21360.00	23710.00	AC	6TI	426D	20F-4R	171.00	15350	C,H,A
8070 PS	60230.00	15300.00	19380.00	21510.00	AC	6TI	426D	12F-2R	171.44	13900	C,H,A
8070 PS 4WD	67880.00	17340.00	21960.00	24380.00	AC	6TI	426D	12F-2R	171.00	15500	C,H,A

HC--High Clearance PD--Power Director PS--Power Shift For later models see DEUTZ-ALLIS and AGCO ALLIS.

Avery

Model	Approx. Retail Price New	Fair	Good	Premium	Make	No. Cyls.	Displ. Cu.-In.	No. Speeds	P.T.O. H.P.	Approx. Shipping Wt.-Lbs.	Cab
1939											
R	......	610.00	1440.00	1830.00		4	165G	4F-1R		2805	No
RO-TRAK	......	700.00	1660.00	2110.00		6	165G	4F-1R		2805	No
1940											
R	......	620.00	1470.00	1870.00		4	165G	4F-1R		2805	No
1941											
R	......	640.00	1520.00	1930.00		4	165G	4F-1R		2805	No
1942											
R	......	660.00	1570.00	1990.00		4	165G	4F-1R		2805	No
1943											
R	......	680.00	1610.00	2030.00		4	165G	4F-1R		2805	No
1944											
R	......	700.00	1660.00	2080.00		4	165G	4F-1R		2805	No
1945											
R	......	720.00	1700.00	2110.00		4	165G	4F-1R		2805	No
1946											
A	......	700.00	1660.00	2040.00		4	133G	3F-1R		2300	No
R	......	740.00	1760.00	2170.00		4	165G	4F-1R		2805	No
V	......	730.00	1730.00	2130.00		4	65G	3F-1R		1802	No
1947											
A	......	720.00	1710.00	2090.00		4	133G	3F-1R		2300	No
R	......	770.00	1820.00	2220.00		4	165G	4F-1R		2805	No
V	......	750.00	1780.00	2170.00		4	65G	3F-1R		1802	No
1948											
A	......	760.00	1740.00	2120.00		4	133G	3F-1R		2300	No
R	......	830.00	1900.00	2320.00		4	165G	4F-1R		2805	No
V	......	800.00	1830.00	2230.00		4	65G	3F-1R		1802	No
1949											
A	......	810.00	1780.00	2170.00		4	133G	3F-1R		2300	No
R	......	880.00	1940.00	2370.00		4	165G	4F-1R		2805	No
V	......	850.00	1880.00	2290.00		4	65G	3F-1R		1802	No

Model	Approx. Retail Price New	Estimated Average Value Less Repairs Fair	Good	Premium	Engine Make	No. Cyls.	Displ. Cu.-In.	No. Speeds	P.T.O. H.P.	Approx. Shipping Wt.-Lbs.	Cab
Avery (Cont.)											
			1950								
A	......	850.00	1810.00	2210.00		4	133G	3F-1R		2300	No
BF	......	880.00	1870.00	2280.00		4	133G	4F-1R		2798	No
R	......	930.00	1980.00	2420.00		4	165G	4F-1R		2805	No
V	......	900.00	1920.00	2340.00		4	65G	3F-1R		1802	No
			1951								
A	......	900.00	1860.00	2270.00		4	133G	3F-1R		2300	No
BF	......	930.00	1910.00	2330.00		4	133G	4F-1R		2798	No
R	......	980.00	2030.00	2480.00		4	165G	4F-1R		2805	No
V	......	960.00	1980.00	2420.00		4	65G	3F-1R		1802	No
			1952								
A	......	950.00	1900.00	2320.00		4	133G	3F-1R		2300	No
BF	......	980.00	1960.00	2390.00		4	133G	4F-1R		2798	No
R	......	1040.00	2080.00	2540.00		4	165G	4F-1R		2805	No
V	......	1020.00	2040.00	2490.00		4	65G	3F-1R		1802	No
			1953								
BF	......	1050.00	2030.00	2480.00		4	133G	4F-1R		2798	No
BFD	......	1030.00	1990.00	2430.00		4	133G	4F-1R		2895	No
BFH	......	1120.00	2170.00	2650.00		4	133G	4F-1R		2895	No
BFS	......	1080.00	2100.00	2560.00		4	133G	4F-1R		2798	No
BG	......	1120.00	2180.00	2660.00		4	133G	4F-1R		2805	No
R	......	1100.00	2130.00	2600.00		4	165G	4F-1R		2805	No
V	......	1070.00	2070.00	2530.00		4	65G	3F-1R		1802	No
			1954								
BF	......	1110.00	2080.00	2540.00		4	133G	4F-1R		2798	No
BFD	......	1120.00	2120.00	2590.00		4	133G	4F-1R		2895	No
BFS	......	1090.00	2050.00	2500.00		4	133G	4F-1R		2798	No
BG	......	1190.00	2230.00	2720.00		4	133G	4F-1R		2805	No
R	......	1160.00	2180.00	2660.00		4	165G	4F-1R		2805	No
V	......	1120.00	2110.00	2570.00		4	65G	3F-1R		1802	No
			1955								
BF	......	1160.00	2130.00	2600.00		4	133G	4F-1R		2798	No
BFS	......	1190.00	2180.00	2660.00		4	133G	4F-1R		2798	No
BG	......	1260.00	2290.00	2790.00		4	133G	4F-1R		2805	No
V	......	1180.00	2160.00	2640.00		4	65G	3F-1R		1802	No
			1956								
BF	......	1200.00	2190.00	2670.00		4	133G	4F-1R		2798	No
BFS	......	1260.00	2300.00	2810.00		4	133G	4F-1R		2798	No
BG	......	1280.00	2330.00	2840.00		4	133G	4F-1R		2805	No
			1957								
BF	......	1230.00	2240.00	2730.00		4	133G	4F-1R		2798	No
BFS	......	1290.00	2370.00	2890.00		4	133G	4F-1R		2798	No
BG	......	1310.00	2400.00	2930.00		4	133G	4F-1R		2805	No
			1958								
BF	......	1280.00	2340.00	2860.00		4	133G	4F-1R		2798	No
			1959								
Big MO 400	......	1370.00	2510.00	3060.00				4F-1R		1622	No
			1960								
Big MO 400	......	1440.00	2560.00	3120.00				4F-1R		1622	No
			1961								
Big MO 400	......	1510.00	2610.00	3180.00				4F-1R		1622	No
			1962								
Big MO 400	......	1600.00	2690.00	3280.00				4F-1R		1622	No
			1963								
Big MO 400	......	1680.00	2750.00	3360.00				4F-1R		1622	No
			1964								
Big MO 400	......	1780.00	2850.00	3480.00				4F-1R		1622	No
Belarus											
			1988								
250	6500.00	2120.00	2490.00	2660.00	Belarus	2	127D	8F-6R	24.95	3750	No
400	10600.00	2840.00	3430.00	3640.00	Belarus	4	253D	11F-6R	53.0	5027	No
420 4WD	12830.00	3270.00	3950.00	4190.00	Belarus	4	253D	11F-6R	53.0	5530	No
500	12000.00	3050.00	3690.00	3910.00	Belarus	4	290D	9F-2R	63.0	6060	No
502	14600.00	3780.00	4580.00	4860.00	Belarus	4	290D	9F-2R	63.0	7826	C,H
520 4WD	14550.00	3660.00	4420.00	4690.00	Belarus	4	290D	9F-2R	63.0	6500	No
522 4WD	17100.00	4040.00	4890.00	5180.00	Belarus	4	290D	9F-2R	63.0	8377	C,H
560	15100.00	3870.00	4680.00	4960.00	Belarus	4	290D	9F-2R	63.0	6700	C,H
562 4WD	17800.00	4260.00	5150.00	5460.00	Belarus	4	290D	9F-2R	63.0	7145	C,H

Belarus (Cont.)

Model	Approx. Retail Price New	Estimated Average Value Less Repairs Fair	Good	Premium	Engine Make	No. Cyls.	Displ. Cu.-In.	No. Speeds	P.T.O. H.P.	Approx. Shipping Wt.-Lbs.	Cab
1988 (Cont.)											
611	12800.00	4260.00	5150.00	5460.00	Belarus	4	302D	10F-2R	60.0	7048	No
800	15300.00	4090.00	4940.00	5240.00	Belarus	4	290D	18F-4R	74.00	6700	No
802	17300.00	4300.00	5200.00	5510.00	Belarus	4	290D	18F-4R	74.00	8531	C,H
820 4WD	18550.00	4520.00	5460.00	5790.00	Belarus	4	290D	18F-4R	74.00	7150	No
822 4WD	20600.00	4730.00	5720.00	6060.00	Belarus	4	290D	18F-4R	74.00	9082	C,H
1770 4WD	47000.00	12600.00	14700.00	16170.00	Belarus	6T	558D	16F-8R	165.	17768	C,H
1989											
250AS	4395.00	2290.00	2680.00	2870.00	Belarus	2	127D	8F-6R	24.95	4300	No
400AN	6995.00	3080.00	3710.00	3930.00	Belarus	4	253D	11F-6R	53.0	5060	No
420AN 4WD	7995.00	3520.00	4240.00	4490.00	Belarus	4	253D	11F-6R	53.0	5530	No
505	7995.00	3520.00	4240.00	4490.00	Belarus	4	289D	9F-2R	63.0	6060	No
525	8995.00	3960.00	4770.00	5060.00	Belarus	4	289D	9F-2R	63.0	6500	No
562 4WD	10495.00	4620.00	5560.00	5890.00	Belarus	4	289D	9F-2R	63.0	7145	C,H
800	9995.00	4400.00	5300.00	5620.00	Belarus	4	289D	18F-4R	74.80	6700	No
802	10495.00	4620.00	5560.00	5890.00	Belarus	4	289D	18F-4R	74.80	7450	C,H
820 4WD	10995.00	4840.00	5830.00	6180.00	Belarus	4	289D	18F-4R	74.80	7150	C,H
822 4WD	11495.00	5060.00	6090.00	6460.00	Belarus	4	289D	18F-4R	74.80	7870	C,H
1770 4WD	43900.00	13490.00	15620.00	17180.00	Belarus	V6T	558D	12F-4R	167.6	20490	C,H
1990											
250AS	4615.00	2450.00	2860.00	3060.00	Belarus	2	127D	8F-6R	24.95	4300	No
400AN	7415.00	3340.00	4000.00	4240.00	Belarus	4	253D	11F-6R	53.0	5060	No
420AN 4WD	8450.00	3800.00	4560.00	4830.00	Belarus	4	253D	11F-6R	53.00	5530	No
505	8475.00	3810.00	4580.00	4860.00	Belarus	4	289D	9F-2R	63.0	6060	No
525	9445.00	4250.00	5100.00	5410.00	Belarus	4	289D	9F-2R	63.0	6500	No
562 4WD	11000.00	4930.00	5910.00	6270.00	Belarus	4	289D	9F-2R	63.0	7145	C,H
800	10495.00	4720.00	5670.00	6010.00	Belarus	4	289D	18F-4R	74.80	6700	No
802	11020.00	4960.00	5950.00	6310.00	Belarus	4	289D	18F-4R	74.80	7450	C,H
820 4WD	11545.00	5200.00	6230.00	6600.00	Belarus	4	289D	18F-4R	74.80	7150	C,H
822 4WD	11955.00	5380.00	6460.00	6850.00	Belarus	4	289D	18F-4R	74.80	7870	C,H
1770 4WD	43900.00	14400.00	16560.00	18220.00	Belarus	6T	558D	12F-4R	167.6	20490	C,H
1991											
250AS	4995.00	2700.00	3150.00	3340.00	Belarus	2	127D	8F-6R	24.95	4300	No
400A	8495.00	3910.00	4670.00	4950.00	Belarus	4	254D	11F-6R	50.68	6535	No
420A 4WD	9995.00	4600.00	5500.00	5830.00	Belarus	4	254D	18F-4R	50.68	7225	No
570	8495.00	3910.00	4670.00	4950.00	Belarus	4	289D	18F-2R	61.24	10426	No
572	11295.00	5200.00	6210.00	6580.00	Belarus	4	289D	18F-2R	61.24	10426	C,H
820	13995.00	6440.00	7700.00	8160.00	Belarus	4	290D	18F-4R	75.15	11075	C,H
822 4WD	14895.00	6850.00	8190.00	8680.00	Belarus	4	290D	18F-4R	75.15	11075	C,H
925	16950.00	7800.00	9320.00	9880.00	Belarus	6T	290D	18F-4R		9050	C,H
1770	45695.00	15490.00	17700.00	19290.00	Belarus	6T	558D	12F-4R	167.6	20490	C,H
1992											
250AS	5595.00	3130.00	3580.00	3800.00	Belarus	2	127D	8F-6R	24.95	4300	No
400A	9300.00	4460.00	5210.00	5470.00	Belarus	4	254D	11F-6R	50.68	6535	No
420A 4WD	9900.00	4750.00	5540.00	5820.00	Belarus	4	254D	18F-4R	50.68	7225	No
570	9300.00	4460.00	5210.00	5470.00	Belarus	4	289D	18F-2R	61.24	10426	No
572	13950.00	6700.00	7810.00	8200.00	Belarus	4	289D	18F-2R	61.24	10426	C,H
820	14550.00	6980.00	8150.00	8560.00	Belarus	4	290D	18F-4R	75.15	11075	C,H
822 4WD	16750.00	8040.00	9380.00	9850.00	Belarus	4	290D	18F-4R	75.15	11075	C,H
925	18100.00	8690.00	10140.00	10650.00	Belarus	6T	290D	18F-4R		9050	C,H
1770	36880.00	16230.00	18810.00	20320.00	Belarus	6T	558D	12F-4R	167.6	20490	C,H
1993											
250AS	6395.00	3710.00	4160.00	4410.00	Belarus	2	127D	8F-6R	24.95	4300	No
400A	10250.00	5130.00	5950.00	6250.00	Belarus	4	254D	11F-6R	50.68	6535	No
420A 4WD	10895.00	5450.00	6320.00	6640.00	Belarus	4	254D	18F-4R	50.68	7225	No
570	10250.00	5130.00	5950.00	6250.00	Belarus	4	289D	18F-2R	61.24	10426	No
572	14650.00	7330.00	8500.00	8930.00	Belarus	4	289D	18F-2R	61.24	10426	C,H
820	15550.00	7780.00	9020.00	9470.00	Belarus	4	290D	18F-4R	75.15	11075	C,H
822 4WD	17995.00	9000.00	10440.00	10960.00	Belarus	4	290D	18F-4R	75.15	11075	C,H
925	19880.00	9940.00	11530.00	12110.00	Belarus	6T	290D	18F-4R		9050	C,H
1770	36880.00	16970.00	19920.00	21310.00	Belarus	6T	558D	12F-4R	167.6	20490	C,H
1994											
250AS	7345.00	4480.00	4920.00	5170.00	Belarus	2	127D	8F-6R	24.95	4300	No
305	9015.00	4780.00	5410.00	5680.00	Belarus	2	127D	8F-6R	28.5	4700	No
310 4WD	10225.00	5420.00	6140.00	6450.00	Belarus	2	127D	8F-6R	28.5	4750	No
400A	12070.00	6090.00	6900.00	7250.00	Belarus	4	253D	11F-6R	50.68	6535	No
400AN	12410.00	6220.00	7040.00	7390.00	Belarus	4	253D	11F-6R	50.68	6535	No
405A w/Cab	12705.00	6400.00	7250.00	7610.00	Belarus	4	253D	11F-6R	50.68	7630	C,H
405AN w/Cab	13070.00	6930.00	7840.00	8230.00	Belarus	4	253D	11F-6R	50.68	7630	C,H
420A 4WD	13740.00	6940.00	7850.00	8240.00	Belarus	4	253D	18F-4R	50.68	7225	No
420AN 4WD	14310.00	7240.00	8200.00	8610.00	Belarus	4	253D	11F-6R	50.68	7225	No
425A 4WD w/Cab	14465.00	7670.00	8680.00	9110.00	Belarus	4	253D	11F-6R	50.68	8630	C,H
425AN 4WD w/Cab	15040.00	7970.00	9020.00	9470.00	Belarus	4	253D	11F-6R	50.68	8630	C,H
505	14900.00	7900.00	8940.00	9390.00	Belarus	4	289D	9F-2R	58.0	7980	No
525	16770.00	8830.00	10000.00	10500.00	Belarus	4	289D	9F-2R	58.0	8540	No
530	12860.00	6820.00	7720.00	8110.00	Belarus	4	289D	9F-2R	55.0	5908	No
570 w/Cab	15820.00	8390.00	9490.00	9970.00	Belarus	4	289D	18F-4R	61.24	8460	C,H
572 4WD w/Cab	17750.00	9410.00	10650.00	11180.00	Belarus	4	289D	18F-4R	61.24	9210	C,H
615 w/Cab	13585.00	7200.00	8150.00	8560.00	Belarus	4	301D	10F-2R	67.0	8600	C,H

Belarus (Cont.)

Model	Approx. Retail Price New	Estimated Average Value Less Repairs Fair	Good	Premium	Engine Make	No. Cyls.	Displ. Cu.-In.	No. Speeds	P.T.O. H.P.	Approx. Shipping Wt.-Lbs.	Cab
1994 (Cont.)											
800	16250.00	8610.00	9750.00	10240.00	Belarus	4	290D	18F-4R	75.15	7960	No
805 w/Cab	17660.00	9360.00	10600.00	11130.00	Belarus	4	290D	18F-4R	75.15	8560	C,H
820 4WD	18540.00	9830.00	11120.00	11680.00	Belarus	4	290D	18F-4R	75.15	8520	No
825 4WD	19820.00	10510.00	11890.00	12490.00	Belarus	4	290D	18F-4R	75.15	9100	C,H
900	20165.00	10690.00	12100.00	12710.00	Belarus	4T	290D	18F-4R	92.0	7960	No
905 w/Cab	21575.00	11440.00	12950.00	13600.00	Belarus	4T	290D	18F-4R	92.0	8560	C,H
920 4WD	22450.00	11900.00	13470.00	14140.00	Belarus	4T	290D	18F-4R	92.0	8520	No
925 4WD w/Cab	23730.00	12580.00	14240.00	14950.00	Belarus	4T	290D	18F-4R	92.0	9100	C,H
1770 w/Cab	38730.00	18130.00	21090.00	22360.00	Belarus	6T	558D	12F-4R	167.6	19585	C,H
1770 w/Cab	41655.00	18870.00	21950.00	23270.00	Belarus	6T	558D	12F-4R	167.6	19600	C,H,A
1995											
250AS	7495.00	4800.00	5250.00	5510.00	Belarus	2	127D	8F-6R	24.95	4300	No
300	9165.00	5130.00	5770.00	6000.00	Belarus	2	127D	8F-6R	28.5	4300	No
310 4WD	10360.00	5800.00	6530.00	6790.00	Belarus	2	127D	8F-6R	28.5	4750	No
400A	11495.00	6440.00	7240.00	7530.00	Belarus	4	253D	10F-8R	50.68	6535	No
400AN	11730.00	6570.00	7390.00	7690.00	Belarus	4	253D	10F-8R	50.68	6535	No
405A w/Cab	12075.00	6760.00	7610.00	7910.00	Belarus	4	253D	10F-8R	50.68	7630	C,H
405AN w/Cab	13990.00	7830.00	8810.00	9160.00	Belarus	4	253D	10F-8R	50.68	7630	C,H
420A 4WD	13090.00	7330.00	8250.00	8580.00	Belarus	4	253D	10F-8R	50.68	7225	No
420AN 4WD	13660.00	7650.00	8610.00	8950.00	Belarus	4	253D	10F-8R	50.68	7225	No
425A 4WD w/Cab	15250.00	8540.00	9610.00	9990.00	Belarus	4	253D	10F-8R	50.68	8630	C,H
425AN 4WD w/Cab	15820.00	8860.00	9970.00	10370.00	Belarus	4	253D	10F-8R	50.68	8630	C,H
505	15260.00	8550.00	9610.00	9990.00	Belarus	4	289D	9F-2R	58.0	7980	No
525 4WD	16660.00	9330.00	10500.00	10920.00	Belarus	4	289D	9F-2R	58.0	8540	No
530	12935.00	7240.00	8150.00	8480.00	Belarus	4	289D	9F-2R	55.0	5908	No
532 4WD	14868.00	8330.00	9370.00	9750.00	Belarus	4	289D	9F-2R	55.0	6200	No
570 w/Cab	16030.00	8980.00	10100.00	10500.00	Belarus	4	289D	18F-4R	61.24	8460	C,H
572 4WD w/Cab	17990.00	10070.00	11330.00	11780.00	Belarus	4	289D	18F-4R	61.24	9210	C,H
800	16660.00	9330.00	10500.00	10920.00	Belarus	4	290D	18F-4R	75.15	7960	No
805 w/Cab	17990.00	10070.00	11330.00	11780.00	Belarus	4	290D	18F-4R	75.15	8560	C,H
820 4WD	18995.00	10640.00	11970.00	12450.00	Belarus	4	290D	18F-4R	75.15	8520	No
825 4WD	20090.00	11250.00	12660.00	13170.00	Belarus	4	290D	18F-4R	75.15	9100	C,H
902	20960.00	11740.00	13210.00	13740.00	Belarus	4T	290D	18F-4R	92.0	7960	C,H
925 4WD w/Cab	24115.00	13500.00	15190.00	15800.00	Belarus	4T	290D	18F-4R	92.0	9100	C,H
1770 w/Cab	39230.00	20790.00	23930.00	25130.00	Belarus	6T	558D	12F-4R	167.6	19585	C,H
1996											
300	9645.00	6460.00	7040.00	7320.00	Belarus	2	127D	6F-6R	28.5	4500	No
310 4WD	10905.00	7310.00	7960.00	8280.00	Belarus	2	127D	6F-6R	28.5	4750	No
400A	12105.00	7380.00	8110.00	8430.00	Belarus	4	253D	10F-8R	51.0	6535	No
400AN	12455.00	7600.00	8350.00	8680.00	Belarus	4	253D	10F-8R	51.0	6535	No
405A w/Cab	14185.00	8650.00	9500.00	9880.00	Belarus	4	253D	10F-8R	51.0	7630	C,H
405AN w/Cab	14730.00	8990.00	9870.00	10270.00	Belarus	4	253D	10F-8R	51.0	7630	C,H
420A 4WD	13780.00	8410.00	9230.00	9600.00	Belarus	4	253D	10F-8R	51.0	7225	No
420AN 4WD	14325.00	8740.00	9600.00	9980.00	Belarus	4	253D	10F-8R	51.0	7225	No
425A 4WD w/Cab	16050.00	9790.00	10750.00	11180.00	Belarus	4	253D	10F-8R	51.0	8630	C,H
425AN 4WD w/Cab	16645.00	10150.00	11150.00	11600.00	Belarus	4	253D	10F-8R	51.0	8630	C,H
505	16060.00	9800.00	10760.00	11190.00	Belarus	4	289D	9F-2R	59.0	7980	No
525 4WD	17540.00	10700.00	11750.00	12220.00	Belarus	4	289D	9F-2R	59.0	8540	No
530	13615.00	8310.00	9120.00	9490.00	Belarus	4	289D	9F-2R	52.0	5908	No
532 4WD	15650.00	9550.00	10490.00	10910.00	Belarus	4	289D	9F-2R	52.0	6490	No
570 w/Cab	16875.00	10290.00	11310.00	11760.00	Belarus	4	289D	18F-4R	61.24	8460	C,H
572 4WD w/Cab	18940.00	11550.00	12690.00	13200.00	Belarus	4	289D	18F-4R	61.24	8950	C,H
800	17540.00	10700.00	11750.00	12220.00	Belarus	4	289D	18F-4R	75.15	7960	No
805 w/Cab	18935.00	11550.00	12690.00	13200.00	Belarus	4	289D	18F-4R	75.15	8560	C,H
820 4WD	20010.00	12210.00	13410.00	13950.00	Belarus	4	289D	18F-4R	75.15	8520	No
825 4WD w/Cab	21140.00	12900.00	14160.00	14730.00	Belarus	4	289D	18F-4R	75.15	9100	C,H
900	20820.00	12700.00	13950.00	14510.00	Belarus	4T	289D	18F-4R	92.0	7960	No
905 w/Cab	22125.00	13500.00	14820.00	15410.00	Belarus	4T	289D	18F-4R	92.0	7960	C,H
920 4WD	23100.00	14090.00	15480.00	16100.00	Belarus	4T	289D	18F-4R	92.0	8520	No
925 4WD w/Cab	24405.00	14890.00	16350.00	17000.00	Belarus	4T	289D	18F-4R	92.0	9100	C,H
1025 4WD w/Cab	25380.00	15480.00	17010.00	17690.00	Belarus	4T	289D	18F-4R	92.0	9144	C,H
1770 w/Cab	43400.00	24190.00	27060.00	28410.00	Belarus	6T	558D	12F-4R	167.7	19585	C,H
1997											
200	7260.00	5230.00	5590.00	5810.00	Belarus	2	70D	16F-8R	19.0	2600	No
220 4WD	8245.00	5940.00	6350.00	6600.00	Belarus	2	70D	16F-8R	19.0	2700	No
250AS	7885.00	5680.00	6070.00	6310.00	Belarus	4	126D	8F-6R	25.0	4300	No
300	9645.00	6460.00	7040.00	7320.00	Belarus	2	127D	6F-6R	28.5	4500	No
310 4WD	10905.00	7310.00	7960.00	8280.00	Belarus	2	127D	6F-6R	28.5	4750	No
400A	12405.00	8310.00	9060.00	9420.00	Belarus	4	253D	10F-8R	51.0	6535	No
400AN	12755.00	8550.00	9310.00	9680.00	Belarus	4	253D	10F-8R	51.0	6535	No
405A w/Cab	14185.00	9500.00	10360.00	10770.00	Belarus	4	253D	10F-8R	51.0	7630	C,H
405AN w/Cab	14730.00	9870.00	10750.00	11180.00	Belarus	4	253D	10F-8R	51.0	7630	C,H
420A 4WD	13780.00	9230.00	10060.00	10460.00	Belarus	4	253D	10F-8R	51.0	7225	No
420AN 4WD	14325.00	9600.00	10460.00	10880.00	Belarus	4	253D	10F-8R	51.0	7225	No
425A 4WD w/Cab	16645.00	11150.00	12150.00	12640.00	Belarus	4	253D	10F-8R	51.0	8630	C,H
425AN 4WD w/Cab	17245.00	11550.00	12590.00	13090.00	Belarus	4	253D	10F-8R	51.0	8630	C,H
505	16080.00	10770.00	11740.00	12210.00	Belarus	4	290D	9F-2R	59.0	7980	No
525 4WD	17540.00	11750.00	12800.00	13310.00	Belarus	4	290D	9F-2R	59.0	8540	No
530	13816.00	9260.00	10090.00	10490.00	Belarus	4	290D	9F-2R	52.0	5908	No
532 4WD	15650.00	10490.00	11430.00	11890.00	Belarus	4	290D	9F-2R	52.0	6490	No
570 w/Cab	16875.00	11310.00	12320.00	12810.00	Belarus	4	290D	18F-4R	61.24	8460	C,H

Belarus (Cont.)

1997 (Cont.)

Model	Approx. Retail Price New	Estimated Average Value Less Repairs: Fair	Good	Premium	Engine: Make	No. Cyls.	Displ. Cu.-In.	No. Speeds	P.T.O. H.P.	Approx. Shipping Wt.-Lbs.	Cab
572 4WD w/Cab	18940.00	**12690.00**	**13830.00**	**14380.00**	Belarus	4	290D	18F-4R	61.24	8950	C,H
615	13410.00	**8990.00**	**9790.00**	**10180.00**	Belarus	4	301D	10F-2R	61.0	8500	C,H
800	17540.00	**11750.00**	**12800.00**	**13310.00**	Belarus	4	290D	18F-4R	75.15	7960	No
805 w/Cab	18935.00	**12690.00**	**13820.00**	**14370.00**	Belarus	4	290D	18F-4R	75.15	8560	C,H
820 4WD	20010.00	**13410.00**	**14610.00**	**15190.00**	Belarus	4	290D	18F-4R	75.15	8520	No
825 4WD w/Cab	21140.00	**14160.00**	**15430.00**	**16050.00**	Belarus	4	290D	18F-4R	75.15	9100	C,H
900	20820.00	**13950.00**	**15200.00**	**15810.00**	Belarus	4T	290D	18F-4R	92.0	7960	No
905 w/Cab	22125.00	**14820.00**	**16150.00**	**16800.00**	Belarus	4T	290D	18F-4R	92.0	7960	C,H
920 4WD	23100.00	**15480.00**	**16860.00**	**17530.00**	Belarus	4T	290D	18F-4R	92.0	8520	No
925 4WD w/Cab	24650.00	**16520.00**	**18000.00**	**18720.00**	Belarus	4T	290D	18F-4R	92.0	9100	C,H
1025 4WD w/Cab	25380.00	**17010.00**	**18530.00**	**19270.00**	Belarus	4T	290D	18F-4R	92.0	9144	C,H
1770 w/Cab	43400.00	**28210.00**	**30810.00**	**32040.00**	Belarus	6T	558D	12F-4R	167.7	19585	C,H
2011	9625.00	**6450.00**	**7030.00**	**7310.00**	Slavia	2	70D	16F-8R	19.0	2602	No
2045 4WD	10125.00	**6070.00**	**6610.00**	**6870.00**	Slavia	2	70D	16F-8R	19.0	2712	No
6311	19245.00	**12890.00**	**14050.00**	**14610.00**	Belarus	4	290D	18F-4R	59.0	8100	C,H
6345 4WD	22210.00	**14880.00**	**16210.00**	**16860.00**	Belarus	4	290D	18F-4R	59.0	8800	C,H
8011L	22875.00	**15330.00**	**16700.00**	**17370.00**	Belarus	4	290D	9F-2R	72.0	5950	No
8311	22540.00	**15100.00**	**16450.00**	**17110.00**	Belarus	4	290D	14F-4R	75.0	8150	C,H
8345 4WD	26330.00	**16180.00**	**17630.00**	**18340.00**	Belarus	4	290D	14F-4R	75.0	8600	C,H
9011L	24200.00	**16210.00**	**17670.00**	**18380.00**	Belarus	4T	290D	9F-2R	90.0	5975	No
9311	24525.00	**16430.00**	**17900.00**	**18620.00**	Belarus	4T	290D	14F-4R	92.0	8200	C,H
9345 4WD	29390.00	**18800.00**	**20490.00**	**21310.00**	Belarus	4T	290D	14F-4R	92.0	8650	C,H

1998

Model	Approx. Retail Price New	Estimated Average Value Less Repairs: Fair	Good	Premium	Engine: Make	No. Cyls.	Displ. Cu.-In.	No. Speeds	P.T.O. H.P.	Approx. Shipping Wt.-Lbs.	Cab
VST-180D	8830.00	**6890.00**	**7240.00**	**7460.00**	Belarus	3	55D	6F-2R	18.5		No
FS254 w/PS	8480.00	**6610.00**	**6950.00**	**7160.00**	Belarus	3	87D	8F-2R	25.0		No
510 2WD	12250.00	**9070.00**	**9680.00**	**9970.00**	Minsk	4T	289D	9F-2R	53.0	7628	No
2011 2WD	9815.00	**7260.00**	**7750.00**	**7980.00**	Slavia	2	70D	16F-8R	19.0	2602	No
2045 4WD	9060.00	**6700.00**	**7160.00**	**7380.00**	Slavia	2	70D	16F-8R	19.0	2712	No
2145 4WD	9360.00	**6930.00**	**7390.00**	**7610.00**	Slavia	2	70D	16F-8R	19.0	2750	No
3011 2WD	9385.00	**6950.00**	**7410.00**	**7630.00**	Belarus	2	127D	8F-6R	29.0	4425	No
3021 2WD	10585.00	**7830.00**	**8360.00**	**8610.00**	Belarus	2	127D	8F-6R	29.0	4500	No
3045 4WD	11750.00	**8700.00**	**9280.00**	**9560.00**	Belarus	2	127D	8F-6R	29.0	4750	No
5011 2WD	16125.00	**11500.00**	**12270.00**	**12640.00**	Minsk	4	289D	11F-8R	55.0	6060	No
5045 4WD	18259.00	**12680.00**	**13540.00**	**13950.00**	Minsk	4	289D	11F-8R	55.0	7850	No
5111 2WD	16870.00	**11500.00**	**12270.00**	**12640.00**	Minsk	4	289D	9F-2R	53.0	5908	No
5145 4WD	18560.00	**13320.00**	**14220.00**	**14650.00**	Minsk	4	289D	11F-10R	53.0	6490	No
5145 4WD	19690.00	**14060.00**	**15010.00**	**15460.00**	Minsk	4	289D	14F-4R	53.0	6490	No
6311 2WD	18890.00	**13680.00**	**14600.00**	**15040.00**	Belarus	4	289D	18F-4R	59.0	8100	C,H,A
6345 4WD	21510.00	**15230.00**	**16260.00**	**16750.00**	Belarus	4	289D	18F-4R	59.0	8500	C,H,A
6345 4WD	22640.00	**16040.00**	**17130.00**	**17640.00**	Belarus	4	289D	14F-4R	59.0	8500	C,H,A
8011L 2WD	18685.00	**13320.00**	**14220.00**	**14650.00**	Belarus	4	289D	9F-2R	72.0	5950	No
8011L 2WD	26810.00	**19090.00**	**20380.00**	**20990.00**	Belarus	4	289D	9F-2R	72.0	5950	C,H,A
8021 2WD	18800.00	**12920.00**	**13800.00**	**14210.00**	Belarus	4	289D	9F-2R	72.0	5950	No
8311 2WD	23200.00	**15200.00**	**16220.00**	**16710.00**	Belarus	4	289D	14F-4R	75.0	8150	C,H,A
8345 4WD	26820.00	**17880.00**	**19080.00**	**19650.00**	Belarus	4	289D	14F-4R	75.0	8600	C,H,A
9011L 2WD	21660.00	**16030.00**	**17110.00**	**17620.00**	Belarus	4	289D	9F-2R	90.0	5975	No
9011L 2WD	29785.00	**19980.00**	**21330.00**	**21970.00**	Belarus	4	289D	9F-2R	90.0	5975	C,H,A
9021 2WD	23510.00	**15270.00**	**16310.00**	**16800.00**	Belarus	4T	289D	9F-2R	90.0	5975	No
9311 2WD	25110.00	**16610.00**	**17730.00**	**18260.00**	Belarus	4T	289D	14F-4R	92.0	8200	C,H,A
9345 4WD	29730.00	**20770.00**	**22170.00**	**22840.00**	Belarus	4T	289D	14F-4R	92.0	8650	C,H,A

1999

Model	Approx. Retail Price New	Estimated Average Value Less Repairs: Fair	Good	Premium	Engine: Make	No. Cyls.	Displ. Cu.-In.	No. Speeds	P.T.O. H.P.	Approx. Shipping Wt.-Lbs.	Cab
VST-180D	8830.00	**7420.00**	**7770.00**	**7930.00**	Belarus	3	55D	6F-2R	18.5		No
FS254 w/PS	8480.00	**7120.00**	**7460.00**	**7610.00**	Belarus	3	87D	8F-2R	25.0		No
510 2WD	12250.00	**10170.00**	**10660.00**	**10980.00**	Minsk	4	289D	9F-2R	53.0	7628	No
2011 2WD	9815.00	**8150.00**	**8540.00**	**8800.00**	Slavia	2	70D	16F-8R	19.0	2602	No
2045 4WD	9060.00	**7520.00**	**7880.00**	**8120.00**	Slavia	2	70D	16F-8R	19.0	2712	No
2145 4WD	9360.00	**7770.00**	**8140.00**	**8380.00**	Slavia	2	70D	16F-8R	19.0	2750	No
3011 2WD	9385.00	**7790.00**	**8170.00**	**8420.00**	Belarus	2	127D	8F-6R	29.0	4425	No
3021 2WD	10585.00	**8790.00**	**9210.00**	**9490.00**	Belarus	2	127D	8F-6R	29.0	4500	No
3045 4WD	11750.00	**9750.00**	**10220.00**	**10530.00**	Belarus	2	127D	8F-6R	29.0	4750	No
5011 2WD	15535.00	**12890.00**	**13520.00**	**13930.00**	Minsk	4	289D	11F-8R	55.0	6060	No
5045 4WD	17135.00	**14220.00**	**14910.00**	**15360.00**	Minsk	4	289D	11F-8R	55.0	7850	No
5111 2WD	15535.00	**12890.00**	**13520.00**	**13930.00**	Minsk	4	289D	9F-2R	53.0	5908	No
5145 4WD	18465.00	**15330.00**	**16070.00**	**16550.00**	Minsk	4	289D	11F-10R	53.0	6490	No
5145 4WD	19465.00	**16160.00**	**16940.00**	**17450.00**	Minsk	4	289D	14F-4R	53.0	6490	No
6311 2WD	18480.00	**15340.00**	**16080.00**	**16560.00**	Belarus	4	289D	18F-4R	59.0	8100	C,H,A
6345 4WD	21280.00	**17660.00**	**18510.00**	**19070.00**	Belarus	4	289D	18F-4R	59.0	8500	C,H,A
6345 4WD	22280.00	**18490.00**	**19380.00**	**19960.00**	Belarus	4	289D	14F-4R	59.0	8500	C,H,A
8011L 2WD	18600.00	**15440.00**	**16180.00**	**16670.00**	Belarus	4	289D	9F-2R	72.0	5950	No
8021 2WD	17465.00	**14500.00**	**15200.00**	**15660.00**	Belarus	4	289D	9F-2R	72.0	5950	No
8311 2WD	20535.00	**17040.00**	**17870.00**	**18410.00**	Belarus	4	289D	14F-4R	75.0	8150	C,H,A
8345 4WD	24155.00	**20050.00**	**21020.00**	**21650.00**	Belarus	4	289D	14F-4R	75.0	8600	C,H,A
9011L 2WD	21775.00	**18070.00**	**18940.00**	**19510.00**	Belarus	4	289D	9F-2R	90.0	5975	No
9021 2WD	20640.00	**17130.00**	**17960.00**	**18500.00**	Belarus	4T	289D	9F-2R	90.0	5975	No
9311 2WD	22440.00	**18630.00**	**19520.00**	**20110.00**	Belarus	4T	289D	14F-4R	92.0	8200	C,H,A
9345 4WD	28065.00	**23290.00**	**24420.00**	**25150.00**	Belarus	4T	289D	14F-4R	92.0	8650	C,H,A

Big Bud

Model	Approx. Retail Price New	Estimated Average Value Less Repairs: Fair	Good	Premium	Engine: Make	No. Cyls.	Displ. Cu.-In.	No. Speeds	P.T.O. H.P.	Approx. Shipping Wt.-Lbs.	Cab
1979											
360/30 4WD	155000.00	27600.00	38400.00	43010.00	Cummins	6T	855D	6F-1R	360*	32000	C,H,A
400/30 4WD	130000.00	28750.00	40000.00	44800.00	Detroit	V-8T	736D	6F-1R	400*	42000	C,H,A
450/50 4WD	125000.00	31050.00	43200.00	48380.00	Cummins	6T	1150D	6F-1R	450*	42000	C,H,A
525/50 4WD	190000.00	43700.00	60800.00	68100.00	Cummins	6TI	1150D	9F-2R	421.49	48000	C,H,A
600/50 4WD	240000.00	52900.00	73600.00	82430.00	Detroit	V12T	1104D	9F-2R	600*	60000	C,H,A
1980											
360 4WD	90000.00	20400.00	28050.00	31420.00	Cummins	6T	855D	12F-2R	360*	32000	C,H,A
360/20 4WD	105000.00	22800.00	31350.00	35110.00	Cummins	6T	855D	12F-2R	360*	32000	C,H,A
360/30 4WD	160000.00	30000.00	41250.00	46200.00	Cummins	6T	855D	6F-1R	360*	32000	C,H,A
400/30 4WD	150000.00	31200.00	42900.00	48050.00	Detroit	V-8T	736D	6F-1R	400*	42000	C,H,A
450/50 4WD	132000.00	36000.00	49500.00	55440.00	Cummins	6T	1150D	6F-1R	450*	42000	C,H,A
525/50 4WD	200000.00	48000.00	66000.00	73920.00	Cummins	6TI	1150D	9F-2R	421.49	48000	C,H,A
600/50 4WD	255000.00	58800.00	80850.00	90550.00	Detroit	V12T	1104D	9F-2R	600*	60000	C,H,A
650/50 4WD	280000.00	62400.00	85800.00	96100.00	Detroit	V12T	1104D	9F-2R	650*	60000	C,H,A
1981											
360/30 4WD	162000.00	33750.00	45900.00	51410.00	Cummins	6T	855D	6F-1R	360*	32000	C,H,A
400/30 4WD	174000.00	35000.00	47600.00	53310.00	Detroit	V-8T	736D	6F-1R	400*	42000	C,H,A
525/50 4WD	214000.00	51000.00	69360.00	77680.00	Cummins	6TI	1150D	9F-2R	421.49	48000	C,H,A
600/50 4WD	275000.00	66250.00	90100.00	100910.00	Detroit	V12T	1104D	9F-2R	600*	60000	C,H,A
650/50 4WD	298000.00	68750.00	93500.00	104720.00	Detroit	V12T	1104D	9F-2R	650*	60000	C,H,A
1982											
360/30 4WD	162000.00	35100.00	47250.00	52920.00	Cummins	6T	855D	6F-1R	306.00	32000	C,H,A
400/30 4WD	174000.00	36400.00	49000.00	54880.00	Detroit	V8T	736D	6F-1R	340.00	42000	C,H,A
525/50 4WD	214000.00	53040.00	71400.00	79970.00	Cummins	6TI	1150D	9F-2R	421.49	48000	C,H,A
650/50 4WD	298000.00	71500.00	96250.00	107800.00	Detroit	V12T	1104D	9F-2R	552.00	60000	C,H,A
1983											
360/30 4WD	162000.00	36450.00	48600.00	54430.00	Cummins	6T	855D	6F-1R	306.00	32000	C,H,A
400/30 4WD	174000.00	37800.00	50400.00	56450.00	Detroit	V8T	736D	6F-1R	340.00	42000	C,H,A
525/50 4WD	214000.00	55080.00	73440.00	82250.00	Cummins	6TI	1150D	9F-2R	421.49	48000	C,H,A
650/50 4WD	298000.00	74250.00	99000.00	110880.00	Detroit	V12T	1104D	9F-2R	552.00	60000	C,H,A
1984											
360/30 4WD	162000.00	37800.00	49950.00	55940.00	Cummins	6T	855D	6F-1R	306.00	32000	C,H,A
400/30 4WD	174000.00	39200.00	51800.00	58020.00	Detroit	V8T	736D	6F-1R	340.00	42000	C,H,A
525/50 4WD	214000.00	57120.00	75480.00	84540.00	Cummins	6TI	1150D	9F-2R	421.49	48000	C,H,A
650/50 4WD	298000.00	77000.00	101750.00	113960.00	Detroit	V12T	1104D	9F-2R	552.00	60000	C,H,A
1985											
360/30 4WD	162000.00	40500.00	51300.00	56940.00	Cummins	6T	855D	6F-1R	306.00	32000	C,H,A
400/30 4WD	174000.00	43200.00	54720.00	60740.00	Detroit	V8T	736D	6F-1R	340.00	42000	C,H,A
525/50 4WD	214000.00	61200.00	77520.00	86050.00	Cummins	6TI	1150D	9F-2R	421.49	48000	C,H,A
650/50 4WD	298000.00	82500.00	104500.00	116000.00	Detroit	V12T	1104D	9F-2R	552.00	60000	C,H,A
1986											
360/30 4WD	162000.00	43200.00	52650.00	58440.00	Cummins	6T	855D	6F-1R	360	32000	C,H,A
400/30 4WD	174000.00	46080.00	56160.00	62340.00	Detroit	V8T	736D	6F-1R	400	42000	C,H,A
500	150000.00	48000.00	58500.00	64940.00	Komatsu	6	1168D	12F-2R	500	46000	C,H,A
525/50 4WD	214000.00	65280.00	79560.00	88310.00	Cummins	6TI	1150D	9F-2R	525	48000	C,H,A
650/50 4WD	298000.00	88960.00	108420.00	120350.00	Detroit	V12T	1104D	9F-2R	650	60000	C,H,A
1987											
370 4WD	107500.00	32980.00	38800.00	42680.00	Komatsu	6TA	674D	12F-2R	370	37500	C,H,A
440 4WD	122500.00	41650.00	49000.00	53900.00	Komatsu	6TA	930D	12F-2R	440	39800	C,H,A
500	153000.00	51000.00	60000.00	66000.00	Komatsu	6	1168D	12F-2R	500	46000	C,H,A
739 4WD	225000.00	74800.00	88000.00	96800.00	Komatsu	6TA	1413D	9F-2R	740		C,H,A
1988											
370 4WD	139000.00	46440.00	54180.00	59600.00	Komatsu	6TA	674D	12F-2R	370		C,H,A
440 4WD	159000.00	53640.00	62580.00	68840.00	Komatsu	6TA	930D	12F-2R	440		C,H,A
500	155000.00	55800.00	65100.00	71610.00	Komatsu	6	1168D	12F-2R	500	46000	C,H,A
740 4WD	289000.00	97200.00	113400.00	124740.00	Komatsu	6TA	1413D	12F-2R	740		C,H,A
1989											
HN-320	90000.00	30400.00	35200.00	38720.00	Cummins	6	855D	12F-2R	320	33000	C,H,A
HN-360	105000.00	38000.00	44000.00	48400.00	Cummins	6	855D	12F-2R	360	34000	C,H,A
370	129000.00	45220.00	52360.00	57600.00	Cummins	6	855D	12F-2R	370	45000	C,H,A
400/20	135000.00	47500.00	55000.00	60500.00	Cummins	6	1150D	12F-2R	400	44000	C,H,A
450/50	150000.00	57000.00	66000.00	72600.00	Cummins	6	1150D	9F-2R	450	46000	C,H,A
500	159000.00	60420.00	69960.00	76960.00	Komatsu	6	1168D	12F-2R	500	46000	C,H,A
525/50	175000.00	66500.00	77000.00	84700.00	Cummins	6	1150D	9F-2R	525	47000	C,H,A
740	289000.00	102600.00	118800.00	130680.00	Detroit	12	1104D	12F-2R	740	75000	C,H,A
1990											
370 HP	140000.00	54000.00	62100.00	68310.00	Komatsu	6TA	674D	12F-2R	370	43000	C,H,A
400 HP	150000.00	56000.00	64400.00	70840.00	Cat.	6TA	893D	12F-2R	400	46000	C,H,A
440 HP	155000.00	58000.00	66700.00	73370.00	Komatsu	6TA	930D	12F-2R	440	46000	C,H,A
450 HP	150000.00	60000.00	69000.00	75900.00	Cummins	6TA	855D	12F-2R	450	46000	C,H,A

Model	Approx. Retail Price New	Estimated Average Value Less Repairs Fair	Good	Premium	Engine Make	No. Cyls.	Displ. Cu.-In.	No. Speeds	P.T.O. H.P.	Approx. Shipping Wt.-Lbs.	Cab

Big Bud (Cont.)

1990 (Cont.)

Model	Approx. Retail Price New	Fair	Good	Premium	Make	No. Cyls.	Displ. Cu.-In.	No. Speeds	P.T.O. H.P.	Approx. Shipping Wt.-Lbs.	Cab
450 HP	155000.00	62000.00	71300.00	78430.00	Detroit	8TA	736D	12F-2R	450	46000	C,H,A
650 HP	300000.00	104000.00	119600.00	131560.00	Detroit	12TA	1104D	9F-2R	650	55000	C,H,A
740 HP	300000.00	110000.00	126500.00	139150.00	Komatsu	6TA	1413D	12F-2R	740	75000	C,H,A

Bolens-Iseki

1982

Model	Approx. Retail Price New	Fair	Good	Premium	Make	No. Cyls.	Displ. Cu.-In.	No. Speeds	P.T.O. H.P.	Approx. Shipping Wt.-Lbs.	Cab
G152	5228.00	2350.00	2820.00	3050.00	Mitsubishi	3	47D	6F-2R	13.00	1078	No
G154 4WD	5700.00	2570.00	3080.00	3330.00	Mitsubishi	3	47D	6F-2R	13.00	1177	No
G174 4WD	6101.00	2750.00	3300.00	3560.00	Mitsubishi	3	52D	6F-2R	14.80	1177	No
G192	6003.00	2700.00	3240.00	3500.00	Isuzu	2	60D	9F-3R	18.20	1672	No
G194 4WD	6672.00	3000.00	3600.00	3890.00	Isuzu	2	60D	9F-3R	18.20	1903	No
G242	7350.00	3310.00	3970.00	4290.00	Isuzu	2	72D	9F-3R		1672	No
G244 4WD	8967.00	4040.00	4840.00	5230.00	Isuzu	2	72D	9F-3R		1903	No
G292	8036.00	3620.00	4340.00	4690.00	Isuzu	3	89D	8F-2R		2631	No
G294 4WD	10094.00	4540.00	5450.00	5890.00	Isuzu	3	89D	8F-2R		2948	No

1983

Model	Approx. Retail Price New	Fair	Good	Premium	Make	No. Cyls.	Displ. Cu.-In.	No. Speeds	P.T.O. H.P.	Approx. Shipping Wt.-Lbs.	Cab
G152	5335.00	2450.00	2930.00	3160.00	Mitsubishi	3	47D	6F-2R	13.00	1078	No
G154 4WD	5816.00	2680.00	3200.00	3460.00	Mitsubishi	3	47D	6F-2R	13.00	1177	No
G174 4WD	6226.00	2860.00	3420.00	3690.00	Mitsubishi	3	52D	6F-2R	14.80	1177	No
G192	6126.00	2820.00	3370.00	3640.00	Isuzu	2	60D	9F-3R	18.20	1672	No
G194 4WD	6808.00	3130.00	3740.00	4040.00	Isuzu	2	60D	9F-3R	18.20	1903	No
G242	7500.00	3450.00	4130.00	4460.00	Isuzu	2	72D	9F-3R		1672	No
G244 4WD	9150.00	4210.00	5030.00	5430.00	Isuzu	2	72D	9F-3R		1903	No
G292	8200.00	3770.00	4510.00	4870.00	Isuzu	3	89D	8F-2R		2631	No
G294 4WD	10300.00	4740.00	5670.00	6120.00	Isuzu	3	89D	8F-2R		2948	No

1984

Model	Approx. Retail Price New	Fair	Good	Premium	Make	No. Cyls.	Displ. Cu.-In.	No. Speeds	P.T.O. H.P.	Approx. Shipping Wt.-Lbs.	Cab
G1502	5500.00	2590.00	3080.00	3330.00	Mitsubishi	3	47D	6F-2R	13.00		No
G1504 4WD	6010.00	2830.00	3370.00	3640.00	Mitsubishi	3	47D	6F-2R	13.00		No
G1704 4WD	6410.00	3010.00	3590.00	3880.00	Mitsubishi	3	52D	6F-2R	14.00		No
G2102	6595.00	3100.00	3690.00	3990.00	Isuzu	3	71D	12F-4R			No
G2104 4WD	7395.00	3480.00	4140.00	4470.00	Isuzu	3	71D	12F-4R			No
G2702	7895.00	3710.00	4420.00	4770.00	Isuzu	3	79D	18F-6R			No
G2704 4WD	9695.00	4560.00	5430.00	5860.00	Isuzu	3	79D	18F-6R			No

1985

Model	Approx. Retail Price New	Fair	Good	Premium	Make	No. Cyls.	Displ. Cu.-In.	No. Speeds	P.T.O. H.P.	Approx. Shipping Wt.-Lbs.	Cab
G1502	5500.00	2640.00	3140.00	3390.00	Mitsubishi	3	47D	6F-2R	13.00		No
G1504 4WD	6010.00	2890.00	3430.00	3700.00	Mitsubishi	3	47D	6F-2R	13.00		No
G1704 4WD	6410.00	3080.00	3650.00	3940.00	Mitsubishi	3	52D	6F-2R	14.00		No
G2102	6595.00	3170.00	3760.00	4060.00	Isuzu	3	71D	12F-4R			No
G2104 4WD	7395.00	3550.00	4220.00	4560.00	Isuzu	3	71D	12F-4R			No
G2702	7895.00	3790.00	4500.00	4860.00	Isuzu	3	79D	18F-6R			No
G2704 4WD	9695.00	4650.00	5530.00	5970.00	Isuzu	3	79D	18F-6R			No

1986

Model	Approx. Retail Price New	Fair	Good	Premium	Make	No. Cyls.	Displ. Cu.-In.	No. Speeds	P.T.O. H.P.	Approx. Shipping Wt.-Lbs.	Cab
G1502	5700.00	2790.00	3310.00	3580.00	Mitsubishi	3	47D	6F-2R	13.00		No
G1504 4WD	6210.00	3040.00	3600.00	3890.00	Mitsubishi	3	47D	6F-2R	13.00		No
G1704 4WD	6610.00	3240.00	3830.00	4140.00	Mitsubishi	3	52D	6F-2R	14.00		No
G2102	6795.00	3330.00	3940.00	4260.00	Isuzu	3	71D	12F-4R			No
G2104 4WD	7595.00	3720.00	4410.00	4760.00	Isuzu	3	71D	12F-4R			No
G2702	8195.00	4020.00	4750.00	5130.00	Isuzu	3	79D	18F-6R			No
G2704 4WD	9895.00	4850.00	5740.00	6200.00	Isuzu	3	79D	18F-6R			No

1987

Model	Approx. Retail Price New	Fair	Good	Premium	Make	No. Cyls.	Displ. Cu.-In.	No. Speeds	P.T.O. H.P.	Approx. Shipping Wt.-Lbs.	Cab
1502	6099.98	3050.00	3600.00	3890.00	Mitsubishi	3	47D	6F-2R	13.00	1080	No
1502H	6349.98	3180.00	3750.00	4050.00	Mitsubishi	3	47D	Infinite	13.00	1080	No
1704 4WD	7549.98	3780.00	4450.00	4810.00	Mitsubishi	3	52D	6F-2R	14.00	1080	No
1704H 4WD	7749.98	3880.00	4570.00	4940.00	Mitsubishi	3	52D	Infinite		1268	No
2102	7849.98	3930.00	4630.00	5000.00	Isuzu	3	71D	12F-4R		1580	No
2104 4WD	8674.98	4340.00	5120.00	5530.00	Isuzu	3	71D	12F-4R		1657	No
2702	9174.98	4590.00	5410.00	5840.00	Isuzu	3	79D	18F-6R		2250	No
2704 4WD	11124.98	5560.00	6560.00	7090.00	Isuzu	3	79D	18F-6R		2440	No

1988

Model	Approx. Retail Price New	Fair	Good	Premium	Make	No. Cyls.	Displ. Cu.-In.	No. Speeds	P.T.O. H.P.	Approx. Shipping Wt.-Lbs.	Cab
1502	7370.00	3570.00	4200.00	4490.00	Mitsubishi	3	47D	6F-2R		1080	No
1502H	7820.00	3730.00	4390.00	4700.00	Mitsubishi	3	47D	Infinite			No
1704 4WD	9240.00	4200.00	4940.00	5290.00	Mitsubishi	3	52D	6F-2R		1268	No
1704H 4WD	9590.00	4380.00	5150.00	5510.00	Mitsubishi	3	52D	Infinite			No
2102	9630.98	4440.00	5220.00	5590.00	Isuzu	3	71D	12F-4R		1580	No
2104 4WD	10450.00	4850.00	5700.00	6100.00	Isuzu	3	71D	12F-4R		1657	No
2702	11110.00	5100.00	6000.00	6420.00	Isuzu	3	79D	18F-6R		2250	No
2704 4WD	13700.00	6120.00	7200.00	7700.00	Isuzu	3	79D	18F-6R		2401	No

Case

1939

Model	Approx. Retail Price New	Fair	Good	Premium	Make	No. Cyls.	Displ. Cu.-In.	No. Speeds	P.T.O. H.P.	Approx. Shipping Wt.-Lbs.	Cab
D	......	730.00	1250.00	1480.00	Case	4	259G	4F-1R	38	4600	No
V	......	760.00	1310.00	1550.00	Continental	4	127G	4F-1R	15	4290	No

Case (Cont.)

Model	Approx. Retail Price New	Estimated Average Value Less Repairs Fair	Good	Premium	Engine Make	No. Cyls.	Displ. Cu.-In.	No. Speeds	P.T.O. H.P.	Approx. Shipping Wt.-Lbs.	Cab
1940											
D	......	730.00	1270.00	1500.00	Case	4	259G	4F-1R	38	4600	No
V	......	770.00	1330.00	1570.00	Continental	4	127G	4F-1R	15	4290	No
1941											
D	......	750.00	1300.00	1530.00	Case	4	259G	4F-1R	38	4600	No
LA	......	1110.00	1910.00	2250.00	Case	4	403G	4F-1R	62	7621	No
SC	......	770.00	1320.00	1560.00	Case	4	153D	4F-1R	30	4200	No
V	......	800.00	1380.00	1630.00	Continental	4	127G	4F-1R	15	4290	No
1942											
D	......	780.00	1360.00	1610.00	Case	4	259G	4F-1R	38	4600	No
LA	......	1120.00	1940.00	2290.00	Case	4	403G	4F-1R	62	7621	No
SC	......	760.00	1310.00	1550.00	Case	4	153D	4F-1R	30	4200	No
VA	......	800.00	1380.00	1630.00	Continental	4	127G	4F-1R	15	4290	No
1943											
D	......	800.00	1380.00	1630.00	Case	4	259G	4F-1R	38	4600	No
LA	......	1140.00	1970.00	2330.00	Case	4	403G	4F-1R	62	7621	No
SC	......	780.00	1350.00	1590.00	Case	4	153D	4F-1R	30	4200	No
VA	......	830.00	1430.00	1690.00	Continental	4	127G	4F-1R	15	4290	No
1944											
D	......	860.00	1440.00	1700.00	Case	4	259G	4F-1R	38	4600	No
LA	......	1190.00	2000.00	2360.00	Case	4	403G	4F-1R	62	7621	No
SC	......	830.00	1390.00	1640.00	Case	4	153D	4F-1R	30	4200	No
VA	......	870.00	1450.00	1710.00	Continental	4	127G	4F-1R	15	4290	No
1945											
D	......	900.00	1510.00	1780.00	Case	4	259G	4F-1R	38	4600	No
LA	......	1220.00	2050.00	2420.00	Case	4	403G	4F-1R	62	7621	No
SC	......	850.00	1430.00	1690.00	Case	4	153D	4F-1R	30	4200	No
VA	......	880.00	1470.00	1740.00	Continental	4	127G	4F-1R	15	4290	No
1946											
D	......	920.00	1530.00	1810.00	Case	4	259G	4F-1R	38	4600	No
LA	......	1240.00	2070.00	2440.00	Case	4	403G	4F-1R	62	7621	No
SC	......	880.00	1480.00	1750.00	Case	4	153D	4F-1R	30	4200	No
VA	......	920.00	1550.00	1830.00	Continental	4	127G	4F-1R	15	4290	No
1947											
D	......	940.00	1570.00	1850.00	Case	4	259G	4F-1R	38	4600	No
LA	......	1250.00	2100.00	2480.00	Case	4	403G	4F-1R	62	7621	No
SC	......	900.00	1510.00	1780.00	Case	4	153D	4F-1R	30	4200	No
VA	......	950.00	1600.00	1890.00	Continental	4	127G	4F-1R	15	4290	No
1948											
D	......	960.00	1570.00	1840.00	Case	4	259G	4F-1R	38	4600	No
LA	......	1270.00	2100.00	2460.00	Case	4	403G	4F-1R	62	7621	No
S	......	920.00	1510.00	1770.00	Case	4	153D	4F-1R	30	4200	No
VA	......	980.00	1620.00	1900.00	Continental	4	127G	4F-1R	15	4290	No
1949											
D	......	970.00	1570.00	1840.00	Case	4	259G	4F-1R	38	4600	No
DC	......	990.00	1600.00	1870.00	Case	4	259G	4F-1R	38	4600	No
LA	......	1310.00	2130.00	2490.00	Case	4	403G	4F-1R	62	7621	No
SC	......	940.00	1520.00	1780.00	Case	4	153D	4F-1R	30	4200	No
VA	......	1000.00	1620.00	1900.00	Continental	4	127G	4F-1R	15	4290	No
1950											
D	......	1010.00	1600.00	1870.00	Case	4	259G	4F-1R	38	4600	No
DC	......	1030.00	1630.00	1910.00	Case	4	259G	4F-1R	38	4600	No
LA	......	1350.00	2140.00	2500.00	Case	4	403G	4F-1R	62	7621	No
SC	......	940.00	1500.00	1760.00	Case	4	153D	4F-1R	30	4200	No
VA	......	1040.00	1650.00	1930.00	Continental	4	127G	4F-1R	15	4290	No
1951											
D	......	1040.00	1620.00	1880.00	Case	4	259G	4F-1R	38	4600	No
DC	......	1050.00	1640.00	1900.00	Case	4	259G	4F-1R	38	4600	No
LA	......	1390.00	2170.00	2520.00	Case	4	403G	4F-1R	62	7621	No
SC	......	980.00	1530.00	1780.00	Case	4	153D	4F-1R	30	4200	No
VA	......	1090.00	1700.00	1970.00	Continental	4	127G	4F-1R	15	4290	No
1952											
D	......	1100.00	1640.00	1900.00	Case	4	259G	4F-1R	38	4600	No
DC	......	1130.00	1670.00	1940.00	Case	4	259G	4F-1R	38	4600	No
LA	......	1480.00	2190.00	2540.00	Case	4	403G	4F-1R	62	7621	No
SC	......	1050.00	1560.00	1810.00	Case	4	153D	4F-1R	30	4200	No
VA	......	1160.00	1720.00	2000.00	Continental	4	127G	4F-1R	15	4290	No
1953											
D	......	1140.00	1660.00	1930.00	Case	4	259G	4F-1R	38	4600	No
DC	......	1160.00	1680.00	1950.00	Case	4	259G	4F-1R	38	4600	No
LA	......	1510.00	2190.00	2540.00	Case	4	403G	4F-1R	62	7621	No
SC	......	1050.00	1530.00	1780.00	Case	4	153D	4F-1R	30	4200	No

Case (Cont.)

Model	Approx. Retail Price New	Fair	Good	Premium	Make	Engine No. Cyls.	Engine Displ. Cu.-In.	No. Speeds	P.T.O. H.P.	Approx. Shipping Wt.-Lbs.	Cab
			1953 (Cont.)								
VA	......	1240.00	1810.00	2100.00	Continental	4	127G	4F-1R	15	4290	No
500 STD	......	1580.00	2300.00	2670.00	Case	6	377D	4F-1R	65	8128	No
			1954								
SC	......	1120.00	1600.00	1860.00	Case	4	153D	4F-1R	30	4200	No
VA	......	1310.00	1880.00	2180.00	Continental	4	123G	4F-1R	15	4290	No
500 STD	......	1610.00	2300.00	2670.00	Case	6	377D	4F-1R	65	8128	No
			1955								
VA	......	1350.00	1880.00	2180.00	Continental	4	123G	4F-1R	15	4290	No
400	......	1490.00	2080.00	2410.00	Case	4	251D	8F-2R	50	6722	No
500 STD	......	1640.00	2300.00	2670.00	Case	6	377D	4F-1R	65	8128	No
			1956								
300	......	1260.00	2300.00	2810.00	Case	4	148G	12F-3R	34	4300	No
400	......	1510.00	2750.00	3360.00	Case	4	251D	8F-2R	50	6722	No
500 STD	......	1610.00	2940.00	3590.00	Case	6	377D	4F-1R	65	8128	No
			1957								
300	......	1280.00	2340.00	2860.00	Case	4	148G	12F-3R	29	4300	No
300B	......	1240.00	2270.00	2770.00	Continental	4	157D	12F-3R	32.	3235	No
310	......	1190.00	2180.00	2660.00	Case	4	148G	12F-3R		4300	No
400	......	1600.00	2920.00	3560.00	Case	4	251D	8F-2R	50	6722	No
400B	......	1480.00	2700.00	3290.00	Case	4	148G	8F-2R	37	3900	No
500 STD	......	1700.00	3100.00	3780.00	Case	6	377D	4F-1R	65	8128	No
500B	......	1390.00	2540.00	3100.00	Case	4	164G	12F-3R	47	4240	No
600 STD	......	1870.00	3420.00	4170.00	Case	4	164D	6F-1R	45	7600	No
600B	......	1580.00	2880.00	3510.00	Case	4	165G	8F-2R	44.56	4420	No
700	......	1820.00	3330.00	4060.00	Case	4	251G	8F-2R	54	5800	No
800	......	1890.00	3460.00	4220.00	Case	4	251G	8F-1R	54	5940	No
900	......	1960.00	3580.00	4370.00	Case	6	377D	6F-1R	71	7040	No
			1958								
200B	......	1120.00	2050.00	2500.00	Case	4	126G	4F-1R	31	3090	No
210B	......	1190.00	2180.00	2660.00	Case	4	126G	4F-1R	31	3090	No
300B	......	1300.00	2370.00	2890.00	Continental	4	157D	12F-3R	32.	3235	No
310B	......	1260.00	2300.00	2810.00	Case	4	148G	12F-3R	29.	3235	No
400B	......	1500.00	2730.00	3330.00	Case	4	148G	8F-2R	37	3900	No
500 STD	......	1720.00	3140.00	3830.00	Case	6	377D	4F-1R	65	8128	No
500B	......	1450.00	2660.00	3250.00	Case	4	165G	12F-3R	47	4240	No
600B	......	1610.00	2940.00	3590.00	Case	4	165G	8F-2R	44.56	4420	No
700	......	1820.00	3330.00	4060.00	Case	4	251G	8F-2R	54	5800	No
800	......	2000.00	3650.00	4450.00	Case	4	251G	8F-1R	54	5940	No
900	......	2070.00	3780.00	4610.00	Case	6	377D	6F-1R	71	7040	No
			1959								
200B	......	1190.00	2170.00	2650.00	Case	4	126G	4F-1R	31	3090	No
210B	......	1220.00	2230.00	2720.00	Case	4	126G	4F-1R	31	3090	No
300B	......	1330.00	2430.00	2970.00	Continental	4	157D	12F-3R		3235	No
310B	......	1300.00	2370.00	2890.00	Case	4	148G	12F-3R		3235	No
400B	......	1510.00	2750.00	3360.00	Case	4	148G	8F-2R	37	3900	No
500 STD	......	1800.00	3300.00	4030.00	Case	6	377D	4F-1R	65	8128	No
500B	......	1470.00	2690.00	3280.00	Case	4	165G	12F-3R	47	4240	No
600B	......	1650.00	3010.00	3670.00	Case	4	165G	8F-2R	44.56	4420	No
700	......	1860.00	3390.00	4140.00	Case	4	251G	8F-2R	54	5800	No
800	......	2010.00	3680.00	4490.00	Case	4	251G	8F-1R	54	5940	No
900	......	2100.00	3840.00	4690.00	Case	6	377D	6F-1R	71	7040	No
			1960								
430	......	1140.00	2030.00	2480.00	Case	4	188D	8F-2R	34	3800	No
440	......	1010.00	1790.00	2180.00	Case	4	148G	8F-1R	33	3590	No
530	......	1280.00	1680.00	1900.00	Case	4	188D	12F-3R	41.2	3600	No
540	......	1140.00	1500.00	1700.00	Case	4	159G	12F-3R	39.5	3455	No
630	......	1520.00	2000.00	2260.00	Case	4	188D	12F-3R	49	4020	No
640	......	1310.00	1730.00	1960.00	Case	4	188G	12F-3R	50	4315	No
730	......	1800.00	2370.00	2680.00	Case	4	267D	8F-2R	57	6160	No
740	......	1540.00	2020.00	2280.00	Case	4	251G	8F-2R	56	6060	No
830	......	1960.00	2580.00	2920.00	Case	4	301D	8F-2R	64	6240	No
840	......	1700.00	2230.00	2520.00	Case	4	284G	8F-2R	66	6090	No
930	......	2030.00	2670.00	3020.00	Case	6	401D	6F-1R	81	8845	No
940	......	1860.00	2440.00	2760.00	Case	6	371G	6F-1R	71	8190	No
			1961								
430	3400.00	1220.00	2110.00	2570.00	Case	4	188D	8F-2R	34	3800	No
440	2940.00	1060.00	1820.00	2220.00	Case	4	148G	8F-1R	33	3530	No
530	3975.00	1360.00	1780.00	2010.00	Case	4	188D	12F-3R	41.2	3600	No
530 C-O-M	4195.00	1430.00	1880.00	2120.00	Case	4	188D	Infinite	41.2	4225	No
540	3495.00	1190.00	1560.00	1760.00	Case	4	159G	12F-3R	39.5	3455	No
540 C-O-M	3700.00	1260.00	1660.00	1880.00	Case	4	188D	infinite	41.2	4150	No
630	4600.00	1580.00	2070.00	2340.00	Case	4	188D	12F-3R	48	4465	No
630 C-O-M	4810.00	1650.00	2160.00	2440.00	Case	4	188D	Infinite	49	4680	No
640	4000.00	1370.00	1790.00	2020.00	Case	4	188G	12F-3R	50	4315	No
640 C-O-M	4200.00	1440.00	1890.00	2140.00	Case	4	188G	Infinite	49	4590	No
730	5400.00	1860.00	2440.00	2760.00	Case	4	267D	8F-2R	56	6240	No

Case (Cont.)

Model	Approx. Retail Price New	Estimated Average Value Less Repairs Fair	Good	Premium	Engine Make	No. Cyls.	Displ. Cu.-In.	No. Speeds	P.T.O. H.P.	Approx. Shipping Wt.-Lbs.	Cab
			1961 (Cont.)								
730 C-O-M	5600.00	**1930.00**	**2530.00**	**2860.00**	Case	4	267D	Infinite	56	6320	No
740	4635.00	**1590.00**	**2090.00**	**2360.00**	Case	4	251G	8F-2R	58	6100	No
740 C-O-M	4855.00	**1660.00**	**2190.00**	**2480.00**	Case	4	251G	Infinite	57	6180	No
830	5850.00	**2010.00**	**2650.00**	**2990.00**	Case	4	301D	8F-2R	64	6465	No
830 C-O-M	6035.00	**2080.00**	**2730.00**	**3090.00**	Case	4	301D	Infinite	64	6545	No
840	5100.00	**1750.00**	**2300.00**	**2600.00**	Case	4	284G	8F-2R	64	6340	No
840 C-O-M	5315.00	**1830.00**	**2400.00**	**2710.00**	Case	4	284G	Infinite	65	6420	No
930	6875.00	**2130.00**	**2800.00**	**3160.00**	Case	6	401D	6F-1R	81	8400	No
940	6150.00	**1980.00**	**2600.00**	**2940.00**	Case	6	377G	6F-1R	80	8345	No
			1962								
430	3400.00	**1290.00**	**2180.00**	**2660.00**	Case	4	188D	8F-2R	34	3800	No
440	2940.00	**1120.00**	**1880.00**	**2290.00**	Case	4	148G	8F-1R	33	3530	No
530	3975.00	**1390.00**	**1830.00**	**2070.00**	Case	4	188D	12F-3R	41.2	3600	No
530 C-O-M	4195.00	**1470.00**	**1930.00**	**2180.00**	Case	4	188D	Infinite	41.2	4225	No
540	3495.00	**1220.00**	**1610.00**	**1820.00**	Case	4	159G	12F-3R	39.5	3455	No
540 C-O-M	3700.00	**1300.00**	**1700.00**	**1920.00**	Case	4	188D	infinite	41.2	4150	No
630	4600.00	**1610.00**	**2120.00**	**2400.00**	Case	4	188D	12F-3R	48	4465	No
630 C-O-M	4810.00	**1680.00**	**2210.00**	**2500.00**	Case	4	188D	Infinite	49	4680	No
640	4000.00	**1400.00**	**1840.00**	**2080.00**	Case	4	188G	12F-3R	50	4315	No
640 C-O-M	4200.00	**1470.00**	**1930.00**	**2180.00**	Case	4	188G	Infinite	49	4590	No
730	5400.00	**1890.00**	**2480.00**	**2800.00**	Case	4	267D	8F-2R	56	6240	No
730 C-O-M	5600.00	**1960.00**	**2580.00**	**2920.00**	Case	4	267D	Infinite	56	6320	No
740	4635.00	**1620.00**	**2130.00**	**2410.00**	Case	4	251G	8F-2R	58	6100	No
740 C-O-M	4855.00	**1700.00**	**2230.00**	**2520.00**	Case	4	251G	Infinite	57	6180	No
830	5850.00	**2050.00**	**2690.00**	**3040.00**	Case	4	301D	8F-2R	64	6465	No
830 C-O-M	6035.00	**2110.00**	**2780.00**	**3140.00**	Case	4	301D	Infinite	64	6545	No
840	5100.00	**1790.00**	**2350.00**	**2660.00**	Case	4	284G	8F-2R	64	6340	No
840 C-O-M	5315.00	**1860.00**	**2450.00**	**2770.00**	Case	4	284G	Infinite	65	6420	No
930	6875.00	**2200.00**	**2890.00**	**3270.00**	Case	6	401D	6F-1R	81	8400	No
940	6150.00	**2050.00**	**2690.00**	**3040.00**	Case	6	377G	6F-1R	80	8345	No
			1963								
430	3427.00	**1380.00**	**2260.00**	**2760.00**	Case	4	188D	8F-2R	34	3530	No
440	2974.00	**1200.00**	**1970.00**	**2400.00**	Case	4	148G	8F-1R	33	3455	No
530	4037.00	**1450.00**	**1900.00**	**2150.00**	Case	4	188D	12F-3R	41.2	3600	No
530 C-O-M	4244.00	**1520.00**	**2000.00**	**2260.00**	Case	4	188D	Infinite	40	4225	No
540	3538.00	**1270.00**	**1670.00**	**1890.00**	Case	4	159G	12F-3R	39.5	3455	No
540 C-O-M	3745.00	**1350.00**	**1770.00**	**2000.00**	Case	4	159G	Infinite	41.2	4150	No
630	4675.00	**1670.00**	**2200.00**	**2490.00**	Case	4	188D	12F-3R	48	4465	No
630 C-O-M	4880.00	**1740.00**	**2290.00**	**2590.00**	Case	4	188D	Infinite	49	4675	No
640	4047.00	**1450.00**	**1910.00**	**2160.00**	Case	4	188G	12F-3R	50	4315	No
640 C-O-M	4254.00	**1520.00**	**2000.00**	**2260.00**	Case	4	188G	Infinite	49	4590	No
730	5431.00	**1940.00**	**2540.00**	**2870.00**	Case	4	267D	8F-2R	56	6240	No
730 C-O-M	5638.00	**2010.00**	**2640.00**	**2980.00**	Case	4	267D	Infinite	56	6320	No
740	4686.00	**1680.00**	**2200.00**	**2490.00**	Case	4	251G	8F-2R	58	6100	No
740 C-O-M	5330.00	**1900.00**	**2500.00**	**2830.00**	Case	4	251G	Infinite	57	6180	No
830	5862.00	**2090.00**	**2740.00**	**3100.00**	Case	4	301D	8F-2R	64	6465	No
830 C-O-M	6069.00	**2160.00**	**2840.00**	**3210.00**	Case	4	301D	Infinite	63	6545	No
840	5157.00	**1840.00**	**2420.00**	**2740.00**	Case	4	284G	8F-2R	64	6340	No
840 C-O-M	5364.00	**1910.00**	**2510.00**	**2840.00**	Case	4	284G	Infinite	65	6420	No
930	6905.00	**2310.00**	**3040.00**	**3440.00**	Case	6	401D	6F-1R	81	8400	No
940	6515.00	**2140.00**	**2810.00**	**3180.00**	Case	6	371G	6F-1R	80	8345	No
			1964								
430	3615.00	**1450.00**	**2310.00**	**2820.00**	Case	4	188D	8F-2R	34	3565	No
440	3162.00	**1270.00**	**2020.00**	**2460.00**	Case	4	148G	8F-2R	33	3530	No
530	4249.00	**1490.00**	**1960.00**	**2220.00**	Case	4	188D	12F-3R	41.2	3600	No
530	4750.00	**1660.00**	**2190.00**	**2480.00**	Case	4	159G	12F-3R	39.5	3455	No
530 C-O-M	4456.00	**1560.00**	**2050.00**	**2320.00**	Case	4	188D	Infinite	40	3925	No
540	3750.00	**1310.00**	**1730.00**	**1960.00**	Case	4	159G	12F-3R	39.5	3455	No
540 C-O-M	3956.00	**1390.00**	**1820.00**	**2060.00**	Case	4	159G	Infinite	41.2	3780	No
730	5647.00	**1980.00**	**2600.00**	**2940.00**	Case	4	267D	8F-2R	56	6160	No
730 C-O-M	5855.00	**2050.00**	**2690.00**	**3040.00**	Case	4	267D	Infinite	56	6680	No
740	4892.00	**1710.00**	**2250.00**	**2540.00**	Case	4	251G	8F-2R	58	6425	No
740 C-O-M	5390.00	**1890.00**	**2480.00**	**2800.00**	Case	4	251G	Infinite	57	6540	No
830	6087.00	**2130.00**	**2800.00**	**3160.00**	Case	4	301D	8F-2R	64	6090	No
830 C-O-M	6294.00	**2200.00**	**2900.00**	**3280.00**	Case	4	301D	Infinite	63	6875	No
840	5362.00	**1880.00**	**2470.00**	**2790.00**	Case	4	284G	8F-2R	63	6680	No
840 C-O-M	5569.00	**1950.00**	**2560.00**	**2890.00**	Case	4	284G	Infinite	63	6750	No
930	7110.00	**2450.00**	**3230.00**	**3650.00**	Case	6	401D	6F-1R	81	8905	No
940	6696.00	**2310.00**	**3030.00**	**3420.00**	Case	6	377G	6F-1R	71	8850	No
			1965								
430	3786.00	**1550.00**	**2420.00**	**2950.00**	Case	4	188D	8F-2R	34	3565	No
440	3356.00	**1380.00**	**2150.00**	**2620.00**	Case	4	148G	8F-2R	33	3530	No
530	4472.00	**1570.00**	**2060.00**	**2330.00**	Case	4	188D	12F-3R	41.2	3600	No
530 C-O-M	4679.00	**1640.00**	**2150.00**	**2430.00**	Case	4	188D	Infinite	40	3925	No
540	3953.00	**1380.00**	**1820.00**	**2060.00**	Case	4	159G	12F-3R	39.5	3455	No
540 C-O-M	4160.00	**1460.00**	**1910.00**	**2160.00**	Case	4	188D	Infinite	41.2	3780	No
730	5856.00	**2050.00**	**2690.00**	**3040.00**	Case	4	267D	8F-2R	57	6565	No
730 C-O-M	6199.00	**2170.00**	**2850.00**	**3220.00**	Case	4	267D	Infinite	56	6680	No
740	5095.00	**1780.00**	**2340.00**	**2640.00**	Case	4	251G	8F-2R	58	6425	No
740 C-O-M	5435.00	**1900.00**	**2500.00**	**2830.00**	Case	4	251G	8F-2R	57	6540	No

Case (Cont.)

Model	Approx. Retail Price New	Estimated Average Value Less Repairs Fair	Good	Premium	Engine Make	No. Cyls.	Displ. Cu.-In.	No. Speeds	P.T.O. H.P.	Approx. Shipping Wt.-Lbs.	Cab
1965 (Cont.)											
830	6314.00	**2210.00**	**2900.00**	**3280.00**	Case	4	301D	8F-2R	64	6680	No
830 C-O-M	6655.00	**2330.00**	**3060.00**	**3460.00**	Case	4	301D	Infinite	64	6875	No
840 C-O-M	5912.00	**2070.00**	**2720.00**	**3070.00**	Case	4	284G	Infinite	65	6750	No
840	5571.00	**1950.00**	**2560.00**	**2890.00**	Case	4	284G	8F-2R	65	6680	No
930	7246.00	**2540.00**	**3330.00**	**3760.00**	Case	6	401D	6F-1R	85	8385	No
940	6892.00	**2410.00**	**3170.00**	**3580.00**	Case	6	377G	6F-1R	85	8360	No
1966											
430	3938.00	**1650.00**	**2520.00**	**3070.00**	Case	4	188D	8F-2R	34	3565	No
440	3563.00	**1500.00**	**2280.00**	**2780.00**	Case	4	148G	8F-2R	33	3490	No
530	4681.00	**1640.00**	**2150.00**	**2430.00**	Case	4	188D	12F-3R	41.2	3600	No
530 C-O-M	4888.00	**1710.00**	**2250.00**	**2540.00**	Case	4	188D	Infinite	40	3925	No
540	4156.00	**1460.00**	**1910.00**	**2160.00**	Case	4	159G	12F-3R	39	3455	No
540 C-O-M	4363.00	**1530.00**	**2010.00**	**2270.00**	Case	4	188D	Infinite	41.2	3780	No
730	6064.00	**2120.00**	**2790.00**	**3150.00**	Case	4	267D	8F-2R	57	7610	No
730 C-O-M	6405.00	**2240.00**	**2950.00**	**3330.00**	Case	4	267D	Infinite	56	7735	No
740	5324.00	**1860.00**	**2450.00**	**2770.00**	Case	4	251G	8F-2R	58	7415	No
740 C-O-M	5480.00	**1920.00**	**2520.00**	**2850.00**	Case	4	251G	Infinite	57	7540	No
830	6623.00	**2320.00**	**3050.00**	**3450.00**	Case	4	301D	8F-2R	64	7620	No
830 C-O-M	6964.00	**2440.00**	**3200.00**	**3620.00**	Case	4	301D	Infinite	64	7745	No
840	5863.00	**2050.00**	**2700.00**	**3050.00**	Case	4	284G	8F-2R	66	6090	No
840 C-O-M	6204.00	**2170.00**	**2850.00**	**3220.00**	Case	4	284G	Infinite	64	7550	No
930	7365.00	**2580.00**	**3390.00**	**3830.00**	Case	6	401D	6F-1R	85	8845	No
940	7005.00	**2450.00**	**3220.00**	**3640.00**	Case	6	377G	6F-1R	71	8190	No
1200	18200.00	**2240.00**	**3640.00**	**4110.00**	Case	6	451D	8F-2R	120	16585	C
1967											
430	4150.00	**1790.00**	**2660.00**	**3250.00**	Case	4	188D	4F-1R	34	3710	No
440	3750.00	**1610.00**	**2400.00**	**2930.00**	Case	4	148G	8F-2R	33	3530	No
530	4910.00	**1720.00**	**2260.00**	**2550.00**	Case	4	188D	12F-3R	41	3600	No
530 C-O-M	5117.00	**1790.00**	**2350.00**	**2660.00**	Case	4	188D	12F-3R	41	3600	No
540	4410.00	**1540.00**	**2030.00**	**2290.00**	Case	4	159G	12F-3R	39.5	3455	No
540 C-O-M	4617.00	**1620.00**	**2120.00**	**2400.00**	Case	4	188D	Infinite	41.2	3600	No
730	6380.00	**2230.00**	**2940.00**	**3320.00**	Case	4	267D	8F-2R	57	7610	No
730	6721.00	**2350.00**	**3090.00**	**3490.00**	Case	4	267D	Infinite	57	7735	No
740	5630.00	**1970.00**	**2590.00**	**2930.00**	Case	4	251G	8F-2R	58	7415	No
740 C-O-M	5971.00	**2090.00**	**2750.00**	**3110.00**	Case	4	251G	Infinite	57	7540	No
830	6910.00	**2420.00**	**3180.00**	**3590.00**	Case	4	301D	8F-2R	64	7620	No
830 C-O-M	7215.00	**2530.00**	**3320.00**	**3750.00**	Case	4	301D	8F-2R	64	7745	No
840	6140.00	**2150.00**	**2820.00**	**3190.00**	Case	4	284G	8F-2R	65	7425	No
840 C-O-M	6481.00	**2270.00**	**2980.00**	**3370.00**	Case	4	284G	Infinite	64	7550	No
930	7720.00	**2700.00**	**3550.00**	**4010.00**	Case	6	401D	6F-1R	85	8385	No
940	7290.00	**2550.00**	**3350.00**	**3790.00**	Case	6	371G	6F-1R	71	8360	No
1030	8847.00	**3100.00**	**4070.00**	**4600.00**	Case	6	451D	8F-2R	101	9500	No
1200	18300.00	**2240.00**	**3640.00**	**4110.00**	Case	6	451D	8F-2R	120	16585	C
1968											
430	4364.00	**1920.00**	**2790.00**	**3400.00**	Case	4	188D	8F-2R	34	3590	No
440	3944.00	**1740.00**	**2520.00**	**3070.00**	Case	4	148G	8F-2R	33	3530	No
530	5162.00	**1860.00**	**2380.00**	**2690.00**	Case	4	188D	12F-3R	41.2	3600	No
540	4637.00	**1670.00**	**2130.00**	**2410.00**	Case	4	159G	12F-3R	39.5	3455	No
730	6711.00	**2420.00**	**3090.00**	**3490.00**	Case	4	267D	8F-2R	57	7610	No
730 C-O-M	7052.00	**2540.00**	**3240.00**	**3660.00**	Case	4	267D	Infinite	57	7610	No
740	5924.00	**2130.00**	**2730.00**	**3090.00**	Case	4	251G	8F-2R	58	7415	No
740 C-O-M	6275.00	**2260.00**	**2890.00**	**3270.00**	Case	4	267D	Infinite	57	7540	No
830	7290.00	**2620.00**	**3350.00**	**3790.00**	Case	4	301D	8F-2R	64	7620	No
830 C-O-M	7631.00	**2750.00**	**3510.00**	**3970.00**	Case	4	301D	Infinite	64	7745	No
840	6461.00	**2330.00**	**2970.00**	**3360.00**	Case	4	284G	8F-2R	65	7425	No
840 C-O-M	6800.00	**2450.00**	**3130.00**	**3540.00**	Case	4	284G	Infinite	65	7425	No
930	8123.00	**2920.00**	**3740.00**	**4230.00**	Case	6	401D	6F-1R	85	8385	No
940	7641.00	**2750.00**	**3520.00**	**3980.00**	Case	6	377G	6F-1R	71	8360	No
1030	9263.00	**3340.00**	**4260.00**	**4810.00**	Case	6	451D	8F-2R	101	9500	No
1200	18400.00	**2240.00**	**3640.00**	**4080.00**	Case	6	451D	8F-2R	120	16585	C
1969											
430	4486.00	**2020.00**	**2870.00**	**3500.00**	Case	4	188D	8F-2R	34	3800	No
440	4018.00	**1810.00**	**2570.00**	**3140.00**	Case	4	148G	8F-2R	33	3530	No
530	5283.00	**1960.00**	**2430.00**	**2750.00**	Case	4	188D	12F-3R	41.2	3600	No
540	4784.00	**1770.00**	**2200.00**	**2490.00**	Case	4	159G	12F-3R	39.5	3455	No
540	5640.00	**2090.00**	**2590.00**	**2930.00**	Case	4	188D	12F-3R	41.2	3600	No
730	6842.00	**2530.00**	**3150.00**	**3560.00**	Case	4	267D	8F-2R	57	7610	No
730 C-O-M	7183.00	**2660.00**	**3300.00**	**3730.00**	Case	4	267D	Infinite	57	7735	No
740	6060.00	**2240.00**	**2790.00**	**3150.00**	Case	4	251G	8F-2R	58	7415	No
740 C-O-M	6369.00	**2360.00**	**2930.00**	**3310.00**	Case	4	251G	Infinite	57	6505	No
830	7384.00	**2730.00**	**3400.00**	**3840.00**	Case	4	301D	8F-2R	64	7620	No
830 C-O-M	7725.00	**2860.00**	**3550.00**	**4010.00**	Case	4	301D	Infinite	64	7745	No
840	6586.00	**2440.00**	**3030.00**	**3420.00**	Case	4	284G	8F-2R	66	7425	No
840 C-O-M	6927.00	**2560.00**	**3190.00**	**3610.00**	Case	4	284G	Infinite	65	7550	No
930	8268.00	**3060.00**	**3800.00**	**4290.00**	Case	6	401D	6F-1R	85	8385	No
940	7768.00	**2870.00**	**3570.00**	**4030.00**	Case	6	377G	6F-1R	85	8190	No
1030	9678.00	**3580.00**	**4450.00**	**5030.00**	Case	6	451D	8F-2R	101	9500	No
1200	18500.00	**3920.00**	**5460.00**	**6120.00**	Case	6	451D	8F-2R	120	16585	C
1470	20638.00	**4480.00**	**6240.00**	**6990.00**	Case	6T	504D	8F-2R	144.9	15500	C,H,A

Case (Cont.)

Model	Approx. Retail Price New	Estimated Average Value Less Repairs Fair	Good	Premium	Make	Engine No. Cyls.	Displ. Cu.-In.	No. Speeds	P.T.O. H.P.	Approx. Shipping Wt.-Lbs.	Cab
1970											
470	4240.00	**1950.00**	**2710.00**	**3310.00**	Case	4	148G	12F-3R	33.11	3490	No
470	4683.00	**2150.00**	**3000.00**	**3660.00**	Case	4	188D	12F-3R	34.38	3565	No
570	5102.00	**2350.00**	**3270.00**	**3990.00**	Case	4	159G	12F-3R	39.50	3530	No
570	5652.00	**2600.00**	**3620.00**	**4420.00**	Case	4	188D	12F-3R	41.27	3675	No
770	9508.00	**3140.00**	**4180.00**	**4680.00**	Case	4	251G	8F-2R	56.32	7760	C,H
770	10138.00	**3350.00**	**4460.00**	**5000.00**	Case	4	267D	8F-2R	56.36	7900	C,H
770 PS	10158.00	**3350.00**	**4470.00**	**5010.00**	Case	4	251G	12F-4R	53.53	7830	C,H
770 PS	10788.00	**3560.00**	**4750.00**	**5320.00**	Case	4	267D	12F-4R	56.77	7970	C,H
870	10322.00	**3410.00**	**4540.00**	**5090.00**	Case	4	301G	8F-2R	71.06	7960	C,H
870	11062.00	**3650.00**	**4870.00**	**5450.00**	Case	4	336D	8F-2R	70.67	8100	C,H
870 PS	11031.00	**3640.00**	**4850.00**	**5430.00**	Case	4	301G	12F-4R	70.65	8030	C,H
870 PS	11771.00	**3880.00**	**5180.00**	**5800.00**	Case	4	336D	12F-4R	70.53	8170	C,H
970	11019.00	**3640.00**	**4850.00**	**5430.00**	Case	6	377G	8F-2R	85.02	9660	C,H
970	11869.00	**3920.00**	**5220.00**	**5850.00**	Case	6	401D	8F-2R	85.70	9800	C,H
970 PS	12187.00	**4020.00**	**5360.00**	**6000.00**	Case	6	377G	12F-4R	85.23	9730	C,H
970 PS	13037.00	**4300.00**	**5740.00**	**6430.00**	Case	6	401D	12F-4R	85.31	9870	C,H
1070	12613.00	**4160.00**	**5550.00**	**6220.00**	Case	6	451D	8F-2R	100.73	10600	C,H
1070 PS	13781.00	**4550.00**	**6060.00**	**6790.00**	Case	6	451D	12F-4R	100.21	10700	C,H
1090	13870.00	**4580.00**	**6100.00**	**6830.00**	Case	6	451D	8F-2R	100.73	12200	C,H
1090 PS	15038.00	**4960.00**	**6620.00**	**7410.00**	Case	6	451D	12F-4R	100.21	12300	C,H
1170	13842.00	**4570.00**	**6090.00**	**6820.00**	Case	6T	451D	8F-2R	121.93	13800	C,H
1470 4WD	20950.00	**4760.00**	**6630.00**	**7430.00**	Case	6T	504D	8F-4R	144.89	15550	C,H
1971											
470	4465.00	**2100.00**	**2860.00**	**3490.00**	Case	4	148G	12F-3R	33.11	3490	No
470	4920.00	**2310.00**	**3150.00**	**3840.00**	Case	4	188D	12F-3R	34.38	3565	No
570	5320.00	**2500.00**	**3410.00**	**4160.00**	Case	4	159G	12F-3R	39.50	3530	No
570	5890.00	**2770.00**	**3770.00**	**4600.00**	Case	4	188D	12F-3R	41.27	3675	No
770	10183.00	**3460.00**	**4480.00**	**5020.00**	Case	4	251G	8F-2R	56.32	7760	C,H
770	10813.00	**3680.00**	**4760.00**	**5330.00**	Case	4	267D	8F-2R	56.36	7900	C,H
770 PS	10833.00	**3680.00**	**4770.00**	**5340.00**	Case	4	251G	12F-4R	53.53	7830	C,H
770 PS	11463.00	**3900.00**	**5040.00**	**5650.00**	Case	4	267D	12F-4R	56.77	7970	C,H
870	10946.00	**3720.00**	**4820.00**	**5400.00**	Case	4	301G	8F-2R	71.06	7960	C,H
870	11736.00	**3990.00**	**5160.00**	**5780.00**	Case	4	336D	8F-2R	70.67	8100	C,H
870 PS	11655.00	**3960.00**	**5130.00**	**5750.00**	Case	4	301G	12F-4R	70.65	8030	C,H
870 PS	12445.00	**4230.00**	**5480.00**	**6140.00**	Case	4	336D	12F-4R	70.53	8170	C,H
970	11689.00	**3970.00**	**5140.00**	**5760.00**	Case	6	377G	8F-2R	85.02	9660	C,H
970	12609.00	**4290.00**	**5550.00**	**6220.00**	Case	6	401D	8F-2R	85.70	9800	C,H
970 PS	12857.00	**4370.00**	**5660.00**	**6340.00**	Case	6	377G	12F-4R	85.23	9730	C,H
970 PS	13777.00	**4680.00**	**6060.00**	**6790.00**	Case	6	401D	12F-4R	85.31	9870	C,H
1070	13243.00	**4500.00**	**5830.00**	**6530.00**	Case	6	451D	8F-2R	100.73	10600	C,H
1070 PS	14411.00	**4900.00**	**6340.00**	**7100.00**	Case	6	451D	12F-4R	100.21	10700	C,H
1090	14595.00	**4960.00**	**6420.00**	**7190.00**	Case	6	451D	8F-2R	100.73	12200	C,H
1090 PS	15763.00	**5360.00**	**6940.00**	**7770.00**	Case	6	451D	12F-4R	100.21	12300	C,H
1170	14567.00	**4950.00**	**6410.00**	**7180.00**	Case	6T	451D	8F-2R	121.93	13800	C,H
1175	15592.00	**5300.00**	**6860.00**	**7680.00**	Case	6T	451D	8F-2R		10700	C,H
1470	21125.00	**5040.00**	**7020.00**	**7860.00**	Case	6T	504D	8F-4R	144.89	15550	C,H
2470	29186.00	**4670.00**	**7590.00**	**8500.00**	Case	6T	504D	12F-4R	165.00	15800	C,H,A
PS - Power Shift											
1972											
470	4685.00	**2250.00**	**3000.00**	**3630.00**	Case	4	148G	8F-2R	33.11	3490	No
470	5165.00	**2480.00**	**3310.00**	**4010.00**	Case	4	188D	8F-2R	34.38	3565	No
570	5615.00	**2700.00**	**3590.00**	**4340.00**	Case	4	159G	8F-2R	39.50	3530	No
570	6205.00	**2980.00**	**3970.00**	**4800.00**	Case	4	188D	8F-2R	41.27	3675	No
770	10858.00	**3800.00**	**4780.00**	**5350.00**	Case	4	251G	8F-2R	56.32	7760	C,H
770	11488.00	**4020.00**	**5060.00**	**5670.00**	Case	4	267D	8F-2R	63.90	7900	C,H
770 PS	11508.00	**3220.00**	**4490.00**	**5030.00**	Case	4	251G	12F-4R	53.53	7830	C,H
770 PS	12138.00	**3400.00**	**4730.00**	**5300.00**	Case	4	267D	12F-4R	64.56	7970	C,H
870	11540.00	**3230.00**	**4500.00**	**5040.00**	Case	4	301G	8F-2R	71.06	7960	C,H
870	12340.00	**3460.00**	**4810.00**	**5390.00**	Case	4	336D	8F-2R	70.67	8100	C,H
870 PS	12249.00	**3430.00**	**4780.00**	**5350.00**	Case	4	301G	12F-4R	70.65	8030	C,H
870 PS	13049.00	**3650.00**	**5090.00**	**5700.00**	Case	4	336D	12F-4R	70.53	8170	C,H,A
970	12550.00	**3510.00**	**4900.00**	**5490.00**	Case	6	377G	8F-2R	85.02	9660	C,H,A
970	13470.00	**3770.00**	**5250.00**	**5880.00**	Case	6	401D	8F-2R	93.87	9800	C,H,A
970 PS	13718.00	**3840.00**	**5350.00**	**5990.00**	Case	6	377G	12F-4R	85.23	9730	C,H,A
970 PS	14638.00	**4100.00**	**5710.00**	**6400.00**	Case	6	401D	12F-4R	93.41	9870	C,H,A
1070	14022.00	**3930.00**	**5470.00**	**6130.00**	Case	6	451D	8F-2R	107.36	10600	C,H,A
1070 PS	15190.00	**4250.00**	**5920.00**	**6630.00**	Case	6	451D	12F-4R	108.10	10700	C,H,A
1090	15320.00	**4290.00**	**5980.00**	**6700.00**	Case	6	451D	8F-2R	107.36	12200	C,H,A
1090 PS	16488.00	**4620.00**	**6430.00**	**7200.00**	Case	6	451D	12F-4R	108.10	12300	C,H,A
1175	17481.00	**4900.00**	**6820.00**	**7640.00**	Case	6T	451D	8F-2R	121.93	10700	C,H,A
1270	15387.00	**4310.00**	**6000.00**	**6720.00**	Case	6T	451D	12F-3R	126.70	12200	C,H,A
1370	20018.00	**4760.00**	**6630.00**	**7430.00**	Case	6T	504D	12F-3R	142.51	12300	C,H,A
1470 4WD	22014.00	**5320.00**	**7410.00**	**8300.00**	Case	6T	504D	8F-4R	144.89	15550	C,H,A
2470 4WD	30056.00	**4810.00**	**7820.00**	**8760.00**	Case	6T	504D	12F-4R	165.00	15800	C,H,A
PS - Power Shift											
1973											
970	13806.00	**3870.00**	**5380.00**	**6030.00**	Case	6	377G	8F-2R	85.02	9660	C,H,A
970	14876.00	**4170.00**	**5800.00**	**6500.00**	Case	6	401D	8F-2R	93.87	9800	C,H,A
970 PS	14974.00	**4190.00**	**5840.00**	**6540.00**	Case	6	377G	12F-4R	85.23	9730	C,H,A
970 PS	16044.00	**4490.00**	**6260.00**	**7010.00**	Case	6	401D	12F-4R	93.41	9870	C,H,A
1070	14598.00	**4090.00**	**5690.00**	**6370.00**	Case	6	451D	8F-2R	107.36	10600	C,H,A

Case (Cont.)

1973 (Cont.)

Model	Approx. Retail Price New	Estimated Average Value Less Repairs: Fair	Good	Premium	Make	Engine No. Cyls.	Displ. Cu.-In.	No. Speeds	P.T.O. H.P.	Approx. Shipping Wt.-Lbs.	Cab
1070 PS	15766.00	4410.00	6150.00	6890.00	Case	6	451D	12F-4R	108.10	10700	C,H,A
1175	18316.00	5130.00	7140.00	8000.00	Case	6T	451D	8F-2R	121.93	10700	C,H,A
1270	16152.00	4520.00	6300.00	7060.00	Case	6T	451D	12F-3R	126.70	12200	C,H,A
1370	21471.00	5320.00	7410.00	8300.00	Case	6T	504D	12F-3R	142.51	12300	C,H,A
2470 4WD	31182.00	4930.00	7540.00	8450.00	Case	6T	504D	12F-4R	174.20	15800	C,H,A

PS - Power Shift

1974

Model	Approx. Retail Price New	Fair	Good	Premium	Make	No. Cyls.	Displ. Cu.-In.	No. Speeds	P.T.O. H.P.	Approx. Shipping Wt.-Lbs.	Cab
970	16658.00	4830.00	6500.00	7280.00	Case	6	401D	8F-2R	93.87	9240	C,H,A
970 PS	17826.00	5170.00	6950.00	7780.00	Case	6	401D	12F-3R	93.41	9380	C,H,A
1070	17689.00	5130.00	6900.00	7730.00	Case	6	451D	8F-2R	107.36	9320	C,H,A
1070 PS	18857.00	5470.00	7350.00	8230.00	Case	6	451D	12F-3R	108.10	9460	C,H,A
1175	19407.00	5630.00	7570.00	8480.00	Case	6T	451D	8F-2R	121.93	10700	C,H,A
1270	18315.00	5310.00	7140.00	8000.00	Case	6T	451D	12F-3R	126.70	12200	C,H,A
1370	22670.00	5990.00	8060.00	9030.00	Case	6T	504D	12F-3R	142.51	12300	C,H,A
2470 4WD	32256.00	5040.00	7560.00	8470.00	Case	6T	504D	12F-4R	174.20	15800	C,H,A
2670 4WD	37176.00	5400.00	8100.00	9070.00	Case	6TI	504D	12F-4R	216.00	16370	C,H,A

PS - Power Shift

1975

Model	Approx. Retail Price New	Fair	Good	Premium	Make	No. Cyls.	Displ. Cu.-In.	No. Speeds	P.T.O. H.P.	Approx. Shipping Wt.-Lbs.	Cab
970	16658.00	4800.00	6240.00	6930.00	Case	6	401D	8F-2R	93.87	9240	C,H,A
970 PS	17826.00	5040.00	6550.00	7270.00	Case	6	401D	12F-3R	93.41	9380	C,H,A
1070	17689.00	5100.00	6630.00	7360.00	Case	6	451D	8F-2R	107.36	9320	C,H,A
1070 PS	18857.00	5400.00	7020.00	7790.00	Case	6	451D	12F-3R	108.10	9460	C,H,A
1175	19407.00	5580.00	7250.00	8050.00	Case	6T	451D	8F-2R	121.93	10700	C,H,A
1270	20175.00	5700.00	7410.00	8230.00	Case	6T	451D	12F-3R	135.39	12200	C,H,A
1370	23954.00	6170.00	8020.00	8900.00	Case	6T	504D	12F-3R	155.56	12300	C,H,A
1570	28181.00	6620.00	8610.00	9560.00	Case	6T	504D	12F-3R	180.00	13330	C,H,A
2470 4WD	33869.00	5510.00	8120.00	9090.00	Case	6T	504D	12F-4R	174.20	15800	C,H,A
2670 4WD	39035.00	6270.00	9240.00	10350.00	Case	6TI	504D	12F-4R	219.44	16370	C,H,A

PS - Power Shift

1976

Model	Approx. Retail Price New	Fair	Good	Premium	Make	No. Cyls.	Displ. Cu.-In.	No. Speeds	P.T.O. H.P.	Approx. Shipping Wt.-Lbs.	Cab
970	18365.00	5390.00	6960.00	7730.00	Case	6	401D	8F-2R	93.87	9240	C,H,A
970 PS	19533.00	5580.00	7200.00	7990.00	Case	6	401D	12F-3R	93.41	9380	C,H,A
1070	19502.00	5740.00	7400.00	8210.00	Case	6	451D	8F-2R	107.36	9320	C,H,A
1070 PS	20670.00	6050.00	7800.00	8660.00	Case	6	451D	12F-3R	108.10	9460	C,H,A
1175	21323.00	6290.00	8120.00	9010.00	Case	6T	451D	8F-2R	121.93	10700	C,H,A
1270	23210.00	6820.00	8800.00	9770.00	Case	6T	451D	12F-3R	135.39	12800	C,H,A
1370	26158.00	7150.00	9220.00	10230.00	Case	6T	504D	12F-3R	155.56	13170	C,H,A
1570	29646.00	7610.00	9820.00	10900.00	Case	6T	504D	12F-3R	180.00	13330	C,H,A
2470 4WD	35558.00	6060.00	8790.00	9850.00	Case	6T	504D	12F-4R	174.20	15800	C,H,A
2670 4WD	41152.00	7400.00	10730.00	12020.00	Case	6TI	504D	12F-4R	219.44	16370	C,H,A

PS - Power Shift

1977

Model	Approx. Retail Price New	Fair	Good	Premium	Make	No. Cyls.	Displ. Cu.-In.	No. Speeds	P.T.O. H.P.	Approx. Shipping Wt.-Lbs.	Cab
970	20186.00	6080.00	7790.00	8650.00	Case	6	401D	8F-2R	93.87	9240	C,H,A
970 PS	21374.00	6530.00	8360.00	9280.00	Case	6	401D	12F-3R	93.41	9380	C,H,A
1070	21892.00	6720.00	8610.00	9560.00	Case	6	451D	8F-2R	107.36	9320	C,H,A
1070 PS	23060.00	7040.00	9020.00	10010.00	Case	6	451D	12F-3R	108.10	9460	C,H,A
1175	22974.00	6880.00	8820.00	9790.00	Case	6T	451D	8F-2R	121.93	10700	C,H,A
1270	25850.00	7380.00	9450.00	10490.00	Case	6T	451D	12F-3R	135.39	12800	C,H,A
1370	28461.00	7700.00	9870.00	10960.00	Case	6T	504D	12F-3R	155.56	13170	C,H,A
1570	32478.00	8030.00	10280.00	11410.00	Case	6T	504D	12F-3R	180.41	13330	C,H,A
2470 4WD	36874.00	6590.00	9420.00	10550.00	Case	6T	504D	12F-4R	174.20	15800	C,H,A
2670 4WD	42173.00	6850.00	9780.00	10950.00	Case	6TI	504D	12F-4R	219.44	16370	C,H,A
2870 4WD	47383.00	7850.00	11220.00	12570.00	Saab	6T	673D	12F-4R	252.10	18500	C,H,A

PS - Power Shift

1978

Model	Approx. Retail Price New	Fair	Good	Premium	Make	No. Cyls.	Displ. Cu.-In.	No. Speeds	P.T.O. H.P.	Approx. Shipping Wt.-Lbs.	Cab
970	22754.00	6930.00	8820.00	9700.00	Case	6	401D	8F-2R	93.87	9240	C,H,A
970 PS	23922.00	7430.00	9450.00	10400.00	Case	6	401D	12F-3R	93.41	9380	C,H,A
1070	24259.00	7590.00	9660.00	10630.00	Case	6	451D	8F-2R	107.36	9320	C,H,A
1070 PS	25427.00	7920.00	10080.00	11090.00	Case	6	451D	12F-3R	108.10	9460	C,H,A
1175	24882.00	7430.00	9450.00	10400.00	Case	6T	451D	8F-2R	121.93	10700	C,H,A
1270	29582.00	8420.00	10710.00	11780.00	Case	6T	451D	12F-3R	135.39	12800	C,H,A
1370	30663.00	9080.00	11550.00	12710.00	Case	6T	504D	12F-3R	155.56	13170	C,H,A
1570	36174.00	10230.00	13020.00	14320.00	Case	6T	504D	12F-3R	180.41	13330	C,H,A
2090	27384.00	4510.00	6360.00	7120.00	Case	6	504D	8F-4R		10950	C,H,A
2290	30657.00	5170.00	7290.00	8170.00	Case	6T	504D	8F-4R		11070	C,H,A
2390	36156.00	7150.00	10080.00	11290.00	Case	6T	504D	12F-3R		14270	C,H,A
2470 4WD	38819.00	7480.00	10540.00	11810.00	Case	6T	504D	12F-4R	174.20	15800	C,H,A
2590	40060.00	7810.00	11010.00	12330.00	Case	6T	504D	12F-3R		14875	C,H,A
2670 4WD	43413.00	8540.00	12030.00	13470.00	Case	6TI	504D	12F-4R	219.44	16370	C,H,A
2870 4WD	49302.00	9310.00	13110.00	14680.00	Saab	6T	673D	12F-4R	252.10	18500	C,H,A

PS - Power Shift

1979

Model	Approx. Retail Price New	Fair	Good	Premium	Make	No. Cyls.	Displ. Cu.-In.	No. Speeds	P.T.O. H.P.	Approx. Shipping Wt.-Lbs.	Cab
1070	26132.00	8260.00	10450.00	11390.00	Case	6	451D	8F-2R	107.36	9320	C,H,A
1070 PS	27300.00	8500.00	10750.00	11720.00	Case	6	451D	12F-3R	108.10	9460	C,H,A
1175	26131.00	7920.00	10020.00	10920.00	Case	6T	451D	8F-2R	121.93	10700	C,H,A
1270	31015.00	8740.00	11050.00	12050.00	Case	6T	451D	12F-3R	135.39	12800	C,H,A
1370	32715.00	9010.00	11400.00	12430.00	Case	6T	504D	12F-3R	155.56	13170	C,H,A
2090	29468.00	4920.00	6850.00	7670.00	Case	6	504D	8F-4R		10950	C,H,A

Case (Cont.)

1979 (Cont.)

Model	Approx. Retail Price New	Fair	Good	Premium	Engine Make	Engine No. Cyls.	Engine Displ. Cu.-In.	No. Speeds	P.T.O. H.P.	Approx. Shipping Wt.-Lbs.	Cab
2290	33167.00	6000.00	8350.00	9350.00	Case	6T	504D	8F-4R		11070	C,H,A
2390	40107.00	6900.00	9600.00	10750.00	Case	6T	504D	12F-3R		14270	C,H,A
2590	43371.00	7590.00	10560.00	11830.00	Case	6T	504D	12F-3R		14875	C,H,A
2670 4WD	44818.00	8030.00	11170.00	12510.00	Case	6TI	504D	12F-4R	219.44	16370	C,H,A
2870 4WD	51216.00	9550.00	13290.00	14890.00	Saab	6	673D	12F-4R	252.10	18500	C,H,A
4490 4WD	49618.00	9110.00	12680.00	14200.00	Case	6T	504D	12F-4R	175.20	17420	C,H,A
4690 4WD	61381.00	10900.00	15160.00	16980.00	Case	6TI	504D	12F-4R	219.62	17775	C,H,A
4890 4WD	72381.00	12050.00	16760.00	18770.00	Saab	6T	673D	12F-4R	253.41	21250	C,H,A

PS - Power Shift

1980

Model	Approx. Retail Price New	Fair	Good	Premium	Engine Make	Engine No. Cyls.	Engine Displ. Cu.-In.	No. Speeds	P.T.O. H.P.	Approx. Shipping Wt.-Lbs.	Cab
1190	11315.00	4130.00	5190.00	5660.00	David Brown	3	164D	12F-4R	43.00	4620	No
1290	12615.00	4730.00	5940.00	6480.00	David Brown	4	195D	12F-4R	53.00	5390	No
1390	16282.00	5500.00	6910.00	7530.00	David Brown	4	219D	12F-4R	60.00	5500	No
1490	20186.00	6480.00	8140.00	8870.00	David Brown	4T	219D	12F-4R	70.00	7240	No
1690	23192.00	7040.00	8840.00	9640.00	Case	6	329D	12F-4R	90.00	8660	No
2090	32786.00	6480.00	8910.00	9980.00	Case	6	504D	12F-3R	108.29	10950	C,H,A
2290	36082.00	6880.00	9460.00	10600.00	Case	6T	504D	12F-3R	129.08	11070	C,H,A
2390	43231.00	7970.00	10960.00	12280.00	Case	6T	504D	12F-3R	160.72	14270	C,H,A
2590	47182.00	8920.00	12270.00	13740.00	Case	6T	504D	12F-3R	180.38	14875	C,H,A
4490 4WD	53416.00	9700.00	13340.00	14940.00	Case	6T	504D	12F-4R	175.20	17420	C,H,A
4690 4WD	68238.00	11580.00	15920.00	17830.00	Case	6TI	504D	12F-4R	219.62	17775	C,H,A
4890 4WD	79941.00	13210.00	18160.00	20340.00	Saab	6T	673D	12F-4R	253.41	21250	C,H,A

1981

Model	Approx. Retail Price New	Fair	Good	Premium	Engine Make	Engine No. Cyls.	Engine Displ. Cu.-In.	No. Speeds	P.T.O. H.P.	Approx. Shipping Wt.-Lbs.	Cab
1190	12908.00	4540.00	5670.00	6180.00	David Brown	3	164D	12F-4R	43.09	4620	No
1290	14306.00	4790.00	5990.00	6530.00	David Brown	4	195D	12F-4R	53.73	5390	No
1390	17670.00	5940.00	7430.00	8100.00	David Brown	4	219D	12F-4R	60.59	5500	No
1490	22335.00	6960.00	8700.00	9480.00	David Brown	4T	219D	12F-4R	70.51	7240	No
1690	25236.00	8000.00	10000.00	10900.00	Case	6	329D	12F-4R	90.39	8660	No
2090	35992.00	9720.00	12150.00	13240.00	Case	6	504D	12F-3R	108.29	10950	C,H,A
2290	40177.00	7750.00	10540.00	11810.00	Case	6T	504D	12F-3R	129.08	11070	C,H,A
2390	47148.00	9250.00	12580.00	14090.00	Case	6T	504D	12F-3R	160.72	14270	C,H,A
2590	52342.00	10580.00	14380.00	16110.00	Case	6T	504D	12F-3R	180.38	14875	C,H,A
4490 4WD	59636.00	11660.00	15860.00	17760.00	Case	6T	504D	12F-4R	175.20	17420	C,H,A
4690 4WD	75019.00	13510.00	18370.00	20570.00	Case	6TI	504D	12F-4R	219.62	17775	C,H,A
4890 4WD	88518.00	15130.00	20580.00	23050.00	Saab	6T	673D	12F-4R	253.41	21250	C,H,A

1982

Model	Approx. Retail Price New	Fair	Good	Premium	Engine Make	Engine No. Cyls.	Engine Displ. Cu.-In.	No. Speeds	P.T.O. H.P.	Approx. Shipping Wt.-Lbs.	Cab
1190	16475.00	5000.00	6210.00	6710.00	David Brown	3	164D	12F-4R	43.09	4620	No
1290	18222.00	5660.00	7040.00	7600.00	David Brown	4	195D	12F-4R	53.73	5390	No
1390	21440.00	7030.00	8740.00	9440.00	David Brown	4	219D	12F-4R	60.59	5500	No
1390 4WD	26375.00	8280.00	10290.00	11110.00	David Brown	4	219D	12F-4R	60.59	6400	No
1490	25208.00	7840.00	9750.00	10530.00	David Brown	4T	219D	12F-4R	70.51	7240	No
1490 4WD	33820.00	10660.00	13250.00	14310.00	David Brown	4T	219D	12F-4R	70.51	7705	No
1490 High Platform 4WD	40144.00	12630.00	15700.00	16960.00	David Brown	4T	219D	12F-4R	70.00	8900	C,H,A
1490 High Platform PS	33131.00	10040.00	12480.00	13480.00	David Brown	4T	219D	12F-4R	70.00	8900	C,H,A
1690	29813.00	8810.00	10950.00	11830.00	Case	6	329D	12F-4R	90.39	8660	No
1690 4WD	39345.00	11970.00	14880.00	16070.00	Case	6	329D	12F-4R	90.39	8755	No
1690 High Platform 4WD	46016.00	13690.00	17020.00	18380.00	Case	6	329D	12F-4R	90.00	9115	C,H,A
1690 High Platform PS	39810.00	12140.00	15090.00	16300.00	Case	6	329D	12F-4R	90.00	9115	C,H,A
2090	42084.00	8600.00	11580.00	12970.00	Case	6	504D	8F-4R	108.74	15490	C,H,A
2090 PS	44263.00	8840.00	11900.00	13330.00	Case	6	504D	12F-3R	108.29	15600	C,H,A
2090 PS 4WD	52579.00	9780.00	13160.00	14740.00	Case	6	504D	12F-3R	108.00	16500	C,H,A
2290	47316.00	9960.00	13410.00	15020.00	Case	6T	504D	8F-4R	128.80	16000	C,H,A
2290 PS	49495.00	10190.00	13720.00	15370.00	Case	6T	504D	12F-3R	129.08	16600	C,H,A
2290 PS 4WD	57811.00	10920.00	14700.00	16460.00	Case	6T	504D	12F-3R	129.00	17000	C,H,A
2390 PS	57809.00	12350.00	16630.00	18630.00	Case	6T	504D	12F-3R	160.72	16720	C,H,A
2590	64029.00	13520.00	18200.00	20380.00	Case	6T	504D	12F-3R	180.38	16800	C,H,A
4490 4WD	70231.00	13060.00	17580.00	19690.00	Case	6T	504D	12F-4R	175.20	17420	C,H,A
4490 4WD w/3 Pt.	76276.00	14110.00	19000.00	21280.00	Case	6T	504D	12F-4R	175.20	17920	C,H,A
4690 4WD	89460.00	15460.00	20810.00	23310.00	Case	6TI	504D	12F-4R	219.62	17775	C,H,A
4690 4WD w/3 Pt.	95505.00	16900.00	22750.00	25480.00	Case	6TI	504D	12F-4R	219.62	18725	C,H,A
4890 4WD	102922.00	18210.00	24510.00	27450.00	Saab	6T	673D	12F-4R	253.41	21250	C,H,A
4890 4WD w/3 Pt.	109047.00	18990.00	25570.00	28640.00	Saab	6T	673D	12F-4R	253.41	21750	C,H,A

PS - Power Shift

1983

Model	Approx. Retail Price New	Fair	Good	Premium	Engine Make	Engine No. Cyls.	Engine Displ. Cu.-In.	No. Speeds	P.T.O. H.P.	Approx. Shipping Wt.-Lbs.	Cab
1190	17104.00	5510.00	6820.00	7370.00	David Brown	3	164D	12F-4R	43.09	4620	No
1290	20842.00	6310.00	7800.00	8420.00	David Brown	4	195D	12F-4R	53.73	5390	No
1290 4WD	25470.00	8160.00	10090.00	10900.00	David Brown	4	195D	12F-4R	53.73	6100	No
1390	22562.00	7430.00	9190.00	9930.00	David Brown	4	219D	12F-4R	60.59	5500	No
1390 4WD	27644.00	8980.00	11110.00	12000.00	David Brown	4	219D	12F-4R	60.59	6400	No
1490	25687.00	8240.00	10190.00	11010.00	David Brown	4T	219D	12F-4R	70.51	7240	No
1490 4WD	34299.00	10750.00	13300.00	14360.00	David Brown	4T	219D	12F-4R	70.51	7705	No
1490 High Platform	32015.00	10260.00	12690.00	13710.00	David Brown	4T	219D	12F-4R	70.00	8375	C,H,A
1490 High Platform 4WD	40623.00	13530.00	16730.00	18070.00	David Brown	4T	219D	12F-4R	70.00	8900	C,H,A
1490 PS	27378.00	8880.00	10990.00	11870.00	David Brown	4T	219D	12F-4R	70.00	7300	No
1690	29813.00	9420.00	11660.00	12590.00	Case	6	329D	12F-4R	90.39	8660	No
1690 4WD	39345.00	12670.00	15670.00	16920.00	Case	6	329D	12F-4R	90.39	9087	No
1690 High Platform	38215.00	11860.00	14660.00	15830.00	Case	6	329D	12F-4R	90.00	8950	C,H,A
1690 High Platform 4WD	46016.00	14440.00	17860.00	19290.00	Case	6	329D	12F-4R	90.00	10157	C,H,A
1690 PS	31650.00	9750.00	12060.00	13030.00	Case	6	329D	12F-4R	90.00	8710	No
2090	44927.00	9590.00	12780.00	14310.00	Case	6	504D	8F-4R	108.74	15490	C,H,A

Case (Cont.)

1983 (Cont.)

Model	Approx. Retail Price New	Fair	Good	Premium	Make	No. Cyls.	Displ. Cu.-In.	No. Speeds	P.T.O. H.P.	Approx. Shipping Wt.-Lbs.	Cab
2090 PS	46777.00	9900.00	13200.00	14780.00	Case	6	504D	12F-3R	108.29	15600	C,H,A
2090 PS 4WD	55218.00	10850.00	14470.00	16210.00	Case	6	504D	12F-3R	108.00	16500	C,H,A
2290	50238.00	10850.00	14470.00	16210.00	Case	6T	504D	8F-4R	128.80	16000	C,H,A
2290 PS	52088.00	11070.00	14760.00	16530.00	Case	6T	504D	12F-3R	129.08	16600	C,H,A
2290 PS 4WD	60529.00	12020.00	16020.00	17940.00	Case	6T	504D	12F-3R	129.00	17000	C,H,A
2390 PS	58676.00	12600.00	16800.00	18820.00	Case	6T	504D	12F-3R	160.72	16720	C,H,A
2590 PS	64029.00	13230.00	17640.00	19760.00	Case	6T	504D	12F-3R	180.38	16800	C,H,A
4490 4WD	73495.00	14070.00	18750.00	21000.00	Case	6T	504D	12F-4R	175.20	17420	C,H,A
4490 4WD w/3 Pt.	78000.00	14450.00	19260.00	21570.00	Case	6T	504D	12F-4R	175.20	17920	C,H,A
4690 4WD	89000.00	15930.00	21240.00	23790.00	Case	6TI	504D	12F-4R	219.62	17775	C,H,A
4690 4WD w/3 Pt.	93000.00	17010.00	22680.00	25400.00	Case	6TI	504D	12F-4R	219.62	18275	C,H,A
4890 4WD	102022.00	18230.00	24300.00	27220.00	Saab	6T	673D	12F-4R	253.41	21250	C,H,A
4890 4WD w/3 Pt.	108292.00	18930.00	25230.00	28260.00	Saab	6T	673D	12F-4R	253.41	21750	C,H,A

PS - Power Shift

1984

Model	Approx. Retail Price New	Fair	Good	Premium	Make	No. Cyls.	Displ. Cu.-In.	No. Speeds	P.T.O. H.P.	Approx. Shipping Wt.-Lbs.	Cab
1194	17960.00	6440.00	7920.00	8550.00	David Brown	3	164D	12F-4R	43.00	4620	No
1294	21885.00	7760.00	9550.00	10310.00	David Brown	4	219D	12F-4R	55.00	5390	No
1294 4WD	26750.00	9260.00	11400.00	12310.00	David Brown	4	219D	12F-4R	55.00	6100	No
1394	23690.00	8070.00	9930.00	10720.00	David Brown	4T	219D	12F-4R	65.00	5500	No
1394 4WD	29030.00	9750.00	12000.00	12960.00	David Brown	4T	219D	12F-4R	65.00	6400	No
1394 PS	25385.00	8340.00	10270.00	11090.00	David Brown	4T	219D	12F-4R	65.00	5560	No
1394 PS 4WD	30725.00	10420.00	12830.00	13860.00	David Brown	4T	219D	12F-4R	65.00	6460	No
1494	26975.00	8960.00	11030.00	11910.00	David Brown	4T	219D	12F-4R	75.00	7240	No
1494 4WD	36015.00	11700.00	14400.00	15550.00	David Brown	4T	219D	12F-4R	75.00	7705	No
1494 High Platform	33615.00	10530.00	12960.00	14000.00	David Brown	4T	219D	12F-4R	75.00	8375	C,H,A
1494 High Platform 4WD	42655.00	10160.00	12510.00	13510.00	David Brown	4T	219D	12F-4R	75.00	8900	C,H,A
1494 PS	28670.00	9230.00	11360.00	12270.00	David Brown	4T	219D	12F-4R	75.00	7300	No
1494 PS 4WD	37710.00	11310.00	13920.00	15030.00	David Brown	4T	219D	12F-4R	75.00	7765	No
1594	29820.00	9280.00	11420.00	12330.00	Case	6	329D	12F-4R	85.90	8660	No
1594 4WD	39345.00	11720.00	14420.00	15570.00	Case	6	329D	12F-4R	85.00	9090	No
1594 High Platform	38215.00	12170.00	14980.00	16180.00	Case	6	329D	12F-4R	85.00	8950	C,H,A
1594 High Platform 4WD	46020.00	13260.00	16320.00	17630.00	Case	6	329D	12F-4R	85.00	10160	C,H,A
1594 PS	31515.00	9950.00	12240.00	13220.00	Case	6	329D	12F-4R	85.54	8710	No
1594 PS 4WD	41040.00	11700.00	14400.00	15550.00	Case	6	329D	12F-4R	85.00	9150	No
2094	49115.00	10110.00	13360.00	14960.00	Case	6	504D	12F-3R	110.50	15490	C,H,A
2094 4WD	57980.00	11450.00	15130.00	16950.00	Case	6	504D	12F-3R	110.00	16500	C,H,A
2294	54700.00	12520.00	16540.00	18530.00	Case	6T	504D	12F-3R	131.97	16600	C,H,A
2294 4WD	63555.00	13300.00	17580.00	19690.00	Case	6T	504D	12F-3R	131.97	17000	C,H,A
2394	61610.00	14280.00	18870.00	21130.00	Case	6T	504D	12F-3R	162.15	16720	C,H,A
2594	67230.00	14840.00	19610.00	21960.00	Case	6T	504D	12F-3R		16800	C,H,A
3294 4WD	70465.00	16240.00	21460.00	24040.00	Case	6T	504D	12F-3R	162.63	17000	C,H,A
4494 4WD	74000.00	16630.00	21980.00	24620.00	Case	6T	504D	12F-4R	175.20	17420	C,H,A
4494 4WD w/3 Pt.	78200.00	17140.00	22640.00	25360.00	Case	6T	504D	12F-4R	175.20	17920	C,H,A
4694 4WD	89000.00	17920.00	23680.00	26520.00	Case	6TI	504D	12F-4R	219.62	17775	C,H,A
4694 4WD w/3 Pt.	93000.00	18680.00	24680.00	27640.00	Case	6TI	504D	12F-4R	219.62	18275	C,H,A
4894 4WD	102000.00	20160.00	26640.00	29840.00	Saab	6T	673D	12F-4R	253.41	21250	C,H,A
4894 4WD w/3 Pt.	108000.00	20440.00	27010.00	30250.00	Saab	6T	673D	12F-4R	253.41	21750	C,H,A
4994 4WD	132050.00	21010.00	27770.00	31100.00	Case	8	866D	12F-2R	344.04	28000	C,H,A

PS - Power Shift

1985

Model	Approx. Retail Price New	Fair	Good	Premium	Make	No. Cyls.	Displ. Cu.-In.	No. Speeds	P.T.O. H.P.	Approx. Shipping Wt.-Lbs.	Cab
1194	17960.00	6640.00	8130.00	8700.00	David Brown	3	164D	12F-4R	43.00	4620	No
1294	21885.00	7750.00	9500.00	10170.00	David Brown	4	219D	12F-4R	55.00	5390	No
1294 4WD	26750.00	9820.00	12030.00	12870.00	David Brown	4	219D	12F-4R	55.00	6100	No
1394	23690.00	8680.00	10630.00	11370.00	David Brown	4T	219D	12F-4R	65.00	5500	No
1394 4WD	29030.00	10200.00	12500.00	13380.00	David Brown	4T	219D	12F-4R	65.00	6400	No
1394 PS 4WD w/Cab	36875.00	13150.00	16110.00	17240.00	David Brown	4T	219D	12F-4R	65.00	7250	C,H,A
1394 PS w/Cab	32020.00	11200.00	13720.00	14680.00	David Brown	4T	219D	12F-4R	65.00	6350	C,H,A
1494	26975.00	9190.00	11260.00	12050.00	David Brown	4T	219D	12F-4R	75.00	7240	No
1494 4WD	36015.00	12800.00	15680.00	16780.00	David Brown	4T	219D	12F-4R	75.00	7705	No
1494 PS 4WD w/Cab	40870.00	14750.00	18070.00	19340.00	David Brown	4T	219D	12F-4R	75.00	8555	C,H,A
1494 PS w/Cab	35109.00	12440.00	15240.00	16310.00	David Brown	4T	219D	12F-4R	75.00	8150	C,H,A
1594	30725.00	10690.00	13100.00	14020.00	Case	6	329D	12F-4R	85.90	8660	No
1594 4WD PS w/Cab	43700.00	15480.00	18960.00	20290.00	Case	6	329D	12F-4R	85.00	9900	C,H,A
1594 PS w/Cab	37920.00	13160.00	16120.00	17250.00	Case	6	329D	12F-4R	85.54	8710	C,H,A
1896	45075.00	15630.00	19150.00	20490.00	CD	6T	359D	12F-4R	95.92	13320	C,H,A
1896 4WD	54865.00	19150.00	23450.00	25090.00	CD	6T	359D	12F-4R	95.92	14437	C,H,A
2094	49115.00	12330.00	15620.00	17340.00	Case	6	504D	12F-4R	110.50	15490	C,H,A
2094 4WD	57980.00	13500.00	17100.00	18980.00	Case	6	504D	12F-4R	110.50	16500	C,H,A
2096	50160.00	13250.00	16780.00	18630.00	CD	6T	359D	12F-4R	115.67	14005	C,H,A
2096 4WD	59947.00	14100.00	17860.00	19830.00	CD	6T	359D	12F-4R	115.67	15125	C,H,A
2294	54700.00	13500.00	17100.00	18980.00	Case	6	504D	12F-4R	131.97	16600	C,H,A
2294 4WD	63555.00	15620.00	19780.00	21960.00	Case	6	504D	12F-3R	131.97	17000	C,H,A
2394	65485.00	16530.00	20930.00	23230.00	Case	6T	504D	12F-3R	162.15	16720	C,H,A
2594	73380.00	17420.00	22070.00	24500.00	Case	6T	504D	12F-3R		16800	C,H,A
3294 4WD	70465.00	17720.00	22450.00	24920.00	Case	6T	504D	12F-3R	162.63	17000	C,H,A
4494 4WD w/3 Pt.	78000.00	18000.00	22800.00	25310.00	Case	6T	504D	12F-4R	175.20	17920	C,H,A
4694 4WD w/3 Pt.	93000.00	20100.00	25460.00	28260.00	Case	6TI	504D	12F-4R	219.62	18275	C,H,A
4894 4WD w/3 Pt.	106000.00	21600.00	27360.00	30370.00	Scania	6T	673D	12F-4R	253.41	21750	C,H,A
4994 4WD	132050.00	23120.00	29280.00	32500.00	Case	8	866D	12F-2R	344.04	28000	C,H,A

PS - Power Shift CD - Consolidated Diesel Corp.

Case-International

Model	Approx. Retail Price New	Estimated Average Value Less Repairs Fair	Good	Premium	Engine Make	No. Cyls.	Displ. Cu.-In.	No. Speeds	P.T.O. H.P.	Approx. Shipping Wt.-Lbs.	Cab
1986											
234	6500.00	**3840.00**	**4420.00**	**4910.00**	Mitsubishi	3	52D	6F-2R	15.20	1164	No
234 4WD	6900.00	**4070.00**	**4690.00**	**5210.00**	Mitsubishi	3	52D	6F-2R	15.20	1270	No
Hydro 234	7375.00	**4350.00**	**5020.00**	**5570.00**	Mitsubishi	3	52D	Infinite	15.20	1204	No
Hydro 234 4WD	7825.00	**4620.00**	**5320.00**	**5910.00**	Mitsubishi	3	52D	Infinite	15.20	1310	No
244	6780.00	**4000.00**	**4610.00**	**5120.00**	Mitsubishi	3	60D	9F-3R	18.00	1498	No
244 4WD	7665.00	**4520.00**	**5210.00**	**5780.00**	Mitsubishi	3	60D	9F-3R	18.00	1642	No
254	7350.00	**4340.00**	**5000.00**	**5550.00**	Mitsubishi	3	65D	9F-3R	21.00	1493	No
254 4WD	8360.00	**4930.00**	**5690.00**	**6320.00**	Mitsubishi	3	65D	9F-3R	21.00	1622	No
274 Offset	10295.00	**6070.00**	**7000.00**	**7770.00**	Nissan	3	99D	8F-2R	27.00	3151	No
284D	9360.00	**5520.00**	**6370.00**	**7070.00**	Nissan	3	99D	8F-2R	27.47	2456	No
284D 4WD	11185.00	**6600.00**	**7610.00**	**8450.00**	Nissan	3	99D	8F-2R	25.00	2811	No
385	12270.00	**7240.00**	**8340.00**	**9260.00**	IH	3	155D	8F-4R	35.00	5050	No
485	15725.00	**9280.00**	**10690.00**	**11870.00**	IH	3	179D	8F-2R	42.42	5200	No
584 4WD	23273.00	**11400.00**	**13500.00**	**14580.00**	IH	4	206D	8F-4R	52.5	6685	No
584 4WD w/Cab	29254.00	**14330.00**	**16970.00**	**18330.00**	IH	4	206D	8F-4R	52.5	7890	C,H,A
585	18845.00	**9230.00**	**10930.00**	**11800.00**	IH	4	206D	8F-4R	52.54	5640	No
585 4WD	23460.00	**11500.00**	**13610.00**	**14700.00**	IH	4	206D	8F-4R	52.00	6685	No
585 RC	19240.00	**9430.00**	**11160.00**	**12050.00**	IH	4	206D	8F-4R	52.54	5890	No
684 4WD	26348.00	**12910.00**	**15280.00**	**16500.00**	IH	4	239D	8F-4R	62.5	6765	No
684 4WD w/Cab	32329.00	**15190.00**	**17980.00**	**19420.00**	IH	4	239D	8F-4R	62.5	7970	C,H,A
685	21155.00	**10290.00**	**12180.00**	**13150.00**	IH	4	239D	8F-4R	62.52	5720	No
685 4WD	26535.00	**12250.00**	**14500.00**	**15660.00**	IH	4	239D	8F-4R	62.00	6765	No
685 RC	21565.00	**10570.00**	**12510.00**	**13510.00**	IH	4	239D	8F-4R	62.52	5970	No
884 4WD	30228.00	**14810.00**	**17530.00**	**18930.00**	IH	4	268D	16F-8R		7223	No
884 4WD	36209.00	**17150.00**	**20300.00**	**21920.00**	IH	4	268D	16F-8R		8428	No
885	25605.00	**12550.00**	**14850.00**	**16040.00**	IH	4	268D	16F-8R	72.91	6065	No
885 4WD	30415.00	**14210.00**	**16820.00**	**18170.00**	IH	4	268D	16F-8R	72.00	7223	No
885 RC	26235.00	**12860.00**	**15220.00**	**16440.00**	IH	4	268D	16F-8R	72.91	6315	No
1394	21781.00	**8200.00**	**10000.00**	**10700.00**	David Brown	4T	219D	12F-4R	65.00	5658	No
1394 4WD	25245.00	**9640.00**	**11750.00**	**12570.00**	David Brown	4T	219D	12F-4R	65.00	5990	No
1394 PS w/Cab	29998.00	**11070.00**	**13500.00**	**14450.00**	David Brown	4T	219D	12F-4R	65.00	6758	C,H,A
1494	24612.00	**9270.00**	**11300.00**	**12090.00**	David Brown	4T	219D	12F-4R	75.00	7240	No
1494 4WD	31827.00	**11890.00**	**14500.00**	**15520.00**	David Brown	4T	219D	12F-4R	75.00	8327	No
1494 PS 4WD w/Cab	39800.00	**14970.00**	**18250.00**	**19530.00**	David Brown	4T	219D	12F-4R	75.00	8555	C,H,A
1494 PS w/Cab	32714.00	**12300.00**	**15000.00**	**16050.00**	David Brown	4T	219D	12F-4R	75.00	8001	C,H,A
1594	26482.00	**10000.00**	**12200.00**	**13050.00**	Case	6	329D	12F-4R	85.90	7544	No
1594 4WD PS w/Cab	39948.00	**15330.00**	**18700.00**	**20010.00**	Case	6	329D	12F-4R	85.00	10105	C,H,A
1594 PS w/Cab	34683.00	**13240.00**	**16150.00**	**17280.00**	Case	6	329D	12F-4R	85.54	8889	C,H,A
1896	36023.00	**14100.00**	**17200.00**	**18400.00**	CD	6T	359D	12F-4R	95.92	11383	C,H,A
1896 4WD	51956.00	**17020.00**	**20750.00**	**22200.00**	CD	6T	359D	12F-4R	95.92	13475	C,H,A
2096	48771.00	**17710.00**	**21600.00**	**23110.00**	CD	6T	359D	12F-4R	115.67	11966	C,H,A
2096 4WD	56909.00	**19020.00**	**23200.00**	**24820.00**	CD	6T	359D	12F-4R	115.67	13489	C,H,A
2294	52928.00	**15040.00**	**18330.00**	**20350.00**	Case	6	504D	12F-4R	131.97	11586	C,H,A
2294 4WD	61884.00	**16320.00**	**19890.00**	**22080.00**	Case	6	504D	12F-3R	131.97	13892	C,H,A
2394	64752.00	**17280.00**	**21060.00**	**23380.00**	Case	6T	504D	24F-3R	162.92	14080	C,H,A
2594	69711.00	**18240.00**	**22230.00**	**24680.00**	Case	6T	504D	24F-3R	182.07	14443	C,H,A
3294	61943.00	**16320.00**	**19890.00**	**22080.00**	Case	6T	504D	12F-3R	162.00	14515	C,H,A
3394	70671.00	**18750.00**	**22850.00**	**25360.00**	Case	6T	504D	24F-3R	162.86	14820	C,H,A
3594	71900.00	**20130.00**	**24530.00**	**27230.00**	Case	6T	504D	24F-3R	182.27	14860	C,H,A
4494 4WD w/3 Pt.	78010.00	**21440.00**	**26130.00**	**29000.00**	Case	6T	504D	12F-4R	175.20	17920	C,H,A
4694 4WD w/3 Pt.	93388.00	**23160.00**	**28230.00**	**31340.00**	Case	6TI	504D	12F-4R	219.62	18275	C,H,A
4894 4WD w/3 Pt.	106758.00	**26900.00**	**32780.00**	**36390.00**	Scania	6T	673D	12F-4R	253.41	21750	C,H,A
4994 4WD	135024.00	**28810.00**	**35110.00**	**38970.00**	Case	8	866D	12F-2R	344.04	28000	C,H,A
5088	54340.00	**16830.00**	**20520.00**	**21960.00**	IH	6T	436D	18F-6R	136.12	13581	C,H,A
5088 4WD	66260.00	**18640.00**	**22730.00**	**24320.00**	IH	6T	436D	18F-6R	136.00	16749	C,H,A
5288	62335.00	**19680.00**	**24000.00**	**25680.00**	IH	6T	466D	18F-6R	162.60	14624	C,H,A
5288 4WD	74160.00	**21120.00**	**25750.00**	**27550.00**	IH	6T	466D	18F-6R	162.00	17862	C,H,A
5488	66515.00	**20630.00**	**25160.00**	**26920.00**	IH	6TI	466D	18F-6R	187.22	14061	C,H,A
5488 4WD	78340.00	**21960.00**	**26780.00**	**28660.00**	IH	6TI	466D	18F-6R	187.00	17299	C,H,A

PS - Power Shift CD - Consolidated Diesel Corp. RC - Row Crop

Model	Approx. Retail Price New	Fair	Good	Premium	Engine Make	No. Cyls.	Displ. Cu.-In.	No. Speeds	P.T.O. H.P.	Approx. Shipping Wt.-Lbs.	Cab
1987											
235	6916.00	**4150.00**	**4770.00**	**5300.00**	Mitsubishi	3	52D	6F-2R	15.20	1157	No
235 4WD	7651.00	**4590.00**	**5280.00**	**5860.00**	Mitsubishi	3	52D	6F-2R	15.20	1268	No
235 4WD Hydro	8800.00	**5280.00**	**6070.00**	**6740.00**	Mitsubishi	3	52D	Infinite	15.20	1345	No
235 Hydro	8065.00	**4840.00**	**5570.00**	**6180.00**	Mitsubishi	3	52D	Infinite	15.20	1235	No
245	7148.00	**4290.00**	**4930.00**	**5470.00**	Mitsubishi	3	60D	9F-3R	18.00	1620	No
245 4WD	8172.00	**4900.00**	**5640.00**	**6260.00**	Mitsubishi	3	60D	9F-3R	18.00	1742	No
255	7784.00	**4670.00**	**5370.00**	**5960.00**	Mitsubishi	3	65D	9F-3R	21.00	1620	No
255 4WD	8993.00	**5400.00**	**6210.00**	**6890.00**	Mitsubishi	3	65D	9F-3R	21.00	1742	No
265 Offset Tractor	8847.00	**5310.00**	**6100.00**	**6770.00**	Mitsubishi	3	79D	9F-3R	24.00	2105	No
275	9686.00	**5810.00**	**6680.00**	**7420.00**	Nissan	3	91D	9F-3R	27.00	2094	No
275 4WD	12165.00	**7300.00**	**8390.00**	**9310.00**	Nissan	3	91D	9F-3R	27.00	2315	No
385	12997.00	**7800.00**	**8970.00**	**9960.00**	IH	3	155D	8F-4R	36.2	5050	No
385 4WD	16112.00	**9670.00**	**11120.00**	**12340.00**	IH	3	155D	8F-4R	35.00	5050	No
485	15538.00	**9320.00**	**10720.00**	**11900.00**	IH	3	179D	8F-4R	42.00	5200	No
485 4WD	20170.00	**12100.00**	**13920.00**	**15450.00**	IH	3	179D	8F-4R	43.00	6090	No
585	18658.00	**9330.00**	**11010.00**	**11890.00**	IH	4	206D	8F-4R	49.9	5640	No
585	24736.00	**12370.00**	**14590.00**	**15760.00**	IH	4	206D	8F-4R	49.9	6440	C,H,A
585 4WD	23273.00	**11640.00**	**13730.00**	**14830.00**	IH	4	206D	8F-4R	52.00	6685	No
585 4WD	29351.00	**14000.00**	**16520.00**	**17840.00**	IH	4	206D	8F-4R	52.00	7485	C,H,A

Case-International (Cont.)

1987 (Cont.)

Model	Approx. Retail Price New	Estimated Average Value Less Repairs Fair	Good	Premium	Engine Make	No. Cyls.	Displ. Cu.-In.	No. Speeds	P.T.O. H.P.	Approx. Shipping Wt.-Lbs.	Cab
585 RC	19053.00	**9530.00**	**11240.00**	**12140.00**	IH	4	206D	8F-4R	52.00	5890	No
585 RC	25131.00	**12000.00**	**14160.00**	**15290.00**	IH	4	206D	8F-4R	52.00	6690	C,H,A
585 RC 4WD	23668.00	**11830.00**	**13960.00**	**15080.00**	IH	4	206D	8F-4R	52.00	6935	No
585 RC 4WD	29746.00	**14000.00**	**16520.00**	**17840.00**	IH	4	206D	8F-4R	52.00	7735	C,H,A
685	20968.00	**10480.00**	**12370.00**	**13360.00**	IH	4	239D	8F-4R	61.02	5720	No
685	27046.00	**12500.00**	**14750.00**	**15930.00**	IH	4	239D	8F-4R	61.02	6520	C,H,A
685 4WD	26348.00	**13170.00**	**15550.00**	**16790.00**	IH	4	239D	8F-4R	61.02	6785	No
685 4WD	32426.00	**15200.00**	**17940.00**	**19380.00**	IH	4	239D	8F-4R	61.02	7585	C,H,A
685 RC	21378.00	**10690.00**	**12610.00**	**13620.00**	IH	4	239D	8F-4R	61.02	5970	No
685 RC	27456.00	**12650.00**	**14930.00**	**16120.00**	IH	4	239D	8F-4R	61.02	6770	C,H,A
685 RC 4WD	26758.00	**13380.00**	**15790.00**	**17050.00**	IH	4	239D	8F-4R	61.02	7015	No
685 RC 4WD	32836.00	**15400.00**	**18170.00**	**19620.00**	IH	4	239D	8F-4R	61.02	7815	C,H,A
885	25418.00	**12710.00**	**15000.00**	**16200.00**	IH	4	268D	16F-8R	72.00	6065	No
885	31496.00	**15000.00**	**17700.00**	**19120.00**	IH	4	268D	16F-8R	72.00	6865	C,H,A
885 4WD	30228.00	**15110.00**	**17840.00**	**19270.00**	IH	4	268D	16F-8R	73.00	7223	No
885 4WD	36306.00	**17500.00**	**20650.00**	**22300.00**	IH	4	268D	16F-8R	73.00	8023	C,H,A
885 RC	26048.00	**13020.00**	**15370.00**	**16600.00**	IH	4	268D	16F-8R	72.00	6315	No
885 RC	32126.00	**15500.00**	**18290.00**	**19750.00**	IH	4	268D	16F-8R	72.00	7115	C,H,A
885 RC 4WD	30858.00	**15430.00**	**18210.00**	**19670.00**	IH	4	268D	16F-8R	72.00	7473	No
885 RC 4WD	36936.00	**17750.00**	**20950.00**	**22630.00**	IH	4	268D	16F-8R	72.00	8273	C,H,A
1394	21781.00	**8820.00**	**10710.00**	**11460.00**	David Brown	4T	219D	12F-4R	65.00	4890	No
1394 4WD	27245.00	**10500.00**	**12750.00**	**13640.00**	David Brown	4T	219D	12F-4R	65.00	6090	No
1394 PS	29998.00	**11340.00**	**13770.00**	**14730.00**	David Brown	4T	219D	12F-4R	65.00	6758	C,H,A
1494	24612.00	**9240.00**	**11220.00**	**12010.00**	David Brown	4T	219D	12F-4R	75.00	6764	No
1494 PS	32714.00	**11340.00**	**13770.00**	**14730.00**	David Brown	4T	219D	12F-4R	75.00	8001	C,H,A
1494 PS 4WD	32000.00	**11930.00**	**14480.00**	**15490.00**	David Brown	4T	219D	12F-4R	75.00	8347	No
1594	26092.00	**9660.00**	**11730.00**	**12550.00**	Case	6	329D	12F-4R	85.90	7544	No
1594 PS	34293.00	**12600.00**	**15300.00**	**16370.00**	Case	6	329D	12F-4R	85.54	8889	C,H,A
1594 PS 4WD	39558.00	**14700.00**	**17850.00**	**19100.00**	Case	6	329D	12F-4R	85.00	10105	C,H,A
1896	32799.00	**11930.00**	**14480.00**	**15490.00**	CD	6T	360D	12F-3R	95.92	9361	No
1896 4WD	40599.00	**14910.00**	**18110.00**	**19380.00**	CD	6T	360D	12F-3R	95.00	10421	No
1896 4WD w/Cab	47443.00	**16800.00**	**20400.00**	**21830.00**	CD	6T	360D	12F-3R	95.00	10836	C,H,A
1896 w/Cab	39643.00	**14450.00**	**17540.00**	**18770.00**	CD	6T	360D	12F-3R	95.00	9776	C,H,A
2096	37752.00	**15410.00**	**18720.00**	**20030.00**	CD	6TA	360D	12F-3R	115.67	9386	No
2096 4WD	45552.00	**17850.00**	**21680.00**	**23200.00**	CD	6TA	360D	12F-3R	115.00	10446	No
2096 4WD w/Cab	52396.00	**20710.00**	**25140.00**	**26900.00**	CD	6TA	360D	12F-3R	115.00	10861	C,H,A
2096 w/Cab	44596.00	**18270.00**	**22190.00**	**23740.00**	CD	6TA	360D	12F-3R	115.00	9801	C,H,A
2294 RC	52857.00	**17000.00**	**20000.00**	**22000.00**	Case	6T	504D	12F-3R	131.97	11937	C,H,A
2294 RC 4WD	61365.00	**19160.00**	**22550.00**	**24810.00**	Case	6T	504D	12F-3R	131.00	13565	C,H,A
2394 RC	63759.00	**18890.00**	**22220.00**	**24440.00**	Case	6T	504D	24F-3R	162.00	13663	C,H,A
2594 RC	68718.00	**19960.00**	**23490.00**	**25840.00**	Case	6T	504D	24F-3R	182.07	14026	C,H,A
3394 RC 4WD	70671.00	**20630.00**	**24270.00**	**26700.00**	Case	6T	504D	24F-3R	162.86	14527	C,H,A
3594 RC 4WD	74592.00	**21790.00**	**25640.00**	**28200.00**	Case	6T	504D	24F-3R	182.27	14647	C,H,A
4494 RC 4WD	78520.00	**22280.00**	**26210.00**	**28830.00**	Case	6T	504D	12F-4R	175.20	18051	C,H,A
4694 RC 4WD	94513.00	**24650.00**	**29010.00**	**31910.00**	Case	6T	504D	12F-4R	219.62	18504	C,H,A
4894 RC 4WD	102162.00	**27940.00**	**32870.00**	**36160.00**	Scania	6T	674D	12F-4R	253.41	21809	C,H,A
4994 RC/Wheat 4WD	130024.00	**30610.00**	**36010.00**	**39610.00**	Case	8	866D	12F-2R	344.04		C,H,A
9110 Wheatland	76178.00	**32000.00**	**38850.00**	**41570.00**	Case	6T	504D	12F-2R	168.40		C,H,A
9130 Wheatland	81241.00	**34120.00**	**41430.00**	**44330.00**	Case	6T	504D	12F-2R	191.20		C,H,A
9150 Wheatland	103050.00	**41180.00**	**50010.00**	**53510.00**	Cummins	6TI	611D	12F-2R	246.10		C,H,A
9170 Wheatland	116201.00	**43340.00**	**52630.00**	**56310.00**	Cummins	6T	855D	12F-2R	308.10		C,H,A
9180 Wheatland	123997.00	**47040.00**	**57120.00**	**61120.00**	Cummins	6T	855D	12F-2R	344.50		C,H,A
9190 Wheatland	169710.00	**50700.00**	**61560.00**	**65870.00**	Cummins	6T	1150D	24F-4R			C,H,A

PS - Power Shift RC - Row Crop

1988

Model	Approx. Retail Price New	Fair	Good	Premium	Make	No. Cyls.	Displ. Cu.-In.	No. Speeds	P.T.O. H.P.	Approx. Shipping Wt.-Lbs.	Cab
235	7646.00	**4660.00**	**5350.00**	**5940.00**	Mitsubishi	3	52D	6F-2R	15.20	1157	No
235 4WD	8634.00	**5270.00**	**6040.00**	**6700.00**	Mitsubishi	3	52D	6F-2R	15.20	1268	No
235 Hydro	8572.00	**5230.00**	**6000.00**	**6660.00**	Mitsubishi	3	52D	Infinite	15.20	1235	No
235 Hydro 4WD	9560.00	**5830.00**	**6690.00**	**7430.00**	Mitsubishi	3	52D	Infinite	15.20	1345	No
245	8117.00	**4950.00**	**5680.00**	**6310.00**	Mitsubishi	3	60D	9F-3R	18.00	1620	No
245 4WD	9329.00	**5690.00**	**6530.00**	**7250.00**	Mitsubishi	3	60D	9F-3R	18.00	1742	No
255	8585.00	**5240.00**	**6010.00**	**6670.00**	Mitsubishi	3	65D	9F-3R	21.00	1620	No
255 4WD	10019.00	**6110.00**	**7010.00**	**7780.00**	Mitsubishi	3	65D	9F-3R	21.00	1742	No
265 Offset	9201.00	**5610.00**	**6440.00**	**7150.00**	Mitsubishi	3	79D	9F-3R	24.00	2105	No
275	10296.00	**6280.00**	**7210.00**	**8000.00**	Nissan	3	91D	9F-3R	27.00	2094	No
275 4WD	13059.00	**7970.00**	**9140.00**	**10150.00**	Nissan	3	91D	9F-3R	27.00	2315	No
385	12997.00	**7280.00**	**8320.00**	**8900.00**	Case-IH	3	155D	8F-4R	36.20	4920	No
385 4WD	16112.00	**9020.00**	**10310.00**	**11030.00**	Case-IH	3	155D	8F-4R	35.00	5680	No
485	15538.00	**8700.00**	**9940.00**	**10640.00**	Case-IH	3	179D	8F-4R	42.00	4960	No
485 4WD	20170.00	**11300.00**	**12910.00**	**13810.00**	Case-IH	3	179D	8F-4R	43.00	5720	No
585	18658.00	**9520.00**	**11200.00**	**11980.00**	Case-IH	4	206D	8F-4R	49.90	5540	No
585 4WD	23273.00	**11870.00**	**13960.00**	**14940.00**	Case-IH	4	206D	8F-4R	52.00	6240	No
585 4WD w/Cab	29351.00	**14280.00**	**16800.00**	**17980.00**	Case-IH	4	206D	8F-4R	52.00	7485	C,H,A
585 w/Cab	24736.00	**12620.00**	**14840.00**	**15880.00**	Case-IH	4	206D	8F-4R	49.90	6440	C,H,A
685	20968.00	**10690.00**	**12580.00**	**13460.00**	Case-IH	4	239D	8F-4R	62.00	5720	No
685 4WD	26348.00	**12750.00**	**15000.00**	**16050.00**	Case-IH	4	239D	8F-4R	62.00	6340	No
685 4WD w/Cab	32426.00	**15810.00**	**18600.00**	**19900.00**	Case-IH	4	239D	8F-4R	62.00	7585	C,H,A
685 w/Cab	27046.00	**13260.00**	**15600.00**	**16690.00**	Case-IH	4	239D	8F-4R	62.00	6520	C,H,A
885	25418.00	**12500.00**	**14700.00**	**15730.00**	Case-IH	4	268D	16F-8R	72.00	6030	No
885 4WD	30228.00	**14790.00**	**17400.00**	**18620.00**	Case-IH	4	268D	16F-8R	73.00	6440	No
885 4WD w/Cab	36306.00	**17540.00**	**20640.00**	**22090.00**	Case-IH	4	268D	16F-8R	73.00	8023	C,H,A
885 w/Cab	31496.00	**15580.00**	**18330.00**	**19610.00**	Case-IH	4	268D	16F-8R	72.00	6865	C,H,A
1394	21781.00	**9030.00**	**10920.00**	**11580.00**	David Brown	4T	219D	12F-4R	65.00	5658	No

Case-International (Cont.)

1988 (Cont.)

Model	Approx. Retail Price New	Estimated Average Value Less Repairs Fair	Good	Premium	Engine Make	No. Cyls.	Displ. Cu.-In.	No. Speeds	P.T.O. H.P.	Approx. Shipping Wt.-Lbs.	Cab
1394 4WD	27245.00	10840.00	13100.00	13890.00	David Brown	4T	219D	12F-4R	65.00	7159	No
1494	24612.00	10110.00	12220.00	12950.00	David Brown	4T	219D	12F-4R	75.00	6764	No
1494 PS 4WD	32000.00	12040.00	14560.00	15430.00	David Brown	4T	219D	12F-4R	75.00	8347	No
1494 PS 4WD w/Cab	38078.00	14190.00	17160.00	18190.00	David Brown	4T	219D	12F-4R	75.00	9197	C,H,A
1494 PS w/Cab	32714.00	12040.00	14560.00	15430.00	David Brown	4T	219D	12F-4R	75.00	8001	C,H,A
1594	26092.00	9890.00	11960.00	12680.00	Case-IH	6	329D	12F-4R	85.90	7544	No
1594 PS 4WD	33480.00	12470.00	15080.00	15990.00	Case-IH	6	329D	12F-4R	85.54	8760	No
1594 PS 4WD w/Cab	39558.00	14620.00	17680.00	18740.00	Case-IH	6	329D	12F-4R	85.54	10105	C,H,A
1594 PS w/Cab	34293.00	12990.00	15700.00	16640.00	Case-IH	6	329D	12F-4R	85.54	8889	C,H,A
1896 4WD	43691.00	16860.00	20380.00	21600.00	CD	6T	360D	12F-3R	95.92	12453	No
1896 4WD w/Cab	50535.00	18490.00	22360.00	23700.00	CD	6T	360D	12F-3R	95.92	12868	C,H,A
1896 PS	34985.00	13120.00	15860.00	16810.00	CD	6T	360D	12F-3R	95.92	11119	No
1896 w/Cab	41829.00	15570.00	18820.00	19950.00	CD	6T	360D	12F-3R	95.92	12179	C,H,A
2096	40457.00	16770.00	20280.00	21500.00	CD	6TA	360D	12F-3R	115.67	11138	No
2096 4WD	49163.00	20430.00	24700.00	26180.00	CD	6TA	360D	12F-3R	115.00	12494	No
2096 4WD w/Cab	56007.00	22790.00	27560.00	29210.00	CD	6TA	360D	12F-3R	115.00	12909	C,H,A
2096 w/Cab	47301.00	20340.00	24600.00	26080.00	CD	6TA	360D	12F-3R	115.00	11553	C,H,A
4494 Wheatland 4WD	71282.00	22060.00	25740.00	28310.00	Case-IH	6T	504D	12F-4R	175.20	16414	C,H,A
4694 Wheatland 4WD	87449.00	25360.00	29590.00	32550.00	Case-IH	6TI	504D	12F-4R	219.62	17309	C,H,A
4894 Wheatland 4WD	100888.00	28830.00	33640.00	37000.00	Case-IH	6T	674D	12F-4R	253.41	20492	C,H,A
4994 RC/Wheatland 4WD	135024.00	32410.00	37810.00	41590.00	Case-IH	V8	866D	12F-2R	344.00		C,H,A
7110 Wheatland	51024.00	26020.00	30610.00	32750.00	Case-IH	6T	504D	18F-2R	131.97	19015	C,H,A
7110 Wheatland 4WD	59432.00	29580.00	34800.00	37240.00	Case-IH	6T	504D	18F-2R	131.97	19015	C,H,A
7120 Wheatland	56020.00	28570.00	33610.00	35960.00	Case-IH	6T	504D	18F-2R	151.62	19565	C,H,A
7120 Wheatland 4WD	64376.00	31620.00	37200.00	39800.00	Case-IH	6T	504D	18F-2R	151.62	19565	C,H,A
7130 Wheatland	60885.00	31050.00	36530.00	39090.00	Case-IH	6T	504D	18F-2R	172.57		C,H,A
7130 Wheatland 4WD	69946.00	34170.00	40200.00	43010.00	Case-IH	6T	504D	18F-2R	172.57		C,H,A
7140 Wheatland	68729.00	32640.00	38400.00	41090.00	Case-IH	6TA	504D	18F-2R	197.53		C,H,A
7140 Wheatland 4WD	77597.00	36210.00	42600.00	45580.00	Case-IH	6TA	504D	18F-2R	197.53		C,H,A
9110 Wheatland	79997.00	34400.00	41600.00	44100.00	Case-IH	6T	504D	12F-2R	168.40		C,H,A
9130 Wheatland	85262.00	36660.00	44340.00	47000.00	Case-IH	6TA	504D	12F-2R	191.20		C,H,A
9150 Wheatland	107171.00	41780.00	50530.00	53560.00	Cummins	6TI	611D	12F-2R	246.10		C,H,A
9170 Wheatland	121353.00	45730.00	55300.00	58620.00	Cummins	6TI	855D	12F-2R	308.10		C,H,A
9180 Wheatland	128956.00	49000.00	59260.00	62820.00	Cummins	6TI	855D	12F-2R	344.50		C,H,A

PS - Power Shift RC - Row Crop

1989

Model	Approx. Retail Price New	Fair	Good	Premium	Engine Make	No. Cyls.	Displ. Cu.-In.	No. Speeds	P.T.O. H.P.	Approx. Shipping Wt.-Lbs.	Cab
235	8105.00	5030.00	5760.00	6340.00	Mitsubishi	3	52D	6F-2R	15.20	1157	No
235 4WD	9152.00	5670.00	6500.00	7150.00	Mitsubishi	3	52D	6F-2R	15.20	1268	No
235 Hydro	9086.00	5630.00	6450.00	7100.00	Mitsubishi	3	52D	Infinite	15.20	1235	No
235 Hydro 4WD	10134.00	6280.00	7200.00	7920.00	Mitsubishi	3	52D	Infinite	15.20	1345	No
245	8604.00	5330.00	6110.00	6720.00	Mitsubishi	3	60D	9F-3R	18.00	1620	No
245 4WD	9889.00	6130.00	7020.00	7720.00	Mitsubishi	3	60D	9F-3R	18.00	1742	No
255	9100.00	5640.00	6460.00	7110.00	Mitsubishi	3	65D	9F-3R	21.00	1620	No
255 4WD	10620.00	6580.00	7540.00	8290.00	Mitsubishi	3	65D	9F-3R	21.00	1742	No
265 Offset	10121.00	6280.00	7190.00	7910.00	Mitsubishi	3	79D	9F-3R	24.00	2105	No
275	10708.00	6640.00	7600.00	8360.00	Nissan	3	91D	9F-3R	27.00	2094	No
275 4WD	13581.00	8420.00	9640.00	10600.00	Nissan	3	91D	9F-3R	27.00	2315	No
385	12997.00	8060.00	9230.00	10150.00	Case-IH	3	155D	8F-4R	36.20	4920	No
385 4WD	16112.00	9990.00	11440.00	12580.00	Case-IH	3	155D	8F-4R	35.00	5680	No
485	15538.00	9630.00	11030.00	12130.00	Case-IH	3	179D	8F-4R	42.00	4960	No
485 4WD	20170.00	12510.00	14320.00	15750.00	Case-IH	3	179D	8F-4R	43.00	5720	No
585	18658.00	9700.00	11380.00	12180.00	Case-IH	4	206D	8F-4R	49.90	5540	No
585 4WD	23273.00	12100.00	14200.00	15190.00	Case-IH	4	206D	8F-4R	52.00	6240	No
585 4WD w/Cab	29351.00	15260.00	17900.00	19150.00	Case-IH	4	206D	8F-4R	52.00	7485	C,H,A
585 w/Cab	24736.00	12860.00	15090.00	16150.00	Case-IH	4	206D	8F-4R	49.90	6440	C,H,A
685	20968.00	10900.00	12790.00	13690.00	Case-IH	4	239D	8F-4R	62.00	5720	No
685 4WD	26348.00	13700.00	16070.00	17200.00	Case-IH	4	239D	8F-4R	62.00	6340	No
685 4WD w/Cab	32426.00	16860.00	19780.00	21170.00	Case-IH	4	239D	8F-4R	62.00	7585	C,H,A
685 w/Cab	27046.00	14060.00	16500.00	17660.00	Case-IH	4	239D	8F-4R	62.00	6520	C,H,A
885	25418.00	13220.00	15510.00	16600.00	Case-IH	4	268D	16F-8R	72.00	6030	No
885 4WD	30228.00	15720.00	18440.00	19730.00	Case-IH	4	268D	16F-8R	73.00	6440	No
885 4WD w/Cab	36306.00	18880.00	22150.00	23700.00	Case-IH	4	268D	16F-8R	73.00	8023	C,H,A
885 w/Cab	31496.00	16380.00	19210.00	20560.00	Case-IH	4	268D	16F-8R	72.00	6865	C,H,A
1394	21781.00	9240.00	11130.00	11800.00	David Brown	4T	219D	12F-4R	65.00	5658	No
1394 4WD	27245.00	11440.00	13780.00	14610.00	David Brown	4T	219D	12F-4R	65.00	7159	No
1494	24612.00	10120.00	12190.00	12920.00	David Brown	4T	219D	12F-4R	75.00	6764	No
1494 PS 4WD	32000.00	13200.00	15900.00	16850.00	David Brown	4T	219D	12F-4R	75.00	8347	No
1494 PS 4WD w/Cab	38078.00	15840.00	19080.00	20230.00	David Brown	4T	219D	12F-4R	75.00	9197	C,H,A
1494 PS w/Cab	32714.00	13420.00	16170.00	17140.00	David Brown	4T	219D	12F-4R	75.00	8001	C,H,A
1594	26092.00	11000.00	13250.00	14050.00	Case-IH	6	329D	12F-4R	85.90	7544	No
1594 PS 4WD	33480.00	13820.00	16640.00	17640.00	Case-IH	6	329D	12F-4R	85.54	8760	No
1594 PS 4WD w/Cab	39558.00	16500.00	19880.00	21070.00	Case-IH	6	329D	12F-4R	85.54	10105	C,H,A
1594 PS w/Cab	34293.00	14210.00	17120.00	18150.00	Case-IH	6	329D	12F-4R	85.54	8889	C,H,A
1896 4WD	43691.00	17820.00	21470.00	22760.00	CD	6T	360D	12F-3R	95.92	12453	No
1896 4WD w/Cab	50535.00	21120.00	25440.00	26970.00	CD	6T	360D	12F-3R	95.92	12868	C,H,A
1896 PS	34985.00	14520.00	17490.00	18540.00	CD	6T	360D	12F-3R	95.92	11119	No
1896 w/Cab	41829.00	17730.00	21360.00	22640.00	CD	6T	360D	12F-3R	95.92	12179	C,H,A
2096	40457.00	17800.00	21440.00	22730.00	CD	6TA	360D	12F-3R	115.67	11138	No
2096 4WD	49163.00	21120.00	25440.00	26970.00	CD	6TA	360D	12F-3R	115.00	12494	No
2096 4WD w/Cab	56007.00	23760.00	28620.00	30340.00	CD	6TA	360D	12F-3R	115.00	12909	C,H,A
2096 w/Cab	47301.00	20810.00	25070.00	26570.00	CD	6TA	360D	12F-3R	115.67	11553	C,H,A
4494 Wheatland 4WD	71282.00	23290.00	26970.00	29670.00	Case-IH	6T	504D	12F-4R	175.20	16414	C,H,A
4694 Wheatland 4WD	87449.00	28670.00	33200.00	36520.00	Case-IH	6TI	504D	12F-4R	219.62	17309	C,H,A

Model	Approx. Retail Price New	Estimated Average Value Less Repairs Fair	Good	Premium	Engine Make	No. Cyls.	Displ. Cu.-In.	No. Speeds	P.T.O. H.P.	Approx. Shipping Wt.-Lbs.	Cab
1989 (Cont.)											
4894 Wheatland 4WD	100888.00	31500.00	36470.00	40120.00	Case-IH	6T	674D	12F-4R	253.41	20492	C,H,A
4994 RC/Wheatland 4WD	135024.00	38010.00	44010.00	48410.00	Case-IH	V8	866D	12F-2R	344.00		C,H,A
7110 Wheatland	51024.00	26530.00	31130.00	33310.00	Case-IH	6T	504D	18F-2R	131.97	14503	C,H,A
7110 Wheatland 4WD	59432.00	30160.00	35380.00	37860.00	Case-IH	6T	504D	18F-2R	131.97	19015	C,H,A
7120 Wheatland	56020.00	29130.00	34170.00	36560.00	Case-IH	6T	504D	18F-2R	151.62	14743	C,H,A
7120 Wheatland 4WD	64376.00	32500.00	38130.00	40800.00	Case-IH	6T	504D	18F-2R	151.62	15758	C,H,A
7130 Wheatland	60885.00	31660.00	37140.00	39740.00	Case-IH	6T	504D	18F-2R	172.57	15327	C,H,A
7130 Wheatland 4WD	69946.00	35360.00	41480.00	44380.00	Case-IH	6T	504D	18F-2R	172.57	16342	C,H,A
7140 Wheatland	69617.00	33800.00	39650.00	42430.00	Case-IH	6TA	504D	18F-2R	197.53	15617	C,H,A
7140 Wheatland 4WD	78485.00	37960.00	44530.00	47650.00	Case-IH	6TA	504D	18F-2R	197.53	16728	C,H,A
9110 Wheatland	79997.00	41600.00	48800.00	52220.00	Case-IH	6T	504D	12F-2R	168.40		C,H,A
9130 Wheatland	85262.00	37520.00	45190.00	47900.00	Case-IH	6TA	504D	12F-2R	191.20		C,H,A
9150 Wheatland	107171.00	44080.00	53090.00	56280.00	Cummins	6TI	611D	12F-2R	246.10		C,H,A
9170 Wheatland	121353.00	49000.00	59020.00	62560.00	Cummins	6TA	855D	12F-2R	308.10		C,H,A
9180 Wheatland	128956.00	52340.00	63050.00	66830.00	Cummins	6TA	855D	12F-2R	344.50		C,H,A

PS - Power Shift RC - Row Crop

Model	Approx. Retail Price New	Fair	Good	Premium	Make	No. Cyls.	Displ. Cu.-In.	No. Speeds	P.T.O. H.P.	Approx. Shipping Wt.-Lbs.	Cab
1990											
235	9410.00	5460.00	6210.00	6650.00	Mitsubishi	3	52D	6F-2R	15.2	1323	No
235 MFD	10671.00	6190.00	7040.00	7530.00	Mitsubishi	3	52D	6F-2R	15.2	1452	No
245	10295.00	5970.00	6800.00	7280.00	Mitsubishi	3	60D	9F-3R	18.00	1914	No
245 MFD	11752.00	6820.00	7760.00	8300.00	Mitsubishi	3	60D	9F-3R	18.00	2062	No
255	10841.00	6290.00	7160.00	7660.00	Mitsubishi	3	65D	9F-3R	21.00	1914	No
255 MFD	12556.00	7280.00	8290.00	8870.00	Mitsubishi	3	65D	9F-3R	21.00	2062	No
265	12341.00	7160.00	8150.00	8720.00	Mitsubishi	3	79D	9F-3R	24.00	2523	No
275	12921.00	7490.00	8530.00	9130.00	Mitsubishi	3	91D	9F-3R	27.00	2512	No
275 MFD	16134.00	9360.00	10650.00	11400.00	Mitsubishi	3	91D	9F-3R	27.00	2751	No
385	13831.00	8020.00	9130.00	9770.00	Case	3	155D	8F-4R	36.2	4920	No
385 MFD	17140.00	9940.00	11310.00	12100.00	Case	3	155D	8F-4R	36.2	5680	No
485	15794.00	9160.00	10420.00	11150.00	Case	3	179D	8F-4R	43.00	4960	No
485 MFD	20991.00	12180.00	13850.00	14820.00	Case	3	179D	8F-4R	43.00	5720	No
585	19312.00	10240.00	11970.00	12810.00	Case	4	206D	8F-4R	52.7	5540	No
585 MFD	24200.00	12830.00	15000.00	16050.00	Case	4	206D	8F-4R	52.7	6240	No
685	22246.00	11790.00	13790.00	14760.00	Case	4	239D	8F-4R	61.02	5720	No
685 MFD	27420.00	14530.00	17000.00	18190.00	Case	4	239D	8F-4R	61.02	6340	No
685 MFD w/Cab	33843.00	17940.00	20980.00	22450.00	Case	4	239D	8F-4R	61.02		C,H,A
685 w/Cab	28669.00	15200.00	17780.00	19030.00	Case	4	239D	8F-4R	61.02		C,H,A
885	25676.00	13610.00	15920.00	17030.00	Case	4	268D	16F-8R	73.00	6030	No
885 MFD	31146.00	16510.00	19310.00	20660.00	Case	4	268D	16F-8R	73.00	6440	No
885 MFD w/Cab	37281.00	19760.00	23110.00	24730.00	Case	4	268D	16F-8R	73.00		C,H,A
885 w/Cab	31811.00	16860.00	19720.00	21100.00	Case	4	268D	16F-8R	73.00		C,H,A
1896	36023.00	15300.00	18360.00	19460.00	Case	6T	359D	12F-3R	95.92	11135	No
1896	42867.00	18230.00	21870.00	23180.00	Case	6T	359D	12F-3R	95.92		C,H,A
2096	41029.00	18460.00	22160.00	23490.00	Case	6TA	359D	12F-3R	115.67	11191	No
2096	47873.00	21540.00	25850.00	27400.00	Case	6TA	359D	12F-3R	115.67		C,H,A
5120	25930.00	15040.00	17110.00	18310.00	Case	4TA	239D	16F-12R	77.00	8620	No
5120 MFD	32320.00	18750.00	21330.00	22820.00	Case	4TA	239D	16F-12R	77.00		No
5120 MFD w/Cab	38720.00	22460.00	25560.00	27350.00	Case	4TA	239D	16F-12R	77.00	10362	C,H,A
5120 w/Cab	32330.00	18750.00	21340.00	22830.00	Case	4TA	239D	16F-12R	77.00		C,H,A
5130	28280.00	16400.00	18670.00	19980.00	Case	6	359D	16F-12R	86.00	9458	No
5130 MFD	34670.00	20110.00	22880.00	24480.00	Case	6	359D	16F-12R	89.80	10670	No
5130 MFD w/Cab	41070.00	23820.00	27110.00	29010.00	Case	6	359D	16F-12R	89.8	10670	C,H,A
5130 w/Cab	34680.00	20110.00	22890.00	24490.00	Case	6	359D	16F-12R	89.80	10670	C,H,A
5140	31380.00	18200.00	20710.00	22160.00	Case	6T	359D	16F-12R	94.00	9810	No
5140 MFD	37770.00	21910.00	24930.00	26680.00	Case	6T	359D	16F-12R	94.00		No
5140 MFD w/Cab	44170.00	25620.00	29150.00	31190.00	Case	6T	359D	16F-12R	94.00	10825	C,H,A
5140 w/Cab	37780.00	21910.00	24940.00	26690.00	Case	6T	359D	16F-12R	94.00		C,H,A
7110 Magnum	56817.00	29680.00	34720.00	37150.00	Case	6T	505D	18F-4R	131.97	19015	C,H,A
7110 Magnum MFD	65208.00	34030.00	39800.00	42590.00	Case	6T	505D	18F-4R	131.97	19015	C,H,A
7120 Magnum	60090.00	31850.00	37260.00	39870.00	Case	6T	505D	18F-4R	151.62	15920	C,H,A
7120 Magnum MFD	68796.00	35510.00	41540.00	44450.00	Case	6T	505D	18F-4R	151.62		C,H,A
7130 Magnum	67393.00	35720.00	41780.00	44710.00	Case	6T	505D	18F-4R	172.57	16280	C,H,A
7130 Magnum MFD	77140.00	39750.00	46500.00	49760.00	Case	6T	505D	18F-4R	172.57		C,H,A
7140 Magnum	75072.00	37100.00	43400.00	46440.00	Case	6TA	505D	18F-4R	197.53	23780	C,H,A
7140 Magnum MFD	84860.00	40810.00	47740.00	51080.00	Case	6TA	505D	18F-4R	197.53	23780	C,H,A
9110	70422.00	37320.00	43660.00	46720.00	Case	6T	505D	12F-2R	168.40	17000	C,H,A
9130	75687.00	40810.00	47740.00	51080.00	Case	6TA	505D	12F-2R	192.2	17750	C,H,A
9150	94278.00	50350.00	58900.00	63020.00	Cummins	6TA	611D	12F-2R	246.1	23000	C,H,A
9170	118636.00	51750.00	62100.00	65830.00	Cummins	6TA	855D	12F-2R	308.1	29000	C,H,A
9180	127601.00	56250.00	67500.00	71550.00	Cummins	6TA	855D	12F-2R	344.5	29000	C,H,A

MFD - Mechanical Front Drive

Model	Approx. Retail Price New	Fair	Good	Premium	Make	No. Cyls.	Displ. Cu.-In.	No. Speeds	P.T.O. H.P.	Approx. Shipping Wt.-Lbs.	Cab
1991											
235	9410.00	5550.00	6310.00	6690.00	Mitsubishi	3	52D	6F-2R	15.2	1323	No
235 MFD	10671.00	6300.00	7150.00	7580.00	Mitsubishi	3	52D	6F-2R	15.2	1452	No
245	10295.00	6070.00	6900.00	7310.00	Mitsubishi	3	60D	9F-3R	18.00	1914	No
245 MFD	11752.00	6930.00	7870.00	8340.00	Mitsubishi	3	60D	9F-3R	18.00	2062	No
255	10841.00	6400.00	7260.00	7700.00	Mitsubishi	3	65D	9F-3R	21.00	1914	No
255 MFD	12556.00	7410.00	8410.00	8920.00	Mitsubishi	3	65D	9F-3R	21.00	2062	No
265	12341.00	7280.00	8270.00	8770.00	Mitsubishi	3	79D	9F-3R	24.00	2523	No
275	12921.00	7620.00	8660.00	9180.00	Mitsubishi	3	91D	9F-3R	27.00	2512	No
275 MFD	16134.00	9520.00	10810.00	11460.00	Mitsubishi	3	91D	9F-3R	27.00	2751	No
395	15900.00	9380.00	10650.00	11290.00	Case	3	155D	8F-4R	35	4920	No
395 MFD	19900.00	11740.00	13330.00	14130.00	Case	3	155D	8F-4R	35	5680	No

Case-International (Cont.)

1991 (Cont.)

Model	Approx. Retail Price New	Fair	Good	Premium	Make	No. Cyls.	Displ. Cu.-In.	No. Speeds	P.T.O. H.P.	Approx. Shipping Wt.-Lbs.	Cab
495	17900.00	**10560.00**	**11990.00**	**12710.00**	Case	3	179D	8F-4R	42	4960	No
495 MFD	23200.00	**13690.00**	**15540.00**	**16470.00**	Case	3	179D	8F-4R	42	5720	No
595	21400.00	**12630.00**	**14340.00**	**15200.00**	Case	4	206D	8F-4R	52	5540	No
595 MFD	26600.00	**15690.00**	**17820.00**	**18890.00**	Case	4	206D	8F-4R	52	6240	No
595 MFD w/Cab	33200.00	**19590.00**	**22240.00**	**23570.00**	Case	4	206D	8F-4R	52		C,H,A
595 w/Cab	28000.00	**16520.00**	**18760.00**	**19890.00**	Case	4	206D	8F-4R	52		C,H,A
695	24800.00	**14630.00**	**16620.00**	**17620.00**	Case	4	239D	8F-4R	62	5720	No
695 MFD	31400.00	**18530.00**	**21040.00**	**22300.00**	Case	4	239D	8F-4R	62	6340	No
695 MFD w/Cab	36820.00	**21720.00**	**24670.00**	**26150.00**	Case	4	239D	8F-4R	62		C,H,A
695 w/Cab	30223.00	**17830.00**	**20250.00**	**21470.00**	Case	4	239D	8F-4R	62		C,H,A
895	27500.00	**16230.00**	**18430.00**	**19540.00**	Case	4	268D	16F-8R	72	6030	No
895 MFD	34100.00	**20120.00**	**22850.00**	**24220.00**	Case	4	268D	16F-8R	72	6440	No
895 MFD w/Cab	39900.00	**23540.00**	**26730.00**	**28330.00**	Case	4	268D	16F-8R	72		C,H,A
895 w/Cab	33300.00	**19650.00**	**22310.00**	**23650.00**	Case	4	268D	16F-8R	72		C,H,A
995	29550.00	**17440.00**	**19800.00**	**20990.00**	Case	4	268D	16F-8R	85		No
995 MFD	34900.00	**20590.00**	**23380.00**	**24780.00**	Case	4	268D	16F-8R	85		No
5120	26860.00	**15850.00**	**18000.00**	**19080.00**	Case	4TA	239D	16F-12R	77	8620	No
5120 MFD	33480.00	**19290.00**	**21910.00**	**23230.00**	Case	4TA	239D	16F-12R	77.00		No
5120 MFD w/Cab	40110.00	**22600.00**	**25660.00**	**27200.00**	Case	4TA	239D	16F-12R	77.00	10362	C,H,A
5120 w/Cab	33490.00	**19760.00**	**22440.00**	**23790.00**	Case	4TA	239D	16F-12R	77.00		C,H,A
5130	29290.00	**17280.00**	**19620.00**	**20800.00**	Case	6	359D	16F-12R	89.80	9458	No
5130 MFD	35900.00	**20360.00**	**23120.00**	**24510.00**	Case	6	359D	16F-12R	89.8		No
5130 MFD w/Cab	42548.00	**25100.00**	**28510.00**	**30220.00**	Case	6	359D	16F-12R	89.8	10582	C,H,A
5130 w/Cab	35920.00	**21190.00**	**24070.00**	**25510.00**	Case	6	359D	16F-12R	89.8		C,H,A
5140	32500.00	**19180.00**	**21780.00**	**23090.00**	Case	6T	359D	24F-12R	97	9810	No
5140 MFD	39130.00	**23090.00**	**26220.00**	**27790.00**	Case	6T	359D	24F-12R	97		No
5140 MFD w/Cab	45759.00	**27000.00**	**30660.00**	**32500.00**	Case	6T	359D	24F-12R	97	10825	C,H,A
5140 w/Cab	39140.00	**23090.00**	**26220.00**	**27790.00**	Case	6T	359D	24F-12R	97		C,H,A
7110 Magnum	58860.00	**31780.00**	**37080.00**	**39310.00**	Case	6T	505D	18F-4R	131.97	15280	C,H,A
7110 Magnum MFD	67550.00	**36480.00**	**42560.00**	**45110.00**	Case	6T	505D	18F-4R	131.97		C,H,A
7120 Magnum	62250.00	**33620.00**	**39220.00**	**41570.00**	Case	6T	505D	18F-4R	151.62	15920	C,H,A
7120 Magnum MFD	71272.00	**38490.00**	**44900.00**	**47590.00**	Case	6T	505D	18F-4R	151.62		C,H,A
7130 Magnum	69800.00	**37690.00**	**43970.00**	**46610.00**	Case	6T	505D	18F-4R	172.57	16280	C,H,A
7130 Magnum MFD	79900.00	**43150.00**	**50340.00**	**53360.00**	Case	6T	505D	18F-4R	172.57		C,H,A
7140 Magnum	77700.00	**39420.00**	**45990.00**	**48750.00**	Case	6TA	505D	18F-4R	197.53	16480	C,H,A
7140 Magnum MFD	87800.00	**44280.00**	**51660.00**	**54760.00**	Case	6TA	505D	18F-4R	197.53		C,H,A
9210	73422.00	**39650.00**	**46260.00**	**49040.00**	Case	6T	505D	12F-2R	168.40	17000	C,H,A
9230	81125.00	**43810.00**	**51110.00**	**54180.00**	Case	6TA	505D	12F-2R	198.63	24272	C,H,A
9240	89995.00	**48600.00**	**56700.00**	**60100.00**	Case	6TA	505D	12F-2R	200.53	28380	C,H,A
9250	99437.00	**53700.00**	**62650.00**	**66410.00**	Cummins	6TA	611D	12F-2R	266.1	30225	C,H,A
9260	109995.00	**59400.00**	**69300.00**	**73460.00**	Cummins	6TA	611D	12F-2R	265.84	30300	C,H,A
9270	122240.00	**55200.00**	**66000.00**	**69960.00**	Cummins	6TA	855D	12F-2R	308.1	37510	C,H,A
9280	132194.00	**59800.00**	**71500.00**	**75790.00**	Cummins	6TA	855D	12F-2R	344.5	39890	C,H,A

MFD - Mechanical Front Drive

1992

Model	Approx. Retail Price New	Fair	Good	Premium	Make	No. Cyls.	Displ. Cu.-In.	No. Speeds	P.T.O. H.P.	Approx. Shipping Wt.-Lbs.	Cab
235	9785.00	**5870.00**	**6650.00**	**7050.00**	Mitsubishi	3	52D	6F-2R	15.2	1323	No
235 MFD	11095.00	**6660.00**	**7550.00**	**8000.00**	Mitsubishi	3	52D	6F-2R	15.2	1452	No
245	10700.00	**6420.00**	**7280.00**	**7720.00**	Mitsubishi	3	60D	9F-3R	18.00	1914	No
245 MFD	12200.00	**7320.00**	**8300.00**	**8800.00**	Mitsubishi	3	60D	9F-3R	18.00	2062	No
255	11275.00	**6770.00**	**7670.00**	**8130.00**	Mitsubishi	3	65D	9F-3R	21.00	1914	No
255 MFD	13050.00	**7830.00**	**8870.00**	**9400.00**	Mitsubishi	3	65D	9F-3R	21.00	2062	No
265	12840.00	**7700.00**	**8730.00**	**9250.00**	Mitsubishi	3	79D	9F-3R	24.00	2523	No
275	13440.00	**8060.00**	**9140.00**	**9690.00**	Mitsubishi	3	91D	9F-3R	27.00	2512	No
275 MFD	16780.00	**10070.00**	**11410.00**	**12100.00**	Mitsubishi	3	91D	9F-3R	27.00	2751	No
395	16500.00	**9900.00**	**11220.00**	**11890.00**	Case	3	155D	8F-4R	35	4920	No
395 MFD	20695.00	**12420.00**	**14070.00**	**14910.00**	Case	3	155D	8F-4R	35	5680	No
495	18600.00	**11160.00**	**12650.00**	**13410.00**	Case	3	179D	8F-4R	42	4960	No
495 MFD	24120.00	**14470.00**	**16400.00**	**17380.00**	Case	3	179D	8F-4R	42	5720	No
595	22250.00	**13350.00**	**15130.00**	**16040.00**	Case	4	206D	8F-4R	52	5540	No
595 MFD	27660.00	**16600.00**	**18810.00**	**19940.00**	Case	4	206D	8F-4R	52	6240	No
595 MFD w/Cab	34500.00	**20700.00**	**23460.00**	**24870.00**	Case	4	206D	8F-4R	52		C,H,A
595 w/Cab	29120.00	**17470.00**	**19800.00**	**20990.00**	Case	4	206D	8F-4R	52		C,H,A
695	25795.00	**15480.00**	**17540.00**	**18590.00**	Case	4	239D	8F-4R	62	5720	No
695 MFD	32650.00	**19590.00**	**22200.00**	**23530.00**	Case	4	239D	8F-4R	62	6340	No
695 MFD w/Cab	38290.00	**22970.00**	**26040.00**	**27600.00**	Case	4	239D	8F-4R	62		C,H,A
695 w/Cab	31430.00	**18860.00**	**21370.00**	**22650.00**	Case	4	239D	8F-4R	62		C,H,A
895	28600.00	**17160.00**	**19450.00**	**20620.00**	Case	4	268D	16F-8R	72	6030	No
895 MFD	35460.00	**21280.00**	**24110.00**	**25560.00**	Case	4	268D	16F-8R	72	6440	No
895 MFD w/Cab	41495.00	**24900.00**	**28220.00**	**29910.00**	Case	4	268D	16F-8R	72		C,H,A
895 w/Cab	34600.00	**20760.00**	**23530.00**	**24940.00**	Case	4	268D	16F-8R	72		C,H,A
995	30732.00	**18440.00**	**20900.00**	**22150.00**	Case	4	268D	16F-8R	85		No
995 MFD	36295.00	**21780.00**	**24680.00**	**26160.00**	Case	4	268D	16F-8R	85		No
5120	27935.00	**16760.00**	**19000.00**	**20140.00**	Case	4TA	239D	16F-12R	77	8620	No
5120 MFD	34820.00	**20890.00**	**23680.00**	**25100.00**	Case	4TA	239D	16F-12R	77.00		No
5120 MFD w/Cab	41715.00	**25030.00**	**28370.00**	**30070.00**	Case	4TA	239D	16F-12R	77.00	10362	C,H,A
5120 w/Cab	34800.00	**20880.00**	**23660.00**	**25080.00**	Case	4TA	239D	16F-12R	77.00		C,H,A
5130	30315.00	**18190.00**	**20610.00**	**21850.00**	Case	6	359D	16F-12R	89.80	9458	No
5130 MFD	37150.00	**22290.00**	**25260.00**	**26780.00**	Case	6	359D	16F-12R	89.8		No
5130 MFD w/Cab	44040.00	**26420.00**	**29950.00**	**31750.00**	Case	6	359D	16F-12R	89.8	10582	C,H,A
5130 w/Cab	37175.00	**22310.00**	**25280.00**	**26800.00**	Case	6	359D	16F-12R	89.8		C,H,A
5140	33640.00	**20180.00**	**22880.00**	**24250.00**	Case	6T	359D	24F-12R	97	9810	No
5140 MFD	40500.00	**24300.00**	**27540.00**	**29190.00**	Case	6T	359D	24F-12R	97		No
5140 MFD w/Cab	47350.00	**28410.00**	**32200.00**	**34130.00**	Case	6T	359D	24F-12R	97	10825	C,H,A

Case-International (Cont.)

1992 (Cont.)

Model	Approx. Retail Price New	Estimated Average Value Less Repairs Fair	Good	Premium	Engine Make	No. Cyls.	Displ. Cu.-In.	No. Speeds	P.T.O. H.P.	Approx. Shipping Wt.-Lbs.	Cab
5140 w/Cab	40500.00	24300.00	27540.00	29190.00	Case	6T	359D	24F-12R	97		C,H,A
7110 Magnum	60900.00	34100.00	38980.00	41320.00	Case	6T	505D	18F-4R	131.97	15280	C,H,A
7110 Magnum MFD	69900.00	38640.00	44160.00	46810.00	Case	6T	505D	18F-4R	131.97		C,H,A
7120 Magnum	64400.00	36060.00	41220.00	43690.00	Case	6T	505D	18F-4R	151.62	15920	C,H,A
7120 Magnum MFD	73700.00	40880.00	46720.00	49520.00	Case	6T	505D	18F-4R	151.62		C,H,A
7130 Magnum	72200.00	40430.00	46210.00	48980.00	Case	6T	505D	18F-4R	172.57	16280	C,H,A
7130 Magnum MFD	82695.00	45920.00	52480.00	55630.00	Case	6T	505D	18F-4R	172.57		C,H,A
7140 Magnum	80400.00	43900.00	50180.00	53190.00	Case	6TA	505D	18F-4R	197.53	16480	C,H,A
7140 Magnum MFD	90870.00	49730.00	56830.00	60240.00	Case	6TA	505D	18F-4R	197.53		C,H,A
9210	75990.00	42550.00	48630.00	51550.00	Case	6T	505D	12F-2R	168.40	17000	C,H,A
9230	83960.00	47020.00	53730.00	56950.00	Case	6TA	505D	12F-2R	192.2	17750	C,H,A
9240	93995.00	52640.00	60160.00	63770.00	Case	6TA	505D	12F-2R	200.53	28380	C,H,A
9250	102900.00	57620.00	65860.00	69810.00	Cummins	6TA	611D	12F-2R	246.1	23000	C,H,A
9260	112995.00	63280.00	72320.00	76660.00	Cummins	6TA	611D	12F-2R	265.84	30300	C,H,A
9270	126500.00	60720.00	70840.00	74380.00	Cummins	6TA	855D	12F-2R	308.1	29000	C,H,A
9280	136800.00	64800.00	75600.00	79380.00	Cummins	6TA	855D	12F-2R	344.5	29000	C,H,A

MFD - Mechanical Front Drive

1993

Model	Approx. Retail Price New	Fair	Good	Premium	Make	No. Cyls.	Displ. Cu.-In.	No. Speeds	P.T.O. H.P.	Approx. Shipping Wt.-Lbs.	Cab
235	10050.00	6230.00	6940.00	7360.00	Mitsubishi	3	52D	6F-2R	15.2	1323	No
235 MFD	11425.00	7080.00	7880.00	8350.00	Mitsubishi	3	52D	6F-2R	15.2	1452	No
245	11020.00	6830.00	7600.00	8060.00	Mitsubishi	3	60D	9F-3R	18.00	1914	No
245 MFD	12560.00	7790.00	8670.00	9190.00	Mitsubishi	3	60D	9F-3R	18.00	2062	No
255	11610.00	7200.00	8010.00	8490.00	Mitsubishi	3	65D	9F-3R	21.00	1914	No
255 MFD	13440.00	8330.00	9270.00	9830.00	Mitsubishi	3	65D	9F-3R	21.00	2062	No
265	13225.00	8200.00	9130.00	9680.00	Mitsubishi	3	79D	9F-3R	24.00	2523	No
275	13840.00	8580.00	9550.00	10120.00	Mitsubishi	3	91D	9F-3R	27.00	2512	No
275 MFD	17280.00	10710.00	11920.00	12640.00	Mitsubishi	3	91D	9F-3R	27.00	2751	No
395	16995.00	10540.00	11730.00	12430.00	Case	3	155D	8F-4R	35	4920	No
395 MFD	21315.00	13220.00	14710.00	15590.00	Case	3	155D	8F-4R	35	5680	No
495	19150.00	11870.00	13210.00	14000.00	Case	3	179D	8F-4R	42	4960	No
495 MFD	24840.00	15400.00	17140.00	18170.00	Case	3	179D	8F-4R	42	5720	No
595	22900.00	14200.00	15800.00	16750.00	Case	4	206D	8F-4R	52	5540	No
595 MFD	28490.00	17660.00	19660.00	20840.00	Case	4	206D	8F-4R	52	6240	No
595 MFD w/Cab	35500.00	22010.00	24500.00	25970.00	Case	4	206D	8F-4R	52		C,H,A
595 w/Cab	29995.00	18600.00	20700.00	21940.00	Case	4	206D	8F-4R	52		C,H,A
695	26550.00	16460.00	18320.00	19420.00	Case	4	239D	8F-4R	62	5720	No
695 MFD	33600.00	20830.00	23180.00	24570.00	Case	4	239D	8F-4R	62	6340	No
695 MFD w/Cab	39440.00	24450.00	27210.00	28840.00	Case	4	239D	8F-4R	62		C,H,A
695 w/Cab	32370.00	20070.00	22340.00	23680.00	Case	4	239D	8F-4R	62		C,H,A
895	29450.00	18260.00	20320.00	21540.00	Case	4	268D	16F-8R	72	6030	No
895 MFD	36520.00	22640.00	25200.00	26710.00	Case	4	268D	16F-8R	72	6440	No
895 MFD w/Cab	42740.00	26500.00	29490.00	31260.00	Case	4	268D	16F-8R	72		C,H,A
895 w/Cab	35640.00	22100.00	24590.00	26070.00	Case	4	268D	16F-8R	72		C,H,A
995	31650.00	19620.00	21840.00	23150.00	Case	4	268D	16F-8R	85		No
995 MFD	37380.00	23180.00	25790.00	27340.00	Case	4	268D	16F-8R	85		No
5120	28775.00	17840.00	19860.00	21050.00	Case	4TA	239D	16F-12R	77	8620	No
5120 MFD	35850.00	21700.00	24150.00	25600.00	Case	4TA	239D	16F-12R	77.00		No
5120 MFD w/Cab	42950.00	26040.00	28980.00	30720.00	Case	4TA	239D	16F-12R	77.00	10362	C,H,A
5120 w/Cab	35800.00	22200.00	24700.00	26180.00	Case	4TA	239D	16F-12R	77.00		C,H,A
5130	31200.00	19340.00	21530.00	22820.00	Case	6	359D	16F-12R	89.80	9458	No
5130 MFD	38260.00	23720.00	26400.00	27980.00	Case	6	359D	16F-12R	89.8		No
5130 MFD w/Cab	45360.00	28120.00	31300.00	33180.00	Case	6	359D	16F-12R	89.8	10582	C,H,A
5130 w/Cab	38290.00	23740.00	26420.00	28010.00	Case	6	359D	16F-12R	89.8		C,H,A
5140	34649.00	21480.00	23910.00	25350.00	Case	6T	359D	24F-12R	97	9810	No
5140 MFD	41715.00	25860.00	28780.00	30510.00	Case	6T	359D	24F-12R	97		No
5140 MFD w/Cab	48770.00	30240.00	33650.00	35670.00	Case	6T	359D	24F-12R	97	10825	C,H,A
5140 w/Cab	41715.00	25860.00	28780.00	30510.00	Case	6T	359D	24F-12R	97		C,H,A
7110 Magnum	62725.00	36380.00	40770.00	43220.00	Case	6T	505D	18F-4R	131.97	15280	C,H,A
7110 Magnum MFD	71995.00	41760.00	46800.00	49610.00	Case	6T	505D	18F-4R	131.97		C,H,A
7120 Magnum	66330.00	38470.00	43120.00	45710.00	Case	6T	505D	18F-4R	151.62	15920	C,H,A
7120 Magnum MFD	75900.00	44020.00	49340.00	52300.00	Case	6T	505D	18F-4R	151.62		C,H,A
7130 Magnum	74365.00	43130.00	48340.00	51240.00	Case	6T	505D	18F-4R	172.57	16280	C,H,A
7130 Magnum MFD	85175.00	49400.00	55360.00	58680.00	Case	6T	505D	18F-4R	172.57		C,H,A
7140 Magnum	82800.00	46860.00	52520.00	55670.00	Case	6TA	505D	18F-4R	197.53	16480	C,H,A
7140 Magnum MFD	93595.00	52490.00	58830.00	62360.00	Case	6TA	505D	18F-4R	197.53		C,H,A
9210	78270.00	45400.00	50880.00	53930.00	Case	6T	505D	12F-2R	168.40	17000	C,H,A
9230	86475.00	50160.00	56210.00	59580.00	Case	6TA	505D	12F-2R	192.2	17750	C,H,A
9240	96800.00	56140.00	62920.00	66700.00	Case	6TA	505D	12F-2R	200.53	28380	C,H,A
9250	105980.00	61470.00	68890.00	73020.00	Cummins	6TA	611D	12F-2R	246.1	23000	C,H,A
9260	116380.00	58190.00	67500.00	70880.00	Cummins	6TA	611D	12F-2R	265.84	30300	C,H,A
9270	130295.00	62500.00	72500.00	76130.00	Cummins	6TA	855D	12F-2R	308.1	29000	C,H,A
9280	140900.00	66500.00	77140.00	81000.00	Cummins	6TA	855D	12F-2R	344.5	29000	C,H,A

MFD - Mechanical Front Drive

1994

Model	Approx. Retail Price New	Fair	Good	Premium	Make	No. Cyls.	Displ. Cu.-In.	No. Speeds	P.T.O. H.P.	Approx. Shipping Wt.-Lbs.	Cab
1120	10500.00	6720.00	7350.00	7720.00	Mitsubishi	3	65D	6F-2R	16.50	1380	No
1120 MFD	11500.00	7360.00	8050.00	8450.00	Mitsubishi	3	65D	6F-2R	16.50	1480	No
1130	11500.00	7360.00	8050.00	8450.00	Mitsubishi	3	75D	9F-3R	20.00	1900	No
1130 MFD	12620.00	8080.00	8830.00	9270.00	Mitsubishi	3	75D	9F-3R	20.00	2062	No
1140	12000.00	7680.00	8400.00	8820.00	Mitsubishi	3	91D	9F-3R	23.00	1914	No
1140 MFD	13350.00	8540.00	9350.00	9820.00	Mitsubishi	3	91D	9F-3R	23.00	2062	No
3220	19153.00	11680.00	12830.00	13470.00	Case	3	179D	8F-4R	42.00	4960	No
3220 MFD	24277.00	14810.00	16270.00	17080.00	Case	3	179D	8F-4R	42.00	5570	No

Case-International (Cont.)

1994 (Cont.)

Model	Approx. Retail Price New	Estimated Average Value Less Repairs Fair	Good	Premium	Engine Make	No. Cyls.	Displ. Cu.-In.	No. Speeds	P.T.O. H.P.	Approx. Shipping Wt.-Lbs.	Cab
3230	22511.00	**13730.00**	**15080.00**	**15830.00**	Case	4	206D	8F-4R	52.00	5540	No
3230 MFD	28249.00	**17230.00**	**18930.00**	**19880.00**	Case	4	206D	8F-4R	52.00	6150	No
3230 MFD w/Cab	35251.00	**21500.00**	**23620.00**	**24800.00**	Case	4	206D	8F-4R	52.00	6950	C,H,A
3230 w/Cab	29513.00	**18000.00**	**19770.00**	**20760.00**	Case	4	206D	8F-4R	52.00	6340	C,H,A
4210	26412.00	**16110.00**	**17700.00**	**18590.00**	Case	4	239D	8F-4R	62.00	5720	No
4210 MFD	32237.00	**19670.00**	**21600.00**	**22680.00**	Case	4	239D	8F-4R	62.00	6330	No
4210 MFD w/Cab	39239.00	**23940.00**	**26290.00**	**27610.00**	Case	4	239D	8F-4R	62.00	7130	C,H,A
4210 w/Cab	33414.00	**20380.00**	**22390.00**	**23510.00**	Case	4	239D	8F-4R	62.00	6520	C,H,A
4230	29350.00	**17900.00**	**19670.00**	**20650.00**	Case	4	268D	16F-8R	72.00	6030	No
4230 MFD	35132.00	**21430.00**	**23540.00**	**24720.00**	Case	4	268D	16F-8R	72.00	6640	No
4230 MFD w/Cab	42134.00	**25700.00**	**28230.00**	**29640.00**	Case	4	268D	16F-8R	72.00	7440	C,H,A
4230 w/Cab	36351.00	**22170.00**	**24360.00**	**25580.00**	Case	4	268D	16F-8R	72.00	6830	C,H,A
4240	31599.00	**19280.00**	**21170.00**	**22230.00**	Case	4	268D	16F-8R	85.00	6030	No
4240 MFD	37260.00	**22730.00**	**24960.00**	**26210.00**	Case	4	268D	16F-8R	85.00	6640	No
5220	33141.00	**21210.00**	**23200.00**	**24360.00**	Case	4TA	239D	16F-12R	80.00	8818	No
5220 MFD	42381.00	**26240.00**	**28700.00**	**30140.00**	Case	4TA	239D	16F-12R	80.00	9590	No
5220 MFD w/Cab	49661.00	**30720.00**	**33600.00**	**35280.00**	Case	4TA	239D	16F-12R	80.00	9921	C,H,A
5220 w/Cab	40421.00	**24960.00**	**27300.00**	**28670.00**	Case	4TA	239D	16F-12R	80.00	9149	C,H,A
5230	38653.00	**24320.00**	**26600.00**	**27930.00**	Case	6	359D	16F-12R	90.00	9810	No
5230 MFD	46014.00	**28160.00**	**30800.00**	**32340.00**	Case	6	359D	16F-12R	90.00	10582	No
5230 MFD w/Cab	53294.00	**33280.00**	**36400.00**	**38220.00**	Case	6	359D	16F-12R	90.00	10913	C,H,A
5230 w/Cab	45933.00	**28800.00**	**31500.00**	**33080.00**	Case	6	359D	16F-12R	90.00	10141	C,H,A
5240	42332.00	**27090.00**	**29630.00**	**31110.00**	Case	6T	359D	16F-12R	100.	9810	No
5240 MFD	49472.00	**30720.00**	**33600.00**	**35280.00**	Case	6T	359D	16F-12R	100.	10582	No
5240 MFD w/Cab	56752.00	**34880.00**	**38150.00**	**40060.00**	Case	6T	359D	16F-12R	100.	10913	C,H,A
5240 w/Cab	49612.00	**31040.00**	**33950.00**	**35650.00**	Case	6T	359D	16F-12R	100.	10141	C,H,A
5250 MFD w/Cab	64768.00	**40960.00**	**44800.00**	**47040.00**	Case	6T	359D	16F-12R	112.00	10913	C,H,A
5250 w/Cab	56862.00	**35520.00**	**38850.00**	**40790.00**	Case	6T	359D	16F-12R	112.00	10141	C,H,A
7210	70876.00	**37560.00**	**42530.00**	**44660.00**	Case	6T	505D	18F-4R	130.00	15610	C,H,A
7210 MFD	81711.00	**42250.00**	**47830.00**	**50220.00**	Case	6T	505D	18F-4R	130.00	16403	C,H,A
7220	75900.00	**40230.00**	**45540.00**	**47820.00**	Case	6T	505D	18F-4R	155.00	15621	C,H,A
7220 MFD	88887.00	**45850.00**	**51900.00**	**54500.00**	Case	6T	505D	18F-4R	155.00	17319	C,H,A
7230	85752.00	**45450.00**	**51450.00**	**54020.00**	Case	6T	505D	18F-4R	170.00	15965	C,H,A
7230 MFD	102004.00	**51940.00**	**58800.00**	**61740.00**	Case	6T	505D	18F-4R	170.00	18404	C,H,A
7240	93705.00	**49660.00**	**56220.00**	**59030.00**	Case	6TA	505D	18F-4R	195.00	16808	C,H,A
7240 MFD	109776.00	**54470.00**	**61670.00**	**64750.00**	Case	6TA	505D	18F-4R	195.00	18578	C,H,A
7250 MFD	118824.00	**59800.00**	**67690.00**	**71080.00**	Case	6TA	505D	18F-4R	215.00	18745	C,H,A
9210	85491.00	**52150.00**	**57280.00**	**60140.00**	Case	6T	505D	12F-3R	168.00	17000	C,H,A
9230	93841.00	**57240.00**	**62870.00**	**66010.00**	Case	6TA	505D	12F-3R	207.00	22000	C,H,A
9250	117580.00	**65580.00**	**72030.00**	**75630.00**	Cummins	6TA	611D	12F-3R	266.00	27446	C,H,A
9270	130943.00	**65720.00**	**74400.00**	**78120.00**	Cummins	6TA	855D	12F-3R	308.00	33110	C,H,A
9280	146593.00	**72390.00**	**81960.00**	**86060.00**	Cummins	6TA	855D	12F-3R	344.00	34500	C,H,A

MFD - Mechanical Front Drive

1995

Model	Approx. Retail Price New	Fair	Good	Premium	Make	No. Cyls.	Displ. Cu.-In.	No. Speeds	P.T.O. H.P.	Approx. Shipping Wt.-Lbs.	Cab
3220	19153.00	**12260.00**	**13410.00**	**14080.00**	Case	3	179D	8F-4R	42	4960	No
3220 MFD	24277.00	**15540.00**	**16990.00**	**17840.00**	Case	3	179D	8F-4R	42	5570	No
3230	22511.00	**14410.00**	**15760.00**	**16550.00**	Case	4	206D	8F-4R	52	5540	No
3230 MFD	28249.00	**18080.00**	**19770.00**	**20760.00**	Case	4	206D	8F-4R	52	6150	No
3230 MFD w/Cab	35251.00	**22560.00**	**24680.00**	**25910.00**	Case	4	206D	8F-4R	52	6950	C,H,A
3230 w/Cab	29513.00	**18890.00**	**20660.00**	**21690.00**	Case	4	206D	8F-4R	52	6340	C,H,A
4210	26412.00	**16900.00**	**18490.00**	**19420.00**	Case	4	239D	8F-4R	62	5720	No
4210 MFD	32237.00	**20630.00**	**22570.00**	**23700.00**	Case	4	239D	8F-4R	62	6330	No
4210 MFD w/Cab	39239.00	**25110.00**	**27470.00**	**28840.00**	Case	4	239D	8F-4R	62	7130	C,H,A
4210 w/Cab	33414.00	**21390.00**	**23390.00**	**24560.00**	Case	4	239D	8F-4R	62	6520	C,H,A
4230	29856.00	**19110.00**	**20900.00**	**21950.00**	Case	4	268D	16F-8R	72	6030	No
4230 MFD	35744.00	**22880.00**	**25020.00**	**26270.00**	Case	4	268D	16F-8R	72	6640	No
4230 MFD w/Cab	42886.00	**27450.00**	**30020.00**	**31520.00**	Case	4	268D	16F-8R	72	7440	C,H,A
4230 w/Cab	36998.00	**23680.00**	**25900.00**	**27200.00**	Case	4	268D	16F-8R	72	6830	C,H,A
4240	32144.00	**20570.00**	**22500.00**	**23630.00**	Case	4	268D	16F-8R	85	6030	No
4240 MFD	37911.00	**24260.00**	**26540.00**	**27870.00**	Case	4	268D	16F-8R	85	6640	No
5220	33638.00	**21780.00**	**24090.00**	**25300.00**	Case	4TA	239D	16F-12R	80	8818	No
5220 MFD	43017.00	**27060.00**	**29930.00**	**31430.00**	Case	4TA	239D	16F-12R	80	9590	No
5220 MFD w/Cab	50406.00	**31940.00**	**35330.00**	**37100.00**	Case	4TA	239D	16F-12R	80	9921	C,H,A
5220 w/Cab	41027.00	**26400.00**	**29200.00**	**30660.00**	Case	4TA	239D	16F-12R	80	9149	C,H,A
5230	39233.00	**25740.00**	**28470.00**	**29890.00**	Case	6	359D	16F-12R	90	9810	No
5230 MFD	46700.00	**29500.00**	**32630.00**	**34260.00**	Case	6	359D	16F-12R	90	10582	No
5230 MFD w/Cab	54094.00	**34320.00**	**37960.00**	**39860.00**	Case	6	359D	16F-12R	90	10913	C,H,A
5230 w/Cab	46622.00	**30030.00**	**33220.00**	**34880.00**	Case	6	359D	16F-12R	90	10141	C,H,A
5240	42968.00	**28050.00**	**31030.00**	**32580.00**	Case	6T	359D	16F-12R	100	9810	No
5240 MFD	50215.00	**31810.00**	**35190.00**	**36950.00**	Case	6T	359D	16F-12R	100	10582	No
5240 MFD w/Cab	57604.00	**36700.00**	**40590.00**	**42620.00**	Case	6T	359D	16F-12R	100	10913	C,H,A
5240 w/Cab	50357.00	**32570.00**	**36030.00**	**37830.00**	Case	6T	359D	16F-12R	100	10141	C,H,A
5250 MFD w/Cab	65739.00	**41910.00**	**46360.00**	**48680.00**	Case	6T	359D	16F-12R	112	10913	C,H,A
5250 w/Cab	57714.00	**36960.00**	**40880.00**	**42920.00**	Case	6T	359D	16F-12R	112	10141	C,H,A
7210	72181.00	**40420.00**	**45470.00**	**47290.00**	Case	6T	505D	18F-4R	130	15610	C,H,A
7210 MFD	83221.00	**46040.00**	**51800.00**	**53870.00**	Case	6T	505D	18F-4R	130	16403	C,H,A
7220	77286.00	**43280.00**	**48690.00**	**50640.00**	Case	6T	505D	18F-4R	155	15621	C,H,A
7220 MFD	91285.00	**50560.00**	**56880.00**	**59160.00**	Case	6T	505D	18F-4R	155	17319	C,H,A
7230	87328.00	**48340.00**	**54390.00**	**56570.00**	Case	6T	505D	18F-4R	170	15965	C,H,A
7230 MFD	103823.00	**56460.00**	**63520.00**	**66060.00**	Case	6T	505D	18F-4R	170	18404	C,H,A
7240	94572.00	**52400.00**	**58950.00**	**61310.00**	Case	6TA	505D	18F-4R	195	16808	C,H,A
7240 MFD	110765.00	**59230.00**	**66630.00**	**69300.00**	Case	6TA	505D	18F-4R	195	18578	C,H,A
7250 MFD	119913.00	**64350.00**	**72400.00**	**75300.00**	Case	6TA	505D	18F-4R	215	18745	C,H,A

Case-International (Cont.)

1995 (Cont.)

Model	Approx. Retail Price New	Estimated Average Value Less Repairs Fair	Good	Premium	Engine Make	No. Cyls.	Displ. Cu.-In.	No. Speeds	P.T.O. H.P.	Approx. Shipping Wt.-Lbs.	Cab
9210	85491.00	54710.00	59840.00	62830.00	Case	6T	505D	12F-3R	168	17000	C,H,A
9230	93841.00	60060.00	65690.00	68980.00	Case	6TA	505D	12F-3R	207	22000	C,H,A
9250	117580.00	69760.00	76300.00	80120.00	Cummins	6TA	611D	12F-3R	266	27446	C,H,A
9270	130943.00	70000.00	78750.00	81900.00	Cummins	6TA	855D	12F-3R	308	33110	C,H,A
9280	146593.00	76160.00	85680.00	89110.00	Cummins	6TA	855D	12F-3R	344	34500	C,H,A

MFD - Mechanical Front Drive

1996

Model	Approx. Retail Price New	Fair	Good	Premium	Make	No. Cyls.	Displ. Cu.-In.	No. Speeds	P.T.O. H.P.	Approx. Shipping Wt.-Lbs.	Cab
3220	19447.00	13030.00	14200.00	14770.00	Case	3	179D	8F-4R	42	4960	No
3220 MFD	24775.00	16600.00	18090.00	18810.00	Case	3	179D	8F-4R	42	5570	No
3230	22447.00	15040.00	16390.00	17050.00	Case	4	206D	8F-4R	52	5540	No
3230 MFD	28209.00	18900.00	20590.00	21410.00	Case	4	206D	8F-4R	52	6150	No
3230 MFD w/Cab	35210.00	23590.00	25700.00	26730.00	Case	4	206D	8F-4R	52	6950	C,H,A
3230 w/Cab	29448.00	19730.00	21500.00	22360.00	Case	4	206D	8F-4R	52	6340	C,H,A
4210	25630.00	17170.00	18710.00	19460.00	Case	4	239D	8F-4R	62	5720	No
4210 MFD	31392.00	21030.00	22920.00	23840.00	Case	4	239D	8F-4R	62	6330	No
4210 MFD w/Cab	38394.00	25720.00	28030.00	29150.00	Case	4	239D	8F-4R	62	7130	C,H,A
4210 w/Cab	32631.00	21860.00	23820.00	24770.00	Case	4	239D	8F-4R	62	6520	C,H,A
4230	29535.00	19790.00	21560.00	22420.00	Case	4	268D	16F-8R	72	6030	No
4230 MFD	35836.00	24010.00	26160.00	27210.00	Case	4	268D	16F-8R	72	6640	No
4230 MFD w/Cab	43551.00	29180.00	31790.00	33060.00	Case	4	268D	16F-8R	72	7440	C,H,A
4230 w/Cab	37250.00	24960.00	27190.00	28280.00	Case	4	268D	16F-8R	72	6830	C,H,A
4240	31697.00	21240.00	23140.00	24070.00	Case	4	268D	16F-8R	85	6030	No
4240 MFD	37997.00	25460.00	27740.00	28850.00	Case	4	268D	16F-8R	85	6640	No
5220	35442.00	24810.00	26940.00	28020.00	Case	4TA	239D	16F-12R	80	8818	No
5220 MFD	43573.00	28700.00	31160.00	32410.00	Case	4TA	239D	16F-12R	80	9590	No
5220 MFD w/Cab	51370.00	34300.00	37240.00	38730.00	Case	4TA	239D	16F-12R	80	9921	C,H,A
5220 w/Cab	43240.00	29400.00	31920.00	33200.00	Case	4TA	239D	16F-12R	80	9149	C,H,A
5230	38640.00	27050.00	29370.00	30550.00	Case	6	359D	16F-12R	90	9810	No
5230 MFD	46469.00	30430.00	33040.00	34360.00	Case	6	359D	16F-12R	90	10582	No
5230 MFD w/Cab	54265.00	35890.00	38960.00	40520.00	Case	6	359D	16F-12R	90	10913	C,H,A
5230 w/Cab	46435.00	31110.00	33770.00	35120.00	Case	6	359D	16F-12R	90	10141	C,H,A
5240	42286.00	29600.00	32140.00	33430.00	Case	6T	359D	16F-12R	100	9810	No
5240 MFD	50122.00	33600.00	36480.00	37940.00	Case	6T	359D	16F-12R	100	10582	No
5240 MFD w/Cab	57917.00	38850.00	42180.00	43870.00	Case	6T	359D	16F-12R	100	10913	C,H,A
5240 w/Cab	50080.00	34300.00	37240.00	38730.00	Case	6T	359D	16F-12R	100	10141	C,H,A
5250 MFD w/Cab	67817.00	45850.00	49780.00	51770.00	Case	6T	359D	16F-12R	112	10913	C,H,A
5250 w/Cab	59315.00	41520.00	45080.00	46880.00	Case	6T	359D	16F-12R	112	10141	C,H,A
7210	76510.00	46060.00	50590.00	52610.00	Case	6T	505D	18F-4R	130	15610	C,H,A
7210 MFD	88215.00	52590.00	57760.00	60070.00	Case	6T	505D	18F-4R	130	16403	C,H,A
7220	81925.00	49360.00	54220.00	56390.00	Case	6T	505D	18F-4R	155	15621	C,H,A
7220 MFD	96760.00	57190.00	62820.00	65330.00	Case	6T	505D	18F-4R	155	17319	C,H,A
7230	95265.00	55670.00	61150.00	63600.00	Case	6T	505D	18F-4R	170	15965	C,H,A
7230 MFD	110050.00	63470.00	69710.00	72500.00	Case	6T	505D	18F-4R	170	18404	C,H,A
7240	100245.00	59930.00	65820.00	68450.00	Case	6TA	505D	18F-4R	195	16808	C,H,A
7240 MFD	117410.00	67350.00	73980.00	76940.00	Case	6TA	505D	18F-4R	195	18578	C,H,A
7250 MFD	127110.00	73270.00	80470.00	83690.00	Case	6TA	505D	18F-4R	215	18745	C,H,A
9330 (1)	99470.00	60680.00	66650.00	69320.00	Case	6TA	505D	12F-3R	235	22000	C,H,A
9350 (1)	124635.00	76030.00	83510.00	86850.00	Cummins	6TA	611D	12F-3R	310	27446	C,H,A
9370 (1)	138800.00	79300.00	87100.00	90580.00	Cummins	6TA	855D	12F-3R	360	33110	C,H,A
9380 (1)	155390.00	93330.00	102510.00	106610.00	Cummins	6TA	855D	12F-3R	400	34500	C,H,A

MFD - Mechanical Front Drive
(1) Gross engine horsepower.

1997

Model	Approx. Retail Price New	Fair	Good	Premium	Make	No. Cyls.	Displ. Cu.-In.	No. Speeds	P.T.O. H.P.	Approx. Shipping Wt.-Lbs.	Cab
3220	19447.00	14000.00	14970.00	15570.00	Case	3	179D	8F-4R	42	4960	C,H,A
3220 MFD	24775.00	17840.00	19080.00	19840.00	Case	3	179D	8F-4R	42	5570	No
3230	22447.00	16160.00	17280.00	17970.00	Case	4	206D	8F-4R	52	5540	No
3230 MFD	28209.00	20310.00	21720.00	22590.00	Case	4	206D	8F-4R	52	6150	No
3230 MFD w/Cab	35210.00	25350.00	27110.00	28190.00	Case	4	206D	8F-4R	52	6950	C,H,A
3230 w/Cab	29448.00	21200.00	22680.00	23590.00	Case	4	206D	8F-4R	52	6340	C,H,A
4210	25630.00	18450.00	19740.00	20530.00	Case	4	239D	8F-4R	62	5720	No
4210 MFD	31392.00	22600.00	24170.00	25140.00	Case	4	239D	8F-4R	62	6330	No
4210 MFD w/Cab	38394.00	27640.00	29560.00	30740.00	Case	4	239D	8F-4R	62	7130	C,H,A
4210 w/Cab	32631.00	23490.00	25130.00	26140.00	Case	4	239D	8F-4R	62	6520	C,H,A
4230	29535.00	21270.00	22740.00	23650.00	Case	4	268D	16F-8R	72	6030	No
4230 MFD	35836.00	25800.00	27590.00	28690.00	Case	4	268D	16F-8R	72	6640	No
4230 MFD w/Cab	43551.00	31360.00	33530.00	34870.00	Case	4	268D	16F-8R	72	7440	C,H,A
4230 w/Cab	37250.00	26820.00	28680.00	29830.00	Case	4	268D	16F-8R	72	6830	C,H,A
4240	31697.00	22820.00	24410.00	25390.00	Case	4	268D	16F-8R	85	6030	No
4240 MFD	37997.00	27360.00	29260.00	30430.00	Case	4	268D	16F-8R	85	6640	No
4240 MFD w/Cab	45650.00	32870.00	35150.00	36560.00	Case	4	268D	16F-8R	85		C,H,A
4240 w/Cab	39350.00	28330.00	30300.00	31510.00	Case	4	268D	16F-8R	85		C,H,A
5220	35442.00	26580.00	28350.00	29480.00	Case	4TA	239D	16F-12R	80	8818	No
5220 MFD	43573.00	31130.00	33200.00	34530.00	Case	4TA	239D	16F-12R	80	9590	No
5220 MFD w/Cab	51370.00	36750.00	39200.00	40770.00	Case	4TA	239D	16F-12R	80	9921	C,H,A
5220 w/Cab	43240.00	32430.00	34590.00	35970.00	Case	4TA	239D	16F-12R	80	9149	C,H,A
5230	38640.00	28980.00	30910.00	32150.00	Case	6	359D	16F-12R	90	9810	No
5230 MFD	46469.00	33380.00	35600.00	37020.00	Case	6	359D	16F-12R	90	10582	No
5230 MFD w/Cab	54265.00	39000.00	41600.00	43260.00	Case	6	359D	16F-12R	90	10913	C,H,A
5230 w/Cab	46435.00	34830.00	37150.00	38640.00	Case	6	359D	16F-12R	90	10141	C,H,A
5240	42286.00	31720.00	33830.00	35180.00	Case	6T	359D	16F-12R	100	9810	No
5240 MFD	50122.00	36000.00	38400.00	39940.00	Case	6T	359D	16F-12R	100	10582	No
5240 MFD w/Cab	57917.00	42000.00	44800.00	46590.00	Case	6T	359D	16F-12R	100	10913	C,H,A

Case-International (Cont.)

1997 (Cont.)

Model	Approx. Retail Price New	Estimated Average Value Less Repairs: Fair	Good	Premium	Engine: Make	No. Cyls.	Displ. Cu.-In.	No. Speeds	P.T.O. H.P.	Approx. Shipping Wt.-Lbs.	Cab
5240 w/Cab	50100.00	37580.00	40080.00	41680.00	Case	6T	359D	16F-12R	100	10141	C,H,A
5250	51520.00	38640.00	41220.00	42870.00	Case	6T	359D	16F-8R	112		No
5250 MFD	60025.00	44250.00	47200.00	49090.00	Case	6T	359D	16F-8R	112		No
5250 MFD w/Cab	67817.00	48750.00	52000.00	54080.00	Case	6T	359D	16F-12R	112	10913	C,H,A
5250 w/Cab	59315.00	43730.00	46640.00	48510.00	Case	6T	359D	16F-12R	112	10141	C,H,A
8910	75478.00	50570.00	55100.00	57300.00	Case	6T	505D	18F-4R	130	15610	C,H,A
8910 MFD	87095.00	57620.00	62780.00	65290.00	Case	6T	505D	18F-4R	130	16403	C,H,A
8920	82610.00	55350.00	60310.00	62720.00	Case	6T	505D	18F-4R	155	15621	C,H,A
8920 MFD	96100.00	62310.00	67890.00	70610.00	Case	6T	505D	18F-4R	155	17319	C,H,A
8930	90695.00	60770.00	66210.00	68860.00	Case	6T	505D	18F-4R	170	15965	C,H,A
8930 MFD	104750.00	67000.00	73000.00	75920.00	Case	6T	505D	18F-4R	170	18404	C,H,A
8940	101687.00	68130.00	74230.00	77200.00	Case	6TA	505D	18F-4R	195	16808	C,H,A
8940 MFD	115800.00	73700.00	80300.00	83510.00	Case	6TA	505D	18F-4R	195	18578	C,H,A
8950 MFD	129080.00	82410.00	89790.00	93380.00	Case	6TA	505D	18F-4R	215	18745	C,H,A
9310 w/3pt, PTO	106425.00	70350.00	76650.00	79720.00	Case	6TA	505D	12F-3R	205(1)		C,H,A
9330 w/3pt, PTO	115495.00	76380.00	83220.00	86550.00	Case	6TA	505D	12F-3R	240(1)		C,H,A
9350 w/3pto, PTO	133577.00	86150.00	93860.00	97610.00	Case	6TA	661D	12F-3R	310(1)		C,H,A
9370	133431.00	88440.00	96360.00	100210.00	Case	6TA	855D	12F-3R	360(1)		C,H,A
9370 w/3pt, PTO	151051.00	97150.00	105850.00	110080.00	Case	6TA	855D	12F-3R	360(1)		C,H,A
9380	149335.00	99160.00	108040.00	112360.00	Case	6TA	855D	12F-3R	400(1)		C,H,A
9380 w/pto	156095.00	101840.00	110960.00	115400.00	Case	6TA	855D	12F-3R	400(1)		C,H,A
9390	154411.00	103460.00	112720.00	117230.00	Case	6TA	855D	12F-3R	425(1)		C,H,A
9390 w/pto	161170.00	105190.00	114610.00	119190.00	Case	6TA	855D	12F-3R	425(1)		C,H,A

MFD - Mechanical Front Drive
(1) Gross engine horsepower.

1998

Model	Approx. Retail Price New	Fair	Good	Premium	Make	No. Cyls.	Displ. Cu.-In.	No. Speeds	P.T.O. H.P.	Approx. Shipping Wt.-Lbs.	Cab
C50	19900.00	15720.00	16720.00	17220.00	Case	3	165D	8F-8R	40	5335	No
C50 4WD	25000.00	19750.00	21000.00	21630.00	Case	3	165D	8F-8R	40	6063	No
CX50	24200.00	19120.00	20330.00	20940.00	Case	3	165D	8F-8R	40	7286	C,H,A
CX50 4WD	29250.00	23110.00	24570.00	25310.00	Case	3	165D	8F-8R	40	7970	C,H,A
C60	22500.00	17780.00	18900.00	19470.00	Case	3T	165D	8F-8R	50	5357	No
C60 4WD	27800.00	21960.00	23350.00	24050.00	Case	3T	165D	8F-8R	50	6096	No
CX60	25200.00	19910.00	21170.00	21810.00	Case	3T	165D	8F-8R	50	7286	C,H,A
CX60 4WD	30300.00	23940.00	25450.00	26210.00	Case	3T	165D	8F-8R	50	7970	C,H,A
C70	23750.00	18760.00	19950.00	20550.00	Case	4	258D	8F-8R	60	5941	No
C70 4WD	29000.00	22910.00	24360.00	25090.00	Case	4	258D	8F-8R	60	6658	No
CX70	27000.00	21330.00	22680.00	23360.00	Case	4	258D	8F-8R	60	7396	C,H,A
CX70 4WD	33500.00	26470.00	28140.00	28980.00	Case	4	258D	8F-8R	60	8466	C,H,A
C80	25800.00	20380.00	21670.00	22320.00	Case	4T	244D	8F-8R	67	5941	No
C80 4WD	30000.00	23700.00	25200.00	25960.00	Case	4T	244D	8F-8R	67	6658	No
CX80	29200.00	23070.00	24530.00	25270.00	Case	4T	244D	8F-8R	67	7396	C,H,A
CX80 4WD	35300.00	27890.00	29650.00	30540.00	Case	4T	244D	8F-8R	67	8466	C,H,A
MX80C	53000.00	41870.00	44520.00	45860.00	Case	4T	244D	16F-12R	67	9921	C,H,A
C90	28256.00	22320.00	23740.00	24450.00	Case	4T	244D	8F-8R	74	5963	No
C90 4WD	34500.00	27260.00	28980.00	29850.00	Case	4T	244D	8F-8R	74	6691	No
CX90	31500.00	24890.00	26460.00	27250.00	Case	4T	244D	8F-8R	74	7396	C,H,A
CX90 4WD	37800.00	29860.00	31750.00	32700.00	Case	4T	244D	8F-8R	74	8466	C,H,A
MX90C	56000.00	44240.00	47040.00	48450.00	Case	4T	244D	16F-12R	74	10472	C,H,A
C100	30500.00	24100.00	25620.00	26390.00	Case	4T	244D	8F-8R	83	5963	No
C100 4WD	36900.00	29150.00	31000.00	31930.00	Case	4T	244D	8F-8R	83	6691	No
CX100	33800.00	26700.00	28390.00	29240.00	Case	4T	244D	8F-8R	83	7396	C,H,A
CX100 4WD	40300.00	31840.00	33850.00	34870.00	Case	4T	244D	8F-8R	83	8466	C,H,A
MX100	47700.00	37680.00	40070.00	41270.00	Case	6T	359D	16F-12R	85	11300	C,H,A
MX100 4WD	52750.00	41670.00	44310.00	45640.00	Case	6T	359D	16F-12R	85	12460	C,H,A
MX100C	51350.00	40570.00	43130.00	44420.00	Case	4T	244D	16F-12R	83	10472	C,H,A
MX110	48800.00	38550.00	40990.00	42220.00	Case	6T	359D	16F-12R	95	11300	C,H,A
MX110 4WD	56660.00	44760.00	47590.00	49020.00	Case	6T	359D	16F-12R	95	12460	C,H,A
MX120	50570.00	39950.00	42480.00	43750.00	Case	6T	359D	16F-12R	105	11300	C,H,A
MX120 4WD	58800.00	46450.00	49390.00	50870.00	Case	6T	359D	16F-12R	105	12460	C,H,A
MX135	59200.00	46770.00	49730.00	51220.00	Case	6T	359D	16F-12R	115	11300	C,H,A
MX135 4WD	67200.00	53090.00	56450.00	58140.00	Case	6T	359D	16F-12R	115	12460	C,H,A
MX150	68250.00	53920.00	57330.00	59050.00	Case	6TA	359D	16F-12R	130	13911	C,H,A
MX150 4WD	77330.00	61090.00	64960.00	66910.00	Case	6TA	359D	16F-12R	130	14616	C,H,A
MX170	73650.00	58180.00	61870.00	63730.00	Case	6TA	359D	16F-12R	145	14076	C,H,A
MX170 4WD	82440.00	65130.00	69250.00	71330.00	Case	6TA	359D	16F-12R	145	14782	C,H,A
8910	79000.00	56980.00	60830.00	62660.00	Case	6T	505D	18F-4R	135	15215	C,H,A
8910 4WD	89000.00	63640.00	67940.00	69980.00	Case	6T	505D	18F-4R	135	16575	C,H,A
8920	86000.00	62160.00	66360.00	68350.00	Case	6T	505D	18F-4R	155	15630	C,H,A
8920 4WD	99000.00	69190.00	73870.00	76090.00	Case	6T	505D	18F-4R	155	16750	C,H,A
8930	96000.00	69560.00	74260.00	76490.00	Case	6T	505D	18F-4R	180	15750	C,H,A
8930 4WD	110000.00	74000.00	79000.00	81370.00	Case	6T	505D	18F-4R	180	16750	C,H,A
8940	106000.00	76960.00	82160.00	84630.00	Case	6T	505D	18F-4R	205	15825	C,H,A
8940 4WD	120000.00	82140.00	87690.00	90320.00	Case	6T	505D	18F-4R	205	16845	C,H,A
8950 4WD	135000.00	92500.00	98750.00	101710.00	Case	6T	505D	18F-4R	225	17445	C,H,A
9330	108000.00	78440.00	83740.00	86250.00	Case	6TA	505D	12F-3R	240*	21026	C,H,A
9330 Row Crop	116000.00	83620.00	89270.00	91950.00	Case	6TA	505D	12F-3R	240*	21026	C,H,A
9350	128000.00	92500.00	98750.00	101710.00	Cummins	6TA	661D	12F-3R	310*	26533	C,H,A
9350 Row Crop	138000.00	96200.00	102700.00	105780.00	Cummins	6TA	661D	12F-3R	310*	29600	C,H,A
9370	145000.00	101380.00	108230.00	111480.00	Cummins	6TA	855D	12F-3R	360*	30416	C,H,A
9380	158000.00	111740.00	119290.00	122870.00	Cummins	6TA	855D	12F-3R	400*	32500	C,H,A
9390	165000.00	117660.00	125610.00	129380.00	Cummins	6TA	855D	12F-3R	425*	32500	C,H,A
QUADTRAC	194000.00	125060.00	133510.00	137520.00	Cummins	6TA	855D	12F-3R	360*	43750	C,H,A

***Engine Horsepower**

Case-International (Cont.)

1999

Model	Approx. Retail Price New	Estimated Average Value Less Repairs Fair	Good	Premium	Engine Make	No. Cyls.	Displ. Cu.-In.	No. Speeds	P.T.O. H.P.	Approx. Shipping Wt.-Lbs.	Cab
C50	19600.00	16660.00	17440.00	17790.00	Case	3	165D	8F-8R	40	5335	No
C50 4WD	24750.00	21040.00	22030.00	22470.00	Case	3	165D	8F-8R	40	6063	No
CX50	23220.00	19740.00	20670.00	21080.00	Case	3	165D	8F-8R	40	7286	C,H,A
CX50 4WD	28300.00	24060.00	25190.00	25690.00	Case	3	165D	8F-8R	40	7970	C,H,A
C60	22225.00	18890.00	19780.00	20180.00	Case	3T	165D	8F-8R	50	5357	No
C60 4WD	27600.00	23460.00	24560.00	25050.00	Case	3T	165D	8F-8R	50	6096	No
CX60	25300.00	21510.00	22520.00	22970.00	Case	3T	165D	8F-8R	50	7286	C,H,A
CX60 4WD	30450.00	25880.00	27100.00	27640.00	Case	3T	165D	8F-8R	50	7970	C,H,A
C70	23750.00	20190.00	21140.00	21560.00	Case	4	258D	8F-8R	60	5941	No
C70 4WD	28900.00	24570.00	25720.00	26230.00	Case	4	258D	8F-8R	60	6658	No
CX70	27000.00	22950.00	24030.00	24510.00	Case	4	258D	8F-8R	60	7396	C,H,A
CX70 4WD	32500.00	27630.00	28930.00	29510.00	Case	4	258D	8F-8R	60	8466	C,H,A
C80	25900.00	22020.00	23050.00	23510.00	Case	4T	244D	8F-8R	67	5941	No
C80 4WD	31000.00	26350.00	27590.00	28140.00	Case	4T	244D	8F-8R	67	6658	No
CX80	29730.00	25270.00	26460.00	26990.00	Case	4T	244D	8F-8R	67	7396	C,H,A
CX80 4WD	34950.00	29710.00	31110.00	31730.00	Case	4T	244D	8F-8R	67	8466	C,H,A
MX80C	52150.00	44330.00	46410.00	47340.00	Case	4T	244D	16F-12R	67	9921	C,H,A
C90	28255.00	24020.00	25150.00	25650.00	Case	4T	244D	8F-8R	74	5963	No
C90 4WD	33550.00	28520.00	29860.00	30460.00	Case	4T	244D	8F-8R	74	6691	No
CX90	32140.00	27320.00	28610.00	29180.00	Case	4T	244D	8F-8R	74	7396	C,H,A
CX90 4WD	37650.00	32000.00	33510.00	34180.00	Case	4T	244D	8F-8R	74	8466	C,H,A
MX90C	54825.00	46600.00	48790.00	49770.00	Case	4T	244D	16F-12R	74	10472	C,H,A
C100	30465.00	25900.00	27110.00	27650.00	Case	4T	244D	8F-8R	83	5963	No
C100 4WD	35975.00	30580.00	32020.00	32660.00	Case	4T	244D	8F-8R	83	6691	No
CX100	34390.00	29230.00	30610.00	31220.00	Case	4T	244D	8F-8R	83	7396	C,H,A
CX100 4WD	39880.00	33900.00	35490.00	36200.00	Case	4T	244D	8F-8R	83	8466	C,H,A
MX100 W/Cab	42300.00	35960.00	37650.00	38400.00	Case	6T	359D	16F-12R	85	11300	C,H,A
MX100 W/Cab 4WD	50825.00	43200.00	45230.00	46140.00	Case	6T	359D	16F-12R	85	12460	C,H,A
MX100C	58100.00	49390.00	51710.00	52740.00	Case	4T	244D	16F-12R	83	10472	C,H,A
MX110 W/Cab	44050.00	37440.00	39210.00	39990.00	Case	6T	359D	16F-12R	95	11300	C,H,A
MX110 W/Cab 4WD	52350.00	44500.00	46590.00	47520.00	Case	6T	359D	16F-12R	95	12460	C,H,A
MX120 W/Cab	48100.00	40890.00	42810.00	43670.00	Case	6T	359D	16F-12R	105	11300	C,H,A
MX120 W/Cab 4WD	56250.00	47810.00	50060.00	51060.00	Case	6T	359D	16F-12R	105	12460	C,H,A
MX135 W/Cab	58255.00	49520.00	51850.00	52890.00	Case	6T	359D	16F-12R	115	11300	C,H,A
MX135 W/Cab 4WD	66450.00	56480.00	59140.00	60320.00	Case	6T	359D	16F-12R	115	12460	C,H,A
MX150	75790.00	64420.00	67450.00	68800.00	Case	6TA	359D	16F-12R	130	13911	C,H,A
MX150 4WD	83950.00	71360.00	74720.00	76210.00	Case	6TA	359D	16F-12R	130	14616	C,H,A
MX170	82100.00	69790.00	73070.00	74530.00	Case	6TA	359D	16F-12R	145	14076	C,H,A
MX170 4WD	90720.00	77110.00	80740.00	82360.00	Case	6TA	359D	16F-12R	145	14782	C,H,A
MX180	86175.00	73250.00	76700.00	78230.00	Case	6T	505D	18F-4R	145	17700	C,H,A
MX180 4WD	94875.00	80640.00	84440.00	86130.00	Case	6T	505D	18F-4R	145	18600	C,H,A
MX200	92280.00	78440.00	82130.00	83770.00	Case	6TA	505D	18F-4R	165	18700	C,H,A
MX200 4WD	101350.00	86150.00	90200.00	92000.00	Case	6TA	505D	18F-4R	165	19700	C,H,A
MX220	102640.00	87240.00	91350.00	93180.00	Case	6TA	505D	18F-4R	185	18700	C,H,A
MX220 4WD	110455.00	93890.00	98310.00	100280.00	Case	6TA	505D	18F-4R	185	19700	C,H,A
MX240 4WD	128000.00	108800.00	113920.00	116200.00	Case	6TA	505D	18F-4R	205	20200	C,H,A
MX270 4WD	140150.00	119130.00	124730.00	127230.00	Case	6TA	505D	18F-4R	235	20200	C,H,A
8910	77745.00	64530.00	67640.00	69670.00	Case	6T	505D	18F-4R	135	15215	C,H,A
8910 4WD	85950.00	71340.00	74780.00	77020.00	Case	6T	505D	18F-4R	135	16230	C,H,A
8920	85000.00	70550.00	73950.00	76170.00	Case	6T	505D	18F-4R	155	15630	C,H,A
8920 4WD	93840.00	77890.00	81640.00	84090.00	Case	6T	505D	18F-4R	155	16575	C,H,A
8930	94325.00	78290.00	82060.00	84520.00	Case	6T	505D	18F-4R	180	15750	C,H,A
8930 4WD	102925.00	85430.00	89550.00	92240.00	Case	6T	505D	18F-4R	180	16750	C,H,A
8940	104740.00	86930.00	91120.00	93850.00	Case	6T	505D	18F-4R	205	15825	C,H,A
8940 4WD	113850.00	91300.00	95700.00	98570.00	Case	6T	505D	18F-4R	205	16845	C,H,A
8950 4WD	132955.00	103750.00	108750.00	112010.00	Case	6T	505D	18F-4R	225	17445	C,H,A
9330	106080.00	88050.00	92290.00	95060.00	Case	6TA	505D	12F-3R	240*	21026	C,H,A
9330 Row Crop	114000.00	92960.00	97440.00	100360.00	Case	6TA	505D	12F-3R	240*	21026	C,H,A
9350	123620.00	101260.00	106140.00	109320.00	Cummins	6TA	661D	12F-3R	310*	26533	C,H,A
9350 Row Crop	133500.00	107900.00	113100.00	116490.00	Cummins	6TA	661D	12F-3R	310*	29600	C,H,A
9370	138810.00	113710.00	119190.00	122770.00	Cummins	6TA	855D	12F-3R	360*	30416	C,H,A
9380	155355.00	128650.00	134850.00	138900.00	Cummins	6TA	855D	12F-3R	400*	32500	C,H,A
9390	159075.00	132030.00	138400.00	142550.00	Cummins	6TA	855D	12F-3R	425*	32500	C,H,A
QUADTRAC	189650.00	145250.00	152250.00	156820.00	Cummins	6TA	855D	12F-3R	360*	43750	C,H,A

*Engine Horsepower

Caterpillar

Model	Approx. Retail Price New	Fair	Good	Premium	Engine Make	No. Cyls.	Displ. Cu.-In.	No. Speeds	P.T.O. H.P.	Approx. Shipping Wt.-Lbs.	Cab
1986											
Challenger 65	......	48380.00	59000.00	63130.00		6T	638D	10F-2R	256	31100	C,H,A
1987											
Challenger 65	......	50820.00	61710.00	66030.00		6T	638D	10F-2R	256	31100	C,H,A
1988											
Challenger 65	......	53750.00	65000.00	68900.00		6T	638D	10F-2R	256	31100	C,H,A
1989											
Challenger 65	......	55880.00	67310.00	71350.00		6T	638D	10F-2R	256	31100	C,H,A
1990											
Challenger 65	......	57600.00	69120.00	73270.00		6T	638D	10F-2R	256	31100	C,H,A
Challenger 75	......	58950.00	70740.00	74980.00		6	629D	10F-2R	281	32000	C,H,A

Model	Approx. Retail Price New	Fair	Estimated Average Value Less Repairs Good	Premium	Engine Make	No. Cyls.	Displ. Cu.-In.	No. Speeds	P.T.O. H.P.	Approx. Shipping Wt.-Lbs.	Cab
Caterpillar (Cont.)											
			1991								
Challenger 65B	......	60440.00	72270.00	76610.00		6T	638D	10F-2R	271	31100	C,H,A
Challenger 75	......	61960.00	74090.00	78540.00		6	629D	10F-2R	281	32000	C,H,A
			1992								
Challenger 65B	......	62400.00	72800.00	76440.00		6T	638D	10F-2R	271	31100	C,H,A
Challenger 65C	......	63840.00	74480.00	78200.00		6T	638D	10F-2R	250	32880	C,H,A
Challenger 75	......	66100.00	77110.00	80970.00		6	629D	10F-2R	281	32000	C,H,A
Challenger 75C	......	67250.00	78460.00	82380.00		6	629D	10F-2R	280	32000	C,H,A
			1993								
Challenger 65B	......	66500.00	77140.00	81000.00		6T	638D	10F-2R	271	31100	C,H,A
Challenger 65C	......	68750.00	79750.00	83740.00		6T	638D	10F-2R	250	32880	C,H,A
Challenger 75C	......	71050.00	82420.00	86540.00		6	629D	10F-2R	280	32000	C,H,A
Challenger 85C	......	76500.00	88740.00	93180.00		6	629D	10F-2R	305	33250	C,H,A
			1994								
Challenger 35	......	63600.00	72000.00	75600.00		6	403D	16F-9R	175	22450	C,H,A
Challenger 45	......	71020.00	80400.00	84420.00		6T	403D	16F-9R	200	22750	C,H,A
Challenger 65C	......	74730.00	84600.00	88830.00		6T	638D	10F-2R	250	32880	C,H,A
Challenger 75C	......	77430.00	87660.00	92040.00		6	629D	10F-2R	280	32000	C,H,A
Challenger 85C	......	84800.00	96000.00	100800.00		6	629D	10F-2R	305	33250	C,H,A
			1995								
Challenger 35	......	68880.00	77490.00	80590.00		6	403D	16F-9R	175	22450	C,H,A
Challenger 45	......	76160.00	85680.00	89110.00		6T	403D	16F-9R	200	22750	C,H,A
Challenger 65C	......	80080.00	90090.00	93690.00		6T	638D	10F-2R	250	32880	C,H,A
Challenger 70C	......	81480.00	91670.00	95340.00		6	638D	10F-2R	250	35270	C,H,A
Challenger 75C	......	84060.00	94560.00	98340.00		6	629D	10F-2R	280	32000	C,H,A
Challenger 85C	......	92400.00	103950.00	108110.00		6	629D	10F-2R	305	33250	C,H,A
			1996								
Challenger 35	133166.00	80010.00	87880.00	91400.00		6	403D	16F-9R	175	22450	C,H,A
Challenger 45	138950.00	84760.00	93100.00	96820.00		6T	403D	16F-9R	200	22750	C,H,A
Challenger 55	147750.00	89060.00	97820.00	101730.00		6	442D	16F-9R	225	25550	C,H,A
Challenger 65D	161700.00	97600.00	107200.00	111490.00		6T	638D	10F-2R	300	32880	C,H,A
Challenger 75C	171000.00	101260.00	111220.00	115670.00		6	629D	10F-2R	280	32000	C,H,A
Challenger 85C	189500.00	109190.00	119930.00	124730.00		6	629D	10F-2R	305	33250	C,H,A
			1997								
Challenger 35	135830.00	88980.00	96940.00	100820.00		6	403D	16F-9R	175	22450	C,H,A
Challenger 45	142215.00	95280.00	103820.00	107970.00		6T	403D	16F-9R	200	22750	C,H,A
Challenger 55	151110.00	100570.00	109570.00	113950.00		6	442D	16F-9R	225	25550	C,H,A
Challenger 65D	157500.00	105530.00	114980.00	119580.00		6T	638D	10F-2R	300	32880	C,H,A
Challenger 75D	165000.00	108540.00	118260.00	122990.00		6	629D	10F-2R	285	33500	C,H,A
Challenger 85D	182750.00	117250.00	127750.00	132860.00		6	732D	10F-2R	310	33650	C,H,A
			1998								
Challenger 35	138088.00	99970.00	106720.00	109920.00		6	403D	16F-9R	175	23350	C,H,A
Challenger 45	147813.00	107890.00	115180.00	118640.00		6T	403D	16F-9R	200	23430	C,H,A
Challenger 55	154205.00	111150.00	118660.00	122220.00		6	442D	16F-9R	225	23430	C,H,A
Challenger 65E	156558.00	114700.00	122450.00	126120.00		6	629D	10F-2R	310	31950	C,H,A
Challenger 75E	176960.00	125770.00	134270.00	138300.00		6	629D	10F-2R	302	34122	C,H,A
Challenger 85E	191911.00	136160.00	145360.00	149720.00		6	732D	10F-2R	375	34987	C,H,A
Challenger 95E	205803.00	144300.00	154050.00	158670.00		6	732D	10F-2R	401	36171	C,H,A
			1999								
Challenger 35	140850.00	116910.00	122540.00	126220.00		6	403D	16F-9R	175	23350	C,H,A
Challenger 45	150770.00	125140.00	131170.00	135110.00		6T	403D	16F-9R	200	23430	C,H,A
Challenger 55	157290.00	130550.00	136840.00	140950.00		6	442D	16F-9R	225	23430	C,H,A
Challenger 65E	160710.00	133390.00	139820.00	144020.00		6	629D	10F-2R	310	31950	C,H,A
Challenger 75E	180500.00	145250.00	152250.00	156820.00		6	629D	10F-2R	302	34122	C,H,A
Challenger 85E	195750.00	158320.00	165950.00	170930.00		6	732D	10F-2R	375	34987	C,H,A
Challenger 95E	209920.00	170070.00	178260.00	183610.00		6	732D	10F-2R	401	36171	C,H,A
Cockshutt											
			1946								
30 RC	......	720.00	1700.00	2090.00	Buda	4	153G	4F-1R	32.9	3609	No
			1947								
30 RC	......	730.00	1730.00	2110.00	Buda	4	153G	4F-1R	32.9	3609	No
			1948								
30 RC	......	780.00	1780.00	2170.00	Buda	4	153G	4F-1R	32.9	3609	No
			1949								
30 D	......	850.00	1880.00	2290.00	Buda	4	153D	4F-1R	28.1	3703	No
30 RC	......	830.00	1830.00	2230.00	Buda	4	153G	4F-1R	32.9	3609	No
			1950								
30 D	......	920.00	1960.00	2390.00	Buda	4	153D	4F-1R	28.1	3703	No
30 RC	......	890.00	1890.00	2310.00	Buda	4	153G	4F-1R	32.9	3609	No
40	......	960.00	2050.00	2500.00	Buda	4	229G	6F-2R	43	5305	No

Cockshutt (Cont.)

Model	Approx. Retail Price New	Estimated Average Value Less Repairs Fair	Good	Premium	Engine Make	No. Cyls.	Displ. Cu.-In.	No. Speeds	P.T.O. H.P.	Approx. Shipping Wt.-Lbs.	Cab
1951											
30 D	......	980.00	2020.00	2460.00	Buda	4	153D	4F-1R	28.1	3703	No
30 RC	......	950.00	1950.00	2380.00	Buda	4	153G	4F-1R	32.9	3609	No
40	......	1020.00	2110.00	2570.00	Buda	6	229G	6F-2R	43	5305	No
1952											
20	......	1020.00	2050.00	2500.00	Continental	4	124G	4F-1R	26.7	2813	No
30 D	......	1040.00	2070.00	2530.00	Buda	4	153D	4F-1R	28.1	3703	No
30 RC	......	1010.00	2020.00	2460.00	Buda	4	153G	4F-1R	32.9	3609	No
40	......	1090.00	2180.00	2660.00	Buda	6	229G	6F-2R	43	5305	No
1953											
20	......	1090.00	2110.00	2570.00	Continental	4	124G	4F-1R	26.7	2813	No
30 D	......	1110.00	2150.00	2620.00	Buda	4	153D	4F-1R	28.1	3703	No
30 RC	......	1070.00	2080.00	2540.00	Buda	4	153G	4F-1R	32.9	3609	No
40	......	1160.00	2240.00	2730.00	Buda	6	229G	6F-2R	43	5305	No
50 RC	......	1120.00	2180.00	2660.00	Buda	6	273G	6F-2R	58	5856	No
50 RC	......	1210.00	2340.00	2860.00	Buda	6	273D	6F-2R	58	6040	No
50 STD	......	1290.00	2500.00	3050.00	Buda	6	273G	6F-2R	58	5856	No
50 STD	......	1340.00	2590.00	3160.00	Buda	6	273D	6F-2R	51	5400	No
1954											
Golden Eagle	......	1210.00	2270.00	2770.00	Perkins	4	270D	6F-1R	39	3758	No
20	......	1160.00	2180.00	2660.00	Continental	4	124G	4F-1R	26.7	2813	No
30 D	......	1170.00	2210.00	2700.00	Buda	4	153D	4F-1R	28.1	3703	No
30 RC	......	1140.00	2140.00	2610.00	Buda	4	153G	4F-1R	32.9	3609	No
40	......	1220.00	2300.00	2810.00	Buda	6	229G	6F-2R	43	5305	No
40 D	......	1260.00	2370.00	2890.00	Perkins	4	269D	6F-2R	45.5	4943	No
50 RC	......	1190.00	2240.00	2730.00	Buda	6	273G	6F-2R	58	5856	No
50 RC	......	1280.00	2400.00	2930.00	Buda	6	273D	6F-2R	58	6040	No
50 STD	......	1360.00	2560.00	3120.00	Buda	6	273G	6F-2R	58	5856	No
50 STD	......	1410.00	2660.00	3250.00	Buda	6	273D	6F-2R	51	5400	No
1955											
Golden Eagle	......	1280.00	2340.00	2860.00	Perkins	4	270D	6F-1R	39	3758	No
20	......	1230.00	2240.00	2730.00	Continental	4	124G	4F-1R	26.7	2813	No
30	......	1240.00	2280.00	2780.00	Buda	4	153D	4F-1R	28.1	3703	No
30 RC	......	1200.00	2190.00	2670.00	Buda	4	153G	4F-1R	32.9	3609	No
40	......	1300.00	2370.00	2890.00	Buda	6	229G	6F-2R	43	5305	No
40 D	......	1340.00	2450.00	2990.00	Perkins	4	269D	6F-2R	45.5	4943	No
50 RC	......	1260.00	2300.00	2810.00	Buda	6	273G	6F-2R	58	5856	No
50 RC	......	1350.00	2470.00	3010.00	Buda	6	273D	6F-2R	58	6040	No
50 STD	......	1440.00	2630.00	3210.00	Buda	6	273G	6F-2R	58	5856	No
50 STD	......	1510.00	2770.00	3380.00	Buda	6	273D	6F-2R	51	5400	No
1956											
Golden Eagle	......	1310.00	2400.00	2930.00	Perkins	4	270D	6F-1R	39	3758	No
20	......	1260.00	2300.00	2810.00	Continental	4	124G	4F-1R	26.7	2813	No
30 D	......	1280.00	2340.00	2860.00	Buda	4	153D	4F-1R	28.1	3703	No
30 RC	......	1240.00	2280.00	2780.00	Buda	4	153G	4F-1R	32.9	3609	No
35 Deluxe	......	1310.00	2400.00	2930.00	Herc.	4	198G	6F-2R	39	4183	No
40	......	1330.00	2430.00	2970.00	Buda	6	229G	6F-2R	43	5305	No
40 D	......	1370.00	2510.00	3060.00	Perkins	4	269D	6F-2R	45.5	4943	No
50 RC	......	1300.00	2370.00	2890.00	Buda	6	273G	6F-2R	58	5856	No
50 RC	......	1400.00	2560.00	3120.00	Buda	6	273D	6F-2R	58	6040	No
50 STD	......	1470.00	2690.00	3280.00	Buda	6	273G	6F-2R	58	5856	No
50 STD	......	1560.00	2850.00	3480.00	Buda	6	273D	6F-2R	51	5400	No
1957											
Golden Eagle	......	1350.00	2470.00	3010.00	Perkins	4	270D	6F-1R	39	3758	No
20	......	1300.00	2370.00	2890.00	Continental	4	124G	4F-1R	26.7	2813	No
30 D	......	1320.00	2420.00	2950.00	Buda	4	153D	4F-1R	28.1	3703	No
30 RC	......	1280.00	2340.00	2860.00	Buda	4	153G	4F-1R	32.9	3609	No
35 Deluxe	......	1350.00	2470.00	3010.00	Herc.	4	198G	6F-1R	39	4183	No
40	......	1370.00	2500.00	3050.00	Buda	6	229G	6F-2R	43	5305	No
40 D	......	1420.00	2600.00	3170.00	Perkins	4	269D	6F-2R	45.5	4943	No
50 RC	......	1350.00	2460.00	3000.00	Buda	6	273G	6F-2R	58	5856	No
50 RC	......	1440.00	2620.00	3200.00	Buda	6	273D	6F-2R	58	6040	No
50 STD	......	1510.00	2750.00	3360.00	Buda	6	273G	6F-2R	58	5856	No
50 STD	......	1600.00	2930.00	3580.00	Buda	6	273D	6F-2R	51	5400	No
1958											
Golden Arrow	......	1380.00	2530.00	3090.00	Herc.	6	198G	6F-2R	40.1	4665	No
20	......	1340.00	2450.00	2990.00	Continental	4	124G	4F-1R	26.7	2813	No
40	......	1400.00	2570.00	3140.00	Buda	6	229G	6F-2R	43	5305	No
40 D	......	1450.00	2660.00	3250.00	Perkins	4	269D	6F-2R	45.5	4943	No
50 RC	......	1380.00	2530.00	3090.00	Buda	6	273G	6F-2R	58	5856	No
50 RC	......	1470.00	2690.00	3280.00	Buda	6	273D	6F-2R	58	6040	No
540 Wide Adj.	......	1120.00	2050.00	2500.00	Continental	4	162G	6F-2R		4415	No
550 STD	......	1210.00	2210.00	2700.00	Herc.	6	198G	6F-2R	40.1	4769	No
550 STD	......	1400.00	2560.00	3120.00	Herc.	6	198D	6F-2R	40.1	4865	No
560 STD	......	1560.00	2850.00	3480.00	Perkins	4	269D	6F-2R	50	6150	No
570 STD	......	1580.00	2880.00	3510.00	Herc.	6	298G	6F-2R	60	6728	No
570 STD	......	1750.00	3210.00	3920.00	Herc.	6	298D	6F-2R	64	6628	No

Cockshutt (Cont.)

Model	Approx. Retail Price New	Estimated Average Value Less Repairs Fair	Good	Premium	Engine Make	No. Cyls.	Displ. Cu.-In.	No. Speeds	P.T.O. H.P.	Approx. Shipping Wt.-Lbs.	Cab
			1959								
Golden Arrow	......	1420.00	2590.00	3160.00	Herc.	6	198G	6F-2R	40.1	4665	No
540 Wide Adj.	......	1160.00	2110.00	2570.00	Continental	4	162G	6F-2R		4415	No
550 STD	......	1250.00	2280.00	2780.00	Herc.	6	198G	6F-2R	40.1	4769	No
550 STD	......	1440.00	2620.00	3200.00	Herc.	6	198D	6F-2R	40.1	4865	No
560 STD	......	1590.00	2910.00	3550.00	Perkins	4	269D	6F-2R	50	6150	No
570 STD	......	1610.00	2940.00	3590.00	Herc.	6	298G	6F-2R	60	6728	No
570 STD	......	1800.00	3300.00	4030.00	Herc.	6	298D	6F-2R	64	6628	No
			1960								
Golden Arrow	......	1490.00	2660.00	3250.00	Herc.	6	198G	6F-2R	40.1	4665	No
540 Wide Adj.	......	1220.00	2180.00	2660.00	Continental	4	162G	6F-2R		4415	No
550 STD	......	1320.00	2350.00	2870.00	Herc.	6	198G	6F-2R	40.1	4769	No
550 STD	......	1530.00	2720.00	3320.00	Herc.	6	198D	6F-2R	40.1	4865	No
560 STD	......	1670.00	2980.00	3640.00	Perkins	4	269D	6F-2R	50	6150	No
570 STD	......	1690.00	3010.00	3670.00	Herc.	6	298D	6F-2R	64	6628	No
570 STD	......	1890.00	3360.00	4100.00	Herc.	6	298G	6F-2R	60	6728	No
			1961								
Golden Arrow	......	1590.00	2750.00	3360.00	Herc.	6	198G	6F-2R	40.1	4665	No
540 Wide Adj.	......	1300.00	2240.00	2730.00	Continental	4	162G	6F-2R		4415	No
550 STD	......	1440.00	2490.00	3040.00	Herc.	6	198G	6F-2R	40.1	4769	No
550 STD	......	1610.00	2780.00	3390.00	Herc.	6	198D	6F-2R	40.1	4865	No
560 STD	......	1780.00	3070.00	3750.00	Perkins	4	269D	6F-2R	50	6150	No
570 Super	......	1980.00	3420.00	4170.00	Herc.	6	339D	6F-2R	65	6728	No
			1962								
Golden Arrow	......	1700.00	2860.00	3490.00	Herc.	6	198G	6F-2R	40.1	4665	No
540 Wide AdJ.	......	1370.00	2300.00	2810.00	Continental	4	162G	6F-2R		4415	No
550 STD	......	1560.00	2620.00	3200.00	Herc.	6	198G	6F-2R	40.1	4769	No
550 STD	......	1690.00	2850.00	3480.00	Herc.	6	198D	6F-2R	40.1	4865	No
560 STD	......	1860.00	3140.00	3830.00	Perkins	4	269D	6F-2R	50	6150	No
570 Super	......	2090.00	3510.00	4280.00	Herc.	6	339D	6F-2R	65	6728	No

Cub Cadet by MTD

Model	Approx. Retail Price New	Fair	Good	Premium	Make	No. Cyls.	Displ. Cu.-In.	No. Speeds	P.T.O. H.P.	Approx. Shipping Wt.-Lbs.	Cab
			1994								
7192 2WD	10899.00	6980.00	7630.00	8010.00	Mitsubishi	3	64D	6	16.5		No
7194 4WD	11849.00	7580.00	8290.00	8710.00	Mitsubishi	3	64D	6	16.5		No
7195 4WD	13389.00	8570.00	9370.00	9840.00	Mitsubishi	3	64D	Variable	15		No
7232 2WD	11899.00	7620.00	8330.00	8750.00	Mitsubishi	3	75D	9	20		No
7234 4WD	12889.00	8250.00	9020.00	9470.00	Mitsubishi	3	75D	9	20		No
7235 4WD	14569.00	9320.00	10200.00	10710.00	Mitsubishi	3	75D	Variable	18		No
7272 2WD	13299.00	8510.00	9310.00	9780.00	Mitsubishi	3	91D	9	23		No
7274 4WD	14749.00	9440.00	10320.00	10840.00	Mitsubishi	3	91D	9	23		No
7275 4WD	16069.00	10280.00	11250.00	11810.00	Mitsubishi	3	91D	Variable	21		No
			1995								
7192 2WD	11449.00	7560.00	8360.00	8780.00	Mitsubishi	3	64D	6	16.5		No
7194 4WD	12449.00	8220.00	9090.00	9550.00	Mitsubishi	3	64D	6	16.5		No
7195H 4WD	14069.00	9290.00	10270.00	10780.00	Mitsubishi	3	64D	Variable	15		No
7232 2WD	12499.00	8250.00	9120.00	9580.00	Mitsubishi	3	75D	9	20		No
7234 4WD	13549.00	8940.00	9890.00	10390.00	Mitsubishi	3	75D	9	20		No
7235H 4WD	15329.00	10120.00	11190.00	11750.00	Mitsubishi	3	75D	Variable	18		No
7272 2WD	13969.00	9220.00	10200.00	10710.00	Mitsubishi	3	91D	9	23		No
7274 4WD	15489.00	10220.00	11310.00	11880.00	Mitsubishi	3	91D	9	23		No
7275H 4WD	16849.00	11120.00	12300.00	12920.00	Mitsubishi	3	91D	Variable	21		No
			1996								
7192 2WD	12809.00	8330.00	9040.00	9400.00	Mitsubishi	3	64D	6	16.5		No
7193H 2WD	14439.00	9450.00	10260.00	10670.00	Mitsubishi	3	64D	Variable	15		No
7194 4WD	13979.00	9030.00	9800.00	10190.00	Mitsubishi	3	64D	6	16.5		No
7195H 4WD	15679.00	10220.00	11100.00	11540.00	Mitsubishi	3	64D	Variable	15		No
7232 2WD	14089.00	9100.00	9880.00	10280.00	Mitsubishi	3	75D	9	20		No
7233H 2WD	16019.00	10430.00	11320.00	11770.00	Mitsubishi	3	75D	Variable	18		No
7234 4WD	15309.00	9910.00	10750.00	11180.00	Mitsubishi	3	75D	9	20		No
7235H 4WD	17149.00	11130.00	12080.00	12560.00	Mitsubishi	3	75D	Variable	18		No
7272 2WD	15849.00	10220.00	11100.00	11540.00	Mitsubishi	3	91D	9	23		No
7273H 2WD	17299.00	11200.00	12160.00	12650.00	Mitsubishi	3	91D	Variable	21		No
7274 4WD	17539.00	11340.00	12310.00	12800.00	Mitsubishi	3	91D	9	23		No
7275H 4WD	18949.00	12250.00	13300.00	13830.00	Mitsubishi	3	91D	Variable	21		No
			1997								
7192 2WD	11969.00	8980.00	9580.00	9960.00	Mitsubishi	3	64D	6	16.5		No
7193H 2WD	13599.00	10200.00	10880.00	11320.00	Mitsubishi	3	64D	Variable	15		No
7194 4WD	12999.00	9750.00	10400.00	10820.00	Mitsubishi	3	64D	6	16.5		No
7195H 4WD	14699.00	11020.00	11760.00	12230.00	Mitsubishi	3	64D	Variable	15		No
7232 2WD	12999.00	9750.00	10400.00	10820.00	Mitsubishi	3	75D	9	20		No
7233H 2WD	14929.00	11200.00	11940.00	12420.00	Mitsubishi	3	75D	Variable	18		No
7234 4WD	14159.00	10620.00	11330.00	11780.00	Mitsubishi	3	75D	9	20		No
7235H 4WD	15999.00	12000.00	12800.00	13310.00	Mitsubishi	3	75D	Variable	18		No
7272 2WD	14599.00	10950.00	11680.00	12150.00	Mitsubishi	3	91D	9	23		No
7273H 2WD	15999.00	12000.00	12800.00	13310.00	Mitsubishi	3	91D	Variable	21		No
7274 4WD	16189.00	12140.00	12950.00	13470.00	Mitsubishi	3	91D	9	23		No

Cub Cadet by MTD (Cont.)

Model	Approx. Retail Price New	Estimated Average Value Less Repairs Fair	Good	Premium	Engine Make	No. Cyls.	Displ. Cu.-In.	No. Speeds	P.T.O. H.P.	Approx. Shipping Wt.-Lbs.	Cab
1997 (Cont.)											
7275H 4WD	17599.00	13200.00	14080.00	14640.00	Mitsubishi	3	91D	Variable	21		No
1998											
7000	11719.00	9260.00	9840.00	10140.00	Mitsubishi	3	68D	6F-2R	17.5		No
7200 4WD	12809.00	10120.00	10760.00	11080.00	Mitsubishi	3	68D	6F-2R	17.5		No
7205 4WD	14069.00	11120.00	11820.00	12180.00	Mitsubishi	3	68D	Variable	16.0		No
7260 4WD	14410.00	11380.00	12100.00	12460.00	Mitsubishi	3	80D	9F-3R	23.0		No
7265 4WD	15970.00	12620.00	13420.00	13820.00	Mitsubishi	3	80D	Variable	21.1		No
7300 4WD	16489.00	13030.00	13850.00	14270.00	Mitsubishi	3	91D	9F-3R	26.0		No
7305 4WD	17789.00	14050.00	14940.00	15390.00	Mitsubishi	3	91D	Variable	24.		No

David Brown

Model	Approx. Retail Price New	Fair	Good	Premium	Make	No. Cyls.	Displ. Cu.-In.	No. Speeds	P.T.O. H.P.	Approx. Shipping Wt.-Lbs.	Cab
1961											
880	3699.00	1760.00	3040.00	3710.00	David Brown	3	143D	12F-4R	40.42	4470	No
990	4095.00	2090.00	3620.00	4420.00	David Brown	4	185D	12F-4R	51.6	4770	No
1962											
880	3750.00	1840.00	3100.00	3780.00	David Brown	3	143D	12F-4R	40.42	4470	No
990	4130.00	2190.00	3680.00	4490.00	David Brown	4	185D	12F-4R	51.6	4770	No
1963											
880	3861.00	1930.00	3170.00	3870.00	David Brown	3	143D	12F-4R	40.42	4470	No
990	4260.00	2280.00	3740.00	4560.00	David Brown	4	185D	12F-4R	51.6	4770	No
1964											
880	3985.00	2020.00	3230.00	3940.00	David Brown	3	143D	12F-4R	40.42	4470	No
990	4473.00	2380.00	3810.00	4650.00	David Brown	4	185D	12F-4R	51.6	4770	No
1965											
880	4310.00	2110.00	3300.00	4030.00	David Brown	3	143D	12F-4R	40.42	4470	No
990	4619.00	2480.00	3870.00	4720.00	David Brown	4	185D	12F-4R	51.6	4770	No
1966											
880	4310.00	2210.00	3360.00	4100.00	David Brown	3	143D	12F-4R	40.42	4470	No
990	4871.00	2580.00	3940.00	4810.00	David Brown	4	185D	12F-4R	51.6	4770	No
1967											
780	3937.00	1940.00	2880.00	3510.00	David Brown	3	146D	12F-4R	36	3710	No
880	4524.00	2300.00	3420.00	4170.00	David Brown	3	143D	12F-4R	40.42	4470	No
990	5014.00	2690.00	4000.00	4880.00	David Brown	4	185D	12F-4R	51.6	4770	No
1200	7046.00	2780.00	3660.00	4140.00	David Brown	4	219D	12F-4R	65.2	6585	No
1968											
780	4371.00	2020.00	2940.00	3590.00	David Brown	3	146D	12F-4R	36	3710	No
880	4736.00	2400.00	3490.00	4260.00	David Brown	3	143D	12F-4R	40.42	4470	No
990	5292.00	2790.00	4060.00	4950.00	David Brown	4	185D	12F-4R	51.6	4770	No
1200	7375.00	2880.00	3680.00	4160.00	David Brown	4	219D	12F-4R	65.2	6585	No
1969											
780	4424.00	2120.00	3010.00	3670.00	David Brown	3	146D	12F-4R	36	3710	No
880	4922.00	2500.00	3550.00	4330.00	David Brown	3	143D	12F-4R	40.42	4470	No
990	5616.00	2900.00	4130.00	5040.00	David Brown	4	185D	12F-4R	51.6	4770	No
1200	7763.00	2980.00	3700.00	4180.00	David Brown	4	219D	12F-4R	65.2	6585	No
3800	4041.00	1890.00	2690.00	3280.00	David Brown	3	146G	12F-4R	39.16	3370	No
4600	4843.00	2180.00	3100.00	3780.00	David Brown	3	164G	12F-4R	46.05	3850	No
1970											
780	4650.00	2210.00	3070.00	3750.00	David Brown	3	164D	12F-4R		3370	No
880	5166.00	2600.00	3620.00	4420.00	David Brown	3	164D	12F-4R	42.29	3850	No
990	6112.00	3010.00	4190.00	5110.00	David Brown	4	195D	12F-4R	52.07	4230	No
1200	8095.00	3080.00	3720.00	4200.00	David Brown	4	219D	12F-4R	65.23	5530	No
3800	4371.00	2010.00	2800.00	3420.00	David Brown	3	146G	12F-4R	39.16	3370	No
4600	5062.00	2330.00	3240.00	3950.00	David Brown	3	164G	12F-4R	46.05	3850	No
1971											
780	4903.00	2300.00	3140.00	3830.00	David Brown	3	164D	12F-4R		3370	No
880	5421.00	2700.00	3680.00	4490.00	David Brown	3	164D	12F-4R	42.29	3850	No
885	5637.00	2650.00	3610.00	4400.00	David Brown	3	146G	12F-4R	41.00	3600	No
885	5940.00	2790.00	3800.00	4640.00	David Brown	3	164D	12F-4R	43.00	3740	No
990	6674.00	3140.00	4270.00	5210.00	David Brown	4	195D	12F-4R	52.07	4230	No
1200	8416.00	3280.00	3960.00	4480.00	David Brown	4	219D	12F-4R	65.23	5530	No
1210	8736.00	3410.00	4110.00	4640.00	David Brown	4	219D	12F-4R	65.00	5530	No
1212	10187.00	3970.00	4790.00	5410.00	David Brown	4	219D	12F-4R	65.00	5660	No
3800	4592.00	2160.00	2940.00	3590.00	David Brown	3	146G	12F-4R	39.16	3370	No
4600	5386.00	2530.00	3450.00	4210.00	David Brown	3	164G	12F-4R	46.05	3850	No
1972											
885	5910.00	2840.00	3780.00	4570.00	David Brown	3	146G	12F-4R	41.00	3600	No
885	6312.00	3030.00	4040.00	4890.00	David Brown	3	164D	12F-4R	43.00	3740	No
990	7234.00	3470.00	4630.00	5600.00	David Brown	4	195D	12F-4R	53.00	4230	No
995	8946.00	3580.00	4290.00	4850.00	David Brown	4	219D	12F-4R	58.00	4600	No
1210	9123.00	3120.00	3930.00	4400.00	David Brown	4	219D	12F-4R	65.00	5530	No

David Brown (Cont.)

Model	Approx. Retail Price New	Estimated Average Value Less Repairs: Fair	Good	Premium	Engine: Make	No. Cyls.	Displ. Cu.-In.	No. Speeds	P.T.O. H.P.	Approx. Shipping Wt.-Lbs.	Cab
1972 (Cont.)											
1212	10543.00	3340.00	4200.00	4700.00	David Brown	4	219D	12F-4R	65.00	5660	No
1973											
885	6235.00	3060.00	3990.00	4790.00	David Brown	3	146G	12F-4R	41.00	3600	No
885	6543.00	3210.00	4190.00	5030.00	David Brown	3	164D	12F-4R	43.00	3740	No
990	7615.00	3730.00	4870.00	5840.00	David Brown	4	195D	12F-4R	53.00	4230	No
995	9417.00	3860.00	4610.00	5210.00	David Brown	4	219D	12F-4R	58.00	4600	No
1210	9517.00	3250.00	4060.00	4510.00	David Brown	4	219D	12F-4R	65.00	5530	No
1212	10856.00	3550.00	4440.00	4930.00	David Brown	4	219D	12F-4R	65.00	5660	No
1974											
885	6506.00	3250.00	4160.00	4950.00	David Brown	3	146G	12F-4R	39.26	3600	No
885	6946.00	3470.00	4450.00	5300.00	David Brown	3	164D	12F-4R	43.20	3740	No
990	8191.00	4100.00	5240.00	6240.00	David Brown	4	195D	12F-4R	53.77	4230	No
995	9531.00	4000.00	4770.00	5340.00	David Brown	4	219D	12F-4R	58.77	4600	No
1210	9943.00	3310.00	4110.00	4560.00	David Brown	4	219D	12F-4R	65.98	5530	No
1212	11194.00	3400.00	4230.00	4700.00	David Brown	4	219D	12F-4R	65.38	5660	No
1975											
885	6832.00	3480.00	4370.00	5160.00	David Brown	3	146G	12F-4R	39.26	4100	No
885	7399.00	3720.00	4670.00	5510.00	David Brown	3	164D	12F-4R	43.20	4290	No
990	8792.00	4480.00	5630.00	6640.00	David Brown	4	195D	12F-4R	53.77	4600	No
995	9951.00	4280.00	5080.00	5690.00	David Brown	4	219D	12F-4R	58.77	4780	No
1210	10604.00	3420.00	4230.00	4700.00	David Brown	4	219D	12F-4R	65.98	5900	No
1212	12216.00	3800.00	4700.00	5220.00	David Brown	4	219D	12F-4R	65.38	6100	No
1412	13944.00	4160.00	5140.00	5710.00	David Brown	4T	219D	12F-4R	80.00	7310	No
1976											
885	7099.00	3620.00	4540.00	5310.00	David Brown	3	146G	12F-4R	39.26	4100	No
885	7689.00	3830.00	4800.00	5620.00	David Brown	3	164D	12F-4R	43.20	4290	No
990	9216.00	4700.00	5900.00	6900.00	David Brown	4	195D	12F-4R	53.77	4600	No
995	10520.00	4630.00	5470.00	6130.00	David Brown	4	219D	12F-4R	58.77	4780	No
1210	11623.00	3710.00	4570.00	5030.00	David Brown	4	219D	12F-4R	65.98	5900	No
1410	13209.00	3980.00	4900.00	5390.00	David Brown	4T	219D	12F-4R	80.00	7150	No
1412	14615.00	4530.00	5580.00	6140.00	David Brown	4T	219D	12F-4R	80.00	7310	No
1977											
885	7345.00	3750.00	4700.00	5450.00	David Brown	3	146G	12F-4R	39.26	4100	No
885	8072.00	4120.00	5170.00	6000.00	David Brown	3	164D	12F-4R	43.20	4290	No
990	9824.00	5010.00	6290.00	7300.00	David Brown	4	195D	12F-4R	53.77	4600	No
995	11272.00	5070.00	5970.00	6630.00	David Brown	4	219D	12F-4R	58.77	4780	No
1210	12528.00	3850.00	4720.00	5190.00	David Brown	4	219D	12F-4R	65.98	5900	No
1410	14559.00	4620.00	5660.00	6230.00	David Brown	4T	219D	12F-4R	80.80	7150	No
1412	15812.00	5130.00	6280.00	6910.00	David Brown	4T	219D	12F-4R	80.60	7310	No
1978											
885	8561.00	4370.00	5480.00	6300.00	David Brown	3	164D	12F-4R	43.20	4290	No
990	10432.00	5320.00	6680.00	7680.00	David Brown	4	195D	12F-4R	53.77	4600	No
995	12068.00	5550.00	6520.00	7170.00	David Brown	4	219D	12F-4R	58.77	4780	No
1210	13455.00	4290.00	5230.00	5750.00	David Brown	4	219D	12F-4R	65.98	5900	No
1410	15910.00	5290.00	6460.00	7110.00	David Brown	4T	219D	12F-4R	80.80	7150	No
1979											
885	8840.00	4600.00	5570.00	6350.00	David Brown	3	164D	12F-4R	43.20	4290	No
990	10874.00	5650.00	6850.00	7810.00	David Brown	4	195D	12F-4R	53.77	4600	No
1210	13986.00	4610.00	5600.00	6100.00	David Brown	4	219D	12F-4R	65.98	5900	No
1410	16617.00	5720.00	6950.00	7580.00	David Brown	4T	219D	12F-4R	80.80	7150	No

Deutz-Allis

Model	Approx. Retail Price New	Estimated Average Value Less Repairs: Fair	Good	Premium	Engine: Make	No. Cyls.	Displ. Cu.-In.	No. Speeds	P.T.O. H.P.	Approx. Shipping Wt.-Lbs.	Cab
1986											
5015	6550.00	3540.00	4060.00	4390.00	Toyosha	3	61D	9F-3R	15.00	1387	No
5015 4WD	7150.00	3860.00	4430.00	4780.00	Toyosha	3	61D	9F-3R	15.00	1557	No
5220	8499.00	4590.00	5270.00	5690.00	Toyosha	3	87D	14F-4R	21.00	2433	No
5220 4WD	9699.00	5240.00	6010.00	6490.00	Toyosha	3	87D	14F-4R	21.00	2604	No
5230	9699.00	5240.00	6010.00	6490.00	Toyosha	3	92D	14F-4R	26.00	2892	No
5230 4WD	10799.00	5830.00	6700.00	7240.00	Toyosha	3	92D	14F-4R	26.00	3050	No
6060	21460.00	8800.00	10730.00	11480.00	AC	4T	433D	8F-2R	64.90	5869	No
6060	26335.00	10800.00	13170.00	14090.00	AC	4T	433D	8F-2R	64.90	6200	C,H
6060 4WD	26263.00	10770.00	13130.00	14050.00	AC	4T	433D	8F-2R	83.66	6669	No
6060 4WD	31138.00	12770.00	15570.00	16660.00	AC	4T	433D	8F-2R	83.66	7000	C,H
6070	24225.00	9930.00	12110.00	12960.00	AC	4T	200D	12F-3R	71.01	5900	No
6070 4WD	29225.00	11980.00	14610.00	15630.00	AC	4T	200D	12F-3R	70.00	6700	No
6070 4WD w/Cab	34100.00	13980.00	17050.00	18240.00	AC	4T	200D	12F-3R	70.00	7800	C,H,A
6070 w/Cab	29100.00	11930.00	14550.00	15570.00	AC	4T	200D	12F-3R	71.01	7050	C,H,A
6080	28625.00	11740.00	14310.00	15310.00	AC	4TI	200D	12F-3R	83.66	7170	No
6080 4WD	34100.00	13980.00	17050.00	18240.00	AC	4TI	200D	12F-3R		7600	No
6080 4WD w/Cab	38975.00	15980.00	19490.00	20850.00	AC	4TI	200D	12F-3R	83.00	8750	C,H,A
6080 w/Cab	33500.00	13740.00	16750.00	17920.00	AC	4TI	200D	12F-3R	83.66	8070	C,H,A
6140	15895.00	7790.00	9220.00	9960.00	Toyosha	3	142D	10F-2R	41.08	4228	No
6140 4WD	19790.00	9700.00	11480.00	12400.00	Toyosha	3	142D	10F-2R	41.08	4628	No
6240	16250.00	6660.00	8130.00	8700.00	Deutz	3	173D	8F-4R	44.00	5776	No
6240 4WD	20150.00	8260.00	10080.00	10790.00	Deutz	3	173D	8F-4R	44.00	6173	No

Model	Approx. Retail Price New	Estimated Average Value Less Repairs Fair	Good	Premium	Engine Make	No. Cyls.	Displ. Cu.-In.	No. Speeds	P.T.O. H.P.	Approx. Shipping Wt.-Lbs.	Cab

Deutz-Allis (Cont.)

1986 (Cont.)

Model	Approx. Retail Price New	Fair	Good	Premium	Make	No. Cyls.	Displ. Cu.-In.	No. Speeds	P.T.O. H.P.	Approx. Shipping Wt.-Lbs.	Cab
6250	17625.00	7230.00	8810.00	9430.00	Deutz	3	173D	8F-4R	50.70	6020	No
6250 4WD	22020.00	9030.00	11010.00	11780.00	Deutz	3	173D	8F-4R	50.70	6459	No
6260	20400.00	8360.00	10200.00	10910.00	Deutz	3	187D	8F-4R	57.09	6020	No
6260 4WD	25000.00	10250.00	12500.00	13380.00	Deutz	3	187D	8F-4R	57.09	6878	No
6260 4WD w/Cab	31612.00	12960.00	15810.00	16920.00	Deutz	3	187D	8F-4R	57.09	7319	C,H,A
6260 w/Cab	27091.00	11110.00	13550.00	14500.00	Deutz	3	187D	8F-4R	57.09	6459	C,H,A
6265	22100.00	9060.00	11050.00	11820.00	Deutz	4	230D	12F-4R	65.80	6222	No
6265 4WD	27265.00	11180.00	13630.00	14580.00	Deutz	4	230D	12F-4R	65.80	7429	No
6265 4WD w/Cab	33890.00	13900.00	16950.00	18140.00	Deutz	4	230D	12F-4R	65.80	8204	C,H,A
6265 w/Cab	28715.00	11770.00	14360.00	15370.00	Deutz	4	230D	12F-4R	65.80	6997	C,H,A
6275	24855.00	10190.00	12430.00	13300.00	Deutz	4	249D	12F-4R	70.90	6922	No
6275 4WD	30420.00	12470.00	15210.00	16280.00	Deutz	4	249D	12F-4R	70.90	7429	No
6275 4WD w/Cab	37050.00	14350.00	17500.00	18730.00	Deutz	4	249D	12F-4R	70.90	8204	C,H,A
6275 w/Cab	31500.00	12920.00	15750.00	16850.00	Deutz	4	249D	12F-4R	70.90	7697	C,H,A
8010 PD	46175.00	14140.00	17230.00	19130.00	AC	6T	301D	20F-4R	109.00	11850	C,H,A
8010 PD 4WD	54055.00	16660.00	20300.00	22530.00	AC	6T	301D	20F-4R	109.00	13450	C,H,A
8010 PS	47710.00	14630.00	17830.00	19790.00	AC	6T	301D	12F-2R	109.55	12000	C,H,A
8010 PS 4WD	55590.00	17150.00	20900.00	23200.00	AC	6T	301D	12F-2R	109.00	13600	C,H,A
8010 PS HC	55335.00	17030.00	20760.00	23040.00	AC	6T	301D	12F-2R	109.00	12500	C,H,A
8030 PD	52398.00	16130.00	19660.00	21820.00	AC	6T	426D	20F-4R	134.00	12450	C,H,A
8030 PD 4WD	60278.00	18650.00	22730.00	25230.00	AC	6T	426D	20F-4R	134.00	14050	C,H,A
8030 PS	53982.00	16630.00	20270.00	22500.00	AC	6T	426D	12F-2R	134.42	12600	C,H,A
8030 PS 4WD	61862.00	19160.00	23350.00	25920.00	AC	6T	426D	12F-2R	134.00	14200	C,H,A
8030 PS HC	61604.00	19070.00	23250.00	25810.00	AC	6T	426D	12F-2R	134.00	13000	C,H,A
8050 PD	58411.00	18050.00	22000.00	24420.00	AC	6TI	426D	20F-4R	155.00	12750	C,H,A
8050 PD 4WD	66291.00	20570.00	25070.00	27830.00	AC	6TI	426D	20F-4R	155.00	14350	C,H,A
8050 PS	60111.00	18600.00	22660.00	25150.00	AC	6TI	426D	12F-3R	155.15	12900	C,H,A
8050 PS 4WD	67990.00	21120.00	25740.00	28570.00	AC	6TI	426D	12F-3R	155.00	14500	C,H,A
8050 PS HC	67773.00	21050.00	25650.00	28470.00	AC	6TI	426D	12F-3R	155.00	13600	C,H,A
8070 PD	60337.00	18350.00	22360.00	24820.00	AC	6TI	426D	20F-4R	171.00	13750	C,H,A
8070 PD 4WD	68217.00	20870.00	25440.00	28240.00	AC	6TI	426D	20F-4R	171.00	15350	C,H,A
8070 PS	62037.00	18890.00	23020.00	25550.00	AC	6TI	426D	12F-2R	171.44	13900	C,H,A
8070 PS 4WD	69916.00	21410.00	26100.00	28970.00	AC	6TI	426D	12F-2R	171.00	15500	C,H,A
4W-305 4WD	93685.00	24540.00	29910.00	33200.00	AC	6T	731D	20F-4R	250.00	21826	C,H,A

HC - High Clearance PD - Power Director PS - Power Shift

1987

Model	Approx. Retail Price New	Fair	Good	Premium	Make	No. Cyls.	Displ. Cu.-In.	No. Speeds	P.T.O. H.P.	Approx. Shipping Wt.-Lbs.	Cab
5215 HST	7990.00	4400.00	5030.00	5430.00	Toyosha	3	61D	Infinite	14.00		No
5215 HST 4WD	8799.00	4840.00	5540.00	5980.00	Toyosha	3	61D	Infinite	14.00		No
5220	8999.00	4950.00	5670.00	6120.00	Toyosha	3	87D	12F-4R	21.00	2433	No
5220 4WD	10299.00	5660.00	6490.00	7010.00	Toyosha	3	87D	12F-4R	21.00	2605	No
5230	10299.00	5660.00	6490.00	7010.00	Toyosha	3	87D	12F-4R	26.00	2892	No
5230 4WD	11799.00	6490.00	7430.00	8020.00	Toyosha	3	87D	12F-4R	26.00	3050	No
6035	11705.00	5850.00	6910.00	7460.00	Deutz	2	115D	8F-2R	33.00	4255	No
6070	24225.00	10180.00	12360.00	13230.00	AC	4T	433D	12F-3R	83.00		No
6070 w/Cab	29100.00	12220.00	14840.00	15880.00	AC	4T	433D	12F-3R	83.00		C,H
6080 4WD	34098.00	14320.00	17390.00	18610.00	AC	4TI	433D	12F-3R			No
6080 w/Cab	33496.00	14070.00	17080.00	18280.00	AC	4TI	433D	12F-3R			C,H
6140	15891.00	7950.00	9380.00	10130.00	Toyosha	3	142D	10F-2R	41.08	4228	No
6140 4WD	19790.00	9900.00	11680.00	12610.00	Toyosha	3	142D	10F-2R	41.08	4628	No
6240	16738.00	7030.00	8540.00	9140.00	Deutz	3	172D	8F-4R	43.00	5776	No
6240 4WD	20755.00	8720.00	10590.00	11330.00	Deutz	3	172D	8F-4R	43.00	6173	No
6250	18154.00	7630.00	9260.00	9910.00	Deutz	3	172D	8F-4R	51.00	6018	No
6250 4WD	22676.00	9520.00	11570.00	12380.00	Deutz	3	172D	8F-4R	51.00	6459	No
6260	21012.00	8830.00	10720.00	11470.00	Deutz	3	187D	8F-4R	57.09	6018	No
6260 4WD	25647.00	10770.00	13080.00	14000.00	Deutz	3	187D	8F-4R	57.09	6459	No
6260 4WD w/Cab	32560.00	13680.00	16610.00	17770.00	Deutz	3	187D	8F-4R	57.09	7319	C,H,A
6260 w/Cab	27904.00	11720.00	14230.00	15230.00	Deutz	3	187D	8F-4R	57.09	6878	C,H,A
6265	22750.00	9560.00	11600.00	12410.00	Deutz	3	230D	12F-4R	65.80	6922	No
6265 4WD	28082.00	11790.00	14320.00	15320.00	Deutz	3	230D	12F-4R	65.80	7429	No
6265 4WD w/Cab	34904.00	14660.00	17800.00	19050.00	Deutz	3	230D	12F-4R	65.80	8333	C,H,A
6265 w/Cab	29572.00	12420.00	15080.00	16140.00	Deutz	3	230D	12F-4R	65.80	7826	C,H,A
6275	25600.00	10750.00	13060.00	13970.00	Deutz	4	249D	12F-4R	70.90	6922	No
6275 4WD	31333.00	13160.00	15980.00	17100.00	Deutz	4	249D	12F-4R	70.90	7429	No
6275 4WD w/Cab	38154.00	16030.00	19460.00	20820.00	Deutz	4	249D	12F-4R	70.90	8429	C,H,A
6275 w/Cab	32421.00	13620.00	16540.00	17700.00	Deutz	4	249D	12F-4R	70.90	7920	C,H,A
7085	31552.00	10730.00	12620.00	13880.00	Deutz	4T	249D	15F-5R	85.18	8466	No
7085 4WD	39318.00	13370.00	15730.00	17300.00	Deutz	4T	249D	15F-5R	85.18	9193	No
7085 4WD w/Cab	44653.00	15180.00	17860.00	19650.00	Deutz	4T	249D	15F-5R	85.18	9193	C,H,A
7085 w/Cab	36887.00	12540.00	14760.00	16240.00	Deutz	4T	249D	15F-5R	85.18	8466	C,H,A
7110	44800.00	15230.00	17920.00	19710.00	Deutz	6	374D	15F-5R	110.00	9702	C,H,A
7110 4WD	54400.00	18500.00	21760.00	23940.00	Deutz	6	374D	15F-5R	110.00	10672	C,H,A
7120	47700.00	16220.00	19080.00	20990.00	Deutz	6T	374D	24F-8R	123.15	11246	C,H,A
7120 4WD	57920.00	19690.00	23170.00	25490.00	Deutz	6T	374D	24F-8R	123.15	12083	C,H,A
7145	57617.00	19590.00	23050.00	25360.00	Deutz	6T	374D	36F-12R	144.60	11905	C,H,A
7145 4WD	68143.00	23170.00	27260.00	29990.00	Deutz	6T	374D	36F-12R	144.60	12897	C,H,A
8010 PD	46176.00	15020.00	17670.00	19440.00	AC	6T	301D	20F-4R	109.00	11850	C,H,A
8010 PD 4WD	54055.00	17700.00	20820.00	22900.00	AC	6T	301D	20F-4R	109.00	13450	C,H,A
8010 PS	47710.00	15540.00	18280.00	20110.00	AC	6T	301D	12F-2R	109.55	12000	C,H,A
8010 PS 4WD	55589.00	18220.00	21440.00	23580.00	AC	6T	301D	12F-2R	109.00	13600	C,H,A
8030 PD	52398.00	17140.00	20160.00	22180.00	AC	6T	426D	20F-4R	134.00	12450	C,H,A
8030 PD 4WD	60278.00	19820.00	23310.00	25640.00	AC	6T	426D	20F-4R	134.00	14050	C,H,A
8030 PS	53982.00	17670.00	20790.00	22870.00	AC	6T	426D	12F-2R	134.42	12600	C,H,A
8030 PS 4WD	61862.00	20350.00	23950.00	26350.00	AC	6T	426D	12F-2R	134.42	14200	C,H,A

Deutz-Allis (Cont.)

1987 (Cont.)

Model	Approx. Retail Price New	Estimated Average Value Less Repairs Fair	Good	Premium	Engine Make	No. Cyls.	Displ. Cu.-In.	No. Speeds	P.T.O. H.P.	Approx. Shipping Wt.-Lbs.	Cab
8050 PD	58411.00	**19180.00**	22560.00	24820.00	AC	6TI	426D	20F-4R	155.00	12750	C,H,A
8050 PD 4WD	66291.00	**21860.00**	25720.00	28290.00	AC	6TI	426D	20F-4R	155.00	14350	C,H,A
8050 PS	60111.00	**19760.00**	23240.00	25560.00	AC	6TI	426D	12F-3R	155.15	12900	C,H,A
8050 PS 4WD	67990.00	**22440.00**	26400.00	29040.00	AC	6TI	426D	12F-3R	155.15	14500	C,H,A
8070 PD	60337.00	**19840.00**	23340.00	25670.00	AC	6TI	426D	20F-4R	171.00	13750	C,H,A
8070 PD 4WD	68217.00	**22510.00**	26490.00	29140.00	AC	6TI	426D	20F-4R	171.00	15350	C,H,A
8070 PS	62037.00	**20410.00**	24020.00	26420.00	AC	6TI	426D	12F-2R	171.44	13900	C,H,A
8070 PS 4WD	69916.00	**23090.00**	27170.00	29890.00	AC	6TI	426D	12F-2R	171.44	15500	C,H,A
4W-305 4WD	93685.00	**26750.00**	31470.00	34620.00	AC	6T	731D	20F-4R	250.00	21876	C,H,A

HST - Hydrostatic Transmission PD - Power Director PS - Power Shift

1988

Model	Approx. Retail Price New	Estimated Average Value Less Repairs Fair	Good	Premium	Engine Make	No. Cyls.	Displ. Cu.-In.	No. Speeds	P.T.O. H.P.	Approx. Shipping Wt.-Lbs.	Cab
5215	7739.00	**4330.00**	4950.00	5300.00	Toyosha	3	61D	9F-3R	15.00	1384	No
5215 4WD	8719.00	**4880.00**	5580.00	5970.00	Toyosha	3	61D	9F-3R	15.00	1597	No
5215 Hydro	8899.00	**4980.00**	5700.00	6100.00	Toyosha	3	61D	Infinite	14.00	1668	No
5215 Hydro 4WD	9899.00	**5540.00**	6340.00	6780.00	Toyosha	3	61D	Infinite	14.00	1877	No
5220	9899.00	**5540.00**	6340.00	6780.00	Toyosha	3	87D	12F-4R	21.00	2433	No
5220 4WD	11499.00	**6440.00**	7360.00	7880.00	Toyosha	3	87D	12F-4R	21.00	2605	No
5230	11499.00	**6440.00**	7360.00	7880.00	Toyosha	3	92D	12F-4R	26.00	2892	No
5230 4WD	12899.00	**7220.00**	8260.00	8840.00	Toyosha	3	92D	12F-4R	26.00	3050	No
6240	16738.00	**7200.00**	8700.00	9220.00	Deutz	3	172D	8F-4R	44.00	5776	No
6240 4WD	20755.00	**8930.00**	10790.00	11440.00	Deutz	3	172D	8F-4R	44.00	6173	No
6250	18154.00	**7810.00**	9440.00	10010.00	Deutz	3	172D	8F-4R	50.70	6018	No
6250 4WD	22778.00	**9800.00**	11850.00	12560.00	Deutz	3	172D	8F-4R	50.70	6459	No
6260	21012.00	**9040.00**	10930.00	11590.00	Deutz	3	187D	8F-4R	57.00	6018	No
6260 4WD	26647.00	**11460.00**	13860.00	14690.00	Deutz	3	187D	8F-4R	57.00	6459	No
6260 4WD w/Cab	33830.00	**14550.00**	17590.00	18650.00	Deutz	3	187D	8F-4R	57.00	7319	C,H,A
6260 w/Cab	27904.00	**12000.00**	14510.00	15380.00	Deutz	3	187D	8F-4R	57.00	6878	C,H,A
6265	22750.00	**9780.00**	11830.00	12540.00	Deutz	4	230D	12F-4R	65.80	6922	No
6265 4WD	28082.00	**12080.00**	14600.00	15480.00	Deutz	4	230D	12F-4R	65.80	7429	No
6265 4WD w/Cab	34904.00	**15010.00**	18150.00	19240.00	Deutz	4	230D	12F-4R	65.80	8333	C,H,A
6265 w/Cab	29572.00	**12720.00**	15380.00	16300.00	Deutz	4	230D	12F-4R	65.80	7826	C,H,A
6275	25600.00	**11010.00**	13310.00	14110.00	Deutz	4	249D	12F-4R	70.90	6922	No
6275 4WD	31333.00	**13470.00**	16290.00	17270.00	Deutz	4	249D	12F-4R	70.90	7429	No
6275 4WD w/Cab	38154.00	**16410.00**	19840.00	21030.00	Deutz	4	249D	12F-4R	70.90	8100	C,H,A
6275 w/Cab	32421.00	**13940.00**	16860.00	17870.00	Deutz	4	249D	12F-4R	70.90	7700	C,H,A
7085	31552.00	**11360.00**	13250.00	14580.00	Deutz	4T	249D	20F-5R	85.00	8466	No
7085 4WD	36802.00	**13250.00**	15460.00	17010.00	Deutz	4T	249D	20F-5R	85.00	9193	No
7085 4WD w/Cab	41784.00	**15040.00**	17550.00	19310.00	Deutz	4T	249D	20F-5R	85.00		C,H,A
7085 w/Cab	36887.00	**13280.00**	15490.00	17040.00	Deutz	4T	249D	20F-5R	85.00		C,H,A
7110	45680.00	**16450.00**	19190.00	21110.00	Deutz	6	374D	15F-5R	110.00	9702	C,H,A
7110 4WD	54400.00	**19580.00**	22850.00	25140.00	Deutz	6	374D	15F-5R	110.00	10672	C,H,A
7120	48920.00	**17610.00**	20550.00	22610.00	Deutz	6	374D	24F-8R	122.00	11246	C,H,A
7120 4WD	57920.00	**20850.00**	24330.00	26760.00	Deutz	6	374D	24F-8R	122.00	12083	C,H,A
7145	57617.00	**20740.00**	24200.00	26620.00	Deutz	6T	374D	36F-12R	144.60	11905	C,H,A
7145 4WD	61473.00	**22130.00**	25820.00	28400.00	Deutz	6T	374D	36F-12R	144.60	12897	C,H,A
8010 PD	46176.00	**15900.00**	18550.00	20410.00	AC	6T	301D	20F-4R		11850	C,H,A
8010 PD 4WD	54055.00	**18740.00**	21860.00	24050.00	AC	6T	301D	20F-4R		13450	C,H,A
8030 PD	52398.00	**18140.00**	21170.00	23290.00	AC	6T	426D	20F-4R		12450	C,H,A
8030 PD 4WD	60278.00	**20980.00**	24480.00	26930.00	AC	6T	426D	20F-4R		12600	C,H,A
8050 PD	58411.00	**20310.00**	23690.00	26060.00	AC	6TI	426D	20F-4R		12750	C,H,A
8050 PD 4WD	66291.00	**23150.00**	27000.00	29700.00	AC	6TI	426D	20F-4R		14350	C,H,A
8070 PD	60337.00	**21000.00**	24500.00	26950.00	AC	6TI	426D	20F-4R		13750	C,H,A
8070 PD 4WD	68217.00	**23840.00**	27810.00	30590.00	AC	6TI	426D	20F-4R		15350	C,H,A
4W-305 4WD	93685.00	**29050.00**	33890.00	37280.00	AC	6TI	731D	20F-4R		21826	C,H,A

PD - Power Director

1989

Model	Approx. Retail Price New	Estimated Average Value Less Repairs Fair	Good	Premium	Engine Make	No. Cyls.	Displ. Cu.-In.	No. Speeds	P.T.O. H.P.	Approx. Shipping Wt.-Lbs.	Cab
5215	8739.00	**4980.00**	5680.00	6080.00	Toyosha	3	61D	9F-3R	15.00	1384	No
5215 4WD	9719.00	**5540.00**	6320.00	6760.00	Toyosha	3	61D	9F-3R	15.00	1597	No
5215 Hydro	9899.00	**5640.00**	6430.00	6880.00	Toyosha	3	61D	Infinite	14.00	1668	No
5215 Hydro 4WD	10899.00	**6210.00**	7080.00	7580.00	Toyosha	3	61D	Infinite	14.00	1877	No
5220	10899.00	**6210.00**	7080.00	7580.00	Toyosha	3	87D	12F-4R	21.00	2433	No
5220 4WD	11499.00	**6550.00**	7470.00	7990.00	Toyosha	3	87D	12F-4R	21.00	2605	No
5220 w/Cab	12199.00	**6950.00**	7930.00	8490.00	Toyosha	3	87D	12F-4R	21.00	3043	C,H
5230	11499.00	**6550.00**	7470.00	7990.00	Toyosha	3	92D	12F-4R	26.00	2892	No
5230 4WD	12899.00	**7350.00**	8380.00	8970.00	Toyosha	3	92D	12F-4R	26.00	3050	No
6240	17156.00	**7550.00**	9090.00	9640.00	Deutz	3	172D	8F-4R	43.00	6173	No
6250	18608.00	**8190.00**	9860.00	10450.00	Deutz	3	172D	8F-4R	50.70	6459	No
6260	21537.00	**9480.00**	11420.00	12110.00	Deutz	3	187D	8F-4R	57.09	6459	No
6260 w/Cab	28537.00	**12560.00**	15130.00	16040.00	Deutz	3	187D	8F-4R	57.09		C,H,A
6265	23319.00	**10260.00**	12360.00	13100.00	Deutz	4	230D	12F-4R	65.08	7429	No
6265 w/Cab	30319.00	**13340.00**	16070.00	17030.00	Deutz	4	230D	12F-4R	65.08		C,H,A
6275	26240.00	**11550.00**	13910.00	14750.00	Deutz	4	249D	12F-4R	70.90	7429	No
6275 w/Cab	33240.00	**14630.00**	17620.00	18680.00	Deutz	4	249D	12F-4R	70.90		C,H,A
7085	32749.00	**12450.00**	14410.00	15850.00	Deutz	4T	249D	20F-5R	85.18	9193	No
7085 w/Cab	38249.00	**14540.00**	16830.00	18510.00	Deutz	4T	249D	20F-5R	85.18		C,H,A
7110	46882.00	**17820.00**	20630.00	22690.00	Deutz	6	374D	15F-5R	110.00	10670	C,H,A
7120	50143.00	**19050.00**	22060.00	24270.00	Deutz	6T	374D	24F-8R	122.06	12081	C,H,A
7145	59057.00	**22440.00**	25990.00	28590.00	Deutz	6T	374D	36F-12R	144.60	12987	C,H,A
9150	56174.00	**21350.00**	24720.00	27190.00	Deutz	6TA	374D	18F-6R	151.07	14880	C,H,A
9170	59525.00	**22620.00**	26190.00	28810.00	Deutz	6T	584D	18F-6R	173.37	16040	C,H,A
9190 4WD	79854.00	**28500.00**	33000.00	36300.00	Deutz	6T	584D	18F-6R	193.55	16600	C,H,A

Deutz-Allis (Cont.)

1990

Model	Approx. Retail Price New	Fair	Good	Premium	Engine Make	No. Cyls.	Displ. Cu.-In.	No. Speeds	P.T.O. H.P.	Approx. Shipping Wt.-Lbs.	Cab
5215 Hydro	10025.00	5820.00	6620.00	7080.00	Toyosha	3	61D	Infinite	14.00	1668	No
5215 Hydro 4WD	11285.00	6550.00	7450.00	7970.00	Toyosha	3	61D	Infinite	14.00	1877	No
5215 Synchro	8850.00	5130.00	5840.00	6250.00	Toyosha	3	61D	9F	15.00	1384	No
5215 Synchro 4WD	9900.00	5740.00	6530.00	6990.00	Toyosha	3	61D	9F	15.00	1597	No
5220 Hydro	11495.00	6670.00	7590.00	8120.00	Toyosha	3	83D	Infinite	17.00	1985	No
5220 Hydro 4WD	12760.00	7400.00	8420.00	9010.00	Toyosha	3	83D	Infinite	17.00	2194	No
5220 Synchro	10920.00	6330.00	7210.00	7720.00	Toyosha	3	87D	12F	21.00	2433	No
5220 Synchro 4WD	12700.00	7370.00	8380.00	8970.00	Toyosha	3	87D	12F	21.00	2605	No
5230 Synchro	12700.00	7370.00	8380.00	8970.00	Toyosha	3	92D	12F	26.00	2892	No
5230 Synchro 4WD	14280.00	8280.00	9430.00	10090.00	Toyosha	3	92D	12F	26.00	3050	No
6150	17909.00	8060.00	9670.00	10250.00	Deutz	3	187D	8F-4R	54.00	4935	No
6240	17156.00	7720.00	9260.00	9820.00	Deutz	3	172D	8F-4R	43.00	5776	No
6240 4WD	21274.00	9570.00	11490.00	12180.00	Deutz	3	172D	8F-4R	43.00	6173	No
6250	18608.00	8370.00	10050.00	10650.00	Deutz	3	172D	8F-4R	51.00	6018	No
6250 4WD	23347.00	10510.00	12610.00	13370.00	Deutz	3	172D	8F-4R	51.00	6459	No
6250V	21663.00	9750.00	11700.00	12400.00	Deutz	3	172D	8F-4R	51.00		No
6250V 4WD	24605.00	11070.00	13290.00	14090.00	Deutz	3	172D	8F-4R	51.00		No
6260	21537.00	9690.00	11630.00	12330.00	Deutz	3	187D	8F-4R	57.09	6018	No
6260 4WD	27313.00	12290.00	14750.00	15640.00	Deutz	3	187D	8F-4R	57.09	6459	No
6260 4WD w/Cab	34670.00	15600.00	18720.00	19840.00	Deutz	3	187D	8F-4R	57.09	7319	C,H,A
6260 w/Cab	28602.00	12870.00	15450.00	16380.00	Deutz	3	187D	8F-4R	57.09	6878	C,H,A
6260F	22473.00	10110.00	12140.00	12870.00	Deutz	3	187D	8F-4R	57.00		No
6260F 4WD	25517.00	11480.00	13780.00	14610.00	Deutz	3	187D	8F-4R	57.00		No
6260F 4WD w/Cab	29756.00	13390.00	16070.00	17030.00	Deutz	3	187D	8F-4R	57.00		C,H,A
6260F w/Cab	26655.00	12000.00	14390.00	15250.00	Deutz	3	187D	8F-4R	57.00		C,H,A
6260L	22750.00	10240.00	12290.00	13030.00	Deutz	3	187D	8F-4R	57.00		No
6260L 4WD	25656.00	11550.00	13850.00	14680.00	Deutz	3	187D	8F-4R	57.00		No
6260L 4WD w/Cab	29894.00	13450.00	16140.00	17110.00	Deutz	3	187D	8F-4R	57.00		C,H,A
6260L w/Cab	26932.00	12120.00	14540.00	15410.00	Deutz	3	187D	8F-4R	57.00		C,H,A
6265	23319.00	10490.00	12590.00	13350.00	Deutz	4	230D	12F-4R	65.80	6922	No
6265 4WD	28784.00	12950.00	15540.00	16470.00	Deutz	4	230D	12F-4R	65.80	7429	No
6265 4WD w/Cab	35777.00	16100.00	19320.00	20480.00	Deutz	4	230D	12F-4R	65.80	8333	C,H,A
6265 w/Cab	30311.00	13640.00	16370.00	17350.00	Deutz	4	230D	12F-4R	65.80	7826	C,H,A
6275	26240.00	11810.00	14170.00	15020.00	Deutz	4	249D	12F-4R	70.90	6922	No
6275 4WD	32116.00	14450.00	17340.00	18380.00	Deutz	4	249D	12F-4R	70.90	7429	No
6275 4WD w/Cab	39108.00	17600.00	21120.00	22390.00	Deutz	4	249D	12F-4R	70.90		C,H,A
6275 w/Cab	33232.00	14950.00	17950.00	19030.00	Deutz	4	249D	12F-4R	70.90		C,H,A
6275F	26814.00	12070.00	14480.00	15350.00	Deutz	4	249D	8F-4R	71.00		No
6275F 4WD	29976.00	13490.00	16190.00	17160.00	Deutz	4	249D	8F-4R	71.00		No
6275F 4WD w/Cab	34363.00	15460.00	18560.00	19670.00	Deutz	4	249D	8F-4R	71.00		C,H,A
6275F w/Cab	31134.00	14010.00	16810.00	17820.00	Deutz	4	249D	8F-4R	71.00		C,H,A
6275L	26958.00	12130.00	14560.00	15430.00	Deutz	4	249D	8F-4R	71.00		No
6275L 4WD	30120.00	13550.00	16270.00	17250.00	Deutz	4	249D	8F-4R	71.00		No
6275L 4WD w/Cab	34507.00	15530.00	18630.00	19750.00	Deutz	4	249D	8F-4R	71.00		C,H,A
6275L w/Cab	31278.00	14080.00	16890.00	17900.00	Deutz	4	249D	8F-4R	71.00		C,H,A
7085	32749.00	13100.00	15070.00	16580.00	Deutz	4T	249D	20F-5R	85.18		No
7085 4WD	37722.00	15090.00	17350.00	19090.00	Deutz	4T	249D	20F-5R	85.18		No
7085 4WD w/Cab	42829.00	17130.00	19700.00	21670.00	Deutz	4T	249D	20F-5R	85.18		C,H,A
7085 w/Cab	38217.00	15290.00	17580.00	19340.00	Deutz	4T	249D	20F-5R	85.18		C,H,A
7110	46882.00	18750.00	21570.00	23730.00	Deutz	6	374D	15F-5R	122.00	9702	C,H,A
7110 4WD	55760.00	22300.00	25650.00	28220.00	Deutz	6	374D	15F-5R	122.00	10672	C,H,A
7120	50143.00	20060.00	23070.00	25380.00	Deutz	6T	374D	24F-8R	122.06	11246	C,H,A
7120 4WD	59370.00	23750.00	27310.00	30040.00	Deutz	6T	374D	24F-8R	122.06	12083	C,H,A
7145	59057.00	23620.00	27170.00	29890.00	Deutz	6T	374D	36F-12R	144.60	11905	C,H,A
7145 4WD	63010.00	25200.00	28990.00	31890.00	Deutz	6T	374D	36F-12R	144.60	12897	C,H,A
9150	56174.00	22470.00	25840.00	28420.00	Deutz	6TA	374D	18F-6R	158.67	13520	C,H,A
9150 4WD	66353.00	26540.00	30520.00	33570.00	Deutz	6T	374D	18F-6R	158.67	14880	C,H,A

1991

Model	Approx. Retail Price New	Fair	Good	Premium	Engine Make	No. Cyls.	Displ. Cu.-In.	No. Speeds	P.T.O. H.P.	Approx. Shipping Wt.-Lbs.	Cab
5215 Hydro	10520.00	6210.00	7050.00	7470.00	Toyosha	3	61D	Infinite	14.00	1668	No
5215 Hydro 4WD	11850.00	6990.00	7940.00	8420.00	Toyosha	3	61D	Infinite	14.00	1877	No
5215 Synchro	9200.00	5430.00	6160.00	6530.00	Toyosha	3	61D	9F	15.00	1384	No
5215 Synchro 4WD	10395.00	6130.00	6970.00	7390.00	Toyosha	3	61D	9F	15.00	1597	No
5220 Hydro	12070.00	7120.00	8090.00	8580.00	Toyosha	3	83D	Infinite	17.00	1985	No
5220 Hydro 4WD	13395.00	7900.00	8980.00	9520.00	Toyosha	3	83D	Infinite	17.00	2194	No
5220 Synchro	11465.00	6760.00	7680.00	8140.00	Toyosha	3	87D	12F	21.00	2433	No
5220 Synchro 4WD	13300.00	7850.00	8910.00	9450.00	Toyosha	3	87D	12F	21.00	2605	No
5230 Synchro	13300.00	7850.00	8910.00	9450.00	Toyosha	3	92D	12F	26.00	2892	No
5230 Synchro 4WD	14995.00	8850.00	10050.00	10650.00	Toyosha	3	92D	12F	26.00	3050	No
6150	17909.00	9670.00	11280.00	11960.00	Deutz	3	187D	8F-4R	54.00	4935	No
6240	18114.00	9780.00	11410.00	12100.00	Deutz	3	172D	8F-4R	44.00	5776	No
6240 4WD	22338.00	12060.00	14070.00	14910.00	Deutz	3	172D	8F-4R	44.00	6173	No
6250	19538.00	8990.00	10750.00	11400.00	Deutz	3	172D	8F-4R	50.70	6018	No
6250 4WD	24514.00	11280.00	13480.00	14290.00	Deutz	3	172D	8F-4R	50.70	6459	No
6260	22614.00	10400.00	12440.00	13190.00	Deutz	3	187D	8F-4R	57.09	6018	No
6260 4WD	28679.00	13190.00	15770.00	16720.00	Deutz	3	187D	8F-4R	57.09	6459	No
6260 4WD w/Cab	36097.00	16610.00	19850.00	21040.00	Deutz	3	187D	8F-4R	57.09	7319	C,H,A
6260 w/Cab	30032.00	13820.00	16520.00	17510.00	Deutz	3	187D	8F-4R	57.09	6878	C,H,A
6265	23319.00	10730.00	12830.00	13600.00	Deutz	4	230D	12F-4R	65.80	6922	No
6265 4WD	28784.00	13240.00	15830.00	16780.00	Deutz	4	230D	12F-4R	65.80	7429	No
6265 4WD w/Cab	35777.00	16460.00	19680.00	20860.00	Deutz	4	230D	12F-4R	65.80	8333	C,H,A
6265 w/Cab	30311.00	13940.00	16670.00	17670.00	Deutz	4	230D	12F-4R	65.80	7826	C,H,A
6275	26240.00	12070.00	14430.00	15300.00	Deutz	4	249D	12F-4R	70.90	6922	No
6275 4WD	32116.00	14770.00	17660.00	18720.00	Deutz	4	249D	12F-4R	70.90	7429	No

Deutz-Allis (Cont.)

1991 (Cont.)

Model	Approx. Retail Price New	Fair	Good	Premium	Engine Make	Engine No. Cyls.	Engine Displ. Cu.-In.	No. Speeds	P.T.O. H.P.	Approx. Shipping Wt.-Lbs.	Cab
6275 4WD w/Cab	39108.00	17990.00	21510.00	22800.00	Deutz	4	249D	12F-4R	70.90		C,H,A
6275 w/Cab	33232.00	15290.00	18280.00	19380.00	Deutz	4	249D	12F-4R	70.90		C,H,A
7085	34386.00	14440.00	16510.00	18000.00	Deutz	4T	249D	20F-5R	85.18	9900	No
7085 4WD	39608.00	16640.00	19010.00	20720.00	Deutz	4T	249D	20F-5R	85.18		No
7085 4WD w/Cab	45350.00	19050.00	21770.00	23730.00	Deutz	4T	249D	20F-5R	85.18		C,H,A
7085 w/Cab	40128.00	16850.00	19260.00	20990.00	Deutz	4T	249D	20F-5R	85.18		C,H,A
7110	49163.00	20650.00	23600.00	25720.00	Deutz	6	374D	20F-5R	110.00	9702	C,H,A
7110 4WD	58548.00	24590.00	28100.00	30630.00	Deutz	6	374D	20F-5R	110.00	10672	C,H,A
7120	52650.00	22110.00	25270.00	27540.00	Deutz	6T	374D	24F-8R	122.06	11246	C,H,A
7120 4WD	62339.00	26180.00	29920.00	32610.00	Deutz	6T	374D	24F-8R	122.06	12083	C,H,A
9130	56973.00	23930.00	27350.00	29810.00	Deutz	6TI	374D	18F-6R	135.00	14285	C,H,A
9130 4WD	66622.00	27980.00	31980.00	34860.00	Deutz	6TI	374D	18F-6R	135.00	14285	C,H,A
9150	58983.00	24770.00	28310.00	30860.00	Deutz	6TI	374D	18F-6R	158.67	13520	C,H,A
9150 4WD	69671.00	29260.00	33440.00	36450.00	Deutz	6TI	374D	18F-6R	158.67	14880	C,H,A
9170	62501.00	26250.00	30000.00	32700.00	Deutz	6T	584D	18F-6R	173.37	15837	C,H,A
9170 4WD	76670.00	31500.00	36000.00	39240.00	Deutz	6T	584D	18F-6R	173.37		C,H,A
9190 4WD	83847.00	34020.00	38880.00	42380.00	Deutz	6T	584D	18F-6R	193.55		C,H,A

Deutz-Fahr

1970

Model	Approx. Retail Price New	Fair	Good	Premium	Engine Make	Engine No. Cyls.	Engine Displ. Cu.-In.	No. Speeds	P.T.O. H.P.	Approx. Shipping Wt.-Lbs.	Cab
D2506	2917.00	1280.00	1710.00	1920.00	Deutz	2	115D	8F-2R	23.00	3545	No
D3006	3418.00	1440.00	1930.00	2160.00	Deutz	2	115D	8F-2R	32.00	3785	No
D4006	4068.00	1650.00	2200.00	2460.00	Deutz	3	173D	8F-2R	38.00	3950	No
D6006	6247.00	2380.00	3170.00	3550.00	Deutz	4	231D	9F-3R	66.00	5450	No
D9006	8282.00	3040.00	4050.00	4540.00	Deutz	6	345D	12F-6R	96.00	7910	No

1971

Model	Approx. Retail Price New	Fair	Good	Premium	Engine Make	Engine No. Cyls.	Engine Displ. Cu.-In.	No. Speeds	P.T.O. H.P.	Approx. Shipping Wt.-Lbs.	Cab
D2506	2917.00	1360.00	1760.00	1970.00	Deutz	2	115D	8F-2R	23.00	3820	No
D3006	3418.00	1530.00	1980.00	2220.00	Deutz	2	115D	8F-2R	32.00	3980	No
D4006	4068.00	1760.00	2270.00	2540.00	Deutz	3	173D	8F-2R	38.00	4180	No
D4006A 4WD	5445.00	2260.00	2920.00	3270.00	Deutz	3	173D	8F-2R	38.00	5005	No
D5506	5692.00	2310.00	2990.00	3350.00	Deutz	4	231D	8F-4R	55.00	4630	No
D6006	6247.00	2530.00	3280.00	3670.00	Deutz	4	231D	9F-3R	66.00	5700	No
D6006A 4WD	8269.00	3250.00	4210.00	4720.00	Deutz	4	231D	9F-3R	66.00	6700	No
D9006	8282.00	3160.00	4080.00	4570.00	Deutz	6	345D	12F-6R	96.00	8060	No
D9006A 4WD	10718.00	3000.00	4180.00	4680.00	Deutz	6	345D	12F-6R	96.00	8650	No

1972

Model	Approx. Retail Price New	Fair	Good	Premium	Engine Make	Engine No. Cyls.	Engine Displ. Cu.-In.	No. Speeds	P.T.O. H.P.	Approx. Shipping Wt.-Lbs.	Cab
D2506	3048.00	1450.00	1830.00	2050.00	Deutz	2	115D	8F-2R	23.00	3820	No
D3006	3572.00	1640.00	2060.00	2310.00	Deutz	2	115D	8F-2R	32.00	3980	No
D4006	4312.00	1890.00	2380.00	2670.00	Deutz	3	173D	8F-2R	36.95	4180	No
D4006A 4WD	6066.00	2510.00	3150.00	3530.00	Deutz	3	173D	8F-2R	36.95	5005	No
D5506	5989.00	2520.00	3160.00	3540.00	Deutz	4	231D	8F-4R	55.00	4630	No
D6006	6776.00	2690.00	3380.00	3790.00	Deutz	4	231D	9F-3R	66.00	5700	No
D6006A 4WD	8871.00	3460.00	4340.00	4860.00	Deutz	4	231D	9F-3R	66.00	6700	No
D8006	8364.00	3280.00	4120.00	4610.00	Deutz	6	345D	16F-7R	85.51	6665	No
D8006A 4WD	10951.00	3070.00	4270.00	4780.00	Deutz	6	345D	16F-7R	85.51	7590	No
D9006	8944.00	2670.00	3720.00	4170.00	Deutz	6	345D	16F-7R	96.00	8060	No
D9006A 4WD	11531.00	3230.00	4500.00	5040.00	Deutz	6	345D	16F-7R	96.00	8650	No
D10006	9922.00	1590.00	2580.00	2890.00	Deutz	6	345D	16F-7R	105.00	8395	No
D10006A 4WD	12742.00	1920.00	3120.00	3490.00	Deutz	6	345D	16F-7R	105.00	8790	No
D13006	12500.00	1860.00	3020.00	3380.00	Deutz	6T	345D	16F-7R	125.00	9020	No
D13006A 4WD	15448.00	2240.00	3640.00	4080.00	Deutz	6T	345D	16F-7R	125.00	10120	No

1973

Model	Approx. Retail Price New	Fair	Good	Premium	Engine Make	Engine No. Cyls.	Engine Displ. Cu.-In.	No. Speeds	P.T.O. H.P.	Approx. Shipping Wt.-Lbs.	Cab
D3006	4578.00	1830.00	2290.00	2540.00	Deutz	2	115D	8F-2R	32.00	3980	No
D4006	5197.00	2050.00	2560.00	2840.00	Deutz	3	173D	8F-2R	36.95	4180	No
D4006A 4WD	7806.00	2990.00	3740.00	4150.00	Deutz	3	173D	8F-2R	36.95	5005	No
D4506	5878.00	2300.00	2870.00	3190.00	Deutz	3	173D	12F-4R	43.15	4180	No
D4506A 4WD	6763.00	2620.00	3270.00	3630.00	Deutz	3	173D	12F-4R	43.15	5070	No
D5506	7606.00	2920.00	3650.00	4050.00	Deutz	4	231D	12F-4R	56.08	4630	No
D6006	8368.00	3190.00	3990.00	4430.00	Deutz	4	231D	9F-3R	65.30	5700	No
D6006A 4WD	11790.00	2880.00	4010.00	4490.00	Deutz	4	231D	9F-3R	65.30	6700	No
D8006	9990.00	2800.00	3900.00	4370.00	Deutz	6	345D	16F-7R	85.51	6665	No
D8006A 4WD	10951.00	3070.00	4270.00	4780.00	Deutz	6	345D	16F-7R	85.51	7590	No
D10006	11772.00	2000.00	3060.00	3430.00	Deutz	6	345D	16F-7R	105.04	8395	No
D10006A 4WD	15780.00	2260.00	3450.00	3860.00	Deutz	6	345D	16F-7R	105.04	8790	No
D13006	12977.00	2210.00	3370.00	3770.00	Deutz	6T	345D	16F-7R	125.71	9020	No
D13006A 4WD	19084.00	2560.00	3920.00	4390.00	Deutz	6T	345D	16F-7R	125.71	10120	No

1974

Model	Approx. Retail Price New	Fair	Good	Premium	Engine Make	Engine No. Cyls.	Engine Displ. Cu.-In.	No. Speeds	P.T.O. H.P.	Approx. Shipping Wt.-Lbs.	Cab
D3006	4927.00	2010.00	2500.00	2780.00	Deutz	2	115D	8F-2R	32.00	3980	No
D4006	5847.00	2350.00	2920.00	3240.00	Deutz	3	173D	8F-2R	36.95	4180	No
D4006A 4WD	8400.00	2440.00	3280.00	3670.00	Deutz	3	173D	8F-2R	36.95	5005	No
D4506	6387.00	2550.00	3170.00	3520.00	Deutz	3	173D	8F-4R	43.15	4180	No
D4506A 4WD	6763.00	2160.00	2910.00	3260.00	Deutz	3	173D	12F-4R	43.15	5070	No
D5506	8334.00	3120.00	3880.00	4310.00	Deutz	4	231D	8F-4R	56.08	4630	No
D6006	9427.00	3490.00	4340.00	4820.00	Deutz	4	231D	12F-4R	65.30	5700	No
D6006A 4WD	12920.00	3750.00	5040.00	5650.00	Deutz	4	231D	12F-4R	65.30	6700	No
D8006	11707.00	3400.00	4570.00	5120.00	Deutz	6	345D	16F-7R	85.51	6665	No
D8006A 4WD	15987.00	2610.00	3920.00	4390.00	Deutz	6	345D	16F-7R	85.51	7590	No
D10006	12820.00	2160.00	3240.00	3630.00	Deutz	6	345D	16F-7R	105.04	8395	No

Deutz-Fahr (Cont.)

Model	Approx. Retail Price New	Estimated Average Value Less Repairs: Fair	Good	Premium	Engine: Make	No. Cyls.	Displ. Cu.-In.	No. Speeds	P.T.O. H.P.	Approx. Shipping Wt.-Lbs.	Cab
1974 (Cont.)											
D10006A 4WD	17314.00	2790.00	4190.00	4690.00	Deutz	6	345D	16F-7R	105.04	8790	No
D13006	16160.00	2700.00	4050.00	4540.00	Deutz	6T	345D	16F-7R	125.77	9020	No
D13006A 4WD	20987.00	3240.00	4860.00	5440.00	Deutz	6T	345D	16F-7R	125.77	10120	No
1975											
D3006	5757.00	2570.00	3180.00	3530.00	Deutz	2	115D	8F-2R	32.00	3980	No
D4006	6576.00	2880.00	3560.00	3950.00	Deutz	3	173D	8F-2R	36.95	4180	No
D4006A 4WD	9449.00	3610.00	4470.00	4960.00	Deutz	3	173D	8F-2R	36.95	5005	No
D4506	7394.00	3190.00	3950.00	4390.00	Deutz	3	173D	8F-4R	43.15	4180	No
D4506A 4WD	10902.00	3270.00	4250.00	4720.00	Deutz	3	173D	8F-4R	43.15	5070	No
D5206	8822.00	2770.00	3600.00	4000.00	Deutz	3	173D	8F-4R	52.00	4345	No
D5206A 4WD	11909.00	3300.00	4290.00	4760.00	Deutz	3	173D	8F-4R	52.00	5225	No
D6206	9834.00	1870.00	2750.00	3080.00	Deutz	4	231D	8F-4R	60.00	4660	No
D6206A 4WD	13096.00	2340.00	3440.00	3850.00	Deutz	4	231D	8F-4R	60.00	5355	No
D6806	10902.00	2070.00	3050.00	3420.00	Deutz	4	231D	12F-4R	68.00	5700	No
D6806A 4WD	15279.00	2700.00	3980.00	4460.00	Deutz	4	231D	12F-4R	68.00	6700	No
D7206	12083.00	2300.00	3380.00	3790.00	Deutz	4	231D	12F-4R	71.00	5890	No
D8006	13293.00	2390.00	3530.00	3950.00	Deutz	6	345D	16F-7R	85.51	6665	No
D8006A 4WD	18328.00	3330.00	4900.00	5490.00	Deutz	6	345D	16F-7R	85.51	7590	No
D10006	15270.00	2790.00	4120.00	4610.00	Deutz	6	345D	16F-7R	105.04	8395	No
D10006A 4WD	20620.00	3330.00	4900.00	5490.00	Deutz	6	345D	16F-7R	105.04	8790	No
D13006	18351.00	3170.00	4680.00	5240.00	Deutz	6T	345D	16F-7R	125.77	9020	No
D13006A 4WD	24059.00	3810.00	5620.00	6290.00	Deutz	6T	345D	16F-7R	125.77	10120	No
1976											
D3006	6289.00	2840.00	3500.00	3850.00	Deutz	2	115D	8F-2R	32.00	3980	No
D4006	6944.00	3100.00	3810.00	4190.00	Deutz	3	173D	8F-2R	36.95	4180	No
D4006A 4WD	9979.00	3780.00	4660.00	5130.00	Deutz	3	173D	8F-2R	36.95	5005	No
D4506	7691.00	3390.00	4170.00	4590.00	Deutz	3	173D	8F-4R	43.15	4180	No
D4506A 4WD	11068.00	3430.00	4430.00	4920.00	Deutz	3	173D	8F-4R	43.15	5070	No
D5206	9358.00	2930.00	3780.00	4200.00	Deutz	3	173D	8F-4R	52.00	4345	No
D5206A 4WD	12637.00	2530.00	3670.00	4110.00	Deutz	3	173D	8F-4R	52.00	5225	No
D6206	10741.00	2150.00	3120.00	3490.00	Deutz	4	231D	8F-4R	60.00	4660	No
D6206A 4WD	14556.00	2700.00	3920.00	4390.00	Deutz	4	231D	8F-4R	60.00	5355	No
D6806	11824.00	2370.00	3430.00	3840.00	Deutz	4	231D	12F-4R	68.00	5700	No
D6806A 4WD	16212.00	3000.00	4350.00	4870.00	Deutz	4	231D	12F-4R	68.00	6700	No
D7206	13069.00	2500.00	3630.00	4070.00	Deutz	4	231D	12F-4R	71.00	5890	No
D8006	15343.00	2860.00	4150.00	4650.00	Deutz	6	345D	16F-7R	85.51	6665	No
D8006A 4WD	20215.00	3600.00	5220.00	5850.00	Deutz	6	345D	16F-7R	85.51	7590	No
D10006	16940.00	3100.00	4500.00	5040.00	Deutz	6	345D	16F-7R	105.04	8390	No
D10006A 4WD	22309.00	3660.00	5310.00	5950.00	Deutz	6	345D	16F-7R	105.04	8790	No
D13006	19378.00	3460.00	5020.00	5620.00	Deutz	6T	345D	16F-7R	125.77	9020	No
D13006A 4WD	25316.00	4060.00	5890.00	6600.00	Deutz	6T	345D	16F-7R	125.77	10120	No
1977											
D3006	6787.00	3120.00	3820.00	4200.00	Deutz	2	115D	8F-2R	32.00	3980	No
D4006	7101.00	3240.00	3970.00	4370.00	Deutz	3	173D	8F-2R	36.95	4180	No
D4006A 4WD	9719.00	3890.00	4760.00	5240.00	Deutz	3	173D	8F-2R	36.95	5005	No
D4506	8601.00	3520.00	4310.00	4740.00	Deutz	3	173D	8F-4R	43.15	4180	No
D4506A 4WD	11166.00	3570.00	4580.00	5080.00	Deutz	3	173D	8F-4R	43.15	5070	No
D5206	9727.00	3110.00	3990.00	4430.00	Deutz	3	173D	8F-4R	52.00	4345	No
D5206A 4WD	12678.00	4060.00	5200.00	5770.00	Deutz	3	173D	8F-4R	52.00	5225	No
D6206	10986.00	2310.00	3300.00	3700.00	Deutz	4	231D	8F-4R	60.23	4660	No
D6206A 4WD	14178.00	2980.00	4250.00	4760.00	Deutz	4	231D	8F-4R	60.23	5355	No
D6806	12455.00	2620.00	3740.00	4190.00	Deutz	4	231D	12F-4R	68.18	5700	No
D6806A 4WD	16747.00	3520.00	5020.00	5620.00	Deutz	4	231D	12F-4R	68.18	6700	No
D7206	13112.00	2750.00	3930.00	4400.00	Deutz	4	231D	12F-4R	71.00	5890	No
D8006	16330.00	3260.00	4650.00	5210.00	Deutz	6	345D	16F-7R	85.51	6835	No
D8006A 4WD	21429.00	4200.00	6000.00	6720.00	Deutz	6	345D	16F-7R	85.51	7590	No
D10006	18361.00	3630.00	5190.00	5810.00	Deutz	6	345D	16F-7R	105.04	8060	No
D10006A 4WD	23117.00	4250.00	6070.00	6800.00	Deutz	6	345D	16F-7R	105.04	8790	No
D13006	20632.00	3840.00	5490.00	6150.00	Deutz	6T	345D	16F-7R	125.77	9020	No
D13006A 4WD	26856.00	4530.00	6470.00	7250.00	Deutz	6T	345D	16F-7R	125.77	10185	No
1978											
D3006	7465.00	3310.00	4030.00	4430.00	Deutz	2	115D	8F-2R	32.00	3980	No
D4506	9035.00	3700.00	4520.00	4970.00	Deutz	3	173D	8F-2R	43.15	4180	No
D4506A 4WD	12520.00	4510.00	5500.00	6050.00	Deutz	3	173D	8F-2R	43.15	5070	No
D6206	12580.00	2770.00	3900.00	4370.00	Deutz	4	231D	8F-4R	60.23	4660	No
D6206A 4WD	16300.00	3590.00	5050.00	5660.00	Deutz	4	231D	8F-4R	60.23	5355	No
D6806	14199.00	3120.00	4400.00	4930.00	Deutz	4	231D	12F-4R	68.18	5700	No
D6806A 4WD	19530.00	4070.00	5740.00	6430.00	Deutz	4	231D	12F-4R	68.18	6700	No
D8006	16658.00	3520.00	4960.00	5560.00	Deutz	6	345D	16F-7R	85.51	6835	No
D8006A 4WD	21429.00	4400.00	6200.00	6940.00	Deutz	6	345D	16F-7R	85.51	7590	No
D10006	18729.00	3960.00	5580.00	6250.00	Deutz	6	345D	16F-7R	105.04	8060	No
D10006A 4WD	23990.00	4420.00	6230.00	6980.00	Deutz	6	345D	16F-7R	105.04	8790	No
D13006	21046.00	4180.00	5890.00	6600.00	Deutz	6T	345D	16F-7R	125.77	9020	No
D13006A 4WD	28008.00	5060.00	7130.00	7990.00	Deutz	6T	345D	16F-7R	125.77	10185	No
1979											
DX90	21847.00	4420.00	6140.00	6880.00	Deutz	5	287D	15F-5R	84.47	10045	No
DX90A 4WD	28458.00	5410.00	7520.00	8420.00	Deutz	5	287D	15F-5R	84.47	10835	No
DX110	28282.00	5290.00	7360.00	8240.00	Deutz	6	345D	15F-5R	100.29	10485	C,H,A
DX110A 4WD	35193.00	6900.00	9600.00	10750.00	Deutz	6	345D	15F-5R	100.29	11050	C,H,A

Deutz-Fahr (Cont.)

Model	Approx. Retail Price New	Estimated Average Value Less Repairs Fair	Good	Premium	Engine Make	No. Cyls.	Displ. Cu.-In.	No. Speeds	P.T.O. H.P.	Approx. Shipping Wt.-Lbs.	Cab
1979 (Cont.)											
DX140	34121.00	**6690.00**	**9310.00**	**10430.00**	Deutz	6T	374D	24F-8R	131.00	12380	C,H,A
DX140A 4WD	42310.00	**8280.00**	**11520.00**	**12900.00**	Deutz	6T	374D	24F-8R	131.00	13395	C,H,A
DX160	36445.00	**6970.00**	**9700.00**	**10860.00**	Deutz	6T	374D	24F-8R	145.41	12440	C,H,A
DX160A 4WD	44952.00	**9040.00**	**12580.00**	**14090.00**	Deutz	6T	374D	24F-8R	145.41	13450	C,H,A
D3006	7465.00	**2810.00**	**3550.00**	**3870.00**	Deutz	2	115D	8F-2R	32.00	3980	No
D4506	10535.00	**3240.00**	**4100.00**	**4470.00**	Deutz	3	173D	8F-2R	43.15	4180	No
D4506A 4WD	14468.00	**4580.00**	**5790.00**	**6310.00**	Deutz	3	173D	8F-2R	43.15	5070	No
D6206	14002.00	**3220.00**	**4480.00**	**5020.00**	Deutz	4	231D	8F-4R	60.23	4660	No
D6206A 4WD	18143.00	**4170.00**	**5810.00**	**6510.00**	Deutz	4	231D	8F-4R	60.23	5355	No
D6806	16105.00	**3700.00**	**5150.00**	**5770.00**	Deutz	4	231D	12F-4R	68.18	5700	No
D6806A 4WD	22152.00	**5100.00**	**7090.00**	**7940.00**	Deutz	4	231D	12F-4R	68.18	6700	No
D8006	16658.00	**3830.00**	**5330.00**	**5970.00**	Deutz	6	345D	16F-7R	85.51	6835	No
D8006A 4WD	21429.00	**4460.00**	**6210.00**	**6960.00**	Deutz	6	345D	16F-7R	85.51	7590	No
10006A 4WD	23990.00	**4950.00**	**6880.00**	**7710.00**	Deutz	6	345D	16F-7R	105.04	8790	No
D10006	18729.00	**4070.00**	**5660.00**	**6340.00**	Deutz	6	345D	16F-7R	105.04	8060	No
D13006	21046.00	**4600.00**	**6400.00**	**7170.00**	Deutz	6T	345D	16F-7R	125.77	9020	No
D13006A 4WD	28008.00	**5360.00**	**7460.00**	**8360.00**	Deutz	6T	345D	16F-7R	125.77	10185	No
1980											
DX90	23722.00	**5040.00**	**6930.00**	**7760.00**	Deutz	5	287D	15F-5R	84.47	10045	No
DX90A 4WD	30895.00	**6240.00**	**8580.00**	**9610.00**	Deutz	5	287D	15F-5R	84.47	10835	No
DX110	30138.00	**6100.00**	**8380.00**	**9390.00**	Deutz	6	345D	15F-5R	100.29	10485	C,H,A
DX110A 4WD	37474.00	**7490.00**	**10300.00**	**11540.00**	Deutz	6	345D	15F-5R	100.29	11050	C,H,A
DX120	32197.00	**6360.00**	**8750.00**	**9800.00**	Deutz	6	374D	15F-5R	111.29	9790	C,H,A
DX120A 4WD	39871.00	**7750.00**	**10660.00**	**11940.00**	Deutz	6	374D	15F-5R	111.00	10850	C,H,A
DX130	35243.00	**6960.00**	**9570.00**	**10720.00**	Deutz	6T	374D	24F-8R	121.27	11490	C,H,A
DX130A 4WD	43507.00	**8880.00**	**12210.00**	**13680.00**	Deutz	6T	374D	24F-8R	121.00	12680	C,H,A
DX140	36370.00	**7490.00**	**10300.00**	**11540.00**	Deutz	6T	374D	24F-8R	131.00	12380	C,H,A
DX140A 4WD	46402.00	**9600.00**	**13200.00**	**14780.00**	Deutz	6T	374D	24F-8R	131.00	13395	C,H,A
DX160	39998.00	**7990.00**	**10990.00**	**12310.00**	Deutz	6T	374D	24F-8R	145.41	12440	C,H,A
DX160A 4WD	49290.00	**10370.00**	**14260.00**	**15970.00**	Deutz	6T	374D	24F-8R	145.41	13450	C,H,A
D4506	11312.00	**4860.00**	**5880.00**	**6350.00**	Deutz	3	173D	8F-2R	43.15	4180	No
D4506A 4WD	15538.00	**6680.00**	**8080.00**	**8730.00**	Deutz	3	173D	8F-2R	43.15	5070	No
D6206	14886.00	**3570.00**	**4910.00**	**5500.00**	Deutz	4	231D	8F-4R	60.23	4660	No
D6206A 4WD	19322.00	**4640.00**	**6380.00**	**7150.00**	Deutz	4	231D	8F-4R	60.23	5355	No
D6806	16957.00	**4070.00**	**5600.00**	**6270.00**	Deutz	4	231D	12F-4R	68.18	5700	No
D6806A 4WD	23326.00	**5600.00**	**7700.00**	**8620.00**	Deutz	4	231D	12F-4R	68.18	6700	No
1981											
DX90	26683.00	**6080.00**	**8260.00**	**9250.00**	Deutz	5	287D	15F-5R	84.47	10045	No
DX90A 4WD	32836.00	**7010.00**	**9530.00**	**10670.00**	Deutz	5	287D	15F-5R	84.47	10835	No
DX120	38344.00	**8090.00**	**11000.00**	**12320.00**	Deutz	6	374D	15F-5R	111.29	9790	C,H,A
DX120A 4WD	46373.00	**10090.00**	**13730.00**	**15380.00**	Deutz	6	374D	15F-5R	111.00	10850	C,H,A
DX130	40019.00	**8510.00**	**11570.00**	**12960.00**	Deutz	6T	374D	24F-8R	121.27	11490	C,H,A
DX130A 4WD	48154.00	**10540.00**	**14330.00**	**16050.00**	Deutz	6T	374D	24F-8R	121.00	12680	C,H,A
DX160	44561.00	**9640.00**	**13110.00**	**14680.00**	Deutz	6T	374D	24F-8R	145.41	12440	C,H,A
DX160A 4WD	53131.00	**11280.00**	**15350.00**	**17190.00**	Deutz	6T	374D	24F-8R	145.41	13450	C,H,A
D4507	13877.00	**3380.00**	**4590.00**	**5140.00**	Deutz	3	173D	8F-2R	43.00	4420	No
D4507A 4WD	18423.00	**4500.00**	**6120.00**	**6850.00**	Deutz	3	173D	8F-2R	43.00	5080	No
D5207	15747.00	**3940.00**	**5350.00**	**5990.00**	Deutz	3	173D	8F-4R	51.00	4595	No
D5207A 4WD	19979.00	**4600.00**	**6260.00**	**7010.00**	Deutz	3	173D	8F-4R	51.00	5260	No
D6206	15928.00	**3980.00**	**5420.00**	**6070.00**	Deutz	4	231D	8F-4R	60.23	4660	No
D6206A 4WD	20675.00	**4750.00**	**6460.00**	**7240.00**	Deutz	4	231D	8F-4R	60.23	5355	No
D6207	17329.00	**4330.00**	**5890.00**	**6600.00**	Deutz	4	231D	8F-4R	60.00	4660	No
D6207A 4WD	21983.00	**5000.00**	**6800.00**	**7620.00**	Deutz	4	231D	8F-4R	60.00	5355	No
D6806	16957.00	**4240.00**	**5770.00**	**6460.00**	Deutz	4	231D	12F-4R	68.18	5700	No
D6806A 4WD	23326.00	**5500.00**	**7480.00**	**8380.00**	Deutz	4	231D	12F-4R	68.18	6700	No
D6807	19927.00	**4550.00**	**6190.00**	**6930.00**	Deutz	4	231D	12F-4R	68.00	5700	No
D6807A 4WD	26325.00	**6000.00**	**8160.00**	**9140.00**	Deutz	4	231D	12F-4R	68.00	6700	No
1982											
DX90	26217.00	**5770.00**	**7770.00**	**8700.00**	Deutz	5	287D	15F-5R	84.47	10045	No
DX90A 4WD	33493.00	**7540.00**	**10150.00**	**11370.00**	Deutz	5	287D	15F-5R	84.47	10835	No
DX120	39111.00	**8840.00**	**11900.00**	**13330.00**	Deutz	6	374D	15F-5R	111.29	9790	C,H,A
DX120A 4WD	47300.00	**10660.00**	**14350.00**	**16070.00**	Deutz	6	374D	15F-5R	111.00	10850	C,H,A
DX130	40819.00	**9230.00**	**12430.00**	**13920.00**	Deutz	6T	374D	24F-8R	121.27	11490	C,H,A
DX130A 4WD	49117.00	**10690.00**	**14390.00**	**16120.00**	Deutz	6T	374D	24F-8R	121.00	12680	C,H,A
DX160	45452.00	**10240.00**	**13790.00**	**15450.00**	Deutz	6T	374D	24F-8R	145.41	12440	C,H,A
DX160A 4WD	54194.00	**11990.00**	**16140.00**	**18080.00**	Deutz	6T	374D	24F-8R	145.41	13450	C,H,A
D4507	14155.00	**3640.00**	**4900.00**	**5490.00**	Deutz	3	173D	8F-2R	43.00	4420	No
D4507A 4WD	18791.00	**4680.00**	**6300.00**	**7060.00**	Deutz	3	173D	8F-2R	43.00	5080	No
D5207	16062.00	**4180.00**	**5620.00**	**6290.00**	Deutz	3	173D	8F-4R	51.00	4595	No
D5207A 4WD	20379.00	**5020.00**	**6760.00**	**7570.00**	Deutz	3	173D	8F-4R	51.00	5260	No
D6206	16247.00	**4220.00**	**5690.00**	**6370.00**	Deutz	4	231D	8F-4R	60.23	4660	No
D6206A 4WD	21089.00	**5200.00**	**7000.00**	**7840.00**	Deutz	4	231D	8F-4R	60.23	5355	No
D6207	17676.00	**4600.00**	**6190.00**	**6930.00**	Deutz	4	231D	8F-4R	60.00	4660	No
D6207A 4WD	22423.00	**5490.00**	**7390.00**	**8280.00**	Deutz	4	231D	8F-4R	60.00	5355	No
D6806	17296.00	**4500.00**	**6050.00**	**6780.00**	Deutz	4	231D	12F-4R	68.18	5700	No
D6806A 4WD	23792.00	**5770.00**	**7770.00**	**8700.00**	Deutz	4	231D	12F-4R	68.18	6700	No
D6807	19927.00	**4890.00**	**6580.00**	**7370.00**	Deutz	4	231D	12F-4R	68.00	5700	No
D6807A 4WD	26852.00	**6500.00**	**8750.00**	**9800.00**	Deutz	4	231D	12F-4R	68.00	6700	No

Model	Approx. Retail Price New	Estimated Average Value Less Repairs Fair	Good	Premium	Make	Engine No. Cyls.	Displ. Cu.-In.	No. Speeds	P.T.O. H.P.	Approx. Shipping Wt.-Lbs.	Cab
Deutz-Fahr (Cont.)											
			1983								
DX90	26741.00	6130.00	8170.00	9150.00	Deutz	5	287D	15F-5R	84.47	10045	No
DX90A 4WD	34163.00	8400.00	11200.00	12540.00	Deutz	5	287D	15F-5R	84.00	10835	No
DX120	39893.00	9560.00	12740.00	14270.00	Deutz	6	374D	15F-5R	111.29	10030	C,H,A
DX120A 4WD	48246.00	11340.00	15120.00	16930.00	Deutz	6	374D	15F-5R	111.00	10850	C,H,A
DX130	41635.00	9610.00	12820.00	14360.00	Deutz	6T	374D	24F-8R	121.27	11490	C,H,A
DX130 4WD	50099.00	11880.00	15840.00	17740.00	Deutz	6T	374D	24F-8R	121.00	12680	C,H,A
DX160	46361.00	11340.00	15120.00	16930.00	Deutz	6T	374D	24F-8R	145.41	12440	C,H,A
DX160A 4WD	55278.00	12960.00	17280.00	19350.00	Deutz	6T	374D	24F-8R	145.00	13450	C,H,A
D4507	14438.00	3780.00	5040.00	5650.00	Deutz	3	173D	8F-2R	43.00	4420	No
D4507A 4WD	19167.00	4860.00	6480.00	7260.00	Deutz	3	173D	8F-2R	43.00	5080	No
D5207	16383.00	4420.00	5900.00	6610.00	Deutz	3	173D	8F-4R	51.00	4595	No
D5207A 4WD	20786.00	5180.00	6910.00	7740.00	Deutz	3	173D	8F-4R	51.00	5260	No
D6206	16572.00	4190.00	5580.00	6250.00	Deutz	4	231D	8F-4R	60.23	4660	No
D6206A 4WD	21511.00	5400.00	7200.00	8060.00	Deutz	4	231D	8F-4R	60.00	5355	No
D6207	18030.00	4590.00	6120.00	6850.00	Deutz	4	231D	8F-4R	60.00	4660	No
D6207A 4WD	22871.00	5670.00	7560.00	8470.00	Deutz	4	231D	8F-4R	60.00	5355	No
D6806	17642.00	4460.00	5940.00	6650.00	Deutz	4	231D	12F-4R	68.18	5700	No
D6806A 4WD	24268.00	5940.00	7920.00	8870.00	Deutz	4	231D	12F-4R	68.00	6700	No
D6807	20326.00	4910.00	6550.00	7340.00	Deutz	4	231D	12F-4R	68.00	5700	No
D6807A 4WD	27389.00	6290.00	8390.00	9400.00	Deutz	4	231D	12F-4R	68.00	6700	No
D7807	23500.00	5540.00	7380.00	8270.00	Deutz	4	249D	12F-4R	73.00	6460	No
D7807A 4WD	25550.00	5810.00	7740.00	8670.00	Deutz	4	249D	12F-4R	73.00	7276	No
			1984								
DX4.70	30005.00	7000.00	9250.00	10360.00	Deutz	4T	249D	15F-5R	85.18	8466	No
DX4.70 4WD	37542.00	8960.00	11840.00	13260.00	Deutz	4T	249D	15F-5R	85.18	9193	No
DX4.70 4WD w/Cab	42930.00	10530.00	13910.00	15580.00	Deutz	4T	249D	15F-5R	85.18	9968	C,H,A
DX4.70 w/Cab	35393.00	8480.00	11210.00	12560.00	Deutz	4T	249D	15F-5R	85.18	9241	C,H,A
DX6.30	42272.00	10360.00	13690.00	15330.00	Deutz	6	374D	15F-5R	110.00	12787	C,H,A
DX6.30 4WD	51739.00	12740.00	16840.00	18860.00	Deutz	6	374D	15F-5R	110.00	14991	C,H,A
DX6.50	45884.00	11060.00	14620.00	16370.00	Deutz	6T	374D	24F-8R	123.15	16975	C,H,A
DX6.50 4WD	55972.00	13720.00	18130.00	20310.00	Deutz	6T	374D	24F-8R	123.15	17637	C,H,A
DX7.10	51091.00	12600.00	16650.00	18650.00	Deutz	6T	374D	36F-12R	144.60	11905	C,H,A
DX7.10 4WD	60916.00	14560.00	19240.00	21550.00	Deutz	6T	374D	36F-12R	144.60	12897	C,H,A
DX90	28851.00	6520.00	8620.00	9650.00	Deutz	5	287D	15F-5R	84.47	8780	No
DX90 w/Cab	34031.00	8120.00	10730.00	12020.00	Deutz	5	287D	15F-5R	84.47	9880	C,H,A
DX90A 4WD	35504.00	8480.00	11210.00	12560.00	Deutz	5	287D	15F-5R	84.00	9600	No
DX90A 4WD w/Cab	40684.00	9690.00	12800.00	14340.00	Deutz	5	287D	15F-5R	84.00	10700	C,H,A
DX120	40646.00	9970.00	13170.00	14750.00	Deutz	6	374D	15F-5R	111.29	10030	C,H,A
DX120A 4WD	49156.00	12040.00	15910.00	17820.00	Deutz	6	374D	15F-5R	111.00	10850	C,H,A
DX130	44119.00	10670.00	14100.00	15790.00	Deutz	6T	374D	24F-8R	121.27	11490	C,H,A
DX130A 4WD	53087.00	12740.00	16840.00	18860.00	Deutz	6T	374D	24F-8R	121.00	12680	C,H,A
DX160	49126.00	11760.00	15540.00	17410.00	Deutz	6T	374D	24F-8R	145.41	12440	C,H,A
DX160A 4WD	58573.00	14140.00	18690.00	20930.00	Deutz	6T	374D	24F-8R	145.00	13450	C,H,A
D4507	16064.00	4500.00	5940.00	6650.00	Deutz	3	173D	8F-2R	43.00	4420	No
D4507 4WD	21077.00	5600.00	7400.00	8290.00	Deutz	3	173D	8F-2R	43.00	5080	No
D5207	18229.00	4760.00	6290.00	7050.00	Deutz	3	173D	8F-2R	51.00	4595	No
D5207A 4WD	23067.00	6160.00	8140.00	9120.00	Deutz	3	173D	8F-2R	51.00	5260	No
D6507	21060.00	5600.00	7400.00	8290.00	Deutz	4	230D	8F-2R	60.00	4550	No
D6507 w/Cab	27812.00	7280.00	9620.00	10770.00	Deutz	4	230D	8F-2R	60.00	5650	C,H,A
D6507A 4WD	26250.00	7000.00	9250.00	10360.00	Deutz	4	230D	8F-2R	60.00	5250	No
D6507A 4WD w/Cab	33002.00	8400.00	11100.00	12430.00	Deutz	4	230D	8F-2R	60.00	6350	C,H,A
D7007	23993.00	6160.00	8140.00	9120.00	Deutz	4	230D	12F-4R	68.00	5920	No
D7007 w/Cab	30747.00	7900.00	10430.00	11680.00	Deutz	4	230D	12F-4R	68.00	7080	C,H,A
D7007A 4WD	30698.00	7760.00	10250.00	11480.00	Deutz	4	230D	12F-4R	68.00	6680	No
D7007A 4WD w/Cab	37450.00	9630.00	12730.00	14260.00	Deutz	4	230D	12F-4R	68.00	7782	C,H,A
D7807	25919.00	6270.00	8290.00	9290.00	Deutz	4	249D	12F-4R	73.00	6460	No
D7807 w/Cab	32671.00	8010.00	10580.00	11850.00	Deutz	4	249D	12F-4R	73.00	7560	C,H,A
D7807A 4WD	32434.00	7950.00	10510.00	11770.00	Deutz	4	249D	12F-4R	73.00	7276	No
D7807A 4WD w/Cab	39186.00	9550.00	12620.00	14130.00	Deutz	4	249D	12F-4R	73.00	8376	C,H,A
			1985								
DX3.10	16890.00	4170.00	5280.00	5860.00	Deutz	3	173D	8F-4R	44.00	5776	No
DX3.10A 4WD	21100.00	5100.00	6460.00	7170.00	Deutz	3	173D	8F-4R	44.00	6173	No
DX3.30	17625.00	4380.00	5550.00	6160.00	Deutz	3	173D	8F-4R	50.70	6020	No
DX3.30A 4WD	22020.00	5550.00	7030.00	7800.00	Deutz	3	173D	8F-4R	50.70	6060	No
DX3.50	20500.00	4950.00	6270.00	6960.00	Deutz	3	173D	8F-4R	57.09	6020	No
DX3.50 w/Cab	27095.00	6600.00	8360.00	9280.00	Deutz	3	187D	8F-4R	57.09	6795	C,H,A
DX3.50A 4WD	25000.00	6000.00	7600.00	8440.00	Deutz	3	187D	8F-4R	57.09	6060	No
DX3.50A 4WD w/Cab	31615.00	7980.00	10110.00	11220.00	Deutz	3	187D	8F-4R	57.09	6835	C,H,A
DX3.70	22100.00	5400.00	6840.00	7590.00	Deutz	4	230D	12F-4R	65.80	6222	No
DX3.70 w/Cab	28715.00	7050.00	8930.00	9910.00	Deutz	4	230D	12F-4R	65.80	6997	C,H,A
DX3.70A 4WD	27265.00	6660.00	8440.00	9370.00	Deutz	4	230D	12F-4R	65.80	7429	No
DX3.70A 4WD w/Cab	33890.00	8250.00	10450.00	11600.00	Deutz	4	230D	12F-4R	65.80	8204	C,H,A
DX3.90	24855.00	5940.00	7520.00	8350.00	Deutz	4	249D	12F-4R	70.90	6922	No
DX3.90 w/Cab	31500.00	7950.00	10070.00	11180.00	Deutz	4	249D	12F-4R	70.90	7697	C,H,A
DX3.90A 4WD	30420.00	7620.00	9650.00	10710.00	Deutz	4	249D	12F-4R	70.90	7429	No
DX3.90A 4WD w/Cab	37050.00	9450.00	11970.00	13290.00	Deutz	4	249D	12F-4R	70.90	8204	C,H,A
DX4.70	30005.00	7500.00	9500.00	10550.00	Deutz	4T	249D	15F-5R	85.18	8466	No
DX4.70 4WD	37545.00	9750.00	12350.00	13710.00	Deutz	4T	249D	15F-5R	85.18	9193	No
DX4.70 4WD w/Cab	42930.00	11250.00	14250.00	15820.00	Deutz	4T	249D	15F-5R	85.18	9968	C,H,A
DX4.70 w/Cab	35395.00	9090.00	11510.00	12780.00	Deutz	4T	249D	15F-5R	85.18	9241	C,H,A
DX6.30	42275.00	11100.00	14060.00	15610.00	Deutz	6	374D	15F-5R	110.00	12787	C,H,A
DX6.30 4WD	51740.00	13800.00	17480.00	19400.00	Deutz	6	374D	15F-5R	110.00	14991	C,H,A

Model	Approx. Retail Price New	Estimated Average Value Less Repairs Fair	Good	Premium	Engine Make	No. Cyls.	Displ. Cu.-In.	No. Speeds	P.T.O. H.P.	Approx. Shipping Wt.-Lbs.	Cab
Deutz-Fahr (Cont.)											
1985 (Cont.)											
DX6.50	45885.00	12150.00	15390.00	17080.00	Deutz	6T	374D	24F-8R	123.15	16975	C,H,A
DX6.50 4WD	55975.00	15000.00	19000.00	21090.00	Deutz	6T	374D	24F-8R	123.15	17637	C,H,A
DX7.10	51095.00	13800.00	17480.00	19400.00	Deutz	6T	374D	24F-8R	144.60	11905	C,H,A
DX7.10 4WD	60920.00	16200.00	20520.00	22780.00	Deutz	6T	374D	32F-8R	144.60	12897	C,H,A
DX8.30A 4WD	82200.00	19500.00	24700.00	27420.00	Deutz	6T	584D		190.00		C,H,A
D3607	11375.00	4550.00	5570.00	5960.00	Deutz	3	115D		33.00		No
D4507	16100.00	6440.00	7890.00	8440.00	Deutz	3	173D	8F-2R	43.00	4420	No
Ferguson											
1948											
TE20	......	1010.00	2300.00	2810.00	Continental	4	120G	4F-1R	27	2600	No
TO20 STD	......	970.00	2220.00	2710.00	Continental	4	120G	4F-1R	26.5	2497	No
1949											
TE20	......	1070.00	2370.00	2890.00	Continental	4	120G	4F-1R	27	2600	No
TO20 STD	......	1030.00	2280.00	2780.00	Continental	4	120G	4F-1R	26.5	2497	No
1950											
TE20	......	1140.00	2430.00	2970.00	Continental	4	120G	4F-1R	27	2600	No
TO20 STD	......	1100.00	2340.00	2860.00	Continental	4	120G	4F-1R	26.5	2497	No
1951											
TE20	......	1200.00	2470.00	3010.00	Continental	4	120G	4F-1R	27	2600	No
TO20 STD	......	1170.00	2420.00	2950.00	Continental	4	120G	4F-1R	26.5	2497	No
TO30	......	1240.00	2560.00	3120.00	Continental	4	129G	4F-1R	30.2	2843	No
1952											
TO30	......	1300.00	2600.00	3170.00	Continental	4	129G	4F-1R	30.2	2843	No
1953											
TO30	......	1370.00	2650.00	3230.00	Continental	4	129G	4F-1R	30.2	2843	No
1954											
TO30	......	1450.00	2740.00	3340.00	Continental	4	129G	4F-1R	30.2	2843	No
TO35 STD	......	1470.00	2770.00	3380.00	Continental	4	134G	6F-1R	33	2980	No
TO35 Deluxe	......	1550.00	2910.00	3550.00	Perkins	4	137D	6F-1R	37	3211	No
1955											
TO35 STD	......	1540.00	2820.00	3440.00	Continental	4	134G	6F-1R	33	2980	No
TO35 Deluxe	......	1620.00	2960.00	3610.00	Perkins	4	137D	6F-1R	37	3211	No
1956											
TO35 STD	......	1580.00	2890.00	3530.00	Continental	4	134G	6F-1R	33	2980	No
TO35 Deluxe	......	1670.00	3050.00	3720.00	Perkins	4	137D	6F-1R	37	3211	No
F40	......	1440.00	2640.00	3220.00	Continental	4	134G	6F-1R	34	3100	No
1957											
F40	......	1500.00	2740.00	3340.00	Continental	4	134G	6F-1R	34	3100	No
Ford											
1939											
9N	......	1040.00	2380.00	2950.00	Ford	4	119G	3F-1R	23.07	3375	No
1940											
9N	......	1040.00	2380.00	2950.00	Ford	4	119G	3F-1R	23.07	3375	No
1941											
9N	......	1050.00	2420.00	3000.00	Ford	4	119G	3F-1R	23.07	3375	No
1942											
9N	......	1070.00	2450.00	3040.00	Ford	4	119G	3F-1R	23.07	3375	No
1943											
2N	......	1130.00	2510.00	3110.00	Ford	4	120G	3F-1R	24	3070	No
9N	......	1120.00	2480.00	3080.00	Ford	4	119G	3F-1R	23.07	3375	No
1944											
2N	......	1180.00	2550.00	3160.00	Ford		120G	3F-1R	24	3070	No
1945											
2N	......	1250.00	2570.00	3190.00	Ford	4	119G	3F-1R	24	3070	No
1946											
2N	......	1310.00	2620.00	3250.00	Ford	4	119G	3F-1R	24	3070	No
1947											
2N	......	1370.00	2670.00	3310.00	Ford	4	119G	3F-1R	24	3070	No
8N	......	1420.00	2750.00	3410.00	Ford	4	119G	4F-1R	21.06	2714	No

Ford (Cont.)

Model	Approx. Retail Price New	Fair	Good	Premium	Engine Make	Engine No. Cyls.	Engine Displ. Cu.-In.	No. Speeds	P.T.O. H.P.	Approx. Shipping Wt.-Lbs.	Cab
1948											
8N	......	1480.00	2790.00	3460.00	Ford	4	119G	4F-1R	21.06	2714	No
1949											
8N	......	1550.00	2860.00	3550.00	Ford	4	119G	4F-1R	21.06	2714	No
1950											
8N	......	1630.00	2920.00	3620.00	Ford	4	119G	4F-1R	21.06	2714	No
1951											
8N	......	1720.00	2990.00	3710.00	Ford	4	119G	4F-1R	21.06	2714	No
1952											
NAA	......	1840.00	3130.00	3880.00	Ford	4	134G	4F-1R	30.15	2841	No
8N	......	1810.00	3080.00	3820.00	Ford	4	119G	4F-1R	21.06	2714	No
1953											
Fordson Major	......	1440.00	2090.00	2420.00	Ford	4	220D	6F-2R	48	5515	No
NAA	......	1930.00	3200.00	3970.00	Ford	4	134G	4F-1R	30.15	2841	No
1954											
Fordson Major	......	1490.00	2130.00	2470.00	Ford	4	220D	6F-2R	48	5515	No
NAA	......	1910.00	3100.00	3840.00	Ford	4	134G	4F-1R	30.15	2841	No
600 Series	......	1620.00	3040.00	3710.00	Ford	4	134G	4F-1R	32	2462	No
700 Series	......	1630.00	3070.00	3750.00	Ford	4	134G	4F-1R	28.06	3390	No
800 Series	......	1670.00	3140.00	3830.00	Ford	4	172G	5F-1R	45	2640	No
800 Series	......	1730.00	3260.00	3980.00	Ford	4	172D	4F-1R	46	2960	No
900 Series	......	1700.00	3200.00	3900.00	Ford	4	172G	5F-1R	47	3355	No
1955											
Fordson Major	......	1540.00	2160.00	2510.00	Ford	4	220D	6F-2R	48	5515	No
600 Series	......	1700.00	3100.00	3780.00	Ford	4	134G	4F-1R	34	2462	No
700 Series	......	1720.00	3140.00	3830.00	Ford	4	134G	4F-1R	35	3175	No
800 Series	......	1750.00	3200.00	3900.00	Ford	4	172G	5F-1R	46	2985	No
800 Series	......	1820.00	3330.00	4060.00	Ford	4	172D	4F-1R	46	2960	No
900 Series	......	1800.00	3300.00	4030.00	Ford	4	172G	5F-1R	47	3355	No
1956											
Fordson Major	......	1580.00	2160.00	2480.00	Ford	4	220D	6F-2R	41	5425	No
600 Series	......	1720.00	3140.00	3830.00	Ford	4	134G	4F-1R	32	2462	No
700 Series	......	1730.00	3170.00	3870.00	Ford	4	134G	4F-1R	35	3175	No
800 Series	......	1770.00	3240.00	3950.00	Ford	4	172G	5F-1R	46	2985	No
800 Series	......	1850.00	3380.00	4120.00	Ford	4	172D	5F-1R	47	2995	No
900 Series	......	1820.00	3330.00	4060.00	Ford	4	172G	5F-1R	47	3355	No
1957											
Fordson Dexta	......	1630.00	2190.00	2520.00	Perkins	3	144D	6F-2R	31.4	3030	No
Fordson Major	......	1590.00	2140.00	2460.00	Ford	4	220D	6F-2R	48	5515	No
601 Series	......	1650.00	3010.00	3670.00	Ford	4	131G	10F-2R	37	2820	No
601 Series	......	1710.00	3120.00	3810.00	Ford	4	141D	10F-2R	37	2996	No
701 Series	......	1660.00	3040.00	3710.00	Ford	4	134G	4F-1R	35	3175	No
701 Series	......	1760.00	3210.00	3920.00	Ford	4	144D	4F-1R	32	3350	No
801 Series	......	1710.00	3120.00	3810.00	Ford	4	172G	5F-1R	46	2985	No
801 Series	......	1820.00	3330.00	4060.00	Ford	4	172D	10F-2R	44	3010	No
901 Series	......	1790.00	3260.00	3980.00	Ford	4	172G	4F-1R	47	3270	No
901 Series	......	1870.00	3430.00	4190.00	Ford	4	172D	4F-1R	45	3450	No
1958											
Fordson Dexta	......	1660.00	2190.00	2500.00	Perkins	3	144D	6F-2R	31.4	3030	No
Fordson Major	......	1610.00	2120.00	2420.00	Ford	4	220D	6F-2R	41	5425	No
Fordson Power Major	......	2000.00	2620.00	2990.00	Ford	4	220D	6F-2R	48	5515	No
601 Series	......	1680.00	3070.00	3750.00	Ford	4	134G	10F-2R	37	2820	No
601 Series	......	1750.00	3200.00	3900.00	Ford	4	144D	10F-2R	37	2996	No
701 Series	......	1720.00	3140.00	3830.00	Ford	4	134G	4F-1R	35	3175	No
701 Series	......	1820.00	3330.00	4060.00	Ford	4	144D	4F-4R	32	3350	No
801 Series	......	1730.00	3170.00	3870.00	Ford	4	172G	10F-2R	50	2836	No
801 Series	......	1870.00	3420.00	4170.00	Ford	4	172D	10F-2R	44	3010	No
901 Series	......	1810.00	3310.00	4040.00	Ford	4	172G	4F-1R	47	3270	No
901 Series	......	1910.00	3490.00	4260.00	Ford	4	172D	4F-1R	45	3450	No
1959											
Fordson Dexta	......	1680.00	2210.00	2520.00	Perkins	3	144D	6F-2R	31.4	3030	No
Fordson Power Major	......	2030.00	2670.00	3040.00	Ford	4	220D	6F-2R	48	5515	No
501 Series	......	1690.00	3090.00	3770.00	Ford	4	134G	4F-1R	35	3530	No
601 Series	......	1750.00	3200.00	3900.00	Ford	4	131G	10F-2R	37	2820	No
601 Series	......	1820.00	3330.00	4060.00	Ford	4	141D	10F-2R	37	2996	No
701 Series	......	1790.00	3270.00	3990.00	Ford	4	134G	4F-1R	35	3175	No
701 Series	......	1890.00	3460.00	4220.00	Ford	4	144D	4F-4R	32	3350	No
801 Series	......	1820.00	3330.00	4060.00	Ford	4	172G	10F-2R	50	2836	No
801 Series	......	1940.00	3550.00	4330.00	Ford	4	172D	10F-2R	44	3010	No
901 Series	......	1880.00	3440.00	4200.00	Ford	4	172G	4F-1R	47	3270	No
901 Series	......	1940.00	3550.00	4330.00	Ford	4	172D	4F-1R	45	3450	No

Model	Approx. Retail Price New	Estimated Average Value Less Repairs Fair	Good	Premium	Engine Make	No. Cyls.	Displ. Cu.-In.	No. Speeds	P.T.O. H.P.	Approx. Shipping Wt.-Lbs.	Cab
Ford (Cont.)											
			1960								
Fordson Dexta	......	1720.00	2250.00	2540.00	Perkins	3	144D	6F-2R	31.4	3030	No
Fordson Power Major	......	2070.00	2710.00	3060.00	Ford	4	220D	6F-2R	48	5515	No
501 Series	......	1780.00	3170.00	3870.00	Ford	4	134G	4F-1R	35	3530	No
501 Series	......	1910.00	3390.00	4140.00	Ford	4	144D	4F-1R	31.7	3710	No
601 Series	......	1840.00	3260.00	3980.00	Ford	4	131G	4F-1R	37	2623	No
601 Series	......	1940.00	3440.00	4200.00	Ford	4	141D	4F-1R	37	2799	No
701 Series	......	1870.00	3330.00	4060.00	Ford	4	134G	4F-1R	35	3175	No
701 Series	......	1980.00	3520.00	4290.00	Ford	4	144D	4F-4R	32	3350	No
801 Series	......	1930.00	3420.00	4170.00	Ford	4	172G	10F-2R	50	2836	No
801 Series	......	2030.00	3620.00	4420.00	Ford	4	172D	10F-2R	44	3010	No
901 Series	......	1960.00	3490.00	4260.00	Ford	4	172G	4F-1R	47	3165	No
901 Series	......	2070.00	3680.00	4490.00	Ford	4	172D	4F-1R	45	3450	No
			1961								
Fordson Dexta	......	1750.00	2300.00	2600.00	Perkins	3	144D	6F-2R	31.4	3030	No
Fordson Power Major	......	2080.00	2740.00	3100.00	Ford	4	220D	6F-2R	48	5515	No
Fordson Super Major	......	2000.00	2620.00	2960.00	Ford	4	220D	6F-2R	49	4609	No
501 Series	......	1890.00	3260.00	3980.00	Ford	4	134G	4F-1R	35	3530	No
501 Series	......	2040.00	3520.00	4290.00	Ford	4	144D	4F-1R	37	3710	No
601 Series	......	1940.00	3360.00	4100.00	Ford	4	131G	4F-1R	37	2623	No
601 Series	......	2020.00	3490.00	4260.00	Ford	4	141D	4F-1R	37	2799	No
701 Series	......	1980.00	3430.00	4190.00	Ford	4	134G	4F-1R	35	3175	No
701 Series	......	2070.00	3580.00	4370.00	Ford	4	144D	4F-4R	32	3350	No
801 Series	......	2060.00	3560.00	4340.00	Ford	4	172G	4F-1R	50	3487	No
801 Series	......	2130.00	3680.00	4490.00	Ford	4	172D	4F-1R	45	3657	No
901 Series	......	2090.00	3620.00	4420.00	Ford	4	172G	4F-1R	47	3270	No
901 Series	......	2170.00	3740.00	4560.00	Ford	4	172D	4F-1R	45	3450	No
6000	......	2350.00	3080.00	3480.00	Ford	6	223G	10F-2R	66.1	6893	No
6000	......	2630.00	3460.00	3910.00	Ford	6	241D	10F-2R	66.26	6875	No
			1962								
Fordson Dexta	......	1790.00	2350.00	2660.00	Perkins	3	144D	6F-2R	31.4	3030	No
Fordson Super Dexta	......	1840.00	2420.00	2740.00	Perkins	4	144D	6F-2R	32	3150	No
Fordson Super Major	......	2020.00	2660.00	3010.00	Ford	4	220D	6F-2R	49	4609	No
501 Series	......	2000.00	3370.00	4110.00	Ford	4	134G	4F-1R	35	3530	No
501 Series	......	2130.00	3580.00	4370.00	Ford	4	144D	4F-1R	31.7	3710	No
601 Series	......	2110.00	3560.00	4340.00	Ford	4	131G	10F-2R	37	2820	No
601 Series	......	2150.00	3620.00	4420.00	Ford	4	141D	10F-2R	37	2996	No
701 Series	......	2070.00	3490.00	4260.00	Ford	4	134G	4F-1R	35	3175	No
701 Series	......	2170.00	3650.00	4450.00	Ford	4	144D	4F-4R	32	3350	No
801 Series	......	2150.00	3620.00	4420.00	Ford	4	172G	4F-1R	50	3487	No
801 Series	......	2220.00	3740.00	4560.00	Ford	4	172D	4F-1R	45	3657	No
901 Series	......	2190.00	3680.00	4490.00	Ford	4	172G	4F-1R	47	3270	No
901 Series	......	2260.00	3810.00	4650.00	Ford	4	172D	4F-1R	45	3450	No
2000	......	2530.00	3740.00	4640.00	Ford	3	158G		30.52	3358	No
2000	......	2620.00	3880.00	4810.00	Ford	3	158D		38.8	3853	No
4000	......	2900.00	4290.00	5320.00	Ford	4	172G		46.3	3279	No
4000	......	3040.00	4500.00	5580.00	Ford	4	172D		46.7	3474	No
5000 Super Major	......	2620.00	4420.00	5390.00	Ford	4	220D	6F-2R	47.5	5565	No
6000	......	2610.00	4390.00	5360.00	Ford	6	223G	10F-2R	66.1	6893	No
6000	......	2890.00	4860.00	5930.00	Ford	6	241D	10F-2R	66.26	6875	No
			1963								
Fordson Dexta	2950.00	1820.00	2390.00	2700.00	Perkins	3	144D	6F-2R	31.4	3030	No
Fordson Super Dexta	3250.00	2120.00	2780.00	3140.00	Perkins	4	152D	6F-2R	32	3150	No
Fordson Super Major	3780.00	2300.00	3020.00	3410.00	Ford	4	220D	6F-2R	49	4609	No
2000	2856.00	2580.00	3810.00	4720.00	Ford	3	158G		38.8	3026	No
2000	3413.00	2690.00	3980.00	4940.00	Ford	3	158D		38.8	3557	No
4000	3815.00	3000.00	4430.00	5490.00	Ford	4	172G	10F-2R	46	2987	No
4000	3900.00	3110.00	4600.00	5700.00	Ford	4	172D	10F-2R	41	3182	No
5000	4893.00	3310.00	4900.00	6080.00	Ford	4	233D	10F-2R	54.1	5260	No
5000	......	3150.00	4660.00	5780.00	Ford	4	233G	8F-2R	53.09	5218	No
5000 Super Major	4154.00	2740.00	4490.00	5480.00	Ford	4	220D	6F-2R	47.5	5565	No
6000	5140.00	2790.00	4570.00	5580.00	Ford	6	223G	10F-2R	62	6498	No
6000	5735.00	3020.00	4950.00	6040.00	Ford	6	242D	10F-2R	62	6589	No
			1964								
Fordson Dexta	2950.00	1840.00	2420.00	2740.00	Perkins	3	144D	6F-2R	31.4	3030	No
2000	2913.00	2620.00	3880.00	4810.00	Ford	3	158G		30.51	2712	No
2000	3481.00	2740.00	4050.00	5020.00	Ford	3	158D		38.8	3089	No
4000	4000.00	3060.00	4530.00	5620.00	Ford	4	172G	5F-1R	46	3104	No
4000	4000.00	3130.00	4630.00	5740.00	Ford	4	172D	5F-1R	44	3280	No
5000	4893.00	3310.00	4900.00	6080.00	Ford	4	233D	10F-2R	54.1	5260	No
5000	......	3240.00	4790.00	5940.00	Ford	4	233G	8F-2R	53.09	5218	No
5000 Super Major	4239.00	2860.00	4570.00	5580.00	Ford	4	220D	6F-2R	47.5	4469	No
6000	5243.00	3020.00	4830.00	5890.00	Ford	6	223G	10F-2R	62	6498	No
6000	5850.00	3220.00	5150.00	6280.00	Ford	6	242D	10F-2R	62	6589	No
			1965								
5000 Super Major	4325.00	2960.00	4620.00	5640.00	Ford	4	220D	6F-2R	47.5	4469	No
2000	2750.00	2670.00	3940.00	4890.00	Ford	3	158G	4F-1R	30	3280	No
2000	3442.00	2810.00	4150.00	5150.00	Ford	3	158D	8F-2R	36.0	3560	No
3000	2986.00	2830.00	4180.00	5180.00	Ford	3	158G	8F-2R	38	3480	No
3000	3595.00	2990.00	4420.00	5480.00	Ford	3	175D	8F-2R	38	3920	No

Ford (Cont.)

Model	Approx. Retail Price New	Estimated Average Value Less Repairs Fair	Good	Premium	Make	Engine No. Cyls.	Displ. Cu.-In.	No. Speeds	P.T.O. H.P.	Approx. Shipping Wt.-Lbs.	Cab
1965 (Cont.)											
4000	4200.00	3090.00	4560.00	5650.00	Ford	3	192G	10F-2R	45.4	4210	No
4000	4214.00	3170.00	4690.00	5820.00	Ford	3	201D	10F-2R	45.6	4450	No
5000	4893.00	3500.00	5180.00	6420.00	Ford	4	233D	10F-2R	54.1	5260	No
5000	......	3340.00	4930.00	6110.00	Ford	4	233G	8F-2R	53.09	5218	No
6000	5349.00	3160.00	4930.00	6020.00	Ford	6	223G	10F-2R	62	6498	No
6000	5967.00	3360.00	5250.00	6410.00	Ford	6	242D	10F-2R	62	6589	No
1966											
2000	2842.00	2820.00	4080.00	5060.00	Ford	3	157G	4F-1R	30	3280	No
2000	3642.00	2960.00	4280.00	5310.00	Ford	3	158D	8F-2R	36.0	3560	No
3000	3135.00	2930.00	4240.00	5260.00	Ford	3	158G	8F-2R	39	3480	No
3000	3600.00	3130.00	4530.00	5620.00	Ford	3	175D	8F-2R	38	3920	No
4000	4196.00	3200.00	4620.00	5730.00	Ford	3	192G	10F-2R	45.6	4210	No
4000	4436.00	3300.00	4770.00	5920.00	Ford	3	201D	10F-2R	45.6	4450	No
5000	4893.00	3530.00	5100.00	6320.00	Ford	4	233G	10F-2R	58	5218	No
5000	5151.00	3670.00	5310.00	6580.00	Ford	4	233D	10F-2R	54	5318	No
5000 Super Major	4500.00	2630.00	3450.00	3900.00	Ford	4	220D	6F-2R	47.5	4469	No
6000	5456.00	3260.00	4960.00	6050.00	Ford	6	223G	10F-2R	66	6498	No
6000	6086.00	3560.00	5430.00	6630.00	Ford	6	242D	10F-2R	66	6589	No
1967											
2000	2900.00	2910.00	4220.00	5230.00	Ford	3	158G	4F-1R	30.51	3280	No
2000	3642.00	3010.00	4350.00	5390.00	Ford	3	158D	8F-2R	36.0	3560	No
3000	3292.00	3010.00	4360.00	5410.00	Ford	3	158G	8F-2R	37.8	3480	No
3000	3633.00	3200.00	4620.00	5730.00	Ford	3	175D	8F-2R	36.1	3805	No
4000	4417.00	3250.00	4700.00	5830.00	Ford	3	192G	10F-2R	45.4	4210	No
4000	4669.00	3340.00	4830.00	5990.00	Ford	3	201D	10F-2R	45.6	4450	No
5000	5142.00	3570.00	5170.00	6410.00	Ford	4	233G	10F-2R	58.5	5410	No
5000	5422.00	3720.00	5390.00	6680.00	Ford	4	233D	10F-2R	54.1	5810	No
6000	5565.00	3380.00	5030.00	6140.00	Ford	6	223G	10F-2R	66	6498	No
6000	6208.00	3680.00	5470.00	6670.00	Ford	6	242D	10F-2R	66	6875	No
1968											
2000	3240.00	3080.00	4370.00	5420.00	Ford	3	158G	4F-R	30	3380	No
2000	3642.00	3170.00	4500.00	5580.00	Ford	3	158D	8F-2R	36.0	3560	No
3000	3457.00	3100.00	4390.00	5440.00	Ford	3	158G	8F-2R	37.8	3480	No
3000	3814.00	3270.00	4630.00	5740.00	Ford	3	158D	8F-2R	39.2	3805	No
4000	4908.00	3340.00	4730.00	5870.00	Ford	3	192G	10F-2R	39.9	4210	No
4000	5188.00	3450.00	4890.00	6060.00	Ford	3	201D	10F-2R	45.6	4450	No
5000	5713.00	3800.00	5380.00	6670.00	Ford	4	256G	10F-2R	65.69	5410	No
5000	6024.00	3950.00	5590.00	6930.00	Ford	4	256D	10F-2R	66.5	5810	No
6000	5738.00	3670.00	5340.00	6520.00	Ford	6	223G	10F-2R	66.1	6920	No
6000	6396.00	3870.00	5630.00	6870.00	Ford	6	242D	10F-2R	66.26	7100	No
8000	8051.00	3920.00	5700.00	6950.00	Ford	6	401D	8F-2R	105	9070	No
1969											
2000	3573.00	3190.00	4420.00	5480.00	Ford	3	158G	8F-2R	30.57	3300	No
2000	3642.00	3310.00	4590.00	5690.00	Ford	3	158D	8F-2R	36.0	3560	No
3000	3630.00	3380.00	4690.00	5820.00	Ford	3	158G	8F-2R	37.8	3100	No
3000	4005.00	3580.00	4970.00	6160.00	Ford	3	158D	8F-2R	39.2	3805	No
4000	5589.00	3720.00	5160.00	6400.00	Ford	3	201G	10F-2R	50.1	5118	No
4000	5883.00	3860.00	5360.00	6650.00	Ford	3	201D	10F-2R	51.0	5368	No
5000	6391.00	4160.00	5770.00	7160.00	Ford	4	256G	10F-2R	65.6	6280	No
5000	6569.00	4300.00	5960.00	7390.00	Ford	4	256D	10F-2R	66.5	6580	No
6000	5960.00	3720.00	5290.00	6450.00	Ford	6	223G	10F-2R	66.1	6200	No
6000	6648.00	3980.00	5660.00	6910.00	Ford	6	242D	10F-2R	66	6585	No
8000	8861.00	4280.00	6080.00	7420.00	Ford	6	401D	16F-4R	105	10845	No
County Super 4	11676.00	3740.00	5140.00	5760.00	Ford	4	256D	8F-2R	67	8930	No
County Super 6	14700.00	4700.00	6470.00	7250.00	Ford	6	401D	8F-2R	113	9990	No
1970											
2000	3600.00	3330.00	4520.00	5610.00	Ford	3	158G	6F-2R	30.58	3296	No
2000	3700.00	3480.00	4730.00	5870.00	Ford	3	158D	6F-2R	31.97	3562	No
3000	3812.00	3600.00	4900.00	6080.00	Ford	3	158G	8F-2R	37.87	3480	No
3000	4205.00	3850.00	5240.00	6500.00	Ford	3	175D	8F-2R	39.20	3805	No
4000	5883.00	4090.00	5560.00	6890.00	Ford	3	201G	10F-2R	50.16	5118	No
4000	6194.00	4200.00	5710.00	7080.00	Ford	3	201D	10F-2R	51.00	5368	No
5000	6727.00	4700.00	6390.00	7920.00	Ford	4	256G	10F-2R	65.64	6280	No
5000	6904.00	4900.00	6660.00	8260.00	Ford	4	256D	10F-2R	66.49	6580	No
8000	8951.00	4580.00	6370.00	7770.00	Ford	6	401D	16F-4R	105.73	10845	No
9000	10458.00	4810.00	6690.00	8160.00	Ford	6T	401D	16F-4R	131.22	10995	No
County Super 4	12290.00	4060.00	5410.00	6060.00	Ford	4	256D	8F-2R	67.00	8930	No
County Super 6	15475.00	5110.00	6810.00	7630.00	Ford	6	363D	8F-2R	113.00	9990	No
1971											
2000	3720.00	3470.00	4620.00	5730.00	Ford	3	158G	8F-2R	30.83	3507	No
2000	3876.00	3670.00	4900.00	6080.00	Ford	3	158D	8F-2R	31.19	3546	No
3000	4003.00	3800.00	5070.00	6290.00	Ford	3	158G	8F-2R	37.84	3664	No
3000	4415.00	4060.00	5410.00	6710.00	Ford	3	175D	8F-2R	39.30	3801	No
4000	6193.00	4430.00	5910.00	7330.00	Ford	3	201G	10F-2R	50.16	4898	No
4000	6520.00	4540.00	6050.00	7500.00	Ford	3	201D	10F-2R	51.00	5118	No
5000	7081.00	4950.00	6600.00	8180.00	Ford	4	256G	10F-2R	65.64	6280	No
5000	7267.00	5080.00	6770.00	8400.00	Ford	4	256D	10F-2R	66.49	6580	No
8000	9422.00	4700.00	6400.00	7810.00	Ford	6	401D	16F-4R	105.73	10845	No

Ford (Cont.)

1971 (Cont.)

Model	Approx. Retail Price New	Fair	Good	Premium	Engine Make	Engine No. Cyls.	Engine Displ. Cu.-In.	No. Speeds	P.T.O. H.P.	Approx. Shipping Wt.-Lbs.	Cab
9000	10755.00	5060.00	6880.00	8390.00	Ford	6T	401D	16F-4R	131.22	11515	No
County Super 4	12937.00	4400.00	5690.00	6370.00	Ford	4	256D	8F-2R	67.00	8930	No
County Super 6	16289.00	5540.00	7170.00	8030.00	Ford	6	363D	8F-2R	113.00	9990	No

1972

Model	Approx. Retail Price New	Fair	Good	Premium	Engine Make	Engine No. Cyls.	Engine Displ. Cu.-In.	No. Speeds	P.T.O. H.P.	Approx. Shipping Wt.-Lbs.	Cab
2000	3796.00	3640.00	4760.00	5860.00	Ford	3	158G	8F-2R	30.83	3507	No
2000	3955.00	3850.00	5030.00	6190.00	Ford	3	158D	8F-2R	31.19	3546	No
3000	4305.00	4000.00	5240.00	6450.00	Ford	3	158G	8F-2R	37.84	3664	No
3000	4636.00	4260.00	5580.00	6860.00	Ford	3	175D	8F-2R	39.30	3801	No
4000	6519.00	4530.00	5930.00	7290.00	Ford	3	201G	10F-2R	50.16	4898	No
4000	6863.00	4650.00	6090.00	7490.00	Ford	3	201D	10F-2R	51.00	5118	No
5000	7454.00	5070.00	6630.00	8160.00	Ford	4	256G	10F-2R	65.64	6280	No
5000	7650.00	5300.00	6940.00	8540.00	Ford	4	256D	10F-2R	66.49	6580	No
7000	9282.00	5040.00	6720.00	8130.00	Ford	4T	256D	8F-2R	83.49	5806	No
8000	11218.00	5280.00	7040.00	8520.00	Ford	6	401D	16F-4R	105.73	10845	C,H
9000	12887.00	5710.00	7610.00	9210.00	Ford	6T	401D	16F-4R	131.22	10995	C,H
County Super 4	13618.00	4770.00	5990.00	6710.00	Ford	4	256D	8F-2R	67.00	8930	No
County Super 6	17147.00	6000.00	7550.00	8460.00	Ford	6	363D	8F-2R	113.00	9990	No

1973

Model	Approx. Retail Price New	Fair	Good	Premium	Engine Make	Engine No. Cyls.	Engine Displ. Cu.-In.	No. Speeds	P.T.O. H.P.	Approx. Shipping Wt.-Lbs.	Cab
1000	3054.00	2300.00	3010.00	3610.00	Shibaura	2	78D	9F-3R	23.00	2300	No
2000	3873.00	3840.00	4930.00	6020.00	Ford	3	158G	8F-2R	30.85	3507	No
2000	4036.00	4060.00	5200.00	6340.00	Ford	3	158D	8F-2R	31.19	3546	No
3000	4520.00	4240.00	5440.00	6640.00	Ford	3	158G	8F-2R	37.84	3664	No
3000	4867.00	4510.00	5780.00	7050.00	Ford	3	175D	8F-2R	39.30	3801	No
4000	6862.00	4700.00	6030.00	7360.00	Ford	3	201G	10F-2R	50.16	4898	No
4000	7224.00	4360.00	5590.00	6820.00	Ford	3	201D	10F-2R	51.00	5118	No
5000	7819.00	4780.00	6130.00	7480.00	Ford	4	256G	10F-2R	65.64	6280	No
5000	8023.00	4940.00	6340.00	7740.00	Ford	4	256D	10F-2R	66.49	6580	No
7000	9771.00	5280.00	6890.00	8270.00	Ford	4T	256D	8F-2R	83.49	5806	No
8000	10836.00	5390.00	7040.00	8450.00	Ford	6	401D	16F-4R	105.73	10495	C,H
8600	11808.00	5790.00	7560.00	9070.00	Ford	6	401D	16F-4R	105.73	10845	C,H
9000	13568.00	6160.00	8040.00	9650.00	Ford	6T	401D	16F-4R	131.22	10995	C,H
County Super 4	14335.00	5160.00	6450.00	7160.00	Ford	4	256D	8F-2R	67.00	8930	No
County Super 6	18049.00	6500.00	8120.00	9010.00	Ford	6	401D	8F-2R	96.00	9990	No

1974

Model	Approx. Retail Price New	Fair	Good	Premium	Engine Make	Engine No. Cyls.	Engine Displ. Cu.-In.	No. Speeds	P.T.O. H.P.	Approx. Shipping Wt.-Lbs.	Cab
1000	3215.00	2500.00	3200.00	3810.00	Shibaura	2	78D	9F-3R	23.00	2300	No
2000	4841.00	4050.00	5100.00	6170.00	Ford	3	158G	8F-2R	30.85	3507	No
2000	5045.00	4270.00	5370.00	6500.00	Ford	3	158D	8F-2R	31.19	3546	No
3000	5424.00	4480.00	5640.00	6820.00	Ford	3	158G	8F-2R	37.84	3664	No
3000	5840.00	4750.00	5980.00	7240.00	Ford	3	175D	8F-2R	39.30	3801	No
4000	8456.00	5100.00	6430.00	7780.00	Ford	3	201G	10F-2R	50.16	4504	No
4000	8672.00	5220.00	6580.00	7960.00	Ford	3	201D	10F-2R	51.00	4754	No
5000	9274.00	5550.00	6990.00	8460.00	Ford	4	256G	10F-2R	65.64	6280	No
5000	9529.00	5690.00	7160.00	8660.00	Ford	4	256D	10F-2R	66.49	6580	No
7000	11495.00	5750.00	7360.00	8760.00	Ford	4T	256D	8F-2R	83.49	5806	No
8600	17088.00	4960.00	6660.00	7460.00	Ford	6	401D	16F-4R	110.69	10800	C,H
9600	19441.00	5640.00	7580.00	8490.00	Ford	6T	401D	16F-4R	135.46	10900	C,H
County Super 4	17919.00	5200.00	6990.00	7830.00	Ford	4	256D	8F-2R	67.00	8930	No
County Super 6	22562.00	6540.00	8800.00	9860.00	Ford	6	401D	8F-2R	96.00	9990	No

1975

Model	Approx. Retail Price New	Fair	Good	Premium	Engine Make	Engine No. Cyls.	Engine Displ. Cu.-In.	No. Speeds	P.T.O. H.P.	Approx. Shipping Wt.-Lbs.	Cab
1000	4233.00	2650.00	3330.00	3930.00	Shibaura	2	78D	9F-3R	23.00	2300	No
2000	5695.00	4240.00	5240.00	6290.00	Ford	3	158G	8F-2R	30.85	3507	No
2000	5935.00	4400.00	5440.00	6530.00	Ford	3	158D	8F-2R	31.19	3546	No
3000	6509.00	4680.00	5780.00	6940.00	Ford	3	158G	8F-2R	37.84	3664	No
3000	7008.00	4950.00	6120.00	7340.00	Ford	3	175D	8F-2R	39.30	3801	No
4000	9395.00	5720.00	7070.00	8480.00	Ford	3	201G	10F-2R	50.16	4504	No
4000	9635.00	5850.00	7230.00	8680.00	Ford	3	201D	10F-2R	51.00	4754	No
5000	11389.00	6540.00	8090.00	9710.00	Ford	4	256G	10F-2R	65.64	5218	No
5000	11689.00	6650.00	8220.00	9860.00	Ford	4	256D	10F-2R	66.49	5468	No
7000	12100.00	6380.00	8000.00	9440.00	Ford	4T	256D	8F-2R	83.49	5806	No
8600	17987.00	5400.00	7020.00	7790.00	Ford	6	401D	16F-4R	110.69	10800	C,H
9600	20464.00	6140.00	7980.00	8860.00	Ford	6T	401D	16F-4R	135.46	10900	C,H
County Super 4	18862.00	5660.00	7360.00	8170.00	Ford	4	256D	8F-2R	67.00	8930	No
County Super 6	23749.00	7130.00	9260.00	10280.00	Ford	6	401D	8F-2R	96.00	9990	No

1976

Model	Approx. Retail Price New	Fair	Good	Premium	Engine Make	Engine No. Cyls.	Engine Displ. Cu.-In.	No. Speeds	P.T.O. H.P.	Approx. Shipping Wt.-Lbs.	Cab
1000	4445.00	2380.00	2810.00	3150.00	Shibaura	2	78D	9F-3R	23.00	2300	No
2600	6209.00	3670.00	4610.00	5390.00	Ford	3	158G	8F-2R	34.18	3507	No
2600	6469.00	3810.00	4780.00	5590.00	Ford	3	158D	8F-2R	32.47	3546	No
3600	6960.00	4060.00	5090.00	5960.00	Ford	3	175G	8F-2R	40.62	4400	No
3600	7200.00	4180.00	5250.00	6140.00	Ford	3	175D	8F-2R	40.55	4590	No
4100	8662.00	4930.00	6180.00	7230.00	Ford	3	183D	8F-2R	45.46	4910	No
4600	8740.00	4970.00	6230.00	7290.00	Ford	3	201G	10F-2R	50.16	4439	No
4600	9100.00	4640.00	5820.00	6810.00	Ford	3	201D	10F-2R	51.00	4710	No
5600	11967.00	6100.00	7660.00	8960.00	Ford	4	233D	16F-4R	58.46	5500	No
6600	12654.00	6450.00	8100.00	9480.00	Ford	4	256G	16F-4R	68.00	5580	No
6600	12980.00	6620.00	8310.00	9720.00	Ford	4	256D	16F-4R	68.10	5780	No
7600	14071.00	7180.00	9010.00	10540.00	Ford	4T	256D	16F-4R	84.79	5800	No
8600	18934.00	5870.00	7570.00	8400.00	Ford	6	401D	16F-4R	110.69	10800	C,H
9600	21541.00	6680.00	8620.00	9570.00	Ford	6T	401D	16F-4R	135.36	10900	C,H
County Super 4	19855.00	6160.00	7940.00	8810.00	Ford	4	256D	8F-2R	67.00	8930	No

Ford (Cont.)

Model	Approx. Retail Price New	Estimated Average Value Less Repairs: Fair	Good	Premium	Engine Make	No. Cyls.	Displ. Cu.-In.	No. Speeds	P.T.O. H.P.	Approx. Shipping Wt.-Lbs.	Cab
1976 (Cont.)											
County Super 6	24999.00	7750.00	10000.00	11100.00	Ford	6	401D	8F-2R	96.00	9990	No
RC--Row Crop SU--Low Profile											
1977											
1600	4550.00	2830.00	3550.00	4120.00	Shibaura	2	78D	9F-3R	22.02	2260	No
2600	7305.00	4240.00	5320.00	6170.00	Ford	3	158G	8F-2R	34.18	3507	No
2600	7611.00	4390.00	5510.00	6390.00	Ford	3	158D	8F-2R	32.47	3546	No
3600	8484.00	4840.00	6070.00	7040.00	Ford	3	175G	8F-2R	40.62	4400	No
3600	8777.00	4990.00	6260.00	7260.00	Ford	3	175D	8F-2R	40.55	4590	No
4100	10190.00	5200.00	6520.00	7560.00	Ford	3	183D	8F-2R	45.46	4910	No
4600	10045.00	5120.00	6430.00	7460.00	Ford	3	201G	8F-2R	52.18	4480	No
4600	10466.00	5340.00	6700.00	7770.00	Ford	3	201D	8F-2R	52.44	4710	No
5600	13297.00	6780.00	8510.00	9870.00	Ford	4	233D	16F-4R	58.46	5500	No
6600	14060.00	7170.00	9000.00	10440.00	Ford	4	256G	16F-4R	68.00	5580	No
6600	14422.00	7360.00	9230.00	10710.00	Ford	4	256D	16F-4R	68.10	5780	No
6700	19474.00	8760.00	10320.00	11460.00	Ford	4	256G	16F-4R	68.00	5780	C,H,A
6700	19854.00	8930.00	10520.00	11680.00	Ford	4	256D	16F-4R	68.94	5980	C,H,A
7600	15634.00	7040.00	8290.00	9200.00	Ford	4T	256D	16F-4R	84.79	5800	No
7700	20696.00	8550.00	10070.00	11180.00	Ford	4T	256D	16F-4R	84.38	6000	No
8700	21819.00	6980.00	8950.00	9940.00	Ford	6	401D	16F-4R	110.58	10900	C,H,A
9700	25466.00	8150.00	10440.00	11590.00	Ford	6T	401D	16F-4R	135.64	11000	C,H,A
County Super 4	20900.00	6690.00	8570.00	9510.00	Ford	4	256D	8F-2R	67.00	8930	No
County Super 6	26315.00	8420.00	10790.00	11980.00	Ford	6	401D	8F-2R	96.00	9990	No
FW-20 4WD	47267.00	8880.00	12680.00	14200.00	Cummins	V8	555D	20F-4R		24775	C,H,A
FW-30 4WD	57269.00	9930.00	14180.00	15880.00	Cummins	V8	903D	20F-4R	105.31	25320	C,H,A
FW-40 4WD	61867.00	10890.00	15560.00	17430.00	Cummins	V8	903D	20F-4R		26132	C,H,A
FW-60 4WD	67781.00	12130.00	17330.00	19410.00	Cummins	V8T	903D	20F-4R		26171	C,H,A
RC--Row Crop SU--Low Profile											
1978											
1600	4830.00	2960.00	3710.00	4270.00	Shibaura	2	78D	9F-3R	22.02	2260	No
2600	7689.00	4430.00	5560.00	6390.00	Ford	3	158G	8F-2R	34.18	3507	No
2600	8012.00	4600.00	5770.00	6640.00	Ford	3	158D	8F-2R	32.47	3546	No
3600	8908.00	5050.00	6340.00	7290.00	Ford	3	175G	8F-2R	40.62	4400	No
3600	9216.00	5210.00	6540.00	7520.00	Ford	3	175D	8F-2R	40.55	4590	No
4100	10726.00	5470.00	6870.00	7900.00	Ford	3	183D	8F-2R	45.46	4910	No
4600	10574.00	5390.00	6770.00	7790.00	Ford	3	201G	8F-2R	52.18	4480	No
4600	11017.00	5620.00	7050.00	8110.00	Ford	3	201D	8F-2R	52.44	4710	No
5600	13997.00	7140.00	8960.00	10300.00	Ford	4	233D	16F-4R	58.46	5500	No
6600	14800.00	7550.00	9470.00	10890.00	Ford	4	256G	16F-4R	68.00	5580	No
6600	15181.00	7740.00	9720.00	11180.00	Ford	4	256D	16F-4R	68.10	5780	No
6700	20499.00	9430.00	11070.00	12180.00	Ford	4	256G	16F-4R	68.00	5780	C,H,A
6700	20899.00	9610.00	11290.00	12420.00	Ford	4	256D	16F-4R	68.94	5980	C,H,A
7600	16457.00	7570.00	8890.00	9780.00	Ford	4T	256D	16F-4R	84.79	5800	No
7700	21785.00	9200.00	10800.00	11880.00	Ford	4T	256D	16F-4R	84.38	6000	C,H,A
8700	22967.00	7580.00	9650.00	10620.00	Ford	6	401D	16F-4R	110.58	10900	C,H,A
9700	26806.00	8850.00	11260.00	12390.00	Ford	6T	401D	16F-4R	135.64	11000	C,H,A
County Super 4	22000.00	7260.00	9240.00	10160.00	Ford	4	256D	8F-2R	67.00	8930	No
County Super 6	27700.00	9140.00	11630.00	12790.00	Ford	6	401D	8F-2R	96.00	9990	No
FW-20 4WD	49755.00	9830.00	13860.00	15520.00	Cummins	V8	555D	20F-4R		24775	C,H,A
FW-30 4WD	60283.00	11000.00	15500.00	17360.00	Cummins	V8	903D	20F-4R	105.31	25320	C,H,A
FW-40 4WD	65123.00	12100.00	17050.00	19100.00	Cummins	V8	903D	20F-4R		26132	C,H,A
FW-60 4WD	71348.00	13420.00	18910.00	21180.00	Cummins	V8T	903D	20F-4R		26171	C,H,A
RC--Row Crop SU--Low Profile											
1979											
1600	5084.00	3120.00	3780.00	4310.00	Shibaura	2	78D	9F-3R	22.02	2260	No
2600	8225.00	4800.00	5810.00	6620.00	Ford	3	158G	8F-2R	34.18	3507	No
2600	8549.00	4970.00	6020.00	6860.00	Ford	3	158D	8F-2R	32.47	3546	No
3600	9393.00	5300.00	6420.00	7320.00	Ford	3	175G	8F-2R	40.62	4400	No
3600	9716.00	5470.00	6630.00	7560.00	Ford	3	175D	8F-2R	40.55	4590	No
4100	11628.00	6000.00	7260.00	8280.00	Ford	3	183D	8F-2R	45.46	4910	No
4600	11981.00	6180.00	7490.00	8540.00	Ford	3	201G	8F-2R	52.18	4480	No
4600	12297.00	6340.00	7680.00	8760.00	Ford	3	201D	8F-2R	52.44	4710	No
5600	14729.00	7610.00	9220.00	10510.00	Ford	4	233D	16F-4R	58.46	5500	No
6600	16020.00	7470.00	8750.00	9540.00	Ford	4	256D	16F-4R	68.10	5780	No
6700	21712.00	10160.00	11890.00	12960.00	Ford	4	256D	16F-4R	68.94	6900	C,H,A
7600	17527.00	8190.00	9590.00	10450.00	Ford	4T	256D	16F-4R	84.79	5800	No
7700	22688.00	9240.00	11220.00	12230.00	Ford	4T	256D	16F-4R	84.38	7000	C,H,A
TW10	27982.00	9510.00	12030.00	13110.00	Ford	6	401D	16F-4R	110.24	10900	C,H,A
TW20	30918.00	10510.00	13300.00	14500.00	Ford	6T	401D	16F-4R	135.60	12000	C,H,A
TW30	35327.00	12010.00	15190.00	16560.00	Ford	6TI	401D	16F-4R	163.28	13050	C,H,A
FW-20 4WD	52374.00	10900.00	15160.00	16980.00	Cummins	V8	555D	20F-4R		24775	C,H,A
FW-30 4WD	63458.00	12300.00	17110.00	19160.00	Cummins	V8	903D	20F-4R	105.31	25320	C,H,A
FW-40 4WD	68550.00	13460.00	18720.00	20970.00	Cummins	V8	903D	20F-4R		26132	C,H,A
FW-60 4WD	75103.00	14950.00	20800.00	23300.00	Cummins	V8T	903D	20F-4R		26171	C,H,A
RC--Row Crop SU--Low Profile											
1980											
1100	4563.00	3000.00	3510.00	4040.00	Shibaura	2	43D	10F-2R	11.00	1131	No
1100 4WD	5033.00	3270.00	3830.00	4410.00	Shibaura	2	43D	10F-2R	11.00	1244	No
1200 4WD	5556.00	3570.00	4190.00	4820.00	Shibaura	2	43D	20F-2R	13.00	1294	No
1300	5388.00	3470.00	4070.00	4680.00	Shibaura	2	49D	12F-4R	13.50	1723	No
1300 4WD	5898.00	3770.00	4420.00	5080.00	Shibaura	2	49D	12F-4R	13.50	1984	No

Ford (Cont.)

1980 (Cont.)

Model	Approx. Retail Price New	Estimated Average Value Less Repairs Fair	Good	Premium	Engine Make	No. Cyls.	Displ. Cu.-In.	No. Speeds	P.T.O. H.P.	Approx. Shipping Wt.-Lbs.	Cab
1500	5865.00	**3690.00**	**4330.00**	**4980.00**	Shibaura	2	62D	12F-4R	17.00	1958	No
1500 4WD	6543.00	**4090.00**	**4790.00**	**5510.00**	Shibaura	2	62D	12F-4R	17.00	2205	No
1700	6460.00	**4040.00**	**4730.00**	**5440.00**	Shibaura	2	78D	12F-4R	23.26	2276	No
1700 4WD	7347.00	**4550.00**	**5340.00**	**6140.00**	Shibaura	2	78D	12F-4R	23.00	2513	No
1900	7523.00	**4600.00**	**5390.00**	**6200.00**	Shibaura	3	87D	12F-4R	26.88	2518	No
1900 4WD	9069.00	**5260.00**	**6170.00**	**7100.00**	Shibaura	3	87D	12F-4R	26.00	2750	No
2600	8479.00	**5020.00**	**5880.00**	**6640.00**	Ford	3	158G	8F-2R	34.18	3507	No
2600	8802.00	**5200.00**	**6080.00**	**6870.00**	Ford	3	158D	8F-2R	32.47	3546	No
3600	10307.00	**5990.00**	**7010.00**	**7920.00**	Ford	3	175G	8F-2R	40.62	4400	No
3600	10853.00	**6280.00**	**7350.00**	**8310.00**	Ford	3	175D	8F-2R	40.55	4590	No
4100	12536.00	**6500.00**	**7580.00**	**8190.00**	Ford	3	183D	8F-2R	45.46	4910	No
4600	13059.00	**6750.00**	**7870.00**	**8500.00**	Ford	3	201G	8F-2R	52.18	4480	No
4600	13402.00	**6910.00**	**8070.00**	**8720.00**	Ford	3	201D	8F-2R	52.44	4710	No
5600	16755.00	**8040.00**	**9380.00**	**10130.00**	Ford	4	233D	16F-4R	58.46	5500	No
5600 4WD	22122.00	**10620.00**	**12390.00**	**13380.00**	Ford	4	233D	16F-4R	60.00	6175	No
6600	18265.00	**7850.00**	**9500.00**	**10260.00**	Ford	4	256D	16F-4R	68.10	5780	No
6600 4WD	23632.00	**10160.00**	**12290.00**	**13270.00**	Ford	4	256D	16F-4R	68.00	6280	No
6700	24688.00	**10620.00**	**12840.00**	**13870.00**	Ford	4	256D	16F-4R	68.94	6900	C,H,A
6700 4WD	29903.00	**12860.00**	**15550.00**	**16790.00**	Ford	4	256D	16F-4R	68.00	7400	C,H,A
7600	19897.00	**8560.00**	**10350.00**	**11180.00**	Ford	4T	256D	16F-4R	84.79	5800	No
7600 4WD	25264.00	**10750.00**	**13000.00**	**14040.00**	Ford	4T	256D	16F-4R	84.00	6400	No
7700	25857.00	**11120.00**	**13450.00**	**14530.00**	Ford	4T	256D	16F-4R	84.38	7000	C,H,A
7700 4WD	31072.00	**12470.00**	**15080.00**	**16290.00**	Ford	4T	256D	16F-4R	84.00	7600	C,H,A
TW10	32777.00	**10850.00**	**13640.00**	**14870.00**	Ford	6	401D	16F-4R	110.24	10900	C,H,A
TW10 4WD	40389.00	**13300.00**	**16720.00**	**18230.00**	Ford	6	401D	16F-4R	110.00	13350	C,H,A
TW20	36738.00	**12250.00**	**15400.00**	**16790.00**	Ford	6T	401D	16F-4R	135.60	12000	C,H,A
TW20 4WD	44257.00	**15050.00**	**18920.00**	**20620.00**	Ford	6T	401D	16F-4R	135.00	14600	C,H,A
TW30	41108.00	**14000.00**	**17600.00**	**19180.00**	Ford	6TI	401D	16F-4R	163.28	14050	C,H,A
TW30 4WD	48627.00	**16450.00**	**20680.00**	**22540.00**	Ford	6TI	401D	16F-4R	163.00	14800	C,H,A
FW-20 4WD	60453.00	**12110.00**	**16650.00**	**18650.00**	Cummins	V8	555D	20F-4R		24775	C,H,A
FW-30 4WD	73017.00	**14400.00**	**19810.00**	**22190.00**	Cummins	V8	903D	20F-4R	105.31	25320	C,H,A
FW-60 4WD	86502.00	**15960.00**	**21950.00**	**24580.00**	Cummins	V8T	903D	20F-4R		26171	C,H,A

RC--Row Crop SU--Low Profile

1981

Model	Approx. Retail Price New	Fair	Good	Premium	Engine Make	No. Cyls.	Displ. Cu.-In.	No. Speeds	P.T.O. H.P.	Approx. Shipping Wt.-Lbs.	Cab
1100	5145.00	**3450.00**	**3980.00**	**4540.00**	Shibaura	2	43D	10F-2R	11.00	1131	No
1100 4WD	5669.00	**3760.00**	**4330.00**	**4940.00**	Shibaura	2	43D	10F-2R	11.00	1244	No
1200 4WD	6080.00	**3940.00**	**4540.00**	**5180.00**	Shibaura	2	43D	20F-2R	13.00	1294	No
1300	5941.00	**3860.00**	**4450.00**	**5070.00**	Shibaura	2	49D	12F-4R	13.00	1723	No
1300 4WD	6528.00	**4210.00**	**4850.00**	**5530.00**	Shibaura	2	49D	12F-4R	13.00	1984	No
1500	6409.00	**4080.00**	**4700.00**	**5360.00**	Shibaura	2	69D	12F-4R	17.00	1958	No
1500 4WD	7137.00	**4510.00**	**5190.00**	**5920.00**	Shibaura	2	69D	12F-4R	17.00	2205	No
1700	6996.00	**4420.00**	**5100.00**	**5810.00**	Shibaura	2	78D	12F-4R	23.26	2276	No
1700 4WD	7953.00	**4690.00**	**5410.00**	**6170.00**	Shibaura	2	78D	12F-4R	23.00	2513	No
1900	7587.00	**4480.00**	**5160.00**	**5880.00**	Shibaura	3	87D	12F-4R	26.88	2518	No
1900 4WD	9232.00	**5450.00**	**6280.00**	**7160.00**	Shibaura	3	87D	12F-4R	26.00	2750	No
2600	11673.00	**6480.00**	**7560.00**	**8470.00**	Ford	3	158D	8F-2R	32.47	3546	No
2600	11673.00	**6300.00**	**7350.00**	**8230.00**	Ford	3	158G	8F-2R	34.18	3507	No
3600	14267.00	**7700.00**	**8990.00**	**10070.00**	Ford	3	175G	8F-2R	40.62	4400	No
3600	14289.00	**7720.00**	**9000.00**	**10080.00**	Ford	3	175D	8F-2R	40.55	4590	No
4100	15680.00	**7680.00**	**8940.00**	**9660.00**	Ford	3	183D	8F-2R	45.46	4910	No
4600	16085.00	**7880.00**	**9170.00**	**9900.00**	Ford	3	201G	8F-2R	52.18	4480	No
4600	16108.00	**7890.00**	**9180.00**	**9910.00**	Ford	3	201D	8F-2R	52.44	4710	No
5600	19172.00	**9390.00**	**10930.00**	**11800.00**	Ford	4	233D	16F-4R	58.46	5500	No
5600 4WD	24880.00	**12190.00**	**14180.00**	**15310.00**	Ford	4	233D	16F-4R	58.00	6175	No
6600	20824.00	**10200.00**	**11870.00**	**12820.00**	Ford	4	256D	16F-4R	68.10	5780	No
6600 4WD	26301.00	**12890.00**	**14990.00**	**16190.00**	Ford	4	256D	16F-4R	68.00	6280	No
6700	28668.00	**14050.00**	**16340.00**	**17650.00**	Ford	4	256D	16F-4R	68.94	6900	C,H,A
6700 4WD	34387.00	**16850.00**	**19600.00**	**21170.00**	Ford	4	256D	16F-4R	68.00	7400	C,H,A
7600	22576.00	**11060.00**	**12870.00**	**13900.00**	Ford	4T	256D	16F-4R	84.79	5800	No
7600 4WD	28284.00	**12840.00**	**14930.00**	**16120.00**	Ford	4T	256D	16F-4R	84.79	6400	No
7700	29883.00	**13150.00**	**15840.00**	**17110.00**	Ford	4T	256D	16F-4R	84.38	7000	C,H,A
7700 4WD	35602.00	**14960.00**	**18020.00**	**19460.00**	Ford	4T	256D	16F-4R	84.38	7600	C,H,A
TW10	36890.00	**12600.00**	**15750.00**	**17170.00**	Ford	6	401D	16F-4R	110.24	11900	C,H,A
TW10 4WD	45439.00	**15840.00**	**19800.00**	**21580.00**	Ford	6	401D	16F-4R	110.00	13350	C,H,A
TW20	41344.00	**14880.00**	**18610.00**	**20290.00**	Ford	6T	401D	16F-4R	135.60	13000	C,H,A
TW20 4WD	49789.00	**17280.00**	**21600.00**	**23540.00**	Ford	6T	401D	16F-4R	135.00	14600	C,H,A
TW30	46300.00	**16200.00**	**20250.00**	**22070.00**	Ford	6TI	401D	16F-4R	163.28	14050	C,H,A
TW30 4WD	54775.00	**18280.00**	**22850.00**	**24910.00**	Ford	6TI	401D	16F-4R	163.00	14800	C,H,A
FW-20 4WD	66385.00	**20300.00**	**25370.00**	**27650.00**	Cummins	V8	555D	20F-4R		24775	C,H,A
FW-30 4WD	80497.00	**23580.00**	**29470.00**	**32120.00**	Cummins	V8	903D	20F-4R		25320	C,H,A
FW-60 4WD	95680.00	**27250.00**	**34060.00**	**37130.00**	Cummins	V8T	903D	20F-4R		26171	C,H,A

RC--Row Crop SU--Low Profile

1982

Model	Approx. Retail Price New	Fair	Good	Premium	Engine Make	No. Cyls.	Displ. Cu.-In.	No. Speeds	P.T.O. H.P.	Approx. Shipping Wt.-Lbs.	Cab
1100	5609.00	**3730.00**	**4220.00**	**4770.00**	Shibaura	2	43D	10F-2R	11.00	1131	No
1100 4WD	6126.00	**4040.00**	**4570.00**	**5160.00**	Shibaura	2	43D	10F-2R	11.00	1244	No
1200 4WD	6513.00	**4270.00**	**4840.00**	**5470.00**	Shibaura	2	43D	20F-2R	13.00	1294	No
1300	6257.00	**4050.00**	**4600.00**	**5200.00**	Shibaura	2	49D	12F-4R	13.00	1723	No
1300 4WD	6860.00	**4420.00**	**5010.00**	**5660.00**	Shibaura	2	49D	12F-4R	13.00	1984	No
1500	6745.00	**4350.00**	**4930.00**	**5570.00**	Shibaura	2	69D	12F-4R	17.00	1958	No
1500 4WD	7521.00	**4630.00**	**5250.00**	**5930.00**	Shibaura	2	69D	12F-4R	17.00	2205	No
1700	7353.00	**4530.00**	**5140.00**	**5810.00**	Shibaura	2	78D	12F-4R	23.26	2276	No
1700 4WD	8348.00	**5010.00**	**5680.00**	**6420.00**	Shibaura	2	78D	12F-4R	23.00	2513	No

Ford (Cont.)

1982 (Cont.)

Model	Approx. Retail Price New	Estimated Average Value Less Repairs Fair	Good	Premium	Engine Make	No. Cyls.	Displ. Cu.-In.	No. Speeds	P.T.O. H.P.	Approx. Shipping Wt.-Lbs.	Cab
1900	8356.00	5130.00	5820.00	6580.00	Shibaura	3	87D	12F-4R	26.88	2518	No
1900 4WD	10006.00	6000.00	6800.00	7680.00	Shibaura	3	87D	12F-4R	26.00	2750	No
2310	11391.00	5700.00	6610.00	7140.00	Ford	3	158D	8F-2R	32.00	3300	No
2610	13000.00	6500.00	7540.00	8140.00	Ford	3	158G	8F-4R	34.00	3507	No
2610	13900.00	6950.00	8060.00	8710.00	Ford	3	175D	8F-2R	36.69	3545	No
3610	15300.00	7650.00	8870.00	9580.00	Ford	3	175G	8F-4R	40.00	3715	No
3610	15613.00	7810.00	9060.00	9790.00	Ford	3	192D	8F-4R	42.47	3895	No
4110	16949.00	8480.00	9830.00	10620.00	Ford	3	201D	8F-4R	49.26	4390	No
4610	17400.00	8700.00	10090.00	10900.00	Ford	3	201G	8F-4R	52.00	4530	No
4610	17640.00	8820.00	10230.00	11050.00	Ford	3	201D	8F-4R	52.32	4760	No
5610	20653.00	9290.00	11150.00	12040.00	Ford	4	256D	16F-4R	62.54	6075	No
5610 4WD	26704.00	12020.00	14420.00	15570.00	Ford	4	256D	16F-4R	62.54	6600	No
6610	22632.00	10180.00	12220.00	13200.00	Ford	4	268D	16F-4R	72.13	6075	No
6610 4WD	28683.00	12910.00	15490.00	16730.00	Ford	4	268D	16F-4R	72.13	6600	No
6710	30962.00	13930.00	16720.00	18060.00	Ford	4	268D	16F-8R	72.00	7950	C,H,A
6710 4WD	36196.00	16290.00	19550.00	21110.00	Ford	4	268D	16F-4R	72.00	8425	C,H,A
7610	24165.00	10870.00	13050.00	14090.00	Ford	4T	268D	16F-4R	86.95	6180	No
7610 4WD	30216.00	13600.00	16320.00	17630.00	Ford	4T	268D	16F-4R	86.95	6705	No
7710	32432.00	14590.00	17510.00	18910.00	Ford	4T	268D	16F-4R	86.00	8700	C,H,A
7710 4WD	38580.00	17360.00	20830.00	22500.00	Ford	4T	268D	16F-4R	86.00	9250	C,H,A
TW10	39915.00	14770.00	18360.00	19830.00	Ford	6	401D	16F-4R	110.24	11900	C,H,A
TW10 4WD	48867.00	18080.00	22480.00	24280.00	Ford	6	401D	16F-4R	110.00	13350	C,H,A
TW20	44187.00	16350.00	20330.00	21960.00	Ford	6T	401D	16F-4R	135.60	13000	C,H,A
TW20 4WD	53139.00	18920.00	23520.00	25400.00	Ford	6T	401D	16F-4R	135.00	14600	C,H,A
TW30	49720.00	17290.00	21490.00	23210.00	Ford	6TI	401D	16F-4R	163.28	14050	C,H,A
TW30 4WD	54775.00	19530.00	24280.00	26220.00	Ford	6TI	401D	16F-4R	163.00	14800	C,H,A
FW-20 4WD	71688.00	25790.00	32060.00	34630.00	Cummins	V8	555D	20F-4R		24775	C,H,A
FW-30 4WD	86165.00	28920.00	35960.00	38840.00	Cummins	V8	903D	20F-4R		25320	C,H,A
FW-60 4WD	100313.00	31570.00	39240.00	42380.00	Cummins	V8T	903D	20F-4R		26171	C,H,A

RC--Row Crop SU--Low Profile

1983

Model	Approx. Retail Price New	Fair	Good	Premium	Make	No. Cyls.	Displ. Cu.-In.	No. Speeds	P.T.O. H.P.	Approx. Shipping Wt.-Lbs.	Cab
1110	5889.00	3860.00	4480.00	5020.00	Shibaura	2	43D	10F-2R	11.50	1282	No
1110 4WD	6432.00	4160.00	4830.00	5410.00	Shibaura	2	43D	10F-2R	11.50	1395	No
1110 H	6239.00	4050.00	4710.00	5280.00	Shibaura	2	43D	Infinite	11.50	1290	No
1110 H 4WD	6782.00	4360.00	5060.00	5670.00	Shibaura	2	43D	Infinite	11.50	1403	No
1210	6478.00	4190.00	4860.00	5440.00	Shibaura	3	54D	10F-2R	13.50	1334	No
1210 4WD	7075.00	4520.00	5250.00	5880.00	Shibaura	3	54D	10F-2R	13.50	1439	No
1210 H	6828.00	4380.00	5090.00	5700.00	Shibaura	3	54D	Infinite	13.50	1342	No
1210 H 4WD	7425.00	4720.00	5480.00	6140.00	Shibaura	3	54D	Infinite	13.50	1447	No
1310	6589.00	4250.00	4930.00	5520.00	Shibaura	3	58D	12F-4R	16.50	2064	No
1310 4WD	7203.00	4590.00	5330.00	5970.00	Shibaura	3	58D	12F-4R	16.50	2262	No
1510	7082.00	4530.00	5250.00	5880.00	Shibaura	3	68D	12F-4R	20.45	2218	No
1510 4WD	7897.00	4980.00	5780.00	6470.00	Shibaura	3	68D	12F-4R	19.50	2428	No
1710	7726.00	4890.00	5670.00	6350.00	Shibaura	3	85D	12F-4R	23.88	2340	No
1710 4WD	8765.00	5470.00	6350.00	7110.00	Shibaura	3	85D	12F-4R	23.50	2560	No
1910	8774.00	5530.00	6420.00	7190.00	Shibaura	3	104D	12F-4R	28.60	2600	No
1910 4WD	10506.00	5880.00	6830.00	7650.00	Shibaura	3	104D	12F-4R	28.60	2830	No
2310	12467.00	6360.00	7360.00	7950.00	Ford	3	158D	8F-2R	32.00	3300	No
2610	13767.00	7020.00	8120.00	8770.00	Ford	3	175D	8F-2R	36.69	3545	No
3610	15446.00	7880.00	9110.00	9840.00	Ford	3	192D	8F-2R	42.26	3845	No
4110	17124.00	8730.00	10100.00	10910.00	Ford	3	201D	8F-2R	48.33	4340	No
4610	17807.00	9080.00	10510.00	11350.00	Ford	3	201D	8F-2R	52.52	4710	No
5610	22565.00	10380.00	12410.00	13400.00	Ford	4	256D	16F-8R	62.57	6125	No
5610 4WD	27378.00	12590.00	15060.00	16270.00	Ford	4	256D	8F-2R		6000	No
5610 4WD	28368.00	13050.00	15600.00	16850.00	Ford	4	256D	16F-4R	62.54	6000	No
5610 4WD w/Cab	34492.00	15870.00	18970.00	20490.00	Ford	4	256D	16F-4R	62.54	7100	C,H,A
5610 w/Cab	28694.00	13200.00	15780.00	17040.00	Ford	4	256D	16F-8R	62.57	7225	C,H,A
6610	23914.00	11000.00	13150.00	14200.00	Ford	4	268D	16F-4R	72.13	6075	No
6610 4WD	30267.00	13920.00	16650.00	17980.00	Ford	4	268D	16F-4R	72.13	6600	No
6610 4WD w/Cab	36396.00	16740.00	20020.00	21620.00	Ford	4	268D	16F-4R	72.13	6600	C,H,A
6610 w/Cab	30043.00	13820.00	16520.00	17840.00	Ford	4	268D	16F-4R	72.13	6075	C,H,A
6710	25383.00	11680.00	13960.00	15080.00	Ford	4	268D	16F-4R	72.00	6800	No
6710 4WD	31839.00	14650.00	17510.00	18910.00	Ford	4	268D	16F-4R	72.00	7325	No
6710 w/Cab	31403.00	14450.00	17270.00	18650.00	Ford	4	268D	16F-4R	72.00	7900	C,H,A
7610	24423.00	11240.00	13430.00	14500.00	Ford	4T	268D	8F-2R	86.00	5880	No
7610 4WD	31767.00	14610.00	17470.00	18870.00	Ford	4T	268D	16F-4R	86.95	6705	No
7610 4WD w/Cab	36158.00	16630.00	19890.00	21480.00	Ford	4T	268D	16F-4R	86.95	6705	C,H
7610 w/Cab	29805.00	13710.00	16390.00	17700.00	Ford	4T	268D	16F-4R	86.95	7280	C,H
7710	27638.00	12710.00	15200.00	16420.00	Ford	4T	268D	16F-4R	86.00	7600	No
7710 4WD	34094.00	15680.00	18750.00	20250.00	Ford	4T	268D	16F-4R	86.00	8150	No
7710 4WD w/Cab	40114.00	18450.00	22060.00	23830.00	Ford	4T	268D	16F-4R	86.00	8150	C,H,A
7710 w/Cab	33658.00	15480.00	18510.00	19990.00	Ford	4T	268D	16F-4R	86.00	8700	C,H,A
TW-10	36160.00	13740.00	17000.00	18360.00	Ford	6	401D	16F-4R	110.24	10800	No
TW-10 4WD	45560.00	17310.00	21410.00	23120.00	Ford	6	401D	16F-4R	110.00	12250	No
TW-10 4WD w/Cab	51413.00	19540.00	24160.00	26090.00	Ford	6	401D	16F-4R	110.00	13350	C,H,A
TW-10 w/Cab	42013.00	15970.00	19750.00	21330.00	Ford	6	401D	16F-4R	110.00	11900	C,H,A
TW-20	40648.00	15450.00	19110.00	20640.00	Ford	6T	401D	16F-4R	135.60	11900	No
TW-20 4WD	50048.00	18260.00	22580.00	24390.00	Ford	6T	401D	16F-4R	135.00	13500	No
TW-20 4WD w/Cab	55901.00	20480.00	25330.00	27360.00	Ford	6T	401D	16F-4R	135.00	14600	C,H,A
TW-20 w/Cab	46501.00	17670.00	21860.00	23610.00	Ford	6T	401D	16F-4R	135.60	13000	C,H,A
TW-30	52277.00	17970.00	22220.00	24000.00	Ford	6TI	401D	16F-4R	163.28	14050	C,H,A
TW-30 4WD	61677.00	20780.00	25700.00	27760.00	Ford	6TI	401D	16F-4R	163.00	14800	C,H,A

RC--Row Crop SU--Low Profile H--Hydrostatic Transmission SMS--Synchronized Manual Shuttle Transmission

Ford (Cont.)

Model	Approx. Retail Price New	Estimated Average Value Less Repairs Fair	Good	Premium	Engine Make	No. Cyls.	Displ. Cu.-In.	No. Speeds	P.T.O. H.P.	Approx. Shipping Wt.-Lbs.	Cab
1984											
1110	5889.00	3930.00	4550.00	5100.00	Shibaura	2	43D	10F-2R	11.50	1282	No
1110 4WD	6432.00	4240.00	4910.00	5500.00	Shibaura	2	43D	10F-2R	11.50	1395	No
1110 H	6239.00	4130.00	4780.00	5350.00	Shibaura	2	43D	Infinite	11.50	1290	No
1110 H 4WD	6782.00	4440.00	5140.00	5760.00	Shibaura	2	43D	Infinite	11.50	1403	No
1210	6478.00	4260.00	4940.00	5530.00	Shibaura	3	54D	10F-2R	13.50	1334	No
1210 4WD	7075.00	4600.00	5330.00	5970.00	Shibaura	3	54D	10F-2R	13.50	1439	No
1210 H	6828.00	4460.00	5170.00	5790.00	Shibaura	3	54D	Infinite	13.50	1342	No
1210 H 4WD	7425.00	4800.00	5560.00	6230.00	Shibaura	3	54D	Infinite	13.50	1447	No
1310	6817.00	4460.00	5160.00	5780.00	Shibaura	3	58D	12F-4R	16.50	2064	No
1310 4WD	7567.00	4880.00	5650.00	6330.00	Shibaura	3	58D	12F-4R	16.50	2262	No
1510	7360.00	4770.00	5520.00	6180.00	Shibaura	3	68D	12F-4R	20.45	2218	No
1510 4WD	8242.00	5270.00	6100.00	6830.00	Shibaura	3	68D	12F-4R	19.50	2428	No
1710	7865.00	5050.00	5850.00	6550.00	Shibaura	3	85D	12F-4R	23.88	2340	No
1710 4WD	9012.00	5650.00	6540.00	7330.00	Shibaura	3	85D	12F-4R	23.50	2560	No
1910	9145.00	5780.00	6700.00	7500.00	Shibaura	3	104D	12F-4R	28.60	2600	No
1910 4WD	10994.00	6440.00	7450.00	8340.00	Shibaura	3	104D	12F-4R	28.60	2830	No
2110	11684.00	6830.00	7910.00	8860.00	Shibaura	4	139D	12F-4R	34.91	3460	No
2110 4WD	13454.00	7730.00	8950.00	10020.00	Shibaura	4	139D	12F-4R	34.91	3590	No
2810	12315.00	6400.00	7390.00	7980.00	Ford	3	158D	8F-2R	32.83	4363	No
2910	14128.00	7350.00	8480.00	9160.00	Ford	3	175D	8F-2R	36.62	4395	No
3910	16031.00	8340.00	9620.00	10390.00	Ford	3	192D	8F-2R	42.62	4505	No
4610	18326.00	9530.00	11000.00	11880.00	Ford	3	201D	8F-2R	52.52	4710	No
5610	22490.00	10570.00	12590.00	13600.00	Ford	4	256D	16F-4R	62.54	6075	No
5610 4WD	28015.00	13170.00	15690.00	16950.00	Ford	4	256D	16F-4R	62.54	6100	No
5610 4WD w/Cab	34328.00	16130.00	19220.00	20760.00	Ford	4	256D	16F-4R	62.54	7100	C,H,A
5610 w/Cab	28803.00	13540.00	16130.00	17420.00	Ford	4	256D	16F-4R	62.54	7175	C,H,A
6610	24177.00	11360.00	13540.00	14620.00	Ford	4	268D	8F-4R	72.00	5525	No
6610 4WD	30306.00	14240.00	16970.00	18330.00	Ford	4	268D	16F-4R	72.13	6600	No
6610 4WD w/Cab	36619.00	17210.00	20510.00	22150.00	Ford	4	268D	16F-4R	72.13	6600	C,H,A
6610 w/Cab	30944.00	14540.00	17330.00	18720.00	Ford	4	268D	16F-4R	72.13	6075	C,H,A
6710	26711.00	12550.00	14960.00	16160.00	Ford	4	268D	16F-4R	72.00	6800	No
6710 4WD	32385.00	15220.00	18140.00	19590.00	Ford	4	268D	16F-4R	72.00	7325	No
6710 w/Cab	33271.00	15640.00	18630.00	20120.00	Ford	4	268D	16F-4R	72.00	7900	C,H,A
7610	26176.00	12300.00	14660.00	15830.00	Ford	4T	268D	16F-4R	86.95	6180	No
7610 4WD	31851.00	14970.00	17840.00	19270.00	Ford	4T	268D	16F-4R	86.95	6705	No
7610 4WD w/Cab	36373.00	17100.00	20370.00	22000.00	Ford	4T	268D	16F-4R	86.95	6705	C,H
7610 w/Cab	31264.00	14690.00	17510.00	18910.00	Ford	4T	268D	16F-8R	86.00	7330	C,H
7710	27500.00	12930.00	15400.00	16630.00	Ford	4T	268D	16F-4R	86.00	7600	No
7710 4WD	33900.00	15930.00	18980.00	20500.00	Ford	4T	268D	16F-4R	86.00	8150	No
7710 4WD w/Cab	39100.00	18380.00	21900.00	23650.00	Ford	4T	268D	16F-4R	86.00	8150	C,H,A
7710 w/Cab	33800.00	15890.00	18930.00	20440.00	Ford	4T	268D	16F-4R	86.00	8700	C,H,A
TW-5	36254.00	14140.00	17400.00	18790.00	Ford	6	401D	16F-4R	105.74	10400	No
TW-5 w/Cab	42400.00	16540.00	20350.00	21980.00	Ford	6	401D	16F-4R	105.74	11500	C,H,A
TW-5 4WD	46124.00	17990.00	22140.00	23910.00	Ford	6	401D	16F-4R	105.00	11850	No
TW-5 4WD w/Cab	51300.00	18840.00	23180.00	25030.00	Ford	6	401D	16F-4R	105.00	12950	C,H,A
TW-15	40453.00	15780.00	19420.00	20970.00	Ford	6T	401D	16F-4R	121.40	11250	No
TW-15 w/Cab	46600.00	17390.00	21410.00	23120.00	Ford	6T	401D	16F-4R	121.40	12350	C,H,A
TW-15 4WD	50323.00	18850.00	23200.00	25060.00	Ford	6T	401D	16F-4R	121.25	12700	No
TW-15 4WD w/Cab	56475.00	19690.00	24230.00	26170.00	Ford	6T	401D	16F-4R	121.25	13800	C,H,A
TW-25	43731.00	16280.00	20030.00	21630.00	Ford	6T	401D	16F-4R	140.68	12250	No
TW-25 w/Cab	49877.00	18280.00	22500.00	24300.00	Ford	6T	401D	16F-4R	140.68	13350	C,H,A
TW-25 4WD	53601.00	20120.00	24770.00	26750.00	Ford	6T	401D	16F-4R	140.00	13700	No
TW-25 4WD w/Cab	59747.00	20960.00	25800.00	27860.00	Ford	6T	401D	16F-4R	140.00	14800	C,H,A
TW-35	56097.00	19540.00	24050.00	25970.00	Ford	6TI	401D	16F-4R	170.30	13800	C,H,A
TW-35 4WD	65967.00	21440.00	26380.00	28490.00	Ford	6TI	401D	16F-4R	171.12	14900	C,H,A

RC--Row Crop SU--Low Profile H--Hydrostatic Transmission SMS--Synchronized Manual Shuttle Transmission

Model	Approx. Retail Price New	Fair	Good	Premium	Make	No. Cyls.	Displ. Cu.-In.	No. Speeds	P.T.O. H.P.	Approx. Shipping Wt.-Lbs.	Cab
1985											
1110	5960.00	4040.00	4660.00	5170.00	Shibaura	2	43D	10F-2R	11.50	1282	No
1110 4WD	6475.00	4340.00	5010.00	5560.00	Shibaura	2	43D	10F-2R	11.50	1395	No
1110 H	6805.00	4530.00	5230.00	5810.00	Shibaura	2	43D	Infinite	11.50	1290	No
1110 H 4WD	6990.00	4630.00	5350.00	5940.00	Shibaura	2	43D	Infinite	11.50	1403	No
1210	6480.00	4340.00	5010.00	5560.00	Shibaura	3	54D	10F-2R	13.50	1334	No
1210 4WD	7050.00	4670.00	5390.00	5980.00	Shibaura	3	54D	10F-2R	13.50	1439	No
1210 H	7480.00	4920.00	5680.00	6310.00	Shibaura	3	54D	Infinite	13.50	1342	No
1210 H 4WD	7620.00	5000.00	5780.00	6420.00	Shibaura	3	54D	Infinite	13.50	1447	No
1310	6990.00	4630.00	5350.00	5940.00	Shibaura	3	58D	12F-4R	16.50	2064	No
1310 4WD	7760.00	4680.00	5400.00	5990.00	Shibaura	3	58D	12F-4R	16.50	2262	No
1510	7370.00	4860.00	5610.00	6230.00	Shibaura	3	68D	12F-4R	20.45	2218	No
1510 4WD	8305.00	5390.00	6230.00	6920.00	Shibaura	3	68D	12F-4R	19.50	2428	No
1710	7865.00	5140.00	5940.00	6590.00	Shibaura	3	85D	12F-4R	23.88	2340	No
1710 4WD	9015.00	5750.00	6640.00	7370.00	Shibaura	3	85D	12F-4R	23.50	2560	No
1910	9145.00	5880.00	6800.00	7550.00	Shibaura	3	104D	12F-4R	28.60	2600	No
1910 4WD	10995.00	6670.00	7700.00	8550.00	Shibaura	3	104D	12F-4R	28.60	2830	No
2110	11685.00	7070.00	8160.00	9060.00	Shibaura	4	139D	12F-4R	34.91	3460	No
2110 4WD	13455.00	7980.00	9220.00	10230.00	Shibaura	4	139D	12F-4R	34.91	3590	No
2810	12315.00	6530.00	7510.00	8110.00	Ford	3	158D	8F-2R	32.83	4363	No
2810 4WD	16725.00	8860.00	10200.00	11020.00	Ford	3	158D	6F-4R	32.00	4570	No
2910	14555.00	7710.00	8880.00	9590.00	Ford	3	175D	8F-4R	36.40	4400	No
2910 4WD	18670.00	9900.00	11390.00	12300.00	Ford	3	175D	8F-2R	36.83	4545	No
3910	16390.00	8690.00	10000.00	10800.00	Ford	3	192D	8F-4R	42.67	4510	No
3910 4WD	20860.00	11060.00	12730.00	13750.00	Ford	3	192D	8F-4R	43.25	4660	No
4610	18685.00	9900.00	11400.00	12310.00	Ford	3	201D	8F-4R	52.32	4760	No
4610 4WD	23155.00	12270.00	14130.00	15260.00	Ford	3	201D	8F-4R	52.32	4910	No

Ford (Cont.)

Model	Approx. Retail Price New	Estimated Average Value Less Repairs Fair	Good	Premium	Engine Make	No. Cyls.	Displ. Cu.-In.	No. Speeds	P.T.O. H.P.	Approx. Shipping Wt.-Lbs.	Cab
1985 (Cont.)											
5610	22490.00	10800.00	12820.00	13850.00	Ford	4	256D	16F-4R	62.54	6075	No
5610 4WD	27715.00	13300.00	15800.00	17060.00	Ford	4	256D	16F-4R	62.54	6100	No
5610 4WD w/Cab	34330.00	16480.00	19570.00	21140.00	Ford	4	256D	16F-4R	62.54	7100	C,H,A
5610 w/Cab	29375.00	14100.00	16740.00	18080.00	Ford	4	256D	16F-8R	62.57	7225	C,H,A
6610	24635.00	11830.00	14040.00	15160.00	Ford	4	268D	16F-4R	72.13	6075	No
6610 4WD	30310.00	14550.00	17280.00	18660.00	Ford	4	268D	16F-4R	72.13	6600	No
6610 4WD w/Cab	37265.00	17890.00	21240.00	22940.00	Ford	4	268D	16F-4R	72.13	6600	C,H,A
6610 w/Cab	30950.00	14860.00	17640.00	19050.00	Ford	4	268D	16F-4R	72.13	6075	C,H,A
6710	26715.00	12820.00	15230.00	16450.00	Ford	4	268D	16F-4R	72.00	6800	No
6710 4WD	32390.00	15550.00	18460.00	19940.00	Ford	4	268D	16F-4R	72.00	7325	No
6710 w/Cab	33275.00	15970.00	18970.00	20490.00	Ford	4	268D	16F-4R	72.00	7900	C,H,A
7610	26180.00	12570.00	14920.00	16110.00	Ford	4T	268D	16F-4R	86.95	6180	No
7610 4WD	31855.00	15290.00	18160.00	19610.00	Ford	4T	268D	16F-4R	86.95	6705	No
7610 4WD w/Cab	36380.00	17460.00	20740.00	22400.00	Ford	4T	268D	16F-4R	86.95	6705	C,H
7610 w/Cab	30705.00	14740.00	17500.00	18900.00	Ford	4T	268D	16F-4R	86.95	7280	C,H
7710	27500.00	13200.00	15680.00	16930.00	Ford	4T	268D	16F-4R	86.00	7600	No
7710 4WD	33900.00	16270.00	19320.00	20870.00	Ford	4T	268D	16F-4R	86.00	8150	No
7710 4WD w/Cab	39160.00	18800.00	22320.00	24110.00	Ford	4T	268D	16F-4R	86.00	8150	C,H,A
7710 w/Cab	33800.00	16220.00	19270.00	20810.00	Ford	4T	268D	16F-4R	86.00	8700	C,H,A
TW-5	36255.00	14000.00	17150.00	18350.00	Ford	6	401D	16F-4R	105.74	10400	No
TW-5 w/Cab	42400.00	16160.00	19800.00	21190.00	Ford	6	401D	16F-4R	105.74	11500	C,H,A
TW-5 4WD	46125.00	18000.00	22050.00	23590.00	Ford	6	401D	16F-4R	105.74	11850	No
TW-5 4WD w/Cab	51300.00	20000.00	24500.00	26220.00	Ford	6	401D	16F-4R	105.74	12950	C,H,A
TW-15	40455.00	15760.00	19310.00	20660.00	Ford	6T	401D	16F-4R	121.40	11250	No
TW-15 w/Cab	46605.00	18000.00	22050.00	23590.00	Ford	6T	401D	16F-4R	121.40	12350	C,H,A
TW-15 4WD	50325.00	19400.00	23770.00	25430.00	Ford	6T	401D	16F-4R	121.25	12700	No
TW-15 4WD w/Cab	56475.00	20990.00	25710.00	27510.00	Ford	6T	401D	16F-4R	121.25	13800	C,H,A
TW-25	43735.00	17490.00	21430.00	22930.00	Ford	6T	401D	16F-4R	140.68	12250	No
TW-25 w/Cab	49880.00	19550.00	23950.00	25630.00	Ford	6T	401D	16F-4R	140.68	13350	C,H,A
TW-25 4WD	53605.00	21040.00	25770.00	27570.00	Ford	6T	401D	16F-4R	140.00	13700	No
TW-25 4WD w/Cab	59750.00	21900.00	26830.00	28710.00	Ford	6T	401D	16F-4R	140.00	14800	C,H,A
TW-35	56100.00	20040.00	24550.00	26270.00	Ford	6T	401D	16F-4R	170.30	13800	C,H,A
TW-35 4WD	65970.00	22390.00	27430.00	29350.00	Ford	6T	401D	16F-4R	171.12	14900	C,H,A

RC--Row Crop SU--Low Profile H--Hydrostatic Transmission SMS--Synchronized Manual Shuttle Transmission

Model	Approx. Retail Price New	Fair	Good	Premium	Engine Make	No. Cyls.	Displ. Cu.-In.	No. Speeds	P.T.O. H.P.	Approx. Shipping Wt.-Lbs.	Cab
1986											
1110	5960.00	4110.00	4730.00	5250.00	Shibaura	2	43D	10F-2R	11.50	1223	No
1110 4WD	6475.00	4410.00	5080.00	5640.00	Shibaura	2	43D	10F-2R	11.50	1395	No
1110 H	6805.00	4610.00	5310.00	5890.00	Shibaura	2	43D	Infinite	11.50	1231	No
1110 H 4WD	6990.00	4710.00	5430.00	6030.00	Shibaura	2	43D	Infinite	11.50	1403	No
1210	6765.00	4580.00	5280.00	5860.00	Shibaura	3	54D	10F-2R	13.50	1323	No
1210 4WD	7560.00	4520.00	5210.00	5780.00	Shibaura	3	54D	10F-2R	13.50	1439	No
1210 H	7884.00	5240.00	6040.00	6700.00	Shibaura	3	54D	Infinite	13.50	1342	No
1210 H 4WD	8679.00	5710.00	6580.00	7300.00	Shibaura	3	54D	Infinite	13.50	1447	No
1310	7428.00	4970.00	5730.00	6360.00	Shibaura	3	58D	12F-4R	16.50	2063	No
1310 4WD	8249.00	5460.00	6290.00	6980.00	Shibaura	3	58D	12F-4R	16.50	2262	No
1510	7500.00	5020.00	5780.00	6420.00	Shibaura	3	68D	12F-4R	20.45	2230	No
1510 4WD	8432.00	5570.00	6410.00	7120.00	Shibaura	3	68D	12F-4R	19.50	2440	No
1710	8430.00	5640.00	6500.00	7220.00	Shibaura	3	85D	12F-4R	23.88	2470	No
1710 4WD	9636.00	6280.00	7230.00	8030.00	Shibaura	3	85D	12F-4R	23.50	2640	No
1910	9369.00	6120.00	7050.00	7830.00	Shibaura	3	104D	12F-4R	28.60	2980	No
1910 4WD	11515.00	7030.00	8100.00	8990.00	Shibaura	3	104D	12F-4R	28.60	3245	No
2110	11917.00	7270.00	8380.00	9300.00	Shibaura	4	139D	12F-4R	34.91	3635	No
2110 4WD	13722.00	8270.00	9540.00	10590.00	Shibaura	4	139D	12F-4R	34.91	3946	No
2810	12845.00	6940.00	7960.00	8600.00	Ford	3	158D	8F-2R	32.83	4333	No
2810 4WD	16969.00	9160.00	10520.00	11360.00	Ford	3	158D	8F-2R	32.00	4868	No
2910	14585.00	7880.00	9040.00	9760.00	Ford	3	175D	8F-4R	36.40	4485	No
2910 4WD	19050.00	10290.00	11810.00	12760.00	Ford	3	175D	8F-4R	36.66	5020	No
3910	16350.00	8830.00	10140.00	10950.00	Ford	3	192D	8F-4R	42.67	4547	No
3910 4WD	20800.00	11230.00	12900.00	13930.00	Ford	3	192D	8F-4R	43.25	5182	No
4610	18737.00	10120.00	11620.00	12550.00	Ford	3	201D	8F-4R	52.32	4914	No
4610 4WD	23205.00	12530.00	14390.00	15540.00	Ford	3	201D	8F-4R	52.32	5449	No
5610	22040.00	10800.00	12780.00	13800.00	Ford	4	256D	8F-4R	62.00	6041	No
5610 4WD	27363.00	13410.00	15870.00	17140.00	Ford	4	256D	8F-4R	62.00	6593	No
5610 4WD w/Cab	34733.00	17020.00	20150.00	21760.00	Ford	4	256D	16F-8R	62.00	8016	C,H,A
5610 w/Cab	29908.00	14660.00	17350.00	18740.00	Ford	4	256D	16F-8R	62.57	7479	C,H,A
6610	25300.00	12400.00	14670.00	15840.00	Ford	4	268D	16F-8R	72.30	6146	No
6610 4WD	30975.00	15180.00	17970.00	19410.00	Ford	4	268D	16F-8R	72.00	6683	No
6610 4WD w/Cab	37200.00	18230.00	21580.00	23310.00	Ford	4	268D	16F-8R	72.13	8013	C,H,A
6610 w/Cab	31515.00	15440.00	18280.00	19740.00	Ford	4	268D	16F-8R	72.30	7476	C,H,A
7610	26925.00	13190.00	15620.00	16870.00	Ford	4T	268D	16F-8R	86.00	6356	No
7610 4WD	32600.00	15970.00	18910.00	20420.00	Ford	4T	268D	16F-8R	86.00	6967	No
7710	28028.00	13730.00	16260.00	17560.00	Ford	4T	268D	16F-8R	86.62	7234	No
7710 4WD	33861.00	16590.00	19640.00	21210.00	Ford	4T	268D	16F-8R	86.62	7835	No
7710 4WD w/Cab	40276.00	19740.00	23360.00	25230.00	Ford	4T	268D	16F-8R	86.62	8865	C,H,A
7710 w/Cab	34443.00	16880.00	19980.00	21580.00	Ford	4T	268D	16F-8R	86.62	8264	C,H,A
8210 4WD	36623.00	15020.00	18310.00	19590.00	Ford	6	401D	16F-8R	95.00	8395	No
8210 4WD w/Cab	42356.00	17370.00	21180.00	22660.00	Ford	6	401D	16F-8R	95.00	9425	C,H,A
TW-5	36529.00	14980.00	18270.00	19550.00	Ford	6	401D	16F-4R	105.74	11722	No
TW-5 w/Cab	42465.00	17220.00	21000.00	22470.00	Ford	6	401D	16F-4R	105.74	12510	C,H,A
TW-5 4WD w/Cab	51324.00	20500.00	25000.00	26750.00	Ford	6	401D	16F-4R	105.74	13609	C,H,A
TW-15	40719.00	16700.00	20360.00	21790.00	Ford	6T	401D	16F-4R	121.40	11754	No
TW-15 w/Cab	46655.00	18450.00	22500.00	24080.00	Ford	6T	401D	16F-4R	121.40	12542	C,H,A
TW-15 4WD	50325.00	20090.00	24500.00	26220.00	Ford	6T	401D	16F-4R	121.25	12813	No

Ford (Cont.)

1986 (Cont.)

Model	Approx. Retail Price New	Estimated Average Value Less Repairs: Fair	Good	Premium	Engine Make	No. Cyls.	Displ. Cu.-In.	No. Speeds	P.T.O. H.P.	Approx. Shipping Wt.-Lbs.	Cab
TW-15 4WD w/Cab	56475.00	22340.00	27240.00	29150.00	Ford	6T	401D	16F-4R	121.25	13661	C,H,A
TW-25	44573.00	18280.00	22290.00	23850.00	Ford	6T	401D	16F-4R	140.68	13649	No
TW-25 w/Cab	50509.00	20710.00	25260.00	27030.00	Ford	6T	401D	16F-4R	140.68	14437	C,H,A
TW-25 4WD	53605.00	21440.00	26150.00	27980.00	Ford	6T	401D	16F-4R	140.00	14300	No
TW-25 4WD w/Cab	59750.00	22860.00	27880.00	29830.00	Ford	6T	401D	16F-4R	140.00	14746	C,H,A
TW-35	56620.00	21160.00	25810.00	27620.00	Ford	6T	401D	16F-4R	170.30	14383	C,H,A
TW-35 4WD	66491.00	23160.00	28250.00	30230.00	Ford	6T	401D	16F-4R	171.12	15652	C,H,A

RC--Row Crop SU--Low Profile H--Hydrostatic Transmission SMS--Synchronized Manual Shuttle Transmission
See New Holland/Ford for later models.

Hesston-Fiat

1981

Model	Approx. Retail Price New	Fair	Good	Premium	Make	No. Cyls.	Displ. Cu.-In.	No. Speeds	P.T.O. H.P.	Approx. Shipping Wt.-Lbs.	Cab
480-8	13050.00	3260.00	4440.00	4970.00	Fiat	3	158D	8F-2R	42.58	4215	No
480-8 DT	17205.00	4300.00	5850.00	6550.00	Fiat	3	158D	8F-2R	42.58	4835	No
580	16320.00	4080.00	5550.00	6220.00	Fiat	3	168D	8F-2R	51.61	5110	No
580 DT	21000.00	5250.00	7140.00	8000.00	Fiat	3	168D	8F-2R	51.61	5670	No
640	16685.00	4170.00	5670.00	6350.00	Fiat	4	211D	8F-2R	62.00	4790	No
640 DT	21650.00	5250.00	7140.00	8000.00	Fiat	4	211D	8F-2R	62.00	5410	No
680	18200.00	4550.00	6190.00	6930.00	Fiat	4	211D	8F-2R	62.47	5405	No
680 DT	23395.00	5500.00	7480.00	8380.00	Fiat	4	211D	8F-2R	62.47	5965	No
780	20245.00	4800.00	6530.00	7310.00	Fiat	4	224D	8F-2R	70.57	5495	No
780 DT	26075.00	6250.00	8500.00	9520.00	Fiat	4	224D	8F-2R	70.57	6055	No
880-5	28065.00	6500.00	8840.00	9900.00	Fiat	5	280D	12F-3R	81.32	6935	C,H,A
880-5 DT	33970.00	7250.00	9860.00	11040.00	Fiat	5	280D	12F-3R	81.32	7910	C,H,A
980	29940.00	6750.00	9180.00	10280.00	Fiat	6	316D	12F-3R	91.12	7310	C,H,A
980 DT	37645.00	8500.00	11560.00	12950.00	Fiat	6	316D	12F-3R	91.12	8440	C,H,A
1180	33250.00	7300.00	9930.00	11120.00	Fiat	6	335D	12F-4R	102.00	11730	C,H,A
1180 DT	41250.00	9000.00	12240.00	13710.00	Fiat	6	335D	12F-4R	102.00	13030	C,H,A
1380	36800.00	7550.00	10270.00	11500.00	Fiat	6T	335D	12F-4R	123.16	12015	C,H,A
1380 DT	44950.00	9750.00	13260.00	14850.00	Fiat	6T	335D	12F-4R	123.16	13890	C,H,A
1880	47200.00	10550.00	14350.00	16070.00	Fiat	6T	494D	12F-4R	162.48	13445	C,H,A
1880 DT	55600.00	12080.00	16420.00	18390.00	Fiat	6T	494D	12F-4R	162.48	14440	C,H,A

1982

Model	Approx. Retail Price New	Fair	Good	Premium	Make	No. Cyls.	Displ. Cu.-In.	No. Speeds	P.T.O. H.P.	Approx. Shipping Wt.-Lbs.	Cab
480-8	13900.00	3610.00	4870.00	5450.00	Fiat	3	158D	8F-2R	42.58	4215	No
480-8 DT	18100.00	4710.00	6340.00	7100.00	Fiat	3	158D	8F-2R	42.58	4835	No
580	16320.00	4240.00	5710.00	6400.00	Fiat	3	168D	8F-2R	51.61	5110	No
580 DT	21000.00	5460.00	7350.00	8230.00	Fiat	3	168D	8F-2R	51.61	5670	No
640	16685.00	4340.00	5840.00	6540.00	Fiat	4	211D	8F-2R	62.00	4790	No
640 DT	21650.00	5630.00	7580.00	8490.00	Fiat	4	211D	8F-2R	62.00	5410	No
680	19100.00	4970.00	6690.00	7490.00	Fiat	4	211D	8F-2R	62.47	5405	No
680 DT	24600.00	6080.00	8190.00	9170.00	Fiat	4	211D	8F-2R	62.47	5965	No
780	20990.00	5460.00	7350.00	8230.00	Fiat	4	224D	8F-2R	70.57	5495	No
780 DT	24500.00	5980.00	8050.00	9020.00	Fiat	4	224D	8F-2R	70.57	6055	No
880-5	29400.00	7020.00	9450.00	10580.00	Fiat	5	280D	12F-3R	81.32	6935	C,H,A
880-5 DT	35900.00	8110.00	10920.00	12230.00	Fiat	5	280D	12F-3R	81.32	7910	C,H,A
980	32980.00	7540.00	10150.00	11370.00	Fiat	6	316D	12F-3R	91.12	7310	C,H,A
980 DT	40200.00	8890.00	11970.00	13410.00	Fiat	6	316D	12F-3R	91.12	8440	C,H,A
1180	33250.00	7070.00	9520.00	10660.00	Fiat	6	335D	12F-4R	102.00	11730	C,H,A
1180 DT	41250.00	9150.00	12320.00	13800.00	Fiat	6	335D	12F-4R	102.00	13030	C,H,A
1180 Turbo	36900.00	7900.00	10640.00	11920.00	Fiat	6T	335D	12F-4R		11880	C,H,A
1180 DT Turbo	44900.00	10140.00	13650.00	15290.00	Fiat	6T	335D	12F-4R		13180	C,H,A
1380	39650.00	8840.00	11900.00	13330.00	Fiat	6T	335D	12F-4R	123.16	12015	C,H,A
1380 DT	48650.00	10920.00	14700.00	16460.00	Fiat	6T	335D	12F-4R	123.16	13890	C,H,A
1580	41900.00	9200.00	12390.00	13880.00	Fiat	6	494D	12F-4R	138.00	13225	C,H,A
1580 DT	49900.00	11260.00	15160.00	16980.00	Fiat	6	494D	12F-4R	138.00	14220	C,H,A
1880	51500.00	11830.00	15930.00	17840.00	Fiat	6T	494D	12F-4R	162.48	13445	C,H,A
1880 DT	59500.00	13130.00	17680.00	19800.00	Fiat	6T	494D	12F-4R	162.48	14440	C,H,A

1983

Model	Approx. Retail Price New	Fair	Good	Premium	Make	No. Cyls.	Displ. Cu.-In.	No. Speeds	P.T.O. H.P.	Approx. Shipping Wt.-Lbs.	Cab
466	14870.00	4020.00	5350.00	5990.00	Fiat	3	158D	12F-4R	45.13	4851	No
466	15320.00	4140.00	5520.00	6180.00	Fiat	3	158D	20F-8R	45.00	5101	No
466	15535.00	4190.00	5590.00	6260.00	Fiat	3	158D	12F-12R	45.00	5101	No
466 DT 4WD	19240.00	5200.00	6930.00	7760.00	Fiat	3	158D	12F-4R	45.13	5402	No
480-8	13900.00	3750.00	5000.00	5600.00	Fiat	3	158D	8F-2R	42.58	4215	No
480-8 DT 4WD	18100.00	4890.00	6520.00	7300.00	Fiat	3	158D	8F-2R	42.58	4835	No
566	16065.00	4340.00	5780.00	6470.00	Fiat	3	168D	12F-4R	51.00	4901	No
566 DT 4WD	20400.00	5510.00	7340.00	8220.00	Fiat	3	168D	12F-4R	51.00	5452	No
580	17300.00	4670.00	6230.00	6980.00	Fiat	3	168D	8F-2R	51.61	5110	No
580 DT 4WD	21800.00	5620.00	7490.00	8390.00	Fiat	3	168D	8F-2R	51.61	5670	No
580 DT 4WD w/Cab	27550.00	6890.00	9180.00	10280.00	Fiat	3	168D	8F-2R	51.61	6770	C,H,A
580 w/Cab	23050.00	5940.00	7920.00	8870.00	Fiat	3	168D	8F-2R	51.61	6210	C,H,A
640	16685.00	4510.00	6010.00	6730.00	Fiat	4	211D	8F-2R	62.00	4790	No
640 DT 4WD	21650.00	5450.00	7270.00	8140.00	Fiat	4	211D	8F-2R	62.00	5410	No
666	18065.00	4880.00	6500.00	7280.00	Fiat	4	211D	12F-4R	62.40	5689	No
666 DT 4WD	22800.00	5750.00	7670.00	8590.00	Fiat	4	211D	12F-4R	62.40	6350	No
680	19900.00	5130.00	6840.00	7660.00	Fiat	4	211D	8F-2R	62.47	5405	No
680 DT 4WD	24600.00	6290.00	8390.00	9400.00	Fiat	4	211D	8F-2R	62.47	5965	No
680 DT 4WD w/Cab	30350.00	7290.00	9720.00	10890.00	Fiat	4	211D	8F-2R	62.47	7065	C,H,A
680 w/Cab	25650.00	6480.00	8640.00	9680.00	Fiat	4	211D	8F-2R	62.47	6505	C,H,A
780	21900.00	5450.00	7270.00	8140.00	Fiat	4	224D	8F-2R	70.57	5495	No
780 DT 4WD	27500.00	6800.00	9070.00	10160.00	Fiat	4	224D	8F-2R	70.57	6055	No

Hesston-Fiat (Cont.)

1983 (Cont.)

Model	Approx. Retail Price New	Fair	Good	Premium	Make	Engine No. Cyls.	Engine Displ. Cu.-In.	No. Speeds	P.T.O. H.P.	Approx. Shipping Wt.-Lbs.	Cab
780 DT 4WD w/Cab	33250.00	7910.00	10550.00	11820.00	Fiat	4	224D	8F-2R	70.57	7155	C,H,A
780 w/Cab	27650.00	6480.00	8640.00	9680.00	Fiat	4	224D	8F-2R	70.57	6595	C,H,A
880-5	30900.00	6860.00	9140.00	10240.00	Fiat	5	280D	12F-3R	81.32	6935	C,H,A
880-5 DT 4WD	35900.00	8100.00	10800.00	12100.00	Fiat	5	280D	12F-3R	81.32	7910	C,H,A
980	34795.00	7830.00	10440.00	11690.00	Fiat	6	316D	12F-3R	91.12	7310	C,H,A
980 DT 4WD	40200.00	9180.00	12240.00	13710.00	Fiat	6	316D	12F-3R	91.12	8440	C,H,A
1180	39670.00	8420.00	11230.00	12580.00	Fiat	6T	335D	12F-4R	107.48	11730	C,H,A
1180 DT 4WD	48270.00	10800.00	14400.00	16130.00	Fiat	6T	335D	12F-4R	107.48	13030	C,H,A
1380	42625.00	8690.00	11590.00	12980.00	Fiat	6T	335D	12F-4R	123.16	12015	C,H,A
1380 DT 4WD	52300.00	12150.00	16200.00	18140.00	Fiat	6T	335D	12F-4R	123.16	13890	C,H,A
1580	43000.00	9720.00	12960.00	14520.00	Fiat	6	494D	12F-4R	141.44	13225	C,H,A
1580 DT 4WD	53000.00	11880.00	15840.00	17740.00	Fiat	6	494D	12F-4R	141.44	14220	C,H,A
1880	53820.00	12020.00	16020.00	17940.00	Fiat	6T	494D	12F-4R	162.48	13445	C,H,A
1880 DT 4WD	62900.00	14090.00	18790.00	21050.00	Fiat	6T	494D	12F-4R	162.48	14440	C,H,A

1984

Model	Approx. Retail Price New	Fair	Good	Premium	Make	Engine No. Cyls.	Engine Displ. Cu.-In.	No. Speeds	P.T.O. H.P.	Approx. Shipping Wt.-Lbs.	Cab
466	14870.00	4160.00	5500.00	6160.00	Fiat	3	158D	12F-4R	45.13	4851	No
466 DT 4WD	19240.00	5390.00	7120.00	7970.00	Fiat	3	158D	12F-4R	45.13	5402	No
566	16065.00	4500.00	5940.00	6650.00	Fiat	3	168D	12F-4R	51.00	4901	No
566 DT 4WD	20400.00	5710.00	7550.00	8460.00	Fiat	3	168D	12F-4R	51.00	5452	No
580	17300.00	4840.00	6400.00	7170.00	Fiat	3	168D	8F-2R	51.61	5110	No
580 DT 4WD	21800.00	6100.00	8070.00	9040.00	Fiat	3	168D	8F-2R	51.61	5670	No
580 DT 4WD w/Cab	27550.00	7140.00	9440.00	10570.00	Fiat	3	168D	8F-2R	51.61	6770	C,H,A
580 w/Cab	23050.00	6160.00	8140.00	9120.00	Fiat	3	168D	8F-2R	51.61	6210	C,H,A
666	18065.00	5060.00	6680.00	7480.00	Fiat	4	211D	12F-4R	62.40	5689	No
666 DT 4WD	22800.00	5990.00	7920.00	8870.00	Fiat	4	211D	12F-4R	62.40	6350	No
680	19900.00	5260.00	6960.00	7800.00	Fiat	4	211D	8F-2R	62.47	5405	No
680 DT 4WD	24600.00	6610.00	8730.00	9780.00	Fiat	4	211D	8F-2R	62.47	5965	No
680 DT 4WD w/Cab	30350.00	7900.00	10430.00	11680.00	Fiat	4	211D	8F-2R	62.47	7065	C,H,A
680 w/Cab	25650.00	6860.00	9070.00	10160.00	Fiat	4	211D	8F-2R	62.47	6505	C,H,A
766	21500.00	5660.00	7470.00	8370.00	Fiat	4	224D	12F-4R	70.00	5800	No
766 DT 4WD	26235.00	7000.00	9250.00	10360.00	Fiat	4	224D	12F-4R	70.00	6200	No
780	21900.00	5660.00	7470.00	8370.00	Fiat	4	224D	8F-2R	70.57	5495	No
780 DT 4WD	27500.00	7000.00	9250.00	10360.00	Fiat	4	224D	8F-2R	70.57	6055	No
780 DT 4WD w/Cab	33250.00	8400.00	11100.00	12430.00	Fiat	4	224D	8F-2R	70.57	7155	C,H,A
780 w/Cab	27650.00	6830.00	9030.00	10110.00	Fiat	4	224D	8F-2R	70.57	6595	C,H,A
880-5	30900.00	7560.00	9990.00	11190.00	Fiat	5	280D	12F-3R	81.32	6935	C,H,A
880-5 DT 4WD	35900.00	8960.00	11840.00	13260.00	Fiat	5	280D	12F-3R	81.32	7910	C,H,A
980	34795.00	8680.00	11470.00	12850.00	Fiat	6	316D	12F-3R	91.12	7310	C,H,A
980 DT 4WD	40200.00	10080.00	13320.00	14920.00	Fiat	6	316D	12F-3R	91.12	8440	C,H,A
1180 DT Turbo 4WD	48270.00	12320.00	16280.00	18230.00	Fiat	6T	335D	12F-4R	107.48	13030	C,H,A
1180 Turbo	39670.00	9800.00	12950.00	14500.00	Fiat	6T	335D	12F-4R	107.48	11730	C,H,A
1180 Turbo	40395.00	10080.00	13320.00	14920.00	Fiat	6T	335D	12F-12R	107.00	11980	C,H,A
1380	42625.00	10530.00	13910.00	15580.00	Fiat	6T	335D	12F-4R	123.16	12015	C,H,A
1380 DT 4WD	52300.00	12880.00	17020.00	19060.00	Fiat	6T	335D	12F-4R	123.16	13890	C,H,A
1580 DT Turbo 4WD	53000.00	13160.00	17390.00	19480.00	Fiat	6	494D	12F-4R	141.44	14220	C,H,A
1580 DT Turbo 4WD	53725.00	13330.00	17610.00	19720.00	Fiat	6	494D	12F-4R	141.00	14470	C,H,A
1580 Turbo	43000.00	10420.00	13760.00	15410.00	Fiat	6	494D	12F-4R	141.44	13225	C,H,A
1880	53820.00	12320.00	16280.00	18230.00	Fiat	6T	494D	12F-4R	162.48	13445	C,H,A
1880 DT 4WD	62900.00	14560.00	19240.00	21550.00	Fiat	6T	494D	12F-4R	162.48	14440	C,H,A

1985

Model	Approx. Retail Price New	Fair	Good	Premium	Make	Engine No. Cyls.	Engine Displ. Cu.-In.	No. Speeds	P.T.O. H.P.	Approx. Shipping Wt.-Lbs.	Cab
45-66	14500.00	4350.00	5510.00	6120.00	Fiat	3	158D	12F-4R	39.00	4850	No
45-66 DT 4WD	18800.00	5640.00	7140.00	7930.00	Fiat	3	158D	12F-4R	39.00	5450	No
55-66	17395.00	5220.00	6610.00	7340.00	Fiat	3	165D	12F-4R	45.78	4850	No
55-66 DT 4WD	22080.00	6300.00	7980.00	8860.00	Fiat	3	165D	12F-4R	45.00	5450	No
60-66	18980.00	5690.00	7210.00	8000.00	Fiat	3	179D	12F-4R	51.49	4900	No
60-66 DT 4WD	23310.00	6600.00	8360.00	9280.00	Fiat	3	179D	12F-4R	51.49	5455	No
60-90	27300.00	7590.00	9610.00	10670.00	Fiat	3	179D	12F-4R	51.00	6295	C,H,A
60-90 DT 4WD	31440.00	8820.00	11170.00	12400.00	Fiat	3	179D	12F-4R	51.00	6755	C,H,A
70-66	21140.00	6060.00	7680.00	8530.00	Fiat	4	220D	12F-4R	62.72	5690	No
70-66 DT 4WD	25910.00	7020.00	8890.00	9870.00	Fiat	4	220D	12F-4R	62.72	6350	No
70-90	29835.00	8100.00	10260.00	11390.00	Fiat	4	220D	12F-4R	62.25	6800	C,H,A
70-90 DT 4WD	34680.00	9300.00	11780.00	13080.00	Fiat	4	220D	12F-4R	62.00	7440	C,H,A
80-66	24220.00	6660.00	8440.00	9370.00	Fiat	4	238D	12F-4R	70.43	5800	No
80-66 DT 4WD	30075.00	8190.00	10370.00	11510.00	Fiat	4	238D	12F-4R	70.43	6450	No
80-90	32200.00	8820.00	11170.00	12400.00	Fiat	4	238D	12F-4R	70.86	6800	C,H,A
80-90 DT 4WD	37940.00	10020.00	12690.00	14090.00	Fiat	4	238D	12F-4R	70.00	7640	C,H,A
90-90	28945.00	7800.00	9880.00	10970.00	Fiat	5	298D	15F-3R	81.00	7410	C,H,A
90-90 DT 4WD	34630.00	9300.00	11780.00	13080.00	Fiat	5	298D	15F-3R	81.00	8125	C,H,A
100-90	31310.00	8190.00	10370.00	11510.00	Fiat	6	331D	15F-3R	91.52	7780	C,H,A
100-90 DT 4WD	37075.00	9900.00	12540.00	13920.00	Fiat	6	331D	15F-3R	91.52	8625	C,H,A
130-90	46875.00	12420.00	15730.00	17460.00	Fiat	6	358D	16F-16R	107.48	11800	C,H,A
130-90 DT 4WD	57040.00	15600.00	19760.00	21930.00	Fiat	6	358D	16F-16R	107.48	13100	C,H,A
140-90	51345.00	13800.00	17480.00	19400.00	Fiat	6T	358D	16F-16R	123.35	12015	C,H,A
140-90 DT 4WD	61800.00	16500.00	20900.00	23200.00	Fiat	6T	358D	16F-16R	123.35	13340	C,H,A
160-90	54050.00	14520.00	18390.00	20410.00	Fiat	6T	494D	16F-16R	143.91	13350	C,H,A
160-90	54790.00	14700.00	18620.00	20670.00	Fiat	6T	494D	24F-8R	143.91	13400	C,H,A
160-90 DT 4WD	64435.00	16320.00	20670.00	22940.00	Fiat	6T	494D	16F-16R	143.91	14220	C,H,A
160-90 DT 4WD PS	66785.00	16800.00	21280.00	23620.00	Fiat	6T	494D	16F-16R	143.91	14370	C,H,A
160-90 PS	56400.00	14100.00	17860.00	19830.00	Fiat	6T	494D	16F-16R	142.64	13500	C,H,A
180-90	61160.00	15330.00	19420.00	21560.00	Fiat	6T	494D	16F-16R	162.15	13450	C,H,A
180-90 DT 4WD	72180.00	18600.00	23560.00	26150.00	Fiat	6T	494D	16F-16R	162.87	14320	C,H,A
180-90 DT 4WD PS	74530.00	19200.00	24320.00	27000.00	Fiat	6T	494D	16F-16R	162.15	14470	C,H,A

Hesston-Fiat (Cont.)

1985 (Cont.)

Model	Approx. Retail Price New	Estimated Average Value Less Repairs Fair	Good	Premium	Engine Make	No. Cyls.	Displ. Cu.-In.	No. Speeds	P.T.O. H.P.	Approx. Shipping Wt.-Lbs.	Cab
180-90 PS	63510.00	15900.00	20140.00	22360.00	Fiat	6T	494D	16F-16R	162.87	13600	C,H,A

PS--Power Shift

1986

Model	Approx. Retail Price New	Estimated Average Value Less Repairs Fair	Good	Premium	Engine Make	No. Cyls.	Displ. Cu.-In.	No. Speeds	P.T.O. H.P.	Approx. Shipping Wt.-Lbs.	Cab
45-66	14500.00	4640.00	5660.00	6280.00	Fiat	3	165D	12F-4R	39.49	3674	No
45-66 DT 4WD	18800.00	6020.00	7330.00	8140.00	Fiat	3	165D	12F-4R	39.49	4114	No
55-66	17395.00	5570.00	6780.00	7530.00	Fiat	3	165D	12F-4R	45.78	4850	No
55-66 DT 4WD	22080.00	7070.00	8610.00	9560.00	Fiat	3	165D	12F-4R	45.00	5450	No
60-66	18980.00	6070.00	7400.00	8210.00	Fiat	3	179D	12F-4R	51.49	4900	No
60-66 DT 4WD	23310.00	6780.00	8270.00	9180.00	Fiat	3	179D	12F-4R	51.49	5455	No
60-90	27300.00	8000.00	9750.00	10820.00	Fiat	3	179D	12F-4R	51.00	6295	C,H,A
60-90 DT 4WD	31440.00	8960.00	10920.00	12120.00	Fiat	3	179D	12F-4R	51.00	6755	C,H,A
70-66	21140.00	6400.00	7800.00	8660.00	Fiat	4	220D	12F-4R	62.72	5690	No
70-66 DT 4WD	25910.00	7520.00	9170.00	10180.00	Fiat	4	220D	12F-4R	62.72	6350	No
70-66 DT 4WD	26450.00	7840.00	9560.00	10610.00	Fiat	4	220D	20F-8R	62.00	6400	No
70-90	29835.00	8640.00	10530.00	11690.00	Fiat	4	220D	12F-4R	62.25	6800	C,H,A
70-90 DT 4WD	34680.00	9920.00	12090.00	13420.00	Fiat	4	220D	12F-4R	62.00	7440	C,H,A
80-66	24220.00	7100.00	8660.00	9610.00	Fiat	4	238D	12F-4R	70.43	5800	No
80-66 DT 4WD	30075.00	8640.00	10530.00	11690.00	Fiat	4	238D	12F-4R	70.43	6450	No
80-90	32200.00	8960.00	10920.00	12120.00	Fiat	4	238D	12F-4R	70.86	6800	C,H,A
80-90 DT 4WD	37940.00	10340.00	12600.00	13990.00	Fiat	4	238D	12F-4R	70.00	7640	C,H,A
90-90	35322.00	9660.00	11780.00	13080.00	Fiat	5	298D	15F-3R	81.00	7410	C,H,A
90-90 DT 4WD	41003.00	11840.00	14430.00	16020.00	Fiat	5	298D	15F-3R	81.00	8125	C,H,A
100-90	37298.00	10560.00	12870.00	14290.00	Fiat	6	331D	15F-3R	91.52	7780	C,H,A
100-90 DT 4WD	43061.00	12480.00	15210.00	16880.00	Fiat	6	331D	15F-3R	91.52	8625	C,H,A
130-90	46875.00	13120.00	15990.00	17750.00	Fiat	6	358D	16F-16R	107.48	11800	C,H,A
130-90 DT 4WD	57040.00	16320.00	19890.00	22080.00	Fiat	6	358D	16F-16R	107.48	13100	C,H,A
140-90	51345.00	14720.00	17940.00	19910.00	Fiat	6T	358D	16F-16R	123.35	12015	C,H,A
140-90 DT 4WD	61800.00	18180.00	22150.00	24590.00	Fiat	6T	358D	16F-16R	123.35	13340	C,H,A
160-90	54050.00	15680.00	19110.00	21210.00	Fiat	6T	494D	16F-16R	143.91	13350	C,H,A
160-90 PS	56400.00	16450.00	20050.00	22260.00	Fiat	6T	494D	16F-16R	142.64	13500	C,H,A
160-90 PS 4WD	66783.00	19100.00	23280.00	25840.00	Fiat	6T	494D	16F-16R	142.64	13500	C,H,A
180-90 4WD	72915.00	19840.00	24180.00	26840.00	Fiat	6T	494D	24F-8R	162.00	13500	C,H,A
180-90 PS	63507.00	17120.00	20870.00	23170.00	Fiat	6T	494D	16F-16R	162.15	13500	C,H,A

PS--Power Shift

1987

Model	Approx. Retail Price New	Estimated Average Value Less Repairs Fair	Good	Premium	Engine Make	No. Cyls.	Displ. Cu.-In.	No. Speeds	P.T.O. H.P.	Approx. Shipping Wt.-Lbs.	Cab
45-66	14500.00	4930.00	5800.00	6380.00	Fiat	3	165D	12F-4R	39.49	3674	No
45-66 DT 4WD	18800.00	6390.00	7520.00	8270.00	Fiat	3	165D	12F-4R	39.49	4114	No
55-66	17395.00	5910.00	6960.00	7660.00	Fiat	3	165D	12F-4R	45.78	4850	No
55-66 DT 4WD	22080.00	7510.00	8830.00	9710.00	Fiat	3	165D	12F-4R	45.00	5450	No
60-66	18980.00	6450.00	7590.00	8350.00	Fiat	3	179D	12F-4R	51.49	4900	No
60-66 DT 4WD	23310.00	7480.00	8800.00	9680.00	Fiat	3	179D	12F-4R	51.49	5455	No
60-90	27300.00	8600.00	10120.00	11130.00	Fiat	3	179D	12F-4R	51.00	6295	C,H,A
60-90 DT 4WD	31440.00	9930.00	11680.00	12850.00	Fiat	3	179D	12F-4R	51.00	6755	C,H,A
70-66	21140.00	6800.00	8000.00	8800.00	Fiat	4	220D	12F-4R	62.72	5690	No
70-66 DT 4WD	25910.00	8160.00	9600.00	10560.00	Fiat	4	220D	12F-4R	62.72	6350	No
70-66 DT 4WD	26450.00	8500.00	10000.00	11000.00	Fiat	4	220D	20F-8R	62.00	6400	No
70-90	29835.00	9180.00	10800.00	11880.00	Fiat	4	220D	12F-4R	62.25	6800	C,H,A
70-90 DT 4WD	34680.00	10610.00	12480.00	13730.00	Fiat	4	220D	12F-4R	62.00	7440	C,H,A
80-66	24220.00	7550.00	8880.00	9770.00	Fiat	4	238D	12F-4R	70.43	5800	No
80-66 DT 4WD	30075.00	9380.00	11040.00	12140.00	Fiat	4	238D	12F-4R	70.43	6450	No
80-90	32200.00	10100.00	11880.00	13070.00	Fiat	4	238D	12F-4R	70.86	6800	C,H,A
80-90 DT 4WD	37940.00	11120.00	13080.00	14390.00	Fiat	4	238D	12F-4R	70.00	7640	C,H,A
90-90	35322.00	10300.00	12120.00	13330.00	Fiat	5	298D	15F-3R	81.00	7410	C,H,A
90-90 DT 4WD	41003.00	12240.00	14400.00	15840.00	Fiat	5	298D	15F-3R	81.00	8125	C,H,A
100-90	37298.00	10950.00	12880.00	14170.00	Fiat	6	331D	15F-3R	91.52	7780	C,H,A
100-90 DT 4WD	43061.00	12920.00	15200.00	16720.00	Fiat	6	331D	15F-3R	91.52	8625	C,H,A
130-90	46875.00	13600.00	16000.00	17600.00	Fiat	6	358D	16F-16R	107.48	11800	C,H,A
130-90 DT 4WD	57040.00	17000.00	20000.00	22000.00	Fiat	6	358D	16F-16R	107.48	13100	C,H,A
140-90	51345.00	15300.00	18000.00	19800.00	Fiat	6T	358D	16F-16R	123.35	12015	C,H,A
140-90 DT 4WD	61800.00	18700.00	22000.00	24200.00	Fiat	6T	358D	16F-16R	123.35	13340	C,H,A
160-90	54050.00	16660.00	19600.00	21560.00	Fiat	6T	494D	16F-16R	143.91	13350	C,H,A
160-90 PS	56400.00	17170.00	20200.00	22220.00	Fiat	6T	494D	16F-16R	142.64	13500	C,H,A
160-90 PS 4WD	66783.00	20060.00	23600.00	25960.00	Fiat	6T	494D	16F-16R	142.64	13500	C,H,A
180-90 4WD	72915.00	21080.00	24800.00	27280.00	Fiat	6T	494D	24F-8R	162.00	13500	C,H,A
180-90 PS	63507.00	19480.00	22920.00	25210.00	Fiat	6T	494D	16F-16R	162.15	13500	C,H,A

PS--Power Shift

1988

Model	Approx. Retail Price New	Estimated Average Value Less Repairs Fair	Good	Premium	Engine Make	No. Cyls.	Displ. Cu.-In.	No. Speeds	P.T.O. H.P.	Approx. Shipping Wt.-Lbs.	Cab
45-66	14500.00	5220.00	6090.00	6700.00	Fiat	3	165D	12F-4R	37.00	3674	No
45-66DT 4WD	18800.00	6770.00	7900.00	8690.00	Fiat	3	165D	12F-4R	39.49	4114	No
55-46	14800.00	5330.00	6220.00	6840.00	Fiat	3	165D	8F-2R	45.00	4080	No
55-46 DT 4WD	19400.00	6980.00	8150.00	8970.00	Fiat	3	165D	8F-2R	45.00		No
55-66	17394.00	6260.00	7310.00	8040.00	Fiat	3	165D	12F-4R	45.78	4851	No
55-66DT 4WD	22077.00	7950.00	9270.00	10200.00	Fiat	3	165D	12F-4R	45.00	5402	No
60-66	18978.00	6830.00	7970.00	8770.00	Fiat	3	179D	12F-4R	51.49	4900	No
60-66 Orchard	18363.00	6610.00	7710.00	8480.00	Fiat	3	179D	12F-4R	51.00		No
60-66 Orchard 4WD	22692.00	7780.00	9070.00	9980.00	Fiat	3	179D	12F-4R	51.00		No
60-66DT 4WD	23642.00	8030.00	9370.00	10310.00	Fiat	3	179D	12F-4R	51.49	5450	No
65-46	19500.00	6660.00	7770.00	8550.00	Fiat	3	220D	8F-2R	58.00		No
70-66	21139.00	7200.00	8400.00	9240.00	Fiat	4	220D	12F-4R	62.72	5689	No
70-66 4WD	26686.00	8860.00	10330.00	11360.00	Fiat	4	220D	12F-4R	62.00	6350	No
70-66 High Clearance	23094.00	7560.00	8820.00	9700.00	Fiat	4	220D	12F-4R	62.00	5689	No

Hesston-Fiat (Cont.)

1988 (Cont.)

Model	Approx. Retail Price New	Fair	Good	Premium	Make	No. Cyls.	Displ. Cu.-In.	No. Speeds	P.T.O. H.P.	Approx. Shipping Wt.-Lbs.	Cab
70-66 Orchard	20593.00	6550.00	7640.00	8400.00	Fiat	4	220D	12F-4R	62.00		No
70-66DT 4WD	29783.00	9720.00	11340.00	12470.00	Fiat	4	220D	12F-4R	62.72	7290	No
70-66DT Orchard 4WD	25184.00	8280.00	9660.00	10630.00	Fiat	4	220D	12F-4R	62.00		No
70-90	30130.00	10080.00	11760.00	12940.00	Fiat	4	220D	12F-4R	62.25	6798	C,H,A
70-90DT 4WD	35023.00	11160.00	13020.00	14320.00	Fiat	4	220D	12F-4R	62.00	7436	C,H,A
80-66	24462.00	7340.00	8570.00	9430.00	Fiat	4	238D	12F-4R	70.43	5800	No
80-66 High Clearance	25214.00	7630.00	8900.00	9790.00	Fiat	4	238D	12F-4R	70.00	5800	No
80-66 Orchard	23735.00	7020.00	8190.00	9010.00	Fiat	4	238D	12F-4R	70.00		No
80-66 Orchard 4WD	28078.00	8280.00	9660.00	10630.00	Fiat	4	238D	12F-4R	70.00		No
80-66DT 4WD	30674.00	9140.00	10670.00	11740.00	Fiat	4	238D	12F-4R	70.43	6450	No
80-66DT H.C. 4WD	32225.00	9720.00	11340.00	12470.00	Fiat	4	238D	12F-4R	70.43	7290	No
80-90	32521.00	9830.00	11470.00	12620.00	Fiat	4	238D	12F-4R	70.86	6930	C,H,A
80-90DT 4WD	38318.00	11880.00	13860.00	15250.00	Fiat	4	238D	12F-4R	70.00	7634	C,H,A
100-90	30808.00	9070.00	10580.00	11640.00	Fiat	6	331D	15F-3R	91.52		No
100-90	36496.00	11250.00	13130.00	14440.00	Fiat	6	331D	15F-3R	91.52	7595	C,H,A
100-90 DT 4WD	36200.00	11160.00	13020.00	14320.00	Fiat	6	331D	15F-3R	91.52		No
100-90 DT 4WD	41888.00	12960.00	15120.00	16630.00	Fiat	6	331D	15F-3R	91.52	8439	C,H,A
130-90 Turbo	48278.00	14400.00	16800.00	18480.00	Fiat	6T	358D	16F-16R	107.48	11800	C,H,A
130-90 Turbo PS	50699.00	15840.00	18480.00	20330.00	Fiat	6T	358D	16F-16R	107.00	11800	C,H,A
130-90DT Turbo 4WD	54590.00	17420.00	20330.00	22360.00	Fiat	6T	358D	16F-16R	107.48	13100	C,H,A
130-90DT PS 4WD	57010.00	18000.00	21000.00	23100.00	Fiat	6T	358D	16F-16R	107.00	13100	C,H,A
140-90 Turbo	52881.00	16920.00	19740.00	21710.00	Fiat	6T	358D	16F-16R	123.35	12015	C,H,A
140-90 Turbo PS	55302.00	18000.00	21000.00	23100.00	Fiat	6T	358D	16F-16R	123.00	12015	C,H,A
140-90 Turbo PS 4WD	62244.00	20160.00	23520.00	25870.00	Fiat	6T	358D	16F-16R	123.00	13338	C,H,A
140-90DT Turbo 4WD	59800.00	19190.00	22390.00	24630.00	Fiat	6T	358D	16F-16R	123.35	13338	C,H,A
160-90 Turbo	54080.00	17640.00	20580.00	22640.00	Fiat	6T	494D	16F-16R	141.71	13350	C,H,A
160-90 Turbo PS	56524.00	18430.00	21500.00	23650.00	Fiat	6T	494D	16F-16R	142.64	13350	C,H,A
160-90DT Turbo 4WD	63440.00	20300.00	23690.00	26060.00	Fiat	6T	494D	16F-16R	141.71	14220	C,H,A
160-90DT PS 4WD	65884.00	21350.00	24910.00	27400.00	Fiat	6T	494D	16F-16R	142.64	14220	C,H,A
180-90 Turbo	61425.00	18720.00	21840.00	24020.00	Fiat	6T	494D	16F-16R	162.87	13448	C,H,A
180-90DT Turbo 4WD	71925.00	21960.00	25620.00	28180.00	Fiat	6T	494D	16F-16R	162.87	14318	C,H,A
180-90DT Turbo PS	63893.00	20520.00	23940.00	26330.00	Fiat	6T	494D	16F-16R	162.15	13448	C,H,A

PS--Power Shift

1989

Model	Approx. Retail Price New	Fair	Good	Premium	Make	No. Cyls.	Displ. Cu.-In.	No. Speeds	P.T.O. H.P.	Approx. Shipping Wt.-Lbs.	Cab
45-66	14950.00	5680.00	6580.00	7240.00	Fiat	3	165D	12F-4R	37.00	3674	No
45-66DT 4WD	19400.00	7370.00	8540.00	9390.00	Fiat	3	165D	12F-4R	39.49	4114	No
55-46	15010.00	5700.00	6600.00	7260.00	Fiat	3	165D	8F-2R	45.00	4080	No
55-46 DT 4WD	19788.00	7520.00	8710.00	9580.00	Fiat	3	165D	8F-2R	45.00		No
55-66	17394.00	6610.00	7650.00	8420.00	Fiat	3	165D	12F-4R	45.78	4851	No
55-66DT 4WD	22077.00	8390.00	9710.00	10680.00	Fiat	3	165D	12F-4R	45.00	5402	No
60-66 Orchard	18800.00	7140.00	8270.00	9100.00	Fiat	3	179D	12F-4R	51.00		No
60-66 Orchard 4WD	23400.00	8890.00	10300.00	11330.00	Fiat	3	179D	12F-4R	51.00		No
60-66DT 4WD	24351.00	9250.00	10710.00	11780.00	Fiat	3	179D	12F-4R	51.49	5450	No
65-46	19890.00	7560.00	8750.00	9630.00	Fiat	4	220D	8F-2R	58.00		No
70-66 4WD	27487.00	9880.00	11440.00	12580.00	Fiat	4	220D	12F-4R	62.00	6350	No
70-66 High Clearance	24000.00	8740.00	10120.00	11130.00	Fiat	4	220D	12F-4R	62.00	5689	No
70-66 Orchard	21000.00	7600.00	8800.00	9680.00	Fiat	4	220D	12F-4R	62.00		No
70-66DT 4WD	30500.00	10640.00	12320.00	13550.00	Fiat	4	220D	12F-4R	62.72	7290	No
70-66DT Orchard 4WD	26000.00	9120.00	10560.00	11620.00	Fiat	4	220D	12F-4R	62.00		No
70-90	31034.00	11020.00	12760.00	14040.00	Fiat	4	220D	12F-12R	62.25	6798	C,H,A
70-90DT 4WD	36074.00	12540.00	14520.00	15970.00	Fiat	4	220D	12F-12R	62.00	7436	C,H,A
80-66	25000.00	8360.00	9680.00	10650.00	Fiat	4	238D	12F-4R	70.43	5800	No
80-66 High Clearance	26000.00	8740.00	10120.00	11130.00	Fiat	4	238D	12F-4R	70.00	5800	No
80-66 Orchard	24500.00	8930.00	10340.00	11370.00	Fiat	4	238D	12F-4R	70.00		No
80-66 Orchard 4WD	29000.00	9880.00	11440.00	12580.00	Fiat	4	238D	12F-4R	70.00		No
80-66DT 4WD	31800.00	10720.00	12410.00	13650.00	Fiat	4	238D	12F-4R	70.43	6450	No
80-66DT H.C. 4WD	32800.00	11210.00	12980.00	14280.00	Fiat	4	238D	12F-4R	70.43	7290	No
80-90	33000.00	11400.00	13200.00	14520.00	Fiat	4	238D	12F-4R	70.86	6930	C,H,A
80-90DT 4WD	39000.00	12920.00	14960.00	16460.00	Fiat	4	238D	12F-4R	70.00	7634	C,H,A
100-90	31500.00	10260.00	11880.00	13070.00	Fiat	6	331D	15F-3R	91.52		No
100-90	37200.00	12160.00	14080.00	15490.00	Fiat	6	331D	15F-3R	91.52	7595	C,H,A
100-90 DT 4WD	37300.00	13870.00	16060.00	17670.00	Fiat	6	331D	15F-3R	91.52		No
100-90 DT 4WD	43100.00	14440.00	16720.00	18390.00	Fiat	6	331D	15F-3R	91.52	8439	C,H,A
130-90 Turbo	48278.00	16340.00	18920.00	20810.00	Fiat	6T	358D	16F-16R	107.48	11800	C,H,A
130-90DT Turbo 4WD	54590.00	18620.00	21560.00	23720.00	Fiat	6T	358D	16F-16R	107.48	13100	C,H,A
140-90 Turbo	52881.00	17860.00	20680.00	22750.00	Fiat	6T	358D	16F-16R	123.35	12015	C,H,A
140-90 Turbo PS	55302.00	19000.00	22000.00	24200.00	Fiat	6T	358D	16F-16R	123.00	12015	C,H,A
140-90 Turbo PS 4WD	62244.00	20900.00	24200.00	26620.00	Fiat	6T	358D	16F-16R	123.00	13338	C,H,A
140-90DT Turbo 4WD	59800.00	20140.00	23320.00	25650.00	Fiat	6T	358D	16F-16R	123.35	13338	C,H,A
160-90 Turbo	54080.00	18810.00	21780.00	23960.00	Fiat	6T	494D	16F-16R	141.71	13350	C,H,A
160-90 Turbo PS	56524.00	19460.00	22530.00	24780.00	Fiat	6T	494D	16F-16R	142.64	13350	C,H,A
160-90DT Turbo 4WD	63440.00	21280.00	24640.00	27100.00	Fiat	6T	494D	16F-16R	141.71	14220	C,H,A
160-90DT PS 4WD	65884.00	22420.00	25960.00	28560.00	Fiat	6T	494D	16F-16R	142.64	14220	C,H,A
180-90 Turbo	61425.00	20980.00	24290.00	26720.00	Fiat	6T	494D	16F-16R	162.87	13448	C,H,A
180-90DT Turbo 4WD	71925.00	24320.00	28160.00	30980.00	Fiat	6T	494D	16F-16R	162.87	14318	C,H,A
180-90DT Turbo PS	63893.00	22150.00	25650.00	28220.00	Fiat	6T	494D	16F-16R	162.15	13448	C,H,A

PS--Power Shift

1990

Model	Approx. Retail Price New	Fair	Good	Premium	Make	No. Cyls.	Displ. Cu.-In.	No. Speeds	P.T.O. H.P.	Approx. Shipping Wt.-Lbs.	Cab
45-66	15500.00	6200.00	7130.00	7840.00	Fiat	3	165D	12F-4R	39.00	3674	No
45-66DT 4WD	19800.00	7920.00	9110.00	10020.00	Fiat	3	165D	12F-4R	39.49	4114	No
55-56	15549.00	6220.00	7150.00	7870.00	Fiat	3	165D	8F-2R	45.00	4420	No
55-56 DT 4WD	20382.00	8150.00	9380.00	10320.00	Fiat	3	165D	8F-2R	45.00	5000	No

Hesston-Fiat (Cont.)

1990 (Cont.)

Model	Approx. Retail Price New	Estimated Average Value Less Repairs Fair	Good	Premium	Engine Make	No. Cyls.	Displ. Cu.-In.	No. Speeds	P.T.O. H.P.	Approx. Shipping Wt.-Lbs.	Cab
60-66 Orchard	19481.00	7790.00	8960.00	9860.00	Fiat	3	179D	12F-4R	51.00		No
60-66 Orchard 4WD	24074.00	9630.00	11070.00	12180.00	Fiat	3	179D	12F-4R	51.00		No
60-66DT 4WD	25082.00	10030.00	11540.00	12690.00	Fiat	3	179D	12F-4R	51.49	5450	No
60-76DTF Orchard 4WD	25300.00	10120.00	11640.00	12800.00	Fiat	3	179D	12F-4R	51.00		No
60-76F Orchard	20300.00	8120.00	9340.00	10270.00	Fiat	3	179D	12F-4R	51.00		No
65-56	20487.00	8200.00	9420.00	10360.00	Fiat	4	220D	8F-2R	60.00	4860	No
65-56 DT 4WD	24980.00	9990.00	11490.00	12640.00	Fiat	4	220D	8F-2R	60.00	5400	No
70-66 4WD	28315.00	11330.00	13030.00	14330.00	Fiat	4	220D	12F-12R	62.00	6350	No
70-66 High Clearance	24976.00	9990.00	11490.00	12640.00	Fiat	4	220D	12F-12R	62.00	5689	No
70-66 Orchard	21847.00	8740.00	10050.00	11060.00	Fiat	4	220D	12F-4R	62.00		No
70-66DT 4WD	31300.00	12520.00	14400.00	15840.00	Fiat	4	220D	12F-12R	62.72	7290	No
70-66DT Orchard 4WD	26718.00	10690.00	12290.00	13520.00	Fiat	4	220D	12F-4R	62.00		No
70-76DTF Orchard 4WD	28000.00	11200.00	12880.00	14170.00	Fiat	4	220D	12F-4R	62.00		No
70-76F Orchard	22600.00	9040.00	10400.00	11440.00	Fiat	4	220D	12F-4R	62.00		No
80-66	25952.00	10380.00	11940.00	13130.00	Fiat	4	238D	12F-12R	70.43	5800	No
80-66 High Clearance	27270.00	10910.00	12540.00	13790.00	Fiat	4	238D	12F-12R	70.00	5800	No
80-66 Orchard	25180.00	10070.00	11580.00	12740.00	Fiat	4	238D	12F-4R	70.00		No
80-66 Orchard 4WD	29788.00	11600.00	13340.00	14670.00	Fiat	4	238D	12F-4R	70.00		No
80-66DT 4WD	32542.00	12400.00	14260.00	15690.00	Fiat	4	238D	12F-4R	70.43	6450	No
80-66DT H.C. 4WD	33941.00	12800.00	14720.00	16190.00	Fiat	4	238D	12F-12R	70.43	7290	No
80-76DTF Orchard 4WD	29788.00	11200.00	12880.00	14170.00	Fiat	4	238D	12F-4R	70.00		No
80-76F Orchard	25180.00	10070.00	11580.00	12740.00	Fiat	4	238D	12F-4R	70.00		No
80-90	34166.00	12800.00	14720.00	16190.00	Fiat	4	238D	12F-12R	70.86	6930	C,H,A
80-90DT 4WD	40257.00	15200.00	17480.00	19230.00	Fiat	4	238D	12F-12R	70.00	7634	C,H,A
100-90	32684.00	12000.00	13800.00	15180.00	Fiat	6	331D	15F-3R	91.52	7420	No
100-90	38719.00	14560.00	16740.00	18410.00	Fiat	6	331D	15F-3R	91.52	8240	C,H,A
100-90 DT 4WD	38405.00	14400.00	16560.00	18220.00	Fiat	6	331D	15F-3R	91.52	8264	No
100-90 DT 4WD	44439.00	16800.00	19320.00	21250.00	Fiat	6	331D	15F-3R	91.52	9080	C,H,A
100-90 DT	42117.00	16000.00	18400.00	20240.00	Fiat	6	331D	20F-4R	91.00	8710	No
130-90 Turbo PS	50669.00	18800.00	21620.00	23780.00	Fiat	6T	358D	16F-16R	107.48	11800	C,H,A
130-90DT Turbo 4WD	57010.00	21600.00	24840.00	27320.00	Fiat	6T	358D	16F-16R	107.48	13100	C,H,A
140-90 Turbo PS	55302.00	20800.00	23920.00	26310.00	Fiat	6T	358D	16F-16R	123.00	12015	C,H,A
140-90 Turbo PS 4WD	62244.00	23200.00	26680.00	29350.00	Fiat	6T	358D	16F-16R	123.00	13338	C,H,A
160-90 Turbo PS	56524.00	21200.00	24380.00	26820.00	Fiat	6T	494D	16F-16R	142.64	13350	C,H,A
180-90DT Turbo PS	63893.00	23320.00	26820.00	29500.00	Fiat	6T	494D	16F-16R	162.15	13448	C,H,A
180-90DT Turbo 4WD	74393.00	26400.00	30360.00	33400.00	Fiat	6T	494D	16F-16R	162.87	14318	C,H,A

PS--Power Shift

1991

Model	Approx. Retail Price New	Fair	Good	Premium	Make	No. Cyls.	Displ. Cu.-In.	No. Speeds	P.T.O. H.P.	Approx. Shipping Wt.-Lbs.	Cab
45-66	15810.00	6640.00	7590.00	8270.00	Fiat	3	165D	12F-4R	39.00	3674	No
45-66DT 4WD	20196.00	8480.00	9690.00	10560.00	Fiat	3	165D	12F-4R	39.49	4114	No
55-56	15860.00	6660.00	7610.00	8300.00	Fiat	3	165D	8F-2R	45.00	4420	No
55-56 DT 4WD	20803.00	8740.00	9990.00	10890.00	Fiat	3	165D	8F-2R	45.00	5000	No
55-76F Orchard	19085.00	8020.00	9160.00	9980.00	Fiat	3	165D	12F-4R	45.00		No
55-76FDT Orchard 4WD	23552.00	9890.00	11310.00	12330.00	Fiat	3	165D	12F-4R	45.00		No
60-66	20600.00	8650.00	9890.00	10780.00	Fiat	3	179D	12F-4R	51.00	4900	No
60-66DT 4WD	25597.00	10750.00	12290.00	13400.00	Fiat	3	179D	12F-4R	51.49	5450	No
60-76DTF Orchard 4WD	25875.00	10870.00	12420.00	13540.00	Fiat	3	179D	12F-4R	51.00		No
60-76F Orchard	20775.00	8730.00	9970.00	10870.00	Fiat	3	179D	12F-4R	51.00		No
65-56	20897.00	8780.00	10030.00	10930.00	Fiat	4	220D	8F-2R	60.00	4860	No
65-56DT 4WD	25493.00	10710.00	12240.00	13340.00	Fiat	4	220D	8F-2R	60.00	5400	No
70-66	23200.00	9740.00	11140.00	12140.00	Fiat	4	220D	12F-12R	62.72	5689	No
70-66 High Clearance	25476.00	10700.00	12230.00	13330.00	Fiat	4	220D	12F-12R	62.00	5689	No
70-66DT 4WD	28323.00	11900.00	13600.00	14820.00	Fiat	4	220D	12F-12R	62.00	6350	No
70-66DT 4WD	31926.00	13410.00	15320.00	16700.00	Fiat	4	220D	12F-12R	62.72	7290	No
70-76 Orchard	23052.00	9680.00	11070.00	12070.00	Fiat	4	220D	12F-4R	62.00		No
70-76DTF Orchard 4WD	28119.00	11810.00	13500.00	14720.00	Fiat	4	220D	12F-4R	62.00		No
70-76F Orchard	23121.00	9710.00	11100.00	12100.00	Fiat	4	220D	12F-4R	62.00		No
80-66	26471.00	11120.00	12710.00	13850.00	Fiat	4	238D	12F-12R	70.43	5800	No
80-66 High Clearance	27815.00	11680.00	13350.00	14550.00	Fiat	4	238D	12F-12R	70.00	5800	No
80-66DT 4WD	33253.00	13970.00	15960.00	17400.00	Fiat	4	238D	12F-4R	70.43	6450	No
80-66DT H.C. 4WD	34620.00	14540.00	16620.00	18120.00	Fiat	4	238D	12F-12R	70.43	7290	No
80-76DTF Orchard 4WD	30453.00	12790.00	14620.00	15940.00	Fiat	4	238D	12F-4R	70.00		No
80-90	34849.00	14640.00	16730.00	18240.00	Fiat	4	238D	12F-12R	70.86	6930	C,H,A
80-90DT 4WD	41122.00	17270.00	19740.00	21520.00	Fiat	4	238D	12F-12R	70.00	7634	C,H,A
100-90	33338.00	13570.00	15500.00	16900.00	Fiat	6	331D	15F-3R	91.52	7420	No
100-90	39493.00	15750.00	18000.00	19620.00	Fiat	6	331D	15F-3R	91.52	8240	C,H,A
100-90 DT 4WD	39304.00	15540.00	17760.00	19360.00	Fiat	6	331D	15F-3R	91.52	8264	No
100-90 DT 4WD	45458.00	18060.00	20640.00	22500.00	Fiat	6	331D	15F-3R	91.52	9080	C,H,A
100-90 DT	42959.00	17220.00	19680.00	21450.00	Fiat	6	331D	20F-4R	91.00	8710	No
F110	40200.00	16040.00	18340.00	19990.00	Fiat	6	358D	16F-16R	98.00	9570	C,H,A
F110DT 4WD	46500.00	18480.00	21120.00	23020.00	Fiat	6	358D	16F-16R	98.00	10230	C,H,A
F130	48500.00	19320.00	22080.00	24070.00	Fiat	6T	358D	32F-16R	115.00	11120	C,H,A
F130DT 4WD	56300.00	22260.00	25440.00	27730.00	Fiat	6T	358D	32F-16R	115.00	12000	C,H,A
140-90 Turbo PS 4WD	62244.00	24780.00	28320.00	30870.00	Fiat	6T	358D	16F-16R	123.00	13338	C,H,A
160-90 Turbo PS	56524.00	22260.00	25440.00	27730.00	Fiat	6T	494D	16F-16R	142.64	13350	C,H,A
160-90 Turbo PS 4WD	65884.00	26040.00	29760.00	32440.00	Fiat	6T	494D	16F-16R	142.00	14220	C,H,A
180-90DT Turbo 4WD	74393.00	28560.00	32640.00	35580.00	Fiat	6T	494D	16F-16R	162.87	14318	C,H,A

PS--Power Shift

Model	Approx. Retail Price New	Estimated Average Value Less Repairs Fair	Good	Premium	Engine Make	No. Cyls.	Displ. Cu.-In.	No. Speeds	P.T.O. H.P.	Approx. Shipping Wt.-Lbs.	Cab

Huber

Model	Approx. Retail Price New	Fair	Good	Premium	Make	No. Cyls.	Displ. Cu.-In.	No. Speeds	P.T.O. H.P.	Approx. Shipping Wt.-Lbs.	Cab
1939											
L Modern Farmer STD	1600.00	**740.00**	**1760.00**	**2240.00**		4	338	3F-1R		4050	No
LC Modern Farmer	1330.00	**660.00**	**1560.00**	**1980.00**		4	338	3F-1R		4200	No
1940											
L Modern Farmer STD	1620.00	**760.00**	**1810.00**	**2300.00**		4	338	3F-1R		4050	No
LC Modern Farmer	1350.00	**680.00**	**1620.00**	**2060.00**		4	338	3F-1R		4200	No
1941											
L Modern Farmer STD	1645.00	**780.00**	**1860.00**	**2360.00**		4	338	3F-1R		4050	No
LC Modern Farmer	1365.00	**700.00**	**1660.00**	**2110.00**		4	338	3F-1R		4200	No
1942											
L Modern Farmer STD	1675.00	**800.00**	**1900.00**	**2410.00**		4	338	3F-1R		4050	No
LC Modern Farmer	1380.00	**720.00**	**1720.00**	**2180.00**		4	338	3F-1R		4200	No

Hurlimann

Model	Approx. Retail Price New	Fair	Good	Premium	Make	No. Cyls.	Displ. Cu.-In.	No. Speeds	P.T.O. H.P.	Approx. Shipping Wt.-Lbs.	Cab
1998											
H-305 XE 2WD	23479.00	**18310.00**	**19250.00**	**19830.00**	Hurlimann	3	183D	12F-12R	45	4277	No
H-305 XE 4WD	26773.00	**20880.00**	**21950.00**	**22610.00**	Hurlimann	3	183D	12F-12R	45	4740	No
H-306 XE 4WD	30320.00	**23650.00**	**24860.00**	**25610.00**	Hurlimann	3	183D	12F-12R	54	5071	No
Prince 325 DT 4WD	16623.00	**12480.00**	**13120.00**	**13510.00**	Mitsubishi	3	68D	12F-12R	23	2138	No
Prince 435 DT 4WD	19789.00	**14560.00**	**15300.00**	**15760.00**	Mitsubishi	4	90D	12F-12R	32	2271	No
Prince 445 DT 4WD	21989.00	**16630.00**	**17490.00**	**18020.00**	Mitsubishi	4	90D	12F-12R	37	2535	No
Prince 445 DT 4WD	26449.00	**20480.00**	**21530.00**	**22180.00**	Mitsubishi	4	90D	12F-12R	37	2535	C,H
XA-606 DT 4WD	34872.00	**25810.00**	**27550.00**	**28380.00**	Hurlimann	3	183D	45F-45R	54	5622	No
XA-606 DT 4WD	39063.00	**28910.00**	**30860.00**	**31790.00**	Hurlimann	3	183D	45F-45R	54	5997	C,H
XA-607 DT 4WD	37582.00	**27810.00**	**29690.00**	**30580.00**	Hurlimann	4	244D	45F-45R	63	6041	No
XA-607 DT 4WD	40942.00	**30300.00**	**32340.00**	**33310.00**	Hurlimann	4	244D	45F-45R	63	6415	C,H
909 XT DT 4WD	44273.00	**32760.00**	**34980.00**	**36030.00**	Hurlimann	4T	244D	45F-45R	85	8047	No
909 XT DT 4WD	47688.00	**35290.00**	**37670.00**	**38800.00**	Hurlimann	4T	244D	45F-45R	85	4598	C,H
910.6 XT DT 4WD	51713.00	**38270.00**	**40850.00**	**42080.00**	Hurlimann	6	366D	45F-45R	94	9370	C,H
6135 XB DT 4WD	75075.00	**55310.00**	**59050.00**	**60820.00**	Hurlimann	6T	366D	54F-54R	119	10803	C,H,A
H-6165 Master DT 4WD	89414.00	**62900.00**	**67150.00**	**69170.00**	Hurlimann	6TA	366D	26F-25R	149	12787	C,H,A
1999											
H-305 XE 2WD	23995.00	**20160.00**	**21120.00**	**21540.00**	Hurlimann	3	183D	12F-12R	45	4277	No
H-305 XE 4WD	27995.00	**23520.00**	**24640.00**	**25130.00**	Hurlimann	3	183D	12F-12R	45	4740	No
H-306 XE 4WD	30660.00	**25750.00**	**26980.00**	**27520.00**	Hurlimann	3	183D	12F-12R	54	5071	No
Prince 325 DT 4WD	15995.00	**13440.00**	**14080.00**	**14360.00**	Mitsubishi	3	68D	12F-12R	23	2138	No
Prince 435 DT 4WD	18660.00	**15670.00**	**16420.00**	**16750.00**	Mitsubishi	4	90D	12F-12R	32	2271	No
Prince 445 DT 4WD	21325.00	**17910.00**	**18770.00**	**19150.00**	Mitsubishi	4	90D	12F-12R	37	2535	No
Prince 445 DT 4WD	26260.00	**22060.00**	**23110.00**	**23570.00**	Mitsubishi	4	90D	12F-12R	37	2535	C,H
XA-607 DT 4WD	46225.00	**38370.00**	**40220.00**	**41430.00**	Hurlimann	4	244D	45F-45R	63	6415	C,H
909 XT DT 4WD	50660.00	**42050.00**	**44070.00**	**45390.00**	Hurlimann	4T	244D	45F-45R	85	4598	C,H
910.6 XT DT 4WD	58995.00	**48970.00**	**51330.00**	**52870.00**	Hurlimann	6	366D	45F-45R	94	9370	C,H
6135 XB DT 4WD	74745.00	**62040.00**	**65030.00**	**66980.00**	Hurlimann	6T	366D	54F-54R	119	10803	C,H,A
H-6165 Master DT 4WD	95445.00	**74700.00**	**78300.00**	**80650.00**	Hurlimann	6TA	366D	26F-25R	149	12787	C,H,A

IMT

Model	Approx. Retail Price New	Fair	Good	Premium	Make	No. Cyls.	Displ. Cu.-In.	No. Speeds	P.T.O. H.P.	Approx. Shipping Wt.-Lbs.	Cab
1991											
IMT 539	8000.00	**3360.00**	**3840.00**	**4190.00**	IMR	3	152D	6F-2R	34.00	3400	No
IMT 542	9100.00	**3820.00**	**4370.00**	**4760.00**	IMR	3	152D	6F-2R	36.00	4000	No
IMT 549 DV 4WD	11900.00	**4620.00**	**5280.00**	**5760.00**	IMR	3	152D	10F-2R	39.00	4600	No
IMT 560	11200.00	**4410.00**	**5040.00**	**5490.00**	IMR	4	203D	6F-2R	50.00	5600	No
IMT 565 DV 4WD	14500.00	**5460.00**	**6240.00**	**6800.00**	IMR	4	203D	6F-2R	55.00	6640	No
IMT 577	13800.00	**5120.00**	**5860.00**	**6390.00**	IMR	4	248D	10F-2R	64.00	8000	No
IMT 577 DV 4WD	17200.00	**5960.00**	**6820.00**	**7430.00**	IMR	4	248D	10F-2R	64.00	8900	No
1992											
539 P/S	9300.00	**4090.00**	**4740.00**	**5120.00**	IMR	3	152D	6F-2R	35.00	3200	No
539 ST.	8500.00	**3740.00**	**4340.00**	**4690.00**	IMR	3	152D	6F-2R	35.00	3200	No
542	9900.00	**4360.00**	**5050.00**	**5450.00**	IMR	3	152D	6F-2R	38.00	4000	No
542 HY	10600.00	**4660.00**	**5410.00**	**5840.00**	IMR	3	152D	6F-2R	38.00	4000	No
549 DV 4WD	12900.00	**5240.00**	**6070.00**	**6560.00**	IMR	3	152D	10F-2R	40.00	4800	No
560	12500.00	**5060.00**	**5870.00**	**6340.00**	IMR	4	203D	6F-2R	54.00	6150	No
565 DV 4WD	15700.00	**6160.00**	**7140.00**	**7710.00**	IMR	4	203D	6F-2R	55.00	6850	No
577	14750.00	**5850.00**	**6780.00**	**7320.00**	IMR	4	248D	10F-2R	64.00	7000	No
577 DV 4WD	17900.00	**7040.00**	**8160.00**	**8810.00**	IMR	4	248D	10F-2R	64.00	7800	No

Int. Harvester-Farmall

Model	Approx. Retail Price New	Fair	Good	Premium	Make	No. Cyls.	Displ. Cu.-In.	No. Speeds	P.T.O. H.P.	Approx. Shipping Wt.-Lbs.	Cab
1939											
A	......	**540.00**	**1280.00**	**1630.00**	IH	4	113G	4F-1R	16.1	2014	No
B	......	**550.00**	**1310.00**	**1660.00**	IH	4	113G	4F-1R	16.1	2014	No
H	......	**570.00**	**1340.00**	**1700.00**	IH	4	164G	5F-1R	30.2	3875	No
M	......	**670.00**	**1600.00**	**2030.00**	IH	4	248D	5F-1R	36.0	4964	No

Model	Approx. Retail Price New	Estimated Average Value Less Repairs Fair	Good	Premium	Make	Engine No. Cyls.	Displ. Cu.-In.	No. Speeds	P.T.O. H.P.	Approx. Shipping Wt.-Lbs.	Cab

Int. Harvester-Farmall (Cont.)

Model	Approx. Retail Price New	Fair	Good	Premium	Make	No. Cyls.	Displ. Cu.-In.	No. Speeds	P.T.O. H.P.	Approx. Shipping Wt.-Lbs.	Cab
1940											
A	......	560.00	1320.00	1680.00	IH	4	113G	4F-1R	16.1	2014	No
B	......	570.00	1340.00	1700.00	IH	4	113G	4F-1R	16.1	2014	No
H	......	580.00	1380.00	1750.00	IH	4	164G	5F-1R	30.2	3875	No
M	......	690.00	1640.00	2080.00	IH	4	248D	5F-1R	36.0	4964	No
O-4	......	610.00	1450.00	1840.00	IH	4	152G	5F-1R	25.6	3816	No
I-6	......	860.00	2050.00	2600.00	IH	4	264D	5F-1R	48.0	5510	No
O-6	......	630.00	1490.00	1890.00	IH	4	248G	5F-1R	36.0	4858	No
W-6	......	650.00	1550.00	1970.00	IH	4	248G	5F-1R	36.0	4858	No
WD6	......	710.00	1680.00	2130.00	IH	4	248D	5F-1R	32.0	4858	No
I-9	......	1200.00	2850.00	3620.00	IH	4	350D	5F-1R	52.6	7200	No
W-9	......	860.00	2030.00	2580.00	IH	4	335G	5F-1R	49.3	6425	No
WD-9	......	890.00	2110.00	2680.00	IH	4	335D	5F-1R	52.6	6650	No
1941											
A	......	570.00	1340.00	1700.00	IH	4	113G	4F-1R	16.1	2014	No
B	......	580.00	1380.00	1750.00	IH	4	113G	4F-1R	16.1	2014	No
H	......	590.00	1410.00	1790.00	IH	4	164G	5F-1R	30.2	3875	No
M	......	710.00	1680.00	2130.00	IH	4	248D	5F-1R	36.0	4964	No
O-4	......	640.00	1510.00	1920.00	IH	4	152G	5F-1R	25.6	3816	No
W4	......	660.00	1570.00	1990.00	IH	4	152G	5F-1R	30.8	3816	No
I-6	......	890.00	2110.00	2680.00	IH	4	264D	5F-1R	48.0	5510	No
O-6	......	650.00	1550.00	1970.00	IH	4	248G	5F-1R	36.0	4858	No
W6	......	680.00	1610.00	2050.00	IH	4	248G	5F-1R	36.0	4858	No
WD6	......	730.00	1740.00	2210.00	IH	4	248D	5F-1R	32.0	4858	No
I-9	......	1230.00	2910.00	3700.00	IH	4	350D	5F-1R	52.6	7200	No
W-9	......	870.00	2060.00	2620.00	IH	4	335G	5F-1R	49.3	6425	No
WD-9	......	920.00	2170.00	2760.00	IH	4	335D	5F-1R	52.6	6650	No
1942											
A	......	580.00	1380.00	1750.00	IH	4	113G	4F-1R	16.1	2014	No
B	......	590.00	1410.00	1790.00	IH	4	113G	4F-1R	16.1	2014	No
H	......	610.00	1440.00	1830.00	IH	4	164G	5F-1R	30.2	3875	No
M	......	740.00	1750.00	2220.00	IH	4	248D	5F-1R	36.0	4964	No
O-4	......	670.00	1580.00	2010.00	IH	4	152G	5F-1R	25.6	3816	No
W4	......	690.00	1640.00	2080.00	IH	4	152G	5F-1R	30.8	3816	No
I-6	......	920.00	2170.00	2760.00	IH	4	264D	5F-1R	48.0	5510	No
O-6	......	670.00	1580.00	2010.00	IH	4	248G	5F-1R	36.0	4858	No
W6	......	730.00	1730.00	2200.00	IH	4	248G	5F-1R	36.0	4858	No
WD6	......	760.00	1810.00	2300.00	IH	4	248D	5F-1R	32.0	4858	No
I-9	......	1250.00	2970.00	3770.00	IH	4	350D	5F-1R	52.6	7200	No
W-9	......	890.00	2120.00	2690.00	IH	4	335G	5F-1R	49.3	6425	No
WD-9	......	930.00	2210.00	2810.00	IH	4	335D	5F-1R	52.6	6650	No
1943											
A	......	600.00	1410.00	1780.00	IH	4	113G	4F-1R	16.1	2014	No
B	......	610.00	1440.00	1810.00	IH	4	113G	4F-1R	16.1	2014	No
H	......	620.00	1480.00	1870.00	IH	4	164G	5F-1R	30.2	3875	No
M	......	770.00	1820.00	2290.00	IH	4	248D	5F-1R	36.0	4964	No
O-4	......	690.00	1640.00	2070.00	IH	4	152G	5F-1R	25.6	3816	No
W4	......	720.00	1700.00	2140.00	IH	4	152G	5F-1R	30.8	3816	No
I-6	......	940.00	2240.00	2820.00	IH	4	264D	5F-1R	48.0	5510	No
O-6	......	710.00	1680.00	2120.00	IH	4	248G	5F-1R	36.0	4858	No
W6	......	760.00	1810.00	2280.00	IH	4	248G	5F-1R	36.0	4858	No
WD6	......	790.00	1870.00	2360.00	IH	4	248D	5F-1R	32.0	4858	No
I-9	......	1280.00	3040.00	3830.00	IH	4	350D	5F-1R	52.6	7200	No
W-9	......	910.00	2170.00	2730.00	IH	4	335G	5F-1R	49.3	6425	No
WD-9	......	970.00	2300.00	2900.00	IH	4	335D	5F-1R	52.6	6650	No
1944											
A	......	610.00	1440.00	1800.00	IH	4	113G	4F-1R	16.1	2014	No
B	......	620.00	1470.00	1840.00	IH	4	113G	4F-1R	16.1	2014	No
H	......	640.00	1510.00	1890.00	IH	4	164G	5F-1R	30.2	3875	No
M	......	780.00	1860.00	2330.00	IH	4	248D	5F-1R	36.0	4964	No
O-4	......	720.00	1700.00	2130.00	IH	4	152G	5F-1R	25.6	3816	No
W4	......	750.00	1770.00	2210.00	IH	4	152G	5F-1R	30.8	3816	No
I-6	......	920.00	2170.00	2710.00	IH	4	264D	5F-1R	48.0	5510	No
O-6	......	730.00	1740.00	2180.00	IH	4	248G	5F-1R	36.0	4858	No
W6	......	820.00	1930.00	2410.00	IH	4	248G	5F-1R	36.0	4858	No
WD6	......	860.00	2050.00	2560.00	IH	4	248D	5F-1R	32.0		No
I-9	......	1310.00	3100.00	3880.00	IH	4	350D	5F-1R	52.6	7200	No
W-9	......	930.00	2210.00	2760.00	IH	4	335G	5F-1R	49.3	6425	No
WD9	......	990.00	2340.00	2930.00	IH	4	335D	5F-1R	52.6	6650	No
1945											
A	......	620.00	1470.00	1820.00	IH	4	113G	4F-1R	16.1	2014	No
B	......	640.00	1510.00	1870.00	IH	4	113G	4F-1R	16.1	2014	No
H	......	660.00	1550.00	1920.00	IH	4	152G	5F-1R	30.2	3875	No
M	......	800.00	1900.00	2360.00	IH	4	248G	5F-1R	36.0	4964	No
O4	......	740.00	1750.00	2170.00	IH	4	152G	5F-1R	25.6	3816	No
W4	......	780.00	1850.00	2290.00	IH	4	152G	5F-1R	30.8	3816	No
O6	......	760.00	1790.00	2220.00	IH	4	248G	5F-1R	36.0	4858	No
W6	......	860.00	2030.00	2520.00	IH	4	248G	5F-1R	36.0	4858	No
WD6	......	910.00	2150.00	2670.00	IH	4	248D	5F-1R	32.0		No
W9	......	960.00	2280.00	2830.00	IH	4	335G	5F-1R	49.3	6425	No

Int. Harvester-Farmall (Cont.)

Model	Approx. Retail Price New	Estimated Average Value Less Repairs Fair	Good	Premium	Make	Engine No. Cyls.	Displ. Cu.-In.	No. Speeds	P.T.O. H.P.	Approx. Shipping Wt.-Lbs.	Cab
1945 (Cont.)											
WD9	......	1000.00	2380.00	2950.00	IH	4	335D	5F-1R	52.6	6650	No
1946											
A	......	640.00	1510.00	1860.00	IH	4	113G	4F-1R	16.1	2014	No
B	......	650.00	1550.00	1910.00	IH	4	113G	4F-1R	16.1	2014	No
H	......	660.00	1570.00	1930.00	IH	4	164G	5F-1R	30.2	3875	No
M	......	820.00	1950.00	2400.00	IH	4	248G	5F-1R	36.0	4964	No
MD	......	890.00	2110.00	2600.00	IH	4	248D	5F-1R	36.0	4964	No
O4, OS4	......	760.00	1810.00	2230.00	IH	4	152G	5F-1R	25.6	3816	No
W4	......	800.00	1910.00	2350.00	IH	4	152G	5F-1R	30.8	3816	No
O6, OS6	......	810.00	1930.00	2370.00	IH	4	248G	5F-1R	36.0	4858	No
W6	......	820.00	1930.00	2370.00	IH	4	247G	5F-1R	31.4	4858	No
WD6	......	890.00	2110.00	2600.00	IH	4	248D	5F-1R	32.0		No
W9	......	1000.00	2370.00	2920.00	IH	4	335G	5F-1R	49.3	6425	No
WD9	......	1030.00	2430.00	2990.00	IH	4	335D	5F-1R	52.6	6650	No
1947											
A	......	650.00	1550.00	1890.00	IH	4	113G	4F-1R	16.1	2014	No
B	......	660.00	1570.00	1920.00	IH	4	113G	4F-1R	16.1	2014	No
Cub	......	690.00	1340.00	1660.00	IH	4	60G	3F-1R	10.8	1620	No
H	......	680.00	1600.00	1950.00	IH	4	152G	5F-1R	30.2	3875	No
M	......	850.00	2020.00	2460.00	IH	4	248G	5F-1R	36.0	4964	No
MD	......	910.00	2150.00	2620.00	IH	4	248D	5F-1R	36.0	4964	No
Super A	......	670.00	1590.00	1940.00	IH	4	113G	4F-1R	18.0	2360	No
O4, OS4	......	790.00	1860.00	2270.00	IH	4	152G	5F-1R	25.6	3816	No
W4	......	830.00	1960.00	2390.00	IH	4	152G	5F-1R	30.8	3816	No
O6, OS6	......	840.00	2000.00	2440.00	IH	4	248G	5F-1R	36.0	4858	No
W6	......	900.00	2130.00	2600.00	IH	4	248G	5F-1R	36.0	4858	No
WD6	......	950.00	2240.00	2730.00	IH	4	248D	5F-1R	32.0		No
W9	......	1010.00	2400.00	2930.00	IH	4	335G	5F-1R	49.3	6425	No
WD9	......	1050.00	2480.00	3030.00	IH	4	335D	5F-1R	52.6	6650	No
1948											
C	......	710.00	1630.00	1990.00	IH	4	113G	4F-1R	20.9	2761	No
Cub	......	720.00	1370.00	1700.00	IH	4	60G	3F-1R	10.8	1620	No
H	......	720.00	1650.00	2010.00	IH	4	152G	5F-1R	30.2	3875	No
M	......	910.00	2080.00	2540.00	IH	4	248G	5F-1R	36.0	4964	No
MD	......	1000.00	2280.00	2780.00	IH	4	248D	5F-1R	36.0	4964	No
Super A	......	720.00	1640.00	2000.00	IH	4	113G	4F-1R	18.0	2360	No
O4, OS4	......	840.00	1920.00	2340.00	IH	4	152G	5F-1R	25.6	3816	No
W4	......	870.00	1980.00	2420.00	IH	4	152G	5F-1R	30.8	3816	No
O6, OS6	......	920.00	2100.00	2560.00	IH	4	248G	5F-1R	36.0	4858	No
W6	......	970.00	2210.00	2700.00	IH	4	248G	5F-1R	36.0	4858	No
WD6	......	1010.00	2300.00	2810.00	IH	4	248D	5F-1R	32.0		No
W9	......	1100.00	2510.00	3060.00	IH	4	335G	5F-1R	49.3	6425	No
WD9	......	1120.00	2560.00	3120.00	IH	4	335D	5F-1R	52.6	6650	No
1949											
C	......	760.00	1680.00	2050.00	IH	4	113G	4F-1R	20.9	2761	No
Cub	......	760.00	1410.00	1750.00	IH	4	60G	3F-1R	10.8	1620	No
H	......	770.00	1700.00	2070.00	IH	4	152G	5F-1R	30.2	3875	No
M	......	970.00	2140.00	2610.00	IH	4	248G	5F-1R	36.0	4964	No
MD	......	1050.00	2310.00	2820.00	IH	4	248D	5F-1R	36.0	4964	No
Super A	......	760.00	1690.00	2060.00	IH	4	113G	4F-1R	18.0	2360	No
O4, OS4	......	900.00	1980.00	2420.00	IH	4	152G	5F-1R	25.6	3816	No
W4	......	930.00	2050.00	2500.00	IH	4	152G	5F-1R	30.8	3816	No
O6, OS6	......	990.00	2180.00	2660.00	IH	4	248G	5F-1R	36.0	4858	No
W6	......	1030.00	2270.00	2770.00	IH	4	248G	5F-1R	36.0	4858	No
WD6	......	1070.00	2350.00	2870.00	IH	4	248D	5F-1R	32.0		No
W9	......	1160.00	2560.00	3120.00	IH	4	335G	5F-1R	49.3	6425	No
WD9	......	1190.00	2620.00	3200.00	IH	4	335D	5F-1R	52.6	6650	No
1950											
C	......	810.00	1740.00	2120.00	IH	4	113G	4F-1R	20.9	2761	No
Cub	......	800.00	1440.00	1790.00	IH	4	60G	3F-1R	10.8	1620	No
H	......	830.00	1760.00	2150.00	IH	4	152G	5F-1R	30.2	3875	No
M	......	1030.00	2190.00	2670.00	IH	4	248G	5F-1R	36.0	4964	No
MD	......	1110.00	2370.00	2890.00	IH	4	248D	5F-1R	36.0	4964	No
Super A	......	810.00	1730.00	2110.00	IH	4	113G	4F-1R	18.0	2360	No
O4, OS4	......	950.00	2020.00	2460.00	IH	4	152G	5F-1R	25.6	3816	No
W4	......	980.00	2080.00	2540.00	IH	4	152G	5F-1R	30.8	3816	No
O6, OS6	......	1070.00	2270.00	2770.00	IH	4	248G	5F-1R	36.0	4858	No
W6	......	1100.00	2340.00	2860.00	IH	4	248G	5F-1R	36.0	4858	No
WD6	......	1130.00	2420.00	2950.00	IH	4	248D	5F-1R	32.0		No
W9	......	1250.00	2660.00	3250.00	IH	4	335G	5F-1R	49.3	6425	No
WD9	......	1280.00	2720.00	3320.00	IH	4	335D	5F-1R	52.6	6650	No
1951											
C	......	870.00	1810.00	2210.00	IH	4	113G	4F-1R	20.9	2761	No
Cub	......	850.00	1470.00	1820.00	IH	4	60G	3F-1R	10.8	1620	No
H	......	870.00	1800.00	2200.00	IH	4	152G	5F-1R	30.2	3875	No
M	......	1090.00	2250.00	2750.00	IH	4	248G	5F-1R	36.0	4964	No
MD	......	1190.00	2460.00	3000.00	IH	4	248D	5F-1R	36.0	4964	No
Super A	......	870.00	1790.00	2180.00	IH	4	113G	4F-1R	18.0	2360	No

Model	Approx. Retail Price New	Estimated Average Value Less Repairs Fair	Good	Premium	Engine Make	No. Cyls.	Displ. Cu.-In.	No. Speeds	P.T.O. H.P.	Approx. Shipping Wt.-Lbs.	Cab

Int. Harvester-Farmall (Cont.)

Model	Approx. Retail Price New	Fair	Good	Premium	Make	No. Cyls.	Displ. Cu.-In.	No. Speeds	P.T.O. H.P.	Approx. Shipping Wt.-Lbs.	Cab
1951 (Cont.)											
Super C	......	900.00	1860.00	2270.00	IH	4	123G	4F-1R	23.7	2890	No
O4, OS4	......	1000.00	2070.00	2530.00	IH	4	152G	5F-1R	25.6	3816	No
W4	......	1040.00	2150.00	2620.00	IH	4	152G	5F-1R	30.8	3816	No
O6, OS6	......	1120.00	2310.00	2820.00	IH	4	248G	5F-1R	36.0	4858	No
W6	......	1160.00	2400.00	2930.00	IH	4	248G	5F-1R	36.0	4858	No
WD6	......	1210.00	2500.00	3050.00	IH	4	248D	5F-1R	32.0		No
W9	......	1320.00	2720.00	3320.00	IH	4	335G	5F-1R	49.3	6425	No
WD9	......	1330.00	2750.00	3360.00	IH	4	335D	5F-1R	52.6	6650	No
1952											
Cub	......	890.00	1510.00	1870.00	IH	4	60G	3F-1R	10.8	1620	No
H	......	930.00	1860.00	2270.00	IH	4	152G	5F-1R	30.2	3875	No
M	......	1150.00	2300.00	2810.00	IH	4	248G	5F-1R	36.0	4964	No
MD	......	1250.00	2500.00	3050.00	IH	4	248D	5F-1R	36.0	4964	No
Super A	......	920.00	1850.00	2260.00	IH	4	113G	4F-1R	18.0	2360	No
Super C	......	940.00	1890.00	2310.00	IH	4	123G	4F-1R	23.7	2890	No
Super M	......	1180.00	2370.00	2890.00	IH	4	264G	5F-1R	43.5	5140	No
Super MD	......	1270.00	2530.00	3090.00	IH	4	264D	5F-1R	43.6	5470	No
Super MTA	......	1360.00	2720.00	3320.00	IH	4	264G	10F-2R	43.5	5898	No
Super MTA	......	1450.00	2890.00	3530.00	IH	4	264D	10F-2R	43.6	5898	No
O4, OS4	......	1080.00	2150.00	2620.00	IH	4	152G	5F-1R	25.6	3816	No
W4	......	1120.00	2240.00	2730.00	IH	4	152G	5F-1R	30.8	3816	No
O6, OS6	......	1200.00	2400.00	2930.00	IH	4	248G	5F-1R	36.0	4858	No
W6	......	1230.00	2470.00	3010.00	IH	4	264G	5F-1R	47.9	4838	No
W6TA	......	1270.00	2550.00	3110.00	IH	4	264G	5F-1R	47.9	4838	No
WD6	......	1290.00	2580.00	3150.00	IH	4	264D	5F-1R	47.9	4838	No
WD6TA	......	1370.00	2740.00	3340.00	IH	4	264D	5F-1R	32.0	4838	No
W9	......	1380.00	2750.00	3360.00	IH	4	335G	5F-1R	49.3	6425	No
WD9	......	1410.00	2820.00	3440.00	IH	4	335D	5F-1R	49.3	6650	No
1953											
Cub	......	930.00	1550.00	1920.00	IH	4	60G	3F-1R	10.8	1620	No
H	......	1000.00	1930.00	2360.00	IH	4	152G	5F-1R	30.2	3875	No
Super A	......	980.00	1890.00	2310.00	IH	4	113G	4F-1R	18.0	2360	No
Super C	......	1020.00	1980.00	2420.00	IH	4	123G	4F-1R	23.7	2890	No
Super H	......	1090.00	2110.00	2570.00	IH	4	164G	5F-1R	30.2	3875	No
Super M	......	1280.00	2490.00	3040.00	IH	4	264G	5F-1R	43.5	5140	No
Super MD	......	1340.00	2600.00	3170.00	IH	4	264D	5F-1R	43.6	5470	No
Super MTA	......	1420.00	2750.00	3360.00	IH	4	264G	10F-2R	43.5	5898	No
Super MTA	......	1520.00	2950.00	3600.00	IH	4	264D	10F-2R	43.6	5898	No
O4, OS4	......	1140.00	2210.00	2700.00	IH	4	152G	5F-1R	25.6	3816	No
Super W4	......	1220.00	2370.00	2890.00	IH	4	164G	5F-1R	30.2	3814	No
W4	......	1200.00	2320.00	2830.00	IH	4	152G	5F-1R	30.8	3816	No
O6, OS6	......	1260.00	2450.00	2990.00	IH	4	248G	5F-1R	36.0	4858	No
Super W6	......	1300.00	2530.00	3090.00	IH	4	248G	5F-1R	36.0	4858	No
Super W6TA	......	1390.00	2690.00	3280.00	IH	4	264G	5F-1R	47.9	4838	No
Super WD6	......	1400.00	2720.00	3320.00	IH	4	264G	5F-1R	47.9	4838	No
Super WD6TA	......	1470.00	2850.00	3480.00	IH	4	264D	5F-1R	47.9	4838	No
W6	......	1320.00	2560.00	3120.00	IH	4	248G	5F-1R	36.0	4858	No
WD6	......	1360.00	2640.00	3220.00	IH	4	264G	5F-1R	47.9	4838	No
Super WD9	......	1530.00	2970.00	3620.00	IH	4	335D	5F-1R	49.3	6722	No
W9	......	1450.00	2810.00	3430.00	IH	4	335G	5F-1R	49.3	6425	No
WD9	......	1490.00	2880.00	3510.00	IH	4	335D	5F-1R	52.6	6650	No
1954											
Cub	......	980.00	1580.00	1960.00	IH	4	60G	3F-1R	10.8	1620	No
Super A	......	1030.00	1940.00	2370.00	IH	4	113G	4F-1R	18.0	2360	No
Super C	......	1090.00	2040.00	2490.00	IH	4	123G	4F-1R	23.7	2890	No
Super H	......	1140.00	2140.00	2610.00	IH	4	164G	5F-1R	30.2	3875	No
Super M	......	1340.00	2520.00	3070.00	IH	4	264G	5F-1R	43.6	5140	No
Super MD	......	1410.00	2660.00	3250.00	IH	4	264D	5F-1R	43.6	5470	No
Super MTA	......	1520.00	2870.00	3500.00	IH	4	264G	10F-2R	43.5	5898	No
Super MTA	......	1600.00	3020.00	3680.00	IH	4	264D	10F-2R	43.6	5898	No
Super W4	......	1300.00	2440.00	2980.00	IH	4	164G	5F-1R	30.2	3814	No
Super W6	......	1380.00	2590.00	3160.00	IH	4	248G	5F-1R	36.0	4858	No
Super W6TA	......	1470.00	2770.00	3380.00	IH	4	264G	5F-1R	47.9	4838	No
Super WD6	......	1460.00	2750.00	3360.00	IH	4	264G	5F-1R	47.9	4838	No
Super WD6TA	......	1550.00	2920.00	3560.00	IH	4	264D	5F-1R	47.9	4838	No
Super WD9, WDR9	......	1600.00	3010.00	3670.00	IH	4	335D	5F-1R	49.3	6722	No
100	......	750.00	1410.00	1720.00	IH	6	123G	4F-1R	20.8	2600	No
200	......	830.00	1570.00	1920.00	IH	4	123G	4F-1R	24.2	3160	No
300	......	1000.00	1890.00	2310.00	IH	4	169G	5F-1R	37.9	4143	No
400	......	1210.00	2280.00	2780.00	IH	4	264G	5F-1R	48.3	5240	No
400	......	1280.00	2400.00	2930.00	IH	4	264D	5F-1R	43.6	5650	No
1955											
Cub	......	1010.00	1600.00	1980.00	IH	4	60G	3F-1R	10.8	1620	No
Cub Low-Boy	......	1050.00	1660.00	2060.00	IH	4	60G	3F-1R	10.8	1655	No
Super WD6TA	......	1620.00	2960.00	3610.00	IH	4	264D	5F-1R	47.9	4838	No
Super WD9, WDR9	......	1670.00	3060.00	3730.00	IH	4	350D	5F-1R	59.4	6651	No
100	......	840.00	1540.00	1880.00	IH	6	123G	4F-1R	20.8	2600	No
200	......	930.00	1700.00	2070.00	IH	4	123G	4F-1R	24.2	3160	No
300	......	1140.00	2090.00	2550.00	IH	4	169G	5F-1R	37.9	4143	No
300 U	......	1100.00	2020.00	2460.00	IH	4	169G	5F-1R	37.9	3511	No

Int. Harvester-Farmall (Cont.)

Model	Approx. Retail Price New	Estimated Average Value Less Repairs Fair	Good	Premium	Engine Make	No. Cyls.	Displ. Cu.-In.	No. Speeds	P.T.O. H.P.	Approx. Shipping Wt.-Lbs.	Cab
1955 (Cont.)											
400	......	1270.00	2330.00	2840.00	IH	4	264G	5F-1R	48.3	5240	No
400	......	1350.00	2470.00	3010.00	IH	4	264D	5F-1R	43.6	5650	No
1956											
Cub	......	1070.00	1650.00	2050.00	IH	4	60G	3F-1R	10.8	1620	No
Cub Low-Boy	......	1100.00	1700.00	2110.00	IH	4	60G	3F-1R	10.8	1655	No
Super WD9, WDR9	......	1710.00	3130.00	3820.00	IH	4	350D	5F-1R	59.4	6651	No
100	......	840.00	1540.00	1880.00	IH	4	123G	4F-1R	20.8	2600	No
130	......	890.00	1630.00	1990.00	IH	4	123G	4F-1R	21.8	2680	No
200	......	930.00	1700.00	2070.00	IH	4	123G	4F-1R	24.2	3160	No
230	......	1000.00	1820.00	2220.00	IH	4	123G	4F-1R	27.0	3200	No
300	......	1180.00	2150.00	2620.00	IH	4	169G	5F-1R	37.9	4143	No
300 U	......	1240.00	2270.00	2770.00	IH	4	169G	5F-1R	37.9	3511	No
350	......	1310.00	2400.00	2930.00	IH	4	175G	10F-2R	38.8	4100	No
350	......	1410.00	2570.00	3140.00	IH	4	193D	10F-2R	37.9	4187	No
400	......	1370.00	2510.00	3060.00	IH	4	264G	5F-1R	48.3	5240	No
400	......	1480.00	2700.00	3290.00	IH	4	264D	5F-1R	43.6	5650	No
450	......	1400.00	2560.00	3120.00	IH	6	281G	5F-1R	51.1	5800	No
450	......	1450.00	2660.00	3250.00	IH	6	281D	5F-1R	47.4	6180	No
650	......	1810.00	2480.00	2850.00	IH	6	350G		60.6	4880	No
650	......	2030.00	2780.00	3200.00	IH	6	350D		61.6	5123	No
1957											
Cub	......	1110.00	1680.00	2080.00	IH	4	60G	3F-1R	10.8	1620	No
Cub Low-Boy	......	1160.00	1750.00	2170.00	IH	4	60G	3F-1R	10.8	1655	No
130	......	1310.00	2400.00	2930.00	IH	4	123G	4F-1R	20.8	2680	No
230	......	1210.00	2210.00	2700.00	IH	4	123G	4F-1R	27.0	3200	No
330 U	......	1280.00	2340.00	2860.00	IH	4	135G	10F-2R	37.9	3920	No
350	......	1440.00	2640.00	3220.00	IH	4	175G	10F-2R	38.8	4100	No
350	......	1520.00	2780.00	3390.00	IH	4	193D	10F-2R	37.9	4187	No
450	......	1440.00	2620.00	3200.00	IH	6	281G	5F-1R	51.1	5800	No
450	......	1510.00	2750.00	3360.00	IH	6	281D	5F-1R	47.4	6180	No
650	......	1850.00	2480.00	2850.00	IH	6	350G		60.6	4880	No
650	......	2140.00	2870.00	3300.00	IH	6	350D		61.6	5123	No
1958											
Cub	......	1130.00	1700.00	2110.00	IH	4	60G	3F-1R	10.8	1620	No
Cub Low-Boy	......	1180.00	1780.00	2210.00	IH	4	60G	3F-1R	10.8	1655	No
130	......	1350.00	2460.00	3000.00	IH	4	123G	4F-1R	20.8	2680	No
140	......	1800.00	2720.00	3370.00	IH	4	123G	4F-1R	23.7	3107	No
230	......	1060.00	1950.00	2380.00	IH	4	123G	4F-1R	27.0	3200	No
240	......	1170.00	2140.00	2610.00	IH	4	123G	4F-1R	31	3360	No
330 U	......	1320.00	2410.00	2940.00	IH	4	135G	10F-2R	37.9	3920	No
340	......	1330.00	2430.00	2970.00	IH	4	135G	5F-1R	36	4405	No
340	......	1540.00	2820.00	3440.00	IH	4	135D	5F-1R	36	4510	No
350	......	1520.00	2770.00	3380.00	IH	4	175G	10F-2R	42.6	4785	No
350	......	1550.00	2840.00	3470.00	IH	4	193D	10F-2R	37.9	4187	No
450	......	1590.00	2910.00	3550.00	IH	6	281G	5F-1R	51.1	5800	No
450	......	1630.00	2980.00	3640.00	IH	6	281D	5F-1R	47.4	6180	No
460	......	1510.00	2750.00	3360.00	IH	6	221G	5F-1R	50	5265	No
460	......	1680.00	3070.00	3750.00	IH	6	236D	5F-1R	50	5485	No
560	......	1650.00	3010.00	3670.00	IH	6	263G	5F-1R	62	5898	No
560	......	2020.00	3690.00	4500.00	IH	6	282D	5F-1R	62	6172	No
650	......	1920.00	2520.00	2870.00	IH	6	350G		60.6	4880	No
650	......	2170.00	2850.00	3250.00	IH	6	350D		61.6	5123	No
1959											
Cub	......	1180.00	1740.00	2160.00	IH	4	60G	3F-1R	10.8	1620	No
Cub Low-Boy	......	1230.00	1820.00	2260.00	IH	4	60G	3F-1R	10.8	1655	No
140	......	1860.00	2750.00	3410.00	IH	4	123G	4F-1R	23.7	3107	No
240	......	1370.00	2500.00	3050.00	IH	4	123G	4F-1R	31	3360	No
B-275	......	1330.00	2430.00	2970.00	IH	4	144D	8F-2R	32.8	3520	No
340	......	1380.00	2530.00	3090.00	IH	4	135G	5F-1R	36	4405	No
340	......	1580.00	2880.00	3510.00	IH	4	135D	5F-1R	36	4510	No
450	......	1620.00	2970.00	3620.00	IH	4	281G	10F-2R	51.1	5912	No
460	......	1440.00	2630.00	3210.00	IH	6	221G	5F-1R	52	5265	No
460	......	1750.00	3200.00	3900.00	IH	6	236D	5F-1R	52	5485	No
560	......	1730.00	3170.00	3870.00	IH	6	263G	5F-1R	42	5961	No
560	......	2100.00	3840.00	4690.00	IH	6	282D	5F-1R	62	6172	No
660	......	1720.00	2250.00	2570.00	IH	6	263G	5F-1R	80	7925	No
660	......	1960.00	2580.00	2940.00	IH	6	281D	5F-1R	80	8190	No
1960											
Cub	......	1200.00	1770.00	2200.00	IH	4	60G	3F-1R	10.8	1620	No
Cub Low-Boy	......	1250.00	1850.00	2290.00	IH	4	60G	3F-1R	10.8	1655	No
140	......	1890.00	2790.00	3460.00	IH	4	123G	4F-1R	23.7	3107	No
240	......	1330.00	2370.00	2890.00	IH	4	123G	4F-1R	31.	3360	No
B-275	......	1400.00	2500.00	3050.00	IH	4	144D	8F-2R	32.8	3520	No
340D	......	1670.00	2980.00	3640.00	IH	4	135D	5F-1R	36	4510	No
340G	......	1480.00	2620.00	3200.00	IH	4	135G	5F-1R	36	4405	No
404	......	1350.00	2400.00	2930.00	IH	4	135G	4F-1R	36.7	3427	No
460	......	1550.00	2750.00	3360.00	IH	6	221G	5F-1R	50	5265	No
460	......	1870.00	3330.00	4060.00	IH	6	236D	5F-1R	50	5485	No
560	......	1840.00	3280.00	4000.00	IH	6	263G	5F-1R	62	5898	No

Model	Approx. Retail Price New	Estimated Average Value Less Repairs Fair	Good	Premium	Engine Make	No. Cyls.	Displ. Cu.-In.	No. Speeds	P.T.O. H.P.	Approx. Shipping Wt.-Lbs.	Cab

Int. Harvester-Farmall (Cont.)

Model	Approx. Retail Price New	Fair	Good	Premium	Make	No. Cyls.	Displ. Cu.-In.	No. Speeds	P.T.O. H.P.	Approx. Shipping Wt.-Lbs.	Cab
1960 (Cont.)											
560	......	2240.00	3980.00	4860.00	IH	6	281D	5F-1R	62	6172	No
660	......	1790.00	2350.00	2660.00	IH	6	263G	5F-1R	80	7925	No
660	......	2030.00	2670.00	3020.00	IH	6	281D	5F-1R	80	8190	No
1961											
Cub	......	1220.00	1800.00	2230.00	IH	4	60G	3F-1R	10.8	1620	No
Cub Low-Boy	......	1270.00	1880.00	2330.00	IH	4	60G	3F-1R	10.8	1655	No
140	......	1960.00	2890.00	3580.00	IH	4	123G	4F-1R	23.7	3107	No
240	......	1430.00	2460.00	3000.00	IH	4	123G	4F-1R	31.0	3360	No
B-275	......	1690.00	2920.00	3560.00	IH	4	144D	8F-2R	32.8	3520	No
340D	......	1780.00	3070.00	3750.00	IH	4	135D	5F-1R	36	4510	No
340G	......	1570.00	2720.00	3320.00	IH	4	135G	5F-1R	36	4405	No
404	......	1460.00	2530.00	3090.00	IH	4	135G	4F-1R	36.7	3560	No
460	......	1850.00	3200.00	3900.00	IH	6	221D	5F-1R	50	4835	No
460	......	2150.00	3710.00	4530.00	IH	6	221G	5F-1R	50	5265	No
504	......	1680.00	2910.00	3550.00	IH	4	153G	10F-2R	46.0	4453	No
504	......	1950.00	3380.00	4120.00	IH	4	188D	10F-2R	46.2	4608	No
560	......	2060.00	3560.00	4340.00	IH	6	263G	5F-1R	62	5898	No
560	......	2350.00	4070.00	4970.00	IH	6	281D	5F-1R	62	6172	No
660	......	1860.00	2440.00	2760.00	IH	6	263G	5F-1R	80	7925	No
660	......	2100.00	2760.00	3120.00	IH	6	281D	5F-1R	80	8190	No
1962											
Cub	1650.00	1240.00	1840.00	2280.00	IH	4	60G	3F-1R	10.8	1620	No
Cub Low-Boy	1675.00	1300.00	1920.00	2380.00	IH	4	60G	3F-1R	10.8	1655	No
140	2400.00	2020.00	2990.00	3710.00	IH	4	123G	4F-1R	20.8	3031	No
240	2670.00	1400.00	2350.00	2870.00	IH	4	123G	4F-1R	32	3360	No
340	3600.00	1750.00	2940.00	3590.00	IH	4	135G	5F-1R	36	4405	No
340	4300.00	2010.00	3390.00	4140.00	IH	4	166D	5F-1R	38.9	4510	No
404	2960.00	1510.00	2530.00	3090.00	IH	4	135G	4F-1R	36.7	3560	No
B414	2720.00	1410.00	2380.00	2900.00	IH	4	143G	8F-2R	36.9	3600	No
B414	3020.00	1530.00	2570.00	3140.00	IH	4	154D	8F-2R	35.9	3650	No
460	4725.00	1990.00	3340.00	4080.00	IH	6	236G	5F-1R	50	5265	No
460	5400.00	2240.00	3780.00	4610.00	IH	6	236D	5F-1R	50	5485	No
504	3820.00	1830.00	3090.00	3770.00	IH	4	153G	10F-2R	46.0	4608	No
504	4400.00	2050.00	3460.00	4220.00	IH	4	188D	10F-2R	46.2	4453	No
560	5430.00	2180.00	3670.00	4480.00	IH	6	263G	5F-1R	62	5898	No
560	6220.00	2480.00	4170.00	5090.00	IH	6	281D	5F-1R	62	6172	No
606	4500.00	1770.00	2320.00	2620.00	IH	6	221G	10F-2R	53.8	4880	No
606	5300.00	2050.00	2690.00	3040.00	IH	6	236D	10F-2R	54.3	5123	No
660	5950.00	2240.00	2940.00	3320.00	IH	6	263G	5F-1R	82	7925	No
660	6650.00	2490.00	3270.00	3700.00	IH	6	281D	5F-1R	80	8190	No
1963											
Cub	1675.00	1260.00	1870.00	2320.00	IH	4	60G	3F-1R	10.8	1620	No
Cub Low-Boy	1700.00	1330.00	1960.00	2430.00	IH	4	60G	3F-1R	10.8	1655	No
140	2450.00	2050.00	3030.00	3760.00	IH	4	122G	4F-1R	20.8	2750	No
340	3605.00	1790.00	2940.00	3590.00	IH	4	135G	5F-1R	36	4400	No
340	4355.00	2070.00	3390.00	4140.00	IH	4	166D	5F-1R	38.9	4515	No
404	2970.00	1550.00	2540.00	3100.00	IH	4	135G	4F-1R	36.7	3750	No
B414	2770.00	1470.00	2410.00	2940.00	IH	4	144G	8F-2R	36	3700	No
B414	3065.00	1590.00	2600.00	3170.00	IH	4	154D	8F-2R	36	3770	No
460	4780.00	2250.00	3700.00	4510.00	IH	6	236G	5F-1R	50	5255	No
460	5500.00	2540.00	4160.00	5080.00	IH	6	236D	5F-1R	50	5420	No
504	3865.00	1900.00	3110.00	3790.00	IH	4	153G	10F-2R	46.0	4880	No
504	4430.00	2120.00	3480.00	4250.00	IH	4	188D	10F-2R	46.2	4430	No
560	5470.00	2250.00	3690.00	4500.00	IH	6	263G	5F-1R	62	5900	No
560	6260.00	2560.00	4200.00	5120.00	IH	6	281D	5F-1R	62	6175	No
606	4600.00	1750.00	2300.00	2600.00	IH	6	221G	10F-2R	53.8	4880	No
606	5320.00	1680.00	2210.00	2500.00	IH	6	236D	10F-2R	54.3	5123	No
660	5980.00	2000.00	2620.00	2960.00	IH	6	263G	5F-1R	82	7925	No
660	6700.00	2280.00	2990.00	3380.00	IH	6	281D	5F-1R	80	8190	No
706	5940.00	2710.00	4440.00	5420.00	IH	6	263G	8F-4R	70	7620	No
706	6720.00	3010.00	4940.00	6030.00	IH	6	282D	8F-4R	70	7900	No
806	6690.00	3000.00	4920.00	6000.00	IH	6	301G	16F-8R	90	7930	No
806	7480.00	3310.00	5430.00	6630.00	IH	6	361D	16F-8R	90	8690	No
1964											
Cub	1680.00	1290.00	1900.00	2360.00	IH	4	60G	3F-1R	10.8	1620	No
Cub Low-Boy	1710.00	1350.00	1990.00	2470.00	IH	4	60G	3F-1R	10.8	1655	No
140	2520.00	2080.00	3070.00	3810.00	IH	4	122G	4F-1R	20.8	2520	No
404	3110.00	1640.00	2620.00	3200.00	IH	4	135G	4F-1R	36.7	3750	No
B414	2800.00	1520.00	2430.00	2970.00	IH	4	143G	8F-2R	36.9	3700	No
B414	3100.00	1660.00	2660.00	3250.00	IH	4	154D	8F-2R	35.9	3770	No
424	3000.00	1600.00	2560.00	3120.00	IH	4	146G	8F-2R	35	3700	No
424	3320.00	1740.00	2780.00	3390.00	IH	4	154D	8F-2R	36.5	3820	No
504	3920.00	1970.00	3150.00	3840.00	IH	4	188G	10F-2R	46.2	4310	No
504	4485.00	2190.00	3510.00	4280.00	IH	4	153D	10F-2R	46.0	4510	No
606	4775.00	2310.00	3700.00	4510.00	IH	6	221G	10F-2R	53.8	4880	No
606	5500.00	2600.00	4160.00	5080.00	IH	6	236D	10F-2R	54.3	5123	No
706	6010.00	2920.00	4680.00	5710.00	IH	6	263G	8F-4R	70	7620	No
706	6800.00	3120.00	4990.00	6090.00	IH	6	282D	8F-4R	70	8360	No
806	6930.00	3170.00	5080.00	6200.00	IH	6	301G	16F-8R	90	7930	No
806	7730.00	3490.00	5590.00	6820.00	IH	6	361D	16F-8R	90	8690	No

Int. Harvester-Farmall (Cont.)

Model	Approx. Retail Price New	Estimated Average Value Less Repairs Fair	Good	Premium	Engine Make	No. Cyls.	Displ. Cu.-In.	No. Speeds	P.T.O. H.P.	Approx. Shipping Wt.-Lbs.	Cab
1965											
Cub	1750.00	1310.00	1940.00	2410.00	IH	4	60G	3F-1R	10.8	1620	No
Cub Low-Boy	1770.00	1380.00	2040.00	2530.00	IH	4	60G	3F-1R	10.8	1655	No
140	2610.00	2120.00	3140.00	3890.00	IH	4	122G	4F-1R	24	2750	No
404	3210.00	1720.00	2690.00	3280.00	IH	4	135G	4F-1R	36.7	3760	No
B414	2910.00	1600.00	2500.00	3050.00	IH	4	143G	8F-2R	36.9	3700	No
B414	3210.00	1730.00	2690.00	3280.00	IH	4	154D	8F-2R	36	3770	No
424	3095.00	1680.00	2620.00	3200.00	IH	4	146G	8F-2R	36.5	3730	No
424	3410.00	1800.00	2820.00	3440.00	IH	4	154D	8F-2R	36.5	3880	No
504	4030.00	2060.00	3220.00	3930.00	IH	4	153G	10F-2R	46.0	4880	No
504	4595.00	2290.00	3580.00	4370.00	IH	4	188D	10F-2R	46.2	5080	No
606	4860.00	2400.00	3750.00	4580.00	IH	6	221G	10F-2R	53.8	4880	No
606	5595.00	2700.00	4220.00	5150.00	IH	6	236D	10F-2R	54.3	5120	No
656	5400.00	2620.00	4100.00	5000.00	IH	6	263G	10F-2R	63.5	6530	No
656	6130.00	2920.00	4560.00	5560.00	IH	6	282D	10F-2R	61.5	6800	No
706	6160.00	2900.00	4520.00	5510.00	IH	6	282G	8F-4R	73	8100	No
706	6955.00	3260.00	5090.00	6210.00	IH	6	282D	8F-4R	72	8360	No
806	7055.00	3300.00	5160.00	6300.00	IH	6	361G	16F-8R	93	7930	No
806	7880.00	3640.00	5680.00	6930.00	IH	6	361D	16F-8R	94.9	8690	No
1206	9100.00	4140.00	6460.00	7880.00	IH	6T	361D	16F-8R	112.5	9500	No
1966											
Cub	1790.00	1370.00	1980.00	2460.00	IH	4	60G	3F-1R	10.8	1620	No
Cub Low-Boy	1830.00	1440.00	2080.00	2580.00	IH	4	60G	3F-1R	10.8	1655	No
140	2700.00	2210.00	3200.00	3970.00	IH	4	123G	4F-1R	23.7	2640	No
404	3320.00	1810.00	2770.00	3380.00	IH	4	135G	4F-1R	36.7	3460	No
B414	2930.00	1640.00	2500.00	3050.00	IH	4	143G	8F-2R	36.9	3700	No
B414	3230.00	1780.00	2710.00	3310.00	IH	4	154D	8F-2R	35.9	3750	No
424	3180.00	1760.00	2680.00	3270.00	IH	4	146G	8F-2R	36	3730	No
424	3500.00	1890.00	2880.00	3510.00	IH	4	154D	8F-2R	36.5	3820	No
504	4120.00	2150.00	3280.00	4000.00	IH	4	153G	10F-2R	46.2	4880	No
504	4650.00	2370.00	3620.00	4420.00	IH	4	188D	10F-2R	46.2	5080	No
606	4940.00	2500.00	3800.00	4640.00	IH	6	221G	10F-2R	53.8	4880	No
606	5670.00	2800.00	4270.00	5210.00	IH	6	236D	10F-2R	54.3	5123	No
656	5650.00	2840.00	4320.00	5270.00	IH	6	263G	10F-2R	63.5	6550	No
656	6410.00	3110.00	4740.00	5780.00	IH	6	282D	10F-2R	61.5	6800	No
706	6310.00	3070.00	4670.00	5700.00	IH	6	310G	8F-4R	76	7620	No
706	7105.00	3400.00	5180.00	6320.00	IH	6	291D	8F-4R	76.5	7900	No
806	7180.00	3350.00	5110.00	6230.00	IH	6	361G	16F-8R	90	7930	No
806	8040.00	3800.00	5790.00	7060.00	IH	6	361D	16F-8R	90	8690	No
1206	9450.00	4390.00	6690.00	8160.00	IH	6T	361D	16F-8R	112.5	10500	No
4100	18000.00	5040.00	7020.00	7930.00	IH	6T	429D	8F-2R	110.0	13940	No
4300	24000.00	3840.00	6240.00	7050.00	IH	6T	817D	8F-2R	203.0	27620	No
1967											
Cub	1980.00	1400.00	2030.00	2520.00	IH	4	60G	3F-1R	10.8	1620	No
Cub Low-Boy	2020.00	1470.00	2130.00	2640.00	IH	4	60G	3F-1R	10.8	1655	No
140	2790.00	2300.00	3330.00	4130.00	IH	4	122G	4F-1R	20.8	2750	No
404	3340.00	1870.00	2780.00	3390.00	IH	4	135G	4F-1R	36.7	3470	No
B414	2950.00	1700.00	2530.00	3090.00	IH	4	144G	8F-2R	36	3710	No
B414	3250.00	1790.00	2660.00	3250.00	IH	4	154D	8F-2R	36	3770	No
424	3270.00	1870.00	2780.00	3390.00	IH	4	146G	8F-2R	37	3700	No
424	3600.00	1980.00	2940.00	3590.00	IH	4	154D	8F-2R	37	3820	No
444	3480.00	1930.00	2870.00	3500.00	IH	4	144G	8F-2R	38	3700	No
444	3850.00	2090.00	3100.00	3780.00	IH	4	154D	8F-2R	37	3820	No
504	4200.00	2240.00	3330.00	4060.00	IH	4	153G	10F-2R	46	4880	No
504	4765.00	2480.00	3690.00	4500.00	IH	4	188D	10F-2R	46	5080	No
606	4975.00	2570.00	3820.00	4660.00	IH	6	221G	10F-2R	54	4880	No
606	5700.00	2880.00	4290.00	5230.00	IH	6	236D	10F-2R	54	5123	No
656	5900.00	2970.00	4420.00	5390.00	IH	6	263G	10F-2R	63	6550	No
656	6680.00	3300.00	4920.00	6000.00	IH	6	282D	10F-2R	61	6800	No
706	6460.00	3210.00	4770.00	5820.00	IH	6	310G	8F-4R	76	8070	No
706	7330.00	3580.00	5330.00	6500.00	IH	6	310D	8F-4R	76	8390	No
756	7130.00	3500.00	5200.00	6340.00	IH	6	291G	8F-4R	76	8070	No
756	7960.00	3850.00	5730.00	6990.00	IH	6	310D	8F-4R	76	8350	No
806	7260.00	3550.00	5290.00	6450.00	IH	6	361G	16F-8R	93	7930	No
806	8125.00	3920.00	5840.00	7130.00	IH	6	361D	16F-8R	94	8690	No
856	7870.00	3810.00	5680.00	6930.00	IH	6	301G	8F-4R	93	8510	No
856	9040.00	4320.00	6430.00	7850.00	IH	6	407D	8F-4R	100.4	9270	No
1206	9825.00	4660.00	6930.00	8460.00	IH	6	361D	8F-4R	112.6	9500	No
1256	10500.00	4950.00	7360.00	8980.00	IH	6	407D	16F-8R	116.1	11030	No
4100	18250.00	5110.00	7120.00	7970.00	IH	6T	429D	8F-2R	110.0	13940	No
4300	24200.00	3870.00	6290.00	7110.00	IH	6T	817D	8F-2R	203.0	27620	No
1968											
Cub	2070.00	1470.00	2090.00	2590.00	IH	4	60G	3F-1R	10.8	1620	No
Cub Low-Boy	2100.00	1530.00	2160.00	2680.00	IH	4	60G	3F-1R	10.8	1655	No
Cub 154 Low-Boy	1980.00	1000.00	1410.00	1750.00	IH	4	60G	3F-1R	13.5	1480	No
140	2950.00	2380.00	3370.00	4180.00	IH	4	122G	4F-1R	20.8	2750	No
404	3440.00	1950.00	2840.00	3470.00	IH	4	135G	4F-1R	36.7	3460	No
444	3725.00	2080.00	3020.00	3680.00	IH	4	144G	8F-2R	36.5	3738	No
444	4105.00	2250.00	3270.00	3990.00	IH	4	154D	8F-2R	36.5	3888	No
504	4270.00	2320.00	3370.00	4110.00	IH	4	153G	10F-2R	46.0	4808	No
504	4835.00	2570.00	3730.00	4550.00	IH	4	188D	10F-2R	46.2	4553	No
544	5340.00	2790.00	4060.00	4950.00	IH	4	200G	10F-2R	53	6342	No

Int. Harvester-Farmall (Cont.)

1968 (Cont.)

Model	Approx. Retail Price New	Estimated Average Value Less Repairs: Fair	Good	Premium	Engine: Make	No. Cyls.	Displ. Cu.-In.	No. Speeds	P.T.O. H.P.	Approx. Shipping Wt.-Lbs.	Cab
544	5595.00	2860.00	4160.00	5080.00	IH	4	123D	10F-2R	53	6442	No
656	6200.00	3170.00	4610.00	5620.00	IH	6	263G	10F-2R	63.5	6350	No
656	7020.00	3530.00	5130.00	6260.00	IH	6	282D	10F-2R	61.5	6800	No
656H	7020.00	2890.00	3690.00	4170.00	IH	6	282D	Infinite	66	6500	No
656H	7120.00	2920.00	3740.00	4230.00	IH	6	263G	Infinite	63.5	6900	No
756	7380.00	3690.00	5360.00	6540.00	IH	6	291G	16F-8R	76.5	9619	No
756	8210.00	4050.00	5890.00	7190.00	IH	6	310D	8F-4R	76	9561	No
756 4WD	10180.00	4700.00	6840.00	8350.00	IH	6	291G	16F-8R	76.5	8970	No
756 4WD	11000.00	5060.00	7360.00	8980.00	IH	6	310D	16F-8R	76	9500	No
856	8210.00	3830.00	5570.00	6800.00	IH	6	301G	16F-8R	93	8890	No
856	9290.00	4530.00	6590.00	8040.00	IH	6	407D	16F-8R	100.5	9760	No
856 4WD	9290.00	4310.00	6270.00	7650.00	IH	6	407D	16F-8R	100.5	10170	No
856 4WD	10940.00	4810.00	7000.00	8540.00	IH	6	301G	16F-8R	93	9410	No
1256	10720.00	4940.00	7180.00	8760.00	IH	6T	407D	8F-4R	116.0	9525	No
4100 4WD	18500.00	5180.00	7220.00	8090.00	IH	6T	429D	8F-4R	110.0	13940	No
4300 4WD	24500.00	3920.00	6370.00	7130.00	IH	6T	817D	8F-4R	203.0	27620	No

H--Hydrostatic Transmission

1969

Model	Approx. Retail Price New	Fair	Good	Premium	Make	No. Cyls.	Displ. Cu.-In.	No. Speeds	P.T.O. H.P.	Approx. Shipping Wt.-Lbs.	Cab
Cub	2140.00	1540.00	2140.00	2650.00	IH	4	60G	3F-1R	10.8	1620	No
Cub 154 Low-Boy	2060.00	1080.00	1500.00	1860.00	IH	4	60G	3F-1R	13.5	1480	No
140	3180.00	2540.00	3520.00	4370.00	IH	4	122G	4F-1R	20.8	2640	No
444	3970.00	2240.00	3180.00	3880.00	IH	4	144G	8F-2R	36.5	3700	No
444	4360.00	2410.00	3430.00	4190.00	IH	4	154D	8F-2R	36.5	3888	No
544	6180.00	3200.00	4540.00	5540.00	IH	4	239D	10F-2R	53.0	6342	No
656	6435.00	3330.00	4740.00	5780.00	IH	6	263G	10F-2R	63.5	6550	No
656	7260.00	3720.00	5290.00	6450.00	IH	6	282D	10F-2R	61.5	6800	No
656H	7310.00	2890.00	3590.00	4060.00	IH	6	263G	Infinite	65.5	6200	No
656H	8055.00	3170.00	3940.00	4450.00	IH	6	282D	Infinite	66	6500	No
756	7630.00	3880.00	5520.00	6730.00	IH	6	291G	8F-4R	76.5	8070	No
756	8460.00	4260.00	6050.00	7380.00	IH	6	310D	8F-4R	76	8350	No
756 4WD	10430.00	4690.00	6680.00	8150.00	IH	6	291G	8F-4R	76.5	8970	No
756 4WD	11260.00	5070.00	7210.00	8800.00	IH	6	310D	16F-8R	76	9250	No
826	9210.00	4600.00	6530.00	7970.00	IH	6	358D	16F-8R	92.0	8930	No
826 4WD	11810.00	5320.00	7560.00	9220.00	IH	6	358D	16F-8R	92.0	8930	No
826H	9420.00	3670.00	4560.00	5150.00	IH	6	301G	Infinite	84.1	9000	No
826H	10220.00	4040.00	5020.00	5670.00	IH	6	358D	Infinite	84.1	9000	No
856	8650.00	4120.00	5860.00	7150.00	IH	6	301G	8F-4R	93.0	8620	No
856	10080.00	4760.00	6770.00	8260.00	IH	6	407D	8F-4R	100.5	9260	No
856 4WD	11380.00	5120.00	7280.00	8880.00	IH	6	301G	8F-4R	93.0	9420	No
856 4WD	12470.00	5840.00	8300.00	10130.00	IH	6	407D	8F-4R	100.5	10000	No
1256	10925.00	5140.00	7310.00	8920.00	IH	6T	407D	8F-4R	116.0	9925	No
1456	12050.00	4830.00	6000.00	6780.00	IH	6T	407D	16F-8R	131.5	10700	No
1456 4WD	14900.00	5510.00	6850.00	7740.00	IH	6	407D	16F-8R	131.5	14649	No
4156 4WD	19000.00	5320.00	7410.00	8300.00	IH	6T	429D	8F-4R	140	13940	No
4300 4WD	25000.00	4000.00	6500.00	7280.00	IH	6T	817D	8F-2R	203.0	27620	No

H--Hydrostatic Transmission

1970

Model	Approx. Retail Price New	Fair	Good	Premium	Make	No. Cyls.	Displ. Cu.-In.	No. Speeds	P.T.O. H.P.	Approx. Shipping Wt.-Lbs.	Cab
Cub	2230.00	1620.00	2200.00	2730.00	IH	4	60G	3F-1R	10.75	1620	No
Cub 154 Lo Boy	2110.00	1130.00	1530.00	1900.00	IH	4	60G	3F-1R	13.50	1480	No
140	3300.00	2650.00	3600.00	4460.00	IH	4	123G	4F-1R	24.30	2750	No
444	4215.00	2400.00	3340.00	4080.00	IH	4	153G	8F-2R	38.09	3700	No
444	4615.00	2580.00	3590.00	4380.00	IH	4	154D	8F-2R	36.91	3820	No
544	5840.00	3150.00	4380.00	5340.00	IH	4	200G	10F-2R	52.84	6300	No
544	6430.00	3420.00	4760.00	5810.00	IH	4	239D	10F-2R	52.95	6500	No
544H	6600.00	2890.00	3500.00	3960.00	IH	4	200G	Infinite	53.87	6400	No
544H	7190.00	3110.00	3770.00	4260.00	IH	4	239D	Infinite	55.52	6600	No
574	5515.00	3000.00	4170.00	5090.00	IH	4	200G	8F-4R	52.97	4700	No
574	6310.00	3360.00	4680.00	5710.00	IH	4	239D	8F-4R	52.55	4800	No
656	6670.00	3530.00	4910.00	5990.00	IH	6	263G	10F-2R	63.85	6530	No
656	7545.00	3930.00	5470.00	6670.00	IH	6	282D	10F-2R	61.42	6800	No
656H	7505.00	3040.00	3680.00	4160.00	IH	6	263G	Infinite	65.80	6900	No
656H	8340.00	3320.00	4020.00	4540.00	IH	6	282D	Infinite	66.06	7170	No
756	7880.00	4090.00	5680.00	6930.00	IH	6	291G	16F-8R	76.56	8070	No
756	8710.00	4470.00	6210.00	7580.00	IH	6	310D	16F-8R	76.09	8350	No
756 4WD	10680.00	5140.00	7160.00	8740.00	IH	6	291G	16F-8R	76.00	8970	No
756 4WD	11510.00	5530.00	7690.00	9380.00	IH	6	310D	16F-8R	76.00	9250	No
826	9430.00	4800.00	6680.00	8150.00	IH	6	358D	16F-8R	92.19	8830	No
826 4WD	12080.00	5560.00	7730.00	9430.00	IH	6	358D	16F-8R	92.00	9730	No
826H	9640.00	3850.00	4660.00	5270.00	IH	6	301G	Infinite	84.15	8900	No
826H	10310.00	4110.00	4970.00	5620.00	IH	6	358D	Infinite	84.66	9000	No
856	9090.00	4640.00	6460.00	7880.00	IH	6	301G	16F-8R	93.27	8510	No
856	10190.00	5150.00	7160.00	8740.00	IH	6	407D	16F-8R	100.49	9270	No
856 4WD	11890.00	5470.00	7610.00	9280.00	IH	6	301G	16F-8R	93.00	9410	No
856 4WD	12990.00	5980.00	8310.00	10140.00	IH	6	407D	16F-8R	100.	10170	No
1026H	11080.00	4400.00	5330.00	6020.00	IH	6T	407D	Infinite	112.45	9500	No
1026H 4WD	13730.00	5220.00	6320.00	7140.00	IH	6T	407D	Infinite	112.00	10950	No
1456	12220.00	4830.00	5850.00	6610.00	IH	6T	407D	16F-8R	131.80	10600	No
1456 4WD	15320.00	5820.00	7050.00	7970.00	IH	6T	407D	16F-8R	131.00	12050	No
4156 4WD	19300.00	5400.00	7530.00	8430.00	IH	6T	429D	8F-4R	116.1	13940	No
4300 4WD	25300.00	4050.00	6580.00	7370.00	IH	6T	817D	8F-4R	214.2	27620	No

H--Hydrostatic Transmission

Int. Harvester-Farmall (Cont.)

1971

Model	Approx. Retail Price New	Estimated Average Value Less Repairs: Fair	Good	Premium	Engine: Make	No. Cyls.	Displ. Cu.-In.	No. Speeds	P.T.O. H.P.	Approx. Shipping Wt.-Lbs.	Cab
Cub	2400.00	1730.00	2310.00	2860.00	IH	4	60G	3F-1R	10.75	1620	No
Cub 154 Lo Boy	2260.00	1190.00	1580.00	1960.00	IH	4	60G	3F-1R	13.50	1480	No
140	3410.00	2760.00	3680.00	4560.00	IH	4	123G	4F-1R	24.30	2750	No
444	4470.00	2570.00	3500.00	4270.00	IH	4	153G	8F-2R	38.09	3700	No
444	4880.00	2760.00	3760.00	4590.00	IH	4	154D	8F-2R	36.91	3820	No
454	4265.00	2480.00	3370.00	4110.00	IH	4	157G	8F-4R	40.86	4240	No
454	4705.00	2680.00	3650.00	4450.00	IH	3	179D	8F-4R	40.47	4560	No
544	6090.00	3330.00	4540.00	5540.00	IH	4	200G	10F-2R	52.84	6300	No
544	6680.00	3610.00	4920.00	6000.00	IH	4	239D	10F-2R	52.95	6500	No
544H	6850.00	3060.00	3690.00	4170.00	IH	4	200G	Infinite	53.87	6400	No
544H	7440.00	3290.00	3970.00	4490.00	IH	4	239D	Infinite	55.52	6600	No
574	5760.00	3180.00	4330.00	5280.00	IH	4	200G	8F-4R	52.97	4700	No
574	6570.00	3560.00	4850.00	5920.00	IH	4	239D	8F-4R	52.55	4800	No
656	6905.00	3720.00	5060.00	6170.00	IH	6	263G	10F-2R	63.85	6530	No
656	7745.00	4110.00	5600.00	6830.00	IH	6	282D	10F-2R	61.42	6800	No
656H	7695.00	3390.00	4090.00	4620.00	IH	6	263G	Infinite	65.80	6900	No
656H	8545.00	3530.00	4250.00	4800.00	IH	6	282D	Infinite	66.06	7170	No
756	8130.00	4290.00	5840.00	7130.00	IH	6	291G	16F-8R	76.56	8070	No
756	8960.00	4450.00	6050.00	7380.00	IH	6	310D	16F-8R	76.09	8350	No
756 4WD	10930.00	5370.00	7320.00	8930.00	IH	6	291G	16F-8R	76.00	8970	No
756 4WD	11760.00	5760.00	7850.00	9580.00	IH	6	310D	16F-8R	76.00	9250	No
766	8210.00	3400.00	4090.00	4620.00	IH	6	291G	16F-8R	79.73	9000	No
766	8760.00	3610.00	4350.00	4920.00	IH	6	360D	16F-8R	85.45	9500	No
826	9650.00	4770.00	6500.00	7930.00	IH	6	358D	16F-8R	92.19	8830	No
826 4WD	12840.00	6040.00	8220.00	10030.00	IH	6	358D	16F-8R	92.00	9730	No
826H	9860.00	4040.00	4870.00	5500.00	IH	6	301G	Infinite	84.15	8900	No
826H	10400.00	4250.00	5120.00	5790.00	IH	6	358D	Infinite	84.66	9000	No
826H 4WD	13050.00	5090.00	6130.00	6930.00	IH	6	301G	Infinite	84.00	9800	No
826H 4WD	13590.00	5300.00	6390.00	7220.00	IH	6	358D	Infinite	84.00	9900	No
856	9640.00	4770.00	6490.00	7920.00	IH	6	301G	16F-8R	93.27	8510	No
856	10640.00	5240.00	7130.00	8700.00	IH	6	407D	16F-8R	100.49	9270	No
856 4WD	13480.00	6340.00	8630.00	10530.00	IH	6	301G	16F-8R	93.00	9410	No
856 4WD	14480.00	6810.00	9270.00	11310.00	IH	6	407D	16F-8R	100.	10170	No
966	10038.00	3920.00	4720.00	5330.00	IH	6	414D	16F-8R	96.01	9130	No
966 4WD	13538.00	5280.00	6360.00	7190.00	IH	6	414D	16F-8R	96.00	10030	No
966H	10628.00	4150.00	5000.00	5650.00	IH	6	414D	Infinite	91.38	9300	No
966H 4WD	14128.00	5510.00	6640.00	7500.00	IH	6	414D	Infinite	91.00	10200	No
1026H	11780.00	4590.00	5540.00	6260.00	IH	6T	407D	Infinite	112.45	9500	No
1026H	12170.00	4750.00	5720.00	6460.00	IH	6T	407D	Infinite	112.45	9600	No
1026H 4WD	14970.00	5840.00	7040.00	7960.00	IH	6T	407D	Infinite	112.00	10400	No
1026H 4WD	15360.00	5990.00	7220.00	8160.00	IH	6T	407D	Infinite	112.00	10500	No
1066	10899.00	4250.00	5120.00	5790.00	IH	6T	414D	16F-8R	116.23	9550	No
1066 4WD	14089.00	5500.00	6620.00	7480.00	IH	6T	414D	16F-8R	116.00	10450	No
1066H	11494.00	4480.00	5400.00	6100.00	IH	6T	414D	Infinite	113.58	9720	No
1066H 4WD	14684.00	5730.00	6900.00	7800.00	IH	6T	414D	Infinite	113.00	10620	No
1456	12390.00	5610.00	6760.00	7640.00	IH	6T	407D	16F-8R	131.80	10600	No
1456 4WD	15580.00	6080.00	7320.00	8270.00	IH	6T	407D	16F-8R	131.00	11500	No
1466	12705.00	4960.00	5970.00	6750.00	IH	6T	436D	16F-8R	133.40	10700	No
1466 4WD	15895.00	6200.00	7470.00	8440.00	IH	6T	436D	16F-8R	133.00	11600	No
1468	13675.00	4650.00	6020.00	6740.00	IH	V-8	550D	16F-8R	145.49	11200	No

H--Hydrostatic Transmission

1972

Model	Approx. Retail Price New	Estimated Average Value Less Repairs: Fair	Good	Premium	Engine: Make	No. Cyls.	Displ. Cu.-In.	No. Speeds	P.T.O. H.P.	Approx. Shipping Wt.-Lbs.	Cab
Cub	2545.00	1840.00	2410.00	2960.00	IH	4	60G	3F-1R	10.75	1620	No
Cub 154 Lo Boy	2335.00	1290.00	1680.00	2070.00	IH	4	60G	3F-1R	13.50	1480	No
140	3530.00	2880.00	3760.00	4630.00	IH	4	123G	4F-1R	24.30	2750	No
354	3815.00	2170.00	2890.00	3500.00	IH	4	144G	8F-2R	32.58	3600	No
354	4221.00	2600.00	3470.00	4200.00	IH	4	144D	8F-2R	32.00	3700	No
454	4445.00	2470.00	3290.00	3980.00	IH	4	157G	8F-2R	40.86	4240	No
454	4863.00	2670.00	3560.00	4310.00	IH	3	179D	8F-2R	40.47	4560	No
544	6340.00	3520.00	4700.00	5690.00	IH	4	200G	10F-2R	52.84	6300	No
544	6930.00	3810.00	5080.00	6150.00	IH	4	239D	10F-2R	52.95	6500	No
544H	7100.00	3240.00	3890.00	4400.00	IH	4	200G	Infinite	53.87	6400	No
544H	7690.00	3480.00	4170.00	4710.00	IH	4	239D	Infinite	55.52	6600	No
574	6005.00	3360.00	4480.00	5420.00	IH	4	200G	8F-4R	52.97	4700	No
574	6830.00	3760.00	5010.00	6060.00	IH	4	239D	8F-4R	52.55	4800	No
656	7140.00	3670.00	4890.00	5920.00	IH	6	263G	10F-2R	63.85	6350	No
656	7990.00	4000.00	5340.00	6460.00	IH	6	282D	10F-2R	61.42	6800	No
656H	7895.00	3360.00	4030.00	4550.00	IH	6	263G	Infinite	65.80	6900	No
656H	8745.00	3600.00	4320.00	4880.00	IH	6	282D	Infinite	66.06	7170	No
664	6795.00	3120.00	3740.00	4230.00	IH	4	239D	10F-2R	61.56	5950	No
666	7020.00	3210.00	3850.00	4350.00	IH	6	291G	10F-2R	66.30	7000	No
666	7765.00	3310.00	3970.00	4490.00	IH	6	312D	10F-2R	66.29	7220	No
766	8360.00	3540.00	4250.00	4800.00	IH	6	291G	16F-8R	79.73	9000	No
766	8985.00	3590.00	4310.00	4870.00	IH	6	360D	16F-8R	85.45	9500	No
966	10489.00	4200.00	5040.00	5700.00	IH	6	414D	16F-8R	96.01	9130	C,H
966 4WD	13679.00	5470.00	6570.00	7420.00	IH	6	414D	16F-8R	96.00	10030	C,H
966H	11079.00	4430.00	5320.00	6010.00	IH	6	414D	Infinite	91.38	9300	C,H
966H 4WD	14269.00	5710.00	6850.00	7740.00	IH	6	414D	Infinite	91.00	10200	C,H
1066	11555.00	4620.00	5550.00	6270.00	IH	6T	414D	16F-8R	116.23	10550	C,H,A
1066 4WD	14745.00	5900.00	7080.00	8000.00	IH	6T	414D	16F-8R	116.00	11450	C,H,A
1066H	12150.00	4860.00	5830.00	6590.00	IH	6T	414D	Infinite	113.58	10720	C,H,A
1066H 4WD	15340.00	6140.00	7360.00	8320.00	IH	6T	414D	Infinite	113.00	11620	C,H,A
1466	13455.00	5380.00	6460.00	7300.00	IH	6T	436D	16F-8R	133.40	11700	C,H,A

Int. Harvester-Farmall (Cont.)

1972 (Cont.)

Model	Approx. Retail Price New	Estimated Average Value Less Repairs Fair	Good	Premium	Engine Make	No. Cyls.	Displ. Cu.-In.	No. Speeds	P.T.O. H.P.	Approx. Shipping Wt.-Lbs.	Cab
1466 4WD	16645.00	6660.00	7990.00	9030.00	IH	6T	436D	16F-8R	133.00	12600	C,H,A
1468	14435.00	5050.00	6350.00	7110.00	IH	V8	550D	16F-8R	145.49	11200	C,H,A
4166 4WD	16995.00	5950.00	7480.00	8380.00	IH	6T	436D	8F-4R	150.63	15300	C,H

H--Hydrostatic Transmission

1973

Model	Approx. Retail Price New	Fair	Good	Premium	Make	No. Cyls.	Displ. Cu.-In.	No. Speeds	P.T.O. H.P.	Approx. Shipping Wt.-Lbs.	Cab
Cub	2645.00	1840.00	2400.00	2880.00	IH	4	60G	3F-1R	10.75	1620	No
Cub 154 Lo Boy	2405.00	1420.00	1860.00	2230.00	IH	4	60G	3F-1R	13.50	1480	No
Hydro 70	8855.00	3370.00	4210.00	4670.00	IH	6	291G	Infinite	69.61	6980	No
Hydro 70	9720.00	3680.00	4600.00	5110.00	IH	6	312D	Infinite	69.51	7420	No
Hydro 100	11215.00	4220.00	5270.00	5850.00	IH	6	436D	Infinite	104.17	10170	C,H,A
140	3460.00	2890.00	3710.00	4530.00	IH	4	123G	4F-1R	24.30	2640	No
354	4018.00	2210.00	2890.00	3470.00	IH	4	144G	8F-2R	32.58	3600	No
354	4378.00	2390.00	3120.00	3740.00	IH	4	144D	8F-2R	32.00	3700	No
454	4650.00	2520.00	3300.00	3960.00	IH	4	157G	8F-2R	40.86	4240	No
454	5065.00	2730.00	3560.00	4270.00	IH	3	179D	8F-2R	40.47	4560	No
464	4896.00	2640.00	3450.00	4140.00	IH	4	175G	8F-2R	45.74	4200	No
464	5293.00	2840.00	3710.00	4450.00	IH	3	179D	8F-2R	44.42	4520	No
544	6595.00	3720.00	4860.00	5830.00	IH	4	200G	10F-2R	52.84	6300	No
544	7185.00	4010.00	5240.00	6290.00	IH	4	239D	10F-2R	52.95	6500	No
544H	7350.00	3420.00	4090.00	4620.00	IH	4	200G	Infinite	53.87	6400	No
544H	7945.00	3670.00	4380.00	4950.00	IH	4	239D	Infinite	55.52	6600	No
574	6250.00	3310.00	4320.00	5180.00	IH	4	200G	8F-4R	52.97	4700	No
574	7090.00	3720.00	4860.00	5830.00	IH	4	239D	8F-4R	52.55	4800	No
664	7305.00	3200.00	3820.00	4320.00	IH	4	239D	10F-2R	61.56	5950	No
666	7625.00	3330.00	3980.00	4500.00	IH	6	291G	10F-2R	66.30	7000	No
666	8445.00	3670.00	4380.00	4950.00	IH	6	312D	10F-2R	66.29	7220	No
674	5844.00	3110.00	4060.00	4870.00	IH	4	200G	8F-4R	58.53	4430	No
674	6636.00	3500.00	4570.00	5480.00	IH	4	239D	8F-4R	61.56	4680	No
766	8815.00	3820.00	4560.00	5150.00	IH	6	291G	16F-8R	79.73	9000	No
766	9665.00	4170.00	4980.00	5630.00	IH	6	360D	16F-8R	85.45	9500	No
966	11595.00	4960.00	5930.00	6700.00	IH	6	414D	16F-8R	96.01	9130	C,H
966 4WD	14795.00	6270.00	7500.00	8480.00	IH	6	414D	16F-8R	96.00	10030	C,H
966H	12660.00	5400.00	6450.00	7290.00	IH	6	414D	Infinite	91.38	9300	C,H
966H 4WD	15860.00	6710.00	8020.00	9060.00	IH	6	414D	Infinite	91.00	10200	C,H
1066	12840.00	5470.00	6540.00	7390.00	IH	6T	414D	16F-8R	116.23	10550	C,H,A
1066 4WD	16040.00	6780.00	8110.00	9160.00	IH	6T	414D	16F-8R	166.00	11450	C,H,A
1066H	13920.00	5910.00	7070.00	7990.00	IH	6T	414D	Infinite	113.58	10720	C,H,A
1066H 4WD	17120.00	7020.00	8390.00	9480.00	IH	6T	414D	Infinite	113.00	11620	C,H,A
1466	14795.00	5330.00	6660.00	7390.00	IH	6T	436D	16F-8R	133.40	10700	C,H,A
1466 4WD	17995.00	6480.00	8100.00	8990.00	IH	6T	436D	16F-8R	133.00	12600	C,H,A
1468	15845.00	4580.00	6380.00	7150.00	IH	V8	550D	16F-8R	145.49	11200	C,H,A
4166 4WD	18350.00	3120.00	4770.00	5340.00	IH	6T	436D	8F-4R	150.63	15300	C,H
4366 4WD	25057.00	4260.00	6520.00	7300.00	IH	6T	466D	10F-2R	163.9	19500	C,H,A

H--Hydrostatic Transmission RC--Row Crop

1974

Model	Approx. Retail Price New	Fair	Good	Premium	Make	No. Cyls.	Displ. Cu.-In.	No. Speeds	P.T.O. H.P.	Approx. Shipping Wt.-Lbs.	Cab
Cub	2775.00	1760.00	2250.00	2680.00	IH	4	60G	3F-1R	10.75	1620	No
Cub 154 Lo Boy	2485.00	1940.00	2490.00	2960.00	IH	4	60G	3F-1R	13.50	1480	No
Cub 185 Lo Boy	2990.00	1810.00	2320.00	2760.00	IH	4	60G	6F-2R	13.5	1480	No
Hydro 70	10105.00	3740.00	4650.00	5160.00	IH	6	291G	Infinite	69.61	6980	No
Hydro 70	11105.00	4110.00	5110.00	5670.00	IH	6	312D	Infinite	69.51	7420	No
Hydro 100	14120.00	5220.00	6500.00	7220.00	IH	6	436D	Infinite	104.17	10170	C,H,A
140	3587.00	3020.00	3800.00	4600.00	IH	4	123G	4F-1R	24.30	2640	No
354	4218.00	2360.00	3020.00	3590.00	IH	4	144G	8F-2R	32.58	3600	No
354	4535.00	2520.00	3220.00	3830.00	IH	4	144D	8F-2R	32.00	3700	No
464	5273.00	2890.00	3700.00	4400.00	IH	4	175G	8F-2R	45.74	4200	No
464	5859.00	3180.00	4070.00	4840.00	IH	3	179D	8F-2R	44.42	4520	No
574	6498.00	3500.00	4480.00	5330.00	IH	4	200G	8F-2R	52.97	4700	No
574	7350.00	3930.00	5020.00	5970.00	IH	4	239D	8F-2R	52.55	4800	No
666	8585.00	3610.00	4290.00	4810.00	IH	6	291G	10F-2R	66.30	7000	No
666	9605.00	4030.00	4800.00	5380.00	IH	6	312D	10F-2R	66.29	7220	No
674	6840.00	3670.00	4700.00	5590.00	IH	4	200G	8F-4R	58.53	4430	No
674	7655.00	4080.00	5220.00	6210.00	IH	4	239D	8F-4R	61.56	4680	No
766	9910.00	3670.00	4560.00	5060.00	IH	6	291G	16F-8R	79.73	9000	No
766	10895.00	4030.00	5010.00	5560.00	IH	6	360D	16F-8R	85.45	9500	No
966	13965.00	5170.00	6420.00	7130.00	IH	6	414D	16F-8R	100.80	10130	C,H,A
966 4WD	17765.00	5150.00	6930.00	7760.00	IH	6	414D	16F-8R	100.	11030	C,H,A
966H	14525.00	5370.00	6680.00	7420.00	IH	6	414D	Infinite	91.38	10300	C,H,A
966H 4WD	18325.00	5310.00	7150.00	8010.00	IH	6	414D	Infinite	91.00	11200	C,H,A
1066	14890.00	5510.00	6850.00	7600.00	IH	6T	414D	16F-8R	125.68	10550	C,H,A
1066 4WD	18690.00	6920.00	8600.00	9550.00	IH	6T	414D	16F-8R	125.00	11450	C,H,A
1066H	15970.00	4630.00	6230.00	6980.00	IH	6T	414D	Infinite	113.58	10720	C,H,A
1066H 4WD	19770.00	5730.00	7710.00	8640.00	IH	6T	414D	Infinite	113.00	11620	C,H,A
1466	17410.00	6440.00	8010.00	8890.00	IH	6T	436D	16F-8R	145.77	10700	C,H,A
1466 4WD	21210.00	7850.00	9760.00	10830.00	IH	6T	436D	16F-8R	145.00	12600	C,H,A
1468	18425.00	5340.00	7190.00	8050.00	IH	V8	550D	16F-8R	145.49	11800	C,H,A
1566	18570.00	5390.00	7240.00	8110.00	IH	6T	436D	12F-6R	161.01	12750	C,H,A
1568	19301.00	5600.00	7530.00	8430.00	IH	V8	550D	12F-6R	150.70	13200	C,H,A
4166 4WD	20050.00	3610.00	5410.00	6060.00	IH	6T	436D	8F-4R	150.63	15300	C,H
4366 4WD	26947.00	4590.00	6890.00	7720.00	IH	6T	466D	10F-2R	163.9	19500	C,H,A

H--Hydrostatic Transmission RC--Row Crop

Int. Harvester-Farmall (Cont.)

1975

Model	Approx. Retail Price New	Estimated Average Value Less Repairs Fair	Good	Premium	Engine Make	No. Cyls.	Displ. Cu.-In.	No. Speeds	P.T.O. H.P.	Approx. Shipping Wt.-Lbs.	Cab
Cub	3529.00	2000.00	2520.00	2970.00	IH	4	60G	3F-1R	10.75	1620	No
Cub 185 Lo Boy	3648.00	1890.00	2370.00	2800.00	IH	4	60G	6F-2R	13.5	1480	No
Hydro 70	11375.00	4320.00	5350.00	5940.00	IH	6	291G	Infinite	69.61	6980	No
Hydro 70	12510.00	4750.00	5880.00	6530.00	IH	6	312D	Infinite	69.51	7420	No
Hydro 100	17025.00	5110.00	6640.00	7370.00	IH	6	436D	Infinite	104.17	10170	C,H,A
140	4285.00	3180.00	3930.00	4720.00	IH	4	123G	4F-1R	24.30	2640	No
354	4419.00	2510.00	3150.00	3720.00	IH	4	144G	8F-2R	32.58	3600	No
354	4695.00	2650.00	3330.00	3930.00	IH	4	144D	8F-2R	32.00	3700	No
464	5450.00	3040.00	3810.00	4500.00	IH	4	175G	8F-2R	45.74	4200	No
464	6225.00	3430.00	4300.00	5070.00	IH	3	179D	8F-2R	44.42	4520	No
574	7532.00	3840.00	4820.00	5690.00	IH	4	200G	8F-2R	52.97	4700	No
574	8599.00	4390.00	5500.00	6490.00	IH	4	239D	8F-2R	52.55	4800	No
666	9545.00	3630.00	4490.00	4980.00	IH	6	291G	10F-2R	66.30	7000	No
666	10765.00	4090.00	5060.00	5620.00	IH	6	312D	10F-2R	66.29	7220	No
674	7865.00	4270.00	5350.00	6310.00	IH	4	200G	8F-4R	58.53	4430	No
674	8925.00	4810.00	6030.00	7120.00	IH	4	239D	8F-4R	61.56	4680	No
766	11825.00	4490.00	5560.00	6170.00	IH	6	291G	16F-8R	79.73	9000	No
766	12981.00	4930.00	6100.00	6770.00	IH	6	360D	16F-8R	85.45	9500	No
966	15331.00	5830.00	7210.00	8000.00	IH	6	414D	16F-8R	100.80	10130	C,H,A
966 4WD	19331.00	7350.00	9090.00	10090.00	IH	6	414D	16F-8R	100.	11030	C,H
966H	16396.00	6230.00	7710.00	8560.00	IH	6	414D	Infinite	91.38	10300	C,H
966H 4WD	20396.00	7750.00	9590.00	10650.00	IH	6	414D	Infinite	91.00	11200	C,H
1066	16939.00	6440.00	7960.00	8840.00	IH	6T	414D	16F-8R	125.68	10550	C,H,A
1066 4WD	20939.00	7960.00	9840.00	10920.00	IH	6T	414D	16F-8R	125.00	11450	C,H,A
1066H	18019.00	5410.00	7030.00	7800.00	IH	6T	414D	Infinite	113.58	10720	C,H,A
1066H 4WD	22019.00	6610.00	8590.00	9540.00	IH	6T	414D	Infinite	113.00	11620	C,H,A
1466	20027.00	7610.00	9410.00	10450.00	IH	6T	436D	16F-8R	145.77	10700	C,H,A
1466 4WD	24027.00	7210.00	9370.00	10400.00	IH	6T	436D	16F-8R	145.00	12600	C,H,A
1566	22677.00	6800.00	8840.00	9810.00	IH	6T	436D	12F-6R	161.01	12750	C,H,A
1568	23408.00	7020.00	9130.00	10130.00	IH	V8	550D	12F-6R	150.70	13200	C,H,A
4166 4WD	26582.00	4750.00	7000.00	7840.00	IH	6T	436D	8F-4R	150.63	15300	C,H,A
4366 4WD	32007.00	5320.00	7840.00	8780.00	IH	6T	466D	10F-2R	163.9	19500	C,H,A
4568 4WD	43528.00	6650.00	9800.00	10980.00	IH	V8	798D	10F-2R	235.7	21900	C,H,A

H--Hydrostatic Transmission RC--Row Crop

1976

Model	Approx. Retail Price New	Estimated Average Value Less Repairs Fair	Good	Premium	Engine Make	No. Cyls.	Displ. Cu.-In.	No. Speeds	P.T.O. H.P.	Approx. Shipping Wt.-Lbs.	Cab
Cub	3799.00	2040.00	2560.00	3000.00	IH	4	60G	3F-1R	10.75	1620	No
Cub 185 Lo Boy	3820.00	1950.00	2450.00	2870.00	IH	4	60G	6F-2R	13.5	1480	No
Hydro 70	14160.00	5520.00	6800.00	7480.00	IH	6	291G	Infinite	69.61	7330	No
Hydro 70	14820.00	5780.00	7110.00	7820.00	IH	6	312D	Infinite	69.51	7770	No
Hydro 86	13665.00	5330.00	6560.00	7220.00	IH	6	291G	Infinite	69.61	7330	No
Hydro 86	14180.00	5530.00	6810.00	7490.00	IH	6	312D	Infinite	69.51	7770	No
Hydro 100	21722.00	6730.00	8690.00	9650.00	IH	6	436D	Infinite	104.17	10170	C,H,A
140	4999.00	3300.00	4010.00	4770.00	IH	4	123G	4F-1R	24.30	2640	No
Hydro 186	20755.00	8090.00	9960.00	10960.00	IH	6	436D	Infinite	105.02	11160	C,H,A
284	4920.00	2510.00	3150.00	3690.00	Toyo-Kogyo	4	71G	8F-2R	25.75	2050	No
364	6700.00	3420.00	4290.00	5020.00	IH	4	154D	8F-2R	39.00	3840	No
464	7235.00	3690.00	4630.00	5420.00	IH	4	175G	8F-2R	45.74	4200	No
464	8005.00	4080.00	5120.00	5990.00	IH	3	179D	8F-2R	44.42	4520	No
574	8525.00	4350.00	5460.00	6390.00	IH	4	200G	8F-2R	52.97	4700	No
574	9335.00	4760.00	5970.00	6990.00	IH	4	239D	8F-2R	52.55	4800	No
574 RC	8875.00	4530.00	5680.00	6650.00	IH	4	200G	8F-2R	52.97	5170	No
574 RC	9685.00	4940.00	6200.00	7250.00	IH	4	239D	8F-2R	52.55	5270	No
666	10545.00	4640.00	5480.00	6140.00	IH	6	291G	10F-2R	66.30	7000	No
666	11765.00	5180.00	6120.00	6850.00	IH	6	312D	10F-2R	66.29	7220	No
674	9945.00	5070.00	6370.00	7450.00	IH	4	200G	8F-4R	58.53	5210	No
674	10855.00	5540.00	6950.00	8130.00	IH	4	239D	8F-4R	61.56	5320	No
674 RC	10295.00	5250.00	6590.00	7710.00	IH	4	200G	8F-4R	58.53	5075	No
674 RC	11195.00	5710.00	7170.00	8390.00	IH	4	239D	8F-4R	61.56	5460	No
686	10940.00	4810.00	5690.00	6370.00	IH	6	291G	10F-2R	66.31	7055	No
686	11435.00	5030.00	5950.00	6660.00	IH	6	312D	10F-2R	66.29	7570	No
766	13825.00	5390.00	6640.00	7300.00	IH	6	291G	16F-8R	79.73	9000	No
766	14981.00	5840.00	7190.00	7910.00	IH	6	360D	16F-8R	85.45	9500	No
886	17730.00	6920.00	8510.00	9360.00	IH	6	360D	16F-8R	86.14	10600	C,H,A
966	17331.00	6760.00	8320.00	9150.00	IH	6	414D	16F-8R	100.80	10130	C,H,A
966 4WD	20331.00	7930.00	9760.00	10740.00	IH	6	414D	16F-8R	100.	11030	C,H
986	19525.00	6050.00	7810.00	8670.00	IH	6	436D	16F-8R	105.68	10900	C,H,A
1066	17939.00	7000.00	8610.00	9470.00	IH	6T	414D	16F-8R	125.68	10550	C,H,A
1066 4WD	21939.00	8560.00	10530.00	11580.00	IH	6T	414D	16F-8R	125.00	11450	C,H,A
1086	21595.00	8420.00	10370.00	11410.00	IH	6T	414D	16F-8R	131.41	11700	C,H,A
1466	23027.00	8980.00	11050.00	12160.00	IH	6T	436D	16F-8R	145.77	10700	C,H,A
1466 4WD	26027.00	9750.00	12000.00	13200.00	IH	6T	436D	16F-8R	145.00	12600	C,H,A
1486	24235.00	9450.00	11630.00	12790.00	IH	6T	436D	16F-8R	145.77	11800	C,H,A
1566	24677.00	7010.00	9040.00	10030.00	IH	6T	436D	12F-6R	161.01	12750	C,H,A
1568	25408.00	7130.00	9200.00	10210.00	IH	V8	550D	12F-6R	150.70	13200	C,H,A
1568	27515.00	7440.00	9600.00	10660.00	IH	V8	550D	12F-6R	150.70	13200	C,H,A
1586	27160.00	8060.00	10400.00	11540.00	IH	6T	436D	12F-6R	161.55	12750	C,H,A
4166 4WD	28582.00	5400.00	7830.00	8770.00	IH	6T	436D	8F-4R	150.63	15300	C,H,A
4186 4WD	32210.00	5800.00	8410.00	9420.00	IH	6T	436D	8F-4R	150.63	15300	C,H,A
4366 4WD	34007.00	6400.00	9280.00	10390.00	IH	6T	466D	10F-2R	163.9	19500	C,H,A
4386 4WD	41850.00	7000.00	10150.00	11370.00	IH	6TI	466D	10F-2R	175.3	20000	C,H,A
4586 4WD	48090.00	8000.00	11600.00	12990.00	IH	V8	798D	10F-2R	235.7	21900	C,H,A

RC--Row Crop

Model	Approx. Retail Price New	Estimated Average Value Less Repairs Fair	Good	Premium	Engine Make	No. Cyls.	Displ. Cu.-In.	No. Speeds	P.T.O. H.P.	Approx. Shipping Wt.-Lbs.	Cab

Int. Harvester-Farmall (Cont.)

1977

Model	Approx. Retail Price New	Fair	Good	Premium	Make	No. Cyls.	Displ. Cu.-In.	No. Speeds	P.T.O. H.P.	Approx. Shipping Wt.-Lbs.	Cab
Cub	4755.00	2300.00	2700.00	3000.00	IH	4	60G	3F-1R	10.75	1620	No
Hydro 86	15425.00	6170.00	7560.00	8320.00	IH	6	291G	Infinite	69.61	7330	No
Hydro 86	16005.00	6400.00	7840.00	8620.00	IH	6	312D	Infinite	69.51	7770	No
140	6003.00	3300.00	4080.00	4810.00	IH		123G	4F-1R	24.30	2640	No
Hydro 186	23515.00	7530.00	9640.00	10700.00	IH	6	436D	Infinite	105.02	11160	C,H,A
Hydro 186 4WD	28520.00	9130.00	11690.00	12980.00	IH	6	436D	Infinite	105.00	12060	C,H,A
284	5414.00	2440.00	2870.00	3190.00	Toyo-Kogyo	4	71G	8F-2R	25.75	2050	No
364	7105.00	3200.00	3770.00	4190.00	IH	4	154D	8F-2R	39.00	3840	No
464	8455.00	3810.00	4480.00	4970.00	IH	4	175G	8F-2R	45.74	4200	No
464	9270.00	4170.00	4910.00	5450.00	IH	3	179D	8F-2R	44.42	4520	No
574	10005.00	4500.00	5300.00	5880.00	IH	4	200G	8F-2R	52.97	4700	No
574	10910.00	4910.00	5780.00	6420.00	IH	4	239D	8F-2R	52.55	4800	No
574 RC	10410.00	4690.00	5520.00	6130.00	IH	4	200G	8F-2R	52.97	5170	No
574 RC	11315.00	5090.00	6000.00	6660.00	IH	4	239D	8F-2R	52.55	5270	No
674	11255.00	5070.00	5970.00	6630.00	IH	4	200G	8F-2R	58.53	5210	No
674	12335.00	5550.00	6540.00	7260.00	IH	4	239D	8F-2R	61.56	5320	No
674 RC	11665.00	5250.00	6180.00	6860.00	IH	4	200G	8F-2R	58.53	5075	No
674 RC	12735.00	5730.00	6750.00	7490.00	IH	4	239D	8F-2R	61.56	5460	No
686	12825.00	5130.00	6280.00	6910.00	IH	6	291G	10F-2R	66.31	7055	No
686	13405.00	5360.00	6570.00	7230.00	IH	6	312D	10F-2R	66.29	7570	No
886	20045.00	6240.00	8000.00	8880.00	IH	6	360D	16F-8R	86.14	10600	C,H,A
886 4WD	25050.00	7840.00	10050.00	11160.00	IH	6	360D	16F-8R	86.00	11500	C,H,A
986	22030.00	6880.00	8820.00	9790.00	IH	6	436D	16F-8R	105.68	10900	C,H,A
986 4WD	27035.00	8480.00	10870.00	12070.00	IH	6	436D	16F-8R	105.00	11800	C,H,A
1086	24645.00	7680.00	9840.00	10920.00	IH	6T	414D	16F-8R	131.41	11700	C,H,A
1086 4WD	29650.00	8960.00	11480.00	12740.00	IH	6T	414D	16F-8R	131.00	12600	C,H,A
1486	26525.00	8320.00	10660.00	11830.00	IH	6T	436D	16F-8R	145.77	11800	C,H,A
1486 4WD	31530.00	9600.00	12300.00	13650.00	IH	6T	436D	16F-8R	145.00	12700	C,H,A
1586	29835.00	8960.00	11480.00	12740.00	IH	6T	436D	12F-6R	161.55	12750	C,H,A
1586 4WD	31840.00	9760.00	12510.00	13890.00	IH	6T	436D	12F-6R	161.00	13650	C,H,A
4186 4WD	32535.00	6090.00	8700.00	9740.00	IH	6T	436D	8F-4R	150.63	15300	C,H,A
4386 4WD	42273.00	7350.00	10500.00	11760.00	IH	6TI	466D	10F-2R	175.3	20000	C,H,A
4586 4WD	50950.00	8190.00	11700.00	13100.00	IH	V8	798D	10F-2R	235.7	22400	C,H,A

RC--Row Crop

1978

Model	Approx. Retail Price New	Fair	Good	Premium	Make	No. Cyls.	Displ. Cu.-In.	No. Speeds	P.T.O. H.P.	Approx. Shipping Wt.-Lbs.	Cab
Cub	5066.00	2360.00	2770.00	3050.00	IH	4	60G	3F-1R	10.75	1620	No
Hydro 84	13830.00	5670.00	6920.00	7610.00	IH	4	246D	Infinite	58.73	5160	No
Hydro 86	17185.00	7050.00	8590.00	9450.00	IH	6	291G	Infinite	69.61	7330	No
Hydro 86	17830.00	7310.00	8920.00	9810.00	IH	6	312D	Infinite	69.51	7770	No
140	7010.00	3580.00	4490.00	5160.00	IH	4	123G	4F-1R	24.30	2720	No
Hydro 186	26275.00	8670.00	11040.00	12140.00	IH	6	436D	Infinite	105.02	11160	C,H,A
284	5910.00	2720.00	3190.00	3510.00	Toyo-Kogyo	4	71G	8F-2R	25.75	2050	No
384	7775.00	3580.00	4200.00	4620.00	IH	4	154D	8F-2R	39.00	3770	No
484	9580.00	3930.00	4790.00	5270.00	IH	3	179D	8F-4R	42.42	4660	No
584	11730.00	4810.00	5870.00	6460.00	IH	4	206D	8F-4R	52.54	4850	No
584 RC	12115.00	4970.00	6060.00	6670.00	IH	4	206D	8F-4R	52.54	5380	No
684	13020.00	5340.00	6510.00	7160.00	IH	4	239D	8F-4R	62.52	5220	No
684 RC	13165.00	5400.00	6580.00	7240.00	IH	4	239D	8F-4R	62.52	5670	No
686	14710.00	6770.00	7940.00	8730.00	IH	6	291G	10F-2R	66.31	7055	No
686	15375.00	7070.00	8300.00	9130.00	IH	6	312D	10F-2R	66.29	7570	No
784	13970.00	6430.00	7540.00	8290.00	IH	4	246D	8F-4R	65.47	5410	No
784 RC	14115.00	6490.00	7620.00	8380.00	IH	4	246D	8F-4R	65.47	5950	No
886	22360.00	8820.00	10750.00	11830.00	IH	6	360D	16F-8R	86.14	10600	C,H,A
886 4WD	27860.00	11070.00	13500.00	14850.00	IH	6	360D	16F-8R	86.00	11500	C,H,A
986	24575.00	9550.00	11650.00	12820.00	IH	6	436D	16F-8R	105.68	10900	C,H,A
986 4WD	30075.00	11480.00	14000.00	15400.00	IH	6	436D	16F-8R	105.00	11800	C,H,A
1086	27725.00	11070.00	13500.00	14850.00	IH	6T	414D	16F-8R	131.41	11700	C,H,A
1086 4WD	33225.00	12300.00	15000.00	16500.00	IH	6T	414D	16F-8R	131.00	12600	C,H,A
1486	29815.00	11890.00	14500.00	15950.00	IH	6T	436D	16F-8R	145.77	11800	C,H,A
1486 4WD	35315.00	13120.00	16000.00	17600.00	IH	6T	436D	16F-8R	145.00	12700	C,H,A
1586	33510.00	10230.00	13020.00	14320.00	IH	6T	436D	12F-6R	161.55	12750	C,H,A
1586 4WD	39010.00	11220.00	14280.00	15710.00	IH	6T	436D	12F-6R	161.00	13650	C,H,A
3388 4WD	38930.00	7260.00	10230.00	11460.00	IH	6T	436D	16F-8R	130.61	15960	C,H,A
3588 4WD	43685.00	8140.00	11470.00	12850.00	IH	6T	466D	16F-8R	150.41	16315	C,H,A
4186 4WD	32535.00	6380.00	8990.00	10070.00	IH	6T	436D	8F-4R	150.63	15300	C,H,A
4386 4WD	42273.00	7920.00	11160.00	12500.00	IH	6TI	466D	10F-2R	175.3	20000	C,H,A
4586 4WD	50950.00	8580.00	12090.00	13540.00	IH	V8	798D	10F-2R	235.7	22400	C,H,A
4786 4WD	70655.00	9680.00	13640.00	15280.00	IH	V8	798D	10F-2R	265.5	23600	C,H,A

RC--Row Crop

1979

Model	Approx. Retail Price New	Fair	Good	Premium	Make	No. Cyls.	Displ. Cu.-In.	No. Speeds	P.T.O. H.P.	Approx. Shipping Wt.-Lbs.	Cab
Cub	5350.00	2520.00	2940.00	3210.00	IH	4	60G	3F-1R	10.75	1620	No
Hydro 84	14965.00	6290.00	7630.00	8320.00	IH	4	246D	Infinite	58.73	5160	No
Hydro 86	20240.00	8500.00	10320.00	11250.00	IH	6	310D	Infinite	70.89	7710	No
140	7370.00	3830.00	4640.00	5290.00	IH	4	123G	4F-1R	24.30	2720	No
Hydro 186	29235.00	9940.00	12570.00	13700.00	IH	6	436D	Infinite	105.02	11160	C,H,A
Hydro 186 4WD	35795.00	12170.00	15390.00	16780.00	IH	6	436D	Infinite	105.00	12060	C,H,A
284	6460.00	3040.00	3550.00	3870.00	Toyo-Kogyo	4	71G	8F-2R	25.75	2050	No
384	8495.00	3990.00	4670.00	5090.00	IH	4	154D	8F-2R	39.00	3770	No
484	10265.00	4310.00	5240.00	5710.00	IH	3	179D	8F-4R	42.42	4660	No
584	12445.00	5230.00	6350.00	6920.00	IH	4	206D	8F-4R	52.54	4850	No
584 RC	12855.00	5400.00	6560.00	7150.00	IH	4	206D	8F-4R	52.54	5380	No
684	13800.00	5800.00	7040.00	7670.00	IH	4	239D	8F-4R	62.52	5220	No

Int. Harvester-Farmall (Cont.)

Model	Approx. Retail Price New	Fair	Estimated Average Value Less Repairs Good	Premium	Engine Make	No. Cyls.	Displ. Cu.-In.	No. Speeds	P.T.O. H.P.	Approx. Shipping Wt.-Lbs.	Cab
			1979 (Cont.)								
684 RC	13955.00	5860.00	7120.00	7760.00	IH	4	239D	8F-4R	62.52	5670	No
686	17450.00	7330.00	8900.00	9700.00	IH	6	310D	10F-2R	66.36	7500	No
784	14390.00	6040.00	7340.00	8000.00	IH	4	246D	8F-4R	65.47	5410	No
784 RC	14540.00	6110.00	7420.00	8090.00	IH	4	246D	8F-4R	65.47	5950	No
886	24420.00	8300.00	10500.00	11450.00	IH	6	358D	16F-8R	90.56	10475	C,H,A
886 4WD	31200.00	10610.00	13420.00	14630.00	IH	6	358D	16F-8R	90.00	11500	C,H,A
986	26835.00	9120.00	11540.00	12580.00	IH	6	436D	16F-8R	105.68	10900	C,H,A
986 4WD	33395.00	11350.00	14360.00	15650.00	IH	6	436D	16F-8R	105.00	11800	C,H,A
1086	30845.00	10490.00	13260.00	14450.00	IH	6T	414D	16F-8R	131.41	11700	C,H,A
1086 4WD	37405.00	12240.00	15480.00	16870.00	IH	6T	414D	16F-8R	131.00	12600	C,H,A
1486	33175.00	11280.00	14270.00	15550.00	IH	6T	436D	16F-8R	145.77	11800	C,H,A
1486 4WD	39540.00	12580.00	15910.00	17340.00	IH	6T	436D	16F-8R	145.00	12700	C,H,A
1586	38080.00	12240.00	15480.00	16870.00	IH	6T	436D	12F-6R	161.55	12750	C,H,A
1586 4WD	44305.00	13260.00	16770.00	18280.00	IH	6T	436D	12F-6R	161.00	13650	C,H,A
3388 4WD	38930.00	7820.00	10880.00	12190.00	IH	6T	436D	16F-8R	130.61	15960	C,H,A
3588 4WD	43685.00	8740.00	12160.00	13620.00	IH	6T	466D	16F-8R	150.41	16315	C,H,A
4386 4WD	52920.00	9430.00	13120.00	14690.00	IH	6TI	466D	10F-2R	175.3	20000	C,H,A
4586 4WD	66410.00	10580.00	14720.00	16490.00	IH	V8	798D	10F-2R	235.7	22400	C,H,A
4786 4WD	76310.00	11160.00	15520.00	17380.00	IH	V8	798D	10F-2R	265.5	23600	C,H,A
RC--Row Crop											
			1980								
Hydro 84	17060.00	7340.00	8870.00	9580.00	IH	4	246D	Infinite	58.73	5160	No
Hydro 86	22620.00	9730.00	11760.00	12700.00	IH	6	310D	Infinite	70.89	7710	No
140	7840.00	4160.00	4860.00	5490.00	IH	4	123G	4F-1R	24.30	2720	No
Hydro 186	32670.00	11440.00	14380.00	15670.00	IH	6	436D	Infinite	105.02	11160	C,H,A
Hydro 186 4WD	39270.00	13750.00	17280.00	18840.00	IH	6	436D	Infinite	105.00	12060	C,H,A
284	6910.00	3320.00	3870.00	4180.00	Toyo-Kogyo	4	71G	8F-2R	25.75	2050	No
384	9515.00	4570.00	5330.00	5760.00	IH	4	154D	8F-2R	39.00	3770	No
484	11700.00	5030.00	6080.00	6570.00	IH	3	179D	8F-4R	42.42	4660	No
584	14190.00	6100.00	7380.00	7970.00	IH	4	206D	8F-4R	52.54	4850	No
584 RC	14660.00	6300.00	7620.00	8230.00	IH	4	206D	8F-4R	52.54	5380	No
684	15735.00	6770.00	8180.00	8830.00	IH	4	239D	8F-4R	62.52	5220	No
684 RC	15915.00	6840.00	8280.00	8940.00	IH	4	239D	8F-4R	62.52	5670	No
686	18500.00	7960.00	9620.00	10390.00	IH	6	310D	10F-2R	66.36	7500	No
784	16410.00	7060.00	8530.00	9210.00	IH	4	246D	8F-4R	65.47	5410	No
784 RC	16575.00	7130.00	8620.00	9310.00	IH	4	246D	8F-4R	65.47	5950	No
786	17000.00	7310.00	8840.00	9550.00	IH	6	258D	16F-8R	80.20	10200	No
884	20240.00	8700.00	10530.00	11370.00	IH	4	268D	16F-8R	72.91	5650	No
884 RC	20360.00	8760.00	10590.00	11440.00	IH	4	268D	16F-8R	72.91	6065	No
886	26540.00	9290.00	11680.00	12730.00	IH	6	358D	16F-8R	90.56	10475	C,H,A
886 4WD	33340.00	11670.00	14670.00	15990.00	IH	6	358D	16F-8R	90.00	11500	C,H,A
986	29990.00	10500.00	13200.00	14390.00	IH	6	436D	16F-8R	105.68	10900	C,H,A
986 4WD	36590.00	12250.00	15400.00	16790.00	IH	6	436D	16F-8R	105.00	11800	C,H,A
1086	34470.00	11270.00	14170.00	15450.00	IH	6T	414D	16F-8R	131.41	11700	C,H,A
1086 4WD	41070.00	13300.00	16720.00	18230.00	IH	6T	414D	16F-8R	131.00	12600	C,H,A
1486	37070.00	12250.00	15400.00	16790.00	IH	6T	436D	16F-8R	145.77	11800	C,H,A
1486 4WD	43470.00	13650.00	17160.00	18700.00	IH	6T	436D	16F-8R	145.00	12700	C,H,A
1586	41770.00	14000.00	17600.00	19180.00	IH	6T	436D	12F-6R	161.55	12750	C,H,A
1586 4WD	48070.00	15400.00	19360.00	21100.00	IH	6T	436D	12F-6R	161.00	13650	C,H,A
3388 4WD	43500.00	8880.00	12210.00	13680.00	IH	6T	436D	16F-8R	130.61	15960	C,H,A
3588 4WD	48815.00	9120.00	12550.00	14060.00	IH	6T	466D	16F-8R	150.41	16315	C,H,A
3788 4WD	56990.00	9600.00	13200.00	14780.00	IH	6T	466D	12F-6R	170.57	16920	C,H,A
4386 4WD	57485.00	9960.00	13700.00	15340.00	IH	6TI	466D	10F-2R	175.3	20000	C,H,A
4586 4WD	72005.00	10560.00	14520.00	16260.00	IH	V8	798D	10F-2R	235.7	22400	C,H,A
4786 4WD	82660.00	11520.00	15840.00	17740.00	IH	V8	798D	10F-2R	265.5	23600	C,H,A
RC--Row Crop											
			1981								
Hydro 84	18310.00	6590.00	8240.00	8980.00	IH	4	246D	Infinite	58.73	5160	No
Hydro 84 4WD	24590.00	7410.00	9270.00	10100.00	IH	4	246D	Infinite	58.00	6060	No
Hydro 86	23812.00	8570.00	10720.00	11690.00	IH	6	310D	Infinite	70.89	7710	No
140	8240.00	4450.00	5190.00	5810.00	IH	4	123G	4F-1R	24.30	2720	No
Hydro 186	36745.00	13230.00	16540.00	18030.00	IH	6	436D	Infinite	105.02	11160	C,H,A
Hydro 186 4WD	44160.00	14460.00	18070.00	19700.00	IH	6	436D	Infinite	105.00	12060	C,H,A
274	8145.00	4090.00	4760.00	5140.00	Nissan	3	99D	8F-2R	27.47	2270	No
284	7335.00	3690.00	4300.00	4640.00	Toyo-Kogyo	4	71G	8F-2R	25.75	2050	No
284	7990.00	4010.00	4670.00	5040.00	Nissan	3	99D	8F-2R	27.47	2270	No
384	10590.00	5190.00	6040.00	6520.00	IH	4	154D	8F-2R	39.00	3770	No
484	12720.00	5600.00	6740.00	7280.00	IH	3	179D	8F-4R	42.42	4660	No
584	15490.00	6820.00	8210.00	8870.00	IH	4	206D	8F-4R	52.54	4850	No
584 4WD	20605.00	9070.00	10920.00	11790.00	IH	4	206D	8F-4R	52.00	5880	No
584 RC	15795.00	6950.00	8370.00	9040.00	IH	4	206D	8F-4R	52.54	5380	No
684	16815.00	7400.00	8910.00	9620.00	IH	4	239D	8F-4R	62.52	5220	No
684 4WD	23215.00	10220.00	12300.00	13280.00	IH	4	239D	8F-4R	62.00	6170	No
684 RC	17140.00	7540.00	9080.00	9810.00	IH	4	239D	8F-4R	62.52	5670	No
686	19650.00	8650.00	10420.00	11250.00	IH	6	310D	10F-2R	66.36	7500	No
784	18145.00	7980.00	9620.00	10390.00	IH	4	246D	8F-4R	65.47	5410	No
784 4WD	24545.00	10800.00	13010.00	14050.00	IH	4	246D	8F-4R	65.00	6310	No
784 RC	18660.00	8210.00	9890.00	10680.00	IH	4	246D	8F-4R	65.47	5950	No
786	19000.00	8360.00	10070.00	10880.00	IH	6	358D	16F-8R	80.20	10200	No
884	20240.00	8910.00	10730.00	11590.00	IH	4	268D	16F-8R	72.91	5650	No
884 4WD	26520.00	11670.00	14060.00	15190.00	IH	4	268D	16F-8R	72.00	6550	No
884 RC	20360.00	8960.00	10790.00	11650.00	IH	4	268D	16F-8R	72.91	6065	No

Int. Harvester-Farmall (Cont.)

1981 (Cont.)

Model	Approx. Retail Price New	Estimated Average Value Less Repairs Fair	Good	Premium	Engine Make	No. Cyls.	Displ. Cu.-In.	No. Speeds	P.T.O. H.P.	Approx. Shipping Wt.-Lbs.	Cab
886	30360.00	**10930.00**	**13660.00**	**14890.00**	IH	6	358D	16F-8R	90.56	10475	C,H,A
886 4WD	37910.00	**12960.00**	**16200.00**	**17660.00**	IH	6	358D	16F-8R	90.00	11500	C,H,A
986	33860.00	**11880.00**	**14850.00**	**16190.00**	IH	6	436D	16F-8R	105.68	10900	C,H,A
986 4WD	41275.00	**13680.00**	**17100.00**	**18640.00**	IH	6	436D	16F-8R	105.00	11800	C,H,A
1086	38610.00	**12600.00**	**15750.00**	**17170.00**	IH	6T	414D	16F-8R	131.41	11700	C,H,A
1086 4WD	45910.00	**14900.00**	**18630.00**	**20310.00**	IH	6T	414D	16F-8R	131.00	12600	C,H,A
1486	42580.00	**14040.00**	**17550.00**	**19130.00**	IH	6T	436D	16F-8R	145.77	11800	C,H,A
1486 4WD	49660.00	**15840.00**	**19800.00**	**21580.00**	IH	6T	436D	16F-8R	145.00	12700	C,H,A
1586	47425.00	**15120.00**	**18900.00**	**20600.00**	IH	6T	436D	12F-6R	161.55	12750	C,H,A
1586 4WD	54385.00	**15840.00**	**19800.00**	**21580.00**	IH	6T	436D	12F-6R	161.00	13650	C,H,A
3388 4WD	47960.00	**10500.00**	**14280.00**	**15990.00**	IH	6T	436D	16F-8R	130.61	15960	C,H,A
3588 4WD	53825.00	**11210.00**	**15240.00**	**17070.00**	IH	6T	466D	16F-8R	150.41	16315	C,H,A
3788 4WD	59840.00	**11700.00**	**15910.00**	**17820.00**	IH	6T	466D	12F-6R	170.57	16920	C,H,A
4386 4WD	57845.00	**11250.00**	**15300.00**	**17140.00**	IH	6TI	466D	10F-2R	175.3	20000	C,H,A
4586 4WD	72005.00	**12500.00**	**17000.00**	**19040.00**	IH	V8	798D	10F-2R	235.7	22400	C,H,A
4786 4WD	82660.00	**14000.00**	**19040.00**	**21330.00**	IH	V8	798D	10F-2R	265.5	23600	C,H,A

RC--Row Crop

1982

Model	Approx. Retail Price New	Fair	Good	Premium	Engine Make	No. Cyls.	Displ. Cu.-In.	No. Speeds	P.T.O. H.P.	Approx. Shipping Wt.-Lbs.	Cab
Hydro 84	20385.00	**7170.00**	**8920.00**	**9630.00**	IH	4	246D	Infinite	58.73	5720	No
Hydro 84 4WD	26665.00	**8390.00**	**10430.00**	**11260.00**	IH	4	246D	Infinite	58.00	6620	No
234	6235.00	**3370.00**	**3910.00**	**4220.00**	Mitsubishi	3	52D	6F-2R	15.20	1260	No
234 4WD	6775.00	**3640.00**	**4220.00**	**4560.00**	Mitsubishi	3	52D	6F-2R	15.20	1370	No
Hydro 234	7090.00	**3800.00**	**4400.00**	**4750.00**	Mitsubishi	3	52D	Infinite	15.20	1375	No
Hydro 234 4WD	7630.00	**4070.00**	**4720.00**	**5100.00**	Mitsubishi	3	52D	Infinite	15.20	1445	No
244	6755.00	**3630.00**	**4210.00**	**4550.00**	Mitsubishi	3	60D	9F-3R	18.00	1665	No
244 4WD	7605.00	**4050.00**	**4700.00**	**5080.00**	Mitsubishi	3	60D	9F-3R	18.00	1870	No
254	7435.00	**3970.00**	**4600.00**	**4970.00**	Mitsubishi	3	65D	9F-3R	21.00	1705	No
254 4WD	8425.00	**4460.00**	**5180.00**	**5590.00**	Mitsubishi	3	65D	9F-3R	21.00	1865	No
274	9105.00	**4800.00**	**5570.00**	**6020.00**	Nissan	3	99D	8F-2R	27.47	2270	No
284 4WD	9265.00	**4880.00**	**5660.00**	**6110.00**	Nissan	3	99D	8F-2R	27.00	2950	No
284D	8100.00	**4300.00**	**4990.00**	**5390.00**	Nissan	3	99D	8F-2R	27.47	2270	No
284G	7635.00	**4070.00**	**4720.00**	**5100.00**	Toyo-Kogyo	4	71G	8F-2R	25.75	2050	No
383	11432.00	**5720.00**	**6630.00**	**7160.00**	IH	4	132D	8F-2R	37.00	3480	No
383 4WD	13102.00	**6550.00**	**7600.00**	**8210.00**	IH	4	132D	8F-2R	37.00	4380	No
484	13932.00	**6970.00**	**8080.00**	**8730.00**	IH	4	179D	8F-2R	42.42	3540	No
484 4WD	17892.00	**8950.00**	**10380.00**	**11210.00**	IH	4	179D	8F-2R	42.00	4440	No
584	17080.00	**7690.00**	**9220.00**	**9960.00**	IH	4	206D	8F-4R	52.54	5640	No
584 4WD	22195.00	**9990.00**	**11990.00**	**12950.00**	IH	4	206D	8F-4R	52.00	6540	No
584 RC	17415.00	**7840.00**	**9400.00**	**10150.00**	IH	4	206D	8F-4R	52.54	5890	No
684	18720.00	**8420.00**	**10110.00**	**10920.00**	IH	4	239D	8F-4R	62.52	5720	No
684 4WD	25120.00	**11300.00**	**13570.00**	**14660.00**	IH	4	239D	8F-4R	62.00	6620	No
684 RC	19080.00	**8590.00**	**10300.00**	**11120.00**	IH	4	239D	8F-4R	62.52	5970	No
784	20200.00	**9090.00**	**10910.00**	**11780.00**	IH	4	246D	8F-4R	65.47	5950	No
784 4WD	26600.00	**11970.00**	**14360.00**	**15510.00**	IH	4	246D	8F-4R	65.00	6950	No
784 RC	21150.00	**9520.00**	**11420.00**	**12330.00**	IH	4	246D	8F-4R	65.47	6200	No
884	22530.00	**10140.00**	**12170.00**	**13140.00**	IH	4	268D	16F-8R	72.91	6065	No
884 4WD	28810.00	**12970.00**	**15560.00**	**16810.00**	IH	4	268D	16F-8R	72.00	6965	No
884 RC	23090.00	**10390.00**	**12470.00**	**13470.00**	IH	4	268D	16F-8R	72.91	6315	No
3088	25609.00	**6660.00**	**8960.00**	**10040.00**	IH	6	358D	16F-8R	81.35	10600	C,H,A
3288	35355.00	**8320.00**	**11200.00**	**12540.00**	IH	6	358D	16F-8R	90.46	11100	C,H,A
3488 Hydro	38500.00	**9100.00**	**12250.00**	**13720.00**	IH	6	466D	Infinite	112.56	11225	C,H,A
3688	39160.00	**9490.00**	**12780.00**	**14310.00**	IH	6	436D	16F-8R	113.72	11300	C,H,A
5088	44755.00	**14060.00**	**17480.00**	**18880.00**	IH	6T	436D	18F-6R	136.12	13765	C,H,A
5288	51945.00	**15360.00**	**19090.00**	**20620.00**	IH	6T	466D	18F-6R	162.60	1461	C,H,A
5488	56175.00	**15980.00**	**19870.00**	**21460.00**	IH	6TI	466D	18F-6R	187.22	14710	C,H,A
6388 4WD	53805.00	**11910.00**	**16030.00**	**17950.00**	IH	6T	436D	16F-8R	130.61	15960	C,H,A
6588 4WD	60905.00	**13130.00**	**17680.00**	**19800.00**	IH	6T	466D	16F-8R	150.41	16320	C,H,A
6788 4WD	68925.00	**13650.00**	**18380.00**	**20590.00**	IH	6T	466D	12F-6R	170.00	16920	C,H,A
7388 4WD	65505.00	**14300.00**	**19250.00**	**21560.00**	IH	6TI	466D	10F-2R	181.0	19875	C,H,A
7588 4WD	84260.00	**14950.00**	**20130.00**	**22550.00**	IH	V8	798D	18F-4R	265.0	22600	C,H,A
7788 4WD	93320.00	**15860.00**	**21350.00**	**23910.00**	IH	V8	798D	20F-4R	265.0	23800	C,H,A

RC--Row Crop

1983

Model	Approx. Retail Price New	Fair	Good	Premium	Engine Make	No. Cyls.	Displ. Cu.-In.	No. Speeds	P.T.O. H.P.	Approx. Shipping Wt.-Lbs.	Cab
Hydro 84	22581.00	**7820.00**	**9670.00**	**10440.00**	IH	4	246D	Infinite	58.73	5720	No
Hydro 84 4WD	27686.00	**9000.00**	**11130.00**	**12020.00**	IH	4	246D	Infinite	58.00	6620	No
234	6559.00	**3600.00**	**4170.00**	**4500.00**	Mitsubishi	3	52D	6F-2R	15.20	1260	No
234 4WD	7124.00	**3890.00**	**4500.00**	**4860.00**	Mitsubishi	3	52D	6F-2R	15.20	1370	No
Hydro 234	7449.00	**4050.00**	**4690.00**	**5070.00**	Mitsubishi	3	52D	Infinite	15.20	1375	No
Hydro 234 4WD	8014.00	**4340.00**	**5020.00**	**5420.00**	Mitsubishi	3	52D	Infinite	15.20	1445	No
244	7394.00	**4030.00**	**4660.00**	**5030.00**	Mitsubishi	3	60D	9F-3R	18.00	1665	No
244 4WD	8274.00	**4480.00**	**5180.00**	**5590.00**	Mitsubishi	3	60D	9F-3R	18.00	1870	No
254	8099.00	**4390.00**	**5070.00**	**5480.00**	Mitsubishi	3	65D	9F-3R	21.00	1705	No
254 4WD	9129.00	**4910.00**	**5680.00**	**6130.00**	Mitsubishi	3	65D	9F-3R	21.00	1865	No
274 Offset	9981.00	**5350.00**	**6180.00**	**6670.00**	Nissan	3	99D	8F-2R	27.00	2270	No
284D	8695.00	**4690.00**	**5430.00**	**5860.00**	Nissan	3	99D	8F-2R	27.47	2270	No
284D 4WD	10930.00	**5830.00**	**6740.00**	**7280.00**	Nissan	3	99D	8F-2R	25.00	2657	No
284G	7635.00	**4150.00**	**4800.00**	**5180.00**	Toyo-Kogyo	4	71G	8F-2R	25.75	2050	No
484	15488.00	**7900.00**	**9140.00**	**9870.00**	IH	3	179D	8F-2R	42.42	3540	No
584	18487.00	**8500.00**	**10170.00**	**10980.00**	IH	4	206D	8F-4R	52.54	5640	No
584 4WD	22640.00	**10410.00**	**12450.00**	**13450.00**	IH	4	206D	8F-4R	52.00	6540	No
584 RC	18866.00	**8680.00**	**10380.00**	**11210.00**	IH	4	206D	8F-4R	52.54	5890	No
684	20761.00	**9550.00**	**11420.00**	**12330.00**	IH	4	239D	8F-4R	62.52	5720	No

Int. Harvester-Farmall (Cont.)

1983 (Cont.)

Model	Approx. Retail Price New	Fair	Good	Premium	Make	Engine No. Cyls.	Engine Displ. Cu.-In.	No. Speeds	P.T.O. H.P.	Approx. Shipping Wt.-Lbs.	Cab
684 4WD	25986.00	11950.00	14290.00	15430.00	IH	4	239D	8F-4R	62.00	6620	No
684 RC	21261.00	9780.00	11690.00	12630.00	IH	4	239D	8F-4R	62.52	5970	No
784	21869.00	10060.00	12030.00	12990.00	IH	4	246D	8F-4R	65.47	5950	No
784 4WD	27496.00	12650.00	15120.00	16330.00	IH	4	246D	8F-4R	65.00	6950	No
784 RC	22897.00	10530.00	12590.00	13600.00	IH	4	246D	8F-4R	65.47	6200	No
884	25082.00	11540.00	13800.00	14900.00	IH	4	268D	16F-8R	72.91	6065	No
884 4WD	29751.00	13690.00	16360.00	17670.00	IH	4	268D	16F-8R	72.00	6965	No
884 RC	25696.00	11820.00	14130.00	15260.00	IH	4	268D	16F-8R	72.91	6315	No
3088	30700.00	8020.00	10690.00	11970.00	IH	6	358D	16F-8R	81.35	10600	C,H,A
3088 4WD	42123.00	9990.00	13320.00	14920.00	IH	6	358D	16F-8R	81.35	11500	C,H,A
3288	40190.00	10290.00	13720.00	15370.00	IH	6	358D	16F-8R	90.46	11100	C,H,A
3288 4WD	50940.00	12150.00	16200.00	18140.00	IH	6	358D	16F-8R	90.00	12000	C,H,A
3488 Hydro	49370.00	12420.00	16560.00	18550.00	IH	6	466D	Infinite	112.56	11225	C,H,A
3488 Hydro 4WD	60120.00	13500.00	18000.00	20160.00	IH	6	466D	Infinite	112.00	12200	C,H,A
3688	44975.00	11070.00	14760.00	16530.00	IH	6	436D	16F-8R	113.72	11300	C,H,A
3688 4WD	55725.00	12690.00	16920.00	18950.00	IH	6	436D	16F-8R	113.00	12200	C,H,A
3688 High Clear	51440.00	12040.00	16060.00	17990.00	IH	6	436D	16F-8R	113.00	11500	C,H,A
5088	53720.00	14830.00	18340.00	19810.00	IH	6T	436D	18F-6R	136.12	13765	C,H,A
5088 4WD	64110.00	16450.00	20350.00	21980.00	IH	6T	436D	18F-6R	136.00	14700	C,H,A
5288	59935.00	15400.00	19050.00	20570.00	IH	6T	466D	18F-6R	162.60	14610	C,H,A
5288 4WD	70235.00	16720.00	20680.00	22330.00	IH	6T	466D	18F-6R	162.00	15500	C,H,A
5488	66156.00	17020.00	21060.00	22750.00	IH	6TI	466D	18F-6R	187.22	14710	C,H,A
5488 4WD	76456.00	17780.00	22000.00	23760.00	IH	6TI	466D	18F-6R	187.00	15700	C,H,A
6388 4WD	62180.00	11660.00	15550.00	17420.00	IH	6T	436D	16F-8R	130.61	15960	C,H,A
6588 4WD	67855.00	12710.00	16940.00	18970.00	IH	6T	466D	16F-8R	150.41	16320	C,H,A
6788 4WD	73265.00	14330.00	19100.00	21390.00	IH	6T	466D	12F-6R	170.00	16920	C,H,A

RC--Row Crop

1984

Model	Approx. Retail Price New	Fair	Good	Premium	Make	Engine No. Cyls.	Engine Displ. Cu.-In.	No. Speeds	P.T.O. H.P.	Approx. Shipping Wt.-Lbs.	Cab
Hydro 84	22585.00	8420.00	10360.00	11190.00	IH	4	246D	Infinite	58.73	5720	No
Hydro 84 4WD	27690.00	9630.00	11850.00	12800.00	IH	4	246D	Infinite	58.00	6620	No
234	6560.00	3670.00	4240.00	4580.00	Mitsubishi	3	52D	6F-2R	15.20	1260	No
234 4WD	7125.00	3970.00	4580.00	4950.00	Mitsubishi	3	52D	6F-2R	15.20	1370	No
Hydro 234	7450.00	4130.00	4770.00	5150.00	Mitsubishi	3	52D	Infinite	15.20	1375	No
Hydro 234 4WD	8015.00	4430.00	5110.00	5520.00	Mitsubishi	3	52D	Infinite	15.20	1445	No
244	7395.00	4110.00	4740.00	5120.00	Mitsubishi	3	60D	9F-3R	18.00	1665	No
244 4WD	8275.00	4560.00	5270.00	5690.00	Mitsubishi	3	60D	9F-3R	18.00	1870	No
254	8100.00	4470.00	5160.00	5570.00	Mitsubishi	3	65D	9F-3R	21.00	1705	No
254 4WD	9130.00	5010.00	5780.00	6240.00	Mitsubishi	3	65D	9F-3R	21.00	1865	No
274 Offset	9985.00	5450.00	6290.00	6790.00	Nissan	3	99D	8F-2R	27.00	2270	No
284D	8695.00	4780.00	5520.00	5960.00	Nissan	3	99D	8F-2R	27.47	2270	No
284D 4WD	10930.00	5940.00	6860.00	7410.00	Nissan	3	99D	8F-2R	25.00	2657	No
284G	7635.00	4230.00	4880.00	5270.00	Toyo-Kogyo	4	71G	8F-2R	25.75	2050	No
484	15490.00	8060.00	9290.00	10030.00	IH	3	179D	8F-2R	42.42	3540	No
584	18490.00	8690.00	10350.00	11180.00	IH	4	206D	8F-4R	52.54	5640	No
584 4WD	22640.00	10640.00	12680.00	13690.00	IH	4	206D	8F-4R	52.00	6540	No
584 RC	18870.00	8870.00	10570.00	11420.00	IH	4	206D	8F-4R	52.54	5890	No
684	20765.00	9760.00	11630.00	12560.00	IH	4	239D	8F-4R	62.52	5720	No
684 4WD	25990.00	12220.00	14550.00	15710.00	IH	4	239D	8F-4R	62.00	6620	No
684 RC	21265.00	10000.00	11910.00	12860.00	IH	4	239D	8F-4R	62.52	5970	No
784	21870.00	10280.00	12250.00	13230.00	IH	4	246D	8F-4R	65.47	5950	No
784 4WD	27500.00	12930.00	15400.00	16630.00	IH	4	246D	8F-4R	65.00	6950	No
784 RC	22900.00	10760.00	12820.00	13850.00	IH	4	246D	8F-4R	65.47	6200	No
884	25085.00	11790.00	14050.00	15170.00	IH	4	268D	16F-8R	72.91	6065	No
884 4WD	25755.00	12110.00	14420.00	15570.00	IH	4	268D	16F-8R	72.00	6965	No
884 RC	25670.00	12070.00	14380.00	15530.00	IH	4	268D	16F-8R	72.91	6315	No
3088	30700.00	8400.00	11100.00	12430.00	IH	6	358D	16F-8R	81.35	10600	C,H,A
3088 4WD	42125.00	10360.00	13690.00	15330.00	IH	6	358D	16F-8R	81.35	11500	C,H,A
3288	40190.00	10640.00	14060.00	15750.00	IH	6	358D	16F-8R	90.46	11100	C,H,A
3288 4WD	50940.00	12600.00	16650.00	18650.00	IH	6	358D	16F-8R	90.00	12000	C,H,A
3488 Hydro	49370.00	12040.00	15910.00	17820.00	IH	6	466D	Infinite	112.56	11225	C,H,A
3488 Hydro 4WD	60120.00	13160.00	17390.00	19480.00	IH	6	466D	Infinite	112.00	12200	C,H,A
3688	44975.00	11200.00	14800.00	16580.00	IH	6	436D	16F-8R	113.72	11300	C,H,A
3688 4WD	55725.00	11960.00	15800.00	17700.00	IH	6	436D	16F-8R	113.00	12200	C,H,A
3688 High Clear	51440.00	12430.00	16430.00	18400.00	IH	6	436D	16F-8R	113.00	11500	C,H,A
5088	53720.00	15210.00	18720.00	20220.00	IH	6T	436D	18F-6R	136.12	13765	C,H,A
5088 4WD	64110.00	17200.00	21170.00	22860.00	IH	6T	436D	18F-6R	136.00	14700	C,H,A
5288	59935.00	16580.00	20400.00	22030.00	IH	6T	466D	18F-6R	162.60	14610	C,H,A
5288 4WD	70235.00	18140.00	22320.00	24110.00	IH	6T	466D	18F-6R	162.00	15500	C,H,A
5488	66160.00	17220.00	21200.00	22900.00	IH	6TI	466D	18F-6R	187.22	14710	C,H,A
5488 4WD	76460.00	18980.00	23360.00	25230.00	IH	6TI	466D	18F-6R	187.00	15700	C,H,A
6388 4WD	62180.00	14610.00	19310.00	21630.00	IH	6T	436D	16F-8R	130.61	15960	C,H,A
6588 4WD	67855.00	15640.00	20670.00	23150.00	IH	6T	466D	16F-8R	150.41	16320	C,H,A
6788 4WD	73265.00	16260.00	21480.00	24060.00	IH	6T	466D	12F-6R	170.00	16920	C,H,A

RC--Row Crop

1985

Model	Approx. Retail Price New	Fair	Good	Premium	Make	Engine No. Cyls.	Engine Displ. Cu.-In.	No. Speeds	P.T.O. H.P.	Approx. Shipping Wt.-Lbs.	Cab
Hydro 84	22585.00	8600.00	10540.00	11280.00	IH	4	246D	Infinite	58.73	5720	No
Hydro 84 4WD	27690.00	10000.00	12250.00	13110.00	IH	4	246D	Infinite	58.00	6620	No
234	6560.00	3740.00	4310.00	4660.00	Mitsubishi	3	52D	6F-2R	15.20	1260	No
234 4WD	7125.00	4040.00	4650.00	5020.00	Mitsubishi	3	52D	6F-2R	15.20	1370	No
Hydro 234	7450.00	4210.00	4850.00	5240.00	Mitsubishi	3	52D	Infinite	15.20	1375	No
Hydro 234 4WD	8015.00	4510.00	5190.00	5610.00	Mitsubishi	3	52D	Infinite	15.20	1445	No
244	7395.00	4180.00	4820.00	5210.00	Mitsubishi	3	60D	9F-3R	18.00	1665	No

Model	Approx. Retail Price New	Estimated Average Value Less Repairs Fair	Good	Premium	Engine Make	No. Cyls.	Displ. Cu.-In.	No. Speeds	P.T.O. H.P.	Approx. Shipping Wt.-Lbs.	Cab

Int. Harvester-Farmall (Cont.)

1985 (Cont.)

Model	Approx. Retail Price New	Fair	Good	Premium	Make	No. Cyls.	Displ. Cu.-In.	No. Speeds	P.T.O. H.P.	Approx. Shipping Wt.-Lbs.	Cab
244 4WD	8275.00	**4650.00**	**5350.00**	**5780.00**	Mitsubishi	3	60D	9F-3R	18.00	1870	No
254	8100.00	**4560.00**	**5250.00**	**5670.00**	Mitsubishi	3	65D	9F-3R	21.00	1705	No
254 4WD	9130.00	**5100.00**	**5870.00**	**6340.00**	Mitsubishi	3	65D	9F-3R	21.00	1865	No
274 Offset	9985.00	**5560.00**	**6400.00**	**6910.00**	Nissan	3	99D	8F-2R	27.00	2270	No
284D	8695.00	**4870.00**	**5610.00**	**6060.00**	Nissan	3	99D	8F-2R	27.47	2270	No
284D 4WD	10930.00	**6060.00**	**6970.00**	**7530.00**	Nissan	3	99D	8F-2R	25.00	2657	No
484	15490.00	**8210.00**	**9450.00**	**10210.00**	IH	3	179D	8F-2R	42.42	3540	No
584	18490.00	**8880.00**	**10540.00**	**11380.00**	IH	4	206D	8F-4R	52.54	5640	No
584 4WD	22640.00	**10870.00**	**12910.00**	**13940.00**	IH	4	206D	8F-4R	52.00	6540	No
584 RC	18870.00	**9060.00**	**10760.00**	**11620.00**	IH	4	206D	8F-4R	52.54	5890	No
684	20765.00	**9970.00**	**11840.00**	**12790.00**	IH	4	239D	8F-4R	62.52	5720	No
684 4WD	25990.00	**12480.00**	**14810.00**	**16000.00**	IH	4	239D	8F-4R	62.00	6620	No
684 RC	21265.00	**10210.00**	**12120.00**	**13090.00**	IH	4	239D	8F-4R	62.52	5970	No
784	21870.00	**10500.00**	**12470.00**	**13470.00**	IH	4	246D	8F-4R	65.47	5950	No
784 4WD	27500.00	**13200.00**	**15680.00**	**16930.00**	IH	4	246D	8F-4R	65.00	6950	No
784 RC	22900.00	**10990.00**	**13050.00**	**14090.00**	IH	4	246D	8F-4R	65.47	6200	No
884	25085.00	**12040.00**	**14300.00**	**15440.00**	IH	4	268D	16F-8R	72.91	6065	No
884 4WD	25755.00	**12360.00**	**14680.00**	**15850.00**	IH	4	268D	16F-8R	72.00	6965	No
884 RC	25670.00	**12320.00**	**14630.00**	**15800.00**	IH	4	268D	16F-8R	72.91	6315	No
3088	30700.00	**9000.00**	**11400.00**	**12650.00**	IH	6	358D	16F-8R	81.35	10600	C,H,A
3088 4WD	42125.00	**11400.00**	**14440.00**	**16030.00**	IH	6	358D	16F-8R	81.35	11500	C,H,A
3288	40190.00	**11100.00**	**14060.00**	**15610.00**	IH	6	358D	16F-8R	90.46	11100	C,H,A
3288 4WD	50940.00	**13260.00**	**16800.00**	**18650.00**	IH	6	358D	16F-8R	90.00	12000	C,H,A
3488 Hydro	49370.00	**12690.00**	**16070.00**	**17840.00**	IH	6	466D	Infinite	112.56	11225	C,H,A
3488 Hydro 4WD	60120.00	**14400.00**	**18240.00**	**20250.00**	IH	6	466D	Infinite	112.00	12200	C,H,A
3688	44975.00	**12300.00**	**15580.00**	**17290.00**	IH	6	436D	16F-8R	113.72	11300	C,H,A
3688 4WD	55725.00	**14700.00**	**18620.00**	**20670.00**	IH	6	436D	16F-8R	113.00	12200	C,H,A
3688 High Clear	51440.00	**13920.00**	**17630.00**	**19570.00**	IH	6	436D	16F-8R	113.00	11500	C,H,A
5088	53720.00	**16210.00**	**19860.00**	**21250.00**	IH	6T	436D	18F-6R	136.12	13765	C,H,A
5088 4WD	64110.00	**17680.00**	**21660.00**	**23180.00**	IH	6T	436D	18F-6R	136.00	14700	C,H,A
5288	59935.00	**17200.00**	**21070.00**	**22550.00**	IH	6T	466D	18F-6R	162.60	14610	C,H,A
5288 4WD	70235.00	**18610.00**	**22800.00**	**24400.00**	IH	6T	466D	18F-6R	162.00	15500	C,H,A
5488	66160.00	**18220.00**	**22320.00**	**23880.00**	IH	6TI	466D	18F-6R	187.22	14710	C,H,A
5488 4WD	76460.00	**20020.00**	**24530.00**	**26250.00**	IH	6TI	466D	18F-6R	187.00	15700	C,H,A

RC--Row Crop

John Deere

1939

Model	Approx. Retail Price New	Fair	Good	Premium	Make	No. Cyls.	Displ. Cu.-In.	No. Speeds	P.T.O. H.P.	Approx. Shipping Wt.-Lbs.	Cab
A	......	**910.00**	**2090.00**	**2590.00**	JD		321G	4F-1R	35.3	5100	No
AO	......	**980.00**	**2250.00**	**2790.00**	JD		321D	6F-1R	35.3	4800	No
AO	......	**980.00**	**2250.00**	**2790.00**	JD		321D	6F-1R	35.3	4800	No
AR	......	**970.00**	**2220.00**	**2750.00**	JD		321D	4F-1R	35.3	4800	No
BO	......	**1040.00**	**2400.00**	**2980.00**	JD	2	190G	6F-1R	27	4030	No
BR	......	**1090.00**	**2490.00**	**3090.00**	JD		190G	4F-1R	25	4030	No
D	......	**900.00**	**2080.00**	**2580.00**	JD		501D	2F-1R	38	8125	No
G	......	**1130.00**	**2590.00**	**3210.00**	JD		413G	4F-1R	36	5800	No
H	......	**760.00**	**1750.00**	**2170.00**	JD		99D	3F-1R	12	3035	No
L	......	**740.00**	**1690.00**	**2100.00**	JD		66G	3F-1R	9	2180	No

1940

Model	Approx. Retail Price New	Fair	Good	Premium	Make	No. Cyls.	Displ. Cu.-In.	No. Speeds	P.T.O. H.P.	Approx. Shipping Wt.-Lbs.	Cab
A	......	**910.00**	**2090.00**	**2590.00**	JD		321G	4F-1R	35.3	5100	No
AN	......	**1000.00**	**2290.00**	**2840.00**	JD		321G	6F-1R	35.3	5100	No
AO	......	**980.00**	**2250.00**	**2790.00**	JD		321D	6F-1R	35.3	4800	No
AR	......	**970.00**	**2220.00**	**2750.00**	JD		321D	4F-1R	35.3	4800	No
B	......	**940.00**	**2160.00**	**2680.00**	JD		190G	4F-1R	25	4130	No
BO	......	**1040.00**	**2400.00**	**2980.00**	JD	2	190G	6F-1R	27	4030	No
BR	......	**1090.00**	**2490.00**	**3090.00**	JD		190G	4F-1R	25	4030	No
D	......	**900.00**	**2080.00**	**2580.00**	JD		501D	2F-1R	38	8125	No
G	......	**1130.00**	**2590.00**	**3210.00**	JD		413G	4F-1R	36	5800	No
H	......	**760.00**	**1750.00**	**2170.00**	JD		99D	3F-1R	12	3035	No
L	......	**740.00**	**1690.00**	**2100.00**	JD		66G	3F-1R	9	2180	No

1941

Model	Approx. Retail Price New	Fair	Good	Premium	Make	No. Cyls.	Displ. Cu.-In.	No. Speeds	P.T.O. H.P.	Approx. Shipping Wt.-Lbs.	Cab
A	......	**920.00**	**2130.00**	**2640.00**	JD		321G	4F-1R	35.3	5100	No
AN	......	**1020.00**	**2350.00**	**2910.00**	JD		321G	6F-1R	35.3	5100	No
AO	......	**990.00**	**2280.00**	**2830.00**	JD		321D	6F-1R	35.3	4800	No
AR	......	**980.00**	**2260.00**	**2800.00**	JD		321D	4F-1R	35.3	4800	No
B	......	**950.00**	**2190.00**	**2720.00**	JD		190G	4F-1R	25	4130	No
BO	......	**1060.00**	**2440.00**	**3030.00**	JD		190G	6F-1R	25	4030	No
BR	......	**1100.00**	**2530.00**	**3140.00**	JD		190G	4F-1R	25	4030	No
D	......	**920.00**	**2120.00**	**2630.00**	JD		501D	2F-1R	38	8125	No
G	......	**1150.00**	**2640.00**	**3270.00**	JD		413G	4F-1R	36	5800	No
H	......	**780.00**	**1790.00**	**2220.00**	JD		99D	3F-1R	12	3035	No
L	......	**750.00**	**1730.00**	**2150.00**	JD		66G	3F-1R	9	2180	No

1942

Model	Approx. Retail Price New	Fair	Good	Premium	Make	No. Cyls.	Displ. Cu.-In.	No. Speeds	P.T.O. H.P.	Approx. Shipping Wt.-Lbs.	Cab
A	......	**940.00**	**2170.00**	**2690.00**	JD		321G	4F-1R	35.3	5100	No
AN	......	**1020.00**	**2350.00**	**2910.00**	JD		321G	6F-1R	35.3	5100	No
AO	......	**1000.00**	**2290.00**	**2840.00**	JD		321D	6F-1R	35.3	4800	No
AR	......	**990.00**	**2280.00**	**2830.00**	JD		321D	4F-1R	35.3	4800	No
B	......	**970.00**	**2230.00**	**2770.00**	JD		190G	4F-1R	25	4130	No
BO	......	**1080.00**	**2480.00**	**3080.00**	JD		190G	6F-1R	25	4030	No

Model	Approx. Retail Price New	Estimated Average Value Less Repairs Fair	Good	Premium	Engine Make	No. Cyls.	Displ. Cu.-In.	No. Speeds	P.T.O. H.P.	Approx. Shipping Wt.-Lbs.	Cab
John Deere (Cont.)											
1942 (Cont.)											
BR	......	1120.00	2560.00	3170.00	JD		190G	4F-1R	25	4030	No
D	......	940.00	2150.00	2670.00	JD		501D	2F-1R	38	8125	No
G	......	1170.00	2680.00	3320.00	JD		413G	4F-1R	36	5800	No
H	......	800.00	1850.00	2290.00	JD		99D	3F-1R	12	3035	No
L	......	770.00	1760.00	2180.00	JD		66G	3F-1R	9	2180	No
1943											
A	......	990.00	2210.00	2740.00	JD		321G	4F-1R	35.3	5100	No
AN	......	1070.00	2380.00	2950.00	JD		321G	6F-1R	35.3	5100	No
AO	......	1050.00	2330.00	2890.00	JD		321D	6F-1R	35.3	4800	No
AR	......	1040.00	2310.00	2860.00	JD		321D	4F-1R	35.3	4800	No
B	......	1020.00	2260.00	2800.00	JD		190G	4F-1R	25	4130	No
BO	......	1130.00	2520.00	3130.00	JD		190G	6F-1R	25	4030	No
BR	......	1170.00	2600.00	3220.00	JD		190G	4F-1R	25	4030	No
D	......	980.00	2180.00	2700.00	JD		501D	2F-1R	38	8125	No
G	......	1250.00	2780.00	3450.00	JD		413G	4F-1R	36	5800	No
H	......	850.00	1900.00	2360.00	JD		99D	3F-1R	12	3035	No
L	......	810.00	1790.00	2220.00	JD		66G	3F-1R	9	2180	No
1944											
A	......	1040.00	2250.00	2790.00	JD		321G	4F-1R	35.3	5100	No
AN	......	1120.00	2420.00	3000.00	JD		321G	6F-1R	35.3	5100	No
AO	......	1090.00	2350.00	2910.00	JD		321D	6F-1R	35.3	4800	No
AR	......	1080.00	2330.00	2890.00	JD		321D	4F-1R	35.3	4800	No
B	......	1070.00	2310.00	2860.00	JD		190G	4F-1R	25	4130	No
BO	......	1190.00	2560.00	3170.00	JD		190G	6F-1R	25	4030	No
BR	......	1220.00	2640.00	3270.00	JD		190G	4F-1R	25	4030	No
D	......	1030.00	2220.00	2750.00	JD		501D	2F-1R	38	8125	No
G	......	1310.00	2820.00	3500.00	JD		413G	4F-1R	36	5800	No
H	......	900.00	1950.00	2420.00	JD		99D	3F-1R	12	3035	No
L	......	850.00	1840.00	2280.00	JD		66G	3F-1R	9	2180	No
1945											
A	......	1090.00	2240.00	2780.00	JD	2	321G	4F-1R	35.3	5100	No
AN	......	1180.00	2420.00	3000.00	JD	2	321G	6F-1R	35.3	5100	No
AR	......	1130.00	2330.00	2890.00	JD	2	321D	4F-1R	35.3	4800	No
B	......	1120.00	2300.00	2850.00	JD	2	190G	4F-1R	25	4130	No
BO	......	1250.00	2570.00	3190.00	JD	2	190G	6F-1R	25	4030	No
BR	......	1290.00	2650.00	3290.00	JD	2	190G	4F-1R	25	4030	No
D	......	1080.00	2220.00	2750.00	JD	2	501D	2F-1R	38	8125	No
G	......	1360.00	2800.00	3470.00	JD	2	413G	4F-1R	36	5800	No
H	......	950.00	1960.00	2430.00	JD	2	99D	3F-1R	12	3035	No
LA	......	910.00	1870.00	2320.00		2	66G	3F-1R		2180	No
1946											
A	......	1140.00	2280.00	2830.00	JD	2	321G	4F-1R	35.3	5100	No
AN	......	1230.00	2460.00	3050.00	JD	2	321G	6F-1R	35.3	5100	No
AR	......	1190.00	2380.00	2950.00	JD	2	321D	4F-1R	35.3	4800	No
B	......	1180.00	2350.00	2910.00	JD	2	190G	4F-1R	25	4130	No
BO	......	1290.00	2580.00	3200.00	JD	2	190G	6F-1R	25	4030	No
BR	......	1340.00	2680.00	3320.00	JD	2	190G	4F-1R	25	4030	No
D	......	1130.00	2260.00	2800.00	JD	2	501D	2F-1R	38	8125	No
G	......	1420.00	2840.00	3520.00	JD	2	413G	4F-1R	36	5800	No
H	......	1010.00	2010.00	2490.00	JD	2	99D	3F-1R	12	3035	No
LA	......	960.00	1920.00	2380.00		2	66G	3F-1R		2180	No
1947											
A	......	1190.00	2310.00	2860.00	JD	2	321G	4F-1R	35.3	5100	No
AN	......	1290.00	2500.00	3100.00	JD	2	321G	6F-1R	35.3	5100	No
AR	......	1240.00	2410.00	2990.00	JD	2	321D	4F-1R	35.3	4800	No
B	......	1230.00	2380.00	2950.00	JD	2	190G	4F-1R	25	4130	No
BO	......	1350.00	2620.00	3250.00	JD	2	190G	4F-1R	25	4130	No
BR	......	1400.00	2710.00	3360.00	JD	2	190G	4F-1R	25	4130	No
D	......	1190.00	2310.00	2860.00	JD	2	501D	2F-1R	38	8125	No
G	......	1490.00	2890.00	3580.00	JD	2	413G	4F-1R	36	5800	No
H	......	1060.00	2050.00	2540.00	JD	2	99D	3F-1R	12	3035	No
M	......	1260.00	2450.00	3040.00	JD	2	100G	4F-1R	18	2700	No
1948											
A	......	1240.00	2350.00	2910.00	JD	2	321G	4F-1R	35.3	5100	No
AN	......	1340.00	2530.00	3140.00	JD	2	321G	6F-1R	35.3	5100	No
AR	......	1300.00	2450.00	3040.00	JD	2	321D	4F-1R	35.3	4800	No
B	......	1270.00	2410.00	2990.00	JD	2	190G	4F-1R	25	4130	No
D	......	1240.00	2340.00	2900.00	JD	2	501D	2F-1R	38	8125	No
G	......	1560.00	2940.00	3650.00	JD	2	413G	4F-1R	36	5800	No
M	......	1320.00	2490.00	3090.00	JD	2	100G	4F-1R	18	2700	No
1949											
A	......	1300.00	2380.00	2950.00	JD	2	321G	4F-1R	35.3	5100	No
AN	......	1400.00	2560.00	3170.00	JD	2	321G	6F-1R	35.3	5100	No
AR	......	1350.00	2490.00	3090.00	JD	2	321D	4F-1R	35.3	4800	No
B	......	1320.00	2430.00	3010.00	JD	2	190G	4F-1R	25	4130	No
D	......	1300.00	2380.00	2950.00	JD	2	501D	2F-1R	38	8125	No
G	......	1630.00	2990.00	3710.00	JD	2	413G	4F-1R	36	5800	No

John Deere (Cont.)

Model	Approx. Retail Price New	Estimated Average Value Less Repairs Fair	Good	Premium	Engine Make	No. Cyls.	Displ. Cu.-In.	No. Speeds	P.T.O. H.P.	Approx. Shipping Wt.-Lbs.	Cab
1949 (Cont.)											
M	......	1380.00	2530.00	3140.00	JD	2	100G	4F-1R	18	2700	No
MT	......	1470.00	2690.00	3340.00	JD	2	100G	4F-1R	18	2800	No
R	......	1090.00	2010.00	2490.00	JD	2	415D	5F-1R	51	7100	No
1950											
A	......	1350.00	2420.00	3000.00	JD	2	321G	4F-1R	35.3	5100	No
AN	......	1460.00	2600.00	3220.00	JD	2	321G	6F-1R	35.3	5100	No
AR	......	1410.00	2530.00	3140.00	JD	2	321D	4F-1R	35.3	4800	No
B	......	1380.00	2470.00	3060.00	JD	2	190G	4F-1R	25	4130	No
D	......	1350.00	2420.00	3000.00	JD	2	501D	2F-1R	38	8125	No
G	......	1700.00	3040.00	3770.00	JD	2	413G	4F-1R	36	5800	No
M	......	1440.00	2580.00	3200.00	JD	2	100G	4F-1R	18	2700	No
MT	......	1530.00	2730.00	3390.00	JD	2	100G	4F-1R	18	2800	No
R	......	1140.00	2040.00	2530.00	JD	2	415D	5F-1R	51	7100	No
1951											
A	......	1410.00	2460.00	3050.00	JD	2	321G	4F-1R	35.3	5100	No
AN	......	1520.00	2650.00	3290.00	JD	2	321G	6F-1R	35.3	5100	No
AR	......	1470.00	2570.00	3190.00	JD	2	321D	4F-1R	35.3	4800	No
B	......	1430.00	2500.00	3100.00	JD	2	190G	4F-1R	25	4130	No
D	......	1410.00	2460.00	3050.00	JD	2	501D	2F-1R	38	8125	No
G	......	1780.00	3100.00	3840.00	JD	2	413G	4F-1R	36	5800	No
M	......	1510.00	2630.00	3260.00	JD	2	100G	4F-1R	18	2700	No
MT	......	1610.00	2800.00	3470.00	JD	2	100G	4F-1R	18	2800	No
R	......	1190.00	2080.00	2580.00	JD	2	415D	5F-1R	51	7100	No
1952											
A	......	1500.00	2550.00	3160.00	JD	2	321G	4F-1R	35.3	5100	No
AN	......	1630.00	2770.00	3440.00	JD	2	321G	6F-1R	35.3	5100	No
AR	......	1580.00	2690.00	3340.00	JD	2	321D	4F-1R	35.3	4800	No
B	......	1530.00	2600.00	3220.00	JD	2	190G	4F-1R	25	4130	No
D	......	1500.00	2540.00	3150.00	JD	2	501D	2F-1R	38	8125	No
G	......	1890.00	3210.00	3980.00	JD	2	413G	4F-1R	36	5800	No
M	......	1640.00	2790.00	3460.00	JD	2	100G	4F-1R	18	2700	No
MT	......	1730.00	2940.00	3650.00	JD	2	100G	4F-1R	18	2800	No
R	......	1290.00	2190.00	2720.00	JD	2	415D	5F-1R	51	7100	No
50	......	1340.00	2280.00	2830.00	JD	2	190G	6F-1R	31	4200	No
60	......	1400.00	2380.00	2950.00	JD	2	321G	6F-1R	42	5357	No
1953											
D	......	1580.00	2620.00	3250.00	JD	2	501D	2F-1R	38	8125	No
G	......	1960.00	3260.00	4040.00	JD	2	413G	4F-1R	36	5800	No
R	......	1360.00	2250.00	2790.00	JD	2	415D	5F-1R	51	7100	No
40	......	1340.00	2210.00	2740.00	JD	2	101G	4F-1R	19	2636	No
50	......	1460.00	2420.00	3000.00	JD	2	190G	6F-1R	31	4200	No
60	......	1500.00	2490.00	3090.00	JD	2	321G	6F-1R	42	5357	No
70	......	1520.00	2520.00	3130.00	JD	2	376D	6F-1R	51	7352	No
70	......	1950.00	3230.00	4010.00	JD	2	376D	6F-1R	51	7352	No
1954											
R	......	1360.00	2190.00	2720.00	JD	2	415D	5F-1R	51	7100	No
40	......	1410.00	2280.00	2830.00	JD	2	101G	4F-1R	19	2636	No
50	......	1510.00	2450.00	3040.00	JD	2	190G	6F-1R	31	4200	No
60	......	1570.00	2550.00	3160.00	JD	2	321G	6F-1R	42	5357	No
70	......	1600.00	2600.00	3220.00	JD	2	379G	6F-1R	51	7352	No
70	......	2060.00	3330.00	4130.00	JD	2	376D	6F-1R	51	7352	No
1955											
40	......	1510.00	2390.00	2960.00	JD	2	101G	4F-1R	22.8	2970	No
50	......	1580.00	2500.00	3100.00	JD	2	190G	6F-1R	31	4200	No
60	......	1650.00	2600.00	3220.00	JD	2	321G	6F-1R	42	5357	No
70	......	1690.00	2680.00	3320.00	JD	2	379G	6F-1R	51	7352	No
70	......	2190.00	3470.00	4300.00	JD	2	376D	6F-1R	51	7352	No
80	......	2300.00	3640.00	4510.00	JD	2	471D	6F-1R	68	7900	No
1956											
50	......	1700.00	2620.00	3250.00	JD	2	190G	6F-1R	31	4200	No
60	......	1770.00	2740.00	3400.00	JD	2	321G	6F-1R	42	5357	No
70	......	1830.00	2820.00	3500.00	JD	2	379G	6F-1R	51	7352	No
70	......	2370.00	3660.00	4540.00	JD	2	376D	6F-1R	51	7352	No
80	......	2450.00	3790.00	4700.00	JD	2	471D	6F-1R	68	7900	No
320	......	1820.00	2810.00	3480.00	JD	2	100G	4F-1R	27	2670	No
420	......	2060.00	3190.00	3960.00	JD	2	113G	4F-1R	29	2793	No
520	......	2140.00	3310.00	4100.00	JD	2	190G	6F-1R	39	5325	No
620	......	2210.00	3420.00	4240.00	JD	2	302G	6F-1R	49	6460	No
720	......	2320.00	3580.00	4440.00	JD	2	361G	6F-1R	59	7220	No
720	......	2440.00	3770.00	4680.00	JD	2	376D	6F-1R	59	7700	No
820	......	2580.00	3980.00	4940.00	JD	2	472D	6F-1R	76	8300	No
1957											
320	......	1960.00	2960.00	3670.00	JD	2	100G	4F-1R	27	2670	No
420	......	2220.00	3350.00	4150.00	JD	2	113G	4F-1R	29	2793	No
520	......	2250.00	3400.00	4220.00	JD	2	190G	6F-1R	39	5325	No
620	......	2300.00	3470.00	4300.00	JD	2	302G	6F-1R	49	6460	No

Model	Approx. Retail Price New	Estimated Average Value Less Repairs Fair	Good	Premium	Make	Engine No. Cyls.	Displ. Cu.-In.	No. Speeds	P.T.O. H.P.	Approx. Shipping Wt.-Lbs.	Cab
John Deere (Cont.)											
			1957 (Cont.)								
720	......	2390.00	3600.00	4460.00	JD	2	361G	6F-1R	59	7220	No
720	......	2590.00	3910.00	4850.00	JD	2	376D	6F-1R	59	7700	No
820	......	2770.00	4180.00	5180.00	JD	2	472D	6F-1R	76	8300	No
			1958								
320	......	1900.00	2880.00	3570.00	JD	2	100G	4F-1R	27	2670	No
330	......	2000.00	3020.00	3750.00	JD	2	100G	4F-1R		2722	No
420	......	2280.00	3440.00	4270.00	JD	2	113G	4F-1R	29	2793	No
430	......	2050.00	3100.00	3840.00	JD	2	113G	5F-1R	30	3210	No
520	......	2380.00	3590.00	4450.00	JD	2	190G	6F-1R	39	5325	No
530	......	2460.00	3710.00	4600.00	JD	2	190G	6F-1R	41	5440	No
620	......	2400.00	3630.00	4500.00	JD	2	302G	6F-1R	49	6460	No
630	......	2510.00	3790.00	4700.00	JD	2	302G	6F-1R	49	6670	No
720	......	2490.00	3760.00	4660.00	JD	2	361G	6F-1R	59	7220	No
720	......	2700.00	4080.00	5060.00	JD	2	376D	6F-1R	59	7700	No
730	......	2580.00	3900.00	4840.00	JD	2	361G	6F-1R	59	7270	No
730	......	2730.00	4130.00	5120.00	JD	2	376D	6F-1R	59	7830	No
820	......	2860.00	4320.00	5360.00	JD	2	472D	6F-1R	76	8300	No
830	......	3090.00	4680.00	5800.00	JD	2	472D	6F-1R	81	8140	No
			1959								
330	......	2110.00	3120.00	3870.00	JD	2	100G	4F-1R		2722	No
430	......	2190.00	3240.00	4020.00	JD	2	113G	5F-1R	30	3210	No
435D	......	2440.00	3600.00	4460.00	JD	2	106D	5F-1R	33	3560	No
530	......	2560.00	3780.00	4690.00	JD	2	190G	6F-1R	41	5440	No
630	......	2620.00	3870.00	4800.00	JD	2	302G	6F-1R	49	6670	No
730	......	2720.00	4030.00	5000.00	JD	2	361G	6F-1R	59	7270	No
730	......	2970.00	4390.00	5440.00	JD	2	376D	6F-1R	59	7830	No
830	......	3250.00	4800.00	5950.00	JD	2	472D	6F-1R	81	8140	No
			1960								
330	......	2160.00	3190.00	3960.00	JD	2	100G	4F-1R		2722	No
430	......	2280.00	3370.00	4180.00	JD	2	113G	5F-1R	30	3210	No
435D	......	2570.00	3800.00	4710.00	JD	2	106D	5F-1R	33	3560	No
530	......	2590.00	3840.00	4760.00	JD	2	190G	6F-1R	41	5440	No
630	......	2700.00	3990.00	4950.00	JD	2	302G	6F-1R	49	6670	No
730	......	2780.00	4110.00	5100.00	JD	2	361G	6F-1R	59	7270	No
730	......	3000.00	4430.00	5490.00	JD	2	376D	6F-1R	59	7830	No
830	......	3340.00	4930.00	6110.00	JD	2	472D	6F-1R	81	8140	No
1010	......	2450.00	3610.00	4480.00	JD	4	115G	5F-1R	36	3615	No
1010	......	2670.00	3940.00	4890.00	JD	4	145D	5F-1R	36	3700	No
2010	......	2810.00	4150.00	5150.00	JD	4	202D	8F-3R	46.8	4700	No
2010	......	3020.00	4460.00	5530.00	JD	4	180G	8F-3R	46	4600	No
			1961								
1010	......	2500.00	3700.00	4590.00	JD	4	115G	5F-1R	36	3615	No
1010	......	2730.00	4030.00	5000.00	JD	4	145D	5F-1R	36	3700	No
2010	......	2860.00	4230.00	5250.00	JD	4	180G	8F-3R	46	4600	No
2010	......	3110.00	4600.00	5700.00	JD	4	202D	8F-3R	46.8	4700	No
3010	......	3220.00	4750.00	5890.00	JD	4	201G	8F-3R	55	6220	No
3010	......	3520.00	5210.00	6460.00	JD	4	254D	8F-3R	59	6340	No
4010	......	3810.00	5640.00	6990.00	JD	6	302G	8F-3R	81	6800	No
4010	......	4260.00	6300.00	7810.00	JD	6	380D	8F-3R	84	7130	No
			1962								
1010	2480.00	2540.00	3760.00	4660.00	JD	4	115G	5F-1R	36	3615	No
1010	2880.00	2760.00	4080.00	5060.00	JD	4	145D	5F-1R	36	3700	No
2010	3400.00	2900.00	4280.00	5310.00	JD	4	180G	8F-3R	46	4600	No
2010	3950.00	3160.00	4680.00	5800.00	JD	4	202D	8F-3R	46.8	4700	No
3010	4100.00	3390.00	5010.00	6210.00	JD	4	201G	8F-3R	55	6220	No
3010	4800.00	3720.00	5490.00	6810.00	JD	4	254D	8F-3R	59	6340	No
4010	5000.00	3910.00	5780.00	7170.00	JD	6	302G	8F-3R	81	6800	No
4010	5820.00	4610.00	6810.00	8440.00	JD	6	380D	8F-3R	84	7130	No
			1963								
1010	2506.00	2580.00	3810.00	4720.00	JD	4	115G	5F-1R	36	3750	No
1010	2908.00	2810.00	4150.00	5150.00	JD	4	145D	5F-1R	36	3830	No
2010	3432.00	2960.00	4380.00	5430.00	JD	4	180G	8F-3R	46	4400	No
2010	3987.00	3200.00	4730.00	5870.00	JD	4	202D	8F-3R	46.8	4700	No
3010	4134.00	3410.00	5040.00	6250.00	JD	4	201G	8F-3R	55	6340	No
3010	4843.00	3710.00	5480.00	6800.00	JD	4	254D	8F-3R	59	6550	No
4010	5042.00	4160.00	6150.00	7630.00	JD	6	302G	8F-3R	80	8090	No
4010	5856.00	4910.00	7250.00	8990.00	JD	6	380D	8F-3R	84	8450	No
5010	9186.00	4230.00	6250.00	7750.00	JD	6	531D	8F-3R	121.1	13200	No
			1964								
1010	2638.00	3080.00	4550.00	5640.00	JD	4	115G	5F-1R	36	3615	No
1010	3061.00	3230.00	4770.00	5920.00	JD	4	145D	5F-1R	36	3700	No
2010 Utility	3596.00	3470.00	5120.00	6350.00	JD	4	180G	8F-3R	46	4600	No
2010 Utility	4197.00	3730.00	5520.00	6850.00	JD	4	202D	8F-3R	46.8	4700	No
3020	5259.00	3480.00	5140.00	6370.00	JD	4	227G	8F-2R	70	7930	No
3020	5959.00	3780.00	5580.00	6920.00	JD	4	270D	8F-2R	71	8120	No
3020 HC	6035.00	3830.00	5670.00	7030.00	JD	4	241G	8F-2R	70	8020	No
3020 HC	6735.00	4110.00	6080.00	7540.00	JD	4	270D	8F-2R	71.2	8210	No

John Deere (Cont.)

1964 (Cont.)

Model	Approx. Retail Price New	Estimated Average Value Less Repairs: Fair	Good	Premium	Make	Engine No. Cyls.	Displ. Cu.-In.	No. Speeds	P.T.O. H.P.	Approx. Shipping Wt.-Lbs.	Cab
4020	6100.00	**4550.00**	**6730.00**	**8350.00**	JD	6	360G	8F-2R	95	8400	No
4020	6922.00	**5020.00**	**7430.00**	**9210.00**	JD	6	404D	8F-2R	95	8585	No
4020 HC	5630.00	**4250.00**	**6280.00**	**7790.00**	JD	6	360G	8F-2R	95	8625	No
4020 HC	6450.00	**4810.00**	**7110.00**	**8820.00**	JD	6	404D	8F-2R	95	9335	No
5010	9670.00	**4600.00**	**6800.00**	**8430.00**	JD	6	531D	8F-3R	121.1	13200	No

H, HC, HU--High Clearance LU--Low Profile PS--Power Shift RC--Row Crop

1965

Model	Approx. Retail Price New	Fair	Good	Premium	Make	No. Cyls.	Displ. Cu.-In.	No. Speeds	P.T.O. H.P.	Approx. Shipping Wt.-Lbs.	Cab
1010	2993.00	**3220.00**	**4760.00**	**5900.00**	JD	3	115G	5F-1R	36	3750	No
1010	3418.00	**3410.00**	**5040.00**	**6250.00**	JD	3	145D	5F-1R	36	3700	No
1020 Utility	3292.00	**3350.00**	**4960.00**	**6150.00**	JD	3	135G	8F-4R	38.8	4355	No
1020 Utility	3585.00	**3490.00**	**5160.00**	**6400.00**	JD	3	152D	8F-4R	39	4405	No
2010 Utility	3649.00	**3520.00**	**5200.00**	**6450.00**	JD	4	180G	8F-3R	46	4600	No
2010 Utility	4239.00	**3790.00**	**5600.00**	**6940.00**	JD	4	202D	8F-3R	46.8	4700	No
2020 Utility	4248.00	**3750.00**	**5540.00**	**6870.00**	JD	4	180G	16F-8R	53.9	4565	No
2020 Utility	4657.00	**3980.00**	**5890.00**	**7300.00**	JD	4	202D	16F-8R	54	4645	No
3020	5577.00	**3720.00**	**5490.00**	**6810.00**	JD	4	227G	8F-2R	70	7930	No
3020	6297.00	**4010.00**	**5930.00**	**7350.00**	JD	4	270D	8F-2R	71	8120	No
3020 HC	6348.00	**3840.00**	**5680.00**	**7040.00**	JD	4	241G	8F-2R	70	8020	No
3020 HC	7069.00	**4170.00**	**6170.00**	**7650.00**	JD	4	270D	8F-2R	71	8210	No
4020	6516.00	**4610.00**	**6810.00**	**8440.00**	JD	6	360G	8F-2R	95.5	8400	No
4020	7360.00	**5230.00**	**7730.00**	**9590.00**	JD	6	404D	8F-2R	94.8	8585	No
4020 HC	7076.00	**4960.00**	**7330.00**	**9090.00**	JD	6	360G	8F-2R	95	8625	No
4020 HC	7920.00	**5480.00**	**8110.00**	**10060.00**	JD	6	404D	8F-2R	95	9335	No
5010	10045.00	**5060.00**	**7480.00**	**9280.00**	JD	6	531D	8F-3R	121.1	13200	No

H, HC, HU--High Clearance LU--Low Profile PS--Power Shift RC--Row Crop

1966

Model	Approx. Retail Price New	Fair	Good	Premium	Make	No. Cyls.	Displ. Cu.-In.	No. Speeds	P.T.O. H.P.	Approx. Shipping Wt.-Lbs.	Cab
1020 Utility	3325.00	**3440.00**	**4980.00**	**6180.00**	JD	3	135G	8F-4R	38.8	4100	No
1020 Utility	3621.00	**3580.00**	**5180.00**	**6420.00**	JD	3	152D	8F-4R	39	4150	No
2020 Utility	4472.00	**3980.00**	**5760.00**	**7140.00**	JD	4	180G	16F-8R	53	4565	No
2020 Utility	4902.00	**4200.00**	**6080.00**	**7540.00**	JD	4	202D	16F-8R	54	4645	No
2510	4783.00	**4130.00**	**5970.00**	**7400.00**	JD	4	180G	8F-2R	53.7	6015	No
2510	5297.00	**4370.00**	**6320.00**	**7840.00**	JD	4	202D	8F-2R	54	6095	No
2510 HC	5991.00	**4700.00**	**6790.00**	**8420.00**	JD	4	180G	8F-2R	53.7	6945	No
2510 HC	6506.00	**4940.00**	**7140.00**	**8850.00**	JD	4	202D	8F-2R	54.9	7250	No
3020	5766.00	**3650.00**	**5280.00**	**6550.00**	JD	4	227G	8F-2R	70.5	7930	No
3020	6300.00	**3920.00**	**5670.00**	**7030.00**	JD	4	270D	8F-2R	71.5	8120	No
3020 HC	6602.00	**4040.00**	**5850.00**	**7250.00**	JD	4	241G	8F-2R	70.5	8020	No
3020 HC	7347.00	**4390.00**	**6360.00**	**7890.00**	JD	4	270D	8F-2R	71.2	8210	No
4020	6747.00	**4820.00**	**6970.00**	**8640.00**	JD	6	360G	8F-2R	95	8400	No
4020	7620.00	**5460.00**	**7900.00**	**9800.00**	JD	6	404D	8F-2R	95	8585	No
4020 HC	7354.00	**5200.00**	**7520.00**	**9330.00**	JD	6	360G	8F-2R	95	8625	No
4020 HC	8227.00	**5750.00**	**8310.00**	**10300.00**	JD	6	404D	8F-2R	94.8	9335	No
5020	10585.00	**4870.00**	**7410.00**	**9040.00**	JD	6	531D	8F-2R	133.2	13430	No

H, HC, HU--High Clearance LU--Low Profile PS--Power Shift RC--Row Crop

1967

Model	Approx. Retail Price New	Fair	Good	Premium	Make	No. Cyls.	Displ. Cu.-In.	No. Speeds	P.T.O. H.P.	Approx. Shipping Wt.-Lbs.	Cab
1020 Utility	3358.00	**3460.00**	**5000.00**	**6200.00**	JD	3	135G	8F-4R	38.8	4100	No
1020 Utility	3657.00	**3600.00**	**5210.00**	**6460.00**	JD	3	152D	8F-4R	39	4150	No
2020 Utility	4517.00	**4000.00**	**5790.00**	**7180.00**	JD	4	180G	16F-8R	53.9	4565	No
2020 Utility	4951.00	**4210.00**	**6090.00**	**7550.00**	JD	4	202D	16F-8R	54	4645	No
2510	5166.00	**4310.00**	**6230.00**	**7730.00**	JD	4	180G	8F-2R	53.7	6015	No
2510	5721.00	**4570.00**	**6610.00**	**8200.00**	JD	4	202D	8F-2R	54.9	6095	No
2510 HC	6470.00	**4450.00**	**6440.00**	**7990.00**	JD	4	180G	8F-2R	53.7	6945	No
2510 HC	7026.00	**4710.00**	**6820.00**	**8460.00**	JD	4	202D	8F-2R	54.9	7250	No
3020	5777.00	**3800.00**	**5490.00**	**6810.00**	JD	4	227G	8F-2R	70.5	7420	No
3020	6559.00	**4160.00**	**6020.00**	**7470.00**	JD	4	270D	8F-2R	71.5	8120	No
3020 HC	6932.00	**4340.00**	**6280.00**	**7790.00**	JD	4	241G	8F-2R	70.5	8020	No
3020 HC	7714.00	**4710.00**	**6810.00**	**8440.00**	JD	4	270D	8F-2R	71.2	8210	No
4020	7084.00	**4890.00**	**7070.00**	**8770.00**	JD	6	360G	8F-2R	95.5	8400	No
4020	8000.00	**5550.00**	**8020.00**	**9950.00**	JD	6	404D	8F-2R	94.8	8585	No
4020 HC	7720.00	**5370.00**	**7770.00**	**9640.00**	JD	6	360G	8F-2R	95	8625	No
4020 HC	8638.00	**5940.00**	**8590.00**	**10650.00**	JD	6	404D	8F-2R	94	9335	No
5020	11113.00	**5200.00**	**7740.00**	**9440.00**	JD	6	531D	8F-2R	133.2	13430	No

H, HC, HU--High Clearance LU--Low Profile PS--Power Shift RC--Row Crop

1968

Model	Approx. Retail Price New	Fair	Good	Premium	Make	No. Cyls.	Displ. Cu.-In.	No. Speeds	P.T.O. H.P.	Approx. Shipping Wt.-Lbs.	Cab
820 (3 Cyl)	3580.00	**3160.00**	**4470.00**	**5540.00**	JD	3	152D	8F-4R	34	4060	No
1020 Utility	3418.00	**3560.00**	**5040.00**	**6250.00**	JD	3	135G	8F-4R	38.8	4100	No
1020 Utility	3783.00	**3740.00**	**5290.00**	**6560.00**	JD	3	152D	8F-4R	39	4150	No
1520	4073.00	**3870.00**	**5480.00**	**6800.00**	JD	3	164G	8F-4R	47.8	4100	No
1520	4455.00	**3580.00**	**5070.00**	**6290.00**	JD	3	164D	8F-4R	46.5	4150	No
2020 Utility	4865.00	**4260.00**	**6030.00**	**7480.00**	JD	4	180G	8F-4R	53.9	4495	No
2020 Utility	5359.00	**4010.00**	**5680.00**	**7040.00**	JD	4	202D	8F-4R	54	4575	No
2510	5723.00	**4190.00**	**5930.00**	**7350.00**	JD	4	180G	8F-2R	53.7	6015	No
2510	6295.00	**4460.00**	**6320.00**	**7840.00**	JD	4	202D	8F-2R	54.9	6095	No
2510 HC	6671.00	**4640.00**	**6580.00**	**8160.00**	JD	4	180G	8F-2R	53.7	6945	No
2510 HC	7245.00	**4920.00**	**6970.00**	**8640.00**	JD	4	202D	8F-2R	54.9	7250	No
3020	5985.00	**3830.00**	**5430.00**	**6730.00**	JD	4	227G	8F-2R	70.5	7420	No
3020	6785.00	**4220.00**	**5970.00**	**7400.00**	JD	4	270D	8F-2R	71.5	7610	No
3020 HC	7156.00	**4400.00**	**6230.00**	**7730.00**	JD	4	241G	8F-2R	70.5	8020	No
3020 HC	7956.00	**4780.00**	**6770.00**	**8400.00**	JD	4	270D	8F-2R	71.2	8210	No
4020	7500.00	**5140.00**	**7280.00**	**9030.00**	JD	6	360G	8F-2R	95.5	8400	No

John Deere (Cont.)

1968 (Cont.)

Model	Approx. Retail Price New	Estimated Average Value Less Repairs: Fair	Good	Premium	Engine: Make	No. Cyls.	Displ. Cu.-In.	No. Speeds	P.T.O. H.P.	Approx. Shipping Wt.-Lbs.	Cab
4020	8500.00	5810.00	8230.00	10210.00	JD	6	404D	8F-2R	94.8	8630	No
4020 HC	8050.00	5640.00	7990.00	9910.00	JD	6	360G	8F-2R	96.6	8625	No
4020 HC	8940.00	6210.00	8800.00	10910.00	JD	6	404D	8F-2R	94.8	9335	No
5020	11503.00	5500.00	8000.00	9760.00	JD	6	531D	8F-2R	133.2	13430	No

H, HC, HU--High Clearance LU--Low Profile PS--Power Shift RC--Row Crop

1969

Model	Approx. Retail Price New	Fair	Good	Premium	Make	No. Cyls.	Displ. Cu.-In.	No. Speeds	P.T.O. H.P.	Approx. Shipping Wt.-Lbs.	Cab
820 (3 Cyl)	3545.00	3700.00	5130.00	6360.00	JD	3	152D	8F-4R	34	4060	No
1020 Utility	3823.00	3830.00	5320.00	6600.00	JD	3	135G	8F-4R	38.8	4100	No
1020 Utility	4203.00	3970.00	5510.00	6830.00	JD	3	152D	8F-4R	39	4150	No
1520	4226.00	4030.00	5590.00	6930.00	JD	3	164G	8F-4R	47.8	4100	No
1520	4750.00	4230.00	5880.00	7290.00	JD	3	164D	8F-4R	46.5	4150	No
2020 Utility	4946.00	4380.00	6080.00	7540.00	JD	4	180G	16F-8R	53.9	4495	No
2020 Utility	5441.00	4820.00	6690.00	8300.00	JD	4	202D	16F-8R	54	4575	No
2520	6394.00	4600.00	6390.00	7920.00	JD	4	203G	8F-2R	60	6500	No
2520	6995.00	4900.00	6800.00	8430.00	JD	4	219D	8F-2R	61	6600	No
2520 HC	7417.00	5100.00	7080.00	8780.00	JD	4	203G	8F-2R	60.1	7125	No
2520 HC	7918.00	5350.00	7420.00	9200.00	JD	4	219D	8F-2R	61.2	7225	No
3020	6909.00	4360.00	6060.00	7510.00	JD	4	227G	8F-2R	70.5	7420	No
3020	7709.00	4760.00	6600.00	8180.00	JD	4	270D	8F-2R	71.5	7610	No
3020 HC	7729.00	4770.00	6620.00	8210.00	JD	4	241G	8F-2R	70.5	8020	No
3020 HC	8529.00	5160.00	7160.00	8880.00	JD	4	270D	8F-2R	71.2	8210	No
4000	7815.00	4220.00	5860.00	7270.00	JD	6	360G	8F-2R	97.2	7560	No
4000	8615.00	4710.00	6540.00	8110.00	JD	6	404D	8F-2R	96.8	7900	No
4020	7760.00	5420.00	7520.00	9330.00	JD	6	360G	8F-2R	95.5	8400	No
4020	8649.00	6200.00	8600.00	10660.00	JD	6	404D	8F-2R	94.8	8585	No
4020 HC	8425.00	5890.00	8180.00	10140.00	JD	6	360G	8F-2R	96.6	8625	No
4020 HC	9315.00	6520.00	9050.00	11220.00	JD	6	404D	8F-2R	94.8	9335	No
4520	11200.00	5880.00	8160.00	10120.00	JD	6	404D	8F-2R	123.3	12285	No
5020	12780.00	5750.00	8180.00	9980.00	JD	6	531D	8F-2R	133.2	13400	No

H, HC, HU--High Clearance LU--Low Profile PS--Power Shift RC--Row Crop

1970

Model	Approx. Retail Price New	Fair	Good	Premium	Make	No. Cyls.	Displ. Cu.-In.	No. Speeds	P.T.O. H.P.	Approx. Shipping Wt.-Lbs.	Cab
820	3580.00	3290.00	4470.00	5540.00	JD	3	152D	8F-4R		4060	No
1020	3861.00	3930.00	5350.00	6630.00	JD	3	135G	8F-4R	38.82	4100	No
1020	4245.00	4120.00	5610.00	6960.00	JD	3	152D	8F-4R	38.92	4150	No
1520	4343.00	4170.00	5670.00	7030.00	JD	3	165G	8F-4R	47.86	4100	No
1520	4808.00	4400.00	5990.00	7430.00	JD	3	165D	8F-4R	46.52	4150	No
2020	4995.00	4500.00	6120.00	7590.00	JD	4	180G	8F-4R	53.91	4495	No
2020	5495.00	4740.00	6440.00	7990.00	JD	4	202D	8F-4R	54.09	4575	No
2520 HC	7491.00	5250.00	7130.00	8840.00	JD	4	203G	8F-2R	60.00	7125	No
2520 HC	7997.00	5500.00	7480.00	9280.00	JD	4	219D	8F-2R	61.00	7225	No
2520 RC	6458.00	5230.00	7110.00	8820.00	JD	4	203G	8F-2R	60.16	6500	No
2520 RC	7064.00	5030.00	6840.00	8480.00	JD	4	219D	8F-2R	61.29	6600	No
3020	7281.00	4270.00	5940.00	7250.00	JD	4	241G	8F-2R	71.37	7930	No
3020	8106.00	5050.00	6870.00	8520.00	JD	4	270D	8F-2R	71.26	8120	No
3020 HC	8115.00	5060.00	6880.00	8530.00	JD	4	241G	8F-2R	71.00	8020	No
3020 HC	8955.00	5480.00	7450.00	9240.00	JD	4	270D	8F-2R	71.00	8210	No
4000	8205.00	4500.00	6120.00	7590.00	JD	6	360G	8F-2R		7560	No
4000	9045.00	5020.00	6830.00	8470.00	JD	6	404D	8F-2R	96.89	7900	No
4020	8969.00	5640.00	7660.00	9500.00	JD	6	360G	8F-2R	96.66	8400	No
4020	9894.00	6450.00	8770.00	10880.00	JD	6	404D	8F-2R	94.88	8585	No
4020 4WD	10844.00	6570.00	8940.00	11090.00	JD	6	360G	8F-2R	96.00	9510	No
4020 4WD	11780.00	7390.00	10050.00	12460.00	JD	6	404D	8F-2R	94.00	9695	No
4020 HC	9443.00	6070.00	8260.00	10240.00	JD	6	360G	8F-2R	96.00	8625	No
4020 HC	10377.00	6690.00	9100.00	11280.00	JD	6	404D	8F-2R	94.00	9335	No
4520	11723.00	6000.00	8160.00	10120.00	JD	6T	404D	8F-2R	123.39	12285	No
5020	13550.00	6230.00	8670.00	10580.00	JD	6	531D	8F-2R	141.34	13400	No

H, HC, HU--High Clearance LU--Low Profile PS--Power Shift RC--Row Crop

1971

Model	Approx. Retail Price New	Fair	Good	Premium	Make	No. Cyls.	Displ. Cu.-In.	No. Speeds	P.T.O. H.P.	Approx. Shipping Wt.-Lbs.	Cab
820	3775.00	3250.00	4340.00	5380.00	JD	3	152D	8F-4R		4060	No
1020	4111.00	3680.00	4900.00	6080.00	JD	3	135G	8F-4R	38.82	4100	No
1020	4491.00	3870.00	5160.00	6400.00	JD	3	152D	8F-4R	38.92	4150	No
1520	4654.00	3900.00	5200.00	6450.00	JD	3	165G	8F-4R	47.86	4100	No
1520	5119.00	4140.00	5520.00	6850.00	JD	3	165D	8F-4R	46.52	4150	No
2020	5290.00	3970.00	5300.00	6570.00	JD	4	180G	8F-4R	53.91	4495	No
2020	5790.00	4230.00	5640.00	6990.00	JD	4	202D	8F-4R	54.09	4575	No
2520 HC	7788.00	4990.00	6660.00	8260.00	JD	4	203G	8F-2R	60.00	7125	No
2520 HC	8314.00	5260.00	7010.00	8690.00	JD	4	219D	8F-2R	61.00	7225	No
2520 RC	6714.00	4450.00	5930.00	7350.00	JD	4	203G	8F-2R	60.16	6500	No
2520 RC	7344.00	4770.00	6350.00	7870.00	JD	4	219D	8F-2R	61.29	6600	No
3020	7405.00	4800.00	6400.00	7940.00	JD	4	241G	8F-2R	71.37	7930	No
3020	8230.00	5220.00	6960.00	8630.00	JD	4	270D	8F-2R	71.26	8120	No
3020 4WD	9720.00	5980.00	7970.00	9880.00	JD	4	241G	8F-2R	71.00	8640	No
3020 4WD	10599.00	6430.00	8570.00	10630.00	JD	4	270D	8F-2R	71.00	8830	No
3020 HC	8239.00	5220.00	6960.00	8630.00	JD	4	241G	8F-2R	71.00	8020	No
3020 HC	9079.00	5650.00	7530.00	9340.00	JD	4	270D	8F-2R	71.00	8210	No
4000	8210.00	4850.00	6470.00	8020.00	JD	6	360G	8F-2R		7560	No
4000	9385.00	5550.00	7400.00	9180.00	JD	6	404D	8F-2R	96.89	7900	No
4020	9148.00	5920.00	7890.00	9780.00	JD	6	360G	8F-2R	96.66	8400	No
4020	10092.00	6730.00	8970.00	11120.00	JD	6	404D	8F-2R	94.88	8585	No
4020 4WD	11061.00	6870.00	9150.00	11350.00	JD	6	360G	8F-2R	96.00	9510	No
4020 4WD	12016.00	7710.00	10280.00	12750.00	JD	6	404D	8F-2R	94.00	9695	No

John Deere (Cont.)

1971 (Cont.)

Model	Approx. Retail Price New	Estimated Average Value Less Repairs Fair	Good	Premium	Make	Engine No. Cyls.	Displ. Cu.-In.	No. Speeds	P.T.O. H.P.	Approx. Shipping Wt.-Lbs.	Cab
4020 HC	9632.00	**6290.00**	**8390.00**	**10400.00**	JD	6	360G	8F-2R	96.00	8625	No
4020 HC	10585.00	**6980.00**	**9310.00**	**11540.00**	JD	6	404D	8F-2R	94.00	9335	No
4320	11086.00	**6160.00**	**8220.00**	**10190.00**	JD	6T	404D	8F-2R	116.55	10500	No
4320 4WD	13299.00	**6780.00**	**9040.00**	**11210.00**	JD	6T	404D	8F-2R	116.00	10675	No
4620	13020.00	**6640.00**	**8850.00**	**10970.00**	JD	6TI	404D	8F-2R	135.76	12680	No
4620 4WD	15292.00	**7800.00**	**10400.00**	**12900.00**	JD	6TI	404D	8F-2R	135.00	13010	No
5020	13900.00	**6530.00**	**8900.00**	**10860.00**	JD	6	531D	8F-2R	141.34	15600	No
7020 4WD	15975.00	**7040.00**	**9580.00**	**11690.00**	JD	6TI	404D	8F-2R	146.00	14325	C

H, HC, HU--High Clearance LU--Low Profile PS--Power Shift RC--Row Crop

1972

Model	Approx. Retail Price New	Estimated Average Value Less Repairs Fair	Good	Premium	Make	Engine No. Cyls.	Displ. Cu.-In.	No. Speeds	P.T.O. H.P.	Approx. Shipping Wt.-Lbs.	Cab
820	3937.00	**3400.00**	**4450.00**	**5470.00**	JD	3	152D	8F-4R		4060	No
1020	4378.00	**3840.00**	**5020.00**	**6180.00**	JD	3	135G	8F-4R	38.82	4100	No
1020	4791.00	**4050.00**	**5300.00**	**6520.00**	JD	3	152D	8F-4R	38.92	4150	No
1520	5044.00	**4130.00**	**5400.00**	**6640.00**	JD	3	165G	8F-4R	47.86	4100	No
1520	5530.00	**4380.00**	**5730.00**	**7050.00**	JD	3	165D	8F-4R	46.52	4150	No
2030	6281.00	**4830.00**	**6310.00**	**7760.00**	JD	4	219G	16F-8R	60.34	4405	No
2030	6815.00	**5100.00**	**6670.00**	**8200.00**	JD	4	219D	16F-8R	60.65	4845	No
2520 HC	8034.00	**5220.00**	**6820.00**	**8390.00**	JD	4	203G	8F-2R	60.00	7125	No
2520 HC	8687.00	**5560.00**	**7270.00**	**8940.00**	JD	4	219D	8F-2R	61.00	7225	No
2520 RC	7003.00	**4680.00**	**6120.00**	**7530.00**	JD	4	203G	8F-2R	60.16	6500	No
2520 RC	7656.00	**5020.00**	**6570.00**	**8080.00**	JD	4	219D	8F-2R	61.29	6600	No
3020	7608.00	**5520.00**	**7210.00**	**8870.00**	JD	4	241G	8F-2R	71.00	7420	No
3020	8475.00	**5970.00**	**7800.00**	**9590.00**	JD	4	270D	8F-2R	71.26	7610	No
3020 4WD	9871.00	**6690.00**	**8750.00**	**10760.00**	JD	4	241G	8F-2R	71.00	8640	No
3020 4WD	10733.00	**7140.00**	**9340.00**	**11490.00**	JD	4	270D	8F-2R	71.00	8830	No
3020 HC	8450.00	**5950.00**	**7790.00**	**9580.00**	JD	4	241G	8F-2R	71.00	8020	No
3020 HC	9452.00	**6480.00**	**8470.00**	**10420.00**	JD	4	270D	8F-2R	71.00	8210	No
4000	8422.00	**5320.00**	**6950.00**	**8550.00**	JD	6	360G	8F-2R		7560	No
4000	9389.00	**6180.00**	**8090.00**	**9950.00**	JD	6	404D	8F-2R	96.89	7900	No
4020	9378.00	**6330.00**	**8280.00**	**10180.00**	JD	6	360G	8F-2R	96.66	8445	No
4020	10345.00	**7300.00**	**9550.00**	**11750.00**	JD	6	404D	8F-2R	94.88	8630	No
4020 4WD	11636.00	**7510.00**	**9820.00**	**12080.00**	JD	6	360G	8F-2R	96.00	9510	No
4020 4WD	12603.00	**8320.00**	**10880.00**	**13380.00**	JD	6	404D	8F-2R	94.00	9695	No
4020 HC	9996.00	**6710.00**	**8770.00**	**10790.00**	JD	6	360G	8F-2R	96.00	8625	No
4020 HC	10963.00	**7260.00**	**9500.00**	**11690.00**	JD	6	404D	8F-2R	94.00	9335	No
4320	11312.00	**6610.00**	**8640.00**	**10630.00**	JD	6T	404D	8F-2R	116.55	10500	No
4320 4WD	13570.00	**7060.00**	**9230.00**	**11350.00**	JD	6T	404D	8F-2R	116.00	10675	No
4620	13286.00	**6910.00**	**9030.00**	**11110.00**	JD	6TI	404D	8F-2R	135.76	12680	No
4620 4WD	15604.00	**8110.00**	**10610.00**	**13050.00**	JD	6TI	404D	8F-2R	135.00	13010	No
5020	14550.00	**6980.00**	**9310.00**	**11270.00**	JD	6	531D	8F-2R	141.34	15600	No
6030	16649.00	**7460.00**	**9950.00**	**12040.00**	JD	6TI	531D	8F-2R	175.00	15800	No
6030	19074.00	**8440.00**	**11250.00**	**13610.00**	JD	6TI	531D	8F-2R	175.00	17300	C,H,A
7020 4WD	16703.00	**7300.00**	**9730.00**	**11770.00**	JD	6TI	404D	8F-2R	146.00	14325	C
7520 4WD	19374.00	**8580.00**	**11440.00**	**13840.00**	JD	6TI	531D	8F-2R	175.00	16535	C

H, HC, HU--High Clearance LU--Low Profile PS--Power Shift RC--Row Crop

1973

Model	Approx. Retail Price New	Estimated Average Value Less Repairs Fair	Good	Premium	Make	Engine No. Cyls.	Displ. Cu.-In.	No. Speeds	P.T.O. H.P.	Approx. Shipping Wt.-Lbs.	Cab
820	3957.00	**3530.00**	**4530.00**	**5530.00**	JD	3	152D	8F-4R	31.00	4060	No
1020	4551.00	**4000.00**	**5140.00**	**6270.00**	JD	3	135G	8F-4R	38.82	4100	No
1020	4964.00	**4220.00**	**5420.00**	**6610.00**	JD	3	152D	8F-4R	38.92	4150	No
1520	5044.00	**4260.00**	**5470.00**	**6670.00**	JD	3	165G	8F-4R	47.86	4100	No
1520	5530.00	**4520.00**	**5800.00**	**7080.00**	JD	3	165D	8F-4R	46.52	4150	No
2030	6361.00	**5230.00**	**6710.00**	**8190.00**	JD	4	219G	16F-8R	60.34	4405	No
2030	6896.00	**5510.00**	**7070.00**	**8630.00**	JD	4	219D	16F-8R	60.65	4845	No
2520	7003.00	**5570.00**	**7140.00**	**8710.00**	JD	4	203G	8F-2R	60.16	6500	No
2520	7656.00	**5910.00**	**7590.00**	**9260.00**	JD	4	219D	8F-2R	61.29	6600	No
2520 HC	8511.00	**6100.00**	**7830.00**	**9550.00**	JD	4	203G	8F-2R	60.00	7125	No
2520 HC	9164.00	**6450.00**	**8270.00**	**10090.00**	JD	4	219D	8F-2R	61.00	7225	No
4030	7726.00	**7170.00**	**9200.00**	**11220.00**	JD	6	303G	8F-2R		7542	No
4030	8588.00	**7730.00**	**9920.00**	**12100.00**	JD	6	329D	8F-2R	80.00	7805	No
4030 4WD	9860.00	**8090.00**	**10380.00**	**12660.00**	JD	6	303G	8F-2R		8042	No
4030 4WD	10722.00	**8330.00**	**10690.00**	**13040.00**	JD	6	329D	8F-2R	80.00	8305	No
4030 4WD QR	10255.00	**8300.00**	**10650.00**	**12990.00**	JD	6	303G	16F-6R		8502	No
4030 4WD QR	11117.00	**8540.00**	**10960.00**	**13370.00**	JD	6	329D	16F-6R	80.00	8765	No
4030 QR	8121.00	**7170.00**	**9190.00**	**11210.00**	JD	6	303G	16F-6R		8002	No
4030 QR	8983.00	**7940.00**	**10190.00**	**12430.00**	JD	6	329D	16F-6R	80.33	8265	No
4230	9340.00	**7810.00**	**10020.00**	**12220.00**	JD	6	303G	8F-2R		8318	No
4230	10307.00	**8640.00**	**11090.00**	**13530.00**	JD	6	404D	8F-2R	100.	9242	No
4230 4WD	11598.00	**9060.00**	**11630.00**	**14190.00**	JD	6	303G	8F-2R		9600	No
4230 4WD	12565.00	**9840.00**	**12620.00**	**15400.00**	JD	6	404D	8F-2R	100.	10550	No
4230 4WD PS	13348.00	**10250.00**	**13160.00**	**16060.00**	JD	6	404D	8F-4R	100.	10700	No
4230 4WD QR	11993.00	**9270.00**	**11900.00**	**14520.00**	JD	6	303G	16F-6R		10200	No
4230 4WD QR	12960.00	**10050.00**	**12890.00**	**15730.00**	JD	6	404D	16F-6R	100.	10950	No
4230 HC	10054.00	**8220.00**	**10540.00**	**12860.00**	JD	6	303G	8F-2R		9600	No
4230 HC	11021.00	**8490.00**	**10890.00**	**13290.00**	JD	6	404D	8F-2R	100.	10530	No
4230 HC PS	11804.00	**8910.00**	**11430.00**	**13950.00**	JD	6	404D	8F-4R	100.	10700	No
4230 HC QR	10445.00	**8130.00**	**10440.00**	**12740.00**	JD	6	303G	16F-6R		10000	No
4230 HC QR	11416.00	**8700.00**	**11160.00**	**13620.00**	JD	6	404D	16F-6R	100.	10930	No
4230 PS	11090.00	**9060.00**	**11620.00**	**14180.00**	JD	6	404D	8F-4R	100.	9400	No
4230 QR	9735.00	**8390.00**	**10770.00**	**13140.00**	JD	6	303G	16F-6R		8718	No
4230 QR	10702.00	**8850.00**	**11360.00**	**13860.00**	JD	6	404D	16F-6R	100.32	9650	No
4430 4WD	13570.00	**9840.00**	**12630.00**	**15410.00**	JD	6T	404D	8F-2R	125.00	11300	No
4430 4WD PS	14353.00	**10260.00**	**13160.00**	**16060.00**	JD	6T	404D	8F-4R	125.00	11500	No

John Deere (Cont.)

1973 (Cont.)

Model	Approx. Retail Price New	Estimated Average Value Less Repairs Fair	Good	Premium	Engine Make	No. Cyls.	Displ. Cu.-In.	No. Speeds	P.T.O. H.P.	Approx. Shipping Wt.-Lbs.	Cab
4430 4WD QR	13965.00	**10050.00**	**12900.00**	**15740.00**	JD	6T	404D	16F-6R	125.00	11720	No
4430 HC	12026.00	**9550.00**	**12260.00**	**14960.00**	JD	6T	404D	8F-2R	125.00	10815	No
4430 HC PS	12809.00	**9970.00**	**12790.00**	**15600.00**	JD	6T	404D	8F-4R	125.00	11000	No
4430 HC QR	12421.00	**9230.00**	**11850.00**	**14460.00**	JD	6T	404D	16F-6R	125.00	11235	No
4430 PS	12095.00	**9590.00**	**12310.00**	**15020.00**	JD	6T	404D	8F-4R	125.00	9900	No
4430 QR	11707.00	**9380.00**	**12040.00**	**14690.00**	JD	6T	404D	16F-6R	125.88	10155	No
4630	13578.00	**9850.00**	**12630.00**	**15410.00**	JD	6TI	404D	8F-2R	150.00	12800	No
4630 4WD	15896.00	**11080.00**	**14210.00**	**17340.00**	JD	6TI	404D	8F-2R	150.00	14300	No
4630 4WD PS	16679.00	**11490.00**	**14740.00**	**17980.00**	JD	6TI	404D	8F-4R	150.00	14600	No
4630 PS	14361.00	**10260.00**	**13170.00**	**16070.00**	JD	6TI	404D	8F-4R	150.66	13100	No
6030	16650.00	**7870.00**	**10270.00**	**12320.00**	JD	6TI	531D	8F-2R	175.99	15800	No
6030	19075.00	**8860.00**	**11570.00**	**13880.00**	JD	6TI	531D	8F-2R	175.99	17300	C,H,A
7020 4WD	17613.00	**8140.00**	**10630.00**	**12760.00**	JD	6TI	404D	8F-2R	146.00	14725	C,H,A
7520 4WD	20284.00	**8960.00**	**11700.00**	**14040.00**	JD	6TI	531D	8F-2R	175.00	16935	C,H,A

H, HC, HU--High Clearance LU--Low Profile PS--Power Shift QR--Quad Range

1974

Model	Approx. Retail Price New	Estimated Average Value Less Repairs Fair	Good	Premium	Engine Make	No. Cyls.	Displ. Cu.-In.	No. Speeds	P.T.O. H.P.	Approx. Shipping Wt.-Lbs.	Cab
830	5288.00	**3940.00**	**4960.00**	**6000.00**	JD	3	152D	8F-4R	35.30	4060	No
1530	6765.00	**4730.00**	**5960.00**	**7210.00**	JD	3	164D	16F-8R	45.38	4605	No
2030	8498.00	**5670.00**	**7140.00**	**8640.00**	JD	4	219D	16F-8R	60.65	4845	No
2630	9259.00	**6080.00**	**7660.00**	**9270.00**	JD	4	276D	16F-8R	70.00	5300	No
4030	10004.00	**8640.00**	**10880.00**	**13170.00**	JD	6	329D	8F-2R	80.00	7805	No
4030 QR	10480.00	**8950.00**	**11270.00**	**13640.00**	JD	6	329D	16F-6R	80.33	8265	No
4230 4WD	15005.00	**10260.00**	**12920.00**	**15630.00**	JD	6	404D	8F-2R	100.	10550	No
4230 4WD PS	15949.00	**10770.00**	**13570.00**	**16420.00**	JD	6	404D	8F-4R	100.	10800	No
4230 4WD QR	15519.00	**10540.00**	**13270.00**	**16060.00**	JD	6	404D	16F-6R	100.	10950	No
4230 HC	12996.00	**9180.00**	**11560.00**	**13990.00**	JD	6	404D	8F-2R	100.	10530	No
4230 HC PS	13940.00	**9690.00**	**12200.00**	**14760.00**	JD	6	404D	8F-4R	100.	10700	No
4230 HC QR	13510.00	**9460.00**	**11910.00**	**14410.00**	JD	6	404D	16F-6R	100.	10930	No
4230 PS	13011.00	**9720.00**	**12240.00**	**14810.00**	JD	6	404D	8F-4R	100.	9400	No
4230 QR	12581.00	**9490.00**	**11960.00**	**14470.00**	JD	6	404D	16F-6R	100.32	9650	No
4430 4WD	16643.00	**11150.00**	**14040.00**	**16990.00**	JD	6T	404D	8F-2R	125.00	11300	No
4430 4WD PS	17663.00	**11700.00**	**14730.00**	**17820.00**	JD	6T	404D	8F-4R	125.00	11500	No
4430 4WD QR	17157.00	**11430.00**	**14390.00**	**17410.00**	JD	6T	404D	16F-6R	125.00	11720	No
4430 HC	14635.00	**10060.00**	**12670.00**	**15330.00**	JD	6T	404D	8F-2R	125.00	10815	No
4430 HC PS	15654.00	**10610.00**	**13370.00**	**16180.00**	JD	6T	404D	8F-4R	125.00	11000	No
4430 HC QR	15148.00	**10340.00**	**13020.00**	**15750.00**	JD	6T	404D	16F-6R	125.00	11235	No
4430 PS	14725.00	**10650.00**	**13410.00**	**16230.00**	JD	6T	404D	8F-4R	125.00	9900	No
4430 QR	14219.00	**10380.00**	**13070.00**	**15820.00**	JD	6T	404D	16F-6R	125.88	10155	No
4630 4WD	19903.00	**11830.00**	**14890.00**	**18020.00**	JD	6TI	404D	8F-2R	150.00	14300	No
4630 4WD PS	20923.00	**12380.00**	**15590.00**	**18860.00**	JD	6TI	404D	8F-4R	150.00	14450	No
4630 4WD QR	20714.00	**12270.00**	**15450.00**	**18700.00**	JD	6TI	404D	16F-6R	150.00	14600	No
4630 PS	17908.00	**11290.00**	**14220.00**	**17210.00**	JD	6TI	404D	8F-4R	150.00	13250	No
4630 QR	17402.00	**11020.00**	**13870.00**	**16780.00**	JD	6TI	404D	16F-6R	150.00	13100	No
6030	20663.00	**8330.00**	**10660.00**	**12690.00**	JD	6TI	531D	8F-2R	175.99	15800	No
6030	23847.00	**9520.00**	**12190.00**	**14510.00**	JD	6TI	531D	8F-2R	175.99	17300	C,H,A
7020 4WD	22907.00	**8700.00**	**11140.00**	**13260.00**	JD	6TI	404D	8F-2R	146.00	14725	C,H,A
7520 4WD	26372.00	**9690.00**	**12400.00**	**14760.00**	JD	6TI	531D	8F-2R	175.00	16935	C,H,A

H, HC, HU--High Clearance LU--Low Profile PS--Power Shift QR--Quad Range

1975

Model	Approx. Retail Price New	Estimated Average Value Less Repairs Fair	Good	Premium	Engine Make	No. Cyls.	Displ. Cu.-In.	No. Speeds	P.T.O. H.P.	Approx. Shipping Wt.-Lbs.	Cab
830	5711.00	**4240.00**	**5240.00**	**6290.00**	JD	3	152D	8F-4R	35.30	4060	No
1530	7260.00	**5370.00**	**6640.00**	**7970.00**	JD	3	164D	16F-8R	45.38	4605	No
2030	9151.00	**6410.00**	**7920.00**	**9500.00**	JD	4	219D	16F-8R	60.65	4845	No
2630	9991.00	**6870.00**	**8500.00**	**10200.00**	JD	4	276D	16F-8R	70.37	5300	No
4030	10863.00	**9280.00**	**11470.00**	**13760.00**	JD	6	329D	8F-2R	80.00	7805	No
4030 QR	11377.00	**9560.00**	**11820.00**	**14180.00**	JD	6	329D	16F-6R	80.33	8265	No
4230 4WD	16029.00	**9920.00**	**12260.00**	**14710.00**	JD	6	404D	8F-2R	100.	10550	No
4230 4WD PS	17049.00	**11300.00**	**13970.00**	**16760.00**	JD	6	404D	8F-4R	100.	10800	No
4230 4WD QR	16543.00	**11000.00**	**13600.00**	**16320.00**	JD	6	404D	16F-6R	100.	10950	No
4230 HC	14020.00	**9360.00**	**11570.00**	**13880.00**	JD	6	404D	8F-2R	100.	10530	No
4230 HC PS	15040.00	**9920.00**	**12270.00**	**14720.00**	JD	6	404D	8F-4R	100.	10700	No
4230 HC QR	14534.00	**9640.00**	**11920.00**	**14300.00**	JD	6	404D	16F-6R	100.	10930	No
4230 PS	14111.00	**11060.00**	**13680.00**	**16420.00**	JD	6	404D	8F-4R	100.	9400	No
4230 QR	13605.00	**10780.00**	**13330.00**	**16000.00**	JD	6	404D	16F-6R	100.32	9650	No
4430 4WD	17798.00	**11990.00**	**14820.00**	**17780.00**	JD	6T	404D	8F-2R	125.00	11300	No
4430 4WD PS	18818.00	**12550.00**	**15520.00**	**18620.00**	JD	6T	404D	8F-4R	125.00	11500	No
4430 4WD QR	18312.00	**12270.00**	**15170.00**	**18200.00**	JD	6T	404D	16F-6R	125.00	11720	No
4430 HC	15789.00	**10880.00**	**13460.00**	**16150.00**	JD	6T	404D	8F-2R	125.00	10815	No
4430 HC PS	16809.00	**11450.00**	**14150.00**	**16980.00**	JD	6T	404D	8F-4R	125.00	11000	No
4430 HC QR	16303.00	**11170.00**	**13810.00**	**16570.00**	JD	6T	404D	16F-6R	125.00	11235	No
4430 PS	15880.00	**12030.00**	**14880.00**	**17860.00**	JD	6T	404D	8F-4R	125.00	9900	No
4430 QR	15374.00	**11210.00**	**13860.00**	**16630.00**	JD	6T	404D	16F-6R	125.88	10155	No
4630 4WD	20792.00	**12540.00**	**15500.00**	**18600.00**	JD	6TI	404D	8F-2R	150.00	14300	No
4630 4WD PS	21812.00	**13100.00**	**16190.00**	**19430.00**	JD	6TI	404D	8F-4R	150.00	14450	No
4630 4WD QR	21306.00	**12540.00**	**15510.00**	**18610.00**	JD	6TI	404D	16F-6R	150.00	14600	No
4630 PS	18797.00	**11990.00**	**14820.00**	**17780.00**	JD	6TI	404D	8F-4R	150.00	13250	No
4630 QR	18219.00	**11120.00**	**13750.00**	**16500.00**	JD	6TI	404D	16F-6R	150.00	13100	No
6030	21750.00	**9180.00**	**11520.00**	**13590.00**	JD	6TI	531D	8F-2R	175.99	15800	No
6030	24934.00	**10220.00**	**12820.00**	**15130.00**	JD	6TI	531D	8F-2R	175.99	17300	C,H,A
7020 4WD	22907.00	**10150.00**	**12740.00**	**15030.00**	JD	6TI	404D	8F-2R	146.00	14725	C,H,A
7520 4WD	26372.00	**10900.00**	**13680.00**	**16140.00**	JD	6TI	531D	8F-2R	175.00	16935	C,H,A
8430 4WD	37290.00	**14550.00**	**18000.00**	**19980.00**	JD	6TI	466D	16F-4R	178.16	22010	C,H,A
8630 4WD	44570.00	**15960.00**	**19740.00**	**21910.00**	JD	6TI	619D	16F-4R	225.59	24150	C,H,A

H, HC, HU--High Clearance LU--Low Profile PS--Power Shift QR--Quad Range

John Deere (Cont.)

1976

Model	Approx. Retail Price New	Estimated Average Value Less Repairs: Fair	Good	Premium	Make	Engine No. Cyls.	Displ. Cu.-In.	No. Speeds	P.T.O. H.P.	Approx. Shipping Wt.-Lbs.	Cab
2040	7705.00	**4880.00**	**5920.00**	**7050.00**	JD	3	164D	8F-4R	40.86	4060	No
2240	9529.00	**5900.00**	**7160.00**	**8520.00**	JD	3	179D	16F-8R	50.37	4255	No
2440	10435.00	**6400.00**	**7780.00**	**9260.00**	JD	4	219D	8F-4R	60.00	4600	No
2640	11439.00	**6970.00**	**8460.00**	**10070.00**	JD	4	276D	8F-4R	70.00	5045	No
4030	16343.00	**11390.00**	**13830.00**	**16460.00**	JD	6	329D	8F-2R	80.00	8805	C,H,A
4030 QR	16962.00	**12300.00**	**14930.00**	**17770.00**	JD	6	329D	16F-6R	80.33	9265	C,H,A
4230 4WD	22483.00	**12880.00**	**15640.00**	**18610.00**	JD	6	404D	8F-2R	100.	11550	C,H,A
4230 4WD PS	23819.00	**13440.00**	**16320.00**	**19420.00**	JD	6	404D	8F-4R	100.	11800	C,H,A
4230 4WD QR	23101.00	**13160.00**	**15980.00**	**19020.00**	JD	6	404D	16F-6R	100.	11950	C,H,A
4230 HC	16426.00	**10320.00**	**12530.00**	**14910.00**	JD	6	404D	8F-2R	100.	10530	No
4230 HC PS	17762.00	**11070.00**	**13440.00**	**15990.00**	JD	6	404D	8F-4R	100.	10700	No
4230 HC QR	17044.00	**10670.00**	**12950.00**	**15410.00**	JD	6	404D	16F-6R	100.	10930	No
4230 PS	19888.00	**12820.00**	**15560.00**	**18520.00**	JD	6	404D	8F-4R	100.	10400	C,H,A
4230 QR	19170.00	**12420.00**	**15080.00**	**17950.00**	JD	6	404D	16F-6R	100.32	10650	C,H,A
4430 4WD	24929.00	**14560.00**	**17680.00**	**21040.00**	JD	6T	404D	8F-2R	125.00	12300	C,H,A
4430 4WD PS	26366.00	**15120.00**	**18360.00**	**21850.00**	JD	6T	404D	8F-4R	125.00	12500	C,H,A
4430 4WD QR	25547.00	**14780.00**	**17950.00**	**21360.00**	JD	6T	404D	16F-6R	125.00	12720	C,H,A
4430 HC	18892.00	**10580.00**	**12850.00**	**15290.00**	JD	6T	404D	8F-2R	125.00	10815	No
4430 HC PS	20309.00	**11370.00**	**13810.00**	**16430.00**	JD	6T	404D	8F-4R	125.00	11000	No
4430 HC QR	19490.00	**10910.00**	**13250.00**	**15770.00**	JD	6T	404D	16F-6R	125.00	11235	No
4430 PS	22435.00	**13440.00**	**16320.00**	**19420.00**	JD	6T	404D	8F-4R	125.00	10900	C,H,A
4430 QR	21616.00	**13780.00**	**16730.00**	**19910.00**	JD	6T	404D	16F-6R	125.88	11155	C,H,A
4630 4WD	29023.00	**14800.00**	**18580.00**	**21740.00**	JD	6TI	404D	8F-2R	150.00	15300	C,H,A
4630 4WD PS	30494.00	**15550.00**	**19520.00**	**22840.00**	JD	6TI	404D	8F-4R	150.00	15450	C,H,A
4630 4WD QR	29641.00	**15120.00**	**18970.00**	**22200.00**	JD	6TI	404D	16F-6R	150.00	15600	C,H,A
4630 PS	26450.00	**14000.00**	**17570.00**	**20560.00**	JD	6TI	404D	8F-4R	150.00	14250	C,H,A
4630 QR	25597.00	**13520.00**	**16960.00**	**19840.00**	JD	6TI	404D	16F-6R	150.00	14100	C,H,A
6030	30243.00	**13090.00**	**15470.00**	**17330.00**	JD	6TI	531D	8F-2R	175.99	17300	C,H,A
8430 4WD	41175.00	**16060.00**	**19760.00**	**21740.00**	JD	6TI	466D	16F-4R	178.16	22010	C,H,A
8630 4WD	46150.00	**16460.00**	**20260.00**	**22290.00**	JD	6TI	619D	16F-4R	225.59	24150	C,H,A

H, HC, HU--High Clearance LU--Low Profile PS--Power Shift QR--Quad Range

1977

Model	Approx. Retail Price New	Estimated Average Value Less Repairs: Fair	Good	Premium	Make	Engine No. Cyls.	Displ. Cu.-In.	No. Speeds	P.T.O. H.P.	Approx. Shipping Wt.-Lbs.	Cab
2040	8392.00	**4890.00**	**6050.00**	**7140.00**	JD	3	164D	8F-4R	40.86	4060	No
2240	10387.00	**5710.00**	**7060.00**	**8330.00**	JD	3	179D	16F-8R	50.37	4255	No
2440	11244.00	**6180.00**	**7650.00**	**9030.00**	JD	4	219D	16F-8R	60.00	4855	No
2640	12426.00	**6830.00**	**8450.00**	**9970.00**	JD	4	276D	8F-4R	70.00	5045	No
2840 RCU	15570.00	**8560.00**	**10590.00**	**12500.00**	JD	6	329D	12F-6R	80.65	8500	No
4030	17481.00	**10670.00**	**13190.00**	**15560.00**	JD	6	329D	8F-2R	80.00	8805	C,H,A
4030 QR	18154.00	**11000.00**	**13600.00**	**16050.00**	JD	6	329D	16F-6R	80.33	9265	C,H,A
4230 4WD	24187.00	**13300.00**	**16450.00**	**19410.00**	JD	6	404D	8F-2R	100.	11550	C,H,A
4230 4WD PS	25523.00	**14040.00**	**17360.00**	**20490.00**	JD	6	404D	8F-4R	100.	11800	C,H,A
4230 4WD QR	24860.00	**13670.00**	**16910.00**	**19950.00**	JD	6	404D	16F-6R	100.	11950	C,H,A
4230 PS	21242.00	**12540.00**	**15500.00**	**18290.00**	JD	6	404D	8F-4R	100	10400	C,H,A
4230 QR	20579.00	**12930.00**	**15980.00**	**18860.00**	JD	6	404D	16F-6R	100.32	10650	C,H,A
4230HC	21122.00	**11220.00**	**14080.00**	**16330.00**	JD	6	404D	8F-2R	100.	10530	No
4230HC PS	22503.00	**11480.00**	**14400.00**	**16700.00**	JD	6	404D	8F-4R	100.	10700	No
4230HC QR	21795.00	**11120.00**	**13950.00**	**16180.00**	JD	6	404D	16F-6R	100.	10930	No
4430 4WD	26857.00	**14770.00**	**18260.00**	**21550.00**	JD	6T	404D	8F-2R	125.00	12300	C,H,A
4430 4WD PS	28422.00	**15630.00**	**19330.00**	**22810.00**	JD	6T	404D	8F-4R	125.00	12500	C,H,A
4430 4WD QR	27530.00	**15140.00**	**18720.00**	**22090.00**	JD	6T	404D	16F-6R	125.00	12720	C,H,A
4430 PS	24141.00	**13750.00**	**17000.00**	**20060.00**	JD	6T	404D	8F-4R	125.00	10900	C,H,A
4430 QR	23249.00	**13340.00**	**16490.00**	**19460.00**	JD	6T	404D	16F-6R	125.88	11155	C,H,A
4430HC	20549.00	**10480.00**	**13150.00**	**15250.00**	JD	6T	404D	8F-2R	125.00	10815	No
4430HC PS	22114.00	**11280.00**	**14150.00**	**16410.00**	JD	6T	404D	8F-4R	125.00	11000	No
4430HC QR	21222.00	**10820.00**	**13580.00**	**15750.00**	JD	6T	404D	16F-6R	125.00	11235	No
4630 4WD	32041.00	**16340.00**	**20510.00**	**23790.00**	JD	6TI	404D	8F-2R	150.00	15300	C,H,A
4630 4WD PS	33643.00	**17160.00**	**21530.00**	**24980.00**	JD	6TI	404D	8F-4R	150.00	15450	C,H,A
4630 4WD QR	32714.00	**16680.00**	**20940.00**	**24290.00**	JD	6TI	404D	16F-6R	150.00	15600	C,H,A
4630 PS	29239.00	**14910.00**	**18710.00**	**21700.00**	JD	6TI	404D	8F-4R	150.00	14250	C,H,A
4630 QR	28310.00	**14440.00**	**18120.00**	**21020.00**	JD	6TI	404D	16F-6R	150.00	14100	C,H,A
6030	32913.00	**13690.00**	**16120.00**	**17890.00**	JD	6TI	531D	8F-2R	175.99	17300	C,H,A
8430 4WD	41442.00	**16000.00**	**19600.00**	**21560.00**	JD	6TI	466D	16F-4R	178.16	22010	C,H,A
8630 4WD	50016.00	**17600.00**	**21560.00**	**23720.00**	JD	6TI	619D	16F-4R	225.59	24150	C,H,A

H, HC, HU--High Clearance LU--Low Profile PS--Power Shift QR--Quad Range

1978

Model	Approx. Retail Price New	Estimated Average Value Less Repairs: Fair	Good	Premium	Make	Engine No. Cyls.	Displ. Cu.-In.	No. Speeds	P.T.O. H.P.	Approx. Shipping Wt.-Lbs.	Cab
850	4852.00	**3090.00**	**3870.00**	**4450.00**	Yanmar	3	78D	8F-2R	22.3	3225	No
950	5438.00	**3130.00**	**3930.00**	**4520.00**	Yanmar	3	104D	8F-2R	27.3	3169	No
2040	9702.00	**5600.00**	**6800.00**	**7960.00**	JD	3	164D	8F-4R	40.86	4060	No
2240	11652.00	**6530.00**	**7920.00**	**9270.00**	JD	3	179D	16F-8R	50.37	4255	No
2440	13621.00	**7630.00**	**9260.00**	**10830.00**	JD	4	219D	16F-8R	60.00	4855	No
2640	14102.00	**7900.00**	**9590.00**	**11220.00**	JD	4	276D	8F-4R	70.00	5045	No
2840 RCU	16971.00	**9500.00**	**11540.00**	**13500.00**	JD	6	329D	12F-6R	80.65	8500	No
4040 4WD	27513.00	**15410.00**	**18710.00**	**21890.00**	JD	6	404D	8F-2R	90.00	10944	C,H,A
4040 4WD PS	29133.00	**16310.00**	**19810.00**	**23180.00**	JD	6	404D	8F-4R	90.00	10961	C,H,A
4040 4WD QR	28233.00	**15810.00**	**19200.00**	**22460.00**	JD	6	404D	16F-6R	90.00	11394	C,H,A
4040 PS	24193.00	**13550.00**	**16450.00**	**19250.00**	JD	6	404D	8F-4R	90.79	9960	C,H,A
4040 QR	23293.00	**13040.00**	**15840.00**	**18530.00**	JD	6	404D	16F-6R	90.80	10393	C,H,A
4240 4WD	28727.00	**16090.00**	**19530.00**	**22850.00**	JD	6	466D	8F-2R	110.00	11572	C,H,A
4240 4WD PS	30347.00	**16990.00**	**20640.00**	**24150.00**	JD	6	466D	8F-4R	111.00	11585	C,H,A
4240 4WD QR	29447.00	**16490.00**	**20020.00**	**23420.00**	JD	6	466D	16F-6R	110.00	11157	C,H,A
4240 PS	26846.00	**15030.00**	**18260.00**	**21360.00**	JD	6	466D	8F-4R	111.06	10581	C,H,A
4240 QR	25946.00	**14530.00**	**17640.00**	**20640.00**	JD	6	466D	16F-6R	110.94	11156	C,H,A

John Deere (Cont.)

1978 (Cont.)

Model	Approx. Retail Price New	Fair	Good	Premium	Engine Make	No. Cyls.	Displ. Cu.-In.	No. Speeds	P.T.O. H.P.	Approx. Shipping Wt.-Lbs.	Cab
4240HC	23787.00	**12130.00**	**15220.00**	**17500.00**	JD	6	466D	8F-2R	110.00	10333	No
4240HC PS	25407.00	**12960.00**	**16260.00**	**18700.00**	JD	6	466D	8F-4R	111.00	10343	No
4240HC QR	24507.00	**12500.00**	**15680.00**	**18030.00**	JD	6	466D	16F-6R	110.00	10918	No
4440 4WD PS	35271.00	**19750.00**	**23980.00**	**28060.00**	JD	6T	446D	8F-4R	130.00	11889	C,H,A
4440 4WD QR	34245.00	**19180.00**	**23290.00**	**27250.00**	JD	6T	466D	16F-6R	130.00	12474	C,H,A
4440 PS	30331.00	**16990.00**	**20630.00**	**24140.00**	JD	6T	466D	8F-4R	130.41	10901	C,H,A
4440 QR	29305.00	**16410.00**	**19930.00**	**23320.00**	JD	6T	466D	16F-6R	130.58	11473	C,H,A
4440HC PS	28737.00	**14660.00**	**18390.00**	**21150.00**	JD	6T	466D	8F-4R	130.00	10500	No
4440HC QR	27697.00	**14130.00**	**17730.00**	**20390.00**	JD	6T	466D	16F-6R	130.00	11072	No
4640 4WD PS	40185.00	**20490.00**	**25720.00**	**29580.00**	JD	6TI	466D	8F-4R	155.00	13715	C,H,A
4640 4WD QR	39116.00	**19950.00**	**25030.00**	**28780.00**	JD	6TI	466D	16F-6R	155.00	14300	C,H,A
4640 PS	35245.00	**17980.00**	**22560.00**	**25940.00**	JD	6TI	466D	8F-4R	155.96	12614	C,H,A
4640 QR	34176.00	**17430.00**	**21870.00**	**25150.00**	JD	6TI	466D	16F-6R	155.00	13199	C,H,A
4840 PS	38289.00	**17610.00**	**20680.00**	**22750.00**	JD	6TI	466D	8F-4R	180.63	14317	C,H,A
8430 4WD	44746.00	**17220.00**	**21000.00**	**23100.00**	JD	6TI	466D	16F-4R	178.16	22010	C,H,A
8630 4WD	54077.00	**18040.00**	**22000.00**	**24200.00**	JD	6TI	619D	16F-4R	225.59	24150	C,H,A

H, HC, HU--High Clearance LU--Low Profile PS--Power Shift QR--Quad Range

1979

Model	Approx. Retail Price New	Fair	Good	Premium	Engine Make	No. Cyls.	Displ. Cu.-In.	No. Speeds	P.T.O. H.P.	Approx. Shipping Wt.-Lbs.	Cab
850	5002.00	**3230.00**	**3910.00**	**4460.00**	Yanmar	3	78D	8F-2R	22.3	3225	No
950	5606.00	**3280.00**	**3970.00**	**4530.00**	Yanmar	3	104D	8F-2R	27.3	3169	No
2040	10020.00	**5710.00**	**6810.00**	**7900.00**	JD	3	164D	8F-4R	40.86	4060	No
2040 4WD	15246.00	**8690.00**	**10370.00**	**12030.00**	JD	3	164D	8F-4R	40.00	4260	No
2240	12222.00	**6970.00**	**8310.00**	**9640.00**	JD	3	179D	16F-8R	50.37	4255	No
2240 4WD	16864.00	**9610.00**	**11470.00**	**13310.00**	JD	3	179D	8F-4R	50.90	5422	No
2440	13486.00	**7690.00**	**9170.00**	**10640.00**	JD	4	219D	8F-4R	60.00	4600	No
2640	15206.00	**8670.00**	**10340.00**	**11990.00**	JD	4	276D	8F-4R	70.00	5045	No
2840 RCU	17565.00	**10010.00**	**11940.00**	**13850.00**	JD	6	329D	12F-6R	80.65	8500	No
2940	18994.00	**10830.00**	**12920.00**	**14990.00**	JD	6	329D	16F-8R	81.00	9347	No
2940 4WD	22944.00	**13080.00**	**15600.00**	**18100.00**	JD	6	329D	16F-8R	81.17	9799	No
4040 4WD	28961.00	**16510.00**	**19690.00**	**22840.00**	JD	6	404D	8F-2R	90.00	11944	C,H,A
4040 4WD PS	30656.00	**17470.00**	**20850.00**	**24190.00**	JD	6	404D	8F-4R	90.00	11961	C,H,A
4040 4WD QR	29710.00	**16940.00**	**20200.00**	**23430.00**	JD	6	404D	16F-6R	90.00	12391	C,H,A
4040 PS	25508.00	**14540.00**	**17350.00**	**20130.00**	JD	6	404D	8F-4R	90.79	9960	C,H,A
4040 QR	24572.00	**14010.00**	**16710.00**	**19380.00**	JD	6	404D	16F-6R	90.80	11393	C,H,A
4240 4WD	31703.00	**18070.00**	**21560.00**	**25010.00**	JD	6	466D	8F-2R	110.00	11572	C,H,A
4240 4WD PS	33392.00	**19030.00**	**22710.00**	**26340.00**	JD	6	466D	8F-4R	111.00	11585	C,H,A
4240 4WD QR	32456.00	**18500.00**	**22070.00**	**25600.00**	JD	6	466D	16F-6R	110.00	11157	C,H,A
4240 PS	28254.00	**16110.00**	**19210.00**	**22280.00**	JD	6	466D	8F-4R	111.06	10581	C,H,A
4240 QR	27318.00	**15570.00**	**18580.00**	**21550.00**	JD	6	466D	16F-6R	110.94	11156	C,H,A
4240HC	24625.00	**12810.00**	**15510.00**	**17680.00**	JD	6	466D	8F-2R	110.00	10333	No
4240HC PS	26310.00	**13680.00**	**16580.00**	**18900.00**	JD	6	466D	8F-4R	111.00	10343	No
4240HC QR	25374.00	**13190.00**	**15990.00**	**18230.00**	JD	6	466D	16F-6R	110.00	10918	No
4440 4WD PS	36758.00	**20950.00**	**25000.00**	**29000.00**	JD	6T	466D	8F-4R	130.00	11889	C,H,A
4440 4WD QR	35691.00	**20340.00**	**24270.00**	**28150.00**	JD	6T	466D	16F-6R	130.00	12474	C,H,A
4440 PS	31620.00	**18020.00**	**21500.00**	**24940.00**	JD	6T	466D	8F-4R	130.41	10901	C,H,A
4440 QR	30553.00	**17420.00**	**20780.00**	**24110.00**	JD	6T	466D	16F-6R	130.58	11473	C,H,A
4440HC PS	29743.00	**15470.00**	**18740.00**	**21360.00**	JD	6T	466D	8F-4R	130.00	10500	No
4440HC QR	28676.00	**14910.00**	**18070.00**	**20600.00**	JD	6T	466D	16F-6R	130.00	11072	No
4640 4WD PS	41844.00	**21760.00**	**26360.00**	**30050.00**	JD	6TI	466D	8F-4R	155.00	13715	C,H,A
4640 4WD QR	40732.00	**21180.00**	**25660.00**	**29250.00**	JD	6TI	466D	16F-6R	155.00	14300	C,H,A
4640 PS	36706.00	**19090.00**	**23130.00**	**26370.00**	JD	6TI	466D	8F-4R	155.96	12614	C,H,A
4640 QR	35594.00	**18510.00**	**22420.00**	**25560.00**	JD	6TI	466D	16F-6R	155.00	13199	C,H,A
4840 PS	39629.00	**18630.00**	**21800.00**	**23760.00**	JD	6TI	466D	8F-4R	180.63	14317	C,H,A
8440 4WD	53920.00	**18330.00**	**23190.00**	**25280.00**	JD	6TI	466D	16F-4R	179.83	22210	C,H,A
8640 4WD	65424.00	**22240.00**	**28130.00**	**30660.00**	JD	6TI	619D	16F-4R	228.75	24750	C,H,A

H, HC, HU--High Clearance LU--Low Profile PS--Power Shift QR--Quad Range

1980

Model	Approx. Retail Price New	Fair	Good	Premium	Engine Make	No. Cyls.	Displ. Cu.-In.	No. Speeds	P.T.O. H.P.	Approx. Shipping Wt.-Lbs.	Cab
850	5885.00	**3340.00**	**3910.00**	**4420.00**	Yanmar	3	78D	8F-2R	22.3	3225	No
950	6495.00	**3440.00**	**4030.00**	**4550.00**	Yanmar	3	104D	8F-2R	27.3	3169	No
1050	8355.00	**4430.00**	**5180.00**	**5850.00**	Yanmar	3T	105D	8F-2R	33.4	3592	No
1050 4WD	9730.00	**5160.00**	**6030.00**	**6810.00**	Yanmar	3T	105D	8F-2R	33.4	3814	No
2040	12091.00	**6940.00**	**8120.00**	**9180.00**	JD	3	179D	8F-4R	41.25	4376	No
2040 4WD	17431.00	**9770.00**	**11430.00**	**12920.00**	JD	3	179D	8F-4R	40.44	4580	No
2240	14153.00	**8030.00**	**9400.00**	**10620.00**	JD	3	179D	16F-8R	50.37	4740	No
2240 4WD	18425.00	**10300.00**	**12040.00**	**13610.00**	JD	3	179D	8F-4R	50.90	5422	No
2240 4WD	19191.00	**10700.00**	**12520.00**	**14150.00**	JD	3	179D	16F-8R	50.00	5677	No
2440	16609.00	**9330.00**	**10920.00**	**12340.00**	JD	4	219D	16F-8R	60.00	4855	No
2640	19004.00	**10600.00**	**12400.00**	**14010.00**	JD	4	276D	16F-8R	70.00	5400	No
2940	21466.00	**11910.00**	**13930.00**	**15740.00**	JD	6	359D	16F-8R	81.00	9347	No
2940 4WD	25949.00	**14280.00**	**16710.00**	**18880.00**	JD	6	359D	16F-8R	81.17	9799	No
4040 4WD	35741.00	**18940.00**	**22160.00**	**25040.00**	JD	6	404D	8F-2R	90.00	11944	C,H,A
4040 4WD PS	38816.00	**20570.00**	**24070.00**	**27200.00**	JD	6	404D	8F-4R	90.00	11961	C,H,A
4040 4WD QR	36663.00	**19430.00**	**22730.00**	**25690.00**	JD	6	404D	16F-6R	90.00	12391	C,H,A
4040 PS	31481.00	**16690.00**	**19520.00**	**22060.00**	JD	6	404D	8F-4R	90.79	9960	C,H,A
4040 QR	30328.00	**16070.00**	**18800.00**	**21240.00**	JD	6	404D	16F-6R	90.80	11393	C,H,A
4240 4WD	39091.00	**20720.00**	**24240.00**	**27390.00**	JD	6	466D	8F-2R	110.00	11572	C,H,A
4240 4WD PS	41166.00	**21820.00**	**25520.00**	**28840.00**	JD	6	466D	8F-4R	111.00	11585	C,H,A
4240 4WD QR	40013.00	**21210.00**	**24810.00**	**28040.00**	JD	6	466D	16F-6R	110.00	11157	C,H,A
4240 PS	34831.00	**18460.00**	**21600.00**	**24410.00**	JD	6	466D	8F-4R	111.06	10581	C,H,A
4240 QR	33678.00	**17850.00**	**20880.00**	**23590.00**	JD	6	466D	16F-6R	110.94	11156	C,H,A
4240HC	35186.00	**16890.00**	**19700.00**	**21280.00**	JD	6	466D	8F-2R	110.00	10333	C,H,A
4240HC PS	37261.00	**17890.00**	**20870.00**	**22540.00**	JD	6	466D	8F-4R	111.00	10343	C,H,A

John Deere (Cont.)

1980 (Cont.)

Model	Approx. Retail Price New	Estimated Average Value Less Repairs: Fair	Good	Premium	Engine: Make	No. Cyls.	Displ. Cu.-In.	No. Speeds	P.T.O. H.P.	Approx. Shipping Wt.-Lbs.	Cab
4240HC QR	36108.00	**17330.00**	**20220.00**	**21840.00**	JD	6	466D	16F-6R	110.00	10918	C,H,A
4440 4WD PS	46936.00	**24880.00**	**29100.00**	**32880.00**	JD	6T	466D	8F-4R	130.00	11889	C,H,A
4440 4WD QR	45619.00	**24180.00**	**28280.00**	**31960.00**	JD	6T	466D	16F-6R	130.00	12474	C,H,A
4440 PS	38909.00	**20620.00**	**24120.00**	**27260.00**	JD	6T	466D	8F-4R	130.41	10901	C,H,A
4440 QR	37592.00	**19920.00**	**23310.00**	**26340.00**	JD	6T	466D	16F-6R	130.58	11473	C,H,A
4440HC PS	41422.00	**21950.00**	**25680.00**	**29020.00**	JD	6T	466D	8F-4R	130.00	10500	C,H,A
4440HC QR	40105.00	**21260.00**	**24870.00**	**28100.00**	JD	6T	466D	16F-6R	130.00	11072	C,H,A
4640 4WD PS	52213.00	**25060.00**	**29240.00**	**31580.00**	JD	6TI	466D	8F-4R	155.00	13715	C,H,A
4640 4WD QR	50841.00	**24400.00**	**28470.00**	**30750.00**	JD	6TI	466D	16F-6R	155.00	14300	C,H,A
4640 PS	45877.00	**22020.00**	**25690.00**	**27750.00**	JD	6TI	466D	8F-4R	155.96	12614	C,H,A
4640 QR	44506.00	**21360.00**	**24920.00**	**26910.00**	JD	6TI	466D	16F-6R	155.00	13199	C,H,A
4840 PS	49890.00	**21450.00**	**25940.00**	**28020.00**	JD	6TI	466D	8F-4R	180.63	14317	C,H,A
8440 4WD	61268.00	**21440.00**	**26960.00**	**29390.00**	JD	6TI	466D	16F-4R	179.83	22210	C,H,A
8640 4WD	74323.00	**24850.00**	**31240.00**	**34050.00**	JD	6TI	619D	16F-4R	228.75	24750	C,H,A

H, HC, HU--High Clearance LU--Low Profile PS--Power Shift QR--Quad Range

1981

Model	Approx. Retail Price New	Estimated Average Value Less Repairs: Fair	Good	Premium	Engine: Make	No. Cyls.	Displ. Cu.-In.	No. Speeds	P.T.O. H.P.	Approx. Shipping Wt.-Lbs.	Cab
650	5345.00	**3430.00**	**4000.00**	**4480.00**	Yanmar	2	52D	8F-2R	14.5	1968	No
650 4WD	5840.00	**3260.00**	**3810.00**	**4270.00**	Yanmar	2	52D	8F-2R	14.5	1968	No
750	6265.00	**3380.00**	**3950.00**	**4420.00**	Yanmar	3	78D	8F-2R	18.5	2455	No
750 4WD	6915.00	**3730.00**	**4360.00**	**4880.00**	Yanmar	3	78D	8F-2R	18.0	2455	No
850	6751.00	**3650.00**	**4250.00**	**4760.00**	Yanmar	3	78D	8F-2R	22.3	3225	No
950	7826.00	**4230.00**	**4930.00**	**5520.00**	Yanmar	3	104D	8F-2R	27.3	3169	No
950 4WD	9266.00	**5000.00**	**5840.00**	**6540.00**	Yanmar	3	104D	8F-2R	27.3	3405	No
1050	9409.00	**5080.00**	**5930.00**	**6640.00**	Yanmar	3T	105D	8F-2R	33.4	3592	No
1050 4WD	10904.00	**5400.00**	**6300.00**	**7060.00**	Yanmar	3T	105D	8F-2R	33.4	3814	No
2040	13638.00	**7370.00**	**8590.00**	**9620.00**	JD	3	179D	8F-4R	41.25	4376	No
2040 4WD	19459.00	**10510.00**	**12260.00**	**13730.00**	JD	3	179D	8F-4R	40.44	4580	No
2240	15657.00	**8460.00**	**9860.00**	**11040.00**	JD	3	179D	16F-8R	50.37	4740	No
2240 4WD	20502.00	**11070.00**	**12920.00**	**14470.00**	JD	3	179D	8F-4R	50.90	5422	No
2440	18828.00	**10170.00**	**11860.00**	**13280.00**	JD	4	219D	16F-8R	60.00	4855	No
2640	20194.00	**10910.00**	**12720.00**	**14250.00**	JD	4	276D	8F-4R	70.00	5145	No
2940	23695.00	**12800.00**	**14930.00**	**16720.00**	JD	6	359D	16F-8R	81.00	9347	No
2940 4WD	28515.00	**15400.00**	**17960.00**	**20120.00**	JD	6	359D	16F-8R	81.17	9931	No
4040 4WD	38852.00	**20980.00**	**24480.00**	**27420.00**	JD	6	404D	8F-2R	90.00	11944	C,H,A
4040 4WD PS	41019.00	**22150.00**	**25840.00**	**28940.00**	JD	6	404D	8F-4R	90.00	11961	C,H,A
4040 4WD QR	39774.00	**21480.00**	**25060.00**	**28070.00**	JD	6	404D	16F-6R	90.00	12391	C,H,A
4040 PS	34177.00	**18460.00**	**21530.00**	**24110.00**	JD	6	404D	8F-4R	90.79	9960	C,H,A
4040 QR	32932.00	**17780.00**	**20750.00**	**23240.00**	JD	6	404D	16F-6R	90.80	11393	C,H,A
4240 4WD	42467.00	**22930.00**	**26750.00**	**29960.00**	JD	6	466D	8F-2R	110.00	11572	C,H,A
4240 4WD PS	44542.00	**24050.00**	**28060.00**	**31430.00**	JD	6	466D	8F-4R	111.00	11585	C,H,A
4240 4WD QR	43385.00	**23430.00**	**27330.00**	**30610.00**	JD	6	466D	16F-6R	110.00	11157	C,H,A
4240 PS	37700.00	**20360.00**	**23750.00**	**26600.00**	JD	6	466D	8F-4R	111.06	10581	C,H,A
4240 QR	36547.00	**19740.00**	**23030.00**	**25790.00**	JD	6	466D	16F-6R	110.94	11156	C,H,A
4240HC	38249.00	**18740.00**	**21800.00**	**23540.00**	JD	6	466D	8F-2R	110.00	10333	C,H,A
4240HC PS	40324.00	**19760.00**	**22990.00**	**24830.00**	JD	6	466D	8F-4R	111.00	10343	C,H,A
4240HC QR	39171.00	**19190.00**	**22330.00**	**24120.00**	JD	6	466D	16F-6R	110.00	10918	C,H,A
4440 4WD PS	49039.00	**24030.00**	**27950.00**	**30190.00**	JD	6T	466D	8F-4R	130.00	11889	C,H,A
4440 4WD QR	47617.00	**23330.00**	**27140.00**	**29310.00**	JD	6T	466D	16F-6R	130.00	12474	C,H,A
4440 PS	42197.00	**20680.00**	**24050.00**	**25970.00**	JD	6T	466D	8F-4R	130.41	10901	C,H,A
4440 QR	40775.00	**19980.00**	**23240.00**	**25100.00**	JD	6T	466D	16F-6R	130.58	11473	C,H,A
4440HC PS	44911.00	**22010.00**	**25600.00**	**27650.00**	JD	6T	466D	8F-4R	130.00	10500	C,H,A
4440HC QR	43489.00	**21310.00**	**24790.00**	**26770.00**	JD	6T	466D	16F-6R	130.00	11072	C,H,A
4640 4WD PS	56451.00	**27660.00**	**32180.00**	**34750.00**	JD	6TI	466D	8F-4R	155.00	13715	C,H,A
4640 4WD QR	55080.00	**26990.00**	**31400.00**	**33910.00**	JD	6TI	466D	16F-6R	155.00	14300	C,H,A
4640 PS	49609.00	**24310.00**	**28280.00**	**30540.00**	JD	6TI	466D	8F-4R	155.96	12614	C,H,A
4640 QR	48238.00	**23640.00**	**27500.00**	**29700.00**	JD	6TI	466D	16F-6R	155.00	13199	C,H,A
4840 PS	53880.00	**23710.00**	**28560.00**	**30850.00**	JD	6TI	466D	8F-4R	180.63	14317	C,H,A
8440 4WD	66158.00	**23820.00**	**29770.00**	**32450.00**	JD	6TI	466D	16F-4R	179.83	22210	C,H,A
8640 4WD	80268.00	**28080.00**	**35100.00**	**38260.00**	JD	6TI	619D	16F-4R	228.75	24750	C,H,A

H, HC, HU--High Clearance LU--Low Profile PS--Power Shift QR--Quad Range

1982

Model	Approx. Retail Price New	Estimated Average Value Less Repairs: Fair	Good	Premium	Engine: Make	No. Cyls.	Displ. Cu.-In.	No. Speeds	P.T.O. H.P.	Approx. Shipping Wt.-Lbs.	Cab
650	6030.00	**3430.00**	**3990.00**	**4470.00**	Yanmar	2	52D	8F-2R	14.5	1968	No
650 4WD	6610.00	**3640.00**	**4230.00**	**4740.00**	Yanmar	2	52D	8F-2R	14.5	1968	No
750	7070.00	**3890.00**	**4530.00**	**5070.00**	Yanmar	3	78D	8F-2R	18.5	2455	No
750 4WD	7820.00	**4300.00**	**5010.00**	**5610.00**	Yanmar	3	78D	8F-2R	18.0	2455	No
850	7670.00	**4220.00**	**4910.00**	**5500.00**	Yanmar	3	78D	8F-2R	22.3	3225	No
950	8670.00	**4770.00**	**5550.00**	**6220.00**	Yanmar	3	104D	8F-2R	27.3	3169	No
950 4WD	10335.00	**5680.00**	**6610.00**	**7400.00**	Yanmar	3	104D	8F-2R	27.3	3405	No
1050	10415.00	**5730.00**	**6670.00**	**7470.00**	Yanmar	3T	105D	8F-2R	33.4	3592	No
1050 4WD	12125.00	**6600.00**	**7680.00**	**8600.00**	Yanmar	3T	105D	8F-2R	33.4	3814	No
1250	14735.00	**6500.00**	**7540.00**	**8140.00**	Yanmar	3	143D	9F-2R	40.7	4125	No
1250 4WD	18735.00	**8500.00**	**9860.00**	**10650.00**	Yanmar	3	143D	9F-2R	40.7	4875	No
2040	13970.00	**7680.00**	**8940.00**	**10010.00**	JD	3	179D	8F-4R	41.25	4376	No
2040 4WD	19000.00	**10450.00**	**12160.00**	**13620.00**	JD	3	179D	8F-4R	40.44	4580	No
2240	16423.00	**9030.00**	**10510.00**	**11770.00**	JD	3	179D	16F-8R	50.37	4740	No
2240 4WD	21038.00	**11570.00**	**13460.00**	**15080.00**	JD	3	179D	16F-8R	50.00	5677	No
2440	19647.00	**10810.00**	**12570.00**	**14080.00**	JD	4	219D	16F-8R	60.00	4855	No
2640	22214.00	**12220.00**	**14220.00**	**15930.00**	JD	4	276D	16F-8R	70.00	5400	No
2940 4WD	30226.00	**16620.00**	**19350.00**	**21670.00**	JD	6	359D	16F-8R	81.17	9931	No
4040 4WD	41930.00	**23060.00**	**26840.00**	**30060.00**	JD	6	404D	8F-2R	90.00	11944	C,H,A
4040 4WD PS	44306.00	**24370.00**	**28360.00**	**31760.00**	JD	6	404D	8F-4R	90.00	11961	C,H,A
4040 4WD QR	42986.00	**23640.00**	**27510.00**	**30810.00**	JD	6	404D	16F-6R	90.00	12391	C,H,A

John Deere (Cont.)

1982 (Cont.)

Model	Approx. Retail Price New	Fair	Estimated Average Value Less Repairs Good	Premium	Make	Engine No. Cyls.	Engine Displ. Cu.-In.	No. Speeds	P.T.O. H.P.	Approx. Shipping Wt.-Lbs.	Cab
4040 PS	36549.00	**20100.00**	**23390.00**	**26200.00**	JD	6	404D	8F-4R	90.79	9960	C,H,A
4040 QR	35229.00	**19380.00**	**22550.00**	**25260.00**	JD	6	404D	16F-6R	90.80	11393	C,H,A
4240 4WD	46216.00	**25420.00**	**29580.00**	**33130.00**	JD	6	466D	8F-2R	110.00	11572	C,H,A
4240 4WD PS	48592.00	**26730.00**	**31100.00**	**34830.00**	JD	6	466D	8F-4R	111.00	11585	C,H,A
4240 4WD QR	47272.00	**26000.00**	**30250.00**	**33880.00**	JD	6	466D	16F-6R	110.00	11157	C,H,A
4240 PS	40926.00	**22510.00**	**26190.00**	**29330.00**	JD	6	466D	8F-4R	111.06	10581	C,H,A
4240 QR	39606.00	**21780.00**	**25350.00**	**28390.00**	JD	6	466D	16F-6R	110.94	11156	C,H,A
4240HC	36208.00	**19910.00**	**23170.00**	**25950.00**	JD	6	466D	8F-2R	110.00	10333	No
4240HC PS	38584.00	**21220.00**	**24690.00**	**27650.00**	JD	6	466D	8F-4R	111.00	10343	No
4240HC QR	37264.00	**20500.00**	**23850.00**	**26710.00**	JD	6	466D	16F-6R	110.00	10918	No
4440 4WD PS	52701.00	**26350.00**	**30570.00**	**33020.00**	JD	6T	466D	8F-4R	130.00	11889	C,H,A
4440 4WD QR	51212.00	**25610.00**	**29700.00**	**32080.00**	JD	6T	466D	16F-6R	130.00	12474	C,H,A
4440 PS	45123.00	**22560.00**	**26170.00**	**28260.00**	JD	6T	466D	8F-4R	130.41	10901	C,H,A
4440 QR	43634.00	**21820.00**	**25310.00**	**27340.00**	JD	6T	466D	16F-6R	130.58	11473	C,H,A
4440HC PS	42826.00	**21410.00**	**24840.00**	**26830.00**	JD	6T	466D	8F-4R	130.00	10500	No
4440HC QR	41319.00	**20660.00**	**23970.00**	**25890.00**	JD	6T	466D	16F-6R	130.00	11072	No
4640 4WD PS	60755.00	**30380.00**	**35240.00**	**38060.00**	JD	6TI	466D	8F-4R	155.00	13715	C,H,A
4640 4WD QR	59185.00	**29590.00**	**34330.00**	**37080.00**	JD	6TI	466D	16F-6R	155.00	14300	C,H,A
4640 PS	53123.00	**26560.00**	**30810.00**	**33280.00**	JD	6TI	466D	8F-4R	155.96	12614	C,H,A
4640 QR	51553.00	**25780.00**	**29900.00**	**32290.00**	JD	6TI	466D	16F-6R	155.00	13199	C,H,A
4840 PS	57648.00	**25940.00**	**31130.00**	**33620.00**	JD	6TI	466D	8F-4R	180.63	14317	C,H,A
8440 4WD	66158.00	**29770.00**	**35730.00**	**38590.00**	JD	6TI	466D	16F-4R	179.83	22210	C,H,A
8440 4WD w/3 Pt.	70846.00	**31500.00**	**37800.00**	**40820.00**	JD	6TI	466D	16F-4R	179.83	22710	C,H,A
8450 4WD	74368.00	**27520.00**	**34210.00**	**36950.00**	JD	6TI	466D	16F-4R	186.98	22300	C,H,A
8450 4WD w/3 Pt.	80012.00	**29230.00**	**36340.00**	**39250.00**	JD	6TI	466D	16F-4R	186.98	22700	C,H,A
8640 4WD	80268.00	**29700.00**	**36920.00**	**39870.00**	JD	6TI	619D	16F-4R	228.75	24750	C,H,A
8640 4WD w/3 Pt.	84956.00	**30340.00**	**37720.00**	**40740.00**	JD	6TI	619D	16F-4R	228.75	25250	C,H,A
8650 4WD	90673.00	**23580.00**	**31740.00**	**35550.00**	JD	6TI	619D	16F-4R	238.56	25000	C,H,A
8650 4WD w/3 Pt.	96317.00	**24700.00**	**33250.00**	**37240.00**	JD	6TI	619D	16F-4R	238.56	26000	C,H,A
8850 4WD	115830.00	**27300.00**	**36750.00**	**41160.00**	JD	V8TI	955D	16F-4R	303.99	36074	C,H,A
8850 4WD w/3 Pt.	123250.00	**29900.00**	**40250.00**	**45080.00**	JD	V8TI	955D	16F-4R	303.99	36574	C,H,A

H, HC, HU--High Clearance LU--Low Profile PS--Power Shift QR--Quad Range

1983

Model	Approx. Retail Price New	Fair	Estimated Average Value Less Repairs Good	Premium	Make	Engine No. Cyls.	Engine Displ. Cu.-In.	No. Speeds	P.T.O. H.P.	Approx. Shipping Wt.-Lbs.	Cab
650	6030.00	**3600.00**	**4180.00**	**4680.00**	Yanmar	2	52D	8F-2R	14.5	1968	No
650 4WD	6610.00	**3860.00**	**4490.00**	**5030.00**	Yanmar	2	52D	8F-2R	14.5	1968	No
750	7070.00	**4090.00**	**4750.00**	**5320.00**	Yanmar	3	78D	8F-2R	18.5	2455	No
750 4WD	7820.00	**4380.00**	**5080.00**	**5690.00**	Yanmar	3	78D	8F-2R	18.0	2455	No
850	7670.00	**4350.00**	**5050.00**	**5660.00**	Yanmar	3	78D	8F-2R	22.3	3225	No
950	8670.00	**4860.00**	**5640.00**	**6320.00**	Yanmar	3	104D	8F-2R	27.3	3169	No
950 4WD	12125.00	**6160.00**	**7150.00**	**8010.00**	Yanmar	3	104D	8F-2R	27.3	3405	No
1050	10415.00	**5830.00**	**6770.00**	**7580.00**	Yanmar	3T	105D	8F-2R	33.4	3592	No
1050 4WD	12125.00	**6720.00**	**7800.00**	**8740.00**	Yanmar	3T	105D	8F-2R	33.4	3814	No
1250	14735.00	**6630.00**	**7670.00**	**8280.00**	Yanmar	3	143D	9F-2R	40.7	4125	No
1250 4WD	19235.00	**8670.00**	**10030.00**	**10830.00**	Yanmar	3	143D	9F-2R	40.7	4875	No
2150	17419.00	**9760.00**	**11320.00**	**12680.00**	JD	3	179D	16F-8R	46.47	4950	No
2150 4WD	22449.00	**12570.00**	**14590.00**	**16340.00**	JD	3	179D	16F-8R	46.00	5670	No
2350	20149.00	**11280.00**	**13100.00**	**14670.00**	JD	4	239D	16F-8R	56.18	7120	No
2350 4WD	24764.00	**13870.00**	**16100.00**	**18030.00**	JD	4	239D	16F-8R	56.00	8250	No
2350 4WD w/Cab	30764.00	**17230.00**	**20000.00**	**22400.00**	JD	4	239D	16F-8R	56.00	8850	C,H,A
2350 w/Cab	26149.00	**14640.00**	**17000.00**	**19040.00**	JD	4	239D	16F-8R	56.18	7620	C,H,A
2550	22354.00	**12520.00**	**14530.00**	**16270.00**	JD	4	239D	16F-8R	65.94	7230	No
2550 4WD	26817.00	**15020.00**	**17430.00**	**19520.00**	JD	4	239D	16F-8R	65.00	8360	No
2550 4WD w/Cab	32817.00	**18380.00**	**21330.00**	**23890.00**	JD	4	239D	16F-8R	65.00	8950	C,H,A
2550 w/Cab	28354.00	**15880.00**	**18430.00**	**20640.00**	JD	4	239D	16F-8R	65.94	7730	C,H,A
2750	24874.00	**13930.00**	**16170.00**	**18110.00**	JD	4T	239D	16F-8R	75.35	7810	No
2750 4WD	30859.00	**17280.00**	**20060.00**	**22470.00**	JD	4T	239D	16F-8R	75.00	9020	No
2750 4WD w/Cab	36859.00	**20640.00**	**23960.00**	**26840.00**	JD	4T	239D	16F-8R	75.00	9520	C,H,A
2750 w/Cab	30874.00	**17290.00**	**20070.00**	**22480.00**	JD	4T	239D	16F-8R	75.35	8310	C,H,A
2950	27870.00	**15610.00**	**18120.00**	**20290.00**	JD	6	359D	16F-8R	85.37	10300	No
2950 4WD	33278.00	**18640.00**	**21630.00**	**24230.00**	JD	6	359D	16F-8R	85.00	10410	No
2950 4WD w/Cab	39278.00	**22000.00**	**25530.00**	**28590.00**	JD	6	359D	16F-8R	85.00	10910	C,H,A
2950 w/Cab	33780.00	**18920.00**	**21960.00**	**24600.00**	JD	6	359D	16F-8R	85.37	10800	C,H,A
4050 4WD PS Cab	55895.00	**26520.00**	**30680.00**	**33130.00**	JD	6	466D	15F-4R	105.69	13389	C,H,A
4050 HC PS	50779.00	**24480.00**	**28320.00**	**30590.00**	JD	6	466D	15F-4R	101.00	12703	C,H,A
4050 HC QR Cab	46735.00	**22440.00**	**25960.00**	**28040.00**	JD	6	466D	16F-6R	101.00	13133	C,H,A
4050 PS Cab	46970.00	**22950.00**	**26550.00**	**28670.00**	JD	6	466D	15F-4R	100.95	12489	C,H,A
4050 QR Cab	42927.00	**20910.00**	**24190.00**	**26130.00**	JD	6	466D	16F-6R	101.09	12919	C,H,A
4250 4WD PS Cab	60568.00	**28050.00**	**32450.00**	**35050.00**	JD	6T	466D	15F-4R	123.00	14685	C,H,A
4250 PS Cab	51170.00	**24990.00**	**28910.00**	**31220.00**	JD	6T	466D	15F-4R	123.32	13155	C,H,A
4250 QR Cab	47127.00	**23210.00**	**26850.00**	**29000.00**	JD	6T	466D	16F-6R	123.06	13585	C,H,A
4250HC PS Cab	55176.00	**27030.00**	**31270.00**	**33770.00**	JD	6T	466D	15F-4R	123.00	13369	C,H,A
4250HC QR Cab	51136.00	**25040.00**	**28970.00**	**31290.00**	JD	6T	466D	16F-6R	123.00	13799	C,H,A
4450 4WD PS Cab	58078.00	**28050.00**	**32450.00**	**35050.00**	JD	6T	466D	15F-4R	140.00	15245	C,H,A
4450 PS Cab	54530.00	**26780.00**	**30980.00**	**33460.00**	JD	6T	466D	15F-4R	140.43	14145	C,H,A
4450 QR Cab	50382.00	**24630.00**	**28500.00**	**30780.00**	JD	6T	466D	16F-6R	140.33	14575	C,H,A
4650 4WD PS Cab	72443.00	**31280.00**	**37400.00**	**40390.00**	JD	6TI	466D	15F-4R	165.00	19803	C,H,A
4650 PS Cab	62153.00	**27600.00**	**33000.00**	**35640.00**	JD	6TI	466D	15F-4R	165.52	18703	C,H,A
4650 QR Cab	58005.00	**26220.00**	**31350.00**	**33860.00**	JD	6TI	466D	16F-6R	165.70	19133	C,H,A
4850 4WD PS Cab	77719.00	**32200.00**	**38500.00**	**41580.00**	JD	6TI	466D	15F-4R	192.00	20078	C,H,A
4850 PS Cab	67429.00	**29440.00**	**35200.00**	**38020.00**	JD	6TI	466D	15F-4R	192.99	18978	C,H,A
8450 4WD	74296.00	**26980.00**	**33370.00**	**36040.00**	JD	6TI	466D	16F-4R	186.98	22300	C,H,A
8450 4WD w/3 Pt.	81596.00	**29640.00**	**36660.00**	**39590.00**	JD	6TI	466D	16F-4R	186.98	22700	C,H,A
8650 4WD	93151.00	**23760.00**	**31680.00**	**35480.00**	JD	6TI	619D	16F-4R	238.56	24750	C,H,A

John Deere (Cont.)

1983 (Cont.)

Model	Approx. Retail Price New	Estimated Average Value Less Repairs Fair	Good	Premium	Engine Make	No. Cyls.	Displ. Cu.-In.	No. Speeds	P.T.O. H.P.	Approx. Shipping Wt.-Lbs.	Cab
8650 4WD w/3 Pt.	100451.00	**25110.00**	**33480.00**	**37500.00**	JD	6TI	619D	16F-4R	238.56	25250	C,H,A
8850 4WD	118609.00	**26730.00**	**35640.00**	**39920.00**	JD	V8TI	955D	16F-4R	303.99	36074	C,H,A
8850 4WD w/3 Pt.	127859.00	**30510.00**	**40680.00**	**45560.00**	JD	V8TI	955D	16F-4R	303.99	36574	C,H,A

H, HC, HU--High Clearance LU--Low Profile PS--Power Shift QR--Quad Range

1984

Model	Approx. Retail Price New	Fair	Good	Premium	Make	No. Cyls.	Displ. Cu.-In.	No. Speeds	P.T.O. H.P.	Approx. Shipping Wt.-Lbs.	Cab
650	6315.00	**3710.00**	**4290.00**	**4810.00**	Yanmar	2	52D	8F-2R	14.5	1968	No
650 4WD	6910.00	**3940.00**	**4560.00**	**5110.00**	Yanmar	2	52D	8F-2R	14.5	1968	No
750	7070.00	**4030.00**	**4670.00**	**5230.00**	Yanmar	3	78D	8F-2R	18.5	2455	No
750 4WD	7820.00	**4460.00**	**5160.00**	**5780.00**	Yanmar	3	78D	8F-2R	18.0	2455	No
850	7870.00	**4490.00**	**5190.00**	**5810.00**	Yanmar	3	78D	8F-2R	22.3	3225	No
950	9245.00	**5270.00**	**6100.00**	**6830.00**	Yanmar	3	104D	8F-2R	27.3	3169	No
950 4WD	12310.00	**6270.00**	**7260.00**	**8130.00**	Yanmar	3	104D	8F-2R	27.3	3405	No
1050	10660.00	**6080.00**	**7040.00**	**7890.00**	Yanmar	3T	105D	8F-2R	33.4	3592	No
1050 4WD	12310.00	**6450.00**	**7470.00**	**8370.00**	Yanmar	3T	105D	8F-2R	33.4	3814	No
1250	14735.00	**7660.00**	**8840.00**	**9550.00**	Yanmar	3	143D	9F-2R	40.7	4125	No
1250 4WD	19235.00	**9360.00**	**10800.00**	**11660.00**	Yanmar	3	143D	9F-2R	40.7	4875	No
1450	16309.00	**8480.00**	**9790.00**	**10570.00**	Yanmar	4	190D	9F-2R	51.4	4410	No
1450 4WD	20609.00	**9880.00**	**11400.00**	**12310.00**	Yanmar	4	190D	9F-2R	51.4	5070	No
1650	18457.00	**9600.00**	**11070.00**	**11960.00**	Yanmar	4T	190D	9F-2R	62.2	4630	No
1650 4WD	22809.00	**10400.00**	**12000.00**	**12960.00**	Yanmar	4T	190D	9F-2R	62.2	5290	No
2150	17942.00	**10230.00**	**11840.00**	**13260.00**	JD	3	179D	16F-8R	46.47	4950	No
2150 4WD	23132.00	**13190.00**	**15270.00**	**17100.00**	JD	3	179D	16F-8R	46.00	5670	No
2255	17866.00	**10180.00**	**11790.00**	**13210.00**	JD	3	179D	16F-8R	50.00	5150	No
2350	20754.00	**11830.00**	**13700.00**	**15340.00**	JD	4	239D	16F-8R	56.18	7120	No
2350 4WD	29236.00	**16670.00**	**19300.00**	**21620.00**	JD	4	239D	16F-8R	56.00	8250	No
2350 4WD w/Cab	31687.00	**18060.00**	**20910.00**	**23420.00**	JD	4	239D	16F-8R	56.00	8850	C,H,A
2350 w/Cab	26934.00	**15350.00**	**17780.00**	**19910.00**	JD	4	239D	16F-8R	56.18	7620	C,H,A
2550	23024.00	**13120.00**	**15200.00**	**17020.00**	JD	4	239D	16F-8R	65.94	7230	No
2550 4WD	27622.00	**15750.00**	**18230.00**	**20420.00**	JD	4	239D	16F-8R	65.00	8360	No
2550 4WD w/Cab	34826.00	**19850.00**	**22990.00**	**25750.00**	JD	4	239D	16F-8R	65.00	8950	C,H,A
2550 w/Cab	29204.00	**16650.00**	**19280.00**	**21590.00**	JD	4	239D	16F-8R	65.94	7730	C,H,A
2750	25620.00	**14600.00**	**16910.00**	**18940.00**	JD	4T	239D	16F-8R	75.35	7810	No
2750 4WD	31805.00	**18130.00**	**20990.00**	**23510.00**	JD	4T	239D	16F-8R	75.00	9020	No
2750 4WD w/Cab	32809.00	**18700.00**	**21650.00**	**24250.00**	JD	4T	239D	16F-8R	75.00	9520	C,H,A
2750 w/Cab	26644.00	**15190.00**	**17590.00**	**19700.00**	JD	4T	239D	16F-8R	75.35	8310	C,H,A
2950	28706.00	**16360.00**	**18950.00**	**21220.00**	JD	6	359D	16F-8R	85.37	10300	No
2950 4WD	34276.00	**19540.00**	**22620.00**	**25330.00**	JD	6	359D	16F-8R	85.00	10410	No
2950 4WD w/Cab	40456.00	**23060.00**	**26700.00**	**29900.00**	JD	6	359D	16F-8R	85.00	10910	C,H,A
2950 w/Cab	34886.00	**19890.00**	**23030.00**	**25790.00**	JD	6	359D	16F-8R	85.37	10800	C,H,A
4050 PS	43176.00	**21320.00**	**24600.00**	**26570.00**	JD	6	466D	15F-4R	100.95	11350	No
4050 PS 4WD	56792.00	**27560.00**	**31800.00**	**34340.00**	JD	6	466D	15F-4R	105.69	12250	No
4050 PS 4WD Cab	62935.00	**30160.00**	**34800.00**	**37580.00**	JD	6	466D	15F-4R	105.69	13389	C,H,A
4050 PS Cab	49319.00	**24440.00**	**28200.00**	**30460.00**	JD	6	466D	15F-4R	100.95	12489	C,H,A
4050 QR	38931.00	**18980.00**	**21900.00**	**23650.00**	JD	6	466D	16F-6R	101.09	11850	No
4050 QR Cab	45074.00	**22360.00**	**25800.00**	**27860.00**	JD	6	466D	16F-6R	101.09	12919	C,H,A
4250 PS	47586.00	**23090.00**	**26640.00**	**28770.00**	JD	6T	466D	15F-4R	123.32	12050	No
4250 PS 4WD	57454.00	**28080.00**	**32400.00**	**34990.00**	JD	6T	466D	15F-4R	123.00	13550	No
4250 PS 4WD Cab	63597.00	**29640.00**	**34200.00**	**36940.00**	JD	6T	466D	15F-4R	123.00	14685	C,H,A
4250 PS Cab	53729.00	**26520.00**	**30600.00**	**33050.00**	JD	6T	466D	15F-4R	123.32	13155	C,H,A
4250 QR	43341.00	**22000.00**	**25380.00**	**27410.00**	JD	6T	466D	16F-6R	123.06	12450	No
4250 QR Cab	49484.00	**24180.00**	**27900.00**	**30130.00**	JD	6T	466D	16F-6R	123.06	13585	C,H,A
4450 PS	51025.00	**25480.00**	**29400.00**	**31750.00**	JD	6T	466D	15F-4R	140.43	13050	No
4450 PS 4WD	65221.00	**30680.00**	**35400.00**	**38230.00**	JD	6T	466D	15F-4R	140.00	14150	No
4450 PS 4WD Cab	71364.00	**33280.00**	**38400.00**	**41470.00**	JD	6T	466D	15F-4R	140.00	15245	C,H,A
4450 PS Cab	57168.00	**28340.00**	**32700.00**	**35320.00**	JD	6T	466D	15F-4R	140.43	14145	C,H,A
4450 QR	46670.00	**23400.00**	**27000.00**	**29160.00**	JD	6T	466D	16F-6R	140.33	13475	No
4450 QR Cab	52813.00	**26310.00**	**30360.00**	**32790.00**	JD	6T	466D	16F-6R	140.33	14575	C,H,A
4650 PS	59118.00	**26930.00**	**32090.00**	**34660.00**	JD	6TI	466D	15F-4R	165.52	17600	No
4650 PS 4WD	74278.00	**33370.00**	**39760.00**	**42940.00**	JD	6TI	466D	15F-4R	165.00	18700	No
4650 PS 4WD Cab	80421.00	**35720.00**	**42560.00**	**45970.00**	JD	6TI	466D	15F-4R	165.00	19803	C,H,A
4650 PS Cab	65261.00	**29730.00**	**35430.00**	**38260.00**	JD	6TI	466D	15F-4R	165.52	18703	C,H,A
4650 QR	54763.00	**25240.00**	**30070.00**	**32480.00**	JD	6TI	466D	16F-6R	165.70	18000	No
4650 QR Cab	60906.00	**27260.00**	**32480.00**	**35080.00**	JD	6TI	466D	16F-6R	165.70	19133	C,H,A
4850 PS	69800.00	**31020.00**	**36960.00**	**39920.00**	JD	6TI	466D	15F-4R	192.99	18978	C,H,A
4850 PS 4WD Cab	79605.00	**34310.00**	**40880.00**	**44150.00**	JD	6TI	466D	15F-4R	192.00	20078	C,H,A
8450 4WD	74296.00	**27690.00**	**34080.00**	**36810.00**	JD	6TI	466D	16F-4R	186.98	22300	C,H,A
8450 4WD w/3 Pt.	81596.00	**30420.00**	**37440.00**	**40440.00**	JD	6TI	466D	16F-4R	186.98	22700	C,H,A
8650 4WD	93151.00	**24640.00**	**32560.00**	**36470.00**	JD	6TI	619D	16F-4R	238.56	24750	C,H,A
8650 4WD w/3 Pt.	100451.00	**26600.00**	**35150.00**	**39370.00**	JD	6TI	619D	16F-4R	238.56	25250	C,H,A
8850 4WD	118609.00	**28840.00**	**38110.00**	**42680.00**	JD	V8TI	955D	16F-4R	303.99	36074	C,H,A
8850 4WD w/3 Pt.	127859.00	**31920.00**	**42180.00**	**47240.00**	JD	V8TI	955D	16F-4R	303.99	36574	C,H,A

H, HC, HU--High Clearance LU--Low Profile PS--Power Shift QR--Quad Range

1985

Model	Approx. Retail Price New	Fair	Good	Premium	Make	No. Cyls.	Displ. Cu.-In.	No. Speeds	P.T.O. H.P.	Approx. Shipping Wt.-Lbs.	Cab
650	6315.00	**3860.00**	**4460.00**	**4950.00**	Yanmar	2	52D	8F-2R	14.5	1968	No
650 4WD	6910.00	**4180.00**	**4820.00**	**5350.00**	Yanmar	2	52D	8F-2R	14.5	1968	No
750	7070.00	**4100.00**	**4740.00**	**5260.00**	Yanmar	3	78D	8F-2R	18.5	2455	No
750 4WD	7820.00	**4540.00**	**5240.00**	**5820.00**	Yanmar	3	78D	8F-2R	18.0	2455	No
850	7870.00	**4570.00**	**5270.00**	**5850.00**	Yanmar	3	78D	8F-2R	22.3	3225	No
950	9245.00	**5360.00**	**6190.00**	**6870.00**	Yanmar	3	104D	8F-2R	27.3	3169	No
950 4WD	12310.00	**6560.00**	**7580.00**	**8410.00**	Yanmar	3	104D	8F-2R	27.3	3405	No
1050	10660.00	**6180.00**	**7140.00**	**7930.00**	Yanmar	3T	105D	8F-2R	33.4	3592	No
1050 4WD	12310.00	**6960.00**	**8040.00**	**8920.00**	Yanmar	3T	105D	8F-2R	33.4	3814	No

John Deere (Cont.)

Model	Approx. Retail Price New	Estimated Average Value Less Repairs Fair	Good	Premium	Engine Make	No. Cyls.	Displ. Cu.-In.	No. Speeds	P.T.O. H.P.	Approx. Shipping Wt.-Lbs.	Cab
1985 (Cont.)											
1250	14735.00	**7810.00**	**8990.00**	**9710.00**	Yanmar	3	143D	9F-2R	40.7	4125	No
1250 4WD	19235.00	**9010.00**	**10370.00**	**11200.00**	Yanmar	3	143D	9F-2R	40.7	4875	No
1450	16309.00	**7950.00**	**9150.00**	**9880.00**	Yanmar	4	190D	9F-2R	51.4	4410	No
1450 4WD	20609.00	**9540.00**	**10980.00**	**11860.00**	Yanmar	4	190D	9F-2R	51.4	5070	No
1650	18457.00	**9280.00**	**10680.00**	**11530.00**	Yanmar	4T	190D	9F-2R	62.2	4630	No
1650 4WD	22809.00	**10600.00**	**12200.00**	**13180.00**	Yanmar	4T	190D	9F-2R	62.2	5290	No
2150	17942.00	**10410.00**	**12020.00**	**13340.00**	JD	3	179D	16F-8R	46.47	4950	No
2150 4WD	23132.00	**13050.00**	**15080.00**	**16740.00**	JD	3	179D	16F-8R	46.00	5670	No
2255	17866.00	**10360.00**	**11970.00**	**13290.00**	JD	3	179D	16F-8R	50.00	5150	No
2350	20754.00	**12040.00**	**13910.00**	**15440.00**	JD	4	239D	16F-8R	56.18	7120	No
2350 4WD	29236.00	**16960.00**	**19590.00**	**21750.00**	JD	4	239D	16F-8R	56.00	8250	No
2350 4WD w/Cab	31687.00	**18380.00**	**21230.00**	**23570.00**	JD	4	239D	16F-8R	56.00	8850	C,H,A
2350 w/Cab	26934.00	**15620.00**	**18050.00**	**20040.00**	JD	4	239D	16F-8R	56.18	7620	C,H,A
2550	23024.00	**13350.00**	**15430.00**	**17130.00**	JD	4	239D	16F-8R	65.94	7230	No
2550 4WD	27622.00	**16020.00**	**18510.00**	**20550.00**	JD	4	239D	16F-8R	65.00	8360	No
2550 4WD w/Cab	34826.00	**20200.00**	**23330.00**	**25900.00**	JD	4	239D	16F-8R	65.00	8950	C,H,A
2550 w/Cab	29204.00	**16940.00**	**19570.00**	**21720.00**	JD	4	239D	16F-8R	65.94	7730	C,H,A
2750	25620.00	**14860.00**	**17170.00**	**19060.00**	JD	4T	239D	16F-8R	75.35	7810	No
2750 4WD	31805.00	**18450.00**	**21310.00**	**23650.00**	JD	4T	239D	16F-8R	75.00	9020	No
2750 4WD w/Cab	32809.00	**19030.00**	**21980.00**	**24400.00**	JD	4T	239D	12F-8R	75.00	9520	C,H,A
2750 w/Cab	26644.00	**15450.00**	**17850.00**	**19810.00**	JD	4T	239D	16F-8R	75.35	8310	C,H,A
2750HC 4WD	32400.00	**18790.00**	**21710.00**	**24100.00**	JD	4T	239D	12F-8R	75.00	10000	No
2950	28706.00	**16650.00**	**19230.00**	**21350.00**	JD	6	359D	16F-8R	85.37	10300	No
2950 4WD	34276.00	**19880.00**	**22970.00**	**25500.00**	JD	6	359D	16F-8R	85.00	10410	No
2950 4WD w/Cab	40456.00	**23460.00**	**27110.00**	**30090.00**	JD	6	359D	16F-8R	85.00	10910	C,H,A
2950 w/Cab	34886.00	**20230.00**	**23370.00**	**25940.00**	JD	6	359D	16F-8R	85.37	10800	C,H,A
4050 PS	43176.00	**21730.00**	**25010.00**	**27010.00**	JD	6	466D	15F-4R	100.95	11350	No
4050 PS	49319.00	**24650.00**	**28370.00**	**30640.00**	JD	6	466D	15F-4R	100.95	12489	C,H,A
4050 PS 4WD	56792.00	**28090.00**	**32330.00**	**34920.00**	JD	6	466D	15F-4R	105.69	12250	No
4050 PS 4WD	62935.00	**30210.00**	**34770.00**	**37550.00**	JD	6	466D	15F-4R	105.69	13389	C,H,A
4050 QR	38931.00	**19400.00**	**22330.00**	**24120.00**	JD	6	466D	16F-6R	101.09	11850	No
4050 QR	45074.00	**22370.00**	**25740.00**	**27800.00**	JD	6	466D	16F-6R	101.09	12919	C,H,A
4250 PS	47586.00	**22950.00**	**26410.00**	**28520.00**	JD	6T	466D	15F-4R	123.32	12050	No
4250 PS	53729.00	**26240.00**	**30200.00**	**32620.00**	JD	6T	466D	15F-4R	123.32	13155	C,H,A
4250 PS 4WD	57454.00	**28620.00**	**32940.00**	**35580.00**	JD	6T	466D	15F-4R	123.00	13550	No
4250 PS 4WD	63597.00	**31270.00**	**35990.00**	**38870.00**	JD	6T	466D	15F-4R	123.00	14685	C,H,A
4250 QR	43341.00	**21840.00**	**25130.00**	**27140.00**	JD	6T	466D	16F-6R	123.06	12450	No
4250 QR	49484.00	**24910.00**	**28670.00**	**30960.00**	JD	6T	466D	16F-6R	123.06	13585	C,H,A
4450 PS	51025.00	**25970.00**	**29890.00**	**32280.00**	JD	6T	466D	15F-4R	140.43	13050	No
4450 PS	57168.00	**28620.00**	**32940.00**	**35580.00**	JD	6T	466D	15F-4R	140.43	14145	C,H,A
4450 QR	52895.00	**26770.00**	**30810.00**	**33280.00**	JD	6T	466D	16F-6R	140.33	13475	C,H,A
4650 PS	65496.00	**30720.00**	**36480.00**	**39400.00**	JD	6TI	466D	15F-4R	165.52	18703	C,H,A
4650 PS 4WD	80676.00	**36000.00**	**42750.00**	**46170.00**	JD	6TI	466D	15F-4R	165.00	19803	C,H,A
4650 QR	61146.00	**28800.00**	**34200.00**	**36940.00**	JD	6TI	466D	16F-6R	165.70	19133	C,H,A
4850 PS	70840.00	**31680.00**	**37620.00**	**40630.00**	JD	6TI	466D	15F-4R	192.99	18978	C,H,A
4850 PS 4WD	80293.00	**35040.00**	**41610.00**	**44940.00**	JD	6TI	466D	15F-4R	192.00	20078	C,H,A
8450 4WD	74296.00	**28400.00**	**34790.00**	**37230.00**	JD	6TI	466D	16F-4R	186.98	22300	C,H,A
8450 4WD w/3 Pt.	81596.00	**31200.00**	**38220.00**	**40900.00**	JD	6TI	466D	16F-4R	186.98	22700	C,H,A
8650 4WD	93151.00	**26130.00**	**33100.00**	**36740.00**	JD	6TI	619D	16F-4R	238.56	24750	C,H,A
8650 4WD w/3 Pt.	100451.00	**28500.00**	**36100.00**	**40070.00**	JD	6TI	619D	16F-4R	238.56	25250	C,H,A
8850 4WD	118609.00	**30900.00**	**39140.00**	**43450.00**	JD	V8TI	955D	16F-4R	303.99	36074	C,H,A
8850 4WD w/3 Pt.	127859.00	**34200.00**	**43320.00**	**48090.00**	JD	V8TI	955D	16F-4R	303.99	36574	C,H,A

H, HC, HU--High Clearance LU--Low Profile PS--Power Shift QR--Quad Range

Model	Approx. Retail Price New	Estimated Average Value Less Repairs Fair	Good	Premium	Engine Make	No. Cyls.	Displ. Cu.-In.	No. Speeds	P.T.O. H.P.	Approx. Shipping Wt.-Lbs.	Cab
1986											
650	6315.00	**4040.00**	**4660.00**	**5170.00**	Yanmar	2	52D	8F-2R	14.5	1968	No
650 4WD	6910.00	**4370.00**	**5030.00**	**5580.00**	Yanmar	2	52D	8F-2R	14.5	1968	No
655	7800.00	**4600.00**	**5300.00**	**5880.00**	Yanmar	3	40D	Variable	10.6	1757	No
655 4WD	8600.00	**5070.00**	**5850.00**	**6490.00**	Yanmar	3	40D	Variable	10.6	1700	No
750	7070.00	**4170.00**	**4810.00**	**5340.00**	Yanmar	3	78D	8F-2R	18.5	2455	No
750 4WD	7820.00	**4610.00**	**5320.00**	**5910.00**	Yanmar	3	78D	8F-2R	18.0	2455	No
755	8800.00	**5190.00**	**5980.00**	**6640.00**	Yanmar	3	54D	Variable	20.0	1817	No
755 4WD	9700.00	**5720.00**	**6600.00**	**7330.00**	Yanmar	3	54D	Variable	20.0	1921	No
850	7870.00	**4640.00**	**5350.00**	**5940.00**	Yanmar	3	78D	8F-2R	22.3	3225	No
855	9800.00	**5780.00**	**6660.00**	**7390.00**	Yanmar	3	61D	Variable	19.0	1876	No
950	9245.00	**5460.00**	**6290.00**	**6980.00**	Yanmar	3	104D	8F-2R	27.3	3169	No
950 4WD	12310.00	**7260.00**	**8370.00**	**9290.00**	Yanmar	3	104D	8F-2R	27.3	3405	No
1050	10660.00	**6290.00**	**7250.00**	**8050.00**	Yanmar	3T	105D	8F-2R	33.4	3592	No
1050 4WD	12310.00	**7260.00**	**8370.00**	**9290.00**	Yanmar	3T	105D	8F-2R	33.4	3814	No
1250	14220.00	**7680.00**	**8820.00**	**9530.00**	Yanmar	3	143D	9F-2R	40.7	4125	No
1250 4WD	18720.00	**10110.00**	**11610.00**	**12540.00**	Yanmar	3	143D	9F-2R	40.7	4875	No
1450	16234.00	**8770.00**	**10070.00**	**10880.00**	Yanmar	4	190D	9F-2R	51.4	4410	No
1450 4WD	20534.00	**11090.00**	**12730.00**	**13750.00**	Yanmar	4	190D	9F-2R	51.4	5070	No
1650	18382.00	**9930.00**	**11400.00**	**12310.00**	Yanmar	4T	190D	9F-2R	62.2	4630	No
1650 4WD	22734.00	**12280.00**	**14100.00**	**15230.00**	Yanmar	4T	190D	9F-2R	62.2	5290	No
2150	18135.00	**10700.00**	**12330.00**	**13690.00**	JD	3	179D	16F-8R	46.47	4950	No
2150 4WD	22000.00	**12980.00**	**14960.00**	**16610.00**	JD	3	179D	8F-4R	46.00	5650	No
2150 4WD	22935.00	**13530.00**	**15600.00**	**17320.00**	JD	3	179D	16F-8R	46.00	5670	No
2255	17866.00	**10540.00**	**12150.00**	**13490.00**	JD	3	179D	16F-8R	50.00	5150	No
2350	20565.00	**12130.00**	**13980.00**	**15520.00**	JD	4	239D	16F-8R	56.18	7120	No
2350 4WD	25320.00	**14940.00**	**17220.00**	**19110.00**	JD	4	239D	16F-8R	56.00	8250	No
2350 4WD w/Cab	32002.00	**18880.00**	**21760.00**	**24150.00**	JD	4	239D	16F-8R	56.00	8850	C,H,A
2350 w/Cab	27249.00	**16080.00**	**18530.00**	**20570.00**	JD	4	239D	16F-8R	56.18	7620	C,H,A
2550	22840.00	**13480.00**	**15530.00**	**17240.00**	JD	4	239D	16F-8R	65.94	7230	No

John Deere (Cont.)

1986 (Cont.)

Model	Approx. Retail Price New	Estimated Average Value Less Repairs Fair	Good	Premium	Engine Make	No. Cyls.	Displ. Cu.-In.	No. Speeds	P.T.O. H.P.	Approx. Shipping Wt.-Lbs.	Cab
2550 4WD	27435.00	16190.00	18660.00	20710.00	JD	4	239D	16F-8R	65.00	8360	No
2550 4WD w/Cab	34826.00	20550.00	23680.00	26290.00	JD	4	239D	16F-8R	65.00	8950	C,H,A
2550 w/Cab	29519.00	17420.00	20070.00	22280.00	JD	4	239D	16F-8R	65.94	7730	C,H,A
2750	25433.00	15010.00	17290.00	19190.00	JD	4T	239D	16F-8R	75.35	7810	No
2750 4WD	31598.00	18640.00	21490.00	23850.00	JD	4T	239D	16F-8R	75.00	9020	No
2750 4WD w/Cab	38280.00	22590.00	26030.00	28890.00	JD	4T	239D	12F-8R	75.00	9520	C,H,A
2750 w/Cab	32115.00	18950.00	21840.00	24240.00	JD	4T	239D	16F-8R	75.35	8310	C,H,A
2750HC 4WD	32400.00	19120.00	22030.00	24450.00	JD	4T	239D	12F-8R	75.00	10000	No
2950	28519.00	16830.00	19390.00	21520.00	JD	6	359D	16F-8R	85.37	10300	No
2950 4WD	34089.00	20110.00	23180.00	25730.00	JD	6	359D	16F-8R	85.00	10410	No
2950 4WD w/Cab	40269.00	23760.00	27380.00	30390.00	JD	6	359D	16F-8R	85.00	10910	C,H,A
2950 w/Cab	34699.00	20470.00	23600.00	26200.00	JD	6	359D	16F-8R	85.37	10800	C,H,A
3150 4WD	37300.00	22010.00	25360.00	28150.00	JD	6	359D	16F-8R	96.06	11039	No
3150 4WD	43000.00	25370.00	29240.00	32460.00	JD	6	359D	16F-8R	96.06	11382	C,H,A
4050 PS	42331.00	21600.00	24800.00	26780.00	JD	6	466D	15F-4R	100.95	11350	No
4050 PS	48916.00	24840.00	28520.00	30800.00	JD	6	466D	15F-4R	100.95	12489	C,H,A
4050 PS 4WD	50542.00	25380.00	29140.00	31470.00	JD	6	466D	15F-4R	105.69	12250	No
4050 PS 4WD	57126.00	29160.00	33480.00	36160.00	JD	6	466D	15F-4R	105.69	13389	C,H,A
4050 QR	38086.00	19980.00	22940.00	24780.00	JD	6	466D	16F-6R	101.50	11850	No
4050 QR	44670.00	22680.00	26040.00	28120.00	JD	6	466D	16F-6R	101.50	12919	C,H,A
4250 PS	46741.00	23220.00	26660.00	28790.00	JD	6T	466D	15F-4R	120.86	12050	No
4250 PS	53325.00	26460.00	30380.00	32810.00	JD	6T	466D	15F-4R	120.20	13155	C,H,A
4250 PS 4WD	55449.00	28080.00	32240.00	34820.00	JD	6T	466D	15F-4R	123.00	13550	No
4250 PS 4WD	62033.00	30780.00	35340.00	38170.00	JD	6T	466D	15F-4R	123.00	14685	C,H,A
4250 QR	42496.00	21870.00	25110.00	27120.00	JD	6T	466D	16F-6R	120.20	12450	No
4250 QR	49080.00	24840.00	28520.00	30800.00	JD	6T	466D	16F-6R	120.20	13585	C,H,A
4450 PS	50280.00	25380.00	29140.00	31470.00	JD	6T	466D	15F-4R	140.43	13050	No
4450 PS	56864.00	28620.00	32860.00	35490.00	JD	6T	466D	15F-4R	140.43	14145	C,H,A
4450 QR	52409.00	26680.00	30630.00	33080.00	JD	6T	466D	16F-6R	140.33	13475	C,H,A
4650 PS	65619.00	31120.00	36830.00	39780.00	JD	6T	466D	15F-5R	165.52	18703	C,H,A
4650 QR	61264.00	29400.00	34800.00	37580.00	JD	6T	466D	16F-6R	165.70	18803	C,H,A
4850	70800.00	32340.00	38280.00	41340.00	JD	6T	466D	15F-4R	192.99	18978	C,H,A
4850 4WD	80293.00	36260.00	42920.00	46350.00	JD	6T	466D	15F-4R	192.99	19500	C,H,A
8450 4WD	74296.00	29110.00	35500.00	37990.00	JD	6TI	466D	16F-4R	186.98	22300	C,H,A
8450 4WD w/3 Pt.	81596.00	31980.00	39000.00	41730.00	JD	6TI	466D	16F-4R	186.98	22700	C,H,A
8650 4WD	93151.00	27520.00	33540.00	37230.00	JD	6TI	619D	16F-4R	238.56	24750	C,H,A
8650 4WD w/3 Pt.	100451.00	30400.00	37050.00	41130.00	JD	6TI	619D	16F-4R	238.56	25250	C,H,A
8850 4WD w/3 Pt.	127859.00	36480.00	44460.00	49350.00	JD	V8TI	955D	16F-4R	303.99	36574	C,H,A

H, HC, HU--High Clearance LU--Low Profile PS--Power Shift QR--Quad Range

1987

Model	Approx. Retail Price New	Fair	Good	Premium	Make	No. Cyls.	Displ. Cu.-In.	No. Speeds	P.T.O. H.P.	Approx. Shipping Wt.-Lbs.	Cab
650	7050.00	4350.00	5000.00	5550.00	Yanmar	2	52D	8F-2R	14.5	1968	No
650 4WD	7855.00	4710.00	5420.00	6020.00	Yanmar	2	52D	8F-2R	14.5	1968	No
655	8384.00	5030.00	5790.00	6430.00	Yanmar	3	40D	Variable	10.6	1757	No
655 4WD	9196.00	5520.00	6350.00	7050.00	Yanmar	3	40D	Variable	10.6	1700	No
750	7900.00	4740.00	5450.00	6050.00	Yanmar	3	78D	8F-2R	18.5	2455	No
750 4WD	8980.00	5390.00	6200.00	6880.00	Yanmar	3	78D	8F-2R	18.0	2455	No
755	9324.00	5590.00	6430.00	7140.00	Yanmar	3	54D	Variable	20.0	1817	No
755	9324.00	5590.00	6430.00	7140.00	Yanmar	3	54D	Variable	20.0	1817	No
755 4WD	10218.00	6130.00	7050.00	7830.00	Yanmar	3	54D	Variable	20.0	1921	No
850	8595.00	5160.00	5930.00	6580.00	Yanmar	3	78D	8F-2R	22.3	3225	No
850 4WD	10100.00	6060.00	6970.00	7740.00	Yanmar	3	78D	8F-2R	22.3	3232	No
855	10220.00	6130.00	7050.00	7830.00	Yanmar	3	61D	Variable	19.0	1876	No
950	10015.00	6010.00	6910.00	7670.00	Yanmar	3	104D	8F-2R	27.3	3169	No
950 4WD	12030.00	7220.00	8300.00	9210.00	Yanmar	3	104D	8F-2R	27.3	3405	No
1050	11670.00	7000.00	8050.00	8940.00	Yanmar	3T	105D	8F-2R	33.4	3592	No
1050 4WD	13550.00	8130.00	9350.00	10380.00	Yanmar	3T	105D	8F-2R	33.4	3814	No
1250	14220.00	7820.00	8960.00	9680.00	Yanmar	3	143D	9F-2R	40.7	4125	No
1250 4WD	18720.00	10300.00	11790.00	12730.00	Yanmar	3	143D	9F-2R	40.7	4875	No
1450	16234.00	8930.00	10230.00	11050.00	Yanmar	4	190D	9F-2R	51.4	4410	No
1450 4WD	20534.00	11290.00	12940.00	13980.00	Yanmar	4	190D	9F-2R	51.4	5070	No
1650	18382.00	10110.00	11580.00	12510.00	Yanmar	4T	190D	9F-2R	62.2	4630	No
1650 4WD	22734.00	12500.00	14320.00	15470.00	Yanmar	4T	190D	9F-2R	62.2	5290	No
2150	16731.00	10040.00	11540.00	12810.00	JD	3	179D	8F-4R	45.00	4970	No
2150 4WD	21912.00	13150.00	15120.00	16780.00	JD	3	179D	8F-4R	45.00	5670	No
2255	17142.00	10290.00	11830.00	13130.00	JD	3	179D	8F-4R	50.00	5115	No
2350	19543.00	11730.00	13490.00	14970.00	JD	4	239D	8F-4R	55.00	6490	No
2350 4WD	24296.00	14580.00	16760.00	18600.00	JD	4	239D	8F-4R	55.00	7620	No
2350 4WD w/Cab	30978.00	18590.00	21380.00	23730.00	JD	4	239D	8F-4R	55.00	8220	C,H,A
2350 w/Cab	26225.00	15740.00	18100.00	20090.00	JD	4	239D	8F-4R	55.00	7520	C,H,A
2550	21813.00	13090.00	15050.00	16710.00	JD	4	239D	8F-4R	65.00	7500	No
2550 4WD	26411.00	15850.00	18220.00	20220.00	JD	4	239D	8F-4R	65.00	8100	No
2550 4WD w/Cab	33985.00	20390.00	23450.00	26030.00	JD	4	239D	8F-4R	65.00	8230	C,H,A
2550 w/Cab	28495.00	17100.00	19660.00	21820.00	JD	4	239D	8F-4R	65.00	7630	C,H,A
2750	24410.00	14650.00	16840.00	18690.00	JD	4T	239D	8F-4R	75.00	7700	No
2750 4WD	30575.00	18350.00	21100.00	23420.00	JD	4T	239D	8F-4R	75.00	8910	No
2750 4WD w/Cab	37256.00	22350.00	25710.00	28540.00	JD	4T	239D	8F-4R	75.00	9410	C,H,A
2750 w/Cab	31091.00	18660.00	21450.00	23810.00	JD	4T	239D	8F-4R	75.00	8200	C,H,A
2750HC 4WD	32400.00	19440.00	22360.00	24820.00	JD	4T	239D	12F-8R	75.00	10000	No
2950	28519.00	17110.00	19680.00	21850.00	JD	6	359D	16F-8R	85.37	9100	No
2950 4WD	34089.00	20450.00	23520.00	26110.00	JD	6	359D	16F-8R	85.00	10410	No
2950 4WD w/Cab	40269.00	24160.00	27790.00	30850.00	JD	6	359D	16F-8R	85.00	10900	C,H,A
2950 w/Cab	34699.00	20820.00	23940.00	26570.00	JD	6	359D	16F-8R	85.37	10800	C,H,A
3150 4WD	37300.00	22380.00	25740.00	28570.00	JD	6	359D	16F-8R	96.06	11039	No

John Deere (Cont.)

1987 (Cont.)

Model	Approx. Retail Price New	Estimated Average Value Less Repairs Fair	Good	Premium	Engine Make	No. Cyls.	Displ. Cu.-In.	No. Speeds	P.T.O. H.P.	Approx. Shipping Wt.-Lbs.	Cab
3150 4WD	43000.00	25800.00	29670.00	32930.00	JD	6	359D	16F-8R	96.06	11382	C,H,A
4050 PS	42331.00	22170.00	25390.00	27420.00	JD	6T	359D	15F-4R	105.69	11350	No
4050 PS	48916.00	25300.00	28980.00	31300.00	JD	6T	359D	15F-4R	105.69	12489	C,H,A
4050 PS 4WD	50542.00	25850.00	29610.00	31980.00	JD	6T	359D	15F-4R	105.69	12250	No
4050 PS 4WD	57126.00	29700.00	34020.00	36740.00	JD	6T	359D	15F-4R	105.69	13389	C,H,A
4050 QR	38086.00	20350.00	23310.00	25180.00	JD	6T	359D	16F-6R	105.89	11850	No
4050 QR	44670.00	23380.00	26780.00	28920.00	JD	6T	359D	16F-6R	105.89	12919	C,H,A
4250 PS	46741.00	24200.00	27720.00	29940.00	JD	6T	466D	15F-4R	120.86	12050	No
4250 PS	53325.00	28050.00	32130.00	34700.00	JD	6T	466D	15F-4R	120.20	13155	C,H,A
4250 PS 4WD	55449.00	28600.00	32760.00	35380.00	JD	6T	466D	15F-4R	123.00	13550	No
4250 PS 4WD	62033.00	31080.00	35600.00	38450.00	JD	6T	466D	15F-4R	123.00	14685	C,H,A
4250 QR	42496.00	22110.00	25330.00	27360.00	JD	6T	466D	16F-6R	120.20	12450	No
4250 QR	49080.00	25580.00	29300.00	31640.00	JD	6T	466D	16F-6R	120.20	13585	C,H,A
4450 PS	50280.00	25850.00	29610.00	31980.00	JD	6T	466D	15F-4R	140.43	13050	No
4450 PS	56864.00	29430.00	33710.00	36410.00	JD	6T	466D	15F-4R	140.43	14145	C,H,A
4450 QR	52409.00	27720.00	31750.00	34290.00	JD	6T	466D	16F-6R	140.33	13475	C,H,A
4650 PS	65619.00	31200.00	36820.00	39770.00	JD	6T	466D	15F-5R	165.52	18703	C,H,A
4650 QR	61264.00	29150.00	34400.00	37150.00	JD	6T	466D	16F-6R	165.70	18803	C,H,A
4850	70800.00	34000.00	40120.00	43330.00	JD	6T	466D	15F-4R	192.99	18978	C,H,A
4850 4WD	80293.00	38000.00	44840.00	48430.00	JD	6T	466D	15F-4R	192.99	19500	C,H,A
8450 4WD	74296.00	30240.00	36720.00	39290.00	JD	6TI	466D	16F-4R	186.98	22300	C,H,A
8450 4WD w/3 Pt.	81596.00	32760.00	39780.00	42570.00	JD	6TI	466D	16F-4R	186.98	22700	C,H,A
8650 4WD	93151.00	30600.00	36000.00	39600.00	JD	6TI	619D	16F-4R	238.56	24750	C,H,A
8650 4WD w/3 Pt.	100451.00	32300.00	38000.00	41800.00	JD	6TI	619D	16F-4R	238.56	25250	C,H,A
8850 4WD	118609.00	35020.00	41200.00	45320.00	JD	V8TI	955D	16F-4R	303.99	36074	C,H,A
8850 4WD w/3 Pt.	127859.00	39100.00	46000.00	50600.00	JD	V8TI	955D	16F-4R	303.99	36574	C,H,A

H, HC, HU--High Clearance LU--Low Profile PS--Power Shift QR--Quad Range

1988

Model	Approx. Retail Price New	Fair	Good	Premium	Make	No. Cyls.	Displ. Cu.-In.	No. Speeds	P.T.O. H.P.	Approx. Shipping Wt.-Lbs.	Cab
650	7485.00	4690.00	5380.00	5970.00	Yanmar	2	52D	8F-2R	14.5	1968	No
650 4WD	8385.00	5120.00	5870.00	6520.00	Yanmar	2	52D	8F-2R	14.5	1968	No
655	8559.00	5220.00	5990.00	6650.00	Yanmar	3	40D	Variable	10.6	1757	No
655 4WD	9379.00	5720.00	6570.00	7290.00	Yanmar	3	40D	Variable	10.6	1700	No
750	8466.00	5160.00	5930.00	6580.00	Yanmar	3	78D	8F-2R	18.5	2455	No
750 4WD	9619.00	5870.00	6730.00	7470.00	Yanmar	3	78D	8F-2R	18.0	2455	No
755	9805.00	5980.00	6860.00	7620.00	Yanmar	3	54D	Variable	20.0	1817	No
755 4WD	10742.00	6550.00	7520.00	8350.00	Yanmar	3	54D	Variable	20.0	1921	No
850	9036.00	5510.00	6330.00	7030.00	Yanmar	3	78D	8F-2R	22.0	3225	No
850 4WD	10617.00	6480.00	7430.00	8250.00	Yanmar	3	78D	8F-2R	22.3	3232	No
855	10742.00	6550.00	7520.00	8350.00	Yanmar	3	61D	Variable	19.0	1876	No
900HC	10939.00	6130.00	7000.00	7490.00	Yanmar	3	78D	8F-2R	22.0	1876	No
950	10319.00	5780.00	6600.00	7060.00	Yanmar	3	104D	8F-2R	27.3	3169	No
950 4WD	12599.00	7060.00	8060.00	8620.00	Yanmar	3	104D	8F-2R	27.3	3405	No
1050	12266.00	6870.00	7850.00	8400.00	Yanmar	3T	105D	8F-2R	33.4	3592	No
1050 4WD	14250.00	7980.00	9120.00	9760.00	Yanmar	3T	105D	8F-2R	33.4	3814	No
1250	14220.00	7400.00	8460.00	9050.00	Yanmar	3	143D	9F-2R	40.7	4125	No
1250 4WD	18720.00	9360.00	10700.00	11450.00	Yanmar	3	143D	9F-2R	40.7	4875	No
1450	16234.00	8530.00	9750.00	10430.00	Yanmar	4	190D	9F-2R	51.4	4410	No
1450 4WD	20534.00	10380.00	11860.00	12690.00	Yanmar	4	190D	9F-2R	51.4	5070	No
1650	18382.00	9730.00	11120.00	11900.00	Yanmar	4T	190D	9F-2R	62.2	4630	No
1650 4WD	22734.00	11610.00	13270.00	14200.00	Yanmar	4T	190D	9F-2R	62.2	5290	No
2155	15939.00	9720.00	11160.00	12390.00	JD	3	179D	8F-4R	45.60	5269	No
2155 4WD	22340.00	13630.00	15640.00	17360.00	JD	3	179D	8F-4R	45.60	5986	No
2355	18312.00	11170.00	12820.00	14230.00	JD	4	239D	8F-4R	55.90	6261	No
2355 4WD	25370.00	15480.00	17760.00	19710.00	JD	4	239D	8F-4R		6878	No
2355 4WD w/Cab	32052.00	19550.00	22440.00	24910.00	JD	4	239D	8F-4R		7793	C,H,A
2355 w/Cab	27244.00	16620.00	19070.00	21170.00	JD	4	239D	8F-4R	55.90	7187	C,H,A
2355N	18825.00	11480.00	13180.00	14630.00	JD	3	179D	8F-4R	55.00		No
2355N 4WD	24783.00	15120.00	17350.00	19260.00	JD	3	179D	8F-4R	55.00		No
2555	21375.00	13040.00	14960.00	16610.00	JD	4	239D	8F-4R	66.00	6515	No
2555 4WD	27697.00	16900.00	19390.00	21520.00	JD	4	239D	8F-4R	65.00	7286	No
2555 4WD Cab	34379.00	20970.00	24070.00	26720.00	JD	4	239D	8F-4R	65.00	7959	C,H,A
2555 Cab	29726.00	18130.00	20810.00	23100.00	JD	4	239D	8F-4R	66.00	7441	C,H,A
2755	24170.00	14740.00	16920.00	18780.00	JD	4T	239D	8F-4R	75.00	6558	No
2755 4WD	32213.00	19650.00	22550.00	25030.00	JD	4T	239D	8F-4R	75.00	7374	No
2755 4WD Cab	38895.00	23730.00	27230.00	30230.00	JD	4T	239D	8F-4R	75.00	8433	C,H,A
2755 Cab	32675.00	19930.00	22870.00	25390.00	JD	4T	239D	8F-4R	75.00	7441	C,H,A
2755HC 4WD	33824.00	20630.00	23680.00	26290.00	JD	4T	239D	12F-8R	75.00	7750	No
2855N	24925.00	15200.00	17450.00	19370.00	JD	4T	239D	8F-4R	80.00		No
2855N 4WD	31527.00	19230.00	22070.00	24500.00	JD	4T	239D	8F-4R	80.00		No
2955	27602.00	16840.00	19320.00	21450.00	JD	6	359D	8F-4R	85.00	8444	No
2955 4WD	34357.00	20960.00	24050.00	26700.00	JD	6	359D	8F-4R	85.00	8973	No
2955 4WD Cab	42063.00	24400.00	28000.00	31080.00	JD	6	359D	8F-4R	85.00	9590	C,H,A
2955 Cab	36438.00	22230.00	25510.00	28320.00	JD	6	359D	8F-4R	85.00	9083	C,H,A
2955HC 4WD	35732.00	21800.00	25010.00	27760.00	JD	6	359D	12F-8R	85.00	9140	No
2955HC 4WD Cab	42433.00	25620.00	29400.00	32630.00	JD	6	359D	12F-8R	85.00	9835	C,H,A
3155 4WD	38329.00	21460.00	24530.00	26250.00	JD	6	359D	16F-8R	96.06	10207	No
3155 4WD Cab	44029.00	24660.00	28180.00	30150.00	JD	6	359D	16F-8R	96.06	10571	C,H,A
4050 PS	42331.00	23130.00	26430.00	28280.00	JD	6T	359D	15F-4R	105.69	11350	No
4050 PS 4WD	42331.00	23130.00	26430.00	28280.00	JD	6T	359D	15F-4R	105.69	11350	No
4050 PS 4WD Cab	45000.00	24640.00	28160.00	30130.00	JD	6T	359D	15F-4R	105.69	12489	C,H,A
4050 PS Cab	48916.00	26600.00	30400.00	32530.00	JD	6T	359D	15F-4R	105.69	12489	C,H,A
4050 QR	38086.00	20720.00	23680.00	25340.00	JD	6T	359D	16F-6R	105.89	10811	No
4050 QR 4WD	46297.00	24640.00	28160.00	30130.00	JD	6T	359D	15F-4R	105.00		No

John Deere (Cont.)

1988 (Cont.)

Model	Approx. Retail Price New	Fair	Good	Premium	Engine Make	No. Cyls.	Displ. Cu.-In.	No. Speeds	P.T.O. H.P.	Approx. Shipping Wt.-Lbs.	Cab
4050 QR 4WD Cab	52881.00	28000.00	32000.00	34240.00	JD	6T	359D	16F-6R	105.00		C,H,A
4050 QR Cab	44670.00	24080.00	27520.00	29450.00	JD	6T	359D	16F-6R	105.89		C,H,A
4250 PS	46741.00	24920.00	28480.00	30470.00	JD	6T	466D	15F-4R	120.86	12050	No
4250 PS 4WD	55449.00	29120.00	33280.00	35610.00	JD	6T	466D	15F-4R	123.00	13550	No
4250 PS 4WD Cab	62033.00	31360.00	35840.00	38350.00	JD	6T	466D	15F-4R	123.00	14685	C,H,A
4250 PS Cab	53321.00	28560.00	32640.00	34930.00	JD	6T	466D	15F-4R	120.86	13155	C,H,A
4250 QR	42496.00	22400.00	25600.00	27390.00	JD	6T	466D	16F-6R	120.21	11140	No
4250 QR 4WD	51204.00	27440.00	31360.00	33560.00	JD	6T	466D	16F-6R	120.86		No
4250 QR 4WD Cab	57788.00	30800.00	35200.00	37660.00	JD	6T	466D	16F-6R	120.86		C,H,A
4250 QR Cab	49080.00	26320.00	30080.00	32190.00	JD	6T	466D	16F-6R	120.21		C,H,A
4450 4WD	54616.00	29400.00	33600.00	35950.00	JD	6T	466D	15F-4R	140.00		No
4450 4WD Cab	61200.00	33150.00	37890.00	40540.00	JD	6T	466D	15F-4R	140.00		C,H,A
4450 PS	50280.00	26990.00	30850.00	33010.00	JD	6T	466D	15F-4R	140.43	13050	No
4450 PS	56864.00	31080.00	35520.00	38010.00	JD	6T	466D	15F-4R	140.43	14145	C,H,A
4450 QR	45825.00	24640.00	28160.00	30130.00	JD	6T	466D	16F-6R	140.33	11326	No
4450 QR w/Cab	52409.00	28000.00	32000.00	34240.00	JD	6T	466D	16F-6R	140.33		C,H,A
4650	54763.00	28730.00	32830.00	35130.00	JD	6T	466D	16F-6R	165.70	14310	No
4650 4WD	64256.00	34270.00	39170.00	41910.00	JD	6T	466D	16F-6R	165.70		No
4650 4WD Cab	70757.00	37520.00	42880.00	45880.00	JD	6T	466D	16F-6R	165.70		C,H,A
4650 Cab	61264.00	33150.00	37890.00	40540.00	JD	6T	466D	16F-6R	165.70		C,H,A
4650 PS	65619.00	32280.00	37980.00	40640.00	JD	6T	466D	15F-4R	165.52	18703	C,H,A
4850	70800.00	34680.00	40800.00	43660.00	JD	6TI	466D	15F-4R	192.99	15371	C,H,A
4850 4WD	80293.00	38250.00	45000.00	48150.00	JD	6TI	466D	15F-4R	190.00		C,H,A
8450 4WD	74296.00	30100.00	36400.00	38580.00	JD	6TI	466D	16F-6R	186.98	23522	C,H,A
8450 4WD 3 Pt	81596.00	33110.00	40040.00	42440.00	JD	6TI	466D	16F-6R	186.98	25003	C,H,A
8650 4WD	93151.00	32400.00	37800.00	41580.00	JD	6TI	619D	16F-6R	238.56	26425	C,H,A
8650 4WD 3Pt	100451.00	34200.00	39900.00	43890.00	JD	6TI	619D	16F-6R	238.56	27906	C,H,A
8850 4WD	118609.00	37080.00	43260.00	47590.00	JD	6TI	955D	16F-6R	303.99	32125	C,H,A
8850 4WD 3Pt	127859.00	41400.00	48300.00	53130.00	JD	8TI	955D	16F-6R	303.99	34250	C,H,A

H, HC, HU--High Clearance LU--Low Profile PS--Power Shift QR--Quad Range

1989

Model	Approx. Retail Price New	Fair	Good	Premium	Engine Make	No. Cyls.	Displ. Cu.-In.	No. Speeds	P.T.O. H.P.	Approx. Shipping Wt.-Lbs.	Cab
650	8408.00	5340.00	6110.00	6720.00	Yanmar	2	52D	8F-2R	14.5	1968	No
650 4WD	9334.00	5790.00	6630.00	7290.00	Yanmar	2	52D	8F-2R	14.5	1968	No
655	9344.00	5790.00	6630.00	7290.00	Yanmar	3	40D	Variable	10.6	1757	No
655 4WD	10260.00	6360.00	7290.00	8020.00	Yanmar	3	40D	Variable	10.6	1700	No
750	9424.00	5840.00	6690.00	7360.00	Yanmar	3	78D	8F-2R	18.5	2455	No
750 4WD	10605.00	6580.00	7530.00	8280.00	Yanmar	3	78D	8F-2R	18.0	2455	No
755	10811.00	6700.00	7680.00	8450.00	Yanmar	3	54D	Variable	20.0	1817	No
755 4WD	11856.00	7350.00	8420.00	9260.00	Yanmar	3	54D	Variable	20.0	1921	No
850	10157.00	5790.00	6600.00	7060.00	Yanmar	3	78D	8F-2R	22.3	3225	No
850 4WD	11820.00	6740.00	7680.00	8220.00	Yanmar	3	78D	8F-2R	22.3	3232	No
855	11840.00	6750.00	7700.00	8240.00	Yanmar	3	61D	Variable	19.0	1876	No
855 4WD	13026.00	7430.00	8470.00	9060.00	Yanmar	3	61D	Variable	19.0	1876	No
900HC	11943.00	6810.00	7760.00	8300.00	Yanmar	3	78D	8F-2R	22.0	1876	No
950	11598.00	6610.00	7540.00	8070.00	Yanmar	3	104D	8F-2R	27.3	3169	No
950 4WD	13995.00	7980.00	9100.00	9740.00	Yanmar	3	104D	8F-2R	27.3	3405	No
1050	13390.00	7630.00	8700.00	9310.00	Yanmar	3T	105D	8F-2R	33.4	3592	No
1050 4WD	15702.00	8950.00	10210.00	10930.00	Yanmar	3T	105D	8F-2R	33.4	3814	No
1250	14220.00	7540.00	8590.00	9190.00	Yanmar	3	143D	9F-2R	40.7	4125	No
1250 4WD	18720.00	9530.00	10870.00	11630.00	Yanmar	3	143D	9F-2R	40.7	4875	No
1450	16234.00	8680.00	9900.00	10590.00	Yanmar	4	190D	9F-2R	51.4	4410	No
1450 4WD	20534.00	10560.00	12050.00	12890.00	Yanmar	4	190D	9F-2R	51.4	5070	No
1650	18382.00	9910.00	11300.00	12090.00	Yanmar	4T	190D	9F-2R	62.2	4630	No
1650 4WD	22734.00	11820.00	13480.00	14420.00	Yanmar	4T	190D	9F-2R	62.2	5290	No
2155	16539.00	10250.00	11740.00	12910.00	JD	3	179D	8F-4R	45.60	5269	No
2155 4WD	22940.00	14220.00	16290.00	17920.00	JD	3	179D	8F-4R	45.60	5986	No
2355	19252.00	11940.00	13670.00	15040.00	JD	4	239D	8F-4R	55.90	6261	No
2355 4WD	25791.00	15990.00	18310.00	20140.00	JD	4	239D	8F-4R	55.90	6878	No
2355 4WD w/Cab	32361.00	20060.00	22980.00	25280.00	JD	4	239D	8F-4R	55.90	7793	C,H,A
2355 w/Cab	27553.00	17080.00	19560.00	21520.00	JD	4	239D	8F-4R	55.90	7187	C,H,A
2355N	19525.00	12110.00	13860.00	15250.00	JD	3T	179D	8F-4R	55.00		No
2355N 4WD	25783.00	15990.00	18310.00	20140.00	JD	3T	179D	8F-4R	55.00		No
2555	22415.00	13900.00	15920.00	17510.00	JD	4	239D	8F-4R	66.00	6515	No
2555 4WD	28518.00	17680.00	20250.00	22280.00	JD	4	239D	8F-4R	65.00	7286	No
2555 4WD w/Cab	35088.00	21760.00	24910.00	27400.00	JD	4	239D	8F-4R	65.00	7959	C,H,A
2555 w/Cab	30135.00	18680.00	21400.00	23540.00	JD	4	239D	8F-4R	66.00	7441	C,H,A
2755	25217.00	15640.00	17900.00	19690.00	JD	4T	239D	8F-4R	75.00	6558	No
2755 4WD	32916.00	20410.00	23370.00	25710.00	JD	4T	239D	8F-4R	75.00	7374	No
2755 4WD w/Cab	39486.00	24480.00	28040.00	30840.00	JD	4T	239D	8F-4R	75.00	8433	C,H,A
2755 w/Cab	33266.00	20630.00	23620.00	25980.00	JD	4T	239D	8F-4R	75.00	7441	C,H,A
2755HC 4WD	34936.00	21660.00	24810.00	27290.00	JD	4T	239D	12F-8R	75.00	7750	No
2855N	25907.00	16060.00	18390.00	20230.00	JD	4T	239D	8F-4R	80.00		No
2855N 4WD	32509.00	20160.00	23080.00	25390.00	JD	4T	239D	8F-4R	80.00		No
2955	29530.00	18310.00	20970.00	23070.00	JD	6	359D	8F-4R	85.00	8444	No
2955 4WD	35941.00	21700.00	24850.00	27340.00	JD	6	359D	8F-4R	85.00	8973	No
2955 4WD w/Cab	43145.00	26040.00	29820.00	32800.00	JD	6	359D	8F-4R	85.00	9590	C,H,A
2955 w/Cab	37520.00	23260.00	26640.00	29300.00	JD	6	359D	8F-4R	85.00	9083	C,H,A
2955HC 4WD	37335.00	22940.00	26270.00	28900.00	JD	6	359D	12F-8R	85.00	9140	No
2955HC 4WD w/Cab	43515.00	26040.00	29820.00	32800.00	JD	6	359D	12F-8R	85.00	9835	C,H,A
3155 4WD	39511.00	22520.00	25680.00	27480.00	JD	6	359D	16F-8R	96.06	10207	No
3155 4WD w/Cab	45211.00	25770.00	29390.00	31450.00	JD	6	359D	16F-8R	96.06	10571	C,H,A
4055 PS	44511.00	25370.00	28930.00	30960.00	JD	6T	466D	15F-4R	105.00		No
4055 PS	51291.00	29240.00	33340.00	35670.00	JD	6T	466D	15F-4R	105.00		C,H,A

John Deere (Cont.)

1989 (Cont.)

Model	Approx. Retail Price New	Fair	Good	Premium	Make	No. Cyls.	Displ. Cu.-In.	No. Speeds	P.T.O. H.P.	Approx. Shipping Wt.-Lbs.	Cab
		Estimated Average Value Less Repairs			Engine						
4055 PS 4WD	52722.00	30050.00	34270.00	36670.00	JD	6T	466D	15F-4R	105.00	11350	No
4055 PS 4WD w/Cab	59502.00	32490.00	37050.00	39640.00	JD	6T	466D	15F-4R	105.00	12489	C,H,A
4055 QR	40266.00	22950.00	26170.00	28000.00	JD	6T	466D	16F-6R	105.00		No
4055 QR 4WD	48477.00	27630.00	31510.00	33720.00	JD	6T	466D	16F-6R	105.00		No
4055 QR 4WD w/Cab	55257.00	30780.00	35100.00	37560.00	JD	6T	466D	16F-6R	105.00		C,H,A
4055 QR w/Cab	47046.00	26820.00	30580.00	32720.00	JD	6T	466D	16F-6R	105.00		C,H,A
4255 PS	48796.00	27810.00	31720.00	33940.00	JD	6T	466D	15F-4R	120.00	12050	No
4255 PS 4WD	57504.00	31920.00	36400.00	38950.00	JD	6T	466D	15F-4R	120.00	13550	No
4255 PS 4WD w/Cab	64384.00	34770.00	39650.00	42430.00	JD	6T	466D	15F-4R	120.00	14685	C,H,A
4255 PS w/Cab	55676.00	31350.00	35750.00	38250.00	JD	6T	466D	15F-4R	120.00	13155	C,H,A
4255 QR	45551.00	25960.00	29610.00	31680.00	JD	6T	466D	16F-6R	120.00	11140	No
4255 QR 4WD	53259.00	30360.00	34620.00	37040.00	JD	6T	466D	16F-6R	120.00		No
4255 QR 4WD w/Cab	60139.00	33630.00	38350.00	41040.00	JD	6T	466D	16F-6R	120.00		C,H,A
4255 QR w/Cab	51431.00	29320.00	33430.00	35770.00	JD	6T	466D	16F-6R	120.00		C,H,A
4455 4WD w/Cab	63701.00	35340.00	40300.00	43120.00	JD	6T	466D	16F-4R	140.00		C,H,A
4455 PS	52385.00	29860.00	34050.00	36430.00	JD	6T	466D	15F-4R	140.00	13050	No
4455 PS w/Cab	59265.00	33060.00	37700.00	40340.00	JD	6T	466D	15F-4R	140.00	14145	C,H,A
4455 QR	48030.00	27380.00	31220.00	33410.00	JD	6T	466D	16F-6R	140.00	11326	No
4455 QR 4WD	56821.00	31350.00	35750.00	38250.00	JD	6T	466D	16F-4R	140.00		No
4455 QR w/Cab	54910.00	30780.00	35100.00	37560.00	JD	6T	466D	16F-6R	140.00		C,H,A
4555 PS 4WD	65772.00	35060.00	39980.00	42780.00	JD	6T	466D	15F-4R	155.00		No
4555 PS 4WD w/Cab	72652.00	37620.00	42900.00	45900.00	JD	6T	466D	15F-4R	155.00		C,H,A
4555 PS w/Cab	63159.00	35630.00	40630.00	43470.00	JD	6T	466D	15F-4R	155.00		C,H,A
4555 QR	51924.00	29600.00	33750.00	36110.00	JD	6T	466D	16F-6R	155.00	14310	No
4555 QR w/Cab	58804.00	32490.00	37050.00	39640.00	JD	6T	466D	16F-6R	155.00	18703	C,H,A
4755 PS	71228.00	36400.00	42700.00	45690.00	JD	6TA	466D	15F-4R	175.00		C,H,A
4755 PS 4WD	80721.00	40040.00	46970.00	50260.00	JD	6TA	466D	15F-4R	175.00		C,H,A
4755 QR	66873.00	33280.00	39040.00	41770.00	JD	6TA	466D	16F-6R	175.00		C,H,A
4955 PS	76770.00	37440.00	43920.00	46990.00	JD	6TA	466D	15F-4R	200.00		C,H,A
4955 PS 4WD	86263.00	41080.00	48190.00	51560.00	JD	6TA	466D	15F-4R	200.00		C,H,A
8560 4WD, PTO, 3Pt	94500.00	47060.00	55210.00	59080.00	JD	6TA	466D	12F-3R	256.00		C,H,A
8560 PS 4WD, PTO, 3Pt	99500.00	49920.00	58560.00	62660.00	JD	6TA	466D	24F-6R	256.00		C,H,A
8560 PS 4WD, PTO, 3Pt	109500.00	54600.00	64050.00	68530.00	JD	6TA	466D	12F-2R	256.00		C,H,A
8960 4WD, PTO, 3Pt	125476.00	60010.00	70390.00	75320.00	JD	6TA	855D	12F-3R	322.00		C,H,A
8960 PS 4WD	127676.00	61150.00	71740.00	76760.00	JD	6TA	855D	12F-2R	322.00		C,H,A
8960 PS 4WD, PTO, 3Pt	140476.00	66040.00	77470.00	82890.00	JD	6TA	855D	12F-2R	322.00		C,H,A

H, HC, HU--High Clearance LU--Low Profile PS--Power Shift QR--Quad Range

1990

Model	Approx. Retail Price New	Fair	Good	Premium	Make	No. Cyls.	Displ. Cu.-In.	No. Speeds	P.T.O. H.P.	Approx. Shipping Wt.-Lbs.	Cab
655	9624.00	6060.00	6930.00	7550.00	Yanmar	3	40D	Variable	10.6	1757	No
655 4WD	10568.00	6660.00	7610.00	8300.00	Yanmar	3	40D	Variable	10.6	1700	No
670	9620.00	6060.00	6930.00	7550.00	Yanmar	3	54D	8F-2R	16.0	1980	No
670 4WD	10681.00	6730.00	7690.00	8380.00	Yanmar	3	54D	8F-2R	16.0	2120	No
755	11470.00	7230.00	8260.00	9000.00	Yanmar	3	54D	Variable	20.0	1817	No
755 4WD	12578.00	7920.00	9060.00	9880.00	Yanmar	3	54D	Variable	20.0	1921	No
770	10388.00	6540.00	7480.00	8150.00	Yanmar	3	83D	8F-2R	20.0	2180	No
770 4WD	11608.00	7310.00	8360.00	9110.00	Yanmar	3	83D	8F-2R	24.0	2355	No
855	12561.00	7910.00	9040.00	9850.00	Yanmar	3	61D	Variable	19.0	1876	No
855 4WD	13820.00	8710.00	9950.00	10850.00	Yanmar	3	61D	Variable	19.0	1876	No
870	11412.00	6620.00	7530.00	8060.00	Yanmar	3	87D	9F-3R	25.0	1876	No
870 4WD	13143.00	7620.00	8670.00	9280.00	Yanmar	3	87D	9F-3R	25.0	1876	No
900HC	12301.00	7140.00	8120.00	8690.00	Yanmar	3	78D	8F-2R	22.0	1876	No
955 4WD	15442.00	8960.00	10190.00	10900.00	Yanmar	3	87D	Variable	27.3	1876	No
970	13205.00	7660.00	8720.00	9330.00	Yanmar	3	111D	9F-3R	30.0	1876	No
970 4WD	15543.00	9020.00	10260.00	10980.00	Yanmar	3	111D	9F-3R	30.0	1876	No
1070	15321.00	8890.00	10110.00	10820.00	Yanmar	3	116D	9F-3R	35.0	1876	No
1070 4WD	17867.00	10360.00	11790.00	12620.00	Yanmar	3	116D	9F-3R	35.0	1876	No
2155	17177.00	10820.00	12370.00	13480.00	JD	3	179D	8F-4R	45.60	5269	No
2155 4WD	23834.00	15020.00	17160.00	18700.00	JD	3	179D	8F-4R	45.60	5986	No
2355	19994.00	12600.00	14400.00	15700.00	JD	4	239D	8F-4R	55.90	6261	No
2355 4WD	26795.00	16880.00	19290.00	21030.00	JD	4	239D	8F-4R	55.90	6878	No
2355 4WD w/Cab	33627.00	21190.00	24210.00	26390.00	JD	4	239D	8F-4R	55.90	7793	C,H,A
2355 w/Cab	28627.00	18040.00	20610.00	22470.00	JD	4	239D	8F-4R	55.90	7187	C,H,A
2355N	20278.00	12780.00	14600.00	15910.00	JD	3T	179D	8F-4R	55.00		No
2355N 4WD	26786.00	16880.00	19290.00	21030.00	JD	3T	179D	8F-4R	55.00		No
2555	23280.00	14670.00	16760.00	18270.00	JD	4	239D	8F-4R	66.00	6515	No
2555 4WD	29627.00	18670.00	21330.00	23250.00	JD	4	239D	8F-4R	65.00	7286	No
2555 4WD w/Cab	36460.00	22970.00	26250.00	28610.00	JD	4	239D	8F-4R	65.00	7959	C,H,A
2555 w/Cab	31308.00	19720.00	22540.00	24570.00	JD	4	239D	8F-4R	66.00	7441	C,H,A
2755	26190.00	16500.00	18860.00	20560.00	JD	4T	239D	8F-4R	75.00	6558	No
2755 4WD	34197.00	21540.00	24620.00	26840.00	JD	4T	239D	8F-4R	75.00	7374	No
2755 4WD w/Cab	41029.00	25850.00	29540.00	32200.00	JD	4T	239D	8F-4R	75.00	8433	C,H,A
2755 HC 4WD	36297.00	22870.00	26130.00	28480.00	JD	4T	239D	12F-8R	75.00	7750	No
2755 w/Cab	34561.00	21770.00	24880.00	27120.00	JD	4T	239D	8F-4R	75.00	7441	C,H,A
2855N	26907.00	16950.00	19370.00	21110.00	JD	4T	239D	8F-4R	80.00		No
2855N 4WD	33773.00	21280.00	24320.00	26510.00	JD	4T	239D	8F-4R	80.00		No
2955	30671.00	19320.00	22080.00	24070.00	JD	6	359D	8F-4R	85.00	8444	No
2955 4WD	37339.00	23520.00	26880.00	29300.00	JD	6	359D	8F-4R	85.00	8973	No
2955 4WD w/Cab	44831.00	27720.00	31680.00	34530.00	JD	6	359D	8F-4R	85.00	9590	C,H,A
2955 HC 4WD	38788.00	24440.00	27930.00	30440.00	JD	6	359D	12F-8R	85.00	9140	No
2955 HC 4WD w/Cab	45216.00	27720.00	31680.00	34530.00	JD	6	359D	12F-8R	85.00	9835	C,H,A
2955 w/Cab	38981.00	23940.00	27360.00	29820.00	JD	6	359D	8F-4R	85.00	9083	C,H,A
3155 4WD	41047.00	23810.00	27090.00	28990.00	JD	6	359D	16F-8R	96.06	10207	No
3155 4WD w/Cab	46975.00	27250.00	31000.00	33170.00	JD	6	359D	16F-8R	96.06	10571	C,H,A

John Deere (Cont.)

1990 (Cont.)

Model	Approx. Retail Price New	Estimated Average Value Less Repairs Fair	Good	Premium	Engine Make	No. Cyls.	Displ. Cu.-In.	No. Speeds	P.T.O. H.P.	Approx. Shipping Wt.-Lbs.	Cab
4055 PS	46188.00	26790.00	30480.00	32610.00	JD	6T	466D	15F-4R	109.18		No
4055 PS 4WD	54727.00	30160.00	34320.00	36720.00	JD	6T	466D	15F-4R	109.18	11350	No
4055 PS 4WD w/Cab	61882.00	33060.00	37620.00	40250.00	JD	6T	466D	15F-4R	109.18	12489	C,H,A
4055 PS w/Cab	53343.00	29580.00	33660.00	36020.00	JD	6T	466D	15F-4R	109.18	13955	C,H,A
4055 QR	41773.00	24230.00	27570.00	29500.00	JD	6T	466D	16F-6R	108.70		No
4055 QR 4WD	50312.00	29180.00	33210.00	35540.00	JD	6T	466D	16F-6R	105.00		No
4055 QR 4WD w/Cab	57467.00	31900.00	36300.00	38840.00	JD	6T	466D	16F-6R	105.00		C,H,A
4055 QR w/Cab	48928.00	28380.00	32290.00	34550.00	JD	6T	466D	16F-6R	108.70	12130	C,H,A
4255 PS	50748.00	29430.00	33490.00	35830.00	JD	6T	466D	15F-4R	120.00	12050	No
4255 PS 4WD	59804.00	32480.00	36960.00	39550.00	JD	6T	466D	15F-4R	123.36	13550	No
4255 PS 4WD w/Cab	66959.00	35380.00	40260.00	43080.00	JD	6T	466D	15F-4R	123.36	14685	C,H,A
4255 PS w/Cab	57903.00	33000.00	37550.00	40180.00	JD	6T	466D	15F-4R	120.00	13155	C,H,A
4255 QR	46333.00	26270.00	29900.00	31990.00	JD	6T	466D	16F-6R	123.69	11140	No
4255 QR 4WD	55389.00	31490.00	35840.00	38350.00	JD	6T	466D	16F-6R	120.00		No
4255 QR 4WD w/Cab	62544.00	35380.00	40260.00	43080.00	JD	6T	466D	16F-6R	120.00		C,H,A
4255 QR w/Cab	53488.00	30740.00	34980.00	37430.00	JD	6T	466D	16F-6R	123.69		C,H,A
4455 PS	54481.00	31600.00	35960.00	38480.00	JD	6T	466D	15F-4R	140.00	13050	No
4455 PS w/Cab	61636.00	34800.00	39600.00	42370.00	JD	6T	466D	15F-4R	140.00	14145	C,H,A
4455 QR	49951.00	28300.00	32210.00	34470.00	JD	6T	466D	16F-6R	142.69	11326	No
4455 QR 4WD	59095.00	33640.00	38280.00	40960.00	JD	6T	466D	16F-4R	140.00		No
4455 QR 4WD w/Cab	66249.00	37700.00	42900.00	45900.00	JD	6T	466D	16F-4R	140.00		C,H,A
4455 QR w/Cab	57106.00	32480.00	36960.00	39550.00	JD	6T	466D	16F-6R	142.69		C,H,A
4555 PS 4WD	68698.00	38280.00	43560.00	46610.00	JD	6T	466D	15F-4R	155.00		No
4555 PS 4WD w/Cab	75853.00	41180.00	46860.00	50140.00	JD	6T	466D	15F-4R	155.00		C,H,A
4555 PS w/Cab	65980.00	37350.00	42500.00	45480.00	JD	6T	466D	15F-4R	155.00		C,H,A
4555 QR	54295.00	30740.00	34980.00	37430.00	JD	6T	466D	16F-6R	156.83	14310	No
4555 QR w/Cab	61450.00	34800.00	39600.00	42370.00	JD	6T	466D	16F-6R	156.83	18703	C,H,A
4755 PS	74412.00	38160.00	44640.00	47770.00	JD	6TA	466D	15F-4R	177.06		C,H,A
4755 PS 4WD	84285.00	42400.00	49600.00	53070.00	JD	6TA	466D	15F-4R	177.06		C,H,A
4755 QR	69882.00	36040.00	42160.00	45110.00	JD	6TA	466D	16F-6R	177.11		C,H,A
4955 PS	80225.00	40810.00	47740.00	51080.00	JD	6TA	466D	15F-4R	202.73		C,H,A
4955 PS 4WD	90098.00	45050.00	52700.00	56390.00	JD	6TA	466D	15F-4R	202.73		C,H,A
8560 4WD	82425.00	42400.00	49600.00	53070.00	JD	6TA	466D	12F-3R	198.00		C,H,A
8560 4WD	87675.00	45580.00	53320.00	57050.00	JD	6TA	466D	24F-6R	202.65		C,H,A
8560 4WD w/PTO, 3 Pt.	95340.00	47860.00	55990.00	59910.00	JD	6TA	466D	12F-3R	256.00		C,H,A
8760	99225.00	50350.00	58900.00	63020.00	JD	6TA	619D	12F-3R	260.94		C,H,A
8760 PS	114975.00	57240.00	66960.00	71650.00	JD	6TA	619D	12F-2R	260.94		C,H,A
8960 4WD	118310.00	59890.00	70060.00	74960.00	JD	6TA	855D	12F-3R	322.00		C,H,A
8960 4WD	123560.00	63070.00	73780.00	78950.00	JD	6TA	855D	24F-6R	333.40		C,H,A
8960 4WD PS	134060.00	67310.00	78740.00	84250.00	JD	6TA	855D	12F-2R	332.25		C,H,A

H, HC, HU--High Clearance PS--Power Shift QR--Quad Range

1991

Model	Approx. Retail Price New	Fair	Good	Premium	Engine Make	No. Cyls.	Displ. Cu.-In.	No. Speeds	P.T.O. H.P.	Approx. Shipping Wt.-Lbs.	Cab
670	9860.00	6310.00	7200.00	7780.00	Yanmar	3	54D	8F-2R	16.0	1980	No
670 4WD	10948.00	7010.00	7990.00	8630.00	Yanmar	3	54D	8F-2R	16.0	2120	No
755	11757.00	7520.00	8580.00	9270.00	Yanmar	3	54D	Variable	20.0	1817	No
755 4WD	12893.00	8250.00	9410.00	10160.00	Yanmar	3	54D	Variable	20.0	1921	No
770	10648.00	6820.00	7770.00	8390.00	Yanmar	3	83D	8F-2R	20.0	2180	No
770 4WD	11898.00	7740.00	8830.00	9540.00	Yanmar	3	83D	8F-2R	24.0	2355	No
855	12875.00	8240.00	9400.00	10150.00	Yanmar	3	61D	Variable	19.0	1876	No
855 4WD	14166.00	9070.00	10340.00	11170.00	Yanmar	3	61D	Variable	19.0	1876	No
870	11698.00	6900.00	7840.00	8310.00	Yanmar	3	87D	9F-3R	25.0	1876	No
870 4WD	13472.00	7950.00	9030.00	9570.00	Yanmar	3	87D	9F-3R	25.0	1876	No
955 4WD	15828.00	9340.00	10610.00	11250.00	Yanmar	3	87D	Variable	27.3	1876	No
970	13535.00	7990.00	9070.00	9610.00	Yanmar	3	111D	9F-3R	30.0	1876	No
970 4WD	15932.00	9740.00	11060.00	11720.00	Yanmar	3	111D	9F-3R	30.0	1876	No
1070	15704.00	9270.00	10520.00	11150.00	Yanmar	3	116D	9F-3R	35.0	1876	No
1070 4WD	18314.00	10810.00	12270.00	13010.00	Yanmar	3	116D	9F-3R	35.0	1876	No
2155	17840.00	11420.00	13020.00	14060.00	JD	3	179D	8F-4R	45.60	5269	No
2155 4WD	24763.00	15850.00	18080.00	19530.00	JD	3	179D	8F-4R	45.60	5986	No
2355	20766.00	13290.00	15160.00	16370.00	JD	4	239D	8F-4R	55.90	6261	No
2355 4WD	27839.00	17820.00	20320.00	21950.00	JD	4	239D	8F-4R	55.90	6878	No
2355 4WD w/Cab	34944.00	22360.00	25510.00	27550.00	JD	4	239D	8F-4R	55.90	7793	C,H,A
2355 w/Cab	29744.00	19040.00	21710.00	23450.00	JD	4	239D	8F-4R	55.90	7187	C,H,A
2355N	21061.00	13480.00	15380.00	16610.00	JD	3T	179D	8F-4R	55.00		No
2355N 4WD	27829.00	17810.00	20320.00	21950.00	JD	3T	179D	8F-4R	55.00		No
2555	24179.00	15480.00	17650.00	19060.00	JD	4	239D	8F-4R	66.00	6515	No
2555 4WD	30780.00	19700.00	22470.00	24270.00	JD	4	239D	8F-4R	65.00	7286	No
2555 4WD w/Cab	37886.00	24250.00	27660.00	29870.00	JD	4	239D	8F-4R	65.00	7959	C,H,A
2555 w/Cab	32528.00	20820.00	23750.00	25650.00	JD	4	239D	8F-4R	66.00	7441	C,H,A
2755	27202.00	17410.00	19860.00	21450.00	JD	4T	239D	8F-4R	75.00	6558	No
2755 4WD	35529.00	22740.00	25940.00	28020.00	JD	4T	239D	8F-4R	75.00	7374	No
2755 4WD w/Cab	42634.00	27290.00	31120.00	33610.00	JD	4T	239D	8F-4R	75.00	8433	C,H,A
2755 HC 4WD	37709.00	24130.00	27530.00	29730.00	JD	4T	239D	12F-8R	75.00	7750	No
2755 w/Cab	35907.00	22980.00	26210.00	28310.00	JD	4T	239D	8F-4R	75.00	7441	C,H,A
2855N	27947.00	17890.00	20400.00	22030.00	JD	4T	239D	8F-4R	80.00		No
2855N 4WD	35088.00	22460.00	25610.00	27660.00	JD	4T	239D	8F-4R	80.00		No
2955	31858.00	20390.00	23260.00	25120.00	JD	6	359D	8F-4R	85.00	8444	No
2955 4WD	38793.00	24830.00	28320.00	30590.00	JD	6	359D	8F-4R	85.00	8973	No
2955 4WD w/Cab	46584.00	29810.00	34010.00	36730.00	JD	6	359D	16F-8R	85.00	9590	C,H,A
2955 w/Cab	40500.00	25920.00	29570.00	31940.00	JD	6	359D	16F-8R	85.00	9083	C,H,A
2955HC 4WD	34300.00	21950.00	25040.00	27040.00	JD	6	359D	12F-8R	85.00	9140	No
2955HC 4WD w/Cab	46985.00	30070.00	34300.00	37040.00	JD	6	359D	12F-8R	85.00	9835	C,H,A
3155 4WD	42910.00	25320.00	28750.00	30480.00	JD	6	359D	16F-8R	96.06	10207	No

John Deere (Cont.)

1991 (Cont.)

Model	Approx. Retail Price New	Estimated Average Value Less Repairs: Fair	Good	Premium	Engine: Make	No. Cyls.	Displ. Cu.-In.	No. Speeds	P.T.O. H.P.	Approx. Shipping Wt.-Lbs.	Cab
3155 4WD w/Cab	48610.00	27140.00	30820.00	32670.00	JD	6	359D	16F-8R	96.06	10571	C,H,A
4055 PS	48036.00	28340.00	32180.00	34110.00	JD	6T	466D	15F-4R	109.18		No
4055 PS 4WD	56924.00	32450.00	36850.00	39060.00	JD	6T	466D	15F-4R	109.18	11350	No
4055 PS 4WD w/Cab	64357.00	35400.00	40200.00	42610.00	JD	6T	466D	15F-4R	109.18	12489	C,H,A
4055 PS w/Cab	55477.00	31860.00	36180.00	38350.00	JD	6T	466D	15F-4R	109.18	13955	C,H,A
4055 QR	43444.00	25630.00	29110.00	30860.00	JD	6T	466D	16F-6R	108.70		No
4055 QR w/Cab	50885.00	29500.00	33500.00	35510.00	JD	6T	466D	16F-6R	108.70	12130	C,H,A
4255 PS	52974.00	30680.00	34840.00	36930.00	JD	6T	466D	15F-4R	120.00	12050	No
4255 PS 4WD	62392.00	35580.00	40400.00	42820.00	JD	6T	466D	15F-4R	123.36	13550	No
4255 PS 4WD w/Cab	69638.00	38110.00	43280.00	45880.00	JD	6T	466D	15F-4R	123.36	14685	C,H,A
4255 PS w/Cab	60220.00	34220.00	38860.00	41190.00	JD	6T	466D	15F-4R	120.00	13155	C,H,A
4255 QR	48380.00	27730.00	31490.00	33380.00	JD	6T	466D	16F-6R	123.69	11140	No
4255 QR w/Cab	55628.00	32100.00	36450.00	38640.00	JD	6T	466D	16F-6R	123.69		C,H,A
4455 PS	56660.00	32450.00	36850.00	39060.00	JD	6T	466D	15F-4R	140.00	13050	No
4455 PS w/Cab	64101.00	36580.00	41540.00	44030.00	JD	6T	466D	15F-4R	140.00	14145	C,H,A
4455 QR	51949.00	29800.00	33840.00	35870.00	JD	6T	466D	16F-6R	142.69	11326	No
4455 QR w/Cab	59390.00	33930.00	38530.00	40840.00	JD	6T	466D	16F-6R	142.69		C,H,A
4555 PS 4WD	71446.00	39180.00	44490.00	47160.00	JD	6T	466D	15F-4R	155.00		No
4555 PS 4WD w/Cab	78887.00	41890.00	47570.00	50420.00	JD	6T	466D	15F-4R	155.00		C,H,A
4555 PS w/Cab	68619.00	39880.00	45290.00	48010.00	JD	6T	466D	15F-4R	155.00		C,H,A
4555 QR	56467.00	32690.00	37120.00	39350.00	JD	6T	466D	16F-6R	156.83	14310	No
4555 QR w/Cab	63908.00	36880.00	41880.00	44390.00	JD	6T	466D	16F-6R	156.83	18703	C,H,A
4755 PS	77388.00	40120.00	46810.00	49620.00	JD	6TA	466D	15F-4R	177.06		C,H,A
4755 PS 4WD	87656.00	45360.00	52920.00	56100.00	JD	6TA	466D	15F-4R	177.06		C,H,A
4755 QR	72677.00	37800.00	44100.00	46750.00	JD	6TA	466D	16F-6R	177.11		C,H,A
4955 PS	83434.00	43200.00	50400.00	53420.00	JD	6TA	466D	15F-4R	202.73		C,H,A
4955 PS 4WD	93702.00	45900.00	53550.00	56760.00	JD	6TA	466D	15F-4R	202.73		C,H,A
8560 4WD w/PTO, 3 Pt.	95340.00	48780.00	56910.00	60330.00	JD	6TA	466D	12F-3R	256.00		C,H,A
8560 4WD w/PTO, 3 Pt.	100590.00	52110.00	60800.00	64450.00	JD	6TA	466D	24F-6R	256.00		C,H,A
8760	99225.00	52490.00	61240.00	64910.00	JD	6TA	619D	12F-3R	260.94		C,H,A
8760 PS	114975.00	118800.00	138600.00	146920.00	JD	6TA	619D	12F-2R	260.94		C,H,A
8960 4WD	118310.00	61020.00	71190.00	75460.00	JD	6TA	855D	12F-3R	322.00		C,H,A
8960 4WD	123560.00	64800.00	75600.00	80140.00	JD	6TA	855D	24F-6R	333.40		C,H,A
8960 4WD PS	134060.00	67500.00	78750.00	83480.00	JD	6TA	855D	12F-2R	332.25		C,H,A

H, HC, HU--High Clearance PS--Power Shift QR--Quad Range

1992

Model	Approx. Retail Price New	Estimated Average Value Less Repairs: Fair	Good	Premium	Engine: Make	No. Cyls.	Displ. Cu.-In.	No. Speeds	P.T.O. H.P.	Approx. Shipping Wt.-Lbs.	Cab
670	10250.00	6660.00	7590.00	8120.00	Yanmar	3	54D	8F-2R	16.0	1980	No
670 4WD	11954.00	7770.00	8850.00	9470.00	Yanmar	3	54D	8F-2R	16.0	2120	No
755	12169.00	7910.00	9010.00	9640.00	Yanmar	3	54D	Variable	20.0	1817	No
755 4WD	13346.00	8780.00	9990.00	10690.00	Yanmar	3	54D	Variable	20.0	1921	No
770	11021.00	7160.00	8160.00	8730.00	Yanmar	3	83D	8F-2R	20.0	2180	No
770 4WD	12938.00	8410.00	9570.00	10240.00	Yanmar	3	83D	8F-2R	24.0	2355	No
855	13327.00	8660.00	9860.00	10550.00	Yanmar	3	61D	Variable	19.0	1876	No
855 4WD	14686.00	9550.00	10870.00	11630.00	Yanmar	3	61D	Variable	19.0	1876	No
870	12107.00	7260.00	8230.00	8720.00	Yanmar	3	87D	9F-3R	25.0	1876	No
870 4WD	14785.00	8870.00	10050.00	10650.00	Yanmar	3	87D	9F-3R	25.0	1876	No
955 4WD	16383.00	9830.00	11140.00	11810.00	Yanmar	3	87D	Variable	27.3	1876	No
970	14009.00	8410.00	9530.00	10100.00	Yanmar	3	111D	9F-3R	30.0	1876	No
970 4WD	17331.00	10400.00	11790.00	12500.00	Yanmar	3	111D	9F-3R	30.0	1876	No
1070	16254.00	9750.00	11050.00	11710.00	Yanmar	3	116D	9F-3R	35.0	1876	No
1070 4WD	18955.00	11370.00	12890.00	13660.00	Yanmar	3	116D	9F-3R	35.0	1876	No
2155	17840.00	11600.00	13200.00	14120.00	JD	3	179D	8F-4R	45.60	5269	No
2155 4WD	24763.00	16100.00	18330.00	19610.00	JD	3	179D	8F-4R	45.60	5986	No
2355	20766.00	13500.00	15370.00	16450.00	JD	4	239D	8F-4R	55.90	6261	No
2355 4WD	27839.00	18100.00	20600.00	22040.00	JD	4	239D	8F-4R	55.90	6878	No
2355 4WD w/Cab	34944.00	22710.00	25860.00	27670.00	JD	4	239D	8F-4R	55.90	7793	C,H,A
2355 w/Cab	29744.00	19330.00	22010.00	23550.00	JD	4	239D	8F-4R	55.90	7187	C,H,A
2355N Narrow	21061.00	13690.00	15590.00	16680.00	JD	3T	179D	8F-4R	55.00		No
2355N Narrow 4WD	27829.00	18090.00	20590.00	22030.00	JD	3T	179D	8F-4R	55.00		No
2555	24789.00	16110.00	18340.00	19620.00	JD	4	239D	8F-4R	66.00	6515	No
2555 4WD	31550.00	20510.00	23350.00	24990.00	JD	4	239D	8F-4R	65.00	7286	No
2555 4WD w/Cab	38833.00	25240.00	28740.00	30750.00	JD	4	239D	8F-4R	65.00	7959	C,H,A
2555 w/Cab	33341.00	21670.00	24670.00	26400.00	JD	4	239D	8F-4R	66.00	7441	C,H,A
2755	27882.00	18120.00	20630.00	22070.00	JD	4T	239D	8F-4R	75.00	6558	No
2755 4WD	36417.00	23670.00	26950.00	28840.00	JD	4T	239D	8F-4R	75.00	7374	No
2755 4WD w/Cab	43692.00	28400.00	32330.00	34590.00	JD	4T	239D	8F-4R	75.00	8433	C,H,A
2755 w/Cab	36805.00	23920.00	27240.00	29150.00	JD	4T	239D	8F-4R	75.00	7441	C,H,A
2755HC 4WD	38652.00	25120.00	28600.00	30600.00	JD	4T	239D	12F-8R	75.00	7750	No
2855N	28646.00	18620.00	21200.00	22680.00	JD	4T	239D	8F-4R	80.00		No
2855N 4WD	35965.00	23380.00	26610.00	28470.00	JD	4T	239D	8F-4R	80.00		No
2955	32654.00	21230.00	24160.00	25850.00	JD	6	359D	8F-4R	85.00	8444	No
2955 4WD	39763.00	25850.00	29430.00	31490.00	JD	6	359D	8F-4R	85.00	8973	No
2955 4WD w/Cab	47749.00	29900.00	34040.00	36420.00	JD	6	359D	16F-8R	85.00	9590	C,H,A
2955 w/Cab	41513.00	26980.00	30720.00	32870.00	JD	6	359D	16F-8R	85.00	9083	C,H,A
2955HC 4WD	41308.00	26850.00	30570.00	32710.00	JD	6	359D	12F-8R	85.00	9140	No
2955HC 4WD w/Cab	48160.00	31300.00	35640.00	38140.00	JD	6	359D	12F-8R	85.00	9835	C,H,A
3055	37265.00	22360.00	25340.00	26860.00	JD	6	359D	16F-8R	94.40	14770	No
3055 w/Cab	42965.00	25780.00	29220.00	30970.00	JD	6	359D	16F-8R	94.40	14770	C,H,A
3155 4WD	42910.00	25750.00	29180.00	30930.00	JD	6	359D	16F-8R	96.06	10207	No
3155 4WD w/Cab	48610.00	29170.00	33060.00	35040.00	JD	6	359D	16F-8R	96.06	10571	C,H,A
3255 4WD	45915.00	27550.00	31220.00	33090.00	JD	6T	359D	16F-8R	102.60	18300	No
3255 4WD w/Cab	51615.00	30970.00	35100.00	37210.00	JD	6T	359D	16F-8R	102.60	18300	C,H,A
4055 PS	50299.00	30180.00	34200.00	36250.00	JD	6T	466D	15F-4R	109.18		No

John Deere (Cont.)

Model	Approx. Retail Price New	Estimated Average Value Less Repairs Fair	Good	Premium	Engine Make	No. Cyls.	Displ. Cu.-In.	No. Speeds	P.T.O. H.P.	Approx. Shipping Wt.-Lbs.	Cab
1992 (Cont.)											
4055 PS 4WD	59357.00	34200.00	38760.00	41090.00	JD	6T	466D	15F-4R	109.18	11350	No
4055 PS 4WD w/Cab	66947.00	36600.00	41480.00	43970.00	JD	6T	466D	15F-4R	109.18	12489	C,H,A
4055 PS w/Cab	57889.00	34730.00	39370.00	41730.00	JD	6T	466D	15F-4R	109.18	13955	C,H,A
4055 QR	45615.00	27370.00	31020.00	32880.00	JD	6T	466D	16F-6R	108.70		No
4055 QR w/Cab	53205.00	31920.00	36180.00	38350.00	JD	6T	466D	16F-6R	108.70	12130	C,H,A
4255 PS	55253.00	33150.00	37570.00	39820.00	JD	6T	466D	15F-4R	120.00	12050	No
4255 PS 4WD	64859.00	36000.00	40800.00	43250.00	JD	6T	466D	15F-4R	123.36	13550	No
4255 PS 4WD w/Cab	72449.00	40200.00	45560.00	48290.00	JD	6T	466D	15F-4R	123.36	14685	C,H,A
4255 PS w/Cab	62843.00	37710.00	42730.00	45290.00	JD	6T	466D	15F-5R	120.00	13155	C,H,A
4255 QR	50569.00	30340.00	34390.00	36450.00	JD	6T	466D	16F-6R	123.69	11140	No
4255 QR w/Cab	58159.00	34260.00	38830.00	41160.00	JD	6T	466D	16F-6R	123.69		C,H,A
4455 PS	59308.00	34860.00	39510.00	41880.00	JD	6T	466D	15F-4R	140.00	13050	No
4455 PS 4WD	69007.00	39600.00	44880.00	47570.00	JD	6T	466D	15F-4R	140.00	13050	No
4455 PS 4WD w/Cab	76597.00	42600.00	48280.00	51180.00	JD	6T	466D	15F-4R	140.00	14145	C,H,A
4455 PS w/Cab	66898.00	38400.00	43520.00	46130.00	JD	6T	466D	15F-4R	140.00	14145	C,H,A
4455 QR	54503.00	32700.00	37060.00	39280.00	JD	6T	466D	16F-6R	142.69	11326	No
4455 QR w/Cab	62093.00	37260.00	42220.00	44750.00	JD	6T	466D	16F-6R	142.69		C,H,A
4555 PS 4WD	71446.00	40800.00	46240.00	49010.00	JD	6T	466D	15F-4R	155.00		No
4555 PS 4WD w/Cab	78887.00	44400.00	50320.00	53340.00	JD	6T	466D	15F-4R	155.00		C,H,A
4555 PS w/Cab	68619.00	40200.00	45560.00	48290.00	JD	6T	466D	15F-4R	155.00		C,H,A
4555 QR	56467.00	33000.00	37400.00	39640.00	JD	6T	466D	16F-6R	156.83	14310	No
4555 QR w/Cab	63908.00	37200.00	42160.00	44690.00	JD	6T	466D	16F-6R	156.83	18703	C,H,A
4560	60203.00	35400.00	40120.00	42530.00	JD	6T	466D	16F-6R	155.00		No
4560 PS	65008.00	38400.00	43520.00	46130.00	JD	6T	466D	15F-4R	155.00		No
4560 PS 4WD	75481.00	43800.00	49640.00	52620.00	JD	6T	466D	15F-4R	155.00		No
4560 PS 4WD w/Cab	83071.00	47400.00	53720.00	56940.00	JD	6T	466D	15F-4R	155.00		C,H,A
4560 PS w/Cab	72598.00	41400.00	46920.00	49740.00	JD	6T	466D	15F-4R	155.00		C,H,A
4560 w/Cab	67793.00	39600.00	44880.00	47570.00	JD	6T	466D	16F-6R	155.00		C,H,A
4760 PS	80789.00	43680.00	49920.00	52920.00	JD	6TA	466D	15F-4R	175		C,H,A
4760 PS 4WD	91262.00	48160.00	55040.00	58340.00	JD	6TA	466D	15F-4R	175		C,H,A
4760 QR	75984.00	41440.00	47360.00	50200.00	JD	6TA	466D	16F-6R	175		C,H,A
4960 PS	88506.00	46480.00	53120.00	56310.00	JD	6TA	466D	15F-4R	200		C,H,A
4960 PS 4WD	98979.00	52080.00	59520.00	63090.00	JD	6TA	466D	15F-4R	200		C,H,A
5200	18318.00	12820.00	14110.00	14960.00	JD	3	179D	9F-3R	40		No
5200 4WD	22732.00	15910.00	17500.00	18550.00	JD	3	179D	9F-3R	40		No
5300	19612.00	13730.00	15100.00	16010.00	JD	3	179D	9F-3R	50		No
5300 4WD	23874.00	16710.00	18380.00	19480.00	JD	3	179D	9F-3R	50		No
5400	21756.00	15230.00	16750.00	17760.00	JD	3	179D	9F-3R	60		No
5400 4WD	26080.00	18260.00	20080.00	21290.00	JD	3	179D	9F-3R	60		No
8560 4WD	88277.00	49440.00	56500.00	59890.00	JD	6TA	466D	12F-3R	200.00		C,H,A
8560 4WD	93900.00	51520.00	58880.00	62410.00	JD	6TA	466D	24F-6R	202.65		C,H,A
8760 4WD	106270.00	57680.00	65920.00	69880.00	JD	6TA	619D	12F-3R	260.94		C,H,A
8760 4WD PS	123139.00	63280.00	72320.00	76660.00	JD	6TA	619D	12F-2R	260.94		C,H,A
8960 4WD	126542.00	68320.00	78080.00	82770.00	JD	6TA	855D	12F-3R	322.00		C,H,A
8960 4WD	132165.00	71680.00	81920.00	86840.00	JD	6TA	855D	24F-6R	333.40		C,H,A
8960 4WD PS	143411.00	76160.00	87040.00	92260.00	JD	6TA	855D	12F-2R	332.25		C,H,A

H, HC, HU--High Clearance PS--Power Shift QR--Quad Range

Model	Approx. Retail Price New	Fair	Good	Premium	Engine Make	No. Cyls.	Displ. Cu.-In.	No. Speeds	P.T.O. H.P.	Approx. Shipping Wt.-Lbs.	Cab
1993											
670	10457.00	7010.00	7840.00	8310.00	Yanmar	3	54D	8F-2R	16.0	1980	No
670 4WD	12133.00	8130.00	9100.00	9650.00	Yanmar	3	54D	8F-2R	16.0	2120	No
755	13240.00	8870.00	9930.00	10530.00	Yanmar	3	54D	Variable	20.0	1817	No
755 4WD	14429.00	9670.00	10820.00	11470.00	Yanmar	3	54D	Variable	20.0	1921	No
770	11293.00	7570.00	8470.00	8980.00	Yanmar	3	83D	8F-2R	20.0	2180	No
770 4WD	13132.00	8800.00	9850.00	10440.00	Yanmar	3	83D	8F-2R	24.0	2355	No
855	14085.00	9440.00	10560.00	11190.00	Yanmar	3	61D	Variable	19.0	1876	No
855 4WD	15472.00	10370.00	11600.00	12300.00	Yanmar	3	61D	Variable	19.0	1876	No
870	12406.00	7690.00	8560.00	9070.00	Yanmar	3	87D	9F-3R	25.0	1876	No
870 4WD	15006.00	9300.00	10350.00	10970.00	Yanmar	3	87D	9F-3R	25.0	1876	No
955 4WD	16706.00	10540.00	11730.00	12430.00	Yanmar	3	87D	Variable	27.3	1876	No
970	14355.00	8990.00	10010.00	10610.00	Yanmar	3	111D	9F-3R	30.0	1876	No
970 4WD	17590.00	11160.00	12420.00	13170.00	Yanmar	3	111D	9F-3R	30.0	1876	No
1070	16660.00	10330.00	11500.00	12190.00	Yanmar	3	116D	9F-3R	35.0	1876	No
1070 4WD	19239.00	11930.00	13280.00	14080.00	Yanmar	3	116D	9F-3R	35.0	1876	No
2355 4WD w/Cab	37041.00	24820.00	27780.00	29450.00	JD	4	239D	8F-4R	55.90	7793	C,H,A
2355 w/Cab	31529.00	21120.00	23650.00	25070.00	JD	4	239D	8F-4R	55.90	7187	C,H,A
2355N	21672.00	14520.00	16250.00	17230.00	JD	4	239D	8F-4R	55.90	6261	No
2355N 4WD	28636.00	19190.00	21480.00	22770.00	JD	4	239D	8F-4R	55.90	6878	No
2555	24750.00	16580.00	18560.00	19670.00	JD	4	239D	8F-4R	66.00	6515	No
2555 4WD	30316.00	20310.00	22740.00	24100.00	JD	4	239D	8F-4R	65.00	7286	No
2755	27974.00	18740.00	20980.00	22240.00	JD	4T	239D	8F-4R	75.00		No
2755 4WD	35302.00	23650.00	26480.00	28070.00	JD	4T	239D	8F-4R	75.00		No
2855N Narrow	29463.00	19740.00	22100.00	23430.00	JD	4T	239D	8F-4R	80.00		No
2855N Narrow 4WD	36990.00	24780.00	27740.00	29400.00	JD	4T	239D	8F-4R	80.00		No
3055	36787.00	24650.00	27590.00	29250.00	JD	6	359D	16F-8R	94.40	14770	No
3055 w/Cab	42658.00	28580.00	31990.00	33910.00	JD	6	359D	16F-8R	94.40	14770	C,H,A
3255 4WD	46217.00	30970.00	34660.00	36740.00	JD	6T	359D	16F-8R	102.60	18300	No
3255 4WD w/Cab	52088.00	34900.00	39070.00	41410.00	JD	6T	359D	16F-8R	102.60	18300	C,H,A
4560 PS 4WD w/Cab	85488.00	53000.00	58990.00	62530.00	JD	6T	466D	15F-4R	155.00		C,H,A
4560 PS w/Cab	74690.00	46310.00	51540.00	54630.00	JD	6T	466D	15F-4R	155.00		C,H,A
4560 w/Cab	69741.00	43240.00	48120.00	51010.00	JD	6T	466D	16F-6R	155.00		C,H,A
4560 w/Cab 4WD	80539.00	49930.00	55570.00	58900.00	JD	6T	466D	16F-6R	155.00		C,H,A
4760	78187.00	45350.00	50820.00	53870.00	JD	6TA	466D	16F-6R	175		C,H,A
4760 4WD	88985.00	50460.00	56550.00	59940.00	JD	6TA	466D	16F-6R	175		C,H,A

John Deere (Cont.)

1993 (Cont.)

Model	Approx. Retail Price New	Estimated Average Value Less Repairs Fair	Good	Premium	Engine Make	No. Cyls.	Displ. Cu.-In.	No. Speeds	P.T.O. H.P.	Approx. Shipping Wt.-Lbs.	Cab
4760 PS	83136.00	47560.00	53300.00	56500.00	JD	6TA	466D	15F-4R	175		C,H,A
4760 PS 4WD	93934.00	52200.00	58500.00	62010.00	JD	6TA	466D	15F-4R	175		C,H,A
4960 PS	91086.00	51620.00	57850.00	61320.00	JD	6TA	466D	15F-4R	200		C,H,A
4960 PS 4WD	101884.00	57420.00	64350.00	68210.00	JD	6TA	466D	15F-4R	200		C,H,A
5200	18183.00	12910.00	14180.00	15030.00	JD	3	179D	9F-3R	40		No
5200 4WD	22683.00	16110.00	17690.00	18750.00	JD	3	179D	9F-3R	40		No
5300	19640.00	13940.00	15320.00	16240.00	JD	3	179D	9F-3R	50		No
5300 4WD	24948.00	17710.00	19460.00	20630.00	JD	3	179D	9F-3R	50		No
5400	21945.00	15580.00	17120.00	18150.00	JD	3	179D	9F-3R	60		No
5400 4WD	27254.00	19350.00	21260.00	22540.00	JD	3	179D	9F-3R	60		No
6200	26780.00	17940.00	20090.00	21300.00	JD	4T	239D	12F-4R	66.00		No
6200 w/Cab	34646.00	23210.00	25990.00	27550.00	JD	4T	239D	12F-4R	66.00		C,H,A
6300	28974.00	19410.00	21730.00	23030.00	JD	4T	239D	12F-4R	75.00		No
6300 4WD	36840.00	24680.00	27630.00	29290.00	JD	4T	239D	12F-4R	75.00		No
6400	31206.00	20910.00	23410.00	24820.00	JD	4T	239D	12F-8R	85.00		No
6400 w/Cab	39072.00	26180.00	29300.00	31060.00	JD	4T	239D	12F-4R	85.00		C,H,A
7600	56392.00	37780.00	42290.00	44830.00	JD	6T	414D	16F-12R	110.00		C,H,A
7600 4WD	65975.00	44200.00	49480.00	52450.00	JD	6T	466D	16F-12R	110.00		No
7700	62572.00	41920.00	46930.00	49750.00	JD	6T	466D	16F-12R	125.00		C,H,A
7800	67007.00	44900.00	50260.00	53280.00	JD	6T	466D	16F-12R	145.00		C,H,A
7800 4WD	76590.00	51320.00	57440.00	60890.00	JD	6T	466D	16F-12R	145.00		C,H,A
8570 4WD	89214.00	51740.00	57990.00	61470.00	JD	6TA	466D	12F-3R	200.00		C,H,A
8570 4WD	94837.00	55010.00	61640.00	65340.00	JD	6TA	466D	24F-6R	202.65		C,H,A
8770 4WD	107814.00	62530.00	70080.00	74290.00	JD	6TA	619D	12F-3R	260.94		C,H,A
8770 4WD PS	124683.00	70180.00	78650.00	83370.00	JD	6TA	619D	12F-2R	260.94		C,H,A
8870 4WD	122214.00	60000.00	69600.00	73080.00	JD	6TA	619D	12F-3R			C,H,A
8870 4WD 3Pt.	131188.00	64000.00	74240.00	77950.00	JD	6TA	619D	12F-3R			C,H,A
8970 4WD	137214.00	66500.00	77140.00	81000.00	JD	6TA	855D	12F-3R	322.00		C,H,A
8970 4WD	142837.00	69500.00	80620.00	84650.00	JD	6TA	855D	24F-6R	333.40		C,H,A

H, HC, HU--High Clearance PS--Power Shift QR--Quad Range

1994

Model	Approx. Retail Price New	Fair	Good	Premium	Engine Make	No. Cyls.	Displ. Cu.-In.	No. Speeds	P.T.O. H.P.	Approx. Shipping Wt.-Lbs.	Cab
670	10720.00	7400.00	8150.00	8560.00	Yanmar	3	54D	8F-2R	16.0	1980	No
670 4WD	12440.00	8580.00	9450.00	9920.00	Yanmar	3	54D	8F-2R	16.0	2120	No
755	13570.00	8970.00	9880.00	10370.00	Yanmar	3	54D	Variable	20.0	1817	No
755 4WD	14790.00	9800.00	10790.00	11330.00	Yanmar	3	54D	Variable	20.0	1921	No
770	11575.00	7990.00	8800.00	9240.00	Yanmar	3	83D	8F-2R	20.0	2180	No
770 4WD	13460.00	9290.00	10230.00	10740.00	Yanmar	3	83D	8F-2R	24.0	2355	No
855	14440.00	9960.00	10970.00	11520.00	Yanmar	3	61D	Variable	19.0	1876	No
855 4WD	15858.00	10940.00	12050.00	12650.00	Yanmar	3	61D	Variable	19.0	1876	No
870	12715.00	8140.00	8900.00	9350.00	Yanmar	3	87D	9F-3R	25.0	1876	No
870 4WD	15380.00	9600.00	10500.00	11030.00	Yanmar	3	87D	9F-3R	25.0	1876	No
955 4WD	17120.00	10880.00	11900.00	12500.00	Yanmar	3	87D	Variable	27.3	1876	No
970	14715.00	9420.00	10300.00	10820.00	Yanmar	3	111D	9F-3R	30.0	1876	No
970 4WD	18021.00	11530.00	12620.00	13250.00	Yanmar	3	111D	9F-3R	30.0	1876	No
1070	17075.00	10930.00	11950.00	12550.00	Yanmar	3	116D	9F-3R	35.0	1876	No
1070 4WD	19700.00	12610.00	13790.00	14480.00	Yanmar	3	116D	9F-3R	35.0	1876	No
2355N	22616.00	15610.00	17190.00	18050.00	JD	4	239D	8F-4R	55.90	6261	No
2355N 4WD	29893.00	20630.00	22720.00	23860.00	JD	4	239D	8F-4R	55.90	6878	No
2555 Low Profile	26246.00	18110.00	19950.00	20950.00	JD	4	239D	8F-4R	66.00	6515	No
2555 Low Profile 4WD	32135.00	22170.00	24420.00	25640.00	JD	4	239D	8F-4R	65.00	7286	No
2755 4WD	37432.00	25830.00	28450.00	29870.00	JD	4T	239D	8F-4R	75.00		No
2755 Low Profile	29652.00	20460.00	22540.00	23670.00	JD	4T	239D	8F-4R	75.00		No
2855N Narrow	30754.00	21220.00	23370.00	24540.00	JD	4T	239D	8F-4R	80.00		No
2855N Narrow 4WD	38664.00	26680.00	29390.00	30860.00	JD	4T	239D	8F-4R	80.00		No
4560 4WD w/Cab	83375.00	53360.00	58360.00	61280.00	JD	6T	466D	16F-6R	155.00		C,H,A
4560 PS 4WD w/Cab	88499.00	56640.00	61950.00	65050.00	JD	6T	466D	15F-4R	155.00		C,H,A
4560 PS w/Cab	77300.00	49470.00	54110.00	56820.00	JD	6T	466D	15F-4R	155.00		C,H,A
4560 w/Cab	72176.00	46190.00	50520.00	53050.00	JD	6T	466D	16F-6R	155.00		C,H,A
4760	80915.00	49360.00	54210.00	56920.00	JD	6TA	466D	16F-6R	175		C,H,A
4760 4WD	92114.00	55510.00	60970.00	64020.00	JD	6TA	466D	16F-6R	175		C,H,A
4760 PS	86039.00	51850.00	56950.00	59800.00	JD	6TA	466D	15F-4R	175		C,H,A
4760 PS 4WD	97238.00	58560.00	64320.00	67540.00	JD	6TA	466D	15F-4R	175		C,H,A
4960	94265.00	57340.00	62980.00	66130.00	JD	6TA	466D	15F-4R	200		C,H,A
4960 4WD	105464.00	62220.00	68340.00	71760.00	JD	6TA	466D	15F-4R	200		C,H,A
5200	18638.00	13610.00	14720.00	15460.00	JD	3	179D	9F-3R	40		No
5200 4WD	24455.00	17850.00	19320.00	20290.00	JD	3	179D	9F-3R	40		No
5300	20524.00	14980.00	16210.00	17020.00	JD	3	179D	9F-3R	50		No
5300 4WD	26071.00	19030.00	20600.00	21630.00	JD	3	179D	9F-3R	50		No
5400	23472.00	17140.00	18540.00	19470.00	JD	3	179D	9F-3R	60		No
5400 4WD	28208.00	20590.00	22280.00	23390.00	JD	3	179D	9F-3R	60		No
6200	27717.00	19130.00	21070.00	22120.00	JD	4T	239D	12F-4R	66.00		No
6200 4WD	34113.00	23540.00	25930.00	27230.00	JD	4T	239D	12F-4R	66.00		No
6200 w/Cab	35859.00	24740.00	27250.00	28610.00	JD	4T	239D	12F-4R	66.00		C,H,A
6300	29989.00	20690.00	22790.00	23930.00	JD	4T	239D	12F-4R	75.00		No
6300 4WD	36385.00	25110.00	27650.00	29030.00	JD	4T	239D	12F-4R	75.00		No
6300 w/Cab	38131.00	26310.00	28980.00	30430.00	JD	4T	239D	12F-4R	75.00		C,H,A
6400	32630.00	22520.00	24800.00	26040.00	JD	4T	239D	12F-4R	85.00		No
6400 4WD	39026.00	26930.00	29660.00	31140.00	JD	4T	239D	12F-4R	85.00		No
6400 w/Cab	40772.00	28130.00	30990.00	32540.00	JD	4T	239D	12F-4R	85.00		C,H,A
7200	46034.00	31760.00	34990.00	36740.00	JD	6T	359D	16F-8R	92		C,H,A
7200 4WD	53347.00	36810.00	40540.00	42570.00	JD	6T	359D	16F-8R	92		C,H,A
7400	49656.00	34260.00	37740.00	39630.00	JD	6T	414D	12F-4R	100.		C,H,A
7400 4WD	56969.00	39310.00	43300.00	45470.00	JD	6T	414D	12F-4R	100.		C,H,A

John Deere (Cont.)

1994 (Cont.)

Model	Approx. Retail Price New	Estimated Average Value Less Repairs Fair	Good	Premium	Engine Make	No. Cyls.	Displ. Cu.-In.	No. Speeds	P.T.O. H.P.	Approx. Shipping Wt.-Lbs.	Cab
7600	57802.00	39880.00	43930.00	46130.00	JD	6T	414D	16F-12R	110.00		C,H,A
7600 4WD	67745.00	46740.00	51490.00	54070.00	JD	6T	414D	16F-12R	110.00		C,H,A
7700	64762.00	44690.00	49220.00	51680.00	JD	6T	466D	16F-12R	125.00		C,H,A
7700 4WD	74705.00	51550.00	56780.00	59620.00	JD	6T	466D	16F-12R	125.00		C,H,A
7800	69352.00	47850.00	52710.00	55350.00	JD	6T	466D	16F-12R	145.00		C,H,A
7800 4WD	79295.00	54710.00	60260.00	63270.00	JD	6T	466D	16F-12R	145.00		C,H,A
8570 4WD	89214.00	54420.00	59770.00	62760.00	JD	6TA	466D	12F-3R	200.00		C,H,A
8570 4WD	94837.00	57850.00	63540.00	66720.00	JD	6TA	466D	24F-6R	202.65		C,H,A
8570 4WD PTO, 3Pt.	101671.00	61000.00	67000.00	70350.00	JD	6TA	466D	12F-3R	200.00		C,H,A
8770 4WD	107814.00	64050.00	70350.00	73870.00	JD	6TA	619D	12F-3R	260.94		C,H,A
8870 4WD	122214.00	63600.00	72000.00	75600.00	JD	6TA	619D	12F-3R			C,H,A
8870 4WD 3Pt.	131188.00	67840.00	76800.00	80640.00	JD	6TA	619D	12F-3R			C,H,A
8970 4WD	137214.00	70490.00	79800.00	83790.00	JD	6TA	855D	12F-3R	322.00		C,H,A
8970 4WD	142837.00	73670.00	83400.00	87570.00	JD	6TA	855D	24F-6R	333.40		C,H,A

H, HC, HU--High Clearance PS--Power Shift QR--Quad Range

1995

Model	Approx. Retail Price New	Estimated Average Value Less Repairs Fair	Good	Premium	Engine Make	No. Cyls.	Displ. Cu.-In.	No. Speeds	P.T.O. H.P.	Approx. Shipping Wt.-Lbs.	Cab
670	11342.00	7810.00	8580.00	9010.00	Yanmar	3	54D	8F-2R	16.0	1980	No
670 4WD	13534.00	9230.00	10140.00	10650.00	Yanmar	3	54D	8F-2R	16.0	2120	No
755	13825.00	9820.00	10780.00	11320.00	Yanmar	3	54D	Variable	20.0	1817	No
755 4WD	15485.00	10650.00	11700.00	12290.00	Yanmar	3	54D	Variable	20.0	1921	No
770	12249.00	8520.00	9360.00	9830.00	Yanmar	3	83D	8F-2R	20.0	2180	No
770 4WD	14106.00	10020.00	11000.00	11550.00	Yanmar	3	83D	8F-2R	24.0	2355	No
855	14742.00	10470.00	11500.00	12080.00	Yanmar	3	61D	Variable	19.0	1876	No
855 4WD	16604.00	11360.00	12480.00	13100.00	Yanmar	3	61D	Variable	19.0	1876	No
870	13378.00	8830.00	9770.00	10260.00	Yanmar	3	87D	9F-3R	25.0	1876	No
870 4WD	16080.00	10610.00	11740.00	12330.00	Yanmar	3	87D	9F-3R	25.0	1876	No
955 4WD	18580.00	12000.00	13270.00	13930.00	Yanmar	3	87D	Variable	27.3	1876	No
970	15570.00	10280.00	11370.00	11940.00	Yanmar	3	111D	9F-3R	30.0	1876	No
970 4WD	19508.00	12540.00	13870.00	14560.00	Yanmar	3	111D	9F-3R	30.0	1876	No
1070	18178.00	12000.00	13270.00	13930.00	Yanmar	3	116D	9F-3R	35.0	1876	No
1070 4WD	21200.00	13530.00	14970.00	15720.00	Yanmar	3	116D	9F-3R	35.0	1876	No
5200	20182.00	15140.00	16150.00	16960.00	JD	3	179D	9F-3R	40.00	4250	No
5200 4WD	24164.00	18120.00	19330.00	20300.00	JD	3	179D	9F-3R	40.00	4650	No
5300	21091.00	15820.00	16870.00	17710.00	JD	3	179D	9F-3R	50.00	4350	No
5300 4WD	26792.00	20090.00	21430.00	22500.00	JD	3	179D	9F-3R	50.00	4750	No
5400	24183.00	18140.00	19350.00	20320.00	JD	3	179D	9F-3R	60.00	4600	No
5400 4WD	29030.00	21770.00	23220.00	24380.00	JD	3	179D	9F-3R	60.00	5000	No
5400N	24644.00	18480.00	19720.00	20710.00	JD	3	179D	12F-12R	60.00	4763	No
5400N 4WD	30144.00	22610.00	24120.00	25330.00	JD	3	179D	12F-12R	60.00	5072	No
6200	28410.00	20170.00	22160.00	23270.00	JD	4T	239D	12F-4R	66.00	7420	No
6200 4WD	34966.00	24830.00	27270.00	28630.00	JD	4T	239D	12F-4R	66.00	7916	No
6200 4WD w/Cab	43302.00	30740.00	33780.00	35470.00	JD	4T	239D	12F-4R	66.00	8423	C,H,A
6200 w/Cab	36746.00	26090.00	28660.00	30090.00	JD	4T	239D	12F-4R	66.00	7927	C,H,A
6200L	28410.00	20170.00	22160.00	23270.00	JD	4T	239D	12F-4R	66.00	7420	No
6200L 4WD	34966.00	24830.00	27270.00	28630.00	JD	4T	239D	12F-4R	66.00	7916	No
6300	30695.00	21790.00	23940.00	25140.00	JD	4T	239D	12F-4R	75.00	7497	No
6300 4WD	37525.00	26640.00	29270.00	30730.00	JD	4T	239D	12F-4R	75.00	8004	No
6300 4WD w/Cab	45861.00	32560.00	35770.00	37560.00	JD	4T	239D	12F-4R	75.00	8511	C,H,A
6300 w/Cab	39031.00	27710.00	30440.00	31960.00	JD	4T	239D	12F-4R	75.00	8004	C,H,A
6300L	30695.00	21790.00	23940.00	25140.00	JD	4T	239D	12F-4R	75.00	7497	No
6300L 4WD	37143.00	26370.00	28970.00	30420.00	JD	4T	239D	12F-4R	75.00	8004	No
6400	33677.00	23910.00	26270.00	27580.00	JD	4T	239D	12F-4R	85.00	7607	No
6400 4WD	40625.00	28840.00	31690.00	33280.00	JD	4T	239D	12F-4R	85.00	8246	No
6400 4WD w/Cab	48961.00	34760.00	38190.00	40100.00	JD	4T	239D	12F-4R	85.00	8754	C,H,A
6400 w/Cab	42013.00	29830.00	32770.00	34410.00	JD	4T	239D	12F-4R	85.00	8114	C,H,A
6400L	33677.00	23910.00	26270.00	27580.00	JD	4T	239D	12F-4R	85.00	7607	No
6400L 4WD	40625.00	28840.00	31690.00	33280.00	JD	4T	239D	12F-4R	85.00	8246	No
6500L	38729.00	27500.00	30210.00	31720.00	JD	4T	239D	16F-12R	95.00	7740	No
6500L 4WD	45677.00	32430.00	35630.00	37410.00	JD	4T	239D	16F-12R	95.00	8379	No
7200	46781.00	33220.00	36490.00	38320.00	JD	6T	359D	12F-4R	92.00	10662	C,H,A
7200 4WD	54094.00	38410.00	42190.00	44300.00	JD	6T	359D	12F-4R	92.00	11522	C,H,A
7200HC	46092.00	32730.00	35950.00	37750.00	JD	6T	359D	12F-4R	92.00		No
7200HC 4WD	53405.00	37920.00	41660.00	43740.00	JD	6T	359D	12F-4R	92.00		No
7200HC 4WD w/Cab	61035.00	43340.00	47610.00	49990.00	JD	6T	359D	12F-4R	92.00		C,H,A
7200HC w/Cab	53722.00	38140.00	41900.00	44000.00	JD	6T	359D	12F-4R	92.00		C,H,A
7400	50444.00	35820.00	39350.00	41320.00	JD	6T	414D	12F-4R	100.	10827	C,H,A
7400 4WD	57757.00	41010.00	45050.00	47300.00	JD	6T	414D	12F-4R	100.	11687	C,H,A
7400HC	49767.00	35340.00	38820.00	40760.00	JD	6T	414D	12F-4R	100.		No
7400HC 4WD	57080.00	40530.00	44520.00	46750.00	JD	6T	414D	12F-4R	100.		No
7400HC 4WD w/Cab	64710.00	45940.00	50470.00	52990.00	JD	6T	414D	12F-4R	100.		C,H,A
7400HC w/Cab	57397.00	40750.00	44770.00	47010.00	JD	6T	414D	12F-4R	100.		C,H,A
7600	58734.00	41700.00	45810.00	48100.00	JD	6T	414D	16F-12R	110.00	13160	C,H,A
7600 4WD	68677.00	48760.00	53570.00	56250.00	JD	6T	414D	16F-12R	110.00	15200	C,H,A
7700	65795.00	46710.00	51320.00	53890.00	JD	6T	466D	16F-12R	125.00	13870	C,H,A
7700 4WD	75738.00	53770.00	59080.00	62030.00	JD	6T	466D	16F-12R	125.00	15400	C,H,A
7800	70433.00	50010.00	54940.00	57690.00	JD	6T	466D	16F-12R	145.00	13910	C,H,A
7800 4WD	80376.00	57070.00	62690.00	65830.00	JD	6T	466D	16F-12R	145.00	15480	C,H,A
8100	80010.00	52810.00	58410.00	61330.00	JD	6TA	466D	16F-4R	160.00	16435	C,H,A
8100 4WD	91489.00	59400.00	65700.00	68990.00	JD	6TA	466D	16F-4R	160.00	17876	C,H,A
8200	89334.00	58740.00	64970.00	68220.00	JD	6TA	466D	16F-4R	180.00	16457	C,H,A
8200 4WD	100813.00	63360.00	70080.00	73580.00	JD	6TA	466D	16F-4R	180.00	17898	C,H,A
8300	98110.00	64750.00	71620.00	75200.00	JD	6TA	466D	16F-4R	200.00	17030	C,H,A
8300 4WD	109589.00	67980.00	75190.00	78950.00	JD	6TA	466D	16F-4R	200.00	18523	C,H,A

John Deere (Cont.)

1995 (Cont.)

Model	Approx. Retail Price New	Estimated Average Value Less Repairs Fair	Good	Premium	Engine Make	No. Cyls.	Displ. Cu.-In.	No. Speeds	P.T.O. H.P.	Approx. Shipping Wt.-Lbs.	Cab
8400 4WD	119744.00	72960.00	79800.00	83790.00	JD	6TA	496D	16F-4R	225.00		C,H,A
8570 4WD	95117.00	60880.00	66580.00	69910.00	JD	6TA	466D	12F-3R	206.00	29564	C,H,A
8570 4WD	99729.00	63830.00	69810.00	73300.00	JD	6TA	466D	24F-6R	202.65		C,H,A
8770 4WD	114945.00	71680.00	78400.00	82320.00	JD	6TA	619D	12F-3R	256.00	31438	C,H,A
8770 4WD	119557.00	74880.00	81900.00	86000.00	JD	6TA	619D	24F-6R	256.00		C,H,A
8770 4WD PS	132474.00	80000.00	87500.00	91880.00	JD	6TA	619D	12F-2R	256.00		C,H,A
8870 4WD	126538.00	67200.00	75600.00	78620.00	JD	6TA	619D	12F-3R	300.00	31438	C,H,A
8870 4WD	131150.00	71120.00	80010.00	83210.00	JD	6TA	619D	24F-6R	300.00		C,H,A
8870 4WD PS	142681.00	75600.00	85050.00	88450.00	JD	6TA	619D	12F-2R	300.00		C,H,A
8970 4WD	144175.00	77840.00	87570.00	91070.00	JD	6TA	855D	12F-3R	339.00		C,H,A
8970 4WD	148787.00	80080.00	90090.00	93690.00	JD	6TA	855D	24F-6R	339.00	31879	C,H,A
8970 4WD PS	161704.00	84560.00	95130.00	98940.00	JD	6TA	855D	12F-2R	339.00		C,H,A
8970 4WD PS PTO	168989.00	87360.00	98280.00	102210.00	JD	6TA	855D	12F-2R	339.00		C,H,A
8970 4WD PTO	151460.00	82320.00	92610.00	96310.00	JD	6TA	855D	12F-3R	339.00		C,H,A
8970 4WD PTO	156072.00	84560.00	95130.00	98940.00	JD	6TA	855D	24F-6R	339.00		C,H,A

H, HC, HU--High Clearance PS--Power Shift QR--Quad Range

1996

Model	Approx. Retail Price New	Fair	Good	Premium	Make	No. Cyls.	Displ. Cu.-In.	No. Speeds	P.T.O. H.P.	Approx. Shipping Wt.-Lbs.	Cab
670	11796.00	8140.00	8800.00	9150.00	Yanmar	3	54D	8F-2R	16.0	1980	No
670 4WD	13554.00	9620.00	10400.00	10820.00	Yanmar	3	54D	8F-2R	16.0	2120	No
755	14378.00	10360.00	11200.00	11650.00	Yanmar	3	54D	Variable	20.0	1817	No
755 4WD	15568.00	11100.00	12000.00	12480.00	Yanmar	3	54D	Variable	20.0	1921	No
770	12739.00	9130.00	9870.00	10270.00	Yanmar	3	83D	8F-2R	20.0	2180	No
770 4WD	14670.00	10360.00	11200.00	11650.00	Yanmar	3	83D	8F-2R	24.0	2355	No
855	15332.00	11100.00	12000.00	12480.00	Yanmar	3	61D	Variable	19.0	1876	No
855 4WD	16732.00	11990.00	12960.00	13480.00	Yanmar	3	61D	Variable	19.0	1876	No
870	13994.00	9380.00	10180.00	10590.00	Yanmar	3	87D	9F-3R	25.0	1876	No
870 4WD	16764.00	11200.00	12160.00	12650.00	Yanmar	3	87D	9F-3R	25.0	1876	No
955 4WD	18663.00	12600.00	13680.00	14230.00	Yanmar	3	87D	Variable	27.3	1876	No
970	16193.00	11340.00	12310.00	12800.00	Yanmar	3	111D	9F-3R	30.0	1876	No
970 4WD	19651.00	13300.00	14440.00	15020.00	Yanmar	3	111D	9F-3R	30.0	1876	No
1070	18794.00	12810.00	13910.00	14470.00	Yanmar	3	116D	9F-3R	35.0	1876	No
1070 4WD	21492.00	14700.00	15960.00	16600.00	Yanmar	3	116D	9F-3R	35.0	1876	No
5200	19691.00	15540.00	16550.00	17210.00	JD	3	179D	9F-3R	40.0	4250	No
5200 4WD	24755.00	19060.00	20300.00	21110.00	JD	3	179D	9F-3R	40.0	4650	No
5200 4WD w/Cab	32677.00	25160.00	26800.00	27870.00	JD	3	179D	9F-3R	40.0		C,H,A
5200 w/Cab	27613.00	21260.00	22640.00	23550.00	JD	3	179D	9F-3R	40.0		C,H,A
5300	21610.00	16640.00	17720.00	18430.00	JD	3	179D	9F-3R	50.0	4350	No
5300 4WD	26629.00	20500.00	21840.00	22710.00	JD	3	179D	9F-3R	50.0	4750	No
5300 4WD w/Cab	34551.00	26600.00	28330.00	29460.00	JD	3	179D	9F-3R	50.0		C,H,A
5300 w/Cab	29532.00	22740.00	24220.00	25190.00	JD	3	179D	9F-3R	50.0		C,H,A
5400	24028.00	18620.00	19830.00	20620.00	JD	3	179D	9F-3R	60.0	4600	No
5400 4WD	29040.00	22360.00	23810.00	24760.00	JD	3	179D	9F-3R	60.0	5000	No
5400 4WD w/Cab	36962.00	28460.00	30310.00	31520.00	JD	3T	179D	9F-3R	60.0		C,H,A
5400 w/Cab	31950.00	24600.00	26200.00	27250.00	JD	3T	179D	9F-3R	60.0		C,H,A
5400N	25381.00	19540.00	20810.00	21640.00	JD	3	179D	12F-12R	60.0	4763	No
5400N 4WD	31237.00	24050.00	25610.00	26630.00	JD	3	179D	12F-12R	60.0	5072	No
6200	29177.00	21590.00	23340.00	24270.00	JD	4T	239D	12F-4R	66.0	7420	No
6200	31497.00	23310.00	25200.00	26210.00	JD	4T	239D	16F-16R	66.0		No
6200 4WD	35910.00	26570.00	28730.00	29880.00	JD	4T	239D	12F-4R	66.0	7916	No
6200 4WD	38230.00	28290.00	30580.00	31800.00	JD	4T	239D	16F-16R	66.0		No
6200 4WD w/Cab	44451.00	32890.00	35560.00	36980.00	JD	4T	239D	12F-4R	66.0	8423	C,H,A
6200 w/Cab	37718.00	27910.00	30170.00	31380.00	JD	4T	239D	12F-4R	66.0	7927	C,H,A
6200L	29158.00	21580.00	23330.00	24260.00	JD	4T	239D	12F-4R	66.0	7420	No
6200L	31478.00	23290.00	25180.00	26190.00	JD	4T	239D	16F-16R	66.0		No
6200L 4WD	35891.00	26560.00	28710.00	29860.00	JD	4T	239D	12F-4R	66.0	7916	No
6300	31524.00	23330.00	25220.00	26230.00	JD	4T	239D	12F-4R	75.0	7497	No
6300	33844.00	25050.00	27080.00	28160.00	JD	4T	239D	16F-16R	75.0		No
6300 4WD	38538.00	28520.00	30830.00	32060.00	JD	4T	239D	12F-4R	75.0	8004	No
6300 4WD	40858.00	30240.00	32690.00	34000.00	JD	4T	239D	16F-16R	75.0		No
6300 4WD w/Cab	47074.00	34840.00	37660.00	39170.00	JD	4T	239D	12F-4R	75.0	8511	C,H,A
6300 w/Cab	40060.00	29640.00	32050.00	33330.00	JD	4T	239D	12F-4R	75.0	8004	C,H,A
6300L	31504.00	23310.00	25200.00	26210.00	JD	4T	239D	12F-4R	75.0	7497	No
6300L	33824.00	25030.00	27060.00	28140.00	JD	4T	239D	16F-16R	75.0		No
6300L 4WD	38640.00	28590.00	30910.00	32150.00	JD	4T	239D	12F-4R	75.0	8004	No
6400	34575.00	25590.00	27660.00	28770.00	JD	4T	276D	12F-4R	85.0	7607	No
6400	36895.00	27300.00	29520.00	30700.00	JD	4T	276D	16F-16R	85.0		No
6400 4WD	41711.00	30870.00	33370.00	34710.00	JD	4T	276D	12F-4R	85.0	8246	No
6400 4WD	44031.00	32580.00	35230.00	36640.00	JD	4T	276D	16F-16R	85.0		No
6400 4WD w/Cab	50261.00	37190.00	40210.00	41820.00	JD	4T	276D	12F-4R	85.0	8754	C,H,A
6400 w/Cab	43125.00	31910.00	34500.00	35880.00	JD	4T	276D	12F-4R	85.0	8114	C,H,A
6400L	34567.00	25580.00	27650.00	28760.00	JD	4T	276D	12F-4R	85.0	7607	No
6400L	36887.00	27300.00	29510.00	30690.00	JD	4T	276D	16F-16R	85.0		No
6400L 4WD	41703.00	30860.00	33360.00	34690.00	JD	4T	276D	12F-4R	85.0	8246	No
6500L	39763.00	29430.00	31810.00	33080.00	JD	4T	276D	16F-12R	95.0	7740	No
6500L 4WD	46899.00	34710.00	37520.00	39020.00	JD	4T	276D	16F-12R	95.0	8379	No
7200	47939.00	35480.00	38350.00	39880.00	JD	6T	359D	12F-4R	92.0	10662	C,H,A
7200	50260.00	37190.00	40210.00	41820.00	JD	6T	359D	16F-16R	92.0		C,H,A
7200 4WD	56318.00	41680.00	45050.00	46850.00	JD	6T	359D	12F-4R	92.0	11522	C,H,A
7200 4WD	58638.00	43390.00	46910.00	48790.00	JD	6T	359D	16F-16R	92.0		C,H,A
7200HC	47796.00	35370.00	38240.00	39770.00	JD	6T	359D	12F-4R	92.0		No
7200HC	50116.00	37090.00	40090.00	41690.00	JD	6T	359D	16F-16R	92.0		C,H,A
7200HC 4WD	57403.00	42480.00	45920.00	47760.00	JD	6T	359D	12F-4R	92.0		No
7200HC 4WD w/Cab	65033.00	48120.00	52030.00	54110.00	JD	6T	359D	12F-4R	92.0		C,H,A

John Deere (Cont.)

1996 (Cont.)

Model	Approx. Retail Price New	Estimated Average Value Less Repairs Fair	Good	Premium	Engine Make	No. Cyls.	Displ. Cu.-In.	No. Speeds	P.T.O. H.P.	Approx. Shipping Wt.-Lbs.	Cab
7200HC w/Cab	55426.00	41020.00	44340.00	46110.00	JD	6T	359D	12F-4R	92.0		C,H,A
7400	51697.00	38260.00	41360.00	43010.00	JD	6T	414D	12F-4R	100.0	10827	C,H,A
7400	54017.00	39970.00	43210.00	44940.00	JD	6T	414D	16F-16R	100.0		C,H,A
7400 4WD	60076.00	44460.00	48060.00	49980.00	JD	6T	414D	12F-4R	100.0	11687	C,H,A
7400 4WD	62396.00	46170.00	49920.00	51920.00	JD	6T	414D	16F-16R	100.0		C,H,A
7400HC	50116.00	37090.00	40090.00	41690.00	JD	6T	414D	16F-16R	100.0		C,H,A
7400HC	51608.00	38190.00	41290.00	42940.00	JD	6T	414D	12F-4R	100.0		No
7400HC 4WD	61215.00	45300.00	48970.00	50930.00	JD	6T	414D	12F-4R	100.0		No
7400HC 4WD w/Cab	68845.00	50950.00	55080.00	57280.00	JD	6T	414D	12F-4R	100.0		C,H,A
7400HC w/Cab	59238.00	43840.00	47390.00	49290.00	JD	6T	414D	12F-4R	100.0		C,H,A
7600	60210.00	44560.00	48170.00	50100.00	JD	6T	414D	16F-16R	110.0	13160	C,H,A
7600 4WD	71400.00	52840.00	57120.00	59410.00	JD	6T	414D	16F-16R	110.0	15200	C,H,A
7600 PS	63350.00	46880.00	50680.00	52710.00	JD	6T	414D	19F-7R	110.0		C,H,A
7700	67447.00	49910.00	53960.00	56120.00	JD	6T	466D	16F-12R	125.0	13870	C,H,A
7700 4WD	78637.00	58190.00	62910.00	65430.00	JD	6T	466D	16F-12R	125.0	15400	C,H,A
7700 PS	70587.00	52230.00	56470.00	58730.00	JD	6T	466D	19F-7R	125.0		C,H,A
7800	72226.00	53450.00	57780.00	60090.00	JD	6T	466D	16F-12R	145.0	13910	C,H,A
7800 4WD	83416.00	61730.00	66730.00	69400.00	JD	6T	466D	16F-12R	145.0	15480	C,H,A
7800 PS	75366.00	55770.00	60290.00	62700.00	JD	6T	466D	19F-7R	145.0		C,H,A
8100	81185.00	56830.00	61700.00	64170.00	JD	6TA	466D	16F-4R	160.0	16435	C,H,A
8100 4WD	94009.00	65810.00	71450.00	74310.00	JD	6TA	466D	16F-4R	160.0	17876	C,H,A
8200	90655.00	63460.00	68900.00	71660.00	JD	6TA	466D	16F-4R	180.0	16457	C,H,A
8200 4WD	103479.00	70700.00	76760.00	79830.00	JD	6TA	466D	16F-4R	180.0	17898	C,H,A
8300	99563.00	69690.00	75670.00	78700.00	JD	6TA	466D	16F-4R	200.0	17030	C,H,A
8300 4WD	112387.00	77000.00	83600.00	86940.00	JD	6TA	466D	16F-4R	200.0	18523	C,H,A
8400 4WD	121661.00	79730.00	86870.00	90350.00	JD	6TA	496D	16F-4R	225.0		C,H,A
8570 4WD	95117.00	63730.00	69440.00	72220.00	JD	6TA	466D	12F-3R	206.0	29564	C,H,A
8570 4WD	99729.00	66820.00	72800.00	75710.00	JD	6TA	466D	24F-6R	206.0		C,H,A
8570 4WD PTO, 3Pt.	111238.00	74530.00	81200.00	84450.00	JD	6TA	466D	12F-3R	206.0		C,H,A
8770 4WD	114945.00	75710.00	82490.00	85790.00	JD	6TA	619D	12F-3R	256.0	31438	C,H,A
8770 4WD	119557.00	78060.00	85050.00	88450.00	JD	6TA	619D	24F-6R	256.0		C,H,A
8770 4WD PS	131088.00	85760.00	93440.00	97180.00	JD	6TA	619D	12F-2R	256.0		C,H,A
8870 4WD	126538.00	83750.00	91250.00	94900.00	JD	6TA	619D	12F-3R	300.0	31438	C,H,A
8870 4WD	131150.00	86430.00	94170.00	97940.00	JD	6TA	619D	24F-6R	300.0		C,H,A
8870 4WD PS	142681.00	91790.00	100010.00	104010.00	JD	6TA	619D	12F-2R	300.0		C,H,A
8970 4WD	144175.00	85400.00	93800.00	97550.00	JD	6TA	855D	12F-3R	339.0		C,H,A
8970 4WD	148787.00	87230.00	95810.00	99640.00	JD	6TA	855D	24F-6R	339.0	31879	C,H,A
8970 4WD PS	160318.00	91500.00	100500.00	104520.00	JD	6TA	855D	12F-2R	339.0		C,H,A
8970 4WD PS PTO	167603.00	97600.00	107200.00	111490.00	JD	6TA	855D	12F-2R	339.0		C,H,A
8970 4WD PTO	151460.00	90280.00	99160.00	103130.00	JD	6TA	855D	12F-3R	339.0		C,H,A
8970 4WD PTO	156072.00	92720.00	101840.00	105910.00	JD	6TA	855D	24F-6R	339.0		C,H,A

H, HC, HU--High Clearance PS--Power Shift QR--Quad Range

1997

Model	Approx. Retail Price New	Fair	Good	Premium	Engine Make	No. Cyls.	Displ. Cu.-In.	No. Speeds	P.T.O. H.P.	Approx. Shipping Wt.-Lbs.	Cab
670	11796.00	8470.00	9020.00	9380.00	Yanmar	3	54D	8F-2R	18.5	1980	No
670 4WD	13554.00	10010.00	10660.00	11090.00	Yanmar	3	54D	8F-2R	18.5	2120	No
755	14836.00	10780.00	11480.00	11940.00	Yanmar	3	54D	Variable	20.0	1817	No
755 4WD	16105.00	12400.00	13210.00	13740.00	Yanmar	3	54D	Variable	20.0	1921	No
770	12739.00	9240.00	9840.00	10230.00	Yanmar	3	83D	8F-2R	24.0	2180	No
770 4WD	15191.00	11550.00	12300.00	12790.00	Yanmar	3	83D	8F-2R	24.0	2355	No
855	15790.00	12160.00	12950.00	13470.00	Yanmar	3	61D	Variable	24.0	1876	No
855 4WD	17269.00	13090.00	13940.00	14500.00	Yanmar	3	61D	Variable	24.0	1876	No
870	14952.00	108000.00	115200.00	119810.00	Yanmar	3	87D	9F-3R	28.0	1876	No
870 4WD	17320.00	12990.00	13860.00	14410.00	Yanmar	3	87D	9F-3R	28.0	1876	No
955 4WD	19324.00	14250.00	15200.00	15810.00	Yanmar	3	87D	Variable	33.0	1876	No
970	16750.00	12560.00	13400.00	13940.00	Yanmar	3	111D	9F-3R	30.0	1876	No
970 4WD	20289.00	15000.00	16000.00	16640.00	Yanmar	3	111D	9F-3R	33.0	1876	No
1070	18937.00	13730.00	14640.00	15230.00	Yanmar	3	116D	9F-3R	38.5	1876	No
1070 4WD	22048.00	15900.00	16960.00	17640.00	Yanmar	3	116D	9F-3R	38.5	1876	No
5200	21048.00	16840.00	17680.00	18390.00	JD	3	179D	9F-3R	40.0	4250	No
5200 4WD	26989.00	21590.00	22670.00	23580.00	JD	3	179D	9F-3R	40.0	4650	No
5200 4WD w/Cab	34789.00	27830.00	29220.00	30390.00	JD	3	179D	9F-3R	40.0		C,H,A
5200 w/Cab	29661.00	23730.00	24920.00	25920.00	JD	3	179D	9F-3R	40.0		C,H,A
5300	23212.00	18570.00	19500.00	20280.00	JD	3	179D	9F-3R	50.0	4350	No
5300 4WD	28269.00	22620.00	23750.00	24700.00	JD	3	179D	9F-3R	50.0	4750	No
5300 4WD w/Cab	36915.00	29530.00	31010.00	32250.00	JD	3	179D	9F-3R	50.0		C,H,A
5300 w/Cab	31773.00	25420.00	26690.00	27760.00	JD	3	179D	9F-3R	50.0		C,H,A
5400	26313.00	21050.00	22100.00	22980.00	JD	3	179D	9F-3R	60.0	4600	No
5400 4WD	31471.00	25180.00	26440.00	27500.00	JD	3	179D	9F-3R	60.0	5000	No
5400 4WD w/Cab	39591.00	31670.00	33260.00	34590.00	JD	3T	179D	9F-3R	60.0		C,H,A
5400 w/Cab	34429.00	27540.00	28920.00	30080.00	JD	3T	179D	9F-3R	60.0		C,H,A
5400N	26015.00	20810.00	21850.00	22720.00	JD	3	179D	12F-12R	60.0	4763	No
5400N 4WD	32017.00	25610.00	26890.00	27970.00	JD	3	179D	12F-12R	60.0	5072	No
5400N 4WD w/Cab	40115.00	32090.00	33700.00	35050.00	JD	3T	179D	12F-12R	60.0		C,H,A
5400N w/Cab	34113.00	27290.00	28660.00	29810.00	JD	3T	179D	12F-12R	60.0		C,H,A
5500	29068.00	22380.00	23840.00	24790.00	JD	4T	239D	9F-3R	73.0		No
5500 4WD	34233.00	26360.00	28070.00	29190.00	JD	4T	239D	9F-3R	73.0		No
5500 4WD w/Cab	42353.00	32610.00	34730.00	36120.00	JD	4T	239D	9F-3R	73.0		C,H,A
5500 w/Cab	37188.00	28640.00	30490.00	31710.00	JD	4T	239D	9F-3R	73.0		C,H,A
5500N	28663.00	22070.00	23500.00	24440.00	JD	4T	239D	12F-12R	73.0		No
5500N 4WD	34658.00	26690.00	28420.00	29560.00	JD	4T	239D	12F-12R	73.0		No
5500N 4WD w/Cab	42756.00	32920.00	35060.00	36460.00	JD	4T	239D	12F-12R	73.0		C,H,A
5500N w/Cab	36761.00	28310.00	30140.00	31350.00	JD	4T	239D	12F-12R	73.0		C,H,A
6200	30643.00	23600.00	25130.00	26140.00	JD	4T	239D	12F-4R	66.0	7420	No

John Deere (Cont.)

Model	Approx. Retail Price New	Estimated Average Value Less Repairs Fair	Good	Premium	Engine Make	Engine No. Cyls.	Engine Displ. Cu.-In.	No. Speeds	P.T.O. H.P.	Approx. Shipping Wt.-Lbs.	Cab
			1997 (Cont.)								
6200	33033.00	**25440.00**	**27090.00**	**28170.00**	JD	4T	239D	16F-16R	66.0		No
6200 4WD	37578.00	**28940.00**	**30810.00**	**32040.00**	JD	4T	239D	12F-4R	66.0	7916	No
6200 4WD	39968.00	**30780.00**	**32770.00**	**34080.00**	JD	4T	239D	16F-16R	66.0		No
6200 4WD w/Cab	46376.00	**35710.00**	**38030.00**	**39550.00**	JD	4T	239D	12F-4R	66.0	8423	C,H,A
6200 w/Cab	39441.00	**30370.00**	**32340.00**	**33630.00**	JD	4T	239D	12F-4R	66.0	7927	C,H,A
6200L	30623.00	**23580.00**	**25110.00**	**26110.00**	JD	4T	239D	12F-4R	66.0	7420	No
6200L	33013.00	**25420.00**	**27070.00**	**28150.00**	JD	4T	239D	16F-16R	66.0		No
6200L 4WD	37558.00	**28920.00**	**30800.00**	**32030.00**	JD	4T	239D	12F-4R	66.0	7916	No
6300	33061.00	**25460.00**	**27110.00**	**28190.00**	JD	4T	239D	12F-4R	75.0	7497	No
6300	35451.00	**27300.00**	**29070.00**	**30230.00**	JD	4T	239D	16F-16R	75.0		No
6300 4WD	40285.00	**31460.00**	**33500.00**	**34840.00**	JD	4T	239D	16F-16R	75.0		No
6300 4WD	42675.00	**32860.00**	**34990.00**	**36390.00**	JD	4T	239D	12F-4R	75.0	8004	No
6300 4WD w/Cab	49079.00	**37790.00**	**40250.00**	**41860.00**	JD	4T	239D	12F-4R	75.0	8511	C,H,A
6300 LC	49446.00	**38070.00**	**40550.00**	**42170.00**	JD	4T	239D	16F-16R	75.0		C,H,A
6300 w/Cab	41855.00	**32230.00**	**34320.00**	**35690.00**	JD	4T	239D	12F-4R	75.0	8004	C,H,A
6300L	33039.00	**25440.00**	**27090.00**	**28170.00**	JD	4T	239D	12F-4R	75.0	7497	No
6300L	35429.00	**27280.00**	**29050.00**	**30210.00**	JD	4T	239D	16F-16R	75.0		No
6300L 4WD	40389.00	**31100.00**	**33120.00**	**34450.00**	JD	4T	239D	12F-4R	75.0	8004	No
6300LC 4WD	56670.00	**43640.00**	**46470.00**	**48330.00**	JD	4T	239D	16F-16R	75.0		C,H,A
6400	36809.00	**28340.00**	**30180.00**	**31390.00**	JD	4T	276D	12F-4R	85.0	7607	No
6400	39199.00	**30180.00**	**32140.00**	**33430.00**	JD	4T	276D	16F-16R	85.0		No
6400 4WD	44159.00	**34000.00**	**36210.00**	**37660.00**	JD	4T	276D	12F-4R	85.0	8246	No
6400 4WD	46549.00	**35840.00**	**38170.00**	**39700.00**	JD	4T	276D	16F-16R	85.0		No
6400 4WD w/Cab	52359.00	**40320.00**	**42930.00**	**44650.00**	JD	4T	276D	12F-4R	85.0	8754	C,H,A
6400 w/Cab	45009.00	**34660.00**	**36910.00**	**38390.00**	JD	4T	276D	12F-4R	85.0	8114	C,H,A
6400L	30584.00	**28400.00**	**30250.00**	**31460.00**	JD	4T	276D	16F-16R	85.0		No
6400L	36194.00	**27870.00**	**29680.00**	**30870.00**	JD	4T	276D	12F-4R	85.0	7607	No
6400L 4WD	43544.00	**33530.00**	**35710.00**	**37140.00**	JD	4T	276D	12F-4R	85.0	8246	No
6400LC	52603.00	**40500.00**	**43130.00**	**44860.00**	JD	4T	276D	16F-16R	85.0		C,H,A
6400LC 4WD	59953.00	**46160.00**	**49160.00**	**51130.00**	JD	4T	276D	16F-16R	85.0		C,H,A
6500L	41547.00	**31990.00**	**34070.00**	**35430.00**	JD	4T	276D	16F-12R	95.0	7740	No
6500L 4WD	48897.00	**37650.00**	**40100.00**	**41700.00**	JD	4T	276D	16F-12R	95.0	8379	No
6500LC	54931.00	**42300.00**	**45040.00**	**46840.00**	JD	4T	276D	16F-16R	95.0		C,H,A
6500LC 4WD	62281.00	**47960.00**	**51070.00**	**53110.00**	JD	4T	276D	16F-16R	95.0		C,H,A
7210	49440.00	**38070.00**	**40540.00**	**42160.00**	JD	6T	359D	12F-4R	92.0	10662	C,H,A
7210	51830.00	**39910.00**	**42500.00**	**44200.00**	JD	6T	359D	16F-16R	92.0		C,H,A
7210 4WD	57161.00	**44010.00**	**46870.00**	**48750.00**	JD	6T	359D	12F-4R	92.0	11522	C,H,A
7210 4WD	59551.00	**45850.00**	**48830.00**	**50780.00**	JD	6T	359D	16F-16R	92.0		C,H,A
7210HC	49217.00	**37900.00**	**40360.00**	**41970.00**	JD	6T	359D	12F-4R	92.0		No
7210HC	51607.00	**39740.00**	**42320.00**	**44010.00**	JD	6T	359D	16F-16R	92.0		C,H,A
7210HC 4WD	56938.00	**43840.00**	**46690.00**	**48560.00**	JD	6T	359D	12F-4R	92.0		No
7210HC 4WD w/Cab	64797.00	**50080.00**	**53330.00**	**55460.00**	JD	6T	359D	12F-4R	92.0		C,H,A
7210HC w/Cab	57076.00	**43950.00**	**46800.00**	**48670.00**	JD	6T	359D	12F-4R	92.0		C,H,A
7410	53310.00	**41050.00**	**43710.00**	**45460.00**	JD	6T	414D	12F-4R	100.0	10827	C,H,A
7410	55700.00	**42890.00**	**45670.00**	**47500.00**	JD	6T	414D	16F-16R	100.0		C,H,A
7410 4WD	61031.00	**46990.00**	**50050.00**	**52050.00**	JD	6T	414D	12F-4R	100.0	11687	C,H,A
7410 4WD	63421.00	**48830.00**	**52010.00**	**54090.00**	JD	6T	414D	16F-16R	100.0		C,H,A
7410HC	53145.00	**40920.00**	**43580.00**	**45320.00**	JD	6T	414D	12F-4R	100.0		No
7410HC	55535.00	**42760.00**	**45540.00**	**47360.00**	JD	6T	414D	16F-16R	100.0		C,H,A
7410HC 4WD	60866.00	**46870.00**	**49910.00**	**51910.00**	JD	6T	414D	12F-4R	100.0		No
7410HC 4WD w/Cab	68725.00	**52920.00**	**56360.00**	**58610.00**	JD	6T	414D	12F-4R	100.0		C,H,A
7410HC w/Cab	61004.00	**46970.00**	**50020.00**	**52020.00**	JD	6T	414D	12F-4R	100.0		C,H,A
7610	62076.00	**47800.00**	**50900.00**	**52940.00**	JD	6T	414D	16F-16R	110.0	13160	C,H,A
7610 4WD	72574.00	**55880.00**	**59510.00**	**61890.00**	JD	6T	414D	16F-16R	110.0	15200	C,H,A
7610 PS	65310.00	**50290.00**	**53550.00**	**55690.00**	JD	6T	414D	19F-7R	110.0		C,H,A
7710	69540.00	**53550.00**	**57020.00**	**59300.00**	JD	6T	496D	16F-12R	125.0	13870	C,H,A
7710 4WD	80038.00	**61630.00**	**65630.00**	**68260.00**	JD	6T	496D	16F-12R	125.0	15400	C,H,A
7710 PS	72774.00	**56040.00**	**59680.00**	**62070.00**	JD	6T	496D	19F-7R	125.0		C,H,A
7810	74573.00	**57420.00**	**61150.00**	**63600.00**	JD	6T	496D	16F-12R	145.0	13910	C,H,A
7810 4WD	85071.00	**65510.00**	**69760.00**	**72550.00**	JD	6T	496D	16F-12R	145.0	15480	C,H,A
7810 PS	77807.00	**59910.00**	**63800.00**	**66350.00**	JD	6T	496D	19F-7R	145.0		C,H,A
8100	84084.00	**63060.00**	**67270.00**	**69960.00**	JD	6TA	496D	16F-4R	160.0	16435	C,H,A
8100 4WD	96084.00	**72060.00**	**76870.00**	**79950.00**	JD	6TA	496D	16F-4R	160.0	17876	C,H,A
8200	93335.00	**70000.00**	**74670.00**	**77660.00**	JD	6TA	496D	16F-4R	180.0	16457	C,H,A
8200 4WD	105335.00	**79000.00**	**84270.00**	**87640.00**	JD	6TA	496D	16F-4R	180.0	17898	C,H,A
8300	102510.00	**76880.00**	**82010.00**	**85290.00**	JD	6TA	496D	16F-4R	200.0	17030	C,H,A
8300 4WD	114510.00	**85880.00**	**91610.00**	**95270.00**	JD	6TA	496D	16F-4R	200.0	18523	C,H,A
8400 4WD	124626.00	**90000.00**	**96000.00**	**99840.00**	JD	6TA	496D	16F-4R	225.0		C,H,A
9100	102738.00	**73970.00**	**79110.00**	**82270.00**	JD	6TA	496D	12F-3R	260*		C,H,A
9100	107488.00	**77390.00**	**82770.00**	**86080.00**	JD	6TA	496D	24F-24R	260*		C,H,A
9200	122195.00	**81870.00**	**89200.00**	**92770.00**	JD	6TA	643D	12F-3R	310*		C,H,A
9200	126945.00	**85050.00**	**92670.00**	**96380.00**	JD	6TA	643D	24F-24R	310*		C,H,A
9200 PS	138822.00	**91120.00**	**99280.00**	**103250.00**	JD	6TA	643D	12F-2R	310*		C,H,A
9200 w/PTO, 3Pt.	138948.00	**92460.00**	**100740.00**	**104770.00**	JD	6TA	643D	12F-3R	310*		C,H,A
9300	134077.00	**89110.00**	**97090.00**	**100970.00**	JD	6TA	765D	12F-3R	360*		C,H,A
9300	138827.00	**91120.00**	**99280.00**	**103250.00**	JD	6TA	765D	24F-24R	360*		C,H,A
9300 PS	150704.00	**97820.00**	**106580.00**	**110840.00**	JD	6TA	765D	12F-2R	360*		C,H,A
9300 w/PTO, 3Pt.	150830.00	**99160.00**	**108040.00**	**112360.00**	JD	6TA	765D	12F-3R	360*		C,H,A
9400	158158.00	**103850.00**	**113150.00**	**117680.00**	JD	6TA	765D	12F-3R	425*		C,H,A
9400	162908.00	**107200.00**	**116800.00**	**121470.00**	JD	6TA	765D	24F-24R	425*		C,H,A
9400 PS	174785.00	**114100.00**	**124320.00**	**129290.00**	JD	6TA	765D	12F-2R	425*		C,H,A
9400 w/PTO, 3Pt.	174911.00	**115240.00**	**125560.00**	**130580.00**	JD	6TA	765D	12F-3R	425*		C,H,A

HC--High Clearance L--Low Profile PS--Power Shift
***Engine Horsepower**

John Deere (Cont.)

Model	Approx. Retail Price New	Estimated Average Value Less Repairs Fair	Good	Premium	Engine Make	No. Cyls.	Displ. Cu.-In.	No. Speeds	P.T.O. H.P.	Approx. Shipping Wt.-Lbs.	Cab
1998											
770	13927.00	**11000.00**	**11700.00**	**12050.00**	Yanmar	3	83D	8F-2R	20.0		No
770 4WD	15191.00	**12000.00**	**12760.00**	**13140.00**	Yanmar	3	83D	8F-2R	20.0		No
855	15886.00	**12550.00**	**13340.00**	**13740.00**	Yanmar	3	61D	Variable	19.0		No
855 4WD	17269.00	**13640.00**	**14510.00**	**14950.00**	Yanmar	3	61D	Variable	19.0		No
870	14952.00	**11810.00**	**12560.00**	**12940.00**	Yanmar	3	87D	9F-3R	25.0		No
870 4WD	17320.00	**13680.00**	**14550.00**	**14990.00**	Yanmar	3	87D	9F-3R	25.0		No
955 4WD	19324.00	**15270.00**	**16230.00**	**16720.00**	Yanmar	3	87D	Variable	27.0		No
970	17562.00	**13870.00**	**14750.00**	**15190.00**	Yanmar	3	111D	9F-3R	30.0		No
970 4WD	20289.00	**16030.00**	**17040.00**	**17550.00**	Yanmar	3	111D	9F-3R	30.0		No
1070	18937.00	**14960.00**	**15910.00**	**16390.00**	Yanmar	3	116D	9F-3R	35.0		No
1070 4WD	22048.00	**17420.00**	**18520.00**	**19080.00**	Yanmar	3	116D	9F-3R	35.0		No
5210	21072.00	**17490.00**	**18330.00**	**18880.00**	JD	3	179D	9F-3R	45.0		No
5210 w/Cab	29210.00	**24240.00**	**25410.00**	**26170.00**	JD	3	179D	9F-3R	45.0		C,H,A
5210 4WD	27000.00	**22410.00**	**23490.00**	**24200.00**	JD	3	179D	9F-3R	45.0		No
5210 4WD w/Cab	34278.00	**28450.00**	**29820.00**	**30720.00**	JD	3	179D	9F-3R	45.0		C,H,A
5310	23795.00	**19750.00**	**20700.00**	**21320.00**	JD	3T	179D	9F-3R	55.0		No
5310 w/Cab	32527.00	**27000.00**	**28300.00**	**29150.00**	JD	3T	179D	9F-3R	55.0		C,H,A
5310 4WD	29775.00	**24710.00**	**25900.00**	**26680.00**	JD	3T	179D	9F-3R	55.0		No
5310 4WD w/Cab	37785.00	**31360.00**	**32870.00**	**33860.00**	JD	3T	179D	9F-3R	55.0		C,H,A
5310N	24550.00	**20380.00**	**21360.00**	**22000.00**	JD	3T	179D	9F-3R	55.0		No
5310N w/Cab	33030.00	**27420.00**	**28740.00**	**29600.00**	JD	3T	179D	9F-3R	55.0		C,H,A
5310N 4WD	30500.00	**25320.00**	**26540.00**	**27340.00**	JD	3T	179D	9F-3R	55.0		No
5310N 4WD w/Cab	38985.00	**32360.00**	**33920.00**	**34940.00**	JD	3T	179D	9F-3R	55.0		C,H,A
5410	26435.00	**21940.00**	**23000.00**	**23690.00**	JD	3T	179D	9F-3R	65.0		No
5410 w/Cab	34730.00	**28830.00**	**30220.00**	**31130.00**	JD	3T	179D	9F-3R	65.0		C,H,A
5410 4WD	31752.00	**26350.00**	**27620.00**	**28450.00**	JD	3T	179D	9F-3R	65.0		No
5410 4WD w/Cab	40040.00	**33230.00**	**34840.00**	**35890.00**	JD	3T	179D	9F-3R	65.0		C,H,A
5510	30504.00	**25010.00**	**25930.00**	**26710.00**	JD	4T	239D	9F-3R	75.0		No
5510 w/Cab	37565.00	**30800.00**	**31930.00**	**32890.00**	JD	4T	239D	9F-3R	75.0		C,H,A
5510 4WD	35905.00	**29440.00**	**30520.00**	**31440.00**	JD	4T	239D	9F-3R	75.0		No
5510 4WD w/Cab	44190.00	**36240.00**	**37560.00**	**38690.00**	JD	4T	239D	9F-3R	75.0		C,H,A
5510N	29522.00	**24210.00**	**25090.00**	**25840.00**	JD	4T	239D	12F-12R	75.0		No
5510N w/Cab	38000.00	**31160.00**	**32300.00**	**33270.00**	JD	4T	239D	12F-12R	75.0		C,H,A
5510N 4WD	35592.00	**29190.00**	**30250.00**	**31160.00**	JD	4T	239D	12F-12R	75.0		No
5510N 4WD w/Cab	44075.00	**36140.00**	**37460.00**	**38580.00**	JD	4T	239D	12F-12R	75.0		C,H,A
6110	30290.00	**24840.00**	**25750.00**	**26520.00**	JD	4T	276D	12F-4R	65.0		No
6110 w/Cab	38783.00	**31800.00**	**32970.00**	**33960.00**	JD	4T	276D	12F-4R	65.0		No
6110 4WD	37435.00	**30700.00**	**31820.00**	**32780.00**	JD	4T	276D	12F-4R	65.0		No
6110 4WD w/Cab	45926.00	**37660.00**	**39040.00**	**40210.00**	JD	4T	276D	12F-4R	65.0		No
6110L	29975.00	**24580.00**	**25480.00**	**26240.00**	JD	4T	276D	12F-4R	65.0		No
6110L 4WD	37115.00	**30430.00**	**31550.00**	**32500.00**	JD	4T	276D	12F-4R	65.0		No
6210	31642.00	**25950.00**	**26900.00**	**27710.00**	JD	4T	239D	12F-4R	72.0		No
6210 w/Cab	40975.00	**33600.00**	**34830.00**	**35880.00**	JD	4T	239D	12F-4R	72.0		C,H,A
6210 4WD	38785.00	**31800.00**	**32970.00**	**33960.00**	JD	4T	239D	12F-4R	72.0		No
6210 4WD w/Cab	48120.00	**39460.00**	**40900.00**	**42130.00**	JD	4T	239D	12F-4R	72.0		C,H,A
6210L	31780.00	**26060.00**	**27010.00**	**27820.00**	JD	4T	239D	12F-4R	72.0		No
6210L 4WD	38925.00	**31920.00**	**33090.00**	**34080.00**	JD	4T	239D	12F-4R	72.0		No
6310	34200.00	**28040.00**	**29070.00**	**29940.00**	JD	4T	239D	12F-4R	80.0		No
6310 w/Cab	43496.00	**35670.00**	**36970.00**	**38080.00**	JD	4T	239D	12F-4R	80.0		C,H,A
6310 4WD	41640.00	**34150.00**	**35390.00**	**36450.00**	JD	4T	239D	12F-4R	80.0		No
6310 4WD w/Cab	50940.00	**41770.00**	**43300.00**	**44600.00**	JD	4T	239D	12F-4R	80.0		C,H,A
6310L	33880.00	**27780.00**	**28800.00**	**29660.00**	JD	4T	239D	12F-4R	80.0		No
6310L 4WD	41450.00	**33990.00**	**35230.00**	**36290.00**	JD	4T	239D	12F-4R	80.0		No
6310S	50820.00	**41670.00**	**43200.00**	**44500.00**	JD	4T	239D	16F-16R	80.0		C,H,A
6310S 4WD	58260.00	**47770.00**	**49520.00**	**51010.00**	JD	4T	239D	16F-16R	80.0		C,H,A
6405	33170.00	**26200.00**	**27860.00**	**28700.00**	JD	4T	276D	12F-4R	85.0		No
6405 4WD	40536.00	**32020.00**	**34050.00**	**35070.00**	JD	4T	276D	12F-4R	85.0		No
6410	37116.00	**30440.00**	**31550.00**	**32500.00**	JD	4T	276D	12F-4R	90.0		No
6410 w/Cab	46290.00	**37960.00**	**39350.00**	**40530.00**	JD	4T	276D	12F-4R	90.0		C,H,A
6410 4WD	44690.00	**36650.00**	**37990.00**	**39130.00**	JD	4T	276D	12F-4R	90.0		No
6410 4WD w/Cab	53860.00	**44170.00**	**45780.00**	**47150.00**	JD	4T	276D	12F-4R	90.0		C,H,A
6410L	37146.00	**30460.00**	**31570.00**	**32520.00**	JD	4T	276D	12F-4R	90.0		No
6410L 4WD	44720.00	**36670.00**	**38010.00**	**39150.00**	JD	4T	276D	12F-4R	90.0		No
6410S	54086.00	**44350.00**	**45970.00**	**47350.00**	JD	4T	276D	16F-16R	90.0		C,H,A
6410S 4WD	61660.00	**50560.00**	**52410.00**	**53980.00**	JD	4T	276D	16F-16R	90.0		C,H,A
6510L	42185.00	**34590.00**	**35860.00**	**36940.00**	JD	4T	276D	16F-16R	95.0		No
6510L 4WD	49755.00	**40800.00**	**42290.00**	**43560.00**	JD	4T	276D	16F-16R	95.0		No
6510S	55946.00	**45880.00**	**47550.00**	**48980.00**	JD	4T	276D	12F-4R	95.0		C,H,A
6510S 4WD	63520.00	**52090.00**	**53990.00**	**55610.00**	JD	4T	276D	12F-4R	95.0		C,H,A
6605	36900.00	**29150.00**	**31000.00**	**31930.00**	JD	6T	414D	12F-4R	95.0		No
6605 4WD	44200.00	**34920.00**	**37130.00**	**38240.00**	JD	6T	414D	12F-4R	95.0		No
7210	51630.00	**42340.00**	**43890.00**	**45210.00**	JD	6T	414D	12F-4R	95.0		C,H,A
7210 4WD	59975.00	**49180.00**	**50980.00**	**52510.00**	JD	6T	414D	12F-4R	95.0		C,H,A
7210HC	51400.00	**42150.00**	**43690.00**	**45000.00**	JD	6T	414D	12F-4R	95.0		No
7210HC w/Cab	59500.00	**48790.00**	**50580.00**	**52100.00**	JD	6T	414D	12F-4R	95.0		C,H,A
7210HC 4WD	60890.00	**49930.00**	**51760.00**	**53310.00**	JD	6T	414D	12F-4R	95.0		No
7210HC 4WD w/Cab	68990.00	**56570.00**	**58640.00**	**60400.00**	JD	6T	414D	12F-4R	95.0		C,H,A
7405	43560.00	**34410.00**	**36590.00**	**37690.00**	JD	6T	414D	16F-16R	105.0		No
7405 4WD	51355.00	**40570.00**	**43140.00**	**44430.00**	JD	6T	414D	16F-16R	105.0		No
7405HC 4WD	55305.00	**43690.00**	**46460.00**	**47850.00**	JD	6T	414D	16F-16R	105.0		No
7410	55620.00	**45610.00**	**47280.00**	**48700.00**	JD	6T	414D	12F-4R	105.0		C,H,A
7410 4WD	64665.00	**53030.00**	**54970.00**	**56620.00**	JD	6T	414D	12F-4R	105.0		C,H,A
7410HC	55450.00	**45470.00**	**47130.00**	**48540.00**	JD	6T	414D	12F-4R	105.0		No
7410HC w/Cab	63545.00	**52110.00**	**54010.00**	**55630.00**	JD	6T	414D	12F-4R	105.0		C,H,A

John Deere (Cont.)

Model	Approx. Retail Price New	Estimated Average Value Less Repairs Fair	Good	Premium	Make	Engine No. Cyls.	Displ. Cu.-In.	No. Speeds	P.T.O. H.P.	Approx. Shipping Wt.-Lbs.	Cab
1998 (Cont.)											
7410HC 4WD	65645.00	**53830.00**	**55800.00**	**57470.00**	JD	6T	414D	12F-4R	105.0		No
7410HC 4WD w/Cab	73740.00	**60470.00**	**62680.00**	**64560.00**	JD	6T	414D	12F-4R	105.0		C,H,A
7610	64650.00	**53010.00**	**54950.00**	**56600.00**	JD	6T	414D	16F-16R	115.0		C,H,A
7610 4WD	76560.00	**62780.00**	**65080.00**	**67030.00**	JD	6T	414D	16F-16R	115.0		C,H,A
7610 PS	67980.00	**55740.00**	**57780.00**	**59510.00**	JD	6T	414D	19F-7R	115.0		C,H,A
7610 PS 4WD	78090.00	**64030.00**	**66380.00**	**68370.00**	JD	6T	414D	19F-7R	115.0		C,H,A
7710	72475.00	**59430.00**	**61600.00**	**63450.00**	JD	6T	496D	16F-12R	130.0		C,H,A
7710 4WD	84385.00	**69200.00**	**71730.00**	**73880.00**	JD	6T	496D	16F-12R	130.0		C,H,A
7710 PS	75805.00	**62160.00**	**64430.00**	**66360.00**	JD	6T	496D	19F-7R	130.0		C,H,A
7710 PS 4WD	85780.00	**70340.00**	**72910.00**	**75100.00**	JD	6T	496D	19F-7R	130.0		C,H,A
7810	77520.00	**63570.00**	**65890.00**	**67870.00**	JD	6T	496D	16F-12R	150.0		C,H,A
7810 4WD	89375.00	**73290.00**	**75970.00**	**78250.00**	JD	6T	496D	16F-12R	150.0		C,H,A
7810 PS	80900.00	**66340.00**	**68770.00**	**70830.00**	JD	6T	496D	19F-7R	150.0		C,H,A
7810 PS 4WD	92400.00	**75770.00**	**78540.00**	**80900.00**	JD	6T	496D	19F-7R	150.0		C,H,A
8100	88475.00	**69050.00**	**73420.00**	**75620.00**	JD	6TA	496D	16F-4R	160.0		C,H,A
8100 4WD	101955.00	**79000.00**	**84000.00**	**86520.00**	JD	6TA	496D	16F-4R	160.0		C,H,A
8100T	116360.00	**84240.00**	**88560.00**	**91220.00**	JD	6TA	496D	16F-4R	160.0		C,H,A
8200	99315.00	**77420.00**	**82320.00**	**84790.00**	JD	6TA	496D	16F-4R	180.0		C,H,A
8200 4WD	111560.00	**86900.00**	**92400.00**	**95170.00**	JD	6TA	496D	16F-4R	180.0		C,H,A
8200T	125830.00	**92040.00**	**96760.00**	**99660.00**	JD	6TA	496D	16F-4R	180.0		C,H,A
8300	107477.00	**82950.00**	**88200.00**	**90850.00**	JD	6TA	496D	16F-4R	200.0		C,H,A
8300 4WD	122250.00	**94170.00**	**100130.00**	**103130.00**	JD	6TA	496D	16F-4R	200.0		C,H,A
8300T	133765.00	**95940.00**	**100860.00**	**103890.00**	JD	6TA	496D	16F-4R	200.0		C,H,A
8400 4WD	131050.00	**99540.00**	**105840.00**	**109020.00**	JD	6TA	496D	16F-4R	225.0		C,H,A
8400T	141655.00	**101400.00**	**106600.00**	**109800.00**	JD	6TA	496D	16F-4R	225.0		C,H,A
9100	108520.00	**84650.00**	**88990.00**	**91660.00**	JD	6TA	496D	12F-3R	260*		C,H,A
9100 PS	113415.00	**88460.00**	**93000.00**	**95790.00**	JD	6TA	496D	24F-24R	260*		C,H,A
9200	128560.00	**95130.00**	**101560.00**	**104610.00**	JD	6TA	643D	12F-3R	310*		C,H,A
9200	133455.00	**98760.00**	**105430.00**	**108590.00**	JD	6TA	643D	24F-24R	310*		C,H,A
9200 PS	148686.00	**110030.00**	**117460.00**	**120980.00**	JD	6TA	643D	12F-2R	310*		C,H,A
9300	147380.00	**109060.00**	**116430.00**	**119920.00**	JD	6TA	765D	12F-3R	360*		C,H,A
9300	152270.00	**112680.00**	**120290.00**	**123900.00**	JD	6TA	765D	24F-24R	360*		C,H,A
9300 PS	168135.00	**124420.00**	**132830.00**	**136820.00**	JD	6TA	765D	12F-2R	360*		C,H,A
9400	166135.00	**122940.00**	**131250.00**	**135190.00**	JD	6TA	765D	12F-3R	425*		C,H,A
9400	171026.00	**126560.00**	**135110.00**	**139160.00**	JD	6TA	765D	24F-24R	425*		C,H,A
9400 PS	184735.00	**136700.00**	**145940.00**	**150320.00**	JD	6TA	765D	12F-2R	425*		C,H,A
1999											
790	10290.00	**8950.00**	**9160.00**	**9340.00**	Yanmar	3	91D	8F-2R	25.0		No
790 4WD	12060.00	**10490.00**	**10730.00**	**10950.00**	Yanmar	3	91D	8F-2R	25.0		No
4100 4WD	13150.00	**11440.00**	**11700.00**	**11930.00**	Yanmar	3	61D	8F-4R	17.0		No
4100 4WD Hydro	14850.00	**12920.00**	**13220.00**	**13480.00**	Yanmar	3	61D	8F-2R	16.0		No
4200	14170.00	**12330.00**	**12610.00**	**12860.00**	Yanmar	3	73D	9F-3R	21.5		No
4200 Hydro	15945.00	**13870.00**	**14190.00**	**14470.00**	Yanmar	3	73D	Variable	20.0		No
4200 4WD	15580.00	**13560.00**	**13870.00**	**14150.00**	Yanmar	3	73D	9F-3R	21.5		No
4200 4WD Hydro	17145.00	**14920.00**	**15260.00**	**15570.00**	Yanmar	3	73D	Variable	20.0		No
4300	14930.00	**12990.00**	**13290.00**	**13560.00**	Yanmar	3	91D	9F-3R	27.0		No
4300 Hydro	16700.00	**14530.00**	**14860.00**	**15160.00**	Yanmar	3	91D	Variable	25.5		No
4300 4WD	16130.00	**14030.00**	**14360.00**	**14650.00**	Yanmar	3	91D	9F-3R	27.0		No
4300 4WD Hydro	17900.00	**15570.00**	**15930.00**	**16250.00**	Yanmar	3	91D	9F-3R	25.5		No
4400 4WD	18395.00	**16000.00**	**16370.00**	**16700.00**	Yanmar	3	100D	12F-12R	30.0		No
4400 4WD Hydro	19430.00	**16900.00**	**17290.00**	**17640.00**	Yanmar	3	100D	Variable	28.5		No
4500 4WD	20115.00	**17500.00**	**17900.00**	**18260.00**	Yanmar	4	121D	9F-3R	33.0		No
4600 4WD	21915.00	**19070.00**	**19500.00**	**19890.00**	Yanmar	4	121D	9F-3R	36.0		No
4600 4WD Hydro	23500.00	**20450.00**	**20920.00**	**21340.00**	Yanmar	4	121D	Variable	34.5		No
5210	22115.00	**19460.00**	**20350.00**	**20760.00**	JD	3	179D	9F-3R	45.0		No
5210 w/Cab	30165.00	**26550.00**	**27750.00**	**28310.00**	JD	3	179D	9F-3R	45.0		C,H,A
5210 4WD	27275.00	**24000.00**	**25090.00**	**25590.00**	JD	3	179D	9F-3R	45.0		No
5210 4WD w/Cab	35285.00	**31050.00**	**32460.00**	**33110.00**	JD	3	179D	9F-3R	45.0		C,H,A
5310	24697.00	**21730.00**	**22720.00**	**23170.00**	JD	3T	179D	9F-3R	55.0		No
5310 w/Cab	32855.00	**28910.00**	**30230.00**	**30840.00**	JD	3T	179D	9F-3R	55.0		C,H,A
5310 4WD	30342.00	**26700.00**	**27920.00**	**28480.00**	JD	3T	179D	9F-3R	55.0		No
5310 4WD w/Cab	38162.00	**33580.00**	**35110.00**	**35810.00**	JD	3T	179D	9F-3R	55.0		C,H,A
5310N	24795.00	**21820.00**	**22810.00**	**23270.00**	JD	3T	179D	9F-3R	55.0		No
5310N w/Cab	33360.00	**29360.00**	**30690.00**	**31300.00**	JD	3T	179D	9F-3R	55.0		C,H,A
5310N 4WD	30810.00	**27110.00**	**28350.00**	**28920.00**	JD	3T	179D	9F-3R	55.0		No
5310N 4WD w/Cab	39375.00	**34650.00**	**36230.00**	**36960.00**	JD	3T	179D	9F-3R	55.0		C,H,A
5410	27366.00	**24080.00**	**25180.00**	**25680.00**	JD	3T	179D	9F-3R	65.0		No
5410 w/Cab	35742.00	**31450.00**	**32880.00**	**33540.00**	JD	3T	179D	9F-3R	65.0		C,H,A
5410 4WD	32736.00	**28810.00**	**30120.00**	**30720.00**	JD	3T	179D	9F-3R	65.0		No
5410 4WD w/Cab	41106.00	**36170.00**	**37820.00**	**38580.00**	JD	3T	179D	9F-3R	65.0		C,H,A
5510	30810.00	**26810.00**	**27420.00**	**27970.00**	JD	4T	239D	9F-3R	75.0		No
5510 w/Cab	38605.00	**33590.00**	**34360.00**	**35050.00**	JD	4T	239D	9F-3R	75.0		C,H,A
5510 4WD	36265.00	**31550.00**	**32280.00**	**32930.00**	JD	4T	239D	9F-3R	75.0		No
5510 4WD w/Cab	44635.00	**38830.00**	**39730.00**	**40530.00**	JD	4T	239D	9F-3R	75.0		C,H,A
5510N	29816.00	**25940.00**	**26540.00**	**27070.00**	JD	4T	239D	12F-12R	75.0		No
5510N w/Cab	38385.00	**33400.00**	**34160.00**	**34840.00**	JD	4T	239D	12F-12R	75.0		C,H,A
5510N 4WD	35945.00	**31270.00**	**31990.00**	**32630.00**	JD	4T	239D	12F-12R	75.0		No
5510N 4WD w/Cab	44515.00	**38730.00**	**39620.00**	**40410.00**	JD	4T	239D	12F-12R	75.0		C,H,A
6110	31410.00	**27330.00**	**27960.00**	**28520.00**	JD	4T	276D	12F-4R	65.0		No
6110 w/Cab	39405.00	**34280.00**	**35070.00**	**35770.00**	JD	4T	276D	12F-4R	65.0		No
6110 4WD	38550.00	**33540.00**	**34310.00**	**35000.00**	JD	4T	276D	12F-4R	65.0		No

HC--High Clearance L--Low Profile S--Low Clearance PS--Power Shift
***Engine Horsepower**

John Deere (Cont.)

1999 (Cont.)

Model	Approx. Retail Price New	Estimated Average Value Less Repairs: Fair	Good	Premium	Engine: Make	No. Cyls.	Displ. Cu.-In.	No. Speeds	P.T.O. H.P.	Approx. Shipping Wt.-Lbs.	Cab
6110 4WD w/Cab	46550.00	40500.00	41430.00	42260.00	JD	4T	276D	12F-4R	65.0		No
6110L	31085.00	27040.00	27670.00	28220.00	JD	4T	276D	12F-4R	65.0		No
6110L 4WD	38230.00	33260.00	34030.00	34710.00	JD	4T	276D	12F-4R	65.0		No
6210	32785.00	28520.00	29180.00	29760.00	JD	4T	239D	12F-4R	72.0		No
6210 w/Cab	41630.00	36220.00	37050.00	37790.00	JD	4T	239D	12F-4R	72.0		C,H,A
6210 4WD	39925.00	34740.00	35530.00	36240.00	JD	4T	239D	12F-4R	72.0		No
6210 4WD w/Cab	48775.00	42430.00	43410.00	44280.00	JD	4T	239D	12F-4R	72.0		C,H,A
6210L	32925.00	28650.00	29300.00	29890.00	JD	4T	239D	12F-4R	72.0		No
6210L 4WD	40066.00	34860.00	35660.00	36370.00	JD	4T	239D	12F-4R	72.0		No
6310	35897.00	31230.00	31950.00	32590.00	JD	4T	239D	12F-4R	80.0		No
6310 w/Cab	44710.00	38900.00	39790.00	40590.00	JD	4T	239D	12F-4R	80.0		C,H,A
6310 4WD	43338.00	37700.00	38570.00	39340.00	JD	4T	239D	12F-4R	80.0		No
6310 4WD w/Cab	52150.00	45370.00	46410.00	47340.00	JD	4T	239D	12F-4R	80.0		C,H,A
6310L	35572.00	30950.00	31660.00	32290.00	JD	4T	239D	12F-4R	80.0		No
6310L 4WD	43145.00	37540.00	38400.00	39170.00	JD	4T	239D	12F-4R	80.0		No
6310S	52150.00	45370.00	46410.00	47340.00	JD	4T	239D	16F-16R	80.0		C,H,A
6310S 4WD	59590.00	51840.00	53040.00	54100.00	JD	4T	239D	16F-16R	80.0		C,H,A
6405	33170.00	28200.00	29520.00	30110.00	JD	4T	276D	12F-4R	85.0		No
6405 4WD	40536.00	34460.00	36080.00	36800.00	JD	4T	276D	12F-4R	85.0		No
6410	38345.00	33360.00	34130.00	34810.00	JD	4T	276D	12F-4R	90.0		No
6410 w/Cab	47030.00	40920.00	41860.00	42700.00	JD	4T	276D	12F-4R	90.0		C,H,A
6410 4WD	45915.00	39950.00	40860.00	41680.00	JD	4T	276D	12F-4R	90.0		No
6410 4WD w/Cab	54600.00	47500.00	48590.00	49560.00	JD	4T	276D	12F-4R	90.0		C,H,A
6410L	38375.00	33390.00	34150.00	34830.00	JD	4T	276D	12F-4R	90.0		No
6410L 4WD	45945.00	39970.00	40890.00	41710.00	JD	4T	276D	12F-4R	90.0		No
6410S	54950.00	47810.00	48910.00	49890.00	JD	4T	276D	16F-16R	90.0		C,H,A
6410S 4WD	62525.00	54400.00	55650.00	56760.00	JD	4T	276D	16F-16R	90.0		C,H,A
6510L	43495.00	37840.00	38710.00	39480.00	JD	4T	276D	16F-16R	95.0		No
6510L 4WD	51065.00	44430.00	45450.00	46360.00	JD	4T	276D	16F-16R	95.0		No
6510S	56840.00	49450.00	50590.00	51600.00	JD	4T	276D	12F-4R	95.0		C,H,A
6510S 4WD	64415.00	56040.00	57330.00	58480.00	JD	4T	276D	12F-4R	95.0		C,H,A
6605	36900.00	31370.00	32840.00	33500.00	JD	6T	414D	12F-4R	95.0		No
6605 4WD	44200.00	37570.00	39340.00	40130.00	JD	6T	414D	12F-4R	95.0		No
7210	51740.00	45010.00	46050.00	46970.00	JD	6T	414D	12F-4R	95.0		C,H,A
7210 4WD	60340.00	52500.00	53700.00	54770.00	JD	6T	414D	12F-4R	95.0		C,H,A
7210HC	51510.00	44810.00	45840.00	46760.00	JD	6T	414D	12F-4R	95.0		No
7210HC w/Cab	59735.00	51970.00	53160.00	54220.00	JD	6T	414D	12F-4R	95.0		C,H,A
7210HC 4WD	62000.00	53940.00	55180.00	56280.00	JD	6T	414D	12F-4R	95.0		No
7210HC 4WD w/Cab	70100.00	60990.00	62390.00	63640.00	JD	6T	414D	12F-4R	95.0		C,H,A
7405	43560.00	37030.00	38770.00	39550.00	JD	6T	414D	16F-16R	105.0		No
7405 4WD	51355.00	43650.00	45710.00	46620.00	JD	6T	414D	16F-16R	105.0		No
7405HC 4WD	55305.00	47010.00	49220.00	50200.00	JD	6T	414D	16F-16R	105.0		No
7410	55787.00	48540.00	49650.00	50640.00	JD	6T	414D	12F-4R	105.0		C,H,A
7410 4WD	64980.00	56530.00	57830.00	58990.00	JD	6T	414D	12F-4R	105.0		C,H,A
7410HC	55616.00	48390.00	49500.00	50490.00	JD	6T	414D	12F-4R	105.0		No
7410HC w/Cab	63840.00	55540.00	56820.00	57960.00	JD	6T	414D	12F-4R	105.0		C,H,A
7410HC 4WD	65975.00	57400.00	58720.00	59890.00	JD	6T	414D	12F-4R	105.0		No
7410HC 4WD w/Cab	74200.00	64550.00	66040.00	67360.00	JD	6T	414D	12F-4R	105.0		C,H,A
7610	65565.00	57040.00	58350.00	59520.00	JD	6T	414D	16F-16R	115.0		C,H,A
7610 4WD	77665.00	67570.00	69120.00	70500.00	JD	6T	414D	16F-16R	115.0		C,H,A
7610 PS	68950.00	59990.00	61370.00	62600.00	JD	6T	414D	19F-7R	115.0		C,H,A
7610 PS 4WD	81050.00	70510.00	72140.00	73580.00	JD	6T	414D	19F-7R	115.0		C,H,A
7710	73380.00	63840.00	65310.00	66620.00	JD	6T	496D	16F-12R	130.0		C,H,A
7710 4WD	85480.00	74370.00	76080.00	77600.00	JD	6T	496D	16F-12R	130.0		C,H,A
7710 PS	76765.00	66790.00	68320.00	69690.00	JD	6T	496D	19F-7R	130.0		C,H,A
7710 PS 4WD	88865.00	77310.00	79090.00	80670.00	JD	6T	496D	19F-7R	130.0		C,H,A
7810	82945.00	72160.00	73820.00	75300.00	JD	6T	496D	16F-12R	150.0		C,H,A
7810 4WD	94995.00	82650.00	84550.00	86240.00	JD	6T	496D	16F-12R	150.0		C,H,A
7810 PS	86330.00	75110.00	76830.00	78370.00	JD	6T	496D	19F-7R	150.0		C,H,A
7810 PS WD	98430.00	85630.00	87600.00	89350.00	JD	6T	496D	19F-7R	150.0		C,H,A
8100	95600.00	81260.00	85080.00	86780.00	JD	6TA	496D	16F-4R	160.0		C,H,A
8100 4WD	104000.00	88400.00	92560.00	94410.00	JD	6TA	496D	16F-4R	160.0		C,H,A
8100T	118775.00	93050.00	97480.00	99430.00	JD	6TA	496D	16F-4R	160.0		C,H,A
8200	106567.00	90580.00	94850.00	96750.00	JD	6TA	496D	16F-4R	180.0		C,H,A
8200 4WD	112155.00	95330.00	99820.00	101820.00	JD	6TA	496D	16F-4R	180.0		C,H,A
8200T	128245.00	100800.00	105600.00	107710.00	JD	6TA	496D	16F-4R	180.0		C,H,A
8300	114350.00	97200.00	101770.00	103810.00	JD	6TA	496D	16F-4R	200.0		C,H,A
8300 4WD	129200.00	106250.00	111250.00	113480.00	JD	6TA	496D	16F-4R	200.0		C,H,A
8300T	138300.00	109200.00	114400.00	116690.00	JD	6TA	496D	16F-4R	200.0		C,H,A
8400 4WD	139220.00	116950.00	122510.00	124960.00	JD	6TA	496D	16F-4R	225.0		C,H,A
8400T	145375.00	117600.00	123200.00	125660.00	JD	6TA	496D	16F-4R	225.0		C,H,A
9100	111745.00	93870.00	98340.00	100310.00	JD	6TA	496D	12F-3R	260*		C,H,A
9200	129840.00	107770.00	112960.00	116350.00	JD	6TA	643D	12F-3R	310*		C,H,A
9200	134835.00	111910.00	117310.00	120830.00	JD	6TA	643D	24F-24R	310*		C,H,A
9200 PS	147325.00	122280.00	128170.00	132020.00	JD	6TA	643D	12F-2R	310*		C,H,A
9300	148945.00	123620.00	129580.00	133470.00	JD	6TA	765D	12F-3R	360*		C,H,A
9300	153945.00	127770.00	133930.00	137950.00	JD	6TA	765D	24F-24R	360*		C,H,A
9300 PS	166430.00	138140.00	144790.00	149130.00	JD	6TA	765D	12F-2R	360*		C,H,A
9400	168325.00	139710.00	146440.00	150830.00	JD	6TA	765D	12F-3R	425*		C,H,A
9400	173320.00	143860.00	150790.00	155310.00	JD	6TA	765D	24F-24R	425*		C,H,A
9400 PS	185810.00	154220.00	161660.00	166510.00	JD	6TA	765D	12F-2R	425*		C,H,A

HC--High Clearance L--Low Profile S--Low Clearance PS--Power Shift
***Engine Horsepower**

Kioti

Model	Approx. Retail Price New	Estimated Average Value Less Repairs Fair	Good	Premium	Engine Make	No. Cyls.	Displ. Cu.-In.	No. Speeds	P.T.O. H.P.	Approx. Shipping Wt.-Lbs.	Cab
1988											
LB1714 4WD	6925.00	3880.00	4430.00	4740.00	Daedong	3	57D	8F-7R	14.0	1900	No
LB2202	7250.00	4060.00	4640.00	4970.00	Daedong	3	68D	8F-2R	19.0	2070	No
LB2204 4WD	8300.00	4650.00	5310.00	5680.00	Daedong	3	68D	8F-2R	19.0	2290	No
1989											
LB1714 4WD	7250.00	4130.00	4710.00	5040.00	Daedong	3	57D	8F-8R	14.5	1800	No
LB2202	7450.00	4250.00	4840.00	5180.00	Daedong	3	68D	8F-2R	19.0	1940	No
LB2204 4WD	8495.00	4840.00	5520.00	5910.00	Daedong	3	68D	8F-2R	19.0	2160	No
1990											
LB1714 4WD	7495.00	4350.00	4950.00	5300.00	Daedong	3	57D	8F-8R	14.5	1800	No
LB2202	7695.00	4460.00	5080.00	5440.00	Daedong	3	68D	8F-2R	19.0	1940	No
LB2204 4WD	8995.00	5220.00	5940.00	6360.00	Daedong	3	68D	8F-2R	19.0	2160	No
1991											
LB1914 4WD	9250.00	5460.00	6200.00	6570.00	Daedong	3	57D	8F-8R	16.0	1800	No
LB2214 4WD	10250.00	6050.00	6870.00	7280.00	Daedong	3	68D	8F-8R	19.0	2286	No
LB2614 4WD	11250.00	6640.00	7540.00	7990.00	Daedong	3	80D	8F-8R	22.0	2314	No
1992											
LB1914	9350.00	5610.00	6360.00	6740.00	Daedong	3	57D	8F-8R	19.0	1800	No
LB2214	10350.00	6210.00	7040.00	7460.00	Daedong	3	68D	8F-8R	19.0	2286	No
LB2614	11350.00	6810.00	7720.00	8180.00	Daedong	3	80D	8F-8R	22.0	2314	No
1993											
LB1914	9450.00	5860.00	6520.00	6910.00	Daedong	3	57D	8F-8R	19.0	1800	No
LK2554	10450.00	6480.00	7210.00	7640.00	Daedong	3	79D	8F-2R	22.0	2480	No
LK3054	11750.00	7290.00	8110.00	8600.00	Daedong	3	85D	8F-8R	24.0	2580	No
1994											
LB1914	9550.00	6110.00	6690.00	7030.00	Daedong	3	57D	8F-8R	19.0	1800	No
LK2554	10550.00	6750.00	7390.00	7760.00	Daedong	3	79D	8F-2R	22.0	2480	No
LK3054	12000.00	7680.00	8400.00	8820.00	Daedong	3	85D	8F-8R	24.0	2580	No
1995											
LB1914	9690.00	6400.00	7070.00	7420.00	Daedong	3	57D	8F-8R	16.0	1900	No
LK2554	10694.00	7060.00	7810.00	8200.00	Daedong	3	79D	8F-2R	22.0	2480	No
LK3054	12430.00	8200.00	9070.00	9520.00	Daedong	3	85D	8F-8R	24.0	2580	No
1996											
LB1914	9955.00	6970.00	7570.00	7870.00	Daedong	3	57D	8F-8R	16.0	1900	No
LK2554	10790.00	7550.00	8200.00	8530.00	Daedong	3	79D	8F-2R	22.0	2480	No
LK3054	12695.00	8890.00	9650.00	10040.00	Daedong	3	85D	8F-8R	24.0	2580	No
1997											
LB1914	10145.00	7610.00	8120.00	8450.00	Daedong	3	57D	8F-8R	16.0	1900	No
LK2552	10455.00	7840.00	8360.00	8690.00	Daedong	3	79D	8F-2R	22.0	2400	No
LK2554	11480.00	8610.00	9180.00	9550.00	Daedong	3	79D	8F-2R	22.0	2480	No
LK3054	12990.00	9740.00	10390.00	10810.00	Daedong	3	85D	8F-8R	24.0	2580	No
1998											
LB1914	10575.00	8350.00	8880.00	9150.00	Daedong	3	57D	8F-8R	16.0	1900	No
LK2554	11780.00	9310.00	9900.00	10200.00	Daedong	3	79D	8F-2R	22.0	2480	No
LK3054	13450.00	10630.00	11300.00	11640.00	Daedong	3	85D	8F-8R	24.0	2580	No
1999											
LB1914 4WD	10575.00	8990.00	9410.00	9600.00	Daedong	3	57D	8F-8R	17.5	1900	No
LK2552 2WD	11100.00	9440.00	9880.00	10080.00	Daedong	3	79D	8F-2R	22.0	2395	No
LK2554 4WD	11100.00	9440.00	9880.00	10080.00	Daedong	3	79D	8F-2R	22.0	2480	No
LK3052 2WD	12540.00	10660.00	11160.00	11380.00	Daedong	3	85D	8F-8R	24.0	2580	No
LK3054 4WD	13450.00	11430.00	11970.00	12210.00	Daedong	3	85D	8F-8R	24.0	2675	No
LK3504 4WD	15275.00	12980.00	13600.00	13870.00	Daedong	3	100D	8F-8R	29.0	2795	No

Kubota

Model	Approx. Retail Price New	Fair	Good	Premium	Make	No. Cyls.	Displ. Cu.-In.	No. Speeds	P.T.O. H.P.	Approx. Shipping Wt.-Lbs.	Cab
1976											
L175 C	3295.00	1680.00	2110.00	2470.00	Kubota	2	45D	8F-2R	15.00	1520	No
L175 F	3150.00	1610.00	2020.00	2360.00	Kubota	2	45D	8F-2R	15.00	1430	No
L185 F	3595.00	1830.00	2300.00	2690.00	Kubota	2	45D	8F-2R	15.00	1595	No
L225	3890.00	1980.00	2490.00	2910.00	Kubota	3	68D	8F-2R	20.86	1620	No
L225 DT	4495.00	2290.00	2880.00	3370.00	Kubota	3	68D	8F-2R	20.86	1770	No
L260	4365.00	2230.00	2790.00	3260.00	Kubota	2	78D	8F-2R	24.11	2340	No
L285	4713.00	2400.00	3020.00	3530.00	Kubota	4	91D	8F-2R	26.45	2230	No
L285 W	4837.00	2470.00	3100.00	3630.00	Kubota	4	91D	8F-2R	26.45	2250	No
B6000 C	2995.00	1900.00	2310.00	2750.00	Kubota	2	35D	6F-2R	11.00	860	No
B6000 E	2730.00	1680.00	2040.00	2430.00	Kubota	2	35D	6F-2R	11.00	770	No

C, D, DT--Front Wheel Assist DTSS--Front Wheel Assist, Shuttle Shift E--Two Wheel Drive F--Farm Standard W--Two Row Offset
H, HC--High Clearance HSE--Hydrostatic Transmission, Two Wheel Drive HSD--Hydrostatic Transmission, Four Wheel Drive OC--Orchard L--Low Profile

Kubota (Cont.)

1977

Model	Approx. Retail Price New	Estimated Average Value Less Repairs Fair	Good	Premium	Engine Make	No. Cyls.	Displ. Cu.-In.	No. Speeds	P.T.O. H.P.	Approx. Shipping Wt.-Lbs.	Cab
L175 C	3295.00	**1830.00**	**2300.00**	**2670.00**	Kubota	2	45D	8F-2R	15.00	1520	No
L185 DT	4140.00	**2210.00**	**2780.00**	**3230.00**	Kubota	2	45D	8F-2R	15.00	1740	No
L185 F	3595.00	**1990.00**	**2490.00**	**2890.00**	Kubota	2	45D	8F-2R	15.00	1595	No
L225	3890.00	**2090.00**	**2620.00**	**3040.00**	Kubota	3	68D	8F-2R	20.86	1620	No
L245 DT	4875.00	**2540.00**	**3180.00**	**3690.00**	Kubota	3	68D	8F-2R	22.00	2000	No
L245 F	4445.00	**2420.00**	**3040.00**	**3530.00**	Kubota	3	68D	8F-2R	22.00	1850	No
L285	4995.00	**2700.00**	**3390.00**	**3930.00**	Kubota	4	91D	8F-2R	26.45	2230	No
B6000 C	3175.00	**1970.00**	**2430.00**	**2870.00**	Kubota	2	35D	6F-2R	11.00	860	No
B6000 E	2795.00	**1810.00**	**2240.00**	**2640.00**	Kubota	2	35D	6F-2R	11.00	770	No
B7100 DT	3550.00	**2230.00**	**2750.00**	**3250.00**	Kubota	3	47D	6F-2R		1085	No

C, D, DT--Front Wheel Assist DTSS--Front Wheel Assist, Shuttle Shift E--Two Wheel Drive F--Farm Standard W--Two Row Offset
H, HC--High Clearance HSE--Hydrostatic Transmission, Two Wheel Drive HSD--Hydrostatic Transmission, Four Wheel Drive OC--Orchard L--Low Profile

1978

Model	Approx. Retail Price New	Fair	Good	Premium	Engine Make	No. Cyls.	Displ. Cu.-In.	No. Speeds	P.T.O. H.P.	Approx. Shipping Wt.-Lbs.	Cab
L185 DT	4940.00	**2520.00**	**3160.00**	**3630.00**	Kubota	2	45D	8F-2R	15.00	1740	No
L185 F	4350.00	**2320.00**	**2910.00**	**3350.00**	Kubota	2	45D	8F-2R	15.00	1595	No
L245 DT	5865.00	**3090.00**	**3870.00**	**4450.00**	Kubota	3	68D	8F-2R	22.00	2000	No
L245 F	5120.00	**2780.00**	**3490.00**	**4010.00**	Kubota	3	68D	8F-2R	22.00	1850	No
L245 HC	6290.00	**3410.00**	**4280.00**	**4920.00**	Kubota	3	68D	8F-2R		2345	No
L285	6275.00	**3300.00**	**4140.00**	**4760.00**	Kubota	4	91D	8F-2R	26.45	2230	No
L295 DT	7825.00	**4140.00**	**5200.00**	**5980.00**	Kubota	3	79D	8F-2R		2600	No
M4000 F	9450.00	**3880.00**	**4730.00**	**5200.00**	Kubota	6	136D	16F-4R		4125	No
M4500 DT	14695.00	**6030.00**	**7350.00**	**8090.00**	Kubota	6	159D	16F-4R		4730	No
B5100 DT	3765.00	**2320.00**	**2820.00**	**3300.00**	Kubota	2	31D	6F-2R		895	No
B5100 E	3395.00	**2010.00**	**2450.00**	**2870.00**	Kubota	2	31D	6F-2R		805	No
B6100 DT	3950.00	**2320.00**	**2820.00**	**3300.00**	Kubota	3	41D	6F-2R		1035	No
B6100 E	3625.00	**2210.00**	**2690.00**	**3150.00**	Kubota	3	41D	6F-2R		970	No
B7100 DT	4290.00	**2570.00**	**3120.00**	**3650.00**	Kubota	3	47D	6F-2R		1085	No

C, D, DT--Front Wheel Assist DTSS--Front Wheel Assist, Shuttle Shift E--Two Wheel Drive F--Farm Standard W--Two Row Offset
H, HC--High Clearance HSE--Hydrostatic Transmission, Two Wheel Drive HSD--Hydrostatic Transmission, Four Wheel Drive OC--Orchard L--Low Profile

1979

Model	Approx. Retail Price New	Fair	Good	Premium	Engine Make	No. Cyls.	Displ. Cu.-In.	No. Speeds	P.T.O. H.P.	Approx. Shipping Wt.-Lbs.	Cab
L185 DT	5490.00	**2860.00**	**3460.00**	**3940.00**	Kubota	2	45D	8F-2R	15.45	1785	No
L185 F	4885.00	**2640.00**	**3200.00**	**3650.00**	Kubota	2	45D	8F-2R	15.33	1595	No
L245 DT	6650.00	**3560.00**	**4320.00**	**4930.00**	Kubota	3	68D	8F-2R	22.35	2000	No
L245 F	5830.00	**3150.00**	**3810.00**	**4340.00**	Kubota	3	68D	8F-2R	22.06	1850	No
L245 HC	7135.00	**3770.00**	**4570.00**	**5210.00**	Kubota	3	68D	8F-2R	22.00	2345	No
L285	6675.00	**3470.00**	**4210.00**	**4800.00**	Kubota	4	91D	8F-2R	26.45	2230	No
L295	7200.00	**3740.00**	**4540.00**	**5180.00**	Kubota	3	79D	8F-2R	25.00	2305	No
L295 DT	8875.00	**4620.00**	**5590.00**	**6370.00**	Kubota	3	79D	8F-2R	25.00	2600	No
L345 DT	9595.00	**4990.00**	**6050.00**	**6900.00**	Kubota	4	91D	8F-2R		3155	No
M4000 F	9785.00	**4110.00**	**4990.00**	**5440.00**	Kubota	6	136D	16F-4R	41.00	4125	No
M4500 DT	15795.00	**6630.00**	**8060.00**	**8790.00**	Kubota	6	159D	16F-4R	47.00	4730	No
M4500 F	11500.00	**4830.00**	**5870.00**	**6400.00**	Kubota	6	159D	16F-4R	47.00	4220	No
B5100 DT	4165.00	**2540.00**	**3030.00**	**3520.00**	Kubota	2	31D	6F-2R	10	895	No
B5100 E	3745.00	**2420.00**	**2890.00**	**3350.00**	Kubota	2	31D	6F-2R	10	805	No
B6100 DT	4415.00	**2340.00**	**2790.00**	**3240.00**	Kubota	3	41D	6F-2R	12.00	1035	No
B6100 E	4050.00	**2480.00**	**2960.00**	**3430.00**	Kubota	3	41D	6F-2R	12.00	970	No
B7100 DT	4855.00	**2990.00**	**3570.00**	**4140.00**	Kubota	3	47D	6F-2R	13.60	1085	No
M7500 DT	18900.00	**7940.00**	**9640.00**	**10510.00**	Kubota	4	243D	16F-4R	70.00	5610	No

C, D, DT--Front Wheel Assist DTSS--Front Wheel Assist, Shuttle Shift E--Two Wheel Drive F--Farm Standard W--Two Row Offset
H, HC--High Clearance HSE--Hydrostatic Transmission, Two Wheel Drive HSD--Hydrostatic Transmission, Four Wheel Drive OC--Orchard L--Low Profile

1980

Model	Approx. Retail Price New	Fair	Good	Premium	Engine Make	No. Cyls.	Displ. Cu.-In.	No. Speeds	P.T.O. H.P.	Approx. Shipping Wt.-Lbs.	Cab
L185 DT	5690.00	**3020.00**	**3530.00**	**3990.00**	Kubota	2	45D	8F-2R	15.45	1785	No
L185 F	5195.00	**2750.00**	**3220.00**	**3640.00**	Kubota	2	45D	8F-2R	15.33	1595	No
L245 DT	7095.00	**3760.00**	**4400.00**	**4970.00**	Kubota	3	68D	8F-2R	22.35	2000	No
L245 F	6235.00	**3310.00**	**3870.00**	**4370.00**	Kubota	3	68D	8F-2R	22.06	1850	No
L245 HC	7490.00	**3970.00**	**4640.00**	**5240.00**	Kubota	3	68D	8F-2R	22.00	2345	No
L285	6675.00	**3540.00**	**4140.00**	**4680.00**	Kubota	4	91D	8F-2R	26.45	2230	No
L295	7495.00	**3970.00**	**4650.00**	**5250.00**	Kubota	3	79D	8F-2R	25.00	2305	No
L295 DT	8995.00	**4770.00**	**5580.00**	**6310.00**	Kubota	3	79D	8F-2R	25.00	2600	No
L305 DT	9395.00	**4980.00**	**5830.00**	**6590.00**	Kubota	3	79D	8F-2R	25.00	2855	No
L305 F	7595.00	**4030.00**	**4710.00**	**5320.00**	Kubota	3	79D	8F-2R	25.00	2555	No
L345 DT	9995.00	**5300.00**	**6200.00**	**7010.00**	Kubota	4	91D	8F-2R	28.00	3155	No
L345 F	8710.00	**4620.00**	**5400.00**	**6100.00**	Kubota	4	91D	8F-2R	28.00	2770	No
M4000 F	9785.00	**4210.00**	**5090.00**	**5500.00**	Kubota	6	136D	16F-4R	41.00	4125	No
M4500 DT	15795.00	**6790.00**	**8210.00**	**8870.00**	Kubota	6	159D	16F-4R	47.00	4730	No
M4500 F	12000.00	**5160.00**	**6240.00**	**6740.00**	Kubota	6	159D	16F-4R	47.00	4220	No
M4500 OC	11990.00	**5160.00**	**6240.00**	**6740.00**	Kubota	6	159D	16F-4R	47.00	4400	No
B5100 DT	4195.00	**2670.00**	**3130.00**	**3600.00**	Kubota	2	31D	6F-2R	10	895	No
B5100 E	3795.00	**2430.00**	**2850.00**	**3280.00**	Kubota	2	31D	6F-2R	10	805	No
M5500 DT	17500.00	**7530.00**	**9100.00**	**9830.00**	Kubota	3	182D	16F-4R	53.00	5070	No
M5500 F	13500.00	**5810.00**	**7020.00**	**7580.00**	Kubota	3	182D	16F-4R	53.00	4560	No
B6100 DT	4750.00	**2990.00**	**3500.00**	**4030.00**	Kubota	3	41D	6F-2R	12.00	1035	No
B6100 E	4295.00	**2720.00**	**3190.00**	**3670.00**	Kubota	3	41D	6F-2R	12.00	970	No
B7100 DT	5195.00	**3190.00**	**3740.00**	**4300.00**	Kubota	3	47D	6F-2R	13.60	1085	No
B7100 HSD	5795.00	**3540.00**	**4150.00**	**4770.00**	Kubota	3	47D	Infinite	13.60	1300	No
B7100 HSE	5375.00	**3350.00**	**3930.00**	**4520.00**	Kubota	3	47D	Infinite	13.60	1205	No
M7500 DT	20250.00	**8710.00**	**10530.00**	**11370.00**	Kubota	4	243D	16F-4R	72.00	5610	No
M7500 F	15200.00	**6540.00**	**7900.00**	**8530.00**	Kubota	4	243D	16F-4R	72.00	5085	No

C, D, DT--Front Wheel Assist DTSS--Front Wheel Assist, Shuttle Shift E--Two Wheel Drive F--Farm Standard W--Two Row Offset
HC--High Clearance HSE--Hydrostatic Transmission, Two Wheel Drive HSD--Hydrostatic Transmission, Four Wheel Drive OC--Orchard L--Low Profile

Model	Approx. Retail Price New	Estimated Average Value Less Repairs Fair	Good	Premium	Engine Make	No. Cyls.	Displ. Cu.-In.	No. Speeds	P.T.O. H.P.	Approx. Shipping Wt.-Lbs.	Cab

Kubota (Cont.)

1981

Model	Approx. Retail Price New	Fair	Good	Premium	Make	No. Cyls.	Displ. Cu.-In.	No. Speeds	P.T.O. H.P.	Approx. Shipping Wt.-Lbs.	Cab
L185 DT	5990.00	**3240.00**	**3770.00**	**4220.00**	Kubota	2	45D	8F-2R	15.45	1785	No
L185 F	5450.00	**2940.00**	**3430.00**	**3840.00**	Kubota	2	45D	8F-2R	15.33	1595	No
L245 DT	7450.00	**4020.00**	**4690.00**	**5250.00**	Kubota	3	68D	8F-2R	22.35	2000	No
L245 F	6550.00	**3540.00**	**4130.00**	**4630.00**	Kubota	3	68D	8F-2R	22.06	1850	No
L245 HC	7490.00	**4050.00**	**4720.00**	**5290.00**	Kubota	3	68D	8F-2R	22.00	2345	No
L285	6675.00	**3610.00**	**4210.00**	**4720.00**	Kubota	4	91D	8F-2R	26.45	2230	No
L295	7495.00	**4050.00**	**4720.00**	**5290.00**	Kubota	3	79D	8F-2R	26.46	2305	No
L295 DT	8995.00	**4860.00**	**5670.00**	**6350.00**	Kubota	3	79D	8F-2R	26.46	2600	No
L305 DT	9680.00	**5230.00**	**6100.00**	**6830.00**	Kubota	3	79D	8F-2R	26.21	2855	No
L305 F	8130.00	**4390.00**	**5120.00**	**5730.00**	Kubota	3	79D	8F-2R	26.21	2555	No
L345 DT	10495.00	**5130.00**	**5980.00**	**6700.00**	Kubota	4	91D	8F-2R	29.35	3155	No
M4000 F	9785.00	**4310.00**	**5190.00**	**5610.00**	Kubota	6	136D	16F-4R	41.00	4125	No
M4500 DT	16270.00	**7160.00**	**8620.00**	**9310.00**	Kubota	6	159D	16F-4R	49.72	4730	No
M4500 F	12400.00	**5460.00**	**6570.00**	**7100.00**	Kubota	6	159D	16F-4R	49.72	4220	No
M4500 OC	12900.00	**5680.00**	**6840.00**	**7390.00**	Kubota	6	159D	16F-4R	49.00	4400	No
B5100 DT	4430.00	**2860.00**	**3300.00**	**3760.00**	Kubota	2	31D	6F-2R	10	895	No
B5100 E	3990.00	**2590.00**	**2990.00**	**3410.00**	Kubota	2	31D	6F-2R	10	805	No
M5500 DT	18000.00	**7920.00**	**9540.00**	**10300.00**	Kubota	3	182D	16F-4R	53.99	5070	No
M5500 F	13900.00	**6120.00**	**7370.00**	**7960.00**	Kubota	3	182D	16F-4R	53.99	4560	No
B6100 DT	5180.00	**3230.00**	**3730.00**	**4250.00**	Kubota	3	41D	6F-2R	12.00	1035	No
B6100 E	4690.00	**3000.00**	**3460.00**	**3940.00**	Kubota	3	41D	6F-2R	12.00	970	No
B6100 HSD 4WD	5840.00	**3630.00**	**4180.00**	**4770.00**	Kubota	3	41D	Infinite	12.00	1230	No
B6100 HSE	5330.00	**3330.00**	**3840.00**	**4380.00**	Kubota	3	41D	Infinite	12.00	1140	No
B7100 DT	5670.00	**3530.00**	**4060.00**	**4630.00**	Kubota	3	47D	6F-2R	13.60	1085	No
B7100 HSD 4WD	6320.00	**3910.00**	**4510.00**	**5140.00**	Kubota	3	47D	Infinite	13.60	1300	No
B7100 HSE	5870.00	**3700.00**	**4270.00**	**4870.00**	Kubota	3	47D	Infinite	13.60	1205	No
M7500 DT	20860.00	**9180.00**	**11060.00**	**11950.00**	Kubota	4	243D	16F-4R	72.34	5610	No
M7500 F	15700.00	**6910.00**	**8320.00**	**8990.00**	Kubota	4	243D	16F-4R	72.34	5085	No

C, D, DT--Front Wheel Assist DTSS--Front Wheel Assist, Shuttle Shift E--Two Wheel Drive F--Farm Standard W--Two Row Offset HC--High Clearance HSE--Hydrostatic Transmission, Two Wheel Drive HSD--Hydrostatic Transmission, Four Wheel Drive OC--Orchard L--Low Profile

1982

Model	Approx. Retail Price New	Fair	Good	Premium	Make	No. Cyls.	Displ. Cu.-In.	No. Speeds	P.T.O. H.P.	Approx. Shipping Wt.-Lbs.	Cab
L185 DT	6290.00	**3460.00**	**4030.00**	**4510.00**	Kubota	2	45D	8F-2R	15.45	1785	No
L185 F	5730.00	**3150.00**	**3670.00**	**4110.00**	Kubota	2	45D	8F-2R	15.33	1595	No
L235 DT	7280.00	**4000.00**	**4660.00**	**5220.00**	Kubota	3	68D	8F-2R	19.59	2115	No
L235 F	6450.00	**3550.00**	**4130.00**	**4630.00**	Kubota	3	68D	8F-2R	19.59	1950	No
L245 DT	7680.00	**4220.00**	**4920.00**	**5510.00**	Kubota	3	68D	8F-2R	22.35	2345	No
L245 F	6750.00	**3710.00**	**4320.00**	**4840.00**	Kubota	3	68D	8F-2R	22.06	2000	No
L245 HC	7710.00	**4240.00**	**4930.00**	**5520.00**	Kubota	3	68D	8F-2R	22.00	2345	No
L275 DT	8530.00	**4690.00**	**5460.00**	**6120.00**	Kubota	3	79D	8F-2R	23.42	2315	No
L275 F	7380.00	**4060.00**	**4720.00**	**5290.00**	Kubota	3	79D	8F-2R	23.42	2150	No
L295 DT	8995.00	**4950.00**	**5760.00**	**6450.00**	Kubota	3	79D	8F-2R	26.46	2600	No
L295 F	7495.00	**4120.00**	**4800.00**	**5380.00**	Kubota	3	79D	8F-2R	26.46	2305	No
L305 DT	10270.00	**5650.00**	**6570.00**	**7360.00**	Kubota	3	79D	8F-2R	26.21	2855	No
L305 F	8630.00	**4750.00**	**5520.00**	**6180.00**	Kubota	3	79D	8F-2R	26.21	2555	No
L345 DT	11130.00	**5570.00**	**6480.00**	**7260.00**	Kubota	4	91D	8F-2R	29.35	3155	No
L345 F	9240.00	**5250.00**	**6110.00**	**6840.00**	Kubota	4	91D	8F-2R	29.35	2770	No
L355 DTSS	12130.00	**5570.00**	**6460.00**	**6980.00**	Kubota	4	106D	8F-8R	29.00	2684	No
M4050 DT	16500.00	**7430.00**	**8910.00**	**9620.00**	Kubota	6	159D	8F-2R	42.00	4356	No
M4050 F	12500.00	**5630.00**	**6750.00**	**7290.00**	Kubota	6	159D	8F-2R	42.00	3740	No
M4500 DT	18280.00	**8230.00**	**9870.00**	**10660.00**	Kubota	6	159D	16F-4R	49.72	4730	No
M4500 F	13930.00	**6270.00**	**7520.00**	**8120.00**	Kubota	6	159D	16F-4R	49.72	4220	No
M4500 QC	14490.00	**6520.00**	**7830.00**	**8460.00**	Kubota	6	159D	16F-4R	49.00	4400	No
B5100 DT	4690.00	**3060.00**	**3470.00**	**3920.00**	Kubota	2	31D	6F-2R	10	895	No
B5100 E	4320.00	**2850.00**	**3230.00**	**3650.00**	Kubota	2	31D	6F-2R	10	805	No
M5500 DT	19840.00	**8930.00**	**10710.00**	**11570.00**	Kubota	3	182D	16F-4R	53.99	5070	No
M5500 F	15330.00	**6900.00**	**8280.00**	**8940.00**	Kubota	3	182D	16F-4R	53.99	4560	No
B6100 DT	5610.00	**3600.00**	**4080.00**	**4610.00**	Kubota	3	41D	6F-2R	12.00	1035	No
B6100 E	5080.00	**3290.00**	**3730.00**	**4220.00**	Kubota	3	41D	6F-2R	12.00	970	No
B6100 HSD 4WD	6320.00	**4050.00**	**4590.00**	**5190.00**	Kubota	3	41D	Infinite	12.00	1230	No
B6100 HSE	5770.00	**3710.00**	**4200.00**	**4750.00**	Kubota	3	41D	Infinite	12.00	1140	No
B7100 DT	6070.00	**3880.00**	**4400.00**	**4970.00**	Kubota	3	47D	6F-2R	13.60	1085	No
B7100 HSD 4WD	6910.00	**4350.00**	**4930.00**	**5570.00**	Kubota	3	47D	Infinite	13.60	1300	No
B7100 HSE	6290.00	**3950.00**	**4480.00**	**5060.00**	Kubota	3	47D	Infinite	13.60	1205	No
M7500 DT	23650.00	**10640.00**	**12770.00**	**13790.00**	Kubota	4	243D	16F-4R	72.34	5610	No
M7500 F	17800.00	**8010.00**	**9610.00**	**10380.00**	Kubota	4	243D	16F-4R	72.34	5085	No
B8200 DT	6760.00	**4250.00**	**4810.00**	**5440.00**	Kubota	3	57D	9F-3R	16.00	1565	No
B8200 E	6030.00	**3810.00**	**4320.00**	**4880.00**	Kubota	3	57D	9F-3R	16.00	1420	No

C, D, DT--Front Wheel Assist DTSS--Front Wheel Assist, Shuttle Shift E--Two Wheel Drive F--Farm Standard W--Two Row Offset HC--High Clearance HSE--Hydrostatic Transmission, Two Wheel Drive HSD--Hydrostatic Transmission, Four Wheel Drive OC--Orchard L--Low Profile

1983

Model	Approx. Retail Price New	Fair	Good	Premium	Make	No. Cyls.	Displ. Cu.-In.	No. Speeds	P.T.O. H.P.	Approx. Shipping Wt.-Lbs.	Cab
L235 DT 4WD	7441.00	**4170.00**	**4840.00**	**5420.00**	Kubota	3	68D	8F-2R	19.59	2115	No
L235 F	6579.00	**3680.00**	**4280.00**	**4790.00**	Kubota	3	68D	8F-2R	19.59	1950	No
L245 HC	7864.00	**4400.00**	**5110.00**	**5720.00**	Kubota	3	68D	8F-2R	22.00	2345	No
L275 DT 4WD	8701.00	**4870.00**	**5660.00**	**6340.00**	Kubota	3	79D	8F-2R	23.42	2350	No
L275 F	7528.00	**4220.00**	**4890.00**	**5480.00**	Kubota	3	79D	8F-2R	23.42	2150	No
L305	8803.00	**4930.00**	**5720.00**	**6410.00**	Kubota	3	79D	8F-2R	26.21	2555	No
L305 DT 4WD	10475.00	**5870.00**	**6810.00**	**7630.00**	Kubota	3	79D	8F-2R	26.21	2855	No
L345	9425.00	**5280.00**	**6130.00**	**6870.00**	Kubota	4	91D	8F-2R	29.35	2770	No
L345 DT	11353.00	**6360.00**	**7380.00**	**8270.00**	Kubota	4	91D	8F-2R	29.35	3155	No
L355 DTSS 4WD	12373.00	**6310.00**	**7300.00**	**7880.00**	Kubota	4	105D	8F-8R	29.00	2684	No
M4050 DT 4WD	16500.00	**7590.00**	**9080.00**	**9810.00**	Kubota	6	159D	8F-2R	45.74	4356	No
M4050 F	12500.00	**5750.00**	**6880.00**	**7430.00**	Kubota	6	159D	8F-2R	45.74	3740	No

Kubota (Cont.)

1983 (Cont.)

Model	Approx. Retail Price New	Estimated Average Value Less Repairs Fair	Good	Premium	Engine Make	No. Cyls.	Displ. Cu.-In.	No. Speeds	P.T.O. H.P.	Approx. Shipping Wt.-Lbs.	Cab
M4500 DT 4WD	18280.00	8410.00	10050.00	10850.00	Kubota	6	159D	16F-4R	49.72	4730	No
M4500 F	13930.00	6410.00	7660.00	8270.00	Kubota	6	159D	16F-4R	49.72	4220	No
M4500 OC	14490.00	6670.00	7970.00	8610.00	Kubota	6	159D	16F-4R	49.00	4400	No
M4950 DT 4WD	20265.00	9320.00	11150.00	12040.00	Kubota	6	170D	12F-4R	49.57	5452	No
M4950 DT 4WD w/Cab	24612.00	11320.00	13540.00	14620.00	Kubota	6	170D	12F-4R	49.57	6252	C,H
M4950 F	16465.00	7570.00	9060.00	9790.00	Kubota	6	170D	12F-4R	49.57	4746	No
M4950 F w/Cab	19847.00	9130.00	10920.00	11790.00	Kubota	6	170D	12F-4R	49.57	5546	C,H
B5100 D 4WD	4784.00	3110.00	3470.00	3920.00	Kubota	2	31D	6F-2R	10	895	No
B5100 E	4406.00	2870.00	3200.00	3620.00	Kubota	2	31D	6F-2R	10	805	No
M5500 DT 4WD	19840.00	9130.00	10910.00	11780.00	Kubota	3	182D	16F-4R	53.99	5070	No
M5500 F	15330.00	7050.00	8430.00	9100.00	Kubota	3	182D	16F-4R	53.99	4560	No
M5950 DT 4WD	23065.00	10610.00	12690.00	13710.00	Kubota	3	196D	12F-4R	58.00	5673	No
M5950 DT 4WD w/Cab	27556.00	12680.00	15160.00	16370.00	Kubota	3	196D	12F-4R	58.00	6563	C,H,A
M5950 F	19165.00	8820.00	10540.00	11380.00	Kubota	3	196D	12F-4R	58.00	4989	No
M5950 F w/Cab	23656.00	10880.00	13010.00	14050.00	Kubota	3	196D	12F-4R	58.00	5879	C,H,A
B6100 D 4WD	5722.00	3690.00	4110.00	4640.00	Kubota	3	41D	6F-2R	12.00	1035	No
B6100 E	5182.00	3340.00	3730.00	4220.00	Kubota	3	41D	6F-2R	12.00	970	No
B6100 HSD 4WD	6446.00	4180.00	4660.00	5270.00	Kubota	3	41D	Infinite	12.00	1230	No
B6100 HSE	5885.00	3830.00	4270.00	4830.00	Kubota	3	41D	Infinite	12.00	1140	No
M6950 DT 4WD	25165.00	11580.00	13840.00	14950.00	Kubota	4	243D	12F-4R	66.00	6622	No
M6950 DT 4WD w/Cab	29656.00	13640.00	16310.00	17620.00	Kubota	4	243D	12F-4R	66.00	7512	C,H,A
M6950 F	20765.00	9550.00	11420.00	12330.00	Kubota	4	243D	12F-4R	66.00	5770	No
M6950 F w/Cab	26221.00	12060.00	14420.00	15570.00	Kubota	4	243D	12F-4R	66.00	6590	C,H,A
B7100 DT 4WD	6191.00	3960.00	4410.00	4980.00	Kubota	3	47D	6F-2R	13.60	1085	No
B7100 HSD 4WD	7048.00	4480.00	5000.00	5650.00	Kubota	3	47D	Infinite	13.60	1300	No
B7100 HSE	6416.00	4160.00	4640.00	5240.00	Kubota	3	47D	Infinite	13.60	1205	No
M7500 DT 4WD	23650.00	10880.00	13010.00	14050.00	Kubota	4	243D	16F-4R	72.34	5610	No
M7500 F	17800.00	8190.00	9790.00	10570.00	Kubota	4	243D	16F-4R	72.34	5085	No
M7950 DT 4WD	27865.00	12820.00	15330.00	16560.00	Kubota	4	262D	12F-4R	76.00	6610	No
M7950 DT 4WD w/Cab	33321.00	15330.00	18330.00	19800.00	Kubota	4	262D	12F-4R	76.00	7500	C,H,A
M7950 F	22915.00	10540.00	12600.00	13610.00	Kubota	4	262D	12F-4R	76.00	5840	No
M7950 F w/Cab	27406.00	12610.00	15070.00	16280.00	Kubota	4	262D	12F-4R	76.00	6730	C,H,A
B8200 DT 4WD	6895.00	4390.00	4900.00	5540.00	Kubota	3	57D	9F-3R	16.00	1565	No
B8200 E	6151.00	3940.00	4390.00	4960.00	Kubota	3	57D	9F-3R	16.00	1420	No

C, D, DT--Front Wheel Assist DTSS--Front Wheel Assist, Shuttle Shift E--Two Wheel Drive F--Farm Standard W--Two Row Offset HC--High Clearance HSE--Hydrostatic Transmission, Two Wheel Drive HSD--Hydrostatic Transmission, Four Wheel Drive OC--Orchard L--Low Profile

1984

Model	Approx. Retail Price New	Fair	Good	Premium	Make	No. Cyls.	Displ. Cu.-In.	No. Speeds	P.T.O. H.P.	Approx. Shipping Wt.-Lbs.	Cab
L235 DT 4WD	7445.00	4240.00	4910.00	5500.00	Kubota	3	68D	8F-2R	19.59	2115	No
L235 F	6580.00	3750.00	4340.00	4860.00	Kubota	3	68D	8F-2R	19.59	1950	No
L245 HC	7865.00	4480.00	5190.00	5810.00	Kubota	3	68D	8F-2R	22.00	2345	No
L275 DT 4WD	8705.00	4960.00	5750.00	6440.00	Kubota	3	79D	8F-2R	23.42	2350	No
L275 F	7530.00	4290.00	4970.00	5570.00	Kubota	3	79D	8F-2R	23.42	2150	No
L305	8805.00	5020.00	5810.00	6510.00	Kubota	3	79D	8F-2R	26.21	2555	No
L305 DT 4WD	10475.00	5970.00	6910.00	7740.00	Kubota	3	79D	8F-2R	26.21	2855	No
L345	9425.00	5370.00	6220.00	6970.00	Kubota	4	91D	8F-2R	29.35	2770	No
L345 DT 4WD	11353.00	6470.00	7490.00	8390.00	Kubota	4	91D	8F-2R	29.35	3155	No
L355 DTSS 4WD	12373.00	6430.00	7420.00	8010.00	Kubota	4	105D	8F-8R	29.00	2684	No
M4050 DT 4WD	16500.00	7760.00	9240.00	9980.00	Kubota	6	159D	8F-2R	45.74	4356	No
M4050 F	12500.00	5880.00	7000.00	7560.00	Kubota	6	159D	8F-2R	45.74	3740	No
M4500	13930.00	6550.00	7800.00	8420.00	Kubota	6	159D	16F-4R	49.72	4220	No
M4500 DT 4WD	18280.00	8590.00	10240.00	11060.00	Kubota	6	159D	16F-4R	49.72	4730	No
M4500 OC	14490.00	6810.00	8110.00	8760.00	Kubota	6	159D	16F-4R	49.00	4400	No
M4950 DT 4WD	20265.00	9530.00	11350.00	12260.00	Kubota	6	170D	12F-4R	49.57	5452	No
M4950 DT 4WD w/Cab	24612.00	11570.00	13780.00	14880.00	Kubota	6	170D	12F-4R	49.57	6252	C,H
M4950 F	16465.00	7740.00	9220.00	9960.00	Kubota	6	170D	12F-4R	49.57	4746	No
M4950 F w/Cab	19847.00	9330.00	11110.00	12000.00	Kubota	6	170D	12F-4R	49.57	5546	C,H
B5100 D 4WD	4785.00	3150.00	3510.00	3970.00	Kubota	2	31D	6F-2R	10	895	No
B5100 E	4410.00	2910.00	3240.00	3660.00	Kubota	2	31D	6F-2R	10	805	No
M5500 DT 4WD	19840.00	9330.00	11110.00	12000.00	Kubota	3	182D	16F-4R	53.99	5070	No
M5500 F	15330.00	7210.00	8590.00	9280.00	Kubota	3	182D	16F-4R	53.99	4560	No
M5950 DT 4WD	23065.00	10840.00	12920.00	13950.00	Kubota	3	196D	12F-4R	58.00	5673	No
M5950 DT 4WD w/Cab	27556.00	12950.00	15430.00	16660.00	Kubota	3	196D	12F-4R	58.00	6563	C,H,A
M5950 F	19165.00	9010.00	10730.00	11590.00	Kubota	3	196D	12F-4R	58.00	4989	No
M5950 F w/Cab	23656.00	11120.00	13250.00	14310.00	Kubota	3	196D	12F-4R	58.00	5879	C,H,A
B6100 D 4WD	5725.00	3740.00	4160.00	4700.00	Kubota	3	41D	6F-2R	12.00	1035	No
B6100 E	5185.00	3400.00	3790.00	4280.00	Kubota	3	41D	6F-2R	12.00	970	No
B6100 HSD 4WD	6450.00	4120.00	4590.00	5190.00	Kubota	3	41D	Infinite	12.00	1230	No
B6100 HSE	5885.00	3770.00	4200.00	4750.00	Kubota	3	41D	Infinite	12.00	1140	No
B6200 D 4WD	6300.00	4030.00	4490.00	5070.00	Kubota	3	52D	6F-2R	12.50	1180	No
B6200 E	5705.00	3720.00	4140.00	4680.00	Kubota	3	52D	6F-2R	12.50	1060	No
M6950 DT 4WD	25165.00	11830.00	14090.00	15220.00	Kubota	4	243D	12F-4R	66.44	6622	No
M6950 DT 4WD w/Cab	29656.00	13940.00	16610.00	17940.00	Kubota	4	243D	12F-4R	66.44	7512	C,H,A
M6950 F	20765.00	9760.00	11630.00	12560.00	Kubota	4	243D	12F-4R	66.44	5770	No
M6950 F w/Cab	26225.00	12330.00	14690.00	15870.00	Kubota	4	243D	12F-4R	66.44	6590	C,H,A
B7100 DT 4WD	6195.00	3970.00	4410.00	4980.00	Kubota	3	47D	6F-2R	13.60	1085	No
B7100 HSD 4WD	7050.00	4500.00	5000.00	5650.00	Kubota	3	47D	Infinite	13.60	1300	No
B7100 HSE	6420.00	4110.00	4570.00	5160.00	Kubota	3	47D	Infinite	13.60	1205	No
B7200 D 4WD	6930.00	4430.00	4930.00	5570.00	Kubota	3	57D	6F-2R	14.00	1235	No
B7200 E	6275.00	4020.00	4470.00	5050.00	Kubota	3	57D	6F-2R	14.00	1080	No
M7500 DT 4WD	23650.00	11120.00	13240.00	14300.00	Kubota	4	243D	16F-4R	72.34	5610	No
M7500 F	17800.00	8370.00	9970.00	10770.00	Kubota	4	243D	16F-4R	72.34	5085	No
M7950 DT 4WD	27865.00	13100.00	15600.00	16850.00	Kubota	4	262D	12F-4R	75.44	6610	No
M7950 DT 4WD w/Cab	33321.00	15660.00	18660.00	20150.00	Kubota	4	262D	12F-4R	75.44	7500	C,H,A

Kubota (Cont.)

1984 (Cont.)

Model	Approx. Retail Price New	Estimated Average Value Less Repairs Fair	Good	Premium	Engine Make	No. Cyls.	Displ. Cu.-In.	No. Speeds	P.T.O. H.P.	Approx. Shipping Wt.-Lbs.	Cab
M7950 F	22915.00	10770.00	12830.00	13860.00	Kubota	4	262D	12F-4R	75.44	5840	No
M7950 F w/Cab	27406.00	12880.00	15350.00	16580.00	Kubota	4	262D	12F-4R	75.44	6730	C,H,A
B8200 DT 4WD	6895.00	4400.00	4900.00	5540.00	Kubota	3	57D	9F-3R	16.00	1565	No
B8200 E	6155.00	3940.00	4390.00	4960.00	Kubota	3	57D	9F-3R	16.00	1420	No
B8200 HSD 4WD	7595.00	4830.00	5380.00	6080.00	Kubota	3	57D	Infinite	14.50	1700	No
B8200 HSE	6855.00	4370.00	4870.00	5500.00	Kubota	3	57D	Infinite	14.50	1545	No

C, D, DT--Front Wheel Assist DTSS--Front Wheel Assist, Shuttle Shift E--Two Wheel Drive F--Farm Standard W--Two Row Offset
HC--High Clearance HSE--Hydrostatic Transmission, Two Wheel Drive HSD--Hydrostatic Transmission, Four Wheel Drive OC--Orchard L--Low Profile

1985

Model	Approx. Retail Price New	Fair	Good	Premium	Make	No. Cyls.	Displ. Cu.-In.	No. Speeds	P.T.O. H.P.	Approx. Shipping Wt.-Lbs.	Cab
L235 DT 4WD	8180.00	4740.00	5480.00	6080.00	Kubota	3	68D	8F-2R	19.59	2115	No
L235 F	7300.00	4230.00	4890.00	5430.00	Kubota	3	68D	8F-2R	19.59	1950	No
L245 HC	8610.00	4990.00	5770.00	6410.00	Kubota	3	68D	8F-2R	22.00	2345	No
L275 DT 4WD	9330.00	5410.00	6250.00	6940.00	Kubota	3	79D	8F-2R	23.42	2350	No
L275 F	8150.00	4730.00	5460.00	6060.00	Kubota	3	79D	8F-2R	23.42	2150	No
L305 DT 4WD	10810.00	6270.00	7240.00	8040.00	Kubota	3	79D	8F-2R	26.21	2855	No
L305 F	8805.00	5110.00	5900.00	6550.00	Kubota	3	79D	8F-2R	26.21	2555	No
L345 DT 4WD	11810.00	6850.00	7910.00	8780.00	Kubota	4	91D	8F-2R	29.35	3155	No
L345 F	10100.00	5860.00	6770.00	7520.00	Kubota	4	91D	8F-2R	29.35	2770	No
L345 W	10190.00	5910.00	6830.00	7580.00	Kubota	4	91D	8F-2R	29.35	2530	No
L355 SS	13610.00	7210.00	8300.00	8960.00	Kubota	4	105D	8F-8R	29.00	2684	No
L2250	8375.00	4860.00	5610.00	6230.00	Kubota	3	79D	8F-7R	21.15	2068	No
L2250 4WD	9275.00	5380.00	6210.00	6890.00	Kubota	3	79D	8F-7R	21.15	2321	No
L2550	9075.00	4810.00	5540.00	5980.00	Kubota	3	85D	8F-7R	23.98	2220	No
L2550 4WD	10175.00	5390.00	6210.00	6710.00	Kubota	3	85D	8F-7R	23.98	2464	No
L2850	10075.00	5340.00	6150.00	6640.00	Kubota	4	106D	8F-7R	27.51	2464	No
L2850 4WD	11575.00	6140.00	7060.00	7630.00	Kubota	4	106D	8F-7R	27.51	2705	No
L3750	14550.00	7710.00	8880.00	9590.00	Kubota	5	142D	8F-8R	36.96	3640	No
L3750 4WD	16550.00	8770.00	10100.00	10910.00	Kubota	5	142D	8F-8R	36.96	3860	No
M4050 DT 4WD	18400.00	8830.00	10490.00	11330.00	Kubota	6	159D	8F-2R	45.74	4356	No
M4050 F	14700.00	7060.00	8380.00	9050.00	Kubota	6	159D	8F-2R	45.74	3740	No
L4150	15650.00	8300.00	9550.00	10310.00	Kubota	5	142D	8F-8R	40.64	3750	No
L4150 4WD	18150.00	9620.00	11070.00	11960.00	Kubota	5	142D	8F-8R	40.64	4080	No
M4500	15200.00	7300.00	8660.00	9350.00	Kubota	6	159D	16F-4R	49.72	4220	No
M4500 DT 4WD	18900.00	9070.00	10770.00	11630.00	Kubota	6	159D	16F-4R	49.72	4220	No
M4500 OC	15275.00	7330.00	8710.00	9410.00	Kubota	6	159D	16F-4R	49.00	4400	No
M4950 DT 4WD	21245.00	10200.00	12110.00	13080.00	Kubota	6	170D	12F-4R	49.57	5452	No
M4950 DT 4WD w/Cab	24415.00	11720.00	13920.00	15030.00	Kubota	6	170D	12F-4R	49.57	6252	C,H
M4950 F	17245.00	8280.00	9830.00	10620.00	Kubota	6	170D	12F-4R	49.57	4746	No
M4950 F w/Cab	20715.00	9940.00	11810.00	12760.00	Kubota	6	170D	12F-4R	49.57	5546	C,H
B5200 DT 4WD	5825.00	3670.00	4080.00	4570.00	Kubota	3	46D	6F-2R	11.50	1254	No
B5200 E	5375.00	3390.00	3760.00	4210.00	Kubota	3	46D	6F-2R	11.50	1122	No
M5500 DT 4WD	20480.00	9830.00	11670.00	12600.00	Kubota	3	182D	16F-4R	53.99	5070	No
M5950 DT	24065.00	11550.00	13720.00	14820.00	Kubota	3	196D	12F-4R	58.00	5673	No
M5950 DT 4WD w/Cab	28715.00	13780.00	16370.00	17680.00	Kubota	3	196D	12F-4R	58.00	6563	C,H,A
M5950 F	20065.00	9630.00	11440.00	12360.00	Kubota	3	196D	12F-4R	58.00	4989	No
M5950 F w/Cab	24715.00	11860.00	14090.00	15220.00	Kubota	3	196D	12F-4R	58.00	5879	C,H,A
B6200 DT 4WD	6405.00	4040.00	4480.00	5020.00	Kubota	3	52D	6F-2R	12.50	1232	No
B6200 E	5885.00	3710.00	4120.00	4610.00	Kubota	3	52D	6F-2R	12.50	1333	No
B6200 HSD 4WD	7325.00	4620.00	5130.00	5750.00	Kubota	3	52D	Infinite	12.50	1150	No
B6200 HSE	6725.00	4240.00	4710.00	5280.00	Kubota	3	52D	Infinite	12.50	1100	No
M6950 DT 4WD	25865.00	12420.00	14740.00	15920.00	Kubota	4	243D	12F-4R	66.44	6622	No
M6950 DT 4WD w/Cab	30515.00	14650.00	17390.00	18780.00	Kubota	4	243D	12F-4R	66.44	7512	C,H,A
M6950 F	21365.00	10260.00	12180.00	13150.00	Kubota	4	243D	12F-4R	66.44	5770	No
M6950 F w/Cab	26015.00	12490.00	14830.00	16020.00	Kubota	4	243D	12F-4R	66.44	6590	C,H,A
B7200 DT 4WD	6895.00	4340.00	4830.00	5410.00	Kubota	3	57D	6F-2R	14.00	1320	No
B7200 E	6295.00	3970.00	4410.00	4940.00	Kubota	3	57D	6F-2R	14.00	1215	No
B7200 HSD 4WD	7772.00	4900.00	5440.00	6090.00	Kubota	3	57D	Infinite	14.00	1275	No
B7200 HSE	7175.00	4520.00	5020.00	5620.00	Kubota	3	57D	Infinite	14.00	1225	No
M7500 DT 4WD	25270.00	12130.00	14400.00	15550.00	Kubota	4	243D	16F-4R	72.34	5610	No
M7500 F	19270.00	9250.00	10980.00	11860.00	Kubota	4	243D	16F-4R	72.34	5085	No
M7950 DT 4WD	29055.00	13950.00	16560.00	17890.00	Kubota	4	262D	12F-4R	75.44	6610	No
M7950 DT 4WD w/Cab	33705.00	16180.00	19210.00	20750.00	Kubota	4	262D	12F-4R	75.44	7500	C,H,A
M7950 F	23665.00	11360.00	13490.00	14570.00	Kubota	4	262D	12F-4R	75.44	5840	No
M7950 F w/Cab	28315.00	13590.00	16140.00	17430.00	Kubota	4	262D	12F-4R	75.44	6730	C,H,A
B8200 DT-2 4WD	7695.00	4850.00	5390.00	6040.00	Kubota	3	57D	9F-3R	16.00	1525	No
B8200 F	6895.00	4340.00	4830.00	5410.00	Kubota	3	57D	9F-3R	16.00	1408	No
B8200 HSD 4WD	8595.00	5420.00	6020.00	6740.00	Kubota	3	57D	Infinite	14.50	1525	No
B8200 HSE	7795.00	4910.00	5460.00	6120.00	Kubota	3	57D	Infinite	14.50	1408	No
M8950 DT	32600.00	15650.00	18580.00	20070.00	Kubota	4T	262D	24F-8R	85.63	6853	No
M8950 DT 4WD w/Cab	37250.00	17880.00	21230.00	22930.00	Kubota	4	262D	24F-8R	85.63	7713	C,H,A
M8950 F	27100.00	13010.00	15450.00	16690.00	Kubota	4T	262D	24F-8R	85.63	6093	No
M8950 F w/Cab	31750.00	15240.00	18100.00	19550.00	Kubota	4T	262D	24F-8R	85.63	6953	C,H,A

C, D, DT--Front Wheel Assist DTSS--Front Wheel Assist, Shuttle Shift E--Two Wheel Drive F--Farm Standard W--Two Row Offset
HC--High Clearance HSE--Hydrostatic Transmission, Two Wheel Drive HSD--Hydrostatic Transmission, Four Wheel Drive OC--Orchard L--Low Profile

1986

Model	Approx. Retail Price New	Fair	Good	Premium	Make	No. Cyls.	Displ. Cu.-In.	No. Speeds	P.T.O. H.P.	Approx. Shipping Wt.-Lbs.	Cab
L245 HC	9280.00	5480.00	6310.00	7000.00	Kubota	3	68D	8F-2R	22.00	2345	No
L345 F	10330.00	6100.00	7020.00	7790.00	Kubota	4	90D	8F-2R	29.30	2530	No
L355 SS	13950.00	7530.00	8650.00	9340.00	Kubota	4	105D	8F-8R	29.00	2684	No
L2250 DT-1 4WD	8780.00	5180.00	5970.00	6630.00	Kubota	3	79D	8F-7R	21.15	2321	No
L2250 F-1	7680.00	4530.00	5220.00	5790.00	Kubota	3	79D	8F-7R	21.15	2068	No
L2550 DT-1 4WD	9610.00	5670.00	6540.00	7260.00	Kubota	3	85D	8F-7R	23.98	2464	No
L2550 F-1	8410.00	4960.00	5720.00	6350.00	Kubota	3	85D	8F-7R	23.98	2220	No

Kubota (Cont.)

1986 (Cont.)

Model	Approx. Retail Price New	Estimated Average Value Less Repairs Fair	Good	Premium	Engine Make	No. Cyls.	Displ. Cu.-In.	No. Speeds	P.T.O. H.P.	Approx. Shipping Wt.-Lbs.	Cab
L2850 DT-1 4WD	10850.00	**5860.00**	**6730.00**	**7270.00**	Kubota	4	106D	8F-7R	27.51	2705	No
L2850 F-1	9250.00	**5000.00**	**5740.00**	**6200.00**	Kubota	4	106D	8F-7R	27.51	2464	No
L3350 HDT	15500.00	**8370.00**	**9610.00**	**10380.00**	Kubota	4	113D	8F-8R	32.86	3770	No
L3750 HDT 4WD	17500.00	**9450.00**	**10850.00**	**11720.00**	Kubota	5	142D	8F-8R	36.96	3860	No
L3750 HF	15000.00	**8100.00**	**9300.00**	**10040.00**	Kubota	5	142D	8F-8R	36.96	3640	No
M4030 DT 4WD	19000.00	**9310.00**	**11020.00**	**11900.00**	Kubota	6	159D	8F-2R	44.05	4784	No
M4030 F/L	15600.00	**7640.00**	**9050.00**	**9770.00**	Kubota	6	159D	8F-2R	44.05	4232	No
L4150 HDT 4WD	19200.00	**10370.00**	**11900.00**	**12850.00**	Kubota	5	142D	8F-8R	40.64	4080	No
L4150 HF	15985.00	**8630.00**	**9910.00**	**10700.00**	Kubota	5	142D	8F-8R	40.64	3750	No
M4500 OC	15725.00	**7710.00**	**9120.00**	**9850.00**	Kubota	6	159D	8F-2R	49.70	4004	No
M4950 DT 4WD	21880.00	**10720.00**	**12690.00**	**13710.00**	Kubota	6	170D	12F-4R	49.57	5452	No
M4950 F	17680.00	**8660.00**	**10250.00**	**11070.00**	Kubota	6	170D	12F-4R	49.57	4760	No
M5030 DT 4WD	20100.00	**9850.00**	**11660.00**	**12590.00**	Kubota	6	170D	16F-4R	49.77	4788	C,H
M5030 F	16600.00	**8130.00**	**9630.00**	**10400.00**	Kubota	6	170D	16F-4R	49.77	4232	C,H
B5200 DT 4WD	6450.00	**4130.00**	**4580.00**	**5080.00**	Kubota	3	47D	6F-2R	11.50	1254	No
B5200 E	5800.00	**3710.00**	**4120.00**	**4570.00**	Kubota	3	47D	6F-2R	11.50	1122	No
M5950 DT	24600.00	**12050.00**	**14270.00**	**15410.00**	Kubota	3	196D	12F-4R	58.00	5673	No
M5950 DT 4WD w/Cab	30950.00	**15170.00**	**17950.00**	**19390.00**	Kubota	3	196D	12F-4R	58.00	6563	C,H,A
M5950 F	20500.00	**10050.00**	**11890.00**	**12840.00**	Kubota	3	196D	12F-4R	58.00	4989	No
M5950 F w/Cab	26850.00	**13160.00**	**15570.00**	**16820.00**	Kubota	3	196D	12F-4R	58.00	5879	C,H,A
M6030 DT 4WD	22000.00	**10780.00**	**12760.00**	**13780.00**	Kubota	3	196D	16F-4R	57.75	6300	No
M6030 F/L	18000.00	**8820.00**	**10440.00**	**11280.00**	Kubota	3	196D	16F-4R	57.75	4630	No
B6200 DT 4WD	6950.00	**4450.00**	**4940.00**	**5480.00**	Kubota	3	52D	6F-2R	12.50	1232	No
B6200 E	6300.00	**4030.00**	**4470.00**	**4960.00**	Kubota	3	52D	6F-2R	12.50	1333	No
B6200 HSD 4WD	7950.00	**5090.00**	**5650.00**	**6270.00**	Kubota	3	52D	Infinite	12.50	1150	No
B6200 HSE	7200.00	**4610.00**	**5110.00**	**5670.00**	Kubota	3	52D	Infinite	12.50	1100	No
M6950 DT 4WD	26400.00	**12940.00**	**15310.00**	**16540.00**	Kubota	4	243D	12F-4R	66.44	6622	No
M6950 DT 4WD w/Cab	32750.00	**16050.00**	**19000.00**	**20520.00**	Kubota	4	243D	12F-4R	66.44	7512	C,H,A
M6950 F	21800.00	**10680.00**	**12640.00**	**13650.00**	Kubota	4	243D	12F-4R	66.44	5770	No
M6950 F w/Cab	28150.00	**13790.00**	**16330.00**	**17640.00**	Kubota	4	243D	12F-4R	66.44	5780	C,H,A
M7030 DT 4WD	24900.00	**12200.00**	**14440.00**	**15600.00**	Kubota	4	243D	16F-4R	68.87	5159	No
M7030 F/L	20300.00	**9950.00**	**11770.00**	**12710.00**	Kubota	4	243D	16F-4R	68.87	4607	No
B7200 DT 4WD	7400.00	**4740.00**	**5250.00**	**5830.00**	Kubota	3	57D	6F-2R	14.00	1320	No
B7200 E	6700.00	**4290.00**	**4760.00**	**5280.00**	Kubota	3	57D	6F-2R	14.00	1215	No
B7200 HSD 4WD	8500.00	**5440.00**	**6040.00**	**6700.00**	Kubota	3	57D	Infinite	14.00	1275	No
B7200 HSE	7700.00	**4930.00**	**5470.00**	**6070.00**	Kubota	3	57D	Infinite	14.00	1225	No
M7500 L	20060.00	**9830.00**	**11640.00**	**12570.00**	Kubota	4	243D	16F-4R	72.00	4607	No
M7950 DT 4WD	30000.00	**14700.00**	**17400.00**	**18790.00**	Kubota	4	262D	12F-4R	75.44	6100	No
M7950 DT 4WD w/Cab	36350.00	**17810.00**	**21080.00**	**22770.00**	Kubota	4	262D	12F-4R	75.44	6970	C,H,A
M7950 DTM 4WD	32300.00	**15830.00**	**18730.00**	**20230.00**	Kubota	4	262D	16F-4R	75.44	6100	No
M7950 F	24400.00	**11960.00**	**14150.00**	**15280.00**	Kubota	4	262D	12F-4R	75.44	5950	No
M7950 F w/Cab	30750.00	**15070.00**	**17840.00**	**19270.00**	Kubota	4	262D	12F-4R	75.44		C,H,A
M7950 HC	26600.00	**13030.00**	**15430.00**	**16660.00**	Kubota	4	262D	16F-4R	75.44	5600	No
M7950 W	25600.00	**12540.00**	**14850.00**	**16040.00**	Kubota	4	262D	16F-4R	75.44	5600	No
M8030 DT 4WD	26900.00	**13180.00**	**15600.00**	**16850.00**	Kubota	4	262D	16F-4R	76.91	5710	No
M8030 F/L	21700.00	**10630.00**	**12590.00**	**13600.00**	Kubota	4	262D	16F-4R	76.91	5109	No
B8200 DT-2 4WD	8050.00	**5150.00**	**5720.00**	**6350.00**	Kubota	3	57D	9F-3R	16.00	1525	No
B8200 F	7200.00	**4610.00**	**5110.00**	**5670.00**	Kubota	3	57D	9F-3R	16.00	1408	No
B8200 HSD 4WD	9150.00	**5860.00**	**6500.00**	**7220.00**	Kubota	3	57D	Infinite	14.50	1525	No
B8200 HSE	8300.00	**5310.00**	**5890.00**	**6540.00**	Kubota	3	57D	Infinite	14.50	1408	No
M8950 DT	33600.00	**16460.00**	**19490.00**	**21050.00**	Kubota	4T	262D	24F-8R	85.63	6853	No
M8950 DT 4WD w/Cab	39950.00	**19580.00**	**23170.00**	**25020.00**	Kubota	4	262D	24F-8R	85.63	7713	C,H,A
M8950 F w/Cab	31750.00	**15560.00**	**18420.00**	**19890.00**	Kubota	4T	262D	24F-8R	85.63	6953	C,H,A
M8950 F/L	28000.00	**13720.00**	**16240.00**	**17540.00**	Kubota	4T	262D	24F-8R	85.63	6093	No
B9200 HSD 4WD	9650.00	**6180.00**	**6850.00**	**7600.00**	Kubota	4	75D	Infinite	16.00	4916	No
B9200 HSE	8800.00	**5630.00**	**6250.00**	**6940.00**	Kubota	4	75D	Infinite	16.00	4299	No

C, D, DT--Front Wheel Assist DTSS--Front Wheel Assist, Shuttle Shift E--Two Wheel Drive F--Farm Standard W--Two Row Offset HC--High Clearance HSE--Hydrostatic Transmission, Two Wheel Drive HSD--Hydrostatic Transmission, Four Wheel Drive OC--Orchard L--Low Profile

1987

Model	Approx. Retail Price New	Fair	Good	Premium	Engine Make	No. Cyls.	Displ. Cu.-In.	No. Speeds	P.T.O. H.P.	Approx. Shipping Wt.-Lbs.	Cab
L245 HC	9690.00	**5810.00**	**6690.00**	**7430.00**	Kubota	3	68D	8F-2R	22.00	2345	No
L355 SS	13950.00	**7670.00**	**8790.00**	**9490.00**	Kubota	4	105D	8F-8R	29.00	2684	No
L2250 DT-1 4WD	9600.00	**5760.00**	**6620.00**	**7350.00**	Kubota	3	79D	8F-7R	21.15	2321	No
L2250 F-1	8300.00	**4980.00**	**5730.00**	**6360.00**	Kubota	3	79D	8F-7R	21.15	2068	No
L2550 DT-1 4WD	10400.00	**6240.00**	**7180.00**	**7970.00**	Kubota	3	85D	8F-7R	23.98	2464	No
L2550 F-1	9000.00	**5400.00**	**6210.00**	**6890.00**	Kubota	3	85D	8F-7R	23.98	2220	No
L2850 DT-1 4WD	11800.00	**6490.00**	**7430.00**	**8020.00**	Kubota	4	106D	8F-7R	27.51	2705	No
L2850 F-1	9950.00	**5470.00**	**6270.00**	**6770.00**	Kubota	4	106D	8F-7R	27.51	2464	No
L3350 HDT	17000.00	**9350.00**	**10710.00**	**11570.00**	Kubota	4	113D	8F-8R	32.86	3770	No
L3750 HDT 4WD	19000.00	**10450.00**	**11970.00**	**12930.00**	Kubota	5	142D	8F-8R	36.96	3860	No
L3750 HF	15000.00	**8250.00**	**9450.00**	**10210.00**	Kubota	5	142D	8F-8R	36.96	3640	No
M4030 DT 4WD	20300.00	**10150.00**	**11980.00**	**12940.00**	Kubota	6	159D	8F-2R	44.05	4784	No
M4030 F/L	16300.00	**8150.00**	**9620.00**	**10390.00**	Kubota	6	159D	8F-2R	44.05	4232	No
L4150 DTN	20100.00	**11060.00**	**12660.00**	**13670.00**	Kubota	5	142D	8F-8R	40.00	4145	No
L4150 HDT 4WD	20500.00	**11280.00**	**12920.00**	**13950.00**	Kubota	5	142D	8F-8R	40.64	4080	No
L4150 HF	15985.00	**8790.00**	**10070.00**	**10880.00**	Kubota	5	142D	8F-8R	40.64	3750	No
B4200 DT	6000.00	**3600.00**	**4140.00**	**4600.00**	Kubota	2	35D	6F-2R	10	926	No
M4950 DT 4WD	23000.00	**11500.00**	**13570.00**	**14660.00**	Kubota	6	170D	12F-4R	49.57	5452	No
M4950 F	18600.00	**9300.00**	**10970.00**	**11850.00**	Kubota	6	170D	12F-4R	49.57	4760	No
M5030 DT 4WD	21800.00	**10900.00**	**12860.00**	**13890.00**	Kubota	6	170D	16F-4R	49.77	4788	C,H
M5030 F	17800.00	**8900.00**	**10500.00**	**11340.00**	Kubota	6	170D	16F-4R	49.77	4232	C,H
B5200 DT 4WD	7040.00	**4580.00**	**5070.00**	**5580.00**	Kubota	3	47D	6F-2R	11.50	1254	No
B5200 E	6190.00	**4020.00**	**4460.00**	**4910.00**	Kubota	3	47D	6F-2R	11.50	1122	No
M5950 DT	26800.00	**13400.00**	**15810.00**	**17080.00**	Kubota	3	196D	12F-4R	58.00	5673	No

Model	Approx. Retail Price New	Estimated Average Value Less Repairs Fair	Good	Premium	Engine Make	No. Cyls.	Displ. Cu.-In.	No. Speeds	P.T.O. H.P.	Approx. Shipping Wt.-Lbs.	Cab

Kubota (Cont.)

1987 (Cont.)

Model	Approx. Retail Price New	Fair	Good	Premium	Make	No. Cyls.	Displ. Cu.-In.	No. Speeds	P.T.O. H.P.	Approx. Shipping Wt.-Lbs.	Cab
M5950 DT 4WD w/Cab	33700.00	**16850.00**	**19880.00**	**21470.00**	Kubota	3	196D	12F-4R	58.00	6563	C,H,A
M5950 F	22000.00	**11000.00**	**12980.00**	**14020.00**	Kubota	3	196D	12F-4R	58.00	4989	No
M5950 F w/Cab	28900.00	**14450.00**	**17050.00**	**18410.00**	Kubota	3	196D	12F-4R	58.00	5879	C,H,A
M6030 DT 4WD	23900.00	**11950.00**	**14100.00**	**15230.00**	Kubota	3	196D	16F-4R	57.74	6300	No
M6030 DTN	23810.00	**11910.00**	**14050.00**	**15170.00**	Kubota	3	196D	16F-4R	57.00	4740	No
M6030 F/L	19300.00	**9650.00**	**11390.00**	**12300.00**	Kubota	3	196D	16F-4R	57.74	4630	No
B6200 DT 4WD	7660.00	**4980.00**	**5520.00**	**6070.00**	Kubota	3	52D	6F-2R	12.50	1232	No
B6200 E	6760.00	**4390.00**	**4870.00**	**5360.00**	Kubota	3	52D	6F-2R	12.50	1333	No
B6200 HSD 4WD	8790.00	**5710.00**	**6330.00**	**6960.00**	Kubota	3	52D	Infinite	12.50	1150	No
B6200 HSE	7810.00	**5080.00**	**5620.00**	**6180.00**	Kubota	3	52D	Infinite	12.50	1100	No
M6950 DT 4WD	28500.00	**14250.00**	**16820.00**	**18170.00**	Kubota	4	243D	12F-4R	66.44	6622	No
M6950 DT 4WD w/Cab	35400.00	**17700.00**	**20890.00**	**22560.00**	Kubota	4	243D	12F-4R	66.44	7512	C,H,A
M6950 F	23500.00	**11750.00**	**13870.00**	**14980.00**	Kubota	4	243D	12F-4R	66.44	5770	No
M6950 F w/Cab	30400.00	**15200.00**	**17940.00**	**19380.00**	Kubota	4	243D	12F-4R	66.44	5780	C,H,A
M7030 DT 4WD	27300.00	**13650.00**	**16110.00**	**17400.00**	Kubota	4	243D	16F-4R	68.87	5159	No
M7030 F/L	21800.00	**10900.00**	**12860.00**	**13890.00**	Kubota	4	243D	16F-4R	68.87	4607	No
B7200 DT 4WD	8100.00	**5270.00**	**5830.00**	**6410.00**	Kubota	3	57D	6F-2R	14.00	1320	No
B7200 E	7150.00	**4650.00**	**5150.00**	**5670.00**	Kubota	3	57D	6F-2R	14.00	1215	No
B7200 HSD 4WD	9300.00	**6050.00**	**6700.00**	**7370.00**	Kubota	3	57D	Infinite	14.00	1275	No
B7200 HSE	8340.00	**5420.00**	**6010.00**	**6610.00**	Kubota	3	57D	Infinite	14.00	1225	No
M7950 DT 4WD	32500.00	**16250.00**	**19180.00**	**20710.00**	Kubota	4	262D	12F-4R	75.44	6100	No
M7950 DT 4WD w/Cab	39400.00	**19700.00**	**23250.00**	**25110.00**	Kubota	4	262D	12F-4R	75.44	6970	C,H,A
M7950 DTM 4WD	33300.00	**16650.00**	**19650.00**	**21220.00**	Kubota	4	262D	16F-4R	75.44	6100	No
M7950 F	26000.00	**13000.00**	**15340.00**	**16570.00**	Kubota	4	262D	12F-4R	75.44	5950	No
M7950 F w/Cab	32900.00	**16450.00**	**19410.00**	**20960.00**	Kubota	4	262D	12F-4R	75.44		C,H,A
M7950 HC	27300.00	**13650.00**	**16110.00**	**17400.00**	Kubota	4	262D	16F-4R	75.44	5600	No
M7950 W	26300.00	**13150.00**	**15520.00**	**16760.00**	Kubota	4	262D	16F-4R	75.44	5600	No
M8030 DT 4WD	29300.00	**14650.00**	**17290.00**	**18670.00**	Kubota	4	262D	16F-4R	76.91	5710	No
M8030 F/L	23300.00	**11650.00**	**13750.00**	**14850.00**	Kubota	4	262D	16F-4R	76.91	5109	No
B8200 DT-2 4WD	8800.00	**5720.00**	**6340.00**	**6970.00**	Kubota	3	57D	9F-3R	16.00	1525	No
B8200 F	7800.00	**5070.00**	**5620.00**	**6180.00**	Kubota	3	57D	9F-3R	16.00	1408	No
B8200 HSD 4WD	10100.00	**6570.00**	**7270.00**	**8000.00**	Kubota	3	57D	Infinite	14.50	1525	No
B8200 HSE	9000.00	**5850.00**	**6480.00**	**7130.00**	Kubota	3	57D	Infinite	14.50	1408	No
M8950 DT	36500.00	**18250.00**	**21540.00**	**23260.00**	Kubota	4T	262D	24F-8R	85.63	6853	No
M8950 DT 4WD w/Cab	43400.00	**21700.00**	**25610.00**	**27660.00**	Kubota	4	262D	24F-8R	85.63	7713	C,H,A
M8950 F w/Cab	36900.00	**18450.00**	**21770.00**	**23510.00**	Kubota	4T	262D	24F-8R	85.63	6953	C,H,A
M8950 F/L	30000.00	**15000.00**	**17700.00**	**19120.00**	Kubota	4T	262D	24F-8R	85.63	6093	No
B9200 DT	9300.00	**6050.00**	**6700.00**	**7370.00**	Kubota	3	57D	9F-3R	18.50	1676	No
B9200 F	8300.00	**5400.00**	**5980.00**	**6580.00**	Kubota	3	57D	9F-3R	18.50	1570	No
B9200 HSD 4WD	10600.00	**6890.00**	**7630.00**	**8390.00**	Kubota	4	75D	Infinite	16.00	4916	No
B9200 HSE	9500.00	**6180.00**	**6840.00**	**7520.00**	Kubota	4	75D	Infinite	16.00	4299	No

C, D, DT--Front Wheel Assist DTSS--Front Wheel Assist, Shuttle Shift E--Two Wheel Drive F--Farm Standard W--Two Row Offset
HC--High Clearance HSE--Hydrostatic Transmission, Two Wheel Drive HSD--Hydrostatic Transmission, Four Wheel Drive OC--Orchard L--Low Profile

1988

Model	Approx. Retail Price New	Fair	Good	Premium	Make	No. Cyls.	Displ. Cu.-In.	No. Speeds	P.T.O. H.P.	Approx. Shipping Wt.-Lbs.	Cab
L245 HC	9980.00	**6090.00**	**6990.00**	**7760.00**	Kubota	3	68D	8F-2R	22.00	2345	No
L355 SS	14360.00	**8040.00**	**9190.00**	**9830.00**	Kubota	4	105D	8F-8R	29.00	2684	No
L2250 DT-1 4WD	9880.00	**6030.00**	**6920.00**	**7680.00**	Kubota	3	79D	8F-7R	21.15	2321	No
L2250 F-1	8550.00	**5220.00**	**5990.00**	**6650.00**	Kubota	3	79D	8F-7R	21.15	2068	No
L2550 DT-1 4WD	10700.00	**6530.00**	**7490.00**	**8310.00**	Kubota	3	85D	8F-7R	23.98	2464	No
L2550 F-1	9275.00	**5660.00**	**6490.00**	**7200.00**	Kubota	3	85D	8F-7R	23.98	2220	No
L2850 DT-1 4WD	12150.00	**6800.00**	**7780.00**	**8330.00**	Kubota	4	106D	8F-7R	27.51	2705	No
L2850 F-1	10250.00	**5740.00**	**6560.00**	**7020.00**	Kubota	4	106D	8F-7R	27.51	2464	No
L3350 HDT	17500.00	**9800.00**	**11200.00**	**11980.00**	Kubota	4	113D	8F-8R	32.86	3770	No
L3750 HDT 4WD	19570.00	**10960.00**	**12530.00**	**13410.00**	Kubota	5	142D	8F-8R	36.96	3860	No
L3750 HF	15450.00	**8650.00**	**9890.00**	**10580.00**	Kubota	5	142D	8F-8R	36.96	3640	No
M4030 DT 4WD	20900.00	**10660.00**	**12540.00**	**13420.00**	Kubota	6	159D	8F-2R	44.05	4784	No
M4030 F/L	16790.00	**8560.00**	**10070.00**	**10780.00**	Kubota	6	159D	8F-2R	44.05	4232	No
L4150 DTN	20700.00	**11590.00**	**13250.00**	**14180.00**	Kubota	5	142D	8F-8R	40.00	4145	No
L4150 HDT 4WD	21100.00	**11820.00**	**13500.00**	**14450.00**	Kubota	5	142D	8F-8R	40.64	4080	No
L4150 HF	16450.00	**9210.00**	**10530.00**	**11270.00**	Kubota	5	142D	8F-8R	40.64	3750	No
B4200 DT	6180.00	**3770.00**	**4330.00**	**4810.00**	Kubota	2	35D	6F-2R	10	926	No
M4950 DT 4WD	23600.00	**12040.00**	**14160.00**	**15150.00**	Kubota	6	170D	12F-4R	49.57	5452	No
M4950 F	19150.00	**9770.00**	**11490.00**	**12290.00**	Kubota	6	170D	12F-4R	49.57	4760	No
M5030 DT 4WD	22450.00	**11450.00**	**13470.00**	**14410.00**	Kubota	6	170D	16F-4R	49.77	4788	C,H
M5030 F	18300.00	**9330.00**	**10980.00**	**11750.00**	Kubota	6	170D	16F-4R	49.77	4232	C,H
B5200 DT 4WD	7250.00	**4790.00**	**5290.00**	**5770.00**	Kubota	3	47D	6F-2R	11.50	1254	No
B5200 E	6375.00	**4210.00**	**4650.00**	**5070.00**	Kubota	3	47D	6F-2R	11.50	1122	No
M5950 DT	27600.00	**14080.00**	**16560.00**	**17720.00**	Kubota	3	196D	12F-4R	58.00	5673	No
M5950 DT 4WD w/Cab	34700.00	**17700.00**	**20820.00**	**22280.00**	Kubota	3	196D	12F-4R	58.00	6563	C,H,A
M5950 F	22600.00	**11530.00**	**13560.00**	**14510.00**	Kubota	3	196D	12F-4R	58.00	4989	No
M5950 F w/Cab	29700.00	**15150.00**	**17820.00**	**19070.00**	Kubota	3	196D	12F-4R	58.00	5879	C,H,A
M6030 DT 4WD	24600.00	**12550.00**	**14760.00**	**15790.00**	Kubota	3	196D	16F-4R	57.74	6300	No
M6030 DTN	24500.00	**12500.00**	**14700.00**	**15730.00**	Kubota	3	196D	16F-4R	57.00	4740	No
M6030 F/L	19800.00	**10100.00**	**11880.00**	**12710.00**	Kubota	3	196D	16F-4R	57.74	4630	No
B6200 DT 4WD	7890.00	**5210.00**	**5760.00**	**6280.00**	Kubota	3	52D	6F-2R	12.50	1232	No
B6200 E	6960.00	**4590.00**	**5080.00**	**5540.00**	Kubota	3	52D	6F-2R	12.50	1333	No
B6200 HSD 4WD	9050.00	**5970.00**	**6610.00**	**7210.00**	Kubota	3	52D	Infinite	12.50	1150	No
B6200 HSE	8050.00	**5310.00**	**5880.00**	**6410.00**	Kubota	3	52D	Infinite	12.50	1100	No
M6950 DT 4WD	29300.00	**14940.00**	**17580.00**	**18810.00**	Kubota	4	243D	12F-4R	66.44	6622	No
M6950 DT 4WD w/Cab	36400.00	**18560.00**	**21840.00**	**23370.00**	Kubota	4	243D	12F-4R	66.44	7512	C,H,A
M6950 F	24200.00	**12340.00**	**14520.00**	**15540.00**	Kubota	4	243D	12F-4R	66.44	5770	No
M6950 F w/Cab	31300.00	**15960.00**	**18780.00**	**20100.00**	Kubota	4	243D	12F-4R	66.44	5780	C,H,A
M7030 DT 4WD	28100.00	**14330.00**	**16860.00**	**18040.00**	Kubota	4	243D	16F-4R	68.87	5159	No

Kubota (Cont.)

1988 (Cont.)

Model	Approx. Retail Price New	Estimated Average Value Less Repairs Fair	Good	Premium	Engine Make	No. Cyls.	Displ. Cu.-In.	No. Speeds	P.T.O. H.P.	Approx. Shipping Wt.-Lbs.	Cab
M7030 F/L	22400.00	11420.00	13440.00	14380.00	Kubota	4	243D	16F-4R	68.87	4607	No
B7200 DT 4WD	8350.00	5510.00	6100.00	6650.00	Kubota	3	57D	6F-2R	14.00	1320	No
B7200 E	7360.00	4860.00	5370.00	5850.00	Kubota	3	57D	6F-2R	14.00	1215	No
B7200 HSD 4WD	9580.00	6320.00	6990.00	7620.00	Kubota	3	57D	Infinite	14.00	1275	No
B7200 HSE	8590.00	5670.00	6270.00	6830.00	Kubota	3	57D	Infinite	14.00	1225	No
M7950 DT 4WD	33400.00	17030.00	20040.00	21440.00	Kubota	4	262D	12F-4R	75.44	6100	No
M7950 DT 4WD w/Cab	40500.00	20660.00	24300.00	26000.00	Kubota	4	262D	12F-4R	75.44	6970	C,H,A
M7950 DTM 4WD	34300.00	17490.00	20580.00	22020.00	Kubota	4	262D	16F-4R	75.44	6100	No
M7950 F	26700.00	13620.00	16020.00	17140.00	Kubota	4	262D	12F-4R	75.44	5950	No
M7950 F w/Cab	33800.00	17240.00	20280.00	21700.00	Kubota	4	262D	12F-4R	75.44		C,H,A
M7950 HC	28100.00	14330.00	16860.00	18040.00	Kubota	4	262D	16F-4R	75.44	5600	No
M7950 W	27000.00	13770.00	16200.00	17330.00	Kubota	4	262D	16F-4R	75.44	5600	No
M8030 DT 4WD	30180.00	15390.00	18110.00	19380.00	Kubota	4	262D	16F-4R	76.91	5710	No
M8030 F/L	24000.00	12240.00	14400.00	15410.00	Kubota	4	262D	16F-4R	76.91	5109	No
B8200 DT-2 4WD	9060.00	5980.00	6610.00	7210.00	Kubota	3	57D	9F-3R	16.00	1525	No
B8200 F	8030.00	5300.00	5860.00	6390.00	Kubota	3	57D	9F-3R	16.00	1408	No
B8200 HSD 4WD	10400.00	6860.00	7590.00	8270.00	Kubota	3	57D	Infinite	14.50	1525	No
B8200 HSE	9250.00	6110.00	6750.00	7360.00	Kubota	3	57D	Infinite	14.50	1408	No
M8950 DT	37600.00	19180.00	22560.00	24140.00	Kubota	4T	262D	24F-8R	85.63	6853	No
M8950 DT 4WD w/Cab	44700.00	22800.00	26820.00	28700.00	Kubota	4	262D	24F-8R	85.63	7713	C,H,A
M8950 F w/Cab	38000.00	19380.00	22800.00	24400.00	Kubota	4T	262D	24F-8R	85.63	6953	C,H,A
M8950 F/L	30900.00	15760.00	18540.00	19840.00	Kubota	4T	262D	24F-8R	85.63	6093	No
B9200 DT	9580.00	6320.00	6990.00	7620.00	Kubota	3	57D	9F-3R	18.50	1676	No
B9200 F	8550.00	5640.00	6240.00	6800.00	Kubota	3	57D	9F-3R	18.50	1570	No
B9200 HSD 4WD	10900.00	7190.00	7960.00	8680.00	Kubota	4	75D	Infinite	16.00	4916	No
B9200 HSE	9780.00	6460.00	7140.00	7780.00	Kubota	4	75D	Infinite	16.00	4299	No

C, D, DT--Front Wheel Assist DTSS--Front Wheel Assist, Shuttle Shift E--Two Wheel Drive F--Farm Standard W--Two Row Offset HC--High Clearance HSE--Hydrostatic Transmission, Two Wheel Drive HSD--Hydrostatic Transmission, Four Wheel Drive OC--Orchard L--Low Profile

1989

Model	Approx. Retail Price New	Estimated Average Value Less Repairs Fair	Good	Premium	Engine Make	No. Cyls.	Displ. Cu.-In.	No. Speeds	P.T.O. H.P.	Approx. Shipping Wt.-Lbs.	Cab
L245 HC	9980.00	6190.00	7090.00	7800.00	Kubota	3	68D	8F-2R	22.00	2345	No
L355 SS	14360.00	8190.00	9330.00	9980.00	Kubota	4	105D	8F-8R	29.00	2684	No
L2250 DT-1 4WD	9880.00	6130.00	7020.00	7720.00	Kubota	3	79D	8F-7R	21.15	2321	No
L2250 F-1	8550.00	5300.00	6070.00	6680.00	Kubota	3	79D	8F-7R	21.15	2068	No
L2550 DT-1 4WD	10700.00	6630.00	7600.00	8360.00	Kubota	3	85D	8F-7R	23.98	2464	No
L2550 F-1	9275.00	5750.00	6590.00	7250.00	Kubota	3	85D	8F-7R	23.98	2220	No
L2850 DT-1 4WD	12150.00	7530.00	8630.00	9490.00	Kubota	4	106D	8F-7R	27.51	2705	No
L2850 F-1	10250.00	6360.00	7280.00	8010.00	Kubota	4	106D	8F-7R	27.51	2464	No
L3350 HDT	17500.00	9980.00	11380.00	12180.00	Kubota	4	113D	8F-8R	32.86	3770	No
L3750 HDT 4WD	19570.00	11160.00	12720.00	13610.00	Kubota	5	142D	8F-8R	36.96	3860	No
L3750 HF	15450.00	8810.00	10040.00	10740.00	Kubota	5	142D	8F-8R	36.96	3640	No
M4030 DT 4WD	20900.00	10870.00	12750.00	13640.00	Kubota	6	159D	8F-2R	44.05	4784	No
M4030 F/L	16790.00	8730.00	10240.00	10960.00	Kubota	6	159D	8F-2R	44.05	4232	No
L4150 DTN	20700.00	11800.00	13460.00	14400.00	Kubota	5	142D	8F-8R	40.00	4145	No
L4150 HDT 4WD	21100.00	12030.00	13720.00	14680.00	Kubota	5	142D	8F-8R	40.64	4080	No
L4150 HF	16450.00	9380.00	10690.00	11440.00	Kubota	5	142D	8F-8R	40.64	3750	No
B4200 DT	6180.00	3830.00	4390.00	4830.00	Kubota	2	35D	6F-2R	10	926	No
M4950 DT 4WD	23600.00	12270.00	14400.00	15410.00	Kubota	6	170D	12F-4R	49.57	5452	No
M4950 F	19150.00	9960.00	11680.00	12500.00	Kubota	6	170D	12F-4R	49.57	4760	No
M5030 DT 4WD	22450.00	12800.00	14590.00	15610.00	Kubota	6	170D	16F-4R	49.77	4788	C,H
M5030 F	18300.00	9520.00	11160.00	11940.00	Kubota	6	170D	16F-4R	49.77	4232	C,H
B5200 DT 4WD	7250.00	4860.00	5370.00	5800.00	Kubota	3	47D	6F-2R	11.50	1254	No
B5200 E	6375.00	4270.00	4720.00	5100.00	Kubota	3	47D	6F-2R	11.50	1122	No
M5950 DT	27600.00	14350.00	16840.00	18020.00	Kubota	3	196D	12F-4R	58.00	5673	No
M5950 DT 4WD w/Cab	34700.00	18040.00	21170.00	22650.00	Kubota	3	196D	12F-4R	58.00	6563	C,H,A
M5950 F	22600.00	11750.00	13790.00	14760.00	Kubota	3	196D	12F-4R	58.00	4989	No
M5950 F w/Cab	29700.00	15440.00	18120.00	19390.00	Kubota	3	196D	12F-4R	58.00	5879	C,H,A
M6030 DT 4WD	24600.00	12790.00	15010.00	16060.00	Kubota	3	196D	16F-4R	57.74	6300	No
M6030 DTN	24500.00	12740.00	14950.00	16000.00	Kubota	3	196D	16F-4R	57.00	4740	No
M6030 F/L	19800.00	10300.00	12080.00	12930.00	Kubota	3	196D	16F-4R	57.74	4630	No
B6200 DT 4WD	7890.00	5290.00	5840.00	6310.00	Kubota	3	52D	6F-2R	12.50	1232	No
B6200 E	6960.00	4660.00	5150.00	5560.00	Kubota	3	52D	6F-2R	12.50	1333	No
B6200 HSD 4WD	9050.00	6060.00	6700.00	7240.00	Kubota	3	52D	Infinite	12.50	1150	No
B6200 HSE	8050.00	5390.00	5960.00	6440.00	Kubota	3	52D	Infinite	12.50	1100	No
M6950 DT 4WD	29300.00	15240.00	17870.00	19120.00	Kubota	4	243D	12F-4R	66.44	6622	No
M6950 DT 4WD w/Cab	36400.00	18930.00	22200.00	23750.00	Kubota	4	243D	12F-4R	66.44	7512	C,H,A
M6950 F	24200.00	12580.00	14760.00	15790.00	Kubota	4	243D	12F-4R	66.44	5770	No
M6950 F w/Cab	31300.00	16280.00	19090.00	20430.00	Kubota	4	243D	12F-4R	66.44	5780	C,H,A
M7030 DT 4WD	28100.00	14610.00	17140.00	18340.00	Kubota	4	243D	16F-4R	68.87	5159	No
M7030 F/L	22400.00	11650.00	13660.00	14620.00	Kubota	4	243D	16F-4R	68.87	4607	No
B7200 DT 4WD	8350.00	5600.00	6180.00	6670.00	Kubota	3	57D	6F-2R	14.00	1320	No
B7200 E	7360.00	4930.00	5450.00	5890.00	Kubota	3	57D	6F-2R	14.00	1215	No
B7200 HSD 4WD	9580.00	6420.00	7090.00	7660.00	Kubota	3	57D	Infinite	14.00	1275	No
B7200 HSE	8590.00	5760.00	6360.00	6870.00	Kubota	3	57D	Infinite	14.00	1225	No
M7950 DT 4WD	33400.00	17370.00	20370.00	21800.00	Kubota	4	262D	12F-4R	75.44	6100	No
M7950 DT 4WD w/Cab	40500.00	21060.00	24710.00	26440.00	Kubota	4	262D	12F-4R	75.44	6970	C,H,A
M7950 DTM 4WD	34300.00	17840.00	20920.00	22380.00	Kubota	4	262D	16F-4R	75.44	6100	No
M7950 F	26700.00	13880.00	16290.00	17430.00	Kubota	4	262D	12F-4R	75.44	5950	No
M7950 F w/Cab	33800.00	17580.00	20620.00	22060.00	Kubota	4	262D	12F-4R	75.44		C,H,A
M7950 HC	28100.00	14610.00	17140.00	18340.00	Kubota	4	262D	16F-4R	75.44	5600	No
M7950 W	27000.00	14040.00	16470.00	17620.00	Kubota	4	262D	16F-4R	75.44	5600	No
M8030 DT 4WD	30180.00	15690.00	18410.00	19700.00	Kubota	4	262D	16F-4R	76.91	5710	No
M8030 F/L	24000.00	12480.00	14640.00	15670.00	Kubota	4	262D	16F-4R	76.91	5109	No
B8200 DT-2 4WD	9060.00	6070.00	6700.00	7240.00	Kubota	3	57D	9F-3R	16.00	1525	No

Kubota (Cont.)

Model	Approx. Retail Price New	Estimated Average Value Less Repairs Fair	Good	Premium	Engine Make	No. Cyls.	Displ. Cu.-In.	No. Speeds	P.T.O. H.P.	Approx. Shipping Wt.-Lbs.	Cab
1989 (Cont.)											
B8200 F	8030.00	5380.00	5940.00	6420.00	Kubota	3	57D	9F-3R	16.00	1408	No
B8200 HSD 4WD	10400.00	6970.00	7700.00	8320.00	Kubota	3	57D	Infinite	14.50	1525	No
B8200 HSE	9250.00	6200.00	6850.00	7400.00	Kubota	3	57D	Infinite	14.50	1408	No
M8950 DT	37600.00	19550.00	22940.00	24550.00	Kubota	4T	262D	24F-8R	85.63	6853	No
M8950 DT 4WD w/Cab	44700.00	23240.00	27270.00	29180.00	Kubota	4	262D	24F-8R	85.63	7713	C,H,A
M8950 F w/Cab	38000.00	19760.00	23180.00	24800.00	Kubota	4T	262D	24F-8R	85.63	6953	C,H,A
M8950 F/L	30900.00	16070.00	18850.00	20170.00	Kubota	4T	262D	24F-8R	85.63	6093	No
B9200 DT	9580.00	6420.00	7090.00	7660.00	Kubota	3	57D	9F-3R	18.50	1676	No
B9200 F	8550.00	5730.00	6330.00	6840.00	Kubota	3	57D	9F-3R	18.50	1570	No
B9200 HSD 4WD	10900.00	7300.00	8070.00	8720.00	Kubota	4	75D	Infinite	16.00	4916	No
B9200 HSE	9780.00	6550.00	7240.00	7820.00	Kubota	4	75D	Infinite	16.00	4299	No

C, D, DT--Front Wheel Assist DTSS--Front Wheel Assist, Shuttle Shift E--Two Wheel Drive W--Two Row Offset F--Farm Standard HC--High Clearance HSE--Hydrostatic Transmission, Two Wheel Drive HSD--Hydrostatic Transmission, Four Wheel Drive OC--Orchard L--Low Profile

Model	Approx. Retail Price New	Estimated Average Value Less Repairs Fair	Good	Premium	Engine Make	No. Cyls.	Displ. Cu.-In.	No. Speeds	P.T.O. H.P.	Approx. Shipping Wt.-Lbs.	Cab
1990											
B1550 DT 4WD	10070.00	5840.00	6650.00	7120.00	Kubota	3	52D	6F-2R	14.00	1246	No
B1550 E	8770.00	5090.00	5790.00	6200.00	Kubota	3	52D	6F-2R	14.00	1113	No
B1550 HSD 4WD	11470.00	6650.00	7570.00	8100.00	Kubota	3	52D	Infinite	13.00	1323	No
B1550 HSE	10170.00	5900.00	6710.00	7180.00	Kubota	3	52D	Infinite	13.00	1190	No
B1750 DT 4WD	11090.00	6990.00	7990.00	8710.00	Kubota	3	57D	6F-2R	16.50	1290	No
B1750 E	9790.00	6170.00	7050.00	7690.00	Kubota	3	57D	6F-2R	16.50	1168	No
B1750 HSD 4WD	12490.00	7870.00	8990.00	9800.00	Kubota	3	57D	Infinite	15.50	1367	No
B1750 HSE	11190.00	7050.00	8060.00	8790.00	Kubota	3	57D	Infinite	15.50	1224	No
L2050 DT 4WD	10190.00	6930.00	7640.00	8180.00	Kubota	3	68D	8F-2R	20.00	2093	No
L2050 F	8990.00	6110.00	6740.00	7210.00	Kubota	3	68D	8F-2R	20.00	1781	No
B2150 DT 4WD	12100.00	8230.00	9080.00	9720.00	Kubota	4	75D	9F-3R	20.00	1731	No
B2150 E	10700.00	7280.00	8030.00	8590.00	Kubota	4	75D	9F-3R	20.00	1576	No
B2150 HSD 4WD	13500.00	9180.00	10130.00	10840.00	Kubota	4	75D	Infinite	18.00	1742	No
B2150 HSE	12200.00	8300.00	9150.00	9790.00	Kubota	4	75D	Infinite	18.00	1587	No
L2250 DT-7 4WD	12520.00	8510.00	9390.00	10050.00	Kubota	3	79D	8F-7R	21.00	2380	No
L2250 F-1	9920.00	6750.00	7440.00	7960.00	Kubota	3	79D	8F-7R	21.00	2170	No
L2550 DT-7 4WD	13540.00	8530.00	9750.00	10630.00	Kubota	3	85D	8F-7R	23.50	2485	No
L2550 F-7	12040.00	7590.00	8670.00	9450.00	Kubota	3	85D	8F-7R	23.50	2305	No
L2550 GST 4WD	15000.00	9450.00	10800.00	11770.00	Kubota	3	85D	8F-8R	23.50	2490	No
L2650 DT-W 4WD	13400.00	8440.00	9650.00	10520.00	Kubota	3	85D	8F-8R	23.50	2602	No
L2850 DT-7 4WD	15470.00	9750.00	11140.00	12140.00	Kubota	4	106D	8F-7R	27.00	2680	No
L2850 F-7	13740.00	8660.00	9890.00	10780.00	Kubota	4	106D	8F-7R	27.00	2480	No
L2850 GST 4WD	16900.00	10650.00	12170.00	13270.00	Kubota	4	106D	8F-8R	27.00	2680	No
L2950 DT-W 4WD	14200.00	8950.00	10220.00	11140.00	Kubota	3	89D	8F-8R	26.00	2734	No
L3250 DT 4WD	16590.00	9620.00	10950.00	11720.00	Kubota	4	114D	8F-7R	32.00	2740	No
L3250 F	14590.00	8460.00	9630.00	10300.00	Kubota	4	114D	8F-7R	32.00	2530	No
L3350 DT 4WD	18500.00	10730.00	12210.00	13070.00	Kubota	4	114D	8F-8R	33.00	3770	No
L3450 DT-W 4WD	15400.00	8930.00	10160.00	10870.00	Kubota	4	114D	8F-8R	30.00	2866	No
L3650 DT-W 4WD	16200.00	9400.00	10690.00	11440.00	Kubota	4	114D	8F-8R	33.00	2911	No
L3650 GST 4WD	17100.00	9920.00	11290.00	12080.00	Kubota	4	114D	8F-8R	33.00	2833	No
L3750 DT 4WD	20500.00	11890.00	13530.00	14480.00	Kubota	4	142D	8F-8R	37.00	3860	No
L3750 F	16000.00	9280.00	10560.00	11300.00	Kubota	4	142D	8F-8R	37.00	3640	No
M4030 SU	15990.00	8480.00	9910.00	10600.00	Kubota	5	149D	8F-2R	42.00	3946	No
L4150 DT 4WD	22000.00	12760.00	14520.00	15540.00	Kubota	5	142D	8F-8R	40.00	4080	No
L4150 F	17200.00	9980.00	11350.00	12150.00	Kubota	5	142D	8F-8R	40.00	3750	No
B4200 DT 4WD	7420.00	4680.00	5340.00	5820.00	Kubota	2	35D	6F-2R	10	926	No
L4350 HDT 4WD	21900.00	12700.00	14450.00	15460.00	Kubota	4	134D	8F-8R	38.00	3860	No
L4350 HDT-W 4WD	22600.00	13110.00	14920.00	15960.00	Kubota	4	134D	8F-8R	38.00	3860	No
L4350 MDT 4WD	20900.00	12120.00	13790.00	14760.00	Kubota	4	134D	8F-8R	38.00	3860	No
L4850 HDT-W 4WD	23800.00	13800.00	15710.00	16810.00	Kubota	5	152D	8F-8R	43.00	4080	No
M4950 DT 4WD	26700.00	14150.00	16550.00	17710.00	Kubota	6	170D	12F-4R	49.00	5357	No
M4950 F	21500.00	11400.00	13330.00	14260.00	Kubota	6	170D	12F-4R	49.00	4762	No
M5030 SU	18600.00	9860.00	11530.00	12340.00	Kubota	6	170D	16F-4R	49.00	4185	No
M5030 SU MDT 4WD	23400.00	12400.00	14510.00	15530.00	Kubota	6	170D	8F-8R	49.00	4974	No
B5200 DT 4WD	8520.00	5790.00	6390.00	6840.00	Kubota	3	47D	6F-2R	11.50	1254	No
B5200 E	7520.00	5110.00	5640.00	6040.00	Kubota	3	47D	6F-2R	11.50	1122	No
L5450 HDT-W 4WD	25850.00	14990.00	17060.00	18250.00	Kubota	5	168D	8F-8R	49.00	4410	No
M5950 DT 4WD	30000.00	15900.00	18600.00	19900.00	Kubota	3	196D	12F-4R	58.00	5673	No
M5950 F	24500.00	12990.00	15190.00	16250.00	Kubota	3	196D	12F-4R	58.00	4989	No
M6030 DTN-B 4WD	26000.00	13780.00	16120.00	17250.00	Kubota	3	196D	16F-4R	58.00	5010	No
B6200 DT 4WD	8930.00	6070.00	6700.00	7170.00	Kubota	3	52D	6F-2R	12.50	1232	No
B6200 E	7930.00	5390.00	5950.00	6370.00	Kubota	3	52D	6F-2R	12.50	1333	No
B6200 HSD 4WD	10230.00	6960.00	7670.00	8210.00	Kubota	3	52D	Infinite	12.50	1150	No
B6200 HSE	9230.00	6280.00	6920.00	7400.00	Kubota	3	52D	Infinite	12.50	1100	No
M6950 DT 4WD	31500.00	16700.00	19530.00	20900.00	Kubota	4	243D	12F-4R	66.00	6504	No
M6950 F	26000.00	13780.00	16120.00	17250.00	Kubota	4	243D	12F-4R	66.00	5776	No
M7030 SU	23500.00	12460.00	14570.00	15590.00	Kubota	4	243D	16F-4R	68.00	4586	No
M7030 SUDT 4WD	28300.00	15000.00	17550.00	18780.00	Kubota	4	243D	16F-4R	68.00	5710	No
B7200 DT 4WD	9200.00	6260.00	6900.00	7380.00	Kubota	3	57D	6F-2R	14.00	1320	No
B7200 E	8200.00	5580.00	6150.00	6580.00	Kubota	3	57D	6F-2R	14.00	1215	No
B7200 HSD 4WD	10500.00	7140.00	7880.00	8430.00	Kubota	3	57D	Infinite	14.00	1275	No
B7200 HSE	9450.00	6430.00	7090.00	7590.00	Kubota	3	57D	Infinite	14.00	1225	No
M7950 DT 4WD	34600.00	18340.00	21450.00	22950.00	Kubota	4	262D	12F-4R	75.00	6810	No
M7950 DT 4WD w/Cab	42000.00	22260.00	26040.00	27860.00	Kubota	4	262D	12F-4R	75.00	6810	C,H,A
M7950 F	28100.00	14890.00	17420.00	18640.00	Kubota	4	262D	12F-4R	75.00	5960	No
M7950 F w/Cab	35500.00	18820.00	22010.00	23550.00	Kubota	4	262D	12F-4R	75.00	5960	C,H,A
M8030 F	26200.00	13890.00	16240.00	17380.00	Kubota	4	262D	16F-4R	76.00	5247	No
M8030 MDT 4WD	32800.00	17380.00	20340.00	21760.00	Kubota	4	262D	16F-4R	76.00	6342	No
B8200 DT 4WD	10100.00	6870.00	7580.00	8110.00	Kubota	3	57D	9F-3R	16.00	1525	No

Kubota (Cont.)

1990 (Cont.)

Model	Approx. Retail Price New	Estimated Average Value Less Repairs Fair	Good	Premium	Engine Make	No. Cyls.	Displ. Cu.-In.	No. Speeds	P.T.O. H.P.	Approx. Shipping Wt.-Lbs.	Cab
B8200 F	9000.00	6120.00	6750.00	7220.00	Kubota	3	57D	9F-3R	16.00	1408	No
B8200 HSD 4WD	11400.00	7750.00	8550.00	9150.00	Kubota	3	57D	Infinite	14.50	1525	No
B8200 HSE	10350.00	7040.00	7760.00	8300.00	Kubota	3	57D	Infinite	14.50	1408	No
M8950 DT 4WD	39600.00	20990.00	24550.00	26270.00	Kubota	4	262D	24F-8R	86.00	7726	No
M8950 DT 4WD w/Cab	47000.00	24910.00	29140.00	31180.00	Kubota	4	262D	24F-8R	86.00	7726	C,H,A
M8950 F	32800.00	17380.00	20340.00	21760.00	Kubota	4	262D	24F-8R	86.00	6953	No
M8950 F w/Cab	40200.00	21310.00	24920.00	26660.00	Kubota	4	262D	24F-8R	86.00	6953	C,H,A
B9200 DT 4WD	11000.00	7480.00	8250.00	8830.00	Kubota	3	75D	9F-3R	18.50	1709	No
B9200 F	9900.00	6730.00	7430.00	7950.00	Kubota	3	75D	9F-3R	18.50	1555	No
B9200 HSD 4WD	12300.00	8360.00	9230.00	9880.00	Kubota	4	75D	Infinite	16.00	1720	No
B9200 HSE	11250.00	7650.00	8440.00	9030.00	Kubota	4	75D	Infinite	16.00	1603	No

C, D, DT--Front Wheel Assist DTSS--Front Wheel Assist, Shuttle Shift E--Two Wheel Drive F-Farm Standard W--Two Row Offset H, HC--High Clearance HSE--Hydrostatic Transmission, Two Wheel Drive HSD--Hydrostatic Transmission, Four Wheel Drive OC--Orchard L--Low Profile

1991

Model	Approx. Retail Price New	Estimated Average Value Less Repairs Fair	Good	Premium	Engine Make	No. Cyls.	Displ. Cu.-In.	No. Speeds	P.T.O. H.P.	Approx. Shipping Wt.-Lbs.	Cab
B1550 DT 4WD	10070.00	5940.00	6750.00	7160.00	Kubota	3	52D	6F-2R	14.00	1246	No
B1550 E	8770.00	5170.00	5880.00	6230.00	Kubota	3	52D	6F-2R	14.00	1113	No
B1550 HSD 4WD	11470.00	6770.00	7690.00	8150.00	Kubota	3	52D	Infinite	13.00	1323	No
B1550 HSE	10170.00	6000.00	6810.00	7220.00	Kubota	3	52D	Infinite	13.00	1190	No
B1750 DT 4WD	11090.00	7100.00	8100.00	8750.00	Kubota	3	57D	6F-2R	16.50	1290	No
B1750 E	9790.00	6270.00	7150.00	7720.00	Kubota	3	57D	6F-2R	16.50	1168	No
B1750 HSD 4WD	12490.00	7990.00	9120.00	9850.00	Kubota	3	57D	Infinite	15.50	1367	No
B1750 HSE	11190.00	7160.00	8170.00	8820.00	Kubota	3	57D	Infinite	15.50	1224	No
L2050 DT 4WD	10190.00	6520.00	7440.00	8040.00	Kubota	3	68D	8F-2R	20.00	2093	No
L2050 F	8990.00	5750.00	6560.00	7090.00	Kubota	3	68D	8F-2R	20.00	1781	No
B2150 DT 4WD	12100.00	7740.00	8830.00	9540.00	Kubota	4	75D	9F-3R	20.00	1731	No
B2150 E	10700.00	6850.00	7810.00	8440.00	Kubota	4	75D	9F-3R	20.00	1576	No
B2150 HSD 4WD	13500.00	8640.00	9860.00	10650.00	Kubota	4	75D	Infinite	18.00	1742	No
B2150 HSE	12200.00	7810.00	8910.00	9620.00	Kubota	4	75D	Infinite	18.00	1587	No
L2250 DT-7 4WD	12520.00	8010.00	9140.00	9870.00	Kubota	3	79D	8F-7R	21.00	2380	No
L2250 F-1	9920.00	6350.00	7240.00	7820.00	Kubota	3	79D	8F-7R	21.00	2170	No
L2550 DT-7 4WD	13540.00	8670.00	9880.00	10670.00	Kubota	3	85D	8F-7R	23.50	2485	No
L2550 F-7	12040.00	7710.00	8790.00	9490.00	Kubota	3	85D	8F-7R	23.50	2305	No
L2550 GST 4WD	15000.00	9600.00	10950.00	11830.00	Kubota	3	85D	8F-8R	23.50	2490	No
L2650 DT-W 4WD	13400.00	8580.00	9780.00	10560.00	Kubota	3	85D	8F-8R	23.50	2602	No
L2850 DT-7 4WD	15470.00	9900.00	11290.00	12190.00	Kubota	4	106D	8F-7R	27.00	2680	No
L2850 F-7	13740.00	8790.00	10030.00	10830.00	Kubota	4	106D	8F-7R	27.00	2480	No
L2850 GST 4WD	16900.00	10820.00	12340.00	13330.00	Kubota	4	106D	8F-8R	27.00	2680	No
L2950 DT-W 4WD	14200.00	9090.00	10370.00	11200.00	Kubota	3	89D	8F-8R	26.00	2734	No
L3250 DT 4WD	16590.00	9790.00	11120.00	11790.00	Kubota	4	114D	8F-7R	32.00	2740	No
L3250 F	14590.00	8610.00	9780.00	10370.00	Kubota	4	114D	8F-7R	32.00	2530	No
L3350 DT 4WD	18500.00	10920.00	12400.00	13140.00	Kubota	4	114D	8F-8R	33.00	3770	No
L3450 DT-W 4WD	15400.00	9090.00	10320.00	10940.00	Kubota	4	114D	8F-8R	30.00	2866	No
L3650 DT-W 4WD	16200.00	9560.00	10850.00	11500.00	Kubota	4	114D	8F-8R	33.00	2911	No
L3650 GST 4WD	17100.00	10090.00	11460.00	12150.00	Kubota	4	114D	8F-8R	33.00	2833	No
L3750 DT 4WD	20500.00	12100.00	13740.00	14560.00	Kubota	4	142D	8F-8R	37.00	3860	No
L3750 F	16000.00	9440.00	10720.00	11360.00	Kubota	4	142D	8F-8R	37.00	3640	No
M4030 SU	15990.00	8640.00	10070.00	10670.00	Kubota	5	149D	8F-2R	42.00	3946	No
L4150 DT 4WD	22000.00	12980.00	14740.00	15620.00	Kubota	5	142D	8F-8R	40.00	4080	No
L4150 F	17200.00	10150.00	11520.00	12210.00	Kubota	5	142D	8F-8R	40.00	3750	No
B4200 DT 4WD	7420.00	4750.00	5420.00	5850.00	Kubota	2	35D	6F-2R	10	926	No
L4350 HDT 4WD	21900.00	12920.00	14670.00	15550.00	Kubota	4	134D	8F-8R	38.00	3860	No
L4350 HDT-W 4WD	22600.00	13330.00	15140.00	16050.00	Kubota	4	134D	8F-8R	38.00	3860	No
L4350 MDT 4WD	20900.00	12330.00	14000.00	14840.00	Kubota	4	134D	8F-8R	38.00	3860	No
L4850 HDT-W 4WD	23800.00	14040.00	15950.00	16910.00	Kubota	5	152D	8F-8R	43.00	4080	No
M4950 DT 4WD	26700.00	14420.00	16820.00	17830.00	Kubota	6	170D	12F-4R	49.00	5357	No
M4950 F	21500.00	11610.00	13550.00	14360.00	Kubota	6	170D	12F-4R	49.00	4762	No
M5030 SU	18600.00	10040.00	11720.00	12420.00	Kubota	6	170D	16F-4R	49.00	4185	No
M5030 SU MDT 4WD	23400.00	12640.00	14740.00	15620.00	Kubota	6	170D	8F-8R	49.00	4974	No
B5200 DT 4WD	8520.00	5880.00	6480.00	6930.00	Kubota	3	47D	6F-2R	11.50	1254	No
B5200 E	7520.00	5190.00	5720.00	6120.00	Kubota	3	47D	6F-2R	11.50	1122	No
L5450 HDT-W 4WD	25850.00	15250.00	17320.00	18360.00	Kubota	5	168D	8F-8R	49.00	4410	No
M5950 DT 4WD	30000.00	16200.00	18900.00	20030.00	Kubota	3	196D	12F-4R	58.00	5673	No
M5950 F	24500.00	13230.00	15440.00	16370.00	Kubota	3	196D	12F-4R	58.00	4989	No
M6030 DTN-B 4WD	26000.00	14040.00	16380.00	17360.00	Kubota	3	196D	16F-4R	58.00	5010	No
B6200 DT 4WD	8930.00	6160.00	6790.00	7270.00	Kubota	3	52D	6F-2R	12.50	1232	No
B6200 E	7930.00	5470.00	6030.00	6450.00	Kubota	3	52D	6F-2R	12.50	1333	No
B6200 HSD 4WD	10230.00	7060.00	7780.00	8330.00	Kubota	3	52D	Infinite	12.50	1150	No
B6200 HSE	9230.00	6370.00	7020.00	7510.00	Kubota	3	52D	Infinite	12.50	1100	No
M6950 DT 4WD	31500.00	17010.00	19850.00	21040.00	Kubota	4	243D	12F-4R	66.00	6504	No
M6950 F	26000.00	14040.00	16380.00	17360.00	Kubota	4	243D	12F-4R	66.00	5776	No
M7030 SU	23500.00	12690.00	14810.00	15700.00	Kubota	4	243D	16F-4R	68.00	4586	No
M7030 SUDT 4WD	28300.00	15280.00	17830.00	18900.00	Kubota	4	243D	16F-4R	68.00	5710	No
B7200 DT 4WD	9200.00	6350.00	6990.00	7480.00	Kubota	3	57D	6F-2R	14.00	1320	No
B7200 E	8200.00	5660.00	6230.00	6670.00	Kubota	3	57D	6F-2R	14.00	1215	No
B7200 HSD 4WD	10500.00	7250.00	7980.00	8540.00	Kubota	3	57D	Infinite	14.00	1275	No
B7200 HSE	9450.00	6520.00	7180.00	7680.00	Kubota	3	57D	Infinite	14.00	1225	No
M7950 DT 4WD	34600.00	18680.00	21800.00	23110.00	Kubota	4	262D	12F-4R	75.00	6810	No
M7950 DT 4WD w/Cab	42000.00	22680.00	26460.00	28050.00	Kubota	4	262D	12F-4R	75.00	6810	C,H,A
M7950 F	28100.00	15170.00	17700.00	18760.00	Kubota	4	262D	12F-4R	75.00	5960	No
M7950 F w/Cab	35500.00	19170.00	22370.00	23710.00	Kubota	4	262D	12F-4R	75.00	5960	C,H,A
M8030 F	26200.00	14150.00	16510.00	17500.00	Kubota	4	262D	16F-4R	76.00	5247	No
M8030 MDT 4WD	32800.00	17710.00	20660.00	21900.00	Kubota	4	262D	16F-4R	76.00	6342	No
B8200 DT 4WD	10100.00	6970.00	7680.00	8220.00	Kubota	3	57D	9F-3R	16.00	1525	No

Kubota (Cont.)

1991 (Cont.)

Model	Approx. Retail Price New	Estimated Average Value Less Repairs: Fair	Good	Premium	Engine Make	No. Cyls.	Displ. Cu.-In.	No. Speeds	P.T.O. H.P.	Approx. Shipping Wt.-Lbs.	Cab
B8200 F	9000.00	6210.00	6840.00	7320.00	Kubota	3	57D	9F-3R	16.00	1408	No
B8200 HSD 4WD	11400.00	7870.00	8660.00	9270.00	Kubota	3	57D	Infinite	14.50	1525	No
B8200 HSE	10350.00	7140.00	7870.00	8420.00	Kubota	3	57D	Infinite	14.50	1408	No
M8950 DT 4WD	39600.00	21380.00	24950.00	26450.00	Kubota	4	262D	24F-8R	86.00	7726	No
M8950 DT 4WD w/Cab	47000.00	25380.00	29610.00	31390.00	Kubota	4	262D	24F-8R	86.00	7726	C,H,A
M8950 F	32800.00	17710.00	20660.00	21900.00	Kubota	4	262D	24F-8R	86.00	6953	No
M8950 F w/Cab	40200.00	21710.00	25330.00	26850.00	Kubota	4	262D	24F-8R	86.00	6953	C,H,A
B9200 DT 4WD	11000.00	7590.00	8360.00	8950.00	Kubota	3	75D	9F-3R	18.50	1709	No
B9200 F	9900.00	6830.00	7520.00	8050.00	Kubota	3	75D	9F-3R	18.50	1555	No
B9200 HSD 4WD	12300.00	8490.00	9350.00	10010.00	Kubota	4	75D	Infinite	16.00	1720	No
B9200 HSE	11250.00	7760.00	8550.00	9150.00	Kubota	4	75D	Infinite	16.00	1603	No

C, D, DT--Front Wheel Assist DTSS--Front Wheel Assist, Shuttle Shift E--Two Wheel Drive F--Farm Standard W--Two Row Offset
H, HC--High Clearance HSE--Hydrostatic Transmission, Two Wheel Drive HSD--Hydrostatic Transmission, Four Wheel Drive OC--Orchard L--Low Profile

1992

Model	Approx. Retail Price New	Fair	Good	Premium	Make	No. Cyls.	Displ. Cu.-In.	No. Speeds	P.T.O. H.P.	Approx. Shipping Wt.-Lbs.	Cab
B1550 DT 4WD	10270.00	6160.00	6980.00	7400.00	Kubota	3	52D	6F-2R	14.00	1246	No
B1550 E	8945.00	5370.00	6080.00	6450.00	Kubota	3	52D	6F-2R	14.00	1113	No
B1550 HSD 4WD	11700.00	7020.00	7960.00	8440.00	Kubota	3	52D	Infinite	13.00	1323	No
B1550 HSE	10370.00	6220.00	7050.00	7470.00	Kubota	3	52D	Infinite	13.00	1190	No
B1750 DT 4WD	11310.00	7350.00	8370.00	8960.00	Kubota	3	57D	6F-2R	16.50	1290	No
B1750 E	9985.00	6490.00	7390.00	7910.00	Kubota	3	57D	6F-2R	16.50	1168	No
B1750 HSD 4WD	12740.00	8280.00	9430.00	10090.00	Kubota	3	57D	Infinite	15.50	1367	No
B1750 HSE	11400.00	7410.00	8440.00	9030.00	Kubota	3	57D	Infinite	15.50	1224	No
B2150 DT 4WD	12340.00	8020.00	9130.00	9770.00	Kubota	4	75D	9F-3R	20.00	1731	No
B2150 E	10900.00	7090.00	8070.00	8640.00	Kubota	4	75D	9F-3R	20.00	1576	No
B2150 HSD 4WD	13770.00	8950.00	10190.00	10900.00	Kubota	4	75D	Infinite	18.00	1742	No
B2150 HSE	12400.00	8060.00	9180.00	9820.00	Kubota	4	75D	Infinite	18.00	1587	No
L2350 DT-7 4WD	12770.00	8300.00	9450.00	10110.00	Kubota	3	68D	8F-2R	20.5	2380	No
L2350 F-1	10115.00	6580.00	7490.00	8010.00	Kubota	3	68D	8F-2R	20.5	2170	No
L2650 DT-W 4WD	13660.00	8880.00	10110.00	10820.00	Kubota	3	85D	8F-8R	23.50	2602	No
L2950 DT-W 4WD	14484.00	9420.00	10720.00	11470.00	Kubota	3	89D	8F-8R	26.00	2734	No
L3450 DT-W 4WD	15700.00	9420.00	10680.00	11320.00	Kubota	4	114D	8F-8R	30.00	2866	No
L3650 DT-W 4WD	16524.00	9910.00	11240.00	11910.00	Kubota	4	114D	8F-8R	33.00	2911	No
L3650 GST 4WD	17440.00	10460.00	11860.00	12570.00	Kubota	4	114D	8F-8R	33.00	2833	No
M4030 SU	16300.00	9130.00	10430.00	11060.00	Kubota	5	149D	8F-2R	42.00	3946	No
B4200 DT 4WD	7550.00	4910.00	5590.00	5980.00	Kubota	2	35D	6F-2R	10	926	No
L4350 HDT 4WD	22330.00	13400.00	15180.00	16090.00	Kubota	4	134D	8F-8R	38.00	3860	No
L4350 HDT-W 4WD	23050.00	13830.00	15670.00	16610.00	Kubota	4	134D	8F-8R	38.00	3860	No
L4350 MDT 4WD	21300.00	12780.00	14480.00	15350.00	Kubota	4	134D	8F-8R	38.00	3860	No
L4850 HDT-W 4WD	24275.00	14570.00	16510.00	17500.00	Kubota	5	152D	8F-8R	43.00	4080	No
M4950 DT 4WD	27230.00	15120.00	17280.00	18320.00	Kubota	6	170D	12F-4R	49.00	5357	No
M4950 F	21930.00	12180.00	13920.00	14760.00	Kubota	6	170D	12F-4R	49.00	4762	No
M5030 SU	18970.00	10620.00	12140.00	12870.00	Kubota	6	170D	16F-4R	49.00	4185	No
M5030 SU MDT 4WD	23860.00	13360.00	15270.00	16190.00	Kubota	6	170D	8F-8R	49.00	4974	No
B5200 DT 4WD	8690.00	6080.00	6690.00	7090.00	Kubota	3	47D	6F-2R	11.50	1254	No
B5200 E	7670.00	5370.00	5910.00	6270.00	Kubota	3	47D	6F-2R	11.50	1122	No
L5450 HDT-W 4WD	26360.00	15820.00	17930.00	19010.00	Kubota	5	168D	8F-8R	49.00	4410	No
M5950 DT 4WD	30600.00	16970.00	19390.00	20550.00	Kubota	3	196D	12F-4R	58.00	5673	No
M5950 F	24990.00	13860.00	15840.00	16790.00	Kubota	3	196D	12F-4R	58.00	4989	No
M6030 DTN-B 4WD	26520.00	14850.00	16970.00	17990.00	Kubota	3	196D	16F-4R	58.00	5010	No
B6200 DT 4WD	9100.00	6370.00	7010.00	7430.00	Kubota	3	52D	6F-2R	12.50	1232	No
B6200 E	8080.00	5660.00	6220.00	6590.00	Kubota	3	52D	6F-2R	12.50	1333	No
B6200 HSD 4WD	10430.00	7300.00	8030.00	8510.00	Kubota	3	52D	Infinite	12.50	1150	No
B6200 HSE	9400.00	6580.00	7240.00	7670.00	Kubota	3	52D	Infinite	12.50	1100	No
M6950 DT 4WD	32130.00	17810.00	20350.00	21570.00	Kubota	4	243D	12F-4R	66.00	6504	No
M6950 F	26520.00	14700.00	16800.00	17810.00	Kubota	4	243D	12F-4R	66.00	5776	No
M7030 SU	23970.00	13420.00	15340.00	16260.00	Kubota	4	243D	16F-4R	68.00	4586	No
M7030 SUDT 4WD	28800.00	16130.00	18430.00	19540.00	Kubota	4	243D	16F-4R	68.00	5710	No
B7100 DT 4WD	9200.00	5980.00	6810.00	7290.00	Kubota	3	47D	6F-2R	13.00	1320	No
B7100 E	8200.00	5330.00	6070.00	6500.00	Kubota	3	47D	6F-2R	13.00	1215	No
B7100 HSD 4WD	10500.00	6830.00	7770.00	8310.00	Kubota	3	47D	Infinite	13.00	1275	No
B7100 HSE	9450.00	6140.00	6990.00	7480.00	Kubota	3	47D	Infinite	13.00	1225	No
M7950 DT 4WD	35290.00	19600.00	22400.00	23740.00	Kubota	4	262D	12F-4R	75.00	6810	No
M7950 DT 4WD w/Cab	42840.00	23800.00	27200.00	28830.00	Kubota	4	262D	12F-4R	75.00	6810	C,H,A
M7950 F	28600.00	16020.00	18300.00	19400.00	Kubota	4	262D	12F-4R	75.00	5960	No
M7950 F w/Cab	36200.00	20270.00	23170.00	24560.00	Kubota	4	262D	12F-4R	75.00	5960	C,H,A
M8030 F	26724.00	14970.00	17100.00	18130.00	Kubota	4	262D	16F-4R	76.00	5247	No
M8030 MDT 4WD	33450.00	18730.00	21410.00	22700.00	Kubota	4	262D	16F-4R	76.00	6342	No
M8950 DT 4WD	40390.00	22400.00	25600.00	27140.00	Kubota	4	262D	24F-8R	86.00	7726	No
M8950 DT 4WD w/Cab	47940.00	26600.00	30400.00	32220.00	Kubota	4	262D	24F-8R	86.00	7726	C,H,A
M8950 F	33450.00	18730.00	21410.00	22700.00	Kubota	4	262D	24F-8R	86.00	6953	No
M8950 F w/Cab	41000.00	22960.00	26240.00	27810.00	Kubota	4	262D	24F-8R	86.00	6953	C,H,A

C, D, DT--Front Wheel Assist DTSS--Front Wheel Assist, Shuttle Shift E--Two Wheel Drive F--Farm Standard W--Two Row Offset
H, HC--High Clearance HSE--Hydrostatic Transmission, Two Wheel Drive HSD--Hydrostatic Transmission, Four Wheel Drive OC--Orchard L--Low Profile

1993

Model	Approx. Retail Price New	Fair	Good	Premium	Make	No. Cyls.	Displ. Cu.-In.	No. Speeds	P.T.O. H.P.	Approx. Shipping Wt.-Lbs.	Cab
B1550 DT	10900.00	6760.00	7520.00	7970.00	Kubota	3	52D	6F-2R	14.00	1280	No
B1550 E	9600.00	5950.00	6620.00	7020.00	Kubota	3	52D	6F-2R	14.00	1150	No
B1550 HSD	12400.00	7690.00	8560.00	9070.00	Kubota	3	52D	Infinite	13.00	1325	No
B1550 HSE	11000.00	6820.00	7590.00	8050.00	Kubota	3	52D	Infinite	13.00	1190	No
B1750 DT	12000.00	8040.00	9000.00	9540.00	Kubota	3	57D	6F-2R	16.5	1290	No
B1750 E	10700.00	7170.00	8030.00	8510.00	Kubota	3	57D	6F-2R	16.5	1170	No
B1750 HSD	13500.00	9050.00	10130.00	10740.00	Kubota	3	57D	Infinite	16.5	1365	No
B1750 HSE	12100.00	8110.00	9080.00	9630.00	Kubota	3	57D	Infinite	16.5	1225	No

Kubota (Cont.)

1993 (Cont.)

Model	Approx. Retail Price New	Estimated Average Value Less Repairs Fair	Good	Premium	Engine Make	No. Cyls.	Displ. Cu.-In.	No. Speeds	P.T.O. H.P.	Approx. Shipping Wt.-Lbs.	Cab
B2150 DT	13000.00	**8710.00**	**9750.00**	**10340.00**	Kubota	4	75D	9F-3R	20.1	1675	No
B2150 E	11600.00	**7770.00**	**8700.00**	**9220.00**	Kubota	4	75D	9F-3R	20.1	1570	No
B2150 HSD	14550.00	**9750.00**	**10910.00**	**11570.00**	Kubota	4	75D	Infinite	20.1	1720	No
B2150 HSE	13100.00	**8780.00**	**9830.00**	**10420.00**	Kubota	4	75D	Infinite	20.1	1605	No
L2350 DT	11400.00	**7640.00**	**8550.00**	**9060.00**	Kubota	3	68D	8F-2R	20.5	2095	No
L2350 F	9990.00	**6690.00**	**7490.00**	**7940.00**	Kubota	3	68D	8F-2R	20.5	1780	No
L2650 DT	14900.00	**9980.00**	**11180.00**	**11850.00**	Kubota	3	85D	8F-8R	23.5	2600	No
L2650 F-3	12300.00	**8240.00**	**9230.00**	**9780.00**	Kubota	3	85D	8F-8R	23.5	2380	No
L2650 F-8	13315.00	**8920.00**	**9990.00**	**10590.00**	Kubota	3	85D	8F-8R	23.5	2380	No
L2650 GST	16055.00	**10760.00**	**12040.00**	**12760.00**	Kubota	3	85D	8F-8R	23.5	2655	No
L2950 DT	15900.00	**10650.00**	**11930.00**	**12650.00**	Kubota	3	89D	8F-8R	26.0	2720	No
L2950 F-3	13000.00	**8710.00**	**9750.00**	**10340.00**	Kubota	3	89D	8F-8R	26.0	2445	No
L2950 F-8	14075.00	**9430.00**	**10560.00**	**11190.00**	Kubota	3	89D	8F-8R	26.0	2445	No
L2950 GST	16955.00	**11360.00**	**12720.00**	**13480.00**	Kubota	3	89D	8F-8R	26.0	2780	No
L3450 DT	17300.00	**10730.00**	**11940.00**	**12660.00**	Kubota	4	113D	8F-8R	30.0	2845	No
L3450 F	15100.00	**9360.00**	**10420.00**	**11050.00**	Kubota	4	113D	8F-8R	30.0	2610	No
L3450 GST	18355.00	**11380.00**	**12670.00**	**13430.00**	Kubota	4	113D	8F-8R	30.0	2900	No
L3650 DT	18090.00	**11220.00**	**12480.00**	**13230.00**	Kubota	4	113D	8F-8R	33.0	2910	No
L3650 F	15890.00	**9850.00**	**10960.00**	**11620.00**	Kubota	4	113D	8F-8R	30.0	2700	No
L3650 GST	18910.00	**11720.00**	**13050.00**	**13830.00**	Kubota	4	113D	8F-8R	33.0	2965	No
M4030 SU	17190.00	**9970.00**	**11170.00**	**11840.00**	Kubota	6	158D	8F-8R	44.05	3950	No
B4200 DT	7800.00	**5230.00**	**5850.00**	**6200.00**	Kubota	2	35D	6F-2R	10	926	No
L4350 HDT-W	24000.00	**14880.00**	**16560.00**	**17550.00**	Kubota	4	134D	8F-8R	38.0	3860	No
L4350 MDT	22300.00	**13830.00**	**15390.00**	**16310.00**	Kubota	4	134D	8F-8R	38.0	3860	No
L4850 HDT-W	25300.00	**14670.00**	**16450.00**	**17440.00**	Kubota	5	152D	8F-8R	43.0	4080	No
M4950 DT	27000.00	**15660.00**	**17550.00**	**18600.00**	Kubota	6	170D	12F-4R	49.57	5450	No
M4950 F	21750.00	**12620.00**	**14140.00**	**14990.00**	Kubota	6	170D	12F-4R	49.57	4770	No
M5030 SU	19900.00	**11540.00**	**12940.00**	**13720.00**	Kubota	6	170D	8F-8R	49.77	4185	No
M5030 SU MDT	25000.00	**14500.00**	**16250.00**	**17230.00**	Kubota	6	170D	8F-8R	49.77	4980	No
B5200 DT	8900.00	**6320.00**	**6940.00**	**7360.00**	Kubota	3	47D	6F-2R	11.5	1180	No
B5200 E	7900.00	**5610.00**	**6160.00**	**6530.00**	Kubota	3	47D	6F-2R	11.5	1060	No
L5450 HDT-W	27400.00	**16990.00**	**18910.00**	**20050.00**	Kubota	5	168D	8F-8R	49.0	4410	No
M5950 DT	30000.00	**17400.00**	**19500.00**	**20670.00**	Kubota	3	196D	12F-4R	58.00	5675	No
M5950 F	24500.00	**14210.00**	**15930.00**	**16890.00**	Kubota	3	196D	12F-4R	58.00	4990	No
M6030 DTN	29800.00	**17280.00**	**19370.00**	**20530.00**	Kubota	3	196D	16F-4R	57.74	5010	No
B6200 DT	9300.00	**6600.00**	**7250.00**	**7690.00**	Kubota	3	52D	6F-2R	12.5	1180	No
B6200 E	8300.00	**5890.00**	**6470.00**	**6860.00**	Kubota	3	52D	6F-2R	12.5	1060	No
B6200 HSD	10600.00	**7530.00**	**8270.00**	**8770.00**	Kubota	3	52D	Infinite	12.5	1280	No
B6200 HSE	9600.00	**6820.00**	**7490.00**	**7940.00**	Kubota	3	52D	Infinite	12.5	1160	No
M6950 DT	31800.00	**18440.00**	**20670.00**	**21910.00**	Kubota	4	243D	12F-4R	66.44	6625	No
M6950 F	26250.00	**15230.00**	**17060.00**	**18080.00**	Kubota	4	243D	12F-4R	66.44	5795	No
M7030 DTN	33300.00	**19310.00**	**21650.00**	**22950.00**	Kubota	4	243D	16F-4R	68.86	5710	No
M7030 N	26000.00	**15080.00**	**16900.00**	**17910.00**	Kubota	3	243D	16F-4R	68.86	4586	No
M7030 SU	25200.00	**14620.00**	**16380.00**	**17360.00**	Kubota	4	243D	16F-4R	68.86	4586	No
M7030 SU DT	30200.00	**17520.00**	**19630.00**	**20810.00**	Kubota	4	243D	16F-4R	68.86	5710	No
B7100 HSD	8995.00	**6030.00**	**6750.00**	**7160.00**	Kubota	3	47D	Infinite	13.0	1257	No
M7580 DT	38000.00	**22040.00**	**24700.00**	**26180.00**	Kubota	4	264D	12F-12R	70.00	7430	No
M7580 DTC	45600.00	**26450.00**	**29640.00**	**31420.00**	Kubota	4	264D	12F-12R	70.00		C,H,A
M7950 DT	35000.00	**20300.00**	**22750.00**	**24120.00**	Kubota	4	262D	12F-4R	75.44	6810	No
M7950 DTC	42500.00	**24650.00**	**27630.00**	**29290.00**	Kubota	4	262D	12F-4R	75.44		C,H,A
M7950 F	29000.00	**16820.00**	**18850.00**	**19980.00**	Kubota	4	262D	12F-4R	75.44	5960	No
M7950 FC	36900.00	**21400.00**	**23990.00**	**25430.00**	Kubota	4	262D	12F-4R	75.44		C,H,A
M8030 DT	35000.00	**20300.00**	**22750.00**	**24120.00**	Kubota	4	262D	16F-8R	76.91	6340	No
M8030 DTL	34600.00	**20070.00**	**22490.00**	**23840.00**	Kubota	4	262D	16F-8R	76.91	6340	No
M8030 DTM	35500.00	**20590.00**	**23080.00**	**24470.00**	Kubota	4	262D	16F-8R	76.91	6340	No
M8030 F	28000.00	**16240.00**	**18200.00**	**19290.00**	Kubota	4	262D	16F-8R	76.91	5420	No
M8580 DT	39700.00	**23030.00**	**25810.00**	**27360.00**	Kubota	4	285D	12F-12R	80.00	8975	No
M8580 DTC	47800.00	**27720.00**	**31070.00**	**32930.00**	Kubota	4	285D	12F-12R	80.00		C,H,A
M8950 DT	40000.00	**23200.00**	**26000.00**	**27560.00**	Kubota	4T	262D	24F-8R	85.63	7715	No
M8950 DTC	47500.00	**27550.00**	**30880.00**	**32730.00**	Kubota	4T	262D	24F-8R	85.63		C,H,A
M8950 F	34000.00	**19720.00**	**22100.00**	**23430.00**	Kubota	4T	262D	24F-8R	85.63	6955	No
M8950 FC	41700.00	**24190.00**	**27110.00**	**28740.00**	Kubota	4T	262D	24F-8R	85.63		C,H,A
M9580 DT	45200.00	**26220.00**	**29380.00**	**31140.00**	Kubota	4T	285D	24F-24R	91.00	9085	No
M9580 DTC	52800.00	**30620.00**	**34320.00**	**36380.00**	Kubota	4T	285D	24F-24R	91.00		C,H,A

C, D, DT--Front Wheel Assist DTSS--Front Wheel Assist, Shuttle Shift E--Two Wheel Drive F--Farm Standard W--Two Row Offset
H, HC--High Clearance HSE--Hydrostatic Transmission, Two Wheel Drive HSD--Hydrostatic Transmission, Four Wheel Drive OC--Orchard L--Low Profile

1994

Model	Approx. Retail Price New	Fair	Good	Premium	Engine Make	No. Cyls.	Displ. Cu.-In.	No. Speeds	P.T.O. H.P.	Approx. Shipping Wt.-Lbs.	Cab
B1550 DT 4WD	11500.00	**7360.00**	**8050.00**	**8450.00**	Kubota	3	52D	6F-2R	14.00	1279	No
B1550 E	10000.00	**6400.00**	**7000.00**	**7350.00**	Kubota	3	52D	6F-2R	14.00	1146	No
B1550 HSD 4WD	13000.00	**8320.00**	**9100.00**	**9560.00**	Kubota	3	52D	Infinite	13.00	1356	No
B1550 HSE	11500.00	**7360.00**	**8050.00**	**8450.00**	Kubota	3	52D	Infinite	13.00	1190	No
B1750 DT 4WD	12600.00	**8690.00**	**9580.00**	**10060.00**	Kubota	3	57D	6F-2R	16.50	1323	No
B1750 E	11100.00	**7660.00**	**8440.00**	**8860.00**	Kubota	3	57D	6F-2R	16.50	1201	No
B1750 HSD 4WD	14200.00	**9800.00**	**10790.00**	**11330.00**	Kubota	3	57D	Infinite	15.50	1400	No
B1750 HSE	12700.00	**8760.00**	**9650.00**	**10130.00**	Kubota	3	57D	Infinite	15.50	1257	No
B2150 DT 4WD	13600.00	**9380.00**	**10340.00**	**10860.00**	Kubota	4	75D	9F-3R	20.00	1764	No
B2150 E	12000.00	**8280.00**	**9120.00**	**9580.00**	Kubota	4	75D	9F-3R	20.00	1609	No
B2150 HSD 4WD	15300.00	**10560.00**	**11630.00**	**12210.00**	Kubota	4	75D	Infinite	18.00	1775	No
B2150 HSE	13700.00	**9450.00**	**10410.00**	**10930.00**	Kubota	4	75D	Infinite	18.00	1620	No
L2350 DT 4WD	11400.00	**7870.00**	**8660.00**	**9090.00**	Kubota	3	68D	8F-2R	20.5	2093	No
L2350 F-1	9990.00	**6890.00**	**7590.00**	**7970.00**	Kubota	3	68D	8F-2R	20.5	1781	No
L2650 DT-W 4WD	15240.00	**10520.00**	**11580.00**	**12160.00**	Kubota	3	85D	8F-8R	23.50	2602	No
L2900 DT	16240.00	**11210.00**	**12340.00**	**12960.00**	Kubota	3	91D	8F-8R	25.00	2800	No

Kubota (Cont.)

1994 (Cont.)

Model	Approx. Retail Price New	Estimated Average Value Less Repairs Fair	Good	Premium	Engine Make	No. Cyls.	Displ. Cu.-In.	No. Speeds	P.T.O. H.P.	Approx. Shipping Wt.-Lbs.	Cab
L2900 F	14200.00	9800.00	10790.00	11330.00	Kubota	3	91D	8F-8R	25.00	2645	No
L2900 GST	16550.00	11420.00	12580.00	13210.00	Kubota	3	91D	8F-8R	25.00	2810	No
L3300 DT	17750.00	12250.00	13490.00	14170.00	Kubota	3	100D	8F-8R	28.00	2800	No
L3300 F	15000.00	10350.00	11400.00	11970.00	Kubota	3	100D	8F-8R	28.00	2645	No
L3300 GST	18060.00	12460.00	13730.00	14420.00	Kubota	3	100D	8F-8R	28.00	2810	No
L3600 DT	18870.00	12080.00	13210.00	13870.00	Kubota	4	113D	8F-8R	31.00	3030	No
L3600 GST	19180.00	12280.00	13430.00	14100.00	Kubota	4	113D	8F-8R	31.00	3075	No
M4030 SU	18050.00	11550.00	12640.00	13270.00	Kubota	5	149D	8F-2R	42.00	3946	No
B4200 DT 4WD	8100.00	5590.00	6160.00	6470.00	Kubota	2	35D	6F-2R	10	926	No
L4200 DT	20475.00	13100.00	14330.00	15050.00	Kubota	4	134D	8F-8R	37.00	3030	No
L4200 F	17800.00	11390.00	12460.00	13080.00	Kubota	4	134D	8F-8R	37.00	2875	No
L4200 F GST	18110.00	11590.00	12680.00	13310.00	Kubota	4	134D	8F-8R	37.00	2890	No
L4200 GST	21385.00	13690.00	14970.00	15720.00	Kubota	4	134D	8F-8R	37.00	3055	No
L4350 HDT 4WD	24500.00	15680.00	17150.00	18010.00	Kubota	4	134D	8F-8R	38.00	3860	No
L4350 HDT-W 4WD	25200.00	16130.00	17640.00	18520.00	Kubota	4	134D	8F-8R	38.00	3860	No
L4350 MDT 4WD	23400.00	14980.00	16380.00	17200.00	Kubota	4	134D	8F-8R	38.00	3860	No
L4850 HDT-W 4WD	26600.00	17020.00	18620.00	19550.00	Kubota	5	152D	8F-8R	43.00	4080	No
M4950 DT 4WD	27000.00	17280.00	18900.00	19850.00	Kubota	6	170D	12F-4R	49.00	5357	No
M4950 F	21750.00	13920.00	15230.00	15990.00	Kubota	6	170D	12F-4R	49.00	4762	No
M5030 SU	20900.00	13380.00	14630.00	15360.00	Kubota	6	170D	16F-4R	49.00	4409	No
M5030 SU MDT 4WD	26200.00	16770.00	18340.00	19260.00	Kubota	6	170D	8F-8R	49.00	4978	No
B5200 DT 4WD	8900.00	6500.00	7030.00	7380.00	Kubota	3	47D	6F-2R	11.50	1180	No
B5200 E	8200.00	5990.00	6480.00	6800.00	Kubota	3	47D	6F-2R	11.50	1058	No
L5450 HDT-W 4WD	28800.00	18430.00	20160.00	21170.00	Kubota	5	168D	8F-8R	49.00	4410	No
M5950 DT 4WD	30300.00	18480.00	20300.00	21320.00	Kubota	3	196D	12F-4R	58.00	5673	No
M5950 F	24750.00	15100.00	16580.00	17410.00	Kubota	3	196D	12F-4R	58.00	4989	No
M6030 DTN-B 4WD	31200.00	19030.00	20900.00	21950.00	Kubota	3	196D	16F-4R	57.00	5010	No
B6200 DT 4WD	9300.00	6790.00	7350.00	7720.00	Kubota	3	52D	6F-2R	12.50	1179	No
B6200 E	8300.00	6060.00	6560.00	6890.00	Kubota	3	52D	6F-2R	12.50	1058	No
B6200 HSD 4WD	10600.00	7740.00	8370.00	8790.00	Kubota	3	52D	Infinite	12.50	1279	No
B6200 HSE	9600.00	7010.00	7580.00	7960.00	Kubota	3	52D	Infinite	12.50	1158	No
M6950 DT 4WD	31800.00	19400.00	21310.00	22380.00	Kubota	4	243D	12F-4R	66.00	6504	No
M6950 F	26250.00	16010.00	17590.00	18470.00	Kubota	4	243D	12F-4R	66.00	5776	No
M7030 DTNB	34900.00	21290.00	23380.00	24550.00	Kubota	4	243D	16F-4R	68.00	5004	No
M7030 N	27100.00	16530.00	18160.00	19070.00	Kubota	4	243D	16F-4R	68.00	4410	No
M7030 SU	26400.00	16100.00	17690.00	18580.00	Kubota	4	243D	16F-4R	68.00	5181	No
M7030 SUDT 4WD	31700.00	19340.00	21240.00	22300.00	Kubota	4	243D	16F-4R	68.00	5710	No
B7100 HSD 4WD	9495.00	6930.00	7500.00	7880.00	Kubota	3	47D	Infinite	13.00	1257	No
M7580 DT	39900.00	24340.00	26730.00	28070.00	Kubota	4	264D	12F-12R	70.00	6834	No
M7580 DTC	47900.00	29220.00	32090.00	33700.00	Kubota	4	264D	12F-12R	70.00	7429	C,H,A
M7950 DT 4WD	35000.00	21350.00	23450.00	24620.00	Kubota	4	262D	12F-4R	75.00	6810	No
M7950 DT 4WD w/Cab	42500.00	25930.00	28480.00	29900.00	Kubota	4	262D	12F-4R	75.00	7297	C,H,A
M7950 F	29000.00	17690.00	19430.00	20400.00	Kubota	4	262D	12F-4R	75.00	5960	No
M7950 F w/Cab	36900.00	22510.00	24720.00	25960.00	Kubota	4	262D	12F-4R	75.00	6460	C,H,A
M8030 DTM 4WD	37000.00	22570.00	24790.00	26030.00	Kubota	4	262D	16F-4R	76.00	6342	No
M8030 F	29300.00	17870.00	19630.00	20610.00	Kubota	4	262D	16F-4R	76.00	5417	No
M8580 DT	41600.00	25380.00	27870.00	29260.00	Kubota	4	284D	12F-12R	80.00	8377	No
M8580 DTC	50200.00	30620.00	33630.00	35310.00	Kubota	4	284D	12F-12R	80.00	8973	C,H,A
M8950 DT 4WD	40000.00	24400.00	26800.00	28140.00	Kubota	4	262D	24F-8R	86.00	7226	No
M8950 DT 4WD w/Cab	47500.00	28980.00	31830.00	33420.00	Kubota	4	262D	24F-8R	86.00	8223	C,H,A
M8950 F	34000.00	20740.00	22780.00	23920.00	Kubota	4	262D	24F-8R	86.00	6953	No
M8950 F w/Cab	41700.00	25440.00	27940.00	29340.00	Kubota	4	262D	24F-8R	86.00	7452	C,H,A
M9580 DT	47400.00	28910.00	31760.00	33350.00	Kubota	4T	284D	24F-24R	100.0	8488	No
M9580 DTC	55500.00	33860.00	37190.00	39050.00	Kubota	4T	284D	24F-24R	100.0	9083	No

C, D, DT--Front Wheel Assist DTSS--Front Wheel Assist, Shuttle Shift E--Two Wheel Drive F--Farm Standard W--Two Row Offset H, HC--High Clearance HSE--Hydrostatic Transmission, Two Wheel Drive HSD--Hydrostatic Transmission, Four Wheel Drive OC--Orchard L--Low Profile

1995

Model	Approx. Retail Price New	Fair	Good	Premium	Make	No. Cyls.	Displ. Cu.-In.	No. Speeds	P.T.O. H.P.	Approx. Shipping Wt.-Lbs.	Cab
B1550 DT 4WD	11500.00	7590.00	8400.00	8820.00	Kubota	3	52D	6F-2R	14.00	1279	No
B1550 E	10000.00	6600.00	7300.00	7670.00	Kubota	3	52D	6F-2R	14.00	1146	No
B1550 HSD 4WD	13000.00	8580.00	9490.00	9970.00	Kubota	3	52D	Infinite	13.00	1356	No
B1550 HSE	11500.00	7590.00	8400.00	8820.00	Kubota	3	52D	Infinite	13.00	1190	No
B1750 DT 4WD	12600.00	8950.00	9830.00	10320.00	Kubota	3	57D	6F-2R	16.50	1323	No
B1750 E	11100.00	7880.00	8660.00	9090.00	Kubota	3	57D	6F-2R	16.50	1201	No
B1750 HSD 4WD	14200.00	10080.00	11080.00	11630.00	Kubota	3	57D	Infinite	15.50	1400	No
B1750 HSE	12700.00	9020.00	9910.00	10410.00	Kubota	3	57D	Infinite	15.50	1257	No
B2150 DT 4WD	13600.00	9660.00	10610.00	11140.00	Kubota	4	75D	9F-3R	20.00	1764	No
B2150 E	12000.00	8520.00	9360.00	9830.00	Kubota	4	75D	9F-3R	20.00	1609	No
B2150 HSD 4WD	15300.00	10860.00	11930.00	12530.00	Kubota	4	75D	Infinite	18.00	1775	No
B2150 HSE	13700.00	9730.00	10690.00	11230.00	Kubota	4	75D	Infinite	18.00	1620	No
L2350 DT 4WD	11400.00	8090.00	8890.00	9340.00	Kubota	3	68D	8F-2R	20.5	2093	No
L2350 F-1	9990.00	7090.00	7790.00	8180.00	Kubota	3	68D	8F-2R	20.5	1781	No
L2650 DT-W 4WD	15240.00	10820.00	11890.00	12490.00	Kubota	3	85D	8F-8R	23.50	2602	No
L2900 DT	16240.00	11530.00	12670.00	13300.00	Kubota	3	91D	8F-8R	25.00	2800	No
L2900 F	14200.00	10080.00	11080.00	11630.00	Kubota	3	91D	8F-8R	25.00	2645	No
L2900 GST	16550.00	11750.00	12910.00	13560.00	Kubota	3	91D	8F-8R	25.00	2810	No
L3300 DT	17750.00	12600.00	13850.00	14540.00	Kubota	3	100D	8F-8R	28.00	2800	No
L3300 F	15000.00	10650.00	11700.00	12290.00	Kubota	3	100D	8F-8R	28.00	2645	No
L3300 GST	18060.00	12820.00	14090.00	14800.00	Kubota	3	100D	8F-8R	28.00	2810	No
L3600 DT	18870.00	12450.00	13780.00	14470.00	Kubota	4	113D	8F-8R	31.00	3030	No
L3600 GST	19180.00	12660.00	14000.00	14700.00	Kubota	4	113D	8F-8R	31.00	3075	No
M4030 SU	18050.00	11550.00	12640.00	13270.00	Kubota	5	149D	8F-2R	42.00	3946	No
B4200 DT 4WD	8100.00	5750.00	6320.00	6640.00	Kubota	2	35D	6F-2R	10	926	No
L4200 DT	20475.00	13510.00	14950.00	15700.00	Kubota	4	134D	8F-8R	37.00	3030	No

Kubota (Cont.)

1995 (Cont.)

Model	Approx. Retail Price New	Estimated Average Value Less Repairs Fair	Good	Premium	Engine Make	No. Cyls.	Displ. Cu.-In.	No. Speeds	P.T.O. H.P.	Approx. Shipping Wt.-Lbs.	Cab
L4200 F	17800.00	11750.00	12990.00	13640.00	Kubota	4	134D	8F-8R	37.00	2875	No
L4200 F GST	18110.00	11950.00	13220.00	13880.00	Kubota	4	134D	8F-8R	37.00	2890	No
L4200 GST	21385.00	14110.00	15610.00	16390.00	Kubota	4	134D	8F-8R	37.00	3055	No
L4350 HDT 4WD	24500.00	16170.00	17890.00	18790.00	Kubota	4	134D	8F-8R	38.00	3860	No
L4350 HDT-W 4WD	25200.00	16630.00	18400.00	19320.00	Kubota	4	134D	8F-8R	38.00	3860	No
L4350 MDT 4WD	23400.00	15440.00	17080.00	17930.00	Kubota	4	134D	8F-8R	38.00	3860	No
L4850 HDT-W 4WD	26600.00	17560.00	19420.00	20390.00	Kubota	5	152D	8F-8R	43.00	4080	No
M4950 DT 4WD	27000.00	17280.00	18900.00	19850.00	Kubota	6	170D	12F-4R	49.00	5357	No
M4950 F	21750.00	13920.00	15230.00	15990.00	Kubota	6	170D	12F-4R	49.00	4762	No
M5030 SU	20900.00	13380.00	14630.00	15360.00	Kubota	6	170D	16F-4R	49.00	4409	No
M5030 SU MDT 4WD	26200.00	16770.00	18340.00	19260.00	Kubota	6	170D	8F-8R	49.00	4978	No
B5200 DT 4WD	8900.00	6680.00	7120.00	7480.00	Kubota	3	47D	6F-2R	11.50	1180	No
B5200 E	8200.00	6150.00	6560.00	6890.00	Kubota	3	47D	6F-2R	11.50	1058	No
L5450 HDT-W 4WD	28800.00	19010.00	21020.00	22070.00	Kubota	5	168D	8F-8R	49.00	4410	No
M5950 DT 4WD	30300.00	19390.00	21210.00	22270.00	Kubota	3	196D	12F-4R	58.00	5673	No
M5950 F	24750.00	15840.00	17330.00	18200.00	Kubota	3	196D	12F-4R	58.00	4989	No
M6030 DTN-B 4WD	31200.00	19970.00	21840.00	22930.00	Kubota	3	196D	16F-4R	57.00	5010	No
B6200 DT 4WD	9300.00	6980.00	7440.00	7810.00	Kubota	3	52D	6F-2R	12.50	1179	No
B6200 E	8300.00	6230.00	6640.00	6970.00	Kubota	3	52D	6F-2R	12.50	1058	No
B6200 HSD 4WD	10600.00	7950.00	8480.00	8900.00	Kubota	3	52D	Infinite	12.50	1279	No
B6200 HSE	9600.00	7200.00	7680.00	8060.00	Kubota	3	52D	Infinite	12.50	1158	No
M6950 DT 4WD	31800.00	20350.00	22260.00	23370.00	Kubota	4	243D	12F-4R	66.00	6504	No
M6950 F	26250.00	16800.00	18380.00	19300.00	Kubota	4	243D	12F-4R	66.00	5776	No
M7030 DTNB	34900.00	22340.00	24430.00	25650.00	Kubota	4	243D	16F-4R	68.00	5004	No
M7030 N	27100.00	17340.00	18970.00	19920.00	Kubota	4	243D	16F-4R	68.00	4410	No
M7030 SU	26400.00	16900.00	18480.00	19400.00	Kubota	4	243D	16F-4R	68.00	5181	No
M7030 SUDT 4WD	31700.00	20290.00	22190.00	23300.00	Kubota	4	243D	16F-4R	68.00	5710	No
B7100 HSD 4WD	9495.00	6740.00	7410.00	7780.00	Kubota	3	47D	Infinite	13.00	1257	No
M7580 DT	39900.00	25540.00	27930.00	29330.00	Kubota	4	264D	12F-12R	70.00	6834	No
M7580 DTC	47900.00	30660.00	33530.00	35210.00	Kubota	4	264D	12F-12R	70.00	7429	C,H,A
M7950 DT 4WD	35000.00	22400.00	24500.00	25730.00	Kubota	4	262D	12F-4R	75.00	6810	No
M7950 DT 4WD w/Cab	42500.00	27200.00	29750.00	31240.00	Kubota	4	262D	12F-4R	75.00	7297	C,H,A
M7950 F	29000.00	18560.00	20300.00	21320.00	Kubota	4	262D	12F-4R	75.00	5960	No
M7950 F w/Cab	36900.00	23620.00	25830.00	27120.00	Kubota	4	262D	12F-4R	75.00	6460	C,H,A
M8030 DTM 4WD	37000.00	23680.00	25900.00	27200.00	Kubota	4	262D	16F-4R	76.00	6342	No
M8030 F	29300.00	18750.00	20510.00	21540.00	Kubota	4	262D	16F-4R	76.00	5417	No
M8580 DT	41600.00	26620.00	29120.00	30580.00	Kubota	4	284D	12F-12R	80.00	8377	No
M8580 DTC	50200.00	32130.00	35140.00	36900.00	Kubota	4	284D	12F-12R	80.00	8973	C,H,A
M8950 DT 4WD	40000.00	25600.00	28000.00	29400.00	Kubota	4	262D	24F-8R	86.00	7226	No
M8950 DT 4WD w/Cab	47500.00	30400.00	33250.00	34910.00	Kubota	4	262D	24F-8R	86.00	8223	C,H,A
M8950 F	34000.00	21760.00	23800.00	24990.00	Kubota	4	262D	24F-8R	86.00	6953	No
M8950 F w/Cab	41700.00	26690.00	29190.00	30650.00	Kubota	4	262D	24F-8R	86.00	7452	C,H,A
M9580 DT	47400.00	30340.00	33180.00	34840.00	Kubota	4T	284D	24F-24R	100.0	8488	No
M9580 DTC	55500.00	35520.00	38850.00	40790.00	Kubota	4T	284D	24F-24R	100.0	9083	No

C, D, DT--Front Wheel Assist DTSS--Front Wheel Assist, Shuttle Shift E--Two Wheel Drive F--Farm Standard W--Two Row Offset
H, HC--High Clearance HSE--Hydrostatic Transmission, Two Wheel Drive HSD--Hydrostatic Transmission, Four Wheel Drive OC--Orchard L--Low Profile

1996

Model	Approx. Retail Price New	Fair	Good	Premium	Engine Make	No. Cyls.	Displ. Cu.-In.	No. Speeds	P.T.O. H.P.	Approx. Shipping Wt.-Lbs.	Cab
B1550 DT 4WD	11500.00	8050.00	8740.00	9090.00	Kubota	3	52D	6F-2R	14.00	1279	No
B1550 E	10000.00	7000.00	7600.00	7900.00	Kubota	3	52D	6F-2R	14.00	1146	No
B1550 HSD 4WD	13000.00	9100.00	9880.00	10280.00	Kubota	3	52D	Infinite	13.00	1356	No
B1550 HSE	11500.00	8050.00	8740.00	9090.00	Kubota	3	52D	Infinite	13.00	1190	No
B1750 DT 4WD	12600.00	9320.00	10080.00	10480.00	Kubota	3	57D	6F-2R	16.50	1323	No
B1750 E	11100.00	8210.00	8880.00	9240.00	Kubota	3	57D	6F-2R	16.50	1201	No
B1750 HSD 4WD	14200.00	10510.00	11360.00	11810.00	Kubota	3	57D	Infinite	15.50	1400	No
B1750 HSE	12700.00	9400.00	10160.00	10570.00	Kubota	3	57D	Infinite	15.50	1257	No
B2150 DT 4WD	13600.00	10060.00	10880.00	11320.00	Kubota	4	75D	9F-3R	20.00	1764	No
B2150 E	12000.00	8880.00	9600.00	9980.00	Kubota	4	75D	9F-3R	20.00	1609	No
B2150 HSD 4WD	15300.00	11320.00	12240.00	12730.00	Kubota	4	75D	Infinite	18.00	1775	No
B2150 HSE	13700.00	10140.00	10960.00	11400.00	Kubota	4	75D	Infinite	18.00	1620	No
L2350 DT 4WD	11400.00	8440.00	9120.00	9490.00	Kubota	3	68D	8F-2R	20.5	2093	No
L2350 F-1	9990.00	7390.00	7990.00	8310.00	Kubota	3	68D	8F-2R	20.5	1781	No
L2650 DT-W 4WD	15240.00	11280.00	12190.00	12680.00	Kubota	3	85D	8F-8R	23.50	2602	No
L2900 DT	16240.00	12020.00	12990.00	13510.00	Kubota	3	91D	8F-8R	25.00	2800	No
L2900 F	14200.00	10510.00	11360.00	11810.00	Kubota	3	91D	8F-8R	25.00	2645	No
L2900 GST	16550.00	12250.00	13240.00	13770.00	Kubota	3	91D	8F-8R	25.00	2810	No
L3300 DT	17750.00	13140.00	14200.00	14770.00	Kubota	3	100D	8F-8R	28.00	2800	No
L3300 F	15000.00	11100.00	12000.00	12480.00	Kubota	3	100D	8F-8R	28.00	2645	No
L3300 GST	18060.00	13360.00	14450.00	15030.00	Kubota	3	100D	8F-8R	28.00	2810	No
L3600 DT	18870.00	13210.00	14340.00	14910.00	Kubota	4	113D	8F-8R	31.00	3030	No
L3600 GST	19180.00	13430.00	14580.00	15160.00	Kubota	4	113D	8F-8R	31.00	3075	No
M4030 SU	18050.00	12090.00	13180.00	13710.00	Kubota	5	149D	8F-2R	42.00	3946	No
B4200 DT 4WD	8100.00	5990.00	6480.00	6740.00	Kubota	2	35D	6F-2R	10	926	No
L4200 DT	20475.00	14330.00	15560.00	16180.00	Kubota	4	134D	8F-8R	37.00	3030	No
L4200 F	17800.00	12460.00	13530.00	14070.00	Kubota	4	134D	8F-8R	37.00	2875	No
L4200 F GST	18110.00	12680.00	13760.00	14310.00	Kubota	4	134D	8F-8R	37.00	2890	No
L4200 GST	21385.00	14970.00	16250.00	16900.00	Kubota	4	134D	8F-8R	37.00	3055	No
L4350 HDT 4WD	24500.00	17150.00	18620.00	19370.00	Kubota	4	134D	8F-8R	38.00	3860	No
L4350 HDT-W 4WD	25200.00	17640.00	19150.00	19920.00	Kubota	4	134D	8F-8R	38.00	3860	No
L4350 MDT 4WD	23400.00	16380.00	17780.00	18490.00	Kubota	4	134D	8F-8R	38.00	3860	No
L4850 HDT-W 4WD	26600.00	18620.00	20220.00	21030.00	Kubota	5	152D	8F-8R	43.00	4080	No
M4950 DT 4WD	27000.00	18090.00	19710.00	20500.00	Kubota	6	170D	12F-4R	49.00	5357	No
M4950 F	21750.00	14570.00	15880.00	16520.00	Kubota	6	170D	12F-4R	49.00	4762	No
M5030 SU	20900.00	14000.00	15260.00	15870.00	Kubota	6	170D	16F-4R	49.00	4409	No

Kubota (Cont.)

1996 (Cont.)

Model	Approx. Retail Price New	Estimated Average Value Less Repairs Fair	Good	Premium	Engine Make	No. Cyls.	Displ. Cu.-In.	No. Speeds	P.T.O. H.P.	Approx. Shipping Wt.-Lbs.	Cab
M5030 SU MDT 4WD	26200.00	17550.00	19130.00	19900.00	Kubota	6	170D	8F-8R	49.00	4978	No
B5200 DT 4WD	8900.00	6850.00	7300.00	7590.00	Kubota	3	47D	6F-2R	11.50	1180	No
B5200 E	8200.00	6310.00	6720.00	6990.00	Kubota	3	47D	6F-2R	11.50	1058	No
L5450 HDT-W 4WD	28800.00	19300.00	21020.00	21860.00	Kubota	5	168D	8F-8R	49.00	4410	No
M5950 DT 4WD	30300.00	20300.00	22120.00	23010.00	Kubota	3	196D	12F-4R	58.00	5673	No
M5950 F	24750.00	16580.00	18070.00	18790.00	Kubota	3	196D	12F-4R	58.00	4989	No
M6030 DTN-B 4WD	31200.00	20900.00	22780.00	23690.00	Kubota	3	196D	16F-4R	57.00	5010	No
B6200 DT 4WD	9300.00	7160.00	7630.00	7940.00	Kubota	3	52D	6F-2R	12.50	1179	No
B6200 E	8300.00	6390.00	6810.00	7080.00	Kubota	3	52D	6F-2R	12.50	1058	No
B6200 HSD 4WD	10600.00	8160.00	8690.00	9040.00	Kubota	3	52D	Infinite	12.50	1279	No
B6200 HSE	9600.00	7390.00	7870.00	8190.00	Kubota	3	52D	Infinite	12.50	1158	No
M6950 DT 4WD	31800.00	21310.00	23210.00	24140.00	Kubota	4	243D	12F-4R	66.00	6504	No
M6950 F	26250.00	17590.00	19160.00	19930.00	Kubota	4	243D	12F-4R	66.00	5776	No
M7030 DTNB	34900.00	23380.00	25480.00	26500.00	Kubota	4	243D	16F-4R	68.00	5004	No
M7030 N	27100.00	18160.00	19780.00	20570.00	Kubota	4	243D	16F-4R	68.00	4410	No
M7030 SU	26400.00	17690.00	19270.00	20040.00	Kubota	4	243D	16F-4R	68.00	5181	No
M7030 SUDT 4WD	31700.00	21240.00	23140.00	24070.00	Kubota	4	243D	16F-4R	68.00	5710	No
B7100 HSD 4WD	9495.00	7030.00	7600.00	7900.00	Kubota	3	47D	Infinite	13.00	1257	No
M7580 DT	39900.00	26730.00	29130.00	30300.00	Kubota	4	264D	12F-12R	70.00	6834	No
M7580 DTC	47900.00	32090.00	34970.00	36370.00	Kubota	4	264D	12F-12R	70.00	7429	C,H,A
M7950 DT 4WD	35000.00	23450.00	25550.00	26570.00	Kubota	4	262D	12F-4R	75.00	6810	No
M7950 DT 4WD w/Cab	42500.00	28480.00	31030.00	32270.00	Kubota	4	262D	12F-4R	75.00	7297	C,H,A
M7950 F	29000.00	19430.00	21170.00	22020.00	Kubota	4	262D	12F-4R	75.00	5960	No
M7950 F w/Cab	36900.00	24720.00	26940.00	28020.00	Kubota	4	262D	12F-4R	75.00	6460	C,H,A
M8030 DTM 4WD	37000.00	24790.00	27010.00	28090.00	Kubota	4	262D	16F-4R	76.00	6342	No
M8030 F	29300.00	19630.00	21390.00	22250.00	Kubota	4	262D	16F-4R	76.00	5417	No
M8580 DT	41600.00	27870.00	30370.00	31590.00	Kubota	4	284D	12F-12R	80.00	8377	No
M8580 DTC	50200.00	33630.00	36650.00	38120.00	Kubota	4	284D	12F-12R	80.00	8973	C,H,A
M8950 DT 4WD	40000.00	26800.00	29200.00	30370.00	Kubota	4	262D	24F-8R	86.00	7226	No
M8950 DT 4WD w/Cab	47500.00	31830.00	34680.00	36070.00	Kubota	4	262D	24F-8R	86.00	8223	C,H,A
M8950 F	34000.00	22780.00	24820.00	25810.00	Kubota	4	262D	24F-8R	86.00	6953	No
M8950 F w/Cab	41700.00	27940.00	30440.00	31660.00	Kubota	4	262D	24F-8R	86.00	7452	C,H,A
M9580 DT	47400.00	31760.00	34600.00	35980.00	Kubota	4T	284D	24F-24R	100.0	8488	No
M9580 DTC	55500.00	37190.00	40520.00	42140.00	Kubota	4T	284D	24F-24R	100.0	9083	No

C, D, DT--Front Wheel Assist DTSS--Front Wheel Assist, Shuttle Shift E--Two Wheel Drive F--Farm Standard W--Two Row Offset H, HC--High Clearance HSE--Hydrostatic Transmission, Two Wheel Drive HSD--Hydrostatic Transmission, Four Wheel Drive OC--Orchard L--Low Profile

1997

Model	Approx. Retail Price New	Fair	Good	Premium	Make	No. Cyls.	Displ. Cu.-In.	No. Speeds	P.T.O. H.P.	Approx. Shipping Wt.-Lbs.	Cab
B1700 HSD 4WD	13190.00	10160.00	10820.00	11250.00	Kubota	3	59D	Variable	13.00	1265	No
B1700DT 4WD	11690.00	9000.00	9590.00	9970.00	Kubota	3	59D	6F-2R	14.00	1265	No
B1700E 2WD	10490.00	8080.00	8600.00	8940.00	Kubota	3	59D	6F-2R	14.00	1265	No
B1700HSDB 4WD	13590.00	10460.00	11140.00	11590.00	Kubota	3	59D	Variable	13.00	1265	No
B2100DT 4WD	12890.00	9930.00	10570.00	10990.00	Kubota	3	61D	6F-2R	17.0	1310	No
B2100HSD 4WD	14490.00	11160.00	11880.00	12360.00	Kubota	3	61D	Variable	16.0	1310	No
B2100HSDB 4WD	14890.00	11470.00	12210.00	12700.00	Kubota	3	61D	Variable	16.0	1310	No
B2150HSD 4WD	15490.00	11930.00	12700.00	13210.00	Kubota	4	75D	Variable	18.00	1760	No
L2350DT 4WD	13010.00	10020.00	10670.00	11100.00	Kubota	3	68D	8F-2R	20.50	2149	No
L2350F 2WD	11070.00	8520.00	9080.00	9440.00	Kubota	3	68D	8F-2R	20.50	1740	No
B2400HSD 4WD	14990.00	11540.00	12290.00	12780.00	Kubota	3	68D	Variable	18.00	1325	No
B2400HSDB 4WD	15390.00	11850.00	12620.00	13130.00	Kubota	3	68D	Variable	18.00	1325	No
B2400HSE 2WD	13690.00	10540.00	11230.00	11680.00	Kubota	3	68D	Variable	18.0	1325	No
L2900DT 4WD	17180.00	13230.00	14090.00	14650.00	Kubota	3	91D	8F-2R	25.00	2610	No
L2900F 2WD	15080.00	11610.00	12370.00	12870.00	Kubota	3	91D	8F-2R	25.00	2610	No
L2900GST 4WD	17580.00	13540.00	14420.00	15000.00	Kubota	3	91D	8F-2R	25.00	2610	No
L3300DT 4WD	18830.00	14500.00	15440.00	16060.00	Kubota	3	100D	8F-2R	28.00	2690	No
L3300F 2WD	15880.00	12230.00	13020.00	13540.00	Kubota	3	100D	8F-2R	28.00	2690	No
L3300GST 4WD	19130.00	14730.00	15690.00	16320.00	Kubota	3	100D	8F-2R	28.00	2690	No
L3600DT 4WD	19980.00	15390.00	16380.00	17040.00	Kubota	4	113D	8F-8R	31.0	2890	No
L3600GST 4WD	20230.00	15580.00	16590.00	17250.00	Kubota	4	113D	8F-8R	31.00	2910	No
L3600GSTCA 4WD	28680.00	22080.00	23520.00	24460.00	Kubota	4	113D	16F-16R	31.00	2910	C,H,A
M4030SU 2WD	18340.00	13210.00	14120.00	14690.00	Kubota	5	148D	8F-2R	42.00	4246	No
M4030SU-TF 2WD	19600.00	14110.00	15090.00	15690.00	Kubota	5	148D	16F-4R	42.00	4450	No
L4200DT 4WD	21680.00	16690.00	17780.00	18490.00	Kubota	4	134D	8F-8R	37.00	2930	No
L4200F 2WD	18780.00	14460.00	15400.00	16020.00	Kubota	4	134D	8F-8R	37.00	2853	No
L4200FGST 2WD	19080.00	14690.00	15650.00	16280.00	Kubota	4	134D	8F-8R	37.00	2853	No
L4200GST 4WD	22580.00	17390.00	18520.00	19260.00	Kubota	4	134D	8F-8R	37.00	2853	No
L4200GSTCA 4WD	30180.00	23240.00	24750.00	25740.00	Kubota	4	134D	16F-16R	37.00	3377	C,H,A
L4350HDT 4WD	25780.00	18560.00	19850.00	20640.00	Kubota	4	134D	8F-8R	38.00	3762	No
L4350HDT-W 4WD	26480.00	19070.00	20390.00	21210.00	Kubota	4	134D	8F-8R	38.00	3762	No
L4350MDT 4WD	24580.00	18930.00	20160.00	20970.00	Kubota	4	134D	8F-8R	38.00	3762	No
M4700DT 4WD	23390.00	16840.00	18010.00	18730.00	Kubota	5	167D	8F-4R	42.00	3322	No
M4700F 2WD	18790.00	13530.00	14470.00	15050.00	Kubota	5	167D	8F-4R	42.00	3256	No
M4700F-CS 2WD	19490.00	14030.00	15010.00	15610.00	Kubota	5	167D	12F-4R	42.00	3256	No
M4700S 2WD	19090.00	13750.00	14700.00	15290.00	Kubota	5	167D	8F-4R	42.00	3255	No
M4700SCS 2WD	19190.00	13820.00	14780.00	15370.00	Kubota	5	167D	12F-4R	42.00	3256	No
M4700SD 4WD	23690.00	17060.00	18240.00	18970.00	Kubota	5	167D	8F-4R	42.00	3322	No
L4850HDT-W 4WD	27980.00	20150.00	21550.00	22410.00	Kubota	5	152D	8F-8R	43.00	3762	No
M5030SU 2WD	21190.00	15260.00	16320.00	16970.00	Kubota	6	170D	16F-4R	49.00	4350	No
M5030SU-MDT 4WD	26490.00	19070.00	20400.00	21220.00	Kubota	6	170D	8F-8R	49.00	5556	No
M5400Dt 4WD	25490.00	18350.00	19630.00	20420.00	Kubota	5	167D	8F-4R	50.00	3322	No
M5400F 2WD	20790.00	14970.00	16010.00	16650.00	Kubota	5	167D	8F-4R	50.00	3256	No
M5400S 2WD	21090.00	15190.00	16240.00	16890.00	Kubota	5	167D	8F-4R	50.00	3256	No
M5400SD 4WD	25790.00	18570.00	19860.00	20650.00	Kubota	5	167D	8F-4R	50.00	3322	No
L5450HDT-W 4WD	30230.00	21770.00	23280.00	24210.00	Kubota	5	167D	8F-8R	49.00	4246	No

Kubota (Cont.)

1997 (Cont.)

Model	Approx. Retail Price New	Estimated Average Value Less Repairs Fair	Good	Premium	Engine Make	No. Cyls.	Displ. Cu.-In.	No. Speeds	P.T.O. H.P.	Approx. Shipping Wt.-Lbs.	Cab
M6030 DTN-B 4WD	32790.00	23610.00	25250.00	26260.00	Kubota	3	196D	16F-4R	57.00	4999	No
M7030DTN-B 4WD	36590.00	26350.00	28170.00	29300.00	Kubota	4	243D	16F-4R	68.00	5108	No
M7030N 2WD	28490.00	20510.00	21940.00	22820.00	Kubota	4	243D	16F-4R	68.00	4680	No
M7030SU 2WD	27790.00	20010.00	21400.00	22260.00	Kubota	4	243D	16F-4R	68.00	4932	No
M7030SUDT 4WD	33290.00	23970.00	25630.00	26660.00	Kubota	4	243D	16F-4R	68.00	5884	No
B7100HSD 4WD	10040.00	7730.00	8230.00	8560.00	Kubota	3	46D	Variable	13.00	1265	No
M7580DT-1 4WD	41790.00	30090.00	32180.00	33470.00	Kubota	4	264D	12F-12R	70.00	6890	No
M7580DTC 4WD	50090.00	36070.00	38570.00	40110.00	Kubota	4	264D	12F-12R	70.00	7485	C,H,A
M8030DT 4WD	37990.00	27350.00	29250.00	30420.00	Kubota	4	262D	16F-4R	76.90	6095	No
M8030DTL 4WD	37690.00	27140.00	29020.00	30180.00	Kubota	4	262D	16F-4R	76.90	6600	No
M8030DTM 4WD	38490.00	27710.00	29640.00	30830.00	Kubota	4	262D	16F-4R	76.90	6654	No
M8030F-1	30240.00	21770.00	23290.00	24220.00	Kubota	4	262D	16F-4R	76.90	5138	No
M8580DT 4WD	43590.00	31390.00	33560.00	34900.00	Kubota	4	285D	12F-12R	80.00	8440	No
M8580DTC 4WD	52490.00	37790.00	40420.00	42040.00	Kubota	4	285D	12F-12R	80.00	9210	C,H,A
M9580DT-1 4WD	49590.00	35710.00	38180.00	39710.00	Kubota	4T	285D	24F-24R	91.00	8488	No
M9580DT-1M 4WD	52570.00	37850.00	40480.00	42100.00	Kubota	4T	285D	36F-36R	91.00	8440	No
M9580DTC 4WD	58090.00	41830.00	44730.00	46520.00	Kubota	4T	285D	24F-24R	91.00	9083	No
M9580DTC-M 4WD	60990.00	43910.00	46960.00	48840.00	Kubota	4T	285D	36F-36R	91.00	9210	C,H,A

C, D, DT--Front Wheel Assist DTSS--Front Wheel Assist, Shuttle Shift E--Two Wheel Drive F--Farm Standard W--Two Row Offset H, HC--High Clearance HSE--Hydrostatic Transmission, Two Wheel Drive HSD--Hydrostatic Transmission, Four Wheel Drive OC--Orchard L--Low Profile

1998

Model	Approx. Retail Price New	Fair	Good	Premium	Engine Make	No. Cyls.	Displ. Cu.-In.	No. Speeds	P.T.O. H.P.	Approx. Shipping Wt.-Lbs.	Cab
B1700DT 4WD	11690.00	9590.00	9940.00	10240.00	Kubota	3	59D	6F-2R	14.00	1265	No
B1700E 2WD	10490.00	8600.00	8920.00	9190.00	Kubota	3	59D	6F-2R	14.00	1265	No
B1700HSD 4WD	13190.00	10820.00	11210.00	11550.00	Kubota	3	59D	Variable	13.00	1265	No
B1700HSDB 4WD	13590.00	11140.00	11550.00	11900.00	Kubota	3	59D	Variable	13.00	1265	No
B2100DT 4WD	12890.00	10570.00	10960.00	11290.00	Kubota	3	61D	6F-2R	17.0	1310	No
B2100HSD 4WD	14490.00	11880.00	12320.00	12690.00	Kubota	3	61D	Variable	16.0	1310	No
B2100HSDB 4WD	14890.00	12210.00	12660.00	13040.00	Kubota	3	61D	Variable	16.0	1310	No
B2150HSD 4WD	15490.00	12700.00	13170.00	13570.00	Kubota	4	75D	Variable	18.00	1760	No
L2350DT 4WD	13010.00	10670.00	11060.00	11390.00	Kubota	3	68D	8F-2R	20.50	2149	No
L2350F 2WD	11070.00	9080.00	9410.00	9690.00	Kubota	3	68D	8F-2R	20.50	1740	No
B2400HSD 4WD	14990.00	12290.00	12740.00	13120.00	Kubota	3	68D	Variable	18.00	1325	No
B2400HSDB 4WD	15390.00	12620.00	13080.00	13470.00	Kubota	3	68D	Variable	18.00	1325	No
B2400HSE 2WD	13690.00	11230.00	11640.00	11990.00	Kubota	3	68D	Variable	18.0	1325	No
L2900DT 4WD	17180.00	14090.00	14600.00	15040.00	Kubota	3	91D	8F-2R	25.00	2610	No
L2900F 2WD	15080.00	12370.00	12820.00	13210.00	Kubota	3	91D	8F-2R	25.00	2610	No
L2900GST 4WD	17580.00	14420.00	14940.00	15390.00	Kubota	3	91D	8F-2R	25.00	2610	No
L3300DT 4WD	18830.00	15440.00	16010.00	16490.00	Kubota	3	100D	8F-2R	28.00	2690	No
L3300F 2WD	15880.00	13020.00	13500.00	13910.00	Kubota	3	100D	8F-2R	28.00	2690	No
L3300GST 4WD	19130.00	15690.00	16260.00	16750.00	Kubota	3	100D	8F-2R	28.00	2690	No
L3600DT 4WD	19980.00	16380.00	16980.00	17490.00	Kubota	4	113D	8F-8R	31.0	2890	No
L3600GST 4WD	20230.00	16590.00	17200.00	17720.00	Kubota	4	113D	8F-8R	31.00	2910	No
L3600GSTCA 4WD	28680.00	23520.00	24380.00	25110.00	Kubota	4	113D	16F-16R	31.00	2910	C,H,A
M4030SU 2WD	18340.00	14310.00	15040.00	15490.00	Kubota	5	148D	8F-2R	42.00	4246	No
M4030SU-TF 2WD	19600.00	15290.00	16070.00	16550.00	Kubota	5	148D	16F-4R	42.00	4450	No
L4200DT 4WD	21680.00	17780.00	18430.00	18980.00	Kubota	4	134D	8F-8R	37.00	2930	No
L4200F 2WD	18780.00	15400.00	15960.00	16440.00	Kubota	4	134D	8F-8R	37.00	2853	No
L4200FGST 2WD	19080.00	15650.00	16220.00	16710.00	Kubota	4	134D	8F-8R	37.00	2853	No
L4200GST 4WD	22580.00	18520.00	19190.00	19770.00	Kubota	4	134D	8F-8R	37.00	2853	No
L4200GSTCA 4WD	30180.00	24750.00	25650.00	26420.00	Kubota	4	134D	16F-16R	37.00	3377	C,H,A
L4350HDT 4WD	25780.00	20110.00	21140.00	21770.00	Kubota	4	134D	8F-8R	38.00	3762	No
L4350HDT-W 4WD	26480.00	20650.00	21710.00	22360.00	Kubota	4	134D	8F-8R	38.00	3762	No
L4350MDT 4WD	24580.00	20160.00	20890.00	21520.00	Kubota	4	134D	8F-8R	38.00	3762	No
M4700DT 4WD	23390.00	18240.00	19180.00	19760.00	Kubota	5	167D	8F-4R	42.00	3322	No
M4700F 2WD	18790.00	14660.00	15410.00	15870.00	Kubota	5	167D	8F-4R	42.00	3256	No
M4700F-CS 2WD	19490.00	15200.00	15980.00	16460.00	Kubota	5	167D	12F-4R	42.00	3256	No
M4700S 2WD	19090.00	14890.00	15650.00	16120.00	Kubota	5	167D	8F-4R	42.00	3255	No
M4700SCS 2WD	19190.00	14970.00	15740.00	16210.00	Kubota	5	167D	12F-4R	42.00	3256	No
M4700SD 4WD	23690.00	18480.00	19430.00	20010.00	Kubota	5	167D	8F-4R	42.00	3322	No
L4850HDT-W 4WD	27980.00	21820.00	22940.00	23630.00	Kubota	5	152D	8F-8R	43.00	3762	No
M5030SU 2WD	21190.00	16530.00	17380.00	17900.00	Kubota	6	170D	16F-4R	49.00	4350	No
M5030SU-MDT 4WD	26490.00	20660.00	21720.00	22370.00	Kubota	6	170D	8F-8R	49.00	5556	No
M5400Dt 4WD	25490.00	19880.00	20900.00	21530.00	Kubota	5	167D	8F-4R	50.00	3322	No
M5400F 2WD	20790.00	16220.00	17050.00	17560.00	Kubota	5	167D	8F-4R	50.00	3256	No
M5400S 2WD	21090.00	16450.00	17290.00	17810.00	Kubota	5	167D	8F-4R	50.00	3256	No
M5400SD 4WD	25790.00	20120.00	21150.00	21790.00	Kubota	5	167D	8F-4R	50.00	3322	No
L5450HDT-W 4WD	30230.00	23580.00	24790.00	25530.00	Kubota	5	167D	8F-8R	49.00	4246	No
M6030 DTN-B 4WD	32790.00	25580.00	26890.00	27700.00	Kubota	3	196D	16F-4R	57.00	4999	No
M7030DTN-B 4WD	36590.00	28540.00	30000.00	30900.00	Kubota	4	243D	16F-4R	68.00	5108	No
M7030N 2WD	28490.00	22220.00	23360.00	24060.00	Kubota	4	243D	16F-4R	68.00	4680	No
M7030SU 2WD	27790.00	21680.00	22790.00	23470.00	Kubota	4	243D	16F-4R	68.00	4932	No
M7030SUDT 4WD	33290.00	25970.00	27300.00	28120.00	Kubota	4	243D	16F-4R	68.00	5884	No
B7100HSD 4WD	10040.00	8230.00	8530.00	8790.00	Kubota	3	46D	Variable	13.00	1265	No
M7580DT-1 4WD	41790.00	32600.00	34270.00	35300.00	Kubota	4	264D	12F-12R	70.00	6890	No
M7580DTC 4WD	50090.00	39070.00	41070.00	42300.00	Kubota	4	264D	12F-12R	70.00	7485	C,H,A
M8030DT 4WD	37990.00	29630.00	31150.00	32090.00	Kubota	4	262D	16F-4R	76.90	6095	No
M8030DTL 4WD	37690.00	29400.00	30910.00	31840.00	Kubota	4	262D	16F-4R	76.90	6600	No
M8030DTM 4WD	38490.00	30020.00	31560.00	32510.00	Kubota	4	262D	16F-4R	76.90	6654	No
M8030F-1	30240.00	23590.00	24800.00	25540.00	Kubota	4	262D	16F-4R	76.90	5138	No
M8580DT 4WD	43590.00	34000.00	35740.00	36810.00	Kubota	4	285D	12F-12R	80.00	8440	No
M8580DTC 4WD	52490.00	40940.00	43040.00	44330.00	Kubota	4	285D	12F-12R	80.00	9210	C,H,A
M9580DT-1 4WD	49590.00	38680.00	40660.00	41880.00	Kubota	4T	285D	24F-24R	91.00	8488	No
M9580DT-1M 4WD	52570.00	41010.00	43110.00	44400.00	Kubota	4T	285D	36F-36R	91.00	8440	No

Kubota (Cont.)

1998 (Cont.)

Model	Approx. Retail Price New	Estimated Average Value Less Repairs Fair	Good	Premium	Engine Make	No. Cyls.	Displ. Cu.-In.	No. Speeds	P.T.O. H.P.	Approx. Shipping Wt.-Lbs.	Cab
M9580DTC 4WD	58090.00	**45310.00**	**47630.00**	**49060.00**	Kubota	4T	285D	24F-24R	91.00	9083	No
M9580DTC-M 4WD	60990.00	**47570.00**	**50010.00**	**51510.00**	Kubota	4T	285D	36F-36R	91.00	9210	C,H,A

C, D, DT--Front Wheel Assist DTSS--Front Wheel Assist, Shuttle Shift E--Two Wheel Drive F--Farm Standard W--Two Row Offset H, HC--High Clearance HSE--Hydrostatic Transmission, Two Wheel Drive HSD--Hydrostatic Transmission, Four Wheel Drive OC--Orchard L--Low Profile

1999

Model	Approx. Retail Price New	Fair	Good	Premium	Make	No. Cyls.	Displ. Cu.-In.	No. Speeds	P.T.O. H.P.	Approx. Shipping Wt.-Lbs.	Cab
B7300HSD	10300.00	**8960.00**	**9170.00**	**9350.00**	Kubota	3	44D	Variable	12.5	1312	No
B1700DT 4WD	11690.00	**10170.00**	**10400.00**	**10610.00**	Kubota	3	59D	6F-2R	14.00	1265	No
B1700E 2WD	10490.00	**9130.00**	**9340.00**	**9530.00**	Kubota	3	59D	6F-2R	14.00	1265	No
B1700HSD 4WD	13190.00	**11480.00**	**11740.00**	**11980.00**	Kubota	3	59D	Variable	13.00	1265	No
B1700HSDB 4WD	13590.00	**11820.00**	**12100.00**	**12340.00**	Kubota	3	59D	Variable	13.00	1265	No
B2100DT 4WD	12890.00	**11210.00**	**11470.00**	**11700.00**	Kubota	3	61D	6F-2R	17.0	1310	No
B2100HSD 4WD	14490.00	**12610.00**	**12900.00**	**13160.00**	Kubota	3	61D	Variable	16.0	1310	No
B2100HSDB 4WD	14890.00	**12950.00**	**13250.00**	**13520.00**	Kubota	3	61D	Variable	16.0	1310	No
B2150HSD 4WD	15490.00	**13480.00**	**13790.00**	**14070.00**	Kubota	4	75D	Variable	18.00	1760	No
B2400HSD 4WD	14990.00	**13040.00**	**13340.00**	**13610.00**	Kubota	3	68D	Variable	18.00	1325	No
B2400HSDB 4WD	15390.00	**13390.00**	**13700.00**	**13970.00**	Kubota	3	68D	Variable	18.00	1325	No
B2400HSE 2WD	13690.00	**11910.00**	**12180.00**	**12420.00**	Kubota	3	68D	Variable	18.0	1325	No
L2500F	11400.00	**9920.00**	**10150.00**	**10350.00**	Kubota	3	85D	8F-2R	22.5	1962	No
L2500DT 4WD	13400.00	**11660.00**	**11930.00**	**12170.00**	Kubota	3	85D	8F-2R	22.5	2205	No
B2710HSD	15500.00	**13490.00**	**13800.00**	**14080.00**	Kubota	4	81D	Variable	20.0	1620	No
L3010F	14000.00	**12180.00**	**12460.00**	**12710.00**	Kubota	3	91D	8F-8R	25.5	2610	No
L3010DT 4WD	16100.00	**14010.00**	**14330.00**	**14620.00**	Kubota	3	91D	8F-8R	25.5	2610	No
L3010GST	16650.00	**14490.00**	**14820.00**	**15120.00**	Kubota	3	91D	8F-8R	25.5	2610	No
L3010HST	17150.00	**14920.00**	**15260.00**	**15570.00**	Kubota	3	91D	Variable	24.0	2610	No
L3410DT 4WD	17600.00	**15310.00**	**15660.00**	**15970.00**	Kubota	3	100D	8F-8R	28.5	2690	No
L3410GST	18150.00	**15790.00**	**16150.00**	**16470.00**	Kubota	3	100D	8F-8R	28.5	2690	No
L3410HST	18650.00	**16230.00**	**16600.00**	**16930.00**	Kubota	3	100D	Variable	26.0	2690	No
L3710DT	18850.00	**16400.00**	**16780.00**	**17120.00**	Kubota	4	113D	8F-8R	31.5	2890	No
L3710GST	19350.00	**16840.00**	**17220.00**	**17560.00**	Kubota	4	113D	8F-8R	31.5	2890	No
L3710HST	20050.00	**17440.00**	**17850.00**	**18210.00**	Kubota	4	113D	Variable	30.0	2910	No
L3710HSTC	26450.00	**23010.00**	**23540.00**	**24010.00**	Kubota	4	113D	Variable	30.0	2910	C,H,A
L4310F	16500.00	**14360.00**	**14690.00**	**14980.00**	Kubota	4	134D	8F-8R	37.5	2853	No
L4310DT 4WD	21500.00	**18710.00**	**19140.00**	**19520.00**	Kubota	4	134D	8F-8R	37.5	2930	No
L4310GST	22650.00	**19710.00**	**20160.00**	**20560.00**	Kubota	4	134D	8F-8R	37.5	2853	No
L4310HST	22550.00	**19620.00**	**20070.00**	**20470.00**	Kubota	4	134D	Variable	36.0	2930	No
L4310HSTC	28950.00	**25190.00**	**25770.00**	**26290.00**	Kubota	4	134D	Variable	36.0	2930	C,H,A
M4700	19490.00	**16370.00**	**17150.00**	**17490.00**	Kubota	5	167D	8F-4R	42.0	3255	No
M4700D 4WD	24100.00	**20240.00**	**21210.00**	**21630.00**	Kubota	5	167D	8F-4R	42.0	3322	No
M4700 CS	19890.00	**16710.00**	**17500.00**	**17850.00**	Kubota	5	167D	8F-4R	42.00	3256	No
M5400	21490.00	**18050.00**	**18910.00**	**19290.00**	Kubota	5	167D	8F-4R	50.00	3256	No
M5400D 4WD	26190.00	**22000.00**	**23050.00**	**23510.00**	Kubota	5	167D	8F-4R	50.00	3322	No
M5400D-N 4WD	27100.00	**22760.00**	**23850.00**	**24330.00**	Kubota	5	167D	8F-4R	50.00	3322	No
M6800	23200.00	**19490.00**	**20420.00**	**20830.00**	Kubota	4	202D	8F-4R	62.0	4480	No
M6800DT 4WD	27500.00	**23100.00**	**24200.00**	**24680.00**	Kubota	4	202D	8F-4R	62.0	4480	No
M7580DT-1 4WD	41790.00	**35100.00**	**36780.00**	**37520.00**	Kubota	4	264D	12F-12R	70.00	6890	No
M7580DTC 4WD	50090.00	**42080.00**	**44080.00**	**44960.00**	Kubota	4	264D	12F-12R	70.00	7485	C,H,A
M8200	26300.00	**22090.00**	**23140.00**	**23600.00**	Kubota	4T	202D	8F-8R	73.0	5010	No
M8200DT 4WD	30300.00	**25450.00**	**26660.00**	**27190.00**	Kubota	4T	202D	8F-8R	73.0	5010	No
M8200C	33800.00	**28390.00**	**29740.00**	**30340.00**	Kubota	4T	202D	8F-8R	73.0	5010	C,H,A
M8200DTC 4WD	37800.00	**31750.00**	**33260.00**	**33930.00**	Kubota	4T	202D	8F-8R	73.0	5010	C,H,A
M8200DTN-B	31100.00	**26120.00**	**27370.00**	**27920.00**	Kubota	4T	202D	8F-8R	73.0	5108	No
M8580DT 4WD	43590.00	**36620.00**	**38360.00**	**39130.00**	Kubota	4	285D	12F-12R	80.00	8440	No
M8580DTC 4WD	52490.00	**44090.00**	**46190.00**	**47110.00**	Kubota	4	285D	12F-12R	80.00	9210	C,H,A
M9000	28000.00	**23520.00**	**24640.00**	**25130.00**	Kubota	4TI	202D	8F-8R	80.0	5100	No
M9000DT 4WD	32200.00	**27050.00**	**28340.00**	**28910.00**	Kubota	4TI	202D	8F-8R	80.0	5100	No
M9000C	35500.00	**29820.00**	**31240.00**	**31870.00**	Kubota	4TI	202D	8F-8R	80.0	5100	C,H,A
M9000DTC 4WD	39700.00	**33350.00**	**34940.00**	**35640.00**	Kubota	4TI	202D	8F-8R	80.0	5585	C,H,A
M9000DTL	31600.00	**26540.00**	**27810.00**	**28370.00**	Kubota	4TI	202D	8F-8R	80.0	5200	C,H,A
M-110FC	48000.00	**40320.00**	**42240.00**	**43090.00**	Kubota	5T	356D	16F-16R	88.0	8598	C,H,A
M-110DTC 4WD	54700.00	**45950.00**	**48140.00**	**49100.00**	Kubota	5T	356D	16F-16R	88.0	8598	C,H,A
M-120FC	53000.00	**44520.00**	**46640.00**	**47570.00**	Kubota	5T	356D	16F-16R	98.0	8598	C,H,A
M-120DTC 4WD	60300.00	**50650.00**	**53060.00**	**54120.00**	Kubota	5T	356D	16F-16R	98.0	9259	C,H,A

Landini

1985

Model	Approx. Retail Price New	Fair	Good	Premium	Make	No. Cyls.	Displ. Cu.-In.	No. Speeds	P.T.O. H.P.	Approx. Shipping Wt.-Lbs.	Cab
DT1000S 4WD	42725.00	**12820.00**	**16240.00**	**18030.00**	Perkins	6	354D	12F-4R	92.00	10251	C,H
Platform R1000S	29745.00	**8920.00**	**11300.00**	**12540.00**	Perkins	6	354D	12F-4R	92.00	9056	No
R1000S	36235.00	**10870.00**	**13770.00**	**15290.00**	Perkins	6	354D	12F-4R	92.00	9520	C,H
DT5830 4WD	20205.00	**8080.00**	**9900.00**	**10590.00**	Perkins	3	152D	12F-4R	42.00	4934	No
R5830	15190.00	**6080.00**	**7440.00**	**7960.00**	Perkins	3	152D	12F-4R	42.00	4299	No
DT6530 4WD	22770.00	**9110.00**	**11160.00**	**11940.00**	Perkins	4	236D	12F-4R	57.00	4740	No
R6530 F	17905.00	**7160.00**	**8770.00**	**9380.00**	Perkins	4	236D	12F-4R	57.00	4539	No
DT6830 4WD	22510.00	**9000.00**	**11030.00**	**11800.00**	Perkins	4	236D	12F-4R	57.00	5246	No
R6830	17510.00	**7000.00**	**8580.00**	**9180.00**	Perkins	4	236D	12F-4R	57.00	4630	No
R6830 Row Crop	18060.00	**7220.00**	**8850.00**	**9470.00**	Perkins	4	236D	12F-4R	57.00	4630	No
DT7830 4WD	24395.00	**9760.00**	**11950.00**	**12790.00**	Perkins	4	236D	12F-4R	63.00	5755	No
R7830	19335.00	**7730.00**	**9470.00**	**10130.00**	Perkins	4	236D	12F-4R	63.00	5247	No
DT8550 4WD	34332.00	**13730.00**	**16820.00**	**18000.00**	Perkins	4	248D	12F-4R	68.00	7902	C,H
DT8830 4WD	26385.00	**10550.00**	**12930.00**	**13840.00**	Perkins	4	248D	12F-4R	68.00	6328	No
R8830	21320.00	**8530.00**	**10450.00**	**11180.00**	Perkins	4	248D	12F-4R	68.00	5799	No
DT12500 4WD	46510.00	**13950.00**	**17670.00**	**19610.00**	Perkins	6	354D	12F-4R	100.	11530	C,H

Landini (Cont.)

Model	Approx. Retail Price New	Estimated Average Value Less Repairs Fair	Good	Premium	Engine Make	No. Cyls.	Displ. Cu.-In.	No. Speeds	P.T.O. H.P.	Approx. Shipping Wt.-Lbs.	Cab
1985 (Cont.)											
R12500	38940.00	11680.00	14800.00	16430.00	Perkins	6	354D	12F-4R	100.	10450	C,H
DT14500	49755.00	14930.00	18910.00	20990.00	Perkins	6T	354D	12F-4R	122.00	12500	C,H
R14500	42185.00	12660.00	16030.00	17790.00	Perkins	6T	354D	12F-4R	122.00	11177	C,H
1986											
DT1000S 4WD	42725.00	13670.00	16660.00	18490.00	Perkins	6	354D	12F-4R	92.00	10251	C,H
Platform R1000S	29745.00	9520.00	11600.00	12880.00	Perkins	6	354D	12F-4R	92.00	9056	No
R1000S	36235.00	11600.00	14130.00	15680.00	Perkins	6	354D	12F-4R	92.00	9520	C,H
DT5830 4WD	20205.00	8280.00	10100.00	10810.00	Perkins	3	152D	12F-4R	42.00	4934	No
R5830	15190.00	6230.00	7600.00	8130.00	Perkins	3	152D	12F-4R	42.00	4299	No
DT6530 4WD	22770.00	9340.00	11390.00	12190.00	Perkins	4	236D	12F-4R	57.00	4740	No
R6530 F	17905.00	7340.00	8950.00	9580.00	Perkins	4	236D	12F-4R	57.00	4539	No
DT6830 4WD	22510.00	9230.00	11260.00	12050.00	Perkins	4	236D	12F-4R	57.00	5246	No
R6830	17510.00	7180.00	8760.00	9370.00	Perkins	4	236D	12F-4R	57.00	4630	No
R6830 Row Crop	18060.00	7410.00	9030.00	9660.00	Perkins	4	236D	12F-4R	57.00	4630	No
DT7830 4WD	24395.00	10000.00	12200.00	13050.00	Perkins	4	236D	12F-4R	63.00	5755	No
R7830	19335.00	7930.00	9670.00	10350.00	Perkins	4	236D	12F-4R	63.00	5247	No
R8530 F	21325.00	8740.00	10660.00	11410.00	Perkins	4	248D	12F-4R	68.00	4883	No
R8530 L	21310.00	8740.00	10660.00	11410.00	Perkins	4	248D	12F-4R	68.00	5104	No
DT8550 4WD	34332.00	14080.00	17170.00	18370.00	Perkins	4	248D	12F-4R	68.00	7902	C,H
DT8830 4WD	26385.00	10820.00	13190.00	14110.00	Perkins	4	248D	12F-4R	68.00	6328	No
R8830	21320.00	8740.00	10660.00	11410.00	Perkins	4	248D	12F-4R	68.00	5799	No
DT12500 4WD	46510.00	14880.00	18140.00	20140.00	Perkins	6	354D	12F-4R	100.	11530	C,H
R12500	38940.00	12460.00	15190.00	16860.00	Perkins	6	354D	12F-4R	100.	10450	C,H
DT14500	49755.00	15920.00	19400.00	21530.00	Perkins	6T	354D	12F-4R	122.00	12500	C,H
R14500	42185.00	13500.00	16450.00	18260.00	Perkins	6T	354D	12F-4R	122.00	11177	C,H
1987											
DT1000S 4WD	43325.00	14730.00	17330.00	19060.00	Perkins	6	354D	12F-4R	92.00	10251	C,H
1988											
DT1000S 4WD	43825.00	15780.00	18410.00	20250.00	Perkins	6	354D	12F-4R	92.00	10251	C,H
1989											
DT1000S 4WD	44425.00	16880.00	19550.00	21510.00	Perkins	6	354D	12F-4R	92.00	10251	C,H
1990											
DT1000S 4WD	44725.00	17890.00	20570.00	22630.00	Perkins	6	354D	12F-4R	92.00	10251	C,H
1991											
DT1000S 4WD	45000.00	18900.00	21600.00	23540.00	Perkins	6	354D	12F-4R	92.00	10251	C,H
1992											
DT1000S 4WD	45500.00	20020.00	23210.00	25070.00	Perkins	6	354D	12F-4R	92.00	10251	C,H
1993											
DT1000S 4WD	45950.00	21140.00	24810.00	26550.00	Perkins	6	354D	12F-4R	92.00	10251	C,H
1994											
DT1000S 4WD	46555.00	22810.00	26540.00	28130.00	Perkins	6	354D	12F-4R	92.00	10251	C,H
1995											
DT50	40875.00	17630.00	19830.00	20620.00	Perkins	3	152D	12F-12R	39.0	6770	C,H
R50	35020.00	15100.00	16990.00	17670.00	Perkins	3	152D	12F-12R	39.0	6106	C,H
DT55F	45071.00	19440.00	21860.00	22730.00	Perkins	3	152D	12F-12R	39.0		C,H
R55F	37975.00	16370.00	18420.00	19160.00	Perkins	3	152D	12F-12R	39.0		C,H
DT60	43442.00	18730.00	21070.00	21910.00	Perkins	3T	152D	12F-12R	49.5	7013	C,H
DT60F	46625.00	20100.00	22620.00	23530.00	Perkins	3T	152D	12F-12R	49.5		C,H
R60	37224.00	16050.00	18060.00	18780.00	Perkins	3T	152D	12F-12R	49.5	6239	C,H
R60F	39403.00	16990.00	19110.00	19870.00	Perkins	3T	152D	12F-12R	49.5		C,H
DT65	48030.00	20710.00	23300.00	24230.00	Perkins	4	236D	12F-12R	57.0	7124	C,H,A
DT65F	51084.00	22030.00	24780.00	25770.00	Perkins	4	236D	12F-12R	57.0		C,H,A
R65	41438.00	17870.00	20100.00	20900.00	Perkins	4	236D	12F-12R	57.0	6571	C,H,A
R65F	43311.00	18680.00	21020.00	21860.00	Perkins	4	236D	12F-12R	57.0		C,H,A
C75	46152.00	19900.00	22390.00	23290.00	Perkins	4	236D	16F-8R	61.25	9381	No
CF75	45823.00	19760.00	22230.00	23120.00	Perkins	4	236D	16F-8R	61.25	8230	No
CFL75	46297.00	19960.00	22460.00	23360.00	Perkins	4	236D	16F-8R	61.25		No
DT75	49320.00	21270.00	23930.00	24890.00	Perkins	4	236D	12F-12R	61.25	7677	C,H,A
DT75F	52298.00	22550.00	25370.00	26390.00	Perkins	4	236D	12F-12R	61.25		C,H,A
R75	42940.00	18520.00	20830.00	21660.00	Perkins	4	236D	12F-12R	61.25	7013	C,H,A
R75F	44537.00	19210.00	21610.00	22470.00	Perkins	4	236D	12F-12R	61.25		C,H,A
C85	53497.00	23070.00	25950.00	26990.00	Perkins	4	248D	16F-8R	71.25	9602	No
CF85	51709.00	22300.00	25090.00	26090.00	Perkins	4	248D	16F-8R	71.25	8230	No
CFL85	52269.00	22540.00	25360.00	26370.00	Perkins	4	248D	16F-8R	71.25		No
DT85	50981.00	21980.00	24730.00	25720.00	Perkins	4	248D	12F-12R	71.25	8075	C,H,A
DT85F	53944.00	23260.00	26170.00	27220.00	Perkins	4	248D	12F-12R	71.25		C,H,A
R85	44366.00	19130.00	21520.00	22380.00	Perkins	4	248D	12F-12R	71.25	7412	C,H,A
R85F	46214.00	19930.00	22420.00	23320.00	Perkins	4	248D	12F-12R	71.25		C,H,A
C95	57093.00	24620.00	27700.00	28810.00	Perkins	4T	236D	16F-8R	84.0		No
DT95	53301.00	22990.00	25860.00	26890.00	Perkins	4T	236D	12F-12R	84.0	8186	C,H,A
R95	46244.00	19940.00	22430.00	23330.00	Perkins	4T	236D	12F-12R	84.0	7522	C,H,A
DT1000S 4WD	46955.00	26300.00	29580.00	30760.00	Perkins	6	354D	12F-4R	92.00	10251	C,H
DT5860	33220.00	14330.00	16120.00	16770.00	Perkins	3	152D	12F-4R	39.0	5591	No
R5860	26425.00	11400.00	12820.00	13330.00	Perkins	3	152D	12F-4R	39.00	4971	No

Landini (Cont.)

Model	Approx. Retail Price New	Estimated Average Value Less Repairs Fair	Good	Premium	Engine Make	No. Cyls.	Displ. Cu.-In.	No. Speeds	P.T.O. H.P.	Approx. Shipping Wt.-Lbs.	Cab
			1995 (Cont.)								
DT6060	35689.00	15390.00	17310.00	18000.00	Perkins	3T	152D	12F-4R	49.5	5856	No
R6060	29149.00	12570.00	14140.00	14710.00	Perkins	3T	152D	12F-4R	49.5	5237	No
DT6860	37684.00	16250.00	18280.00	19010.00	Perkins	4	236D	12F-12R	57.0	6122	No
R6860	31138.00	13430.00	15110.00	15710.00	Perkins	4	236D	12F-12R	57.0	5546	No
DT6880	51202.00	22080.00	24840.00	25830.00	Perkins	4	236D	12F-12R	57.0	7611	C,H,A
R6880	43895.00	18930.00	21290.00	22140.00	Perkins	4	236D	12F-12R	57.0	6947	C,H,A
DT7860	39408.00	16990.00	19120.00	19890.00	Perkins	4	236D	12F-12R	61.25	6874	No
DT7860HC	41525.00	17910.00	20140.00	20950.00	Perkins	4	236D	12F-12R	61.25	6891	No
R7860	33839.00	14620.00	16440.00	17100.00	Perkins	4	236D	12F-12R	61.25	6387	No
R7860HC	34070.00	14690.00	16530.00	17190.00	Perkins	4	236D	12F-12R	61.25	6188	No
DT7880	52646.00	22700.00	25540.00	26560.00	Perkins	4	236D	12F-12R	61.25	8075	C,H,A
R7880	45854.00	19770.00	22250.00	23140.00	Perkins	4	236D	12F-12R	61.25	7611	C,H,A
DT8860	43286.00	18670.00	21000.00	21840.00	Perkins	4	248D	12F-12R	71.25	6962	No
DT8860HC	43013.00	18550.00	20870.00	21710.00	Perkins	4	248D	12F-12R	71.25	7102	No
R8860	35855.00	15460.00	17390.00	18090.00	Perkins	4	248D	12F-12R	71.25	6476	No
R8860HC	36084.00	15560.00	17510.00	18210.00	Perkins	4	248D	12F-12R	71.25	6531	No
DT8880	54414.00	23460.00	26400.00	27460.00	Perkins	4	248D	12F-12R	71.25	8451	C,H,A
DT8880HC	55282.00	23840.00	26820.00	27890.00	Perkins	4	248D	12F-12R	71.25	8418	C,H,A
R8880	46458.00	20030.00	22540.00	23440.00	Perkins	4	248D	12F-12R	71.25	7633	C,H,A
DT9880	59819.00	25790.00	29020.00	30180.00	Perkins	4T	236D	12F-12R	84.0	8850	C,H,A
DT9880HC	59853.00	25810.00	29040.00	30200.00	Perkins	4T	236D	12F-12R	84.0	8529	C,H,A
R9880	53004.00	22850.00	25710.00	26740.00	Perkins	4T	236D	12F-12R	84.0	8407	C,H,A
DT10000	68826.00	28090.00	32330.00	33950.00	Perkins	6	354D	12F-4R	88.5	9779	C,H,A
R10000	58602.00	23920.00	27530.00	28910.00	Perkins	6	354D	12F-4R	88.5	9381	C,H,A
DT13000	73228.00	29880.00	34400.00	36120.00	Perkins	6	354D	12F-4R	94.0	9912	C,H,A
R13000	62232.00	25400.00	29230.00	30690.00	Perkins	6	354D	12F-4R	94.0	9513	C,H,A
DT14500	81135.00	33110.00	38110.00	40020.00	Perkins	6T	354D	12F-4R	124.75	12035	C,H,A
R14500	68637.00	28010.00	32240.00	33850.00	Perkins	6T	354D	12F-4R	124.75	11062	C,H,A
			1996								
DT50	44187.00	21020.00	23090.00	24010.00	Perkins	3	152D	12F-12R	42.9	6770	C,H
R50	37630.00	17450.00	19160.00	19930.00	Perkins	3	152D	12F-12R	42.9	6106	C,H
DT55F	47943.00	22230.00	24420.00	25400.00	Perkins	3	152D	12F-12R	42.9		C,H
DT55FP	39833.00	18220.00	20010.00	20810.00	Perkins	3	152D	12F-12R	42.9		No
DT55GE	40300.00	18950.00	20810.00	21640.00	Perkins	3	152D	12F-12R	42.9		No
DT55L	48139.00	22320.00	24510.00	25490.00	Perkins	3	152D	12F-12R	42.9		C,H
DT55LP	39910.00	18340.00	20140.00	20950.00	Perkins	3	152D	12F-12R	42.9		No
DT55V	49288.00	21980.00	24140.00	25110.00	Perkins	3	152D	12F-12R	42.9		C,H
R55F	40275.00	18670.00	20510.00	21330.00	Perkins	3	152D	12F-12R	42.9		C,H
R55FP	31636.00	14720.00	16170.00	16820.00	Perkins	3	152D	12F-12R	42.9		No
R55GE	32541.00	15090.00	16570.00	17230.00	Perkins	3	152D	12F-12R	42.9		No
R55L	40276.00	18670.00	20510.00	21330.00	Perkins	3	152D	12F-12R	42.9		C,H
R55LP	31663.00	14680.00	16120.00	16770.00	Perkins	3	152D	12F-12R	42.9		No
R55V	40300.00	18680.00	20520.00	21340.00	Perkins	3	152D	12F-12R	42.9		C,H
DT60	46466.00	21540.00	23660.00	24610.00	Perkins	3T	152D	12F-12R	54.3	7013	C,H
DT60F	49560.00	22980.00	25240.00	26250.00	Perkins	3T	152D	12F-12R	54.3		C,H
DT60FP	41535.00	18930.00	20790.00	21620.00	Perkins	3T	152D	12F-12R	54.3		No
DT60GE	42060.00	19730.00	21670.00	22540.00	Perkins	3T	152D	12F-12R	54.3		No
DT60L	49558.00	22980.00	25240.00	26250.00	Perkins	3T	152D	12F-12R	54.3		C,H,A
DT60LP	41329.00	18970.00	20830.00	21660.00	Perkins	3T	152D	12F-12R	54.3		No
DT60V	50962.00	22220.00	24410.00	25390.00	Perkins	3T	152D	12F-12R	54.3		C,H,A
R60	39678.00	18400.00	20200.00	21010.00	Perkins	3T	152D	12F-12R	54.3	6239	C,H
R60F	41322.00	19160.00	21040.00	21880.00	Perkins	3T	152D	12F-12R	54.3		C,H
R60FP	32682.00	15190.00	16680.00	17350.00	Perkins	3T	152D	12F-12R	54.3		No
R60GE	33528.00	15550.00	17080.00	17760.00	Perkins	3T	152D	12F-12R	54.3		No
R60L	41545.00	19260.00	21160.00	22010.00	Perkins	3T	152D	12F-12R	54.3		C,H,A
R60LP	32682.00	15150.00	16640.00	17310.00	Perkins	3T	152D	12F-12R	54.3		No
R60V	42017.00	19440.00	21360.00	22210.00	Perkins	3T	152D	12F-12R	54.3		C,H,A
DT65	51563.00	22810.00	25060.00	26060.00	Perkins	4	236D	12F-12R	57.26	7124	C,H,A
DT65F	56000.00	24880.00	27320.00	28410.00	Perkins	4	236D	12F-12R	57.26		C,H,A
DT65FP	42225.00	18980.00	20840.00	21670.00	Perkins	4	236D	12F-12R	57.26		No
DT65GE	44513.00	20060.00	22030.00	22910.00	Perkins	4	236D	12F-12R	57.26		No
DT65L	56000.00	24570.00	26990.00	28070.00	Perkins	4	236D	12F-12R	57.26		C,H,A
DT65LP	43136.00	19020.00	20890.00	21730.00	Perkins	4	236D	12F-12R	57.26		No
DT65V	53952.00	24000.00	26360.00	27410.00	Perkins	4	236D	12F-12R	57.26		C,H,A
R65	44355.00	19620.00	21540.00	22400.00	Perkins	4	236D	12F-12R	57.26	6571	C,H,A
R65F	45686.00	21080.00	23150.00	24080.00	Perkins	4	236D	12F-12R	57.26		C,H,A
R65FP	35010.00	15370.00	16880.00	17560.00	Perkins	4	236D	12F-12R	57.26		No
R65GE	35660.00	16270.00	17870.00	18590.00	Perkins	4	236D	12F-12R	57.26		No
R65L	47575.00	22060.00	24230.00	25200.00	Perkins	4	236D	12F-12R	57.26		C,H,A
R65LP	34820.00	15480.00	17000.00	17680.00	Perkins	4	236D	12F-12R	57.26		No
R65V	45795.00	20630.00	22660.00	23570.00	Perkins	4	236D	12F-12R	57.26		C,H,A
C75	49360.00	22880.00	25140.00	26150.00	Perkins	4	236D	16F-8R	61.25	9381	No
CF75	48065.00	22280.00	24480.00	25460.00	Perkins	4	236D	16F-8R	61.25	8230	No
CFL75	48560.00	22510.00	24730.00	25720.00	Perkins	4	236D	16F-8R	61.25		No
DT75	52970.00	23470.00	25780.00	26810.00	Perkins	4	236D	12F-12R	64.37	7677	C,H,A
DT75F	56880.00	25270.00	27750.00	28860.00	Perkins	4	236D	12F-12R	64.37		C,H,A
DT75FP	42954.00	19300.00	21200.00	22050.00	Perkins	4	236D	12F-12R	64.37		No
DT75GE	46039.00	20650.00	22680.00	23590.00	Perkins	4	236D	12F-12R	64.37		No
DT75L	56880.00	24960.00	27420.00	28520.00	Perkins	4	236D	12F-12R	64.37		C,H,A
DT75LP	43865.00	19340.00	21240.00	22090.00	Perkins	4	236D	12F-12R	64.37		No
DT75V	55886.00	24800.00	27230.00	28320.00	Perkins	4	236D	12F-12R	64.37		C,H,A
R75	45333.00	21640.00	23770.00	24720.00	Perkins	4	236D	12F-12R	64.37	7013	C,H,A
R75F	48989.00	21910.00	24060.00	25020.00	Perkins	4	236D	12F-12R	64.37		C,H,A

Landini (Cont.)

1996 (Cont.)

Model	Approx. Retail Price New	Estimated Average Value Less Repairs Fair	Good	Premium	Engine Make	No. Cyls.	Displ. Cu.-In.	No. Speeds	P.T.O. H.P.	Approx. Shipping Wt.-Lbs.	Cab
R75FP	36380.00	15980.00	17550.00	18250.00	Perkins	4	236D	12F-12R	64.39		No
R75GE	37175.00	17240.00	18930.00	19690.00	Perkins	4	236D	12F-12R	64.37		No
R75L	48989.00	22710.00	24950.00	25950.00	Perkins	4	236D	12F-12R	64.37		C,H,A
R75LP	36187.00	16780.00	18430.00	19170.00	Perkins	4	236D	12F-12R	64.37		No
R75V	47150.00	21060.00	23140.00	24070.00	Perkins	4	236D	12F-12R	64.37		C,H,A
C85	56250.00	26080.00	28640.00	29790.00	Perkins	4	248D	16F-8R	71.25	9602	No
CF85	54390.00	25220.00	27700.00	28810.00	Perkins	4	248D	16F-8R	71.25	8230	No
CFL85	54975.00	25490.00	28000.00	29120.00	Perkins	4	248D	16F-8R	71.25		No
DT85	54698.00	24240.00	26620.00	27690.00	Perkins	4	248D	12F-12R	74.83	8075	C,H,A
DT85F	58593.00	26030.00	28590.00	29730.00	Perkins	4	248D	12F-12R	74.83		C,H,A
DT85FP	45353.00	20600.00	22620.00	23530.00	Perkins	4	248D	12F-12R	74.83		No
DT85GE	49009.00	21970.00	24130.00	25100.00	Perkins	4	248D	12F-12R	74.83		No
DT85L	58593.00	25720.00	28250.00	29380.00	Perkins	4	248D	12F-12R	74.83		C,H,A
DT85LP	46455.00	20400.00	22410.00	23310.00	Perkins	4	248D	12F-12R	74.83		No
R85	46816.00	21330.00	23430.00	24370.00	Perkins	4	248D	12F-12R	74.83	7412	C,H,A
R85F	50510.00	22310.00	24510.00	25490.00	Perkins	4	248D	12F-12R	74.83		C,H,A
R85FP	38505.00	17020.00	18700.00	19450.00	Perkins	4	248D	12F-12R	74.83		No
R85GE	39465.00	18300.00	20100.00	20900.00	Perkins	4	248D	12F-12R	74.83		No
R85L	50510.00	23420.00	25720.00	26750.00	Perkins	4	248D	12F-12R	74.83		C,H,A
R85LP	38785.00	17980.00	19750.00	20540.00	Perkins	4	248D	12F-12R	74.83		No
C95	60190.00	27900.00	30650.00	31880.00	Perkins	4T	236D	16F-8R	84.0		No
DT95	57350.00	25730.00	28260.00	29390.00	Perkins	4T	236D	12F-12R	88.0	8186	C,H,A
R95	49352.00	22880.00	25130.00	26140.00	Perkins	4T	236D	12F-12R	88.0	7522	C,H,A
DT5860	36055.00	16310.00	17910.00	18630.00	Perkins	3	152D	12F-4R	42.9	5591	No
R5860	28750.00	13030.00	14310.00	14880.00	Perkins	3	152D	12F-4R	42.9	4971	No
DT6060	38035.00	17190.00	18880.00	19640.00	Perkins	3T	152D	12F-4R	54.3	5856	No
R6060	31700.00	14260.00	15660.00	16290.00	Perkins	3T	152D	12F-4R	54.3	5237	No
DT6860	39826.00	18340.00	20140.00	20950.00	Perkins	4	236D	12F-12R	57.26	6122	No
R6860	33760.00	15050.00	16530.00	17190.00	Perkins	4	236D	12F-12R	57.26	5546	No
DT6880	54555.00	24980.00	27430.00	28530.00	Perkins	4	236D	12F-12R	57.26	7611	C,H,A
R6880	46985.00	20890.00	22950.00	23870.00	Perkins	4	236D	12F-12R	57.26	6947	C,H,A
DT7860	41755.00	19130.00	21010.00	21850.00	Perkins	4	236D	12F-12R	64.37	6874	No
DT7860HC	43186.00	19700.00	21640.00	22510.00	Perkins	4	236D	12F-12R	64.37	6891	No
R7860	35927.00	15660.00	17200.00	17890.00	Perkins	4	236D	12F-12R	64.37	6387	No
R7860HC	35433.00	16270.00	17870.00	18590.00	Perkins	4	236D	12F-12R	64.37	6188	No
DT7880	56057.00	26080.00	28650.00	29800.00	Perkins	4	236D	12F-12R	64.37	8075	C,H,A
R7880	47215.00	21000.00	23060.00	23980.00	Perkins	4	236D	12F-12R	64.37	7611	C,H,A
DT8860	45565.00	20820.00	22860.00	23770.00	Perkins	4	248D	12F-12R	74.83	6962	No
DT8860HC	46295.00	21490.00	23600.00	24540.00	Perkins	4	248D	12F-12R	74.83	7102	No
R8860	38025.00	16590.00	18220.00	18950.00	Perkins	4	248D	12F-12R	74.83	6476	No
R8860HC	37915.00	17450.00	19170.00	19940.00	Perkins	4	248D	12F-12R	74.83	6531	No
DT8880	58905.00	26900.00	29540.00	30720.00	Perkins	4	248D	12F-12R	74.83	8451	C,H,A
DT8880HC	57405.00	25950.00	28500.00	29640.00	Perkins	4	248D	12F-12R	74.83	8418	C,H,A
R8880	49620.00	21880.00	24030.00	24990.00	Perkins	4	248D	12F-12R	74.83	7633	C,H,A
DT9880	63569.00	28600.00	31410.00	32670.00	Perkins	4T	236D	12F-12R	88.0	8850	C,H,A
DT9880HC	62160.00	28050.00	30810.00	32040.00	Perkins	4T	236D	12F-12R	88.0	8529	C,H,A
R9880	55478.00	24560.00	26980.00	28060.00	Perkins	4T	236D	12F-12R	88.0	8407	C,H,A
DT10000	74307.00	33320.00	37270.00	39130.00	Perkins	6	354D	12F-4R	88.5	9779	C,H,A
R10000	62455.00	28000.00	31330.00	32900.00	Perkins	6	354D	12F-4R	88.5	9381	C,H,A
DT13000	78220.00	35080.00	39240.00	41200.00	Perkins	6	354D	12F-4R	94.0	9912	C,H,A
R13000	66785.00	29950.00	33500.00	35180.00	Perkins	6	354D	12F-4R	94.0	9513	C,H,A
DT14500	88538.00	39700.00	44410.00	46630.00	Perkins	6T	354D	12F-4R	124.75	12035	C,H,A
R14500	74896.00	33590.00	37570.00	39450.00	Perkins	6T	354D	12F-4R	124.75	11062	C,H,A

1997

Model	Approx. Retail Price New	Fair	Good	Premium	Make	No. Cyls.	Displ. Cu.-In.	No. Speeds	P.T.O. H.P.	Approx. Shipping Wt.-Lbs.	Cab
DT55FP	29860.00	20010.00	21800.00	22670.00	Perkins	3	152D	12F-12R	42.9		No
DT55GE	31060.00	20810.00	22670.00	23580.00	Perkins	3	152D	12F-12R	42.9		No
DT55LP	30063.00	20140.00	21950.00	22830.00	Perkins	3	152D	12F-12R	42.9		No
DT55V	36036.00	24140.00	26310.00	27360.00	Perkins	3	152D	12F-12R	42.9		C,H
DT55VP	30705.00	20570.00	22420.00	23320.00	Perkins	3	152D	12F-12R	42.9		No
R55FP	24138.00	16170.00	17620.00	18330.00	Perkins	3	152D	12F-12R	42.9		No
R55V	30630.00	20520.00	22360.00	23250.00	Perkins	3	152D	12F-12R	42.9		C,H
R55VP	25725.00	17240.00	18780.00	19530.00	Perkins	3	152D	12F-12R	42.9		No
DT60FP	31030.00	20790.00	22650.00	23560.00	Perkins	3T	152D	12F-12R	54.3		No
DT60GE	32337.00	21670.00	23610.00	24550.00	Perkins	3T	152D	12F-12R	54.3		No
DT60LP	31095.00	20830.00	22700.00	23610.00	Perkins	3T	152D	12F-12R	54.3		No
DT60V	36425.00	24410.00	26590.00	27650.00	Perkins	3T	152D	12F-12R	54.3		C,H,A
DT60VP	31095.00	20830.00	22700.00	23610.00	Perkins	3T	152D	12F-12R	54.3		No
R60FP	24897.00	16680.00	18180.00	18910.00	Perkins	3T	152D	12F-12R	54.3		No
R60V	31875.00	21360.00	23270.00	24200.00	Perkins	3T	152D	12F-12R	54.3		C,H,A
R60VP	27233.00	18250.00	19880.00	20680.00	Perkins	3T	152D	12F-12R	54.3		No
DT65	37395.00	25060.00	27300.00	28390.00	Perkins	4	236D	12F-12R	57.26	7124	C,H,A
DT65F	40782.00	27320.00	29770.00	30960.00	Perkins	4	236D	12F-12R	57.26		C,H,A
DT65FP	31110.00	20840.00	22710.00	23620.00	Perkins	4	236D	12F-12R	57.26		No
DT65GE	32886.00	22030.00	24010.00	24970.00	Perkins	4	236D	12F-12R	57.26		No
DT65L	40285.00	26990.00	29410.00	30590.00	Perkins	4	236D	12F-12R	57.26		C,H,A
DT65LP	31175.00	20890.00	22760.00	23670.00	Perkins	4	236D	12F-12R	57.26		No
DT65V	39340.00	26360.00	28720.00	29870.00	Perkins	4	236D	12F-12R	57.26		C,H,A
DT65VP	32415.00	21720.00	23660.00	24610.00	Perkins	4	236D	12F-12R	54.26		No
R65	32155.00	21540.00	23470.00	24410.00	Perkins	4	236D	12F-12R	57.26	6571	C,H,A
R65F	34550.00	23150.00	25220.00	26230.00	Perkins	4	236D	12F-12R	57.26		C,H,A
R65FP	25197.00	16880.00	18390.00	19130.00	Perkins	4	236D	12F-12R	57.26		No
R65GE	26670.00	17870.00	19470.00	20250.00	Perkins	4	236D	12F-12R	57.26		No
R65LP	25371.00	17000.00	18520.00	19260.00	Perkins	4	236D	12F-12R	57.26		No

Model	Approx. Retail Price New	Estimated Average Value Less Repairs Fair	Good	Premium	Engine Make	No. Cyls.	Displ. Cu.-In.	No. Speeds	P.T.O. H.P.	Approx. Shipping Wt.-Lbs.	Cab
Landini (Cont.)											
			1997 (Cont.)								
R65V	33817.00	22660.00	24690.00	25680.00	Perkins	4	236D	12F-12R	57.26		C,H,A
R65VP	27498.00	18420.00	20070.00	20870.00	Perkins	4	236D	12F-12R	57.26		No
C75	36321.00	24340.00	26510.00	27570.00	Perkins	4	236D	16F-8R	61.25		No
C75F	35370.00	23700.00	25820.00	26850.00	Perkins	4	236D	16F-8R	61.25		No
C75FL	35730.00	23940.00	26080.00	27120.00	Perkins	4	236D	16F-8R	61.25		No
DT75	38481.00	25780.00	28090.00	29210.00	Perkins	4	236D	12F-12R	64.37	7677	C,H,A
DT75F	41422.00	27750.00	30240.00	31450.00	Perkins	4	236D	12F-12R	64.37		C,H,A
DT75FP	31640.00	21200.00	23100.00	24020.00	Perkins	4	236D	12F-12R	64.37		No
DT75GE	33855.00	22680.00	24710.00	25700.00	Perkins	4	236D	12F-12R	64.37		No
DT75L	40925.00	27420.00	29880.00	31080.00	Perkins	4	236D	12F-12R	64.37		C,H,A
DT75LP	31700.00	21240.00	23140.00	24070.00	Perkins	4	236D	12F-12R	64.37		No
DT75V	40648.00	27230.00	29670.00	30860.00	Perkins	4	236D	12F-12R	64.37		C,H,A
DT75VP	33532.00	22470.00	24480.00	25460.00	Perkins	4	236D	12F-12R	64.37		No
R75	35475.00	23770.00	25900.00	26940.00	Perkins	4	236D	12F-12R	64.37	7013	C,H,A
R75F	35915.00	24060.00	26220.00	27270.00	Perkins	4	236D	12F-12R	64.37		C,H,A
R75FP	26190.00	17550.00	19120.00	19890.00	Perkins	4	236D	12F-12R	64.39		No
R75V	34530.00	23140.00	25210.00	26220.00	Perkins	4	236D	12F-12R	64.37		C,H,A
R75VP	28286.00	18950.00	20650.00	21480.00	Perkins	4	236D	12F-12R	64.37		No
C85	41322.00	27690.00	30170.00	31380.00	Perkins	4	248D	16F-8R	71.25		No
C85F	39963.00	26780.00	29170.00	30340.00	Perkins	4	248D	16F-8R	71.25		No
C85FL	40387.00	27060.00	29480.00	30660.00	Perkins	4	248D	16F-8R	71.25		No
DT85	39736.00	26620.00	29010.00	30170.00	Perkins	4	248D	12F-12R	74.83	8075	C,H,A
DT85F	42664.00	28590.00	31150.00	32400.00	Perkins	4	248D	12F-12R	74.83		C,H,A
DT85FP	33765.00	22620.00	24650.00	25640.00	Perkins	4	248D	12F-12R	74.83		No
DT85GE	36010.00	24130.00	26290.00	27340.00	Perkins	4	248D	12F-12R	74.83		No
DT85L	42167.00	28250.00	30780.00	32010.00	Perkins	4	248D	12F-12R	74.83		C,H,A
DT85LP	33442.00	22410.00	24410.00	25390.00	Perkins	4	248D	12F-12R	74.83		No
R85	34971.00	23430.00	25530.00	26550.00	Perkins	4	248D	12F-12R	74.83	7412	C,H,A
R85F	36580.00	24510.00	26700.00	27770.00	Perkins	4	248D	12F-12R	74.83		C,H,A
R85FP	27905.00	18700.00	20370.00	21190.00	Perkins	4	248D	12F-12R	74.83		No
C95	44183.00	29600.00	32250.00	33540.00	Perkins	4T	236D	16F-8R	84.0		No
DT95	42177.00	28260.00	30790.00	32020.00	Perkins	4T	236D	12F-12R	88.0	8186	C,H,A
DT5860	26737.00	17910.00	19520.00	20300.00	Perkins	3	152D	12F-4R	42.9		No
R5860	21360.00	14310.00	15590.00	16210.00	Perkins	3	152D	12F-4R	42.9	4971	No
DT6060	28175.00	18880.00	20570.00	21390.00	Perkins	3T	152D	12F-4R	54.3	5856	No
R6060	23370.00	15660.00	17060.00	17740.00	Perkins	3T	152D	12F-4R	54.3	5237	No
DT6860	30065.00	20140.00	21950.00	22830.00	Perkins	4	236D	12F-12R	57.26	6122	No
R6860	24670.00	16530.00	18010.00	18730.00	Perkins	4	236D	12F-12R	57.26	5546	No
DT6880	40943.00	27430.00	29890.00	31090.00	Perkins	4	236D	12F-12R	57.26	7611	C,H,A
R6880	34253.00	22950.00	25010.00	26010.00	Perkins	4	236D	12F-12R	57.26	6947	C,H,A
DT7860	31360.00	21010.00	22890.00	23810.00	Perkins	4	236D	12F-12R	64.37	6874	No
DT7860HC	32302.00	21640.00	23580.00	24520.00	Perkins	4	236D	12F-12R	64.37	6891	No
R7860	25677.00	17200.00	18740.00	19490.00	Perkins	4	236D	12F-12R	64.37	6387	No
R7860HC	26675.00	17870.00	19470.00	20250.00	Perkins	4	236D	12F-12R	64.37	6188	No
DT7880	42761.00	28650.00	31220.00	32470.00	Perkins	4	236D	12F-12R	64.37	8075	C,H,A
R7880	34421.00	23060.00	25130.00	26140.00	Perkins	4	236D	12F-12R	64.37	7611	C,H,A
DT8860	35416.00	23730.00	25850.00	26880.00	Perkins	4	248D	12F-12R	74.83	6962	No
DT8860HC	35225.00	23600.00	25710.00	26740.00	Perkins	4	248D	12F-12R	74.83	7102	No
R8860	27200.00	18220.00	19860.00	20650.00	Perkins	4	248D	12F-12R	74.83	6476	No
R8860HC	28787.00	19290.00	21020.00	21860.00	Perkins	4	248D	12F-12R	74.83	6531	No
DT8880	44096.00	29540.00	32190.00	33480.00	Perkins	4	248D	12F-12R	74.83	8451	C,H,A
DT8880HC	42538.00	28500.00	31050.00	32290.00	Perkins	4	248D	12F-12R	74.83	8418	C,H,A
R8880	35863.00	24030.00	26180.00	27230.00	Perkins	4	248D	12F-12R	74.83	7633	C,H,A
DT9880	46887.00	31410.00	34230.00	35600.00	Perkins	4T	236D	12F-12R	88.0	8850	C,H,A
DT9880HC	45988.00	30810.00	33570.00	34910.00	Perkins	4T	236D	12F-12R	88.0	8529	C,H,A
R9880	40264.00	26980.00	29390.00	30570.00	Perkins	4T	236D	12F-12R	88.0	8407	C,H,A
			1998								
DT50 TECHNO	28990.00	21450.00	22900.00	23590.00	Perkins	3	152D	12F-12R	43.0		No
DT55FP	31495.00	23310.00	24880.00	25630.00	Perkins	3	152D	24F-12R	42.9		No
DT55GE	31995.00	23680.00	25280.00	26040.00	Perkins	3	152D	24F-12R	42.9		No
DT55LP	31605.00	23390.00	24970.00	25720.00	Perkins	3	152D	24F-12R	42.9		No
DT55V	38885.00	28780.00	30720.00	31640.00	Perkins	3	152D	24F-12R	42.9		C,H
DT55VP	31195.00	23080.00	24640.00	25380.00	Perkins	3	152D	24F-12R	42.9		No
R55FP	25535.00	18900.00	20170.00	20780.00	Perkins	3	152D	24F-12R	42.9		No
R55V	32455.00	24020.00	25640.00	26410.00	Perkins	3	152D	24F-12R	42.9		C,H
R55VP	26410.00	19540.00	20860.00	21490.00	Perkins	3	152D	24F-12R	42.9		No
DT60 TECHNO	32440.00	24010.00	25630.00	26400.00	Perkins	3T	152D	12F-12R	51.3		No
DT60 TECHNO w/Cab	37085.00	27440.00	29300.00	30180.00	Perkins	3T	152D	12F-12R	51.3		C,H,A
DT60 TOP	33417.00	24730.00	26400.00	27190.00	Perkins	3T	152D	12F-12R	51.3		No
DT60 TOP w/Cab	37796.00	27970.00	29860.00	30760.00	Perkins	3T	152D	12F-12R	51.3		C,H,A
DT60FP	31878.00	23590.00	25180.00	25940.00	Perkins	3T	152D	24F-12R	54.3		No
DT60GE	33060.00	24460.00	26120.00	26900.00	Perkins	3T	152D	24F-12R	54.3		No
DT60LP	32410.00	23980.00	25600.00	26370.00	Perkins	3T	152D	24F-12R	54.3		No
DT60V	40410.00	29900.00	31920.00	32880.00	Perkins	3T	152D	24F-12R	54.3		C,H
DT60VP	31630.00	23410.00	24990.00	25740.00	Perkins	3T	152D	24F-12R	54.3		No
R60FP	26315.00	19470.00	20790.00	21410.00	Perkins	3T	152D	24F-12R	54.3		No
R60V	33675.00	24920.00	26600.00	27400.00	Perkins	3T	152D	24F-12R	54.3		C,H,A
R60VP	27720.00	20510.00	21900.00	22560.00	Perkins	3T	152D	24F-12R	54.3		No
DT65	39020.00	28880.00	30830.00	31760.00	Perkins	4	236D	24F-12R	61.0		C,H,A
DT65F	43200.00	31970.00	34130.00	35150.00	Perkins	4	236D	24F-12R	61.0		C,H,A
DT65FP	32769.00	24250.00	25890.00	26670.00	Perkins	4	236D	24F-12R	61.0		No
DT65GE	33445.00	24750.00	26420.00	27210.00	Perkins	4	236D	24F-12R	61.0		No
DT65L	42985.00	31810.00	33960.00	34980.00	Perkins	4	236D	24F-12R	61.0		C,H,A

Landini (Cont.)

1998 (Cont.)

Model	Approx. Retail Price New	Estimated Average Value Less Repairs Fair	Good	Premium	Engine Make	No. Cyls.	Displ. Cu.-In.	No. Speeds	P.T.O. H.P.	Approx. Shipping Wt.-Lbs.	Cab
DT65LP	32830.00	**24290.00**	**25940.00**	**26720.00**	Perkins	4	236D	24F-12R	61.0		No
DT65V	42282.00	**31290.00**	**33400.00**	**34400.00**	Perkins	4	236D	24F-12R	61.0		C,H,A
DT65VP	32815.00	**24280.00**	**25920.00**	**26700.00**	Perkins	4	236D	24F-12R	61.0		No
R65	33915.00	**25100.00**	**26790.00**	**27590.00**	Perkins	4	236D	24F-12R	61.0		C,H,A
R65F	36535.00	**27040.00**	**28860.00**	**29730.00**	Perkins	4	236D	24F-12R	61.0		C,H,A
R65FP	26872.00	**19890.00**	**21230.00**	**21870.00**	Perkins	4	236D	24F-12R	61.0		No
R65GE	27720.00	**20510.00**	**21900.00**	**22560.00**	Perkins	4	236D	24F-12R	61.0		No
R65LP	27205.00	**20130.00**	**21490.00**	**22140.00**	Perkins	4	236D	24F-12R	61.0		No
R65LP HC	26980.00	**19970.00**	**21310.00**	**21950.00**	Deutz	4T	166D	12F-12R	61.0		No
R65V	35525.00	**26290.00**	**28070.00**	**28910.00**	Perkins	4	236D	24F-12R	61.0		C,H,A
R65VP	28040.00	**20750.00**	**22150.00**	**22820.00**	Perkins	4	236D	24F-12R	61.0		No
DT70 TECHNO	34727.00	**25700.00**	**27430.00**	**28250.00**	Perkins	4	236D	12F-12R	57.8		No
DT70 TECHNO w/Cab	39670.00	**29360.00**	**31340.00**	**32280.00**	Perkins	4	236D	12F-12R	57.8		C,H,A
DT70 TOP	35767.00	**26470.00**	**28260.00**	**29110.00**	Perkins	4	236D	12F-12R	57.2		No
DT70 TOP w/Cab	40432.00	**29920.00**	**31940.00**	**32900.00**	Perkins	4	236D	12F-12R	57.8		C,H,A
C75 W/Blade	50885.00	**37660.00**	**40200.00**	**41410.00**	Perkins	4	236D	16F-8R	61.25		No
C75F	36700.00	**27160.00**	**28990.00**	**29860.00**	Perkins	4	236D	16F-8R	61.25		No
DT75	40870.00	**30240.00**	**32290.00**	**33260.00**	Perkins	4	236D	24F-12R	64.37		C,H,A
DT75F	43835.00	**32440.00**	**34630.00**	**35670.00**	Perkins	4	236D	24F-12R	64.37		C,H,A
DT75FP	33651.00	**24900.00**	**26580.00**	**27380.00**	Perkins	4	236D	24F-12R	64.37		No
DT75GE	34990.00	**25890.00**	**27640.00**	**28470.00**	Perkins	4	236D	24F-12R	64.37		No
DT75L	43620.00	**32280.00**	**34460.00**	**35490.00**	Perkins	4	236D	24F-12R	64.37		C,H,A
DT75LP	33335.00	**24670.00**	**26340.00**	**27130.00**	Perkins	4	236D	24F-12R	64.37		No
DT75V	43680.00	**32320.00**	**34510.00**	**35550.00**	Perkins	4	236D	24F-12R	64.37		C,H,A
DT75VP	36245.00	**26820.00**	**28630.00**	**29490.00**	Perkins	4	236D	24F-12R	64.37		No
R75F	37452.00	**27710.00**	**29590.00**	**30480.00**	Perkins	4	236D	24F-12R	64.37		C,H,A
R75FP	28065.00	**20770.00**	**22170.00**	**22840.00**	Perkins	4	236D	24F-12R	64.37		No
R75V	36470.00	**26990.00**	**28810.00**	**29670.00**	Perkins	4	236D	24F-12R	64.37		C,H,A
R75VP	30535.00	**22600.00**	**24120.00**	**24840.00**	Perkins	4	236D	24F-12R	64.37		No
C85 w/Blade	56371.00	**41720.00**	**44530.00**	**45870.00**	Perkins	4	248D	16F-8R	71.25		No
C85F	41240.00	**30520.00**	**32580.00**	**33560.00**	Perkins	4	248D	16F-8R	71.25		No
DT85	43105.00	**31900.00**	**34050.00**	**35070.00**	Perkins	4	248D	24F-12R	72.1	8075	C,H,A
DT85F	45065.00	**33350.00**	**35600.00**	**36670.00**	Perkins	4	248D	24F-12R	72.1		C,H,A
DT85FP	34856.00	**25790.00**	**27540.00**	**28370.00**	Perkins	4	248D	24F-12R	72.1		No
DT85GE	36520.00	**27030.00**	**28850.00**	**29720.00**	Perkins	4	248D	24F-12R	72.1		No
DT85L	44845.00	**33190.00**	**35430.00**	**36490.00**	Perkins	4	248D	24F-12R	72.1		C,H,A
DT85LP	34537.00	**25560.00**	**27280.00**	**28100.00**	Perkins	4	248D	24F-12R	72.1		No
R85	36765.00	**27210.00**	**29040.00**	**29910.00**	Perkins	4	248D	24F-12R	72.1	7412	C,H,A
R85F	38585.00	**28550.00**	**30480.00**	**31390.00**	Perkins	4	248D	24F-12R	72.1		C,H,A
R85FP	29115.00	**21550.00**	**23000.00**	**23690.00**	Perkins	4	248D	24F-12R	72.1		No
RP85LP HC	29116.00	**21550.00**	**23000.00**	**23690.00**	Deutz	4T	166D	12F-12R	72.1		No
C95 w/Blade	60045.00	**44430.00**	**47440.00**	**48860.00**	Perkins	4T	236D	16F-8R	84.0		No
DT95	44930.00	**33250.00**	**35500.00**	**36570.00**	Perkins	4T	236D	24F-12R	82.6		C,H,A
DT95 GT	50610.00	**37450.00**	**39980.00**	**41180.00**	Perkins	4T	236D	12F-12R	82.6		C,H,A
DT105 TECHNO	50050.00	**37040.00**	**39540.00**	**40730.00**	Perkins	6	366D	18F-18R	95.0		No
DT105 TECHNO w/Cab	52195.00	**38620.00**	**41230.00**	**42470.00**	Perkins	6	366D	18F-18R	95.0		C,H,A
DT105 TOP w/Cab	58610.00	**43370.00**	**46300.00**	**47690.00**	Perkins	6	366D	36F-36R	95.0		C,H,A
DT115 TECHNO	53646.00	**39700.00**	**42380.00**	**43650.00**	Perkins	6	366D	18F-18R	101.0		No
DT115 TECHNO w/Cab	56420.00	**41750.00**	**44570.00**	**45910.00**	Perkins	6	366D	18F-18R	101.0		C,H,A
DT115 TOP w/Cab	62915.00	**46560.00**	**49700.00**	**51190.00**	Perkins	6	366D	36F-36R	101.0		C,H,A
DT130 TECHNO	56660.00	**41930.00**	**44760.00**	**46100.00**	Perkins	6T	366D	18F-18R	117.0		No
DT130 TECHNO w/Cab	59435.00	**43980.00**	**46950.00**	**48360.00**	Perkins	6T	366D	18F-18R	117.0		C,H,A
DT130 TOP	65885.00	**48760.00**	**52050.00**	**53610.00**	Perkins	6T	366D	36F-36R	117.0		No
DT145 TECHNO	71840.00	**53160.00**	**56750.00**	**58450.00**	Perkins	6T	366D	18F-18R	128.0		No
DT145 TECHNO w/Cab	74025.00	**54780.00**	**58480.00**	**60230.00**	Perkins	6T	366D	18F-18R	128.0		C,H,A
DT145 TOP w/Cab	81205.00	**60090.00**	**64150.00**	**66080.00**	Perkins	6T	366D	36F-36R	128.0		C,H,A
DT165 TOP w/Cab	89475.00	**66210.00**	**70690.00**	**72810.00**	Perkins	6T	366D	36F-36R	148.0		C,H,A
DT5860	27865.00	**20620.00**	**22010.00**	**22670.00**	Perkins	3	152D	12F-4R	42.9		No
R5860	22420.00	**16590.00**	**17710.00**	**18240.00**	Perkins	3	152D	12F-4R	42.9	4971	No
DT6060	28755.00	**21280.00**	**22720.00**	**23400.00**	Perkins	3T	152D	12F-4R	54.3	5856	No
R6060	23760.00	**17580.00**	**18770.00**	**19330.00**	Perkins	3T	152D	12F-4R	54.3	5237	No
DT6860	30245.00	**22380.00**	**23890.00**	**24610.00**	Perkins	4	236D	12F-12R	57.26	6122	No
R6860	24915.00	**18440.00**	**19680.00**	**20270.00**	Perkins	4	236D	12F-12R	57.26	5546	No
DT6880	44510.00	**32940.00**	**35160.00**	**36220.00**	Perkins	4	236D	12F-12R	57.26	7611	C,H,A
R6880	35715.00	**26430.00**	**28220.00**	**29070.00**	Perkins	4	236D	12F-12R	57.26	6947	C,H,A
DT7860	32395.00	**23970.00**	**25590.00**	**26360.00**	Perkins	4	236D	12F-12R	64.37	6874	No
DT7860HC	33175.00	**24550.00**	**26210.00**	**27000.00**	Perkins	4	236D	12F-12R	64.37	6891	No
R7860	27140.00	**20080.00**	**21440.00**	**22080.00**	Perkins	4	236D	12F-12R	64.37	6387	No
R7860HC	27870.00	**20620.00**	**22020.00**	**22680.00**	Perkins	4	236D	12F-12R	64.37	6188	No
DT7880	46050.00	**34080.00**	**36380.00**	**37470.00**	Perkins	4	236D	12F-12R	64.37	8075	C,H,A
R7880	39645.00	**29340.00**	**31320.00**	**32260.00**	Perkins	4	236D	12F-12R	64.37	7611	C,H,A
DT8860	36305.00	**26870.00**	**28680.00**	**29540.00**	Perkins	4	248D	12F-12R	74.83	6962	No
DT8860HC	35446.00	**26230.00**	**28000.00**	**28840.00**	Perkins	4	248D	12F-12R	74.83	7102	No
R8860	28990.00	**21450.00**	**22900.00**	**23590.00**	Perkins	4	248D	12F-12R	74.83	6476	No
R8860HC	28820.00	**21330.00**	**22770.00**	**23450.00**	Perkins	4	248D	12F-12R	74.83	6531	No
DT8880	47326.00	**35020.00**	**37390.00**	**38510.00**	Perkins	4	248D	12F-12R	74.83	8451	C,H,A
DT8880HC	46650.00	**34520.00**	**36850.00**	**37960.00**	Perkins	4	248D	12F-12R	74.83	8418	C,H,A
R8880	40737.00	**30150.00**	**32180.00**	**33150.00**	Perkins	4	248D	12F-12R	74.83	7633	C,H,A
RS 9065	32690.00	**24190.00**	**25830.00**	**26610.00**	Deutz	4T	166D	12F-12R	57.0		No
RV 9065	34440.00	**25490.00**	**27210.00**	**28030.00**	Deutz	4T	166D	12F-12R	57.0		No
DT9880	50790.00	**37590.00**	**40120.00**	**41320.00**	Perkins	4T	236D	12F-12R	88.0	8850	C,H,A
DT9880HC	50056.00	**37040.00**	**39540.00**	**40730.00**	Perkins	4T	236D	12F-12R	88.0	8529	C,H,A
R9880	45545.00	**33700.00**	**35980.00**	**37060.00**	Perkins	4T	236D	12F-12R	88.0	8407	C,H,A

Landini (Cont.)

Model	Approx. Retail Price New	Estimated Average Value Less Repairs Fair	Good	Premium	Engine Make	No. Cyls.	Displ. Cu.-In.	No. Speeds	P.T.O. H.P.	Approx. Shipping Wt.-Lbs.	Cab
1999											
DT60 TECHNO	33000.00	27390.00	28710.00	29570.00	Perkins	3T	152D	12F-12R	51.3		No
DT60 TECHNO w/Cab	38265.00	31760.00	33290.00	34290.00	Perkins	3T	152D	12F-12R	51.3		C,H,A
DT60 TOP	34015.00	28230.00	29590.00	30480.00	Perkins	3T	152D	12F-12R	51.3		No
DT60 TOP w/Cab	39000.00	32370.00	33930.00	34950.00	Perkins	3T	152D	12F-12R	51.3		C,H,A
C65 w/Blade	52570.00	43630.00	45740.00	47110.00	Perkins	4	236D	16F-8R	61.0		No
C65F w/Blade	45110.00	37440.00	39250.00	40430.00	Perkins	4	236D	16F-8R	61.0		No
DT65	41420.00	34380.00	36040.00	37120.00	Perkins	4	236D	12F-12R	61.0		C,H,A
DT65F	46345.00	38470.00	40320.00	41530.00	Perkins	4	236D	12F-12R	61.0		C,H,A
DT65FP	33595.00	27880.00	29230.00	30110.00	Perkins	4	236D	12F-12R	61.0		No
DT65GE	34370.00	28530.00	29900.00	30800.00	Perkins	4	236D	12F-12R	61.0		No
DT65V	43370.00	36000.00	37730.00	38860.00	Perkins	4	236D	12F-12R	61.0		C,H,A
R65	36490.00	30290.00	31750.00	32700.00	Perkins	4	236D	24F-12R	61.0		C,H,A
R65F	37495.00	31120.00	32620.00	33600.00	Perkins	4	236D	24F-12R	61.0		C,H,A
R65FP	27830.00	23100.00	24210.00	24940.00	Perkins	4	236D	24F-12R	61.0		No
R65GE	28350.00	23530.00	24670.00	25410.00	Perkins	4	236D	24F-12R	61.0		No
R65LP	29265.00	24290.00	25460.00	26220.00	Perkins	4	236D	24F-12R	61.0		No
R65V	37695.00	31290.00	32800.00	33780.00	Perkins	4	236D	24F-12R	61.0		C,H,A
DT70 TECHNO	35365.00	29350.00	30770.00	31690.00	Perkins	4	236D	12F-12R	57.8		No
DT70 TECHNO w/Cab	40935.00	33980.00	35610.00	36680.00	Perkins	4	236D	12F-12R	57.8		C,H,A
DT70 TOP	36440.00	30250.00	31700.00	32650.00	Perkins	4	236D	12F-12R	57.2		No
DT70 TOP w/Cab	41720.00	34630.00	36300.00	37390.00	Perkins	4	236D	12F-12R	57.8		C,H,A
C85 w/Blade	60860.00	50510.00	52950.00	54540.00	Perkins	4	248D	16F-8R	71.25		No
C85F	51555.00	42790.00	44850.00	46200.00	Perkins	4	248D	16F-8R	71.25		No
DT85	44590.00	37010.00	38790.00	39950.00	Perkins	4	248D	12F-12R	72.1	8075	C,H,A
DT85F	46080.00	38250.00	40090.00	41290.00	Perkins	4	248D	12F-12R	72.1		C,H,A
DT85FP	35770.00	29690.00	31120.00	32050.00	Perkins	4	248D	12F-12R	72.1		No
DT85GE	37385.00	31030.00	32530.00	33510.00	Perkins	4	248D	12F-12R	72.1		No
R85	38370.00	31850.00	33380.00	34380.00	Perkins	4	248D	12F-12R	72.1	7412	C,H,A
R85F	39990.00	33190.00	34790.00	35830.00	Perkins	4	248D	12F-12R	72.1		C,H,A
R85FP	29880.00	24800.00	26000.00	26780.00	Perkins	4	248D	12F-12R	72.1		No
RP85LP HC	31505.00	26150.00	27410.00	28230.00	Deutz	4T	166D	12F-12R	72.1		No
C95 w/Blade	63920.00	53050.00	55610.00	57280.00	Perkins	4T	236D	16F-8R	84.0		No
DT95	47470.00	39400.00	41300.00	42540.00	Perkins	4T	236D	12F-12R	82.6		C,H,A
DT95 GT	53055.00	44040.00	46160.00	47550.00	Perkins	4T	236D	12F-12R	82.6		C,H,A
DT105 TECHNO	50410.00	41840.00	43860.00	45180.00	Perkins	6	366D	18F-18R	95.0		No
DT105 TECHNO w/Cab	53310.00	44250.00	46380.00	47770.00	Perkins	6	366D	18F-18R	95.0		C,H,A
DT105 TOP w/Cab	59685.00	49540.00	51930.00	53490.00	Perkins	6	366D	36F-36R	95.0		C,H,A
DT115 TECHNO	55760.00	46280.00	48510.00	49970.00	Perkins	6	366D	18F-18R	101.0		No
DT115 TECHNO w/Cab	58625.00	48660.00	51000.00	52530.00	Perkins	6	366D	18F-18R	101.0		C,H,A
DT115 TOP w/Cab	65265.00	54170.00	56780.00	58480.00	Perkins	6	366D	36F-36R	101.0		C,H,A
DT130 TECHNO	58875.00	48870.00	51220.00	52760.00	Perkins	6T	366D	18F-18R	117.0		No
DT130 TECHNO w/Cab	61740.00	51240.00	53710.00	55320.00	Perkins	6T	366D	18F-18R	117.0		C,H,A
DT130 TOP w/Cab	69000.00	57270.00	60030.00	61830.00	Perkins	6T	366D	36F-36R	117.0		C,H,A
DT145 TECHNO	72560.00	60230.00	63130.00	65020.00	Perkins	6T	366D	18F-18R	128.0		No
DT145 TECHNO w/Cab	75495.00	62660.00	65680.00	67650.00	Perkins	6T	366D	18F-18R	128.0		C,H,A
DT145 TOP w/Cab	82665.00	68610.00	71920.00	74080.00	Perkins	6T	366D	36F-36R	128.0		C,H,A
DT165 TOP w/Cab	91210.00	75700.00	79350.00	81730.00	Perkins	6T	366D	36F-36R	148.0		C,H,A
DT6860	33085.00	27460.00	28780.00	29640.00	Perkins	4	236D	12F-12R	61.0	6122	No
R6860	28155.00	23370.00	24500.00	25240.00	Perkins	4	236D	12F-12R	61.0	5546	No
DT8860	36690.00	30450.00	31920.00	32880.00	Perkins	4	248D	12F-12R	72.1	6962	No
DT8860HC	37886.00	31450.00	32960.00	33950.00	Perkins	4	248D	12F-12R	72.1	7102	No
R8860	31955.00	26520.00	27800.00	28630.00	Perkins	4	248D	12F-12R	72.1	6476	No
R8860HC	31690.00	25730.00	26970.00	27780.00	Perkins	4	248D	12F-12R	72.1	6531	No
DT8880	46290.00	38420.00	40270.00	41480.00	Perkins	4	248D	12F-12R	72.1	8451	C,H,A
DT8880HC	46540.00	38630.00	40490.00	41710.00	Perkins	4	248D	12F-12R	72.1	8418	C,H,A
R8880	39875.00	33100.00	34690.00	35730.00	Perkins	4	248D	12F-12R	72.1	7633	C,H,A
R9060	34615.00	28730.00	30120.00	31020.00	Perkins	4T	0D	12F-12R	82.6		C,H,A
DT9060	40185.00	33350.00	34960.00	36010.00	Perkins	4T	0D	12F-12R	82.6		C,H,A
R9060HC	34350.00	28510.00	29890.00	30790.00	Perkins	4T	0D	12F-12R	82.6		C,H,A
DT9060HC	42185.00	35010.00	36700.00	37800.00	Perkins	4T	0D	12F-12R	82.6		C,H,A
DT9880	50915.00	42260.00	44300.00	45630.00	Perkins	4T	236D	12F-12R	86.3	8850	C,H,A
DT9880HC	50556.00	41960.00	43980.00	45300.00	Perkins	4T	236D	12F-12R	86.3	8529	C,H,A
R9880	44450.00	36890.00	38670.00	39830.00	Perkins	4T	236D	12F-12R	86.3	8407	C,H,A

Long

Model	Approx. Retail Price New	Fair	Good	Premium	Engine Make	No. Cyls.	Displ. Cu.-In.	No. Speeds	P.T.O. H.P.	Approx. Shipping Wt.-Lbs.	Cab
1972											
445	3547.00	1240.00	1560.00	1750.00	UTB	3	143D	6F-2R	40.00	3880	No
1973											
445	4454.00	1600.00	2000.00	2220.00	UTB	3	143D	6F-2R	41.93	3880	No
445 DT	5087.00	1830.00	2290.00	2540.00	UTB	3	143D	6F-2R	41.90	4420	No
550	5539.00	1990.00	2490.00	2760.00	UTB	4	191D	8F-2R	53.61	4510	No
R9500	9844.00	3540.00	4430.00	4920.00	Perkins	6	354D	12F-4R	97.72	7700	No

DT - Front Wheel Assist

Model	Approx. Retail Price New	Fair	Good	Premium	Engine Make	No. Cyls.	Displ. Cu.-In.	No. Speeds	P.T.O. H.P.	Approx. Shipping Wt.-Lbs.	Cab
1974											
350	4015.00	1490.00	1850.00	2050.00	UTB	3	143D	6F-2R	32.00	3200	No
445	4684.00	1730.00	2160.00	2400.00	UTB	3	143D	6F-2R	41.93	3880	No
445 DT	5341.00	1980.00	2460.00	2730.00	UTB	3	143D	6F-2R	41.90	4420	No
550	5816.00	2150.00	2680.00	2980.00	UTB	4	191D	8F-2R	53.61	4510	No
R9500	11933.00	4420.00	5490.00	6090.00	Perkins	6	354D	12F-4R	97.72	7700	No

DT - Front Wheel Assist

Long (Cont.)

Model	Approx. Retail Price New	Estimated Average Value Less Repairs Fair	Good	Premium	Engine Make	No. Cyls.	Displ. Cu.-In.	No. Speeds	P.T.O. H.P.	Approx. Shipping Wt.-Lbs.	Cab
1975											
350	4567.00	1740.00	2150.00	2390.00	UTB	3	143D	6F-2R	32.00	3200	No
445	5336.00	2030.00	2510.00	2790.00	UTB	3	143D	6F-2R	41.93	3880	No
445 DT	6029.00	2290.00	2830.00	3140.00	UTB	3	143D	6F-2R	41.90	4220	No
550	6598.00	2510.00	3100.00	3440.00	UTB	4	191D	8F-2R	53.61	4510	No
900	10321.00	3920.00	4850.00	5380.00	Zetor	4	285D	16F-8R	72.88	7750	No
1100	11413.00	4340.00	5360.00	5950.00	Zetor	4T	285D	16F-8R	92.00	8500	No
R9500	12888.00	4900.00	6060.00	6730.00	Perkins	6	354D	12F-4R	97.72	770	No
DT - Front Wheel Assist											
1976											
350	5184.00	2020.00	2490.00	2740.00	UTB	3	143D	6F-2R	32.00	3200	No
445	5607.00	2190.00	2690.00	2960.00	UTB	3	143D	6F-2R	41.93	3880	No
445 DT	6899.00	2690.00	3310.00	3640.00	UTB	3	143D	6F-2R	41.90	4420	No
560	7136.00	2780.00	3430.00	3770.00	UTB	4	191D	8F-2R	53.61	4510	No
560 DT	8476.00	3310.00	4070.00	4480.00	UTB	4	191D	8F-2R	53.60	4750	No
900	10321.00	4030.00	4950.00	5450.00	Zetor	4	285D	16F-8R	72.88	7750	No
1100	11413.00	4450.00	5480.00	6030.00	Zetor	4T	285D	16F-8R	92.00	8500	No
1300	14997.00	5850.00	7200.00	7920.00	Zetor	6	417D	16F-8R	105.00	9000	No
DT - Front Wheel Assist											
1977											
360	5737.00	2300.00	2810.00	3090.00	UTB	3	143D	6F-2R	32.00	3750	No
445 DT	7572.00	3030.00	3710.00	4080.00	UTB	3	143D	6F-2R	41.90	4420	No
460	6393.00	2560.00	3130.00	3440.00	UTB	3	143D	6F-2R	41.93	3850	No
560	7826.00	3130.00	3840.00	4220.00	UTB	4	191D	8F-2R	53.61	4510	No
560 DT	9490.00	3800.00	4650.00	5120.00	UTB	4	191D	8F-2R	53.60	4750	No
900	11481.00	4590.00	5630.00	6190.00	Zetor	4	285D	16F-8R	72.88	7750	No
1100	12517.00	5010.00	6130.00	6740.00	Zetor	4T	285D	16F-8R	92.00	8500	No
1300	15447.00	6180.00	7570.00	8330.00	Zetor	6	417D	16F-8R	105.00	9000	No
DT - Front Wheel Assist											
1978											
360	6056.00	2480.00	3030.00	3330.00	UTB	3	143D	6F-2R	32.00	3750	No
460	6763.00	2770.00	3380.00	3720.00	UTB	3	143D	6F-2R	41.93	3850	No
460 DT	8281.00	3400.00	4140.00	4550.00	UTB	3	143D	6F-2R	41.90	4420	No
560	8248.00	3380.00	4120.00	4530.00	UTB	4	191D	8F-2R	53.61	4510	No
560 DT	9965.00	4090.00	4980.00	5480.00	UTB	4	191D	8F-2R	53.60	4750	No
910	12055.00	4940.00	6030.00	6630.00	Zetor	4	278D	16F-8R	72.88	7750	No
910 DT	15415.00	6320.00	7710.00	8480.00	Zetor	4	278D	16F-8R	72.80	8740	No
1110	13143.00	5390.00	6570.00	7230.00	Zetor	4T	285D	16F-8R	92.00	8500	No
1110 DT	16513.00	6770.00	8260.00	9090.00	Zetor	4T	285D	16F-8R	92.00	8890	No
1310	16219.00	6650.00	8110.00	8920.00	Zetor	6	417D	16F-8R	105.00	9000	No
1310 DT	19453.00	7980.00	9730.00	10700.00	Zetor	6	417D	16F-8R	105.00	9990	No
DT - Front Wheel Assist											
1979											
360	7272.00	3050.00	3710.00	4040.00	UTB	3	143D	6F-2R	32.00	3750	No
460	8099.00	3400.00	4130.00	4500.00	UTB	3	143D	8F-2R	41.93	3850	No
460 DT	10597.00	4450.00	5400.00	5890.00	UTB	3	143D	8F-2R	41.90	4420	No
510	8674.00	3640.00	4420.00	4820.00	UTB	3	143D	8F-2R	48.52	3900	No
510 DT	11310.00	4750.00	5770.00	6290.00	UTB	3	143D	8F-2R	48.52	4470	No
560 DT	10047.00	4220.00	5120.00	5580.00	UTB	4	191D	8F-2R	53.60	4750	No
610	10210.00	4290.00	5210.00	5680.00	UTB	4	191D	8F-2R	64.18	4560	No
610 DT	12930.00	5430.00	6590.00	7180.00	UTB	4	191D	8F-2R	64.18	4800	No
910	12537.00	5270.00	6390.00	6970.00	Zetor	4	278D	16F-8R	72.88	7750	No
910 DT	16340.00	6860.00	8330.00	9080.00	Zetor	4	278D	16F-8R	72.88	8740	No
1110	13668.00	5740.00	6970.00	7600.00	Zetor	4T	285D	16F-8R	92.00	8500	No
1110 DT	17504.00	7350.00	8930.00	9730.00	Zetor	4T	285D	16F-8R	92.00	8890	No
1310	16867.00	7080.00	8600.00	9370.00	Zetor	6	417D	16F-8R	105.00	9000	No
1310 DT	20621.00	8660.00	10520.00	11470.00	Zetor	6	417D	16F-8R	105.00	9990	No
DT - Front Wheel Assist											
1980											
260 C	6000.00	2580.00	3120.00	3370.00	UTB	2	95D	6F-2R	24.00	3180	No
310	7000.00	3010.00	3640.00	3930.00	UTB	2	110D	6F-2R	28.00	3250	No
310 DT	8144.00	3500.00	4240.00	4580.00	UTB	2	110D	6F-2R	28.00	3820	No
360	8026.00	3450.00	4170.00	4500.00	UTB	3	143D	6F-2R	36.16	3750	No
460	8800.00	3780.00	4580.00	4950.00	UTB	3	143D	8F-2R	41.93	3850	No
460 DT	11500.00	4950.00	5980.00	6460.00	UTB	3	143D	8F-2R	41.90	4420	No
510	9573.00	4120.00	4980.00	5380.00	UTB	3	165D	8F-2R	49.15	3900	No
510 DT	12100.00	5200.00	6290.00	6790.00	UTB	3	165D	8F-2R	49.35	4470	No
610	11269.00	4850.00	5860.00	6330.00	UTB	4	220D	8F-2R	64.33	4560	No
610 DT	14273.00	6140.00	7420.00	8010.00	UTB	4	220D	8F-2R	64.00	4800	No
910	15495.00	6660.00	8060.00	8710.00	Zetor	4	278D	16F-8R	72.88	7750	No
910 DT	19663.00	8460.00	10230.00	11050.00	Zetor	4	278D	16F-8R	72.88	8740	No
1310	20959.00	9010.00	10900.00	11770.00	Zetor	6	417D	16F-8R	105.00	9000	No
1310 DT	24811.00	10670.00	12900.00	13930.00	Zetor	6	417D	16F-8R	105.00	9990	No
DT - Front Wheel Assist											
1981											
260 C	6000.00	2640.00	3180.00	3430.00	UTB	2	95D	6F-2R	24.00	3195	No
310	7000.00	3080.00	3710.00	4010.00	UTB	2	110D	6F-2R	28.00	3250	No
310 DT	8150.00	3590.00	4320.00	4670.00	UTB	2	110D	6F-2R	28.00	3820	No
360	8040.00	3540.00	4260.00	4600.00	UTB	3	143D	6F-2R	36.16	3750	No

Long (Cont.)

1981 (Cont.)

Model	Approx. Retail Price New	Estimated Average Value Less Repairs Fair	Good	Premium	Engine Make	No. Cyls.	Displ. Cu.-In.	No. Speeds	P.T.O. H.P.	Approx. Shipping Wt.-Lbs.	Cab
460	8800.00	3870.00	4660.00	5030.00	UTB	3	143D	8F-2R	41.93	3850	No
460 DT	11500.00	5060.00	6100.00	6590.00	UTB	3	143D	8F-2R	41.90	4420	No
510	9575.00	4210.00	5080.00	5490.00	UTB	3	165D	8F-2R	49.15	3900	No
510 DT	12100.00	5320.00	6410.00	6920.00	UTB	3	165D	8F-2R	49.35	4470	No
610	11300.00	4970.00	5990.00	6470.00	UTB	4	220D	8F-2R	64.33	4560	No
610 DT	14275.00	6280.00	7570.00	8180.00	UTB	4	220D	8F-2R	64.00	4800	No
910	15500.00	6820.00	8220.00	8880.00	Zetor	4	278D	16F-8R	72.88	7750	No
910 DT	19675.00	8660.00	10430.00	11260.00	Zetor	4	278D	16F-8R	72.88	8740	No
1310	20960.00	9220.00	11110.00	12000.00	Zetor	6	417D	16F-8R	105.00	9000	No
1310 DT	24825.00	10920.00	13160.00	14210.00	Zetor	6	417D	16F-8R	105.00	9990	No

DT - Front Wheel Assist

1982

Model	Approx. Retail Price New	Fair	Good	Premium	Make	No. Cyls.	Displ. Cu.-In.	No. Speeds	P.T.O. H.P.	Approx. Shipping Wt.-Lbs.	Cab
260 C	6000.00	2700.00	3240.00	3500.00	UTB	2	95D	6F-2R	24.00	3195	No
310	7000.00	3150.00	3780.00	4080.00	UTB	2	110D	6F-2R	28.00	3250	No
310 DT	8150.00	3670.00	4400.00	4750.00	UTB	2	110D	6F-2R	28.00	3820	No
360	8050.00	3620.00	4350.00	4700.00	UTB	3	143D	6F-2R	36.16	3750	No
460	8800.00	3960.00	4750.00	5130.00	UTB	3	143D	8F-2R	41.93	3850	No
460 DT	11500.00	5180.00	6210.00	6710.00	UTB	3	143D	8F-2R	41.90	4420	No
510	9575.00	4310.00	5170.00	5580.00	UTB	3	165D	8F-2R	49.15	3900	No
510 DT	12100.00	5450.00	6530.00	7050.00	UTB	3	165D	8F-2R	49.35	4470	No
610	11350.00	5110.00	6130.00	6620.00	UTB	4	220D	8F-2R	64.33	4560	No
610 DT	14300.00	6440.00	7720.00	8340.00	UTB	4	220D	8F-2R	64.00	4800	No
910	15600.00	7020.00	8420.00	9090.00	Zetor	4	278D	16F-8R	72.88	7750	No
910 DT	19700.00	8870.00	10640.00	11490.00	Zetor	4	278D	16F-8R	72.88	8740	No
1310	21000.00	9450.00	11340.00	12250.00	Zetor	6	417D	16F-8R	105.00	9000	No
1310 DT	24900.00	11210.00	13450.00	14530.00	Zetor	6	417D	16F-8R	105.00	9990	No

DT - Front Wheel Assist

1983

Model	Approx. Retail Price New	Fair	Good	Premium	Make	No. Cyls.	Displ. Cu.-In.	No. Speeds	P.T.O. H.P.	Approx. Shipping Wt.-Lbs.	Cab
260 C	6000.00	2760.00	3300.00	3560.00	UTB	2	95D	6F-2R	24.00	3195	No
310 DT 4WD	8200.00	3770.00	4510.00	4870.00	UTB	2	110D	6F-2R	28.00	3820	No
360	8100.00	3730.00	4460.00	4820.00	UTB	3	143D	6F-2R	36.16	3750	No
460	8800.00	4050.00	4840.00	5230.00	UTB	3	143D	8F-2R	41.93	3850	No
460 DT 4WD	11500.00	5290.00	6330.00	6840.00	UTB	3	143D	8F-2R	41.00	4420	No
510	9600.00	4420.00	5280.00	5700.00	UTB	3	165D	8F-2R	49.15	3900	No
510 DT 4WD	12100.00	5570.00	6660.00	7190.00	UTB	3	165D	8F-2R	49.35	4470	No
610	11400.00	5240.00	6270.00	6770.00	UTB	4	220D	8F-2R	64.33	4560	No
610 DT 4WD	14300.00	6580.00	7870.00	8500.00	UTB	4	220D	8F-2R	64.00	4800	No
910	15700.00	7220.00	8640.00	9330.00	Zetor	4	278D	16F-8R	72.88	7750	No
910 DT 4WD	19800.00	9110.00	10890.00	11760.00	Zetor	4	278D	16F-8R	72.00	8740	No
1310	21000.00	9660.00	11550.00	12470.00	Zetor	6	417D	16F-8R	105.00	9000	No
1310 DT 4WD	24900.00	11450.00	13700.00	14800.00	Zetor	6	417D	16F-8R	105.00	9990	No

DT - Front Wheel Assist

1984

Model	Approx. Retail Price New	Fair	Good	Premium	Make	No. Cyls.	Displ. Cu.-In.	No. Speeds	P.T.O. H.P.	Approx. Shipping Wt.-Lbs.	Cab
260	6150.00	2890.00	3440.00	3720.00	UTB	2	95D	8F-2R	24.00	3195	No
260 C	6000.00	2820.00	3360.00	3630.00	UTB	2	95D	6F-2R	24.00	3195	No
310	7000.00	3290.00	3920.00	4230.00	UTB	2	110D	8F-2R	28.00	3750	No
310 DTC 4WD	8250.00	3880.00	4620.00	4990.00	UTB	2	110D	8F-2R	28.00	4430	No
360	8200.00	3850.00	4590.00	4960.00	UTB	3	143D	8F-2R	35.00	3750	No
360 DTC 4WD	9400.00	4420.00	5260.00	5680.00	UTB	3	143D	8F-2R	35.00	4430	No
460	8800.00	4140.00	4930.00	5320.00	UTB	3	143D	8F-2R	41.93	3850	No
460 DTC 4WD	11500.00	5410.00	6440.00	6960.00	UTB	3	143D	8F-2R	41.00	5263	No
510	9640.00	4530.00	5400.00	5830.00	UTB	3	165D	8F-2R	49.15	4113	No
510 DTC 4WD	12800.00	6020.00	7170.00	7740.00	UTB	3	165D	8F-2R	49.35	5263	No
610	11500.00	5410.00	6440.00	6960.00	UTB	4	220D	8F-2R	64.33	4330	No
610 DTC 4WD	14300.00	6720.00	8010.00	8650.00	UTB	4	220D	8F-2R	64.00	5150	No
610 DTE 4WD	14300.00	6720.00	8010.00	8650.00	UTB	4	220D	8F-2R	64.00	5500	No
610 DTE WT 4WD	15800.00	7430.00	8850.00	9560.00	UTB	4	220D	8F-2R	64.00	5700	No

DT - Front Wheel Assist

1985

Model	Approx. Retail Price New	Fair	Good	Premium	Make	No. Cyls.	Displ. Cu.-In.	No. Speeds	P.T.O. H.P.	Approx. Shipping Wt.-Lbs.	Cab
260	6200.00	2980.00	3530.00	3810.00	UTB	2	95D	8F-2R	24.00	3195	No
260 C	6000.00	2880.00	3420.00	3690.00	UTB	2	95D	6F-2R	24.00	3195	No
310	7000.00	3360.00	3990.00	4310.00	UTB	2	110D	8F-2R	28.00	3750	No
310 DTC 4WD	8300.00	3980.00	4730.00	5110.00	UTB	2	110D	8F-2R	28.00	4430	No
360	8250.00	3960.00	4700.00	5080.00	UTB	3	143D	8F-2R	35.00	3750	No
360 DTC 4WD	9450.00	4540.00	5390.00	5820.00	UTB	3	143D	8F-2R	35.00	4430	No
460	8840.00	4240.00	5040.00	5440.00	UTB	3	143D	8F-2R	41.93	3850	No
460 DTC 4WD	11500.00	5520.00	6560.00	7090.00	UTB	3	143D	8F-2R	41.00	5263	No
510	9648.00	4630.00	5500.00	5940.00	UTB	3	165D	8F-2R	49.15	4113	No
510 DTC 4WD	12900.00	6190.00	7350.00	7940.00	UTB	3	165D	8F-2R	49.35	5263	No
610	11550.00	5540.00	6580.00	7110.00	UTB	4	220D	8F-2R	64.33	4330	No
610 DTC 4WD	14300.00	6860.00	8150.00	8800.00	UTB	4	220D	8F-2R	64.00	5150	No
610 DTE 4WD	14400.00	6910.00	8210.00	8870.00	UTB	4	220D	8F-2R	64.00	5500	No
610 DTE WT 4WD	15900.00	7630.00	9060.00	9790.00	UTB	4	220D	8F-2R	64.00	5700	No

DT--Front Wheel Assist

1986

Model	Approx. Retail Price New	Fair	Good	Premium	Make	No. Cyls.	Displ. Cu.-In.	No. Speeds	P.T.O. H.P.	Approx. Shipping Wt.-Lbs.	Cab
260	6200.00	3040.00	3600.00	3890.00	UTB	2	95D	8F-2R	24.00	3195	No
260 C	6000.00	2940.00	3480.00	3760.00	UTB	2	95D	6F-2R	24.00	3195	No
310	7000.00	3430.00	4060.00	4390.00	UTB	2	110D	8F-2R	28.00	3750	No
310 DTC 4WD	8300.00	4070.00	4810.00	5200.00	UTB	2	110D	8F-2R	28.00	4430	No

Long (Cont.)

Model	Approx. Retail Price New	Estimated Average Value Less Repairs Fair	Good	Premium	Engine Make	No. Cyls.	Displ. Cu.-In.	No. Speeds	P.T.O. H.P.	Approx. Shipping Wt.-Lbs.	Cab
			1986 (Cont.)								
360	8250.00	4040.00	4790.00	5170.00	UTB	3	143D	8F-2R	35.00	3750	No
460	8860.00	4340.00	5140.00	5550.00	UTB	3	143D	8F-2R	41.93	3850	No
460 DTC 4WD	11500.00	5640.00	6670.00	7200.00	UTB	3	143D	8F-2R	41.00	5263	No
510	9648.00	4730.00	5600.00	6050.00	UTB	3	165D	8F-2R	49.15	4113	No
510 DTC 4WD	12150.00	5950.00	7050.00	7610.00	UTB	3	165D	8F-2R	49.35	5263	No
610	11730.00	5750.00	6800.00	7340.00	UTB	4	220D	8F-2R	64.33	4330	No
610 DTC 4WD	14315.00	7010.00	8300.00	8960.00	UTB	4	220D	8F-2R	64.00	5150	No
DT--Front Wheel Assist											
			1987								
360	8242.00	4120.00	4860.00	5250.00	UTB	3	143D	8F-2R	35.00	3850	No
460	8855.00	4430.00	5220.00	5640.00	UTB	3	143D	8F-2R	41.93	3850	No
460 DTC	11569.00	5790.00	6830.00	7380.00	UTB	3	143D	8F-2R	41.93	5263	No
460 Manual Shuttle	9660.00	4830.00	5700.00	6160.00	UTB	3	143D	8F-2R	41.93	3850	No
510	9648.00	4820.00	5690.00	6150.00	UTB	3	165D	8F-2R	49.15		No
510 DTC	12157.00	6080.00	7170.00	7740.00	UTB	3	165D	8F-2R	49.15	5350	No
610	11736.00	5870.00	6920.00	7470.00	UTB	4	219D	8F-2R	64.00	4630	No
610 DTC	14315.00	7160.00	8450.00	9130.00	UTB	4	219D	8F-2R	64.00	5892	No
DT - Front Wheel Assist											
			1988								
360	......	4410.00	5190.00	5550.00	UTB	3	143D	6F-2R	35.00	3750	No
460	......	4740.00	5580.00	5970.00	UTB	3	143D	8F-2R	35.00	4013	No
460 DTC 4WD	......	6200.00	7290.00	7800.00	UTB	3	143D	8F-2R	41.90	4653	No
460 SD	......	5180.00	6090.00	6520.00	UTB	3	143D	8F-8R	41.90	4247	No
510	......	5170.00	6080.00	6510.00	UTB	3	165D	8F-2R	49.15	4230	No
510 DTC 4WD	......	6480.00	7620.00	8150.00	UTB	3	165D	8F-2R	49.15	4350	No
610	......	6280.00	7390.00	7910.00	UTB	4	219D	8F-2R	64.00	4630	No
610 DTC 4WD	......	7670.00	9020.00	9650.00	UTB	4	219D	8F-2R	64.00	5892	No
DT - Front Wheel Assist											
			1989								
310	8514.00	4430.00	5190.00	5550.00	UTB	2	110D	8F-2R	28.00	3270	No
360	8981.00	4670.00	5480.00	5860.00	UTB	3	143D	8F-2R	35.00	3750	No
460	9608.00	5000.00	5860.00	6270.00	UTB	3	143D	8F-2R	41.90	3850	No
510	10647.00	5540.00	6500.00	6960.00	UTB	3	165D	8F-2R	49.15	4230	No
610	12333.00	6410.00	7520.00	8050.00	UTB	4	219D	8F-2R	64.00	4630	No
DT - Front Wheel Assist											
			1990								
2360	9530.00	5050.00	5910.00	6320.00	UTB	3	143D	8F-2R	35.00		No
2360 DTC 4WD	12850.00	6360.00	7440.00	7960.00	UTB	3	143D	8F-2R	35.00		No
2460	10060.00	5330.00	6240.00	6680.00	UTB	3	143D	8F-2R	41.90		No
2460 DTC 4WD	13225.00	7010.00	8200.00	8770.00	UTB	3	143D	8F-2R	41.90		No
2460 DTCSD Shuttle	14155.00	7500.00	8780.00	9400.00	UTB	3	143D	8F-2R	41.90		No
2460 SD Shuttle	10995.00	5830.00	6820.00	7300.00	UTB	3	143D	8F-2R	41.90		No
2510	10980.00	5820.00	6810.00	7290.00	UTB	3	165D	8F-2R	49.10		No
2510 DTC 4WD	13910.00	6890.00	8060.00	8620.00	UTB	3	165D	8F-2R	49.10		No
2510 DTCSD Shuttle	14835.00	7420.00	8680.00	9290.00	UTB	3	165D	8F-2R	49.10		No
2510 SD Shuttle	11910.00	6310.00	7380.00	7900.00	UTB	3	165D	8F-2R	49.10		No
2610	12550.00	6650.00	7780.00	8330.00	UTB	4	219D	8F-2R	64.00		No
2610 DTC 4WD	15860.00	7950.00	9300.00	9950.00	UTB	4	219D	8F-2R	64.00		No
2610 DTCSD 4WD	16790.00	8480.00	9920.00	10610.00	UTB	4	219D	8F-2R	64.00		No
2610 SD Shuttle	13480.00	7140.00	8360.00	8950.00	UTB	4	219D	8F-2R	64.00		No
DT - Front Wheel Assist											
			1991								
2360	10030.00	5420.00	6320.00	6700.00	UTB	3	143D	8F-2R	35.00		No
2360 DTC 4WD	13525.00	6760.00	7890.00	8360.00	UTB	3	143D	8F-2R	35.00		No
2460	10592.00	5720.00	6670.00	7070.00	UTB	3	143D	8F-2R	41.90		No
2460 DTC 4WD	13923.00	6980.00	8140.00	8630.00	UTB	3	143D	8F-2R	41.90		No
2460 DTCSD Shuttle	14902.00	7510.00	8760.00	9290.00	UTB	3	143D	8F-2R	41.90		No
2460 SD Shuttle	11572.00	6250.00	7290.00	7730.00	UTB	3	143D	8F-2R	41.90		No
2510	11556.00	6210.00	7250.00	7690.00	UTB	3	165D	8F-2R	49.10		No
2510 DTC 4WD	14639.00	7370.00	8590.00	9110.00	UTB	3	165D	8F-2R	49.10		No
2510 DTCSD Shuttle	15617.00	7890.00	9210.00	9760.00	UTB	3	165D	8F-2R	49.10		No
2510 SD Shuttle	12537.00	6770.00	7900.00	8370.00	UTB	3	165D	8F-2R	49.10		No
2610	13210.00	7130.00	8320.00	8820.00	UTB	4	219D	8F-2R	64.00		No
2610 DTC 4WD	16695.00	8480.00	9890.00	10480.00	UTB	4	219D	8F-2R	64.00		No
2610 DTCSD 4WD	17675.00	9010.00	10510.00	11140.00	UTB	4	219D	8F-2R	64.00		No
2610 SD Shuttle	14190.00	7660.00	8940.00	9480.00	UTB	4	219D	8F-2R	64.00		No
DT - Front Wheel Assist											
			1992								
2360	10350.00	5800.00	6620.00	7020.00	UTB	3	143D	8F-2R	35.00		No
2360 DTC 4WD	13950.00	7250.00	8290.00	8790.00	UTB	3	143D	8F-2R	35.00		No
2460	10900.00	6100.00	6980.00	7400.00	UTB	3	143D	8F-2R	41.90		No
2460 DTC 4WD	14340.00	7470.00	8540.00	9050.00	UTB	3	143D	8F-2R	41.90		No
2460 DTCSD Shuttle	15350.00	8040.00	9180.00	9730.00	UTB	3	143D	8F-2R	41.90		No
2460 SD Shuttle	11920.00	6680.00	7630.00	8090.00	UTB	3	143D	8F-2R	41.90		No
2510	11900.00	6440.00	7360.00	7800.00	UTB	3	165D	8F-2R	49.10		No
2510 DTC 4WD	15078.00	7880.00	9010.00	9550.00	UTB	3	165D	8F-2R	49.10		No
2510 DTCSD Shuttle	16085.00	8450.00	9650.00	10230.00	UTB	3	165D	8F-2R	49.10		No
2510 SD Shuttle	12920.00	7240.00	8270.00	8770.00	UTB	3	165D	8F-2R	49.10		No

Long (Cont.)

1992 (Cont.)

Model	Approx. Retail Price New	Estimated Average Value Less Repairs Fair	Good	Premium	Engine Make	No. Cyls.	Displ. Cu.-In.	No. Speeds	P.T.O. H.P.	Approx. Shipping Wt.-Lbs.	Cab
2610	13600.00	7620.00	8700.00	9220.00	UTB	4	219D	8F-2R	64.00		No
2610 DTC 4WD	17195.00	9070.00	10370.00	10990.00	UTB	4	219D	8F-2R	64.00		No
2610 DTCSD 4WD	18200.00	9630.00	11010.00	11670.00	UTB	4	219D	8F-2R	64.00		No
2610 SD Shuttle	14615.00	8180.00	9350.00	9910.00	UTB	4	219D	8F-2R	64.00		No

DT - Front Wheel Assist

1993

Model	Approx. Retail Price New	Fair	Good	Premium	Make	No. Cyls.	Displ. Cu.-In.	No. Speeds	P.T.O. H.P.	Approx. Shipping Wt.-Lbs.	Cab
2360	10350.00	6000.00	6730.00	7130.00	UTB	3	143D	8F-2R	35.00		No
2360 DTC 4WD	13950.00	8090.00	9070.00	9610.00	UTB	3	143D	8F-2R	35.00		No
2460	10900.00	6320.00	7090.00	7520.00	UTB	3	143D	8F-2R	41.90		No
2460 DTC 4WD	14340.00	8320.00	9320.00	9880.00	UTB	3	143D	8F-2R	41.90		No
2460 DTCSD Shuttle	15350.00	8900.00	9980.00	10580.00	UTB	3	143D	8F-2R	41.90		No
2460 SD Shuttle	11920.00	6910.00	7750.00	8220.00	UTB	3	143D	8F-2R	41.90		No
2510	11900.00	6900.00	7740.00	8200.00	UTB	3	165D	8F-2R	49.10		No
2510 DTC 4WD	15078.00	8750.00	9800.00	10390.00	UTB	3	165D	8F-2R	49.10		No
2510 DTCSD Shuttle	16085.00	9330.00	10460.00	11090.00	UTB	3	165D	8F-2R	49.10		No
2510 SD Shuttle	12920.00	7490.00	8400.00	8900.00	UTB	3	165D	8F-2R	49.10		No
2610	13600.00	7890.00	8840.00	9370.00	UTB	4	219D	8F-2R	64.3		No
2610 DTC 4WD	17195.00	9970.00	11180.00	11850.00	UTB	4	219D	8F-2R	64.3		No
2610 DTCSD 4WD	18200.00	10560.00	11830.00	12540.00	UTB	4	219D	8F-2R	64.3		No
2610 SD Shuttle	14615.00	8480.00	9500.00	10070.00	UTB	4	219D	8F-2R	64.3		No

DT - Front Wheel Assist

1994

Model	Approx. Retail Price New	Fair	Good	Premium	Make	No. Cyls.	Displ. Cu.-In.	No. Speeds	P.T.O. H.P.	Approx. Shipping Wt.-Lbs.	Cab
2260	7829.00	4780.00	5250.00	5510.00	UTB	2	95D	6F-2R	24.0		No
2360	10957.00	6680.00	7340.00	7710.00	UTB	3	143D	8F-2R	35.00		No
2360 DTC 4WD	15050.00	9180.00	10080.00	10580.00	UTB	3	143D	8F-2R	35.00		No
2460	11763.00	7180.00	7880.00	8270.00	UTB	3	143D	8F-2R	41.90		No
2460 DTC 4WD	16050.00	9790.00	10750.00	11290.00	UTB	3	143D	8F-2R	41.90		No
2460 DTCSD Shuttle	17139.00	10460.00	11480.00	12050.00	UTB	3	143D	8F-2R	41.90		No
2460 SD Shuttle	12918.00	7880.00	8660.00	9090.00	UTB	3	143D	8F-2R	41.90		No
2510	12816.00	7820.00	8590.00	9020.00	UTB	3	165D	8F-2R	49.10		No
2510 DTC 4WD	16847.00	10280.00	11290.00	11860.00	UTB	3	165D	8F-2R	49.10		No
2510 DTCSD Shuttle	17935.00	10940.00	12020.00	12620.00	UTB	3	165D	8F-2R	49.10		No
2510 SD Shuttle	13886.00	8470.00	9300.00	9770.00	UTB	3	165D	8F-2R	49.10		No
2610	14846.00	9060.00	9950.00	10450.00	UTB	4	219D	8F-2R	64.3		No
2610 DTC 4WD	18656.00	11380.00	12500.00	13130.00	UTB	4	219D	8F-2R	64.3		No
2610 DTCSD 4WD	19747.00	12050.00	13230.00	13890.00	UTB	4	219D	8F-2R	64.3		No
2610 SD Shuttle	15913.00	9710.00	10660.00	11190.00	UTB	4	219D	8F-2R	64.3		No
2710	19204.00	11710.00	12870.00	13510.00	UTB	4	229D	12F-3R	70.0		No
2710 DTC	23496.00	14330.00	15740.00	16530.00	UTB	4	229D	12F-3R	70.0		No

DT - Front Wheel Assist

1995

Model	Approx. Retail Price New	Fair	Good	Premium	Make	No. Cyls.	Displ. Cu.-In.	No. Speeds	P.T.O. H.P.	Approx. Shipping Wt.-Lbs.	Cab
2260	7829.00	5010.00	5480.00	5750.00	UTB	2	95D	6F-2R	24.0		No
2360	10957.00	7010.00	7670.00	8050.00	UTB	3	143D	8F-2R	35.00		No
2360 DTC 4WD	15050.00	9630.00	10540.00	11070.00	UTB	3	143D	8F-2R	35.00		No
2460	11763.00	7530.00	8230.00	8640.00	UTB	3	143D	8F-2R	41.90		No
2460 DTC 4WD	16050.00	10270.00	11240.00	11800.00	UTB	3	143D	8F-2R	41.90		No
2460 DTCSD Shuttle	17139.00	10970.00	12000.00	12600.00	UTB	3	143D	8F-2R	41.90		No
2460 SD Shuttle	12918.00	8270.00	9040.00	9490.00	UTB	3	143D	8F-2R	41.90		No
2510	12816.00	8200.00	8970.00	9420.00	UTB	3	165D	8F-2R	49.10		No
2510 DTC 4WD	16847.00	10780.00	11790.00	12380.00	UTB	3	165D	8F-2R	49.10		No
2510 DTCSD Shuttle	17935.00	11480.00	12560.00	13190.00	UTB	3	165D	8F-2R	49.10		No
2510 SD Shuttle	13886.00	8890.00	9720.00	10210.00	UTB	3	165D	8F-2R	49.10		No
2610	14846.00	9500.00	10390.00	10910.00	UTB	4	219D	8F-2R	64.3		No
2610 DTC 4WD	18656.00	11940.00	13060.00	13710.00	UTB	4	219D	8F-2R	64.3		No
2610 DTCSD Shuttle	19747.00	12640.00	13820.00	14510.00	UTB	4	219D	8F-2R	64.3		No
2610 SD Shuttle	15913.00	10180.00	11140.00	11700.00	UTB	4	219D	8F-2R	64.3		No
2710	19204.00	12290.00	13440.00	14110.00	UTB	4	229D	12F-3R	70.0		No
2710 DTC	23496.00	15040.00	16450.00	17270.00	UTB	4	229D	12F-3R	70.0		No

DT - Front Wheel Assist

1996

Model	Approx. Retail Price New	Fair	Good	Premium	Make	No. Cyls.	Displ. Cu.-In.	No. Speeds	P.T.O. H.P.	Approx. Shipping Wt.-Lbs.	Cab
2310	8751.00	5860.00	6390.00	6650.00	UTB	2	110D	6F-2R	28.0		No
2360	11275.00	7550.00	8230.00	8560.00	UTB	3	143D	8F-2R	35.00		No
2360 DTC 4WD	15800.00	10590.00	11530.00	11990.00	UTB	3	143D	8F-2R	35.00		No
2460	12115.00	8120.00	8840.00	9190.00	UTB	3	143D	8F-2R	41.90		No
2460 DTC 4WD	16850.00	11290.00	12300.00	12790.00	UTB	3	143D	8F-2R	41.90		No
2460 DTCSD Shuttle	17992.00	12060.00	13130.00	13660.00	UTB	3	143D	8F-2R	41.90		No
2460 SD Shuttle	13217.00	8860.00	9650.00	10040.00	UTB	3	143D	8F-2R	41.90		No
2510	13200.00	8840.00	9640.00	10030.00	UTB	3	165D	8F-2R	49.10		No
2510 DTC 4WD	17685.00	11850.00	12910.00	13430.00	UTB	3	165D	8F-2R	49.10		No
2510 DTCSD Shuttle	18810.00	12600.00	13730.00	14280.00	UTB	3	165D	8F-2R	49.10		No
2510 SD Shuttle	14302.00	9580.00	10440.00	10860.00	UTB	3	165D	8F-2R	49.10		No
2610	14995.00	10050.00	10950.00	11390.00	UTB	4	219D	8F-2R	64.3		No
2610 DTC 4WD	19585.00	13120.00	14300.00	14870.00	UTB	4	219D	8F-2R	64.3		No
2610 DTCSD Shuttle	20730.00	13890.00	15130.00	15740.00	UTB	4	219D	8F-2R	64.3		No
2610 SD Shuttle	16095.00	10780.00	11750.00	12220.00	UTB	4	219D	8F-2R	64.3		No
2710	19780.00	13250.00	14440.00	15020.00	UTB	4	229D	12F-3R	70.0		No
2710 DTC	24670.00	16530.00	18010.00	18730.00	UTB	4	229D	12F-3R	70.0		No

DT - Front Wheel Assist

Long (Cont.)

1997

Model	Approx. Retail Price New	Fair	Good	Premium	Make	No. Cyls.	Displ. Cu.-In.	No. Speeds	P.T.O. H.P.	Approx. Shipping Wt.-Lbs.	Cab
2310	9193.00	6620.00	7080.00	7360.00	UTB	2	110D	6F-2R	28.0	3700	No
2360	11844.00	8530.00	9120.00	9490.00	UTB	3	143D	8F-2R	35.00	4220	No
2360 DTC 4WD	16281.00	11720.00	12540.00	13040.00	UTB	3	143D	8F-2R	35.00	4760	No
2460	12935.00	9310.00	9960.00	10360.00	UTB	3	143D	8F-2R	41.90	4220	No
2460 DTC 4WD	16761.00	12070.00	12910.00	13430.00	UTB	3	143D	8F-2R	41.90	4760	No
2510	14107.00	10160.00	10860.00	11290.00	UTB	3	165D	8F-2R	49.10	4220	No
2510 DTC 4WD	17623.00	12690.00	13570.00	14110.00	UTB	3	165D	8F-2R	49.10	4760	No
2610	16046.00	11550.00	12360.00	12850.00	UTB	4	219D	8F-2R	64.3	4570	No
2610 DTC 4WD	20095.00	14470.00	15470.00	16090.00	UTB	4	219D	8F-2R	64.3	5120	No

DTC- Front Wheel Assist

1998

Model	Approx. Retail Price New	Fair	Good	Premium	Make	No. Cyls.	Displ. Cu.-In.	No. Speeds	P.T.O. H.P.	Approx. Shipping Wt.-Lbs.	Cab
Farmtrac 60	15465.00	12060.00	12680.00	13060.00		3	192D	8F-2R	44.7	4519	No
2310	9193.00	7170.00	7540.00	7770.00	UTB	2	110D	6F-2R	28.0	3700	No
2360	11844.00	9240.00	9710.00	10000.00	UTB	3	143D	8F-2R	35.00	4220	No
2360 DTC 4WD	16281.00	12700.00	13350.00	13750.00	UTB	3	143D	8F-2R	35.00	4760	No
2460	12935.00	10090.00	10610.00	10930.00	UTB	3	143D	8F-2R	41.90	4220	No
2460 DTC 4WD	16761.00	13070.00	13740.00	14150.00	UTB	3	143D	8F-2R	41.90	4760	No
2510	14107.00	11000.00	11570.00	11920.00	UTB	3	165D	8F-2R	49.10	4220	No
2510 DTC 4WD	17623.00	13750.00	14450.00	14880.00	UTB	3	165D	8F-2R	49.10	4760	No
2610	16046.00	12520.00	13160.00	13560.00	UTB	4	219D	8F-2R	64.3	4570	No
2610 DTC 4WD	20095.00	15670.00	16480.00	16970.00	UTB	4	219D	8F-2R	64.3	5120	No

DTC- Front Wheel Assist

1999

Model	Approx. Retail Price New	Fair	Good	Premium	Make	No. Cyls.	Displ. Cu.-In.	No. Speeds	P.T.O. H.P.	Approx. Shipping Wt.-Lbs.	Cab
Landtrac 20 4WD	14386.00	12080.00	12660.00	12910.00	Mitsubishi	4	0D	12F-6R	25	3792	No
Landtrac 30 4WD	17050.00	14320.00	15000.00	15300.00	Mitsubishi	4	0D	12F-6R	34	3770	No
Landtrac 35 4WD	......	VDC	VDC	VDC	Mitsubishi	4	0D	16F-16R	36	4751	No
Landtrac 40 4WD	20646.00	17340.00	18170.00	18530.00	Mitsubishi	4	0D	16F-16R	42	4883	No
Landtrac 45 4WD	21712.00	18240.00	19110.00	19490.00	Mitsubishi	4	0D	16F-16R	46	5137	No
Farmtrac 60	15712.00	13200.00	13830.00	14110.00	Escorts	3	192D	8F-2R	44.7	4519	No
2310	9320.00	7830.00	8200.00	8360.00	UTB	2	110D	6F-2R	28.0	3700	No
2360	12210.00	10260.00	10750.00	10970.00	UTB	3	143D	8F-2R	35.00	4220	No
2360 DTC 4WD	16785.00	14100.00	14770.00	15070.00	UTB	3	143D	8F-2R	35.00	4760	No
2460	13335.00	11200.00	11740.00	11980.00	UTB	3	143D	8F-2R	41.90	4220	No
2460 DTC 4WD	17279.00	14510.00	15210.00	15510.00	UTB	3	143D	8F-2R	41.90	4760	No
2510	14543.00	12220.00	12800.00	13060.00	UTB	3	165D	8F-2R	49.10	4220	No
2510 DTC 4WD	18168.00	15260.00	15990.00	16310.00	UTB	3	165D	8F-2R	49.10	4760	No
2610	17025.00	14300.00	14980.00	15280.00	UTB	4	219D	8F-2R	64.3	4570	No
2610 DTC 4WD	20716.00	17400.00	18230.00	18600.00	UTB	4	219D	8F-2R	64.3	5120	No

DTC- Front Wheel Assist

Mahindra

1997

Model	Approx. Retail Price New	Fair	Good	Premium	Make	No. Cyls.	Displ. Cu.-In.	No. Speeds	P.T.O. H.P.	Approx. Shipping Wt.-Lbs.	Cab
475 DI	9000.00	6480.00	6930.00	7210.00	Own	3	115D	8F-2R	39	3894	No
485 DI	10800.00	7780.00	8320.00	8650.00	Own	4	145D	8F-2R	41	4090	No
575 DI	11400.00	8210.00	8780.00	9130.00	Own	4	154D	8F-2R	42	4085	No

1998

Model	Approx. Retail Price New	Fair	Good	Premium	Make	No. Cyls.	Displ. Cu.-In.	No. Speeds	P.T.O. H.P.	Approx. Shipping Wt.-Lbs.	Cab
475 DI	9850.00	7680.00	8080.00	8320.00	Own	3	115D	8F-2R	39	3894	No
4005 DI	11950.00	9320.00	9800.00	10090.00	Own	4	145D	8F-2R	40	4092	No
4505 DI	12450.00	9710.00	10210.00	10520.00	Own	4	154D	8F-2R	43	4070	No
5005 DI	12950.00	10100.00	10620.00	10940.00	Own	4	154D	8F-2R	50	4258	No

1999

Model	Approx. Retail Price New	Fair	Good	Premium	Make	No. Cyls.	Displ. Cu.-In.	No. Speeds	P.T.O. H.P.	Approx. Shipping Wt.-Lbs.	Cab
475 DI	9850.00	8270.00	8670.00	8840.00	Own	3	115D	8F-2R	39	3894	No
4005 DI	11950.00	10040.00	10520.00	10730.00	Own	4	145D	8F-2R	40	4092	No
4505 DI	12450.00	10460.00	10960.00	11180.00	Own	4	154D	8F-2R	43	4070	No
5005 DI	12950.00	10880.00	11400.00	11630.00	Own	4	154D	8F-2R	50	4258	No

Massey Ferguson

1958

Model	Approx. Retail Price New	Fair	Good	Premium	Make	No. Cyls.	Displ. Cu.-In.	No. Speeds	P.T.O. H.P.	Approx. Shipping Wt.-Lbs.	Cab
MF-50	......	1310.00	2400.00	2930.00	Continental	4	134G	6F-2R	33	3290	No
MF-50	......	1450.00	2660.00	3250.00	Perkins	3	152D	6F-2R	38.33	3490	No
MF-65	......	1520.00	2780.00	3390.00	Continental	4	176G	6F-2R		3843	No
MF-65	......	1700.00	3100.00	3780.00	Perkins	4	203D	6F-1R	61.23	4120	No
MF-85	......	1870.00	2460.00	2800.00	Continental	4	242G	8F-2R	61.23	5085	No
MF-85	......	2150.00	2830.00	3230.00	Perkins	4	276D	8F-2R	62.2	5737	No

1959

Model	Approx. Retail Price New	Fair	Good	Premium	Make	No. Cyls.	Displ. Cu.-In.	No. Speeds	P.T.O. H.P.	Approx. Shipping Wt.-Lbs.	Cab
MF-50	......	1350.00	2470.00	3010.00	Continental	4	134G	6F-2R	33	3290	No
MF-50	......	1490.00	2720.00	3320.00	Perkins	3	152D	6F-2R	38.33	3490	No
MF-65	......	1560.00	2850.00	3480.00	Continental	4	176G	6F-2R		3843	No
MF-65	......	1730.00	3170.00	3870.00	Perkins	4	203D	6F-2R	61.23	4120	No
MF-85	......	1930.00	2530.00	2880.00	Continental	4	242G	8F-2R	61.23	5085	No
MF-85	......	2210.00	2900.00	3310.00	Perkins	4	276D	8F-2R	62.2	5737	No
MF-88	......	1730.00	2280.00	2600.00	Continental	4	276G	8F-2R	63.31	6680	No
MF-88	......	2170.00	2850.00	3250.00	Perkins	4	277D	8F-2R	64	7165	No

Model	Approx. Retail Price New	Fair	Good	Premium	Engine Make	Engine No. Cyls.	Engine Displ. Cu.-In.	No. Speeds	P.T.O. H.P.	Approx. Shipping Wt.-Lbs.	Cab
			Estimated Average Value Less Repairs								

Massey Ferguson (Cont.)

Model	Approx. Retail Price New	Fair	Good	Premium	Make	No. Cyls.	Displ. Cu.-In.	No. Speeds	P.T.O. H.P.	Approx. Shipping Wt.-Lbs.	Cab
1960											
MF-50	......	1420.00	2530.00	3090.00	Continental	4	134G	6F-2R	33	3290	No
MF-50	......	1560.00	2770.00	3380.00	Perkins	3	152D	6F-2R	38.33	3490	No
MF-65	......	1640.00	2910.00	3550.00	Continental	4	176G	6F-2R		3843	No
MF-65	......	1850.00	3290.00	4010.00	Perkins	4	203D	6F-2R	61.23	4120	No
MF-85	......	1940.00	2550.00	2880.00	Continental	4	242G	8F-2R	61.23	5085	No
MF-85	......	2220.00	2920.00	3300.00	Perkins	4	276D	8F-2R	62.2	5737	No
MF-88	......	1750.00	2300.00	2600.00	Continental	4	276G	8F-2R	63.31	6680	No
MF-88	......	2190.00	2880.00	3250.00	Perkins	4	277D	8F-2R	64	7165	No
1961											
MF-50	......	1510.00	2610.00	3180.00	Continental	4	134G	6F-2R	33	3290	No
MF-50	......	1690.00	2920.00	3560.00	Perkins	3	152D	6F-2R	38.33	3490	No
MF-65	......	1720.00	2980.00	3640.00	Continental	4	176G	6F-2R		3843	No
MF-65	......	1920.00	3330.00	4060.00	Perkins	4	203D	6F-2R	61.23	4120	No
MF-85	......	1960.00	2580.00	2920.00	Continental	4	242G	8F-2R	61.23	5085	No
MF-85	......	2230.00	2930.00	3310.00	Perkins	4	276D	8F-2R	62.2	5737	No
MF-88	......	1860.00	2440.00	2760.00	Continental	4	276G	8F-2R	63.31	6680	No
MF-88	......	2560.00	3360.00	3800.00	Perkins	4	277D	8F-2R	64	7165	No
1962											
MF-50	......	1590.00	2670.00	3260.00	Continental	4	134G	6F-2R	33	3290	No
MF-50	......	1770.00	2990.00	3650.00	Perkins	3	152D	6F-2R	38.33	3490	No
MF-65	......	1810.00	3040.00	3710.00	Continental	4	176G	6F-2R		3843	No
MF-65	......	2010.00	3390.00	4140.00	Perkins	4	203D	6F-2R	61.23	4120	No
MF-85	......	1980.00	2600.00	2940.00	Continental	4	242G	8F-2R	61.23	5085	No
MF-85	......	2250.00	2960.00	3350.00	Perkins	4	276D	8F-2R	62.2	5737	No
MF-88	......	1860.00	2450.00	2770.00	Continental	4	276G	8F-2R	63.31	6680	No
MF-88	......	2220.00	2920.00	3300.00	Perkins	4	277D	8F-2R	64	7165	No
MF-90	......	1930.00	2530.00	2860.00	Continental	4	242G	16F-4R	61	5576	No
MF-90	......	2380.00	3130.00	3540.00	Perkins	4	302D	8F-2R	68.53	7245	No
1963											
MF-35	2830.00	1490.00	2450.00	2990.00	Continental	4	134G	6F-2R	34	2790	No
MF-35	3300.00	1680.00	2750.00	3360.00	Perkins	4	153D	6F-2R	37	3200	No
MF-50	3161.00	1620.00	2660.00	3250.00	Continental	4	134G	6F-2R	31	3290	No
MF-50	3620.00	1800.00	2960.00	3610.00	Perkins	3	153D	6F-2R	38.33	3660	No
MF-65	3850.00	1890.00	3100.00	3780.00	Continental	4	176G	6F-2R	48	3843	No
MF-65 Dieselmatic	4410.00	2110.00	3460.00	4220.00	Perkins	4	203D	6F-2R	48	4220	No
MF-90	4970.00	2090.00	2750.00	3110.00	Continental	4	242G	8F-2R	61	5576	No
MF-90	6000.00	2140.00	2820.00	3190.00	Perkins	4	302D	8F-2R	68.53	5737	No
MF-97	6800.00	2380.00	3130.00	3540.00	MM	6	504D	5F-1R	90	7675	No
MF-97 4WD	8555.00	2990.00	3940.00	4450.00	MM	6	504D	5F-1R	90	8600	No
1964											
MF-50	3192.00	1990.00	2940.00	3650.00	Continental	4	134G	6F-2R	31	3290	No
MF-50	3655.00	2140.00	3170.00	3930.00	Perkins	3	153D	6F-2R	38.33	3660	No
MF-65	3890.00	2250.00	3330.00	4130.00	Continental	4	176G	6F-2R	48	3800	No
MF-65 Dieselmatic	4666.00	2610.00	3850.00	4770.00	Perkins	4	203D	12F-4R	50	4200	No
MF-90	5020.00	2770.00	4090.00	5070.00	Continental	4	242G	16F-4R	61	5576	No
MF-90	6057.00	2820.00	4170.00	5170.00	Perkins	4	302D	16F-4R	68.53	5737	No
MF-97	6852.00	3150.00	4660.00	5780.00	MM	6	504D	5F-1R	90	7675	No
MF-97 4WD	8607.00	3960.00	5850.00	7250.00	MM	6	504D	5F-1R	90	8600	No
MF-135	3216.00	1940.00	2870.00	3560.00	Continental	3	145G	6F-2R	35.3	2940	No
MF-135	3555.00	2100.00	3100.00	3840.00	Perkins	3	153D	6F-2R	37.8	3130	No
MF-150	3457.00	2050.00	3030.00	3760.00	Continental	4	145G	6F-2R	35	3500	No
MF-150	3968.00	2290.00	3380.00	4190.00	Perkins	3	153D	6F-2R	37.8	4020	No
MF-165	4200.00	2390.00	3540.00	4390.00	Continental	4	176G	6F-2R	46	4600	No
MF-165	4800.00	2670.00	3940.00	4890.00	Perkins	4	203D	6F-2R	52.4	4855	No
MF-175	5150.00	2830.00	4180.00	5180.00	Continental	4	206G	12F-4R	50	5320	No
MF-175	5850.00	3150.00	4660.00	5780.00	Perkins	4	236D	12F-4R	63.34	5725	No
MF-180	5500.00	2990.00	4420.00	5480.00	Continental	4	236G	12F-4R	62.8	6250	No
MF-180	6200.00	3310.00	4900.00	6080.00	Perkins	4	236D	12F-4R	63.6	6620	No
1965											
MF-85	4620.00	2130.00	3140.00	3890.00	Continental	4	242G	8F-2R	61	5085	No
MF-85	5430.00	2500.00	3690.00	4580.00	Perkins	4	276D	8F-2R	62	5085	No
MF-90	5070.00	2340.00	3470.00	4300.00	Continental	4	242G	8F-2R	61	5576	No
MF-90	6120.00	2820.00	4160.00	5160.00	Perkins	4	302D	16F-4R	68.53	5737	No
MF-135	3248.00	2410.00	3570.00	4430.00	Continental	3	145G	6F-2R	35.3	2940	No
MF-135	3587.00	2570.00	3790.00	4700.00	Perkins	3	153D	6F-2R	37.8	3130	No
MF-150	3583.00	2570.00	3800.00	4710.00	Continental	3	145G	6F-2R	35	3500	No
MF-150	4010.00	2770.00	4090.00	5070.00	Perkins	3	153D	6F-2R	37.8	4020	No
MF-165	4246.00	2410.00	3570.00	4430.00	Continental	4	176G	6F-2R	46	4597	No
MF-165	4850.00	2690.00	3980.00	4940.00	Perkins	4	203D	6F-2R	52.4	4855	No
MF-175	5195.00	2850.00	4210.00	5220.00	Continental	4	206G	12F-4R	50	5320	No
MF-175	5890.00	3170.00	4690.00	5820.00	Perkins	4	236D	12F-4R	63.34	5725	No
MF-180	5555.00	3050.00	4510.00	5590.00	Continental	4	206G	12F-4R	62.8	6250	No
MF-180	6250.00	3340.00	4930.00	6110.00	Perkins	4	236D	12F-4R	63.6	6620	No
MF-1100	6869.00	2820.00	4400.00	5370.00	Perkins	6	354D	12F-4R	93.94	8800	No
MF-1130	7628.00	3130.00	4880.00	5950.00	Perkins	6T	354D	12F-4R	120.51	10000	No
1966											
MF-130	2955.00	2800.00	4050.00	5020.00	Perkins	4	107D	8F-2R	27	2600	No
MF-135	3280.00	2950.00	4270.00	5300.00	Continental	3	145G	6F-2R	35.3	3079	No

Massey Ferguson (Cont.)

Model	Approx. Retail Price New	Estimated Average Value Less Repairs Fair	Good	Premium	Engine Make	No. Cyls.	Displ. Cu.-In.	No. Speeds	P.T.O. H.P.	Approx. Shipping Wt.-Lbs.	Cab
1966 (Cont.)											
MF-135	3623.00	**3110.00**	**4500.00**	**5580.00**	Perkins	3	153D	6F-2R	37.8	3314	No
MF-150	3620.00	**3110.00**	**4500.00**	**5580.00**	Continental	3	145G	6F-2R	35	3940	No
MF-150	4050.00	**3310.00**	**4790.00**	**5940.00**	Perkins	3	153D	6F-2R	37.8	4805	No
MF-165	4290.00	**3430.00**	**4960.00**	**6150.00**	Continental	4	176G	6F-2R	46	4780	No
MF-165	4900.00	**3710.00**	**5370.00**	**6660.00**	Perkins	4	204D	6F-2R	52.4	5100	No
MF-175	5246.00	**3510.00**	**5070.00**	**6290.00**	Continental	4	206G	12F-4R	50	5320	No
MF-175	5950.00	**3740.00**	**5410.00**	**6710.00**	Perkins	4	236D	12F-4R	63.34	6125	No
MF-180	5260.00	**3410.00**	**4940.00**	**6130.00**	Continental	4	206G	12F-4R	50	6250	No
MF-180	5992.00	**3760.00**	**5440.00**	**6750.00**	Perkins	4	236D	12F-4R	63.6	6755	No
MF-1100	7230.00	**3040.00**	**4630.00**	**5650.00**	Perkins	6	354D	6F-2R	93	8800	No
MF-1130	8475.00	**3560.00**	**5420.00**	**6610.00**	Perkins	6T	354D	12F-4R	120.51	9570	No
1967											
MF-130	4065.00	**2850.00**	**4120.00**	**5110.00**	Perkins	4	107D	8F-2R	27	2600	No
MF-135	3922.00	**2780.00**	**4030.00**	**5000.00**	Perkins	3	153D	6F-2R	37.8	3130	No
MF-135	3800.00	**2730.00**	**3940.00**	**4890.00**	Continental	4	145G	6F-2R	35.3	3060	No
MF-150	3780.00	**2720.00**	**3930.00**	**4870.00**	Continental	3	145G	8F-2R	37	3500	No
MF-150	4160.00	**2900.00**	**4190.00**	**5200.00**	Perkins	3	153D	8F-2R	37.8	4020	No
MF-165	4485.00	**3050.00**	**4410.00**	**5470.00**	Continental	4	175G	6F-2R	52	4595	No
MF-165	4915.00	**3250.00**	**4700.00**	**5830.00**	Perkins	4	204D	6F-2R	52.4	4915	No
MF-175	5545.00	**3550.00**	**5130.00**	**6360.00**	Continental	4	206G	8F-2R	50	5545	No
MF-175	6128.00	**3820.00**	**5530.00**	**6860.00**	Perkins	4	236D	8F-2R	63.34	5725	No
MF-180	5781.00	**3660.00**	**5290.00**	**6560.00**	Continental	4	206G	12F-4R	62.8	6250	No
MF-180	6481.00	**3990.00**	**5770.00**	**7160.00**	Perkins	4	236D	12F-4R	63.6	6618	No
MF-1100	7030.00	**3020.00**	**4500.00**	**5490.00**	Waukesha	6	320G	12F-4R	90.2	8850	No
MF-1100	7611.00	**3270.00**	**4870.00**	**5940.00**	Perkins	6	354D	6F-2R	93.94	8800	No
MF-1130	8921.00	**3840.00**	**5710.00**	**6970.00**	Perkins	6T	354D	12F-4R	120.51	10000	No
1968											
MF-130	4100.00	**2930.00**	**4150.00**	**5150.00**	Perkins	4	107D	8F-2R	27	2600	No
MF-135	4358.00	**3060.00**	**4340.00**	**5380.00**	Perkins	3	153D	6F-2R	37.8	3130	No
MF-135	3900.00	**2830.00**	**4010.00**	**4970.00**	Continental	3	145G	6F-2R	35.3	2940	No
MF-150	4200.00	**2980.00**	**4220.00**	**5230.00**	Continental	3	153G	8F-2R	37	3500	No
MF-150	4622.00	**3180.00**	**4500.00**	**5580.00**	Perkins	3	152D	8F-2R	37.8	4020	No
MF-165	4670.00	**3200.00**	**4540.00**	**5630.00**	Continental	4	176G	6F-2R	52	4600	No
MF-165	5080.00	**3400.00**	**4810.00**	**5960.00**	Perkins	4	204D	6F-2R	52.4	4855	No
MF-175	5776.00	**3730.00**	**5290.00**	**6560.00**	Perkins	4	206G	8F-2R	50	5320	No
MF-175	6280.00	**3970.00**	**5630.00**	**6980.00**	Perkins	4	236D	8F-2R	63.34	5725	No
MF-180	6065.00	**3870.00**	**5480.00**	**6800.00**	Continental	4	206G	8F-2R	50	6250	No
MF-180	6594.00	**4130.00**	**5840.00**	**7240.00**	Perkins	4	236D	12F-4R	63.6	6620	No
MF-1100	7400.00	**3260.00**	**4740.00**	**5780.00**	Waukesha	6	320G	12F-4R	90.2	8850	No
MF-1100	8012.00	**3530.00**	**5130.00**	**6260.00**	Perkins	6	354D	6F-2R	93.94	8800	No
MF-1130	9912.00	**4360.00**	**6340.00**	**7740.00**	Perkins	6T	354D	12F-4R	120.51	10000	No
1969											
MF-130	4500.00	**3190.00**	**4420.00**	**5480.00**	Perkins	4	107D	8F-2R	27	2600	No
MF-135	4400.00	**3160.00**	**4380.00**	**5430.00**	Perkins	3	153G	6F-2R	37	2940	No
MF-135	4400.00	**3210.00**	**4460.00**	**5530.00**	Perkins	3	153D	6F-2R	37	3130	No
MF-150	4245.00	**3410.00**	**4730.00**	**5870.00**	Perkins	3	153G	8F-2R	37	3500	No
MF-150	4670.00	**3190.00**	**4420.00**	**5480.00**	Perkins	3	153D	8F-2R	37.8	4020	No
MF-165	4717.00	**3450.00**	**4790.00**	**5940.00**	Perkins	4	212G	6F-2R	52	4597	No
MF-165	5131.00	**3560.00**	**4940.00**	**6130.00**	Perkins	4	204D	6F-2R	52.4	4855	No
MF-175	5834.00	**3700.00**	**5130.00**	**6360.00**	Perkins	4	236G	12F-4R	61	5320	No
MF-175	6343.00	**4210.00**	**5840.00**	**7240.00**	Perkins	4	236D	12F-4R	63.34	6250	No
MF-180	6126.00	**4080.00**	**5660.00**	**7020.00**	Perkins	4	236G	12F-4R	61	6250	No
MF-180	6660.00	**3920.00**	**5440.00**	**6750.00**	Perkins	4	236D	12F-4R	63.3	6618	No
MF-1080	7698.00	**3770.00**	**5240.00**	**6500.00**	Perkins	4	318D	6F-2R	81.23	7010	C,H
MF-1100	8222.00	**4030.00**	**5590.00**	**6930.00**	Waukesha	6	320G	12F-4R	90.2	8850	No
MF-1100	8900.00	**4360.00**	**6050.00**	**7500.00**	Perkins	6	354D	6F-2R	93.94	8800	No
MF-1130	11013.00	**5400.00**	**7490.00**	**9290.00**	Perkins	6T	354D	12F-4R	120.51	10000	No
1970											
MF-130	5000.00	**3500.00**	**4760.00**	**5900.00**	Perkins	4	107D	8F-2R	26.96	2600	No
MF-135	4190.00	**3100.00**	**4210.00**	**5220.00**	Perkins	3	153G	12F-4R	37.55	3060	No
MF-135	4446.00	**3230.00**	**4390.00**	**5440.00**	Perkins	3	153D	6F-2R	37.00	3130	No
MF-135	4500.00	**3490.00**	**4750.00**	**5890.00**	Perkins	3	153G	6F-2R	37.00	2940	No
MF-135	4848.00	**3430.00**	**4660.00**	**5780.00**	Perkins	3	153D	12F-4R	37.82	3250	No
MF-150	4286.00	**3140.00**	**4270.00**	**5300.00**	Perkins	3	153G	6F-2R	37.00	3500	No
MF-150	4667.00	**3330.00**	**4530.00**	**5620.00**	Perkins	3	153G	12F-4R	37.00	3805	No
MF-150	4715.00	**3360.00**	**4570.00**	**5670.00**	Perkins	3	153D	6F-2R	37.00	4020	No
MF-150	5098.00	**3550.00**	**4830.00**	**5990.00**	Perkins	3	153D	12F-4R	37.88	4325	No
MF-165	4914.00	**3460.00**	**4700.00**	**5830.00**	Perkins	4	212G	6F-2R	51.00	4597	No
MF-165	5131.00	**3570.00**	**4850.00**	**6010.00**	Perkins	4	212G	12F-4R	51.91	4780	No
MF-165	5345.00	**3670.00**	**5000.00**	**6200.00**	Perkins	4	204D	6F-2R	52.00	4855	No
MF-165	5428.00	**3760.00**	**5120.00**	**6350.00**	Perkins	4	204D	12F-4R	52.42	5100	No
MF-175	6078.00	**4040.00**	**5490.00**	**6810.00**	Perkins	4	236G	12F-4R	61.89	5319	No
MF-175	6608.00	**4300.00**	**5850.00**	**7250.00**	Perkins	4	236D	12F-4R	63.34	5725	No
MF-180	6382.00	**4190.00**	**5700.00**	**7070.00**	Perkins	4	236G	12F-4R	61.00	6250	No
MF-180	6938.00	**4470.00**	**6080.00**	**7540.00**	Perkins	4	236D	12F-4R	63.68	6618	No
MF-1080 RC	8103.00	**4050.00**	**5510.00**	**6830.00**	Perkins	4	318D	6F-2R	81.00	7010	No
MF-1080 RC	8491.00	**4250.00**	**5770.00**	**7160.00**	Perkins	4	318D	12F-4R	81.23	7450	No
MF-1080 Western	7941.00	**3970.00**	**5400.00**	**6700.00**	Perkins	4	318D	6F-2R	81.00	8275	No
MF-1080 Western	8321.00	**4160.00**	**5660.00**	**7020.00**	Perkins	4	318D	12F-4R	81.00	8380	No
MF-1100 RC	8050.00	**4030.00**	**5470.00**	**6780.00**	Waukesha	6	320G	6F-2R	90.00	8600	No

Massey Ferguson (Cont.)

1970 (Cont.)

Model	Approx. Retail Price New	Estimated Average Value Less Repairs: Fair	Good	Premium	Engine: Make	No. Cyls.	Displ. Cu.-In.	No. Speeds	P.T.O. H.P.	Approx. Shipping Wt.-Lbs.	Cab
MF-1100 RC	8655.00	4330.00	5890.00	7300.00	Waukesha	6	320G	12F-4R	90.29	8850	No
MF-1100 RC	8767.00	4380.00	5960.00	7390.00	Perkins	6	354D	6F-2R	93.00	8500	No
MF-1100 RC	9370.00	4690.00	6370.00	7900.00	Perkins	6	354D	12F-4R	93.00	8800	No
MF-1100 Western	7889.00	3950.00	5370.00	6660.00	Waukesha	6	320G	6F-2R	90.00	9750	No
MF-1100 Western	8482.00	4240.00	5770.00	7160.00	Waukesha	6	320G	12F-4R	90.00	10610	No
MF-1100 Western	8592.00	4300.00	5840.00	7240.00	Perkins	6	354D	6F-2R	93.00	10290	No
MF-1100 Western	9183.00	4590.00	6240.00	7740.00	Perkins	6	354D	12F-4R	93.94	10563	No
MF-1130 RC	11593.00	5330.00	7420.00	9050.00	Perkins	6T	354D	12F-4R	120.00	10500	No
MF-1130 Western	11361.00	5230.00	7270.00	8870.00	Perkins	6T	354D	12F-4R	120.51	10000	No

RC - Row Crop

1971

Model	Approx. Retail Price New	Fair	Good	Premium	Engine: Make	No. Cyls.	Displ. Cu.-In.	No. Speeds	P.T.O. H.P.	Approx. Shipping Wt.-Lbs.	Cab
MF-130	3360.00	3240.00	4330.00	5370.00	Perkins	4	107D	8F-2R	26.96	2700	No
MF-135	4078.00	3610.00	4810.00	5960.00	Perkins	3	153G	6F-2R	37.00	3085	No
MF-135	4269.00	3710.00	4940.00	6130.00	Perkins	3	153G	8F-2R	37.00	3100	No
MF-135	4478.00	3810.00	5090.00	6310.00	Perkins	3	153D	6F-2R	37.00	3260	No
MF-135	4532.00	3840.00	5120.00	6350.00	Perkins	3	153G	12F-4R	37.55	3150	No
MF-135	4543.00	3850.00	5130.00	6360.00	Perkins	3	153D	8F-2R	37.00	3275	No
MF-135	5077.00	4120.00	5490.00	6810.00	Perkins	3	153D	12F-4R	37.82	3325	No
MF-135 Special	3449.00	3290.00	4390.00	5440.00	Perkins	3	153G	6F-2R	37.00	3050	No
MF-150	4329.00	3740.00	4980.00	6180.00	Perkins	3	153G	6F-2R	37.00	3500	No
MF-150	4506.00	3830.00	5100.00	6320.00	Perkins	3	153G	8F-2R	37.00	3725	No
MF-150	4749.00	3950.00	5270.00	6540.00	Perkins	3	153G	12F-4R	37.00	3805	No
MF-150	4763.00	3960.00	5280.00	6550.00	Perkins	3	153D	6F-2R	37.00	4020	No
MF-150	4956.00	4060.00	5410.00	6710.00	Perkins	3	153D	8F-2R	37.00	4200	No
MF-150	5411.00	4290.00	5720.00	7090.00	Perkins	3	153D	12F-4R	37.88	4325	No
MF-165	5058.00	4110.00	5480.00	6800.00	Perkins	3	212G	6F-2R	51.00	4597	No
MF-165	5528.00	4350.00	5800.00	7190.00	Perkins	4	212G	8F-2R	51.00	4597	No
MF-165	5778.00	4480.00	5970.00	7400.00	Perkins	4	204D	6F-2R	52.00	4855	No
MF-165	6020.00	4600.00	6130.00	7600.00	Perkins	4	204D	8F-2R	52.00	4855	No
MF-165	6162.00	4670.00	6230.00	7730.00	Perkins	4	212G	12F-4R	51.91	4780	No
MF-165	6392.00	4790.00	6390.00	7920.00	Perkins	4	204D	12F-4R	52.42	5100	No
MF-175	5820.00	4500.00	6000.00	7440.00	Perkins	4	236G	8F-2R	61.00	5199	No
MF-175	6466.00	4830.00	6440.00	7990.00	Perkins	4	236G	12F-4R	61.89	5319	No
MF-175	7046.00	5120.00	6830.00	8470.00	Perkins	4	236D	8F-2R	63.00	5605	No
MF-175	7348.00	5280.00	7040.00	8730.00	Perkins	4	236D	12F-4R	63.34	5725	No
MF-180	6111.00	4650.00	6200.00	7690.00	Perkins	4	236G	6F-2R	62.00	6130	No
MF-180	6789.00	4990.00	6660.00	8260.00	Perkins	4	236G	12F-4R	62.83	6250	No
MF-180	7398.00	5300.00	7070.00	8770.00	Perkins	4	236D	6F-2R	63.00	6498	No
MF-180	7715.00	5470.00	7290.00	9040.00	Perkins	4	236D	12F-4R	63.68	6618	No
MF-1080 RC	8579.00	4380.00	5830.00	7230.00	Perkins	4	318D	6F-2R	81.00	7010	No
MF-1080 RC	8938.00	4560.00	6080.00	7540.00	Perkins	4	318D	12F-4R	81.33	7450	No
MF-1080 RC	10660.00	5440.00	7250.00	8990.00	Perkins	4	318D	12F-4R	81.33	8550	C,H,A
MF-1080 Western	10127.00	5170.00	6890.00	8540.00	Perkins	4	318D	12F-4R	81.00	8050	C,H,A
MF-1100 RC	8512.00	4340.00	5790.00	7180.00	Waukesha	6	320G	6F-2R	90.00	8600	No
MF-1100 RC	9229.00	4710.00	6280.00	7790.00	Perkins	6	354D	6F-2R	93.00	8500	No
MF-1100 RC	9525.00	4860.00	6480.00	8040.00	Waukesha	6	320G	12F-4R	90.29	8850	No
MF-1100 RC	10242.00	5220.00	6970.00	8640.00	Perkins	6	354D	12F-4R	93.94	8800	No
MF-1100 RC	11187.00	5710.00	7610.00	9440.00	Perkins	6	354D	12F-4R	93.94	9800	C,H,A
MF-1100 Western	8086.00	4120.00	5500.00	6820.00	Waukesha	6	320G	6F-2R	90.00	9750	No
MF-1100 Western	9049.00	4620.00	6150.00	7630.00	Waukesha	6	320G	12F-4R	90.00	10610	No
MF-1100 Western	10628.00	5420.00	7230.00	8970.00	Perkins	6	354D	12F-4R	93.00	9800	C,H,A
MF-1130 RC	12303.00	4800.00	5780.00	6530.00	Perkins	6T	354D	12F-4R	120.51	9500	No
MF-1130 RC	13433.00	5240.00	6310.00	7130.00	Perkins	6T	354D	12F-4R	120.51	10500	C,H,A
MF-1130 Western	12761.00	4980.00	6000.00	6780.00	Perkins	6T	354D	12F-4R	120.00	10000	C,H,A
MF-1150 RC	13993.00	4760.00	6160.00	6900.00	Perkins	V8	511D	12F-4R	135.60	13425	No
MF-1150 RC	15635.00	5320.00	6880.00	7710.00	Perkins	V8	511D	12F-4R	135.60	14450	C,H,A
MF-1150 Western	14853.00	5050.00	6540.00	7330.00	Perkins	V8	511D	12F-4R	135.00	13950	C,H,A
MF-1500 4WD	16156.00	4520.00	6300.00	7060.00	Cat.	V8	573D	12F-4R		14420	C
MF-1800 4WD	19454.00	5450.00	7590.00	8500.00	Cat.	V8	636D	12F-4R		16000	C

RC - Row Crop

1972

Model	Approx. Retail Price New	Fair	Good	Premium	Engine: Make	No. Cyls.	Displ. Cu.-In.	No. Speeds	P.T.O. H.P.	Approx. Shipping Wt.-Lbs.	Cab
MF-130	3500.00	3380.00	4420.00	5440.00	Perkins	4	107D	8F-2R	26.96	2700	No
MF-135	4187.00	3740.00	4890.00	6020.00	Perkins	3	153G	6F-2R	37.00	3085	No
MF-135	4383.00	3840.00	5020.00	6180.00	Perkins	3	153G	8F-2R	37.00	3100	No
MF-135	4678.00	3990.00	5220.00	6420.00	Perkins	3	153D	6F-2R	37.00	3260	No
MF-135	4721.00	4020.00	5250.00	6460.00	Perkins	3	153G	12F-4R	37.55	3150	No
MF-135	4802.00	4060.00	5300.00	6520.00	Perkins	3	153D	8F-2R	37.00	3275	No
MF-135	5101.00	4210.00	5510.00	6780.00	Perkins	3	153D	12F-4R	37.82	3325	No
MF-150	4509.00	3900.00	5100.00	6270.00	Perkins	3	153G	6F-2R	37.00	3500	No
MF-150	4659.00	3980.00	5210.00	6410.00	Perkins	3	153G	8F-2R	37.00	3725	No
MF-150	4910.00	4110.00	5380.00	6620.00	Perkins	3	153G	12F-4R	37.00	3805	No
MF-150	4961.00	4140.00	5410.00	6650.00	Perkins	3	153D	6F-2R	37.00	4020	No
MF-150	5112.00	4220.00	5520.00	6790.00	Perkins	3	153D	8F-2R	37.00	4200	No
MF-150	5364.00	4350.00	5690.00	7000.00	Perkins	3	153D	12F-4R	37.88	4325	No
MF-165	5118.00	4220.00	5520.00	6790.00	Perkins	4	212G	6F-2R	51.00	4597	No
MF-165	5343.00	4340.00	5680.00	6990.00	Perkins	4	212G	12F-4R	51.91	4780	No
MF-165	5566.00	4450.00	5830.00	7170.00	Perkins	4	204D	6F-2R	52.00	4855	No
MF-165	5653.00	4500.00	5880.00	7230.00	Perkins	4	204D	12F-4R	52.42	5100	No
MF-175	5936.00	4650.00	6080.00	7480.00	Perkins	4	236G	6F-2R	61.00	5199	No
MF-175	6595.00	4990.00	6530.00	8030.00	Perkins	4	236G	12F-4R	61.89	5319	No
MF-175	7393.00	5400.00	7070.00	8700.00	Perkins	4	236D	6F-2R	63.00	5605	No
MF-180	6417.00	4900.00	6400.00	7870.00	Perkins	4	236G	6F-2R	62.00	6130	No

Massey Ferguson (Cont.)

1972 (Cont.)

Model	Approx. Retail Price New	Estimated Average Value Less Repairs: Fair	Good	Premium	Engine Make	Engine No. Cyls.	Engine Displ. Cu.-In.	No. Speeds	P.T.O. H.P.	Approx. Shipping Wt.-Lbs.	Cab
MF-180	7768.00	5600.00	7320.00	9000.00	Perkins	4	236D	6F-2R	63.00	6498	No
MF-1080 RC	8665.00	4510.00	5890.00	7250.00	Perkins	4	318D	6F-2R	81.00	7010	No
MF-1080 RC	9027.00	4690.00	6140.00	7550.00	Perkins	4	318D	12F-4R	81.33	7450	No
MF-1080 RC	10767.00	5600.00	7320.00	9000.00	Perkins	4	318D	12F-4R	81.33	8550	C,H,A
MF-1080 Western	10228.00	5320.00	6960.00	8560.00	Perkins	4	318D	12F-4R	81.00	8050	C,H,A
MF-1100 RC	8597.00	4470.00	5850.00	7200.00	Waukesha	6	320G	6F-2R	90.00	8600	No
MF-1100 RC	9321.00	4850.00	6340.00	7800.00	Perkins	6	354D	6F-2R	93.00	8500	No
MF-1100 RC	10001.00	5200.00	6800.00	8360.00	Waukesha	6	320G	12F-4R	90.29	8850	No
MF-1100 RC	10344.00	5380.00	7030.00	8650.00	Perkins	6	354D	12F-4R	93.94	8800	No
MF-1100 RC	11299.00	5880.00	7680.00	9450.00	Perkins	6	354D	12F-4R	93.94	9800	C,H,A
MF-1100 Western	9139.00	4750.00	6220.00	7650.00	Waukesha	6	320G	12F-4R	90.00	10610	No
MF-1100 Western	10734.00	5580.00	7300.00	8980.00	Perkins	6	354D	12F-4R	93.00	9800	C,H,A
MF-1130 RC	12426.00	5960.00	7950.00	9620.00	Perkins	6T	354D	12F-4R	120.51	9500	No
MF-1130 RC	13567.00	6510.00	8680.00	10500.00	Perkins	6T	354D	12F-4R	120.51	10500	C,H,A
MF-1130 Western	12889.00	6190.00	8250.00	9980.00	Perkins	6T	354D	12F-4R	120.00	10000	C,H,A
MF-1150 RC	14133.00	5650.00	6780.00	7660.00	Perkins	V8	511D	12F-4R	135.60	13425	No
MF-1150 RC	15790.00	6320.00	7580.00	8570.00	Perkins	V8	511D	12F-4R	135.60	14450	C,H,A
MF-1150 Western	15002.00	6000.00	7200.00	8140.00	Perkins	V8	511D	12F-4R	135.00	13950	C,H,A
MF-1500 4WD	18088.00	6330.00	7960.00	8920.00	Cat.	V8	573D	12F-4R		14420	C
MF-1800 4WD	20995.00	7350.00	9240.00	10350.00	Cat.	V8	636D	12F-4R		16000	C

RC - Row Crop

1973

Model	Approx. Retail Price New	Fair	Good	Premium	Make	No. Cyls.	Displ. Cu.-In.	No. Speeds	P.T.O. H.P.	Approx. Shipping Wt.-Lbs.	Cab
MF-135	5188.00	3280.00	4210.00	5140.00	Perkins	3	153G	12F-4R	37.55	3370	No
MF-135	5605.00	3500.00	4490.00	5480.00	Perkins	3	153D	12F-4R	37.82	3540	No
MF-150	5776.00	3590.00	4610.00	5620.00	Perkins	3	153G	12F-4R	37.00	3940	No
MF-150	6310.00	3870.00	4970.00	6060.00	Perkins	3	153D	12F-4R	37.88	4325	No
MF-165	6286.00	3860.00	4950.00	6040.00	Perkins	4	212G	12F-4R	51.91	4780	No
MF-165	6651.00	4060.00	5200.00	6340.00	Perkins	4	204D	12F-4R	52.42	5150	No
MF-175	7515.00	4510.00	5790.00	7060.00	Perkins	4	236G	12F-4R	61.89	5319	No
MF-175	8325.00	4940.00	6340.00	7740.00	Perkins	4	236D	12F-4R	63.34	5725	No
MF-180	7622.00	4570.00	5860.00	7150.00	Perkins	4	236G	12F-4R	62.83	6250	No
MF-180	8420.00	4990.00	6410.00	7820.00	Perkins	4	236D	12F-4R	63.68	6618	No
MF-1085 RC	11434.00	4480.00	5600.00	6220.00	Perkins	4	318D	12F-4R	81.58	9400	No
MF-1085 RC w/Cab	14152.00	5460.00	6820.00	7570.00	Perkins	4	318D	12F-4R	81.58	10400	C,H,A
MF-1085 Western	13664.00	5280.00	6600.00	7330.00	Perkins	4	318D	12F-4R	81.00	9900	C,H,A
MF-1105 RC	12978.00	5030.00	6290.00	6980.00	Perkins	6T	354D	12F-4R	100.72	9725	No
MF-1105 RC w/Cab	15534.00	5950.00	7440.00	8260.00	Perkins	6T	354D	12F-4R	100.72	10725	C,H,A
MF-1105 Western	15178.00	5820.00	7280.00	8080.00	Perkins	6T	354D	12F-4R	100.	10000	C,H,A
MF-1135 RC	14107.00	5080.00	6350.00	7050.00	Perkins	6T	354D	12F-4R	120.84	10425	No
MF-1135 RC w/Cab	16898.00	6080.00	7600.00	8440.00	Perkins	6T	354D	12F-4R	120.84	11425	C,H,A
MF-1135 Western	16347.00	5890.00	7360.00	8170.00	Perkins	6T	354D	12F-4R	120.00	11000	C,H,A
MF-1155 RC	16494.00	5940.00	7420.00	8240.00	Perkins	V8	540D	12F-4R	140.97	12750	No
MF-1155 RC w/Cab	19050.00	6860.00	8570.00	9510.00	Perkins	V8	540D	12F-4R	140.97	13750	C,H,A
MF-1155 Western	18020.00	6490.00	8110.00	9000.00	Perkins	V8	540D	12F-4R	140.00	13000	C,H,A
MF-1500 4WD	19040.00	6850.00	8570.00	9510.00	Cat.	V8	573D	12F-4R		14420	C
MF-1800 4WD	22100.00	7960.00	9950.00	11050.00	Cat.	V8	636D	12F-4R		16000	C

RC - Row Crop

1974

Model	Approx. Retail Price New	Fair	Good	Premium	Make	No. Cyls.	Displ. Cu.-In.	No. Speeds	P.T.O. H.P.	Approx. Shipping Wt.-Lbs.	Cab
MF-135	4743.00	3100.00	3910.00	4730.00	Perkins	3	153G	6F-2R	37.00	3305	No
MF-135	4961.00	3220.00	4050.00	4900.00	Perkins	3	153G	6F-2R	37.00	3320	No
MF-135	5217.00	3360.00	4230.00	5120.00	Perkins	3	153D	6F-2R	37.00	3475	No
MF-135	5301.00	3400.00	4280.00	5180.00	Perkins	3	153G	12F-4R	37.55	3370	No
MF-135	5440.00	3480.00	4380.00	5300.00	Perkins	3	153D	8F-2R	37.00	3490	No
MF-135	5775.00	3660.00	4610.00	5580.00	Perkins	3	153D	12F-4R	37.82	3540	No
MF-150	5650.00	4130.00	5200.00	6290.00	Perkins	3	153G	8F-2R	37.00	3860	No
MF-150	5955.00	3760.00	4730.00	5720.00	Perkins	3	153G	12F-4R	37.00	3940	No
MF-150	6200.00	3890.00	4900.00	5930.00	Perkins	3	153D	8F-2R	37.00	4200	No
MF-150	6505.00	4050.00	5100.00	6170.00	Perkins	3	153D	12F-4R	37.88	4325	No
MF-165	6690.00	4150.00	5230.00	6330.00	Perkins	4	212G	8F-2R	51.00	4597	No
MF-165	7040.00	4340.00	5470.00	6620.00	Perkins	4	212G	12F-4R	51.91	4780	No
MF-165	7275.00	4470.00	5630.00	6810.00	Perkins	4	204D	8F-2R	52.00	4855	No
MF-165	7390.00	4530.00	5710.00	6910.00	Perkins	4	204D	12F-4R	52.42	5100	No
MF-175	8000.00	4500.00	5760.00	6850.00	Perkins	4	236G	8F-2R	61.00	5199	No
MF-175	8350.00	4680.00	5980.00	7120.00	Perkins	4	236G	12F-4R	61.89	5319	No
MF-175	8900.00	4950.00	6340.00	7550.00	Perkins	4	236D	8F-2R	63.00	5605	No
MF-175	9250.00	5130.00	6560.00	7810.00	Perkins	4	236D	12F-4R	63.34	5725	No
MF-180	8200.00	4600.00	5890.00	7010.00	Perkins	4	236G	8F-2R	62.00	6200	No
MF-180	8550.00	4780.00	6110.00	7270.00	Perkins	4	236G	12F-4R	62.83	6250	No
MF-180	9000.00	5000.00	6400.00	7620.00	Perkins	4	236D	8F-2R	63.00	6568	No
MF-180	9350.00	5180.00	6620.00	7880.00	Perkins	4	236D	12F-4R	63.68	6618	No
MF-285	12303.00	5170.00	6150.00	6890.00	Perkins	4	318D	8F-2R	81.00	6975	No
MF-285	12867.00	5400.00	6430.00	7200.00	Perkins	4	318D	12F-4R	81.96	7025	No
MF-1085 RC	12889.00	4770.00	5930.00	6580.00	Perkins	4	318D	8F-2R	81.00	8800	No
MF-1085 RC	13453.00	4980.00	6190.00	6870.00	Perkins	4	318D	12F-4R	81.58	9400	No
MF-1085 RC	16084.00	5950.00	7400.00	8210.00	Perkins	4	318D	8F-2R	81.00	9800	C,H,A
MF-1085 RC	16649.00	6160.00	7660.00	8500.00	Perkins	4	318D	12F-4R	81.58	10400	C,H,A
MF-1085 Western	16075.00	5950.00	7400.00	8210.00	Perkins	4	318D	12F-4R	81.00	9900	C,H,A
MF-1105 RC	15596.00	5770.00	7170.00	7960.00	Perkins	6T	354D	8F-2R	100.	9125	No
MF-1105 RC	16222.00	6000.00	7460.00	8280.00	Perkins	6T	354D	12F-4R	100.72	9725	No
MF-1105 RC	18792.00	6950.00	8640.00	9590.00	Perkins	6T	354D	8F-2R	100.	10125	C,H,A
MF-1105 RC	19418.00	7190.00	8930.00	9910.00	Perkins	6T	354D	12F-4R	100.72	10725	C,H,A
MF-1105 Western	18973.00	7020.00	8730.00	9690.00	Perkins	6T	354D	12F-4R	100.	10000	C,H,A

Massey Ferguson (Cont.)

1974 (Cont.)

Model	Approx. Retail Price New	Estimated Average Value Less Repairs Fair	Good	Premium	Engine Make	No. Cyls.	Displ. Cu.-In.	No. Speeds	P.T.O. H.P.	Approx. Shipping Wt.-Lbs.	Cab
MF-1135 RC	17056.00	**6310.00**	**7850.00**	**8710.00**	Perkins	6T	354D	8F-2R	120.00	9825	No
MF-1135 RC	17634.00	**6530.00**	**8110.00**	**9000.00**	Perkins	6T	354D	12F-4R	120.84	10425	No
MF-1135 RC	20342.00	**7530.00**	**9360.00**	**10390.00**	Perkins	6T	354D	8F-2R	120.00	10825	C,H,A
MF-1135 RC	21122.00	**7820.00**	**9720.00**	**10790.00**	Perkins	6T	354D	12F-4R	120.84	11425	C,H,A
MF-1135 Western	20434.00	**7560.00**	**9400.00**	**10430.00**	Perkins	6T	354D	12F-4R	120.00	11000	C,H,A
MF-1155 RC	19991.00	**7400.00**	**9200.00**	**10210.00**	Perkins	V8	540D	8F-2R	140.00	12150	No
MF-1155 RC	20617.00	**7630.00**	**9480.00**	**10520.00**	Perkins	V8	540D	12F-4R	140.97	12750	No
MF-1155 RC	23186.00	**8580.00**	**10670.00**	**11840.00**	Perkins	V8	540D	8F-2R	140.00	13150	C,H,A
MF-1155 RC	23812.00	**8810.00**	**10950.00**	**12160.00**	Perkins	V8	540D	12F-4R	140.97	13750	C,H,A
MF-1155 Western	22525.00	**8330.00**	**10360.00**	**11500.00**	Perkins	V8	540D	12F-4R	140.00	13000	C,H,A
MF-1500 4WD	22400.00	**6500.00**	**8740.00**	**9790.00**	Cat.	V8	573D	12F-4R		14420	C
MF-1505 4WD	26190.00	**7600.00**	**10210.00**	**11440.00**	Cat.	V8	636D	12F-4R		16500	C
MF-1505 4WD w/PTO	27540.00	**7990.00**	**10740.00**	**12030.00**	Cat.	V8	636D	12F-4R	175.96	17000	C
MF-1800 4WD	26000.00	**7540.00**	**10140.00**	**11360.00**	Cat.	V8	636D	12F-4R		16000	C
MF-1805 4WD	27873.00	**8080.00**	**10870.00**	**12170.00**	Cat.	V8	636D	12F-4R		16700	C
MF-1805 4WD w/PTO	29223.00	**8480.00**	**11400.00**	**12770.00**	Cat.	V8	636D	12F-4R	192.65	17200	C

RC - Row Crop

1975

Model	Approx. Retail Price New	Fair	Good	Premium	Make	No. Cyls.	Displ. Cu.-In.	No. Speeds	P.T.O. H.P.	Approx. Shipping Wt.-Lbs.	Cab
MF-230	5809.00	**3470.00**	**4290.00**	**5150.00**	Continental	4	145G	6F-2R	34.34	3200	No
MF-230	6081.00	**3620.00**	**4480.00**	**5380.00**	Perkins	3	152D	6F-2R	34.53	3404	No
MF-235	6721.00	**3970.00**	**4910.00**	**5890.00**	Continental	4	145G	6F-2R	41.00	3119	No
MF-235	6912.00	**4080.00**	**5040.00**	**6050.00**	Continental	4	145G	8F-2R	41.13	3244	No
MF-235	6960.00	**4100.00**	**5070.00**	**6080.00**	Perkins	3	152D	6F-2R	42.00	3200	No
MF-235	7222.00	**4250.00**	**5250.00**	**6300.00**	Continental	4	145G	12F-4R	41.00	3369	No
MF-235	7248.00	**4260.00**	**5270.00**	**6320.00**	Perkins	3	152D	8F-2R	42.39	3325	No
MF-235	7584.00	**4450.00**	**5500.00**	**6600.00**	Perkins	3	152D	12F-4R	42.00	3450	No
MF-255	7812.00	**3980.00**	**5000.00**	**5900.00**	Perkins	4	212G	8F-2R	50.00	5450	No
MF-255	8067.00	**4110.00**	**5160.00**	**6090.00**	Perkins	4	203D	8F-2R	50.00	5650	No
MF-255	8225.00	**4200.00**	**5260.00**	**6210.00**	Perkins	4	212G	12F-4R	50.01	5600	No
MF-255	8480.00	**4330.00**	**5430.00**	**6410.00**	Perkins	4	203D	12F-4R	50.69	5850	No
MF-255 RC	8203.00	**4180.00**	**5250.00**	**6200.00**	Perkins	4	212G	8F-2R	50.00	5950	No
MF-255 RC	8470.00	**4320.00**	**5420.00**	**6400.00**	Perkins	4	203D	8F-2R	50.00	6150	No
MF-255 RC	8636.00	**4400.00**	**5530.00**	**6530.00**	Perkins	4	212G	12F-4R	50.00	6100	No
MF-255 RC	8904.00	**4540.00**	**5700.00**	**6730.00**	Perkins	4	203D	12F-4R	50.00	6350	No
MF-265	9445.00	**4060.00**	**4820.00**	**5400.00**	Perkins	4	236G	8F-2R	60.00	5920	No
MF-265	9700.00	**4170.00**	**4950.00**	**5540.00**	Perkins	4	236D	8F-2R	60.00	6050	No
MF-265	9881.00	**4250.00**	**5040.00**	**5650.00**	Perkins	4	236G	12F-4R	60.00	5970	No
MF-265	10136.00	**4360.00**	**5170.00**	**5790.00**	Perkins	4	236D	12F-4R	60.73	6100	No
MF-265 RC	9917.00	**4260.00**	**5060.00**	**5670.00**	Perkins	4	236G	8F-2R	60.00	6420	No
MF-265 RC	10185.00	**4380.00**	**5190.00**	**5810.00**	Perkins	4	236D	8F-2R	60.00	6550	No
MF-265 RC	10375.00	**4460.00**	**5290.00**	**5930.00**	Perkins	4	236G	12F-4R	60.00	6470	No
MF-265 RC	10643.00	**4580.00**	**5430.00**	**6080.00**	Perkins	4	236D	12F-4R	60.73	6600	No
MF-275	10413.00	**4480.00**	**5310.00**	**5950.00**	Perkins	4	248D	8F-2R	67.00	6370	No
MF-275	10849.00	**4670.00**	**5530.00**	**6190.00**	Perkins	4	248D	12F-4R	67.43	6420	No
MF-275 RC	10937.00	**4700.00**	**5580.00**	**6250.00**	Perkins	4	248D	8F-2R	67.00	6370	No
MF-275 RC	11373.00	**4890.00**	**5800.00**	**6500.00**	Perkins	4	248D	12F-4R	67.00	6420	No
MF-285	12198.00	**5250.00**	**6220.00**	**6970.00**	Perkins	4	318D	8F-2R	81.00	6975	No
MF-285	12755.00	**5490.00**	**6510.00**	**7290.00**	Perkins	4	318D	12F-4R	81.96	7025	No
MF-1085 RC	13567.00	**5160.00**	**6380.00**	**7080.00**	Perkins	4	318D	8F-2R	81.00	8800	No
MF-1085 RC	14161.00	**5380.00**	**6660.00**	**7390.00**	Perkins	4	318D	12F-4R	81.58	9400	No
MF-1085 RC	16930.00	**6430.00**	**7960.00**	**8840.00**	Perkins	4	318D	8F-2R	81.00	9800	C,H,A
MF-1085 RC	17525.00	**6660.00**	**8240.00**	**9150.00**	Perkins	4	318D	12F-4R	81.58	10400	C,H,A
MF-1085 Western	16921.00	**6430.00**	**7950.00**	**8830.00**	Perkins	4	318D	12F-4R	81.00	9900	C,H,A
MF-1105 RC	16417.00	**6240.00**	**7720.00**	**8570.00**	Perkins	6T	354D	8F-2R	100.	9125	No
MF-1105 RC	17076.00	**6490.00**	**8030.00**	**8910.00**	Perkins	6T	354D	12F-4R	100.72	9725	No
MF-1105 RC	19781.00	**7520.00**	**9300.00**	**10320.00**	Perkins	6T	354D	8F-2R	100.	10125	C,H,A
MF-1105 RC	20440.00	**7770.00**	**9610.00**	**10670.00**	Perkins	6T	354D	12F-4R	100.72	10725	C,H,A
MF-1105 Western	19972.00	**7590.00**	**9390.00**	**10420.00**	Perkins	6T	354D	12F-4R	100.	10000	C,H,A
MF-1135 RC	17954.00	**6820.00**	**8440.00**	**9370.00**	Perkins	6T	354D	8F-2R	120.00	9825	No
MF-1135 RC	18562.00	**7050.00**	**8720.00**	**9680.00**	Perkins	6T	354D	12F-4R	120.84	10425	No
MF-1135 RC	21413.00	**8140.00**	**10060.00**	**11170.00**	Perkins	6T	354D	8F-2R	120.00	10825	C,H,A
MF-1135 RC	22234.00	**8450.00**	**10450.00**	**11600.00**	Perkins	6T	354D	12F-4R	120.84	11425	C,H,A
MF-1135 Western	21509.00	**8170.00**	**10110.00**	**11220.00**	Perkins	6T	354D	12F-4R	120.00	11000	C,H,A
MF-1155 RC	21043.00	**6310.00**	**8210.00**	**9110.00**	Perkins	V8	540D	8F-2R	140.00	12150	No
MF-1155 RC	21702.00	**6510.00**	**8460.00**	**9390.00**	Perkins	V8	540D	12F-4R	140.97	12750	No
MF-1155 RC	24406.00	**7320.00**	**9520.00**	**10570.00**	Perkins	V8	540D	8F-2R	140.00	13150	C,H,A
MF-1155 RC	25065.00	**7520.00**	**9780.00**	**10860.00**	Perkins	V8	540D	12F-4R	140.97	13750	C,H,A
MF-1155 Western	23710.00	**7110.00**	**9250.00**	**10270.00**	Perkins	V8	540D	12F-4R	140.00	13000	C,H,A
MF-1505 4WD	30900.00	**8670.00**	**11270.00**	**12510.00**	Cat.	V8	636D	12F-4R		16500	C,H,A
MF-1505 4WD w/PTO	32400.00	**9120.00**	**11860.00**	**13170.00**	Cat.	V8	636D	12F-4R	175.96	17000	C,H,A
MF-1805 4WD	32880.00	**9260.00**	**12040.00**	**13360.00**	Cat.	V8	636D	12F-4R		16700	C,H,A
MF-1805 4WD w/PTO	34380.00	**9710.00**	**12630.00**	**14020.00**	Cat.	V8	636D	12F-4R	192.65	17200	C,H,A

RC - Row Crop

1976

Model	Approx. Retail Price New	Fair	Good	Premium	Make	No. Cyls.	Displ. Cu.-In.	No. Speeds	P.T.O. H.P.	Approx. Shipping Wt.-Lbs.	Cab
MF-230	5809.00	**3530.00**	**4290.00**	**5110.00**	Continental	4	145G	6F-2R	34.34	3200	No
MF-230	6081.00	**3690.00**	**4480.00**	**5330.00**	Perkins	3	153D	6F-2R	34.53	3404	No
MF-235	6683.00	**4020.00**	**4880.00**	**5810.00**	Continental	4	145G	6F-2R	41.00	3119	No
MF-235	6948.00	**4170.00**	**5070.00**	**6030.00**	Perkins	3	153D	6F-2R	42.00	3200	No
MF-235	7148.00	**4280.00**	**5200.00**	**6190.00**	Continental	4	145G	8F-2R	41.13	3244	No
MF-235	7492.00	**4480.00**	**5440.00**	**6470.00**	Continental	4	145G	12F-4R	41.00	3369	No
MF-235	7740.00	**4610.00**	**5600.00**	**6660.00**	Perkins	3	153D	8F-2R	42.39	3325	No
MF-235	8084.00	**4810.00**	**5840.00**	**6950.00**	Perkins	3	153D	12F-4R	42.00	3450	No

Massey Ferguson (Cont.)

1976 (Cont.)

Model	Approx. Retail Price New	Estimated Average Value Less Repairs Fair	Good	Premium	Engine Make	No. Cyls.	Displ. Cu.-In.	No. Speeds	P.T.O. H.P.	Approx. Shipping Wt.-Lbs.	Cab
MF-245	7073.00	**3860.00**	**4850.00**	**5680.00**	Continental	4	145G	6F-2R	41.00	3450	No
MF-245	7343.00	**4000.00**	**5020.00**	**5870.00**	Perkins	3	153D	6F-2R	42.00	3600	No
MF-245	7547.00	**4100.00**	**5150.00**	**6030.00**	Continental	4	145G	8F-2R	41.09	3500	No
MF-245	7898.00	**4280.00**	**5380.00**	**6300.00**	Continental	4	145G	12F-4R	41.00	3540	No
MF-245	8150.00	**4410.00**	**5540.00**	**6480.00**	Perkins	3	153D	8F-2R	42.00	3650	No
MF-245	8501.00	**4590.00**	**5760.00**	**6740.00**	Perkins	3	153D	12F-4R	42.90	3693	No
MF-255	8963.00	**4570.00**	**5740.00**	**6720.00**	Perkins	4	236D	8F-2R	52.00	5650	No
MF-255	9422.00	**4810.00**	**6030.00**	**7060.00**	Perkins	4	236D	12F-4R	52.68	5850	No
MF-255 RC	9514.00	**4850.00**	**6090.00**	**7130.00**	Perkins	4	236D	8F-2R	52.00	6150	No
MF-255 RC	9973.00	**5090.00**	**6380.00**	**7470.00**	Perkins	4	236D	12F-4R	52.00	6350	No
MF-265	10210.00	**4490.00**	**5310.00**	**5950.00**	Perkins	4	236D	8F-2R	60.00	6050	No
MF-265	10669.00	**4690.00**	**5550.00**	**6220.00**	Perkins	4	236D	12F-4R	60.73	6100	No
MF-265 RC	10762.00	**4740.00**	**5600.00**	**6270.00**	Perkins	4	236D	8F-2R	60.00	6550	No
MF-265 RC	11221.00	**4940.00**	**5840.00**	**6540.00**	Perkins	4	236D	12F-4R	60.00	6600	No
MF-275	10961.00	**4820.00**	**5700.00**	**6380.00**	Perkins	4	248D	8F-2R	67.00	6370	No
MF-275	11420.00	**5030.00**	**5940.00**	**6650.00**	Perkins	4	248D	12F-4R	67.43	6420	No
MF-275 RC	11513.00	**5070.00**	**5990.00**	**6710.00**	Perkins	4	248D	8F-2R	67.00	6870	No
MF-275 RC	11972.00	**5270.00**	**6230.00**	**6980.00**	Perkins	4	248D	12F-4R	67.00	6920	No
MF-285	12840.00	**5650.00**	**6680.00**	**7480.00**	Perkins	4	318D	8F-2R	81.00	6975	No
MF-285	13426.00	**5910.00**	**6980.00**	**7820.00**	Perkins	4	318D	12F-4R	81.96	7025	No
MF-1085 RC	13601.00	**5300.00**	**6530.00**	**7180.00**	Perkins	4	318D	8F-2R	81.00	8800	No
MF-1085 RC	14199.00	**5540.00**	**6820.00**	**7500.00**	Perkins	4	318D	12F-4R	81.58	9400	No
MF-1085 RC	17578.00	**6860.00**	**8440.00**	**9280.00**	Perkins	4	318D	12F-4R	81.58	10400	C,H,A
MF-1085 Western	16969.00	**6620.00**	**8150.00**	**8970.00**	Perkins	4	318D	12F-4R	81.00	9900	C,H,A
MF-1105 RC	16581.00	**6470.00**	**7960.00**	**8760.00**	Perkins	6T	354D	8F-2R	100.	9125	No
MF-1105 RC	17246.00	**6730.00**	**8280.00**	**9110.00**	Perkins	6T	354D	12F-4R	100.72	9725	No
MF-1105 RC	20644.00	**8050.00**	**9910.00**	**10900.00**	Perkins	6T	354D	12F-4R	100.72	10725	C,H,A
MF-1105 Western	20171.00	**7870.00**	**9680.00**	**10650.00**	Perkins	6T	354D	12F-4R	100.	10000	C,H,A
MF-1135 RC	18134.00	**7070.00**	**8700.00**	**9570.00**	Perkins	6T	354D	8F-2R	120.00	9825	No
MF-1135 RC	18747.00	**7310.00**	**9000.00**	**9900.00**	Perkins	6T	354D	12F-4R	120.84	10425	No
MF-1135 RC	22345.00	**8720.00**	**10730.00**	**11800.00**	Perkins	6T	354D	12F-4R	120.84	11425	C,H,A
MF-1135 Western	21617.00	**8430.00**	**10380.00**	**11420.00**	Perkins	6T	354D	12F-4R	120.00	11000	C,H,A
MF-1155 RC	21253.00	**6590.00**	**8500.00**	**9440.00**	Perkins	V8	540D	8F-2R	140.00	12150	No
MF-1155 RC	21919.00	**6800.00**	**8770.00**	**9740.00**	Perkins	V8	540D	12F-4R	140.97	12750	No
MF-1155 RC	25316.00	**7850.00**	**10130.00**	**11240.00**	Perkins	V8	540D	12F-4R	140.97	13750	C,H,A
MF-1155 Western	23947.00	**7420.00**	**9580.00**	**10630.00**	Perkins	V8	540D	12F-4R	140.00	13000	C,H,A
MF-1505 4WD	31414.00	**9740.00**	**12570.00**	**13950.00**	Cat.	V8	636D	12F-4R		16500	C,H,A
MF-1505 4WD w/PTO	33191.00	**10290.00**	**13280.00**	**14740.00**	Cat.	V8	636D	12F-4R	175.96	17400	C,H,A
MF-1805 4WD	33352.00	**10340.00**	**13340.00**	**14810.00**	Cat.	V8	636D	12F-4R		16700	C,H,A
MF-1805 4WD w/PTO	35129.00	**10890.00**	**14050.00**	**15600.00**	Cat.	V8	636D	12F-4R	192.65	17600	C,H,A
MF-2800 RC	33030.00	**6610.00**	**9580.00**	**10730.00**	Perkins	V8T	640D	8F-6R	194.00	13545	C,H,A
MF-2800 RC	33872.00	**6770.00**	**9820.00**	**11000.00**	Perkins	V8T	640D	24F-4R	194.00	13890	C,H,A
MF-2800 Western	32278.00	**6460.00**	**9360.00**	**10480.00**	Perkins	V8T	640D	24F-4R	194.00	13243	C,H,A

RC - Row Crop

1977

Model	Approx. Retail Price New	Fair	Good	Premium	Engine Make	No. Cyls.	Displ. Cu.-In.	No. Speeds	P.T.O. H.P.	Approx. Shipping Wt.-Lbs.	Cab
MF-230	6398.00	**3790.00**	**4690.00**	**5530.00**	Continental	4	145G	6F-2R	34.34	3200	No
MF-230	6684.00	**3950.00**	**4890.00**	**5770.00**	Perkins	3	153D	6F-2R	34.53	3404	No
MF-245	7548.00	**4100.00**	**5150.00**	**5970.00**	Continental	4	145G	6F-2R	41.00	3450	No
MF-245	7836.00	**4250.00**	**5340.00**	**6190.00**	Perkins	3	153D	6F-2R	42.00	3600	No
MF-245	7869.00	**4270.00**	**5360.00**	**6220.00**	Continental	4	145G	8F-2R	41.09	3500	No
MF-245	8506.00	**4590.00**	**5760.00**	**6680.00**	Perkins	3	153D	8F-2R	42.00	3650	No
MF-245	8882.00	**4790.00**	**6000.00**	**6960.00**	Perkins	3	153D	12F-4R	42.90	3690	No
MF-255	9507.00	**4280.00**	**5040.00**	**5590.00**	Perkins	4	236D	8F-2R	52.00	5650	No
MF-255	9987.00	**4490.00**	**5290.00**	**5870.00**	Perkins	4	236D	12F-4R	52.68	5850	No
MF-255 RC	10084.00	**4540.00**	**5350.00**	**5940.00**	Perkins	4	236D	8F-2R	52.00	5700	No
MF-255 RC	10564.00	**4750.00**	**5600.00**	**6220.00**	Perkins	4	236D	12F-4R	52.00	5900	No
MF-265	10576.00	**4760.00**	**5610.00**	**6230.00**	Perkins	4	236D	8F-2R	60.00	6050	No
MF-265	11056.00	**4980.00**	**5860.00**	**6510.00**	Perkins	4	236D	12F-4R	60.73	6100	No
MF-265 RC	11151.00	**5020.00**	**5910.00**	**6560.00**	Perkins	4	236D	8F-2R	60.00	6200	No
MF-265 RC	11631.00	**5230.00**	**6160.00**	**6840.00**	Perkins	4	236D	12F-4R	60.00	6250	No
MF-275	11460.00	**5160.00**	**6070.00**	**6740.00**	Perkins	4	248D	8F-2R	67.00	6370	No
MF-275	11940.00	**5370.00**	**6330.00**	**7030.00**	Perkins	4	248D	12F-4R	67.43	6420	No
MF-275 RC	12037.00	**5420.00**	**6380.00**	**7080.00**	Perkins	4	248D	8F-2R	67.00	6520	No
MF-275 RC	12517.00	**5630.00**	**6630.00**	**7360.00**	Perkins	4	248D	12F-4R	67.00	6570	No
MF-285	13367.00	**6020.00**	**7090.00**	**7870.00**	Perkins	4	318D	8F-2R	81.00	6975	No
MF-285	13977.00	**6290.00**	**7410.00**	**8230.00**	Perkins	4	318D	12F-4R	81.96	7025	No
MF-1085 RC	13879.00	**5550.00**	**6800.00**	**7480.00**	Perkins	4	318D	8F-2R	81.00	8800	No
MF-1085 RC	14489.00	**5800.00**	**7100.00**	**7810.00**	Perkins	4	318D	12F-4R	81.58	9400	No
MF-1085 RC	17937.00	**7180.00**	**8790.00**	**9670.00**	Perkins	4	318D	12F-4R	81.58	10400	C,H,A
MF-1085 Western	17315.00	**6930.00**	**8480.00**	**9330.00**	Perkins	4	318D	12F-4R	81.00	9900	C,H,A
MF-1105 RC	16685.00	**6670.00**	**8180.00**	**9000.00**	Perkins	6T	354D	8F-2R	100.	9125	No
MF-1105 RC	17360.00	**6940.00**	**8510.00**	**9360.00**	Perkins	6T	354D	12F-4R	100.72	9725	No
MF-1105 RC	20808.00	**8320.00**	**10200.00**	**11220.00**	Perkins	6T	354D	12F-4R	100.72	10725	C,H,A
MF-1105 Western	20327.00	**8130.00**	**9960.00**	**10960.00**	Perkins	6T	354D	12F-4R	100.	10000	C,H,A
MF-1135 RC	18275.00	**7310.00**	**8960.00**	**9860.00**	Perkins	6T	354D	8F-2R	120.00	9825	No
MF-1135 RC	18950.00	**7580.00**	**9290.00**	**10220.00**	Perkins	6T	354D	12F-4R	120.84	10425	No
MF-1135 RC	22398.00	**8960.00**	**10980.00**	**12080.00**	Perkins	6T	354D	12F-4R	120.84	11425	C,H,A
MF-1135 Western	21917.00	**8770.00**	**10740.00**	**11810.00**	Perkins	6T	354D	12F-4R	120.00	11000	C,H,A
MF-1155 RC	21547.00	**6900.00**	**8830.00**	**9800.00**	Perkins	V8	540D	8F-2R	140.00	12150	No
MF-1155 RC	22222.00	**7110.00**	**9110.00**	**10110.00**	Perkins	V8	540D	12F-4R	140.97	12750	No
MF-1155 RC	25670.00	**8210.00**	**10530.00**	**11690.00**	Perkins	V8	540D	12F-4R	140.97	13750	C,H,A
MF-1155 Western	24282.00	**7770.00**	**9960.00**	**11060.00**	Perkins	V8	540D	12F-4R	140.00	13000	C,H,A
MF-1505 4WD	34862.00	**11160.00**	**14290.00**	**15860.00**	Cat.	V8	636D	12F-4R		16500	C,H,A

Massey Ferguson (Cont.)

1977 (Cont.)

Model	Approx. Retail Price New	Estimated Average Value Less Repairs Fair	Good	Premium	Engine Make	No. Cyls.	Displ. Cu.-In.	No. Speeds	P.T.O. H.P.	Approx. Shipping Wt.-Lbs.	Cab
MF-1505 4WD w/PTO	36783.00	**11770.00**	**15080.00**	**16740.00**	Cat.	V8	636D	12F-4R	175.96	17400	C,H,A
MF-1805 4WD	36958.00	**11830.00**	**15150.00**	**16820.00**	Cat.	V8	636D	12F-4R		16700	C,H,A
MF-1805 4WD w/PTO	38879.00	**12440.00**	**15940.00**	**17690.00**	Cat.	V8	636D	12F-4R	192.65	17600	C,H,A
MF-2800 RC	35232.00	**7400.00**	**10570.00**	**11840.00**	Perkins	V8T	640D	8F-6R	194.00	13545	C,H,A
MF-2800 RC	36125.00	**7590.00**	**10840.00**	**12140.00**	Perkins	V8T	640D	24F-4R	194.00	13890	C,H,A
MF-2800 Western	34434.00	**7230.00**	**10330.00**	**11570.00**	Perkins	V8T	640D	24F-4R	194.00	13243	C,H,A

RC - Row Crop

1978

Model	Approx. Retail Price New	Fair	Good	Premium	Make	No. Cyls.	Displ. Cu.-In.	No. Speeds	P.T.O. H.P.	Approx. Shipping Wt.-Lbs.	Cab
MF-205	4935.00	**3320.00**	**4040.00**	**4730.00**	Toyosha	2	65D	6F-2R	16.56	1849	No
MF-205-4	5514.00	**3650.00**	**4430.00**	**5180.00**	Toyosha	2	65D	6F-2R	16.40	2257	No
MF-210	5820.00	**3820.00**	**4640.00**	**5430.00**	Toyosha	2	77D	12F-3R	21.96	2050	No
MF-210-4	6635.00	**4280.00**	**5190.00**	**6070.00**	Toyosha	2	77D	12F-3R	21.77	2257	No
MF-220	7348.00	**4680.00**	**5680.00**	**6650.00**	Toyosha	2	90D	12F-3R	26.37	2390	No
MF-220-4	8590.00	**5150.00**	**6250.00**	**7310.00**	Toyosha	2	90D	12F-3R	26.48	2700	No
MF-230	7189.00	**4030.00**	**4890.00**	**5720.00**	Continental	4	145G	6F-2R	34.34	3200	No
MF-230	7505.00	**4200.00**	**5100.00**	**5970.00**	Perkins	3	153D	6F-2R	34.53	3404	No
MF-245	8467.00	**3900.00**	**4570.00**	**5030.00**	Continental	4	145G	6F-2R	41.00	3450	No
MF-245	8787.00	**4040.00**	**4750.00**	**5230.00**	Perkins	3	153D	6F-2R	42.00	3600	No
MF-245	8822.00	**4060.00**	**4760.00**	**5240.00**	Continental	4	145G	8F-2R	41.09	3500	No
MF-245	9532.00	**4390.00**	**5150.00**	**5670.00**	Perkins	3	153D	8F-2R	42.00	3650	No
MF-245	9947.00	**4580.00**	**5370.00**	**5910.00**	Perkins	3	153D	12F-4R	42.90	3693	No
MF-255	10930.00	**5030.00**	**5900.00**	**6490.00**	Perkins	4	236D	8F-2R	52.00	5650	No
MF-255	11476.00	**5280.00**	**6200.00**	**6820.00**	Perkins	4	236D	12F-4R	52.68	5850	No
MF-255 RC	11497.00	**5290.00**	**6210.00**	**6830.00**	Perkins	4	236D	8F-2R	52.00	5700	No
MF-255 RC	12131.00	**5580.00**	**6550.00**	**7210.00**	Perkins	4	236D	12F-4R	52.00	5900	No
MF-265	12051.00	**5540.00**	**6510.00**	**7160.00**	Perkins	4	236D	8F-2R	60.00	6050	No
MF-265	12597.00	**5800.00**	**6800.00**	**7480.00**	Perkins	4	236D	12F-4R	60.73	6100	No
MF-265 RC	12618.00	**5800.00**	**6810.00**	**7490.00**	Perkins	4	236D	8F-2R	60.00	6200	No
MF-265 RC	13252.00	**6100.00**	**7160.00**	**7880.00**	Perkins	4	236D	12F-4R	60.00	6250	No
MF-275	13152.00	**6050.00**	**7100.00**	**7810.00**	Perkins	4	248D	8F-2R	67.00	6370	No
MF-275	13698.00	**6300.00**	**7400.00**	**8140.00**	Perkins	4	248D	12F-4R	67.43	6420	No
MF-275 RC	13719.00	**6310.00**	**7410.00**	**8150.00**	Perkins	4	248D	8F-2R	67.00	6520	No
MF-275 RC	14353.00	**6600.00**	**7750.00**	**8530.00**	Perkins	4	248D	12F-4R	67.00	6570	No
MF-285	15189.00	**6230.00**	**7600.00**	**8360.00**	Perkins	4	318D	8F-2R	81.00	6975	No
MF-285	15874.00	**6510.00**	**7940.00**	**8730.00**	Perkins	4	318D	12F-4R	81.96	7025	No
MF-1085 RC	15902.00	**6520.00**	**7950.00**	**8750.00**	Perkins	4	318D	8F-2R	81.00	8800	No
MF-1085 RC	16587.00	**6800.00**	**8290.00**	**9120.00**	Perkins	4	318D	12F-4R	81.58	9400	No
MF-1085 RC	19829.00	**8130.00**	**9920.00**	**10910.00**	Perkins	4	318D	8F-2R	81.00	9800	C,H,A
MF-1085 RC	20514.00	**8410.00**	**10260.00**	**11290.00**	Perkins	4	318D	12F-4R	81.58	10400	C,H,A
MF-1085 Western	19815.00	**8120.00**	**9910.00**	**10900.00**	Perkins	4	318D	12F-4R	81.00	9900	C,H,A
MF-1105 RC	18878.00	**7740.00**	**9440.00**	**10380.00**	Perkins	6T	354D	8F-2R	100.	9125	No
MF-1105 RC	19632.00	**8050.00**	**9820.00**	**10800.00**	Perkins	6T	354D	12F-4R	100.72	9725	No
MF-1105 RC	22747.00	**9330.00**	**11370.00**	**12510.00**	Perkins	6T	354D	8F-2R	100.	10125	C,H,A
MF-1105 RC	23501.00	**9640.00**	**11750.00**	**12930.00**	Perkins	6T	354D	12F-4R	100.72	10725	C,H,A
MF-1105 Western	22966.00	**9420.00**	**11480.00**	**12630.00**	Perkins	6T	354D	12F-4R	100.	10000	C,H,A
MF-1135 RC	20637.00	**8460.00**	**10320.00**	**11350.00**	Perkins	6T	354D	8F-2R	120.00	9825	No
MF-1135 RC	21391.00	**8770.00**	**10700.00**	**11770.00**	Perkins	6T	354D	12F-4R	120.84	10425	No
MF-1135 RC	24506.00	**10050.00**	**12250.00**	**13480.00**	Perkins	6T	354D	8F-2R	120.00	10825	C,H,A
MF-1135 RC	25260.00	**10360.00**	**12630.00**	**13890.00**	Perkins	6T	354D	12F-4R	120.84	11425	C,H,A
MF-1135 Western	24725.00	**10140.00**	**12360.00**	**13600.00**	Perkins	6T	354D	12F-4R	120.00	11000	C,H,A
MF-1155 RC	24293.00	**8020.00**	**10200.00**	**11220.00**	Perkins	V8	540D	8F-2R	140.00	12150	No
MF-1155 RC	25047.00	**8270.00**	**10520.00**	**11570.00**	Perkins	V8	540D	12F-4R	140.97	12750	No
MF-1155 RC	28162.00	**9290.00**	**11830.00**	**13010.00**	Perkins	V8	540D	8F-2R	140.00	13150	C,H,A
MF-1155 RC	28916.00	**9540.00**	**12150.00**	**13370.00**	Perkins	V8	540D	12F-4R	140.97	13750	C,H,A
MF-1155 Western	27365.00	**9030.00**	**11490.00**	**12640.00**	Perkins	V8	540D	12F-4R	140.00	13000	C,H,A
MF-2675 RC	23858.00	**5250.00**	**7400.00**	**8290.00**	Perkins	6	354D	8F-6R	100.84	9000	C,H,A
MF-2675 RC	24800.00	**5460.00**	**7690.00**	**8610.00**	Perkins	6	354D	24F-4R	103.29	9600	C,H,A
MF-2675 Western	23950.00	**5270.00**	**7430.00**	**8320.00**	Perkins	6	354D	24F-4R	103.00	10100	C,H,A
MF-2705 RC	25681.00	**5650.00**	**7960.00**	**8920.00**	Perkins	6T	354D	8F-6R	121.00	11200	C,H,A
MF-2705 RC	26623.00	**5860.00**	**8250.00**	**9240.00**	Perkins	6T	354D	24F-4R	122.20	11800	C,H,A
MF-2705 Western	25773.00	**5670.00**	**7990.00**	**8950.00**	Perkins	6T	354D	24F-4R	122.00	11300	C,H,A
MF-2745 RC	28685.00	**6310.00**	**8890.00**	**9960.00**	Perkins	V8	540D	8F-6R	143.40	12798	C,H,A
MF-2745 RC	29627.00	**6520.00**	**9180.00**	**10280.00**	Perkins	V8	540D	24F-4R	143.40	13398	C,H,A
MF-2745 Western	28227.00	**6210.00**	**8750.00**	**9800.00**	Perkins	V8	540D	24F-4R	143.00	12898	C,H,A
MF-2775 RC	32582.00	**6600.00**	**9300.00**	**10420.00**	Perkins	V8	640D	8F-6R	165.00	12800	C,H,A
MF-2775 RC	33524.00	**6820.00**	**9610.00**	**10760.00**	Perkins	V8	640D	24F-4R	165.95	13400	C,H,A
MF-2775 Western	31740.00	**6380.00**	**8990.00**	**10070.00**	Perkins	V8	640D	24F-4R	165.00	12900	C,H,A
MF-2805 RC	38261.00	**7040.00**	**9920.00**	**11110.00**	Perkins	V8T	640D	8F-6R	194.00	13000	C,H,A
MF-2805 RC	39203.00	**7260.00**	**10230.00**	**11460.00**	Perkins	V8T	640D	24F-4R	194.62	13600	C,H,A
MF-2805 Western	37419.00	**6820.00**	**9610.00**	**10760.00**	Perkins	V8T	640D	24F-4R	194.00	13100	C,H,A
MF-4840 4WD	55472.00	**11090.00**	**15620.00**	**17490.00**	Cummins	V8	903D	12F-4R		24963	C,H,A
MF-4840 4WD	56972.00	**11420.00**	**16090.00**	**18020.00**	Cummins	V8	903D	18F-6R		25638	C,H,A
MF-4840 4WD w/PTO	58972.00	**11860.00**	**16710.00**	**18720.00**	Cummins	V8	903D	18F-6R	210.67	26538	C,H,A
MF-4880 4WD	67425.00	**13200.00**	**18600.00**	**20830.00**	Cummins	V8T	903D	12F-4R		27965	C,H,A
MF-4880 4WD	68925.00	**13620.00**	**19190.00**	**21490.00**	Cummins	V8T	903D	18F-6R		28565	C,H,A
MF-4880 4WD w/PTO	70925.00	**13860.00**	**19530.00**	**21870.00**	Cummins	V8T	903D	18F-6R	272.81	29365	C,H,A

RC - Row Crop

1979

Model	Approx. Retail Price New	Fair	Good	Premium	Make	No. Cyls.	Displ. Cu.-In.	No. Speeds	P.T.O. H.P.	Approx. Shipping Wt.-Lbs.	Cab
MF-184-4	19637.00	**6340.00**	**8010.00**	**8730.00**	Perkins	4	236D	12F-4R	62.45	6130	No
MF-205	5541.00	**3510.00**	**4190.00**	**4860.00**	Toyosha	2	65D	6F-2R	16.56	1849	No
MF-205-4	6165.00	**3910.00**	**4660.00**	**5410.00**	Toyosha	2	65D	6F-2R	16.40	2257	No
MF-210	6483.00	**4110.00**	**4900.00**	**5680.00**	Toyosha	2	77D	12F-3R	21.96	2050	No

Model	Approx. Retail Price New	Estimated Average Value Less Repairs Fair	Good	Premium	Engine Make	No. Cyls.	Displ. Cu.-In.	No. Speeds	P.T.O. H.P.	Approx. Shipping Wt.-Lbs.	Cab

Massey Ferguson (Cont.)

1979 (Cont.)

Model	Approx. Retail Price New	Fair	Good	Premium	Make	No. Cyls.	Displ. Cu.-In.	No. Speeds	P.T.O. H.P.	Approx. Shipping Wt.-Lbs.	Cab
MF-210-4	7259.00	**4600.00**	**5490.00**	**6370.00**	Toyosha	2	77D	12F-3R	21.77	2257	No
MF-220	7795.00	**4940.00**	**5890.00**	**6830.00**	Toyosha	2	90D	12F-3R	26.37	2390	No
MF-220-4	9200.00	**5360.00**	**6390.00**	**7410.00**	Toyosha	2	90D	12F-3R	26.48	2700	No
MF-230	8193.00	**4670.00**	**5570.00**	**6460.00**	Continental	4	145G	6F-2R	34.34	3200	No
MF-230	8553.00	**4880.00**	**5820.00**	**6750.00**	Perkins	3	153D	6F-2R	34.53	3404	No
MF-245	9508.00	**4470.00**	**5230.00**	**5700.00**	Continental	4	145G	6F-2R	41.00	3450	No
MF-245	9991.00	**4700.00**	**5500.00**	**6000.00**	Perkins	3	153D	6F-2R	42.00	3600	No
MF-245	10266.00	**4830.00**	**5650.00**	**6160.00**	Continental	4	145G	8F-2R	41.09	3500	No
MF-245	10971.00	**5160.00**	**6030.00**	**6570.00**	Perkins	3	153D	8F-2R	42.00	3650	No
MF-245	11444.00	**5380.00**	**6290.00**	**6860.00**	Perkins	3	153D	12F-4R	42.90	3693	No
MF-255	12425.00	**5840.00**	**6830.00**	**7450.00**	Perkins	4	236D	8F-2R	52.00	5650	No
MF-255	13038.00	**6130.00**	**7170.00**	**7820.00**	Perkins	4	236D	12F-4R	52.68	5850	No
MF-255 RC	13046.00	**6130.00**	**7180.00**	**7830.00**	Perkins	4	236D	8F-2R	52.00	5700	No
MF-255 RC	13690.00	**6430.00**	**7530.00**	**8210.00**	Perkins	4	236D	12F-4R	52.00	5900	No
MF-265	13555.00	**6370.00**	**7460.00**	**8130.00**	Perkins	4	236D	8F-2R	60.00	6050	No
MF-265	14168.00	**6660.00**	**7790.00**	**8490.00**	Perkins	4	236D	12F-4R	60.73	6100	No
MF-265 RC	14233.00	**6690.00**	**7830.00**	**8540.00**	Perkins	4	236D	8F-2R	60.00	6200	No
MF-265 RC	14876.00	**6990.00**	**8180.00**	**8920.00**	Perkins	4	236D	12F-4R	60.00	6250	No
MF-275	14776.00	**6950.00**	**8130.00**	**8860.00**	Perkins	4	248D	8F-2R	67.00	6370	No
MF-275	15389.00	**7230.00**	**8460.00**	**9220.00**	Perkins	4	248D	12F-4R	67.43	6420	No
MF-275 RC	15515.00	**7290.00**	**8530.00**	**9300.00**	Perkins	4	248D	8F-2R	67.00	6520	No
MF-275 RC	16158.00	**7590.00**	**8890.00**	**9690.00**	Perkins	4	248D	12F-4R	67.00	6570	No
MF-285	17365.00	**7290.00**	**8860.00**	**9660.00**	Perkins	4	318D	8F-2R	81.00	6975	No
MF-285	18141.00	**7620.00**	**9250.00**	**10080.00**	Perkins	4	318D	12F-4R	81.96	7025	No
MF-2675 RC	24708.00	**5680.00**	**7910.00**	**8860.00**	Perkins	6	354D	8F-6R	100.84	9000	No
MF-2675 RC	26820.00	**6170.00**	**8580.00**	**9610.00**	Perkins	6	354D	24F-6R	103.29	9600	No
MF-2675 RC	27762.00	**6390.00**	**8880.00**	**9950.00**	Perkins	6	354D	8F-6R	100.84	10000	C,H,A
MF-2675 RC	29524.00	**6790.00**	**9450.00**	**10580.00**	Perkins	6	354D	24F-6R	103.29	10600	C,H,A
MF-2675 Western	28048.00	**6450.00**	**8980.00**	**10060.00**	Perkins	6	354D	24F-6R	103.00	10100	C,H,A
MF-2705 RC	28862.00	**6640.00**	**9240.00**	**10350.00**	Perkins	6T	354D	8F-6R	121.11	10200	No
MF-2705 RC	31670.00	**7280.00**	**10130.00**	**11350.00**	Perkins	6T	354D	24F-6R	122.20	10800	No
MF-2705 RC	34500.00	**7940.00**	**11040.00**	**12370.00**	Perkins	6T	354D	24F-6R	122.20	11800	C,H,A
MF-2705 Western	32775.00	**7540.00**	**10490.00**	**11750.00**	Perkins	6T	354D	24F-6R	122.00	11300	C,H,A
MF-2745 RC	29578.00	**6800.00**	**9470.00**	**10610.00**	Perkins	V8	540D	8F-6R	143.40	11798	No
MF-2745 RC	32351.00	**7130.00**	**9920.00**	**11110.00**	Perkins	V8	540D	24F-6R	143.40	12398	No
MF-2745 RC	35367.00	**7660.00**	**10660.00**	**11940.00**	Perkins	V8	540D	24F-6R	143.40	13398	C,H,A
MF-2745 Western	33599.00	**7220.00**	**10050.00**	**11260.00**	Perkins	V8	540D	24F-6R	143.00	12898	C,H,A
MF-2775	36716.00	**7820.00**	**10880.00**	**12190.00**	Perkins	V8	640D	8F-6R	165.00	12800	C,H,A
MF-2775	40018.00	**8510.00**	**11840.00**	**13260.00**	Perkins	V8	640D	24F-6R	165.95	13400	C,H,A
MF-2775 Western	38017.00	**8050.00**	**11200.00**	**12540.00**	Perkins	V8	640D	24F-6R	165.00	12900	C,H,A
MF-2805	43076.00	**8280.00**	**11520.00**	**12900.00**	Perkins	V8T	640D	8F-6R	194.00	13000	C,H,A
MF-2805	46075.00	**8740.00**	**12160.00**	**13620.00**	Perkins	V8T	640D	24F-6R	194.62	13600	C,H,A
MF-4840 4WD	60726.00	**12820.00**	**17830.00**	**19970.00**	Cummins	V8	903D	12F-4R		24963	C,H,A
MF-4840 4WD	62620.00	**13250.00**	**18440.00**	**20650.00**	Cummins	V8	903D	18F-6R		25638	C,H,A
MF-4840 4WD w/PTO	64557.00	**13700.00**	**19060.00**	**21350.00**	Cummins	V8	903D	18F-6R	210.67	26538	C,H,A
MF-4880 4WD	73811.00	**15600.00**	**21700.00**	**24300.00**	Cummins	V8T	903D	12F-4R		27965	C,H,A
MF-4880 4WD	75692.00	**16030.00**	**22300.00**	**24980.00**	Cummins	V8T	903D	18F-6R		28565	C,H,A
MF-4880 4WD w/PTO	77642.00	**16480.00**	**22930.00**	**25680.00**	Cummins	V8T	903D	18F-6R	272.81	29365	C,H,A

RC - Row Crop

1980

Model	Approx. Retail Price New	Fair	Good	Premium	Make	No. Cyls.	Displ. Cu.-In.	No. Speeds	P.T.O. H.P.	Approx. Shipping Wt.-Lbs.	Cab
MF-154-4	18687.00	**6540.00**	**8220.00**	**8960.00**	Perkins	3	153D	12F-4R	42.52	4934	No
MF-184-4	23817.00	**8340.00**	**10480.00**	**11420.00**	Perkins	4	236D	12F-4R	62.45	6130	No
MF-205	6157.00	**3690.00**	**4320.00**	**4970.00**	Toyosha	2	65D	6F-2R	16.56	1849	No
MF-205-4	6850.00	**4090.00**	**4790.00**	**5510.00**	Toyosha	2	65D	6F-2R	16.40	2257	No
MF-210	7203.00	**4290.00**	**5040.00**	**5800.00**	Toyosha	2	77D	12F-3R	21.96	2050	No
MF-210-4	8066.00	**4790.00**	**5620.00**	**6460.00**	Toyosha	2	77D	12F-3R	21.77	2257	No
MF-220	8661.00	**5140.00**	**6030.00**	**6930.00**	Toyosha	2	90D	12F-3R	26.37	2390	No
MF-220-4	10222.00	**5470.00**	**6410.00**	**7370.00**	Toyosha	2	90D	12F-3R	26.48	2700	No
MF-230	9500.00	**5040.00**	**5890.00**	**6660.00**	Continental	4	145G	6F-2R	34.34	3200	No
MF-230	11577.00	**6140.00**	**7180.00**	**8110.00**	Perkins	3	153D	6F-2R	34.53	3404	No
MF-245	13702.00	**5890.00**	**7130.00**	**7700.00**	Perkins	3	153D	6F-2R	42.00	3600	No
MF-245	15063.00	**6480.00**	**7830.00**	**8460.00**	Perkins	3	153D	8F-2R	42.00	3650	No
MF-245	15691.00	**6750.00**	**8160.00**	**8810.00**	Perkins	3	153D	12F-4R	42.90	3693	No
MF-255	16684.00	**7170.00**	**8680.00**	**9370.00**	Perkins	4	236D	8F-2R	52.00	5650	No
MF-255	17566.00	**7550.00**	**9130.00**	**9860.00**	Perkins	4	236D	12F-4R	52.68	5850	No
MF-255 RC	17518.00	**7530.00**	**9110.00**	**9840.00**	Perkins	4	236D	8F-2R	52.00	5700	No
MF-255 RC	18444.00	**7930.00**	**9590.00**	**10360.00**	Perkins	4	236D	12F-4R	52.00	5900	No
MF-265	18271.00	**7860.00**	**9500.00**	**10260.00**	Perkins	4	236D	8F-2R	60.00	6050	No
MF-265	19123.00	**8220.00**	**9940.00**	**10740.00**	Perkins	4	236D	12F-4R	60.73	6100	No
MF-265 RC	19185.00	**8250.00**	**9980.00**	**10780.00**	Perkins	4	236D	8F-2R	60.00	6200	No
MF-265 RC	20079.00	**8630.00**	**10440.00**	**11280.00**	Perkins	4	236D	12F-4R	60.00	6250	No
MF-275	20138.00	**8660.00**	**10470.00**	**11310.00**	Perkins	4	248D	8F-2R	67.00	6370	No
MF-275	21020.00	**9040.00**	**10930.00**	**11800.00**	Perkins	4	248D	12F-4R	67.43	6420	No
MF-275 RC	21145.00	**9090.00**	**11000.00**	**11880.00**	Perkins	4	248D	8F-2R	67.00	6520	No
MF-275 RC	22071.00	**9490.00**	**11480.00**	**12400.00**	Perkins	4	248D	12F-4R	67.00	6570	No
MF-285	22842.00	**9820.00**	**11880.00**	**12830.00**	Perkins	4	318D	8F-2R	81.00	6975	No
MF-285	26954.00	**11590.00**	**14020.00**	**15140.00**	Perkins	4	318D	12F-4R	81.96	7025	C,H,A
MF-2675 RC	35977.00	**7200.00**	**9900.00**	**11090.00**	Perkins	6	354D	8F-6R	100.84	10000	C,H,A
MF-2675 RC	37454.00	**7780.00**	**10690.00**	**11970.00**	Perkins	6	354D	24F-6R	103.29	10600	C,H,A
MF-2675 Western	35581.00	**7320.00**	**10070.00**	**11280.00**	Perkins	6	354D	24F-6R	103.00	10100	C,H,A
MF-2705 RC	39372.00	**8020.00**	**11020.00**	**12340.00**	Perkins	6T	354D	8F-6R	121.11	11200	C,H,A
MF-2705 RC	40849.00	**8350.00**	**11480.00**	**12860.00**	Perkins	6T	354D	24F-6R	122.20	11800	C,H,A
MF-2705 Western	38807.00	**7870.00**	**10820.00**	**12120.00**	Perkins	6T	354D	24F-6R	122.00	11300	C,H,A

Massey Ferguson (Cont.)

1980 (Cont.)

Model	Approx. Retail Price New	Estimated Average Value Less Repairs Fair	Good	Premium	Engine Make	No. Cyls.	Displ. Cu.-In.	No. Speeds	P.T.O. H.P.	Approx. Shipping Wt.-Lbs.	Cab
MF-2745 RC	44052.00	9120.00	12540.00	14050.00	Perkins	V8	540D	8F-6R	143.40	12798	C,H,A
MF-2745 RC	45535.00	9480.00	13040.00	14610.00	Perkins	V8	540D	24F-6R	143.40	13398	C,H,A
MF-2745 Western	43258.00	8690.00	11950.00	13380.00	Perkins	V8	540D	24F-6R	143.00	12898	C,H,A
MF-2775 RC	50584.00	9360.00	12870.00	14410.00	Perkins	V8	640D	8F-6R	165.00	12800	C,H,A
MF-2775 RC	52061.00	9840.00	13530.00	15150.00	Perkins	V8	640D	24F-6R	165.95	13400	C,H,A
MF-2775 Western	49458.00	9480.00	13040.00	14610.00	Perkins	V8	640D	24F-6R	165.00	12900	C,H,A
MF-2805 RC	59296.00	10870.00	14950.00	16740.00	Perkins	V8T	640D	8F-6R	194.00	13000	C,H,A
MF-2805 RC	60773.00	11450.00	15740.00	17630.00	Perkins	V8T	640D	24F-6R	194.62	13600	C,H,A
MF-2805 Western	57734.00	10560.00	14520.00	16260.00	Perkins	V8T	640D	24F-6R	194.00	13100	C,H,A
MF-4800 4WD w/PTO	79004.00	14640.00	20130.00	22550.00	Cummins	V8	903D	18F-6R	179.31	24500	C,H,A
MF-4840 4WD w/PTO	91040.00	17530.00	24100.00	26990.00	Cummins	V8	903D	18F-6R	210.67	26538	C,H,A
MF-4880 4WD w/PTO	101886.00	19410.00	26690.00	29890.00	Cummins	V8T	903D	18F-6R	272.81	29365	C,H,A
MF-4900 4WD w/PTO	109755.00	20340.00	27970.00	31330.00	Cummins	V8T	903D	18F-6R	320.55	29500	C,H,A

RC - Row Crop

1981

Model	Approx. Retail Price New	Fair	Good	Premium	Make	No. Cyls.	Displ. Cu.-In.	No. Speeds	P.T.O. H.P.	Approx. Shipping Wt.-Lbs.	Cab
MF-154-4	18874.00	6800.00	8490.00	9250.00	Perkins	3	153D	12F-4R	42.52	4934	No
MF-205	6207.00	3900.00	4490.00	5120.00	Toyosha	2	65D	6F-2R	16.56	1849	No
MF-205-4	6850.00	4280.00	4930.00	5620.00	Toyosha	2	65D	6F-2R	16.40	2257	No
MF-210	7462.00	4640.00	5350.00	6100.00	Toyosha	2	77D	12F-3R	21.96	2050	No
MF-210-4	8486.00	5240.00	6040.00	6890.00	Toyosha	2	77D	12F-3R	21.77	2257	No
MF-220	8661.00	5350.00	6160.00	7020.00	Toyosha	2	90D	12F-3R	26.37	2390	No
MF-220-4	10222.00	5680.00	6540.00	7460.00	Toyosha	2	90D	12F-3R	26.48	2700	No
MF-230	12162.00	6570.00	7660.00	8580.00	Perkins	3	153D	6F-2R	34.53	3404	No
MF-245	14397.00	6340.00	7630.00	8240.00	Perkins	3	153D	6F-2R	42.00	3600	No
MF-245	15826.00	6960.00	8390.00	9060.00	Perkins	3	153D	8F-2R	42.00	3650	No
MF-245	16487.00	7250.00	8740.00	9440.00	Perkins	3	153D	12F-4R	42.90	3693	No
MF-255	13319.00	5860.00	7060.00	7630.00	Perkins	4	236D	8F-2R	52.00	5650	No
MF-255	13980.00	6150.00	7410.00	8000.00	Perkins	4	236D	12F-4R	52.68	5850	No
MF-255 RC	13984.00	6150.00	7410.00	8000.00	Perkins	4	236D	8F-2R	52.00	5700	No
MF-255 RC	14679.00	6460.00	7780.00	8400.00	Perkins	4	236D	12F-4R	52.00	5900	No
MF-265	20658.00	9090.00	10950.00	11830.00	Perkins	4	236D	8F-2R	60.00	6050	No
MF-265	21584.00	9500.00	11440.00	12360.00	Perkins	4	236D	12F-4R	60.73	6100	No
MF-265 RC	21690.00	9540.00	11500.00	12420.00	Perkins	4	236D	8F-2R	60.00	6200	No
MF-265 RC	22663.00	9970.00	12010.00	12970.00	Perkins	4	236D	12F-4R	60.00	6250	No
MF-275	22304.00	9810.00	11820.00	12770.00	Perkins	4	248D	8F-2R	67.00	6370	No
MF-275	23230.00	10220.00	12310.00	13300.00	Perkins	4	248D	12F-4R	67.43	6420	No
MF-275 RC	23419.00	10300.00	12410.00	13400.00	Perkins	4	248D	8F-2R	67.00	6520	No
MF-275 RC	24392.00	10730.00	12930.00	13960.00	Perkins	4	248D	12F-4R	67.00	6570	No
MF-285	24359.00	10720.00	12910.00	13940.00	Perkins	4	318D	8F-2R	81.00	6975	No
MF-285	25530.00	11230.00	13530.00	14610.00	Perkins	4	318D	12F-4R	81.96	7025	No
MF-285 Cab	30659.00	13490.00	16250.00	17550.00	Perkins	4	318D	8F-2R	81.96	8400	C,H,A
MF-285 Cab	31830.00	14010.00	16870.00	18220.00	Perkins	4	318D	12F-4R	81.96	8450	C,H,A
MF-2675 RC	37775.00	8180.00	11120.00	12450.00	Perkins	6	354D	8F-6R	100.84	10000	C,H,A
MF-2675 RC	39327.00	8580.00	11660.00	13060.00	Perkins	6	354D	24F-6R	103.29	10600	C,H,A
MF-2675 Western	37360.00	8000.00	10880.00	12190.00	Perkins	6	354D	24F-6R	103.00	10100	C,H,A
MF-2705 RC	41056.00	9000.00	12240.00	13710.00	Perkins	6T	354D	8F-6R	121.11	11200	C,H,A
MF-2705 RC	42556.00	9380.00	12750.00	14280.00	Perkins	6T	354D	24F-6R	122.20	11800	C,H,A
MF-2705 Western	42130.00	9250.00	12580.00	14090.00	Perkins	6T	354D	24F-6R	122.00	11300	C,H,A
MF-2745 RC	49432.00	11000.00	14960.00	16760.00	Perkins	V8	540D	8F-6R	143.40	12798	C,H,A
MF-2745 RC	51432.00	11600.00	15780.00	17670.00	Perkins	V8	540D	24F-6R	143.40	13398	C,H,A
MF-2745 Western	50918.00	11400.00	15500.00	17360.00	Perkins	V8	540D	24F-6R	143.00	12898	C,H,A
MF-2775 RC	51312.00	11580.00	15740.00	17630.00	Perkins	V8	640D	8F-6R	165.00	12800	C,H,A
MF-2775 RC	53103.00	11800.00	16050.00	17980.00	Perkins	V8	640D	24F-6R	165.95	13400	C,H,A
MF-2775 Western	52572.00	11650.00	15840.00	17740.00	Perkins	V8	640D	24F-6R	165.00	12900	C,H,A
MF-2805 RC	60198.00	12000.00	16320.00	18280.00	Perkins	V8T	640D	8F-6R	194.00	13000	C,H,A
MF-2805 RC	61989.00	12250.00	16660.00	18660.00	Perkins	V8T	640D	24F-6R	194.62	13600	C,H,A
MF-2805 Western	61369.00	12500.00	17000.00	19040.00	Perkins	V8T	640D	24F-6R	194.00	13100	C,H,A
MF-4800 4WD	79086.00	16270.00	22130.00	24790.00	Cummins	V8	903D	18F-6R		24000	C,H,A
MF-4800 4WD w/PTO	82164.00	17040.00	23180.00	25960.00	Cummins	V8	903D	18F-6R	179.08	24500	C,H,A
MF-4840 4WD	91603.00	19400.00	26390.00	29560.00	Cummins	V8	903D	18F-6R		26038	C,H,A
MF-4840 4WD w/PTO	94745.00	20190.00	27450.00	30740.00	Cummins	V8	903D	18F-6R	210.67	26538	C,H,A
MF-4880 4WD	102883.00	21720.00	29540.00	33090.00	Cummins	V8T	903D	18F-6R		28865	C,H,A
MF-4880 4WD w/PTO	105961.00	22490.00	30590.00	34260.00	Cummins	V8T	903D	18F-6R	272.81	29365	C,H,A
MF-4900 4WD	111066.00	23020.00	31300.00	35060.00	Cummins	V8T	903D	18F-6R		29000	C,H,A
MF-4900 4WD w/PTO	114144.00	24540.00	33370.00	37370.00	Cummins	V8T	903D	18F-6R	320.55	29500	C,H,A

RC - Row Crop

1982

Model	Approx. Retail Price New	Fair	Good	Premium	Make	No. Cyls.	Displ. Cu.-In.	No. Speeds	P.T.O. H.P.	Approx. Shipping Wt.-Lbs.	Cab
MF-205	6207.00	4080.00	4630.00	5230.00	Toyosha	2	65D	6F-2R	16.56	1849	No
MF-205-4 4WD	6850.00	4470.00	5070.00	5730.00	Toyosha	2	65D	6F-2R	16.40	2257	No
MF-210	7764.00	4900.00	5550.00	6270.00	Toyosha	2	77D	12F-3R	21.96	2050	No
MF-210-4 4WD	8786.00	5630.00	6380.00	7210.00	Toyosha	2	77D	12F-3R	21.77	2257	No
MF-220	8661.00	5560.00	6300.00	7120.00	Toyosha	2	90D	12F-3R	26.37	2390	No
MF-220-4 4WD	10221.00	5890.00	6680.00	7550.00	Toyosha	2	90D	12F-3R	26.48	2700	No
MF-230	12162.00	6080.00	7050.00	7610.00	Perkins	3	153D	6F-2R	34.53	3404	No
MF-245	14973.00	6740.00	8090.00	8740.00	Perkins	3	153D	6F-2R	42.00	3600	No
MF-245	16459.00	7410.00	8890.00	9600.00	Perkins	3	153D	8F-2R	42.00	3650	No
MF-245	17146.00	7720.00	9260.00	10000.00	Perkins	3	153D	12F-4R	42.90	3693	No
MF-254 4WD	17845.00	8030.00	9640.00	10410.00	Perkins	3	153D	12F-4R	43.36	4595	No
MF-255	13319.00	5990.00	7190.00	7770.00	Perkins	4	236D	8F-2R	52.00	5650	No
MF-255	13980.00	6290.00	7550.00	8150.00	Perkins	4	236D	12F-4R	52.68	5850	No
MF-255 RC	13984.00	6290.00	7550.00	8150.00	Perkins	4	236D	8F-2R	52.00	5700	No
MF-255 RC	14697.00	6610.00	7940.00	8580.00	Perkins	4	236D	12F-4R	52.00	5900	No

Massey Ferguson (Cont.)

1982 (Cont.)

Model	Approx. Retail Price New	Estimated Average Value Less Repairs: Fair	Good	Premium	Engine: Make	No. Cyls.	Displ. Cu.-In.	No. Speeds	P.T.O. H.P.	Approx. Shipping Wt.-Lbs.	Cab
MF-265	20679.00	9310.00	11170.00	12060.00	Perkins	4	236D	8F-2R	60.00	6050	No
MF-265	21642.00	9740.00	11690.00	12630.00	Perkins	4	236D	12F-4R	60.73	6100	No
MF-265 RC	21484.00	9670.00	11600.00	12530.00	Perkins	4	236D	8F-2R	60.00	6200	No
MF-265 RC	22447.00	10100.00	12120.00	13090.00	Perkins	4	236D	12F-4R	60.00	6250	No
MF-274 4WD	19557.00	8800.00	10560.00	11410.00	Perkins	4	236D	12F-4R	55.39	5490	No
MF-275	21529.00	9690.00	11630.00	12560.00	Perkins	4	248D	8F-2R	67.00	6370	No
MF-275	22455.00	10110.00	12130.00	13100.00	Perkins	4	248D	12F-4R	67.43	6420	No
MF-275 RC	22304.00	10040.00	12040.00	13000.00	Perkins	4	248D	8F-2R	67.00	6520	No
MF-275 RC	23230.00	10450.00	12540.00	13540.00	Perkins	4	248D	12F-4R	67.00	6570	No
MF-285	25333.00	11400.00	13680.00	14770.00	Perkins	4	318D	8F-2R	81.00	6975	No
MF-285	26551.00	11950.00	14340.00	15490.00	Perkins	4	318D	12F-4R	81.96	7025	No
MF-285 Cab	33552.00	15100.00	18120.00	19570.00	Perkins	4	318D	12F-4R	81.96	8450	C,H,A
MF-294 4WD	23093.00	10390.00	12470.00	13470.00	Perkins	4	248D	12F-4R	67.39	7300	No
MF-1010	5728.00	3440.00	3900.00	4410.00	Toyosha	3	53D	6F-2R	13.00	1522	No
MF-1010 4WD	6300.00	3780.00	4280.00	4840.00	Toyosha	3	53D	6F-2R	13.00	1720	No
MF-2640	35093.00	7800.00	10500.00	11760.00	Perkins	6	354D	16F-12R	90.95	10940	C,H,A
MF-2640 4WD	42093.00	9620.00	12950.00	14500.00	Perkins	6	354D	16F-12R	90.95	11800	C,H,A
MF-2675 RC	36696.00	8220.00	11060.00	12390.00	Perkins	6	354D	8F-6R	100.84	10000	C,H,A
MF-2675 RC	38203.00	8630.00	11620.00	13010.00	Perkins	6	354D	24F-6R	103.29	10600	C,H,A
MF-2675 Western	35368.00	7900.00	10640.00	11920.00	Perkins	6	354D	8F-6R	100.	9500	C,H,A
MF-2675 Western	36997.00	8320.00	11200.00	12540.00	Perkins	6	354D	24F-6R	103.00	10100	C,H,A
MF-2705 RC	40158.00	9150.00	12320.00	13800.00	Perkins	6T	354D	8F-6R	121.11	11200	C,H,A
MF-2705 RC	41665.00	9520.00	12810.00	14350.00	Perkins	6T	354D	24F-6R	122.20	11800	C,H,A
MF-2705 Western	38920.00	8810.00	11870.00	13290.00	Perkins	6T	354D	8F-6R	121.00	10700	C,H,A
MF-2705 Western	40427.00	9230.00	12420.00	13910.00	Perkins	6T	354D	24F-6R	122.00	11300	C,H,A
MF-2745 RC	44933.00	10370.00	13970.00	15650.00	Perkins	V8	540D	8F-6R	143.40	12798	C,H,A
MF-2745 RC	46440.00	10790.00	14530.00	16270.00	Perkins	V8	540D	24F-6R	143.40	13398	C,H,A
MF-2745 Western	42918.00	9850.00	13270.00	14860.00	Perkins	V8	540D	8F-6R	143.00	12298	C,H,A
MF-2745 Western	44425.00	10240.00	13790.00	15450.00	Perkins	V8	540D	24F-6R	143.00	12898	C,H,A
MF-2775 RC	51596.00	10820.00	14560.00	16310.00	Perkins	V8	640D	8F-6R	165.00	12800	C,H,A
MF-2775 RC	53103.00	11180.00	15050.00	16860.00	Perkins	V8	640D	24F-6R	165.95	13400	C,H,A
MF-2775 Western	48919.00	10110.00	13620.00	15250.00	Perkins	V8	640D	8F-6R	165.00	12300	C,H,A
MF-2775 Western	50426.00	10500.00	14140.00	15840.00	Perkins	V8	640D	24F-6R	165.00	12900	C,H,A
MF-2805 RC	60482.00	12480.00	16800.00	18820.00	Perkins	V8T	640D	8F-6R	194.00	13000	C,H,A
MF-2805 RC	61989.00	13000.00	17500.00	19600.00	Perkins	V8T	640D	24F-6R	194.62	13600	C,H,A
MF-2805 Western	59292.00	12300.00	16560.00	18550.00	Perkins	V8T	640D	8F-6R	194.00	12500	C,H,A
MF-2805 Western	60799.00	12690.00	17080.00	19130.00	Perkins	V8T	640D	24F-6R	194.00	13100	C,H,A
MF-4800 4WD	79086.00	17440.00	23480.00	26300.00	Cummins	V8	903D	18F-6R		24000	C,H,A
MF-4800 4WD w/PTO	82164.00	17980.00	24210.00	27120.00	Cummins	V8	903D	18F-6R	179.08	24500	C,H,A
MF-4840 4WD	91603.00	20440.00	27510.00	30810.00	Cummins	V8	903D	18F-6R		26038	C,H,A
MF-4840 4WD w/PTO	94745.00	20990.00	28260.00	31650.00	Cummins	V8	903D	18F-6R	210.67	26538	C,H,A
MF-4880 4WD	102883.00	23160.00	31180.00	34920.00	Cummins	V8T	903D	18F-6R		28865	C,H,A
MF-4880 4WD w/PTO	105961.00	24170.00	32540.00	36450.00	Cummins	V8T	903D	18F-6R	272.81	29365	C,H,A
MF-4900 4WD	111066.00	25240.00	33970.00	38050.00	Cummins	V8T	903D	18F-6R		29000	C,H,A
MF-4900 4WD w/PTO	114144.00	26040.00	35050.00	39260.00	Cummins	V8T	903D	18F-6R	320.55	29500	C,H,A

RC - Row Crop

1983

Model	Approx. Retail Price New	Fair	Good	Premium	Make	No. Cyls.	Displ. Cu.-In.	No. Speeds	P.T.O. H.P.	Approx. Shipping Wt.-Lbs.	Cab
MF-205	6207.00	4270.00	4770.00	5390.00	Toyosha	2	65D	6F-2R	16.56	1849	No
MF-205-4 4WD	6850.00	4670.00	5200.00	5880.00	Toyosha	2	65D	6F-2R	16.40	2257	No
MF-210	7764.00	5220.00	5820.00	6580.00	Toyosha	2	77D	12F-3R	21.96	2210	No
MF-210-4 4WD	8786.00	5850.00	6520.00	7370.00	Toyosha	2	77D	12F-3R	21.77	2590	No
MF-220	8661.00	5590.00	6230.00	7040.00	Toyosha	2	90D	12F-3R	26.37	2390	No
MF-220-4	10221.00	6100.00	6800.00	7680.00	Toyosha	2	90D	12F-3R	26.48	2700	No
MF-240	11073.00	6200.00	7200.00	8060.00	Perkins	3	152D	8F-2R	34.77	3400	No
MF-250	14983.00	7640.00	8840.00	9550.00	Perkins	3	152D	8F-2R	40.86	3700	No
MF-254 4WD	18202.00	8370.00	10010.00	10810.00	Perkins	3	152D	12F-4R	43.36	5149	No
MF-270	17635.00	8110.00	9700.00	10480.00	Perkins	4	236D	8F-2R	55.85	6050	No
MF-270	19823.00	9120.00	10900.00	11770.00	Perkins	4	236D	12F-4R	55.62	6100	No
MF-270 RC	18419.00	8470.00	10130.00	10940.00	Perkins	4	236D	8F-2R	55.85	6200	No
MF-270 RC	20067.00	9230.00	11040.00	11920.00	Perkins	4	236D	12F-4R	55.62	6250	No
MF-274 4WD	20339.00	9360.00	11190.00	12090.00	Perkins	4	236D	12F-4R	55.39	5490	No
MF-290	20273.00	9330.00	11150.00	12040.00	Perkins	4	248D	8F-2R	65.92	6520	No
MF-290	22461.00	10330.00	12350.00	13340.00	Perkins	4	248D	12F-4R	65.92	6570	No
MF-294 4WD	23555.00	10840.00	12960.00	14000.00	Perkins	4	248D	12F-4R	67.39	6550	No
MF-298	23029.00	10590.00	12670.00	13680.00	Perkins	4	318D	8F-2R	79.54	6975	No
MF-298	23992.00	11040.00	13200.00	14260.00	Perkins	4	318D	12F-4R	79.26	7025	No
MF-670	25950.00	11940.00	14270.00	15410.00	Perkins	4	236D	12F-4R	55.62	7500	C,H
MF-670	27650.00	12720.00	15210.00	16430.00	Perkins	4	236D	12F-4R	55.62	7550	C,H,A
MF-670 4WD	31094.00	14300.00	17100.00	18470.00	Perkins	4	236D	12F-4R	55.62	8900	C,H
MF-670 4WD	32794.00	15090.00	18040.00	19480.00	Perkins	4	236D	12F-4R	55.62	8950	C,H,A
MF-690	27804.00	12790.00	15290.00	16510.00	Perkins	4	248D	12F-4R	65.68	8000	C,H
MF-690	29504.00	13570.00	16230.00	17530.00	Perkins	4	248D	12F-4R	65.68	8050	C,H,A
MF-690 4WD	32948.00	15160.00	18120.00	19570.00	Perkins	4	248D	12F-4R	65.68	9400	C,H
MF-690 4WD	34648.00	15940.00	19060.00	20590.00	Perkins	4	248D	12F-4R	65.68	9450	C,H,A
MF-698	32205.00	14810.00	17710.00	19130.00	Perkins	4	318D	12F-4R	78.83	8285	C,H,A
MF-1010	5728.00	3490.00	3900.00	4410.00	Toyosha	3	53D	6F-2R	13.00	1522	No
MF-1010 4WD	6300.00	3840.00	4280.00	4840.00	Toyosha	3	53D	6F-2R	13.00	1720	No
MF-2640	37900.00	12500.00	15460.00	16700.00	Perkins	6	354D	16F-12R	90.95	10900	C,H,A
MF-2640 4WD	45460.00	15350.00	18990.00	20510.00	Perkins	6	354D	16F-12R	90.95	11800	C,H,A
MF-2675 RC	36696.00	11670.00	14430.00	15580.00	Perkins	6	354D	8F-6R	100.84	10000	C,H,A
MF-2675 RC	38203.00	12240.00	15130.00	16340.00	Perkins	6	354D	24F-6R	103.29	10600	C,H,A
MF-2675 Western	35368.00	11130.00	13770.00	14870.00	Perkins	6	354D	8F-6R	100.	9500	C,H,A
MF-2675 Western	36997.00	11700.00	14480.00	15640.00	Perkins	6	354D	24F-6R	103.00	10100	C,H,A

Massey Ferguson (Cont.)

Model	Approx. Retail Price New	Estimated Average Value Less Repairs: Fair	Good	Premium	Engine: Make	No. Cyls.	Displ. Cu.-In.	No. Speeds	P.T.O. H.P.	Approx. Shipping Wt.-Lbs.	Cab
1983 (Cont.)											
MF-2705 RC	40158.00	9230.00	12310.00	13790.00	Perkins	6T	354D	8F-6R	121.11	11200	C,H,A
MF-2705 RC	41665.00	9720.00	12960.00	14520.00	Perkins	6T	354D	24F-6R	122.20	11800	C,H,A
MF-2705 Western	38920.00	9150.00	12200.00	13660.00	Perkins	6T	354D	8F-6R	121.00	10700	C,H,A
MF-2705 Western	40427.00	12260.00	16340.00	18300.00	Perkins	6T	354D	24F-6R	122.00	11300	C,H,A
MF-2745 RC	44933.00	10260.00	13680.00	15320.00	Perkins	V8	540D	8F-6R	143.40	12798	C,H,A
MF-2745 RC	46440.00	10910.00	14540.00	16290.00	Perkins	V8	540D	24F-6R	143.40	13398	C,H,A
MF-2745 Western	42918.00	9720.00	12960.00	14520.00	Perkins	V8	540D	8F-6R	143.00	12298	C,H,A
MF-2745 Western	44425.00	10370.00	13820.00	15480.00	Perkins	V8	540D	24F-6R	143.00	12898	C,H,A
MF-2775 RC	51596.00	11230.00	14980.00	16780.00	Perkins	V8	640D	8F-6R	165.00	12800	C,H,A
MF-2775 RC	53103.00	11640.00	15520.00	17380.00	Perkins	V8	640D	24F-6R	165.95	13400	C,H,A
MF-2775 Western	48919.00	10500.00	14000.00	15680.00	Perkins	V8	640D	8F-6R	165.00	12300	C,H,A
MF-2775 Western	50426.00	10910.00	14540.00	16290.00	Perkins	V8	640D	24F-6R	165.00	12900	C,H,A
MF-2805 RC	60482.00	12960.00	17280.00	19350.00	Perkins	V8T	640D	8F-6R	194.00	13000	C,H,A
MF-2805 RC	61482.00	13230.00	17640.00	19760.00	Perkins	V8T	640D	24F-6R	194.62	13600	C,H,A
MF-2805 Western	59292.00	12740.00	16990.00	19030.00	Perkins	V8T	640D	8F-6R	194.00	12500	C,H,A
MF-2805 Western	60799.00	13500.00	18000.00	20160.00	Perkins	V8T	640D	24F-6R	194.00	13100	C,H,A
MF-4800 4WD	79086.00	18650.00	24870.00	27850.00	Cummins	V8	903D	18F-6R		24000	C,H,A
MF-4800 4WD w/PTO	82164.00	19480.00	25980.00	29100.00	Cummins	V8	903D	18F-6R	179.08	24500	C,H,A
MF-4840 4WD	91603.00	21490.00	28660.00	32100.00	Cummins	V8	903D	18F-6R		26038	C,H,A
MF-4840 4WD w/PTO	94745.00	22610.00	30150.00	33770.00	Cummins	V8	903D	18F-6R	210.67	26538	C,H,A
MF-4880 4WD	106383.00	24670.00	32900.00	36850.00	Cummins	V8T	903D	18F-6R		28865	C,H,A
MF-4880 4WD w/PTO	109461.00	25500.00	34010.00	38090.00	Cummins	V8T	903D	18F-6R	272.81	29365	C,H,A
MF-4900 4WD	114566.00	26880.00	35840.00	40140.00	Cummins	V8T	903D	18F-6R		29000	C,H,A
MF-4900 4WD w/PTO	117644.00	27710.00	36950.00	41380.00	Cummins	V8T	903D	18F-6R	320.55	29500	C,H,A
RC - Row Crop											
1984											
MF-205	6210.00	4470.00	4980.00	5630.00	Toyosha	2	65D	6F-2R	16.56	1849	No
MF-205-4 4WD	6850.00	4870.00	5420.00	6130.00	Toyosha	2	65D	6F-2R	16.40	2257	No
MF-210	7765.00	5430.00	6050.00	6840.00	Toyosha	2	77D	12F-3R	21.96	2210	No
MF-210-4 4WD	8790.00	6070.00	6760.00	7640.00	Toyosha	2	77D	12F-3R	21.77	2590	No
MF-220	8665.00	5990.00	6670.00	7540.00	Toyosha	2	90D	12F-3R	26.37	2390	No
MF-220-4 4WD	10225.00	6340.00	7060.00	7980.00	Toyosha	2	90D	12F-3R	26.48	2700	No
MF-240	11520.00	6250.00	7210.00	7790.00	Perkins	3	152D	8F-2R	34.77	3560	No
MF-250	15390.00	7470.00	8900.00	9610.00	Perkins	3	152D	8F-2R	40.86	4100	No
MF-254 4WD	19615.00	9220.00	10980.00	11860.00	Perkins	3	152D	12F-4R	43.36	5160	No
MF-270	18180.00	8550.00	10180.00	10990.00	Perkins	4	236D	8F-2R	55.85	6050	No
MF-270	19880.00	9340.00	11130.00	12020.00	Perkins	4	236D	12F-4R	55.62	6100	No
MF-270 RC	18950.00	8910.00	10610.00	11460.00	Perkins	4	236D	8F-2R	55.85	6200	No
MF-270 RC	20645.00	9700.00	11560.00	12490.00	Perkins	4	236D	12F-4R	55.62	6250	No
MF-274 4WD	21440.00	10080.00	12010.00	12970.00	Perkins	4	236D	12F-4R	55.39	5490	No
MF-290	20275.00	9530.00	11350.00	12260.00	Perkins	4	248D	8F-2R	65.92	6520	No
MF-290	22465.00	10560.00	12580.00	13590.00	Perkins	4	248D	12F-4R	65.92	6570	No
MF-290 RC	20851.00	9800.00	11680.00	12610.00	Perkins	4	248D	12F-4R	65.92	6670	No
MF-290 RC	23041.00	10830.00	12900.00	13930.00	Perkins	4	248D	12F-4R	65.92	6720	No
MF-294 4WD	25370.00	11920.00	14210.00	15350.00	Perkins	4	248D	12F-4R	67.39	6550	No
MF-298	23950.00	11260.00	13410.00	14480.00	Perkins	4	318D	8F-2R	79.54	6975	No
MF-298	24955.00	11730.00	13980.00	15100.00	Perkins	4	318D	12F-4R	79.26	7025	No
MF-670	25950.00	12200.00	14530.00	15690.00	Perkins	4	236D	12F-4R	55.62	7500	C,H
MF-670	27650.00	13000.00	15480.00	16720.00	Perkins	4	236D	12F-4R	55.62	7550	C,H,A
MF-670 4WD	31095.00	14620.00	17410.00	18800.00	Perkins	4	236D	12F-4R	55.62	8900	C,H
MF-670 4WD	32795.00	15410.00	18370.00	19840.00	Perkins	4	236D	12F-4R	55.62	8950	C,H,A
MF-690	27805.00	13070.00	15570.00	16820.00	Perkins	4	248D	12F-4R	65.68	8000	C,H
MF-690	29095.00	13680.00	16290.00	17590.00	Perkins	4	248D	12F-4R	65.68	8050	C,H,A
MF-690 4WD	32950.00	14100.00	16800.00	18140.00	Perkins	4	248D	12F-4R	65.68	9400	C,H
MF-690 4WD	34650.00	15280.00	18200.00	19660.00	Perkins	4	248D	12F-4R	65.68	9450	C,H,A
MF-698	25995.00	12220.00	14560.00	15730.00	Perkins	4	318D	12F-4R	78.83	8235	No
MF-698	32205.00	14570.00	17360.00	18750.00	Perkins	4	318D	12F-4R	78.83	8285	C,H,A
MF-698 4WD	32245.00	15160.00	18060.00	19510.00	Perkins	4	318D	12F-4R	78.83	8495	No
MF-698 4WD	38455.00	17160.00	20440.00	22080.00	Perkins	4	318D	12F-4R	78.83	9115	C,H,A
MF-699	27100.00	12740.00	15180.00	16390.00	Perkins	6	354D	12F-4R	85.79	8304	No
MF-699	33310.00	15660.00	18650.00	20140.00	Perkins	6	354D	12F-4R	85.79	9104	C,H,A
MF-699 4WD	32777.00	15410.00	18360.00	19830.00	Perkins	6	354D	12F-4R	85.79	9275	No
MF-699 4WD	38987.00	17390.00	20720.00	22380.00	Perkins	6	354D	12F-4R	85.79	10075	C,H,A
MF-1010	5965.00	3700.00	4120.00	4660.00	Toyosha	3	53D	6F-2R	13.00	1522	No
MF-1010 4WD	6430.00	3990.00	4440.00	5020.00	Toyosha	3	53D	6F-2R	13.00	1720	No
MF-1020	6810.00	4220.00	4700.00	5310.00	Toyosha	3	69D	12F-4R	17.08	1950	No
MF-1020-4 4WD	7450.00	4620.00	5140.00	5810.00	Toyosha	3	69D	12F-4R	17.08	2230	No
MF-1030	7510.00	4660.00	5180.00	5850.00	Toyosha	3	87D	12F-4R	23.35	2210	No
MF-1030-4 4WD	8940.00	5540.00	6170.00	6970.00	Toyosha	3	87D	12F-4R	23.00	2640	No
MF-2640	37900.00	12830.00	15790.00	17050.00	Perkins	6	354D	16F-12R	90.95	10940	C,H,A
MF-2640 4WD	45460.00	15760.00	19390.00	20940.00	Perkins	6	354D	16F-12R	90.95	11800	C,H,A
MF-3505 RC	38000.00	12870.00	15840.00	17110.00	Perkins	6	354D	16F-12R	91.50	11200	C,H,A
MF-3505 RC 4WD	46500.00	16190.00	19920.00	21510.00	Perkins	6	354D	16F-12R	91.50	12600	C,H,A
MF-3525 RC	35872.00	12050.00	14830.00	16020.00	Perkins	6T	354D	16F-12R	108.01	11800	No
MF-3525 RC	42075.00	14510.00	17860.00	19290.00	Perkins	6T	354D	16F-12R	108.01	12900	C,H,A
MF-3525 RC 4WD	44375.00	15410.00	18960.00	20480.00	Perkins	6T	354D	16F-12R	108.01	13200	No
MF-3525 RC 4WD	50575.00	17780.00	21890.00	23640.00	Perkins	6T	354D	16F-12R	108.01	14300	C,H,A
MF-3545 RC	40720.00	13960.00	17180.00	18550.00	Perkins	6TI	354D	16F-12R	126.72	12100	No
MF-3545 RC	46920.00	16340.00	20110.00	21720.00	Perkins	6TI	354D	16F-12R	126.72	13200	C,H,A
MF-3545 RC 4WD	48595.00	17000.00	20930.00	22600.00	Perkins	6TI	354D	16F-12R	126.72	13500	No
MF-3545 RC 4WD	54795.00	19420.00	23900.00	25810.00	Perkins	6TI	354D	16F-12R	126.72	14600	C,H,A
MF-3545 Western	45595.00	15830.00	19490.00	21050.00	Perkins	6TI	354D	16F-12R	126.72	12100	C,H,A
MF-4800 4WD	83040.00	20450.00	27030.00	30270.00	Cummins	V8	903D	18F-6R		24000	C,H,A

Massey Ferguson (Cont.)

1984 (Cont.)

Model	Approx. Retail Price New	Estimated Average Value Less Repairs: Fair	Good	Premium	Engine: Make	No. Cyls.	Displ. Cu.-In.	No. Speeds	P.T.O. H.P.	Approx. Shipping Wt.-Lbs.	Cab
MF-4800 4WD w/PTO	86275.00	**21360.00**	**28220.00**	**31610.00**	Cummins	V8	903D	18F-6R	179.08	24500	C,H,A
MF-4840 4WD	93435.00	**23360.00**	**30870.00**	**34570.00**	Cummins	V8	903D	18F-6R		26038	C,H,A
MF-4840 4WD w/PTO	96575.00	**24240.00**	**32030.00**	**35870.00**	Cummins	V8	903D	18F-6R	210.67	26538	C,H,A
MF-4880 4WD	110235.00	**25270.00**	**33390.00**	**37400.00**	Cummins	V8T	903D	18F-6R		28865	C,H,A
MF-4880 4WD w/PTO	113375.00	**26710.00**	**35290.00**	**39530.00**	Cummins	V8T	903D	18F-6R	272.81	29365	C,H,A
MF-4900 4WD	122015.00	**27440.00**	**36270.00**	**40620.00**	Cummins	V8T	903D	18F-6R		29000	C,H,A
MF-4900 4WD w/PTO	125247.00	**28070.00**	**37090.00**	**41540.00**	Cummins	V8T	903D	18F-6R	320.55	29500	C,H,A

RC - Row Crop

1985

Model	Approx. Retail Price New	Fair	Good	Premium	Make	No. Cyls.	Displ. Cu.-In.	No. Speeds	P.T.O. H.P.	Approx. Shipping Wt.-Lbs.	Cab
MF-240	11925.00	**6320.00**	**7270.00**	**7850.00**	Perkins	3	152D	8F-2R	34.77	3560	No
MF-250	16165.00	**7760.00**	**9210.00**	**9950.00**	Perkins	3	152D	8F-2R	40.86	4100	No
MF-254 4WD	20205.00	**9700.00**	**11520.00**	**12440.00**	Perkins	3	152D	12F-4R	43.36	5160	No
MF-270	19100.00	**9170.00**	**10890.00**	**11760.00**	Perkins	4	236D	8F-2R	55.85	6050	No
MF-270	20895.00	**10030.00**	**11910.00**	**12860.00**	Perkins	4	236D	12F-4R	55.62	6100	No
MF-274 4WD	22520.00	**10810.00**	**12840.00**	**13870.00**	Perkins	4	236D	12F-4R	55.39	5490	No
MF-290	21255.00	**10200.00**	**12120.00**	**13090.00**	Perkins	4	248D	8F-2R	65.92	6520	No
MF-290	23050.00	**11060.00**	**13140.00**	**14190.00**	Perkins	4	248D	12F-4R	65.92	6570	No
MF-294 4WD	26385.00	**12670.00**	**15040.00**	**16240.00**	Perkins	4	248D	12F-4R	67.39	6550	No
MF-298	25390.00	**12190.00**	**14470.00**	**15630.00**	Perkins	4	318D	8F-2R	79.54	6975	No
MF-298	26435.00	**12690.00**	**15070.00**	**16280.00**	Perkins	4	318D	12F-4R	79.26	7025	No
MF-670	27610.00	**13250.00**	**15740.00**	**17000.00**	Perkins	4	236D	12F-4R	55.62	7500	C,H,A
MF-670 4WD	31025.00	**14890.00**	**17680.00**	**19090.00**	Perkins	4	236D	12F-4R	55.62	7550	C,H,A
MF-690	30760.00	**14770.00**	**17530.00**	**18930.00**	Perkins	4	248D	12F-4R	65.68	8000	C,H,A
MF-690 4WD	36045.00	**16800.00**	**19950.00**	**21550.00**	Perkins	4	248D	12F-4R	65.68	9400	C,H,A
MF-698	32205.00	**15460.00**	**18360.00**	**19830.00**	Perkins	4	318D	12F-4R	78.83	8285	C,H,A
MF-698 4WD	38455.00	**17280.00**	**20520.00**	**22160.00**	Perkins	4	318D	12F-4R	78.83	9115	C,H,A
MF-699	33310.00	**15990.00**	**18990.00**	**20510.00**	Perkins	6	354D	12F-4R	85.79	9104	C,H,A
MF-699 4WD	38990.00	**17760.00**	**21090.00**	**22780.00**	Perkins	6	354D	12F-4R	85.79	10075	C,H,A
MF-1010	5965.00	**3760.00**	**4180.00**	**4680.00**	Toyosha	3	53D	6F-2R	13.00	1522	No
MF-1010 4WD	6525.00	**4110.00**	**4570.00**	**5120.00**	Toyosha	3	53D	6F-2R	13.00	1720	No
MF-1020	6980.00	**4400.00**	**4890.00**	**5480.00**	Toyosha	3	69D	12F-4R	17.08	1950	No
MF-1020 4WD	7615.00	**4800.00**	**5330.00**	**5970.00**	Toyosha	3	69D	12F-4R	17.00	2230	No
MF-1030	7865.00	**4960.00**	**5510.00**	**6170.00**	Toyosha	3	87D	12F-4R	23.35	2210	No
MF-1030 4WD	8895.00	**5600.00**	**6230.00**	**6980.00**	Toyosha	3	87D	12F-4R	23.35	2640	No
MF-1040	9635.00	**5590.00**	**6460.00**	**7170.00**	Toyosha	3	122D	12F-4R	27.73	3300	No
MF-1040 4WD	11535.00	**6690.00**	**7730.00**	**8580.00**	Toyosha	3	122D	12F-4R	27.73	3600	No
MF-3505	38000.00	**14400.00**	**17640.00**	**18880.00**	Perkins	6	354D	16F-12R	91.50	11200	C,H,A
MF-3505 4WD	46500.00	**17800.00**	**21810.00**	**23340.00**	Perkins	6	354D	16F-12R	91.50	12600	C,H,A
MF-3525	42195.00	**16000.00**	**19600.00**	**20970.00**	Perkins	6	354D	16F-12R	108.01	12900	C,H,A
MF-3525 4WD	50575.00	**18800.00**	**23030.00**	**24640.00**	Perkins	6T	354D	16F-12R	108.01	14300	C,H,A
MF-3545	47515.00	**17800.00**	**21810.00**	**23340.00**	Perkins	6TI	354D	16F-12R	126.72	13200	C,H,A
MF-3545 4WD	55466.00	**20960.00**	**25680.00**	**27480.00**	Perkins	6TI	354D	16F-12R	126.72	14600	C,H,A
MF-4800 4WD	86275.00	**22280.00**	**28230.00**	**31340.00**	Cummins	V8	903D	18F-6R	179.08	26230	C,H,A
MF-4840 4WD	97545.00	**23260.00**	**29470.00**	**32710.00**	Cummins	V8	903D	18F-6R	210.67	26540	C,H,A
MF-4880 4WD	113375.00	**25610.00**	**32440.00**	**36010.00**	Cummins	V8T	903D	18F-6R	272.81	29365	C,H,A
MF-4900 4WD	126500.00	**30150.00**	**38190.00**	**42390.00**	Cummins	V8T	903D	18F-6R	320.55	29500	C,H,A

RC--Row Crop

1986

Model	Approx. Retail Price New	Fair	Good	Premium	Make	No. Cyls.	Displ. Cu.-In.	No. Speeds	P.T.O. H.P.	Approx. Shipping Wt.-Lbs.	Cab
MF-154 S	16576.00	**8120.00**	**9610.00**	**10380.00**	Perkins	3	152D	12F-4R	42.00	4520	No
MF-154 S 4WD	21000.00	**10290.00**	**12180.00**	**13150.00**	Perkins	3	152D	20F-8R	42.00	4830	No
MF-174 S	18529.00	**9080.00**	**10750.00**	**11610.00**	Perkins	4	236D	12F-4R	57.00	4685	No
MF-174 S 4WD	23519.00	**11520.00**	**13640.00**	**14730.00**	Perkins	4	236D	20F-8R	57.00	4995	No
MF-194 F	20690.00	**10140.00**	**12000.00**	**12960.00**	Perkins	4	248D	12F-4R	68.00	5104	No
MF-194 F 4WD	25690.00	**12590.00**	**14900.00**	**16090.00**	Perkins	4	248D	20F-8R	68.00	5357	No
MF-240	11925.00	**6440.00**	**7390.00**	**7980.00**	Perkins	3	152D	8F-2R	34.77	3560	No
MF-250	16165.00	**7920.00**	**9380.00**	**10130.00**	Perkins	3	152D	8F-2R	40.86	4100	No
MF-254 4WD	20205.00	**9900.00**	**11720.00**	**12660.00**	Perkins	3	152D	12F-4R	43.36	5160	No
MF-270	19576.00	**9590.00**	**11350.00**	**12260.00**	Perkins	4	236D	8F-2R	55.85	5150	No
MF-270	20895.00	**10240.00**	**12120.00**	**13090.00**	Perkins	4	236D	12F-4R	55.62	5160	No
MF-274 4WD	22520.00	**11040.00**	**13060.00**	**14110.00**	Perkins	4	236D	12F-4R	55.39	5490	No
MF-283 4WD	14598.00	**7150.00**	**8470.00**	**9150.00**	Perkins	4	248D	8F-2R	67.00	5700	No
MF-290	21255.00	**10420.00**	**12330.00**	**13320.00**	Perkins	4	248D	8F-2R	65.92	5140	No
MF-290	23050.00	**11300.00**	**13370.00**	**14440.00**	Perkins	4	248D	12F-4R	65.92	5405	No
MF-294 4WD	26385.00	**12930.00**	**15300.00**	**16520.00**	Perkins	4	248D	12F-4R	67.39	6550	No
MF-298	25390.00	**12440.00**	**14730.00**	**15910.00**	Perkins	4	318D	8F-2R	79.54	4126	No
MF-298	26435.00	**12950.00**	**15330.00**	**16560.00**	Perkins	4	318D	12F-4R	79.26	4176	No
MF-670	27610.00	**13530.00**	**16010.00**	**17290.00**	Perkins	4	236D	12F-4R	55.62	7500	C,H,A
MF-670 4WD	32794.00	**16070.00**	**19020.00**	**20540.00**	Perkins	4	236D	12F-4R	55.62	7550	C,H,A
MF-690	30760.00	**15070.00**	**17840.00**	**19270.00**	Perkins	4	248D	12F-4R	65.68	8000	C,H,A
MF-690 4WD	36045.00	**17660.00**	**20910.00**	**22580.00**	Perkins	4	248D	12F-4R	65.68	9400	C,H,A
MF-698	32205.00	**15780.00**	**18680.00**	**20170.00**	Perkins	4	318D	12F-4R	78.83	8285	C,H,A
MF-698 4WD	38455.00	**18840.00**	**22300.00**	**24080.00**	Perkins	4	318D	12F-4R	78.83	9115	C,H,A
MF-699	33310.00	**16320.00**	**19320.00**	**20870.00**	Perkins	6	354D	12F-4R	85.79	9104	C,H,A
MF-699 4WD	38990.00	**19110.00**	**22610.00**	**24420.00**	Perkins	6	354D	12F-4R	85.79	10075	C,H,A
MF-1010	6315.00	**4040.00**	**4480.00**	**4970.00**	Toyosha	3	53D	6F-2R	13.00	1522	No
MF-1010 4WD	6912.00	**4420.00**	**4910.00**	**5450.00**	Toyosha	3	53D	6F-2R	13.00	1720	No
MF-1010 Hydro	7315.00	**4680.00**	**5190.00**	**5760.00**	Toyosha	3	53D	Variable	12.00	1772	No
MF-1010 Hydro 4WD	7912.00	**5060.00**	**5620.00**	**6240.00**	Toyosha	3	53D	Variable	12.00	2000	No
MF-1020	7511.00	**4810.00**	**5330.00**	**5920.00**	Toyosha	3	69D	12F-4R	17.08	2045	No
MF-1020 4WD	8150.00	**5220.00**	**5790.00**	**6430.00**	Toyosha	3	69D	12F-4R	17.08	2285	No
MF-1030	8262.00	**4880.00**	**5620.00**	**6240.00**	Toyosha	3	87D	12F-4R	23.35	2210	No
MF-1030 4WD	9795.00	**5780.00**	**6660.00**	**7390.00**	Toyosha	3	87D	12F-4R	23.00	2640	No

Massey Ferguson (Cont.)

1986 (Cont.)

Model	Approx. Retail Price New	Fair	Good	Premium	Engine Make	Engine No. Cyls.	Engine Displ. Cu.-In.	No. Speeds	P.T.O. H.P.	Approx. Shipping Wt.-Lbs.	Cab
MF-1040	10129.00	**5980.00**	**6890.00**	**7650.00**	Toyosha	3	122D	12F-4R	27.73	3300	No
MF-1040 4WD	12051.00	**7110.00**	**8200.00**	**9100.00**	Toyosha	3	122D	12F-4R	27.73	3600	No
MF-3505	38000.00	**14760.00**	**18000.00**	**19260.00**	Perkins	6	354D	16F-12R	91.50	11200	C,H,A
MF-3505 4WD	46500.00	**18250.00**	**22250.00**	**23810.00**	Perkins	6	354D	16F-12R	91.50	12600	C,H,A
MF-3525	42195.00	**16400.00**	**20000.00**	**21400.00**	Perkins	6	354D	16F-12R	108.01	12900	C,H,A
MF-3525 4WD	50575.00	**19480.00**	**23750.00**	**25410.00**	Perkins	6T	354D	16F-12R	108.01	14300	C,H,A
MF-3545	47515.00	**18450.00**	**22500.00**	**24080.00**	Perkins	6TI	354D	16F-12R	126.72	13200	C,H,A
MF-3545 4WD	55466.00	**21730.00**	**26500.00**	**28360.00**	Perkins	6TI	354D	16F-12R	126.72	14600	C,H,A
MF-4800 4WD	86275.00	**24410.00**	**29750.00**	**33020.00**	Cummins	V8	903D	18F-6R	179.08	26230	C,H,A
MF-4840 4WD	97545.00	**28010.00**	**34140.00**	**37900.00**	Cummins	V8	903D	18F-6R	210.67	26540	C,H,A
MF-4880 4WD	113375.00	**29880.00**	**36420.00**	**40430.00**	Cummins	V8T	903D	18F-6R	272.81	29365	C,H,A
MF-4900 4WD	126500.00	**34080.00**	**41540.00**	**46110.00**	Cummins	V8T	903D	18F-6R	320.55	29500	C,H,A

RC - Row Crop

1987

Model	Approx. Retail Price New	Fair	Good	Premium	Engine Make	Engine No. Cyls.	Engine Displ. Cu.-In.	No. Speeds	P.T.O. H.P.	Approx. Shipping Wt.-Lbs.	Cab
MF-154S 4WD	21420.00	**10710.00**	**12640.00**	**13650.00**	Perkins	3	152D	12F-4R	42.00	4830	No
MF-154S Orchard	16908.00	**8450.00**	**9980.00**	**10780.00**	Perkins	3	152D	12F-4R	42.00	4520	No
MF-174S Orchard	18529.00	**9270.00**	**10930.00**	**11800.00**	Perkins	4	236D	12F-4R	57.00	4685	No
MF-174S Orchard 4WD	23519.00	**11760.00**	**13880.00**	**14990.00**	Perkins	4	236D	12F-4R	57.00	4995	No
MF-194S Orchard	21311.00	**10660.00**	**12570.00**	**13580.00**	Perkins	4	248D	12F-4R	68.00	5104	No
MF-194S Orchard 4WD	26204.00	**13100.00**	**15460.00**	**16700.00**	Perkins	4	248D	12F-4R	68.00	5357	No
MF-240	12909.00	**7100.00**	**8130.00**	**8780.00**	Perkins	3	152D	8F-2R	38.00	3810	No
MF-254 4WD	20551.00	**10280.00**	**12130.00**	**13100.00**	Perkins	3	152D	12F-4R	42.00	5369	No
MF-274 4WD	22867.00	**11430.00**	**13490.00**	**14570.00**	Perkins	4	236D	12F-4R	55.00	5694	No
MF-294 4WD	26734.00	**13370.00**	**15770.00**	**17030.00**	Perkins	4	248D	12F-4R	67.00	6758	No
MF-360	16497.00	**9070.00**	**10390.00**	**11220.00**	Perkins	3	152D	8F-2R	46.10	4910	No
MF-360 4WD	21538.00	**11850.00**	**13570.00**	**14660.00**	Perkins	3	152D	8F-2R	46.10	5346	No
MF-375	19940.00	**9970.00**	**11770.00**	**12710.00**	Perkins	4	236D	12F-4R	58.10	6040	No
MF-375 4WD	24538.00	**12270.00**	**14480.00**	**15640.00**	Perkins	4	236D	12F-4R	58.10	7202	No
MF-383	15695.00	**8630.00**	**9890.00**	**10680.00**	Perkins	4	248D	8F-2R	67.00	6098	No
MF-383 Wide Row Crop	16817.00	**9250.00**	**10600.00**	**11450.00**	Perkins	4	248D	8F-2R	67.00	7166	No
MF-390	22173.00	**12200.00**	**13970.00**	**15090.00**	Perkins	4	248D	12F-4R	67.30	6036	No
MF-390 4WD	27234.00	**14980.00**	**17160.00**	**18530.00**	Perkins	4	248D	12F-4R	67.30	7266	No
MF-398	26844.00	**13420.00**	**15840.00**	**17110.00**	Perkins	4	236D	12F-4R	80.30	7047	No
MF-398 4WD	31884.00	**15940.00**	**18810.00**	**20320.00**	Perkins	4	236D	12F-4R	80.30	7648	No
MF-399	28300.00	**14150.00**	**16700.00**	**18040.00**	Perkins	6	354D	12F-4R	90.50	7233	No
MF-399 4WD	33300.00	**16650.00**	**19650.00**	**21220.00**	Perkins	6	354D	12F-4R	90.50	8029	No
MF-1010	7245.00	**4710.00**	**5220.00**	**5740.00**	Toyosha	3	53D	6F-2R	13.50	1580	No
MF-1010 4WD	7985.00	**5190.00**	**5750.00**	**6330.00**	Toyosha	3	53D	6F-2R	13.50	1800	No
MF-1010 Hydro	8381.00	**5450.00**	**6030.00**	**6630.00**	Toyosha	3	53D	Variable	12.00	1772	No
MF-1010 Hydro 4WD	9166.00	**5960.00**	**6600.00**	**7260.00**	Toyosha	3	53D	Variable	12.00	2000	No
MF-1020	8599.00	**5590.00**	**6190.00**	**6810.00**	Toyosha	3	69D	12F-4R	17.08	2045	No
MF-1020 4WD	9425.00	**6130.00**	**6790.00**	**7470.00**	Toyosha	3	69D	12F-4R	17.08	2285	No
MF-1020 Hydro	9774.00	**6350.00**	**7040.00**	**7740.00**	Toyosha	3	69D	Variable	14.50	2046	No
MF-1020 Hydro 4WD	10600.00	**6890.00**	**7630.00**	**8390.00**	Toyosha	3	69D	Variable	14.50	2266	No
MF-1030	10042.00	**6030.00**	**6930.00**	**7690.00**	Toyosha	3	90D	12F-4R	23.35	2701	No
MF-1030 4WD	11975.00	**7190.00**	**8260.00**	**9170.00**	Toyosha	3	90D	12F-4R	23.35	2832	No
MF-1035	11428.00	**6860.00**	**7890.00**	**8760.00**	Toyosha	3	92D	12F-4R	26.00	2801	No
MF-1035 4WD	13167.00	**7900.00**	**9090.00**	**10090.00**	Toyosha	3	92D	12F-4R	26.00	2932	No
MF-1045	12950.00	**7120.00**	**8160.00**	**8810.00**	Toyosha	3	122D	9F-3R	30.00	3527	No
MF-1045 4WD	14679.00	**8070.00**	**9250.00**	**9990.00**	Toyosha	3	122D	9F-3R	30.00	3825	No
MF-3050	30233.00	**12700.00**	**15420.00**	**16500.00**	Perkins	4	236D	16F-12R	63.00	8565	C,H,A
MF-3050 4WD	35432.00	**14880.00**	**18070.00**	**19340.00**	Perkins	4	236D	16F-12R	63.00	9171	C,H,A
MF-3060	32235.00	**13540.00**	**16440.00**	**17590.00**	Perkins	4	248D	16F-12R	69.70	8565	C,H,A
MF-3060 4WD	37904.00	**15120.00**	**18360.00**	**19650.00**	Perkins	4	248D	16F-12R	69.70	9171	C,H,A
MF-3070	34634.00	**14070.00**	**17090.00**	**18290.00**	Perkins	4T	236D	16F-12R	82.20	9407	C,H,A
MF-3070 4WD	40684.00	**15960.00**	**19380.00**	**20740.00**	Perkins	4T	236D	16F-12R	82.20	10000	C,H,A
MF-3090	38883.00	**15460.00**	**18770.00**	**20080.00**	Perkins	6	354D	16F-12R	100.70	10329	C,H,A
MF-3090 4WD	45064.00	**18060.00**	**21930.00**	**23470.00**	Perkins	6	354D	16F-12R	100.70	10829	C,H,A
MF-3525 4WD	49047.00	**19320.00**	**23460.00**	**25100.00**	Perkins	6T	354D	16F-12R	105.00	15174	C,H,A
MF-3525 RC 4WD	50572.00	**19950.00**	**24230.00**	**25930.00**	Perkins	6T	354D	16F-12R	105.00	13200	C,H,A
MF-3525 Row Crop	42072.00	**16800.00**	**20400.00**	**21830.00**	Perkins	6T	354D	16F-12R	105.00	11800	C,H,A
MF-3525 Western	40547.00	**16170.00**	**19640.00**	**21020.00**	Perkins	6T	354D	16F-12R	105.00	13100	C,H,A
MF-3545 4WD	53818.00	**21340.00**	**25910.00**	**27720.00**	Perkins	6TI	354D	16F-12R	125.00	13500	C,H,A
MF-3545 RC 4WD	55343.00	**21970.00**	**26670.00**	**28540.00**	Perkins	6TI	354D	16F-12R	125.00	13500	C,H,A
MF-3545 Row Crop	47389.00	**18900.00**	**22950.00**	**24560.00**	Perkins	6TI	354D	16F-12R	125.00	12100	C,H,A
MF-3545 Western	45851.00	**18250.00**	**22160.00**	**23710.00**	Perkins	6TI	354D	16F-12R	125.00	11900	C,H,A

RC - Row Crop

1988

Model	Approx. Retail Price New	Fair	Good	Premium	Engine Make	Engine No. Cyls.	Engine Displ. Cu.-In.	No. Speeds	P.T.O. H.P.	Approx. Shipping Wt.-Lbs.	Cab
MF-154S Orchard	17753.00	**9050.00**	**10650.00**	**11400.00**	Perkins	3	152D	12F-4R	42.00	4520	No
MF-154S Orchard 4WD	21420.00	**10920.00**	**12850.00**	**13750.00**	Perkins	3	152D	12F-4R	42.00	4830	No
MF-174S Orchard	19178.00	**9780.00**	**11510.00**	**12320.00**	Perkins	4	236D	12F-4R	57.00	4685	No
MF-174S Orchard 4WD	23519.00	**12000.00**	**14110.00**	**15100.00**	Perkins	4	236D	12F-4R	57.00	4995	No
MF-194F Orchard	21311.00	**10870.00**	**12790.00**	**13690.00**	Perkins	4	248D	12F-4R	68.00	5104	No
MF-194F Orchard 4WD	26204.00	**13360.00**	**15720.00**	**16820.00**	Perkins	4	248D	12F-4R	68.00	5357	No
MF-240	14638.00	**8200.00**	**9370.00**	**10030.00**	Perkins	3	152D	8F-2R	38.00	3810	No
MF-283	13856.00	**7760.00**	**8870.00**	**9490.00**	Perkins	4	248D	8F-2R	67.00	5432	No
MF-360	17982.00	**10070.00**	**11510.00**	**12320.00**	Perkins	3T	152D	8F-2R	46.10	4910	No
MF-360 4WD	24691.00	**13830.00**	**15800.00**	**16910.00**	Perkins	3T	152D	8F-2R	46.10	5346	No
MF-375	21535.00	**10980.00**	**12920.00**	**13820.00**	Perkins	4	236D	12F-4R	58.10	6040	No
MF-375 4WD	27237.00	**13890.00**	**16340.00**	**17480.00**	Perkins	4	236D	12F-4R	58.10	7202	No
MF-383	17139.00	**9600.00**	**10970.00**	**11740.00**	Perkins	4	248D	8F-2R	67.00	6098	No
MF-383 Wide Row	19252.00	**10780.00**	**12320.00**	**13180.00**	Perkins	4	248D	8F-2R	67.00	7166	No

Massey Ferguson (Cont.)

1988 (Cont.)

Model	Approx. Retail Price New	Estimated Average Value Less Repairs: Fair	Good	Premium	Engine Make	No. Cyls.	Displ. Cu.-In.	No. Speeds	P.T.O. H.P.	Approx. Shipping Wt.-Lbs.	Cab
MF-390	23503.00	13160.00	15040.00	16090.00	Perkins	4	248D	12F-4R	67.30	6036	No
MF-390 4WD	29140.00	16320.00	18650.00	19960.00	Perkins	4	248D	12F-4R	67.30	7266	No
MF-398	27381.00	13960.00	16430.00	17580.00	Perkins	4	236D	12F-4R	78.00	7047	No
MF-398 4WD	32841.00	16750.00	19710.00	21090.00	Perkins	4	236D	12F-4R	78.00	7648	No
MF-399	28866.00	14720.00	17320.00	18530.00	Perkins	6	354D	12F-4R	90.50	7233	No
MF-399 4WD	34299.00	17490.00	20580.00	22020.00	Perkins	6	354D	12F-4R	90.50	8029	No
MF-1010	7501.00	4950.00	5480.00	5970.00	Toyosha	3	53D	6F-2R	13.50	1580	No
MF-1010 4WD	8549.00	5640.00	6240.00	6800.00	Toyosha	3	53D	6F-2R	13.50	1800	No
MF-1010 Hydro	8719.00	5760.00	6370.00	6940.00	Toyosha	3	53D	Variable	12.00	1772	No
MF-1010 Hydro 4WD	9627.00	6350.00	7030.00	7660.00	Toyosha	3	53D	Variable	12.00	2000	No
MF-1020	8858.00	5850.00	6470.00	7050.00	Toyosha	3	69D	12F-4R	17.08	2045	No
MF-1020 4WD	9852.00	6500.00	7190.00	7840.00	Toyosha	3	69D	12F-4R	17.08	2285	No
MF-1020 Hydro	10068.00	6650.00	7350.00	8010.00	Toyosha	3	69D	Variable	14.50	2046	No
MF-1020 Hydro 4WD	10921.00	7210.00	7970.00	8690.00	Toyosha	3	69D	Variable	14.50	2266	No
MF-1030	10042.00	6130.00	7030.00	7800.00	Toyosha	3	87D	12F-4R	23.00	2701	No
MF-1030 4WD	12215.00	7450.00	8550.00	9490.00	Toyosha	3	92D	12F-4R	23.00	2832	No
MF-1035	11428.00	6970.00	8000.00	8880.00	Toyosha	3	92D	12F-4R	26.00	2801	No
MF-1035 4WD	14096.00	8600.00	9870.00	10960.00	Toyosha	3	92D	12F-4R	26.00	2932	No
MF-1045	12950.00	7250.00	8290.00	8870.00	Toyosha	3	122D	9F-3R	30.00	3527	No
MF-1045 4WD	15423.00	8640.00	9870.00	10560.00	Toyosha	3	122D	9F-3R	30.00	3825	No
MF-3050	30333.00	13040.00	15770.00	16720.00	Perkins	4	236D	16F-12R	63.00	8565	C,H,A
MF-3050 4WD	35532.00	15280.00	18480.00	19590.00	Perkins	4	236D	16F-12R	63.00	9171	C,H,A
MF-3060	32335.00	13900.00	16810.00	17820.00	Perkins	4	248D	16F-12R	69.70	8565	C,H,A
MF-3060 4WD	38004.00	16340.00	19760.00	20950.00	Perkins	4	248D	16F-12R	69.70	9171	C,H,A
MF-3070	34734.00	14940.00	18060.00	19140.00	Perkins	4T	236D	16F-12R	82.20	9407	C,H,A
MF-3070 4WD	40784.00	17540.00	21210.00	22480.00	Perkins	4T	236D	16F-12R	82.20	10000	C,H,A
MF-3090	38983.00	16760.00	20270.00	21490.00	Perkins	6	354D	16F-12R	100.70	10329	C,H,A
MF-3090 4WD	45164.00	18920.00	22880.00	24250.00	Perkins	6	354D	16F-12R	100.70	10829	C,H,A
MF-3630	47078.00	19780.00	23920.00	25360.00	Perkins	6T	354D	16F-12R	119.50	11729	C,H,A
MF-3630 4WD	55909.00	22790.00	27560.00	29210.00	Perkins	6T	354D	16F-12R	119.50	12809	C,H,A
MF-3650	50195.00	21070.00	25480.00	27010.00	Perkins	6TI	354D	16F-12R	130.00	12037	C,H,A
MF-3650 4WD	59026.00	24080.00	29120.00	30870.00	Perkins	6TI	354D	16F-12R	131.30	13139	C,H,A

1989

Model	Approx. Retail Price New	Estimated Average Value Less Repairs: Fair	Good	Premium	Engine Make	No. Cyls.	Displ. Cu.-In.	No. Speeds	P.T.O. H.P.	Approx. Shipping Wt.-Lbs.	Cab
MF-154S Orchard	18729.00	9740.00	11430.00	12230.00	Perkins	3	152D	12F-4R	42.00	4520	No
MF-154S Orchard 4WD	22384.00	11640.00	13650.00	14610.00	Perkins	3	152D	12F-4R	42.00	4830	No
MF-174S Orchard	20616.00	10720.00	12580.00	13460.00	Perkins	4	236D	12F-4R	57.00	4685	No
MF-174S Orchard 4WD	23872.00	12410.00	14560.00	15580.00	Perkins	4	236D	12F-4R	57.00	4995	No
MF-194F Orchard	21950.00	11410.00	13390.00	14330.00	Perkins	4	248D	12F-4R	68.00	5104	No
MF-194F Orchard 4WD	26597.00	13830.00	16220.00	17360.00	Perkins	4	248D	12F-4R	68.00	5357	No
MF-231	9195.00	5700.00	6530.00	7180.00	Perkins	3	152D	8F-2R	34.00	4065	No
MF-240	14638.00	8340.00	9520.00	10190.00	Perkins	3	152D	8F-2R	38.00	3810	No
MF-253	14950.00	8520.00	9720.00	10400.00	Perkins	3T	152D	8F-2R	45.00	4020	No
MF-283	14703.00	8380.00	9560.00	10230.00	Perkins	4	248D	8F-2R	67.00	5432	No
MF-360	18092.00	10310.00	11760.00	12580.00	Perkins	3T	152D	8F-2R	46.10	4910	No
MF-360 4WD	24712.00	14090.00	16060.00	17180.00	Perkins	3T	152D	8F-2R	46.10	5346	No
MF-364S 4WD	25200.00	13100.00	15370.00	16450.00	Perkins	3	152D	12F-4R	50.00	5082	No
MF-374S	22300.00	11600.00	13600.00	14550.00	Perkins	4	236D	12F-4R	57.00	5145	No
MF-374S 4WD	26500.00	13780.00	16170.00	17300.00	Perkins	4	236D	12F-4R	57.00	5370	No
MF-375	21535.00	11200.00	13140.00	14060.00	Perkins	4	236D	12F-4R	58.10	6040	No
MF-375 4WD	27237.00	14160.00	16620.00	17780.00	Perkins	4	236D	12F-4R	58.10	7202	No
MF-383	17139.00	9770.00	11140.00	11920.00	Perkins	4	248D	8F-2R		6098	No
MF-383 Wide Row	20215.00	11520.00	13140.00	14060.00	Perkins	4	248D	8F-2R		7166	No
MF-384S	23180.00	12050.00	14140.00	15130.00	Perkins	4	236D	12F-4R	65.00	5192	No
MF-384S 4WD	26800.00	13940.00	16350.00	17500.00	Perkins	4	236D	12F-4R	65.00	5412	No
MF-390	23503.00	13400.00	15280.00	16350.00	Perkins	4	248D	12F-4R	67.30	6036	No
MF-390 4WD	29140.00	16610.00	18940.00	20270.00	Perkins	4	248D	12F-4R	67.30	7266	No
MF-390T	24555.00	14000.00	15960.00	17080.00	Perkins	4T	236D	8F-2R	80.00	6051	No
MF-390T 4WD	30192.00	17210.00	19630.00	21000.00	Perkins	4T	236D	8F-2R	80.00	7281	No
MF-394S 4WD	28300.00	14720.00	17260.00	18470.00	Perkins	4	236D				No
MF-398	27381.00	14240.00	16700.00	17870.00	Perkins	4T	236D	12F-4R	80.00	7047	No
MF-398 4WD	32841.00	17080.00	20030.00	21430.00	Perkins	4	236D	12F-4R	80.00	7648	No
MF-399	28866.00	15010.00	17610.00	18840.00	Perkins	6	354D	12F-4R	90.50	7233	No
MF-399 4WD	34299.00	17840.00	20920.00	22380.00	Perkins	6	354D	12F-4R	90.50	8029	No
MF-1010	7728.00	5180.00	5720.00	6180.00	Toyosha	3	53D	6F-2R	13.50	1580	No
MF-1010 4WD	8807.00	5900.00	6520.00	7040.00	Toyosha	3	53D	6F-2R	13.50	1800	No
MF-1010 Hydro	8983.00	6020.00	6650.00	7180.00	Toyosha	3	53D	Variable	12.00	1772	No
MF-1010 Hydro 4WD	9918.00	6650.00	7340.00	7930.00	Toyosha	3	53D	Variable	12.00	2000	No
MF-1020	9125.00	6110.00	6750.00	7290.00	Toyosha	3	69D	12F-4R	17.00	2045	No
MF-1020 4WD	10249.00	6870.00	7580.00	8190.00	Toyosha	3	69D	12F-4R	17.00	2285	No
MF-1020 Hydro	10473.00	7020.00	7750.00	8370.00	Toyosha	3	69D	Variable	14.50	2046	No
MF-1020 Hydro 4WD	11996.00	8040.00	8880.00	9590.00	Toyosha	3	69D	Variable	14.50	2266	No
MF-1030	10042.00	6230.00	7130.00	7840.00	Toyosha	3	87D	12F-4R	23.00	2701	No
MF-1030 4WD	12582.00	7800.00	8930.00	9820.00	Toyosha	3	87D	12F-4R	23.00	2832	No
MF-1035	11428.00	7090.00	8110.00	8920.00	Toyosha	3	92D	12F-4R	26.00	2801	No
MF-1035 4WD	14238.00	8830.00	10110.00	11120.00	Toyosha	3	92D	12F-4R	26.00	2932	No
MF-1045	12950.00	7380.00	8420.00	9010.00	Toyosha	3	122D	9F-3R	30.00	3527	No
MF-1045 4WD	15892.00	9060.00	10330.00	11050.00	Toyosha	3	122D	9F-3R	30.00	3825	No
MF-3050	30333.00	13350.00	16080.00	17050.00	Perkins	4	236D	16F-12R	63.00	8565	C,H,A
MF-3050 4WD	35532.00	15630.00	18830.00	19960.00	Perkins	4	236D	16F-12R	63.00	9171	C,H,A
MF-3060	32335.00	14230.00	17140.00	18170.00	Perkins	4	248D	16F-12R	69.70	8565	C,H,A
MF-3060 4WD	38004.00	16720.00	20140.00	21350.00	Perkins	4	248D	16F-12R	69.70	9171	C,H,A
MF-3070	35776.00	15740.00	18960.00	20100.00	Perkins	4T	236D	16F-12R	82.20	9407	C,H,A
MF-3070 4WD	40784.00	17950.00	21620.00	22920.00	Perkins	4T	236D	16F-12R	82.20	10000	C,H,A

Massey Ferguson (Cont.)

1989 (Cont.)

Model	Approx. Retail Price New	Estimated Average Value Less Repairs Fair	Good	Premium	Engine Make	No. Cyls.	Displ. Cu.-In.	No. Speeds	P.T.O. H.P.	Approx. Shipping Wt.-Lbs.	Cab
MF-3090	38983.00	17150.00	20660.00	21900.00	Perkins	6	354D	16F-12R	100.70	10329	C,H,A
MF-3090 4WD	45164.00	19870.00	23940.00	25380.00	Perkins	6	354D	16F-12R	100.70	10829	C,H,A
MF-3630	47078.00	20710.00	24950.00	26450.00	Perkins	6T	354D	16F-12R	119.50	11729	C,H,A
MF-3630 4WD	55909.00	23320.00	28090.00	29780.00	Perkins	6T	354D	16F-12R	119.50	12809	C,H,A
MF-3650	51700.00	22000.00	26500.00	28090.00	Perkins	6TI	354D	16F-12R	130.00	12037	C,H,A
MF-3650 4WD	60797.00	25520.00	30740.00	32580.00	Perkins	6TI	354D	16F-12R	131.30	13139	C,H,A
MF-3680 4WD	62500.00	26400.00	31800.00	33710.00	Valmet	6T	452D	16F-4R	160.00	13866	C,H,A

1990

Model	Approx. Retail Price New	Fair	Good	Premium	Make	No. Cyls.	Displ. Cu.-In.	No. Speeds	P.T.O. H.P.	Approx. Shipping Wt.-Lbs.	Cab
MF-231	9195.00	5790.00	6620.00	7220.00	Perkins	3	152D	8F-2R	34.00	4065	No
MF-240	14638.00	8490.00	9660.00	10340.00	Perkins	3	152D	8F-2R	42.90	4015	No
MF-253	15700.00	9110.00	10360.00	11090.00	Perkins	3T	152D	8F-2R	45.90	4020	No
MF-283	15070.00	8740.00	9950.00	10650.00	Perkins	4	248D	8F-2R	67.00	5432	No
MF-360	18092.00	10490.00	11940.00	12780.00	Perkins	3T	152D	8F-2R	46.10	4910	No
MF-360 4WD	24712.00	14330.00	16310.00	17450.00	Perkins	3T	152D	8F-2R	49.20	5346	No
MF-362	19900.00	11540.00	13130.00	14050.00	Perkins	4	236D	8F-2R	55.10	6175	No
MF-362 4WD	25200.00	14620.00	16630.00	17790.00	Perkins	4	236D	8F-2R	55.10	6175	No
MF-364S 4WD	25200.00	13360.00	15620.00	16710.00	Perkins	3	152D	12F-4R	50.00	5082	No
MF-374S 4WD	27295.00	14470.00	16920.00	18100.00	Perkins	4	236D	12F-4R	57.00	5370	No
MF-375	21535.00	11410.00	13350.00	14290.00	Perkins	4	236D	12F-4R	58.10	6040	No
MF-375 4WD	27237.00	14440.00	16890.00	18070.00	Perkins	4	236D	12F-4R	58.10	7202	No
MF-383	19265.00	11170.00	12720.00	13610.00	Perkins	4	248D	8F-2R	73.00	6098	No
MF-383 4WD	24060.00	13960.00	15880.00	16990.00	Perkins	4	248D	8F-2R	73.00	7328	No
MF-383 Wide Row	20350.00	11800.00	13430.00	14370.00	Perkins	4	248D	8F-2R	73.00	7166	No
MF-384S	23875.00	12650.00	14800.00	15840.00	Perkins	4	236D	12F-4R	65.00	5192	No
MF-384S 4WD	27604.00	14630.00	17110.00	18310.00	Perkins	4	236D	12F-4R	65.00	5412	No
MF-390	23503.00	13630.00	15510.00	16600.00	Perkins	4	248D	12F-4R	67.30	6036	No
MF-390 4WD	29140.00	16900.00	19230.00	20580.00	Perkins	4	248D	12F-4R	67.30	7266	No
MF-390T	24836.00	14410.00	16390.00	17540.00	Perkins	4T	236D	8F-2R	80.00	6051	No
MF-390T 4WD	30192.00	17510.00	19930.00	21330.00	Perkins	4T	236D	8F-2R	80.00	7281	No
MF-394S	24868.00	13180.00	15420.00	16500.00	Perkins	4	236D	12F-4R	73.00	5258	No
MF-394S 4WD	28866.00	15300.00	17900.00	19150.00	Perkins	4	236D	12F-4R	73.00	5478	No
MF-398	27381.00	14510.00	16980.00	18170.00	Perkins	4T	236D	12F-4R	80.30	7047	No
MF-398 4WD	32841.00	17410.00	20360.00	21790.00	Perkins	4	236D	12F-4R	80.30	7648	No
MF-399	28866.00	15300.00	17900.00	19150.00	Perkins	6	354D	12F-4R	90.50	7233	No
MF-399 4WD	34299.00	18180.00	21270.00	22760.00	Perkins	6	354D	12F-4R	90.50	8029	No
MF-399 4WD w/Cab	40574.00	21500.00	25160.00	26920.00	Perkins	6	354D	12F-4R	90.50	8941	C,H,A
MF-399 w/Cab	35300.00	18710.00	21890.00	23420.00	Perkins	6	354D	12F-4R	90.50	8145	C,H,A
MF-1010	7728.00	5260.00	5800.00	6210.00	Toyosha	3	53D	6F-2R	13.50	1580	No
MF-1010 4WD	8807.00	5990.00	6610.00	7070.00	Toyosha	3	53D	6F-2R	13.50	1800	No
MF-1010 Hydro	8983.00	6110.00	6740.00	7210.00	Toyosha	3	53D	Variable	12.00	1772	No
MF-1010 Hydro 4WD	9918.00	6740.00	7440.00	7960.00	Toyosha	3	53D	Variable	12.00	2000	No
MF-1020	9125.00	6210.00	6840.00	7320.00	Toyosha	3	69D	12F-4R	17.00	2045	No
MF-1020 4WD	10249.00	6970.00	7690.00	8230.00	Toyosha	3	69D	12F-4R	17.00	2285	No
MF-1020 Hydro	10473.00	7120.00	7860.00	8410.00	Toyosha	3	69D	Variable	14.50	2046	No
MF-1020 Hydro 4WD	11996.00	8160.00	9000.00	9630.00	Toyosha	3	69D	Variable	14.50	2296	No
MF-1030	10242.00	6450.00	7370.00	8030.00	Toyosha	3	87D	12F-4R	23.00	2701	No
MF-1030 4WD	12582.00	7930.00	9060.00	9880.00	Toyosha	3	87D	12F-4R	23.00	2832	No
MF-1035	12009.00	7570.00	8650.00	9430.00	Toyosha	3	92D	12F-4R	26.00	2801	No
MF-1035 4WD	14238.00	8970.00	10250.00	11170.00	Toyosha	3	92D	12F-4R	26.00	2932	No
MF-1045 4WD	15892.00	9220.00	10490.00	11220.00	Toyosha	3	122D	9F-3R	30.00	3825	No
MF-3060 4WD	39144.00	17620.00	21140.00	22410.00	Perkins	4	248D	16F-12R	69.70	9310	C,H,A
MF-3070	36849.00	16580.00	19900.00	21090.00	Perkins	4T	236D	16F-12R	82.20	9407	C,H,A
MF-3070 4WD	42008.00	18900.00	22680.00	24040.00	Perkins	4T	236D	16F-12R	82.20	10000	C,H,A
MF-3090	40956.00	18430.00	22120.00	23450.00	Perkins	6	354D	16F-12R	100.70	10329	C,H,A
MF-3090 4WD	47449.00	20700.00	24840.00	26330.00	Perkins	6	354D	16F-12R	100.70	10869	C,H,A
MF-3120	42100.00	18450.00	22140.00	23470.00	Perkins	6	365D	16F-12R	100.	10329	C,H,A
MF-3120 4WD	47200.00	20250.00	24300.00	25760.00	Perkins	6	365D	16F-12R	100.	10869	C,H,A
MF-3140	44300.00	19350.00	23220.00	24610.00	Perkins	6T	365D	16F-12R	115.00	11153	C,H,A
MF-3140 4WD	50000.00	21600.00	25920.00	27480.00	Perkins	6T	365D	16F-12R	115.00	11486	C,H,A
MF-3630	47528.00	20480.00	24570.00	26040.00	Perkins	6T	354D	16F-12R	119.50	11729	C,H,A
MF-3630 4WD	56359.00	24530.00	29430.00	31200.00	Perkins	6T	354D	16F-12R	119.50	12809	C,H,A
MF-3650	53000.00	23850.00	28620.00	30340.00	Perkins	6TI	354D	16F-12R	130.00	12037	C,H,A
MF-3650 4WD	62597.00	27230.00	32670.00	34630.00	Perkins	6TI	354D	16F-12R	131.30	13139	C,H,A
MF-3660	55300.00	24300.00	29160.00	30910.00	Perkins	6T	365D	16F-12R	140.00	12581	C,H,A
MF-3660 4WD	65300.00	28940.00	34720.00	36800.00	Perkins	6T	365D	16F-12R	140.00	13152	C,H,A
MF-3680	59200.00	26640.00	31970.00	33890.00	Valmet	6T	452D	16F-12R	160.00	12786	C,H,A
MF-3680 4WD	68100.00	29700.00	35640.00	37780.00	Valmet	6T	452D	16F-4R	161.90	13866	C,H,A

1991

Model	Approx. Retail Price New	Fair	Good	Premium	Make	No. Cyls.	Displ. Cu.-In.	No. Speeds	P.T.O. H.P.	Approx. Shipping Wt.-Lbs.	Cab
MF-231	9942.00	6360.00	7260.00	7840.00	Perkins	3	152D	8F-2R	34.00	4065	No
MF-240	16140.00	9520.00	10810.00	11460.00	Perkins	3	152D	8F-2R	42.90	4015	No
MF-253	17310.00	10210.00	11600.00	12300.00	Perkins	3T	152D	8F-2R	45.90	4020	No
MF-283	15070.00	8890.00	10100.00	10710.00	Perkins	4	248D	8F-2R	67.00	5432	No
MF-360	20545.00	12120.00	13770.00	14600.00	Perkins	3T	152D	8F-2R	46.10	4910	No
MF-360 4WD	28060.00	16560.00	18800.00	19930.00	Perkins	3T	152D	8F-2R	49.20	5346	No
MF-362	21525.00	12700.00	14420.00	15290.00	Perkins	4	236D	8F-2R	55.00	5305	No
MF-362 4WD	27515.00	16230.00	18440.00	19550.00	Perkins	4	236D	8F-2R	55.00	5930	No
MF-364S 4WD	27720.00	14970.00	17460.00	18510.00	Perkins	3	152D	12F-4R	50.00	5082	No
MF-374S 4WD	29752.00	16070.00	18740.00	19860.00	Perkins	4	236D	12F-4R	57.00	5370	No
MF-375	23740.00	12820.00	14960.00	15860.00	Perkins	4	236D	12F-4R	58.10	6040	No
MF-375	31785.00	17160.00	20030.00	21230.00	Perkins	4	236D	12F-4R	58.10	6967	C,H,A
MF-375 4WD	29460.00	15910.00	18560.00	19670.00	Perkins	4	236D	12F-4R	58.10	7202	No
MF-375 4WD	36600.00	19760.00	23060.00	24440.00	Perkins	4	236D	12F-4R	58.10	8129	C,H,A

Massey Ferguson (Cont.)

1991 (Cont.)

Model	Approx. Retail Price New	Estimated Average Value Less Repairs Fair	Good	Premium	Engine Make	No. Cyls.	Displ. Cu.-In.	No. Speeds	P.T.O. H.P.	Approx. Shipping Wt.-Lbs.	Cab
MF-383	21350.00	**12600.00**	**14310.00**	**15170.00**	Perkins	4	248D	8F-2R	73.00	6098	No
MF-383	28575.00	**16860.00**	**19150.00**	**20300.00**	Perkins	4	248D	8F-2R	73.00	7010	C,H,A
MF-383 4WD	26635.00	**15720.00**	**17850.00**	**18920.00**	Perkins	4	248D	8F-2R	73.00	7328	No
MF-383 4WD	33860.00	**19980.00**	**22690.00**	**24050.00**	Perkins	4	248D	8F-2R	73.00	8240	C,H,A
MF-383 Wide Row	23065.00	**13610.00**	**15450.00**	**16380.00**	Perkins	4	248D	8F-2R	73.00	7166	No
MF-384S	25546.00	**13800.00**	**16090.00**	**17060.00**	Perkins	4	236D	12F-4R	65.00	5192	No
MF-384S 4WD	30640.00	**16550.00**	**19300.00**	**20460.00**	Perkins	4	236D	12F-4R	65.00	5412	No
MF-390	26425.00	**15590.00**	**17710.00**	**18770.00**	Perkins	4	248D	12F-4R	67.30	6036	No
MF-390	34910.00	**20600.00**	**23390.00**	**24790.00**	Perkins	4	248D	12F-8R	70.00	6948	C,H,A.
MF-390 4WD	32150.00	**18970.00**	**21540.00**	**22830.00**	Perkins	4	248D	12F-4R	67.30	7266	No
MF-390 4WD	40070.00	**23640.00**	**26850.00**	**28460.00**	Perkins	4	248D	12F-8R	70.00	8178	C,H,A
MF-390T	27660.00	**16320.00**	**18530.00**	**19640.00**	Perkins	4T	236D	8F-2R	80.00	6051	No
MF-390T	36420.00	**21490.00**	**24400.00**	**25860.00**	Perkins	4T	248D	12F-8R	70.00	6965	C,H,A
MF-390T 4WD	32990.00	**19460.00**	**22100.00**	**23430.00**	Perkins	4T	236D	8F-2R	80.00	7281	No
MF-390T 4WD	42310.00	**24960.00**	**28350.00**	**30050.00**	Perkins	4T	248D	12F-8R	70.00	8193	C,H,A
MF-394S	26110.00	**14100.00**	**16450.00**	**17440.00**	Perkins	4	236D	12F-4R	73.00	5258	No
MF-394S 4WD	31460.00	**16990.00**	**19820.00**	**21010.00**	Perkins	4	236D	12F-4R	73.00	5478	No
MF-398	30490.00	**16470.00**	**19210.00**	**20360.00**	Perkins	4T	236D	12F-4R	80.30	7047	No
MF-398	37990.00	**20520.00**	**23930.00**	**25370.00**	Perkins	4T	236D	12F-8R	80.30	7958	C,H,A
MF-398 4WD	36575.00	**19750.00**	**23040.00**	**24420.00**	Perkins	4	236D	12F-4R	80.30	7648	No
MF-398 4WD	43945.00	**22680.00**	**26460.00**	**28050.00**	Perkins	4	236D	12F-8R	80.30	8560	C,H,A
MF-399	32100.00	**17330.00**	**20220.00**	**21430.00**	Perkins	6	365D	12F-4R	95.00	7233	No
MF-399 4WD	38200.00	**20630.00**	**24070.00**	**25510.00**	Perkins	6	365D	12F-4R	95.00	8029	No
MF-399 4WD w/Cab	46010.00	**23760.00**	**27720.00**	**29380.00**	Perkins	6	365D	12F-4R	95.00	8941	C,H,A
MF-399 w/Cab	39270.00	**19980.00**	**23310.00**	**24710.00**	Perkins	6	365D	12F-4R	95.00	8145	C,H,A
MF-1010	7960.00	**5490.00**	**6050.00**	**6470.00**	Toyosha	3	53D	6F-2R	13.50	1580	No
MF-1010 4WD	9071.00	**6260.00**	**6890.00**	**7370.00**	Toyosha	3	53D	6F-2R	13.50	1800	No
MF-1010 Hydro	9252.00	**6380.00**	**7030.00**	**7520.00**	Toyosha	3	53D	Variable	12.00	1772	No
MF-1010 Hydro 4WD	10216.00	**7050.00**	**7760.00**	**8300.00**	Toyosha	3	53D	Variable	12.00	2000	No
MF-1020	9399.00	**6490.00**	**7140.00**	**7640.00**	Toyosha	3	69D	12F-4R	17.00	2045	No
MF-1020 4WD	10556.00	**7280.00**	**8020.00**	**8580.00**	Toyosha	3	69D	12F-4R	17.00	2285	No
MF-1020 Hydro	10788.00	**7440.00**	**8200.00**	**8770.00**	Toyosha	3	69D	Variable	14.50	2046	No
MF-1020 Hydro 4WD	12356.00	**8530.00**	**9390.00**	**10050.00**	Toyosha	3	69D	Variable	14.50	2296	No
MF-1030	10754.00	**6880.00**	**7850.00**	**8480.00**	Toyosha	3	87D	12F-4R	23.00	2701	No
MF-1030 4WD	12959.00	**8290.00**	**9460.00**	**10220.00**	Toyosha	3	87D	12F-4R	23.00	2832	No
MF-1035	12369.00	**7920.00**	**9030.00**	**9750.00**	Toyosha	3	92D	12F-4R	26.00	2801	No
MF-1035 4WD	14665.00	**9390.00**	**10710.00**	**11570.00**	Toyosha	3	92D	12F-4R	26.00	2932	No
MF-1045 4WD	16369.00	**9660.00**	**10970.00**	**11630.00**	Toyosha	3	122D	9F-3R	30.00	3825	No
MF-1140	12250.00	**7230.00**	**8210.00**	**8700.00**	Toyosha	3	91D	16F-16R	26.20	2590	No
MF-1140 4WD	13900.00	**8200.00**	**9310.00**	**9870.00**	Toyosha	3	91D	16F-16R	26.20	2700	No
MF-1145 4WD	15950.00	**9410.00**	**10690.00**	**11330.00**	Toyosha	3	91D	16F-16R	31.00	2812	No
MF-3070	41786.00	**19220.00**	**22980.00**	**24360.00**	Perkins	4T	236D	16F-12R	82.20	9652	C,H,A
MF-3070 4WD	45369.00	**20470.00**	**24480.00**	**25950.00**	Perkins	4T	236D	16F-12R	82.20	10192	C,H,A
MF-3120	46731.00	**20930.00**	**25030.00**	**26530.00**	Perkins	6	365D	16F-12R	100.	10329	C,H,A
MF-3120 4WD	51448.00	**22770.00**	**27230.00**	**28860.00**	Perkins	6	365D	16F-12R	100.	10869	C,H,A
MF-3140	48287.00	**21160.00**	**25300.00**	**26820.00**	Perkins	6T	365D	16F-12R	115.00	11153	C,H,A
MF-3140 4WD	53500.00	**23460.00**	**28050.00**	**29730.00**	Perkins	6T	365D	16F-12R	115.00	11486	C,H,A
MF-3630 4WD	58459.00	**26890.00**	**32150.00**	**34080.00**	Perkins	6T	354D	16F-12R	119.50	12809	C,H,A
MF-3660	57500.00	**26450.00**	**31630.00**	**33530.00**	Perkins	6T	365D	16F-12R	140.00	12581	C,H,A
MF-3660 4WD	67900.00	**30360.00**	**36300.00**	**38480.00**	Perkins	6T	365D	16F-12R	140.00	13152	C,H,A
MF-3680	64000.00	**29440.00**	**35200.00**	**37310.00**	Valmet	6T	452D	16F-12R	160.00	12786	C,H,A
MF-3680 4WD	73600.00	**32200.00**	**38500.00**	**40810.00**	Valmet	6T	452D	16F-4R	161.90	13152	C,H,A

1992

Model	Approx. Retail Price New	Fair	Good	Premium	Make	No. Cyls.	Displ. Cu.-In.	No. Speeds	P.T.O. H.P.	Approx. Shipping Wt.-Lbs.	Cab
MF-231	10550.00	**6860.00**	**7810.00**	**8360.00**	Perkins	3	152D	8F-2R	34.00	4065	No
MF-240	16140.00	**9680.00**	**10980.00**	**11640.00**	Perkins	3	152D	8F-2R	42.90	4015	No
MF-253	17655.00	**10590.00**	**12010.00**	**12730.00**	Perkins	3T	152D	8F-2R	45.90	4020	No
MF-283	15825.00	**9500.00**	**10760.00**	**11410.00**	Perkins	4	248D	8F-2R	67.00	5432	No
MF-360	20545.00	**12330.00**	**13970.00**	**14810.00**	Perkins	3T	152D	8F-2R	46.10	4910	No
MF-360 4WD	28060.00	**16840.00**	**19080.00**	**20230.00**	Perkins	3T	152D	8F-2R	49.20	5346	No
MF-362	21735.00	**13040.00**	**14780.00**	**15670.00**	Perkins	4	236D	8F-2R	55.00	5335	No
MF-362 4WD	27725.00	**16640.00**	**18850.00**	**19980.00**	Perkins	4	236D	8F-2R	55.00	5960	No
MF-364S 4WD	27720.00	**15520.00**	**17740.00**	**18800.00**	Perkins	3	152D	12F-4R	50.00	5082	No
MF-374S	24117.00	**13510.00**	**15440.00**	**16370.00**	Perkins	4	236D	12F-4R	57.00	5145	No
MF-374S 4WD	29752.00	**16660.00**	**19040.00**	**20180.00**	Perkins	4	236D	12F-4R	57.00	5370	No
MF-375	23780.00	**13320.00**	**15220.00**	**16130.00**	Perkins	4	236D	12F-4R	58.10	6260	No
MF-375 4WD	28295.00	**15850.00**	**18110.00**	**19200.00**	Perkins	4	236D	12F-4R	58.10	6617	No
MF-375 4WD w/Cab	36305.00	**20330.00**	**23240.00**	**24630.00**	Perkins	4	236D	12F-4R	58.10	8129	C,H,A
MF-375 w/Cab	31310.00	**17530.00**	**20040.00**	**21240.00**	Perkins	4	236D	12F-4R	58.10	6967	C,H,A
MF-383	21780.00	**13070.00**	**14810.00**	**15700.00**	Perkins	4	248D	8F-2R	73.00	6098	No
MF-383 4WD	27170.00	**16300.00**	**18480.00**	**19590.00**	Perkins	4	248D	8F-2R	73.00	7328	No
MF-383 4WD w/Cab	34540.00	**20100.00**	**22780.00**	**24150.00**	Perkins	4	248D	8F-2R	73.00	8240	C,H,A
MF-383 w/Cab	29150.00	**17490.00**	**19820.00**	**21010.00**	Perkins	4	248D	8F-2R	73.00	7010	C,H,A
MF-384S	25546.00	**14310.00**	**16350.00**	**17330.00**	Perkins	4	236D	12F-4R	65.00	5192	No
MF-384S 4WD	30640.00	**17160.00**	**19610.00**	**20790.00**	Perkins	4	236D	12F-4R	65.00	5412	No
MF-390	26530.00	**15920.00**	**18040.00**	**19120.00**	Perkins	4	248D	12F-4R	67.30	6295	No
MF-390 4WD	31710.00	**19030.00**	**21560.00**	**22850.00**	Perkins	4	248D	12F-4R	67.30	6902	No
MF-390 4WD w/Cab	39595.00	**22200.00**	**25160.00**	**26670.00**	Perkins	4	248D	12F-8R	67.30	7552	C,H,A
MF-390 w/Cab	34435.00	**20660.00**	**23420.00**	**24830.00**	Perkins	4	248D	12F-8R	67.30	6948	C,H,A
MF-390T	28180.00	**16910.00**	**19160.00**	**20310.00**	Perkins	4T	236D	8F-2R	80.00	6325	No
MF-390T 4WD	33250.00	**19950.00**	**22610.00**	**23970.00**	Perkins	4T	236D	12F-12R	80.00	6952	No
MF-390T 4WD w/Cab	41835.00	**23820.00**	**27000.00**	**28620.00**	Perkins	4T	248D	12F-8R	80.00	7602	C,H,A
MF-390T w/Cab	35945.00	**21570.00**	**24440.00**	**25910.00**	Perkins	4T	248D	12F-8R	80.00	6995	C,H,A
MF-393	24785.00	**14870.00**	**16850.00**	**17860.00**	Perkins	4	236D	8F-2R	83.00	6371	No

Massey Ferguson (Cont.)

1992 (Cont.)

Model	Approx. Retail Price New	Estimated Average Value Less Repairs: Fair	Good	Premium	Engine: Make	No. Cyls.	Displ. Cu.-In.	No. Speeds	P.T.O. H.P.	Approx. Shipping Wt.-Lbs.	Cab
MF-393 4WD	30175.00	18110.00	20520.00	21750.00	Perkins	4	236D	8F-2R	83.00	6986	No
MF-393 4WD w/Cab	37545.00	21600.00	24480.00	25950.00	Perkins	4	236D	8F-2R	83.00	7636	C,H,A
MF-393 w/Cab	32155.00	19290.00	21870.00	23180.00	Perkins	4	236D	8F-2R	83.00	7021	C,H,A
MF-394S	26110.00	14620.00	16710.00	17710.00	Perkins	4	236D	12F-4R	73.00	5258	No
MF-394S 4WD	31460.00	17620.00	20130.00	21340.00	Perkins	4	236D	12F-4R	73.00	5478	No
MF-396	28050.00	16830.00	19070.00	20210.00	Perkins	6	365D	8F-2R	88.00	7120	No
MF-396 4WD	33750.00	20250.00	22950.00	24330.00	Perkins	6	365D	8F-2R	88.00	7690	No
MF-396 4WD w/Cab	42300.00	24720.00	28020.00	29700.00	Perkins	6	365D	12F-4R	88.00	8430	C,H,A
MF-396 Cab	36100.00	21660.00	24550.00	26020.00	Perkins	6	365D	12F-4R	88.00	7831	C,H,A
MF-398	29655.00	16610.00	18980.00	20120.00	Perkins	4	236D	12F-4R	80.30	6405	No
MF-398	37155.00	20810.00	23780.00	25210.00	Perkins	4	236D	12F-8R	80.30	7055	C,H,A
MF-398 4WD	35740.00	20010.00	22870.00	24240.00	Perkins	4	236D	12F-4R	80.30	6915	No
MF-398 4WD	43110.00	23520.00	26880.00	28490.00	Perkins	4	236D	12F-8R	80.30	7565	C,H,A
MF-399	31265.00	17510.00	20010.00	21210.00	Perkins	6	365D	12F-4R	95.00	7400	No
MF-399 4WD	37365.00	20920.00	23910.00	25350.00	Perkins	6	365D	12F-4R	95.00	8029	No
MF-399 4WD w/Cab	45175.00	24640.00	28160.00	29850.00	Perkins	6	365D	12F-4R	95.00	8941	C,H,A
MF-399 w/Cab	38435.00	21520.00	24600.00	26080.00	Perkins	6	365D	12F-4R	95.00	8145	C,H,A
MF-1010	8199.00	5740.00	6310.00	6690.00	Toyosha	3	53D	6F-2R	13.50	1580	No
MF-1010 4WD	9343.00	6540.00	7190.00	7620.00	Toyosha	3	53D	6F-2R	13.50	1800	No
MF-1010 Hydro	9530.00	6670.00	7340.00	7780.00	Toyosha	3	53D	Variable	12.00	1772	No
MF-1010 Hydro 4WD	10523.00	7370.00	8100.00	8590.00	Toyosha	3	53D	Variable	12.00	2000	No
MF-1020	9681.00	6780.00	7450.00	7900.00	Toyosha	3	69D	12F-4R	17.00	2045	No
MF-1020 4WD	10873.00	7610.00	8370.00	8870.00	Toyosha	3	69D	12F-4R	17.00	2285	No
MF-1020 Hydro	11112.00	7780.00	8560.00	9070.00	Toyosha	3	69D	Variable	14.50	2046	No
MF-1020 Hydro 4WD	12727.00	8910.00	9800.00	10390.00	Toyosha	3	69D	Variable	14.50	2296	No
MF-1030	11508.00	7480.00	8520.00	9120.00	Toyosha	3	87D	12F-4R	23.00	2701	No
MF-1030 4WD	13866.00	9010.00	10260.00	10980.00	Toyosha	3	87D	12F-4R	23.00	2832	No
MF-1125	11800.00	7670.00	8730.00	9340.00	Toyosha	3	87D	16F-16R	22.5	2524	No
MF-1125 4WD	13400.00	8710.00	9920.00	10610.00	Toyosha	3	87D	16F-16R	22.5	2634	No
MF-1140	12801.00	7680.00	8710.00	9230.00	Toyosha	3	91D	16F-16R	26.20	2590	No
MF-1140 4WD	14497.00	8700.00	9860.00	10450.00	Toyosha	3	91D	16F-16R	26.20	2700	No
MF-1145 4WD	16588.00	9950.00	11280.00	11960.00	Toyosha	3	91D	16F-16R	31.00	2812	No
MF-1160 4WD	19500.00	11700.00	13260.00	14060.00	Toyosha	4	137D	16F-16R	37.00	3848	No
MF-1180 4WD	22550.00	13530.00	15330.00	16250.00	Toyosha	4	169D	16F-16R	46.00	4773	No
MF-1190 4WD	24050.00	14430.00	16350.00	17330.00	Toyosha	4	169D	16F-16R	53.00	4795	No
MF-3070 4WD	47200.00	22660.00	26430.00	27750.00	Perkins	4T	236D	16F-12R	82.20	10192	C,H,A
MF-3120	47700.00	22900.00	26710.00	28050.00	Perkins	6	365D	16F-12R	100.	10329	C,H,A
MF-3120 4WD	52500.00	25200.00	29400.00	30870.00	Perkins	6	365D	16F-12R	100.	10869	C,H,A
MF-3140	49250.00	22680.00	26460.00	27780.00	Perkins	6T	365D	16F-12R	115.00	11153	C,H,A
MF-3140 4WD	54700.00	25200.00	29400.00	30870.00	Perkins	6T	365D	16F-12R	115.00	11486	C,H,A
MF-3660	60400.00	28990.00	33820.00	35510.00	Perkins	6T	365D	16F-12R	140.00	12581	C,H,A
MF-3660 4WD	70000.00	32640.00	38080.00	39980.00	Perkins	6T	365D	16F-12R	140.00	13152	C,H,A
MF-3680	64000.00	29760.00	34720.00	36460.00	Valmet	6T	452D	16F-12R	160.00	12786	C,H,A
MF-3680 4WD	73600.00	33120.00	38640.00	40570.00	Valmet	6T	452D	16F-4R	161.90	13152	C,H,A

1993

Model	Approx. Retail Price New	Estimated Average Value Less Repairs: Fair	Good	Premium	Engine: Make	No. Cyls.	Displ. Cu.-In.	No. Speeds	P.T.O. H.P.	Approx. Shipping Wt.-Lbs.	Cab
MF-231	10550.00	7070.00	7910.00	8390.00	Perkins	3	152D	8F-2R	34.00	4065	No
MF-240	16140.00	10810.00	12110.00	12840.00	Perkins	3	152D	8F-2R	42.90	4015	No
MF-253	17655.00	10950.00	12180.00	12910.00	Perkins	3T	152D	8F-2R	45.90	4020	No
MF-283	15825.00	9810.00	10920.00	11580.00	Perkins	4	248D	8F-2R	67.00	5432	No
MF-360	20545.00	12740.00	14180.00	15030.00	Perkins	3T	152D	8F-2R	46.10	4910	No
MF-360 4WD	28060.00	17400.00	19360.00	20520.00	Perkins	3T	152D	8F-2R	49.20	5346	No
MF-362	21735.00	13480.00	15000.00	15900.00	Perkins	4	236D	8F-2R	55.00	5335	No
MF-362 4WD	27725.00	17190.00	19130.00	20280.00	Perkins	4	236D	8F-2R	55.00	5960	No
MF-364S 4WD	27720.00	16080.00	18020.00	19100.00	Perkins	3	152D	12F-4R	50.00	5082	No
MF-374S	24117.00	13990.00	15680.00	16620.00	Perkins	4	236D	12F-4R	57.00	5145	No
MF-374S 4WD	29752.00	17260.00	19340.00	20500.00	Perkins	4	236D	12F-4R	57.00	5370	No
MF-375	23780.00	13790.00	15460.00	16390.00	Perkins	4	236D	12F-4R	58.10	6260	No
MF-375	31310.00	18160.00	20350.00	21570.00	Perkins	4	236D	12F-4R	58.10	6967	C,H,A
MF-375 4WD	28295.00	16410.00	18390.00	19490.00	Perkins	4	236D	12F-4R	58.10	6617	No
MF-375 4WD	36305.00	21060.00	23600.00	25020.00	Perkins	4	236D	12F-4R	58.10	8129	C,H,A
MF-383	21780.00	13500.00	15030.00	15930.00	Perkins	4	248D	8F-2R	73.00	6098	No
MF-383	29150.00	18070.00	20110.00	21320.00	Perkins	4	248D	8F-2R	73.00	7010	C,H,A
MF-383 4WD	27170.00	16850.00	18750.00	19880.00	Perkins	4	248D	8F-2R	73.00	7328	No
MF-383 4WD	34540.00	21420.00	23830.00	25260.00	Perkins	4	248D	8F-2R	73.00	8240	C,H,A
MF-384S	25546.00	14820.00	16610.00	17610.00	Perkins	4	236D	12F-4R	65.00	5192	No
MF-384S 4WD	30640.00	17770.00	19920.00	21120.00	Perkins	4	236D	12F-4R	65.00	5412	No
MF-390	26530.00	16450.00	18310.00	19410.00	Perkins	4	248D	12F-4R	67.30	6295	No
MF-390	34435.00	21350.00	23760.00	25190.00	Perkins	4	248D	12F-8R	67.30	6948	C,H,A
MF-390 4WD	31710.00	19660.00	21880.00	23190.00	Perkins	4	248D	12F-4R	67.30	6902	No
MF-390 4WD	39595.00	23560.00	26220.00	27790.00	Perkins	4	248D	12F-8R	67.30	7552	C,H,A
MF-390T	28180.00	17470.00	19440.00	20610.00	Perkins	4T	236D	8F-2R	80.00	6325	No
MF-390T	35945.00	22290.00	24800.00	26290.00	Perkins	4T	248D	12F-8R	80.00	6995	C,H,A
MF-390T 4WD	33250.00	20620.00	22940.00	24320.00	Perkins	4T	236D	12F-12R	80.00	6952	No
MF-390T 4WD	41835.00	25940.00	28870.00	30600.00	Perkins	4T	248D	12F-8R	80.00	7602	C,H,A
MF-393	24785.00	15370.00	17100.00	18130.00	Perkins	4	236D	8F-2R	83.00	6371	No
MF-393 4WD	30175.00	18710.00	20820.00	22070.00	Perkins	4	236D	8F-2R	83.00	6986	No
MF-393 4WD w/Cab	37545.00	22320.00	24840.00	26330.00	Perkins	4	236D	8F-2R	83.00	7636	C,H,A
MF-393 w/Cab	32155.00	19940.00	22190.00	23520.00	Perkins	4	236D	8F-2R	83.00	7021	C,H,A
MF-394S	26110.00	15140.00	16970.00	17990.00	Perkins	4	236D	12F-4R	73.00	5258	No
MF-394S 4WD	31460.00	18250.00	20450.00	21680.00	Perkins	4	236D	12F-4R	73.00	5478	No
MF-396	28050.00	17390.00	19360.00	20520.00	Perkins	6	365D	8F-2R	88.00	7120	No
MF-396 4WD	33750.00	19840.00	22080.00	23410.00	Perkins	6	365D	8F-2R	88.00	7690	No
MF-396 4WD w/Cab	42300.00	24990.00	27810.00	29480.00	Perkins	6	365D	12F-4R	88.00	8430	C,H,A

Massey Ferguson (Cont.)

Model	Approx. Retail Price New	Estimated Average Value Less Repairs Fair	Good	Premium	Engine Make	No. Cyls.	Displ. Cu.-In.	No. Speeds	P.T.O. H.P.	Approx. Shipping Wt.-Lbs.	Cab
1993 (Cont.)											
MF-396 Cab	36100.00	**22380.00**	**24910.00**	**26410.00**	Perkins	6	365D	12F-4R	88.00	7831	C,H,A
MF-398	29655.00	**17200.00**	**19280.00**	**20440.00**	Perkins	4	236D	12F-4R	80.30	6405	No
MF-398	37155.00	**21550.00**	**24150.00**	**25600.00**	Perkins	4	236D	12F-8R	80.30	7055	C,H,A
MF-398 4WD	35740.00	**20730.00**	**23230.00**	**24620.00**	Perkins	4	236D	12F-4R	80.30	6915	No
MF-398 4WD	43110.00	**25000.00**	**28020.00**	**29700.00**	Perkins	4	236D	12F-8R	80.30	7565	C,H,A
MF-399	31265.00	**18130.00**	**20320.00**	**21540.00**	Perkins	6	365D	12F-4R	95.00	7400	No
MF-399 4WD	37365.00	**21670.00**	**24290.00**	**25750.00**	Perkins	6	365D	12F-4R	95.00	8029	No
MF-399 4WD w/Cab	45175.00	**24940.00**	**27950.00**	**29630.00**	Perkins	6	365D	12F-4R	95.00	8941	C,H,A
MF-399 w/Cab	38435.00	**22290.00**	**24980.00**	**26480.00**	Perkins	6	365D	12F-4R	95.00	8145	C,H,A
MF-1010	8445.00	**6000.00**	**6590.00**	**6990.00**	Toyosha	3	53D	6F-2R	13.50	1580	No
MF-1010 4WD	9625.00	**6830.00**	**7510.00**	**7960.00**	Toyosha	3	53D	6F-2R	13.50	1800	No
MF-1010 Hydro	9815.00	**6970.00**	**7660.00**	**8120.00**	Toyosha	3	53D	Variable	12.00	1772	No
MF-1010 Hydro 4WD	10840.00	**7700.00**	**8460.00**	**8970.00**	Toyosha	3	53D	Variable	12.00	2000	No
MF-1020	9970.00	**7080.00**	**7780.00**	**8250.00**	Toyosha	3	69D	12F-4R	17.00	2045	No
MF-1020 4WD	11200.00	**7950.00**	**8740.00**	**9260.00**	Toyosha	3	69D	12F-4R	17.00	2285	No
MF-1020 Hydro	11450.00	**8130.00**	**8930.00**	**9470.00**	Toyosha	3	69D	Variable	14.50	2046	No
MF-1020 Hydro 4WD	13150.00	**9340.00**	**10260.00**	**10880.00**	Toyosha	3	69D	Variable	14.50	2296	No
MF-1030	11850.00	**7940.00**	**8890.00**	**9420.00**	Toyosha	3	87D	12F-4R	23.00	2701	No
MF-1030 4WD	14280.00	**9570.00**	**10710.00**	**11350.00**	Toyosha	3	87D	12F-4R	23.00	2832	No
MF-1125	12150.00	**8140.00**	**9110.00**	**9660.00**	Toyosha	3	87D	16F-16R	22.5	2524	No
MF-1125 4WD	13800.00	**9250.00**	**10350.00**	**10970.00**	Toyosha	3	87D	16F-16R	22.5	2634	No
MF-1140	13185.00	**8180.00**	**9100.00**	**9650.00**	Toyosha	3	91D	16F-16R	26.20	2590	No
MF-1140 4WD	14932.00	**9260.00**	**10300.00**	**10920.00**	Toyosha	3	91D	16F-16R	26.20	2700	No
MF-1145 4WD	17086.00	**10590.00**	**11790.00**	**12500.00**	Toyosha	3	91D	16F-16R	31.00	2812	No
MF-1160 4WD	20888.00	**12950.00**	**14410.00**	**15280.00**	Toyosha	4	137D	16F-16R	37.00	3848	No
MF-1180 4WD	22550.00	**13980.00**	**15560.00**	**16490.00**	Toyosha	4	169D	16F-16R	46.00	4773	No
MF-1190 4WD	24050.00	**14910.00**	**16600.00**	**17600.00**	Toyosha	4	169D	16F-16R	53.00	4795	No
MF-3070 4WD	47200.00	**23600.00**	**27380.00**	**28750.00**	Perkins	4T	236D	16F-12R	82.20	10192	C,H,A
MF-3120	47700.00	**23850.00**	**27670.00**	**29050.00**	Perkins	6	365D	16F-12R	100.	10329	C,H,A
MF-3120 4WD	52500.00	**26250.00**	**30450.00**	**31970.00**	Perkins	6	365D	16F-12R	100.	10869	C,H,A
MF-3140	49250.00	**24000.00**	**27840.00**	**29230.00**	Perkins	6T	365D	16F-12R	115.00	11153	C,H,A
MF-3140 4WD	54700.00	**26500.00**	**30740.00**	**32280.00**	Perkins	6T	365D	16F-12R	115.00	11486	C,H,A
MF-3660	60400.00	**30200.00**	**35030.00**	**36780.00**	Perkins	6T	365D	16F-12R	140.00	12581	C,H,A
MF-3660 4WD	70000.00	**34000.00**	**39440.00**	**41410.00**	Perkins	6T	365D	16F-12R	140.00	13152	C,H,A
MF-3680	64000.00	**31500.00**	**36540.00**	**38370.00**	Valmet	6T	452D	16F-12R	160.00	12786	C,H,A
MF-3680 4WD	73600.00	**35500.00**	**41180.00**	**43240.00**	Valmet	6T	452D	16F-4R	161.90	13152	C,H,A
1994											
MF-231	11080.00	**7650.00**	**8420.00**	**8840.00**	Perkins	3	152D	8F-2R	34.0	4065	No
MF-240	16590.00	**10620.00**	**11610.00**	**12190.00**	Perkins	3	152D	8F-2R	41.0	4015	No
MF-240 4WD	21980.00	**12160.00**	**13300.00**	**13970.00**	Perkins	3	152D	8F-2R	41.0	4585	No
MF-253	19210.00	**12290.00**	**13450.00**	**14120.00**	Perkins	3T	152D	8F-2R	48.0	4265	No
MF-253 4WD	25745.00	**14720.00**	**16100.00**	**16910.00**	Perkins	3T	152D	8F-2R	48.0	4735	No
MF-261	14675.00	**9390.00**	**10270.00**	**10780.00**	Perkins	4	236D	8F-2R	53.0	5280	No
MF-283	17300.00	**11070.00**	**12110.00**	**12720.00**	Perkins	4	248D	8F-2R	67.0	5700	No
MF-283	17300.00	**11070.00**	**12110.00**	**12720.00**	Perkins	4	248D	8F-2R	67.0	5700	No
MF-362	22740.00	**14550.00**	**15920.00**	**16720.00**	Perkins	4	236D	8F-2R	55.0	5335	No
MF-362 4WD	29240.00	**17280.00**	**18900.00**	**19850.00**	Perkins	4	236D	8F-2R	55.0	5960	No
MF-375	25830.00	**15760.00**	**17310.00**	**18180.00**	Perkins	4	236D	12F-4R	60.0	6240	No
MF-375 4WD	31300.00	**17690.00**	**19430.00**	**20400.00**	Perkins	4	236D	12F-4R	60.0	6867	No
MF-375 4WD w/Cab	38280.00	**21350.00**	**23450.00**	**24620.00**	Perkins	4	236D	12F-4R	60.0	7517	C,H,A
MF-375 w/Cab	33635.00	**19520.00**	**21440.00**	**22510.00**	Perkins	4	236D	12F-4R	60.0	6910	C,H,A
MF-383	24040.00	**15390.00**	**16830.00**	**17670.00**	Perkins	4	248D	8F-2R	73.0	6311	No
MF-383 4WD	29835.00	**19090.00**	**20890.00**	**21940.00**	Perkins	4	248D	8F-2R	73.0	6950	No
MF-383 4WD w/Cab	37925.00	**22720.00**	**24850.00**	**26090.00**	Perkins	4	248D	8F-2R	73.0	7552	C,H,A
MF-383 w/Cab	32130.00	**20560.00**	**22490.00**	**23620.00**	Perkins	4	248D	8F-2R	73.0	6957	C,H,A
MF-390	28835.00	**18450.00**	**20190.00**	**21200.00**	Perkins	4	248D	12F-4R	70.0	6275	No
MF-390 4WD	34815.00	**22280.00**	**24370.00**	**25590.00**	Perkins	4	248D	12F-4R	70.0	6902	No
MF-390 4WD w/Cab	42920.00	**26240.00**	**28700.00**	**30140.00**	Perkins	4	248D	12F-4R	70.0	7552	C,H,A
MF-390 w/Cab	38365.00	**24550.00**	**26860.00**	**28200.00**	Perkins	4	248D	12F-12R	70.0	6945	C,H,A
MF-390T	31025.00	**19860.00**	**21720.00**	**22810.00**	Perkins	4T	236D	12F-4R	80.0	6359	No
MF-390T 4WD	36115.00	**23110.00**	**25280.00**	**26540.00**	Perkins	4T	236D	12F-4R	80.0	6952	No
MF-390T 4WD w/Cab	44870.00	**26880.00**	**29400.00**	**30870.00**	Perkins	4T	236D	12F-4R	80.0	7602	C,H,A
MF-390T w/Cab	38675.00	**24750.00**	**27070.00**	**28420.00**	Perkins	4T	236D	12F-4R	80.0	6995	C,H,A
MF-393	27060.00	**17320.00**	**18940.00**	**19890.00**	Perkins	4T	236D	8F-2R	83.0	6371	No
MF-393 4WD	32795.00	**20990.00**	**22960.00**	**24110.00**	Perkins	4T	236D	8F-2R	83.0	6986	No
MF-393 4WD w/Cab	40805.00	**24960.00**	**27300.00**	**28670.00**	Perkins	4T	236D	8F-2R	83.0	7636	C,H,A
MF-393 w/Cab	34555.00	**22120.00**	**24190.00**	**25400.00**	Perkins	4T	236D	8F-2R	83.0	7021	C,H,A
MF-396	30945.00	**19810.00**	**21660.00**	**22740.00**	Perkins	6	365D	8F-2R	104.4	7120	No
MF-396 4WD	37070.00	**23730.00**	**25950.00**	**27250.00**	Perkins	6	365D	8F-2R	104.4	7690	No
MF-396 4WD w/Cab	46180.00	**28160.00**	**30800.00**	**32340.00**	Perkins	6	365D	12F-4R	104.4	8430	C,H,A
MF-398	31995.00	**19520.00**	**21440.00**	**22510.00**	Perkins	4T	236D	12F-4R	80.00	6960	No
MF-398 4WD	38515.00	**23490.00**	**25810.00**	**27100.00**	Perkins	4T	236D	12F-4R	80.00	7395	No
MF-399	33695.00	**20550.00**	**22580.00**	**23710.00**	Perkins	6	365D	12F-4R	95.00	7400	No
MF-399 4WD	41185.00	**25120.00**	**27590.00**	**28970.00**	Perkins	6	365D	12F-4R	95.00	7910	No
MF-399 4WD w/Cab	50620.00	**29890.00**	**32830.00**	**34470.00**	Perkins	6	365D	12F-4R	95.00	8560	C,H,A
MF-399 Mudder	48895.00	**28670.00**	**31490.00**	**33070.00**	Perkins	6	365D	12F-12R	95.00		No
MF-399 Mudder w/Cab	55795.00	**32940.00**	**36180.00**	**37990.00**	Perkins	6	365D	12F-12R	95.00		C,H,A
MF-399 w/Cab	42895.00	**26170.00**	**28740.00**	**30180.00**	Perkins	6	365D	12F-4R	95.00	8050	C,H,A
MF-1120 4WD	9584.00	**6130.00**	**6710.00**	**7050.00**	Isuzu	3	52D	6F-2R	14.2	1360	No
MF-1120 Hydro 4WD	10727.00	**6870.00**	**7510.00**	**7890.00**	Isuzu	3	52D	Variable	13.1	1448	No
MF-1160 4WD	22749.00	**14560.00**	**15920.00**	**16720.00**	Isuzu	4	136D	16F-16R	37.0	4206	No
MF-1180 4WD	24744.00	**15840.00**	**17320.00**	**18190.00**	Isuzu	4	169D	16F-16R	46.0	4773	No
MF-1190 4WD	26464.00	**16940.00**	**18530.00**	**19460.00**	Isuzu	4T	169D	16F-16R	53.0	4795	No

Massey Ferguson (Cont.)

1994 (Cont.)

Model	Approx. Retail Price New	Estimated Average Value Less Repairs Fair	Good	Premium	Engine Make	No. Cyls.	Displ. Cu.-In.	No. Speeds	P.T.O. H.P.	Approx. Shipping Wt.-Lbs.	Cab
MF-1210	10285.00	6580.00	7200.00	7560.00	Iseki	3	61D	6F-2R	15.00	1830	No
MF-1210 4WD	11753.00	7520.00	8230.00	8640.00	Iseki	3	61D	6F-2R	15.00	1984	No
MF-1210 Hydro	11753.00	7520.00	8230.00	8640.00	Iseki	3	61D	Variable	14.00	1852	No
MF-1210 Hydro 4WD	13221.00	8460.00	9260.00	9720.00	Iseki	3	61D	Variable	14.00	2006	No
MF-1220	11647.00	7450.00	8150.00	8560.00	Iseki	3	68D	6F-2R	17.2	1874	No
MF-1220 4WD	13164.00	8430.00	9220.00	9680.00	Iseki	3	68D	6F-2R	17.2	2050	No
MF-1220 Hydro	13013.00	8330.00	9110.00	9570.00	Iseki	3	68D	Variable	16.0	1896	No
MF-1220 Hydro 4WD	14516.00	9290.00	10160.00	10670.00	Iseki	3	68D	Variable	16.0	2072	No
MF-1230	12684.00	8120.00	8880.00	9320.00	Iseki	3	87D	9F-3R	21.0	2227	No
MF-1230 4WD	14244.00	9120.00	9970.00	10470.00	Iseki	3	87D	9F-3R	21.0	2403	No
MF-1230 Hydro	14186.00	9080.00	9930.00	10430.00	Iseki	3	87D	Variable	20.0	2293	No
MF-1230 Hydro 4WD	15745.00	10080.00	11020.00	11570.00	Iseki	3	87D	Variable	20.0	2469	No
MF-1240	13150.00	8420.00	9210.00	9670.00	Iseki	3	87D	16F-16R	22.5	2859	No
MF-1240 4WD	15212.00	9740.00	10650.00	11180.00	Iseki	3	87D	16F-16R	22.5	2960	No
MF-1250	14557.00	9320.00	10190.00	10700.00	Iseki	3	91D	16F-16R	26.2	2933	No
MF-1250 4WD	16686.00	10680.00	11680.00	12260.00	Iseki	3	91D	16F-16R	26.2	3040	No
MF-1260	18979.00	12150.00	13290.00	13960.00	Iseki	3	91D	16F-16R	31.0	3155	No
MF-1260 4WD	19145.00	12250.00	13400.00	14070.00	Iseki	3	91D	16F-16R	31.0	3128	No
MF-3075 4WD	54470.00	28300.00	32040.00	33640.00	Perkins	4T	244D	32F-32R	86.00	10244	C,H,A
MF-3120T	53050.00	27560.00	31200.00	32760.00	Perkins	6T	365D	32F-32R	110.00	11153	C,H,A
MF-3120T 4WD	58830.00	30210.00	34200.00	35910.00	Perkins	6T	365D	32F-32R	110.00	11486	C,H,A
MF-3140	55930.00	28950.00	32770.00	34410.00	Perkins	6T	365D	32F-32R	115.00	11153	C,H,A
MF-3140 4WD	61910.00	31800.00	36000.00	37800.00	Perkins	6T	365D	32F-32R	115.00	11486	C,H,A
MF-3660	64230.00	32970.00	37320.00	39190.00	Perkins	6T	365D	32F-32R	115.00	12581	C,H,A
MF-3660 4WD	75570.00	38980.00	44120.00	46330.00	Perkins	6T	365D	32F-32R	115.00	13152	C,H,A
MF-3670	69680.00	36040.00	40800.00	42840.00	Perkins	6T	403D	32F-32R	154.00	12736	C,H,A
MF-3670 4WD	80150.00	39750.00	45000.00	47250.00	Perkins	6T	403D	32F-32R	154.00	13816	C,H,A
MF-3690	79190.00	40810.00	46200.00	48510.00	Perkins	6T	452D	32F-32R	170.00	13073	C,H,A
MF-3690 4WD	89470.00	44520.00	50400.00	52920.00	Perkins	6T	452D	32F-32R	170.00	14131	C,H,A

1995

Model	Approx. Retail Price New	Estimated Average Value Less Repairs Fair	Good	Premium	Engine Make	No. Cyls.	Displ. Cu.-In.	No. Speeds	P.T.O. H.P.	Approx. Shipping Wt.-Lbs.	Cab
MF-231	11580.00	8220.00	9030.00	9480.00	Perkins	3	152D	8F-2R	34.0	4065	No
MF-240	17340.00	11440.00	12660.00	13290.00	Perkins	3	152D	8F-2R	41.0	4015	No
MF-240 4WD	22970.00	13200.00	14600.00	15330.00	Perkins	3	152D	8F-2R	41.0	4585	No
MF-253	20775.00	13710.00	15170.00	15930.00	Perkins	3T	152D	8F-2R	48.0	4265	No
MF-253 4WD	25975.00	15770.00	17450.00	18320.00	Perkins	3T	152D	8F-2R	48.0	4735	No
MF-261	15335.00	10120.00	11200.00	11760.00	Perkins	4	236D	8F-2R	53.0	5280	No
MF-283	18080.00	11930.00	13200.00	13860.00	Perkins	4	248D	8F-2R	67.0	5700	No
MF-362	23765.00	15690.00	17350.00	18220.00	Perkins	4	236D	8F-2R	55.0	5335	No
MF-362 4WD	30205.00	19140.00	21170.00	22230.00	Perkins	4	236D	8F-2R	55.0	5960	No
MF-375	26890.00	17210.00	18820.00	19760.00	Perkins	4	236D	12F-4R	60.0	6240	No
MF-375 4WD	32705.00	19840.00	21700.00	22790.00	Perkins	4	236D	12F-4R	60.0	6867	No
MF-375 4WD w/Cab	40370.00	24320.00	26600.00	27930.00	Perkins	4	236D	12F-4R	60.0	7517	C,H,A
MF-375 w/Cab	35280.00	21890.00	23940.00	25140.00	Perkins	4	236D	12F-4R	60.0	6910	C,H,A
MF-383	25120.00	16580.00	18340.00	19260.00	Perkins	4	248D	8F-2R	73.0	6311	No
MF-383 4WD	31180.00	20580.00	22760.00	23900.00	Perkins	4	248D	8F-2R	73.0	6950	No
MF-383 4WD w/Cab	39630.00	25080.00	27740.00	29130.00	Perkins	4	248D	8F-2R	73.0	7552	C,H,A
MF-383 w/Cab	33575.00	22160.00	24510.00	25740.00	Perkins	4	248D	8F-2R	73.0	6957	C,H,A
MF-390	30155.00	19900.00	22010.00	23110.00	Perkins	4	248D	12F-4R	70.0	6275	No
MF-390 4WD	36020.00	23770.00	26300.00	27620.00	Perkins	4	248D	12F-4R	70.0	6902	No
MF-390 4WD w/Cab	44465.00	28380.00	31390.00	32960.00	Perkins	4	248D	12F-4R	70.0	7552	C,H,A
MF-390 w/Cab	38380.00	25330.00	28020.00	29420.00	Perkins	4	248D	12F-4R	70.0	6945	C,H,A
MF-390T	31760.00	20960.00	23190.00	24350.00	Perkins	4T	236D	12F-4R	80.0	6359	No
MF-390T 4WD	37380.00	24670.00	27290.00	28660.00	Perkins	4T	236D	12F-4R	80.0	6952	No
MF-390T 4WD w/Cab	46505.00	29700.00	32850.00	34490.00	Perkins	4T	236D	12F-4R	80.0	7602	C,H,A
MF-390T w/Cab	40055.00	26440.00	29240.00	30700.00	Perkins	4T	236D	12F-4R	80.0	6995	C,H,A
MF-393 4WD	34270.00	22620.00	25020.00	26270.00	Perkins	4T	236D	8F-2R	83.0	6986	No
MF-393 4WD w/Cab	42640.00	27390.00	30300.00	31820.00	Perkins	4T	236D	8F-2R	83.0	7636	C,H,A
MF-396	31555.00	20830.00	23040.00	24190.00	Perkins	6	365D	8F-2R	104.4	7120	No
MF-396 4WD	37665.00	24860.00	27500.00	28880.00	Perkins	6	365D	8F-2R	104.4	7690	No
MF-396 4WD w/Cab	47185.00	29700.00	32850.00	34490.00	Perkins	6	365D	12F-4R	104.4	8430	C,H,A
MF-396 w/Cab	40520.00	26740.00	29580.00	31060.00	Perkins	6	365D	12F-4R	104.4	7831	C,H,A
MF-398	33760.00	21610.00	23630.00	24810.00	Perkins	4T	236D	12F-4R	80.00	6960	No
MF-398 4WD	40245.00	25760.00	28170.00	29580.00	Perkins	4T	236D	12F-4R	80.00	7395	No
MF-399	36320.00	23250.00	25420.00	26690.00	Perkins	6	365D	12F-4R	95.00	7400	No
MF-399 4WD	43140.00	27610.00	30200.00	31710.00	Perkins	6	365D	12F-4R	95.00	7910	No
MF-399 4WD w/Cab	52995.00	32640.00	35700.00	37490.00	Perkins	6	365D	12F-4R	95.00	8560	C,H,A
MF-399 Mudder	51095.00	32700.00	35770.00	37560.00	Perkins	6	365D	12F-12R	95.00		No
MF-399 Mudder w/Cab	58305.00	35840.00	39200.00	41160.00	Perkins	6	365D	12F-12R	95.00		C,H,A
MF-399 w/Cab	45265.00	28970.00	31690.00	33280.00	Perkins	6	365D	12F-4R	95.00	8050	C,H,A
MF-1120 4WD	9584.00	6330.00	7000.00	7350.00	Isuzu	3	52D	6F-2R	14.2	1360	No
MF-1120 Hydro 4WD	10727.00	7080.00	7830.00	8220.00	Isuzu	3	52D	Variable	13.1	1448	No
MF-1160 4WD	23886.00	15770.00	17440.00	18310.00	Isuzu	4	136D	16F-16R	37.0	4206	No
MF-1180 4WD	25981.00	17150.00	18970.00	19920.00	Isuzu	4	169D	16F-16R	46.0	4773	No
MF-1190 4WD	27787.00	18340.00	20290.00	21310.00	Isuzu	4T	169D	16F-16R	53.0	4795	No
MF-1210	10285.00	6790.00	7510.00	7890.00	Iseki	3	61D	6F-2R	15.00	1830	No
MF-1210 4WD	11753.00	7760.00	8580.00	9010.00	Iseki	3	61D	6F-2R	15.00	1984	No
MF-1210 Hydro	11753.00	7760.00	8580.00	9010.00	Iseki	3	61D	Variable	14.00	1852	No
MF-1210 Hydro 4WD	13221.00	8730.00	9650.00	10130.00	Iseki	3	61D	Variable	14.00	2006	No
MF-1220	11938.00	7880.00	8720.00	9160.00	Iseki	3	68D	6F-2R	17.2	1874	No
MF-1220 4WD	13493.00	8910.00	9850.00	10340.00	Iseki	3	68D	6F-2R	17.2	2050	No
MF-1220 Hydro	13338.00	8800.00	9740.00	10230.00	Iseki	3	68D	Variable	16.0	1896	No
MF-1220 Hydro 4WD	14879.00	9820.00	10860.00	11400.00	Iseki	3	68D	Variable	16.0	2072	No
MF-1230	13318.00	8790.00	9720.00	10210.00	Iseki	3	87D	9F-3R	21.0	2227	No

Model	Approx. Retail Price New	Estimated Average Value Less Repairs Fair	Good	Premium	Engine Make	No. Cyls.	Displ. Cu.-In.	No. Speeds	P.T.O. H.P.	Approx. Shipping Wt.-Lbs.	Cab
Massey Ferguson (Cont.)											
			1995 (Cont.)								
MF-1230 4WD	14956.00	**9870.00**	**10920.00**	**11470.00**	Iseki	3	87D	9F-3R	21.0	2403	No
MF-1230 Hydro	14895.00	**9830.00**	**10870.00**	**11410.00**	Iseki	3	87D	Variable	20.0	2293	No
MF-1230 Hydro 4WD	16532.00	**10910.00**	**12070.00**	**12670.00**	Iseki	3	87D	Variable	20.0	2469	No
MF-1240	14186.00	**9360.00**	**10360.00**	**10880.00**	Iseki	3	87D	16F-16R	22.5	2859	No
MF-1240 4WD	15973.00	**10540.00**	**11660.00**	**12240.00**	Iseki	3	87D	16F-16R	22.5	2960	No
MF-1250	15285.00	**10090.00**	**11160.00**	**11720.00**	Iseki	3	91D	16F-16R	26.2	2933	No
MF-1250 4WD	17520.00	**11560.00**	**12790.00**	**13430.00**	Iseki	3	91D	16F-16R	26.2	3040	No
MF-1260 4WD	19928.00	**13150.00**	**14550.00**	**15280.00**	Iseki	3	91D	16F-16R	31.0	3128	No
MF-3075 4WD	54470.00	**29900.00**	**33640.00**	**34990.00**	Perkins	4T	244D	32F-32R	86.00	10244	C,H,A
MF-3120T	53460.00	**29400.00**	**33080.00**	**34400.00**	Perkins	6T	365D	32F-32R	110.00	11153	C,H,A
MF-3120T 4WD	59540.00	**32480.00**	**36540.00**	**38000.00**	Perkins	6T	365D	32F-32R	110.00	11486	C,H,A
MF-3140	55620.00	**30460.00**	**34270.00**	**35640.00**	Perkins	6T	365D	32F-32R	115.00	11153	C,H,A
MF-3140 4WD	61910.00	**33880.00**	**38120.00**	**39650.00**	Perkins	6T	365D	32F-32R	115.00	11486	C,H,A
MF-3660	64540.00	**35280.00**	**39690.00**	**41280.00**	Perkins	6T	365D	32F-32R	115.00	12581	C,H,A
MF-3660 4WD	75540.00	**41440.00**	**46620.00**	**48490.00**	Perkins	6T	365D	32F-32R	115.00	13152	C,H,A
MF-3670	69990.00	**38360.00**	**43160.00**	**44890.00**	Perkins	6T	403D	32F-32R	154.00	12736	C,H,A
MF-3670 4WD	80150.00	**42560.00**	**47880.00**	**49800.00**	Perkins	6T	403D	32F-32R	154.00	13816	C,H,A
MF-3690	79190.00	**43120.00**	**48510.00**	**50450.00**	Perkins	6T	452D	32F-32R	170.00	13073	C,H,A
MF-3690 4WD	89470.00	**47600.00**	**53550.00**	**55690.00**	Perkins	6T	452D	32F-32R	170.00	14131	C,H,A
MF-6150	46230.00	**29590.00**	**32360.00**	**33980.00**	Perkins	4T	244D	32F-32R	86.00		C,H,A
MF-6150 4WD	53570.00	**34290.00**	**37500.00**	**39380.00**	Perkins	4T	244D	32F-32R	86.00	10224	C,H,A
MF-6170	50750.00	**32480.00**	**35530.00**	**37310.00**	Perkins	6	365D	32F-32R	97.00	10329	C,H,A
MF-6170 4WD	57800.00	**36990.00**	**40460.00**	**42480.00**	Perkins	6	365D	32F-32R	97.00	10869	C,H,A
MF-6180	55000.00	**35200.00**	**38500.00**	**40430.00**	Perkins	6T	365D	32F-32R	110.00	11153	C,H,A
MF-6180 4WD	61480.00	**39350.00**	**43040.00**	**45190.00**	Perkins	6T	365D	32F-32R	110.00	11486	C,H,A
MF-8120	65160.00	**34540.00**	**39750.00**	**41740.00**	Perkins	6T	365D	32F-32R	130.00	12621	C,H,A
MF-8120 4WD	75100.00	**39800.00**	**45810.00**	**48100.00**	Perkins	6T	365D	32F-32R	130.00	13153	C,H,A
MF-8140	69900.00	**37050.00**	**42640.00**	**44770.00**	Valmet	6T	403D	32F-32R	145.00	13936	C,H,A
MF-8140 4WD	81200.00	**41870.00**	**48190.00**	**50600.00**	Valmet	6T	403D	32F-32R	145.00	15016	C,H,A
MF-8150	74100.00	**39270.00**	**45200.00**	**47460.00**	Valmet	6T	403D	32F-32R	160.00	14273	C,H,A
MF-8150 4WD	85950.00	**44520.00**	**51240.00**	**53800.00**	Valmet	6T	403D	32F-32R	160.00	15331	C,H,A
MF-8160	81950.00	**43430.00**	**49990.00**	**52490.00**	Valmet	6T	452D	32F-32R	180.00	14273	C,H,A
MF-8160 4WD	94850.00	**49710.00**	**57220.00**	**60080.00**	Valmet	6T	452D	32F-32R	180.00	15331	C,H,A
			1996								
MF-231	12175.00	**9010.00**	**9740.00**	**10130.00**	Perkins	3	152D	8F-2R	34.0	4065	No
MF-240	20385.00	**14000.00**	**15200.00**	**15810.00**	Perkins	3	152D	8F-2R	41.0	4015	No
MF-240 4WD	23985.00	**16790.00**	**18230.00**	**18960.00**	Perkins	3	152D	8F-2R	41.0	4585	No
MF-240S	16900.00	**11830.00**	**12840.00**	**13350.00**	Perkins	3	152D	8F-2R	41.0	4015	No
MF-253	22135.00	**15500.00**	**16820.00**	**17490.00**	Perkins	3T	152D	8F-2R	48.0	4265	No
MF-253 4WD	27300.00	**17760.00**	**19350.00**	**20120.00**	Perkins	3T	152D	8F-2R	48.0	4735	No
MF-261	15870.00	**11110.00**	**12060.00**	**12540.00**	Perkins	4	236D	8F-2R	53.0	5280	No
MF-283	19925.00	**13950.00**	**15140.00**	**15750.00**	Perkins	4	248D	8F-2R	67.0	5700	No
MF-283 4WD	25300.00	**17150.00**	**18620.00**	**19370.00**	Perkins	4	248D	8F-2R	67.0		No
MF-354 GE	23550.00	**16490.00**	**17900.00**	**18620.00**	Perkins	3	152D	12F-4R	42.0		No
MF-354 GE 4WD	28795.00	**19390.00**	**21050.00**	**21890.00**	Perkins	3	152D	12F-4R	42.0		No
MF-354S	22655.00	**15860.00**	**17220.00**	**17910.00**	Perkins	3	152D	12F-4R	42.0		No
MF-354S	23270.00	**16290.00**	**17690.00**	**18400.00**	Perkins	3	152D	12F-12R	42.0		No
MF-354S 4WD	28735.00	**20120.00**	**21840.00**	**22710.00**	Perkins	3	152D	12F-4R	42.0		No
MF-354S 4WD w/Cab	35535.00	**24880.00**	**27010.00**	**28090.00**	Perkins	3	152D	12F-12R	42.0		C,H
MF-354S w/Cab	29690.00	**20780.00**	**22560.00**	**23460.00**	Perkins	3	152D	12F-12R	42.0		C,H
MF-354V	31305.00	**21910.00**	**23790.00**	**24740.00**	Perkins	3	152D	12F-12R	42.0		C,H
MF-354V 4WD	36635.00	**25650.00**	**27840.00**	**28950.00**	Perkins	3	152D	12F-12R	42.0		C,H
MF-362	25385.00	**17770.00**	**19290.00**	**20060.00**	Perkins	4	236D	8F-2R	55.0	5335	No
MF-362 4WD	31260.00	**21880.00**	**23760.00**	**24710.00**	Perkins	4	236D	8F-2R	55.0	5960	No
MF-364 GE	24545.00	**17180.00**	**18650.00**	**19400.00**	Perkins	3T	152D	12F-4R	50.0		No
MF-364 GE 4WD	30105.00	**21070.00**	**22880.00**	**23800.00**	Perkins	3T	152D	12F-4R	50.0		No
MF-364S	23450.00	**16420.00**	**17820.00**	**18530.00**	Perkins	3T	152D	12F-4R	50.0		No
MF-364S 4WD	29630.00	**20740.00**	**22520.00**	**23420.00**	Perkins	3T	152D	12F-4R	50.0		No
MF-364S 4WD w/Cab	36810.00	**25770.00**	**27980.00**	**29100.00**	Perkins	3T	152D	12F-12R	50.0		C,H
MF-364S w/Cab	30790.00	**21550.00**	**23400.00**	**24340.00**	Perkins	3T	152D	12F-12R	50.0		C,H
MF-364V	32545.00	**22780.00**	**24730.00**	**25720.00**	Perkins	3T	152D	12F-12R	50.0		C,H
MF-364V 4WD	37880.00	**26520.00**	**28790.00**	**29940.00**	Perkins	3T	152D	12F-12R	50.0		C,H
MF-374 GE	24865.00	**17410.00**	**18900.00**	**19660.00**	Perkins	4	236D	12F-4R	57.0		No
MF-374 GE 4WD	31180.00	**21830.00**	**23700.00**	**24650.00**	Perkins	4	236D	12F-4R	57.0		No
MF-374S	23755.00	**16630.00**	**18050.00**	**18770.00**	Perkins	4	236D	12F-4R	57.0		No
MF-374S 4WD	30420.00	**21290.00**	**23120.00**	**24050.00**	Perkins	4	236D	12F-4R	57.0		No
MF-374S 4WD w/Cab	40365.00	**28260.00**	**30680.00**	**31910.00**	Perkins	4	236D	12F-12R	57.0		C,H,A
MF-374S w/Cab	33815.00	**23670.00**	**25700.00**	**26730.00**	Perkins	4	236D	12F-12R	57.0		C,H,A
MF-374V	33745.00	**23620.00**	**25650.00**	**26680.00**	Perkins	4	236D	12F-12R	57.0		C,H,A
MF-374V 4WD	39090.00	**27360.00**	**29710.00**	**30900.00**	Perkins	4	236D	12F-12R	57.0		C,H,A
MF-375	28625.00	**19180.00**	**20900.00**	**21740.00**	Perkins	4	236D	12F-4R	60.0	6240	No
MF-375 4WD	33850.00	**22680.00**	**24710.00**	**25700.00**	Perkins	4	236D	12F-4R	60.0	6867	No
MF-375 4WD w/Cab	41780.00	**26800.00**	**29200.00**	**30370.00**	Perkins	4	236D	12F-4R	60.0	7517	C,H,A
MF-375 w/Cab	36710.00	**24600.00**	**26800.00**	**27870.00**	Perkins	4	236D	12F-4R	60.0	6910	C,H,A
MF-383	26475.00	**18530.00**	**20120.00**	**20930.00**	Perkins	4	248D	8F-2R	73.0	6311	No
MF-383 4WD	32745.00	**22920.00**	**24890.00**	**25890.00**	Perkins	4	248D	8F-2R	73.0	6950	No
MF-383 4WD w/Cab	41490.00	**27300.00**	**29640.00**	**30830.00**	Perkins	4	248D	8F-2R	73.0	7552	C,H,A
MF-383 w/Cab	35225.00	**24660.00**	**26770.00**	**27840.00**	Perkins	4	248D	8F-2R	73.0	6957	C,H,A
MF-384 GE	25995.00	**18200.00**	**19760.00**	**20550.00**	Perkins	4	236D	12F-4R	65.0		No
MF-384 GE 4WD	31710.00	**22200.00**	**24100.00**	**25060.00**	Perkins	4	236D	12F-4R	65.0		No
MF-384HC	26780.00	**18750.00**	**20350.00**	**21160.00**	Perkins	4	236D	12F-12R	65.0		No
MF-384HC 4WD	32545.00	**22780.00**	**24730.00**	**25720.00**	Perkins	4	236D	12F-12R	65.0		No
MF-384S	24815.00	**17370.00**	**18860.00**	**19610.00**	Perkins	4	236D	12F-4R	65.0		No

Massey Ferguson (Cont.)

Model	Approx. Retail Price New	Estimated Average Value Less Repairs Fair	Good	Premium	Make	Engine No. Cyls.	Displ. Cu.-In.	No. Speeds	P.T.O. H.P.	Approx. Shipping Wt.-Lbs.	Cab
1996 (Cont.)											
MF-384S 4WD	30960.00	21670.00	23530.00	24470.00	Perkins	4	236D	12F-4R	65.0		No
MF-384S 4WD w/Cab	41020.00	28710.00	31180.00	32430.00	Perkins	4	236D	12F-12R	65.0		C,H,A
MF-384S w/Cab	34760.00	24330.00	26420.00	27480.00	Perkins	4	236D	12F-12R	65.0		C,H,A
MF-384V	34755.00	24330.00	26410.00	27470.00	Perkins	4	236D	12F-12R	65.0		C,H,A
MF-384V 4WD	40530.00	28370.00	30800.00	32030.00	Perkins	4	236D	12F-12R	65.0		C,H,A
MF-390	31210.00	21850.00	23720.00	24670.00	Perkins	4	248D	12F-4R	70.0	6275	No
MF-390 4WD	37655.00	26360.00	28620.00	29770.00	Perkins	4	248D	12F-4R	70.0	6902	No
MF-390 4WD w/Cab	46420.00	31500.00	34200.00	35570.00	Perkins	4	248D	12F-4R	70.0	7552	C,H,A
MF-390 w/Cab	40625.00	28440.00	30880.00	32120.00	Perkins	4	248D	12F-4R	70.0	6945	C,H,A
MF-390T	33695.00	23590.00	25610.00	26630.00	Perkins	4T	236D	12F-4R	80.0	6359	No
MF-390T 4WD	39060.00	27340.00	29690.00	30880.00	Perkins	4T	236D	12F-4R	80.0	6952	No
MF-390T 4WD w/Cab	48530.00	32200.00	34960.00	36360.00	Perkins	4T	236D	12F-4R	80.0	7602	C,H,A
MF-390T w/Cab	41965.00	29380.00	31890.00	33170.00	Perkins	4T	236D	12F-4R	80.0	6995	C,H,A
MF-393	29270.00	20490.00	22250.00	23140.00	Perkins	4T	236D	8F-2R	83.0	6986	No
MF-393 4WD	35470.00	24830.00	26960.00	28040.00	Perkins	4T	236D	8F-2R	83.0	6986	No
MF-393 4WD w/Cab	44130.00	29400.00	31920.00	33200.00	Perkins	4T	236D	8F-2R	83.0	7636	C,H,A
MF-393 w/Cab	37375.00	26160.00	28410.00	29550.00	Perkins	4T	236D	8F-2R	83.0	7636	C,H,A
MF-394 4WD w/Cab	42695.00	28700.00	31160.00	32410.00	Perkins	4	248D	24F-12R	73.0		C,H,A
MF-394 GE	27695.00	19390.00	21050.00	21890.00	Perkins	4	248D	12F-4R	73.0		No
MF-394GE 4WD	33865.00	23710.00	25740.00	26770.00	Perkins	4	248D	12F-4R	73.0		No
MF-394HC	28335.00	19840.00	21540.00	22400.00	Perkins	4	248D	12F-12R	73.0		No
MF-394HC 4WD	35405.00	24780.00	26910.00	27990.00	Perkins	4	248D	12F-12R	73.0		No
MF-394S	26395.00	18480.00	20060.00	20860.00	Perkins	4	248D	12F-4R	73.0		No
MF-394S 4WD	32745.00	22920.00	24890.00	25890.00	Perkins	4	248D	12F-4R	73.0		No
MF-394S 4WD w/Cab	42295.00	29610.00	32140.00	33430.00	Perkins	4	248D	12F-12R	73.0		C,H,A
MF-394S w/Cab	35885.00	25120.00	27270.00	28360.00	Perkins	4	248D	12F-12R	73.0		C,H,A
MF-396	32985.00	23090.00	25070.00	26070.00	Perkins	6	365D	8F-2R	88.0	7120	No
MF-396 4WD	39875.00	27910.00	30310.00	31520.00	Perkins	6	365D	8F-2R	88.0	7690	No
MF-396 4WD w/Cab	49725.00	32900.00	35720.00	37150.00	Perkins	6	365D	12F-4R	88.0	8430	C,H,A
MF-396 w/Cab	41935.00	29360.00	31870.00	33150.00	Perkins	6	365D	12F-4R	88.0	7831	C,H,A
MF-398	34940.00	23410.00	25510.00	26530.00	Perkins	4T	236D	12F-4R	80.00	6960	No
MF-398 4WD	41655.00	27910.00	30410.00	31630.00	Perkins	4T	236D	12F-4R	80.00	7395	No
MF-399	37090.00	24850.00	27080.00	28160.00	Perkins	6	365D	12F-4R	95.00	7400	No
MF-399 4WD	44655.00	29920.00	32600.00	33900.00	Perkins	6	365D	12F-4R	95.00	7910	No
MF-399 4WD w/Cab	54855.00	34840.00	37960.00	39480.00	Perkins	6	365D	12F-4R	95.00	8560	C,H,A
MF-399 Mudder	52885.00	34170.00	37230.00	38720.00	Perkins	6	365D	12F-12R	95.00		No
MF-399 Mudder w/Cab	60345.00	38190.00	41610.00	43270.00	Perkins	6	365D	12F-12R	95.00		C,H,A
MF-399 w/Cab	46395.00	29820.00	32490.00	33790.00	Perkins	6	365D	12F-4R	95.00	8050	C,H,A
MF-1120 4WD	9584.00	6710.00	7280.00	7570.00	Isuzu	3	52D	6F-2R	14.2	1360	No
MF-1120 Hydro 4WD	10727.00	7510.00	8150.00	8480.00	Isuzu	3	52D	Variable	13.1	1448	No
MF-1160 4WD	23886.00	16720.00	18150.00	18880.00	Isuzu	4	136D	16F-16R	37.0	4206	No
MF-1180 4WD	25981.00	18190.00	19750.00	20540.00	Isuzu	4	169D	16F-16R	46.0	4773	No
MF-1190 4WD	27787.00	19450.00	21120.00	21970.00	Isuzu	4T	169D	16F-16R	53.0	4795	No
MF-1205 4WD	10200.00	7140.00	7750.00	8060.00	Iseki	3	61D	6F-2R	13.5	1579	No
MF-1205 Hydro 4WD	11400.00	7980.00	8660.00	9010.00	Iseki	3	61D	Variable	13.0	1579	No
MF-1210	10285.00	7200.00	7820.00	8130.00	Iseki	3	61D	6F-2R	15.00	1830	No
MF-1210 4WD	11753.00	8230.00	8930.00	9290.00	Iseki	3	61D	6F-2R	15.00	1984	No
MF-1210 Hydro	11753.00	8230.00	8930.00	9290.00	Iseki	3	61D	Variable	14.00	1852	No
MF-1210 Hydro 4WD	13221.00	9260.00	10050.00	10450.00	Iseki	3	61D	Variable	14.00	2006	No
MF-1215	10654.00	7460.00	8100.00	8420.00	Iseki	3	61D	6F-2R	15.0	1457	No
MF-1215 4WD	11850.00	8300.00	9010.00	9370.00	Iseki	3	61D	6F-2R	15.0	1589	No
MF-1215 Hydro	11869.00	8310.00	9020.00	9380.00	Iseki	3	61D	Variable	14.0	1457	No
MF-1215 Hydro 4WD	13350.00	9350.00	10150.00	10560.00	Iseki	3	61D	Variable	14.0	1589	No
MF-1220	11938.00	8360.00	9070.00	9430.00	Iseki	3	68D	6F-2R	17.2	1874	No
MF-1220 4WD	13493.00	9450.00	10260.00	10670.00	Iseki	3	68D	6F-2R	17.2	2050	No
MF-1220 Hydro	13338.00	9340.00	10140.00	10550.00	Iseki	3	68D	Variable	16.0	1896	No
MF-1220 Hydro 4WD	14879.00	10420.00	11310.00	11760.00	Iseki	3	68D	Variable	16.0	2072	No
MF-1230	13318.00	9320.00	10120.00	10530.00	Iseki	3	87D	9F-3R	21.0	2227	No
MF-1230 4WD	14956.00	10470.00	11370.00	11830.00	Iseki	3	87D	9F-3R	21.0	2403	No
MF-1230 Hydro	14895.00	10430.00	11320.00	11770.00	Iseki	3	87D	Variable	20.0	2293	No
MF-1230 Hydro 4WD	16532.00	11570.00	12560.00	13060.00	Iseki	3	87D	Variable	20.0	2469	No
MF-1240	14186.00	9930.00	10780.00	11210.00	Iseki	3	87D	16F-16R	22.5	2859	No
MF-1240 4WD	15973.00	11180.00	12140.00	12630.00	Iseki	3	87D	16F-16R	22.5	2960	No
MF-1250	15285.00	10700.00	11620.00	12090.00	Iseki	3	91D	16F-16R	26.2	2933	No
MF-1250 4WD	17520.00	12260.00	13320.00	13850.00	Iseki	3	91D	16F-16R	26.2	3040	No
MF-1260 4WD	19928.00	13950.00	15150.00	15760.00	Iseki	3	91D	16F-16R	31.0	3128	No
MF-3075 4WD	54450.00	33220.00	36480.00	37940.00	Perkins	4T	244D	32F-32R	86.00	10244	C,H,A
MF-3120T	53560.00	32670.00	35890.00	37330.00	Perkins	6T	365D	32F-32R	110.00	11153	C,H,A
MF-3120T 4WD	59540.00	36320.00	39890.00	41490.00	Perkins	6T	365D	32F-32R	110.00	11486	C,H,A
MF-3140	55620.00	33930.00	37270.00	38760.00	Perkins	6T	365D	32F-32R	115.00	11153	C,H,A
MF-3140 4WD	61910.00	37770.00	41480.00	43140.00	Perkins	6T	365D	32F-32R	115.00	11486	C,H,A
MF-3660	64540.00	39370.00	43240.00	44970.00	Perkins	6T	365D	32F-32R	140.0	12581	C,H,A
MF-3660 4WD	75050.00	46080.00	50610.00	52630.00	Perkins	6T	365D	32F-32R	140.00	13152	C,H,A
MF-3670	72770.00	44390.00	48760.00	50710.00	Perkins	6T	403D	32F-32R	154.00	12736	C,H,A
MF-3670 4WD	82930.00	50590.00	55560.00	57780.00	Perkins	6T	403D	32F-32R	154.00	13816	C,H,A
MF-3690	84490.00	51540.00	56610.00	58870.00	Perkins	6T	452D	32F-32R	170.00	13073	C,H,A
MF-3690 4WD	94160.00	57440.00	63090.00	65610.00	Perkins	6T	452D	32F-32R	170.00	14131	C,H,A
MF-6150	48680.00	32620.00	35540.00	36960.00	Perkins	4T	244D	32F-32R	86.00		C,H,A
MF-6150 4WD	56610.00	37930.00	41330.00	42980.00	Perkins	4T	244D	32F-32R	86.00	10224	C,H,A
MF-6170	51870.00	34750.00	37870.00	39390.00	Perkins	6	365D	32F-32R	97.00	10329	C,H,A
MF-6170 4WD	59930.00	40150.00	43750.00	45500.00	Perkins	6	365D	32F-32R	97.00	10869	C,H,A
MF-6180	56920.00	38140.00	41550.00	43210.00	Perkins	6T	365D	32F-32R	110.00	11153	C,H,A
MF-6180 4WD	63630.00	42630.00	46450.00	48310.00	Perkins	6T	365D	32F-32R	110.00	11486	C,H,A
MF-8120	68050.00	40150.00	44910.00	47160.00	Perkins	6T	365D	32F-32R	130.00	12621	C,H,A

Model	Approx. Retail Price New	Estimated Average Value Less Repairs Fair	Good	Premium	Engine Make	No. Cyls.	Displ. Cu.-In.	No. Speeds	P.T.O. H.P.	Approx. Shipping Wt.-Lbs.	Cab
Massey Ferguson (Cont.)											
			1996 (Cont.)								
MF-8120 4WD	79110.00	**46020.00**	**51480.00**	**54050.00**	Perkins	6T	365D	32F-32R	130.00	13153	C,H,A
MF-8140	73360.00	**43280.00**	**48420.00**	**50840.00**	Valmet	6T	403D	32F-32R	145.00	13936	C,H,A
MF-8140 4WD	85520.00	**49560.00**	**55440.00**	**58210.00**	Valmet	6T	403D	32F-32R	145.00	15016	C,H,A
MF-8150	82710.00	**48800.00**	**54590.00**	**57320.00**	Valmet	6T	403D	32F-32R	160.00	14273	C,H,A
MF-8150 4WD	90310.00	**52510.00**	**58740.00**	**61680.00**	Valmet	6T	403D	32F-32R	160.00	15331	C,H,A
MF-8160	91640.00	**54070.00**	**60480.00**	**63500.00**	Valmet	6T	452D	32F-32R	180.00	14273	C,H,A
MF-8160 4WD	105250.00	**59000.00**	**66000.00**	**69300.00**	Valmet	6T	452D	32F-32R	180.00	15331	C,H,A
			1997								
MF-231	12540.00	**9410.00**	**10030.00**	**10430.00**	Perkins	3	152D	8F-2R	34.0	4065	No
MF-240	20010.00	**15010.00**	**16010.00**	**16650.00**	Perkins	3	152D	8F-2R	41.0	4015	No
MF-240 4WD	24345.00	**18000.00**	**19200.00**	**19970.00**	Perkins	3	152D	8F-2R	41.0	4585	No
MF-240S	16900.00	**12680.00**	**13520.00**	**14060.00**	Perkins	3	152D	8F-2R	41.0	4015	No
MF-253	22180.00	**16640.00**	**17740.00**	**18450.00**	Perkins	3T	152D	8F-2R	48.0	4265	No
MF-253 4WD	27845.00	**20250.00**	**21600.00**	**22460.00**	Perkins	3T	152D	8F-2R	48.0	4735	No
MF-261	16345.00	**12260.00**	**13080.00**	**13600.00**	Perkins	4	236D	8F-2R	53.0	5280	No
MF-283	20560.00	**15420.00**	**16450.00**	**17110.00**	Perkins	4	248D	8F-2R	67.0	5700	No
MF-283 4WD	26095.00	**19570.00**	**20880.00**	**21720.00**	Perkins	4	248D	8F-2R	67.0		No
MF-354 GE 4WD	29815.00	**22360.00**	**23850.00**	**24800.00**	Perkins	3	152D	12F-4R	42.0		No
MF-354S	23705.00	**17780.00**	**18960.00**	**19720.00**	Perkins	3	152D	12F-4R	42.0		No
MF-354S 4WD	29765.00	**22320.00**	**23810.00**	**24760.00**	Perkins	3	152D	12F-4R	42.0		No
MF-354V	32025.00	**24020.00**	**25620.00**	**26650.00**	Perkins	3	152D	12F-12R	42.0		C,H
MF-354V 4WD	37630.00	**28220.00**	**30100.00**	**31300.00**	Perkins	3	152D	12F-12R	42.0		C,H
MF-362	25540.00	**19160.00**	**20430.00**	**21250.00**	Perkins	4	236D	8F-2R	55.0	5335	No
MF-362 4WD	32490.00	**24370.00**	**25990.00**	**27030.00**	Perkins	4	236D	8F-2R	55.0	5960	No
MF-364 GE 4WD	31170.00	**23380.00**	**24940.00**	**25940.00**	Perkins	3T	152D	12F-4R	50.0		No
MF-364S	24505.00	**18380.00**	**19600.00**	**20380.00**	Perkins	3T	152D	12F-4R	50.0		No
MF-364S 4WD	30840.00	**23130.00**	**24670.00**	**25660.00**	Perkins	3T	152D	12F-4R	50.0		No
MF-364V	33350.00	**25010.00**	**26680.00**	**27750.00**	Perkins	3T	152D	12F-12R	50.0		C,H
MF-364V 4WD	39260.00	**29450.00**	**31410.00**	**32670.00**	Perkins	3T	152D	12F-12R	50.0		C,H
MF-374 GE	25700.00	**19280.00**	**20560.00**	**21380.00**	Perkins	4	236D	12F-4R	57.0		No
MF-374 GE 4WD	32280.00	**24210.00**	**25820.00**	**26850.00**	Perkins	4	236D	12F-4R	57.0		No
MF-374S	24820.00	**18620.00**	**19860.00**	**20650.00**	Perkins	4	236D	12F-4R	57.0		No
MF-374S 4WD	31160.00	**23370.00**	**24930.00**	**25930.00**	Perkins	4	236D	12F-4R	57.0		No
MF-374S 4WD w/Cab	41450.00	**31090.00**	**33160.00**	**34490.00**	Perkins	4	236D	12F-12R	57.0		C,H,A
MF-374S w/Cab	35235.00	**26430.00**	**28190.00**	**29320.00**	Perkins	4	236D	12F-12R	57.0		C,H,A
MF-374V	35510.00	**26630.00**	**28410.00**	**29550.00**	Perkins	4	236D	12F-12R	57.0		C,H,A
MF-374V 4WD	41650.00	**31240.00**	**33320.00**	**34650.00**	Perkins	4	236D	12F-12R	57.0		C,H,A
MF-375	31770.00	**22870.00**	**24460.00**	**25440.00**	Perkins	4	236D	12F-12R	60.0	6240	No
MF-375 4WD	36925.00	**26590.00**	**28430.00**	**29570.00**	Perkins	4	236D	12F-12R	60.0	6867	No
MF-375 4WD Shuttle	34645.00	**24940.00**	**26680.00**	**27750.00**	Perkins	4	236D	8F-8R	60.0	6867	No
MF-375 4WD w/Cab	44590.00	**32110.00**	**34330.00**	**35700.00**	Perkins	4	236D	12F-12R	60.0	7517	C,H,A
MF-375 Shuttle	28970.00	**20860.00**	**22310.00**	**23200.00**	Perkins	4	236D	8F-8R	60.0	6240	No
MF-375 w/Cab	39680.00	**28570.00**	**30550.00**	**31770.00**	Perkins	4	236D	12F-12R	60.0	6910	C,H,A
MF-383	27270.00	**20450.00**	**21820.00**	**22690.00**	Perkins	4	248D	8F-2R	73.0	6311	No
MF-383 4WD	33725.00	**25290.00**	**26980.00**	**28060.00**	Perkins	4	248D	8F-2R	73.0	6950	No
MF-383 4WD w/Cab	42735.00	**32050.00**	**34190.00**	**35560.00**	Perkins	4	248D	8F-2R	73.0	7552	C,H,A
MF-383 w/Cab	36280.00	**27210.00**	**29020.00**	**30180.00**	Perkins	4	248D	8F-2R	73.0	6957	C,H,A
MF-384 GE 4WD	32830.00	**24620.00**	**26260.00**	**27310.00**	Perkins	4	236D	12F-4R	65.0		No
MF-384HC	28275.00	**21210.00**	**22620.00**	**23530.00**	Perkins	4	236D	12F-12R	65.0		No
MF-384HC 4WD	33950.00	**25460.00**	**27160.00**	**28250.00**	Perkins	4	236D	12F-12R	65.0		No
MF-384S	25920.00	**19440.00**	**20740.00**	**21570.00**	Perkins	4	236D	12F-4R	65.0		No
MF-384S 4WD	32010.00	**24010.00**	**25610.00**	**26630.00**	Perkins	4	236D	12F-4R	65.0		No
MF-384S 4WD w/Cab	42420.00	**31820.00**	**33940.00**	**35300.00**	Perkins	4	236D	12F-12R	65.0		C,H,A
MF-384S w/Cab	36210.00	**27160.00**	**28970.00**	**30130.00**	Perkins	4	236D	12F-12R	65.0		C,H,A
MF-384V	36560.00	**27420.00**	**29250.00**	**30420.00**	Perkins	4	236D	12F-12R	65.0		C,H,A
MF-384V 4WD	43140.00	**32360.00**	**34510.00**	**35890.00**	Perkins	4	236D	12F-12R	65.0		C,H,A
MF-390	35475.00	**26610.00**	**28380.00**	**29520.00**	Perkins	4	248D	12F-12R	70.0	6275	No
MF-390 4WD	40850.00	**30640.00**	**32680.00**	**33990.00**	Perkins	4	248D	12F-12R	70.0	6902	No
MF-390 4WD w/Cab	49370.00	**37030.00**	**39500.00**	**41080.00**	Perkins	4	248D	12F-12R	70.0	7552	C,H,A
MF-390 w/Cab	43395.00	**32550.00**	**34720.00**	**36110.00**	Perkins	4	248D	12F-12R	70.0	6945	C,H,A
MF-390T	37150.00	**27860.00**	**29720.00**	**30910.00**	Perkins	4T	236D	12F-12R	80.0	6359	No
MF-390T 4WD	42685.00	**32010.00**	**34150.00**	**35520.00**	Perkins	4T	236D	12F-12R	80.0	6952	No
MF-390T 4WD w/Cab	51535.00	**38650.00**	**41230.00**	**42880.00**	Perkins	4T	236D	12F-12R	80.0	7602	C,H,A
MF-390T w/Cab	44780.00	**33590.00**	**35820.00**	**37250.00**	Perkins	4T	236D	12F-12R	80.0	6995	C,H,A
MF-393	30150.00	**22610.00**	**24120.00**	**25090.00**	Perkins	4T	236D	8F-2R	83.0	6371	No
MF-393 4WD	36535.00	**27400.00**	**29230.00**	**30400.00**	Perkins	4T	236D	8F-2R	83.0	6986	No
MF-393 4WD w/Cab	45455.00	**34090.00**	**36360.00**	**37810.00**	Perkins	4T	236D	8F-2R	83.0	7636	C,H,A
MF-393 w/Cab	38495.00	**28870.00**	**30800.00**	**32030.00**	Perkins	4T	236D	8F-2R	83.0	7021	C,H,A
MF-394 GE 4WD	35060.00	**26300.00**	**28050.00**	**29170.00**	Perkins	4	248D	12F-12R	73.0		No
MF-394HC	29885.00	**22410.00**	**23910.00**	**24870.00**	Perkins	4	248D	12F-12R	73.0		No
MF-394HC 4WD	36340.00	**27260.00**	**29070.00**	**30230.00**	Perkins	4	248D	12F-12R	73.0		No
MF-394S	27555.00	**20670.00**	**22040.00**	**22920.00**	Perkins	4	248D	12F-4R	73.0		No
MF-394S 4WD	33855.00	**25390.00**	**27080.00**	**28160.00**	Perkins	4	248D	12F-4R	73.0		No
MF-394S 4WD w/Cab	43722.00	**31500.00**	**33600.00**	**34940.00**	Perkins	4	248D	12F-12R	73.0		C,H,A
MF-394S w/Cab	37375.00	**28030.00**	**29900.00**	**31100.00**	Perkins	4	248D	12F-12R	73.0		C,H,A
MF-396	34280.00	**25710.00**	**27420.00**	**28520.00**	Perkins	6	365D	8F-2R	88.0	7120	No
MF-396 4WD	41300.00	**30980.00**	**33040.00**	**34360.00**	Perkins	6	365D	8F-2R	88.0	7690	No
MF-396 4WD w/Cab	51445.00	**37500.00**	**40000.00**	**41600.00**	Perkins	6	365D	12F-4R	88.0	8430	C,H,A
MF-396 w/Cab	43835.00	**32880.00**	**35070.00**	**36470.00**	Perkins	6	365D	12F-4R	88.0	7831	C,H,A
MF-398	35645.00	**26730.00**	**28520.00**	**29660.00**	Perkins	4T	236D	12F-4R	80.00	6960	No
MF-398 4WD	42495.00	**31870.00**	**34000.00**	**35360.00**	Perkins	4T	236D	12F-4R	80.00	7395	No
MF-399	38720.00	**27880.00**	**29810.00**	**31000.00**	Perkins	6	365D	12F-4R	95.00	7400	No
MF-399 4WD	45885.00	**33040.00**	**35330.00**	**36740.00**	Perkins	6	365D	12F-4R	95.00	7910	No

Massey Ferguson (Cont.)

1997 (Cont.)

Model	Approx. Retail Price New	Estimated Average Value Less Repairs Fair	Good	Premium	Engine Make	No. Cyls.	Displ. Cu.-In.	No. Speeds	P.T.O. H.P.	Approx. Shipping Wt.-Lbs.	Cab
MF-399 4WD w/Cab	56500.00	38880.00	41580.00	43240.00	Perkins	6	365D	12F-4R	95.00	8560	C,H,A
MF-399 Mudder	54470.00	37730.00	40350.00	41960.00	Perkins	6	365D	12F-12R	95.00		No
MF-399 Mudder w/Cab	62155.00	42480.00	45430.00	47250.00	Perkins	6	365D	12F-12R	95.00		C,H,A
MF-399 w/Cab	48305.00	34780.00	37200.00	38690.00	Perkins	6	365D	12F-4R	95.00	8050	C,H,A
MF-1160 4WD	24100.00	18080.00	19280.00	20050.00	Isuzu	4	136D	16F-16R	37.0	4206	No
MF-1180 4WD	26245.00	19680.00	21000.00	21840.00	Isuzu	4	169D	16F-16R	46.0	4773	No
MF-1190 4WD	28050.00	21040.00	22440.00	23340.00	Isuzu	4T	169D	16F-16R	53.0	4795	No
MF-1205 4WD	10200.00	7650.00	8160.00	8490.00	Iseki	3	61D	6F-2R	13.5	1579	No
MF-1205 Hydro 4WD	11400.00	8550.00	9120.00	9490.00	Iseki	3	61D	Variable	13.0	1579	No
MF-1215	10654.00	7990.00	8520.00	8860.00	Iseki	3	61D	6F-2R	15.0	1457	No
MF-1215 4WD	11850.00	8890.00	9480.00	9860.00	Iseki	3	61D	6F-2R	15.0	1589	No
MF-1215 Hydro	11869.00	8900.00	9500.00	9880.00	Iseki	3	61D	Variable	14.0	1457	No
MF-1215 Hydro 4WD	13350.00	10010.00	10680.00	11110.00	Iseki	3	61D	Variable	14.0	1589	No
MF-1220	12175.00	9130.00	9740.00	10130.00	Iseki	3	68D	6F-2R	17.2	1874	No
MF-1220 4WD	13710.00	10280.00	10970.00	11410.00	Iseki	3	68D	6F-2R	17.2	2050	No
MF-1220 Hydro	13575.00	10180.00	10860.00	11290.00	Iseki	3	68D	Variable	16.0	1896	No
MF-1220 Hydro 4WD	15096.00	11320.00	12080.00	12560.00	Iseki	3	68D	Variable	16.0	2072	No
MF-1230	13468.00	10100.00	10770.00	11200.00	Iseki	3	87D	9F-3R	21.0	2227	No
MF-1230 4WD	15076.00	11310.00	12060.00	12540.00	Iseki	3	87D	9F-3R	21.0	2403	No
MF-1230 Hydro	15045.00	11280.00	12040.00	12520.00	Iseki	3	87D	Variable	20.0	2293	No
MF-1230 Hydro 4WD	16652.00	12490.00	13320.00	13850.00	Iseki	3	87D	Variable	20.0	2469	No
MF-1235 Hydro 4WD	17700.00	13280.00	14160.00	14730.00	Iseki	3	91D	Variable	25.1		No
MF-1240	14522.00	10890.00	11620.00	12090.00	Iseki	3	87D	16F-16R	22.5	2859	No
MF-1240 4WD	16250.00	12190.00	13000.00	13520.00	Iseki	3	87D	16F-16R	22.5	2960	No
MF-1250	15660.00	11750.00	12530.00	13030.00	Iseki	3	91D	16F-16R	26.2	2933	No
MF-1250 4WD	17810.00	13360.00	14250.00	14820.00	Iseki	3	91D	16F-16R	26.2	3040	No
MF-1260 4WD	20100.00	15080.00	16080.00	16720.00	Iseki	3	91D	16F-16R	31.0	3128	No
MF-6150	46620.00	33570.00	35900.00	37340.00	Perkins	4T	244D	16F-16R	86.00		C,H,A
MF-6150	49800.00	35860.00	38350.00	39880.00	Perkins	4T	244D	32F-32R	86.00		C,H,A
MF-6150 4WD	54890.00	39520.00	42270.00	43960.00	Perkins	4T	244D	16F-16R	86.00	10224	C,H,A
MF-6150 4WD	58070.00	41810.00	44710.00	46500.00	Perkins	4T	244D	32F-32R	86.00	10224	C,H,A
MF-6170	53190.00	38300.00	40960.00	42600.00	Perkins	6	365D	16F-16R	97.00	10329	C,H,A
MF-6170	56370.00	40590.00	43410.00	45150.00	Perkins	6	365D	32F-32R	97.00	10329	C,H,A
MF-6170 4WD	60420.00	43500.00	46520.00	48380.00	Perkins	6	365D	16F-16R	97.00	10869	C,H,A
MF-6170 4WD	63600.00	45790.00	48970.00	50930.00	Perkins	6	365D	32F-32R	97.00	10869	C,H,A
MF-6180	59000.00	42480.00	45430.00	47250.00	Perkins	6T	365D	16F-16R	110.00	11153	C,H,A
MF-6180	62180.00	44770.00	47880.00	49800.00	Perkins	6T	365D	32F-32R	110.00	11153	C,H,A
MF-6180 4WD	65480.00	47150.00	50420.00	52440.00	Perkins	6T	365D	16F-16R	110.00	11486	C,H,A
MF-6180 4WD	68660.00	49440.00	52870.00	54990.00	Perkins	6T	365D	32F-32R	110.00	11486	C,H,A
MF-8120	70360.00	45730.00	49960.00	51960.00	Perkins	6T	365D	32F-32R	130.00	12621	C,H,A
MF-8120 4WD	81140.00	52000.00	56800.00	59070.00	Perkins	6T	365D	32F-32R	130.00	13153	C,H,A
MF-8140	75520.00	49090.00	53620.00	55770.00	Valmet	6T	403D	32F-32R	145.00	13936	C,H,A
MF-8140 4WD	87800.00	55250.00	60350.00	62760.00	Valmet	6T	403D	32F-32R	145.00	15016	C,H,A
MF-8150	83260.00	54120.00	59120.00	61490.00	Valmet	6T	403D	32F-32R	160.00	14273	C,H,A
MF-8150 4WD	93550.00	59800.00	65320.00	67930.00	Valmet	6T	403D	32F-32R	160.00	15331	C,H,A
MF-8160	95180.00	61870.00	67580.00	70280.00	Valmet	6T	452D	32F-32R	180.00	14273	C,H,A
MF-8160 4WD	107950.00	66300.00	72420.00	75320.00	Valmet	6T	452D	32F-32R	180.00	15331	C,H,A

1998

Model	Approx. Retail Price New	Fair	Good	Premium	Engine Make	No. Cyls.	Displ. Cu.-In.	No. Speeds	P.T.O. H.P.	Approx. Shipping Wt.-Lbs.	Cab
MF-231	12790.00	10490.00	10870.00	11200.00	Perkins	3	152D	8F-2R	34.0	4065	No
MF-240	20410.00	16120.00	17140.00	17650.00	Perkins	3	152D	8F-2R	41.0	4015	No
MF-240 4WD	24830.00	19200.00	20410.00	21020.00	Perkins	3	152D	8F-2R	41.0	4585	No
MF-240S	17240.00	13620.00	14480.00	14910.00	Perkins	3	152D	8F-2R	41.0	4015	No
MF-253	22615.00	17870.00	19000.00	19570.00	Perkins	3T	152D	8F-2R	48.0	4265	No
MF-253 4WD	27860.00	21170.00	22510.00	23190.00	Perkins	3T	152D	8F-2R	48.0	4735	No
MF-261	16345.00	12910.00	13730.00	14140.00	Perkins	4	236D	8F-2R	53.0	5280	No
MF-263	23565.00	18620.00	19800.00	20390.00	Perkins	3T	152D	8F-2R	53.0	5700	No
MF-263 4WD	29185.00	22120.00	23520.00	24230.00	Perkins	3T	152D	8F-2R	53.0	5700	No
MF-271	17160.00	13560.00	14410.00	14840.00	Perkins	4	236D	8F-2R	57.0		No
MF-281	21075.00	16650.00	17700.00	18230.00	Perkins	4	236D	8F-2R	66.0		No
MF-281 4WD	26745.00	20540.00	21840.00	22500.00	Perkins	4	236D	8F-2R	66.0		No
MF-283	20595.00	16270.00	17300.00	17820.00	Perkins	4	248D	8F-2R	67.0	5700	No
MF-283 4WD	26130.00	20640.00	21950.00	22610.00	Perkins	4	248D	8F-2R	67.0		No
MF-354 GE 4WD	29815.00	23550.00	25050.00	25800.00	Perkins	3	152D		42.0		No
MF-354S	23770.00	18780.00	19970.00	20570.00	Perkins	3	152D	12F-4R	42.0		No
MF-354S 4WD	29855.00	23590.00	25080.00	25830.00	Perkins	3	152D	12F-4R	42.0		No
MF-354V	32175.00	25420.00	27030.00	27840.00	Perkins	3	152D		42.0		C,H
MF-354V 4WD	38645.00	30530.00	32460.00	33430.00	Perkins	3	152D		42.0		C,H
MF-362	25610.00	20230.00	21510.00	22160.00	Perkins	4	236D	8F-2R	55.0	5335	No
MF-362 4WD	32490.00	25670.00	27290.00	28110.00	Perkins	4	236D	8F-2R	55.0	5960	No
MF-364 GE 4WD	31260.00	24700.00	26260.00	27050.00	Perkins	3T	152D		50.0		No
MF-364S	24600.00	19430.00	20660.00	21280.00	Perkins	3T	152D		50.0		No
MF-364S 4WD	30995.00	24490.00	26040.00	26820.00	Perkins	3T	152D		50.0		No
MF-364V	34060.00	26910.00	28610.00	29470.00	Perkins	3T	152D		50.0		C,H
MF-364V 4WD	39935.00	31550.00	33550.00	34560.00	Perkins	3T	152D		50.0		C,H
MF-374 GE	25790.00	20370.00	21660.00	22310.00	Perkins	4	236D		57.0		No
MF-374 GE 4WD	32375.00	25580.00	27200.00	28020.00	Perkins	4	236D		57.0		No
MF-374S	24910.00	19680.00	20920.00	21550.00	Perkins	4	236D		57.0		No
MF-374S 4WD	31215.00	24660.00	26220.00	27010.00	Perkins	4	236D		57.0		No
MF-374S 4WD w/Cab	41450.00	32750.00	34820.00	35870.00	Perkins	4	236D		57.0		C,H,A
MF-374S w/Cab	35105.00	27730.00	29490.00	30380.00	Perkins	4	236D		57.0		C,H,A
MF-374V	36225.00	28620.00	30430.00	31340.00	Perkins	4	236D		57.0		C,H,A
MF-374V 4WD	42320.00	33430.00	35550.00	36620.00	Perkins	4	236D		57.0		C,H,A
MF-375	29130.00	22720.00	23890.00	24610.00	Perkins	4	236D		60.0	6240	No

Massey Ferguson (Cont.)

1998 (Cont.)

Model	Approx. Retail Price New	Estimated Average Value Less Repairs: Fair	Good	Premium	Engine: Make	No. Cyls.	Displ. Cu.-In.	No. Speeds	P.T.O. H.P.	Approx. Shipping Wt.-Lbs.	Cab
MF-375 4WD	35040.00	27330.00	28730.00	29590.00	Perkins	4	236D		60.0	6867	No
MF-375 4WD w/Cab	44590.00	34780.00	36560.00	37660.00	Perkins	4	236D		60.0	7517	C,H,A
MF-375 w/Cab	39680.00	30950.00	32540.00	33520.00	Perkins	4	236D		60.0	6910	C,H,A
MF-383	27270.00	21540.00	22910.00	23600.00	Perkins	4	248D	8F-2R	73.0	6311	No
MF-383 4WD	33725.00	26640.00	28330.00	29180.00	Perkins	4	248D	8F-2R	73.0	6950	No
MF-383 4WD w/Cab	42735.00	33760.00	35900.00	36980.00	Perkins	4	248D	8F-2R	73.0	7552	C,H,A
MF-383 w/Cab	36280.00	28660.00	30480.00	31390.00	Perkins	4	248D	8F-2R	73.0	6957	C,H,A
MF-384 GE 4WD	32915.00	26000.00	27650.00	28480.00	Perkins	4	236D	12F-4R	65.0		No
MF-384HC	28275.00	22340.00	23750.00	24460.00	Perkins	4	236D	12F-12R	65.0		No
MF-384HC 4WD	34100.00	26940.00	28640.00	29500.00	Perkins	4	236D	12F-12R	65.0		No
MF-384S	26180.00	20680.00	21990.00	22650.00	Perkins	4	236D	12F-4R	65.0		No
MF-384S 4WD	32145.00	25400.00	27000.00	27810.00	Perkins	4	236D	12F-4R	65.0		No
MF-384S 4WD w/Cab	42305.00	33420.00	35540.00	36610.00	Perkins	4	236D	12F-12R	65.0		C,H,A
MF-384S w/Cab	36250.00	28640.00	30450.00	31360.00	Perkins	4	236D	12F-12R	65.0		C,H,A
MF-384V	37270.00	29440.00	31310.00	32250.00	Perkins	4	236D	12F-12R	65.0		C,H,A
MF-384V 4WD	43810.00	34610.00	36800.00	37900.00	Perkins	4	236D	12F-12R	65.0		C,H,A
MF-390	32390.00	25590.00	27210.00	28030.00	Perkins	4	248D	12F-4R	70.0	6275	No
MF-390 4WD	38665.00	30550.00	32480.00	33450.00	Perkins	4	248D	12F-4R	70.0	6902	No
MF-390 4WD w/Cab	49370.00	39000.00	41470.00	42710.00	Perkins	4	248D	12F-4R	70.0	7552	C,H,A
MF-390 w/Cab	43260.00	34180.00	36340.00	37430.00	Perkins	4	248D	12F-4R	70.0	6945	C,H,A
MF-390T	37150.00	29350.00	31210.00	32150.00	Perkins	4T	236D	12F-12R	80.0	6359	No
MF-390T 4WD	42685.00	33720.00	35860.00	36940.00	Perkins	4T	236D	12F-12R	80.0	6952	No
MF-390T 4WD w/Cab	51535.00	40710.00	43290.00	44590.00	Perkins	4T	236D	12F-12R	80.0	7602	C,H,A
MF-390T w/Cab	44780.00	35380.00	37620.00	38750.00	Perkins	4T	236D	12F-12R	80.0	6995	C,H,A
MF-393	30150.00	23820.00	25330.00	26090.00	Perkins	4T	236D	8F-2R	83.0	6371	No
MF-393 4WD	36535.00	28860.00	30690.00	31610.00	Perkins	4T	236D	8F-2R	83.0	6986	No
MF-393 4WD w/Cab	45455.00	35910.00	38180.00	39330.00	Perkins	4T	236D	8F-2R	83.0	7636	C,H,A
MF-393 w/Cab	38495.00	30410.00	32340.00	33310.00	Perkins	4T	236D	8F-2R	83.0	7021	C,H,A
MF-394 GE 4WD	35155.00	27770.00	29530.00	30420.00	Perkins	4	248D		73.0		No
MF-394HC	29885.00	23610.00	25100.00	25850.00	Perkins	4	248D	12F-12R	73.0		No
MF-394HC 4WD	36490.00	28830.00	30650.00	31570.00	Perkins	4	248D	12F-12R	73.0		No
MF-394S	27905.00	22050.00	23440.00	24140.00	Perkins	4	248D	12F-4R	73.0		No
MF-394S 4WD	33950.00	26820.00	28520.00	29380.00	Perkins	4	248D	12F-4R	73.0		No
MF-394S 4WD w/Cab	43610.00	34450.00	36630.00	37730.00	Perkins	4	248D	12F-12R	73.0		C,H,A
MF-394S w/Cab	37510.00	29630.00	31510.00	32460.00	Perkins	4	248D	12F-12R	73.0		C,H,A
MF-396	34530.00	27280.00	29010.00	29880.00	Perkins	6	365D	8F-2R	88.0	7120	No
MF-396 4WD	41300.00	32630.00	34690.00	35730.00	Perkins	6	365D	8F-2R	88.0	7690	No
MF-396 4WD w/Cab	51445.00	40640.00	43210.00	44510.00	Perkins	6	365D	12F-4R	88.0	8430	C,H,A
MF-396 w/Cab	44085.00	34830.00	37030.00	38140.00	Perkins	6	365D	12F-4R	88.0	7831	C,H,A
MF-399	40885.00	32300.00	34340.00	35370.00	Perkins	6	365D	12F-4R	95.00	7400	No
MF-399 4WD	48150.00	38040.00	40450.00	41660.00	Perkins	6	365D	12F-4R	95.00	7910	No
MF-399 4WD w/Cab	57600.00	45500.00	48380.00	49830.00	Perkins	6	365D	12F-4R	95.00	8560	C,H,A
MF-399 w/Cab	49215.00	38880.00	41340.00	42580.00	Perkins	6	365D	12F-4R	95.00	8050	C,H,A
MF-1160 4WD	25437.00	20100.00	21370.00	22010.00	Isuzu	4	136D	16F-16R	37.0	4206	No
MF-1180 4WD	27597.00	21800.00	23180.00	23880.00	Isuzu	4	169D	16F-16R	46.0	4773	No
MF-1190 4WD	29457.00	23270.00	24740.00	25480.00	Isuzu	4T	169D	16F-16R	53.0	4795	No
MF-1205 4WD	10300.00	8140.00	8650.00	8910.00	Iseki	3	61D	6F-2R	13.5	1579	No
MF-1205 Hydro 4WD	11535.00	9110.00	9690.00	9980.00	Iseki	3	61D	Variable	13.0	1579	No
MF-1215	10595.00	8370.00	8900.00	9170.00	Iseki	3	61D	6F-2R	15.0	1457	No
MF-1215 4WD	11850.00	9360.00	9950.00	10250.00	Iseki	3	61D	6F-2R	15.0	1589	No
MF-1215 Hydro	11869.00	9380.00	9970.00	10270.00	Iseki	3	61D	Variable	14.0	1457	No
MF-1215 Hydro 4WD	13390.00	10580.00	11250.00	11590.00	Iseki	3	61D	Variable	14.0	1589	No
MF-1220	12300.00	9720.00	10330.00	10640.00	Iseki	3	68D	6F-2R	17.2	1874	No
MF-1220 4WD	13900.00	10980.00	11680.00	12030.00	Iseki	3	68D	6F-2R	17.2	2050	No
MF-1220 Hydro	13740.00	10860.00	11540.00	11890.00	Iseki	3	68D	Variable	16.0	1896	No
MF-1220 Hydro 4WD	15325.00	12110.00	12870.00	13260.00	Iseki	3	68D	Variable	16.0	2072	No
MF-1230	13720.00	10840.00	11530.00	11880.00	Iseki	3	87D	9F-3R	21.0	2227	No
MF-1230 4WD	15380.00	12150.00	12920.00	13310.00	Iseki	3	87D	9F-3R	21.0	2403	No
MF-1230 Hydro	15340.00	12120.00	12890.00	13280.00	Iseki	3	87D	Variable	20.0	2293	No
MF-1230 Hydro 4WD	17000.00	13430.00	14280.00	14710.00	Iseki	3	87D	Variable	20.0	2469	No
MF-1235 Hydro 4WD	17770.00	14040.00	14930.00	15380.00	Iseki	3	91D	Variable	25.1		No
MF-1240	14610.00	11540.00	12270.00	12640.00	Iseki	3	87D	16F-16R	22.5	2859	No
MF-1240 4WD	16455.00	13000.00	13820.00	14240.00	Iseki	3	87D	16F-16R	22.5	2960	No
MF-1250	15745.00	12440.00	13230.00	13630.00	Iseki	3	91D	16F-16R	26.2	2933	No
MF-1250 4WD	18045.00	14260.00	15160.00	15620.00	Iseki	3	91D	16F-16R	26.2	3040	No
MF-1260 4WD	20525.00	16220.00	17240.00	17760.00	Iseki	3	91D	16F-16R	31.0	3128	No
MF-4225	27800.00	21960.00	23350.00	24050.00	Perkins	4	248D		55.		No
MF-4225 4WD	34780.00	27480.00	29220.00	30100.00	Perkins	4	248D		55.		No
MF-4225 4WD w/Cab	44215.00	34930.00	37140.00	38250.00	Perkins	4	248D		55.		C,H,A
MF-4225 w/Cab	38800.00	30650.00	32590.00	33570.00	Perkins	4	248D		55.		C,H,A
MF-4235	33650.00	26580.00	28270.00	29120.00	Perkins	4	248D		65.		No
MF-4235 4WD	39390.00	31120.00	33090.00	34080.00	Perkins	4	248D		65.		No
MF-4235 4WD w/Cab	46500.00	36740.00	39060.00	40230.00	Perkins	4	248D		65.		C,H,A
MF-4235 w/Cab	40720.00	32170.00	34210.00	35240.00	Perkins	4	248D		65.		C,H,A
MF-4243	30070.00	23760.00	25260.00	26020.00	Perkins	4T	244D		75		No
MF-4243 4WD	36455.00	28800.00	30620.00	31540.00	Perkins	4T	244D		75		No
MF-4243 4WD w/Cab	46015.00	36350.00	38650.00	39810.00	Perkins	4T	244D		75		C,H,A
MF-4243 w/Cab	39810.00	31450.00	33440.00	34440.00	Perkins	4T	244D		75		C,H,A
MF-4245	37490.00	29620.00	31490.00	32440.00	Perkins	4T	244D		75		No
MF-4245 4WD	43150.00	34090.00	36250.00	37340.00	Perkins	4T	244D		75		No
MF-4245 4WD w/Cab	51270.00	40500.00	43070.00	44360.00	Perkins	4T	244D		75		C,H,A
MF-4245 w/Cab	45670.00	36080.00	38360.00	39510.00	Perkins	4T	244D		75		C,H,A
MF-4253	33480.00	26450.00	28120.00	28960.00	Perkins	4T	244D		85		No
MF-4253 4WD	39525.00	31230.00	33200.00	34200.00	Perkins	4T	244D		85		No

Massey Ferguson (Cont.)

Model	Approx. Retail Price New	Estimated Average Value Less Repairs Fair	Good	Premium	Engine Make	No. Cyls.	Displ. Cu.-In.	No. Speeds	P.T.O. H.P.	Approx. Shipping Wt.-Lbs.	Cab
			1998 (Cont.)								
MF-4253 4WD w/Cab	48660.00	**38440.00**	**40870.00**	**42100.00**	Perkins	4T	244D		85		C,H,A
MF-4253 w/Cab	41920.00	**33120.00**	**35210.00**	**36270.00**	Perkins	4T	244D		85		C,H,A
MF-4255	39345.00	**31080.00**	**33050.00**	**34040.00**	Perkins	4T	244D		85		No
MF-4255 4WD	44990.00	**35540.00**	**37790.00**	**38920.00**	Perkins	4T	244D		85		No
MF-4255 4WD w/Cab	53010.00	**41880.00**	**44530.00**	**45870.00**	Perkins	4T	244D		85		C,H,A
MF-4255 w/Cab	47285.00	**37360.00**	**39720.00**	**40910.00**	Perkins	4T	244D		85		C,H,A
MF-4263	36160.00	**28570.00**	**30370.00**	**31280.00**	Perkins	6	365D		90		No
MF-4263 4WD	43150.00	**34090.00**	**36250.00**	**37340.00**	Perkins	6	365D		90		No
MF-4263 4WD w/Cab	54465.00	**43030.00**	**45750.00**	**47120.00**	Perkins	6	365D		90		C,H,A
MF-4263 w/Cab	46475.00	**36720.00**	**39040.00**	**40210.00**	Perkins	6	365D		90		C,H,A
MF-4270	43010.00	**33980.00**	**36130.00**	**37210.00**	Perkins	6T	365D		99.		No
MF-4270 4WD	50665.00	**40030.00**	**42560.00**	**43840.00**	Perkins	6T	365D		99.		No
MF-4270 4WD w/Cab	59600.00	**47080.00**	**50060.00**	**51560.00**	Perkins	6T	365D		99.		C,H,A
MF-4270 w/Cab	51545.00	**40720.00**	**43300.00**	**44600.00**	Perkins	6T	365D		99.		C,H,A
MF-6150	50235.00	**39180.00**	**41190.00**	**42430.00**	Perkins	4T	244D	16F-16R	86.00		C,H,A
MF-6150 4WD	58135.00	**45350.00**	**47670.00**	**49100.00**	Perkins	4T	244D	16F-16R	86.00	10224	C,H,A
MF-6170	45545.00	**35530.00**	**37350.00**	**38470.00**	Perkins	6	365D		97.00	10329	No
MF-6170 4WD	53155.00	**41460.00**	**43590.00**	**44900.00**	Perkins	6	365D	16F-16R	97.00	10869	No
MF-6170 4WD w/Cab	61355.00	**47860.00**	**50310.00**	**51820.00**	Perkins	6	365D	16F-16R	97.00	10869	C,H,A
MF-6170 w/Cab	53745.00	**41920.00**	**44070.00**	**45390.00**	Perkins	6	365D	16F-16R	97.00	10329	C,H,A
MF-6180	52160.00	**40690.00**	**42770.00**	**44050.00**	Perkins	6T	365D	16F-16R	110.00	11153	No
MF-6180 4WD	58920.00	**45960.00**	**48310.00**	**49760.00**	Perkins	6T	365D	16F-16R	110.00	11486	No
MF-6180 4WD w/Cab	67120.00	**52350.00**	**55040.00**	**56690.00**	Perkins	6T	365D	16F-16R	110.00	11486	C,H,A
MF-6180 w/Cab	60360.00	**47080.00**	**49500.00**	**50990.00**	Perkins	6T	365D	16F-16R	110.00	11153	C,H,A
MF-8120	72115.00	**51920.00**	**55530.00**	**57200.00**	Perkins	6T	365D	32F-32R	130.00	12621	C,H,A
MF-8120 4WD	83225.00	**59180.00**	**63290.00**	**65190.00**	Perkins	6T	365D	32F-32R	130.00	13153	C,H,A
MF-8140	77405.00	**55730.00**	**59600.00**	**61390.00**	Valmet	6T	403D	32F-32R	145.00	13936	C,H,A
MF-8140 4WD	89995.00	**63940.00**	**68380.00**	**70430.00**	Valmet	6T	403D	32F-32R	145.00	15016	C,H,A
MF-8150	83750.00	**60300.00**	**64490.00**	**66430.00**	Valmet	6T	403D	32F-32R	160.00	14273	C,H,A
MF-8150 4WD	95640.00	**67680.00**	**72380.00**	**74550.00**	Valmet	6T	403D	32F-32R	160.00	15331	C,H,A
MF-8160	100350.00	**71280.00**	**76230.00**	**78520.00**	Valmet	6T	452D	32F-32R	180.00	14273	C,H,A
MF-8160 4WD	108615.00	**74160.00**	**79310.00**	**81690.00**	Valmet	6T	452D	32F-32R	180.00	15331	C,H,A
			1999								
MF-231	13045.00	**11350.00**	**11610.00**	**11840.00**	Perkins	3	152D	8F-2R	34.0	4065	No
MF-240	20575.00	**17490.00**	**18310.00**	**18680.00**	Perkins	3	152D	8F-2R	41.0	4015	No
MF-240 4WD	25325.00	**20830.00**	**21810.00**	**22250.00**	Perkins	3	152D	8F-2R	41.0	4585	No
MF-240S	17240.00	**14650.00**	**15340.00**	**15650.00**	Perkins	3	152D	8F-2R	41.0	4015	No
MF-243	21810.00	**18540.00**	**19410.00**	**19800.00**	Perkins	3	152D	8F-2R	47.0	4015	No
MF-243 4WD	26205.00	**21760.00**	**22780.00**	**23240.00**	Perkins	3	152D	8F-2R	47.0	4015	No
MF-253	23560.00	**20030.00**	**20970.00**	**21390.00**	Perkins	3T	152D	8F-2R	48.0	4265	No
MF-253 4WD	28845.00	**23800.00**	**24920.00**	**25420.00**	Perkins	3T	152D	8F-2R	48.0	4735	No
MF-261	16345.00	**13890.00**	**14550.00**	**14840.00**	Perkins	4	236D	8F-2R	53.0	5280	No
MF-263	26765.00	**22750.00**	**23820.00**	**24300.00**	Perkins	3T	152D	8F-2R	53.0	5700	No
MF-263 4WD	31485.00	**25500.00**	**26700.00**	**27230.00**	Perkins	3T	152D	8F-2R	53.0	5700	No
MF-271	17675.00	**15020.00**	**15730.00**	**16050.00**	Perkins	4	236D	8F-2R	57.0		No
MF-281	21075.00	**17910.00**	**18760.00**	**19140.00**	Perkins	4	236D	8F-2R	66.0		No
MF-281 4WD	26745.00	**22100.00**	**23140.00**	**23600.00**	Perkins	4	236D	8F-2R	66.0		No
MF-283	20595.00	**17510.00**	**18330.00**	**18700.00**	Perkins	4	248D	8F-2R	67.0	5700	No
MF-283 4WD	26130.00	**22210.00**	**23260.00**	**23730.00**	Perkins	4	248D	8F-2R	67.0		No
MF-354 GE 4WD	31825.00	**27050.00**	**28320.00**	**28890.00**	Perkins	3	152D	12F-12R	42.0		No
MF-354S	24955.00	**21210.00**	**22210.00**	**22650.00**	Perkins	3	152D	12F-4R	42.0		No
MF-354S 4WD	31125.00	**26460.00**	**27700.00**	**28250.00**	Perkins	3	152D	12F-4R	42.0		No
MF-354V	31785.00	**27020.00**	**28290.00**	**28860.00**	Perkins	3	152D	12F-12R	42.0		C,H
MF-354V 4WD	37780.00	**32110.00**	**33620.00**	**34290.00**	Perkins	3	152D	12F-12R	42.0		C,H
MF-362	26500.00	**22530.00**	**23590.00**	**24060.00**	Perkins	4	236D	8F-2R	55.0	5335	No
MF-362 4WD	33185.00	**28210.00**	**29540.00**	**30130.00**	Perkins	4	236D	8F-2R	55.0	5960	No
MF-374 GE	29450.00	**25030.00**	**26210.00**	**26730.00**	Perkins	4	236D	12F-12R	57.0		No
MF-374 GE 4WD	36135.00	**30720.00**	**32160.00**	**32800.00**	Perkins	4	236D	12F-12R	57.0		No
MF-374S	27915.00	**23730.00**	**24840.00**	**25340.00**	Perkins	4	236D	12F-4R	57.0		No
MF-374S 4WD	34280.00	**29140.00**	**30510.00**	**31120.00**	Perkins	4	236D	12F-4R	57.0		No
MF-374S 4WD w/Cab	44725.00	**38020.00**	**39810.00**	**40610.00**	Perkins	4	236D	12F-4R	57.0		C,H,A
MF-374S w/Cab	38625.00	**32830.00**	**34380.00**	**35070.00**	Perkins	4	236D	12F-4R	57.0		C,H,A
MF-374V	38110.00	**32390.00**	**33920.00**	**34600.00**	Perkins	4	236D	12F-12R	57.0		C,H,A
MF-374V 4WD	44300.00	**37660.00**	**39430.00**	**40220.00**	Perkins	4	236D	12F-12R	57.0		C,H,A
MF-375	29075.00	**24420.00**	**25590.00**	**26100.00**	Perkins	4	236D	12F-4R	60.0	6240	No
MF-375	32630.00	**27410.00**	**28710.00**	**29280.00**	Perkins	4	236D	18F-6R	60.0	6240	No
MF-375 4WD	34865.00	**29290.00**	**30680.00**	**31290.00**	Perkins	4	236D	12F-4R	60.0	6867	No
MF-375 4WD	37900.00	**31840.00**	**33350.00**	**34020.00**	Perkins	4	236D	18F-6R	60.0	6867	No
MF-375 4WD w/Cab	43035.00	**36150.00**	**37870.00**	**38630.00**	Perkins	4	236D	12F-4R	60.0	7517	C,H,A
MF-375 4WD w/Cab	45175.00	**37950.00**	**39750.00**	**40550.00**	Perkins	4	236D	18F-6R	60.0	7517	C,H,A
MF-375 w/Cab	37810.00	**31760.00**	**33270.00**	**33940.00**	Perkins	4	236D	12F-4R	60.0	6910	C,H,A
MF-375 w/Cab	39945.00	**33550.00**	**35150.00**	**35850.00**	Perkins	4	236D	18F-6R	60.0	6910	C,H,A
MF-383	27270.00	**23180.00**	**24270.00**	**24760.00**	Perkins	4	248D	8F-2R	73.0	6311	No
MF-383 4WD	33725.00	**28670.00**	**30020.00**	**30620.00**	Perkins	4	248D	8F-2R	73.0	6950	No
MF-383 4WD w/Cab	42735.00	**36330.00**	**38030.00**	**38790.00**	Perkins	4	248D	8F-2R	73.0	7552	C,H,A
MF-383 w/Cab	36280.00	**30840.00**	**32290.00**	**32940.00**	Perkins	4	248D	8F-2R	73.0	6957	C,H,A
MF-390	32145.00	**27320.00**	**28610.00**	**29180.00**	Perkins	4	248D	12F-4R	70.0	6275	No
MF-390	35705.00	**30350.00**	**31780.00**	**32420.00**	Perkins	4	248D	18F-6R	70.0	6275	No
MF-390 4WD	38400.00	**32640.00**	**34180.00**	**34860.00**	Perkins	4	248D	12F-4R	70.0	6902	No
MF-390 4WD	41440.00	**35220.00**	**36880.00**	**37620.00**	Perkins	4	248D	18F-6R	70.0	6902	No
MF-390 4WD w/Cab	47815.00	**40640.00**	**42560.00**	**43410.00**	Perkins	4	248D	12F-4R	70.0	7552	C,H,A
MF-390 4WD w/Cab	49950.00	**42460.00**	**44460.00**	**45350.00**	Perkins	4	248D	18F-6R	70.0	7552	C,H,A
MF-390 w/Cab	42095.00	**35780.00**	**37470.00**	**38220.00**	Perkins	4	248D	12F-4R	70.0	6945	C,H,A

Model	Approx. Retail Price New	Estimated Average Value Less Repairs Fair	Good	Premium	Engine Make	No. Cyls.	Displ. Cu.-In.	No. Speeds	P.T.O. H.P.	Approx. Shipping Wt.-Lbs.	Cab

Massey Ferguson (Cont.)

1999 (Cont.)

Model	Approx. Retail Price New	Fair	Good	Premium	Make	No. Cyls.	Displ. Cu.-In.	No. Speeds	P.T.O. H.P.	Approx. Shipping Wt.-Lbs.	Cab
MF-390 w/Cab	44230.00	37600.00	39370.00	40160.00	Perkins	4	248D	18F-6R	70.0	6945	C,H,A
MF-390T	34705.00	29500.00	30890.00	31510.00	Perkins	4T	236D	12F-4R	80.0	6359	No
MF-390T	37740.00	32080.00	33590.00	34260.00	Perkins	4T	236D	18F-6R	80.0	6359	No
MF-390T 4WD	39845.00	33870.00	35460.00	36170.00	Perkins	4T	236D	12F-4R	80.0	6952	No
MF-390T 4WD	42880.00	36450.00	38160.00	38920.00	Perkins	4T	236D	16F-4R	80.0	6952	No
MF-390T 4WD w/Cab	49985.00	42490.00	44490.00	45380.00	Perkins	4T	236D	12F-4R	80.0	7602	C,H,A
MF-390T 4WD w/Cab	52105.00	44290.00	46370.00	47300.00	Perkins	4T	236D	18F-6R	80.0	7602	C,H,A
MF-390T w/Cab	43225.00	36740.00	38470.00	39240.00	Perkins	4T	236D	12F-4R	80.0	6995	C,H,A
MF-390T w/Cab	45365.00	38560.00	40380.00	41190.00	Perkins	4T	236D	18F-6R	80.0	6995	C,H,A
MF-393	30150.00	25630.00	26830.00	27370.00	Perkins	4T	236D	8F-2R	83.0	6371	No
MF-393 4WD	36535.00	31060.00	32520.00	33170.00	Perkins	4T	236D	8F-2R	83.0	6986	No
MF-393 4WD w/Cab	45455.00	38640.00	40460.00	41270.00	Perkins	4T	236D	8F-2R	83.0	7636	C,H,A
MF-393 w/Cab	38495.00	32720.00	34260.00	34950.00	Perkins	4T	236D	8F-2R	83.0	7021	C,H,A
MF-394 GE 4WD	38995.00	33150.00	34710.00	35400.00	Perkins	4	248D	12F-12R	72.0		No
MF-394HC	32280.00	27440.00	28730.00	29310.00	Perkins	4	248D	12F-12R	72.0		No
MF-394HC 4WD	39320.00	33420.00	35000.00	35700.00	Perkins	4	248D	12F-12R	73.0		No
MF-394S	30875.00	26240.00	27480.00	28030.00	Perkins	4	248D	12F-4R	73.0		No
MF-394S 4WD	36795.00	31280.00	32750.00	33410.00	Perkins	4	248D	12F-4R	73.0		No
MF-394S 4WD w/Cab	47160.00	40090.00	41970.00	42810.00	Perkins	4	248D	12F-12R	73.0		C,H,A
MF-394S w/Cab	40875.00	34740.00	36380.00	37110.00	Perkins	4	248D	12F-12R	73.0		C,H,A
MF-396	33320.00	28320.00	29660.00	30250.00	Perkins	6	365D	8F-2R	88.0	7120	No
MF-396 4WD	40920.00	34780.00	36420.00	37150.00	Perkins	6	365D	8F-2R	88.0	7690	No
MF-396 4WD w/Cab	51085.00	43420.00	45470.00	46380.00	Perkins	6	365D	12F-4R	88.0	8430	C,H,A
MF-396 w/Cab	42875.00	36440.00	38160.00	38920.00	Perkins	6	365D	12F-4R	88.0	7831	C,H,A
MF-399	38075.00	32360.00	33890.00	34570.00	Perkins	6	365D	12F-4R	95.00	7400	No
MF-399	41110.00	34940.00	36590.00	37320.00	Perkins	6	365D	18F-6R	95.00	7400	No
MF-399 4WD	45115.00	38350.00	40150.00	40950.00	Perkins	6	365D	12F-4R	95.00	7910	No
MF-399 4WD	48140.00	40920.00	42850.00	43710.00	Perkins	6	365D	18F-6R	95.00	7910	No
MF-399 4WD w/Cab	56045.00	47640.00	49880.00	50880.00	Perkins	6	365D	12F-4R	95.00	8560	C,H,A
MF-399 4WD w/Cab	58185.00	49460.00	51790.00	52830.00	Perkins	6	365D	18F-6R	95.00	8560	C,H,A
MF-399 w/Cab	47660.00	40510.00	42420.00	43270.00	Perkins	6	365D	12F-4R	95.00	8050	C,H,A
MF-399 w/Cab	49800.00	42330.00	44320.00	45210.00	Perkins	6	365D	18F-6R	95.00	8050	C,H,A
MF-1160 4WD	25495.00	21670.00	22690.00	23140.00	Isuzu	4	136D	16F-16R	37.0	4206	No
MF-1165 4WD	26160.00	22240.00	23280.00	23750.00	Isuzu	4	134D	16F-16R	37.0	1874	No
MF-1180 4WD	27600.00	23460.00	24560.00	25050.00	Isuzu	4	169D	16F-16R	46.0	4773	No
MF-1190 4WD	29460.00	25040.00	26220.00	26740.00	Isuzu	4T	169D	16F-16R	53.0	4795	No
MF-1205 4WD	10640.00	9040.00	9470.00	9660.00	Iseki	3	61D	6F-2R	13.5	1579	No
MF-1205 Hydro 4WD	11875.00	10090.00	10570.00	10780.00	Iseki	3	61D	Variable	13.0	1579	No
MF-1215	10935.00	9300.00	9730.00	9930.00	Iseki	3	61D	6F-2R	15.0	1457	No
MF-1215 4WD	11845.00	10070.00	10540.00	10750.00	Iseki	3	61D	6F-2R	15.0	1589	No
MF-1215 Hydro	12185.00	10360.00	10850.00	11070.00	Iseki	3	61D	Variable	14.0	1457	No
MF-1215 Hydro 4WD	13390.00	11380.00	11920.00	12160.00	Iseki	3	61D	Variable	14.0	1589	No
MF-1220	13030.00	11080.00	11600.00	11830.00	Iseki	3	68D	6F-2R	17.2	1874	No
MF-1220 4WD	14640.00	12440.00	13030.00	13290.00	Iseki	3	68D	6F-2R	17.2	2050	No
MF-1220 Hydro	14470.00	12300.00	12880.00	13140.00	Iseki	3	68D	Variable	16.0	1896	No
MF-1220 Hydro 4WD	16055.00	13650.00	14290.00	14580.00	Iseki	3	68D	Variable	16.0	2072	No
MF-1225	12435.00	10570.00	11070.00	11290.00	Iseki	3	68D	6F-2R	19.0	1874	No
MF-1225 4WD	13835.00	11760.00	12310.00	12560.00	Iseki	3	68D	6F-2R	19.0	1874	No
MF-1225 Hydro	13825.00	11730.00	12280.00	12530.00	Iseki	3	68D	Variable	19.0	1874	No
MF-1225 Hydro 4WD	15275.00	12980.00	13600.00	13870.00	Iseki	3	68D	Variable	19.0	1874	No
MF-1230	14450.00	12280.00	12860.00	13120.00	Iseki	3	87D	9F-3R	21.0	2227	No
MF-1230 4WD	16110.00	13690.00	14340.00	14630.00	Iseki	3	87D	9F-3R	21.0	2403	No
MF-1230 Hydro	16070.00	13660.00	14300.00	14590.00	Iseki	3	87D	Variable	20.0	2293	No
MF-1230 Hydro 4WD	17730.00	15070.00	15780.00	16100.00	Iseki	3	87D	Variable	20.0	2469	No
MF-1235 Hydro 4WD	18380.00	15620.00	16360.00	16690.00	Iseki	3	91D	Variable	25.1		No
MF-1240	15385.00	13080.00	13690.00	13960.00	Iseki	3	87D	16F-16R	22.5	2859	No
MF-1240 4WD	17230.00	14650.00	15340.00	15650.00	Iseki	3	87D	16F-16R	22.5	2960	No
MF-1250	16520.00	14040.00	14700.00	14990.00	Iseki	3	91D	16F-16R	26.2	2933	No
MF-1250 4WD	18820.00	16000.00	16750.00	17090.00	Iseki	3	91D	16F-16R	26.2	3040	No
MF-1260 4WD	21300.00	18110.00	18960.00	19340.00	Iseki	3	91D	16F-16R	31.0	3128	No
MF-2210 4WD	33800.00	28390.00	29740.00	30340.00	Perkins	3	165D	12F-12R	49.0		No
MF-2210 4WD	38810.00	32600.00	34150.00	34830.00	Perkins	3	165D	12F-12R	49.0		C,H,A
MF-2220 4WD	36235.00	30440.00	31890.00	32530.00	Perkins	3T	165D	12F-12R	58.0		No
MF-2220 4WD	41540.00	34890.00	36560.00	37290.00	Perkins	3T	165D	12F-12R	58.0		C,H,A
MF-4225	27585.00	23450.00	24550.00	25040.00	Perkins	4	248D	8F-2R	55.		No
MF-4225	32600.00	27710.00	29010.00	29590.00	Perkins	4	248D	12F-12R	55.		No
MF-4225 4WD	34670.00	29470.00	30860.00	31480.00	Perkins	4	248D	8F-2R	55.		No
MF-4225 4WD	39680.00	33730.00	35320.00	36030.00	Perkins	4	248D	12F-12R	55.		No
MF-4225 4WD w/Cab	43440.00	36920.00	38660.00	39430.00	Perkins	4	248D	12F-4R	55.		C,H,A
MF-4225 4WD w/Cab	46735.00	39730.00	41590.00	42420.00	Perkins	4	248D	12F-12R	55.		C,H,A
MF-4225 w/Cab	37945.00	32250.00	33770.00	34450.00	Perkins	4	248D	12F-4R	55.		C,H,A
MF-4225 w/Cab	41240.00	35050.00	36700.00	37430.00	Perkins	4	248D	12F-12R	55.		C,H,A
MF-4233	28465.00	24200.00	25330.00	25840.00	Perkins	4	256D	8F-2R	65.0		No
MF-4233	32375.00	27520.00	28810.00	29390.00	Perkins	4	256D	12F-12R	65.0		No
MF-4233 4WD	34505.00	29330.00	30710.00	31320.00	Perkins	4	256D	8F-2R	65.0		No
MF-4233 4WD	38415.00	32650.00	34190.00	34870.00	Perkins	4	256D	12F-12R	65.0		No
MF-4233 4WD w/Cab	44350.00	37700.00	39470.00	40260.00	Perkins	4	256D	12F-4R	65.0		C,H,A
MF-4233 4WD w/Cab	46645.00	39650.00	41510.00	42340.00	Perkins	4	256D	12F-12R	65.0		C,H,A
MF-4233 w/Cab	38230.00	32500.00	34030.00	34710.00	Perkins	4	256D	12F-4R	65.0		C,H,A
MF-4233 w/Cab	40525.00	34450.00	36070.00	36790.00	Perkins	4	256D	12F-12R	65.0		C,H,A
MF-4235	36420.00	30960.00	32410.00	33060.00	Perkins	4	248D	12F-12R	65.		No
MF-4235 4WD	41470.00	35250.00	36910.00	37650.00	Perkins	4	248D	12F-12R	65.		No
MF-4235 4WD w/Cab	48705.00	41400.00	43350.00	44220.00	Perkins	4	248D	12F-12R	65.		C,H,A
MF-4235 w/Cab	43615.00	37070.00	38820.00	39600.00	Perkins	4	248D	12F-12R	65.		C,H,A

Massey Ferguson (Cont.)

Model	Approx. Retail Price New	Estimated Average Value Less Repairs Fair	Good	Premium	Make	Engine No. Cyls.	Displ. Cu.-In.	No. Speeds	P.T.O. H.P.	Approx. Shipping Wt.-Lbs.	Cab
1999 (Cont.)											
MF-4243	30350.00	**25800.00**	**27010.00**	**27550.00**	Perkins	4T	244D	8F-2R	75		No
MF-4243	34260.00	**29120.00**	**30490.00**	**31100.00**	Perkins	4T	244D	12F-12R	75		No
MF-4243 4WD	37245.00	**31660.00**	**33150.00**	**33810.00**	Perkins	4T	244D	8F-2R	75		No
MF-4243 4WD	41155.00	**34980.00**	**36630.00**	**37360.00**	Perkins	4T	244D	12F-12R	75		No
MF-4243 4WD w/Cab	47500.00	**40380.00**	**42280.00**	**43130.00**	Perkins	4T	244D	12F-4R	75		C,H,A
MF-4243 4WD w/Cab	49795.00	**42330.00**	**44320.00**	**45210.00**	Perkins	4T	244D	12F-12R	75		C,H,A
MF-4243 w/Cab	40175.00	**34150.00**	**35760.00**	**36480.00**	Perkins	4T	244D	12F-4R	75		C,H,A
MF-4243 w/Cab	42470.00	**36100.00**	**37800.00**	**38560.00**	Perkins	4T	244D	12F-12R	75		C,H,A
MF-4245	39900.00	**33920.00**	**35510.00**	**36220.00**	Perkins	4T	244D	12F-12R	75		No
MF-4245 4WD	45325.00	**38530.00**	**40340.00**	**41150.00**	Perkins	4T	244D	12F-12R	75		No
MF-4245 4WD w/Cab	53430.00	**45420.00**	**47550.00**	**48500.00**	Perkins	4T	244D	12F-12R	75		C,H,A
MF-4245 w/Cab	47615.00	**40470.00**	**42380.00**	**43230.00**	Perkins	4T	244D	12F-12R	75		C,H,A
MF-4253	33200.00	**28220.00**	**29550.00**	**30140.00**	Perkins	4T	244D	8F-2R	85		No
MF-4253	37110.00	**31540.00**	**33030.00**	**33690.00**	Perkins	4T	244D	12F-12R	85		No
MF-4253 4WD	40010.00	**34010.00**	**35610.00**	**36320.00**	Perkins	4T	244D	8F-2R	85		No
MF-4253 4WD	43920.00	**37330.00**	**39090.00**	**39870.00**	Perkins	4T	244D	12F-12R	85		No
MF-4253 4WD w/Cab	50215.00	**42680.00**	**44690.00**	**45580.00**	Perkins	4T	244D	12F-12R	85		C,H,A
MF-4253 4WD w/Cab	52500.00	**44630.00**	**46730.00**	**47670.00**	Perkins	4T	244D	12F-12R	85		C,H,A
MF-4253 w/Cab	42435.00	**36070.00**	**37770.00**	**38530.00**	Perkins	4T	244D	12F-12R	85		C,H,A
MF-4253 w/Cab	44725.00	**38020.00**	**39810.00**	**40610.00**	Perkins	4T	244D	12F-12R	85		C,H,A
MF-4255	41795.00	**35530.00**	**37200.00**	**37940.00**	Perkins	4T	244D	12F-12R	85		No
MF-4255 4WD	47900.00	**40720.00**	**42630.00**	**43480.00**	Perkins	4T	244D	12F-12R	85		No
MF-4255 4WD w/Cab	56410.00	**47950.00**	**50210.00**	**51210.00**	Perkins	4T	244D	12F-12R	85		C,H,A
MF-4255 w/Cab	49075.00	**41710.00**	**43680.00**	**44550.00**	Perkins	4T	244D	12F-12R	85		C,H,A
MF-4263	37440.00	**31820.00**	**33320.00**	**33990.00**	Perkins	6	365D	8F-2R	90		No
MF-4263	41350.00	**35150.00**	**36800.00**	**37540.00**	Perkins	6	365D	12F-12R	90		No
MF-4263 4WD	43325.00	**36830.00**	**38560.00**	**39330.00**	Perkins	6	365D	8F-2R	90		No
MF-4263 4WD	47235.00	**40150.00**	**42040.00**	**42880.00**	Perkins	6	365D	12F-12R	90		No
MF-4263 4WD w/Cab	55500.00	**47180.00**	**49400.00**	**50390.00**	Perkins	6	365D	12F-4R	90		C,H,A
MF-4263 4WD w/Cab	57790.00	**49120.00**	**51430.00**	**52460.00**	Perkins	6	365D	12F-12R	90		C,H,A
MF-4263 w/Cab	47305.00	**40210.00**	**42100.00**	**42940.00**	Perkins	6	365D	12F-4R	90		C,H,A
MF-4263 w/Cab	49600.00	**42160.00**	**44140.00**	**45020.00**	Perkins	6	365D	12F-12R	90		C,H,A
MF-4270	45055.00	**38300.00**	**40100.00**	**40900.00**	Perkins	6T	365D	12F-12R	99.		No
MF-4270 4WD	52780.00	**44860.00**	**46970.00**	**47910.00**	Perkins	6T	365D	12F-12R	99.		No
MF-4270 4WD w/Cab	61935.00	**52650.00**	**55120.00**	**56220.00**	Perkins	6T	365D	12F-12R	99.		C,H,A
MF-4270 w/Cab	53255.00	**45270.00**	**47400.00**	**48350.00**	Perkins	6T	365D	12F-12R	99.		C,H,A
MF-6150	51210.00	**43020.00**	**45070.00**	**45970.00**	Perkins	4T	244D	16F-16R	86.00		C,H,A
MF-6150 4WD	58910.00	**49480.00**	**51840.00**	**52880.00**	Perkins	4T	244D	16F-16R	86.00	10224	C,H,A
MF-6170	46520.00	**39080.00**	**40940.00**	**41760.00**	Perkins	6	365D	16F-16R	97.00	10329	No
MF-6170 4WD	53960.00	**45330.00**	**47490.00**	**48440.00**	Perkins	6	365D	16F-16R	97.00	10869	No
MF-6170 4WD w/Cab	62160.00	**52210.00**	**54700.00**	**55790.00**	Perkins	6	365D	16F-16R	97.00	10869	C,H,A
MF-6170 w/Cab	54720.00	**45970.00**	**48150.00**	**49110.00**	Perkins	6	365D	16F-16R	97.00	10329	C,H,A
MF-6180	52510.00	**44110.00**	**46210.00**	**47130.00**	Perkins	6T	365D	16F-16R	110.00		No
MF-6180 4WD	59180.00	**49710.00**	**52080.00**	**53120.00**	Perkins	6T	365D	16F-16R	110.00		No
MF-6180 4WD w/Cab	67380.00	**56600.00**	**59290.00**	**60480.00**	Perkins	6T	365D	16F-16R	110.00		C,H,A
MF-6180 w/Cab	60710.00	**51000.00**	**53430.00**	**54500.00**	Perkins	6T	365D	16F-16R	110.00		C,H,A
MF-6245 4WD	62160.00	**52210.00**	**54700.00**	**55790.00**	Perkins	4T	244D	32F-32R	75.00		C,H,A
MF-6255	55605.00	**46710.00**	**48930.00**	**49910.00**	Perkins	4T	244D	32F-32R	85.00		C,H,A
MF-6255 4WD	63135.00	**53030.00**	**55560.00**	**56670.00**	Perkins	4T	244D	32F-32R	85.00		C,H,A
MF-6265	57905.00	**48640.00**	**50960.00**	**51980.00**	Perkins	4T	244D	32F-32R	95.00		C,H,A
MF-6265 4WD	66105.00	**55530.00**	**58170.00**	**59330.00**	Perkins	4T	244D	32F-32R	85.00		C,H,A
MF-6270	52225.00	**43870.00**	**45960.00**	**46880.00**	Perkins	6T	365D	32F-32R	100.00		No
MF-6270	60765.00	**51040.00**	**53470.00**	**54540.00**	Perkins	6T	365D	32F-32R	100.00		C,H,A
MF-6270 4WD	60145.00	**50520.00**	**52930.00**	**53990.00**	Perkins	6T	365D	32F-32R	100.00		No
MF-6270 4WD	68685.00	**57700.00**	**60440.00**	**61650.00**	Perkins	6T	365D	32F-32R	100.00		C,H,A
MF-6280	55405.00	**46540.00**	**48760.00**	**49740.00**	Perkins	6T	365D	32F-32R	110.00		No
MF-6280	64135.00	**53870.00**	**56440.00**	**57570.00**	Perkins	6T	365D	32F-32R	110.00		C,H,A
MF-6280 4WD	62580.00	**52570.00**	**55070.00**	**56170.00**	Perkins	6T	365D	32F-32R	110.00		No
MF-6280 4WD	71315.00	**59910.00**	**62760.00**	**64020.00**	Perkins	6T	365D	32F-32R	110.00		C,H,A
MF-6290	59400.00	**49900.00**	**52270.00**	**53320.00**	Perkins	6T	365D	32F-32R	120.00		No
MF-6290	75540.00	**63450.00**	**66480.00**	**67810.00**	Perkins	6T	365D	32F-32R	120.00		C,H,A
MF-6290 4WD	66905.00	**56200.00**	**58880.00**	**60060.00**	Perkins	6T	365D	32F-32R	120.00		No
MF-6290 4WD	76250.00	**64050.00**	**67100.00**	**68440.00**	Perkins	6T	365D	32F-32R	120.00		C,H,A
MF-8120	78140.00	**64080.00**	**67200.00**	**68540.00**	Perkins	6T	365D	32F-32R	130.00	12621	C,H,A
MF-8120 4WD	89320.00	**73240.00**	**76820.00**	**78360.00**	Perkins	6T	365D	32F-32R	130.00	13153	C,H,A
MF-8140	83430.00	**68410.00**	**71750.00**	**73190.00**	Valmet	6T	403D	32F-32R	145.00	13936	C,H,A
MF-8140 4WD	96090.00	**78790.00**	**82640.00**	**84290.00**	Valmet	6T	403D	32F-32R	145.00	15016	C,H,A
MF-8150	88570.00	**72630.00**	**76170.00**	**77690.00**	Valmet	6T	403D	32F-32R	160.00	14273	C,H,A
MF-8150 4WD	101400.00	**81510.00**	**85480.00**	**87190.00**	Valmet	6T	403D	32F-32R	160.00	15331	C,H,A
MF-8160	98080.00	**79540.00**	**83420.00**	**85090.00**	Valmet	6T	452D	32F-32R	180.00	14273	C,H,A
MF-8160 4WD	111220.00	**86260.00**	**90470.00**	**92280.00**	Valmet	6T	452D	32F-32R	180.00	15331	C,H,A
MF-8220	77810.00	**63800.00**	**66920.00**	**68260.00**	Perkins	6TA	365D	32F-32R	135.00	12621	C,H,A
MF-8220 4WD	88960.00	**72950.00**	**76510.00**	**78040.00**	Perkins	6TA	365D	32F-32R	135.00	12621	C,H,A
MF-8240	86000.00	**70520.00**	**73960.00**	**75440.00**	Perkins	6TA	402D	32F-32R	145.00	12621	C,H,A
MF-8240 4WD	98390.00	**80680.00**	**84620.00**	**86310.00**	Perkins	6TA	402D	32F-32R	145.00	12621	C,H,A
MF-8245 4WD	102900.00	**82820.00**	**86860.00**	**88600.00**	Perkins	6TA	451D	18F-6R	160.00	12621	C,H,A
MF-8250 4WD	101905.00	**82000.00**	**86000.00**	**87720.00**	Perkins	6TA	451D	32F-32R	165.00	12621	C,H,A
MF-8260 4WD	111190.00	**86920.00**	**91160.00**	**92980.00**	Perkins	6TA	451D	18F-6R	180.00	12621	C,H,A
MF-8270 4WD	119490.00	**93480.00**	**98040.00**	**100000.00**	Perkins	6TA	513D	18F-6R	200.00	12621	C,H,A
MF-8280 4WD	130490.00	**102500.00**	**107500.00**	**109650.00**	Perkins	6TA	513D	18F-6R	225.00	12621	C,H,A

Massey Harris

Model	Approx. Retail Price New	Estimated Average Value Less Repairs Fair	Good	Premium	Engine Make	No. Cyls.	Displ. Cu.-In.	No. Speeds	P.T.O. H.P.	Approx. Shipping Wt.-Lbs.	Cab
			1939								
MH-101 Jr	......	740.00	1740.00	2210.00	Continental	4	139G	4F-1R		2958	No
MH-101 Sr	......	770.00	1820.00	2310.00	Continental	6	226G	4F-1R	33	5725	No
			1940								
MH-101 Jr	......	740.00	1740.00	2210.00	Continental	4	139G	4F-1R		2958	No
MH-101 Sr	......	770.00	1820.00	2310.00	Continental	6	226G	4F-1R	33	5725	No
MH-203	......	680.00	1600.00	2030.00	Continental	6	217G	4F-1R	36.6		No
			1941								
MH-81	......	800.00	1890.00	2400.00	Continental	4	123G	4F-1R	21.6	2560	No
MH-82	......	810.00	1910.00	2430.00	Continental	4	123G	4F-1R	20.7	2560	No
MH-101 Jr	......	760.00	1790.00	2270.00	Continental	4	139G	4F-1R		2958	No
MH-101 Sr	......	780.00	1860.00	2360.00	Continental	6	226G	4F-1R	33	5725	No
MH-102 Sr	......	920.00	2180.00	2770.00	Continental	4	226G	4F-1R	47.9	2958	No
MH-202	......	620.00	1470.00	1870.00	Continental	6	217G	4F-1R	36.6	6600	No
MH-203	......	700.00	1650.00	2100.00	Continental	6	217G	4F-1R	36.6		No
			1942								
MH-81	......	830.00	1960.00	2490.00	Continental	4	123G	4F-1R	21.6	2560	No
MH-82	......	840.00	2000.00	2540.00	Continental	4	123G	4F-1R	20.7	2560	No
MH-101 Jr	......	780.00	1840.00	2340.00	Continental	4	139G	4F-1R		2958	No
MH-101 Sr	......	800.00	1910.00	2430.00	Continental	6	226G	4F-1R	33	5725	No
MH-102 Sr	......	860.00	2030.00	2580.00	Continental	4	226G	4F-1R	47.9	2958	No
MH-202	......	640.00	1510.00	1920.00	Continental	6	217G	4F-1R	36.6	6600	No
MH-203	......	720.00	1700.00	2160.00	Continental	6	217G	4F-1R	36.6		No
			1943								
MH-81	......	860.00	2040.00	2570.00	Continental	4	123G	4F-1R	21.6	2560	No
MH-82	......	870.00	2070.00	2610.00	Continental	4	123G	4F-1R	20.7	2560	No
MH-101 Jr	......	800.00	1890.00	2380.00	Continental	4	139G	4F-1R		2958	No
MH-101 Sr	......	830.00	1960.00	2470.00	Continental	6	226G	4F-1R	33	5725	No
MH-102 Sr	......	880.00	2080.00	2620.00	Continental	4	226G	4F-1R	47.9	2958	No
MH-202	......	650.00	1550.00	1950.00	Continental	6	217G	4F-1R	36.6	6600	No
MH-203	......	740.00	1740.00	2190.00	Continental	6	217G	4F-1R	36.6		No
			1944								
MH-81	......	880.00	2080.00	2600.00	Continental	4	123G	4F-1R	21.6	2560	No
MH-82	......	890.00	2110.00	2640.00	Continental	4	123G	4F-1R	20.7	2560	No
MH-101 Jr	......	820.00	1940.00	2430.00	Continental	4	139G	4F-1R		2958	No
MH-101 Sr	......	850.00	2010.00	2510.00	Continental	6	226G	4F-1R	33	5725	No
MH-102 Sr	......	900.00	2130.00	2660.00	Continental	4	226G	4F-1R	47.9	2958	No
MH-202	......	670.00	1600.00	2000.00	Continental	6	217G	4F-1R	36.6	6600	No
MH-203	......	760.00	1790.00	2240.00	Continental	6	217G	4F-1R	36.6		No
			1945								
MH-81	......	900.00	2130.00	2640.00	Continental	4	123G	4F-1R	21.6	2560	No
MH-82	......	910.00	2170.00	2690.00	Continental	4	123G	4F-1R	20.7	2560	No
MH-101 Jr	......	840.00	1980.00	2460.00	Continental	4	139G	4F-1R		2958	No
MH-101 Sr	......	860.00	2050.00	2540.00	Continental	6	226G	4F-1R	33	5725	No
MH-102 Jr	......	860.00	2030.00	2520.00	Continental	4	162G	4F-1R		5862	No
MH-102 Sr	......	890.00	2110.00	2620.00	Continental	4	226G	4F-1R	47.9	2958	No
MH-203	......	780.00	1840.00	2280.00	Continental	6	217G	4F-1R	36.6		No
			1946								
MH-20	......	750.00	1770.00	2180.00	Continental	4	124G	4F-1R	27	2560	No
MH-30	......	810.00	1910.00	2350.00	Continental	4	134G	5F-2R	33	3475	No
MH-44	......	820.00	1940.00	2390.00	MH	4	260G	5F-1R	41.3	3855	No
MH-44D	......	880.00	2090.00	2570.00	MH	4	260D	5F-1R	39.4	3995	No
MH-55	......	840.00	1980.00	2440.00	MH	4	382G	4F-1R	55.72	6725	No
MH-55D	......	890.00	2110.00	2600.00	MH	4	382D	4F-1R	60.4	7057	No
MH-81	......	910.00	2160.00	2660.00	Continental	4	123G	4F-1R	21.6	2560	No
MH-82	......	930.00	2200.00	2710.00	Continental	4	123G	4F-1R	20.7	2560	No
MH-101 Jr	......	860.00	2030.00	2500.00	Continental	4	162G	4F-1R		2958	No
MH-101 Sr	......	880.00	2090.00	2570.00	Continental	6	226G	4F-1R	33	5725	No
MH-102 Jr	......	910.00	2140.00	2630.00	Continental	4	162G	4F-1R		5862	No
MH-203	......	800.00	1890.00	2330.00	Continental	6	217G	4F-1R	36.6		No
			1947								
MH-11 Pony	......	680.00	1620.00	1980.00	Continental	4	62G	3F-1R	11.1	1550	No
MH-20	......	770.00	1830.00	2230.00	Continental	4	124G	4F-1R	27	2560	No
MH-30	......	820.00	1930.00	2360.00	Continental	4	134G	5F-2R	33	3475	No
MH-44	......	840.00	1990.00	2430.00	MH	4	260G	5F-1R	41.3	3855	No
MH-44-6	......	950.00	2260.00	2760.00	Continental	6	226G	5F-1R	47	4120	No
MH-44D	......	900.00	2130.00	2600.00	MH	4	260D	5F-1R	39.4	3995	No
MH-55	......	850.00	2020.00	2460.00	MH	4	382G	4F-1R	55.72	6725	No
MH-55D	......	910.00	2160.00	2640.00	MH	4	382D	4F-1R	60.4	7057	No
MH-81	......	930.00	2210.00	2700.00	Continental	4	123G	4F-1R	21.6	2560	No
MH-203	......	820.00	1930.00	2360.00	Continental	6	217G	4F-1R	47.9	8750	No

Massey Harris (Cont.)

Model	Approx. Retail Price New	Estimated Average Value Less Repairs Fair	Good	Premium	Engine Make	No. Cyls.	Displ. Cu.-In.	No. Speeds	P.T.O. H.P.	Approx. Shipping Wt.-Lbs.	Cab
1948											
MH-11 Pony	......	730.00	1660.00	2030.00	Continental	4	62G	3F-1R	11.1	1550	No
MH-20	......	830.00	1890.00	2310.00	Continental	4	124G	4F-1R	27	2560	No
MH-22	......	890.00	2040.00	2490.00	Continental	4	139G	4F-1R	17.95	2815	No
MH-30	......	860.00	1960.00	2390.00	Continental	4	134G	5F-2R	33	3475	No
MH-44	......	890.00	2020.00	2460.00	MH	4	260G	5F-1R	41.3	3855	No
MH-44-6	......	1010.00	2300.00	2810.00	Continental	6	226G	5F-1R	47	4120	No
MH-44D	......	960.00	2180.00	2660.00	MH	4	260D	5F-1R	39.4	3995	No
MH-55	......	900.00	2060.00	2510.00	MH	4	382G	4F-1R	55.72	6725	No
MH-55D	......	970.00	2210.00	2700.00	MH	4	382D	4F-1R	60.4	7057	No
MH-81	......	990.00	2260.00	2760.00	Continental	4	123G	4F-1R	21.6	2560	No
1949											
MH-11 Pony	......	780.00	1720.00	2100.00	Continental	4	62G	3F-1R	11.1	1550	No
MH-22	......	940.00	2080.00	2540.00	Continental	4	139G	4F-1R	17.95	2815	No
MH-30	......	910.00	2000.00	2440.00	Continental	4	134G	5F-2R	33	3475	No
MH-44	......	930.00	2060.00	2510.00	MH	4	260G	5F-1R	41.3	3855	No
MH-44-6	......	1070.00	2360.00	2880.00	Continental	6	226G	5F-1R	47	4120	No
MH-44D	......	1010.00	2240.00	2730.00	MH	4	260D	5F-1R	39.4	3995	No
MH-55	......	960.00	2110.00	2570.00	MH	4	382G	4F-1R	55.72	6725	No
MH-55D	......	1020.00	2250.00	2750.00	MH	4	382D	4F-1R	60	7150	No
1950											
MH-11 Pony	......	830.00	1780.00	2170.00	Continental	4	62G	3F-1R	11.1	1550	No
MH-22	......	1000.00	2130.00	2600.00	Continental	4	139G	4F-1R	17.95	2815	No
MH-30	......	960.00	2050.00	2500.00	Continental	4	134G	5F-2R	33	3475	No
MH-44	......	990.00	2110.00	2570.00	MH	4	260G	5F-1R	41.3	3855	No
MH-44-6	......	1120.00	2390.00	2920.00	Continental	6	226G	5F-1R	47	4120	No
MH-44D	......	1070.00	2290.00	2790.00	MH	4	260D	5F-1R	39.4	3995	No
MH-55	......	1020.00	2180.00	2660.00	MH	4	382G	4F-1R	55.72	6725	No
MH-55D	......	1080.00	2310.00	2820.00	MH	4	382D	4F-1R	60	7150	No
1951											
MH-11 Pony	......	890.00	1830.00	2230.00	Continental	4	62G	3F-1R	11.1	1550	No
MH-22	......	1060.00	2190.00	2670.00	Continental	4	139G	4F-1R	17.95	2815	No
MH-30	......	1020.00	2110.00	2570.00	Continental	4	134G	5F-2R	33	3475	No
MH-44	......	1040.00	2150.00	2620.00	MH	4	260G	5F-1R	41.3	3855	No
MH-44D	......	1130.00	2330.00	2840.00	MH	4	260D	5F-1R	39.4	3995	No
MH-55	......	1070.00	2210.00	2700.00	MH	4	382G	4F-1R	55.72	6725	No
MH-55D	......	1150.00	2370.00	2890.00	MH	4	382D	4F-1R	60	7150	No
1952											
MH-11 Pony	......	950.00	1900.00	2320.00	Continental	4	62G	3F-1R	11.1	1550	No
MH-21 Colt	......	1070.00	2140.00	2610.00	Continental	4	124G	4F-1R	25	2550	No
MH-22	......	1120.00	2240.00	2730.00	Continental	4	139G	4F-1R	17.95	2815	No
MH-23 Mustang	......	1140.00	2290.00	2790.00	Continental	4	150G	4F-1R	24	2830	No
MH-30	......	1090.00	2180.00	2660.00	Continental	4	134G	5F-2R	33	3475	No
MH-33	......	1120.00	2230.00	2720.00	MH	4	201G	5F-1R	36.23	5191	No
MH-33D	......	1170.00	2340.00	2860.00	MH	4	201D	5F-1R	46	4190	No
MH-44	......	1100.00	2200.00	2680.00	MH	4	260G	5F-1R	41.3	3855	No
MH-44D	......	1190.00	2380.00	2900.00	MH	4	260D	5F-1R	39.4	3995	No
MH-55	......	1130.00	2250.00	2750.00	MH	4	382G	4F-1R	55.72	6725	No
MH-55D	......	1210.00	2410.00	2940.00	MH	4	382D	4F-1R	60	7150	No
1953											
MH-11 Pony	......	1010.00	1950.00	2380.00	Continental	4	62G	3F-1R	11.1	1550	No
MH-21 Colt	......	1130.00	2190.00	2670.00	Continental	4	124G	4F-1R	25	2550	No
MH-22	......	1180.00	2290.00	2790.00	Continental	4	139G	4F-1R	17.95	2815	No
MH-23 Mustang	......	1210.00	2340.00	2860.00	Continental	4	150G	4F-1R	24	2830	No
MH-30	......	1170.00	2270.00	2770.00	Continental	4	134G	5F-2R	33	3475	No
MH-33	......	1190.00	2300.00	2810.00	MH	4	201G	5F-1R	36.23	5191	No
MH-33D	......	1240.00	2400.00	2930.00	MH	4	201D	5F-1R	46	4190	No
MH-44	......	1160.00	2240.00	2730.00	MH	4	260G	5F-1R	41.3	3855	No
MH-44D	......	1250.00	2430.00	2970.00	MH	4	260D	5F-1R	39.4	3995	No
MH-55	......	1190.00	2300.00	2810.00	MH	4	382G	4F-1R	55.72	6725	No
MH-55D	......	1270.00	2470.00	3010.00	MH	4	382D	4F-1R	60	7150	No
1954											
MH-11 Pony	......	1050.00	1980.00	2420.00	Continental	4	62G	3F-1R	11.1	1550	No
MH-16 Pacer	......	1140.00	2140.00	2610.00	Continental		91G	3F-1R	91	1950	No
MH-21 Colt	......	1210.00	2280.00	2780.00	Continental	4	124G	4F-1R	25	2550	No
MH-22	......	1240.00	2330.00	2840.00	Continental	4	139G	4F-1R	17.95	2815	No
MH-23 Mustang	......	1270.00	2390.00	2920.00	Continental	4	150G	4F-1R	24	2830	No
MH-33	......	1260.00	2370.00	2890.00	MH	4	201G	5F-1R	36.23	5191	No
MH-33D	......	1300.00	2450.00	2990.00	MH	4	201D	5F-1R	46	4190	No
MH-44	......	1220.00	2300.00	2810.00	MH	4	260G	5F-1R	41.3	3855	No
MH-44D	......	1320.00	2490.00	3040.00	MH	4	260D	5F-1R	39.4	3995	No
MH-55	......	1250.00	2350.00	2870.00	MH	4	382G	4F-1R	55.72	6725	No
MH-55D	......	1350.00	2530.00	3090.00	MH	4	382D	4F-1R	60	7150	No
1955											
MH-11 Pony	......	1150.00	2100.00	2560.00	Continental	4	62G	3F-1R	11.1	1550	No
MH-16 Pacer	......	1210.00	2210.00	2700.00	Continental	4	91G	3F-1R	91	1950	No
MH-21 Colt	......	1270.00	2330.00	2840.00	Continental	4	124G	4F-1R	25	2550	No
MH-22	......	1300.00	2370.00	2890.00	Continental	4	139G	4F-1R	17.95	2815	No

Massey Harris (Cont.)

1955 (Cont.)

Model	Approx. Retail Price New	Fair	Good	Premium	Engine Make	Engine No. Cyls.	Engine Displ. Cu.-In.	No. Speeds	P.T.O. H.P.	Approx. Shipping Wt.-Lbs.	Cab
MH-23 Mustang	......	1330.00	2430.00	2970.00	Continental	4	150G	4F-1R	24	2830	No
MH-33	......	1330.00	2420.00	2950.00	MH	4	201G	5F-1R	36.23	5191	No
MH-33D	......	1350.00	2470.00	3010.00	MH	4	201D	5F-1R	46	4190	No
MH-44	......	1280.00	2340.00	2860.00	MH	4	260G	5F-1R	41.3	3855	No
MH-44D	......	1390.00	2530.00	3090.00	MH	4	260D	5F-1R	39.4	3995	No
MH-50	......	1370.00	2500.00	3050.00	Continental	4	134G	6F-2R	31.36	3100	No
MH-55	......	1330.00	2430.00	2970.00	MH	4	382G	4F-1R	55.72	6725	No
MH-55D	......	1430.00	2610.00	3180.00	MH	4	382D	4F-1R	60	7150	No
MH-555	......	1520.00	2780.00	3390.00	MH	4	382G	4F-1R	71	7435	No
MH-555	......	1620.00	2970.00	3620.00	MH	4	382D	4F-1R	72	7525	No

1956

Model	Approx. Retail Price New	Fair	Good	Premium	Engine Make	Engine No. Cyls.	Engine Displ. Cu.-In.	No. Speeds	P.T.O. H.P.	Approx. Shipping Wt.-Lbs.	Cab
MH-11 Pony	......	1190.00	2170.00	2650.00	Continental	4	62G	3F-1R	11.1	1550	No
MH-16 Pacer	......	1240.00	2280.00	2780.00	Continental	4	91G	3F-1R	91	1950	No
MH-21 Colt	......	1310.00	2390.00	2920.00	Continental	4	124G	4F-1R	25	2550	No
MH-23 Mustang	......	1360.00	2490.00	3040.00	Continental	4	150G	4F-1R	24	2830	No
MH-50	......	1420.00	2590.00	3160.00	Continental	4	134G	6F-2R	31.36	3100	No
MH-333	......	1130.00	2070.00	2530.00	MH	4	208G	10F-1R	37.15	4590	No
MH-333	......	1260.00	2300.00	2810.00	MH	4	208D	10F-1R	39	6005	No
MH-444	......	1400.00	2560.00	3120.00	MH	4	277G	10F-1R	52	5780	No
MH-444	......	1540.00	2820.00	3440.00	MH	4	277D	10F-1R	48.21	6499	No
MH-555	......	1490.00	2720.00	3320.00	MH	4	382G	4F-1R	71	7435	No
MH-555	......	1620.00	2960.00	3610.00	MH	4	382D	4F-1R	72	7525	No

1957

Model	Approx. Retail Price New	Fair	Good	Premium	Engine Make	Engine No. Cyls.	Engine Displ. Cu.-In.	No. Speeds	P.T.O. H.P.	Approx. Shipping Wt.-Lbs.	Cab
MH-11 Pony	......	1260.00	2300.00	2810.00	Continental	4	62G	3F-1R	11.1	1550	No
MH-16 Pacer	......	1290.00	2360.00	2880.00	Continental	4	91G	3F-1R	91	1950	No
MH-21 Colt	......	1350.00	2470.00	3010.00	Continental	4	124G	4F-1R	25	2550	No
MH-333	......	1200.00	2200.00	2680.00	MH	4	208G	10F-1R	37.15	4590	No
MH-333	......	1310.00	2400.00	2930.00	MH	4	208D	10F-1R	39	6005	No
MH-444	......	1450.00	2660.00	3250.00	MH	4	277G	10F-1R	52	5780	No
MH-444	......	1590.00	2900.00	3540.00	MH	4	277D	10F-1R	48.21	6499	No
MH-555	......	1530.00	2790.00	3400.00	MH	4	382G	4F-1R	71	7435	No
MH-555	......	1660.00	3030.00	3700.00	MH	4	382D	4F-1R	72	7525	No

1958

Model	Approx. Retail Price New	Fair	Good	Premium	Engine Make	Engine No. Cyls.	Engine Displ. Cu.-In.	No. Speeds	P.T.O. H.P.	Approx. Shipping Wt.-Lbs.	Cab
MH-333	......	1240.00	2270.00	2770.00	MH	4	208G	10F-1R	37.15	4590	No
MH-333	......	1380.00	2530.00	3090.00	MH	4	208D	10F-1R	39	6005	No
MH-444	......	1480.00	2710.00	3310.00	MH	4	277G	10F-1R	52	5780	No
MH-444	......	1610.00	2940.00	3590.00	MH	4	277D	10F-1R	48.21	6499	No
MH-555	......	1560.00	2850.00	3480.00	MH	4	382G	4F-1R	71	7435	No
MH-555	......	1680.00	3070.00	3750.00	MH	4	382D	4F-1R	72	7525	No

Minneapolis-Moline

1939

Model	Approx. Retail Price New	Fair	Good	Premium	Engine Make	Engine No. Cyls.	Engine Displ. Cu.-In.	No. Speeds	P.T.O. H.P.	Approx. Shipping Wt.-Lbs.	Cab
RT	......	540.00	1290.00	1640.00	MM	4	165G	4F-1R	24	3150	No
U	......	730.00	1730.00	2200.00	MM	4	283G	5F-1R	45	8575	No
ZTN	......	610.00	1430.00	1820.00	MM	4	206G	5F-1R	33	3650	No
ZTS	......	580.00	1370.00	1740.00	MM	4	206G	5F-1R	33	3600	No
ZTU	......	640.00	1510.00	1920.00	MM	4	206G	5F-1R	33	3650	No

1940

Model	Approx. Retail Price New	Fair	Good	Premium	Engine Make	Engine No. Cyls.	Engine Displ. Cu.-In.	No. Speeds	P.T.O. H.P.	Approx. Shipping Wt.-Lbs.	Cab
GT	......	670.00	1580.00	2010.00	MM	4	403G	3F-1R		6500	No
RT	......	540.00	1290.00	1640.00	MM	4	165G	4F-1R	24	3150	No
U	......	730.00	1730.00	2200.00	MM	4	283G	5F-1R	45	8575	No
ZTN	......	610.00	1430.00	1820.00	MM	4	206G	5F-1R	33	3650	No
ZTS	......	580.00	1370.00	1740.00	MM	4	206G	5F-1R	33	3600	No
ZTU	......	640.00	1510.00	1920.00	MM	4	206G	5F-1R	33	3650	No

1941

Model	Approx. Retail Price New	Fair	Good	Premium	Engine Make	Engine No. Cyls.	Engine Displ. Cu.-In.	No. Speeds	P.T.O. H.P.	Approx. Shipping Wt.-Lbs.	Cab
GT	......	690.00	1630.00	2070.00	MM	4	403G	3F-1R		6500	No
RT	......	570.00	1340.00	1700.00	MM	4	165G	4F-1R	24	3150	No
U	......	740.00	1760.00	2240.00	MM	4	283G	5F-1R	45	8575	No
ZTN	......	620.00	1470.00	1870.00	MM	4	206G	5F-1R	33	3650	No
ZTS	......	590.00	1410.00	1790.00	MM	4	206G	5F-1R	33	3600	No
ZTU	......	650.00	1540.00	1960.00	MM	4	206G	5F-1R	33	3650	No

1942

Model	Approx. Retail Price New	Fair	Good	Premium	Engine Make	Engine No. Cyls.	Engine Displ. Cu.-In.	No. Speeds	P.T.O. H.P.	Approx. Shipping Wt.-Lbs.	Cab
GTA	......	1090.00	2570.00	3260.00	MM	6	426	5F-1R	65	6730	No
RT	......	590.00	1410.00	1790.00	MM	4	165G	4F-1R	24	3150	No
U	......	760.00	1790.00	2270.00	MM	4	283G	5F-1R	45	8575	No
ZTN	......	640.00	1510.00	1920.00	MM	4	206G	5F-1R	33	3650	No
ZTS	......	610.00	1440.00	1830.00	MM	4	206G	5F-1R	33	3600	No
ZTU	......	670.00	1590.00	2020.00	MM	4	206G	5F-1R	33	3650	No

1943

Model	Approx. Retail Price New	Fair	Good	Premium	Engine Make	Engine No. Cyls.	Engine Displ. Cu.-In.	No. Speeds	P.T.O. H.P.	Approx. Shipping Wt.-Lbs.	Cab
GTA	......	1120.00	2660.00	3350.00	MM	6	426	5F-1R	65	6730	No
RT	......	620.00	1470.00	1850.00	MM	4	165G	4F-1R	24	3150	No
U	......	780.00	1840.00	2320.00	MM	4	283G	5F-1R	45	8575	No
ZTN	......	680.00	1610.00	2030.00	MM	4	206G	5F-1R	33	3650	No
ZTS	......	630.00	1490.00	1880.00	MM	4	206G	5F-1R	33	3600	No
ZTU	......	680.00	1600.00	2020.00	MM	4	206G	5F-1R	33	3650	No

Minneapolis-Moline (Cont.)

Model	Approx. Retail Price New	Estimated Average Value Less Repairs Fair	Good	Premium	Engine Make	No. Cyls.	Displ. Cu.-In.	No. Speeds	P.T.O. H.P.	Approx. Shipping Wt.-Lbs.	Cab
1944											
GTA	......	1160.00	2750.00	3440.00	MM	6	426	5F-1R	65	6730	No
RT	......	650.00	1540.00	1930.00	MM	4	165G	4F-1R	24	3150	No
U	......	790.00	1880.00	2350.00	MM	4	283G	5F-1R	45	8575	No
ZTN	......	700.00	1660.00	2080.00	MM	4	206G	5F-1R	33	3650	No
ZTS	......	650.00	1530.00	1910.00	MM	4	206G	5F-1R	33	3600	No
ZTU	......	700.00	1660.00	2080.00	MM	4	206G	5F-1R	33	3650	No
1945											
GTA	......	1190.00	2810.00	3480.00	MM	6	426	5F-1R	65	6730	No
RT	......	680.00	1610.00	2000.00	MM	4	165G	4F-1R	24	3150	No
U	......	810.00	1920.00	2380.00	MM	4	283G	5F-1R	45	8575	No
ZTN	......	710.00	1690.00	2100.00	MM	4	206G	5F-1R	33	3650	No
ZTS	......	660.00	1570.00	1950.00	MM	4	206G	5F-1R	33	3600	No
ZTU	......	720.00	1710.00	2120.00	MM	4	206G	5F-1R	33	3650	No
1946											
GTA	......	1240.00	2940.00	3620.00	MM	6	426	5F-1R	65	6730	No
RT	......	700.00	1660.00	2040.00	MM	4	165G	4F-1R	24	3150	No
U	......	840.00	2000.00	2460.00	MM	4	283G	5F-1R	45	8575	No
ZTN	......	730.00	1730.00	2130.00	MM	4	206G	5F-1R	33	3650	No
ZTS	......	690.00	1630.00	2010.00	MM	4	206G	5F-1R	33	3600	No
ZTU	......	750.00	1780.00	2190.00	MM	4	206G	5F-1R	33	3650	No
1947											
GTA	......	1300.00	3070.00	3750.00	MM	6	426	5F-1R	65	6730	No
GTB	......	990.00	2340.00	2860.00	MM	4	403G	5F-1R	60	6275	No
GTB	......	950.00	2260.00	2760.00	MM	6	426D	5F-1R	65	7319	No
RT	......	730.00	1730.00	2110.00	MM	4	165G	4F-1R	24	3150	No
U	......	890.00	2100.00	2560.00	MM	4	283G	5F-1R	45	8575	No
V	......	510.00	1220.00	1490.00	Herc.	4	65G	3F-1R		1778	No
ZTN	......	740.00	1760.00	2150.00	MM	4	206G	5F-1R	33	3650	No
ZTS	......	720.00	1700.00	2070.00	MM	4	206G	5F-1R	33	3600	No
ZTU	......	770.00	1820.00	2220.00	MM	4	206G	5F-1R	33	3650	No
1948											
GTB	......	1040.00	2370.00	2890.00	MM	4	403G	5F-1R	60	6275	No
GTB	......	990.00	2270.00	2770.00	MM	6	426D	5F-1R	65	7319	No
RT	......	780.00	1790.00	2180.00	MM	4	165G	4F-1R	24	3150	No
RTE	......	640.00	1470.00	1790.00	MM	4	165G	4F-1R	24	3250	No
RTN	......	700.00	1600.00	1950.00	MM	4	165G	4F-1R	24	3100	No
RTU	......	680.00	1540.00	1880.00	MM	4	165G	4F-1R	24	3100	No
U	......	950.00	2160.00	2640.00	MM	4	283G	5F-1R	45	8575	No
UTC	......	850.00	1950.00	2380.00	MM	4	283G	5F-1R	45	5840	No
UTS	......	870.00	2000.00	2440.00	MM	4	283G	5F-1R	45	6220	No
UTU	......	800.00	1820.00	2220.00	MM	4	283G	5F-1R	45	5850	No
V	......	560.00	1280.00	1560.00	Herc.	4	65G	3F-1R		1778	No
ZTN	......	800.00	1830.00	2230.00	MM	4	206G	5F-1R	33	3650	No
ZTU	......	830.00	1890.00	2310.00	MM	4	206G	5F-1R	33	3650	No
1949											
GTB	......	1070.00	2370.00	2890.00	MM	4	403G	5F-1R	60	6275	No
GTB	......	1100.00	2430.00	2970.00	MM	6	426D	5F-1R	65	7319	No
RT	......	840.00	1860.00	2270.00	MM	4	165G	4F-1R	24	3150	No
RTE	......	710.00	1570.00	1920.00	MM	4	165G	4F-1R	24	3250	No
RTN	......	750.00	1660.00	2030.00	MM	4	165G	4F-1R	24	3100	No
RTS	......	680.00	1500.00	1830.00	MM	4	165G	4F-1R	24	3250	No
RTU	......	730.00	1610.00	1960.00	MM	4	165G	4F-1R	24	3100	No
UTC	......	910.00	2020.00	2460.00	MM	4	283G	5F-1R	45	5840	No
UTS	......	960.00	2110.00	2570.00	MM	4	283G	5F-1R	45	6220	No
UTU	......	860.00	1890.00	2310.00	MM	4	283G	5F-1R	45	5850	No
V	......	610.00	1340.00	1640.00	Herc.	4	65G	3F-1R		1778	No
ZAE	......	700.00	1540.00	1880.00	MM	4	206G	5F-1R	33	3700	No
ZAN	......	750.00	1660.00	2030.00	MM	4	206G	5F-1R	33	3650	No
ZAS	......	780.00	1730.00	2110.00	MM	4	206G	5F-1R	33	3650	No
ZAU	......	820.00	1810.00	2210.00	MM	4	206G	5F-1R	33	3600	No
1950											
BF	......	840.00	1790.00	2180.00	Herc.	4	133G	4F-1R	25.1	4636	No
BG	......	850.00	1810.00	2210.00	Herc.	4	133G	4F-1R	25.1	2880	No
GTB	......	1140.00	2430.00	2970.00	MM	4	403G	5F-1R	60	6275	No
GTB	......	1170.00	2500.00	3050.00	MM	6	426D	5F-1R	65	7319	No
RTE	......	770.00	1630.00	1990.00	MM	4	165G	4F-1R	24	3250	No
RTN	......	810.00	1730.00	2110.00	MM	4	165G	4F-1R	24	3100	No
RTS	......	750.00	1600.00	1950.00	MM	4	165G	4F-1R	24	3250	No
RTU	......	800.00	1700.00	2070.00	MM	4	165G	4F-1R	24	3100	No
UTC	......	960.00	2050.00	2500.00	MM	4	283G	5F-1R	45	5840	No
UTN	......	980.00	2080.00	2540.00	MM	4	283G	5F-1R	45	5840	No
UTS	......	1020.00	2180.00	2660.00	MM	4	283G	5F-1R	45	6220	No
UTU	......	920.00	1950.00	2380.00	MM	4	283G	5F-1R	45	5850	No
V	......	690.00	1470.00	1790.00	Herc.	4	65G	3F-1R		1778	No
ZAE	......	780.00	1660.00	2030.00	MM	4	206G	5F-1R	33	3700	No
ZAN	......	810.00	1730.00	2110.00	MM	4	206G	5F-1R	33	3650	No
ZAS	......	840.00	1790.00	2180.00	MM	4	206G	5F-1R	33	3650	No
ZAU	......	870.00	1860.00	2270.00	MM	4	206G	5F-1R	33	3600	No

Minneapolis-Moline (Cont.)

Model	Approx. Retail Price New	Estimated Average Value Less Repairs Fair	Good	Premium	Engine Make	No. Cyls.	Displ. Cu.-In.	No. Speeds	P.T.O. H.P.	Approx. Shipping Wt.-Lbs.	Cab
1951											
BF	......	900.00	1860.00	2270.00	Herc.	4	133G	4F-1R	25.1	4636	No
BG	......	940.00	1930.00	2360.00	Herc.	4	133G	4F-1R	25.1	2880	No
GTB	......	1270.00	2620.00	3200.00	MM	4	403G	5F-1R	60	6275	No
GTB	......	1210.00	2500.00	3050.00	MM	6	426D	5F-1R	65	7319	No
GTC	......	1090.00	2240.00	2730.00	MM	4	403G	5F-1R	60	6275	No
RTE	......	810.00	1660.00	2030.00	MM	4	165G	4F-1R	24	3250	No
RTN	......	870.00	1790.00	2180.00	MM	4	165G	4F-1R	24	3100	No
RTS	......	820.00	1700.00	2070.00	MM	4	165G	4F-1R	24	3250	No
RTU	......	850.00	1750.00	2140.00	MM	4	165G	4F-1R	24	3100	No
UTC	......	1010.00	2080.00	2540.00	MM	4	283G	5F-1R	45	5840	No
UTE	......	1000.00	2070.00	2530.00	MM	4	283G	5F-1R	45	5840	No
UTN	......	1030.00	2130.00	2600.00	MM	4	283G	5F-1R	45	5840	No
UTS	......	1070.00	2210.00	2700.00	MM	4	283G	5F-1R	45	6220	No
UTU	......	960.00	1990.00	2430.00	MM	4	283G	5F-1R	45	5850	No
V	......	750.00	1540.00	1880.00	Herc.	4	65G	3F-1R		1778	No
ZAE	......	830.00	1720.00	2100.00	MM	4	206G	5F-1R	33	3700	No
ZAN	......	870.00	1790.00	2180.00	MM	4	206G	5F-1R	33	3650	No
ZAS	......	930.00	1920.00	2340.00	MM	4	206G	5F-1R	33	3650	No
ZAU	......	920.00	1890.00	2310.00	MM	4	206G	5F-1R	33	3600	No
1952											
BF	......	970.00	1940.00	2370.00	Herc.	4	133G	4F-1R	25.1	4636	No
BG	......	1010.00	2030.00	2480.00	Herc.	4	133G	4F-1R	25.1	2880	No
GTB	......	1310.00	2620.00	3200.00	MM	6	426D	5F-1R	65	7319	No
GTB	......	1340.00	2690.00	3280.00	MM	4	403G	5F-1R	60	6275	No
GTC	......	1170.00	2340.00	2860.00	MM	4	403G	5F-1R	60	6275	No
RTE	......	860.00	1730.00	2110.00	MM	4	165G	4F-1R	24	3250	No
RTS	......	940.00	1890.00	2310.00	MM	4	165G	4F-1R	24	3250	No
RTU	......	910.00	1820.00	2220.00	MM	4	165G	4F-1R	24	3100	No
UDS	......	1120.00	2240.00	2730.00	MM	4	283D	5F-1R	45	5810	No
UDU	......	1260.00	2520.00	3070.00	MM	4	283D	5F-1R	45	5840	No
UTC	......	1100.00	2210.00	2700.00	MM	4	283G	5F-1R	45	5840	No
UTE	......	1290.00	2580.00	3150.00	MM	4	283G	5F-1R	45	5840	No
UTN	......	1320.00	2640.00	3220.00	MM	4	283G	5F-1R	45	5840	No
UTS	......	1170.00	2340.00	2860.00	MM	4	283G	5F-1R	45	6220	No
UTSD	......	1200.00	2400.00	2930.00	MM	4	283D	5F-1R	45	5810	No
UTU	......	1050.00	2100.00	2560.00	MM	4	283G	5F-1R	45	5850	No
V	......	830.00	1650.00	2010.00	Herc.	4	65G	3F-1R		1778	No
ZAE	......	910.00	1820.00	2220.00	MM	4	206G	5F-1R	33	3700	No
ZAN	......	930.00	1860.00	2270.00	MM	4	206G	5F-1R	33	3650	No
ZAS	......	1020.00	2040.00	2490.00	MM	4	206G	5F-1R	33	3650	No
ZAU	......	980.00	1950.00	2380.00	MM	4	206G	5F-1R	33	3600	No
1953											
BF	......	1030.00	2000.00	2440.00	Herc.	4	133G	4F-1R	25.1	4636	No
BFD	......	890.00	1730.00	2110.00	Herc.	4	133G	4F-1R	25.1	2875	No
BFH	......	920.00	1790.00	2180.00	Herc.	4	133G	4F-1R	25.1	2900	No
BFS	......	880.00	1700.00	2070.00	Herc.	4	133G	4F-1R	25.1	2860	No
BFW	......	910.00	1760.00	2150.00	Herc.	4	133G	4F-1R	25.1	2895	No
BG	......	1060.00	2060.00	2510.00	Herc.	4	133G	4F-1R	25.1	2880	No
GTB	......	1370.00	2660.00	3250.00	MM	4	403G	5F-1R	60	6275	No
GTB	......	1420.00	2750.00	3360.00	MM	6	426D	5F-1R	65	7319	No
GTC	......	1240.00	2400.00	2930.00	MM	4	403G	5F-1R	60	6275	No
RTE	......	940.00	1820.00	2220.00	MM	4	165G	4F-1R	24	3250	No
RTS	......	1010.00	1950.00	2380.00	MM	4	165G	4F-1R	24	3250	No
RTU	......	960.00	1860.00	2270.00	MM	4	165G	4F-1R	24	3100	No
UBE	......	1250.00	2430.00	2970.00	MM	4	283G	5F-1R	45	5840	No
UBG	......	1060.00	2050.00	2500.00	MM	4	283G	5F-1R	45	5840	No
UBN	......	1190.00	2300.00	2810.00	MM	4	283D	5F-1R	45	5850	No
UBU	......	1210.00	2340.00	2860.00	MM	4	283G	5F-1R	45	5750	No
UDS	......	1140.00	2210.00	2700.00	MM	4	283D	5F-1R	45	5810	No
UDU	......	1400.00	2710.00	3310.00	MM	4	283D	5F-1R	45	5840	No
UTC	......	1170.00	2270.00	2770.00	MM	4	283G	5F-1R	45	5840	No
UTE	......	1330.00	2580.00	3150.00	MM	4	283G	5F-1R	45	5840	No
UTS	......	1240.00	2410.00	2940.00	MM	4	283G	5F-1R	45	6220	No
UTSD	......	1270.00	2460.00	3000.00	MM	4	283D	5F-1R	45	5810	No
UTU	......	1150.00	2230.00	2720.00	MM	4	283G	5F-1R	45	5850	No
ZAE	......	960.00	1860.00	2270.00	MM	4	206G	5F-1R	33	3700	No
ZAN	......	990.00	1920.00	2340.00	MM	4	206G	5F-1R	33	3650	No
ZAS	......	1090.00	2100.00	2560.00	MM	4	206G	5F-1R	33	3650	No
ZBE	......	970.00	1890.00	2310.00	MM	4	206G	5F-1R	33	3700	No
ZBU	......	930.00	1810.00	2210.00	MM	4	206G	5F-1R	33	3600	No
ZM	......	1020.00	1970.00	2400.00	MM	4	206G	5F-1R	33	3650	No
1954											
BF	......	1100.00	2070.00	2530.00	Herc.	4	133G	4F-1R	25.1	4636	No
BG	......	1150.00	2170.00	2650.00	Herc.	4	133G	4F-1R	25.1	2880	No
GTB	......	1460.00	2750.00	3360.00	MM	4	403G	5F-1R	60	6275	No
GTB	......	1480.00	2780.00	3390.00	MM	6	426D	5F-1R	65	7319	No
RTU	......	1020.00	1920.00	2340.00	MM	4	165G	4F-1R	24	3100	No
UBE	......	1430.00	2680.00	3270.00	MM	4	283G	5F-1R	45	5840	No
UBE	......	1790.00	3370.00	4110.00	MM	4	283D	5F-1R	45	7600	No
UBG	......	1120.00	2110.00	2570.00	MM	4	283G	5F-1R	45	5840	No
UBN	......	1220.00	2300.00	2810.00	MM	4	283D	5F-1R	45	5850	No

Minneapolis-Moline (Cont.)

1954 (Cont.)

Model	Approx. Retail Price New	Fair	Good	Premium	Make	Engine No. Cyls.	Engine Displ. Cu.-In.	No. Speeds	P.T.O. H.P.	Approx. Shipping Wt.-Lbs.	Cab
UBU	......	1260.00	2370.00	2890.00	MM	4	283G	5F-1R	45	5750	No
UBU	......	1530.00	2870.00	3500.00	MM	4	283D	5F-1R	45	7600	No
UDS	......	1210.00	2270.00	2770.00	MM	4	283D	5F-1R	45	5810	No
UTC	......	1240.00	2340.00	2860.00	MM	4	283G	5F-1R	45	5840	No
UTS	......	1310.00	2470.00	3010.00	MM	4	283G	5F-1R	45	6220	No
UTSD	......	1330.00	2500.00	3050.00	MM	4	283D	5F-1R	45	5810	No
UTU	......	1180.00	2230.00	2720.00	MM	4	283G	5F-1R	45	5850	No
ZAE	......	1000.00	1880.00	2290.00	MM	4	206G	5F-1R	33	3700	No
ZBE	......	1050.00	1970.00	2400.00	MM	4	206G	5F-1R	33	3700	No
ZBN	......	1070.00	2020.00	2460.00	MM	4	206G	5F-1R	33	3650	No
ZBU	......	990.00	1860.00	2270.00	MM	4	206G	5F-1R	33	3600	No
ZM	......	1080.00	2030.00	2480.00	MM	4	206G	5F-1R	33	3650	No

1955

Model	Approx. Retail Price New	Fair	Good	Premium	Make	Engine No. Cyls.	Engine Displ. Cu.-In.	No. Speeds	P.T.O. H.P.	Approx. Shipping Wt.-Lbs.	Cab
BF	......	1170.00	2130.00	2600.00	Herc.	4	133G	4F-1R	25.1	4636	No
BG	......	1220.00	2230.00	2720.00	Herc.	4	133G	4F-1R	25.1	2880	No
GB	......	1420.00	2590.00	3160.00	MM	4	403G	5F-1R	69	6730	No
GB	......	1770.00	3230.00	3940.00	MM	6	425D	5F-1R	65	7600	No
UB Special	......	1190.00	2180.00	2660.00	MM	4	283G	5F-1R	50	5840	No
UBD Special	......	1310.00	2390.00	2920.00	MM	4	283D	5F-1R	45	7600	No
UBE	......	1500.00	2750.00	3360.00	MM	4	283G	5F-1R	45	5840	No
UBE	......	1910.00	3490.00	4260.00	MM	4	283D	5F-1R	45	7600	No
UBG	......	1190.00	2180.00	2660.00	MM	4	283G	5F-1R	45	5840	No
UBU	......	1360.00	2490.00	3040.00	MM	4	283G	5F-1R	45	5750	No
UBU	......	1610.00	2940.00	3590.00	MM	4	283D	5F-1R	45	7600	No
UDS	......	1300.00	2370.00	2890.00	MM	4	283D	5F-1R	45	5810	No
UTC	......	1350.00	2460.00	3000.00	MM	4	283G	5F-1R	45	5840	No
UTS	......	1390.00	2530.00	3090.00	MM	4	283G	5F-1R	45	6220	No
UTSD	......	1400.00	2560.00	3120.00	MM	4	283D	5F-1R	45	5810	No
UTU	......	1290.00	2360.00	2880.00	MM	4	283G	5F-1R	45	5850	No
ZAE	......	1060.00	1940.00	2370.00	MM	4	206G	5F-1R	33	3700	No
ZBE	......	1110.00	2040.00	2490.00	MM	4	206G	5F-1R	33	3700	No
ZBN	......	1140.00	2080.00	2540.00	MM	4	206G	5F-1R	33	3650	No
ZBU	......	1090.00	1980.00	2420.00	MM	4	206G	5F-1R	33	3600	No

1956

Model	Approx. Retail Price New	Fair	Good	Premium	Make	Engine No. Cyls.	Engine Displ. Cu.-In.	No. Speeds	P.T.O. H.P.	Approx. Shipping Wt.-Lbs.	Cab
BF	......	1200.00	2200.00	2680.00	Herc.	4	133G	4F-1R	25.1	4636	No
BG	......	1240.00	2270.00	2770.00	Herc.	4	133G	4F-1R	25.1	2880	No
GB	......	1490.00	2720.00	3320.00	MM	4	403G	5F-1R	69	6730	No
GB	......	1780.00	3260.00	3980.00	MM	6	425D	5F-1R	65	7600	No
UBD Special	......	1340.00	2460.00	3000.00	MM	4	283D	5F-1R	45	7600	No
UBG	......	1230.00	2240.00	2730.00	MM	4	283G	5F-1R	45	5840	No
UDS	......	1320.00	2410.00	2940.00	MM	4	283D	5F-1R	45	5810	No
UTS	......	1420.00	2600.00	3170.00	MM	4	283G	5F-1R	45	6220	No
UTSD	......	1450.00	2660.00	3250.00	MM	4	283D	5F-1R	45	5810	No
ZAE	......	1100.00	2010.00	2450.00	MM	4	206G	5F-1R	33	3700	No
335U Utility	......	1030.00	1890.00	2310.00	MM	4	165G	5F-1R	31.4	3361	No
445 Universal	......	1210.00	2210.00	2700.00	MM	4	206G	5F-1R	40.8	4168	No
445 Universal	......	1230.00	2240.00	2730.00	MM	4	206D	5F-1R	40.8	4770	No
445 Utility	......	1350.00	2460.00	3000.00	MM	4	206D	5F-1R	40.8	4240	No

1957

Model	Approx. Retail Price New	Fair	Good	Premium	Make	Engine No. Cyls.	Engine Displ. Cu.-In.	No. Speeds	P.T.O. H.P.	Approx. Shipping Wt.-Lbs.	Cab
BF	......	1240.00	2260.00	2760.00	Herc.	4	133G	4F-1R	25.1	4636	No
GB	......	1560.00	2850.00	3480.00	MM	4	403G	5F-1R	69	6730	No
GB	......	1920.00	3520.00	4290.00	MM	6	425D	5F-1R	65	7600	No
UBD Special	......	1380.00	2520.00	3070.00	MM	4	283D	5F-1R	45	7600	No
UBG	......	1260.00	2300.00	2810.00	MM	4	283G	5F-1R	45	5840	No
UDS	......	1360.00	2480.00	3030.00	MM	4	283D	5F-1R	45	5810	No
UTS	......	1420.00	2600.00	3170.00	MM	4	283G	5F-1R	45	6220	No
UTSD	......	1480.00	2710.00	3310.00	MM	4	283D	5F-1R	45	5810	No
5 Star Universal	......	1600.00	2930.00	3580.00	MM	4	336D	10F-1R	57	6642	No
5 Star Unviersal	......	1390.00	2550.00	3110.00	MM	4	336G	10F-1R	57	6344	No
335 Universal	......	1100.00	2020.00	2460.00	MM	4	165G	5F-1R	31.4	3481	No
335U Utility	......	1050.00	1920.00	2340.00	MM	4	165G	5F-1R	31.4	3361	No
445 Universal	......	1280.00	2340.00	2860.00	MM	4	206G	5F-1R	40.8	4168	No
445 Universal	......	1350.00	2460.00	3000.00	MM	4	206D	5F-1R	40.8	4770	No
445 Utility	......	1380.00	2530.00	3090.00	MM	4	206D	5F-1R	40.8	4240	No

1958

Model	Approx. Retail Price New	Fair	Good	Premium	Make	Engine No. Cyls.	Engine Displ. Cu.-In.	No. Speeds	P.T.O. H.P.	Approx. Shipping Wt.-Lbs.	Cab
GB	......	1630.00	2980.00	3640.00	MM	6	425D	5F-1R	65	7600	No
GB	......	1920.00	3520.00	4290.00	MM	4	403G	5F-1R	69	6730	No
UBG	......	1260.00	2300.00	2810.00	MM	4	283G	5F-1R	45	5840	No
UDS	......	1390.00	2550.00	3110.00	MM	4	283D	5F-1R	45	5810	No
UTSD	......	1510.00	2760.00	3370.00	MM	4	283D	5F-1R	45	5810	No
ZAE	......	1120.00	2050.00	2500.00	MM	4	206G	5F-1R	33	3700	No
5 Star	......	1510.00	2770.00	3380.00	MM	4	336D	10F-2R	57	6642	No
5 Star	......	1760.00	3210.00	3920.00	MM	4	283G	10F-2R	57	6342	No
5 Star Universal	......	1660.00	3040.00	3710.00	MM	4	336D	10F-1R	57	6642	No
5 Star Unviersal	......	1440.00	2620.00	3200.00	MM	4	336G	10F-1R	57	6344	No
335 Universal	......	1170.00	2140.00	2610.00	MM	4	165G	5F-1R	31.4	3481	No
335U Utility	......	1080.00	1970.00	2400.00	MM	4	165G	5F-1R	31.4	3361	No
445 Universal	......	1350.00	2460.00	3000.00	MM	4	206G	5F-1R	40.8	4168	No
445 Universal	......	1370.00	2500.00	3050.00	MM	4	206D	5F-1R	40.8	4770	No
445 Utility	......	1400.00	2560.00	3120.00	MM	4	206D	5F-1R	40.8	4240	No

Minneapolis-Moline (Cont.)

Model	Approx. Retail Price New	Estimated Average Value Less Repairs Fair	Good	Premium	Engine Make	No. Cyls.	Displ. Cu.-In.	No. Speeds	P.T.O. H.P.	Approx. Shipping Wt.-Lbs.	Cab
1959											
GB	......	1700.00	3100.00	3780.00	MM	4	403G	5F-1R	69	6730	No
GB	......	1990.00	3650.00	4450.00	MM	6	425D	5F-1R	65	7600	No
GVI	......	1800.00	3300.00	4030.00	MM	6	426G	5F-1R	78	7620	No
GVI	......	2120.00	3870.00	4720.00	MM	6	426D	5F-1R	79	7835	No
Jet Star	......	1230.00	2250.00	2750.00	MM	4	206G	10F-2R	44	4550	No
UBG	......	1280.00	2340.00	2860.00	MM	4	283G	5F-1R	45	5840	No
UDS	......	1400.00	2560.00	3120.00	MM	4	283D	5F-1R	45	5810	No
UTSD	......	1540.00	2820.00	3440.00	MM	4	283D	5F-1R	45	5810	No
ZAE	......	1190.00	2180.00	2660.00	MM	4	206G	5F-1R	33	3700	No
5 Star	......	1580.00	2880.00	3510.00	MM	4	336D	10F-2R	57	6642	No
5 Star	......	1840.00	3360.00	4100.00	MM	4	283G	10F-2R	57	6342	No
5 Star Universal	......	1720.00	3150.00	3840.00	MM	4	336D	10F-1R	57	6642	No
5 Star Unviersal	......	1490.00	2720.00	3320.00	MM	4	336G	10F-1R	57	6344	No
335 Universal	......	1050.00	1920.00	2340.00	MM	4	165G	5F-1R	31.4	3481	No
335U Utility	......	1110.00	2030.00	2480.00	MM	4	165G	5F-1R	31.4	3361	No
445 Universal	......	1220.00	2240.00	2730.00	MM	4	206G	5F-1R	40.8	4168	No
445 Universal	......	1260.00	2300.00	2810.00	MM	4	206D	5F-1R	40.8	4770	No
445 Utility	......	1350.00	2460.00	3000.00	MM	4	206D	5F-1R	40.8	4240	No
1960											
GVI	......	1930.00	3420.00	4170.00	MM	6	426G	5F-1R	78	7620	No
GVI	......	2210.00	3940.00	4810.00	MM	6	426D	5F-1R	79	7835	No
JET Star	......	1300.00	2310.00	2820.00	MM	4	206D	10F-2R	45	4600	No
UBG	......	1370.00	2430.00	2970.00	MM	4	283G	5F-1R	45	5840	No
UDS	......	1540.00	2740.00	3340.00	MM	4	283D	5F-1R	45	5810	No
UTSD	......	1650.00	2930.00	3580.00	MM	4	283D	5F-1R	45	5810	No
ZAE	......	1370.00	2430.00	2970.00	MM	4	206G	5F-1R	33	3700	No
5 Star	......	1640.00	2920.00	3560.00	MM	4	283G	10F-2R	57	6342	No
5 Star	......	1910.00	3390.00	4140.00	MM	4	336D	10F-2R	57	6642	No
5 Star Universal	......	1840.00	3280.00	4000.00	MM	4	336D	10F-1R	57	6642	No
5 Star Unviersal	......	1570.00	2780.00	3390.00	MM	4	336G	10F-1R	57	6344	No
M5	......	1450.00	2570.00	3140.00	MM	4	336G	10F-2R	61	6928	No
M5	......	1570.00	2780.00	3390.00	MM	4	336D	10F-2R	58	7078	No
335U Utility	......	1180.00	2090.00	2550.00	MM	4	165G	5F-1R	31.4	3361	No
445 Utility	......	1530.00	2720.00	3320.00	MM	4	206D	5F-1R	40.8	4240	No
1961											
GVI	......	2050.00	3550.00	4330.00	MM	6	426G	5F-1R	78	7620	No
GVI	......	2310.00	4000.00	4880.00	MM	6	426D	5F-1R	79	7835	No
JET Star	......	1370.00	2370.00	2890.00	MM	4	206G	10F-2R	44	4550	No
JET Star	......	1610.00	2780.00	3390.00	MM	4	206D	10F-2R	45	4600	No
UBG	......	1480.00	2560.00	3120.00	MM	4	283G	5F-1R	45	5840	No
UDS	......	1620.00	2810.00	3430.00	MM	4	283D	5F-1R	45	5810	No
UTSD	......	1700.00	2940.00	3590.00	MM	4	283D	5F-1R	45	5810	No
ZAE	......	1440.00	2500.00	3050.00	MM	4	206G	5F-1R	33	3700	No
5 Star Universal	......	1690.00	2920.00	3560.00	MM	4	336G	10F-1R	57	6344	No
5 Star Universal	......	1960.00	3390.00	4140.00	MM	4	336D	10F-1R	57	6642	No
M5	......	1520.00	2640.00	3220.00	MM	4	336G	10F-2R	61	6928	No
M5	......	2030.00	3510.00	4280.00	MM	4	336D	10F-2R	58	7078	No
335U Utility	......	1680.00	2910.00	3550.00	MM	4	165G	5F-1R	31.4	3361	No
1962											
GVI	5700.00	2170.00	3650.00	4450.00	MM	6	426G	5F-1R	78	7620	No
GVI	6405.00	2430.00	4100.00	5000.00	MM	6	426D	5F-1R	79	7835	No
Jet Star	3400.00	1290.00	2180.00	2660.00	MM	4	206G	10F-2R	44	3400	No
Jet Star	4000.00	1520.00	2560.00	3120.00	MM	4	206D	10F-2R	45	3800	No
M5	4200.00	1600.00	2690.00	3280.00	MM	4	336G	10F-2R	61	5928	No
M5	4700.00	1790.00	3010.00	3670.00	MM	4	336D	10F-2R	58	6230	No
M504 4WD	6500.00	2470.00	4160.00	5080.00	MM	4	336G	10R-2R	61	7020	No
M504 4WD	7100.00	2700.00	4540.00	5540.00	MM	4	336D	10F-2R	58	7420	No
G704 4WD	7440.00	2830.00	4760.00	5810.00	MM	6	504LP	5F-1R	101.4	8405	No
G704 4WD	8150.00	3100.00	5220.00	6370.00	MM	6	504D	5F-1R	101.6	8655	No
G705	7600.00	2890.00	4860.00	5930.00	MM	6	504G	5F-1R	101.6	7700	No
G705	7900.00	3000.00	5060.00	6170.00	MM	6	504D	5F-1R	101.4	7900	No
G706 4WD	10000.00	3800.00	6400.00	7810.00	MM	6	504G	5F-1R	101.4	8600	No
G706 4WD	10500.00	3990.00	6720.00	8200.00	MM	6	504D	5F-1R	101.6	8750	No
1963											
Jet Star II	3445.00	1440.00	2370.00	2890.00	MM	4	206G	10F-2R	44	3370	No
Jet Star II	3788.00	1560.00	2560.00	3120.00	MM	4	206LP	10F-2R	44	3570	No
Jet Star II	4125.00	1680.00	2750.00	3360.00	MM	4	206D	10F-2R	44	3770	No
M5	4205.00	1760.00	2880.00	3510.00	MM	4	336G	10F-2R	61	5830	No
M5	4490.00	1790.00	2940.00	3590.00	MM	4	336LP	10F-2R	61	6030	No
M5	4775.00	1950.00	3200.00	3900.00	MM	4	336D	10F-2R	58	6230	No
M504 4WD	6555.00	2560.00	4200.00	5120.00	MM	4	336G	10F-2R	61	7020	No
M504 4WD	6835.00	2670.00	4370.00	5330.00	MM	4	336LP	10F-2R	61	7220	No
M504 4WD	7120.00	2780.00	4560.00	5560.00	MM	4	336D	10F-2R	58	7420	No
M602	4290.00	1950.00	3210.00	3920.00	MM	4	336G	10F-2R	64	6350	No
M602	4580.00	1990.00	3270.00	3990.00	MM	4	336LP	10F-2R	64	6550	No
M602	4870.00	2250.00	3700.00	4510.00	MM	4	336D	10F-2R	64	6750	No
M604 4WD	6590.00	2730.00	4490.00	5480.00	MM	4	336G	10F-2R	73	7020	No
M604 4WD	6880.00	2770.00	4550.00	5550.00	MM	4	336LP	10F-2R	73	7220	No
M604 4WD	7170.00	2850.00	4670.00	5700.00	MM	4	336D	10F-2R	74	7420	No
G705	7650.00	2980.00	4900.00	5980.00	MM	6	504LP	5F-1R	101	7700	No

Minneapolis-Moline (Cont.)

Model	Approx. Retail Price New	Estimated Average Value Less Repairs Fair	Good	Premium	Make	Engine No. Cyls.	Displ. Cu.-In.	No. Speeds	P.T.O. H.P.	Approx. Shipping Wt.-Lbs.	Cab
1963 (Cont.)											
G705	7995.00	3120.00	5120.00	6250.00	MM	6	504D	5F-1R	101	7900	No
G706 4WD	10200.00	3980.00	6530.00	7970.00	MM	6	504LP	5F-1R	101	8600	No
G706 4WD	10540.00	4110.00	6750.00	8240.00	MM	6	504D	5F-1R	101	8800	No
1964											
Jet Star III	3515.00	1490.00	2380.00	2900.00	MM	4	206G	10F-2R	44	3430	No
Jet Star III	3865.00	1620.00	2590.00	3160.00	MM	4	206LP	10F-2R	44	3630	No
Jet Star III	4205.00	1800.00	2880.00	3510.00	MM	4	206D	10F-2R	45	3940	No
U302	3960.00	1690.00	2710.00	3310.00	MM	4	221G	10F-2R	55.8	5425	No
U302	4300.00	1800.00	2880.00	3510.00	MM	4	221LP	10F-2R	55.6	5640	No
M602	4375.00	1840.00	2940.00	3590.00	MM	4	336G	10F-2R	64	6550	No
M602	4675.00	1920.00	3070.00	3750.00	MM	4	336LP	10F-2R	64	6750	No
M602	4966.00	2310.00	3700.00	4510.00	MM	4	336D	10F-2R	64	6950	No
M604 4WD	6721.00	2800.00	4490.00	5480.00	MM	4	336G	10F-2R	73	7020	No
M604 4WD	7017.00	2840.00	4550.00	5550.00	MM	4	336LP	10F-2R	73	7220	No
M604 4WD	7312.00	3110.00	4980.00	6080.00	MM	4	336D	10F-2R	74	7420	No
M670	4900.00	2000.00	3200.00	3900.00	MM	4	336G	10F-2R	73.2	6550	No
M670	5196.00	2120.00	3390.00	4140.00	MM	4	336LP	10F-2R	73.2	6750	No
M670	5491.00	2200.00	3520.00	4290.00	MM	4	336D	10F-2R	71	6950	No
G705	7805.00	3120.00	5000.00	6100.00	MM	6	504LP	5F-1R	101.6	7700	No
G705	8152.00	3260.00	5220.00	6370.00	MM	6	504D	5F-1R	101.4	7900	No
G706 4WD	10400.00	4160.00	6660.00	8130.00	MM	6	504LP	5F-1R	101.4	8600	No
G706 4WD	10750.00	4300.00	6880.00	8390.00	MM	6	504D	5F-1R	101.6	8800	No
1965											
Jet Star III	3582.00	1650.00	2570.00	3140.00	MM	4	206G	10F-2R	44	3430	No
Jet Star III	3941.00	1830.00	2850.00	3480.00	MM	4	206LP	10F-2R	44	3630	No
Jet Star III	4290.00	2010.00	3130.00	3820.00	MM	4	206D	10F-2R	45	3940	No
U302	4040.00	1820.00	2840.00	3470.00	MM	4	221G	10F-2R	55.8	5425	No
U302	4386.00	1890.00	2950.00	3600.00	MM	4	221LP	10F-2R	55.6	5640	No
M670	4990.00	2090.00	3260.00	3980.00	MM	4	336G	10F-2R	73.2	6550	No
M670	5300.00	2260.00	3520.00	4290.00	MM	4	336LP	10F-2R	73.2	6750	No
M670	5600.00	2380.00	3720.00	4540.00	MM	4	336D	10F-2R	71	6950	No
G705	7960.00	3260.00	5090.00	6210.00	MM	6	504LP	5F-1R	101.6	7700	No
G705	8315.00	3410.00	5320.00	6490.00	MM	6	504D	5F-1R	101.4	7900	No
G706 4WD	10615.00	4350.00	6790.00	8280.00	MM	6	504LP	5F-1R	101.4	8600	No
G706 4WD	10966.00	4500.00	7020.00	8560.00	MM	6	504D	5F-1R	101.6	8800	No
G707	8120.00	3330.00	5200.00	6340.00	MM	6	504LP	5F-1R	101	7700	No
G707	8481.00	3480.00	5430.00	6630.00	MM	6	504D	5F-1R	101	7900	No
G708 4WD	10825.00	4440.00	6930.00	8460.00	MM	6	504LP	5F-1R	101	8600	No
G708 4WD	11185.00	4590.00	7160.00	8740.00	MM	6	504D	5F-1R	101	8800	No
G1000	8524.00	3640.00	5690.00	6940.00	MM	6	504LP	10F-2R	110	10000	No
G1000	8905.00	3690.00	5760.00	7030.00	MM	6	504D	10F-2R	110	10200	No
1966											
Jet Star III	3761.00	2110.00	3210.00	3920.00	MM	4	206G	10F-2R	44	3430	No
Jet Star III	4138.00	2080.00	3170.00	3870.00	MM	4	206LP	10F-2R	44	3630	No
Jet Star III	4503.00	2350.00	3580.00	4370.00	MM	4	206D	10F-2R	45	3940	No
U302	4241.00	2020.00	3070.00	3750.00	MM	4	221G	10F-2R	55.8	5425	No
U302	4605.00	2100.00	3200.00	3900.00	MM	4	221LP	10F-2R	55.6	5640	No
M670	5345.00	2440.00	3710.00	4530.00	MM	4	336G	10F-2R	73.2	6550	No
M670	5565.00	2480.00	3780.00	4610.00	MM	4	336LP	10F-2R	73.2	6750	No
M670	5700.00	2520.00	3840.00	4690.00	MM	4	336D	10F-2R	71	6950	No
G1000	8695.00	3770.00	5740.00	7000.00	MM	6	504LP	10F-2R	110.7	10000	No
G1000	9350.00	4200.00	6400.00	7810.00	MM	6	504D	10F-2R	110	10200	No
1967											
Jet Star III	3836.00	2160.00	3210.00	3920.00	MM	4	206G	10F-2R	44	3430	No
Jet Star III	4221.00	2130.00	3170.00	3870.00	MM	4	206LP	10F-2R	44	3630	No
Jet Star III	4595.00	2410.00	3580.00	4370.00	MM	4	206D	10F-2R	45	3940	No
U302	4326.00	2290.00	3410.00	4160.00	MM	4	221G	10F-2R	55.8	5425	No
U302	4697.00	2370.00	3520.00	4290.00	MM	4	221LP	10F-2R	55.6	5640	No
M670	5345.00	2490.00	3710.00	4530.00	MM	4	336G	10F-2R	73.2	6550	No
M670	5843.00	2510.00	3740.00	4560.00	MM	4	336LP	10F-2R	73.2	6750	No
M670	6000.00	2800.00	4170.00	5090.00	MM	4	336D	10F-2R	71	6950	No
G900	6900.00	3150.00	4690.00	5720.00	MM	6	425G	10F-2R	97.8	9200	No
G900	7200.00	3280.00	4880.00	5950.00	MM	6	425LP	10F-2R	97.8	9400	No
G900	7500.00	3450.00	5140.00	6270.00	MM	6	451D	10F-2R	97.7	9600	No
G1000	9130.00	4450.00	6620.00	8080.00	MM	6	504LP	10F-2R	111	10000	No
G1000	9820.00	5230.00	7780.00	9490.00	MM	6	504D	10F-2R	110	10200	No
G1000 Wheatland	8950.00	3850.00	5730.00	6990.00	MM	6	504LP	10F-2R	110.7	10200	No
G1000 Wheatland	9720.00	4180.00	6220.00	7590.00	MM	6	504D	10F-2R	110.8	10400	No
1968											
Jet Star	4432.00	2440.00	3550.00	4330.00	MM	4	206LP	10F-2R	45	3630	No
Jet Star III	4028.00	2210.00	3210.00	3920.00	MM	4	206G	10F-2R	44	3430	No
Jet Star III	4800.00	2460.00	3580.00	4370.00	MM	4	206D	10F-2R	45	3940	No
U302	4545.00	2520.00	3670.00	4480.00	MM	4	221G	10F-2R	55.8	5425	No
U302	4932.00	2520.00	3670.00	4480.00	MM	4	221LP	10F-2R	55.8	5640	No
U302	5250.00	2820.00	4100.00	5000.00	MM		236D	10F-2R	55.6	5840	No
M670	5615.00	2550.00	3710.00	4530.00	MM	4	336G	10F-2R	73.2	6550	No
M670	6135.00	2700.00	3930.00	4800.00	MM	4	336LP	10F-2R	73.2	6750	No
M670	6300.00	3040.00	4430.00	5410.00	MM	4	336D	10F-2R	71	6950	No
G900	7245.00	3360.00	4880.00	5950.00	MM	6	425G	10F-2R	97.8	9200	No

Minneapolis-Moline (Cont.)

1968 (Cont.)

Model	Approx. Retail Price New	Estimated Average Value Less Repairs Fair	Good	Premium	Engine Make	No. Cyls.	Displ. Cu.-In.	No. Speeds	P.T.O. H.P.	Approx. Shipping Wt.-Lbs.	Cab
G900	7560.00	**3360.00**	**4880.00**	**5950.00**	MM	6	425LP	10F-2R	97.8	9400	No
G900	7875.00	**3530.00**	**5140.00**	**6270.00**	MM	6	451D	10F-2R	97.7	9600	No
G1000	9585.00	**4400.00**	**6400.00**	**7810.00**	MM	6	504LP	10F-2R	111	10000	No
G1000	10310.00	**4910.00**	**7140.00**	**8710.00**	MM	6	504D	10F-2R	110	10200	No
G1000 Wheatland	9395.00	**4300.00**	**6260.00**	**7640.00**	MM	6	504LP	10F-2R	110.7	10200	No
G1000 Wheatland	10206.00	**4490.00**	**6530.00**	**7970.00**	MM	6	504D	10F-2R	110.8	10400	No

1969

Model	Approx. Retail Price New	Fair	Good	Premium	Make	No. Cyls.	Displ. Cu.-In.	No. Speeds	P.T.O. H.P.	Approx. Shipping Wt.-Lbs.	Cab
Jet Star III	4110.00	**2260.00**	**3210.00**	**3920.00**	MM	4	206G	10F-2R	45	3630	No
Jet Star III	4520.00	**2490.00**	**3550.00**	**4330.00**	MM	4	206LP	10F-2R	45	3430	No
Jet Star III	4920.00	**2520.00**	**3580.00**	**4370.00**	MM	4	206D	10F-2R	45	3940	No
A4T-1400 4WD	19620.00	**5490.00**	**7650.00**	**8570.00**	MM	6	504D	10F-2R		17300	No
U302	4633.00	**2580.00**	**3670.00**	**4480.00**	MM	4	221G	10F-2R	55.8	5425	No
U302	5031.00	**2580.00**	**3670.00**	**4480.00**	MM	4	221LP	10F-2R	55.8	5640	No
U302	5355.00	**2880.00**	**4100.00**	**5000.00**	MM	4	236D	10F-2R	55.6	5840	No
M670	5725.00	**2610.00**	**3710.00**	**4530.00**	MM	4	336G	10F-2R	73.2	6550	No
M670	6258.00	**2610.00**	**3710.00**	**4530.00**	MM	4	336LP	10F-2R	73.2	6750	No
M670	6425.00	**3110.00**	**4430.00**	**5410.00**	MM	4	336D	10F-2R	71	6950	No
G900	7390.00	**3430.00**	**4880.00**	**5950.00**	MM	6	425G	10F-2R	97.8	9200	No
G900	7712.00	**3430.00**	**4880.00**	**5950.00**	MM	6	425LP	10F-2R	97.8	9400	No
G900	8033.00	**3790.00**	**5400.00**	**6590.00**	MM	6	451D	10F-2R	97.7	9600	No
G950	7538.00	**3880.00**	**5510.00**	**6720.00**	MM	6	425G	10F-2R	98	9950	No
G950	7866.00	**3920.00**	**5570.00**	**6800.00**	MM	6	425LP	10F-2R	98	10550	No
G950	8194.00	**4220.00**	**6000.00**	**7320.00**	MM	6	451D	10F-2R	98	11150	No
G1000	9777.00	**4660.00**	**6620.00**	**8080.00**	MM	6	504LP	10F-2R	111	10000	No
G1000	10515.00	**5470.00**	**7780.00**	**9490.00**	MM	6	504D	10F-2R	110	10200	No
G1000 Wheatland	9581.00	**4400.00**	**6260.00**	**7640.00**	MM	6	504LP	10F-2R	110.7	10200	No
G1000 Wheatland	10410.00	**4340.00**	**6180.00**	**7540.00**	MM	6	504D	10F-2R	110.8	10400	No
G1050	10266.00	**4810.00**	**6840.00**	**8350.00**	MM	6	504LP	10F-2R	110	11050	No
G1050	11041.00	**5300.00**	**7540.00**	**9200.00**	MM	6	585D	10F-2R	141.4	11250	No
G1350	11295.00	**6150.00**	**8750.00**	**10680.00**	MM	6	585D	10F-2R	141.4	12400	No
G1350	11295.00	**6150.00**	**8750.00**	**10680.00**	MM	6	504LP	10F-2R		12200	No

1970

Model	Approx. Retail Price New	Fair	Good	Premium	Make	No. Cyls.	Displ. Cu.-In.	No. Speeds	P.T.O. H.P.	Approx. Shipping Wt.-Lbs.	Cab
Jet Star III	4566.00	**1510.00**	**2010.00**	**2250.00**	MM	4	206LP	10F-2R	45.00	3630	No
Jet Star III	4700.00	**1550.00**	**2070.00**	**2320.00**	MM	4	206G	10F-2R	44.00	3430	No
Jet Star III	4968.00	**1640.00**	**2190.00**	**2450.00**	MM	4	206D	10F-2R		3940	No
A4T-1400 4WD	20136.00	**5640.00**	**7850.00**	**8790.00**	MM	6	504D	10F-2R		17300	No
U302	4679.00	**1540.00**	**2060.00**	**2310.00**	MM	4	221G	10F-2R	55.82	5425	No
U302	5081.00	**1680.00**	**2240.00**	**2510.00**	MM	4	221LP	10F-2R	55.69	5640	No
U302	5409.00	**1790.00**	**2380.00**	**2670.00**	MM	4	236D	10F-2R		5840	No
M670	5781.00	**1910.00**	**2540.00**	**2850.00**	MM	4	336G	10F-2R	73.02	6550	No
M670	6321.00	**2090.00**	**2780.00**	**3110.00**	MM	4	336LP	10F-2R	74.16	6750	No
M670	6489.00	**2140.00**	**2860.00**	**3200.00**	MM	4	336D	10F-2R	71.01	6950	No
G950	7613.00	**2510.00**	**3350.00**	**3750.00**	MM	6	425G	15F-3R		9950	No
G950	7945.00	**2620.00**	**3500.00**	**3920.00**	MM	6	425LP	15F-3R		10550	No
G950	8276.00	**2730.00**	**3640.00**	**4080.00**	MM	6	451D	15F-3R		11150	No
G1000	9973.00	**3290.00**	**4390.00**	**4920.00**	MM	6	504LP	10F-2R	110.94	10000	No
G1000	10725.00	**3540.00**	**4720.00**	**5290.00**	MM	6	504D	10F-2R	111.00	10200	No
G1000 Wheatland	9773.00	**3230.00**	**4300.00**	**4820.00**	MM	6	504LP	10F-2R	110.76	10200	No
G1000 Wheatland	10609.00	**3500.00**	**4670.00**	**5230.00**	MM	6	504D	10F-2R	110.78	10400	No
G1050	10471.00	**3460.00**	**4610.00**	**5160.00**	MM	6	504LP	15F-3R		11450	No
G1050	11262.00	**3720.00**	**4960.00**	**5560.00**	MM	6	504D	15F-3R		11650	No
G1350	11519.00	**3800.00**	**5070.00**	**5680.00**	MM	6	504LP	10F-2R		12200	No
G1350	12388.00	**4090.00**	**5450.00**	**6100.00**	MM	6	585D	10F-2R	141.44	12400	No

1971

Model	Approx. Retail Price New	Fair	Good	Premium	Make	No. Cyls.	Displ. Cu.-In.	No. Speeds	P.T.O. H.P.	Approx. Shipping Wt.-Lbs.	Cab
A4T-1600 4WD	21366.00	**5980.00**	**8330.00**	**9330.00**	MM	6	504D	10F-2R	143.27	17700	No
G350	4883.00	**1660.00**	**2150.00**	**2410.00**	Fiat	3	158D	9F-3R	41.00	3810	No
G350 4WD	6064.00	**2060.00**	**2670.00**	**2990.00**	Fiat	3	158D	9F-3R	41.00	4360	No
G450	6074.00	**2070.00**	**2670.00**	**2990.00**	Fiat	4	211D	12F-3R	54.00	4380	No
G450 4WD	7140.00	**2430.00**	**3140.00**	**3520.00**	Fiat	4	211D	12F-3R	54.00	5120	No
G550	3867.00	**1320.00**	**1700.00**	**1900.00**	MM	4	155G	12F-4R	44.00	3250	No
G550	4744.00	**1610.00**	**2090.00**	**2340.00**	MM	4	155D	12F-4R	39.00	3275	No
G750	7205.00	**2450.00**	**3170.00**	**3550.00**	MM	6	265G	18F-6R	70.00	7380	No
G750	7679.00	**2610.00**	**3380.00**	**3790.00**	MM	6	265LP	18F-6R		7580	No
G750	8065.00	**2740.00**	**3550.00**	**3980.00**	MM	6	283D	18F-6R	70.00	7780	No
G850	7987.00	**2720.00**	**3510.00**	**3930.00**	MM	6	283G	18F-6R	86.00	8870	No
G850	8711.00	**2960.00**	**3830.00**	**4290.00**	MM	6	310D	18F-6R	86.00	9270	No
G940	9000.00	**3060.00**	**3960.00**	**4440.00**	MM	6	310G	18F-6R		8976	No
G940	9960.00	**3390.00**	**4380.00**	**4910.00**	MM	6	310D	18F-6R		9376	No
G950	9460.00	**3220.00**	**4160.00**	**4660.00**	MM	6	425G	15F-3R		9950	No
G950	9722.00	**3310.00**	**4280.00**	**4790.00**	MM	6	425LP	15F-3R		10550	No
G950	10039.00	**3410.00**	**4420.00**	**4950.00**	MM	6	451D	15F-3R		11150	No
G1050	10576.00	**3600.00**	**4650.00**	**5210.00**	MM	6	504LP	15F-3R		11450	No
G1050	11375.00	**3870.00**	**5010.00**	**5610.00**	MM	6	504D	15F-3R		11650	No
G1350	11634.00	**3960.00**	**5120.00**	**5730.00**	MM	6	504LP	10F-2R		12200	No
G1350	12512.00	**4250.00**	**5510.00**	**6170.00**	MM	6	585D	10F-2R	141.44	12400	No

1972

Model	Approx. Retail Price New	Fair	Good	Premium	Make	No. Cyls.	Displ. Cu.-In.	No. Speeds	P.T.O. H.P.	Approx. Shipping Wt.-Lbs.	Cab
A4T-1600 4WD	22416.00	**6280.00**	**8740.00**	**9790.00**	MM	6	504D	10F-2R	143.27	17700	No
G350	4932.00	**1730.00**	**2170.00**	**2430.00**	Fiat	3	158D	9F-3R	41.00	3810	No
G350 4WD	6125.00	**2140.00**	**2700.00**	**3020.00**	Fiat	3	158D	9F-3R	41.00	4360	No
G450	6135.00	**2150.00**	**2700.00**	**3020.00**	Fiat	4	211D	12F-3R	54.00	4380	No

Model	Approx. Retail Price New	Estimated Average Value Less Repairs Fair	Good	Premium	Engine Make	No. Cyls.	Displ. Cu.-In.	No. Speeds	P.T.O. H.P.	Approx. Shipping Wt.-Lbs.	Cab

Minneapolis-Moline (Cont.)

Model	Approx. Retail Price New	Fair	Good	Premium	Make	No. Cyls.	Displ. Cu.-In.	No. Speeds	P.T.O. H.P.	Approx. Shipping Wt.-Lbs.	Cab
			1972 (Cont.)								
G450 4WD	7211.00	2520.00	3170.00	3550.00	Fiat	4	211D	12F-3R	54.00	5120	No
G550	3906.00	1370.00	1720.00	1930.00	MM	4	155G	12F-4R	44.00	6830	No
G550	4791.00	1680.00	2110.00	2360.00	MM	4	155D	12F-4R	39.00	6940	No
G750	7565.00	2650.00	3330.00	3730.00	MM	6	265G	18F-6R	70.00	7380	No
G750	8063.00	2820.00	3550.00	3980.00	MM	6	265LP	18F-6R		7580	No
G750	8468.00	2960.00	3730.00	4180.00	MM	6	283D	18F-6R	70.00	7780	No
G850	8386.00	2940.00	3690.00	4130.00	MM	6	283G	18F-6R	86.00	8870	No
G850	9147.00	3200.00	4030.00	4510.00	MM	6	310D	18F-6R	86.00	9270	No
G940	9300.00	3260.00	4090.00	4580.00	MM	6	310G	18F-6R		8976	No
G940	10000.00	3500.00	4400.00	4930.00	MM	6	310D	18F-6R		9376	No
G950	9555.00	3340.00	4200.00	4700.00	MM	6	425G	15F-3R		9950	No
G950	9812.00	3430.00	4320.00	4840.00	MM	6	425LP	15F-3R		10550	No
G950	10139.00	3550.00	4460.00	5000.00	MM	6	451D	15F-3R		11150	No
G1050	10682.00	3740.00	4700.00	5260.00	MM	6	504LP	15F-3R		11450	No
G1050	11489.00	4020.00	5060.00	5670.00	MM	6	504D	15F-3R		11650	No
G1350	11750.00	4110.00	5170.00	5790.00	MM	6	504LP	10F-2R		12200	No
G1350	12637.00	4420.00	5560.00	6230.00	MM	6	585D	10F-2R	141.44	12400	No
G1355	11985.00	4200.00	5270.00	5900.00	MM	6	504LP	18F-6R	137.00	12600	No
G1355	12890.00	4510.00	5670.00	6350.00	MM	6	585D	18F-6R	142.62	13000	No
			1973								
G350	4981.00	1790.00	2240.00	2490.00	Fiat	3	158D	9F-3R	41.00	3810	No
G350 4WD	6186.00	2230.00	2780.00	3090.00	Fiat	3	158D	9F-3R	41.00	4360	No
G450	6196.00	2230.00	2790.00	3100.00	Fiat	4	211D	12F-3R	54.00	4380	No
G450 4WD	7283.00	2620.00	3280.00	3640.00	Fiat	4	211D	12F-3R	54.00	5120	No
G550	4101.00	1480.00	1850.00	2050.00	MM	4	155G	12F-4R	44.00	6830	No
G550	4839.00	1740.00	2180.00	2420.00	MM	4	155D	12F-4R	39.00	6940	No
G750	7943.00	2860.00	3570.00	3960.00	MM	6	265G	18F-6R	70.00	7380	No
G750	8466.00	3050.00	3810.00	4230.00	MM	6	265LP	18F-6R		7580	No
G750	8891.00	3200.00	4000.00	4440.00	MM	6	283D	18F-6R	70.00	7780	No
G850	8553.00	3080.00	3850.00	4270.00	MM	6	283G	18F-6R	86.00	8870	No
G850	9330.00	3360.00	4200.00	4660.00	MM	6	310D	18F-6R	86.00	9270	No
G940	9400.00	3380.00	4230.00	4700.00	MM	6	310G	18F-6R		8976	No
G940	10100.00	3640.00	4550.00	5050.00	MM	6	310D	18F-6R		9376	No
G955	10303.00	3710.00	4640.00	5150.00	MM	6	425LP	18F-6R	97.00	10612	No
G955	10646.00	3830.00	4790.00	5320.00	MM	6	451D	18F-6R	98.33	10812	No
G1355	12104.00	4360.00	5450.00	6050.00	MM	6	504LP	18F-6R	137.00	12600	No
G1355	13019.00	4690.00	5860.00	6510.00	MM	6	585D	18F-6R	142.62	13000	No
			1974								
G955	10406.00	3850.00	4790.00	5320.00	MM	6	425LP	18F-6R	97.00	10612	No
G955	10752.00	3980.00	4950.00	5500.00	MM	6	451D	18F-6R	98.33	10812	No
G1355	12225.00	4520.00	5620.00	6240.00	MM	6	504LP	18F-6R	137.00	12600	No
G1355	13136.00	4860.00	6040.00	6700.00	MM	6	585D	18F-6R	142.62	13000	No

Mitsubishi-Satoh

Model	Approx. Retail Price New	Fair	Good	Premium	Make	No. Cyls.	Displ. Cu.-In.	No. Speeds	P.T.O. H.P.	Approx. Shipping Wt.-Lbs.	Cab
			1973								
S650G	2914.00	1050.00	1310.00	1450.00	Mazda	4	60G	6F-2R	22.03	2105	No
			1974								
S650G	3232.00	1200.00	1490.00	1650.00	Mazda	4	60G	6F-2R	22.03	2105	No
			1975								
S650G	3550.00	1350.00	1670.00	1850.00	Mazda	4	60G	6F-2R	22.03	2105	No
			1976								
S650G	3668.00	1430.00	1760.00	1940.00	Mazda	4	60G	6F-2R	22.03	2105	No
			1977								
Elk	3590.00	1440.00	1760.00	1940.00	Mazda	4	60G	6F-2R	17.00	1430	No
Beaver S370	3204.00	1280.00	1570.00	1730.00	Mitsubishi	2	41D	6F-2R	12.20	1035	No
Beaver S370D	3518.00	1410.00	1720.00	1890.00	Mitsubishi	2	41D	6F-2R	12.20	1180	No
Bison S650G	4532.00	1810.00	2220.00	2440.00	Mazda	4	60G	6F-2R	22.03	2110	No
Stallion S750	6600.00	2640.00	3230.00	3550.00	Isuzu	3	108D	9F-3R	33.00	2865	No
D--Front Wheel Assist											
			1978								
Bull	5366.00	2200.00	2680.00	2950.00	Mitsubishi	2	76D	9F-3R	22.00	1940	No
Beaver S370	3554.00	1460.00	1780.00	1960.00	Mitsubishi	2	41D	6F-2R	12.20	1035	No
Beaver S370D	3898.00	1600.00	1950.00	2150.00	Mitsubishi	2	41D	6F-2R	12.20	1180	No
Bison S650G	5284.00	2170.00	2640.00	2900.00	Mazda	4	60G	6F-2R	22.03	2110	No
Stallion S750	7414.00	3040.00	3710.00	4080.00	Isuzu	3	108D	9F-3R	33.00	2865	No
D--Front Wheel Assist											
			1979								
Beaver S370	3880.00	1550.00	1880.00	2050.00	Mitsubishi	2	41D	6F-2R	12.20	1035	No
Beaver S370D	4254.00	1700.00	2070.00	2260.00	Mitsubishi	2	41D	6F-2R	12.20	1180	No
Buck S470	4538.00	1820.00	2210.00	2410.00	Mitsubishi	3	52D	6F-2R	15.00	1155	No
Buck S470D	5088.00	2050.00	2490.00	2710.00	Mitsubishi	3	52D	6F-2R	15.00	1265	No
Bull S630	5858.00	2380.00	2890.00	3150.00	Mitsubishi	2	76D	9F-3R	22.00	1940	No
Bull S630D	6712.00	2740.00	3320.00	3620.00	Mitsubishi	2	76D	9F-3R	22.00	2140	No
Bison S650G	5768.00	2340.00	2840.00	3100.00	Mazda	4	60G	6F-2R	22.03	2110	No

Model	Approx. Retail Price New	Estimated Average Value Less Repairs Fair	Good	Premium	Engine Make	No. Cyls.	Displ. Cu.-In.	No. Speeds	P.T.O. H.P.	Approx. Shipping Wt.-Lbs.	Cab

Mitsubishi-Satoh (Cont.)

1979 (Cont.)

Model	Approx. Retail Price New	Fair	Good	Premium	Make	No. Cyls.	Displ. Cu.-In.	No. Speeds	P.T.O. H.P.	Approx. Shipping Wt.-Lbs.	Cab
Stallion S750	8094.00	**2750.00**	**3480.00**	**3790.00**	Isuzu	3	108D	9F-3R	33.00	2865	No
Stallion S750D	10932.00	**3400.00**	**4300.00**	**4690.00**	Isuzu	3	108D	9F-3R	33.00	3440	No

D--Front Wheel Assist

1980

Model	Approx. Retail Price New	Fair	Good	Premium	Make	No. Cyls.	Displ. Cu.-In.	No. Speeds	P.T.O. H.P.	Approx. Shipping Wt.-Lbs.	Cab
Beaver S370	3940.00	**1690.00**	**2050.00**	**2210.00**	Mitsubishi	2	41D	6F-2R	12.20	1035	No
Beaver S370D	4300.00	**1850.00**	**2240.00**	**2420.00**	Mitsubishi	2	41D	6F-2R	12.20	1180	No
Beaver III S373	4500.00	**1940.00**	**2340.00**	**2530.00**	Mitsubishi	3	47D	6F-2R	13.60	1125	No
Beaver III S373D	4860.00	**2090.00**	**2530.00**	**2730.00**	Mitsubishi	3	47D	6F-2R	13.60	1235	No
Buck S470	4860.00	**2090.00**	**2530.00**	**2730.00**	Mitsubishi	3	52D	6F-2R	14.60	1155	No
Buck S470D	5280.00	**2270.00**	**2750.00**	**2970.00**	Mitsubishi	3	52D	6F-2R	14.60	1265	No
Bull S630	5780.00	**2490.00**	**3010.00**	**3250.00**	Mitsubishi	2	76D	9F-3R	22.00	1940	No
Bull S630 4WD	6620.00	**2850.00**	**3440.00**	**3720.00**	Mitsubishi	2	76D	9F-3R	22.00	2140	No
Bison S650G	5975.00	**2570.00**	**3110.00**	**3360.00**	Mazda	4	60G	6F-2R	22.03	2110	No
Bison S670	8580.00	**3000.00**	**3780.00**	**4120.00**	Mitsubishi	4	80D	6F-2R	25.00	2315	No
Bison S670D 4WD	9820.00	**3440.00**	**4320.00**	**4710.00**	Mitsubishi	4	80D	6F-2R	25.00	2535	No
Stallion S750	8840.00	**3090.00**	**3890.00**	**4240.00**	Isuzu	3	108D	9F-3R	33.00	2865	No
Stallion S750D 4WD	10934.00	**3830.00**	**4810.00**	**5240.00**	Isuzu	3	108D	9F-3R	33.00	3440	No

D--Front Wheel Assist

1981

Model	Approx. Retail Price New	Fair	Good	Premium	Make	No. Cyls.	Displ. Cu.-In.	No. Speeds	P.T.O. H.P.	Approx. Shipping Wt.-Lbs.	Cab
Beaver S370	4636.00	**2040.00**	**2460.00**	**2660.00**	Mitsubishi	2	41D	6F-2R	12.20	1035	No
Beaver S370D 4WD	5050.00	**2220.00**	**2680.00**	**2890.00**	Mitsubishi	2	41D	6F-2R	12.20	1180	No
Beaver III S373	5296.00	**2330.00**	**2810.00**	**3040.00**	Mitsubishi	3	47D	6F-2R	13.60	1125	No
Beaver III S373D 4WD	5718.00	**2520.00**	**3030.00**	**3270.00**	Mitsubishi	3	47D	6F-2R	13.60	1235	No
Buck S470	5664.00	**2490.00**	**3000.00**	**3240.00**	Mitsubishi	3	52D	6F-2R	14.60	1155	No
Buck S470D 4WD	6158.00	**2710.00**	**3260.00**	**3520.00**	Mitsubishi	3	52D	6F-2R	14.60	1265	No
Bull S630	6736.00	**2960.00**	**3570.00**	**3860.00**	Mitsubishi	2	76D	9F-3R	22.00	1940	No
Bull S630D 4WD	7716.00	**3400.00**	**4090.00**	**4420.00**	Mitsubishi	2	76D	9F-3R	22.00	2140	No
Bison S650G	7275.00	**3200.00**	**3860.00**	**4170.00**	Mazda	4	60G	6F-2R	22.03	2110	No
Bison S670	9810.00	**3530.00**	**4420.00**	**4820.00**	Mitsubishi	4	80D	6F-2R	25.00	2315	No
Bison S670D 4WD	11228.00	**4040.00**	**5050.00**	**5510.00**	Mitsubishi	4	80D	6F-2R	25.00	2535	No
Stallion S750	10106.00	**3640.00**	**4550.00**	**4960.00**	Isuzu	3	108D	9F-3R	33.00	2865	No
Stallion S750D 4WD	12500.00	**4500.00**	**5630.00**	**6140.00**	Isuzu	3	108D	9F-3R	33.00	3440	No

D--Front Wheel Assist

1982

Model	Approx. Retail Price New	Fair	Good	Premium	Make	No. Cyls.	Displ. Cu.-In.	No. Speeds	P.T.O. H.P.	Approx. Shipping Wt.-Lbs.	Cab
MT180H	7042.00	**3170.00**	**3800.00**	**4100.00**	Mitsubishi	3	55D	Infinite		1268	No
MT180HD 4WD	7521.00	**3380.00**	**4060.00**	**4390.00**	Mitsubishi	3	55D	Infinite		1378	No
MT210	6900.00	**3110.00**	**3730.00**	**4030.00**	Mitsubishi	3	60D	9F-3R		1720	No
MT210D	7857.00	**3540.00**	**4240.00**	**4580.00**	Mitsubishi	3	60D	9F-3R		1852	No
MT250	7854.00	**3530.00**	**4240.00**	**4580.00**	Mitsubishi	3	78D	9F-3R		1940	No
MT250D	8811.00	**3970.00**	**4760.00**	**5140.00**	Mitsubishi	3	78D	9F-3R		2040	No
Beaver S370	5279.00	**2380.00**	**2850.00**	**3080.00**	Mitsubishi	2	41D	6F-2R	12.20	1035	No
Beaver S370D 4WD	5720.00	**2570.00**	**3090.00**	**3340.00**	Mitsubishi	2	41D	6F-2R	12.20	1180	No
MT372	5260.00	**2370.00**	**2840.00**	**3070.00**	Mitsubishi	2	41D	6F-2R	12.20	1069	No
MT372D 4WD	5701.00	**2570.00**	**3080.00**	**3330.00**	Mitsubishi	2	41D	6F-2R	12.20	1177	No
Beaver III S373	5464.00	**2460.00**	**2950.00**	**3190.00**	Mitsubishi	3	47D	6F-2R	13.60	1125	No
Beaver III S373D 4WD	5872.00	**2640.00**	**3170.00**	**3420.00**	Mitsubishi	3	47D	6F-2R	13.60	1235	No
Buck S470	5872.00	**2640.00**	**3170.00**	**3420.00**	Mitsubishi	3	52D	6F-2R	14.60	1155	No
Buck S470D 4WD	6351.00	**2860.00**	**3430.00**	**3700.00**	Mitsubishi	3	52D	6F-2R	14.60	1265	No
Bull S630	6922.00	**3120.00**	**3740.00**	**4040.00**	Mitsubishi	2	76D	9F-3R	22.00	1940	No
Bull S630D 4WD	7879.00	**3550.00**	**4260.00**	**4600.00**	Mitsubishi	2	76D	9F-3R	22.00	2140	No
Bison S650G	7686.00	**3460.00**	**4150.00**	**4480.00**	Mazda	4	60G	6F-2R	22.03	2110	No
Bison S670	10113.00	**3740.00**	**4650.00**	**5020.00**	Mitsubishi	4	80D	6F-2R	25.00	2315	No
Bison S670D 4WD	11526.00	**4270.00**	**5300.00**	**5720.00**	Mitsubishi	4	80D	6F-2R	25.00	2535	No
Stallion S750	10409.00	**3850.00**	**4790.00**	**5170.00**	Isuzu	3	108D	9F-3R	33.00	2865	No
Stallion S750D 4WD	12795.00	**4730.00**	**5890.00**	**6360.00**	Isuzu	3	108D	9F-3R	33.00	3440	No

D--Front Wheel Assist

1983

Model	Approx. Retail Price New	Fair	Good	Premium	Make	No. Cyls.	Displ. Cu.-In.	No. Speeds	P.T.O. H.P.	Approx. Shipping Wt.-Lbs.	Cab
MT180 H	7042.00	**3240.00**	**3870.00**	**4180.00**	Mitsubishi	3	55D	Infinite		1268	No
MT180 HD 4WD	7521.00	**3460.00**	**4140.00**	**4470.00**	Mitsubishi	3	55D	Infinite		1378	No
MT210	6995.00	**3220.00**	**3850.00**	**4160.00**	Mitsubishi	3	60D	9F-3R		1720	No
MT210D 4WD	7857.00	**3610.00**	**4320.00**	**4670.00**	Mitsubishi	3	60D	9F-3R		1852	No
MT250	8095.00	**3720.00**	**4450.00**	**4810.00**	Mitsubishi	3	78D	9F-3R		1940	No
MT250D 4WD	8811.00	**4050.00**	**4850.00**	**5240.00**	Mitsubishi	3	78D	9F-3R		2040	No
Beaver S370	5279.00	**2430.00**	**2900.00**	**3130.00**	Mitsubishi	2	41D	6F-2R	12.20	1136	No
Beaver S370 D 4WD	5720.00	**2630.00**	**3150.00**	**3400.00**	Mitsubishi	2	41D	6F-2R	12.20	1180	No
MT372	5260.00	**2420.00**	**2890.00**	**3120.00**	Mitsubishi	2	41D	6F-2R	12.20	1069	No
MT372 D 4WD	5701.00	**2620.00**	**3140.00**	**3390.00**	Mitsubishi	2	41D	6F-2R	12.20	1177	No
Beaver III S373	5729.00	**2640.00**	**3150.00**	**3400.00**	Mitsubishi	3	47D	6F-2R	13.60	1356	No
Beaver III S373D 4WD	6028.00	**2770.00**	**3320.00**	**3590.00**	Mitsubishi	3	47D	6F-2R	13.60	1433	No
Buck S470	5969.00	**2750.00**	**3280.00**	**3540.00**	Mitsubishi	3	52D	6F-2R	14.60	1367	No
Buck S470D 4WD	6487.00	**2980.00**	**3570.00**	**3860.00**	Mitsubishi	3	52D	6F-2R	14.60	1444	No
Bull S630	7135.00	**3280.00**	**3920.00**	**4230.00**	Mitsubishi	2	76D	9F-3R	22.00	1940	No
Bull S630D 4WD	8037.00	**3700.00**	**4420.00**	**4770.00**	Mitsubishi	2	76D	9F-3R	22.00	2140	No
Bison S650G	7686.00	**3540.00**	**4230.00**	**4570.00**	Mazda	4	60G	6F-2R	22.03	2110	No
Bison S670	10113.00	**3840.00**	**4750.00**	**5130.00**	Mitsubishi	4	80D	6F-2R	25.00	2315	No
Bison S670D 4WD	11526.00	**4380.00**	**5420.00**	**5850.00**	Mitsubishi	4	80D	6F-2R	25.00	2535	No
Stallion S750	12329.00	**4690.00**	**5800.00**	**6260.00**	Isuzu	3	108D	9F-3R	33.00	3417	No
Stallion S750D 4WD	14069.00	**5350.00**	**6610.00**	**7140.00**	Isuzu	3	108D	9F-3R	33.00	3590	No

D--Front Wheel Assist H--Hydrostatic Transmission

Mitsubishi-Satoh (Cont.)

1984

Model	Approx. Retail Price New	Estimated Average Value Less Repairs: Fair	Good	Premium	Engine: Make	No. Cyls.	Displ. Cu.-In.	No. Speeds	P.T.O. H.P.	Approx. Shipping Wt.-Lbs.	Cab
MT160	6305.00	2960.00	3530.00	3810.00	Mitsubishi	3	47D	6F-2R	13.60	1246	No
MT160D 4WD	6835.00	3210.00	3830.00	4140.00	Mitsubishi	3	47D	6F-2R	13.60	1356	No
MT180	6725.00	3160.00	3770.00	4070.00	Mitsubishi	3	55D	6F-2R	15.50	1268	No
MT180D 4WD	7265.00	3420.00	4070.00	4400.00	Mitsubishi	3	55D	6F-2R	15.50	1378	No
MT180H	7560.00	3550.00	4230.00	4570.00	Mitsubishi	3	55D	Infinite	15.50	1268	No
MT180HD 4WD	8100.00	3810.00	4540.00	4900.00	Mitsubishi	3	55D	Infinite	15.50	1378	No
MT210	7270.00	3420.00	4070.00	4400.00	Mitsubishi	3	60D	9F-3R	18.30	1720	No
MT210D 4WD	7960.00	3740.00	4460.00	4820.00	Mitsubishi	3	60D	9F-3R	18.30	1852	No
MT250	8130.00	3820.00	4550.00	4910.00	Mitsubishi	3	78D	9F-3R	22.00	1940	No
MT250D 4WD	8960.00	4210.00	5020.00	5420.00	Mitsubishi	3	78D	9F-3R	22.00	2040	No
MT300	9330.00	4390.00	5230.00	5650.00	Mitsubishi	3	91D	9F-3R	25.00	2337	No
MT300D 4WD	10610.00	4990.00	5940.00	6420.00	Mitsubishi	3	91D	9F-3R	25.00	2558	No
Beaver S370	5280.00	2480.00	2960.00	3200.00	Mitsubishi	2	41D	6F-2R	12.20	1136	No
Beaver S370D 4WD	5720.00	2690.00	3200.00	3460.00	Mitsubishi	2	41D	6F-2R	12.20	1180	No
MT372	5560.00	2610.00	3110.00	3360.00	Mitsubishi	2	41D	6F-2R	12.20	1069	No
MT372D 4WD	6075.00	2860.00	3400.00	3670.00	Mitsubishi	2	41D	6F-2R	12.20	1177	No
Beaver III S373	5915.00	2780.00	3310.00	3580.00	Mitsubishi	3	47D	6F-2R	13.60	1356	No
Beaver III S373D 4WD	6385.00	3000.00	3580.00	3870.00	Mitsubishi	3	47D	6F-2R	13.60	1433	No
Buck S470	6325.00	2970.00	3540.00	3820.00	Mitsubishi	3	52D	6F-2R	14.60	1367	No
Buck S470D 4WD	6875.00	3230.00	3850.00	4160.00	Mitsubishi	3	52D	6F-2R	14.60	1444	No
Bull S630	7720.00	3630.00	4320.00	4670.00	Mitsubishi	2	76D	9F-3R	22.00	1940	No
Bull S630D 4WD	8795.00	4130.00	4930.00	5320.00	Mitsubishi	2	76D	9F-3R	22.00	2140	No
Bison S670	10790.00	4210.00	5180.00	5590.00	Mitsubishi	4	80D	6F-2R	25.00	2315	No
Bison S670D 4WD	12350.00	4820.00	5930.00	6400.00	Mitsubishi	4	80D	6F-2R	25.00	2535	No
Stallion S750	12330.00	4810.00	5920.00	6390.00	Isuzu	3	108D	9F-3R	33.00	3417	No
Stallion S750D 4WD	14560.00	5680.00	6990.00	7550.00	Isuzu	3	108D	9F-3R	33.00	3590	No

D--Front Wheel Assist H--Hydrostatic Transmission

1985

Model	Approx. Retail Price New	Fair	Good	Premium	Make	No. Cyls.	Displ. Cu.-In.	No. Speeds	P.T.O. H.P.	Approx. Shipping Wt.-Lbs.	Cab
MT160	6305.00	3030.00	3590.00	3880.00	Mitsubishi	3	47D	6F-2R	13.60	1246	No
MT160D 4WD	6835.00	3280.00	3900.00	4210.00	Mitsubishi	3	47D	6F-2R	13.60	1356	No
MT180	6725.00	3230.00	3830.00	4140.00	Mitsubishi	3	55D	6F-2R	15.50	1268	No
MT180D 4WD	7265.00	3490.00	4140.00	4470.00	Mitsubishi	3	55D	6F-2R	15.50	1378	No
MT180H	7560.00	3630.00	4310.00	4660.00	Mitsubishi	3	55D	Infinite	15.50	1268	No
MT180HD 4WD	8100.00	3890.00	4620.00	4990.00	Mitsubishi	3	55D	Infinite	15.50	1378	No
MT210	7270.00	3490.00	4140.00	4470.00	Mitsubishi	3	60D	9F-3R	18.30	1720	No
MT210D 4WD	7960.00	3820.00	4540.00	4900.00	Mitsubishi	3	60D	9F-3R	18.30	1852	No
MT250	8130.00	3900.00	4630.00	5000.00	Mitsubishi	3	78D	9F-3R	22.00	1940	No
MT250D 4WD	8960.00	4300.00	5110.00	5520.00	Mitsubishi	3	78D	9F-3R	22.00	2040	No
MT300	9330.00	4480.00	5320.00	5750.00	Mitsubishi	3	91D	9F-3R	25.00	2337	No
MT300D 4WD	10610.00	5090.00	6050.00	6530.00	Mitsubishi	3	91D	9F-3R	25.00	2558	No
MT372	5560.00	2670.00	3170.00	3420.00	Mitsubishi	2	41D	6F-2R	12.20	1069	No
MT372D 4WD	6075.00	2920.00	3460.00	3740.00	Mitsubishi	2	41D	6F-2R	12.20	1177	No

D--Front Wheel Assist H--Hydrostatic Transmission

1986

Model	Approx. Retail Price New	Fair	Good	Premium	Make	No. Cyls.	Displ. Cu.-In.	No. Speeds	P.T.O. H.P.	Approx. Shipping Wt.-Lbs.	Cab
MT160	6305.00	3090.00	3660.00	3950.00	Mitsubishi	3	47D	6F-2R	13.60	1246	No
MT160D 4WD	6835.00	3350.00	3960.00	4280.00	Mitsubishi	3	47D	6F-2R	13.60	1356	No
MT180	6725.00	3300.00	3900.00	4210.00	Mitsubishi	3	55D	6F-2R	15.50	1268	No
MT180D 4WD	7265.00	3560.00	4210.00	4550.00	Mitsubishi	3	55D	6F-2R	15.50	1378	No
MT180H	7560.00	3700.00	4390.00	4740.00	Mitsubishi	3	55D	Infinite	15.50	1268	No
MT180HD 4WD	8100.00	3970.00	4700.00	5080.00	Mitsubishi	3	55D	Infinite	15.50	1378	No
MT210	7270.00	3560.00	4220.00	4560.00	Mitsubishi	3	60D	9F-3R	18.30	1720	No
MT210D 4WD	7960.00	3900.00	4620.00	4990.00	Mitsubishi	3	60D	9F-3R	18.30	1852	No
MT250	8130.00	3980.00	4720.00	5100.00	Mitsubishi	3	78D	9F-3R	22.00	1940	No
MT250D 4WD	8960.00	4390.00	5200.00	5620.00	Mitsubishi	3	78D	9F-3R	22.00	2040	No
MT300	9330.00	4570.00	5410.00	5840.00	Mitsubishi	3	91D	9F-3R	25.00	2337	No
MT300D 4WD	10610.00	5200.00	6150.00	6640.00	Mitsubishi	3	91D	9F-3R	25.00	2558	No
MT372	5560.00	2720.00	3230.00	3490.00	Mitsubishi	2	41D	6F-2R	12.20	1069	No
MT372D 4WD	6075.00	2980.00	3520.00	3800.00	Mitsubishi	2	41D	6F-2R	12.20	1177	No
MT4501	16500.00	6770.00	8250.00	8830.00	Mitsubishi	4	127D	9F-3R	37.30	3144	No
MT4501 4WD	19000.00	7790.00	9500.00	10170.00	Mitsubishi	4	127D	9F-3R	37.30	3446	No

D--Front Wheel Assist H--Hydrostatic Transmission

1987

Model	Approx. Retail Price New	Fair	Good	Premium	Make	No. Cyls.	Displ. Cu.-In.	No. Speeds	P.T.O. H.P.	Approx. Shipping Wt.-Lbs.	Cab
MT160	7679.00	3840.00	4530.00	4890.00	Mitsubishi	3	47D	6F-2R	13.60	1246	No
MT160D 4WD	8253.00	4130.00	4870.00	5260.00	Mitsubishi	3	47D	6F-2R	13.60	1356	No
MT180	8301.00	4150.00	4900.00	5290.00	Mitsubishi	3	55D	6F-2R	15.50	1268	No
MT180D 4WD	8743.00	4370.00	5160.00	5570.00	Mitsubishi	3	55D	6F-2R	15.50	1378	No
MT180H	9250.00	4630.00	5460.00	5900.00	Mitsubishi	3	55D	Infinite	15.50	1268	No
MT180HD 4WD	9873.00	4940.00	5830.00	6300.00	Mitsubishi	3	55D	Infinite	15.50	1378	No
MT210	8643.00	4320.00	5100.00	5510.00	Mitsubishi	3	60D	9F-3R	18.30	1720	No
MT210D 4WD	9530.00	4770.00	5620.00	6070.00	Mitsubishi	3	60D	9F-3R	18.30	1852	No
MT250	9563.00	4780.00	5640.00	6090.00	Mitsubishi	3	78D	9F-3R	22.00	1940	No
MT250D 4WD	10436.00	5220.00	6160.00	6650.00	Mitsubishi	3	78D	9F-3R	22.00	2040	No
MT300	10617.00	5310.00	6260.00	6760.00	Mitsubishi	3	91D	9F-3R	25.00	2337	No
MT300D 4WD	12083.00	6040.00	7130.00	7700.00	Mitsubishi	3	91D	9F-3R	25.00	2558	No
MT372	6778.00	3390.00	4000.00	4320.00	Mitsubishi	2	41D	6F-2R	12.20	1069	No
MT372D 4WD	7429.00	3720.00	4380.00	4730.00	Mitsubishi	2	41D	6F-2R	12.20	1177	No
MT4501	17088.00	7180.00	8720.00	9330.00	Mitsubishi	3	127D	9F-3R	37.30	3144	No
MT4501 4WD	19849.00	8340.00	10120.00	10830.00	Mitsubishi	3	127D	9F-3R	37.30	3446	No

D--Front Wheel Assist H--Hydrostatic Transmission

Mitsubishi-Satoh (Cont.)

1988

Model	Approx. Retail Price New	Estimated Average Value Less Repairs Fair	Good	Premium	Engine Make	No. Cyls.	Displ. Cu.-In.	No. Speeds	P.T.O. H.P.	Approx. Shipping Wt.-Lbs.	Cab
MT160	7679.00	3920.00	4610.00	4930.00	Mitsubishi	3	47D	6F-2R	13.60	1246	No
MT160D 4WD	8253.00	4210.00	4950.00	5300.00	Mitsubishi	3	47D	6F-2R	13.60	1356	No
MT180	8301.00	4230.00	4980.00	5330.00	Mitsubishi	3	55D	6F-2R	15.50	1268	No
MT180D 4WD	8743.00	4460.00	5250.00	5620.00	Mitsubishi	3	55D	6F-2R	15.50	1378	No
MT180H	9250.00	4720.00	5550.00	5940.00	Mitsubishi	3	55D	Infinite	15.50	1268	No
MT180HD 4WD	9873.00	5040.00	5920.00	6330.00	Mitsubishi	3	55D	Infinite	15.50	1378	No
MT210	8643.00	4410.00	5190.00	5550.00	Mitsubishi	3	60D	9F-3R	18.30	1720	No
MT210D 4WD	9530.00	4860.00	5720.00	6120.00	Mitsubishi	3	60D	9F-3R	18.30	1852	No
MT250	9563.00	4880.00	5740.00	6140.00	Mitsubishi	3	78D	9F-3R	22.00	1940	No
MT250D 4WD	10436.00	5320.00	6260.00	6700.00	Mitsubishi	3	78D	9F-3R	22.00	2040	No
MT300	10617.00	5420.00	6370.00	6820.00	Mitsubishi	3	91D	9F-3R	25.00	2337	No
MT300D 4WD	12083.00	6160.00	7250.00	7760.00	Mitsubishi	3	91D	9F-3R	25.00	2558	No
MT372	6778.00	3460.00	4070.00	4360.00	Mitsubishi	2	41D	6F-2R	12.20	1069	No
MT372D 4WD	7429.00	3790.00	4460.00	4770.00	Mitsubishi	2	41D	6F-2R	12.20	1177	No
MT4501	17088.00	7350.00	8890.00	9420.00	Mitsubishi	3	127D	9F-3R	37.30	3144	No
MT4501 4WD	19849.00	8540.00	10320.00	10940.00	Mitsubishi	3	127D	9F-3R	37.30	3446	No

D--Front Wheel Assist H--Hydrostatic Transmission

New Holland/Ford

1987

Model	Approx. Retail Price New	Fair	Good	Premium	Engine Make	No. Cyls.	Displ. Cu.-In.	No. Speeds	P.T.O. H.P.	Approx. Shipping Wt.-Lbs.	Cab
TW-5	35529.00	14500.00	17610.00	18840.00	Own	6	401D	16F-4R	105.74	11722	No
TW-5 4WD	49833.00	20090.00	24400.00	26110.00	Own	6	401D	16F-4R	105.74	13569	C,H,A
TW-15	39719.00	15840.00	19240.00	20590.00	Own	6T	401D	16F-4R	121.40	11754	No
TW-15 4WD	54878.00	20530.00	24930.00	26680.00	Own	6T	401D	16F-4R	121.25	12813	C,H,A
TW-25	43573.00	18720.00	22730.00	24320.00	Own	6T	401D	16F-4R	140.68	13649	No
TW-25 4WD	58726.00	21310.00	25870.00	27680.00	Own	6T	401D	16F-4R	140.68	14918	C,H,A
TW-35	55179.00	21920.00	26610.00	28470.00	Own	6TI	401D	16F-4R	170.30	14343	C,H,A
TW-35 4WD	65049.00	24380.00	29610.00	31680.00	Own	6TI	401D	16F-4R	171.12	15612	C,H,A
1120	6475.00	4490.00	5160.00	5730.00	Shibaura	2	43D	10F-2R	11.50	1283	No
1120 4WD	7262.00	4980.00	5720.00	6350.00	Shibaura	2	43D	10F-2R	11.50	1396	No
1220	7201.00	4920.00	5660.00	6280.00	Shibaura	3	54D	10F-2R	13.50	1329	No
1220 4WD	8155.00	5520.00	6350.00	7050.00	Shibaura	3	54D	10F-2R	13.50	1442	No
1220 H	8516.00	5710.00	6570.00	7290.00	Shibaura	3	54D	Infinite	13.50	1417	No
1220 H 4WD	9470.00	6280.00	7220.00	8010.00	Shibaura	3	54D	Infinite	13.50	1530	No
1320	8025.00	5420.00	6230.00	6920.00	Shibaura	3	58D	12F-4R	16.50	2063	No
1320 4WD	8993.00	6000.00	6900.00	7660.00	Shibaura	3	58D	12F-4R	16.50	2261	No
1520	8249.00	5610.00	6450.00	7160.00	Shibaura	3	68D	12F-4R	20.45	2230	No
1520 4WD	9609.00	6370.00	7320.00	8130.00	Shibaura	3	68D	12F-4R	20.45	2440	No
1720	9120.00	6070.00	6980.00	7750.00	Shibaura	3	85D	12F-4R	23.88	2470	No
1720 4WD	10984.00	6770.00	7790.00	8650.00	Shibaura	3	85D	12F-4R	23.88	2710	No
1920	10072.00	6280.00	7230.00	8030.00	Shibaura	3	104D	12F-4R	28.60	2980	No
1920 4WD	12317.00	7630.00	8780.00	9750.00	Shibaura	3	104D	12F-4R	28.60	3245	No
2120	13103.00	8040.00	9250.00	10270.00	Shibaura	4	139D	12F-4R	34.91	3635	No
2120 4WD	15109.00	9070.00	10430.00	11580.00	Shibaura	4	139D	12F-4R	34.91	3946	No
2810	13288.00	7310.00	8370.00	9040.00	Own	3	158D	8F-2R	32.83	4420	No
2810 4WD	16632.00	9150.00	10480.00	11320.00	Own	3	158D	8F-2R	32.83	4955	No
2910	14094.00	7750.00	8880.00	9590.00	Own	3	175D	8F-2R	36.40	4463	No
2910 4WD	19053.00	10480.00	12000.00	12960.00	Own	3	175D	8F-4R	36.40	5020	No
2910 4WD w/Cab	22187.00	12200.00	13980.00	15100.00	Own	3	175D	8F-2R	36.62	4948	C,H
2910 w/Cab	18074.00	9940.00	11390.00	12300.00	Own	3	175D	8F-4R	36.40	4463	C,H
3910	14675.00	8070.00	9250.00	9990.00	Own	3	192D	6F-4R	42.00	4527	No
3910 4WD	19637.00	10800.00	12370.00	13360.00	Own	3	192D	8F-4R	42.67	5104	No
3910 4WD w/Cab	22504.00	12380.00	14180.00	15310.00	Own	3	192D	8F-2R	42.62	5032	C,H
3910 w/Cab	18524.00	10190.00	11670.00	12600.00	Own	3	192D	8F-4R	42.67	4547	C,H
4610	17404.00	9570.00	10970.00	11850.00	Own	3	201D	8F-4R	52.32	4914	No
4610 4WD	22251.00	12240.00	14020.00	15140.00	Own	3	201D	8F-4R	52.32	5471	No
4610 4WD w/Cab	25384.00	13960.00	15990.00	17270.00	Own	3	201D	8F-2R	52.52	5399	C,H
4610 w/Cab	20916.00	11500.00	13180.00	14230.00	Own	3	201D	8F-2R	52.52	4864	C,H
5610	21620.00	10810.00	12760.00	13780.00	Own	4	256D	16F-8R	62.57	6149	No
5610 4WD	26445.00	13220.00	15600.00	16850.00	Own	4	256D	16F-8R	62.00	6686	No
5610 4WD w/Cab	33733.00	16870.00	19900.00	21490.00	Own	4	256D	16F-8R	62.00	6686	C,H,A
5610 w/Cab	28908.00	14450.00	17060.00	18430.00	Own	4	256D	16F-8R	62.57	6149	C,H,A
5900	14986.00	8240.00	9440.00	10200.00	Own	4	256D	8F-2R	62.00	5760	No
6610	23795.00	11900.00	14040.00	15160.00	Own	4	268D	16F-4R	72.13	6084	No
6610 4WD	29541.00	14770.00	17430.00	18820.00	Own	4	268D	16F-4R	72.13	6528	No
6610 4WD w/Cab	34365.00	17180.00	20280.00	21900.00	Own	4	268D	16F-4R	72.13	6528	C,H,A
6610 w/Cab	28710.00	14360.00	16940.00	18300.00	Own	4	268D	16F-4R	72.13	6084	C,H,A
7610	24305.00	12150.00	14340.00	15490.00	Own	4T	268D	16F-4R	86.95	6251	No
7610 4WD	29992.00	15000.00	17700.00	19120.00	Own	4T	268D	16F-4R	86.95	6902	No
7710	24500.00	12250.00	14460.00	15620.00	Own	4T	268D	16F-4R	86.00	7074	No
7710 4WD	31861.00	15930.00	18800.00	20300.00	Own	4T	268D	16F-4R	86.00	7785	No
7710 4WD w/Cab	38109.00	18500.00	21830.00	23580.00	Own	4T	268D	16F-4R	86.00	7785	C,H,A
7710 w/Cab	30804.00	15400.00	18170.00	19620.00	Own	4T	268D	16F-4R	86.00	7074	C,H,A
8210	42356.00	16800.00	20400.00	21830.00	Own	6	401D	16F-8R	95.00	9425	C,H,A

SU - Low Profile H - Hydrostatic Transmission SMS - Synchronized Manual Shuttle Transmission

1988

Model	Approx. Retail Price New	Fair	Good	Premium	Engine Make	No. Cyls.	Displ. Cu.-In.	No. Speeds	P.T.O. H.P.	Approx. Shipping Wt.-Lbs.	Cab
TW-5	36529.00	15280.00	18480.00	19590.00	Own	6	401D	16F-4R	105.74	11722	No
TW-5 4WD	50833.00	21000.00	25390.00	26910.00	Own	6	401D	16F-4R	105.74	13569	C,H,A
TW-15	40719.00	16650.00	20130.00	21340.00	Own	6T	401D	16F-4R	121.40	11754	No
TW-15 4WD	55878.00	20590.00	24900.00	26390.00	Own	6T	401D	16F-4R	121.25	12813	C,H,A
TW-25	44573.00	18740.00	22660.00	24020.00	Own	6T	401D	16F-4R	140.68	13649	No

New Holland/Ford (Cont.)

1988 (Cont.)

Model	Approx. Retail Price New	Estimated Average Value Less Repairs Fair	Good	Premium	Engine Make	No. Cyls.	Displ. Cu.-In.	No. Speeds	P.T.O. H.P.	Approx. Shipping Wt.-Lbs.	Cab
TW-25 4WD	59726.00	21810.00	26380.00	27960.00	Own	6T	401D	16F-4R	140.68	14918	C,H,A
TW-35	56179.00	22870.00	27650.00	29310.00	Own	6TI	401D	16F-4R	170.30	14343	C,H,A
TW-35 4WD	66049.00	24960.00	30190.00	32000.00	Own	6TI	401D	16F-4R	171.12	15612	C,H,A
1120	7500.00	4760.00	5460.00	6060.00	Shibaura	3	54D	9F-3R	12.50	1338	No
1120 4WD	8495.00	5180.00	5950.00	6610.00	Shibaura	2	43D	10F-2R	11.50	1396	No
1220	7990.00	5240.00	6010.00	6670.00	Shibaura	3	58D	9F-3R	14.50	1338	No
1220 4WD	8875.00	5610.00	6440.00	7150.00	Shibaura	3	54D	10F-2R	13.50	1442	No
1220 H	9046.00	5810.00	6660.00	7390.00	Shibaura	3	54D	Infinite	13.50	1417	No
1220 H 4WD	9990.00	6390.00	7330.00	8140.00	Shibaura	3	54D	Infinite	13.50	1530	No
1320	9505.00	5800.00	6650.00	7380.00	Shibaura	3	77D	9F-3R	17.00	2101	No
1320 4WD	10544.00	6430.00	7380.00	8190.00	Shibaura	3	58D	12F-4R	16.50	2261	No
1520	10045.00	6130.00	7030.00	7800.00	Shibaura	3	81D	9F-3R	19.50	2156	No
1520 4WD	11020.00	6720.00	7710.00	8560.00	Shibaura	3	68D	12F-4R	20.45	2440	No
1720	10475.00	6390.00	7330.00	8140.00	Shibaura	3	91D	12F-4R	23.50	2491	No
1720 4WD	11564.00	7050.00	8100.00	8990.00	Shibaura	3	85D	12F-4R	23.88	2710	No
1920	11920.00	7270.00	8340.00	9260.00	Shibaura	4	122D	12F-4R	28.50	2849	No
1920 4WD	12997.00	7930.00	9100.00	10100.00	Shibaura	3	104D	12F-4R	28.60	3245	No
2120	13734.00	8380.00	9610.00	10670.00	Shibaura	4	139D	12F-4R	34.50	3572	No
2120 4WD	15779.00	9020.00	10350.00	11490.00	Shibaura	4	139D	12F-4R	34.91	3946	No
2810	13288.00	7440.00	8500.00	9100.00	Own	3	158D	8F-2R	32.83	4420	No
2810 4WD	16632.00	9310.00	10640.00	11390.00	Own	3	158D	8F-2R	32.83	4955	No
2910	14091.00	7890.00	9020.00	9650.00	Own	3	175D	6F-4R	36.62	4413	No
2910	17719.00	9920.00	11340.00	12130.00	Own	3	175D	8F-2R	36.62	4413	C,H
2910 4WD	19053.00	10670.00	12190.00	13040.00	Own	3	175D	8F-4R	36.40	5020	No
2910 4WD	22187.00	12430.00	14200.00	15190.00	Own	3	175D	8F-2R	36.62	4948	C,H
3910	15675.00	8780.00	10030.00	10730.00	Own	3	192D	6F-4R	42.00	4527	No
3910	18836.00	10550.00	12060.00	12900.00	Own	3	192D	8F-2R	42.62	4497	C,H
3910 4WD	20637.00	11560.00	13210.00	14140.00	Own	3	192D	8F-4R	42.67	5104	No
3910 4WD	23504.00	13160.00	15040.00	16090.00	Own	3	192D	8F-2R	42.62	5032	C,H
4610	18404.00	10310.00	11780.00	12610.00	Own	3	201D	8F-4R	52.32	4914	No
4610	21916.00	12270.00	14030.00	15010.00	Own	3	201D	8F-2R	52.52	4864	C,H
4610 4WD	23251.00	13020.00	14880.00	15920.00	Own	3	201D	8F-4R	52.32	5471	No
4610 4WD	26384.00	14780.00	16890.00	18070.00	Own	3	201D	8F-2R	52.52	5399	C,H
5610	22620.00	11540.00	13570.00	14520.00	Own	4	256D	16F-4R	62.54	6084	No
5610 w/Cab	29908.00	15250.00	17950.00	19210.00	Own	4	256D	16F-8R	62.57	6149	C,H,A
5610 4WD	27445.00	14000.00	16470.00	17620.00	Own	4	256D	16F-4R	62.54	6621	No
5610 4WD w/Cab	34733.00	17710.00	20840.00	22300.00	Own	4	256D	16F-8R	62.00	6686	C,H,A
5900	14986.00	8390.00	9590.00	10260.00	Own	4	256D	8F-2R	62.00	5760	No
6610	24795.00	12650.00	14880.00	15920.00	Own	4	268D	16F-8R	72.30	6313	No
6610 w/Cab	30710.00	15660.00	18430.00	19720.00	Own	4	268D	16F-4R	72.13	6084	C,H,A
6610 4WD	30541.00	15580.00	18330.00	19610.00	Own	4	268D	16F-4R	72.13	6636	No
6610 4WD w/Cab	35365.00	18040.00	21220.00	22710.00	Own	4	268D	16F-4R	72.13	6636	C,H,A
7610	25305.00	12910.00	15180.00	16240.00	Own	4T	268D	16F-4R	86.95	6251	No
7610 4WD	31992.00	16320.00	19200.00	20540.00	Own	4T	268D	16F-4R	86.95	6902	No
7710	26000.00	13260.00	15600.00	16690.00	Own	4T	268D	16F-8R	86.62	8154	No
7710 w/Cab	33761.00	17220.00	20260.00	21680.00	Own	4T	268D	16F-4R	86.00	6986	C,H,A
7710 4WD	34561.00	17630.00	20740.00	22190.00	Own	4T	268D	16F-4R	86.00	7785	No
7710 4WD	34561.00	17630.00	20740.00	22190.00	Own	4T	268D	16F-4R	86.00	7785	No
7710 4WD w/Cab	40109.00	20460.00	24070.00	25760.00	Own	4T	268D	16F-4R	86.00	7785	C,H,A
8210	42356.00	18210.00	22030.00	23350.00	Own	6	401D	16F-8R	95.00	9425	C,H,A

SU--Low Profile

1989

Model	Approx. Retail Price New	Fair	Good	Premium	Engine Make	No. Cyls.	Displ. Cu.-In.	No. Speeds	P.T.O. H.P.	Approx. Shipping Wt.-Lbs.	Cab
TW5	36529.00	15630.00	18830.00	19960.00	Own	6	401D	16F-4R	105.74	11722	No
TW5 w/Cab	42798.00	17070.00	20560.00	21790.00	Own	6	401D	16F-4R	105.74	11722	C,H,A
TW15	40719.00	17480.00	21050.00	22310.00	Own	6	401D	16F-4R	121.40	11754	No
TW15 w/Cab	46988.00	18960.00	22840.00	24210.00	Own	6	401D	16F-4R	121.40		C,H,A
TW25	44024.00	18490.00	22270.00	23610.00	Own	6T	401D	16F-4R	140.68	13649	No
TW25 w/Cab	50293.00	20370.00	24540.00	26010.00	Own	6T	401D	16F-4R	140.68		C,H,A
TW35	56179.00	22520.00	27130.00	28760.00	Own	6TI	401D	16F-4R	170.30	14343	C,H,A
1120	8178.00	5070.00	5810.00	6390.00	Shibaura	3	54D	9F-3R	12.50	1338	No
1120 4WD	9127.00	5660.00	6480.00	7130.00	Shibaura	3	54D	9F-3R	12.50	1429	No
1120H 4WD Hydro	10132.00	6280.00	7190.00	7910.00	Shibaura	3	54D	Infinite	12.50		No
1120H Hydro	9183.00	5690.00	6520.00	7170.00	Shibaura	3	54D	Infinite	12.50		No
1220	8711.00	5400.00	6190.00	6810.00	Shibaura	3	58D	9F-3R	14.50	1338	No
1220 4WD	9660.00	5990.00	6860.00	7550.00	Shibaura	3	58D	9F-3R	14.50	1429	No
1220H 4WD Hydro	10664.00	6610.00	7570.00	8330.00	Shibaura	3	58D	Infinite	14.50		No
1220H Hydro	9715.00	6020.00	6900.00	7590.00	Shibaura	3	58D	Infinite	14.50		No
1320	10199.00	6320.00	7240.00	7960.00	Shibaura	3	77D	9F-3R	17.00	2101	No
1320 4WD	11270.00	6990.00	8000.00	8800.00	Shibaura	3	77D	9F-3R	17.00	2229	No
1320H 4WD Hydro	12409.00	7690.00	8810.00	9690.00	Shibaura	3	77D	Infinite	17.00		No
1320H Hydro	11338.00	7030.00	8050.00	8860.00	Shibaura	3	77D	Infinite	17.00		No
1520	10710.00	6640.00	7600.00	8360.00	Shibaura	3	81D	9F-3R	19.50	2156	No
1520 4WD	11862.00	7350.00	8420.00	9260.00	Shibaura	3	81D	9F-3R	19.50	2278	No
1520H 4WD Hydro	13146.00	8150.00	9330.00	10260.00	Shibaura	3	81D	Infinite	19.50		No
1520H Hydro	11996.00	7440.00	8520.00	9370.00	Shibaura	3	81D	Variable	19.50		No
1720	11372.00	7050.00	8070.00	8880.00	Shibaura	3	91D	12F-4R	23.50	2491	No
1920	13362.00	8280.00	9490.00	10440.00	Shibaura	4	122D	12F-4R	28.50	2849	No
1920 4WD	15512.00	9620.00	11010.00	12110.00	Shibaura	4	122D	12F-4R	28.50	3089	No
2120	14898.00	9240.00	10580.00	11640.00	Shibaura	4	139D	12F-4R	34.50	3572	No
2120 4WD	17262.00	10080.00	11550.00	12710.00	Shibaura	4	139D	12F-4R	34.50	3858	No
2810	15100.00	8610.00	9820.00	10510.00	Own	3	158D	8F-2R	32.83	4422	No
2910	15400.00	8780.00	10010.00	10710.00	Own	3	175D	8F-2R	36.62	4412	No
2910 w/Cab	19267.00	10980.00	12520.00	13400.00	Own	3	175D	8F-2R	36.62		C,H

New Holland/Ford (Cont.)

Model	Approx. Retail Price New	Estimated Average Value Less Repairs Fair	Good	Premium	Engine Make	No. Cyls.	Displ. Cu.-In.	No. Speeds	P.T.O. H.P.	Approx. Shipping Wt.-Lbs.	Cab
			1989 (Cont.)								
3910	15788.00	**9000.00**	**10260.00**	**10980.00**	Own	3	192D	8F-2R	42.62	4499	No
3910 w/Cab	19655.00	**11200.00**	**12780.00**	**13680.00**	Own	3	192D	8F-4R	42.62		C,H
4610	17713.00	**10100.00**	**11510.00**	**12320.00**	Own	3	201D	8F-2R	52.52	4868	No
4610 w/Cab	22093.00	**12590.00**	**14360.00**	**15370.00**	Own	3	201D	8F-4R	52.52		C,H
5610	23350.00	**12140.00**	**14240.00**	**15240.00**	Own	4	256D	16F-4R	62.54	6084	No
5610 w/Cab	29699.00	**15440.00**	**18120.00**	**19390.00**	Own	4	256D	16F-4R	62.54		C,H,A
5610 4WD	28145.00	**14640.00**	**17170.00**	**18370.00**	Own	4	256D	16F-4R	62.54	6621	No
5610 4WD w/Cab	35133.00	**18270.00**	**21430.00**	**22930.00**	Own	4	256D	16F-8R	62.00	6686	C,H,A
5900	16120.00	**9190.00**	**10480.00**	**11210.00**	Own	4	256D	8F-2R	62.00	5760	No
6610	24776.00	**12880.00**	**15110.00**	**16170.00**	Own	4	268D	16F-4R	72.13	6084	No
6610 w/Cab	31125.00	**16190.00**	**18990.00**	**20320.00**	Own	4	268D	16F-4R	72.13		C,H,A
6610 4WD	30841.00	**16040.00**	**18810.00**	**20130.00**	Own	4	268D	16F-4R	72.13	6636	No
6610 4WD w/Cab	36565.00	**19010.00**	**22310.00**	**23870.00**	Own	4	268D	16F-4R	72.13	6636	C,H,A
7610	26092.00	**13570.00**	**15920.00**	**17030.00**	Own	4T	268D	16F-4R	86.95	6251	No
7610 w/Cab	32773.00	**17040.00**	**19990.00**	**21390.00**	Own	4T	268D	16F-4R	86.95	6902	C,H,A
7710	27464.00	**14280.00**	**16750.00**	**17920.00**	Own	4T	268D	16F-4R	86.62	7074	No
7710 w/Cab	34145.00	**17760.00**	**20830.00**	**22290.00**	Own	4T	268D	16F-4R	86.62		C,H,A
7710 4WD	34344.00	**17860.00**	**20950.00**	**22420.00**	Own	4T	268D	16F-4R	86.62	7074	No
7710 4WD w/Cab	41255.00	**21450.00**	**25170.00**	**26930.00**	Own	4T	268D	16F-4R	86.62		C,H,A
8210	42848.00	**18850.00**	**22710.00**	**24070.00**	Own	6	401D	16F-8R	95.00	9425	C,H,A
***Net Engine Horsepower PS--Power Shift**											
			1990								
1120	8475.00	**5340.00**	**6100.00**	**6650.00**	Shibaura	3	54D	9F-3R	12.50	1338	No
1120 4WD	9481.00	**5970.00**	**6830.00**	**7450.00**	Shibaura	3	54D	9F-3R	12.50	1429	No
1120H 4WD Hydro	10530.00	**6630.00**	**7580.00**	**8260.00**	Shibaura	3	54D	Infinite	12.50	1484	No
1120H Hydro	9525.00	**6000.00**	**6860.00**	**7480.00**	Shibaura	3	54D	Infinite	12.50	1393	No
1220	9117.00	**5740.00**	**6560.00**	**7150.00**	Shibaura	3	58D	9F-3R	14.50	1338	No
1220 4WD	10123.00	**6380.00**	**7290.00**	**7950.00**	Shibaura	3	58D	9F-3R	14.50	1429	No
1220H 4WD Hydro	11074.00	**6980.00**	**7970.00**	**8690.00**	Shibaura	3	58D	Infinite	14.50	1484	No
1220H Hydro	10068.00	**6340.00**	**7250.00**	**7900.00**	Shibaura	3	58D	Infinite	14.50	1393	No
1320	10557.00	**6650.00**	**7600.00**	**8280.00**	Shibaura	3	77D	9F-3R	17.00	2101	No
1320 4WD	11696.00	**7370.00**	**8420.00**	**9180.00**	Shibaura	3	77D	9F-3R	17.00	2229	No
1320H 4WD Hydro	13226.00	**8330.00**	**9520.00**	**10380.00**	Shibaura	3	77D	Infinite	17.00	2297	No
1320H Hydro	12087.00	**7620.00**	**8700.00**	**9480.00**	Shibaura	3	77D	Infinite	17.00	2172	No
1520	11029.00	**6950.00**	**7940.00**	**8660.00**	Shibaura	3	81D	9F-3R	19.50	2156	No
1520 4WD	12247.00	**7720.00**	**8820.00**	**9610.00**	Shibaura	3	81D	9F-3R	19.50	2278	No
1520H 4WD Hydro	13997.00	**8820.00**	**10080.00**	**10990.00**	Shibaura	3	81D	Infinite	19.50	2352	No
1520H Hydro	12779.00	**8050.00**	**9200.00**	**10030.00**	Shibaura	3	81D	Variable	19.50	2233	No
1720	11944.00	**7530.00**	**8600.00**	**9370.00**	Shibaura	3	91D	12F-4R	23.50	2491	No
1720 4WD	13609.00	**8570.00**	**9800.00**	**10680.00**	Shibaura	3	91D	12F-4R	23.50		No
1920	13816.00	**8700.00**	**9950.00**	**10850.00**	Shibaura	4	122D	12F-4R	28.50	2849	No
1920 4WD	16226.00	**10220.00**	**11680.00**	**12730.00**	Shibaura	4	122D	12F-4R	28.50	3089	No
2120	15391.00	**9700.00**	**11080.00**	**12080.00**	Shibaura	4	139D	12F-4R	34.50	3572	No
2120 4WD	17831.00	**11230.00**	**12840.00**	**14000.00**	Shibaura	4	139D	12F-4R	34.50	3858	No
3230	15920.00	**10030.00**	**11460.00**	**12490.00**	Own	3	192D	8F-2R	32.83	4455	No
3230 4WD	19940.00	**12560.00**	**14360.00**	**15650.00**	Own	3	192D	8F-2R	32.83		No
3430	16593.00	**10450.00**	**11950.00**	**13030.00**	Own	3	192D	8F-2R	38.00	4455	No
3430 4WD	20744.00	**13070.00**	**14940.00**	**16290.00**	Own	3	192D	8F-2R	38.00	4983	No
3430 4WD w/Cab	25343.00	**15970.00**	**18250.00**	**19890.00**	Own	3	192D	8F-2R	38.00	5483	C,H
3430 w/Cab	21192.00	**13350.00**	**15260.00**	**16630.00**	Own	3	192D	8F-2R	38.00	4955	C,H
3930	17080.00	**10760.00**	**12300.00**	**13410.00**	Own	3	201D	8F-2R	45.00	4505	No
3930 4WD	21393.00	**13480.00**	**15400.00**	**16790.00**	Own	3	201D	8F-2R	45.00	5033	No
3930 4WD w/Cab	25992.00	**16380.00**	**18710.00**	**20390.00**	Own	3	201D	8F-2R	45.00	5533	C,H
3930 w/Cab	21679.00	**13660.00**	**15610.00**	**17020.00**	Own	3	201D	8F-2R	45.00	5005	C,H
4630	18952.00	**10990.00**	**12510.00**	**13390.00**	Own	3	201D	8F-2R	55.00	4930	No
4630 4WD	23265.00	**13490.00**	**15360.00**	**16440.00**	Own	3	201D	8F-2R	55.00	5458	No
4630 4WD w/Cab	27864.00	**16160.00**	**18390.00**	**19680.00**	Own	3	201D	8F-2R	55.00	5958	C,H
4630 w/Cab	23551.00	**13660.00**	**15540.00**	**16630.00**	Own	3	201D	8F-2R	55.00	5430	C,H
5610	23800.00	**12610.00**	**14760.00**	**15790.00**	Own	4	256D	16F-4R	62.54	6084	No
5610 4WD	28782.00	**15250.00**	**17850.00**	**19100.00**	Own	4	256D	16F-4R	62.00	6621	No
5610 4WD w/Cab	35638.00	**18890.00**	**22100.00**	**23650.00**	Own	4	256D	16F-4R	62.00	7951	C,H,A
5610 Special	18573.00	**10770.00**	**12260.00**	**13120.00**	Own	4	256D	8F-2R	62.00	5800	No
5610 w/Cab	30656.00	**16250.00**	**19010.00**	**20340.00**	Own	4	256D	16F-4R	62.54	7429	C,H,A
5900	17434.00	**10110.00**	**11510.00**	**12320.00**	Own	4	256D	8F-2R	62.00	5760	No
6610	25269.00	**13390.00**	**15670.00**	**16770.00**	Own	4	268D	16F-4R	72.13	6084	No
6610 4WD	31115.00	**16490.00**	**19290.00**	**20640.00**	Own	4	268D	16F-4R	72.13	6621	No
6610 4WD w/Cab	37648.00	**19950.00**	**23340.00**	**24970.00**	Own	4	268D	16F-4R	72.13	7951	C,H,A
6610 w/Cab	31803.00	**16860.00**	**19720.00**	**21100.00**	Own	4	268D	16F-4R	72.13	7414	C,H,A
7610	27709.00	**14690.00**	**17180.00**	**18380.00**	Own	4T	268D	16F-4R	86.95	6291	No
7610 4WD	33554.00	**17780.00**	**20800.00**	**22260.00**	Own	4T	268D	16F-4R	86.95	6902	No
7610 4WD w/Cab	40220.00	**20670.00**	**24180.00**	**25870.00**	Own	4T	268D	16F-4R	86.95	8232	C,H,A
7610 w/Cab	34376.00	**18220.00**	**21310.00**	**22800.00**	Own	4T	268D	16F-4R	86.95	7621	C,H,A
7710	28281.00	**14990.00**	**17530.00**	**18760.00**	Own	4T	268D	16F-4R	86.62	7074	No
7710 4WD	34991.00	**18550.00**	**21690.00**	**23210.00**	Own	4T	268D	16F-4R	86.62	7785	No
7710 4WD w/Cab	41740.00	**22120.00**	**25880.00**	**27690.00**	Own	4T	268D	16F-4R	86.62	8815	C,H,A.
7710 w/Cab	35030.00	**18570.00**	**21720.00**	**23240.00**	Own	4T	268D	16F-4R	86.62	8104	C,H,A
7810	27812.00	**14740.00**	**17240.00**	**18450.00**	Own	6	401D	16F-4R	86.00	7928	No
7810 4WD	33524.00	**17770.00**	**20790.00**	**22250.00**	Own	6	401D	16F-4R	86.00	8465	No
8210	44900.00	**20210.00**	**24250.00**	**25710.00**	Own	6	401D	16F-8R	100.20	9425	C,H,A
8530	37255.00	**19750.00**	**23100.00**	**24720.00**	Own	6	401D	16F-4R	105.74	11722	No
8530 4WD w/Cab	51924.00	**27520.00**	**32190.00**	**34440.00**	Own	6	401D	16F-4R	105.74	11722	C,H,A
8630 4WD	50568.00	**26800.00**	**31350.00**	**33550.00**	Own	6T	401D	16F-4R	121.40	12813	No
8630 4WD w/Cab	56629.00	**30010.00**	**35110.00**	**37570.00**	Own	6T	401D	16F-4R	121.40	13601	C,H,A

New Holland/Ford (Cont.)

Model	Approx. Retail Price New	Estimated Average Value Less Repairs Fair	Good	Premium	Engine Make	No. Cyls.	Displ. Cu.-In.	No. Speeds	P.T.O. H.P.	Approx. Shipping Wt.-Lbs.	Cab
1990 (Cont.)											
8730 4WD	53973.00	28610.00	33460.00	35800.00	Own	6TI	401D	16F-4R	140.68	13649	No
8730 4WD w/Cab	60561.00	32100.00	37550.00	40180.00	Own	6TI	401D	16F-4R	140.68		C,H,A
8830	57303.00	30370.00	35530.00	38020.00	Own	6TI	401D	16F-4R	170.30	14343	C,H,A
8830 4WD	67371.00	35710.00	41770.00	44690.00	Own	6TI	401D	16F-4R	170.30	14343	C,H,A
1156	170107.00	72000.00	86400.00	91580.00	Cummins	6TI	1150D	8F-4R			C,H,A
1991											
1120	8606.00	5510.00	6280.00	6780.00	Shibaura	3	54D	9F-3R	12.50	1338	No
1120 4WD	9635.00	6170.00	7030.00	7590.00	Shibaura	3	54D	9F-3R	12.50	1429	No
1120H 4WD Hydro	10708.00	6850.00	7820.00	8450.00	Shibaura	3	54D	Infinite	12.50	1484	No
1120H Hydro	9679.00	6200.00	7070.00	7640.00	Shibaura	3	54D	Infinite	12.50	1393	No
1220	9160.00	5860.00	6690.00	7230.00	Shibaura	3	58D	9F-3R	14.50	1338	No
1220 4WD	10188.00	6520.00	7440.00	8040.00	Shibaura	3	58D	9F-3R	14.50	1429	No
1220H 4WD Hydro	11160.00	7140.00	8150.00	8800.00	Shibaura	3	58D	Infinite	14.50	1484	No
1220H Hydro	10132.00	6480.00	7400.00	7990.00	Shibaura	3	58D	Infinite	14.50	1393	No
1320	10736.00	6870.00	7840.00	8470.00	Shibaura	3	77D	9F-3R	17.00	2101	No
1320 4WD	12033.00	7700.00	8780.00	9480.00	Shibaura	3	77D	9F-3R	17.00	2229	No
1320H 4WD Hydro	13596.00	8700.00	9930.00	10720.00	Shibaura	3	77D	Infinite	17.00	2297	No
1320H Hydro	12229.00	7830.00	8930.00	9640.00	Shibaura	3	77D	Infinite	17.00	2172	No
1520	11217.00	7180.00	8190.00	8850.00	Shibaura	3	81D	9F-3R	19.50	2156	No
1520 4WD	12595.00	8060.00	9190.00	9930.00	Shibaura	3	81D	9F-3R	19.50	2278	No
1520H 4WD Hydro	14383.00	9210.00	10500.00	11340.00	Shibaura	3	81D	Infinite	19.50	2352	No
1520H Hydro	13005.00	8320.00	9490.00	10250.00	Shibaura	3	81D	Variable	19.50	2233	No
1720	12153.00	7780.00	8870.00	9580.00	Shibaura	3	91D	12F-4R	23.50	2491	No
1720 4WD	13988.00	8950.00	10210.00	11030.00	Shibaura	3	91D	12F-4R	23.50	2690	No
1920	14065.00	9000.00	10270.00	11090.00	Shibaura	4	122D	12F-4R	28.50	2849	No
1920 4WD	16662.00	10660.00	12160.00	13130.00	Shibaura	4	122D	12F-4R	28.50	3069	No
2120	15674.00	10030.00	11440.00	12360.00	Shibaura	4	139D	12F-4R	34.50	3572	No
2120 4WD	18303.00	11710.00	13360.00	14430.00	Shibaura	4	139D	12F-4R	34.50	3858	No
3230	16564.00	10600.00	12090.00	13060.00	Own	3	192D	8F-2R	32.33	5538	No
3230 4WD	20771.00	13290.00	15160.00	16370.00	Own	3	192D	8F-2R	32.33	5538	No
3430	17266.00	11050.00	12600.00	13610.00	Own	3	192D	8F-2R	38.48	5594	No
3430 4WD	21608.00	13830.00	15770.00	17030.00	Own	3	192D	8F-2R	38.48	5594	No
3430 4WD w/Cab	26405.00	16900.00	19280.00	20820.00	Own	3	192D	8F-2R	38.00	5483	C,H
3430 w/Cab	22063.00	14120.00	16110.00	17400.00	Own	3	192D	8F-2R	38.00	4955	C,H
3930	17771.00	11370.00	12970.00	14010.00	Own	3	201D	8F-2R	45.85	5592	No
3930 4WD	22296.00	14270.00	16280.00	17580.00	Own	3	201D	8F-2R	45.85	5592	No
3930 4WD w/Cab	27093.00	17340.00	19780.00	21360.00	Own	3	201D	8F-2R	45.00	5533	C,H
3930 w/Cab	22568.00	14440.00	16480.00	17800.00	Own	3	201D	8F-2R	45.00	5005	C,H
4630	19720.00	12620.00	14400.00	15550.00	Own	3	201D	8F-2R	55.41	5728	No
4630 4WD	24245.00	15520.00	17700.00	19120.00	Own	3	201D	8F-2R	55.41	5728	No
4630 4WD w/Cab	29042.00	18590.00	21200.00	22900.00	Own	3	201D	8F-2R	55.00	5958	C,H
4630 w/Cab	24517.00	15690.00	17900.00	19330.00	Own	3	201D	8F-2R	55.00	5430	C,H
5610	25755.00	15200.00	17260.00	18300.00	Own	4	256D	16F-4R	62.54	6084	No
5610 4WD	31179.00	16840.00	19640.00	20820.00	Own	4	256D	16F-4R	62.00	6621	No
5610 4WD w/Cab	38591.00	20840.00	24310.00	25770.00	Own	4	256D	16F-4R	62.00	7951	C,H,A
5610 Special	19581.00	12530.00	14290.00	15430.00	Own	4	256D	8F-2R	62.00	5800	No
5610 w/Cab	33167.00	19570.00	22220.00	23550.00	Own	4	256D	16F-4R	62.54	7429	C,H,A
6610	27355.00	14770.00	17230.00	18260.00	Own	4	268D	16F-4R	72.13	6084	No
6610 4WD	33674.00	18180.00	21220.00	22490.00	Own	4	268D	16F-4R	72.13	6621	No
6610 4WD w/Cab	40822.00	22040.00	25720.00	27260.00	Own	4	268D	16F-4R	72.13	7951	C,H,A
6610 w/Cab	34504.00	18630.00	21740.00	23040.00	Own	4	268D	16F-4R	72.13	7414	C,H,A
7610	29976.00	16190.00	18890.00	20020.00	Own	4T	268D	16F-4R	86.95	6291	No
7610 4WD	35688.00	19270.00	22480.00	23830.00	Own	4T	268D	16F-4R	86.95	6902	No
7610 4WD w/Cab	43100.00	23270.00	27150.00	28780.00	Own	4T	268D	16F-4R	86.95	8232	C,H,A
7610 w/Cab	37388.00	20190.00	23550.00	24960.00	Own	4T	268D	16F-4R	86.95	7621	C,H,A
7710	30578.00	16510.00	19260.00	20420.00	Own	4T	268D	16F-4R	86.62	7074	No
7710 4WD	37654.00	20330.00	23720.00	25140.00	Own	4T	268D	16F-4R	86.62	7785	No
7710 4WD w/Cab	44975.00	24290.00	28330.00	30030.00	Own	4T	268D	16F-4R	86.62	8815	C,H,A
7710 w/Cab	37899.00	20470.00	23880.00	25310.00	Own	4T	268D	16F-4R	86.62	8104	C,H,A
7810	31404.00	16960.00	19790.00	20980.00	Own	6	401D	16F-4R	86.00	7296	No
7810 4WD	37591.00	20300.00	23680.00	25100.00	Own	6	401D	16F-4R	86.00	7907	No
8210 4WD	48587.00	22350.00	26720.00	28320.00	Own	6	401D	16F-8R	100.20	9891	C,H,A
8530	38830.00	20970.00	24460.00	25930.00	Own	6	401D	16F-4R	105.74	11722	No
8530 4WD w/Cab	54100.00	29210.00	34080.00	36130.00	Own	6	401D	16F-4R	105.74	11722	C,H,A
8630 4WD	52705.00	28460.00	33200.00	35190.00	Own	6T	401D	16F-4R	121.40	12813	No
8630 4WD w/Cab	59023.00	31870.00	37180.00	39410.00	Own	6T	401D	16F-4R	121.40	13601	C,H,A
8730 4WD	56250.00	30380.00	35440.00	37570.00	Own	6TI	401D	16F-4R	140.68	13649	No
8730 4WD w/Cab	63120.00	34090.00	39770.00	42160.00	Own	6TI	401D	16F-4R	140.68		C,H,A
8830	59725.00	32250.00	37630.00	39890.00	Own	6TI	401D	16F-4R	170.30	14343	C,H,A
8830 4WD	70200.00	37910.00	44230.00	46880.00	Own	6TI	401D	16F-4R	170.30	14343	C,H,A
1156	170107.00	73690.00	88110.00	93400.00	Cummins	6TI	1150D	8F-4R			C,H,A
1992											
1120	8908.00	5560.00	6330.00	6770.00	Shibaura	3	54D	9F-3R	12.50	1338	No
1120 4WD	9972.00	6220.00	7080.00	7580.00	Shibaura	3	54D	9F-3R	12.50	1429	No
1120H 4WD Hydro	11082.00	6910.00	7870.00	8420.00	Shibaura	3	54D	Infinite	12.50	1484	No
1120H Hydro	10018.00	6250.00	7110.00	7610.00	Shibaura	3	54D	Infinite	12.50	1393	No
1220	9481.00	5920.00	6730.00	7200.00	Shibaura	3	58D	9F-3R	14.50	1338	No
1220 4WD	10545.00	6580.00	7490.00	8010.00	Shibaura	3	58D	9F-3R	14.50	1429	No
1220H 4WD Hydro	11551.00	7210.00	8210.00	8790.00	Shibaura	3	58D	Infinite	14.50	1484	No
1220H Hydro	10487.00	6540.00	7450.00	7970.00	Shibaura	3	58D	Infinite	14.50	1393	No
1320	11112.00	6930.00	7890.00	8440.00	Shibaura	3	77D	9F-3R	17.00	2101	No
1320 4WD	12704.00	7930.00	9020.00	9650.00	Shibaura	3	77D	9F-3R	17.00	2229	No

Model	Approx. Retail Price New	Estimated Average Value Less Repairs Fair	Good	Premium	Engine Make	No. Cyls.	Displ. Cu.-In.	No. Speeds	P.T.O. H.P.	Approx. Shipping Wt.-Lbs.	Cab
New Holland/Ford (Cont.)											
			1992 (Cont.)								
1320H 4WD Hydro	13940.00	**8700.00**	**9900.00**	**10590.00**	Shibaura	3	77D	Infinite	17.00	2297	No
1320H Hydro	12729.00	**7940.00**	**9040.00**	**9670.00**	Shibaura	3	77D	Infinite	17.00	2172	No
1520	11609.00	**7240.00**	**8250.00**	**8830.00**	Shibaura	3	81D	9F-3R	19.50	2156	No
1520 4WD	13285.00	**8290.00**	**9440.00**	**10100.00**	Shibaura	3	81D	9F-3R	19.50	2278	No
1520H 4WD Hydro	14754.00	**9210.00**	**10480.00**	**11210.00**	Shibaura	3	81D	Infinite	19.50	2352	No
1520H Hydro	13460.00	**8400.00**	**9560.00**	**10230.00**	Shibaura	3	81D	Variable	19.50	2233	No
1620 4WD Hydro	15319.00	**9560.00**	**10880.00**	**11640.00**	Shibaura	3	81D	Infinite	22.00	2352	No
1620 Hydro	13906.00	**8680.00**	**9880.00**	**10570.00**	Shibaura	3	81D	Infinite	22.00	2233	No
1720	12578.00	**7850.00**	**8930.00**	**9560.00**	Shibaura	3	91D	12F-4R	23.50	2491	No
1720 4WD	14346.00	**8950.00**	**10190.00**	**10900.00**	Shibaura	3	91D	12F-4R	23.50	2690	No
1920	14558.00	**9080.00**	**10340.00**	**11060.00**	Shibaura	4	122D	12F-4R	28.50	2849	No
1920 4WD	17106.00	**10670.00**	**12150.00**	**13000.00**	Shibaura	4	122D	12F-4R	28.50	3069	No
2120	16228.00	**10140.00**	**11540.00**	**12350.00**	Shibaura	4	139D	12F-4R	34.50	3572	No
2120 4WD	18805.00	**11750.00**	**13370.00**	**14310.00**	Shibaura	4	139D	12F-4R	34.50	3858	No
3230	16564.00	**9940.00**	**11260.00**	**11940.00**	Own	3	192D	8F-2R	32.83	4455	No
3230 4WD	20771.00	**12460.00**	**14120.00**	**14970.00**	Own	3	192D	8F-2R	32.83	4983	No
3430	17266.00	**10360.00**	**11740.00**	**12440.00**	Own	3	192D	8F-2R	38.00	4455	No
3430 4WD	21608.00	**12970.00**	**14690.00**	**15570.00**	Own	3	192D	8F-2R	38.00	4983	No
3430 4WD w/Cab	26405.00	**15840.00**	**17960.00**	**19040.00**	Own	3	192D	8F-2R	38.00	5483	C,H
3430 w/Cab	22063.00	**13240.00**	**15000.00**	**15900.00**	Own	3	192D	8F-2R	38.00	4955	C,H
3830 4WD	25192.00	**15120.00**	**17130.00**	**18160.00**	Fiat	3	165D	12F-4R	45.00	4000	No
3830 Narrow	19467.00	**11680.00**	**13240.00**	**14030.00**	Fiat	3	165D	12F-4R	45.00	3784	No
3930 4WD w/Cab	27093.00	**16260.00**	**18420.00**	**19530.00**	Own	3	201D	8F-2R	45.00	5533	C,H
3930 w/Cab	22568.00	**13540.00**	**15350.00**	**16270.00**	Own	3	201D	8F-2R	45.00	5005	C,H
4030	21190.00	**12710.00**	**14410.00**	**15280.00**	Fiat	3	179D	12F-4R	51.00	4710	No
4030 4WD	27561.00	**16540.00**	**18740.00**	**19860.00**	Fiat	3	179D	12F-4R	51.00	5060	No
4230	23583.00	**14150.00**	**16040.00**	**17000.00**	Fiat	3	220D	12F-4R	62.00	5430	No
4230 4WD	29850.00	**17910.00**	**20300.00**	**21520.00**	Fiat	3	220D	12F-4R	62.00	5958	No
4430 4WD	32231.00	**19340.00**	**21920.00**	**23240.00**	Fiat	4	238D	12F-4R	70.00	5350	No
5030	22138.00	**13280.00**	**15050.00**	**15950.00**	Own	4	256D	8F-2R	62.00	5742	No
5030 4WD	26663.00	**16000.00**	**18130.00**	**19220.00**	Own	4	256D	8F-2R	62.00	5811	No
5030 4WD w/Cab	31461.00	**18880.00**	**21390.00**	**22670.00**	Own	4	256D	8F-2R	62.00	6311	C,H,A
5030 w/Cab	26936.00	**16160.00**	**18320.00**	**19420.00**	Own	4	256D	8F-2R	62.00	5783	C,H,A
5530	25476.00	**15290.00**	**17320.00**	**18360.00**	Fiat	4	220D	12F-12R	62.00	5689	No
5530 4WD	31926.00	**19160.00**	**21710.00**	**23010.00**	Fiat	4	220D	12F-12R	62.00	7290	No
5610	25755.00	**16740.00**	**19060.00**	**20390.00**	Own	4	256D	16F-4R	62.54	6084	No
5610 4WD Special	28328.00	**18410.00**	**20960.00**	**22430.00**	Own	4	256D	8F-2R	62.00	6435	No
5610 4WD w/Cab	38591.00	**23160.00**	**26240.00**	**27810.00**	Own	4	256D	16F-4R	62.00	7951	C,H,A
5610 Special	21299.00	**13840.00**	**15760.00**	**16860.00**	Own	4	256D	8F-2R	62.00	5800	No
5610 w/Cab	33167.00	**21560.00**	**24540.00**	**26260.00**	Own	4	256D	16F-4R	62.54	7429	C,H,A
5640	24828.00	**14900.00**	**16880.00**	**17890.00**	Own	4	268D	8F-2R	66.00	7306	No
5640 4WD	30646.00	**17160.00**	**19610.00**	**20790.00**	Own	4	268D	8F-2R	66.00	8298	No
5640 4WD w/Cab	39104.00	**21900.00**	**25030.00**	**26530.00**	Own	4	268D	12F-12R	66.00	9380	C,H,A
5640 w/Cab	33286.00	**18640.00**	**21300.00**	**22580.00**	Own	4	268D	12F-12R	66.00	8418	C,H,A
6530	29036.00	**17420.00**	**19740.00**	**20920.00**	Fiat	4	238D	12F-12R	70.00	5689	No
6530 4WD	35841.00	**21510.00**	**24370.00**	**25830.00**	Fiat	4	238D	12F-12R	70.00	7290	No
6610	27355.00	**16410.00**	**18600.00**	**19720.00**	Own	4	268D	16F-4R	72.13	6084	No
6610 4WD	33674.00	**20200.00**	**22900.00**	**24270.00**	Own	4	268D	16F-4R	72.13	6621	No
6610 4WD Special	32231.00	**19340.00**	**21920.00**	**23240.00**	Own	4	268D	8F-2R	72.00	6435	No
6610 4WD w/Cab	40822.00	**24490.00**	**27760.00**	**29430.00**	Own	4	268D	16F-4R	72.13	7951	C,H,A
6610 Special	24702.00	**16060.00**	**18280.00**	**19560.00**	Own	4	268D	8F-2R	72.00	5800	No
6610 w/Cab	34504.00	**20700.00**	**23460.00**	**24870.00**	Own	4	268D	16F-4R	72.13	7414	C,H,A
6640	26822.00	**15020.00**	**17170.00**	**18200.00**	Own	4	304D	8F-2R	76.00	7306	No
6640 4WD	33141.00	**18560.00**	**21210.00**	**22480.00**	Own	4	304D	8F-2R	76.00	8298	No
6640 4WD w/Cab	42162.00	**23610.00**	**26980.00**	**28600.00**	Own	4	304D	12F-12R	76.00	9342	C,H,A
6640 w/Cab	35843.00	**20070.00**	**22940.00**	**24320.00**	Own	4	304D	12F-12R	76.00	8413	C,H,A
7530 4WD	42648.00	**25590.00**	**29000.00**	**30740.00**	Fiat	6	331D	20F-4R	91.00	8074	No
7740	28470.00	**15940.00**	**18220.00**	**19310.00**	Own	4T	304D	8F-2R	86.00	7339	No
7740 4WD	34788.00	**19480.00**	**22260.00**	**23600.00**	Own	4T	304D	8F-2R	86.00	8353	No
7740 4WD w/Cab	44725.00	**25050.00**	**28620.00**	**30340.00**	Own	4T	304D	12F-12R	86.00	9415	C,H,A
7740 w/Cab	38407.00	**21510.00**	**24580.00**	**26060.00**	Own	4T	304D	12F-12R	86.00	8400	C,H,A
7840	33651.00	**20190.00**	**22880.00**	**24250.00**	Own	6	401D	12F-12R	90.00	8342	No
7840 4WD	39970.00	**23980.00**	**27180.00**	**28810.00**	Own	6	401D	12F-12R	90.00	9400	No
7840 4WD w/Cab	47407.00	**28440.00**	**32240.00**	**34170.00**	Own	6	401D	12F-12R	90.00	10445	C,H,A
7840 w/Cab	41088.00	**24650.00**	**27940.00**	**29620.00**	Own	6	401D	12F-12R	90.00	9386	C,H,A
8240	36855.00	**20640.00**	**23590.00**	**25010.00**	Own	6	456D	16F-16R	96.00	8957	No
8240 4WD	43174.00	**24180.00**	**27630.00**	**29290.00**	Own	6	456D	16F-16R	96.00	10015	No
8240 4WD w/Cab	49995.00	**28000.00**	**32000.00**	**33920.00**	Own	6	456D	16F-16R	96.00	11053	C,H,A
8240 w/Cab	43832.00	**24550.00**	**28050.00**	**29730.00**	Own	6	456D	16F-16R	96.00	9995	C,H,A
8340	40197.00	**22510.00**	**25730.00**	**27270.00**	Own	6	456D	16F-16R	106.00	8957	No
8340 4WD	46516.00	**26050.00**	**29770.00**	**31560.00**	Own	6	456D	16F-16R	106.00	10015	No
8340 4WD w/Cab	54150.00	**30320.00**	**34660.00**	**36740.00**	Own	6	456D	16F-16R	106.00	11053	C,H,A
8340 w/Cab	47832.00	**26790.00**	**30610.00**	**32450.00**	Own	6	456D	16F-16R	106.00	9995	C,H,A
8530	38830.00	**21750.00**	**24850.00**	**26340.00**	Own	6	401D	16F-4R	105.74	11722	No
8530 4WD w/Cab	54100.00	**30300.00**	**34620.00**	**36700.00**	Own	6	401D	16F-4R	105.74	11722	C,H,A
8630 4WD Powershift	66967.00	**37500.00**	**42860.00**	**45430.00**	Own	6T	401D	18F-9R	121.40	13300	C,H,A
8630 4WD w/Cab	61358.00	**34360.00**	**39270.00**	**41630.00**	Own	6T	401D	16F-4R	121.40	12500	C,H,A
8730 4WD Powershift	71291.00	**39920.00**	**45630.00**	**48370.00**	Own	6T	401D	16F-4R	140.68	15206	C,H,A
8730 4WD w/Cab	65564.00	**36720.00**	**41960.00**	**44480.00**	Own	6T	401D	16F-4R	140.68	14406	C,H,A
8830	62749.00	**35140.00**	**40160.00**	**42570.00**	Own	6TI	401D	16F-4R	170.30	13043	C,H,A
8830 4WD	71987.00	**40310.00**	**46070.00**	**48830.00**	Own	6TI	401D	16F-4R	170.30	14312	C,H,A
8830 4WD Powershift	75818.00	**42460.00**	**48520.00**	**51430.00**	Own	6TI	401D	18F-9R	170.00	15112	C,H,A
8830 Powershift	66805.00	**37410.00**	**42760.00**	**45330.00**	Own	6TI	401D	18F-9R	170.00	13843	C,H,A
1156	160812.00	**77190.00**	**90060.00**	**94560.00**	Cummins	6TI	1150D	8F-4R	470.00*		C,H,A

*Net SAE HP.

New Holland/Ford (Cont.)

1993

Model	Approx. Retail Price New	Estimated Average Value Less Repairs Fair	Good	Premium	Engine Make	No. Cyls.	Displ. Cu.-In.	No. Speeds	P.T.O. H.P.	Approx. Shipping Wt.-Lbs.	Cab
1120	8549.00	**5730.00**	**6410.00**	**6800.00**	Shibaura	3	54D	9F-3R	12.50	1338	No
1120 4WD	9571.00	**6410.00**	**7180.00**	**7610.00**	Shibaura	3	54D	9F-3R	12.50	1429	No
1120H 4WD Hydro	10636.00	**7130.00**	**7980.00**	**8460.00**	Shibaura	3	54D	Infinite	12.50	1484	No
1120H Hydro	9614.00	**6440.00**	**7210.00**	**7640.00**	Shibaura	3	54D	Infinite	12.50	1393	No
1220	9100.00	**6100.00**	**6830.00**	**7240.00**	Shibaura	3	58D	9F-3R	14.50	1338	No
1220 4WD	10122.00	**6780.00**	**7590.00**	**8050.00**	Shibaura	3	58D	9F-3R	14.50	1429	No
1220H 4WD Hydro	11088.00	**7430.00**	**8320.00**	**8820.00**	Shibaura	3	58D	Infinite	14.50	1484	No
1220H Hydro	10067.00	**6750.00**	**7550.00**	**8000.00**	Shibaura	3	58D	Infinite	14.50	1393	No
1320	10665.00	**7150.00**	**8000.00**	**8480.00**	Shibaura	3	77D	9F-3R	17.00	2101	No
1320 4WD	12194.00	**8170.00**	**9150.00**	**9700.00**	Shibaura	3	77D	9F-3R	17.00	2229	No
1320H 4WD Hydro	13381.00	**8970.00**	**10040.00**	**10640.00**	Shibaura	3	77D	Infinite	17.00	2297	No
1320H Hydro	12219.00	**8190.00**	**9160.00**	**9710.00**	Shibaura	3	77D	Infinite	17.00	2172	No
1520	11142.00	**7470.00**	**8360.00**	**8860.00**	Shibaura	3	81D	9F-3R	19.50	2156	No
1520 4WD	12751.00	**8540.00**	**9560.00**	**10130.00**	Shibaura	3	81D	9F-3R	19.50	2278	No
1520H 4WD Hydro	14162.00	**9490.00**	**10620.00**	**11260.00**	Shibaura	3	81D	Infinite	19.50	2352	No
1520H Hydro	12919.00	**8660.00**	**9690.00**	**10270.00**	Shibaura	3	81D	Variable	19.50	2233	No
1620 4WD Hydro	14705.00	**9850.00**	**11030.00**	**11690.00**	Shibaura	3	81D	Infinite	22.00	2352	No
1620 Hydro	13349.00	**8940.00**	**10010.00**	**10610.00**	Shibaura	3	81D	Infinite	22.00	2233	No
1715	9283.00	**6220.00**	**6960.00**	**7380.00**	Shibaura	3	81D	9F-3R	23.0	2161	No
1715 4WD	10558.00	**7070.00**	**7920.00**	**8400.00**	Shibaura	3	81D	9F-3R	23.0	2280	No
1720	12073.00	**8090.00**	**9060.00**	**9600.00**	Shibaura	3	91D	12F-4R	23.50	2491	No
1720 4WD	13771.00	**9230.00**	**10330.00**	**10950.00**	Shibaura	3	91D	12F-4R	23.50	2690	No
1920	13973.00	**9360.00**	**10480.00**	**11110.00**	Shibaura	4	122D	12F-4R	28.50	2849	No
1920 4WD	16419.00	**11000.00**	**12310.00**	**13050.00**	Shibaura	4	122D	12F-4R	28.50	3069	No
2120	15592.00	**10450.00**	**11690.00**	**12390.00**	Shibaura	4	139D	12F-4R	34.50	3572	No
2120 4WD	18071.00	**12110.00**	**13550.00**	**14360.00**	Shibaura	4	139D	12F-4R	34.50	3858	No
3230	17309.00	**10730.00**	**11940.00**	**12660.00**	Own	3	192D	8F-2R	32.83	4455	No
3415	14477.00	**8980.00**	**9990.00**	**10590.00**	Shibaura	4	135D	12F-4R	38.0	3483	No
3430	18042.00	**11190.00**	**12450.00**	**13200.00**	Own	3	192D	8F-2R	38.00	4455	No
3430 4WD	22580.00	**14000.00**	**15580.00**	**16520.00**	Own	3	192D	8F-2R	38.00	4983	No
3430 4WD w/Cab	27593.00	**17110.00**	**19040.00**	**20180.00**	Own	3	192D	8F-2R	38.00	5483	C,H
3430 w/Cab	23055.00	**14290.00**	**15910.00**	**16870.00**	Own	3	192D	8F-2R	38.00	4955	C,H
3930 4WD w/Cab	28314.00	**17560.00**	**19540.00**	**20710.00**	Own	3	201D	8F-2R	45.00	5533	C,H
3930 w/Cab	23586.00	**14620.00**	**16270.00**	**17250.00**	Own	3	201D	8F-2R	45.00	5005	C,H
4630	20608.00	**12780.00**	**14220.00**	**15070.00**	Own	4	201D	8F-2R	55.0	5194	No
4630 4WD	25337.00	**15710.00**	**17480.00**	**18530.00**	Own	4	201D	8F-2R	55.0	5722	No
4630 4WD w/Cab	30350.00	**18820.00**	**20940.00**	**22200.00**	Own	4	201D	8F-2R	55.0	5958	C,H
4630 LCG	21528.00	**13350.00**	**14850.00**	**15740.00**	Own	4	201D	8F-2R	55.0	4958	No
4630 Low Profile	20612.00	**12780.00**	**14220.00**	**15070.00**	Own	4	201D	8F-2R	55.0	4784	No
4630 Low Profile 4WD	26166.00	**16220.00**	**18060.00**	**19140.00**	Own	4	201D	8F-2R	55.0	5312	No
4630 w/Cab	25621.00	**15890.00**	**17680.00**	**18740.00**	Own	4	201D	8F-2R	55.0	5430	C,H
5030	22034.00	**13660.00**	**15200.00**	**16110.00**	Own	4	256D	8F-2R	62.00	5214	No
5030 4WD	26784.00	**16610.00**	**18480.00**	**19590.00**	Own	4	256D	8F-2R	62.00	5742	No
5030 4WD w/Cab	31797.00	**19710.00**	**21940.00**	**23260.00**	Own	4	256D	8F-2R	62.00	6311	C,H,A
5030 Low Profile	21821.00	**13530.00**	**15060.00**	**15960.00**	Own	4	256D	8F-2R	62.00	5214	No
5030 Low Profile 4WD	27375.00	**16970.00**	**18890.00**	**20020.00**	Own	4	256D	8F-2R	62.00	5742	No
5030 w/Cab	27047.00	**16770.00**	**18660.00**	**19780.00**	Own	4	256D	8F-2R	62.00	5714	C,H,A
5640	25034.00	**15520.00**	**17270.00**	**18310.00**	Own	4	268D	8F-2R	66.00	7306	No
5640 4WD	31814.00	**18450.00**	**20680.00**	**21920.00**	Own	4	268D	8F-2R	66.00	8298	No
5640 4WD w/Cab	41937.00	**24320.00**	**27260.00**	**28900.00**	Own	4	268D	24F-24R	66.00	9380	C,H,A
5640 w/Cab	37261.00	**21610.00**	**24220.00**	**25670.00**	Own	4	268D	16F-16R	66.00	8418	C,H,A
6640	26850.00	**15570.00**	**17450.00**	**18500.00**	Own	4	304D	8F-2R	76.00	7274	No
6640 4WD	34136.00	**19800.00**	**22190.00**	**23520.00**	Own	4	304D	8F-2R	76.00	8298	No
6640 4WD w/Cab	43850.00	**25430.00**	**28500.00**	**30210.00**	Own	4	304D	12F-12R	76.00	9342	C,H,A
6640 w/Cab	37351.00	**21660.00**	**24280.00**	**25740.00**	Own	4	304D	12F-12R	76.00	8413	C,H,A
7740	29324.00	**17010.00**	**19060.00**	**20200.00**	Own	4T	304D	8F-2R	86.00	7339	No
7740 4WD	35832.00	**20780.00**	**23290.00**	**24690.00**	Own	4T	304D	8F-2R	86.00	8353	No
7740 4WD w/Cab	47146.00	**27350.00**	**30650.00**	**32490.00**	Own	4T	304D	24F-24R	86.00	9413	C,H,A
7740 w/Cab	41526.00	**24090.00**	**26990.00**	**28610.00**	Own	4T	304D	16F-16R	86.00	8451	C,H,A
7840	34662.00	**21490.00**	**23920.00**	**25360.00**	Own	6	401D	12F-12R	90.00	8342	No
7840 4WD	41170.00	**25530.00**	**28410.00**	**30120.00**	Own	6	401D	12F-12R	90.00	9400	No
7840 4WD w/Cab	48830.00	**30280.00**	**33690.00**	**35710.00**	Own	6	401D	12F-12R	90.00	10445	C,H,A
7840 w/Cab	42322.00	**26240.00**	**29200.00**	**30950.00**	Own	6	401D	12F-12R	90.00	9386	C,H,A
8240	37962.00	**23540.00**	**26190.00**	**27760.00**	Own	6	456D	16F-16R	96.00	8957	No
8240 4WD	44470.00	**27570.00**	**30680.00**	**32520.00**	Own	6	456D	16F-16R	96.00	10015	No
8240 4WD w/Cab	51655.00	**32030.00**	**35640.00**	**37780.00**	Own	6	456D	16F-16R	96.00	11053	C,H,A
8240 w/Cab	45147.00	**27990.00**	**31150.00**	**33020.00**	Own	6	456D	16F-16R	96.00	9995	C,H,A
8340	41404.00	**25670.00**	**28570.00**	**30280.00**	Own	6	456D	16F-16R	106.00	8957	No
8340 4WD	47912.00	**29710.00**	**33060.00**	**35040.00**	Own	6	456D	16F-16R	106.00	10015	No
8340 4WD w/Cab	55775.00	**34580.00**	**38490.00**	**40800.00**	Own	6	456D	16F-16R	106.00	11053	C,H,A
8340 w/Cab	49267.00	**30550.00**	**33990.00**	**36030.00**	Own	6	456D	16F-16R	106.00	9995	C,H,A
8630 4WD Powershift	66967.00	**38840.00**	**43530.00**	**46140.00**	Own	6T	401D	18F-9R	121.40	13300	C,H,A
8630 4WD w/Cab	61358.00	**35590.00**	**39880.00**	**42270.00**	Own	6T	401D	16F-4R	121.40	12500	C,H,A
8730 4WD Powershift	71291.00	**41350.00**	**46340.00**	**49120.00**	Own	6T	401D	16F-4R	140.68	15206	C,H,A
8730 4WD w/Cab	65564.00	**38030.00**	**42620.00**	**45180.00**	Own	6T	401D	16F-4R	140.68	14406	C,H,A
8830	62749.00	**36390.00**	**40790.00**	**43240.00**	Own	6TI	401D	16F-4R	170.30	13043	C,H,A
8830 4WD	71987.00	**41750.00**	**46790.00**	**49600.00**	Own	6TI	401D	16F-4R	170.30	14312	C,H,A
8830 4WD Powershift	76550.00	**44400.00**	**49760.00**	**52750.00**	Own	6TI	401D	18F-9R	170.00	15112	C,H,A
8830 Powershift	68475.00	**39720.00**	**44510.00**	**47180.00**	Own	6TI	401D	18F-9R	170.00	13843	C,H,A

*Net SAE HP.

1994

Model	Approx. Retail Price New	Fair	Good	Premium	Make	No. Cyls.	Displ. Cu.-In.	No. Speeds	P.T.O. H.P.	Approx. Shipping Wt.-Lbs.	Cab
1120	8806.00	**6080.00**	**6690.00**	**7030.00**	Shibaura	3	54D	9F-3R	12.50	1338	No
1120 4WD	9859.00	**6800.00**	**7490.00**	**7870.00**	Shibaura	3	54D	9F-3R	12.50	1429	No

New Holland/Ford (Cont.)

1994 (Cont.)

Model	Approx. Retail Price New	Estimated Average Value Less Repairs Fair	Good	Premium	Engine Make	No. Cyls.	Displ. Cu.-In.	No. Speeds	P.T.O. H.P.	Approx. Shipping Wt.-Lbs.	Cab
1120H 4WD Hydro	10956.00	**7560.00**	**8330.00**	**8750.00**	Shibaura	3	54D	Infinite	12.50	1484	No
1120H Hydro	9904.00	**6830.00**	**7530.00**	**7910.00**	Shibaura	3	54D	Infinite	12.50	1393	No
1215	7771.00	**5360.00**	**5910.00**	**6210.00**	Shibaura	3	54D	6F-2R	13.50	1338	No
1215 4WD	8685.00	**5990.00**	**6600.00**	**6930.00**	Shibaura	3	54D	6F-2R	13.50	1429	No
1215H 4WD Hydro	9571.00	**6600.00**	**7270.00**	**7630.00**	Shibaura	3	54D	Infinite	13.50	1484	No
1215H Hydro	8656.00	**5970.00**	**6580.00**	**6910.00**	Shibaura	3	54D	Infinite	13.50	1393	No
1220	9374.00	**6470.00**	**7120.00**	**7480.00**	Shibaura	3	58D	9F-3R	14.50	1338	No
1220 4WD	10427.00	**7200.00**	**7930.00**	**8330.00**	Shibaura	3	58D	9F-3R	14.50	1429	No
1220H 4WD Hydro	11423.00	**7880.00**	**8680.00**	**9110.00**	Shibaura	3	58D	Infinite	14.50	1484	No
1220H Hydro	10371.00	**7160.00**	**7880.00**	**8270.00**	Shibaura	3	58D	Infinite	14.50	1393	No
1320	10987.00	**7580.00**	**8350.00**	**8770.00**	Shibaura	3	77D	9F-3R	17.00	2101	No
1320 4WD	12562.00	**8670.00**	**9550.00**	**10030.00**	Shibaura	3	77D	9F-3R	17.00	2271	No
1320H 4WD Hydro	13783.00	**9510.00**	**10480.00**	**11000.00**	Shibaura	3	77D	Infinite	17.00	2297	No
1320H Hydro	12587.00	**8690.00**	**9570.00**	**10050.00**	Shibaura	3	77D	Infinite	17.00	2172	No
1520	11478.00	**7920.00**	**8720.00**	**9160.00**	Shibaura	3	81D	9F-3R	19.50	2156	No
1520 4WD	13136.00	**9060.00**	**9980.00**	**10480.00**	Shibaura	3	81D	9F-3R	19.50	2320	No
1520H 4WD Hydro	14588.00	**10070.00**	**11090.00**	**11650.00**	Shibaura	3	81D	Infinite	19.50	2352	No
1520H Hydro	13309.00	**9180.00**	**10120.00**	**10630.00**	Shibaura	3	81D	Infinite	19.50	2233	No
1620 4WD Hydro	15149.00	**10450.00**	**11510.00**	**12090.00**	Shibaura	3	81D	Infinite	22.00	2352	No
1620 Hydro	13751.00	**9490.00**	**10450.00**	**10970.00**	Shibaura	3	81D	Infinite	22.00	2233	No
1715	9835.00	**6790.00**	**7480.00**	**7850.00**	Shibaura	3	81D	9F-3R	23.00	2161	No
1715 4WD	11185.00	**7720.00**	**8500.00**	**8930.00**	Shibaura	3	81D	9F-3R	23.00	2280	No
1720	12437.00	**8580.00**	**9450.00**	**9920.00**	Shibaura	3	91D	12F-4R	23.50	2491	No
1720 4WD	14186.00	**9790.00**	**10780.00**	**11320.00**	Shibaura	3	91D	12F-4R	23.50	2690	No
1920	14394.00	**9930.00**	**10940.00**	**11490.00**	Shibaura	4	122D	12F-4R	28.50	2849	No
1920 4WD	16913.00	**11670.00**	**12850.00**	**13490.00**	Shibaura	4	122D	12F-4R	28.50	3069	No
2120	16062.00	**11080.00**	**12210.00**	**12820.00**	Shibaura	4	139D	12F-4R	34.50	3572	No
2120 4WD	18614.00	**12840.00**	**14150.00**	**14860.00**	Shibaura	4	139D	12F-4R	34.50	3858	No
3230	17309.00	**11080.00**	**12120.00**	**12730.00**	Own	3	192D	8F-2R	32.83	4455	No
3415	14912.00	**9540.00**	**10440.00**	**10960.00**	Shibaura	4	135D	12F-4R	38.00	3483	No
3430	18158.00	**11620.00**	**12710.00**	**13350.00**	Own	3	192D	8F-2R	38.00	4622	No
3430 4WD	22809.00	**14600.00**	**15970.00**	**16770.00**	Own	3	192D	8F-2R	38.00	5150	No
3430 4WD w/Cab	27593.00	**17660.00**	**19320.00**	**20290.00**	Own	3	192D	8F-2R	38.00	5650	C,H
3430 w/Cab	23055.00	**14760.00**	**16140.00**	**16950.00**	Own	3	192D	8F-2R	38.00	5122	C,H
3830	19800.00	**12670.00**	**13860.00**	**14550.00**	Own	3	165D	12F-4R	45.00	3784	No
3830 4WD	25713.00	**16460.00**	**18000.00**	**18900.00**	Own	3	165D	12F-4R	45.00	4000	No
3930	19096.00	**12220.00**	**13370.00**	**14040.00**	Own	3	201D	8F-2R	45.00	5157	No
3930 4WD	23943.00	**15320.00**	**16760.00**	**17600.00**	Own	3	201D	8F-2R	45.00	5685	No
3930 4WD w/Cab	28314.00	**18120.00**	**19820.00**	**20810.00**	Own	3	201D	8F-2R	45.00	6185	C,H
3930 w/Cab	23586.00	**15100.00**	**16510.00**	**17340.00**	Own	3	201D	8F-2R	45.00	5657	C,H
4030	20818.00	**13320.00**	**14570.00**	**15300.00**	Own	3	179D	12F-4R	51.00	5151	No
4030 4WD	26731.00	**17110.00**	**18710.00**	**19650.00**	Own	3	179D	12F-4R	51.00		No
4030 4WD w/Cab	31656.00	**20260.00**	**22160.00**	**23270.00**	Own	3	179D	12F-4R	51.00		C,H,A
4030 w/Cab	25743.00	**16480.00**	**18020.00**	**18920.00**	Own	3	179D	12F-4R	51.00	5591	C,H,A
4230	21917.00	**14030.00**	**15340.00**	**16110.00**	Own	4	220D	12F-4R	62.00	4860	No
4230 4WD	27830.00	**17810.00**	**19480.00**	**20450.00**	Own	4	220D	12F-4R	62.00	5200	No
4230 4WD w/Cab	32755.00	**20960.00**	**22930.00**	**24080.00**	Own	4	220D	12F-4R	62.00	5640	C,H,A
4230 w/Cab	26842.00	**17180.00**	**18790.00**	**19730.00**	Own	4	220D	12F-4R	62.00	5290	C,H,A
4430	24065.00	**15400.00**	**16850.00**	**17690.00**	Own	4	238D	12F-4R	70.00	5000	No
4430 4WD	29978.00	**19190.00**	**20990.00**	**22040.00**	Own	4	238D	12F-4R	70.00	5350	No
4430 4WD w/Cab	34903.00	**22340.00**	**24430.00**	**25650.00**	Own	4	238D	12F-4R	70.00	5790	C,H,A
4430 w/Cab	28990.00	**18550.00**	**20290.00**	**21310.00**	Own	4	238D	12F-4R	70.00	5440	C,H,A
4630	23122.00	**14800.00**	**16190.00**	**17000.00**	Own	3	201D	16F-8R	55.00	5030	No
4630 4WD	27970.00	**17900.00**	**19580.00**	**20560.00**	Own	3	201D	16F-8R	55.00	5822	No
4630 4WD w/Cab	31993.00	**20480.00**	**22400.00**	**23520.00**	Own	3	201D	16F-8R	55.00	6058	C,H
4630 LCG	21528.00	**13780.00**	**15070.00**	**15820.00**	Own	3	201D	8F-2R	55.00	4958	No
4630 Low Profile	21209.00	**13570.00**	**14850.00**	**15590.00**	Own	3	201D	8F-2R	55.00	4784	No
4630 Low Profile 4WD	26166.00	**16750.00**	**18320.00**	**19240.00**	Own	3	201D	8F-2R	55.00	5312	No
4630 w/Cab	27264.00	**17450.00**	**19090.00**	**20050.00**	Own	3	201D	16F-8R	55.00	5530	C,H
5030	24409.00	**15620.00**	**17090.00**	**17950.00**	Own	4	256D	16F-8R	62.00	5647	No
5030 4WD	29278.00	**18740.00**	**20500.00**	**21530.00**	Own	4	256D	16F-8R	62.00	6175	No
5030 4WD w/Cab	34416.00	**22030.00**	**24090.00**	**25300.00**	Own	4	256D	16F-8R	62.00	6675	C,H
5030 Low Profile	22497.00	**14400.00**	**15750.00**	**16540.00**	Own	4	256D	8F-2R	62.00	5547	No
5030 Low Profile 4WD	28191.00	**18040.00**	**19730.00**	**20720.00**	Own	4	256D	8F-2R	62.00		No
5030 w/Cab	29547.00	**18910.00**	**20680.00**	**21710.00**	Own	4	256D	16F-8R	62.00	6147	C,H
5530	25526.00	**16340.00**	**17870.00**	**18760.00**	Own	4	220D	20F-12R	62.00	5709	No
5530 4WD	31108.00	**19910.00**	**21780.00**	**22870.00**	Own	4	220D	20F-12R	62.00	7310	No
5610S	24611.00	**16130.00**	**17770.00**	**18660.00**	Own	4	268D	8F-2R	66.00	5800	No
5640S	28788.00	**17560.00**	**19290.00**	**20260.00**	Own	4	268D	16F-4R	66.00	7399	No
5640S 4WD	35141.00	**21440.00**	**23540.00**	**24720.00**	Own	4	268D	16F-4R	66.00	8391	No
5640SL	30312.00	**18490.00**	**20310.00**	**21330.00**	Own	4	268D	24F-24R	66.00	7373	No
5640SL 4WD	36664.00	**22370.00**	**24570.00**	**25800.00**	Own	4	268D	24F-24R	66.00	8298	No
5640SL 4WD w/Cab	44687.00	**27260.00**	**29940.00**	**31440.00**	Own	4	268D	24F-24R	66.00	9380	C,H,A
5640SL w/Cab	38334.00	**23380.00**	**25680.00**	**26960.00**	Own	4	268D	24F-24R	66.00	8418	C,H,A
5640SLE	33386.00	**20370.00**	**22370.00**	**23490.00**	Own	4	268D	16F-16R	66.00	7483	No
5640SLE 4WD	39738.00	**24240.00**	**26620.00**	**27950.00**	Own	4	268D	16F-16R	66.00	8475	No
5640SLE 4WD w/Cab	47361.00	**28890.00**	**31730.00**	**33320.00**	Own	4	268D	16F-16R	66.00	9380	C,H,A
5640SLE w/Cab	41008.00	**25020.00**	**27480.00**	**28850.00**	Own	4	268D	16F-16R	66.00	8418	C,H,A
6530	28218.00	**18060.00**	**19750.00**	**20740.00**	Own	4	238D	20F-12R	70.00	5709	No
6530 4WD	35008.00	**22410.00**	**24510.00**	**25740.00**	Own	4	238D	20F-12R	70.00	7310	No
6610S	26900.00	**17630.00**	**19420.00**	**20390.00**	Own	4	304D	8F-2R	76.00	5800	No
6610S 4WD	34841.00	**21180.00**	**23170.00**	**24330.00**	Own	4	304D	8F-2R	76.00	6435	No
6640 Low Profile	30768.00	**18770.00**	**20620.00**	**21650.00**	Own	4	304D	16F-4R	76.00	7354	No
6640 Low Profile 4WD	37667.00	**22980.00**	**25240.00**	**26500.00**	Own	4	304D	16F-4R	76.00	8346	No

New Holland/Ford (Cont.)

1994 (Cont.)

Model	Approx. Retail Price New	Fair	Good	Premium	Engine Make	No. Cyls.	Displ. Cu.-In.	No. Speeds	P.T.O. H.P.	Approx. Shipping Wt.-Lbs.	Cab
6640S	31029.00	18930.00	20790.00	21830.00	Own	4	304D	16F-4R	76.00	7399	No
6640S 4WD	37928.00	23140.00	25410.00	26680.00	Own	4	304D	16F-4R	76.00	8391	No
6640SL	33318.00	20320.00	22320.00	23440.00	Own	4	304D	24F-24R	76.00	7373	C,H,A
6640SL 4WD	40217.00	24530.00	26950.00	28300.00	Own	4	304D	24F-24R	76.00	8304	C,H,A
6640SL 4WD w/Cab	48239.00	29430.00	32320.00	33940.00	Own	4	304D	24F-24R	76.00	9358	C,H,A
6640SL w/Cab	41341.00	25220.00	27700.00	29090.00	Own	4	304D	24F-24R	76.00	8419	C,H,A
6640SLE	34466.00	21020.00	23090.00	24250.00	Own	4	304D	16F-16R	76.00	7483	No
6640SLE 4WD	41364.00	25230.00	27710.00	29100.00	Own	4	304D	16F-16R	76.00	8475	No
6640SLE 4WD w/Cab	49038.00	29910.00	32860.00	34500.00	Own	4	304D	16F-16R	76.00	9380	C,H,A
6640SLE w/Cab	42139.00	25710.00	28230.00	29640.00	Own	4	304D	16F-16R	76.00	8418	C,H,A
7530 4WD	39643.00	25370.00	27750.00	29140.00	Own	6	331D	20F-4R	91.00	8074	No
7610S	29638.00	18020.00	19710.00	20700.00	Own	4T	304D	8F-2R	86.00	5800	No
7610S 4WD	36699.00	21270.00	23360.00	24530.00	Own	4T	304D	8F-2R	86.00	6435	No
7740 Low Profile	32918.00	20080.00	22060.00	23160.00	Own	4T	304D	16F-4R	86.00	7419	No
7740 Low Profile 4WD	39817.00	24290.00	26680.00	28010.00	Own	4T	304D	16F-4R	86.00	8411	No
7740S	33188.00	20250.00	22240.00	23350.00	Own	4T	304D	16F-4R	86.00	7432	No
7740S 4WD	40087.00	24450.00	26860.00	28200.00	Own	4T	304D	16F-4R	86.00	8446	No
7740SL	35236.00	21490.00	23610.00	24790.00	Own	4T	304D	24F-24R	86.00	7432	No
7740SL 4WD	42134.00	25700.00	28230.00	29640.00	Own	4T	304D	24F-24R	86.00	8446	No
7740SL 4WD w/Cab	50870.00	31030.00	34080.00	35780.00	Own	4T	304D	24F-24R	86.00	9413	C,H,A
7740SL w/Cab	43971.00	26820.00	29460.00	30930.00	Own	4T	304D	24F-24R	86.00	8451	C,H,A
7740SLE	35391.00	21590.00	23710.00	24900.00	Own	4T	304D	16F-16R	86.00	7516	No
7740SLE 4WD	42289.00	25800.00	28330.00	29750.00	Own	4T	304D	16F-16R	86.00	8508	No
7740SLE 4WD w/Cab	50625.00	30880.00	33920.00	35620.00	Own	4T	304D	16F-16R	86.00	9413	C,H,A
7740SLE w/Cab	43726.00	26670.00	29300.00	30770.00	Own	4T	304D	16F-16R	86.00	8451	C,H,A
7810S	31957.00	19430.00	21250.00	22310.00	Own	6	401D	8F-2R	90.00	5800	No
7810S 4WD	39017.00	23720.00	25950.00	27250.00	Own	6	401D	8F-2R	90.00	6435	No
7840 Low Profile	35720.00	22860.00	25000.00	26250.00	Own	6	401D	16F-4R	90.00		No
7840 Low Profile 4WD	42618.00	27280.00	29830.00	31320.00	Own	6	401D	16F-4R	90.00		No
7840S	35976.00	23030.00	25180.00	26440.00	Own	6	401D	16F-4R	90.00	8076	No
7840S 4WD	42875.00	27440.00	30010.00	31510.00	Own	6	401D	16F-4R	90.00	9134	No
7840SL	38820.00	24850.00	27170.00	28530.00	Own	6	401D	24F-24R	90.00	8382	No
7840SL 4WD	45718.00	29260.00	32000.00	33600.00	Own	6	401D	24F-24R	90.00	9410	No
7840SL 4WD w/Cab	54988.00	35190.00	38490.00	40420.00	Own	6	401D	24F-24R	90.00	10465	C,H,A
7840SL w/Cab	48089.00	30780.00	33660.00	35340.00	Own	6	401D	24F-24R	90.00	9398	C,H,A
7840SLE	38393.00	24570.00	26880.00	28220.00	Own	6	401D	16F-16R	90.00	8379	No
7840SLE 4WD	45292.00	28990.00	31700.00	33290.00	Own	6	401D	16F-16R	90.00	9437	No
7840SLE 4WD w/Cab	53627.00	34320.00	37540.00	39420.00	Own	6	401D	16F-16R	90.00	10482	C,H,A
7840SLE w/Cab	46729.00	29910.00	32710.00	34350.00	Own	6	401D	16F-16R	90.00	9423	C,H,A
8240SL	39425.00	25230.00	27600.00	28980.00	Own	6	456D	12F-12R	96.00	8883	No
8240SL 4WD	46324.00	29650.00	32430.00	34050.00	Own	6	456D	12F-12R	96.00	9941	No
8240SL 4WD w/Cab	53963.00	34540.00	37770.00	39660.00	Own	6	456D	12F-12R	96.00	10979	C,H,A
8240SL w/Cab	47064.00	30120.00	32950.00	34600.00	Own	6	456D	12F-12R	96.00	9921	C,H,A
8240SLE	40896.00	26170.00	28630.00	30060.00	Own	6	456D	16F-16R	96.00	8957	No
8240SLE 4WD	47795.00	30590.00	33460.00	35130.00	Own	6	456D	16F-16R	96.00	10015	No
8240SLE 4WD w/Cab	55412.00	35460.00	38790.00	40730.00	Own	6	456D	16F-16R	96.00	11053	C,H,A
8240SLE w/Cab	48513.00	31050.00	33960.00	35660.00	Own	6	456D	16F-16R	96.00	9995	C,H,A
8340SL	42322.00	27090.00	29630.00	31110.00	Own	6T	456D	12F-12R	112.00	8883	No
8340SL 4WD	49221.00	31500.00	34460.00	36180.00	Own	6T	456D	12F-12R	112.00	9941	No
8340SL 4WD w/Cab	57579.00	36850.00	40310.00	42330.00	Own	6T	456D	12F-12R	112.00	10979	C,H,A
8340SL w/Cab	50680.00	32440.00	35480.00	37250.00	Own	6T	456D	12F-12R	112.00	9921	C,H,A
8340SLE	45217.00	28940.00	31650.00	33230.00	Own	6T	456D	16F-16R	112.00	8957	No
8340SLE 4WD	52116.00	33350.00	36480.00	38300.00	Own	6T	456D	16F-16R	112.00	10015	No
8340SLE 4WD w/Cab	60451.00	38690.00	42320.00	44440.00	Own	6T	456D	16F-16R	112.00	11053	C,H,A
8340SLE w/Cab	53553.00	34270.00	37490.00	39370.00	Own	6T	456D	16F-16R	112.00	9995	C,H,A
8630	52120.00	31790.00	34920.00	36670.00	Own	6T	401D	16F-4R	121.40	11442	C,H,A
8630 4WD	61358.00	37430.00	41110.00	43170.00	Own	6T	401D	16F-4R	121.40	12501	C,H,A
8630 4WD Powershift	66967.00	40850.00	44870.00	47110.00	Own	6T	401D	18F-9R	121.00		C,H,A
8630 Powershift	57729.00	35220.00	38680.00	40610.00	Own	6T	401D	18F-9R	121.00	12242	C,H,A
8670	72358.00	44140.00	48480.00	50900.00	Own	6T	456D	16F-9R	145.00		C,H,A
8670 4WD	82358.00	50240.00	55180.00	57940.00	Own	6T	456D	16F-9R	145.00		C,H,A
8770	76828.00	46870.00	51480.00	54050.00	Own	6T	456D	16F-9R	160.00		C,H,A
8770 4WD	86828.00	52970.00	58180.00	61090.00	Own	6T	456D	16F-9R	160.00		C,H,A
8870	86037.00	52480.00	57650.00	60530.00	Own	6TA	456D	16F-9R	180.00		C,H,A
8870 4WD	96037.00	58580.00	64350.00	67570.00	Own	6TA	456D	16F-9R	180.00		C,H,A
8970	95193.00	58070.00	63780.00	66970.00	Own	6TI	456D	16F-9R	210.00		C,H,A
8970 4WD	105193.00	64170.00	70480.00	74000.00	Own	6TI	456D	16F-9R	210.00		C,H,A

*Net SAE HP.

1995

Model	Approx. Retail Price New	Fair	Good	Premium	Engine Make	No. Cyls.	Displ. Cu.-In.	No. Speeds	P.T.O. H.P.	Approx. Shipping Wt.-Lbs.	Cab
1215	8978.00	6370.00	7000.00	7350.00	Shibaura	3	54D	6F-2R	13.50	1338	No
1215 4WD	10035.00	7130.00	7830.00	8220.00	Shibaura	3	54D	6F-2R	13.50	1429	No
1215H 4WD Hydro	11058.00	7850.00	8630.00	9060.00	Shibaura	3	54D	Infinite	13.50	1484	No
1215H Hydro	10001.00	7100.00	7800.00	8190.00	Shibaura	3	54D	Infinite	13.50	1393	No
1220	10499.00	7450.00	8190.00	8600.00	Shibaura	3	58D	9F-3R	14.50	1338	No
1220 4WD	11677.00	8290.00	9110.00	9570.00	Shibaura	3	58D	9F-3R	14.50	1429	No
1220H 4WD Hydro	13590.00	9650.00	10600.00	11130.00	Shibaura	3	58D	Infinite	14.50	1484	No
1220H Hydro	11614.00	8250.00	9060.00	9510.00	Shibaura	3	58D	Infinite	14.50	1393	No
1320	12564.00	8920.00	9800.00	10290.00	Shibaura	3	77D	9F-3R	17.00	2145	No
1320 4WD	13887.00	9860.00	10830.00	11370.00	Shibaura	3	77D	9F-3R	17.00	2271	No
1320H 4WD Hydro	15236.00	10820.00	11880.00	12470.00	Shibaura	3	77D	Infinite	17.00	2297	No
1320H Hydro	13913.00	9880.00	10850.00	11390.00	Shibaura	3	77D	Infinite	17.00	2172	No
1520	12947.00	9190.00	10100.00	10610.00	Shibaura	3	81D	9F-3R	19.50	2200	No
1520 4WD	14344.00	10180.00	11190.00	11750.00	Shibaura	3	81D	9F-3R	19.50	2320	No

Model	Approx. Retail Price New	Estimated Average Value Less Repairs Fair	Good	Premium	Engine Make	No. Cyls.	Displ. Cu.-In.	No. Speeds	P.T.O. H.P.	Approx. Shipping Wt.-Lbs.	Cab
New Holland/Ford (Cont.)											
			1995 (Cont.)								
1520H 4WD Hydro	15929.00	11310.00	12430.00	13050.00	Shibaura	3	81D	Infinite	19.50	2352	No
1520H Hydro	14533.00	10320.00	11340.00	11910.00	Shibaura	3	81D	Infinite	19.50	2233	No
1620 4WD Hydro	16701.00	11860.00	13030.00	13680.00	Shibaura	3	81D	Infinite	22.00	2352	No
1715	11124.00	7900.00	8680.00	9110.00	Shibaura	3	81D	9F-3R	23.00	2161	No
1715 4WD	12651.00	8980.00	9870.00	10360.00	Shibaura	3	81D	9F-3R	23.00	2280	No
1720	13450.00	9550.00	10490.00	11020.00	Shibaura	3	91D	12F-4R	23.50	2491	No
1720 4WD	15341.00	10890.00	11970.00	12570.00	Shibaura	3	91D	12F-4R	23.50	2690	No
1920	15269.00	10840.00	11910.00	12510.00	Shibaura	4	122D	12F-4R	28.50	2849	No
1920 4WD	17941.00	12740.00	13990.00	14690.00	Shibaura	4	122D	12F-4R	28.50	3069	No
2120 4WD	21179.00	15040.00	16520.00	17350.00	Shibaura	4	139D	12F-4R	34.50	3858	No
3415	17612.00	11620.00	12860.00	13500.00	Shibaura	4	135D	12F-4R	38.00	3483	No
3430	19193.00	12670.00	14010.00	14710.00	Own	3	192D	8F-2R	38.00	4622	No
3430 4WD	24008.00	15850.00	17530.00	18410.00	Own	3	192D	8F-2R	38.00	5150	No
3830	19800.00	13070.00	14450.00	15170.00	Own	3	165D	12F-4R	45.00	3784	No
3830 4WD	25713.00	16970.00	18770.00	19710.00	Own	3	165D	12F-4R	45.00	4000	No
3930	20236.00	13360.00	14770.00	15510.00	Own	3	201D	8F-2R	45.00	5157	No
3930 4WD	25905.00	17100.00	18910.00	19860.00	Own	3	201D	8F-8R	45.00	5735	No
3930 4WD w/Cab	31224.00	20610.00	22790.00	23930.00	Own	3	201D	8F-8R	45.00	6235	C,H
3930 w/Cab	26207.00	17300.00	19130.00	20090.00	Own	3	201D	8F-8R	45.00	5707	C,H
4030	20818.00	13740.00	15200.00	15960.00	Own	3	179D	12F-4R	51.00	5151	No
4030 4WD	26731.00	17640.00	19510.00	20490.00	Own	3	179D	12F-4R	51.00	5558	No
4030 4WD w/Cab	31656.00	20890.00	23110.00	24270.00	Own	3	179D	12F-4R	51.00	5995	C,H,A
4030 w/Cab	25743.00	16990.00	18790.00	19730.00	Own	3	179D	12F-4R	51.00	5591	C,H,A
4230	21917.00	14470.00	16000.00	16800.00	Own	4	220D	12F-4R	62.00	4860	No
4230 4WD	27830.00	18370.00	20320.00	21340.00	Own	4	220D	12F-4R	62.00	5200	No
4230 4WD w/Cab	32755.00	21620.00	23910.00	25110.00	Own	4	220D	12F-4R	62.00	5640	C,H,A
4230 w/Cab	26842.00	17720.00	19600.00	20580.00	Own	4	220D	12F-4R	62.00	5290	C,H,A
4430	24065.00	15880.00	17570.00	18450.00	Own	4	238D	12F-4R	70.00	5000	No
4430 4WD	29978.00	19790.00	21880.00	22970.00	Own	4	238D	12F-4R	70.00	5350	No
4430 4WD w/Cab	34903.00	23040.00	25480.00	26750.00	Own	4	238D	12F-4R	70.00	5790	C,H,A
4430 w/Cab	28990.00	19130.00	21160.00	22220.00	Own	4	238D	12F-4R	70.00	5440	C,H,A
4630	24045.00	15870.00	17550.00	18430.00	Own	3	201D	16F-8R	55.00	5030	No
4630 4WD	29062.00	19180.00	21220.00	22280.00	Own	3	201D	16F-8R	55.00	5822	No
4630 4WD w/Cab	33289.00	21970.00	24300.00	25520.00	Own	3	201D	8F-8R	55.00	6272	C,H
4630 w/Cab	28272.00	18660.00	20640.00	21670.00	Own	3	201D	8F-8R	55.00	5744	C,H
5030	26076.00	17210.00	19040.00	19990.00	Own	4	256D	16F-8R	62.00	5647	No
5030 4WD	31116.00	20540.00	22720.00	23860.00	Own	4	256D	16F-8R	62.00	6175	No
5030 4WD w/Cab	36434.00	24050.00	26600.00	27930.00	Own	4	256D	16F-8R	62.00	6675	C,H
5030 w/Cab	31395.00	20720.00	22920.00	24070.00	Own	4	256D	16F-8R	62.00	6147	C,H
5530	25742.00	16990.00	18790.00	19730.00	Own	4	220D	20F-12R	62.00	5709	No
5530 4WD	31323.00	20670.00	22870.00	24010.00	Own	4	220D	20F-12R	62.00	7310	No
5610S	24432.00	17350.00	19060.00	20010.00	Own	4	268D	8F-2R	66.00	5995	No
5640S	28362.00	18150.00	19850.00	20840.00	Own	4	268D	8F-2R	66.00	7306	No
5640S 4WD	34905.00	22340.00	24430.00	25650.00	Own	4	268D	8F-2R	66.00	8298	No
5640SL	31222.00	19980.00	21860.00	22950.00	Own	4	268D	24F-24R	66.00	7373	No
5640SL 4WD	37766.00	24170.00	26440.00	27760.00	Own	4	268D	24F-24R	66.00	8298	No
5640SL 4WD w/Cab	46029.00	29460.00	32220.00	33830.00	Own	4	268D	24F-24R	66.00	9380	C,H,A
5640SL w/Cab	39486.00	25270.00	27640.00	29020.00	Own	4	268D	24F-24R	66.00	8418	C,H,A
5640SLE	34389.00	22010.00	24070.00	25270.00	Own	4	268D	16F-16R	66.00	7483	No
5640SLE 4WD	40933.00	26200.00	28650.00	30080.00	Own	4	268D	16F-16R	66.00	8475	No
5640SLE 4WD w/Cab	48784.00	31220.00	34150.00	35860.00	Own	4	268D	16F-16R	66.00	9380	C,H,A
5640SLE w/Cab	42241.00	27030.00	29570.00	31050.00	Own	4	268D	16F-16R	66.00	8418	C,H,A
6530	28434.00	18770.00	20760.00	21800.00	Own	4	238D	20F-12R	70.00	5709	No
6530 4WD	35223.00	23250.00	25710.00	27000.00	Own	4	238D	20F-12R	70.00	7310	No
6610S	26705.00	18960.00	20830.00	21870.00	Own	4	304D	8F-2R	76.00	5995	No
6610S 4WD	34589.00	22830.00	25250.00	26510.00	Own	4	304D	8F-2R	76.00	6925	No
6640 Low Profile	31691.00	20280.00	22180.00	23290.00	Own	4	304D	16F-4R	76.00	7354	No
6640 Low Profile 4WD	38796.00	24830.00	27160.00	28520.00	Own	4	304D	16F-4R	76.00	8346	No
6640S	31957.00	20450.00	22370.00	23490.00	Own	4	304D	16F-4R	76.00	7399	No
6640S 4WD	39062.00	25000.00	27340.00	28710.00	Own	4	304D	16F-4R	76.00	8391	No
6640SL	34316.00	21960.00	24020.00	25220.00	Own	4	304D	24F-24R	76.00	7373	No
6640SL 4WD	41421.00	26510.00	29000.00	30450.00	Own	4	304D	24F-24R	76.00	8304	No
6640SL 4WD w/Cab	49684.00	31800.00	34780.00	36520.00	Own	4	304D	24F-24R	76.00	9358	C,H,A
6640SL w/Cab	42579.00	27250.00	29810.00	31300.00	Own	4	304D	24F-24R	76.00	8419	C,H,A
6640SLE	35550.00	22750.00	24890.00	26140.00	Own	4	304D	16F-16R	76.00	7483	No
6640SLE 4WD	42655.00	27300.00	29860.00	31350.00	Own	4	304D	16F-16R	76.00	8475	No
6640SLE 4WD w/Cab	50507.00	32320.00	35360.00	37130.00	Own	4	304D	16F-16R	76.00	9380	C,H,A
6640SLE w/Cab	43401.00	27780.00	30380.00	31900.00	Own	4	304D	16F-16R	76.00	8418	C,H,A
7530 4WD	39643.00	26160.00	28940.00	30390.00	Own	6	331D	20F-4R	91.00	8074	No
7610S	29424.00	19420.00	21480.00	22550.00	Own	4T	304D	8F-2R	86.00	6375	No
7610S 4WD	36434.00	23320.00	25500.00	26780.00	Own	4T	304D	8F-2R	86.00	7305	No
7740 Low Profile	33905.00	21700.00	23730.00	24920.00	Own	4T	304D	16F-4R	86.00	7419	No
7740 Low Profile 4WD	41011.00	26250.00	28710.00	30150.00	Own	4T	304D	16F-4R	86.00	8411	No
7740S	34184.00	21880.00	23930.00	25130.00	Own	4T	304D	16F-4R	86.00	7432	No
7740S 4WD	41289.00	26430.00	28900.00	30350.00	Own	4T	304D	16F-4R	86.00	8446	No
7740SL	36293.00	23230.00	25410.00	26680.00	Own	4T	304D	24F-24R	86.00	7432	No
7740SL 4WD	43399.00	27780.00	30380.00	31900.00	Own	4T	304D	24F-24R	86.00	8446	No
7740SL 4WD w/Cab	52396.00	32000.00	35000.00	36750.00	Own	4T	304D	24F-24R	86.00	9413	C,H,A
7740SL w/Cab	45291.00	28990.00	31700.00	33290.00	Own	4T	304D	24F-24R	86.00	8400	C,H,A
7740SLE	36453.00	23330.00	25520.00	26800.00	Own	4T	304D	16F-16R	86.00	7516	No
7740SLE 4WD	43558.00	27880.00	30490.00	32020.00	Own	4T	304D	16F-16R	86.00	8508	No
7740SLE 4WD w/Cab	52143.00	32640.00	35700.00	37490.00	Own	4T	304D	16F-16R	86.00	9413	C,H,A
7740SLE w/Cab	45038.00	28820.00	31530.00	33110.00	Own	4T	304D	16F-16R	86.00	8451	C,H,A
7810S	31721.00	20940.00	23160.00	24320.00	Own	6	401D	8F-2R	90.00	6625	No

Model	Approx. Retail Price New	Estimated Average Value Less Repairs Fair	Good	Premium	Engine Make	No. Cyls.	Displ. Cu.-In.	No. Speeds	P.T.O. H.P.	Approx. Shipping Wt.-Lbs.	Cab

New Holland/Ford (Cont.)

1995 (Cont.)

Model	Approx. Retail Price New	Fair	Good	Premium	Make	No. Cyls.	Displ. Cu.-In.	No. Speeds	P.T.O. H.P.	Approx. Shipping Wt.-Lbs.	Cab
7810S 4WD	38732.00	25560.00	28270.00	29680.00	Own	6	401D	8F-2R	90.00	7555	No
7840 Low Profile	36434.00	23320.00	25500.00	26780.00	Own	6	401D	16F-4R	90.00		No
7840 Low Profile 4WD	43471.00	27820.00	30430.00	31950.00	Own	6	401D	16F-4R	90.00		No
7840S	36696.00	23490.00	25690.00	26980.00	Own	6	401D	16F-4R	90.00	8076	No
7840S 4WD	43733.00	27990.00	30610.00	32140.00	Own	6	401D	16F-4R	90.00	9134	No
7840SL	39596.00	25340.00	27720.00	29110.00	Own	6	401D	24F-24R	90.00	8382	No
7840SL 4WD	46633.00	29850.00	32640.00	34270.00	Own	6	401D	24F-24R	90.00	9410	No
7840SL 4WD w/Cab	56087.00	35200.00	38500.00	40430.00	Own	6	401D	24F-24R	90.00	10465	C,H,A
7840SL w/Cab	49050.00	31390.00	34340.00	36060.00	Own	6	401D	24F-24R	90.00	9398	C,H,A
7840SLE	39162.00	25060.00	27410.00	28780.00	Own	6	401D	16F-16R	90.00	8379	No
7840SLE 4WD	46199.00	29570.00	32340.00	33960.00	Own	6	401D	16F-16R	90.00	9437	No
7840SLE 4WD w/Cab	54701.00	34560.00	37800.00	39690.00	Own	6	401D	16F-16R	90.00	10482	C,H,A
7840SLE w/Cab	47664.00	30510.00	33370.00	35040.00	Own	6	401D	16F-16R	90.00	9423	C,H,A
8160	43698.00	27970.00	30590.00	32120.00	Own	6	456D	17F-6R	90.0		No
8160 4WD	52506.00	33600.00	36750.00	38590.00	Own	6	456D	17F-6R	90.0		No
8160 4WD w/Cab	60206.00	38530.00	42140.00	44250.00	Own	6	456D	17F-6R	90.0		C,H,A
8160 w/Cab	51398.00	32900.00	35980.00	37780.00	Own	6	456D	17F-6R	90.0		C,H,A
8240SL	40214.00	26540.00	29360.00	30830.00	Own	6	456D	12F-12R	96.00	8883	No
8240SL 4WD	47251.00	31190.00	34490.00	36220.00	Own	6	456D	12F-12R	96.00	9941	No
8240SL 4WD w/Cab	55043.00	36330.00	40180.00	42190.00	Own	6	456D	12F-12R	96.00	10979	C,H,A
8240SL w/Cab	48007.00	31690.00	35050.00	36800.00	Own	6	456D	12F-12R	96.00	9921	C,H,A
8240SLE	41726.00	27540.00	30460.00	31980.00	Own	6	456D	16F-16R	96.00	8957	No
8240SLE 4WD	48763.00	32180.00	35600.00	37380.00	Own	6	456D	16F-16R	96.00	10015	No
8240SLE 4WD w/Cab	56533.00	37310.00	41270.00	43330.00	Own	6	456D	16F-16R	96.00	11053	C,H,A
8240SLE w/Cab	49496.00	32670.00	36130.00	37940.00	Own	6	456D	16F-16R	96.00	9995	C,H,A
8260	47250.00	30240.00	33080.00	34730.00	Own	6	456D	17F-6R	100.0		No
8260 4WD	56057.00	35880.00	39240.00	41200.00	Own	6	456D	17F-6R	100.0		No
8260 4WD w/Cab	63757.00	40800.00	44630.00	46860.00	Own	6	456D	17F-6R	100.0		C,H,A
8260 w/Cab	54950.00	35170.00	38470.00	40390.00	Own	6	456D	17F-6R	100.0		C,H,A
8340SL	43168.00	28490.00	31510.00	33090.00	Own	6T	456D	12F-12R	112.00	8883	No
8340SL 4WD	50205.00	33140.00	36650.00	38480.00	Own	6T	456D	12F-12R	112.00	9941	No
8340SL 4WD w/Cab	58730.00	38760.00	42870.00	45010.00	Own	6T	456D	12F-12R	112.00	10979	C,H,A
8340SL w/Cab	51693.00	34120.00	37740.00	39630.00	Own	6T	456D	12F-12R	112.00	9921	C,H,A
8340SLE	46121.00	30440.00	33670.00	35350.00	Own	6T	456D	16F-16R	112.00	8957	No
8340SLE 4WD	53158.00	35080.00	38810.00	40750.00	Own	6T	456D	16F-16R	112.00	10015	No
8340SLE 4WD w/Cab	61661.00	40700.00	45010.00	47260.00	Own	6T	456D	16F-16R	112.00	11053	C,H,A
8340SLE w/Cab	54624.00	36050.00	39880.00	41870.00	Own	6T	456D	16F-16R	112.00	9995	C,H,A
8360	54346.00	34780.00	38040.00	39940.00	Own	6T	456D	17F-6R	115.0		No
8360 4WD	66134.00	42330.00	46290.00	48610.00	Own	6T	456D	17F-6R	115.0		No
8360 4WD w/Cab	73828.00	46400.00	50750.00	53290.00	Own	6T	456D	17F-6R	115.0		C,H,A
8360 w/Cab	62040.00	39710.00	43430.00	45600.00	Own	6T	456D	17F-6R	115.0		C,H,A
8560 4WD w/Cab	81084.00	51200.00	56000.00	58800.00	Own	6T	456D	18F-6R	130.0		C,H,A
8560 w/Cab	69252.00	44320.00	48480.00	50900.00	Own	6T	456D	17F-6R	130.0		C,H,A
8670	73888.00	47290.00	51720.00	54310.00	Own	6T	456D	16F-9R	145.00	14632	C,H,A
8670 4WD	83888.00	52480.00	57400.00	60270.00	Own	6T	456D	16F-9R	145.00	15188	C,H,A
8770	76828.00	49170.00	53780.00	56470.00	Own	6T	456D	16F-9R	160.00	16925	C,H,A
8770 4WD	86828.00	54400.00	59500.00	62480.00	Own	6T	456D	16F-9R	160.00	17481	C,H,A
8870	86099.00	55100.00	60270.00	63280.00	Own	6TI	456D	16F-9R	180.00	17101	C,H,A
8870 4WD	96099.00	61500.00	67270.00	70630.00	Own	6TI	456D	16F-9R	180.00	17657	C,H,A
8970	95255.00	60960.00	66680.00	70010.00	Own	6TI	456D	16F-9R	210.00	17333	C,H,A
8970 4WD	105255.00	67360.00	73680.00	77360.00	Own	6TI	456D	16F-9R	210.00	17889	C,H,A

*Net SAE HP.

1996

Model	Approx. Retail Price New	Fair	Good	Premium	Make	No. Cyls.	Displ. Cu.-In.	No. Speeds	P.T.O. H.P.	Approx. Shipping Wt.-Lbs.	Cab
1215	8978.00	6640.00	7180.00	7470.00	Shibaura	3	54D	6F-2R	13.5	1338	No
1215 4WD	10035.00	7430.00	8030.00	8350.00	Shibaura	3	54D	6F-2R	13.5	1429	No
1215H 4WD Hydro	11058.00	8180.00	8850.00	9200.00	Shibaura	3	54D	Infinite	13.5	1484	No
1215H Hydro	10001.00	7400.00	8000.00	8320.00	Shibaura	3	54D	Infinite	13.5	1393	No
1220 4WD	11817.00	8750.00	9450.00	9830.00	Shibaura	3	58D	9F-3R	14.5	1429	No
1220H 4WD Hydro	13730.00	10160.00	10980.00	11420.00	Shibaura	3	58D	Infinite	14.5	1484	No
1320	12564.00	9300.00	10050.00	10450.00	Shibaura	3	77D	9F-3R	17.0	2145	No
1320 4WD	13887.00	10280.00	11110.00	11550.00	Shibaura	3	77D	9F-3R	17.0	2271	No
1320H 4WD Hydro	15236.00	11280.00	12190.00	12680.00	Shibaura	3	77D	Infinite	17.0	2297	No
1320H Hydro	13913.00	10300.00	11130.00	11580.00	Shibaura	3	77D	Infinite	17.0	2172	No
1520	13005.00	9620.00	10400.00	10820.00	Shibaura	3	81D	9F-3R	19.5	2200	No
1520 4WD	14430.00	10680.00	11540.00	12000.00	Shibaura	3	81D	9F-3R	19.5	2320	No
1520H 4WD Hydro	16015.00	11850.00	12810.00	13320.00	Shibaura	3	81D	Infinite	19.5	2352	No
1520H Hydro	14590.00	10800.00	11670.00	12140.00	Shibaura	3	81D	Infinite	19.5	2233	No
1620 4WD Hydro	16787.00	12420.00	13430.00	13970.00	Shibaura	3	81D	Infinite	22.0	2352	No
1715	11207.00	8290.00	8970.00	9330.00	Shibaura	3	81D	9F-3R	23.0	2161	No
1715 4WD	12737.00	9430.00	10190.00	10600.00	Shibaura	3	81D	9F-3R	23.0	2280	No
1720	13772.00	10190.00	11020.00	11460.00	Shibaura	3	91D	12F-4R	23.5	2491	No
1720 4WD	15680.00	11600.00	12540.00	13040.00	Shibaura	3	91D	12F-4R	23.5	2690	No
1920	15814.00	11700.00	12650.00	13160.00	Shibaura	4	122D	12F-4R	28.5	2849	No
1920 4WD	18390.00	13610.00	14710.00	15300.00	Shibaura	4	122D	12F-4R	28.5	3069	No
2120 4WD	21510.00	15920.00	17210.00	17900.00	Shibaura	4	139D	12F-4R	34.5	3858	No
3010S	17016.00	12590.00	13610.00	14150.00	Own	3	165D	8F-2R	42.0		No
3010S 4WD	24095.00	17830.00	19280.00	20050.00	Own	3	165D	8F-2R	42.0		No
3415	18032.00	12620.00	13700.00	14250.00	Shibaura	4	135D	12F-4R	38.00	3483	No
3430	19650.00	13760.00	14930.00	15530.00	Own	3	192D	8F-2R	40.00	4622	No
3430 4WD	24225.00	16960.00	18410.00	19150.00	Own	3	192D	8F-2R	40.00	5150	No
3830	21237.00	14870.00	16140.00	16790.00	Own	3	165D	12F-12R	45.00	3804	No
3830 4WD	27335.00	19140.00	20780.00	21610.00	Own	3	165D	12F-12R	45.00	4020	No
3930	20835.00	14590.00	15840.00	16470.00	Own	3	192D	8F-2R	45.00	5157	No

New Holland/Ford (Cont.)

1996 (Cont.)

Model	Approx. Retail Price New	Estimated Average Value Less Repairs: Fair	Good	Premium	Engine: Make	No. Cyls.	Displ. Cu.-In.	No. Speeds	P.T.O. H.P.	Approx. Shipping Wt.-Lbs.	Cab
3930 4WD	25933.00	**18150.00**	**19710.00**	**20500.00**	Own	3	192D	8F-2R	45.00	5685	No
3930 4WD w/Cab	32842.00	**22990.00**	**24960.00**	**25960.00**	Own	3	192D	8F-8R	45.00	6235	C,H
3930 w/Cab	26435.00	**18510.00**	**20090.00**	**20890.00**	Own	3	192D	8F-8R	45.00	5707	C,H
4030	22880.00	**16020.00**	**17390.00**	**18090.00**	Own	3	179D	12F-12R	51.00	5171	No
4030 4WD	28560.00	**19990.00**	**21710.00**	**22580.00**	Own	3	179D	12F-12R	51.00	5578	No
4030 4WD w/Cab	33633.00	**23540.00**	**25560.00**	**26580.00**	Own	3	179D	12F-12R	51.00	6015	C,H,A
4030 w/Cab	27360.00	**19150.00**	**20790.00**	**21620.00**	Own	3	179D	12F-12R	51.00	5611	C,H,A
4230	24010.00	**16810.00**	**18250.00**	**18980.00**	Own	4	220D	12F-12R	62.00	4880	No
4230 4WD	30030.00	**21020.00**	**22820.00**	**23730.00**	Own	4	220D	12F-12R	62.00	5230	No
4230 4WD w/Cab	34765.00	**24340.00**	**26420.00**	**27480.00**	Own	4	220D	12F-12R	62.00	5670	C,H,A
4230 w/Cab	28643.00	**20050.00**	**21770.00**	**22640.00**	Own	4	220D	12F-12R	62.00	5230	C,H,A
4430	26223.00	**18360.00**	**19930.00**	**20730.00**	Own	4	238D	12F-12R	70.00	5030	No
4430 4WD	32245.00	**22570.00**	**24510.00**	**25490.00**	Own	4	238D	12F-12R	70.00	5380	No
4430 4WD w/Cab	36977.00	**25880.00**	**28100.00**	**29220.00**	Own	4	238D	12F-12R	70.00	5820	C,H,A
4430 w/Cab	30855.00	**21600.00**	**23450.00**	**24390.00**	Own	4	238D	12F-12R	70.00	5470	C,H,A
4630	24045.00	**16830.00**	**18270.00**	**19000.00**	Own	3T	192D	16F-8R	55.00	5030	No
4630 4WD	30290.00	**21200.00**	**23020.00**	**23940.00**	Own	3T	192D	16F-8R	55.00	5822	No
4630 4WD w/Cab	35610.00	**24930.00**	**27060.00**	**28140.00**	Own	3T	192D	16F-8R	55.00		C,H
4630 w/Cab	29668.00	**20770.00**	**22550.00**	**23450.00**	Own	3T	192D	8F-8R	55.00	5744	C,H
4835	26700.00	**18690.00**	**20290.00**	**21100.00**	Own	4	220D	24F-12R	56.00		No
4835 4WD	33667.00	**23570.00**	**25590.00**	**26610.00**	Own	4	220D	24F-12R	56.00		No
4835 4WD w/Cab	41540.00	**29080.00**	**31570.00**	**32830.00**	Own	4	220D	24F-12R	56.00		C,H,A
4835 w/Cab	34600.00	**24220.00**	**26300.00**	**27350.00**	Own	4	220D	24F-12R	56.00		C,H,A
5030	27473.00	**19230.00**	**20880.00**	**21720.00**	Own	4	256D	16F-8R	62.00	5647	No
5030 4WD	32343.00	**22640.00**	**24580.00**	**25560.00**	Own	4	256D	16F-8R	62.00	6175	No
5030 4WD w/Cab	36570.00	**25600.00**	**27790.00**	**28900.00**	Own	4	256D	8F-8R	62.00	6625	C,H
5030 w/Cab	31700.00	**22190.00**	**24090.00**	**25050.00**	Own	4	256D	8F-8R	62.00	6097	C,H
5530	26515.00	**18560.00**	**20150.00**	**20960.00**	Own	4	220D	20F-12R	62.00	5709	No
5530 4WD	32265.00	**22590.00**	**24520.00**	**25500.00**	Own	4	220D	20F-12R	62.00	7310	No
5610S	24432.00	**18080.00**	**19550.00**	**20330.00**	Own	4	268D	8F-2R	66.00	5995	No
5635	31215.00	**21850.00**	**23720.00**	**24670.00**	Own	4	238D	24F-12R	66.00		No
5635 4WD	38535.00	**26980.00**	**29290.00**	**30460.00**	Own	4	238D	24F-12R	66.00		No
5635 4WD w/Cab	46644.00	**32650.00**	**35450.00**	**36870.00**	Own	4	238D	24F-12R	66.00		C,H,A
5635 w/Cab	39325.00	**27530.00**	**29890.00**	**31090.00**	Own	4	238D	24F-12R	66.00		C,H,A
5640S	30883.00	**21620.00**	**23470.00**	**24410.00**	Own	4	268D	16F-4R	66.00	7399	No
5640S 4WD	38123.00	**25540.00**	**27830.00**	**28940.00**	Own	4	268D	16F-4R	66.00	8391	No
5640SL	32935.00	**22070.00**	**24040.00**	**25000.00**	Own	4	268D	24F-24R	66.00	7373	No
5640SL 4WD	39923.00	**26750.00**	**29140.00**	**30310.00**	Own	4	268D	24F-24R	66.00	8298	No
5640SL 4WD w/Cab	47783.00	**30150.00**	**32850.00**	**34160.00**	Own	4	268D	24F-24R	66.00	9380	C,H,A
5640SL w/Cab	40795.00	**27330.00**	**29780.00**	**30970.00**	Own	4	268D	24F-24R	66.00	8418	C,H,A
5640SLE	34670.00	**23230.00**	**25310.00**	**26320.00**	Own	4	268D	16F-16R	66.00	7483	No
5640SLE 4WD	41630.00	**26800.00**	**29200.00**	**30370.00**	Own	4	268D	16F-16R	66.00	8475	No
5640SLE 4WD w/Cab	49716.00	**31490.00**	**34310.00**	**35680.00**	Own	4	268D	16F-16R	66.00	9380	C,H,A
5640SLE w/Cab	42755.00	**28650.00**	**31210.00**	**32460.00**	Own	4	268D	16F-16R	66.00	8418	C,H,A
6530	29285.00	**20500.00**	**22260.00**	**23150.00**	Own	4	238D	20F-12R	70.00	5709	No
6530 4WD	36280.00	**25400.00**	**27570.00**	**28670.00**	Own	4	238D	20F-12R	70.00	7310	No
6610S	26705.00	**18690.00**	**20300.00**	**21110.00**	Own	4	304D	8F-2R	76.00	5995	No
6610S 4WD	34590.00	**24210.00**	**26290.00**	**27340.00**	Own	4	304D	8F-2R	76.00	6925	No
6635	34122.00	**23890.00**	**25930.00**	**26970.00**	Own	4T	238D	24F-12R	76.00		No
6635 4WD	41772.00	**29240.00**	**31750.00**	**33020.00**	Own	4T	238D	24F-12R	76.00		No
6635 4WD w/Cab	48445.00	**33910.00**	**36820.00**	**38290.00**	Own	4T	238D	24F-12R	76.00		C,H,A
6635 w/Cab	40795.00	**28560.00**	**31000.00**	**32240.00**	Own	4T	238D	24F-12R	76.00		C,H,A
6640S	33840.00	**22670.00**	**24700.00**	**25690.00**	Own	4	304D	16F-4R	76.00	7399	No
6640S 4WD	41605.00	**27880.00**	**30370.00**	**31590.00**	Own	4	304D	16F-4R	76.00	8391	No
6640SL	35575.00	**23840.00**	**25970.00**	**27010.00**	Own	4	304D	24F-24R	76.00	7373	No
6640SL 4WD	43873.00	**29400.00**	**32030.00**	**33310.00**	Own	4	304D	24F-24R	76.00	8304	No
6640SL 4WD w/Cab	51732.00	**34660.00**	**37760.00**	**39270.00**	Own	4	304D	24F-24R	76.00	9358	C,H,A
6640SL w/Cab	43435.00	**29100.00**	**31710.00**	**32980.00**	Own	4	304D	24F-24R	76.00	8419	C,H,A
6640SLE	36210.00	**24260.00**	**26430.00**	**27490.00**	Own	4	304D	16F-16R	76.00	7483	No
6640SLE 4WD	44442.00	**29780.00**	**32440.00**	**33740.00**	Own	4	304D	16F-16R	76.00	8475	No
6640SLE 4WD w/Cab	52530.00	**35200.00**	**38350.00**	**39880.00**	Own	4	304D	16F-16R	76.00	9380	C,H,A
6640SLE w/Cab	44297.00	**29680.00**	**32340.00**	**33630.00**	Own	4	304D	16F-16R	76.00	8418	C,H,A
7010 LP	35809.00	**25070.00**	**27220.00**	**28310.00**	Own	4T	304D	16F-4R	86.0		No
7010 LP 4WD	44630.00	**31240.00**	**33920.00**	**35280.00**	Own	4T	304D	16F-4R	86.0		No
7530 4WD	40830.00	**28580.00**	**31030.00**	**32270.00**	Own	6	331D	20F-4R	91.00	8074	No
7610S	29425.00	**20600.00**	**22360.00**	**23250.00**	Own	4T	304D	8F-2R	86.00	6375	No
7610S 4WD	36435.00	**24410.00**	**26600.00**	**27660.00**	Own	4T	304D	8F-2R	86.00	7305	No
7635	34330.00	**24030.00**	**26090.00**	**27130.00**	Own	4T	238D	24F-12R	86.00		No
7635 4WD	41980.00	**28130.00**	**30650.00**	**31880.00**	Own	4T	238D	24F-12R	86.00		No
7635 4WD w/Cab	50090.00	**33560.00**	**36570.00**	**38030.00**	Own	4T	238D	24F-12R	86.00		C,H,A
7635 w/Cab	42438.00	**29710.00**	**32250.00**	**33540.00**	Own	4T	238D	24F-12R	86.00		C,H,A
7740S	36832.00	**25780.00**	**27990.00**	**29110.00**	Own	4T	304D	16F-4R	86.00	7432	No
7740S 4WD	44343.00	**31040.00**	**33700.00**	**35050.00**	Own	4T	304D	16F-4R	86.00	8446	No
7740SL	38633.00	**27040.00**	**29360.00**	**30530.00**	Own	4T	304D	24F-24R	86.00	7432	No
7740SL 4WD	46145.00	**31500.00**	**34200.00**	**35570.00**	Own	4T	304D	24F-24R	86.00	8446	No
7740SL 4WD w/Cab	54760.00	**36400.00**	**39520.00**	**41100.00**	Own	4T	304D	24F-24R	86.00	9413	C,H,A
7740SL w/Cab	47250.00	**33080.00**	**35910.00**	**37350.00**	Own	4T	304D	24F-24R	86.00	8400	C,H,A
7740SLE	38792.00	**27150.00**	**29480.00**	**30660.00**	Own	4T	304D	16F-16R	86.00	7516	No
7740SLE 4WD	47065.00	**32950.00**	**35770.00**	**37200.00**	Own	4T	304D	16F-16R	86.00	8508	No
7740SLE 4WD w/Cab	55910.00	**37100.00**	**40280.00**	**41890.00**	Own	4T	304D	16F-16R	86.00	9413	C,H,A
7740SLE w/Cab	47635.00	**33350.00**	**36200.00**	**37650.00**	Own	4T	304D	16F-16R	86.00	8451	C,H,A
7810S	31721.00	**22210.00**	**24110.00**	**25070.00**	Own	6	401D	8F-2R	90.00	6625	No
7810S 4WD	38732.00	**27110.00**	**29440.00**	**30620.00**	Own	6	401D	8F-2R	90.00	7555	No
7840S	37797.00	**26460.00**	**28730.00**	**29880.00**	Own	6	401D	16F-4R	90.00	8076	No

New Holland/Ford (Cont.)

1996 (Cont.)

Model	Approx. Retail Price New	Estimated Average Value Less Repairs Fair	Good	Premium	Engine Make	No. Cyls.	Displ. Cu.-In.	No. Speeds	P.T.O. H.P.	Approx. Shipping Wt.-Lbs.	Cab
7840SL	39393.00	**27580.00**	**29940.00**	**31140.00**	Own	6	401D	12F-12R	90.00	8342	No
7840SL 4WD	48330.00	**33830.00**	**36730.00**	**38200.00**	Own	6	401D	24F-24R	90.00	9410	No
7840SL 4WD w/Cab	58070.00	**39200.00**	**42560.00**	**44260.00**	Own	6	401D	24F-24R	90.00	10465	C,H,A
7840SL w/Cab	47925.00	**33550.00**	**36420.00**	**37880.00**	Own	6	401D	12F-12R	90.00	9386	C,H,A
7840SLE	40482.00	**28340.00**	**30770.00**	**32000.00**	Own	6	401D	16F-16R	90.00	8379	No
7840SLE 4WD	48078.00	**33660.00**	**36540.00**	**38000.00**	Own	6	401D	16F-16R	90.00	9437	No
7840SLE 4WD w/Cab	57591.00	**40310.00**	**43770.00**	**45520.00**	Own	6	401D	16F-16R	90.00	10482	C,H,A
7840SLE w/Cab	49995.00	**35000.00**	**38000.00**	**39520.00**	Own	6	401D	16F-16R	90.00	9423	C,H,A
8010 HC	45782.00	**32050.00**	**34790.00**	**36180.00**	Own	6	456D	16F-4R	96.0		No
8010 LP	38245.00	**26770.00**	**29070.00**	**30230.00**	Own	6	456D	16F-4R	96.0		No
8010 LP 4WD	46922.00	**32850.00**	**35660.00**	**37090.00**	Own	6	456D	16F-4R	96.0		No
8160	42353.00	**28380.00**	**30920.00**	**32160.00**	Own	6	456D	23F-12R	90.0		No
8160 4WD	51023.00	**34190.00**	**37250.00**	**38740.00**	Own	6	456D	23F-12R	90.0		No
8160 4WD w/Cab	58725.00	**39350.00**	**42870.00**	**44590.00**	Own	6	456D	23F-12R	90.0		C,H,A
8160 w/Cab	50053.00	**33540.00**	**36540.00**	**38000.00**	Own	6	456D	23F-12R	90.0		C,H,A
8240SL	41567.00	**29100.00**	**31590.00**	**32850.00**	Own	6	456D	12F-12R	96.00	8883	No
8240SL 4WD	49163.00	**34410.00**	**37360.00**	**38850.00**	Own	6	456D	12F-12R	96.00	9941	No
8240SL 4WD w/Cab	57190.00	**40030.00**	**43460.00**	**45200.00**	Own	6	456D	12F-12R	96.00	10979	C,H,A
8240SL w/Cab	49593.00	**34720.00**	**37690.00**	**39200.00**	Own	6	456D	12F-12R	96.00	9921	C,H,A
8240SLE	43245.00	**30270.00**	**32870.00**	**34190.00**	Own	6	456D	16F-16R	96.00	8957	No
8240SLE 4WD w/Cab	58725.00	**41110.00**	**44630.00**	**46420.00**	Own	6	456D	16F-16R	96.00	11053	C,H,A
8240SLE w/Cab	51248.00	**35870.00**	**38950.00**	**40510.00**	Own	6	456D	16F-16R	96.00	9995	C,H,A
8260	45905.00	**30760.00**	**33510.00**	**34850.00**	Own	6	456D	23F-12R	100.0		No
8260 4WD	54574.00	**36570.00**	**39840.00**	**41430.00**	Own	6	456D	23F-12R	100.0		No
8260 4WD w/Cab	62275.00	**41720.00**	**45460.00**	**47280.00**	Own	6	456D	23F-12R	100.0		C,H,A
8260 w/Cab	53540.00	**35870.00**	**39080.00**	**40640.00**	Own	6	456D	23F-12R	100.0		C,H,A
8340SL	44585.00	**31210.00**	**33890.00**	**35250.00**	Own	6T	456D	12F-12R	112.00	8883	No
8340SL 4WD	52205.00	**36540.00**	**39680.00**	**41270.00**	Own	6T	456D	12F-12R	112.00	9941	No
8340SL 4WD w/Cab	60985.00	**42690.00**	**46350.00**	**48200.00**	Own	6T	456D	12F-12R	112.00	10979	C,H,A
8340SL w/Cab	53365.00	**37360.00**	**40560.00**	**42180.00**	Own	6T	456D	12F-12R	112.00	9921	C,H,A
8340SLE	47730.00	**33410.00**	**36280.00**	**37730.00**	Own	6T	456D	16F-16R	112.00	8957	No
8340SLE 4WD	55245.00	**38670.00**	**41990.00**	**43670.00**	Own	6T	456D	16F-16R	112.00	10015	No
8340SLE 4WD w/Cab	64003.00	**44800.00**	**48640.00**	**50590.00**	Own	6T	456D	16F-16R	112.00	11053	C,H,A
8340SLE w/Cab	56488.00	**39540.00**	**42930.00**	**44650.00**	Own	6T	456D	16F-16R	112.00	9995	C,H,A
8360	52863.00	**35420.00**	**38590.00**	**40130.00**	Own	6T	456D	23F-12R	115.0		No
8360 4WD	64652.00	**43320.00**	**47200.00**	**49090.00**	Own	6T	456D	23F-12R	115.0		No
8360 4WD w/Cab	72345.00	**48470.00**	**52810.00**	**54920.00**	Own	6T	456D	23F-12R	115.0		C,H,A
8360 w/Cab	60557.00	**40570.00**	**44210.00**	**45980.00**	Own	6T	456D	23F-12R	115.0		C,H,A
8560 4WD w/Cab	81085.00	**53600.00**	**58400.00**	**60740.00**	Own	6T	456D	18F-6R	130.0		C,H,A
8560 w/Cab	69295.00	**46430.00**	**50590.00**	**52610.00**	Own	6T	456D	17F-6R	130.0		C,H,A
8670	79240.00	**53090.00**	**57850.00**	**60160.00**	Own	6T	456D	16F-9R	145.00	14632	C,H,A
8670 4WD	94385.00	**61640.00**	**67160.00**	**69850.00**	Own	6T	456D	16F-9R	145.00	15188	C,H,A
8770	85552.00	**57320.00**	**62450.00**	**64950.00**	Own	6T	456D	16F-9R	160.00	16925	C,H,A
8770 4WD	98657.00	**66100.00**	**72020.00**	**74900.00**	Own	6T	456D	16F-9R	160.00	17481	C,H,A
8870	96757.00	**64830.00**	**70630.00**	**73460.00**	Own	6TI	456D	16F-9R	180.00	17101	C,H,A
8870 4WD	109958.00	**70350.00**	**76650.00**	**79720.00**	Own	6TI	456D	16F-9R	180.00	17657	C,H,A
8970 4WD	119292.00	**77050.00**	**83950.00**	**87310.00**	Own	6TI	456D	16F-9R	210.00	17889	C,H,A

***Net SAE HP.**
LP-Low Profile, HC-High Clearance

1997

Model	Approx. Retail Price New	Estimated Average Value Less Repairs Fair	Good	Premium	Engine Make	No. Cyls.	Displ. Cu.-In.	No. Speeds	P.T.O. H.P.	Approx. Shipping Wt.-Lbs.	Cab
1215	8978.00	**6910.00**	**7360.00**	**7650.00**	Shibaura	3	54D	6F-2R	13.5	1338	No
1215 4WD	10035.00	**7730.00**	**8230.00**	**8560.00**	Shibaura	3	54D	6F-2R	13.5	1429	No
1215H 4WD Hydro	11058.00	**8520.00**	**9070.00**	**9430.00**	Shibaura	3	54D	Variable	13.5	1484	No
1215H Hydro	10001.00	**7700.00**	**8200.00**	**8530.00**	Shibaura	3	54D	Variable	13.5	1393	No
1220 4WD	11823.00	**9100.00**	**9700.00**	**10090.00**	Shibaura	3	58D	9F-3R	14.5	1429	No
1220H 4WD Hydro	13736.00	**10580.00**	**11260.00**	**11710.00**	Shibaura	3	58D	Variable	14.5	1484	No
1320	12636.00	**9730.00**	**10360.00**	**10770.00**	Shibaura	3	77D	9F-3R	17.0	2145	No
1320 4WD	13995.00	**10780.00**	**11480.00**	**11940.00**	Shibaura	3	77D	9F-3R	17.0	2271	No
1320H 4WD Hydro	15344.00	**11820.00**	**12580.00**	**13080.00**	Shibaura	3	77D	Variable	17.0	2297	No
1320H Hydro	13985.00	**10770.00**	**11470.00**	**11930.00**	Shibaura	3	77D	Variable	17.0	2172	No
1530	13782.00	**10610.00**	**11300.00**	**11750.00**	Shibaura	3	81D	9F-3R	21.7	2200	No
1530 4WD	15300.00	**11780.00**	**12550.00**	**13050.00**	Shibaura	3	81D	9F-3R	21.7	2320	No
1530H 4WD Hydro	16820.00	**12950.00**	**13790.00**	**14340.00**	Shibaura	3	81D	Variable	21.7	2352	No
1630 4WD	16165.00	**12450.00**	**13260.00**	**13790.00**	Shibaura	3	81D	9F-3R	24.0		No
1630 4WD Hydro	17557.00	**13520.00**	**14400.00**	**14980.00**	Shibaura	3	81D	Variable	24.0		No
1720	13772.00	**10600.00**	**11290.00**	**11740.00**	Shibaura	3	91D	12F-4R	23.5	2491	No
1720 4WD	15680.00	**12070.00**	**12860.00**	**13370.00**	Shibaura	3	91D	12F-4R	23.5	2690	No
1725	12410.00	**9560.00**	**10180.00**	**10590.00**	Shibaura	3	81D	9F-3R	25.1		No
1725 4WD	13924.00	**10720.00**	**11420.00**	**11880.00**	Shibaura	3	81D	9F-3R	25.1		No
1920	15814.00	**12180.00**	**12970.00**	**13490.00**	Shibaura	4	122D	12F-4R	28.5	2849	No
1920 4WD	18390.00	**14160.00**	**15080.00**	**15680.00**	Shibaura	4	122D	12F-4R	28.5	3069	No
1925 4WD Hydro	17257.00	**13290.00**	**14150.00**	**14720.00**	Shibaura	3	91D	Variable	29.3		No
2120 4WD	21510.00	**16560.00**	**17640.00**	**18350.00**	Shibaura	4	139D	12F-4R	34.5	3858	No
3010S	17257.00	**13290.00**	**14150.00**	**14720.00**	Own	3	165D	8F-2R	42.0		No
3010S 4WD	24358.00	**18760.00**	**19970.00**	**20770.00**	Own	3	165D	8F-2R	42.0		No
3415	18032.00	**13520.00**	**14430.00**	**15010.00**	Shibaura	4	135D	12F-4R	38.0	3483	No
3430	20417.00	**15310.00**	**16330.00**	**16980.00**	Own	3	192D	8F-2R	40.0	4622	No
3430 4WD	25291.00	**18970.00**	**20230.00**	**21040.00**	Own	3	192D	8F-2R	40.0	5150	No
3830	22099.00	**16570.00**	**17680.00**	**18390.00**	Own	3	165D	12F-12R	45.0	3804	No
3830 4WD	28940.00	**21710.00**	**23150.00**	**24080.00**	Own	3	165D	12F-12R	45.0	4020	No
3930	21315.00	**15990.00**	**17050.00**	**17730.00**	Own	3	192D	8F-2R	45.0	5157	No
3930 4WD	26568.00	**19930.00**	**21250.00**	**22100.00**	Own	3	192D	8F-2R	45.0	5685	No
3930 4WD w/Cab	33684.00	**25260.00**	**26950.00**	**28030.00**	Own	3	192D	8F-8R	45.0	6235	C,H

New Holland/Ford (Cont.)

1997 (Cont.)

Model	Approx. Retail Price New	Estimated Average Value Less Repairs Fair	Good	Premium	Engine Make	No. Cyls.	Displ. Cu.-In.	No. Speeds	P.T.O. H.P.	Approx. Shipping Wt.-Lbs.	Cab
3930 w/Cab	26993.00	20250.00	21590.00	22450.00	Own	3	192D	8F-8R	45.0	5707	C,H
4030	23471.00	17600.00	18780.00	19530.00	Own	3	179D	12F-12R	51.0	5171	No
4030 4WD	30255.00	22690.00	24200.00	25170.00	Own	3	179D	12F-12R	51.0	5578	No
4030 4WD w/Cab	35480.00	26610.00	28380.00	29520.00	Own	3	179D	12F-12R	51.0	6015	C,H,A
4030 w/Cab	28242.00	21180.00	22590.00	23490.00	Own	3	179D	12F-12R	51.0	5611	C,H,A
4230	24827.00	18620.00	19860.00	20650.00	Own	4	220D	12F-12R	62.0		No
4230 4WD	31767.00	23830.00	25410.00	26430.00	Own	4	220D	12F-12R	62.0		No
4230 4WD w/Cab	36641.00	27480.00	29310.00	30480.00	Own	4	220D	12F-12R	62.0		C,H,A
4230 w/Cab	29598.00	22200.00	23680.00	24630.00	Own	4	220D	12F-12R	62.0		C,H,A
4330V	24520.00	18390.00	19620.00	20410.00	Own	4	220D	12F-12R	62.0	3935	No
4330V 4WD	31800.00	23850.00	25440.00	26460.00	Own	4	220D	12F-12R	62.0	4122	No
4330V 4WD w/Cab	37025.00	27770.00	29620.00	30810.00	Own	4	220D	12F-12R	62.0		C,H,A
4330V w/Cab	29745.00	22310.00	23800.00	24750.00	Own	4	220D	12F-12R	62.0		C,H,A
4430	27141.00	20360.00	21710.00	22580.00	Own	4	238D	12F-12R	70.0	5030	No
4430 4WD	34076.00	25560.00	27260.00	28350.00	Own	4	238D	12F-12R	70.0	5380	No
4430 4WD w/Cab	38950.00	29210.00	31160.00	32410.00	Own	4	238D	12F-12R	70.0	5820	C,H,A
4430 w/Cab	34076.00	25560.00	27260.00	28350.00	Own	4	238D	12F-12R	70.0	5470	C,H,A
4630	24767.00	18580.00	19810.00	20600.00	Own	3T	192D	16F-8R	55.0	5030	No
4630 4WD	31199.00	23400.00	24960.00	25960.00	Own	3T	192D	16F-8R	55.0	5822	No
4835	27716.00	20790.00	22170.00	23060.00	Own	4	220D	24F-12R	56.0		No
4835 4WD	34677.00	26010.00	27740.00	28850.00	Own	4	220D	24F-12R	56.0		No
4835 4WD w/Cab	42787.00	32090.00	34230.00	35600.00	Own	4	220D	24F-12R	56.0		C,H,A
4835 w/Cab	33507.00	25130.00	26810.00	27880.00	Own	4	220D	12F-12R	56.0		C,H,A
4835 w/Cab	35575.00	26680.00	28460.00	29600.00	Own	4	220D	24F-12R	56.0		C,H,A
5030	25730.00	19300.00	20580.00	21400.00	Own	4	256D	8F-2R	62.0	5547	No
5030 4WD	30738.00	23050.00	24590.00	25570.00	Own	4	256D	8F-2R	62.0	6075	No
5610S	25165.00	19380.00	20640.00	21470.00	Own	4	268D	8F-2R	66.0	5995	No
5635	32150.00	24110.00	25720.00	26750.00	Own	4	238D	24F-12R	66.0		No
5635 4WD	39692.00	29770.00	31750.00	33020.00	Own	4	238D	24F-12R	66.0		No
5635 4WD w/Cab	48044.00	36030.00	38440.00	39980.00	Own	4	238D	24F-12R	66.0		C,H,A
5635 w/Cab	40504.00	30380.00	32400.00	33700.00	Own	4	238D	24F-12R	66.0		C,H,A
5640S	31810.00	23860.00	25450.00	26470.00	Own	4	268D	16F-4R	66.0	7399	No
5640S 4WD	39200.00	28220.00	30180.00	31390.00	Own	4	268D	16F-4R	66.0	8391	No
5640SL	34210.00	25660.00	27370.00	28470.00	Own	4	268D	24F-24R	66.0	7373	No
5640SL 4WD	41058.00	29560.00	31620.00	32890.00	Own	4	268D	24F-24R	66.0	8298	No
5640SL 4WD w/Cab	49150.00	35390.00	37850.00	39360.00	Own	4	268D	24F-24R	66.0	9380	C,H,A
5640SL w/Cab	42305.00	30460.00	32580.00	33880.00	Own	4	268D	24F-24R	66.0	8418	C,H,A
6530	30165.00	22620.00	24130.00	25100.00	Own	4	238D	20F-12R	70.0	5709	No
6530 4WD	37368.00	28030.00	29890.00	31090.00	Own	4	238D	20F-12R	70.0	7310	No
6610S	27506.00	20630.00	22010.00	22890.00	Own	4	304D	8F-2R	76.0	5995	No
6610S 4WD	35628.00	26720.00	28500.00	29640.00	Own	4	304D	8F-2R	76.0	6925	No
6635	33363.00	25020.00	26690.00	27760.00	Own	4T	238D	24F-12R	76.0		No
6635 4WD	41499.00	31120.00	33200.00	34530.00	Own	4T	238D	24F-12R	76.0		No
6635 4WD w/Cab	49851.00	36000.00	38400.00	39940.00	Own	4T	238D	24F-12R	76.0		C,H,A
6635 w/Cab	41715.00	31290.00	33370.00	34710.00	Own	4T	238D	24F-12R	76.0		C,H,A
6640S	34855.00	25100.00	26840.00	27910.00	Own	4	304D	16F-4R	76.0	7399	No
6640S 4WD	43178.00	31090.00	33250.00	34580.00	Own	4	304D	16F-4R	76.0	8391	No
6640SL	36967.00	26620.00	28470.00	29610.00	Own	4	304D	24F-24R	76.0	7373	No
6640SL 4WD	44705.00	32190.00	34420.00	35800.00	Own	4	304D	24F-24R	76.0	8304	No
6640SL 4WD w/Cab	52798.00	36000.00	38500.00	40040.00	Own	4	304D	24F-24R	76.0	9358	C,H,A
6640SL w/Cab	45060.00	32440.00	34700.00	36090.00	Own	4	304D	24F-24R	76.0	8419	C,H,A
6640SLE	37293.00	26850.00	28720.00	29870.00	Own	4	304D	16F-16R	76.0	7483	No
6640SLE 4WD	45290.00	32610.00	34870.00	36270.00	Own	4	304D	16F-16R	76.0	8475	No
6640SLE 4WD w/Cab	53620.00	36720.00	39270.00	40840.00	Own	4	304D	16F-16R	76.0	9380	C,H,A
6640SLE w/Cab	45623.00	32850.00	35130.00	36540.00	Own	4	304D	16F-16R	76.0	8418	C,H,A
7010 LP	35738.00	25730.00	27520.00	28620.00	Own	4T	304D	16F-4R	86.0		No
7010 LP 4WD	43147.00	31070.00	33220.00	34550.00	Own	4T	304D	16F-4R	86.0		No
7610S	30127.00	21690.00	23200.00	24130.00	Own	4T	304D	8F-2R	86.0	6375	No
7610S 4WD	37527.00	27020.00	28900.00	30060.00	Own	4T	304D	8F-2R	86.0	7305	No
7635	36620.00	27470.00	29300.00	30470.00	Own	4T	238D	20F-12R	86.0		No
7635 4WD	44673.00	33510.00	35740.00	37170.00	Own	4T	238D	20F-12R	86.0		No
7635 4WD w/Cab	52230.00	39170.00	41780.00	43450.00	Own	4T	238D	20F-12R	86.0		C,H,A
7635 w/Cab	44175.00	33130.00	35340.00	36750.00	Own	4T	238D	20F-12R	86.0		C,H,A
7740S	37197.00	26780.00	28640.00	29790.00	Own	4T	304D	16F-4R	86.0	7432	No
7740S 4WD	45521.00	32780.00	35050.00	36450.00	Own	4T	304D	16F-4R	86.0	8446	No
7740SL	39640.00	28540.00	30520.00	31740.00	Own	4T	304D	24F-24R	86.0	7432	No
7740SL 4WD	47375.00	34110.00	36480.00	37940.00	Own	4T	304D	24F-24R	86.00	8446	No
7740SL 4WD w/Cab	56250.00	40500.00	43310.00	45040.00	Own	4T	304D	24F-24R	86.0	9413	C,H,A
7740SL w/Cab	48515.00	34930.00	37360.00	38850.00	Own	4T	304D	24F-24R	86.0	8400	C,H,A
7740SLE	39803.00	28660.00	30650.00	31880.00	Own	4T	304D	16F-16R	86.0	7516	No
7740SLE 4WD	47695.00	34340.00	36730.00	38200.00	Own	4T	304D	16F-16R	86.0	8508	No
7740SLE 4WD w/Cab	56803.00	40900.00	43740.00	45490.00	Own	4T	304D	16F-16R	86.0	9413	C,H,A
7740SLE w/Cab	48912.00	35220.00	37660.00	39170.00	Own	4T	304D	16F-16R	86.0	8451	C,H,A
7810S	32673.00	24510.00	26140.00	27190.00	Own	6	401D	8F-2R	90.0	6625	No
7810S 4WD	39894.00	29920.00	31920.00	33200.00	Own	6	401D	8F-2R	90.0	7555	No
8010 HC	45987.00	34490.00	36790.00	38260.00	Own	6	456D	16F-4R	96.0		No
8010 LP	38173.00	28630.00	30540.00	31760.00	Own	6	456D	16F-4R	96.0		No
8010 LP 4WD	45438.00	34080.00	36350.00	37800.00	Own	6	456D	16F-4R	96.0		No
8160	42990.00	30490.00	32610.00	33910.00	Own	6	456D	23F-12R	90.0		No
8160 4WD	51458.00	37050.00	39620.00	41210.00	Own	6	456D	23F-12R	90.0		No
8160 4WD w/Cab	59158.00	42590.00	45550.00	47370.00	Own	6	456D	23F-12R	90.0		C,H,A
8160 w/Cab	50690.00	36500.00	39030.00	40590.00	Own	6	456D	23F-12R	90.0		C,H,A
8260	46795.00	33690.00	36030.00	37470.00	Own	6	456D	23F-12R	100.0		No
8260 4WD	55262.00	39790.00	42550.00	44250.00	Own	6	456D	23F-12R	100.0		No

New Holland/Ford (Cont.)

Model	Approx. Retail Price New	Estimated Average Value Less Repairs Fair	Good	Premium	Engine Make	No. Cyls.	Displ. Cu.-In.	No. Speeds	P.T.O. H.P.	Approx. Shipping Wt.-Lbs.	Cab
1997 (Cont.)											
8260 4WD w/Cab	62962.00	45330.00	48480.00	50420.00	Own	6	456D	23F-12R	100.0		C,H,A
8260 w/Cab	54495.00	39240.00	41960.00	43640.00	Own	6	456D	23F-12R	100.0		C,H,A
8360	54866.00	39500.00	42250.00	43940.00	Own	6T	456D	23F-12R	115.0		No
8360 4WD	66310.00	47740.00	51060.00	53100.00	Own	6T	456D	23F-12R	115.0		No
8360 w/Cab	62320.00	44870.00	47990.00	49910.00	Own	6T	456D	23F-12R	115.0		C,H,A
8560 4WD w/Cab	82146.00	57600.00	61600.00	64060.00	Own	6T	456D	18F-6R	130.0		C,H,A
8560 w/Cab	70461.00	50730.00	54260.00	56430.00	Own	6T	456D	17F-6R	130.0		C,H,A
8670	82335.00	59280.00	63400.00	65940.00	Own	6T	456D	16F-9R	145.0	14632	C,H,A
8670 4WD	99504.00	69840.00	74690.00	77680.00	Own	6T	456D	16F-9R	145.0	15188	C,H,A
8770	90055.00	64840.00	69340.00	72110.00	Own	6T	456D	16F-9R	160.0	16925	C,H,A
8770 4WD	104181.00	73440.00	78540.00	81680.00	Own	6T	456D	16F-9R	160.0	17481	C,H,A
8870	101627.00	73170.00	78250.00	81380.00	Own	6TI	456D	16F-9R	180.0	17101	C,H,A
8870 4WD	115820.00	80640.00	86240.00	89690.00	Own	6TI	456D	16F-9R	180.0	17657	C,H,A
8970 4WD	127453.00	87840.00	93940.00	97700.00	Own	6TI	456D	16F-9R	210.0	17889	C,H,A

*Net SAE HP.
LP-Low Profile, HC-High Clearance, PS Power Shift

Model	Approx. Retail Price New	Fair	Good	Premium	Make	No. Cyls.	Displ. Cu.-In.	No. Speeds	P.T.O. H.P.	Approx. Shipping Wt.-Lbs.	Cab
1998											
TN65F	26740.00	21130.00	22460.00	23130.00	Own	4	238D	16F-16R	57.0		No
TN65F w/Cab	34710.00	27420.00	29160.00	30040.00	Own	4	238D	16F-16R	57.0		C,H,A
TN65F 4WD	34190.00	27010.00	28720.00	29580.00	Own	4	238D	16F-16R	57.0		No
TN65F 4WD w/Cab	42165.00	33310.00	35420.00	36480.00	Own	4	238D	16F-16R	57.0		C,H,A
TN75F	28300.00	22360.00	23770.00	24480.00	Own	4	238D	16F-16R	67.0		No
TN75F w/Cab	36270.00	28650.00	30470.00	31380.00	Own	4	238D	16F-16R	67.0		C,H,A
TN75F 4WD	35860.00	28330.00	30120.00	31020.00	Own	4	238D	16F-16R	67.0		No
TN75F 4WD w/Cab	43830.00	34630.00	36820.00	37930.00	Own	4	238D	16F-16R	67.0		C,H,A
TN90F	30445.00	24050.00	25570.00	26340.00	Own	4T	238D	16F-16R	80.0		No
TN90F w/Cab	38415.00	30350.00	32270.00	33240.00	Own	4T	238D	16F-16R	80.0		C,H,A
TN90F 4WD	38000.00	30020.00	31920.00	32880.00	Own	4T	238D	16F-16R	80.0		No
TN90F 4WD w/Cab	45975.00	36320.00	38620.00	39780.00	Own	4T	238D	16F-16R	80.0		C,H,A
TS90	33360.00	26350.00	28020.00	28860.00	Own	4	304D	24F-24R	70.0		No
TS90 w/Cab	43964.00	34730.00	36930.00	38040.00	Own	4	304D	24F-24R	70.0		C,H,A
TS90 4WD	42980.00	33950.00	36100.00	37180.00	Own	4	304D	24F-24R	70.0		No
TS90 4WD w/Cab	51585.00	40750.00	43330.00	44630.00	Own	4	304D	24F-24R	70.0		C,H,A
TS100	39017.00	30820.00	32770.00	33750.00	Own	4T	304D	24F-24R	80.0		No
TS100 4WD	46686.00	36880.00	39220.00	40400.00	Own	4T	304D	24F-24R	80.0		No
TS100 4WD w/Cab	55290.00	43680.00	46440.00	47830.00	Own	4T	304D	24F-24R	80.0		C,H,A
TS100 w/Cab	47621.00	37620.00	40000.00	41200.00	Own	4T	304D	24F-24R	80.0		C,H,A
TS110	42111.00	33270.00	35370.00	36430.00	Own	4T	304D	24F-24R	90.0		No
TS110 4WD	49780.00	39330.00	41820.00	43080.00	Own	4T	304D	24F-24R	90.0		No
TS110 4WD w/Cab	58385.00	46120.00	49040.00	50510.00	Own	4T	304D	24F-24R	90.0		C,H,A
TS110 w/Cab	50715.00	40070.00	42600.00	43880.00	Own	4T	304D	24F-24R	90.0		C,H,A
1215	8978.00	7360.00	7630.00	7860.00	Shibaura	3	54D	6F-2R	13.5	1338	No
1215 4WD	10035.00	8230.00	8530.00	8790.00	Shibaura	3	54D	6F-2R	13.5	1429	No
1215H 4WD Hydro	11058.00	9070.00	9400.00	9680.00	Shibaura	3	54D	Variable	13.5	1484	No
1215H Hydro	10000.00	8200.00	8500.00	8760.00	Shibaura	3	54D	Variable	13.5	1393	No
1220 4WD	11823.00	9700.00	10050.00	10350.00	Shibaura	3	58D	9F-3R	14.5	1429	No
1220H 4WD Hydro	13736.00	11260.00	11680.00	12030.00	Shibaura	3	58D	Variable	14.5	1484	No
1320	12636.00	10360.00	10740.00	11060.00	Shibaura	3	77D	9F-3R	17.0	2145	No
1320 4WD	13995.00	11480.00	11900.00	12260.00	Shibaura	3	77D	9F-3R	17.0	2271	No
1320H 4WD Hydro	15344.00	12580.00	13040.00	13430.00	Shibaura	3	77D	Variable	17.0	2297	No
1320H Hydro	13985.00	11470.00	11890.00	12250.00	Shibaura	3	77D	Variable	17.0	2172	No
1530	13782.00	11300.00	11720.00	12070.00	Shibaura	3	81D	9F-3R	21.7	2200	No
1530 4WD	15300.00	12550.00	13010.00	13400.00	Shibaura	3	81D	9F-3R	21.7	2320	No
1530H 4WD Hydro	16820.00	13790.00	14300.00	14730.00	Shibaura	3	81D	Variable	21.7	2352	No
1630 4WD	16165.00	13260.00	13740.00	14150.00	Shibaura	3	81D	9F-3R	24.0		No
1630 4WD Hydro	17557.00	14400.00	14920.00	15370.00	Shibaura	3	81D	Variable	24.0		No
1720	13816.00	11330.00	11740.00	12090.00	Shibaura	3	91D	12F-4R	23.5	2491	No
1720 4WD	15680.00	12860.00	13330.00	13730.00	Shibaura	3	91D	12F-4R	23.5	2690	No
1725	12410.00	10180.00	10550.00	10870.00	Shibaura	3	81D	9F-3R	25.1		No
1725 4WD	13924.00	11420.00	11840.00	12200.00	Shibaura	3	81D	9F-3R	25.1		No
1920	15814.00	12970.00	13440.00	13840.00	Shibaura	4	122D	12F-4R	28.5	2849	No
1920 4WD	18390.00	15080.00	15630.00	16100.00	Shibaura	4	122D	12F-4R	28.5	3069	No
1925 4WD Hydro	17257.00	14150.00	14670.00	15110.00	Shibaura	3	91D	Variable	29.3		No
2120 4WD	21510.00	17640.00	18280.00	18830.00	Shibaura	4	139D	12F-4R	34.5	3858	No
3010S	18062.00	14270.00	15170.00	15630.00	Own	3	165D	8F-2R	42.0		No
3010S 4WD	25090.00	20570.00	21330.00	21970.00	Own	3	165D	8F-2R	42.0		No
3415	18032.00	14250.00	15150.00	15610.00	Shibaura	4	135D	12F-4R	38.0	3483	No
3430	20467.00	16170.00	17190.00	17710.00	Own	3	192D	8F-2R	40.0	4622	No
3430 4WD	25450.00	20110.00	21380.00	22020.00	Own	3	192D	8F-2R	40.0	5150	No
3830	22773.00	17990.00	19130.00	19700.00	Own	3	165D	12F-12R	45.0	3804	No
3830 4WD	29815.00	23550.00	25050.00	25800.00	Own	3	165D	12F-12R	45.0	4020	No
3830 4WD w/Cab	35197.00	27810.00	29570.00	30460.00	Own	3	165D	12F-12R	45.0		C,H
3830 w/Cab	28145.00	22240.00	23640.00	24350.00	Own	3	165D	12F-12R	45.0		C,H
3930	23650.00	18680.00	19870.00	20470.00	Own	3	192D	8F-8R	45.0	5207	No
3930 4WD	29067.00	22960.00	24420.00	25150.00	Own	3	192D	8F-8R	45.0	5735	No
3930 4WD w/Cab	34710.00	27420.00	29160.00	30040.00	Own	3	192D	8F-8R	45.0	6235	C,H
3930 w/Cab	27810.00	21970.00	23360.00	24060.00	Own	3	192D	8F-8R	45.0	5707	C,H
4330V	25255.00	19950.00	21210.00	21850.00	Own	4	220D	12F-12R	62.0	3935	No
4330V 4WD	31845.00	25160.00	26750.00	27550.00	Own	4	220D	12F-12R	62.0	4122	No
4330V 4WD w/Cab	37068.00	29280.00	31140.00	32070.00	Own	4	220D	12F-12R	62.0		C,H,A
4330V w/Cab	30636.00	24200.00	25730.00	26500.00	Own	4	220D	12F-12R	62.0		C,H,A
4630	25520.00	20160.00	21440.00	22080.00	Own	3T	192D	16F-8R	55.0	5030	No
4630 4WD	32150.00	25400.00	27010.00	27820.00	Own	3T	192D	16F-8R	55.0	5822	No

New Holland/Ford (Cont.)

Model	Approx. Retail Price New	Estimated Average Value Less Repairs: Fair	Good	Premium	Engine: Make	No. Cyls.	Displ. Cu.-In.	No. Speeds	P.T.O. H.P.	Approx. Shipping Wt.-Lbs.	Cab
1998 (Cont.)											
4835	28217.00	**22290.00**	**23700.00**	**24410.00**	Own	4	220D	24F-12R	56.0		No
4835 4WD	35610.00	**28130.00**	**29910.00**	**30810.00**	Own	4	220D	24F-12R	56.0		No
4835 4WD w/Cab	43984.00	**34750.00**	**36950.00**	**38060.00**	Own	4	220D	24F-12R	56.0		C,H,A
4835 w/Cab	36620.00	**28930.00**	**30760.00**	**31680.00**	Own	4	220D	24F-12R	56.0		C,H,A
5030	27996.00	**22120.00**	**23520.00**	**24230.00**	Own	4	256D	8F-8R	62.0	5597	No
5030 4WD	33356.00	**26350.00**	**28020.00**	**28860.00**	Own	4	256D	8F-8R	62.0	6125	No
5610S	25920.00	**21250.00**	**22030.00**	**22690.00**	Own	4	268D	8F-2R	70.0	5995	No
5635	32937.00	**26020.00**	**27670.00**	**28500.00**	Own	4	238D	24F-12R	66.0		No
5635 4WD	40290.00	**31830.00**	**33840.00**	**34860.00**	Own	4	238D	24F-12R	66.0		No
5635 4WD w/Cab	48893.00	**38630.00**	**41070.00**	**42300.00**	Own	4	238D	24F-12R	66.0		C,H,A
5635 w/Cab	41540.00	**32820.00**	**34890.00**	**35940.00**	Own	4	238D	24F-12R	66.0		C,H,A
6610S	28331.00	**22380.00**	**23800.00**	**24510.00**	Own	4	304D	8F-2R	80.0	5995	No
6610S 4WD	36697.00	**28990.00**	**30830.00**	**31760.00**	Own	4	304D	8F-2R	80.0	6925	No
6635	34185.00	**27010.00**	**28720.00**	**29580.00**	Own	4T	238D	24F-12R	76.0		No
6635 4WD	42615.00	**33670.00**	**35800.00**	**36870.00**	Own	4T	238D	24F-12R	76.0		No
6635 4WD w/Cab	51220.00	**40460.00**	**43030.00**	**44320.00**	Own	4T	238D	24F-12R	76.0		C,H,A
6635 w/Cab	42790.00	**33800.00**	**35940.00**	**37020.00**	Own	4T	238D	24F-12R	76.0		C,H,A
7010 LP	37495.00	**29620.00**	**31500.00**	**32450.00**	Own	4T	304D	16F-4R	90.0		No
7010 LP 4WD	45775.00	**35710.00**	**37540.00**	**38670.00**	Own	4T	304D	16F-4R	90.0		No
7610S	31216.00	**24660.00**	**26220.00**	**27010.00**	Own	4T	304D	8F-2R	90.0	6375	No
7610S 4WD	38653.00	**30540.00**	**32470.00**	**33440.00**	Own	4T	304D	8F-2R	90.0	7305	No
7635	35930.00	**28390.00**	**30180.00**	**31090.00**	Own	4T	238D	24F-12R	86.0		No
7635 4WD	44312.00	**35010.00**	**37220.00**	**38340.00**	Own	4T	238D	24F-12R	86.0		No
7635 4WD w/Cab	52916.00	**39500.00**	**42000.00**	**43260.00**	Own	4T	238D	24F-12R	86.0		C,H,A
7635 w/Cab	44535.00	**35180.00**	**37410.00**	**38530.00**	Own	4T	238D	24F-12R	86.0		C,H,A
8010 HC	47366.00	**37420.00**	**39790.00**	**40980.00**	Own	6	456D	16F-4R	96.0		No
8010 LP	39900.00	**31520.00**	**33520.00**	**34530.00**	Own	6	456D	16F-4R	96.0		No
8010 LP 4WD	47637.00	**35550.00**	**37800.00**	**38930.00**	Own	6	456D	16F-4R	96.0		No
8160	44038.00	**34350.00**	**36110.00**	**37190.00**	Own	6	456D	23F-12R	90.0		No
8160 4WD	53000.00	**41340.00**	**43460.00**	**44760.00**	Own	6	456D	23F-12R	90.0		No
8160 4WD w/Cab	61142.00	**46800.00**	**49200.00**	**50680.00**	Own	6	456D	23F-12R	90.0		C,H,A
8160 w/Cab	52150.00	**40680.00**	**42760.00**	**44040.00**	Own	6	456D	23F-12R	90.0		C,H,A
8260	48200.00	**37600.00**	**39520.00**	**40710.00**	Own	6	456D	23F-12R	100.0		No
8260 4WD	57130.00	**44560.00**	**46850.00**	**48260.00**	Own	6	456D	23F-12R	100.0		No
8260 4WD w/Cab	65060.00	**50750.00**	**53350.00**	**54950.00**	Own	6	456D	23F-12R	100.0		C,H,A
8260 w/Cab	56066.00	**43730.00**	**45970.00**	**47350.00**	Own	6	456D	23F-12R	100.0		C,H,A
8360	56265.00	**43890.00**	**46140.00**	**47520.00**	Own	6T	456D	23F-12R	115.0		No
8360 4WD	68300.00	**53270.00**	**56010.00**	**57690.00**	Own	6T	456D	23F-12R	115.0		No
8360 w/Cab	64190.00	**50070.00**	**52640.00**	**54220.00**	Own	6T	456D	23F-12R	115.0		C,H,A
8560 4WD w/Cab	84611.00	**66000.00**	**69380.00**	**71460.00**	Own	6T	456D	18F-6R	130.0		C,H,A
8560 w/Cab	72575.00	**56610.00**	**59510.00**	**61300.00**	Own	6T	456D	17F-6R	130.0		C,H,A
8670	84990.00	**66290.00**	**69690.00**	**71780.00**	Own	6TI	456D	16F-9R	145.0	14632	C,H,A
8670 4WD	102290.00	**76440.00**	**80360.00**	**82770.00**	Own	6TI	456D	16F-9R	145.0	15188	C,H,A
8770	93390.00	**72840.00**	**76580.00**	**78880.00**	Own	6TI	456D	16F-9R	160.0	16925	C,H,A
8770 4WD	106217.00	**81900.00**	**86100.00**	**88680.00**	Own	6TI	456D	16F-9R	160.0	17481	C,H,A
8870	103670.00	**80860.00**	**85010.00**	**87560.00**	Own	6TI	456D	16F-9R	180.0	17101	C,H,A
8870 4WD	117605.00	**89700.00**	**94300.00**	**97130.00**	Own	6TI	456D	16F-9R	180.0	17657	C,H,A
8970 4WD	127575.00	**97500.00**	**102500.00**	**105580.00**	Own	6TI	456D	16F-9R	210.0	17889	C,H,A

*Net SAE HP.
LP-Low Profile, HC-High Clearance, PS Power Shift

Model	Approx. Retail Price New	Fair	Good	Premium	Make	No. Cyls.	Displ. Cu.-In.	No. Speeds	P.T.O. H.P.	Approx. Shipping Wt.-Lbs.	Cab
1999											
TC18	8780.00	**7640.00**	**7810.00**	**7970.00**	Shibaura	3	58D	6F-2R	15.0		No
TC18 4WD	9840.00	**8560.00**	**8760.00**	**8940.00**	Shibaura	3	58D	6F-2R	15.0		No
TC18 4WD Hydro	10995.00	**9570.00**	**9790.00**	**9990.00**	Shibaura	3	58D	Variable	14.0		No
TC21	13145.00	**11440.00**	**11700.00**	**11930.00**	Shibaura	3	61D	9F-3R	17.0		No
TC21D 4WD Hydro	14875.00	**12940.00**	**13240.00**	**13510.00**	Shibaura	3	61D	Variable	16.0		No
TC25	12415.00	**10800.00**	**11050.00**	**11270.00**	Shibaura	3	81D	9F-3R	21.7		No
TC25 4WD	13700.00	**11920.00**	**12190.00**	**12430.00**	Shibaura	3	81D	9F-3R	21.7		No
TC25D 4WD Hydro	16160.00	**14060.00**	**14380.00**	**14670.00**	Shibaura	3	81D	Variable	20.3		No
TC29	13185.00	**11470.00**	**11740.00**	**11980.00**	Shibaura	3	81D	9F-3R	25.1		No
TC29 4WD	14470.00	**12590.00**	**12880.00**	**13140.00**	Shibaura	3	81D	9F-3R	25.1		No
TC29D 4WD Hydro	16930.00	**14730.00**	**15070.00**	**15370.00**	Shibaura	3	81D	Variable	23.5		No
TC33	13955.00	**12140.00**	**12420.00**	**12670.00**	Shibaura	3	91D	9F-3R	28.6		No
TC33 4WD	15236.00	**13260.00**	**13560.00**	**13830.00**	Shibaura	3	91D	9F-3R	28.6		No
TC33D 4WD Hydro	17700.00	**15400.00**	**15750.00**	**16070.00**	Shibaura	3	91D	Variable	26.9		No
TN55D	32640.00	**27740.00**	**29050.00**	**29630.00**	Own	3	179D	8F-8R	42.0		C,H,A
TN55D 4WD	37860.00	**32180.00**	**33700.00**	**34370.00**	Own	3	179D	8F-8R	42.0		C,H,A
TN55S	31630.00	**26890.00**	**28150.00**	**28710.00**	Own	3	179D	8F-8R	42.0		No
TN55S w/Cab	39195.00	**33320.00**	**34880.00**	**35580.00**	Own	3	179D	8F-8R	42.0		C,H,A
TN65D	35495.00	**30170.00**	**31590.00**	**32220.00**	Own	3	179D	8F-8R	52.0		C,H,A
TN65D 4WD	40815.00	**34690.00**	**36330.00**	**37060.00**	Own	3	179D	8F-8R	52.0		C,H,A
TN65S	34590.00	**29400.00**	**30790.00**	**31410.00**	Own	3	179D	8F-8R	52.0		No
TN65S w/Cab	42150.00	**35830.00**	**37510.00**	**38260.00**	Own	3	179D	8F-8R	52.0		C,H,A
TN65F	27590.00	**23450.00**	**24560.00**	**25050.00**	Own	4	238D	16F-16R	57.0		No
TN65F	30635.00	**26040.00**	**27270.00**	**27820.00**	Own	4	238D	32F-16R	57.0		No
TN65F w/Cab	35680.00	**30330.00**	**31760.00**	**32400.00**	Own	4	238D	16F-16R	57.0		C,H,A
TN65F w/Cab	38730.00	**32920.00**	**34470.00**	**35160.00**	Own	4	238D	32F-16R	57.0		C,H,A
TN65F 4WD	35230.00	**29950.00**	**31360.00**	**31990.00**	Own	4	238D	16F-16R	57.0		No
TN65F 4WD	38280.00	**32540.00**	**34070.00**	**34750.00**	Own	4	238D	32F-16R	57.0		No
TN65F 4WD w/Cab	43320.00	**36820.00**	**38560.00**	**39330.00**	Own	4	238D	16F-16R	57.0		C,H,A
TN65F 4WD w/Cab	46370.00	**39420.00**	**41270.00**	**42100.00**	Own	4	238D	32F-16R	57.0		C,H,A
TN75D	37965.00	**32270.00**	**33790.00**	**34470.00**	Own	3T	179D	8F-8R	62.0		C,H,A
TN75D 4WD	43290.00	**36800.00**	**38530.00**	**39300.00**	Own	3T	179D	8F-8R	62.0		C,H,A

Model	Approx. Retail Price New	Estimated Average Value Less Repairs Fair	Good	Premium	Engine Make	No. Cyls.	Displ. Cu.-In.	No. Speeds	P.T.O. H.P.	Approx. Shipping Wt.-Lbs.	Cab

New Holland/Ford (Cont.)

1999 (Cont.)

Model	Approx. Retail Price New	Fair	Good	Premium	Make	No. Cyls.	Displ. Cu.-In.	No. Speeds	P.T.O. H.P.	Approx. Shipping Wt.-Lbs.	Cab
TN75S	37060.00	31500.00	32980.00	33640.00	Own	3T	179D	8F-8R	62.0		No
TN75S w/Cab	44625.00	37930.00	39720.00	40510.00	Own	3T	179D	8F-8R	62.0		C,H,A
TN75F	29085.00	24720.00	25890.00	26410.00	Own	4	238D	16F-16R	67.0		No
TN75F	32135.00	27320.00	28600.00	29170.00	Own	4	238D	32F-16R	67.0		No
TN75F w/Cab	37175.00	31600.00	33090.00	33750.00	Own	4	238D	16F-16R	67.0		C,H,A
TN75F w/Cab	40225.00	34190.00	35800.00	36520.00	Own	4	238D	32F-16R	67.0		C,H,A
TN75F 4WD	36756.00	31240.00	32710.00	33360.00	Own	4	238D	16F-16R	67.0		No
TN75F 4WD	39805.00	33830.00	35430.00	36140.00	Own	4	238D	32F-16R	67.0		No
TN75F 4WD w/Cab	44850.00	38120.00	39920.00	40720.00	Own	4	238D	16F-16R	67.0		C,H,A
TN75F 4WD w/Cab	47900.00	40720.00	42630.00	43480.00	Own	4	238D	32F-16R	67.0		C,H,A
TN90F	31370.00	26670.00	27920.00	28480.00	Own	4T	238D	16F-16R	80.0		No
TN90F	34420.00	29260.00	30630.00	31240.00	Own	4T	238D	32F-16R	80.0		No
TN90F w/Cab	39460.00	33540.00	35120.00	35820.00	Own	4T	238D	16F-16R	80.0		C,H,A
TN90F w/Cab	42505.00	36130.00	37830.00	38590.00	Own	4T	238D	32F-16R	80.0		C,H,A
TN90F 4WD	39275.00	33150.00	34710.00	35400.00	Own	4T	238D	16F-16R	80.0		No
TN90F 4WD	42000.00	35700.00	37380.00	38130.00	Own	4T	238D	32F-16R	80.0		No
TN90F 4WD w/Cab	47370.00	40270.00	42160.00	43000.00	Own	4T	238D	16F-16R	80.0		C,H,A
TN90F 4WD w/Cab	50075.00	42560.00	44570.00	45460.00	Own	4T	238D	32F-16R	80.0		C,H,A
TS90	36555.00	31070.00	32530.00	33180.00	Own	4	304D	24F-24R	70.0		No
TS90 w/Cab	45285.00	38490.00	40300.00	41110.00	Own	4	304D	24F-24R	70.0		C,H,A
TS90 4WD	45265.00	38250.00	40050.00	40850.00	Own	4	304D	24F-24R	70.0		No
TS90 4WD w/Cab	53995.00	45900.00	48060.00	49020.00	Own	4	304D	24F-24R	70.0		C,H,A
TS100	37350.00	31750.00	33240.00	33910.00	Own	4T	304D	16F-4R	80.0		No
TS100	40265.00	34000.00	35600.00	36310.00	Own	4T	304D	24F-24R	80.0		No
TS100	40710.00	34600.00	36230.00	36960.00	Own	4T	304D	16F-16R	80.0		No
TS100 w/Cab	48995.00	41650.00	43610.00	44480.00	Own	4T	304D	24F-24R	80.0		C,H,A
TS100 w/Cab	50265.00	42730.00	44740.00	45640.00	Own	4T	304D	16F-16R	80.0		C,H,A
TS100 4WD	49025.00	41670.00	43630.00	44500.00	Own	4T	304D	24F-24R	80.0		No
TS100 4WD	49425.00	42010.00	43990.00	44870.00	Own	4T	304D	16F-16R	80.0		No
TS100 4WD w/Cab	57775.00	49110.00	51420.00	52450.00	Own	4T	304D	24F-24R	80.0		C,H,A
TS100 4WD w/Cab	58980.00	50130.00	52490.00	53540.00	Own	4T	304D	16F-16R	80.0		C,H,A
TS110	41330.00	35130.00	36780.00	37520.00	Own	4T	304D	16F-4R	90.0		No
TS110	43375.00	36870.00	38600.00	39370.00	Own	4T	304D	24F-24R	90.0		No
TS110 w/Cab	52110.00	44290.00	46380.00	47310.00	Own	4T	304D	24F-24R	90.0		C,H,A
TS110 w/Cab	53515.00	45490.00	47630.00	48580.00	Own	4T	304D	16F-16R	90.0		C,H,A
TS110 4WD	49255.00	41870.00	43840.00	44720.00	Own	4T	304D	16F-4R	90.0		No
TS110 4WD	51290.00	43600.00	45650.00	46560.00	Own	4T	304D	24F-24R	90.0		No
TS110 4WD	52255.00	44420.00	46510.00	47440.00	Own	4T	304D	16F-16R	90.0		No
TS110 4WD w/Cab	60025.00	51020.00	53420.00	54490.00	Own	4T	304D	24F-24R	90.0		C,H,A
TS110 4WD w/Cab	61810.00	52540.00	55010.00	56110.00	Own	4T	304D	16F-16R	90.0		C,H,A
TL70	28420.00	24730.00	25290.00	25800.00	Own	4	220D	12F-12R	56.0		No
TL70 w/Cab	36100.00	31410.00	32130.00	32770.00	Own	4	220D	12F-12R	56.0		C,H,A
TL70 4WD	36155.00	31460.00	32180.00	32820.00	Own	4	220D	12F-12R	56.0		No
TL70 4WD w/Cab	43825.00	38130.00	39000.00	39780.00	Own	4	220D	12F-12R	56.0		C,H,A
TL80	31500.00	27410.00	28040.00	28600.00	Own	4	238D	12F-12R	66.0		No
TL80 w/Cab	39620.00	34470.00	35260.00	35970.00	Own	4	238D	12F-12R	66.0		C,H,A
TL80 4WD	40580.00	35310.00	36120.00	36840.00	Own	4	238D	12F-12R	66.0		No
TL80 4WD w/Cab	48700.00	42370.00	43340.00	44210.00	Own	4	238D	12F-12R	66.0		C,H,A
TL90	33845.00	29450.00	30120.00	30720.00	Own	4T	238D	12F-12R	76.0		No
TL90 w/Cab	41745.00	36320.00	37150.00	37890.00	Own	4T	238D	12F-12R	76.0		C,H,A
TL90 4WD	41490.00	36100.00	36930.00	37670.00	Own	4T	238D	12F-12R	76.0		No
TL90 4WD w/Cab	49390.00	42970.00	43960.00	44840.00	Own	4T	238D	12F-12R	76.0		C,H,A
TL100	36725.00	31950.00	32690.00	33340.00	Own	4T	238D	24F-12R	82.0		No
TL100 w/Cab	45455.00	39550.00	40460.00	41270.00	Own	4T	238D	24F-12R	82.0		C,H,A
TL100 4WD	45200.00	39320.00	40230.00	41040.00	Own	4T	238D	24F-12R	82.0		No
TL100 4WD w/Cab	53100.00	46200.00	47260.00	48210.00	Own	4T	238D	24F-12R	82.0		C,H,A
1720	14365.00	12500.00	12790.00	13050.00	Shibaura	3	91D	12F-4R	23.5		No
1720 4WD	16350.00	14230.00	14550.00	14840.00	Shibaura	3	91D	12F-4R	23.5		No
1920	15860.00	13800.00	14120.00	14400.00	Shibaura	4	122D	12F-4R	28.5		No
1920 4WD	18980.00	16510.00	16890.00	17230.00	Shibaura	4	122D	12F-4R	28.5		No
2120 4WD	22195.00	19310.00	19750.00	20150.00	Shibaura	4	139D	12F-4R	34.5		No
3010S	18535.00	15760.00	16500.00	16830.00	Own	3	165D	8F-2R	42.0		No
3010S 4WD	25565.00	21730.00	22750.00	23210.00	Own	3	165D	8F-2R	42.0		No
3415	18720.00	15910.00	16660.00	16990.00	Shibaura	4	135D	12F-4R	38.0		No
3830	23455.00	20410.00	20880.00	21300.00	Own	3	165D	12F-12R	45.0		No
3830 4WD	30625.00	26640.00	27260.00	27810.00	Own	3	165D	12F-12R	45.0		No
3830 4WD w/Cab	36085.00	31390.00	32120.00	32760.00	Own	3	165D	12F-12R	45.0		C,H
3830 w/Cab	28920.00	25160.00	25740.00	26260.00	Own	3	165D	12F-12R	45.0		C,H
3930	24400.00	21230.00	21720.00	22150.00	Own	3T	192D	8F-8R	45.0		No
3930 4WD	29905.00	26020.00	26620.00	27150.00	Own	3T	192D	8F-8R	45.0		No
4330V	26000.00	22100.00	23140.00	23600.00	Own	4	220D	12F-12R	62.0		No
4330V 4WD	32685.00	27780.00	29090.00	29670.00	Own	4	220D	12F-12R	62.0		No
4330V 4WD w/Cab	37990.00	32290.00	33810.00	34490.00	Own	4	220D	12F-12R	62.0		C,H,A
4330V w/Cab	31460.00	26740.00	28000.00	28560.00	Own	4	220D	12F-12R	62.0		C,H,A
4630	26235.00	22300.00	23350.00	23820.00	Own	3T	192D	16F-8R	55.0		No
4630 4WD	31655.00	26910.00	28170.00	28730.00	Own	3T	192D	16F-8R	55.0		No
5610S	25920.00	22030.00	23070.00	23530.00	Own	4	268D	8F-2R	70.0		No
6610S	28331.00	24080.00	25220.00	25720.00	Own	4	304D	8F-2R	80.0		No
6610S 4WD	36697.00	31190.00	32660.00	33310.00	Own	4	304D	8F-2R	80.0		No
7010 LP	37720.00	32820.00	33570.00	34240.00	Own	4T	304D	16F-4R	90.0		No
7010 LP 4WD	45625.00	39690.00	40610.00	41420.00	Own	4T	304D	16F-4R	90.0		No
7610S	31216.00	27160.00	27780.00	28340.00	Own	4T	304D	8F-2R	90.0		No
7610S 4WD	38653.00	33630.00	34400.00	35090.00	Own	4T	304D	8F-2R	90.0		No
8010 HC	49440.00	41530.00	43510.00	44380.00	Own	6	456D	8F-2R	96.0		No

New Holland/Ford (Cont.)

1999 (Cont.)

Model	Approx. Retail Price New	Estimated Average Value Less Repairs Fair	Good	Premium	Engine Make	No. Cyls.	Displ. Cu.-In.	No. Speeds	P.T.O. H.P.	Approx. Shipping Wt.-Lbs.	Cab
8010 LP	42326.00	**35980.00**	**37670.00**	**38420.00**	Own	6	456D	16F-4R	96.0		No
8010 LP 4WD	49997.00	**42000.00**	**44000.00**	**44880.00**	Own	6	456D	16F-4R	96.0		No
8160	47300.00	**39730.00**	**41620.00**	**42450.00**	Own	6	456D	23F-12R	90.0		No
8160 4WD	56350.00	**47330.00**	**49590.00**	**50580.00**	Own	6	456D	23F-12R	90.0		No
8160 4WD w/Cab	64535.00	**54210.00**	**56790.00**	**57930.00**	Own	6	456D	23F-12R	90.0		C,H,A
8160 w/Cab	55480.00	**46600.00**	**48820.00**	**49800.00**	Own	6	456D	23F-12R	90.0		C,H,A
8260	51275.00	**43070.00**	**45120.00**	**46020.00**	Own	6	456D	23F-12R	100.0		No
8260 4WD	60330.00	**50680.00**	**53090.00**	**54150.00**	Own	6	456D	23F-12R	100.0		No
8260 4WD w/Cab	68510.00	**57550.00**	**60290.00**	**61500.00**	Own	6	456D	23F-12R	100.0		C,H,A
8260 w/Cab	59445.00	**49930.00**	**52310.00**	**53360.00**	Own	6	456D	23F-12R	100.0		C,H,A
8360	59465.00	**49560.00**	**51920.00**	**52960.00**	Own	6T	456D	23F-12R	115.0		No
8360 4WD	71775.00	**60290.00**	**63160.00**	**64420.00**	Own	6T	456D	23F-12R	115.0		No
8360 4WD w/Cab	81390.00	**68370.00**	**71620.00**	**73050.00**	Own	6T	456D	23F-12R	115.0		C,H,A
8360 w/Cab	69075.00	**58020.00**	**60790.00**	**62010.00**	Own	6T	456D	23F-12R	115.0		C,H,A
8560 4WD w/Cab	88465.00	**74310.00**	**77850.00**	**79410.00**	Own	6T	456D	18F-6R	130.0		C,H,A
8560 w/Cab	76040.00	**63870.00**	**66920.00**	**68260.00**	Own	6T	456D	17F-6R	130.0		C,H,A
8670	86125.00	**72350.00**	**75790.00**	**77310.00**	Own	6TI	456D	16F-9R	145.0		C,H,A
8670 4WD	102505.00	**86100.00**	**90200.00**	**92000.00**	Own	6TI	456D	16F-9R	145.0		C,H,A
8770	94266.00	**79180.00**	**82950.00**	**84610.00**	Own	6TI	456D	16F-9R	160.0		C,H,A
8770 4WD	109380.00	**91880.00**	**96250.00**	**98180.00**	Own	6TI	456D	16F-9R	160.0		C,H,A
8870	108320.00	**90990.00**	**95320.00**	**97230.00**	Own	6TI	456D	16F-9R	180.0		C,H,A
8870 4WD	122480.00	**100800.00**	**105600.00**	**107710.00**	Own	6TI	456D	16F-9R	180.0		C,H,A
8970 4WD	132490.00	**107520.00**	**112640.00**	**114890.00**	Own	6TI	456D	16F-9R	210.0		C,H,A

***Net SAE HP.**
LP-Low Profile, HC-High Clearance, PS Power Shift

New Holland/Versatile

1988

Model	Approx. Retail Price New	Fair	Good	Premium	Make	No. Cyls.	Displ. Cu.-In.	No. Speeds	P.T.O. H.P.	Approx. Shipping Wt.-Lbs.	Cab
256 w/3 Pt. & PTO	41900.00	**24020.00**	**27460.00**	**29380.00**	Cummins	4T	239D	Infinite	85.14	9000	C,H,A
276	45100.00	**25820.00**	**29500.00**	**31570.00**	Cummins	4T	239D	Infinite	100.45	9000	C,H,A
836	70000.00	**35700.00**	**42000.00**	**44940.00**	Cummins	6T	611D	15F-5R	192.54	21000	C,H,A
856	85800.00	**43760.00**	**51480.00**	**55080.00**	Cummins	6T	611D	12F-4R	209.28	21000	C,H,A
876	95200.00	**44880.00**	**52800.00**	**56500.00**	Cummins	6T	611D	12F-4R		21000	C,H,A
936	105000.00	**39130.00**	**47320.00**	**50160.00**	Cummins	6T	855D	12F-4R		22000	C,H,A
956	107300.00	**40550.00**	**49040.00**	**51980.00**	Cummins	6T	855D	12F-4R		22000	C,H,A
976	115300.00	**43000.00**	**52000.00**	**55120.00**	Cummins	6TA	855D	12F-4R		22000	C,H,A
1156	151400.00	**50760.00**	**59220.00**	**65140.00**	Cummins	6TA	1150D	8F-2R		33000	C,H,A

1989

Model	Approx. Retail Price New	Fair	Good	Premium	Make	No. Cyls.	Displ. Cu.-In.	No. Speeds	P.T.O. H.P.	Approx. Shipping Wt.-Lbs.	Cab
276	45391.00	**27010.00**	**30800.00**	**32960.00**	Cummins	4T	239D	Infinite	100.45	9000	C,H,A
276 3 Pt. & PTO	52029.00	**29660.00**	**33820.00**	**36190.00**	Cummins	4T	239D	Infinite	100.45	9000	C,H,A
846	77183.00	**40140.00**	**47080.00**	**50380.00**	Cummins	6T	611D	12F-4R	230*		C,H,A
846 PS w/PTO	90643.00	**44200.00**	**51850.00**	**55480.00**	Cummins	6T	611D	12F-4R	230*		C,H,A
876	97942.00	**47270.00**	**55450.00**	**59330.00**	Cummins	6TI	611D	12F-4R	280*	21000	C,H,A
876 PS w/PTO	99450.00	**48050.00**	**56360.00**	**60310.00**	Cummins	6TI	611D	12F-3R	280*	21000	C,H,A
946	99775.00	**43900.00**	**52880.00**	**56050.00**	Cummins	6TI	855D	12F-4R	325*	22000	C,H,A
946 PS	112314.00	**47210.00**	**56870.00**	**60280.00**	Cummins	6TI	855D	12F-2R	325*	22000	C,H,A
976	107374.00	**44880.00**	**54060.00**	**57300.00**	Cummins	6TA	855D	12F-4R	360*	22000	C,H,A
976 PS	120414.00	**48400.00**	**58300.00**	**61800.00**	Cummins	6TI	855D	12F-2R	360*	22000	C,H,A
1156	164107.00	**54760.00**	**63410.00**	**69750.00**	Cummins	6TI	1150D	8F-4R	470*	33000	C,H,A

***Net SAE horsepower.**

1990

Model	Approx. Retail Price New	Fair	Good	Premium	Make	No. Cyls.	Displ. Cu.-In.	No. Speeds	P.T.O. H.P.	Approx. Shipping Wt.-Lbs.	Cab
9030	49058.00	**30160.00**	**34320.00**	**36720.00**	Own	4T	268D	Infinite	100.	8500	C,H,A
9030 w/3 Pt. & PTO	54328.00	**33640.00**	**38280.00**	**40960.00**	Own	4T	268D	Infinite	100.	9300	C,H,A
846 w/3 Pt.	83265.00	**45580.00**	**53320.00**	**57050.00**	Cummins	6T	611D	12F-4R	230*		C,H,A
876 w/3 Pt.	98029.00	**50350.00**	**58900.00**	**63020.00**	Cummins	6TA	611D	12F-4R	280*		C,H,A
946 w/3 Pt.	109368.00	**46800.00**	**56160.00**	**59530.00**	Cummins	6TA	855D	12F-4R	325*		C,H,A
976 w/3 Pt.	117243.00	**49500.00**	**59400.00**	**62960.00**	Cummins	6TA	855D	12F-4R	360*		C,H,A

***Net SAE Horsepower.**

1991

Model	Approx. Retail Price New	Fair	Good	Premium	Make	No. Cyls.	Displ. Cu.-In.	No. Speeds	P.T.O. H.P.	Approx. Shipping Wt.-Lbs.	Cab
9030	53161.00	**31860.00**	**36180.00**	**38350.00**	Own	4T	268D	Infinite	102.00	10750	C,H,A
9030 w/3 Pt. & PTO	60008.00	**35990.00**	**40870.00**	**43320.00**	Own	4T	268D	Infinite	100.	12150	C,H,A
846 w/3 Pt. & PTO	87815.00	**47520.00**	**55440.00**	**58770.00**	Cummins	6T	611D	15F-5R	230*		C,H,A
876 w/3 Pt. & PTO	113137.00	**54540.00**	**63630.00**	**67450.00**	Cummins	6TI	611D	12F-2R	280*		C,H,A
946 w/3 Pt. & PTO	118804.00	**50050.00**	**59840.00**	**63430.00**	Cummins	6TI	855D	12F-2R	325*		C,H,A
976 w/3 Pt. & PTO	127197.00	**53910.00**	**64460.00**	**68330.00**	Cummins	6TI	855D	12F-2R	360*		C,H,A

***Net SAE Horsepower.**

1992

Model	Approx. Retail Price New	Fair	Good	Premium	Make	No. Cyls.	Displ. Cu.-In.	No. Speeds	P.T.O. H.P.	Approx. Shipping Wt.-Lbs.	Cab
9030	55415.00	**33600.00**	**38080.00**	**40370.00**	Own	4T	268D	Infinite	102.00	10750	C,H,A
9030 w/3 Pt. & PTO	62262.00	**37360.00**	**42340.00**	**44880.00**	Own	4T	268D	Infinite	100.	12150	C,H,A
846 w/3 Pt. & PTO	90458.00	**49280.00**	**56320.00**	**59700.00**	Cummins	6T	611D	15F-5R	230.00*		C,H,A
876 w/3 Pt. & PTO	115400.00	**58970.00**	**67390.00**	**71430.00**	Cummins	6TI	611D	12F-2R	280.00*		C,H,A
946 w/3 Pt. & PTO	127952.00	**67700.00**	**77370.00**	**82010.00**	Cummins	6TI	855D	12F-2R	325.00*		C,H,A
976 w/3 Pt. & PTO	136504.00	**60700.00**	**70820.00**	**74360.00**	Cummins	6TI	855D	12F-2R	360.00*		C,H,A

***Net SAE Horsepower.**

1993

Model	Approx. Retail Price New	Fair	Good	Premium	Make	No. Cyls.	Displ. Cu.-In.	No. Speeds	P.T.O. H.P.	Approx. Shipping Wt.-Lbs.	Cab
9030	52960.00	**35900.00**	**39950.00**	**42350.00**	Own	4T	268D	Infinite	102.00	10750	C,H,A
9030 w/3 Pt. & PTO	59503.00	**39990.00**	**44510.00**	**47180.00**	Own	4T	268D	Infinite	100.	12150	C,H,A

Model	Approx. Retail Price New	Estimated Average Value Less Repairs Fair	Good	Premium	Engine Make	No. Cyls.	Displ. Cu.-In.	No. Speeds	P.T.O. H.P.	Approx. Shipping Wt.-Lbs.	Cab
New Holland/Versatile (Cont.)											
			1993 (Cont.)								
846	77825.00	**46400.00**	**52000.00**	**55120.00**	Cummins	6T	611D	12F-4R	230.00*	15560	C,H,A
846 w/3 Pt. & PTO	83353.00	**51040.00**	**57200.00**	**60630.00**	Cummins	6T	611D	15F-5R	230.00*		C,H,A
876 Mechanical Shift	89197.00	**51730.00**	**57980.00**	**61460.00**	Cummins	6TI	611D	12F-4R	280.00*	15800	C,H,A
876 w/3 Pt. & PTO	108295.00	**60320.00**	**67600.00**	**71660.00**	Cummins	6TI	611D	12F-2R	280.00*		C,H,A
876 Powershift	101362.00	**56260.00**	**63050.00**	**66830.00**	Cummins	6TI	611D	12F-2R	280.00*		C,H,A
946 Mechanical Shift	101706.00	**57420.00**	**64350.00**	**68210.00**	Cummins	6TI	855D	12F-4R	325.00*	18300	C,H,A
946 w/3 Pt. & PTO	121894.00	**66700.00**	**74750.00**	**79240.00**	Cummins	6TI	855D	12F-2R	325.00*		C,H,A
946 Powershift	114962.00	**63220.00**	**70850.00**	**75100.00**	Cummins	6TI	855D	12F-2R	325.00*	18750	C,H,A
976 w/3 Pt. & PTO	130456.00	**70180.00**	**78650.00**	**83370.00**	Cummins	6TI	855D	12F-2R	360.00*		C,H,A
976 Mechanical Shift	109739.00	**61330.00**	**68730.00**	**72850.00**	Cummins	6TI	855D	12F-4R	360.00*	18300	C,H,A
976 Powershift	123523.00	**68440.00**	**76700.00**	**81300.00**	Cummins	6TI	855D	12F-2R	360.00*	18750	C,H,A
***Net SAE Horsepower.**											
			1994								
9030	52960.00	**37060.00**	**40530.00**	**42560.00**	Own	4T	268D	Infinite	102.00	10750	C,H,A
9030 w/3 Pt. & PTO	59503.00	**41280.00**	**45150.00**	**47410.00**	Own	4T	268D	Infinite	100.	12150	C,H,A
9280	85131.00	**51930.00**	**57040.00**	**59890.00**	Cummins	6T	611D	12F-4R	250.00*	17722	C,H,A
9280 w/PTO, 3Pt.	96140.00	**58650.00**	**64410.00**	**67630.00**	Cummins	6T	611D	12F-4R	250.00*	20295	C,H,A
9480	98547.00	**60110.00**	**66030.00**	**69330.00**	Cummins	6TA	855D	12F-4R	300.00*	18697	C,H,A
9480 PS	102212.00	**61000.00**	**67000.00**	**70350.00**	Cummins	6TA	855D	12F-2R	300.00*	19232	C,H,A
9480 PS w/PTO, 3Pt.	111121.00	**66490.00**	**73030.00**	**76680.00**	Cummins	6TA	855D	12F-2R	300.00*	21805	C,H,A
9480 w/PTO, 3Pt.	104156.00	**62220.00**	**68340.00**	**71760.00**	Cummins	6TA	855D	12F-4R	300.00*	21270	C,H,A
9680	103461.00	**61850.00**	**67940.00**	**71340.00**	Cummins	6TA	855D	12F-4R	350.00*	19730	C,H,A
9680 PS	113306.00	**67280.00**	**73900.00**	**77600.00**	Cummins	6TA	855D	12F-2R	350.00*	20065	C,H,A
9680 PS w/PTO, 3Pt.	120915.00	**71070.00**	**78060.00**	**81960.00**	Cummins	6TA	855D	12F-2R	350.00*	22638	C,H,A
9680 w/PTO, 3Pt.	111070.00	**65880.00**	**72360.00**	**75980.00**	Cummins	6TA	855D	12F-4R	350.00*	22303	C,H,A
9880	113284.00	**67710.00**	**74370.00**	**78090.00**	Cummins	6TA	855D	12F-4R	400.00*	20230	C,H,A
9880 w/3Pt.	121524.00	**72900.00**	**80070.00**	**84070.00**	Cummins	6TA	855D	12F-4R	400.00*	21803	C,H,A
***Net SAE Horsepower.**											
			1995								
9030	58361.00	**41580.00**	**45990.00**	**48290.00**	Own	4T	268D	Infinite	102.00	9190	C,H,A
9030 Utility	59443.00	**42530.00**	**47040.00**	**49390.00**	Own	4T	268D	Infinite	102.00	9260	C,H,A
9030 Utility PTO, 3Pt.	66796.00	**47380.00**	**52410.00**	**55030.00**	Own	4T	268D	Infinite	102.00	10330	C,H,A
9030 w/3Pt. & PTO	65714.00	**46660.00**	**51610.00**	**54190.00**	Own	4T	268D	Infinite	100.	10261	C,H,A
9280	85631.00	**54800.00**	**59940.00**	**62940.00**	Cummins	6T	611D	12F-4R	250.00*	17722	C,H,A
9280 w/PTO	90770.00	**58090.00**	**63540.00**	**66720.00**	Cummins	6T	611D	12F-4R	250.00*	18722	C,H,A
9280 w/PTO, 3Pt.	99140.00	**63450.00**	**69400.00**	**72870.00**	Cummins	6T	611D	12F-4R	250.00*	20295	C,H,A
9480	101747.00	**65120.00**	**71220.00**	**74780.00**	Cummins	6TA	855D	12F-4R	300.00*	18697	C,H,A
9480 PS	107612.00	**68870.00**	**75330.00**	**79100.00**	Cummins	6TA	855D	12F-2R	300.00*	19232	C,H,A
9480 PS w/PTO, 3Pt.	121121.00	**74880.00**	**81900.00**	**86000.00**	Cummins	6TA	855D	12F-2R	300.00*	21805	C,H,A
9480 w/PTO, 3Pt.	115256.00	**71680.00**	**78400.00**	**82320.00**	Cummins	6TA	855D	12F-4R	300.00*	21270	C,H,A
9680	108561.00	**69480.00**	**75990.00**	**79790.00**	Cummins	6TA	855D	12F-4R	350.00*	19730	C,H,A
9680 PS	118406.00	**73600.00**	**80500.00**	**84530.00**	Cummins	6TA	855D	12F-2R	350.00*	20065	C,H,A
9680 PS w/PTO, 3Pt.	131915.00	**80000.00**	**87500.00**	**91880.00**	Cummins	6TA	855D	12F-2R	350.00*	22638	C,H,A
9680 w/PTO, 3Pt.	122070.00	**75520.00**	**82600.00**	**86730.00**	Cummins	6TA	855D	12F-4R	350.00*	22303	C,H,A
9880	124284.00	**76990.00**	**84210.00**	**88420.00**	Cummins	6TA	855D	12F-4R	400.00*	20230	C,H,A
9880 w/3Pt.	130524.00	**80320.00**	**87850.00**	**92240.00**	Cummins	6TA	855D	12F-4R	400.00*	21803	C,H,A
***Net SAE Horsepower.**											
			1996								
9030	66590.00	**49410.00**	**53650.00**	**55800.00**	Own	4T	268D	Infinite	102.00	9190	C,H,A
9030 Utility	67475.00	**50730.00**	**55080.00**	**57280.00**	Own	4T	268D	Infinite	102.00	9260	C,H,A
9030 Utility PTO, 3 Pt.	74903.00	**55930.00**	**60720.00**	**63150.00**	Own	4T	268D	Infinite	102.00	10330	C,H,A
9030 w/3 Pt. & PTO	73789.00	**54390.00**	**59050.00**	**61410.00**	Own	4T	268D	Infinite	100.	10261	C,H,A
9282	106442.00	**63710.00**	**69980.00**	**72780.00**	Cummins	6TA	505D	12F-4R	260.00*	17722	C,H,A
9282 w/PTO	113938.00	**68260.00**	**74970.00**	**77970.00**	Cummins	6TA	505D	12F-4R	260.00*	18722	C,H,A
9282 w/PTO, 3 Pt.	120627.00	**71980.00**	**79060.00**	**82220.00**	Cummins	6TA	505D	12F-4R	260.00*	20295	C,H,A
9482	122634.00	**73200.00**	**80400.00**	**83620.00**	Cummins	6TA	660D	12F-4R	310.00*	18697	C,H,A
9482 PS	132970.00	**76860.00**	**84420.00**	**87800.00**	Cummins	6TA	660D	12F-2R	310.00*	19232	C,H,A
9482 PS w/PTO	140466.00	**80220.00**	**88110.00**	**91630.00**	Cummins	6TA	660D	12F-2R	310.00*	20232	C,H,A
9482 PS w/PTO, 3 Pt.	147155.00	**84280.00**	**92560.00**	**96260.00**	Cummins	6TA	660D	12F-2R	310.00*	21805	C,H,A
9482 w/PTO	130130.00	**76250.00**	**83750.00**	**87100.00**	Cummins	6TA	660D	12F-4R	310.00*	19697	C,H,A
9482 w/PTO, 3 Pt.	136820.00	**79800.00**	**87650.00**	**91160.00**	Cummins	6TA	660D	12F-4R	310.00*	21270	C,H,A
9682	139648.00	**80520.00**	**88440.00**	**91980.00**	Cummins	6TA	855D	12F-4R	360.00*	19730	C,H,A
9682 PS	148005.00	**83570.00**	**91790.00**	**95460.00**	Cummins	6TA	855D	12F-2R	360.00*	20065	C,H,A
9682 PS w/PTO	155500.00	**85400.00**	**93800.00**	**97550.00**	Cummins	6TA	855D	12F-2R	360.00*	21065	C,H,A
9682 PS w/PTO, 3 Pt.	162190.00	**88510.00**	**97220.00**	**101110.00**	Cummins	6TA	855D	12F-2R	360.00*	22638	C,H,A
9682 w/PTO	147145.00	**83020.00**	**91190.00**	**94840.00**	Cummins	6TA	855D	12F-4R	360.00*	20730	C,H,A
9682 w/PTO, 3 Pt.	153833.00	**86620.00**	**95140.00**	**98950.00**	Cummins	6TA	855D	12F-4R	360.00*	22303	C,H,A
9882	155990.00	**89000.00**	**97750.00**	**101660.00**	Cummins	6TA	855D	12F-4R	425.00*	20230	C,H,A
9882 w/3 Pt.	162543.00	**93030.00**	**102180.00**	**106270.00**	Cummins	6TA	855D	12F-4R	425.00*	21803	C,H,A
***Net SAE Horsepower.**											
			1997								
9030	68588.00	**53250.00**	**56800.00**	**59070.00**	Own	4T	268D	Variable	102.0	9930	C,H,A
9030 Utility	63063.00	**52110.00**	**55580.00**	**57800.00**	Own	4T	268D	Variable	102.0	9260	C,H,A
9030 Utility w/Loader	70500.00	**56630.00**	**60400.00**	**62820.00**	Own	4T	268D	Variable	102.0		C,H,A
9030 Utility w/Loader, 3Pt	77150.00	**60110.00**	**64120.00**	**66690.00**	Own	4T	268D	Variable	102.0	10330	C,H,A
9030 w/3 Pt & PTO	76000.00	**58880.00**	**62800.00**	**65310.00**	Own	4T	268D	Variable	100.0	10975	C,H,A
9282	110316.00	**73030.00**	**79570.00**	**82750.00**	Cummins	6TA	505D	12F-4R	260.0*	17722	C,H,A
9282 w/PTO	117925.00	**75710.00**	**82490.00**	**85790.00**	Cummins	6TA	505D	12F-4R	260.0*	18722	C,H,A
9282 w/PTO, 3 Pt.	124713.00	**79530.00**	**86650.00**	**90120.00**	Cummins	6TA	505D	12F-4R	260.0*	20295	C,H,A
9482	124615.00	**80400.00**	**87600.00**	**91100.00**	Cummins	6TA	660D	12F-4R	310.0*	18697	C,H,A

New Holland/Versatile (Cont.)

1997 (Cont.)

Model	Approx. Retail Price New	Fair	Good	Premium	Engine Make	Engine No. Cyls.	Engine Displ. Cu.-In.	No. Speeds	P.T.O. H.P.	Approx. Shipping Wt.-Lbs.	Cab
9482 PS	135106.00	85830.00	93510.00	97250.00	Cummins	6TA	660D	12F-2R	310.0*	19232	C,H,A
9482 PS w/PTO	142714.00	90920.00	99060.00	103020.00	Cummins	6TA	660D	12F-2R	310.0*	20232	C,H,A
9482 PS w/PTO, 3 Pt.	149503.00	93470.00	101840.00	105910.00	Cummins	6TA	660D	12F-2R	310.0*	21805	C,H,A
9482 w/PTO	132222.00	87100.00	94900.00	98700.00	Cummins	6TA	660D	12F-4R	310.0*	19697	C,H,A
9482 w/PTO, 3 Pt.	139011.00	89780.00	97820.00	101730.00	Cummins	6TA	660D	12F-4R	310.0*	21270	C,H,A
9682	140785.00	87570.00	95410.00	99230.00	Cummins	6TA	855D	12F-4R	360.0*	19730	C,H,A
9682 PS	150267.00	93930.00	102350.00	106440.00	Cummins	6TA	855D	12F-2R	360.0*	20065	C,H,A
9682 PS w/PTO	157875.00	96820.00	105490.00	109710.00	Cummins	6TA	855D	12F-2R	360.0*	21065	C,H,A
9682 PS w/PTO, 3 Pt.	164665.00	100900.00	109940.00	114340.00	Cummins	6TA	855D	12F-2R	360.0*	22638	C,H,A
9682 w/PTO	148393.00	92660.00	100960.00	105000.00	Cummins	6TA	855D	12F-4R	360.0*	20730	C,H,A
9682 w/PTO, 3 Pt.	155182.00	97150.00	105850.00	110080.00	Cummins	6TA	855D	12F-4R	360.0*	22303	C,H,A
9882	164120.00	103250.00	112490.00	116990.00	Cummins	6TA	855D	12F-4R	425.0*	20230	C,H,A
9882 w/3 Pt.	170770.00	107200.00	116800.00	121470.00	Cummins	6TA	855D	12F-4R	425.0*	21803	C,H,A

*Net SAE Horsepower.

1998

Model	Approx. Retail Price New	Fair	Good	Premium	Engine Make	Engine No. Cyls.	Engine Displ. Cu.-In.	No. Speeds	P.T.O. H.P.	Approx. Shipping Wt.-Lbs.	Cab
TV140	77890.00	63200.00	67200.00	69220.00	Own	6T	456D	Variable	105.0		C,H,A
9030E Loader	70646.00	58180.00	61860.00	63720.00	Own	4T	304D	Variable	102.0		C,H,A
9030E Loader, PTO, 3Pt	78285.00	62810.00	66780.00	68780.00	Own	4T	304D	Variable	102.0	10330	C,H,A
9282	114690.00	84870.00	90610.00	93330.00	Cummins	6TA	505D	12F-4R	260.0*	17722	C,H,A
9282 w/PTO	122525.00	88800.00	94800.00	97640.00	Cummins	6TA	505D	12F-4R	260.0*	18722	C,H,A
9482	127441.00	92500.00	98750.00	101710.00	Cummins	6TA	660D	12F-4R	310.0*	18697	C,H,A
9482 PS	138250.00	97090.00	103650.00	106760.00	Cummins	6TA	660D	12F-4R	310.0*	19697	C,H,A
9682	147752.00	103380.00	110360.00	113670.00	Cummins	6TA	855D	12F-4R	360.0*	19730	C,H,A
9682 PS	157390.00	107300.00	114550.00	117990.00	Cummins	6TA	855D	12F-2R	360.0*	20065	C,H,A
9882	175775.00	122100.00	130350.00	134260.00	Cummins	6TA	855D	12F-4R	425.0*	20230	C,H,A

*Net SAE Horsepower.

1999

Model	Approx. Retail Price New	Fair	Good	Premium	Engine Make	Engine No. Cyls.	Engine Displ. Cu.-In.	No. Speeds	P.T.O. H.P.	Approx. Shipping Wt.-Lbs.	Cab
TV140	83785.00	72250.00	75650.00	77160.00	Own	6T	456D	Variable	105.0		C,H,A
9282	115175.00	96750.00	101350.00	103380.00	Cummins	6TA	505D	12F-4R	260.0*	17722	C,H,A
9282 w/PTO	123015.00	103330.00	108250.00	110420.00	Cummins	6TA	505D	12F-4R	260.0*	18722	C,H,A
9282 w/PTO, 3-Pt.	130000.00	106680.00	111760.00	114000.00	Cummins	6TA	505D	12F-4R	260.0*	18722	C,H,A
9482	130825.00	108360.00	113520.00	115790.00	Cummins	6TA	660D	12F-4R	310.0*	18697	C,H,A
9482 w/PTO, 3-Pt.	145655.00	117600.00	123200.00	125660.00	Cummins	6TA	660D	12F-4R	310.0*	18697	C,H,A
9482 PS	141630.00	115920.00	121440.00	123870.00	Cummins	6TA	660D	12F-4R	310.0*	19697	C,H,A
9482 PS w/PTO, 3-Pt.	156460.00	126000.00	132000.00	134640.00	Cummins	6TA	660D	12F-4R	310.0*	19697	C,H,A
9682	144450.00	117860.00	123540.00	127250.00	Cummins	6TA	855D	12F-4R	360.0*	19730	C,H,A
9682 w/PTO, 3-Pt.	159280.00	125330.00	131370.00	135310.00	Cummins	6TA	855D	12F-4R	360.0*	19730	C,H,A
9682 PS	154085.00	122010.00	127890.00	131730.00	Cummins	6TA	855D	12F-2R	360.0*	20065	C,H,A
9682 PS w/PTO, 3-Pt.	163915.00	126990.00	133110.00	137100.00	Cummins	6TA	855D	12F-2R	360.0*	20065	C,H,A
9882	168040.00	131140.00	137460.00	141580.00	Cummins	6TA	855D	12F-4R	425.0*	20230	C,H,A
9882 w/3Pt.	169890.00	132630.00	139030.00	143200.00	Cummins	6TA	855D	12F-4R	425.0*	20230	C,H,A

*Net SAE Horsepower.

Oliver

1939

Model	Approx. Retail Price New	Fair	Good	Premium	Engine Make	Engine No. Cyls.	Engine Displ. Cu.-In.	No. Speeds	P.T.O. H.P.	Approx. Shipping Wt.-Lbs.	Cab
70 RC	......	630.00	1450.00	1800.00	Oliver	6	201G	6F-2R	22.6	4370	No
70 Standard	......	650.00	1480.00	1840.00	Oliver	6	201G	6F-2R	22.6	6538	No
80 RC	......	660.00	1520.00	1890.00	Oliver	4	334D	4F-1R	23.2	4930	No
80 Standard	......	650.00	1500.00	1860.00	Oliver	4	334D	4F-1R	23.2	5130	No
90 Standard	......	660.00	1520.00	1890.00	Oliver	4	443G	4F-1R	29.9	6797	No

1940

Model	Approx. Retail Price New	Fair	Good	Premium	Engine Make	Engine No. Cyls.	Engine Displ. Cu.-In.	No. Speeds	P.T.O. H.P.	Approx. Shipping Wt.-Lbs.	Cab
60 RC	......	570.00	1310.00	1620.00	Oliver	4	120G	4F-1R	18.35	2450	No
70 RC	......	590.00	1350.00	1670.00	Oliver	6	201G	6F-2R	22.6	4370	No
70 Standard	......	630.00	1460.00	1810.00	Oliver	6	201G	6F-2R	22.6	6538	No
80 RC	......	650.00	1490.00	1850.00	Oliver	4	334D	4F-1R	23.2	4930	No
80 Standard	......	630.00	1450.00	1800.00	Oliver	4	334D	4F-1R	23.2	5130	No
90 Standard	......	680.00	1550.00	1920.00	Oliver	4	443G	4F-1R	29.9	6797	No
90 Standard	......	690.00	1590.00	1970.00	Oliver	4	443D	4F-1R		6962	No

1941

Model	Approx. Retail Price New	Fair	Good	Premium	Engine Make	Engine No. Cyls.	Engine Displ. Cu.-In.	No. Speeds	P.T.O. H.P.	Approx. Shipping Wt.-Lbs.	Cab
60 RC	......	570.00	1310.00	1620.00	Oliver	4	120G	4F-1R	18.35	2450	No
70 RC	......	640.00	1480.00	1840.00	Oliver	6	201G	6F-2R	22.6	4370	No
70 Standard	......	630.00	1450.00	1800.00	Oliver	6	201G	6F-2R	22.6	6538	No
80 RC	......	710.00	1620.00	2010.00	Oliver	4	334D	4F-1R	23.2	4930	No
80 Standard	......	690.00	1590.00	1970.00	Oliver	4	334D	4F-1R	23.2	5130	No
90 Standard	......	720.00	1660.00	2060.00	Oliver	4	443G	4F-1R	29.9	6797	No
90 Standard	......	750.00	1730.00	2150.00	Oliver	4	443D	4F-1R		6962	No

1942

Model	Approx. Retail Price New	Fair	Good	Premium	Engine Make	Engine No. Cyls.	Engine Displ. Cu.-In.	No. Speeds	P.T.O. H.P.	Approx. Shipping Wt.-Lbs.	Cab
60 RC	......	600.00	1370.00	1700.00	Oliver	4	120G	4F-1R	18.35	2450	No
60 Standard	......	630.00	1450.00	1800.00	Oliver	4	120G	4F-1R	18.35	2650	No
70 RC	......	670.00	1550.00	1920.00	Oliver	6	201G	6F-2R	22.6	4370	No
70 Standard	......	660.00	1520.00	1890.00	Oliver	6	201G	6F-2R	22.6	6538	No
80 RC	......	750.00	1730.00	2150.00	Oliver	4	334D	4F-1R	23.2	4930	No
80 Standard	......	720.00	1660.00	2060.00	Oliver	4	334D	4F-1R	23.2	5130	No
90 Standard	......	750.00	1730.00	2150.00	Oliver	4	443G	4F-1R	29.9	6797	No
90 Standard	......	780.00	1790.00	2220.00	Oliver	4	443D	4F-1R		6962	No

Oliver (Cont.)

Model	Approx. Retail Price New	Estimated Average Value Less Repairs Fair	Good	Premium	Engine Make	No. Cyls.	Displ. Cu.-In.	No. Speeds	P.T.O. H.P.	Approx. Shipping Wt.-Lbs.	Cab
1943											
60 RC	......	620.00	1380.00	1710.00	Oliver	4	120G	4F-1R	18.35	2450	No
60 Standard	......	680.00	1520.00	1890.00	Oliver	4	120G	4F-1R	18.35	2650	No
70 RC	......	730.00	1620.00	2010.00	Oliver	6	201G	6F-2R	22.6	4370	No
70 Standard	......	710.00	1590.00	1970.00	Oliver	6	201G	6F-2R	22.6	6538	No
80 RC	......	810.00	1790.00	2220.00	Oliver	4	334D	4F-1R	23.2	4930	No
80 Standard	......	780.00	1730.00	2150.00	Oliver	4	334D	4F-1R	23.2	5130	No
90 Standard	......	810.00	1790.00	2220.00	Oliver	4	443G	4F-1R	29.9	6797	No
90 Standard	......	840.00	1860.00	2310.00	Oliver	4	443D	4F-1R		6962	No
1944											
60 RC	......	670.00	1450.00	1800.00	Oliver	4	120G	4F-1R	18.35	2450	No
60 Standard	......	740.00	1590.00	1970.00	Oliver	4	120G	4F-1R	18.35	2650	No
70 RC	......	780.00	1690.00	2100.00	Oliver	6	201G	6F-2R	22.6	4370	No
70 Standard	......	770.00	1660.00	2060.00	Oliver	6	201G	6F-2R	22.6	6538	No
80 RC	......	860.00	1860.00	2310.00	Oliver	4	334D	4F-1R	23.2	4930	No
80 Standard	......	830.00	1790.00	2220.00	Oliver	4	334D	4F-1R	23.2	5130	No
90 Standard	......	860.00	1860.00	2310.00	Oliver	4	443G	4F-1R	29.9	6797	No
90 Standard	......	900.00	1930.00	2390.00	Oliver	4	443D	4F-1R		6962	No
1945											
60 RC	......	730.00	1500.00	1860.00	Oliver	4	120G	4F-1R	18.35	2450	No
60 Standard	......	790.00	1630.00	2020.00	Oliver	4	120G	4F-1R	18.35	2650	No
70 RC	......	840.00	1730.00	2150.00	Oliver	6	201G	6F-2R	22.6	4370	No
70 Standard	......	830.00	1700.00	2110.00	Oliver	6	201G	6F-2R	22.6	6538	No
80 RC	......	920.00	1900.00	2360.00	Oliver	4	334D	4F-1R	23.2	4930	No
80 Standard	......	920.00	1890.00	2340.00	Oliver	4	334D	4F-1R	23.2	5130	No
90 Standard	......	990.00	2040.00	2530.00	Oliver	4	443G	4F-1R	29.9	6797	No
90 Standard	......	1020.00	2110.00	2620.00	Oliver	4	443D	4F-1R		6962	No
1946											
60 RC	......	780.00	1560.00	1930.00	Oliver	4	120G	4F-1R	18.35	2450	No
60 Standard	......	850.00	1700.00	2110.00	Oliver	4	120G	4F-1R	18.35	2650	No
70 RC	......	900.00	1800.00	2230.00	Oliver	6	201G	6F-2R	22.6	4370	No
70 Standard	......	880.00	1770.00	2200.00	Oliver	6	201G	6F-2R	22.6	6538	No
80 RC	......	990.00	1970.00	2440.00	Oliver	4	334D	4F-1R	23.2	4930	No
80 Standard	......	980.00	1960.00	2430.00	Oliver	4	334D	4F-1R	23.2	5130	No
90 Standard	......	1050.00	2110.00	2620.00	Oliver	4	443G	4F-1R	29.9	6797	No
90 Standard	......	1090.00	2180.00	2700.00	Oliver	4	443D	4F-1R		6962	No
1947											
60 RC	......	840.00	1630.00	2020.00	Oliver	4	120G	4F-1R	18.35	2450	No
60 Standard	......	910.00	1770.00	2200.00	Oliver	4	120G	4F-1R	18.35	2650	No
70 RC	......	940.00	1820.00	2260.00	Oliver	6	201G	6F-2R	22.6	4370	No
70 Standard	......	950.00	1840.00	2280.00	Oliver	6	201G	6F-2R	22.6	6538	No
80 RC	......	1050.00	2040.00	2530.00	Oliver	4	334D	4F-1R	23.2	4930	No
80 Standard	......	1020.00	1970.00	2440.00	Oliver	4	334D	4F-1R	23.2	5130	No
88 RC	......	790.00	1530.00	1900.00	Oliver	6	230G	6F-2R	28.96	5147	No
88 Standard	......	810.00	1560.00	1930.00	Oliver	6	231D	6F-2R	28.96	5451	No
88 Standard	......	840.00	1630.00	2020.00	Oliver	6	230G	6F-2R	41.07	5285	No
90 Standard	......	1100.00	2140.00	2650.00	Oliver	4	443G	4F-1R	29.9	6797	No
90 Standard	......	1140.00	2210.00	2740.00	Oliver	4	443D	4F-1R		6962	No
1948											
60 RC	......	900.00	1700.00	2110.00	Oliver	4	120G	4F-1R	18.35	2450	No
60 Standard	......	970.00	1840.00	2280.00	Oliver	4	120G	4F-1R	18.35	2650	No
70 RC	......	970.00	1840.00	2280.00	Oliver	6	201G	6F-2R	22.6	4370	No
70 Standard	......	1010.00	1900.00	2360.00	Oliver	6	201G	6F-2R	22.6	6538	No
77 RC	......	790.00	1500.00	1860.00	Oliver	6	194G	6F-2R	32.51	6976	No
77 Standard	......	1010.00	1900.00	2360.00	Oliver	6	194D	6F-2R	25.79	7246	No
80 RC	......	1100.00	2070.00	2570.00	Oliver	4	334D	4F-1R	23.2	4930	No
80 Standard	......	1080.00	2040.00	2530.00	Oliver	4	334D	4F-1R	23.2	5130	No
88 Standard	......	860.00	1630.00	2020.00	Oliver	6	230G	6F-2R	41.07	5285	No
88 RC	......	850.00	1600.00	1980.00	Oliver	6	230G	6F-2R	28.96	5147	No
88 Standard	......	860.00	1630.00	2020.00	Oliver	6	231D	6F-2R	28.96	5451	No
90 Standard	......	1150.00	2180.00	2700.00	Oliver	4	443G	4F-1R	29.9	6797	No
90 Standard	......	1210.00	2280.00	2830.00	Oliver	4	443D	4F-1R		6962	No
1949											
66 RC	......	670.00	1220.00	1510.00	Oliver	4	145G	6F-2R	23.92	3193	No
66 Standard	......	740.00	1360.00	1690.00	Oliver	4	145G	6F-2R	23.92	3193	No
66 Standard	......	1000.00	1840.00	2280.00	Oliver	4	129D	6F-2R	16.81	3293	No
77 RC	......	850.00	1560.00	1930.00	Oliver	6	194G	6F-2R	32.51	6976	No
77 Standard	......	1070.00	1970.00	2440.00	Oliver	6	194D	6F-2R	25.79	7246	No
88 Standard	......	930.00	1700.00	2110.00	Oliver	6	230G	6F-2R	41.07	5285	No
88 RC	......	910.00	1670.00	2070.00	Oliver	6	230G	6F-2R	28.96	5147	No
88 Standard	......	930.00	1700.00	2110.00	Oliver	6	231D	6F-2R	28.96	5451	No
90 Standard	......	1200.00	2210.00	2740.00	Oliver	4	443G	4F-1R	29.9	6797	No
90 Standard	......	1250.00	2310.00	2860.00	Oliver	4	443D	4F-1R		6962	No
1950											
66 RC	......	720.00	1290.00	1600.00	Oliver	4	145G	6F-2R	23.92	3193	No
66 Standard	......	800.00	1430.00	1770.00	Oliver	4	145G	6F-2R	23.92	3193	No
66 Standard	......	1060.00	1900.00	2360.00	Oliver	4	129D	6F-2R	16.81	3293	No
77 RC	......	910.00	1630.00	2020.00	Oliver	6	194G	6F-2R	32.51	6976	No

Model	Approx. Retail Price New	Estimated Average Value Less Repairs Fair	Good	Premium	Make	Engine No. Cyls.	Engine Displ. Cu.-In.	No. Speeds	P.T.O. H.P.	Approx. Shipping Wt.-Lbs.	Cab
Oliver (Cont.)											
1950 (Cont.)											
77 Standard	......	1140.00	2040.00	2530.00	Oliver	6	194D	6F-2R	25.79	7246	No
88 Standard	......	990.00	1770.00	2200.00	Oliver	6	230G	6F-2R	41.07	5285	No
88 RC	......	970.00	1730.00	2150.00	Oliver	6	230G	6F-2R	28.96	5147	No
88 Standard	......	990.00	1770.00	2200.00	Oliver	6	231D	6F-2R	28.96	5451	No
90 Standard	......	1250.00	2240.00	2780.00	Oliver	4	443G	4F-1R	29.9	6797	No
90 Standard	......	1520.00	2720.00	3370.00	Oliver	4	443D	4F-1R		6962	No
1951											
66 RC	......	780.00	1360.00	1690.00	Oliver	4	145G	6F-2R	23.92	3193	No
66 Standard	......	880.00	1530.00	1900.00	Oliver	4	145G	6F-2R	23.92	3193	No
66 Standard	......	1130.00	1970.00	2440.00	Oliver	4	129D	6F-2R	16.81	3293	No
77 RC	......	950.00	1660.00	2060.00	Oliver	6	194G	6F-2R	32.51	6976	No
77 Standard	......	1240.00	2170.00	2690.00	Oliver	6	194D	6F-2R	25.79	7246	No
88 Standard	......	1050.00	1840.00	2280.00	Oliver	6	230G	6F-2R	41.07	5285	No
88 RC	......	1030.00	1800.00	2230.00	Oliver	6	230G	6F-2R	28.96	5147	No
88 Standard	......	1050.00	1840.00	2280.00	Oliver	6	231D	6F-2R	28.96	5451	No
90 Standard	......	1310.00	2280.00	2830.00	Oliver	4	443G	4F-1R	29.9	6797	No
90 Standard	......	1580.00	2750.00	3410.00	Oliver	4	443D	4F-1R		6962	No
1952											
66 Standard	......	810.00	1380.00	1710.00	Oliver	4	145G	6F-2R	23.92	3193	No
66 Standard	......	1200.00	2040.00	2530.00	Oliver	4	129D	6F-2R	16.81	3293	No
77 RC	......	1020.00	1730.00	2150.00	Oliver	6	194G	6F-2R	32.51	6976	No
77 Standard	......	1310.00	2230.00	2770.00	Oliver	6	194D	6F-2R	25.79	7246	No
88 Standard	......	1120.00	1900.00	2360.00	Oliver	6	230G	6F-2R	41.07	5285	No
88 RC	......	1100.00	1880.00	2330.00	Oliver	6	230G	6F-2R	28.96	5147	No
88 Standard	......	1120.00	1900.00	2360.00	Oliver	6	231D	6F-2R	28.96	5451	No
99 Standard	......	1460.00	2480.00	3080.00	Oliver	4	443G	4F-1R	54.52	7281	No
1953											
66	......	960.00	1580.00	1960.00	Oliver	4	145G	6F-2R	23.92	3193	No
66	......	1220.00	2030.00	2520.00	Oliver	4	129D	6F-2R	16.81	3293	No
77	......	880.00	1460.00	1810.00	Oliver	6	193G	6F-2R	32.51	7081	No
77	......	1300.00	2160.00	2680.00	Oliver	6	194D	6F-2R	25.79	7246	No
88 Standard	......	1190.00	1970.00	2440.00	Oliver	6	230G	6F-2R	41.07	5285	No
99 Standard	......	1600.00	2650.00	3290.00	Oliver	4	443G	4F-1R	54.52	7281	No
550	......	1320.00	2200.00	2730.00	Oliver	4	155G	6F-2R	41.39	3229	No
550	......	1470.00	2440.00	3030.00	Oliver	4	155D	6F-2R	35.36	3245	No
1954											
Super 55	......	840.00	1360.00	1690.00	Oliver	4	144G	6F-2R	32.65	3369	No
Super 55	......	1050.00	1700.00	2110.00	Oliver	4	144D	6F-2R	34	3469	No
66	......	1020.00	1650.00	2050.00	Oliver	4	145G	6F-2R	23.92	3193	No
66	......	1380.00	2230.00	2770.00	Oliver	4	129D	6F-2R	16.81	3293	No
Super 66	......	820.00	1330.00	1650.00	Oliver	6	144G	6F-2R	32.83	3943	No
Super 66	......	1030.00	1670.00	2070.00	Oliver	6	144D	6F-2R	35	4043	No
77	......	1320.00	2140.00	2650.00	Oliver	6	193G	6F-2R	32.51	7081	No
77	......	1380.00	2230.00	2770.00	Oliver	6	194D	6F-2R	25.79	7246	No
Super 77	......	1180.00	1900.00	2360.00	Oliver	6	216G	6F-2R	41.48	4915	No
Super 77	......	1470.00	2380.00	2950.00	Oliver	6	216D	6F-2R	46	5009	No
88 Standard	......	1250.00	2020.00	2510.00	Oliver	6	230G	6F-2R	41.07	5285	No
Super 88	......	1340.00	2180.00	2700.00	Oliver	6	265G	6F-2R	53.4	4700	No
Super 88	......	1680.00	2720.00	3370.00	Oliver	6	265D	6F-2R	56	5390	No
99 Standard	......	1680.00	2720.00	3370.00	Oliver	4	443G	4F-1R	54.52	7281	No
Super 99	......	1620.00	2620.00	3250.00	Oliver	6	302G	6F-2R	62.2	7337	No
Super 99	......	1930.00	3130.00	3880.00	Oliver	6	302D	6F-2R	62.4	7347	No
550	......	1380.00	2240.00	2780.00	Oliver	4	155G	6F-2R	41.39	3229	No
550	......	1530.00	2480.00	3080.00	Oliver	4	155D	6F-2R	35.36	3245	No
1955											
Super 55	......	860.00	1360.00	1690.00	Oliver	4	144G	6F-2R	32.65	3369	No
Super 55	......	1100.00	1730.00	2150.00	Oliver	4	144D	6F-2R	34	3469	No
Super 66	......	880.00	1390.00	1720.00	Oliver	6	144G	6F-2R	32.83	3943	No
Super 66	......	1140.00	1800.00	2230.00	Oliver	6	144D	6F-2R	35	4043	No
Super 77	......	1290.00	2040.00	2530.00	Oliver	6	216G	6F-2R	41.48	4915	No
Super 77	......	1550.00	2450.00	3040.00	Oliver	6	216D	6F-2R	46	5009	No
Super 88	......	1510.00	2380.00	2950.00	Oliver	6	265G	6F-2R	53.4	4700	No
Super 88	......	1760.00	2790.00	3460.00	Oliver	6	265D	6F-2R	56	5390	No
99 Standard	......	1790.00	2820.00	3500.00	Oliver	4	443G	4F-1R	54.52	7281	No
Super 99	......	1720.00	2720.00	3370.00	Oliver	6	302G	6F-2R	62.2	7337	No
Super 99	......	2040.00	3230.00	4010.00	Oliver	6	302D	6F-2R	62.4	7347	No
550	......	1440.00	2270.00	2820.00	Oliver	4	155G	6F-2R	41.39	3229	No
550	......	1590.00	2510.00	3110.00	Oliver	4	155D	6F-2R	35.36	3245	No
1956											
Super 55	......	1210.00	1870.00	2320.00	Oliver	4	144D	6F-2R	34	3469	No
Super 55	......	840.00	1300.00	1610.00	Oliver	4	144G	6F-2R	32.65	3369	No
Super 66	......	990.00	1530.00	1900.00	Oliver	6	144G	6F-2R	32.83	3943	No
Super 66	......	1250.00	1940.00	2410.00	Oliver	6	144D	6F-2R	35	4043	No
Super 77	......	1410.00	2180.00	2700.00	Oliver	6	216G	6F-2R	41.48	4915	No
Super 77	......	1650.00	2550.00	3160.00	Oliver	6	216D	6F-2R	46	5009	No
Super 88	......	1570.00	2420.00	3000.00	Oliver	6	265G	6F-2R	53.4	4700	No
Super 88	......	1850.00	2860.00	3550.00	Oliver	6	265D	6F-2R	56	5390	No
99 Standard	......	1850.00	2860.00	3550.00	Oliver	4	443G	4F-1R	54.52	7281	No

Model	Approx. Retail Price New	Estimated Average Value Less Repairs Fair	Good	Premium	Engine Make	No. Cyls.	Displ. Cu.-In.	No. Speeds	P.T.O. H.P.	Approx. Shipping Wt.-Lbs.	Cab
Oliver (Cont.)											
			1956 (Cont.)								
Super 99	......	1850.00	2860.00	3550.00	Oliver	6	302G	6F-2R	62.2	7337	No
Super 99	......	2180.00	3370.00	4180.00	Oliver	6	302D	6F-2R	62.4	7347	No
550	......	1490.00	2310.00	2860.00	Oliver	4	155G	6F-2R	41.39	3229	No
550	......	1650.00	2550.00	3160.00	Oliver	4	155D	6F-2R	35.36	3245	No
			1957								
Super 44	......	1370.00	2070.00	2570.00	Continental		302G	4F-1R	28	2386	No
Super 55	......	1520.00	2300.00	2850.00	Oliver	4	144D	6F-2R	34	3469	No
Super 55	......	1580.00	2380.00	2950.00	Oliver	4	144G	6F-2R	32.65	3369	No
Super 66	......	1670.00	2520.00	3130.00	Oliver	6	144D	6F-2R	35	4043	No
Super 66	......	1760.00	2650.00	3290.00	Oliver	6	144G	6F-2R	32.83	3943	No
Super 77	......	1630.00	2470.00	3060.00	Oliver	6	216G	6F-2R	41.48	4915	No
Super 77	......	1820.00	2750.00	3410.00	Oliver	6	216D	6F-2R	46	5009	No
Super 88	......	1710.00	2580.00	3200.00	Oliver	6	265G	6F-2R	53.4	4700	No
Super 88	......	2030.00	3060.00	3790.00	Oliver	6	265D	6F-2R	56	5390	No
99 Standard	......	1940.00	2920.00	3620.00	Oliver	4	443G	4F-1R	54.52	7281	No
Super 99	......	2000.00	3030.00	3760.00	Oliver	6	302G	6F-2R	62.2	7337	No
Super 99	......	2250.00	3400.00	4220.00	Oliver	6	302D	6F-2R	62.4	7347	No
550	......	1550.00	2340.00	2900.00	Oliver	4	155D	6F-2R	35.36	3245	No
550	......	1720.00	2600.00	3220.00	Oliver	4	155G	6F-2R	41.39	3229	No
			1958								
Super 44	......	1400.00	2110.00	2620.00	Continental		302G	4F-1R	28	2386	No
Super 55	......	1310.00	1970.00	2440.00	Oliver	4	144G	6F-2R	32.65	3369	No
Super 55	......	1380.00	2090.00	2590.00	Oliver	4	144D	6F-2R	34	3469	No
Super 66	......	1450.00	2190.00	2720.00	Oliver	6	144G	6F-2R	32.83	3943	No
Super 66	......	1530.00	2310.00	2860.00	Oliver	6	144D	6F-2R	35	4043	No
Super 77	......	1590.00	2400.00	2980.00	Oliver	6	216G	6F-2R	41.48	4915	No
Super 77	......	1870.00	2820.00	3500.00	Oliver	6	216D	6F-2R	46	5009	No
Super 88	......	1780.00	2690.00	3340.00	Oliver	6	265G	6F-2R	53.4	4700	No
Super 88	......	2080.00	3150.00	3910.00	Oliver	6	265D	6F-2R	56	5390	No
Super 99	......	2100.00	3180.00	3940.00	Oliver	6	302G	6F-2R	62.2	7337	No
Super 99	......	2480.00	3740.00	4640.00	Oliver	6	302D	6F-2R	62.4	7347	No
550	......	1590.00	2400.00	2980.00	Oliver	4	155G	6F-2R	41.39	3229	No
550	......	1800.00	2720.00	3370.00	Oliver	4	155D	6F-2R	35.36	3245	No
770	......	2230.00	3370.00	4180.00	Oliver	6	216G	6F-2R	47.59	5286	No
770	......	2410.00	3640.00	4510.00	Oliver	6	216D	6F-2R	52	5425	No
880	......	2270.00	3430.00	4250.00	Oliver	6	265G	12F-2R	57.43	5492	No
880	......	2520.00	3810.00	4720.00	Oliver	6	265D	12F-2R	62	5631	No
950	......	2250.00	3400.00	4220.00	Oliver	6	302G	6F-2R	59.75	7303	No
950	......	2660.00	4030.00	5000.00	Oliver	6	302D	6F-2R	70	10415	No
990	......	4000.00	6040.00	7490.00	GM	3T	213D	6F-2R	84.10	10980	No
995	......	4000.00	6040.00	7490.00	GM	3T	213D	6F-2R	85.37	11245	No
			1959								
Super 44	......	1500.00	2210.00	2740.00	Continental		302G	4F-1R	28	2386	No
550	......	1660.00	2460.00	3050.00	Oliver	4	155G	6F-2R	41.39	3229	No
550	......	1920.00	2840.00	3520.00	Oliver	4	155D	6F-2R	35.36	3245	No
660	......	1760.00	2600.00	3220.00	Oliver	4	155G	6F-2R	40	4047	No
660	......	2000.00	2950.00	3660.00	Oliver	6	155D	6F-2R	41	4147	No
770	......	2340.00	3450.00	4280.00	Oliver	6	216G	6F-2R	47.59	5286	No
770	......	2490.00	3680.00	4560.00	Oliver	6	216D	6F-2R	52	5425	No
880	......	2350.00	3470.00	4300.00	Oliver	6	265G	12F-2R	57.43	5492	No
880	......	2610.00	3850.00	4770.00	Oliver	6	265D	12F-2R	62	5631	No
950	......	2340.00	3450.00	4280.00	Oliver	6	302G	6F-2R	59.75	7303	No
950	......	2770.00	4090.00	5070.00	Oliver	6	302D	6F-2R	70	10415	No
990	......	4140.00	6120.00	7590.00	GM	3T	213D	6F-2R	84.10	10980	No
995	......	4140.00	6120.00	7590.00	GM	3T	213D	6F-2R	85.37	11245	No
			1960								
440	......	1520.00	2240.00	2780.00	Oliver	4	140G	4F-1R	28	2497	No
550	......	1690.00	2500.00	3100.00	Oliver	4	155G	6F-2R	41.39	3229	No
550	......	1960.00	2890.00	3580.00	Oliver	4	155D	6F-2R	35.36	3245	No
660	......	1790.00	2640.00	3270.00	Oliver	4	155G	6F-2R	40	4047	No
660	......	2020.00	2990.00	3710.00	Oliver	6	155D	6F-2R	41	4147	No
770	......	2340.00	3460.00	4290.00	Oliver	6	216G	6F-2R	47.59	5286	No
770	......	2520.00	3730.00	4630.00	Oliver	6	216D	6F-2R	52	5425	No
880	......	2370.00	3510.00	4350.00	Oliver	6	265G	12F-2R	57.43	5492	No
880	......	2630.00	3890.00	4820.00	Oliver	6	265D	12F-2R	62	5631	No
950	......	2430.00	3590.00	4450.00	Oliver	6	302G	6F-2R	59.75	7303	No
950	......	2860.00	4230.00	5250.00	Oliver	6	302D	6F-2R	70	10415	No
990	......	4240.00	6270.00	7780.00	GM	3T	213D	6F-2R	84.10	10980	No
995	......	4240.00	6270.00	7780.00	GM	3T	213D	6F-2R	85.37	11245	No
1800 4WD	......	2590.00	4610.00	5620.00	Oliver	6	265G	18F-6R	86.98	9680	No
1800 4WD	......	2860.00	5090.00	6210.00	Oliver	6	283D	6F-2R	77	9810	No
1800 Tricycle	......	1950.00	3460.00	4220.00	Oliver	6	265G	6F-2R	73.92	8410	No
1800 Tricycle	......	2260.00	4010.00	4890.00	Oliver	6	283D	6F-2R	77	8670	No
1800 Wheatland	......	2070.00	3680.00	4490.00	Oliver	6	265G	6F-2R	73.92	10280	No
1800 Wheatland	......	2310.00	4100.00	5000.00	Oliver	6	283D	6F-2R	77	10420	No
1900 2WD	......	3030.00	5390.00	6580.00	Oliver	4	212D	12F-4R	89.35	11925	No
1900 4WD	......	3850.00	5060.00	5720.00	GM	4	212D	6F-2R	89.35	12050	No
1900 Wheatland	......	3070.00	5450.00	6650.00	GM	4	212G	10F-2R	101	10870	No
1900 Wheatland	......	3110.00	5540.00	6760.00	GM	4T	212D	10F-2R	89.35	10990	No

Oliver (Cont.)

Model	Approx. Retail Price New	Estimated Average Value Less Repairs Fair	Good	Premium	Engine Make	No. Cyls.	Displ. Cu.-In.	No. Speeds	P.T.O. H.P.	Approx. Shipping Wt.-Lbs.	Cab
1961											
440	......	1550.00	2290.00	2840.00	Oliver	4	140G	4F-1R	28	2497	No
550	......	1720.00	2540.00	3150.00	Oliver	4	155D	6F-2R	35.36	3245	No
550	......	1980.00	2920.00	3620.00	Oliver	4	155G	6F-2R	41.39	3229	No
660	......	1810.00	2680.00	3320.00	Oliver	6	155D	6F-2R	41	4147	No
660	......	2050.00	3030.00	3760.00	Oliver	4	155G	6F-2R	40	4047	No
770	......	2370.00	3500.00	4340.00	Oliver	6	216D	6F-2R	52	5425	No
770	......	2550.00	3770.00	4680.00	Oliver	6	216G	6F-2R	47.59	5286	No
880	......	2400.00	3550.00	4400.00	Oliver	6	265D	12F-2R	62	5631	No
880	......	2650.00	3920.00	4860.00	Oliver	6	265G	12F-2R	57.43	5492	No
950	......	2520.00	3720.00	4610.00	Oliver	6	302G	6F-2R	59.75	7303	No
950	......	2910.00	4300.00	5330.00	Oliver	6	302D	6F-2R	70	10415	No
990	......	4320.00	6380.00	7910.00	GM	3T	213D	6F-2R	84.10	10980	No
995	......	4320.00	6380.00	7910.00	GM	3T	213D	6F-2R	85.37	11245	No
1800 4WD	......	2700.00	4670.00	5700.00	Oliver	6	265G	18F-6R	86.98	9680	No
1800 4WD	......	2980.00	5150.00	6280.00	Oliver	6	283D	6F-2R	77	9810	No
1800 Tricycle	......	2080.00	3590.00	4380.00	Oliver	6	265G	6F-2R	73.92	8410	No
1800 Tricycle	......	2360.00	4080.00	4980.00	Oliver	6	283D	6F-2R	77	8670	No
1800 Wheatland	......	2170.00	3740.00	4560.00	Oliver	6	265G	6F-2R	73.92	10280	No
1800 Wheatland	......	2450.00	4230.00	5160.00	Oliver	6	283D	6F-2R	77	10420	No
1900 2WD	......	3160.00	5470.00	6670.00	Oliver	4	212D	12F-4R	89.35	11925	No
1900 4WD	......	3890.00	5110.00	5770.00	GM	4	212D	6F-2R	89.35	12050	No
1900 Wheatland	......	3230.00	5580.00	6810.00	GM	4	212G	10F-2R	101	10870	No
1900 Wheatland	......	3270.00	5650.00	6890.00	GM	4T	212D	10F-2R	89.35	10990	No
1962											
440	2420.00	1570.00	2330.00	2890.00	Oliver	4	140G	4F-1R	28	2497	No
550	2675.00	1750.00	2580.00	3200.00	Oliver	4	155G	6F-2R	41.39	3229	No
550	3430.00	2000.00	2960.00	3670.00	Oliver	4	155D	6F-2R	39.2	3245	No
660	3000.00	1840.00	2720.00	3370.00	Oliver	4	155G	6F-2R	40	3362	No
660	3420.00	2030.00	3010.00	3730.00	Oliver	6	155D	6F-2R	39	3378	No
770	3750.00	2390.00	3540.00	4390.00	Oliver	6	216G	6F-2R	51.6	4686	No
770	4620.00	2580.00	3810.00	4720.00	Oliver	6	216D	6F-2R	50	4864	No
880	4870.00	2700.00	3990.00	4950.00	Oliver	6	265G	12F-2R	64.2	5069	No
880	5450.00	2970.00	4390.00	5440.00	Oliver	6	265D	12F-2R	62	5274	No
1600	4650.00	2600.00	3840.00	4760.00	Oliver	6	231G	6F-2R	57	6240	No
1600	5250.00	2880.00	4250.00	5270.00	Oliver	6	265D	6F-2R	57.95	6360	No
1600 4WD	7250.00	3140.00	5280.00	6440.00	Oliver	6	231G	6F-2R	57	8020	No
1600 4WD	7850.00	3360.00	5660.00	6910.00	Oliver	6	265D	6F-2R	57.95	8140	No
1800	5310.00	2400.00	4040.00	4930.00	Oliver	6	265G	6F-2R	80.1	8208	No
1800	5940.00	2640.00	4440.00	5420.00	Oliver	6	283D	6F-2R	77	8493	No
1800 4WD	7450.00	3210.00	5410.00	6600.00	Oliver	6	265G	18F-6R	80.	9728	No
1800 4WD	8150.00	3480.00	5860.00	7150.00	Oliver	6	283D	6F-2R	77	9848	No
1900	8650.00	3670.00	6180.00	7540.00	Oliver	4	212D	12F-4R	98	11500	No
1900 4WD	11200.00	3920.00	5150.00	5820.00	GM	4	212D	6F-2R	100	12340	No
1900 Wheatland	......	3350.00	5650.00	6890.00	GM	4	212G	10F-2R	101	10870	No
1900 Wheatland	......	3390.00	5710.00	6970.00	GM	4T	212D	10F-2R	89.35	10990	No
1963											
550	2700.00	1770.00	2620.00	3250.00	Oliver	4	155G	6F-2R	41.39	3229	No
550	3460.00	2020.00	2990.00	3710.00	Oliver	4	155D	6F-2R	39.2	3245	No
660	3008.00	1870.00	2760.00	3420.00	Oliver	4	155G	6F-2R	40	3362	No
660	3455.00	2070.00	3060.00	3790.00	Oliver	6	155D	6F-2R	39	3378	No
770	3788.00	2430.00	3600.00	4460.00	Oliver	6	216G	6F-2R	51.6	4686	No
770	4653.00	2600.00	3840.00	4760.00	Oliver	6	216D	6F-2R	50.7	4864	No
880	4900.00	2710.00	4010.00	4970.00	Oliver	6	265G	6F-2R	64.2	5069	No
880	5475.00	2980.00	4400.00	5460.00	Oliver	6	265D	6F-2R	62	5274	No
1600	4675.00	2610.00	3860.00	4790.00	Oliver	6	231G	12F-4R	57	6240	No
1600	5267.00	2880.00	4260.00	5280.00	Oliver	6	265D	12F-4R	57.95	6360	No
1600 4WD	7267.00	3220.00	5290.00	6450.00	Oliver	6	231G	12F-4R	57	8020	No
1600 4WD	7861.00	3460.00	5670.00	6920.00	Oliver	6	265D	12F-4R	57.95	8140	No
1800	5330.00	2470.00	4050.00	4940.00	Oliver	6	265G	12F-4R	80.16	8208	No
1800	5953.00	2710.00	4450.00	5430.00	Oliver	6	283D	12F-4R	77	8493	No
1800 4WD	7488.00	3310.00	5430.00	6630.00	Oliver	6	265G	12F-4R	80.8	9728	No
1800 4WD	8172.00	3580.00	5870.00	7160.00	Oliver	6	283D	12F-4R	77	9848	No
1900	8678.00	3770.00	6190.00	7550.00	Oliver	4	212D	12F-4R	98.	11500	No
1900 4WD	11230.00	4020.00	5290.00	5980.00	GM	4	212D	12F-4R	98.	12340	No
1964											
550	2970.00	1790.00	2650.00	3290.00	Oliver	4	155G	6F-2R	41.39	3229	No
550	3806.00	2050.00	3030.00	3760.00	Oliver	4	155D	6F-2R	39.2	3245	No
660	3265.00	1960.00	2900.00	3600.00	Oliver	4	155G	6F-2R	40	3362	No
660	3760.00	2190.00	3240.00	4020.00	Oliver	6	155D	6F-2R	39	3378	No
770	3864.00	2470.00	3650.00	4530.00	Oliver	6	216G	6F-2R	51.6	4686	No
770	4746.00	2650.00	3910.00	4850.00	Oliver	6	216D	6F-2R	50.7	4864	No
1650	5192.00	2850.00	4210.00	5220.00	Oliver	6	265G	12F-4R	66.7	6727	No
1650	5852.00	3150.00	4660.00	5780.00	Oliver	6	283D	12F-4R	66.2	7063	No
1650 4WD	8075.00	3670.00	5870.00	7160.00	Oliver	6	265G	12F-4R	66.7	8451	No
1650 4WD	8735.00	3950.00	6320.00	7710.00	Oliver	6	283D	12F-4R	66.2	8538	No
1750	5720.00	2690.00	4300.00	5250.00	Oliver	6	283G	12F-4R	80.3	8530	No
1750	6320.00	2930.00	4690.00	5720.00	Oliver	6	310D	12F-4R	80	8660	No
1850	6220.00	2890.00	4620.00	5640.00	Oliver	6	310G	12F-4R	92.43	8888	No
1850	6980.00	3190.00	5110.00	6230.00	Perkins	6	352D	12F-4R	92.9	9000	No
1850 4WD	8710.00	3400.00	4470.00	5050.00	Oliver	6	310G	12F-4R	92.43	10843	No
1850 4WD	9470.00	3670.00	4820.00	5450.00	Perkins	6	352D	12F-4R	92.9	11012	No

Oliver (Cont.)

Model	Approx. Retail Price New	Estimated Average Value Less Repairs: Fair	Good	Premium	Engine Make	No. Cyls.	Displ. Cu.-In.	No. Speeds	P.T.O. H.P.	Approx. Shipping Wt.-Lbs.	Cab
			1964 (Cont.)								
1950	9657.00	**3730.00**	**4900.00**	**5540.00**	GM	4T	212D	12F-4R	105.79	11500	No
1950 4WD	12147.00	**4250.00**	**5590.00**	**6320.00**	GM	4T	212D	12F-4R	105.79	12340	No
			1965								
550	3000.00	**1820.00**	**2690.00**	**3340.00**	Oliver	4	155G	6F-2R	41.39	3229	No
550	3844.00	**2070.00**	**3060.00**	**3790.00**	Oliver	4	155D	6F-2R	39.2	3245	No
770	3903.00	**2490.00**	**3670.00**	**4550.00**	Oliver	6	216G	6F-2R	51.6	4686	No
770	4795.00	**2690.00**	**3980.00**	**4940.00**	Oliver	6	216D	6F-2R	52	4864	No
1250	2878.00	**1780.00**	**2640.00**	**3270.00**	Oliver	4	116G	6F-2R	35	3548	No
1250	3135.00	**1900.00**	**2810.00**	**3480.00**	Oliver	4	138D	6F-2R	35	3666	No
1250 4WD	3850.00	**2230.00**	**3300.00**	**4090.00**	Oliver	4	116G	6F-2R	35	4060	No
1250 4WD	4107.00	**2350.00**	**3470.00**	**4300.00**	Oliver	4	138D	6F-2R	35	4176	No
1550	4980.00	**2750.00**	**4070.00**	**5050.00**	Oliver	6	232G	12F-4R	53.3	6822	No
1550	5555.00	**3020.00**	**4460.00**	**5530.00**	Oliver	6	232D	12F-4R	53.5	5556	No
1650	5245.00	**2870.00**	**4250.00**	**5270.00**	Oliver	6	265G	12F-4R	66.7	7022	No
1650	5911.00	**3180.00**	**4700.00**	**5830.00**	Oliver	6	283D	12F-4R	66.2	7143	No
1650 4WD	8155.00	**3750.00**	**5860.00**	**7150.00**	Oliver	6	265G	12F-4R	66.7	8418	No
1650 4WD	8821.00	**4030.00**	**6290.00**	**7670.00**	Oliver	6	283D	12F-4R	66.2	8538	No
1750	5777.00	**2780.00**	**4340.00**	**5300.00**	Oliver	6	283G	12F-4R	80.3	8530	No
1750	6383.00	**3030.00**	**4730.00**	**5770.00**	Oliver	6	310D	12F-4R	80	8660	No
1850	6282.00	**2990.00**	**4660.00**	**5690.00**	Oliver	6	310G	12F-4R	92.43	8883	No
1850	7050.00	**3300.00**	**5150.00**	**6280.00**	Perkins	6	352D	12F-4R	92.9	9000	No
1850 4WD	8797.00	**3430.00**	**4510.00**	**5100.00**	Oliver	6	310G	12F-4R	92.43	9265	No
1850 4WD	9565.00	**3700.00**	**4860.00**	**5490.00**	Perkins	6	352D	12F-4R	92.9	10485	No
1950	9755.00	**3760.00**	**4950.00**	**5590.00**	GM	4T	212D	12F-4R	105.79	10500	No
1950 4WD	12268.00	**4290.00**	**5640.00**	**6370.00**	GM	4T	212D	12F-4R	105.79	12340	No
			1966								
550	3150.00	**1880.00**	**2720.00**	**3370.00**	Oliver	4	155G	6F-2R	41.39	3229	No
550	4017.00	**2140.00**	**3100.00**	**3840.00**	Oliver	4	155D	6F-2R	35.36	3245	No
770	4078.00	**2620.00**	**3790.00**	**4700.00**	Oliver	6	216G	6F-2R	45	4686	No
770	5009.00	**2820.00**	**4090.00**	**5070.00**	Oliver	6	216D	6F-2R	50	4864	No
1250	3000.00	**1880.00**	**2720.00**	**3370.00**	Oliver	4	116G	6F-2R	35	3548	No
1250	3277.00	**2010.00**	**2910.00**	**3610.00**	Oliver	4	138D	6F-2R	35	3666	No
1250 4WD	4023.00	**2360.00**	**3420.00**	**4240.00**	Oliver	4	116G	6F-2R	35	4060	No
1250 4WD	4295.00	**2490.00**	**3600.00**	**4460.00**	Oliver	4	138D	6F-2R	35	4176	No
1550	5230.00	**2930.00**	**4240.00**	**5260.00**	Oliver	6	232G	12F-4R	53.3	6822	No
1550	5835.00	**3210.00**	**4650.00**	**5770.00**	Oliver	6	232D	12F-4R	53.5	6941	No
1650	5506.00	**3060.00**	**4420.00**	**5480.00**	Oliver	6	265G	12F-4R	66.7	7022	No
1650	6207.00	**3390.00**	**4900.00**	**6080.00**	Oliver	6	283D	12F-4R	66.2	7143	No
1650 4WD	8563.00	**4020.00**	**6120.00**	**7470.00**	Oliver	6	265G	12F-4R	66.7	8420	No
1650 4WD	9262.00	**4230.00**	**6440.00**	**7860.00**	Oliver	6	283D	12F-4R	66.2	8538	No
1750	6056.00	**2960.00**	**4520.00**	**5510.00**	Oliver	6	283G	12F-4R	80.3	8530	No
1750	6705.00	**3240.00**	**4930.00**	**6020.00**	Oliver	6	310D	12F-4R	80	8660	No
1850	6596.00	**3190.00**	**4860.00**	**5930.00**	Oliver	6	310G	12F-4R	92.43	8888	No
1850	7405.00	**3530.00**	**5380.00**	**6560.00**	Perkins	6	352D	12F-4R	92.9	9000	No
1850 4WD	9237.00	**3510.00**	**4620.00**	**5220.00**	Oliver	6	310G	12F-4R	92.43	10843	No
1850 4WD	10045.00	**3690.00**	**4850.00**	**5480.00**	Perkins	6	352D	12F-4R	92.9	11012	No
1950	9852.00	**3800.00**	**4990.00**	**5640.00**	GM	4T	212D	12F-4R	105.79	10500	No
1950 4WD	12390.00	**4340.00**	**5700.00**	**6440.00**	GM	4T	212D	12F-4R	105.79	12800	No
			1967								
550	3182.00	**1900.00**	**2750.00**	**3410.00**	Oliver	4	155G	6F-2R	41.39	3229	No
550	4057.00	**2160.00**	**3130.00**	**3880.00**	Oliver	4	155D	6F-2R	35.36	3245	No
770	4120.00	**2680.00**	**3880.00**	**4810.00**	Oliver	6	216G	6F-2R	47.59	4686	No
770	5060.00	**2900.00**	**4190.00**	**5200.00**	Oliver	6	216D	6F-2R	52	4864	No
1250	3038.00	**1900.00**	**2750.00**	**3410.00**	Oliver	4	116G	6F-2R	35	3510	No
1250	3310.00	**2030.00**	**2930.00**	**3630.00**	Oliver	4	138D	6F-2R	35	3666	No
1250 4WD	4063.00	**2380.00**	**3440.00**	**4270.00**	Oliver	4	116G	6F-2R	35	4060	No
1250 4WD	4335.00	**2510.00**	**3630.00**	**4500.00**	Oliver	4	138D	6F-2R	35	4176	No
1450	5292.00	**2960.00**	**4280.00**	**5310.00**	Oliver	4	268D	14F-4R	55	5520	No
1450 4WD	6705.00	**3620.00**	**5240.00**	**6500.00**	Oliver	4	268D	14F-4R	55	6118	No
1550	5492.00	**3050.00**	**4420.00**	**5480.00**	Oliver	6	232G	12F-4R	53.3	6822	No
1550	6126.00	**3350.00**	**4850.00**	**6010.00**	Oliver	6	232D	12F-4R	53.5	6941	No
1650	5781.00	**3190.00**	**4610.00**	**5720.00**	Oliver	6	265G	12F-4R	66.7	7022	No
1650	6517.00	**3530.00**	**5110.00**	**6340.00**	Oliver	6	283D	12F-4R	66.2	7145	No
1650 4WD	8990.00	**4300.00**	**6390.00**	**7800.00**	Oliver	6	265G	12F-4R	66.7	8418	No
1650 4WD	9725.00	**4400.00**	**6540.00**	**7980.00**	Oliver	6	283D	12F-4R	66.2	8538	No
1750	6359.00	**3160.00**	**4710.00**	**5750.00**	Oliver	6	283G	12F-4R	80.3	8530	No
1750	7037.00	**3460.00**	**5140.00**	**6270.00**	Oliver	6	310D	12F-4R	80	8660	No
1850	6926.00	**3410.00**	**5070.00**	**6190.00**	Oliver	6	310G	12F-4R	92.43	8888	No
1850	7775.00	**3770.00**	**5620.00**	**6860.00**	Perkins	6	352D	12F-4R	92.9	9000	No
1850 4WD	9700.00	**3570.00**	**4690.00**	**5300.00**	Oliver	6	310G	12F-4R	92.43	9699	No
1850 4WD	10545.00	**3760.00**	**4940.00**	**5580.00**	Perkins	6	352D	12F-4R	92.9	11012	No
1950	10345.00	**3620.00**	**4760.00**	**5380.00**	GM	4T	212D	12F-4R	105.79	11500	No
1950 4WD	13010.00	**4550.00**	**5990.00**	**6770.00**	GM	4T	212D	12F-4R	105.79	12800	No
1950T	10797.00	**3780.00**	**4970.00**	**5620.00**	Oliver	6T	212D	18F-6R	105.2	11100	No
1950T 4WD	13475.00	**4720.00**	**6200.00**	**7010.00**	Oliver	6T	310D	18F-6R	105.79	13200	No
			1968								
550	3341.00	**1970.00**	**2790.00**	**3460.00**	Oliver	4	155G	6F-2R	41.39	3229	No
550	4260.00	**2230.00**	**3160.00**	**3920.00**	Oliver	4	155D	6F-2R	35.36	3245	No
1250	3190.00	**2010.00**	**2850.00**	**3530.00**	Oliver	4	116G	6F-2R	35	3510	No
1250	3476.00	**2150.00**	**3040.00**	**3770.00**	Oliver	4	138D	6F-2R	35	3666	No

Oliver (Cont.)

1968 (Cont.)

Model	Approx. Retail Price New	Fair	Estimated Average Value Less Repairs Good	Premium	Engine Make	No. Cyls.	Displ. Cu.-In.	No. Speeds	P.T.O. H.P.	Approx. Shipping Wt.-Lbs.	Cab
1250 4WD	4266.00	2430.00	3450.00	4280.00	Oliver	4	116G	6F-2R	35	4060	No
1250 4WD	4552.00	2670.00	3780.00	4690.00	Oliver	4	138D	6F-2R	35	4176	No
1450	5557.00	3150.00	4460.00	5530.00	Oliver	4	268D	7F-2R	55	5520	No
1450 4WD	7040.00	3860.00	5470.00	6780.00	Oliver	4	268D	14F-4R	55	6120	No
1550	5767.00	3250.00	4600.00	5700.00	Oliver	6	232G	6F-2R	53.3	6822	No
1550	6432.00	3570.00	5050.00	6260.00	Oliver	6	232D	6F-2R	53.5	6940	No
1650	6995.00	3820.00	5420.00	6720.00	Oliver	6	265G	12F-2R	66.7	7022	No
1650	7725.00	4190.00	5930.00	7350.00	Oliver	6	283D	12F-2R	66.2	7143	No
1650 4WD	9155.00	4250.00	6180.00	7540.00	Oliver	6	265G	12F-2R	66.7	8418	No
1650 4WD	9875.00	4520.00	6580.00	8030.00	Oliver	6	283D	12F-2R	66.2	8538	No
1750	7150.00	3590.00	5220.00	6370.00	Oliver	6	283G	12F-4R	80.3	8530	No
1750	7900.00	3920.00	5700.00	6950.00	Oliver	6	310D	12F-4R	80	8660	No
1750 4WD	10200.00	4580.00	6660.00	8130.00	Oliver	6	283G	12F-4R	80.3	10550	No
1750 4WD	11000.00	4840.00	7040.00	8590.00	Oliver	6	310D	12F-4R	80	10660	No
1850	8000.00	3960.00	5760.00	7030.00	Oliver	6	310G	12F-4R	92.43	8880	No
1850	8900.00	4360.00	6340.00	7740.00	Perkins	6	352D	12F-4R	92.9	9000	No
1850 4WD	10600.00	4660.00	6780.00	8270.00	Oliver	6	310G	12F-4R	92.43	10843	No
1850 4WD	11600.00	5100.00	7420.00	9050.00	Perkins	6	352D	12F-4R	92.9	11012	No
1950	10448.00	3760.00	4810.00	5440.00	GM	4T	212D	5F-5R	105.79	11500	No
1950 4WD	13140.00	4730.00	6040.00	6830.00	GM	4T	212D	5F-5R	105.79	12800	No
1950T	10900.00	3920.00	5010.00	5660.00	Oliver	6T	212D	6F-2R	105.2	10860	No
1950T 4WD	13600.00	4900.00	6260.00	7070.00	Oliver	6T	310D	6F-2R	105.79	13200	No
1955	10115.00	3680.00	4700.00	5310.00	Oliver	6T	310D	18F-6R	108.16	10750	No
1955 4WD	14000.00	5040.00	6440.00	7280.00	Oliver	6T	310D	18F-6R	108.1	12850	No
2050	12820.00	4620.00	5900.00	6670.00	Oliver	6	478D	6F-2R	118.8	12900	No
2050 4WD	14256.00	5130.00	6560.00	7410.00	Oliver	6	478D	18F-6R	118.8	15000	No
2150	13523.00	4870.00	6220.00	7030.00	Oliver	6T	478D	18F-6R	131.48	12815	No
2150 4WD	14969.00	5390.00	6890.00	7790.00	Oliver	6T	478D	18F-6R	131.48	15100	No

1969

Model	Approx. Retail Price New	Fair	Good	Premium	Make	No. Cyls.	Displ. Cu.-In.	No. Speeds	P.T.O. H.P.	Approx. Shipping Wt.-Lbs.	Cab
550	3508.00	2060.00	2860.00	3550.00	Oliver	4	155G	6F-2R	41.39	3229	No
550	4303.00	2330.00	3230.00	4010.00	Oliver	4	155D	6F-2R	39.2	3245	No
1250	3350.00	2130.00	2960.00	3670.00	Oliver	4	116G	6F-2R	35	3548	No
1250	3650.00	2280.00	3160.00	3920.00	Oliver	4	138D	6F-2R	35	3666	No
1250 4WD	4480.00	2690.00	3730.00	4630.00	Oliver	4	116G	6F-2R	35	4060	No
1250 4WD	4780.00	2830.00	3930.00	4870.00	Oliver	4	138D	6F-2R	35	4176	No
1255	4185.00	2540.00	3530.00	4380.00	Oliver	3	143D	9F-3R	38.5	3906	No
1255 4WD	5200.00	2940.00	4080.00	5060.00	Oliver	3	143D	9F-3R	38.5	4456	No
1355	5210.00	3090.00	4280.00	5310.00	Oliver	4	190D	12F-3R	51	4566	No
1355 4WD	6120.00	3390.00	4710.00	5840.00	Oliver	4	190D	12F-3R	51	5116	No
1450	5880.00	3370.00	4680.00	5800.00	Oliver	4	268D	7F-2R	55	5520	No
1450 4WD	7450.00	4040.00	5610.00	6960.00	Oliver	4	268D	14F-4R	55	6120	No
1550	6226.00	3540.00	4910.00	6090.00	Oliver	6	232G	6F-2R	53.3	6822	No
1550	6945.00	3890.00	5400.00	6700.00	Oliver	6	232D	6F-2R	53.5	6940	No
1555	5682.00	3270.00	4540.00	5630.00	Oliver	6	232G	12F-4R	53	6770	No
1555	6745.00	3800.00	5270.00	6540.00	Oliver	6	232D	12F-4R	53	6999	No
1655	6795.00	3830.00	5320.00	6600.00	Oliver	6	265G	6F-2R	70.2	7023	No
1655	7605.00	4220.00	5860.00	7270.00	Oliver	6	283D	6F-2R	70.5	7315	No
1655 4WD	10333.00	3820.00	4750.00	5370.00	Oliver	6	265G	18F-3R	70.2	8733	No
1655 4WD	11145.00	4120.00	5130.00	5800.00	Oliver	6	283D	18F-3R	70.5	8850	No
1750	7430.00	3790.00	5400.00	6590.00	Oliver	6	283G	12F-4R	80.3	8530	No
1750	8140.00	4110.00	5850.00	7140.00	Oliver	6	310D	12F-4R	80	8660	No
1750 4WD	10700.00	3960.00	4920.00	5560.00	Oliver	6	283G	12F-4R	80.3	10550	No
1750 4WD	11455.00	4240.00	5270.00	5960.00	Oliver	6	310D	12F-4R	80	10660	No
1850	8270.00	4170.00	5930.00	7240.00	Oliver	6	310G	12F-4R	92.43	8880	No
1850	9210.00	4510.00	6410.00	7820.00	Perkins	6	352D	12F-4R	92.9	9000	No
1850 4WD	10950.00	4050.00	5040.00	5700.00	Oliver	6	310G	12F-4R	92.43	10843	No
1850 4WD	11880.00	4400.00	5470.00	6180.00	Perkins	6	352D	12F-4R	92.9	11012	No
1855	9105.00	4550.00	6470.00	7890.00	Oliver	6	310G	6F-2R	98.6	9190	No
1855	10090.00	4770.00	6780.00	8270.00	Oliver	6T	310D	6F-2R	99	9315	No
1855 4WD	11918.00	4410.00	5480.00	6190.00	Oliver	6	310G	18F-6R	99	11943	No
1855 4WD	12894.00	4770.00	5930.00	6700.00	Oliver	6T	310D	18F-6R	98.6	12236	No
1950	10970.00	4240.00	5280.00	5970.00	GM	4T	212D	5F-5R	105.79	11500	No
1950 4WD	13800.00	5110.00	6350.00	7180.00	GM	4T	212D	5F-5R	105.79	12800	No
1950T	11432.00	4230.00	5260.00	5940.00	Oliver	6T	310D	6F-2R	105.79	10860	No
1950T 4WD	14275.00	5280.00	6570.00	7420.00	Oliver	6T	310D	6F-2R	105.79	13200	No
1955	11100.00	4110.00	5110.00	5770.00	Oliver	6T	310D	18F-6R	108.16	10750	No
1955 4WD	14100.00	5220.00	6490.00	7330.00	Oliver	6T	310D	18F-6R	108.1	12850	No
2050	12950.00	4790.00	5960.00	6740.00	Oliver	6	478D	18F-6R	118.8	12900	No
2050 4WD	14400.00	5330.00	6620.00	7480.00	Oliver	6	478D	18F-6R	118.8	15000	No
2150	13660.00	5050.00	6280.00	7100.00	Oliver	6T	478D	18F-6R	131.48	12815	No
2150 4WD	15120.00	5590.00	6960.00	7870.00	Oliver	6T	478D	18F-6R	131.48	15100	No

1970

Model	Approx. Retail Price New	Fair	Good	Premium	Make	No. Cyls.	Displ. Cu.-In.	No. Speeds	P.T.O. H.P.	Approx. Shipping Wt.-Lbs.	Cab
550	3683.00	2110.00	2870.00	3560.00	Oliver	4	155G	4F-4R	44.00	3229	No
550	4518.00	2410.00	3280.00	4070.00	Oliver	4	155D	4F-4R	39.00	3245	No
1255	4285.00	2640.00	3590.00	4450.00	Fiat	3	143D	9F-3R	38.00	3750	No
1255 4WD	5458.00	3130.00	4260.00	5280.00	Fiat	3	143D	9F-3R	38.00	4456	No
1355	5467.00	3250.00	4420.00	5480.00	Oliver	4	190D	12F-3R	51.00	4566	No
1355 4WD	6426.00	3610.00	4910.00	6090.00	Oliver	4	190D	12F-3R	51.00	5116	No
1555	6116.00	3560.00	4840.00	6000.00	Oliver	6	232G	12F-4R	53.00	6880	No
1555	6811.00	3910.00	5310.00	6580.00	Oliver	6	232D	12F-4R	53.00	6999	No
1655	7134.00	4070.00	5530.00	6860.00	Oliver	6	265G	18F-6R	70.27	7023	No
1655	7985.00	4490.00	6110.00	7580.00	Oliver	6	283D	18F-6R	70.57	7315	No

Oliver (Cont.)

1970 (Cont.)

Model	Approx. Retail Price New	Estimated Average Value Less Repairs: Fair	Good	Premium	Engine Make	No. Cyls.	Displ. Cu.-In.	No. Speeds	P.T.O. H.P.	Approx. Shipping Wt.-Lbs.	Cab
1655 4WD	10850.00	5080.00	7070.00	8630.00	Oliver	6	265G	18F-6R	70.00	8733	No
1655 4WD	11699.00	5380.00	7490.00	9140.00	Oliver	6	283D	18F-6R	70.00	8850	No
1755	7908.00	4450.00	6060.00	7510.00	Oliver	6	283G	18F-6R	86.98	8739	No
1755	8625.00	4810.00	6550.00	8120.00	Oliver	6	310D	18F-6R	86.93	8873	No
1755 4WD	11211.00	5160.00	7180.00	8760.00	Oliver	6	283G	18F-6R	86.00	10732	No
1755 4WD	11974.00	5510.00	7660.00	9350.00	Oliver	6	310D	18F-6R	86.00	10873	No
1855	9195.00	4510.00	6270.00	7650.00	Oliver	6	310G	18F-6R		9190	No
1855	10192.00	4780.00	6650.00	8110.00	Oliver	6T	310D	18F-6R	98.60	9315	No
1855 4WD	12037.00	5540.00	7700.00	9390.00	Oliver	6	310G	18F-6R		11943	No
1855 4WD	13023.00	5990.00	8340.00	10180.00	Oliver	6T	310D	18F-6R	98.00	12236	No
1950	11081.00	4290.00	5190.00	5870.00	GM	4	212D	12F-4R	105.79	11500	No
1950 4WD	13936.00	5300.00	6410.00	7240.00	GM	4	212D	12F-4R	105.78	12800	No
1955	11546.00	4460.00	5400.00	6100.00	Oliver	6T	310D	18F-6R	108.16	10750	No
1955 4WD	14416.00	5480.00	6630.00	7490.00	Oliver	6T	310D	18F-6R	108.00	12850	No

1971

Model	Approx. Retail Price New	Fair	Good	Premium	Make	No. Cyls.	Displ. Cu.-In.	No. Speeds	P.T.O. H.P.	Approx. Shipping Wt.-Lbs.	Cab
550	3867.00	2210.00	2940.00	3650.00	Oliver	4	155G	6F-2R	44.00	3229	No
550	4744.00	2500.00	3330.00	4130.00	Oliver	4	155D	6F-2R	39.00	3245	No
1255	4650.00	2880.00	3840.00	4760.00	Fiat	3	143D	9F-3R	38.00	3906	No
1255 4WD	5775.00	3350.00	4470.00	5540.00	Fiat	3	143D	9F-3R	38.00	4456	No
1265	4883.00	3000.00	4000.00	4960.00	Fiat	3	158D	9F-3R	41.00	3806	No
1265 4WD	6064.00	3500.00	4670.00	5790.00	Fiat	3	158D	9F-3R	41.00	4456	No
1355	5785.00	3460.00	4610.00	5720.00	Oliver	4	190D	12F-3R	51.00	4566	No
1355 4WD	6800.00	3880.00	5170.00	6410.00	Oliver	4	190D	12F-3R	51.00	5116	No
1365	6074.00	3610.00	4810.00	5960.00	Fiat	4	211D	12F-3R	54.00	4606	No
1365 4WD	7140.00	4050.00	5400.00	6700.00	Fiat	4	211D	12F-3R	54.00	5056	No
1555	6422.00	3790.00	5050.00	6260.00	Oliver	6	232G	12F-4R	53.00	6880	No
1555	7152.00	4160.00	5540.00	6870.00	Oliver	6	232D	12F-4R	53.00	6999	No
1655	7205.00	4190.00	5590.00	6930.00	Oliver	6	265G	18F-6R	70.27	7023	No
1655	8065.00	4620.00	6160.00	7640.00	Oliver	6	283D	18F-6R	70.57	7315	No
1655 4WD	10959.00	5150.00	7010.00	8550.00	Oliver	6	265G	18F-6R	70.00	8733	No
1655 4WD	11816.00	5550.00	7560.00	9220.00	Oliver	6	283D	18F-6R	70.00	8850	No
1755	7987.00	4220.00	5750.00	7020.00	Oliver	6	283G	18F-6R	86.98	8739	No
1755	8711.00	4560.00	6220.00	7590.00	Oliver	6	310D	18F-6R	86.93	8873	No
1755 4WD	11323.00	5320.00	7250.00	8850.00	Oliver	6	283G	18F-6R	86.00	10732	No
1755 4WD	12094.00	5680.00	7740.00	9440.00	Oliver	6	310D	18F-6R	86.00	10873	No
1855	9287.00	4600.00	6260.00	7640.00	Oliver	6	310G	18F-6R		9190	No
1855	10294.00	4840.00	6590.00	8040.00	Oliver	6	310D	18F-6R	98.60	9315	No
1855 4WD	12157.00	5710.00	7780.00	9490.00	Oliver	6	310G	18F-6R		11943	No
1855 4WD	13153.00	6180.00	8420.00	10270.00	Oliver	6T	310D	18F-6R	98.00	12236	No
1955	11661.00	5480.00	7460.00	9100.00	Oliver	6T	310D	18F-6R	108.16	10750	No
1955 4WD	14560.00	6840.00	9320.00	11370.00	Oliver	6T	310D	18F-6R	108.00	12850	No
2655 4WD	22000.00	7480.00	9680.00	10840.00	MM	6	585D	10F-2R	143.30	17300	No

1972

Model	Approx. Retail Price New	Fair	Good	Premium	Make	No. Cyls.	Displ. Cu.-In.	No. Speeds	P.T.O. H.P.	Approx. Shipping Wt.-Lbs.	Cab
550	3906.00	2550.00	3340.00	4110.00	Oliver	4	155G	6F-2R	44.00	3229	No
550	4791.00	3010.00	3940.00	4850.00	Oliver	4	155D	6F-2R	39.00	3245	No
1265	4932.00	3350.00	4370.00	5380.00	Oliver	3	158D	9F-3R	41.00	3806	No
1265 4WD	6125.00	3800.00	4960.00	6100.00	Oliver	3	158D	9F-3R	41.00	4456	No
1365	6135.00	3950.00	5170.00	6360.00	Oliver	4	211D	12F-3R	54.00	4606	No
1365 4WD	7211.00	4270.00	5580.00	6860.00	Oliver	4	211D	12F-3R	54.00	5056	No
1555	6486.00	4140.00	5420.00	6670.00	Oliver	6	232G	12F-4R	53.00	6880	No
1555	7224.00	4540.00	5930.00	7290.00	Oliver	6	232D	12F-4R	53.00	6999	No
1655	7565.00	4710.00	6160.00	7580.00	Oliver	6	265G	18F-6R	70.27	7023	No
1655	8468.00	5180.00	6780.00	8340.00	Oliver	6	283D	18F-6R	70.57	7315	No
1655 4WD	11507.00	5520.00	7360.00	8910.00	Oliver	6	265G	18F-6R	70.00	8733	No
1655 4WD	12407.00	5960.00	7940.00	9610.00	Oliver	6	283D	18F-6R	70.00	8850	No
1755	8386.00	4750.00	6330.00	7660.00	Oliver	6	283G	18F-6R	86.98	8739	No
1755	9147.00	4870.00	6490.00	7850.00	Oliver	6	310D	18F-6R	86.93	8873	No
1755 4WD	11889.00	5710.00	7610.00	9210.00	Oliver	6	283G	18F-6R	86.00	10732	No
1755 4WD	12699.00	6100.00	8130.00	9840.00	Oliver	6	310D	18F-6R	86.00	10873	No
1855	9380.00	5030.00	6710.00	8120.00	Oliver	6	310G	18F-6R		9190	No
1855	10397.00	5180.00	6910.00	8360.00	Oliver	6T	310D	18F-6R	98.60	9315	No
1855 4WD	12279.00	5890.00	7860.00	9510.00	Oliver	6	310G	18F-6R		11943	No
1855 4WD	13285.00	6380.00	8500.00	10290.00	Oliver	6T	310D	18F-6R	98.00	12236	No
1955	11778.00	5650.00	7540.00	9120.00	Oliver	6T	310D	18F-6R	108.16	10750	No
1955 4WD	14706.00	7060.00	9410.00	11390.00	Oliver	6T	310D	18F-6R	108.00	12850	No
2155	13670.00	5470.00	6560.00	7410.00	MM	6	585D	10F-3R	141.44	12600	No
2255	14900.00	5960.00	7150.00	8080.00	Cat.	V-8	573D	18F-6R	146.72	13500	No
2255 4WD	17830.00	7130.00	8560.00	9670.00	Cat.	V-8	573D	18F-6R	146.00	15300	No
2655 4WD	22962.00	8040.00	10100.00	11310.00	MM	6	585D	10F-2R	143.30	17300	No

1973

Model	Approx. Retail Price New	Fair	Good	Premium	Make	No. Cyls.	Displ. Cu.-In.	No. Speeds	P.T.O. H.P.	Approx. Shipping Wt.-Lbs.	Cab
550	4101.00	2700.00	3470.00	4230.00	Oliver	4	155G	6F-2R	44.00	3229	No
550	4839.00	3100.00	3970.00	4840.00	Oliver	4	155D	6F-2R	39.00	3245	No
1265	4981.00	3440.00	4410.00	5380.00	Fiat	3	158D	9F-3R	41.00	3806	No
1265 4WD	6186.00	3920.00	5020.00	6120.00	Fiat	3	158D	9F-3R	41.00	4456	No
1365	6196.00	4080.00	5230.00	6380.00	Fiat	4	211D	12F-3R	54.00	4606	No
1365 4WD	7283.00	4810.00	6180.00	7540.00	Fiat	4	211D	12F-3R	54.00	5056	No
1465	8000.00	5040.00	6460.00	7880.00	Oliver	4	278D	7F-2R	70.00	6460	No
1555	6810.00	4400.00	5650.00	6890.00	Oliver	6	232G	12F-4R	53.00	6880	No
1555	7585.00	4820.00	6180.00	7540.00	Oliver	6	232D	12F-4R	53.00	6999	No
1655	7943.00	5010.00	6420.00	7830.00	Oliver	6	265G	18F-6R	70.27	7023	No
1655	8891.00	5510.00	7070.00	8630.00	Oliver	6	283D	18F-6R	70.57	7315	No

Oliver (Cont.)

1973 (Cont.)

Model	Approx. Retail Price New	Fair	Good	Premium	Engine Make	No. Cyls.	Displ. Cu.-In.	No. Speeds	P.T.O. H.P.	Approx. Shipping Wt.-Lbs.	Cab
1655 4WD	11737.00	**5750.00**	**7510.00**	**9010.00**	Oliver	6	265G	18F-6R	70.00	8733	No
1655 4WD	12655.00	**6200.00**	**8100.00**	**9720.00**	Oliver	6	283D	18F-6R	70.00	8850	No
1755	8553.00	**5170.00**	**6750.00**	**8100.00**	Oliver	6	283G	18F-6R	86.98	8739	No
1755	9330.00	**5210.00**	**6800.00**	**8160.00**	Oliver	6	310D	18F-6R	86.93	8873	No
1755 4WD	12127.00	**5940.00**	**7760.00**	**9310.00**	Oliver	6	283G	18F-6R	86.00	10732	No
1755 4WD	12953.00	**6350.00**	**8290.00**	**9950.00**	Oliver	6	310D	18F-6R	86.00	10873	No
1855	9568.00	**5180.00**	**6760.00**	**8110.00**	Oliver	6	310G	18F-6R		9190	No
1855	10605.00	**5390.00**	**7040.00**	**8450.00**	Oliver	6T	310D	18F-6R	98.60	9315	No
1855 4WD	12525.00	**6140.00**	**8020.00**	**9620.00**	Oliver	6	310G	18F-6R		11943	No
1855 4WD	13551.00	**6640.00**	**8670.00**	**10400.00**	Oliver	6T	310D	18F-6R	98.00	12236	No
1955	12014.00	**5890.00**	**7690.00**	**9230.00**	Oliver	6T	310D	18F-6R	108.15	10750	No
1955 4WD	15000.00	**7350.00**	**9600.00**	**11520.00**	Oliver	6T	310D	18F-6R	108.00	12850	No
2255	15198.00	**6560.00**	**7840.00**	**8860.00**	Cat.	V-8	573D	18F-6R	146.72	13500	No
2255 4WD	18186.00	**7460.00**	**8910.00**	**10070.00**	Cat.	V-8	573D	18F-6R	146.00	15300	No
2655 4WD	26421.00	**9510.00**	**11890.00**	**13200.00**	MM	6	585D	10F-2R	143.30	17300	No

1974

Model	Approx. Retail Price New	Fair	Good	Premium	Engine Make	No. Cyls.	Displ. Cu.-In.	No. Speeds	P.T.O. H.P.	Approx. Shipping Wt.-Lbs.	Cab
550	4306.00	**2870.00**	**3610.00**	**4370.00**	Oliver	4	155G	6F-2R	44.00	3229	No
550	5081.00	**3280.00**	**4140.00**	**5010.00**	Oliver	4	155D	6F-2R	39.00	3245	No
1265	5230.00	**3630.00**	**4580.00**	**5540.00**	Fiat	3	158D	9F-3R	41.00	3806	No
1265 4WD	6495.00	**4160.00**	**5230.00**	**6330.00**	Fiat	3	158D	9F-3R	41.00	4456	No
1270	5230.00	**3630.00**	**4580.00**	**5540.00**	Fiat	3	158D	9F-2R	41.00	3806	No
1270 4WD	6495.00	**4160.00**	**5230.00**	**6330.00**	Fiat	3	158D	9F-2R	41.00	4456	No
1365	6506.00	**4320.00**	**5440.00**	**6580.00**	Fiat	4	211D	12F-3R	54.00	4606	No
1365 4WD	7647.00	**4780.00**	**6020.00**	**7280.00**	Fiat	4	211D	12F-3R	54.00	5056	No
1370	6506.00	**4360.00**	**5490.00**	**6640.00**	Fiat	4	211D	12F-3R	54.00	4606	No
1370 4WD	7647.00	**4830.00**	**6080.00**	**7360.00**	Fiat	4	211D	12F-3R	54.00	5056	No
1465	8400.00	**5350.00**	**6730.00**	**8140.00**	Oliver	4	278D	7F-2R	70.00	6460	No
1555	7151.00	**4670.00**	**5890.00**	**7130.00**	Oliver	6	232G	12F-4R	53.00	6880	No
1555	7964.00	**5110.00**	**6440.00**	**7790.00**	Oliver	6	232D	12F-4R	53.00	6999	No
1655	8340.00	**5310.00**	**6690.00**	**8100.00**	Oliver	6	265G	18F-6R	70.27	7023	No
1655	9336.00	**5690.00**	**7160.00**	**8660.00**	Oliver	6	283D	18F-6R	70.57	7315	No
1655 4WD	12324.00	**6160.00**	**7890.00**	**9390.00**	Oliver	6	265G	18F-6R	70.00	8733	No
1655 4WD	13288.00	**6640.00**	**8500.00**	**10120.00**	Oliver	6	283D	18F-6R	70.00	8850	No
1755	8981.00	**5240.00**	**6710.00**	**7990.00**	Oliver	6	283G	18F-6R	86.98	8739	No
1755	9797.00	**5500.00**	**7040.00**	**8380.00**	Oliver	6	310D	18F-6R	86.93	8873	No
1755 4WD	12733.00	**6370.00**	**8150.00**	**9700.00**	Oliver	6	283G	18F-6R	86.00	10732	No
1755 4WD	13601.00	**6800.00**	**8710.00**	**10370.00**	Oliver	6	310D	18F-6R	86.00	10873	No
1855	10046.00	**5420.00**	**6940.00**	**8260.00**	Oliver	6	310G	18F-6R		9190	No
1855	11135.00	**5820.00**	**7450.00**	**8870.00**	Oliver	6T	310D	18F-6R	98.60	9315	No
1855 4WD	13151.00	**6580.00**	**8420.00**	**10020.00**	Oliver	6	310G	18F-6R		11943	No
1855 4WD	14229.00	**7120.00**	**9110.00**	**10840.00**	Oliver	6T	310D	18F-6R	98.00	12236	No
1870	10400.00	**5480.00**	**7010.00**	**8340.00**	MM	6	425LP	18F-6R	97.00	10612	No
1870	11000.00	**5600.00**	**7170.00**	**8530.00**	MM	6	451D	18F-6R	98.00	10812	No
1955	12615.00	**6310.00**	**8070.00**	**9600.00**	Oliver	6T	310D	18F-6R	108.15	10750	No
1955 4WD	15750.00	**7880.00**	**10080.00**	**12000.00**	Oliver	6T	310D	18F-6R	108.00	12850	No
2255	15958.00	**6970.00**	**8300.00**	**9300.00**	Cat.	V-8	573D	18F-6R	146.72	13500	No
2255 4WD	19095.00	**8020.00**	**9550.00**	**10700.00**	Cat.	V-8	573D	18F-6R	146.00	15300	No
2270	13000.00	**5460.00**	**6500.00**	**7280.00**	MM	6	504LP	18F-6R	137.00	12600	No
2270	13600.00	**5710.00**	**6800.00**	**7620.00**	MM	6	585D	18F-6R	142.00	13000	No

1975

Model	Approx. Retail Price New	Fair	Good	Premium	Engine Make	No. Cyls.	Displ. Cu.-In.	No. Speeds	P.T.O. H.P.	Approx. Shipping Wt.-Lbs.	Cab
550	4392.00	**2970.00**	**3670.00**	**4400.00**	Oliver	4	155G	6F-2R	44.00	3229	No
550	5183.00	**3400.00**	**4200.00**	**5040.00**	Oliver	4	155D	6F-2R	39.00	3245	No
1265	5335.00	**3760.00**	**4650.00**	**5580.00**	Fiat	3	158D	9F-3R	41.00	3806	No
1265 4WD	6625.00	**4360.00**	**5390.00**	**6470.00**	Fiat	3	158D	9F-3R	41.00	4456	No
1365	6636.00	**4500.00**	**5570.00**	**6680.00**	Fiat	4	211D	12F-3R	54.00	4606	No
1365 4WD	7800.00	**4950.00**	**6120.00**	**7340.00**	Fiat	4	211D	12F-3R	54.00	5056	No
1465	8568.00	**5590.00**	**6910.00**	**8290.00**	Oliver	4	278D	7F-2R	70.00	6460	No
1555	7294.00	**4840.00**	**5980.00**	**7180.00**	Oliver	6	232G	12F-4R	53.00	6880	No
1555	8123.00	**5290.00**	**6550.00**	**7860.00**	Oliver	6	232D	12F-4R	53.00	6999	No
1655	8507.00	**5450.00**	**6740.00**	**8090.00**	Oliver	6	265G	18F-6R	70.27	7023	No
1655	9523.00	**5790.00**	**7160.00**	**8590.00**	Oliver	6	283D	18F-6R	70.57	7315	No
1655 4WD	12570.00	**6410.00**	**8050.00**	**9500.00**	Oliver	6	265G	18F-6R	70.00	8733	No
1655 4WD	13554.00	**6910.00**	**8680.00**	**10240.00**	Oliver	6	283D	18F-6R	70.00	8850	No
1755	9160.00	**5440.00**	**6820.00**	**8050.00**	Oliver	6	283G	18F-6R	86.98	8739	No
1755	9993.00	**5810.00**	**7290.00**	**8600.00**	Oliver	6	310D	18F-6R	86.93	8873	No
1755 4WD	12988.00	**6620.00**	**8310.00**	**9810.00**	Oliver	6	283G	18F-6R	86.00	10732	No
1755 4WD	13873.00	**7080.00**	**8880.00**	**10480.00**	Oliver	6	310D	18F-6R	86.00	10873	No
1855	10247.00	**5740.00**	**7200.00**	**8500.00**	Oliver	6	310G	18F-6R		9190	No
1855	11358.00	**6300.00**	**7910.00**	**9330.00**	Oliver	6T	310D	18F-6R	98.60	9315	No
1855 4WD	13414.00	**6890.00**	**8640.00**	**10200.00**	Oliver	6	310G	18F-6R		11943	No
1855 4WD	14514.00	**7400.00**	**9290.00**	**10960.00**	Oliver	6T	310D	18F-6R	98.00	12236	No
2255	16277.00	**6190.00**	**7650.00**	**8490.00**	Cat.	V-8	573D	18F-6R	146.72	13500	No
2255	17800.00	**6760.00**	**8370.00**	**9290.00**	Cat.	V-8	573D	18F-6R	146.72	14600	C
2255 4WD	19477.00	**7400.00**	**9150.00**	**10160.00**	Cat.	V-8	573D	18F-6R	146.00	15300	No
2255 4WD	21000.00	**7980.00**	**9870.00**	**10960.00**	Cat.	V-8	573D	18F-6R	146.72	16400	C

Same

1982

Model	Approx. Retail Price New	Estimated Average Value Less Repairs: Fair	Good	Premium	Engine: Make	No. Cyls.	Displ. Cu.-In.	No. Speeds	P.T.O. H.P.	Approx. Shipping Wt.-Lbs.	Cab
Delfino 35 4WD	9441.00	3490.00	4340.00	4690.00	SAME	2	110D	6F-2R	32.00	3046	No
Falcon 50 4WD	18345.00	6790.00	8440.00	9120.00	SAME	3	165D	8F-4R	50.00	4140	No
Minitaurus 60	16499.00	6110.00	7590.00	8200.00	SAME	3	190D	14F-7R	59.00	4654	No
Minitaurus 60 4WD	21492.00	7950.00	9890.00	10680.00	SAME	3	190D	14F-7R	59.00	4982	No
Vigneron 60 4WD	22149.00	8200.00	10190.00	11010.00	SAME	3	190D	14F-7R	60.00	5000	No
Corsaro 70	17270.00	6390.00	7940.00	8580.00	SAME	4	221D	14F-7R	64.00	5730	No
Corsaro 70 4WD	22277.00	8240.00	10250.00	11070.00	SAME	4	221D	14F-7R	64.00	6330	No
Saturno 80 4WD	23485.00	8690.00	10800.00	11660.00	SAME	4	254D	14F-7R	75.00	6460	No
Leopard 85 Export 4WD	30823.00	11410.00	14180.00	15310.00	SAME	4	254D	24F-6R	79.00	7700	No
Mercury 85 Export	24261.00	8980.00	11160.00	12050.00	SAME	4	254D	16F-16R	79.00	6877	No
Mercury 85 Export 4WD	28922.00	10700.00	13300.00	14360.00	SAME	4	254D	16F-16R	79.00	7516	No
Mercury 85 Special	20609.00	7630.00	9480.00	10240.00	SAME	4	254D	12F-12R	79.00	5684	No
Mercury 85 Special 4WD	24323.00	9000.00	11190.00	12090.00	SAME	4	254D	12F-12R	79.00	6345	No
Jaguar 95	30079.00	11130.00	13840.00	14950.00	SAME	5	317D	24F-6R		7750	C,H
Jaguar 95 4WD	38208.00	14140.00	17580.00	18990.00	SAME	5	317D	24F-6R		8360	C,H
Panther 95	28160.00	10420.00	12950.00	13990.00	SAME	5	317D	24F-6R		7310	No
Panther 95 4WD	31363.00	11600.00	14430.00	15580.00	SAME	5	317D	24F-6R		7890	No
Tiger Six 105	35785.00	13240.00	16460.00	17780.00	SAME	6	331D	24F-6R	102.00	8510	C,H
Tiger Six 105 4WD	40552.00	15000.00	18650.00	20140.00	SAME	6	331D	24F-6R	102.00	9460	C,H
Buffalo 130	40048.00	14820.00	18420.00	19890.00	SAME	6	380D	24F-8R	116.00	10760	C,H
Buffalo 130 4WD	44178.00	16350.00	20320.00	21950.00	SAME	6	380D	24F-8R	116.00	11660	C,H
Hercules 160 4WD	57751.00	21370.00	26570.00	28700.00	SAME	6T	380D	12F-4R		13730	C,H,A

1983

Model	Approx. Retail Price New	Fair	Good	Premium	Make	No. Cyls.	Displ. Cu.-In.	No. Speeds	P.T.O. H.P.	Approx. Shipping Wt.-Lbs.	Cab
Delfino 35 4WD	9630.00	3660.00	4530.00	4890.00	SAME	2	110D	6F-2R	32.00	3046	No
Falcon 50 4WD	18712.00	7110.00	8800.00	9500.00	SAME	3	165D	8F-4R	50.00	4140	No
Minitaurus 60	16829.00	6400.00	7910.00	8540.00	SAME	3	190D	14F-7R	59.00	4654	No
Minitaurus 60 4WD	22592.00	8590.00	10620.00	11470.00	SAME	3	190D	14F-7R	59.00	4984	No
Vigneron 60 4WD	22592.00	8590.00	10620.00	11470.00	SAME	3	190D	14F-7R	60.00	5000	No
Corsaro 70	17620.00	6700.00	8280.00	8940.00	SAME	4	221D	14F-7R	64.00	5730	No
Corsaro 70 4WD	22723.00	8640.00	10680.00	11530.00	SAME	4	221D	14F-7R	64.00	6330	No
Saturno 80 4WD	23955.00	9100.00	11260.00	12160.00	SAME	4	254D	14F-7R	75.00	6460	No
Leopard 85 Export 4WD	31439.00	11950.00	14780.00	15960.00	SAME	4	254D	24F-6R	79.00	7700	No
Mercury 85 Export	24746.00	9400.00	11630.00	12560.00	SAME	4	254D	16F-16R	79.00	6877	No
Mercury 85 Export 4WD	29500.00	11210.00	13870.00	14980.00	SAME	4	254D	16F-16R	79.00	7516	No
Mercury 85 Spec. 4WD	24809.00	9430.00	11660.00	12590.00	SAME	4	254D	12F-12R	79.00	6345	No
Mercury 85 Special	21021.00	7990.00	9880.00	10670.00	SAME	4	254D	12F-12R	79.00	5684	No
Jaguar 95	30681.00	11660.00	14420.00	15570.00	SAME	5	317D	24F-6R		7750	C,H
Jaguar 95 4WD	38972.00	14810.00	18320.00	19790.00	SAME	5	317D	24F-6R		8360	C,H
Panther 95	28723.00	10920.00	13500.00	14580.00	SAME	5	317D	24F-6R		7310	No
Panther 95 4WD	31990.00	12160.00	15040.00	16240.00	SAME	5	317D	24F-6R		7890	No
Tiger Six 105	36501.00	13870.00	17160.00	18530.00	SAME	6	331D	24F-6R	102.00	8510	C,H
Tiger Six 105 4WD	41363.00	15720.00	19440.00	21000.00	SAME	6	331D	24F-6R	102.00	9460	C,H
Buffalo 130	40849.00	15520.00	19200.00	20740.00	SAME	6	380D	24F-8R	116.00	10760	C,H
Buffalo 130 4WD	45062.00	17120.00	21180.00	22870.00	SAME	6	380D	24F-8R	116.00	11660	C,H
Hercules 160 4WD	58906.00	22380.00	27690.00	29910.00	SAME	6T	380D	12F-4R		13730	C,H,A

1984

Model	Approx. Retail Price New	Fair	Good	Premium	Make	No. Cyls.	Displ. Cu.-In.	No. Speeds	P.T.O. H.P.	Approx. Shipping Wt.-Lbs.	Cab
Delfino 35 4WD	10000.00	3900.00	4800.00	5180.00	SAME	2	110D	6F-2R	32.00	3046	No
Falcon 50 4WD	19621.00	7650.00	9420.00	10170.00	SAME	3	165D	8F-4R	45.00	4585	No
Minitaurus 60	16829.00	6560.00	8080.00	8730.00	SAME	3	190D	14F-7R	59.00	4654	No
Minitaurus 60 4WD	23397.00	9130.00	11230.00	12130.00	SAME	3	190D	14F-7R	59.00	4984	No
Vigneron 60 4WD	22595.00	8810.00	10850.00	11720.00	SAME	3	190D	8F-4R	56.00	5000	No
Corsaro 70 Orchard	17620.00	6870.00	8460.00	9140.00	SAME	4	221D	8F-4R	68.00	5730	No
Corsaro 70 Orchard 4WD	22723.00	8860.00	10910.00	11780.00	SAME	4	221D	8F-4R	68.00	6330	No
Leopard 85 4WD	32692.00	12750.00	15690.00	16950.00	SAME	4	254D	24F-6R	79.00	7700	No
Mercury 85 Export	24750.00	9650.00	11880.00	12830.00	SAME	4	254D	12F-12R	79.00	6877	No
Mercury 85 Export	28475.00	11110.00	13670.00	14760.00	SAME	4	254D	16F-16R	79.00	7275	No
Mercury 85 Export 4WD	29500.00	11510.00	14160.00	15290.00	SAME	4	254D	12F-12R	79.00	7015	No
Mercury 85 Export 4WD	33225.00	12960.00	15950.00	17230.00	SAME	4	254D	16F-16R	79.00	7516	No
Mercury 85 Special	21021.00	8200.00	10090.00	10900.00	SAME	4	254D	12F-12R	79.00	5684	No
Mercury 85 Special	24746.00	9650.00	11880.00	12830.00	SAME	4	254D	16F-16R	79.00	6185	No
Mercury 85 Special 4WD	24810.00	9680.00	11910.00	12860.00	SAME	4	254D	12F-12R	79.00	6345	No
Mercury 85 Special 4WD	28535.00	11130.00	13700.00	14800.00	SAME	4	254D	16F-16R	79.00	6845	No
Row Crop 85	23838.00	9300.00	11440.00	12360.00	SAME	4	254D	12F-12R	80.00	7160	C,H
Row Crop 85 4WD	27005.00	10530.00	12960.00	14000.00	SAME	4	254D	12F-12R	80.00	7500	No
Leopard 90 4WD	35372.00	13800.00	16980.00	18340.00	SAME	4	254D	24F-6R	79.00	8000	No
Jaguar 95	23838.00	9300.00	11440.00	12360.00	SAME	5	317D	24F-6R	88.00	6850	No
Jaguar 95	30681.00	11970.00	14730.00	15910.00	SAME	5	317D	24F-6R	88.00	7750	C,H
Jaguar 95 4WD	27005.00	10530.00	12960.00	14000.00	SAME	5	317D	24F-6R	88.00	7460	No
Jaguar 95 4WD	38972.00	15200.00	18710.00	20210.00	SAME	5	317D	24F-6R	88.00	8360	C,H
Panther 95	30160.00	11760.00	14480.00	15640.00	SAME	5	317D	24F-6R	88.00	7310	No
Panther 95 4WD	33590.00	13100.00	16120.00	17410.00	SAME	5	317D	24F-6R	88.00	7890	No
Jaguar 100	32215.00	12560.00	15460.00	16700.00	SAME	5	317D	24F-6R	88.00	8000	C,H
Jaguar 100 4WD	40920.00	15960.00	19640.00	21210.00	SAME	5	317D	24F-6R	88.00	8610	C,H
Tiger Six 105	36501.00	14240.00	17520.00	18920.00	SAME	6	331D	24F-6R	102.00	8510	C,H
Tiger Six 105 4WD	41363.00	16130.00	19850.00	21440.00	SAME	6	331D	24F-6R	102.00	9460	C,H
Buffalo 130 4WD	42032.00	16390.00	20180.00	21790.00	SAME	6T	380D	24F-8R	116.00	10760	C,H
Hercules 160 4WD	60910.00	23760.00	29240.00	31580.00	SAME	6T	380D	24F-8R	150.00	13730	C,H,A

Same (Cont.)

Model	Approx. Retail Price New	Estimated Average Value Less Repairs Fair	Good	Premium	Engine Make	No. Cyls.	Displ. Cu.-In.	No. Speeds	P.T.O. H.P.	Approx. Shipping Wt.-Lbs.	Cab
1985											
Mercury Export	25053.00	10020.00	12280.00	13140.00	SAME	4	254D	12F-12R	79.00	6877	No
Mercury Export	25888.00	10360.00	12690.00	13580.00	SAME	4	254D	16F-16R	79.00	7275	No
Mercury Special	21021.00	8410.00	10300.00	11020.00	SAME	4	254D	12F-12R	79.00	5684	No
Mercury Special	24746.00	9900.00	12130.00	12980.00	SAME	4	254D	16F-16R	79.00	6185	No
Mercury Export 4WD	27888.00	11160.00	13670.00	14630.00	SAME	4	254D	12F-12R	79.00	7015	No
Mercury Export 4WD	28723.00	11490.00	14070.00	15060.00	SAME	4	254D	16F-16R	79.00	7516	No
Mercury Special 4WD	24810.00	9920.00	12160.00	13010.00	SAME	4	254D	12F-12R	79.00	6345	No
Mercury Special 4WD	28535.00	11410.00	13980.00	14960.00	SAME	4	254D	16F-16R	79.00	6845	No
Delfino 35 4WD	11945.00	4780.00	5850.00	6260.00	SAME	2	110D	6F-2R	32.00	3046	No
Falcon 50 4WD	19621.00	7850.00	9610.00	10280.00	SAME	3	165D	8F-4R	45.00	4585	No
Minitaurus 60	16829.00	6730.00	8250.00	8830.00	SAME	3	190D	14F-7R	59.00	4654	No
Minitaurus 60 4WD	23397.00	9360.00	11470.00	12270.00	SAME	3	190D	14F-7R	59.00	4984	No
Vigneron 60 4WD	22595.00	9040.00	11070.00	11850.00	SAME	3	190D	8F-4R	56.00	5000	No
Orchard 70	19196.00	7680.00	9410.00	10070.00	SAME	4	221D	8F-4R	68.00	5730	No
Orchard 70 4WD	22723.00	9090.00	11130.00	11910.00	SAME	4	221D	8F-4R	68.00	6330	No
Mercury 75	24388.00	9760.00	11950.00	12790.00	SAME	4	254D	12F-12R	68.00	6256	No
Mercury 75	25223.00	10090.00	12360.00	13230.00	SAME	4	254D	16F-16R	68.00	6300	No
Mercury 75 4WD	26804.00	10720.00	13130.00	14050.00	SAME	4	254D	12F-12R	68.00	6895	No
Mercury 75 4WD	27639.00	11060.00	13540.00	14490.00	SAME	4	254D	16F-16R	68.00	6940	No
Row Crop 85	23838.00	9540.00	11680.00	12500.00	SAME	4	254D	12F-12R	80.00	7160	No
Row Crop 85 4WD	27005.00	10800.00	13230.00	14160.00	SAME	4	254D	12F-12R	80.00	7500	No
Leapord 90 4WD	34469.00	13790.00	16890.00	18070.00	SAME	4	254D	12F-3R	82.00	6680	No
Leapord 90 4WD	35094.00	14040.00	17200.00	18400.00	SAME	4	254D	24F-6R	82.00	6700	No
Leapord 90 4WD	35304.00	14120.00	17300.00	18510.00	SAME	4	254D	20F-5R	82.00	6700	No
Jaguar 100	30341.00	12140.00	14870.00	15910.00	SAME	5	317D	12F-3R	92.00	8000	No
Jaguar 100	30966.00	12390.00	15170.00	16230.00	SAME	5	317D	24F-6R	92.00	8000	No
Jaguar 100	31176.00	12470.00	15280.00	16350.00	SAME	5	317D	20F-5R	92.00	8000	No
Jaguar 100 4WD	37781.00	15110.00	18510.00	19810.00	SAME	5	317D	12F-3R	92.00	8610	No
Jaguar 100 4WD	38406.00	15360.00	18820.00	20140.00	SAME	5	317D	24F-6R	92.00	8610	No
Jaguar 100 4WD	38616.00	15450.00	18920.00	20240.00	SAME	5	317D	20F-5R	92.00	8610	No
Tiger 105	38999.00	15600.00	19110.00	20450.00	SAME	6	331D	12F-3R	100.	7910	No
Tiger 105	39624.00	15850.00	19420.00	20780.00	SAME	6	331D	24F-6R	100.	8000	No
Tiger 105	39834.00	15930.00	19520.00	20890.00	SAME	6	331D	20F-5R	100.	8100	No
Tiger 105 4WD	44791.00	17920.00	21950.00	23490.00	SAME	6	331D	12F-3R	100.	8770	No
Tiger 105 4WD	45416.00	18170.00	22250.00	23810.00	SAME	6	331D	24F-6R	100.	8860	No
Tiger 105 4WD	45626.00	18250.00	22360.00	23930.00	SAME	6	331D	20F-5R	100.	8960	No
Buffalo 130 4WD	41616.00	16650.00	20390.00	21820.00	SAME	6T	380D	12F-4R	128.00	10500	No
Buffalo 130 4WD	42451.00	16980.00	20800.00	22260.00	SAME	6T	380D	24F-8R	128.00	10760	No
Hercules 160 4WD	61197.00	24480.00	29990.00	32090.00	SAME	6T	380D	12F-4R	150.00	13558	No
Hercules 160 4WD	62032.00	24810.00	30400.00	32530.00	SAME	6T	380D	24F-8R	150.00	13700	No
1986											
Mercury Export	25053.00	10270.00	12530.00	13410.00	SAME	4	254D	12F-12R	79.00	6877	No
Mercury Export	25888.00	10610.00	12940.00	13850.00	SAME	4	254D	16F-16R	79.00	7275	No
Mercury Special	21021.00	8620.00	10510.00	11250.00	SAME	4	254D	12F-12R	79.00	5684	No
Mercury Special	24746.00	10150.00	12370.00	13240.00	SAME	4	254D	16F-16R	79.00	6185	No
Mercury Export4WD	27888.00	11430.00	13940.00	14920.00	SAME	4	254D	12F-12R	79.00	7015	No
Mercury Export4WD	28723.00	11780.00	14360.00	15370.00	SAME	4	254D	16F-16R	79.00	7516	No
Mercury Special 4WD	24810.00	10170.00	12410.00	13280.00	SAME	4	254D	12F-12R	79.00	6345	No
Mercury Special 4WD	28535.00	11700.00	14270.00	15270.00	SAME	4	254D	16F-16R	79.00	6845	No
Delfino 35 4WD	11945.00	4900.00	5970.00	6390.00	SAME	2	110D	6F-2R	32.00	3046	No
Falcon 50 4WD	19621.00	8050.00	9810.00	10500.00	SAME	3	165D	8F-4R	45.00	4585	No
Minitaurus 60	16829.00	6900.00	8420.00	9010.00	SAME	3	190D	14F-7R	59.00	4654	No
Minitaurus 60 4WD	23397.00	9590.00	11700.00	12520.00	SAME	3	190D	14F-7R	59.00	4984	No
Vigneron 60 4WD	22595.00	9260.00	11300.00	12090.00	SAME	3	190D	8F-4R	56.00	5000	No
Orchard 70	19196.00	7870.00	9600.00	10270.00	SAME	4	221D	8F-4R	68.00	5730	No
Orchard 70 4WD	22723.00	9320.00	11360.00	12160.00	SAME	4	221D	8F-4R	68.00	6330	No
Mercury 75	24388.00	10000.00	12190.00	13040.00	SAME	4	254D	12F-12R	68.00	6256	No
Mercury 75	25223.00	10340.00	12610.00	13490.00	SAME	4	254D	16F-16R	68.00	6300	No
Mercury 75 4WD	26804.00	10990.00	13400.00	14340.00	SAME	4	254D	12F-12R	68.00	6895	No
Mercury 75 4WD	27639.00	11330.00	13820.00	14790.00	SAME	4	254D	16F-16R	68.00	6940	No
Row Crop 85	23838.00	9770.00	11920.00	12750.00	SAME	4	254D	12F-12R	80.00	7160	No
Row Crop 85 4WD	27005.00	11070.00	13500.00	14450.00	SAME	4	254D	12F-12R	80.00	7500	No
Leapord 90 4WD	34469.00	14130.00	17240.00	18450.00	SAME	4	254D	12F-3R	82.00	6680	No
Leapord 90 4WD	35094.00	14390.00	17550.00	18780.00	SAME	4	254D	24F-6R	82.00	6700	No
Leapord 90 4WD	35304.00	14480.00	17650.00	18890.00	SAME	4	254D	20F-5R	82.00	6700	No
Jaguar 100	30341.00	12440.00	15170.00	16230.00	SAME	5	317D	12F-3R	92.00	8000	No
Jaguar 100	30966.00	12700.00	15480.00	16560.00	SAME	5	317D	24F-6R	92.00	8000	No
Jaguar 100	31176.00	12780.00	15590.00	16680.00	SAME	5	317D	20F-5R	92.00	8000	No
Jaguar 100 4WD	37781.00	15490.00	18890.00	20210.00	SAME	5	317D	12F-3R	92.00	8610	No
Jaguar 100 4WD	38406.00	15750.00	19200.00	20540.00	SAME	5	317D	24F-6R	92.00	8610	No
Jaguar 100 4WD	38616.00	15830.00	19310.00	20660.00	SAME	5	317D	20F-5R	92.00	8610	No
Tiger 105	38999.00	15990.00	19500.00	20870.00	SAME	6	331D	12F-3R	100.	7910	No
Tiger 105	39624.00	16250.00	19810.00	21200.00	SAME	6	331D	24F-6R	100.	8000	No
Tiger 105	39834.00	16330.00	19920.00	21310.00	SAME	6	331D	20F-5R	100.	8100	No
Tiger 105 4WD	44791.00	18360.00	22400.00	23970.00	SAME	6	331D	12F-3R	100.	8770	No
Tiger 105 4WD	45416.00	18620.00	22710.00	24300.00	SAME	6	331D	24F-6R	100.	8860	No
Tiger 105 4WD	45626.00	18710.00	22810.00	24410.00	SAME	6	331D	20F-5R	100.	8960	No
Buffalo 130 4WD	41616.00	17060.00	20810.00	22270.00	SAME	6T	380D	12F-4R	128.00	10500	No
Buffalo 130 4WD	42451.00	17410.00	21230.00	22720.00	SAME	6T	380D	24F-8R	128.00	10760	No
Hercules 160 4WD	61197.00	25090.00	30600.00	32740.00	SAME	6T	380D	12F-4R	150.00	13558	No
Hercules 160 4WD	62032.00	25430.00	31020.00	33190.00	SAME	6T	380D	24F-8R	150.00	13700	No

Same (Cont.)

1987

Model	Approx. Retail Price New	Estimated Average Value Less Repairs Fair	Good	Premium	Engine Make	No. Cyls.	Displ. Cu.-In.	No. Speeds	P.T.O. H.P.	Approx. Shipping Wt.-Lbs.	Cab
Minitaurus 60	16829.00	7070.00	8580.00	9180.00	SAME	3	190D	14F-7R	59.00	4820	No
Minitaurus 60 4WD	23397.00	9830.00	11930.00	12770.00	SAME	3	190D	14F-7R	59.00	5240	No
Solar 60	17400.00	7310.00	8870.00	9490.00	SAME	3	190D	12F-3R	59.00	4585	No
Solar 60 4WD	23995.00	10080.00	12240.00	13100.00	SAME	3	190D	12F-3R	59.00	5202	No
85 Special 4WD	24810.00	10420.00	12650.00	13540.00	SAME	4	253D	12F-12R	79.00	6680	No
Mercury 85 Special	21021.00	8830.00	10720.00	11470.00	SAME	4	253D	12F-12R	79.00	6019	No
100	30341.00	12740.00	15470.00	16550.00	SAME	5	317D	12F-3R	92.00	8355	No
100 4WD	37781.00	15870.00	19270.00	20620.00	SAME	5	317D	12F-3R	92.00	9501	No
110 4WD	45000.00	18900.00	22950.00	24560.00	SAME	6	345D	12F-3R		10317	No
130 4WD w/Cab	50000.00	21000.00	25500.00	27290.00	SAME	6	380D	24F-12R		11397	C,H,A
150 4WD w/Cab	53000.00	22260.00	27030.00	28920.00	SAME	6T	380D	24F-12R		12566	C,H,A

1988

Model	Approx. Retail Price New	Fair	Good	Premium	Make	No. Cyls.	Displ. Cu.-In.	No. Speeds	P.T.O. H.P.	Approx. Shipping Wt.-Lbs.	Cab
Solar 50	19500.00	8390.00	10140.00	10750.00	SAME	3	166D	12F-3R		4409	No
Solar 50 4WD	19500.00	8390.00	10140.00	10750.00	SAME	3	166D	12F-3R		5026	No
Solar 60 4WD	23500.00	10110.00	12220.00	12950.00	SAME	3	190D	12F-3R		5202	No
Vigneron 60 4WD	25000.00	10750.00	13000.00	13780.00	SAME	3	190D	8F-4R		4519	No
Explorer 70 4WD	29000.00	12470.00	15080.00	15990.00	SAME	4	244D	12F-12R		6701	C,H
Explorer 80 4WD	31000.00	13330.00	16120.00	17090.00	SAME	4	244D	12F-12R		7385	C,H
Row Crop 85 4WD	29000.00	12470.00	15080.00	15990.00	SAME	4	253D	12F-4R		7519	No
Explorer 90 4WD	38000.00	16340.00	19760.00	20950.00	SAME	4	244D	12F-12R		7385	C,H
100 4WD	43000.00	18490.00	22360.00	23700.00	SAME	5	317D	12F-3R		9832	C,H,A
110 4WD	45000.00	19350.00	23400.00	24800.00	SAME	6	345D	12F-3R		10758	C,H,A
130 4WD	50000.00	21500.00	26000.00	27560.00	SAME	6	381D	24F-12R		11397	C,H,A
150 4WD	53000.00	22790.00	27560.00	29210.00	SAME	6	380D	24F-12R		12566	C,H,A

1989

Model	Approx. Retail Price New	Fair	Good	Premium	Make	No. Cyls.	Displ. Cu.-In.	No. Speeds	P.T.O. H.P.	Approx. Shipping Wt.-Lbs.	Cab
Turbo 4WD	38072.00	16750.00	20180.00	21390.00	SAME	4T	244D	12F-12R	86.00	7275	C,H,A
Solar 50 4WD	21585.00	9500.00	11440.00	12130.00	SAME	3	166D	12F-3R	46.00	5027	No
Orchard 60 4WD	26676.00	11740.00	14140.00	14990.00	SAME	3	183D	12F-12R	54.00	4629	C,H,A
Solar 60 4WD	23565.00	10370.00	12490.00	13240.00	SAME	3	190D	12F-3R	54.00	5203	No
Vineyard 62 4WD	25932.00	11410.00	13740.00	14560.00	SAME	3	183D	12F-12R	57.00	4629	No
Explorer 70 4WD	29353.00	12920.00	15560.00	16490.00	SAME	4	244D	12F-12R	64.00	6437	C,H
Orchard 75 4WD	27845.00	12250.00	14760.00	15650.00	SAME	4	244D	12F-12R	69.00	5070	C,H,A
Vineyard 75 4WD	27090.00	11920.00	14360.00	15220.00	SAME	4	183D	12F-12R	69.00	5070	No
Explorer 80 4WD	31885.00	14030.00	16900.00	17910.00	SAME	4	244D	12F-12R	74.00	7275	C,H,A
Mudder 85 4WD	29007.00	12760.00	15370.00	16290.00	SAME	4	254D	12F-12R	79.00	7519	No
100 4WD	43233.00	19020.00	22910.00	24290.00	SAME	5	317D	12F-3R	92.00	9833	C,H,A
110 4WD	45251.00	19910.00	23980.00	25420.00	SAME	6	345D	12F-3R	102.00	10758	C,H,A
130 4WD	50093.00	22040.00	26550.00	28140.00	SAME	6	381D	24F-12R	119.00	11398	C,H,A
150 4WD Turbo	53851.00	23690.00	28540.00	30250.00	SAME	6T	381D	24F-12R	138.00	12566	C,H,A
170 4WD Turbo	64110.00	28210.00	33980.00	36020.00	SAME	6TI	381D	24F-12R	155.00	13624	C,H,A

1994

Model	Approx. Retail Price New	Fair	Good	Premium	Make	No. Cyls.	Displ. Cu.-In.	No. Speeds	P.T.O. H.P.	Approx. Shipping Wt.-Lbs.	Cab
Frutteto 60II	28416.00	15060.00	17050.00	17900.00	SAME	3	183D	12F-12R	52.00		No
Frutteto 60II	28646.00	15180.00	17190.00	18050.00	SAME	3	183D	16F-16R	52.00		No
Frutteto 60II w/Cab	33770.00	17900.00	20260.00	21270.00	SAME	3	183D	12F-12R	52.00	5050	C,H,A
Frutteto 60II w/Cab	34000.00	18020.00	20400.00	21420.00	SAME	3	183D	16F-16R	52.00	5050	C,H,A
Vigneron 62	28109.00	14900.00	16870.00	17710.00	SAME	3	183D	12F-12R	52.00	4300	No
Vigneron 62	28351.00	15030.00	17010.00	17860.00	SAME	3	183D	16F-16R	52.00	4300	No
Explorer 70C	32382.00	17160.00	19430.00	20400.00	SAME	4	244D	8F-8R	71.00*	7716	No
Frutteto 75II	29882.00	15840.00	17930.00	18830.00	SAME	4	244D	12F-12R	65.00		No
Frutteto 75II	30112.00	15960.00	18070.00	18970.00	SAME	4	244D	16F-16R	65.00		No
Frutteto 75II w/Cab	35237.00	18680.00	21140.00	22200.00	SAME	4	244D	12F-12R	65.00	5450	C,H,A
Frutteto 75II w/Cab	35467.00	18800.00	21280.00	22340.00	SAME	4	244D	16F-16R	65.00	5450	C,H,A
Vigneron 75	29570.00	15670.00	17740.00	18630.00	SAME	4	244D	12F-12R	65.00	4520	No
Vigneron 75	29814.00	15800.00	17890.00	18790.00	SAME	4	244D	16F-16R	65.00	4520	No
Explorer 80C	34273.00	18170.00	20560.00	21590.00	SAME	4	244D	8F-8R	80.00*	9259	No
Frutteto 85II	32226.00	17080.00	19340.00	20310.00	SAME	4T	244D	12F-12R	78.00		No
Frutteto 85II	32456.00	17200.00	19470.00	20440.00	SAME	4T	244D	16F-16R	78.00		No
Frutteto 85II w/Cab	37621.00	19940.00	22570.00	23700.00	SAME	4T	244D	12F-12R	78.00		C,H,A
Frutteto 85II w/Cab	37851.00	20060.00	22710.00	23850.00	SAME	4T	244D	16F-16R	78.00		C,H,A
Explorer 90 Low Profile	30540.00	16190.00	18320.00	19240.00	SAME	4T	244D	12F-12R	81.00		No
Explorer 90 Low Profile	30705.00	16270.00	18420.00	19340.00	SAME	4T	244D	24F-12R	81.00		No
Explorer 90C	36414.00	19300.00	21850.00	22940.00	SAME	4T	244D	8F-8R	88.00*	10590	No
Row Crop 90	30495.00	16160.00	18300.00	19220.00	SAME	4T	244D	20F-20R	81.00		No
Row Crop 90 4WD	35129.00	18620.00	21080.00	22130.00	SAME	4T	244D	20F-20R	81.00	7831	No

*Engine Horsepower

1995

Model	Approx. Retail Price New	Fair	Good	Premium	Make	No. Cyls.	Displ. Cu.-In.	No. Speeds	P.T.O. H.P.	Approx. Shipping Wt.-Lbs.	Cab
Frutteto 60II	29533.00	16540.00	18610.00	19350.00	SAME	3	183D	12F-12R	52.00		No
Frutteto 60II	29792.00	16680.00	18770.00	19520.00	SAME	3	183D	16F-16R	52.00		No
Frutteto 60II w/Cab	35121.00	19670.00	22130.00	23020.00	SAME	3	183D	12F-12R	52.00	5050	C,H,A
Frutteto 60II w/Cab	35360.00	19800.00	22280.00	23170.00	SAME	3	183D	16F-16R	52.00	5050	C,H,A
Vigneron 62	29233.00	16370.00	18420.00	19160.00	SAME	3	183D	12F-12R	52.00	4300	No
Vigneron 62	29485.00	16510.00	18580.00	19320.00	SAME	3	183D	16F-16R	52.00	4300	No
Explorer 70C	33677.00	18860.00	21220.00	22070.00	SAME	4	244D	8F-8R	71.00*	7716	No
Frutteto 75II	31077.00	17400.00	19580.00	20360.00	SAME	4	244D	12F-12R	65.00		No
Frutteto 75II	31316.00	17540.00	19730.00	20520.00	SAME	4	244D	16F-16R	65.00		No
Frutteto 75II w/Cab	36646.00	20520.00	23090.00	24010.00	SAME	4	244D	12F-12R	65.00	5450	C,H,A
Frutteto 75II w/Cab	36886.00	20660.00	23240.00	24170.00	SAME	4	244D	16F-16R	65.00	5450	C,H,A
Vigneron 75	30753.00	17220.00	19370.00	20150.00	SAME	4	244D	12F-12R	65.00	4520	No
Vigneron 75	31007.00	17360.00	19530.00	20310.00	SAME	4	244D	16F-16R	65.00	4520	No
Explorer 80C	35644.00	19960.00	22460.00	23360.00	SAME	4	244D	8F-8R	80.00*	9259	No

Same (Cont.)

1995 (Cont.)

Model	Approx. Retail Price New	Estimated Average Value Less Repairs Fair	Good	Premium	Engine Make	No. Cyls.	Displ. Cu.-In.	No. Speeds	P.T.O. H.P.	Approx. Shipping Wt.-Lbs.	Cab
Frutteto 85II	33515.00	**18770.00**	**21110.00**	**21950.00**	SAME	4T	244D	12F-12R	78.00		No
Frutteto 85II	33754.00	**18900.00**	**21270.00**	**22120.00**	SAME	4T	244D	16F-16R	78.00		No
Frutteto 85II w/Cab	39126.00	**21910.00**	**24650.00**	**25640.00**	SAME	4T	244D	12F-12R	78.00		C,H,A
Frutteto 85II w/Cab	39365.00	**22040.00**	**24800.00**	**25790.00**	SAME	4T	244D	16F-16R	78.00		C,H,A
Explorer 90 Low Profile	31888.00	**17860.00**	**20090.00**	**20890.00**	SAME	4T	244D	16F-16R	81.00		No
Explorer 90 Low Profile	31933.00	**17880.00**	**20120.00**	**20930.00**	SAME	4T	244D	12F-12R	81.00		No
Explorer 90C	37871.00	**21210.00**	**23860.00**	**24810.00**	SAME	4T	244D	8F-8R	88.00*	10590	No
Row Crop 90	31715.00	**17760.00**	**19980.00**	**20780.00**	SAME	4T	244D	20F-20R	81.00		No
Row Crop 90 4WD	36534.00	**20460.00**	**23020.00**	**23940.00**	SAME	4T	244D	20F-20R	81.00	7831	No

*Engine Horsepower

1996

Model	Approx. Retail Price New	Estimated Average Value Less Repairs Fair	Good	Premium	Engine Make	No. Cyls.	Displ. Cu.-In.	No. Speeds	P.T.O. H.P.	Approx. Shipping Wt.-Lbs.	Cab
Frutteto 60II	27360.00	**18000.00**	**19770.00**	**20560.00**	SAME	3	183D	12F-12R	52.00		No
Frutteto 60II	27860.00	**18120.00**	**19900.00**	**20700.00**	SAME	3	183D	16F-16R	52.00		No
Frutteto 60II 4WD	31185.00	**19020.00**	**20890.00**	**21730.00**	SAME	3	183D	12F-12R	52.00	5050	C,H,A
Frutteto 60II 4WD	31435.00	**19180.00**	**21060.00**	**21900.00**	SAME	3	183D	16F-16R	52.00	5050	C,H,A
Frutteto 60II 4WD	37000.00	**22570.00**	**24790.00**	**25780.00**	SAME	3	183D	12F-12R	52.00	5050	C,H,A
Frutteto 60II 4WD	37250.00	**22720.00**	**24960.00**	**25960.00**	SAME	3	183D	16F-16R	52.00	5050	C,H,A
Frutteto 60II w/Cab	33185.00	**21410.00**	**23520.00**	**24460.00**	SAME	3	183D	12F-12R	52.00	5050	C,H,A
Frutteto 60II w/Cab	33685.00	**21530.00**	**23650.00**	**24600.00**	SAME	3	183D	16F-16R	52.00	5050	C,H,A
Vigneron 62	30850.00	**18820.00**	**20670.00**	**21500.00**	SAME	3	183D	12F-12R	52.00	4300	No
Vigneron 62	31110.00	**18980.00**	**20840.00**	**21670.00**	SAME	3	183D	16F-16R	52.00	4300	No
Explorer 70C	35490.00	**21650.00**	**23780.00**	**24730.00**	SAME	4	244D	8F-8R	71.00*	7716	No
Frutteto 75II	28950.00	**18910.00**	**20770.00**	**21600.00**	SAME	4	244D	12F-12R	65.00		No
Frutteto 75II	29450.00	**19090.00**	**20970.00**	**21810.00**	SAME	4	244D	16F-16R	65.00		No
Frutteto 75II w/Cab	34775.00	**22330.00**	**24520.00**	**25500.00**	SAME	4	244D	12F-12R	65.00	5450	C,H,A
Frutteto 75II w/Cab	35275.00	**22500.00**	**24710.00**	**25700.00**	SAME	4	244D	16F-16R	65.00	5450	C,H,A
Vigneron 75	32435.00	**19790.00**	**21730.00**	**22600.00**	SAME	4	244D	12F-12R	65.00	4520	No
Vigneron 75	32700.00	**19950.00**	**21910.00**	**22790.00**	SAME	4	244D	16F-16R	65.00	4520	No
Explorer 80C	37550.00	**22910.00**	**25160.00**	**26170.00**	SAME	4	244D	8F-8R	80.00*	9259	No
Frutteto 85II	35325.00	**21550.00**	**23670.00**	**24620.00**	SAME	4T	244D	12F-12R	78.00		No
Frutteto 85II	35575.00	**21700.00**	**23840.00**	**24790.00**	SAME	4T	244D	16F-16R	78.00		No
Frutteto 85II w/Cab	41185.00	**25120.00**	**27590.00**	**28690.00**	SAME	4T	244D	12F-12R	78.00		C,H,A
Frutteto 85II w/Cab	41435.00	**25280.00**	**27760.00**	**28870.00**	SAME	4T	244D	16F-16R	78.00		C,H,A
Explorer 90 Low Profile	33625.00	**20510.00**	**22530.00**	**23430.00**	SAME	4T	244D	16F-16R	81.00		No
Explorer 90 Low Profile	33670.00	**20540.00**	**22560.00**	**23460.00**	SAME	4T	244D	24F-12R	81.00		No
Explorer 90C	39875.00	**24320.00**	**26720.00**	**27790.00**	SAME	4T	244D	8F-8R	88.00*	10590	No
Row Crop 90	33440.00	**20400.00**	**22410.00**	**23310.00**	SAME	4T	244D	20F-20R	81.00		No
Row Crop 90 4WD	38480.00	**23470.00**	**25780.00**	**26810.00**	SAME	4T	244D	20F-20R	81.00	7831	No

*Engine Horsepower

1997

Model	Approx. Retail Price New	Estimated Average Value Less Repairs Fair	Good	Premium	Engine Make	No. Cyls.	Displ. Cu.-In.	No. Speeds	P.T.O. H.P.	Approx. Shipping Wt.-Lbs.	Cab
Frutteto 60II	30140.00	**20190.00**	**22000.00**	**22880.00**	SAME	3	183D	12F-12R	52.00		No
Frutteto 60II 4WD	33840.00	**22670.00**	**24700.00**	**25690.00**	SAME	3	183D	12F-12R	52.00	5050	No
Frutteto 60II 4WD	39860.00	**26710.00**	**29100.00**	**30260.00**	SAME	3	183D	12F-12R	52.00	5050	C,H,A
Frutteto 60II w/Cab	36170.00	**24230.00**	**26400.00**	**27460.00**	SAME	3	183D	12F-12R	52.00	5050	C,H,A
Vigneron 62	33385.00	**22370.00**	**24370.00**	**25350.00**	SAME	3	183D	12F-12R	52.00	4300	No
Explorer 70C	36720.00	**24600.00**	**26810.00**	**27880.00**	SAME	4	244D	8F-8R	71.00*	7716	No
Frutteto 75II	31785.00	**21300.00**	**23200.00**	**24130.00**	SAME	4	244D	12F-12R	65.00		No
Frutteto 75II 4WD	35485.00	**23780.00**	**25900.00**	**26940.00**	SAME	4	244D	12F-12R	65.0		No
Frutteto 75II 4WD	41510.00	**27810.00**	**30300.00**	**31510.00**	SAME	4	244D	12F-12R	65.0		C,H,A
Frutteto 75II w/Cab	37810.00	**25330.00**	**27600.00**	**28700.00**	SAME	4	244D	12F-12R	65.00	5450	C,H,A
Vigneron 75	35030.00	**23470.00**	**25570.00**	**26590.00**	SAME	4	244D	12F-12R	65.00	4520	No
Explorer 80C	38855.00	**26030.00**	**28360.00**	**29490.00**	SAME	4	244D	8F-8R	80.00*	9259	No
Frutteto 85II	37825.00	**25340.00**	**27610.00**	**28710.00**	SAME	4T	244D	12F-12R	78.00		No
Frutteto 85II	39615.00	**26540.00**	**28920.00**	**30080.00**	SAME	4T	244D	30F-30R	78.00		No
Frutteto 85II w/Cab	44190.00	**29610.00**	**32260.00**	**33550.00**	SAME	4T	244D	12F-12R	78.00		C,H,A
Frutteto 85II w/Cab	45615.00	**30560.00**	**33300.00**	**34630.00**	SAME	4T	244D	30F-30R	78.00		C,H,A
Explorer 90 Low Profile	34910.00	**23390.00**	**25480.00**	**26500.00**	SAME	4T	244D	12F-12R	81.00		No
Explorer 90 Low Profile	34955.00	**23420.00**	**25520.00**	**26540.00**	SAME	4T	244D	24F-12R	81.00		No
Explorer 90C	41260.00	**27640.00**	**30120.00**	**31330.00**	SAME	4T	244D	8F-8R	88.00*	10590	No
Row Crop 90	37480.00	**25110.00**	**27360.00**	**28450.00**	SAME	4T	244D	20F-20R	81.00		No
Row Crop 90 4WD	43620.00	**29230.00**	**31840.00**	**33110.00**	SAME	4T	244D	20F-20R	81.00	7831	No

*Engine Horsepower

Steiger

1971

Model	Approx. Retail Price New	Estimated Average Value Less Repairs Fair	Good	Premium	Engine Make	No. Cyls.	Displ. Cu.-In.	No. Speeds	P.T.O. H.P.	Approx. Shipping Wt.-Lbs.	Cab
Bearcat	22945.00	**6430.00**	**8950.00**	**10020.00**	Cat.	V8	636D	10F-2R		15700	C,H,A
Super Wildcat	20400.00	**5710.00**	**7960.00**	**8920.00**	Cat.	V8	573D	10F-2R		15400	C,H,A
Tiger	33000.00	**9240.00**	**12870.00**	**14410.00**	Cummins	V8	903D	10F-2R		24350	C,H,A
Wildcat	19000.00	**5320.00**	**7410.00**	**8300.00**	Cat.	V8	522D	10F-2R		15400	C,H,A

1972

Model	Approx. Retail Price New	Estimated Average Value Less Repairs Fair	Good	Premium	Engine Make	No. Cyls.	Displ. Cu.-In.	No. Speeds	P.T.O. H.P.	Approx. Shipping Wt.-Lbs.	Cab
Bearcat	24100.00	**6750.00**	**9400.00**	**10530.00**	Cat.	V8	636D	10F-2R		17500	C,H,A
Cougar	31800.00	**8900.00**	**12400.00**	**13890.00**	Cat.	6T	525D	10F-2R		22000	C,H,A
Super Wildcat	21300.00	**5960.00**	**8310.00**	**9310.00**	Cat.	V8	573D	10F-2R		17000	C,H,A
Tiger	37625.00	**10540.00**	**14670.00**	**16430.00**	Cummins	V8	903D	10F-2R		24350	C,H,A
Wildcat	21005.00	**5880.00**	**8190.00**	**9170.00**	Cat.	V8	522D	10F-2R		17000	C,H,A

1973

Model	Approx. Retail Price New	Estimated Average Value Less Repairs Fair	Good	Premium	Engine Make	No. Cyls.	Displ. Cu.-In.	No. Speeds	P.T.O. H.P.	Approx. Shipping Wt.-Lbs.	Cab
Bearcat	25575.00	**6720.00**	**9360.00**	**10480.00**	Cat.	V8	636D	10F-2R		17500	C,H,A
Cougar	33525.00	**8400.00**	**11700.00**	**13100.00**	Cat.	6T	525D	10F-2R		22000	C,H,A

Steiger (Cont.)

Model	Approx. Retail Price New	Estimated Average Value Less Repairs Fair	Good	Premium	Engine Make	No. Cyls.	Displ. Cu.-In.	No. Speeds	P.T.O. H.P.	Approx. Shipping Wt.-Lbs.	Cab
			1973 (Cont.)								
Super Wildcat	22975.00	5600.00	7800.00	8740.00	Cat.	V8	573D	10F-2R		17000	C,H,A
Tiger	39500.00	9800.00	13650.00	15290.00	Cummins	V8T	903D	10F-2R		24000	C,H,A
			1974								
Bearcat	28500.00	7540.00	10140.00	11360.00	Cat.	V8	636D	10F-2R		18000	C,H,A
Cougar	37600.00	10150.00	13650.00	15290.00	Cat.	6T	525D	10F-2R		22000	C,H,A
Super Wildcat	27200.00	7250.00	9750.00	10920.00	Cat.	V8	573D	10F-2R		18000	C,H,A
Tiger	41700.00	11600.00	15600.00	17470.00	Cummins	V8T	903D	10F-2R		24000	C,H,A
			1975								
Bearcat	34200.00	6500.00	9580.00	10730.00	Cat.	V8	636D	10F-2R		18000	C,H,A
Cougar II	46300.00	8800.00	12960.00	14520.00	Cat.	6T	638D	10F-2R		26690	C,H,A
Panther	52000.00	9880.00	14560.00	16310.00	Cummins	6T	855D	10F-2R		24000	C,H,A
Super Wildcat	33100.00	6290.00	9270.00	10380.00	Cat.	V8	573D	10F-2R		18000	C,H,A
Tiger II	54000.00	10260.00	15120.00	16930.00	Cummins	V8T	903D	10F-2R		27600	C,H,A
			1976								
Bearcat II	38900.00	7780.00	11280.00	12630.00	Cat.	V8	636D	10F-2R		18000	C,H,A
Cougar II	49400.00	9880.00	14330.00	16050.00	Cat.	6T	638D	10F-2R		26690	C,H,A
Panther II	54000.00	10800.00	15660.00	17540.00	Cummins	6T	855D	10F-2R		26000	C,H,A
Tiger II	56300.00	11260.00	16330.00	18290.00	Cummins	V8T	903D	10F-2R		27600	C,H,A
			1977								
Wildcat RC-210	41700.00	8760.00	12510.00	14010.00	Cat.	V8	636D	10F-2R		18000	C,H,A
Wildcat ST-210	41700.00	8760.00	12510.00	14010.00	Cat.	V8	636D	10F-2R		18000	C,H,A
Bearcat ST-220	48400.00	10160.00	14520.00	16260.00	Cummins	6T	855D	10F-2R		26000	C,H,A
Cougar ST-250	53000.00	11130.00	15900.00	17810.00	Cat.	6T	638D	10F-2R		26000	C,H,A
Cougar ST-251	54800.00	11510.00	16440.00	18410.00	Cummins	6T	855D	10F-2R		26000	C,H,A
Cougar ST-270	55200.00	11590.00	16560.00	18550.00	Cat.	6T	638D	10F-2R		26000	C,H,A
Panther 310	61600.00	12940.00	18480.00	20700.00	Cummins	6T	855D	10F-2R		26000	C,H,A
Panther 320	63800.00	13400.00	19140.00	21440.00	Cummins	V8T	903D	10F-2R		26000	C,H,A
Panther 325	67200.00	14110.00	20160.00	22580.00	Cat.	6TA	893D	10F-2R		26000	C,H,A
			1978								
Wildcat RC-210	42400.00	9330.00	13140.00	14720.00	Cat.	V8	636D	10F-2R		19070	C,H,A
Wildcat ST-210	42400.00	9330.00	13140.00	14720.00	Cat.	V8	636D	10F-2R		19070	C,H,A
Bearcat ST-220	51700.00	11370.00	16030.00	17950.00	Cummins	6T	855D	20F-4R		24540	C,H,A
Bearcat PT-225	52600.00	11570.00	16310.00	18270.00	Cat.	6T	638D	20F-4R		25225	C,H,A
Cougar ST-250	53800.00	11840.00	16680.00	18680.00	Cat.	6T	638D	20F-4R		24540	C,H,A
Cougar ST-251	55900.00	12300.00	17330.00	19410.00	Cummins	6T	855D	10F-2R		24540	C,H,A
Cougar PT-270	59200.00	13020.00	18350.00	20550.00	Cat.	6TA	638D	20F-4R		25225	C,H,A
Cougar ST-270	56700.00	12470.00	17580.00	19690.00	Cat.	6TA	638D	20F-4R		24540	C,H,A
Panther ST-310	65200.00	14340.00	20210.00	22640.00	Cummins	6T	855D	20F-4R		24540	C,H,A
Panther ST-320	66200.00	14560.00	20520.00	22980.00	Cummins	V8T	903D	20F-4R		24540	C,H,A
Panther ST-325	69400.00	15270.00	21510.00	24090.00	Cat.	6TA	893D	20F-4R		24540	C,H,A
Panther PT-350	73300.00	16130.00	22720.00	25450.00	Cummins	V8T	903D	20F-4R		25225	C,H,A
Tiger ST-450	112000.00	24640.00	34720.00	38890.00	Cummins	6TA	1150D	20F-4R		41975	C,H,A
			1979								
Wildcat III RC-210	48600.00	11180.00	15550.00	17420.00	Cat.	V8	636D	10F-2R		22000	C,H,A
Bearcat III PT-225	60200.00	13850.00	19260.00	21570.00	Cat.	6T	638D	20F-4R		26700	C,H,A
Cougar III ST-251	62470.00	14370.00	19990.00	22390.00	Cummins	6T	855D	10F-2R		26700	C,H,A
Cougar III PT-270	69200.00	15920.00	22140.00	24800.00	Cat.	6TA	638D	20F-4R		26830	C,H,A
Cougar III ST-270	63330.00	14570.00	20270.00	22700.00	Cat.	6TA	638D	20F-4R		25970	C,H,A
Panther III PTA-297	83700.00	19250.00	26780.00	29990.00	Cummins	V8T	903D	8F-2R		27350	C,H,A
Panther III ST-310	71540.00	16450.00	22890.00	25640.00	Cummins	6TA	855D	20F-4R		26850	C,H,A
Panther III ST-325	73820.00	16980.00	23620.00	26450.00	Cat.	6TA	893D	20F-4R		26950	C,H,A
Panther III PT-350	79570.00	18300.00	25460.00	28520.00	Cummins	V8T	903D	20F-4R		27330	C,H,A
Panther III ST-350	74430.00	17120.00	23820.00	26680.00	Cummins	V8T	903D	20F-4R		26670	C,H,A
Tiger III ST-450	129670.00	29820.00	41490.00	46470.00	Cummins	6TA	1150D	6F-1R		43060	C,H,A
			1980								
Bearcat III PT-225	67150.00	16120.00	22160.00	24820.00	Cat.	6T	638D	20F-4R		26700	C,H,A
Cougar III ST-251	68700.00	16490.00	22670.00	25390.00	Cummins	6T	855D	10F-2R		26700	C,H,A
Cougar III PT-270	75800.00	18190.00	25010.00	28010.00	Cat.	6TA	638D	20F-4R		26830	C,H,A
Cougar III ST-270	69300.00	16630.00	22870.00	25610.00	Cat.	6TA	638D	20F-4R		25970	C,H,A
Panther III PTA-297	89150.00	21400.00	29420.00	32950.00	Cummins	V8T	903D	8F-2R		27350	C,H,A
Panther III PTA-310	87750.00	21060.00	28960.00	32440.00	Cummins	6TA	855D	10F-2R		25615	C,H,A
Panther III ST-310	80900.00	19420.00	26700.00	29900.00	Cummins	6TA	855D	20F-4R		26850	C,H,A
Panther III PTA-325	91200.00	21600.00	29700.00	33260.00	Cat.	6TA	893D	10F-2R		29605	C,H,A
Panther III ST-325	83500.00	20040.00	27560.00	30870.00	Cat.	6T	893D	20F-4R		26950	C,H,A
Panther III PT-350	87400.00	20980.00	28840.00	32300.00	Cummins	V8T	903D	20F-4R		27330	C,H,A
Tiger III ST-450	145700.00	32400.00	44550.00	49900.00	Cummins	6TA	1150D	6F-1R		43060	C,H,A
			1981								
Bearcat III PT-225	70500.00	17630.00	23970.00	26850.00	Cat.	6T	638D	20F-4R		26700	C,H,A
Bearcat III ST-225	64750.00	16190.00	22020.00	24660.00	Cat.	6T	638D	20F-4R		25265	C,H,A
Cougar III ST-251	74400.00	18600.00	25300.00	28340.00	Cummins	6T	855D	10F-4R		26700	C,H,A
Cougar III PTA-270	86600.00	21650.00	29440.00	32970.00	Cat.	6TA	638D	10F-2R		25500	C,H,A
Cougar III ST-270	77600.00	19400.00	26380.00	29550.00	Cat.	6TA	638D	20F-4R		25970	C,H,A
Panther III PTA-310	97700.00	23750.00	32300.00	36180.00	Cummins	6TA	855D	10F-2R		25615	C,H,A
Panther III ST-310	88700.00	22180.00	30160.00	33780.00	Cummins	6TA	855D	20F-4R		26850	C,H,A
Panther III PTA-325	100500.00	24250.00	32980.00	36940.00	Cat.	6TA	893D	10F-2R		29605	C,H,A
Panther III ST-325	91500.00	22880.00	31110.00	34840.00	Cat.	6T	893D	20F-4R		26950	C,H,A

Steiger (Cont.)

Model	Approx. Retail Price New	Estimated Average Value Less Repairs Fair	Good	Premium	Engine Make	No. Cyls.	Displ. Cu.-In.	No. Speeds	P.T.O. H.P.	Approx. Shipping Wt.-Lbs.	Cab
1981 (Cont.)											
Tiger III ST-450	157900.00	36750.00	49980.00	55980.00	Cummins	6TA	1150D	6F-1R		43060	C,H,A
1982											
Cougar ST-250	78950.00	20530.00	27630.00	30950.00	Cat.	6TA	638D	20F-4R		25010	C,H,A
Cougar III PTA-280	99600.00	25610.00	34480.00	38620.00	Cat.	6T	893D	10F-2R		25905	C,H,A
Cougar III PTA-280	99600.00	25900.00	34860.00	39040.00	Cummins	6T	855D	10F-2R		25905	C,H,A
Cougar III ST-280	86451.00	22230.00	29930.00	33520.00	Cat.	6T	893D	20F-4R		25580	C,H,A
Cougar III ST-280	86451.00	22480.00	30260.00	33890.00	Cummins	6T	855D	20F-4R		25580	C,H,A
Panther III PTA-310	108900.00	26780.00	36050.00	40380.00	Cummins	6TA	855D	10F-2R		26965	C,H,A
Panther III ST-310	95800.00	24910.00	33530.00	37550.00	Cummins	6TA	855D	20F-4R		26660	C,H,A
Panther III PTA-325	112300.00	27560.00	37100.00	41550.00	Cat.	6T	893D	10F-2R		27225	C,H,A
Panther III ST-325	99800.00	25950.00	34930.00	39120.00	Cat.	6T	893D	20F-4R		26905	C,H,A
Tiger III ST-450	171500.00	39390.00	53030.00	59390.00	Cat.	V8TA	1099D	6F-1R		40245	C,H,A
Tiger III ST-470	176200.00	40560.00	54600.00	61150.00	Cummins	6TA	1150D	6F-1R		40720	C,H,A
1983											
Bearcat III ST-225	77407.00	20900.00	27870.00	31210.00	Cat.	6T	638D	20F-4R		24711	C,H,A
Cougar ST-250	83679.00	22590.00	30120.00	33730.00	Cat.	6TA	638D	20F-4R		25011	C,H,A
Cougar III PTA-280	106078.00	27000.00	36000.00	40320.00	Cat.	6T	893D	10F-2R		25905	C,H,A
Cougar III PTA-280	106078.00	27540.00	36720.00	41130.00	Cummins	6T	855D	10F-2R		25905	C,H,A
Cougar III ST-280	92078.00	24570.00	32760.00	36690.00	Cat.	6T	893D	20F-4R		25580	C,H,A
Cougar III ST-280	92078.00	24860.00	33150.00	37130.00	Cummins	6T	855D	20F-4R		25580	C,H,A
Panther III ST-310	103012.00	27270.00	36360.00	40720.00	Cummins	6TA	855D	20F-4R		26658	C,H,A
Panther III ST-325	106640.00	27810.00	37080.00	41530.00	Cat.	6T	893D	20F-4R		26905	C,H,A
Tiger III ST-450	182004.00	43740.00	58320.00	65320.00	Cat.	V8TA	1099D	6F-1R		40245	C,H,A
Tiger III ST-470	186896.00	44960.00	59940.00	67130.00	Cummins	6TA	1150D	6F-1R		40720	C,H,A
Panther CP 1325	124742.00	31860.00	42480.00	47580.00	Cat.	6T	893D	12F-2R	299.79	28330	C,H,A
Panther KP 1325	124742.00	32130.00	42840.00	47980.00	Cummins	6TA	855D	12F-2R	301.21	28330	C,H,A
Panther CP 1360	135957.00	34560.00	46080.00	51610.00	Cat.	6TA	893D	12F-2R	334.33	31732	C,H,A
Panther CP 1400	144892.00	36180.00	48240.00	54030.00	Cat.	6TA	893D	12F-2R		35802	C,H,A
Panther KP 1400	144892.00	36720.00	48960.00	54840.00	Cummins	6TA	855D	12F-2R		35802	C,H,A
1984											
Bearcat IV CM-225	76981.00	21280.00	28120.00	31490.00	Cat.	6T	638D	20F-4R		24711	C,H,A
Bearcat IV KM-225	76981.00	21560.00	28480.00	31900.00	Cummins	6T	611D	20F-4R		24411	C,H,A
Cougar IV CM-250	83679.00	23430.00	30960.00	34680.00	Cat.	6TA	638D	20F-4R		25011	C,H,A
Cougar IV CM-280	91094.00	25200.00	33300.00	37300.00	Cat.	6T	893D	20F-4R		25931	C,H,A
Cougar IV CS-280	104357.00	28000.00	37000.00	41440.00	Cat.	6T	893D	10F-2R		26252	C,H,A
Cougar IV KM-280	91094.00	25510.00	33710.00	37760.00	Cummins	6T	855D	20F-4R		25581	C,H,A
Cougar IV KS-280	104357.00	28280.00	37370.00	41850.00	Cummins	6T	855D	10F-2R		25902	C,H,A
Panther IV CS-325	120640.00	31920.00	42180.00	47240.00	Cat.	6T	893D	10F-2R	272.55	26900	C,H,A
Panther IV KS-325	120640.00	32200.00	42550.00	47660.00	Cummins	6T	855D	10F-2R		26900	C,H,A
Panther IV CM-360	112420.00	30240.00	39960.00	44760.00	Cat.	6T	893D	20F-4R		26993	C,H,A
Panther IV CS-360	126420.00	34160.00	45140.00	50560.00	Cat.	6T	893D	10F-2R		26900	C,H,A
Panther IV KM-360	112420.00	30520.00	40330.00	45170.00	Cummins	6T	855D	20F-4R		26653	C,H,A
Panther IV KS-360	126420.00	33880.00	44770.00	50140.00	Cummins	6T	855D	10F-2R		26900	C,H,A
Tiger IV KP-525	186896.00	46480.00	61420.00	68790.00	Cummins	6TA	1150D	24F-4R		40720	C,H,A
Panther CP 1325	124742.00	33320.00	44030.00	49310.00	Cat.	6T	893D	12F-2R	299.79	28330	C,H,A
Panther KP 1325	124742.00	33600.00	44400.00	49730.00	Cummins	6TA	855D	12F-2R	301.21	28330	C,H,A
Panther CP 1360	135957.00	35840.00	47360.00	53040.00	Cat.	6TA	893D	12F-2R	334.33	31732	C,H,A
Panther KP 1360	135957.00	36120.00	47730.00	53460.00	Cummins	6TA	855D	12F-2R	326.12	31732	C,H,A
Panther CP 1400	144892.00	38360.00	50690.00	56770.00	Cat.	6TA	893D	12F-2R		35802	C,H,A
Panther KP 1400	144892.00	38920.00	51430.00	57600.00	Cummins	6TA	855D	12F-2R		35802	C,H,A
1985											
Bearcat IV CM-225	77000.00	22800.00	28880.00	32060.00	Cat.	6T	638D	20F-4R		24711	C,H,A
Bearcat IV KM-225	77000.00	23100.00	29260.00	32480.00	Cummins	6T	611D	20F-4R		24411	C,H,A
Cougar IV CM-250	83700.00	25110.00	31810.00	35310.00	Cat.	6TA	638D	20F-4R		25011	C,H,A
Cougar IV CM-280	91100.00	27000.00	34200.00	37960.00	Cat.	6T	893D	20F-4R		25931	C,H,A
Cougar IV CS-280	104360.00	30000.00	38000.00	42180.00	Cat.	6T	893D	10F-2R		26252	C,H,A
Cougar IV KM-280	91100.00	27330.00	34620.00	38430.00	Cummins	6T	855D	20F-4R		25581	C,H,A
Cougar IV KS-280	104360.00	30300.00	38380.00	42600.00	Cummins	6T	855D	10F-2R		25902	C,H,A
Panther IV CM-325	115500.00	33000.00	41800.00	46400.00	Cat.	6T	893D	20F-4R		26903	C,H,A
Panther IV CS-325	120640.00	34500.00	43700.00	48510.00	Cat.	6T	893D	10F-2R		26900	C,H,A
Panther IV KM-325	115500.00	33300.00	42180.00	46820.00	Cummins	6T	855D	20F-4R		26653	C,H,A
Panther IV KM-325	126420.00	36000.00	45600.00	50620.00	Cummins	6T	855D	10F-2R		26900	C,H,A
Panther IV SM-325	115500.00	33600.00	42560.00	47240.00	Komatsu	6TI	674D	20F-4R		26216	C,H,A
Panther IV CM-360	112500.00	32400.00	41040.00	45550.00	Cat.	6T	893D	20F-4R		26993	C,H,A
Panther IV CS-360	126420.00	36600.00	46360.00	51460.00	Cat.	6T	893D	10F-2R		26900	C,H,A
Panther IV KM360	112500.00	32280.00	40890.00	45390.00	Cummins	6T	855D	20F-4R		26653	C,H,A
Panther IV KS 360	126420.00	36600.00	46360.00	51460.00	Cummins	6T	855D	10F-2R		26900	C,H,A
Tiger IV KP-525	186900.00	49800.00	63080.00	70020.00	Cummins	6TA	1150D	24F-4R		40720	C,H,A
Panther CP 1325	124750.00	35700.00	45220.00	50190.00	Cat.	6T	893D	12F-2R	299.79	28330	C,H,A
Panther KP 1325	124750.00	36000.00	45600.00	50620.00	Cummins	6TA	855D	12F-2R	301.21	28330	C,H,A
Panther CP 1360	136000.00	38100.00	48260.00	53570.00	Cat.	6TA	893D	12F-2R	334.33	31732	C,H,A
Panther KP 1360	136000.00	39000.00	49400.00	54830.00	Cummins	6TA	855D	12F-2R	326.12	31732	C,H,A
Panther CP-1400	144900.00	41100.00	52060.00	57790.00	Cat.	6TA	893D	12F-2R		35802	C,H,A
Panther KP-1400	144900.00	41700.00	52820.00	58630.00	Cummins	6TA	855D	12F-2R		35802	C,H,A
1986											
Bearcat IV CM-225	77000.00	24000.00	29250.00	32470.00	Cat.	6T	638D	20F-4R		24711	C,H,A
Bearcat IV KM-225	77000.00	24640.00	30030.00	33330.00	Cummins	6T	611D	20F-4R		24411	C,H,A
Cougar IV CM-280	91100.00	28480.00	34710.00	38530.00	Cat.	6T	893D	20F-4R		25931	C,H,A
Cougar IV CS-280	104360.00	32000.00	39000.00	43290.00	Cat.	6T	893D	10F-2R		26252	C,H,A

Steiger (Cont.)

1986 (Cont.)

Model	Approx. Retail Price New	Fair	Good	Premium	Engine Make	No. Cyls.	Displ. Cu.-In.	No. Speeds	P.T.O. H.P.	Approx. Shipping Wt.-Lbs.	Cab
Cougar IV KM-280	91100.00	28800.00	35100.00	38960.00	Cummins	6T	855D	20F-4R		25581	C,H,A
Cougar IV KS-280	104360.00	32640.00	39780.00	44160.00	Cummins	6T	855D	10F-2R		25902	C,H,A
Panther IV CM-325	115500.00	34560.00	42120.00	46750.00	Cat.	6T	893D	20F-4R		26903	C,H,A
Panther IV CS-325	120640.00	36800.00	44850.00	49780.00	Cat.	6T	893D	10F-2R		26900	C,H,A
Panther IV KM-325	115500.00	35200.00	42900.00	47620.00	Cummins	6T	855D	20F-4R		26653	C,H,A
Panther IV KM-325	126420.00	38400.00	46800.00	51950.00	Cummins	6T	855D	10F-2R		26900	C,H,A
Panther IV SM-325	115500.00	32320.00	39390.00	43720.00	Komatsu	6TI	674D	20F-4R		26216	C,H,A
Panther IV CM-360	112500.00	33600.00	40950.00	45460.00	Cat.	6T	893D	20F-4R		26993	C,H,A
Panther IV CS-360	126420.00	38720.00	47190.00	52380.00	Cat.	6T	893D	10F-2R		26900	C,H,A
Panther IV KM360	112500.00	34080.00	41540.00	46110.00	Cummins	6T	855D	20F-4R		26653	C,H,A
Panther IV KS 360	126420.00	39040.00	47580.00	52810.00	Cummins	6T	855D	10F-2R		26900	C,H,A
Tiger IV KP-525	186900.00	53410.00	65090.00	72250.00	Cummins	6TA	1150D	24F-4R		40720	C,H,A
Panther CP 1325	124750.00	37760.00	46020.00	51080.00	Cat.	6T	893D	12F-2R	299.79	28330	C,H,A
Panther KP 1325	124750.00	38080.00	46410.00	51520.00	Cummins	6TA	855D	12F-2R	301.21	28330	C,H,A
Panther CP 1360	136000.00	41280.00	50310.00	55840.00	Cat.	6TA	893D	12F-2R	334.33	31732	C,H,A
Panther KP 1360	136000.00	41600.00	50700.00	56280.00	Cummins	6TA	855D	12F-2R	326.12	31732	C,H,A
Panther CP-1400	144900.00	43840.00	53430.00	59310.00	Cat.	6TA	893D	12F-2R		35802	C,H,A
Panther KP-1400	144900.00	44290.00	53980.00	59920.00	Cummins	6TA	855D	12F-2R		35802	C,H,A

1989

Model	Approx. Retail Price New	Fair	Good	Premium	Engine Make	No. Cyls.	Displ. Cu.-In.	No. Speeds	P.T.O. H.P.	Approx. Shipping Wt.-Lbs.	Cab
Panther 9170	118650.00	42940.00	49720.00	54690.00	Cummins	6TA	855D	12F-2R		28500	C,H,A
Lion 9180	127500.00	46360.00	53680.00	59050.00	Cummins	6TA	855D	12F-2R		28200	C,H,A

1990

Model	Approx. Retail Price New	Fair	Good	Premium	Engine Make	No. Cyls.	Displ. Cu.-In.	No. Speeds	P.T.O. H.P.	Approx. Shipping Wt.-Lbs.	Cab
Panther 9170	118650.00	45200.00	51980.00	57180.00	Cummins	6TA	855D	12F-2R		28500	C,H,A
Lion 9180	127500.00	48800.00	56120.00	61730.00	Cummins	6TA	855D	12F-2R		28200	C,H,A

Tafe

1995

Model	Approx. Retail Price New	Fair	Good	Premium	Engine Make	No. Cyls.	Displ. Cu.-In.	No. Speeds	P.T.O. H.P.	Approx. Shipping Wt.-Lbs.	Cab
25 DI	8600.00	4820.00	5420.00	5640.00	Simpson	2	102D	8F-2R	23	3274	No
35 DI	10800.00	6050.00	6800.00	7070.00	Simpson	3	144D	8F-2R	30	3561	No
45 DI	11900.00	6660.00	7500.00	7800.00	Simpson	3	152D	8F-2R	41	3748	No

1996

Model	Approx. Retail Price New	Fair	Good	Premium	Engine Make	No. Cyls.	Displ. Cu.-In.	No. Speeds	P.T.O. H.P.	Approx. Shipping Wt.-Lbs.	Cab
25 DI	8600.00	5250.00	5760.00	5990.00	Simpson	2	102D	8F2R	23	3450	No
35 DI	10800.00	6590.00	7240.00	7530.00	Simpson	3	144D	8F2R	30	3700	No
45 DI	11900.00	7260.00	7970.00	8290.00	Simpson	3	152D	8F2R	41	3900	No
45 DI 4WD	18600.00	11350.00	12460.00	12960.00	Simpson	3	152D	8F2R	41	4700	No

1997

Model	Approx. Retail Price New	Fair	Good	Premium	Engine Make	No. Cyls.	Displ. Cu.-In.	No. Speeds	P.T.O. H.P.	Approx. Shipping Wt.-Lbs.	Cab
25 DI	8900.00	5960.00	6500.00	6760.00	Simpson	2	102D	8F2R	23	3450	No
35 DI	11100.00	7440.00	8100.00	8420.00	Simpson	3	144D	8F2R	30	3700	No
45 DI	12200.00	8170.00	8910.00	9270.00	Simpson	3	152D	8F2R	41	3900	No
45 DI 4WD	18600.00	12460.00	13580.00	14120.00	Simpson	3	152D	8F2R	41	4700	No

1998

Model	Approx. Retail Price New	Fair	Good	Premium	Engine Make	No. Cyls.	Displ. Cu.-In.	No. Speeds	P.T.O. H.P.	Approx. Shipping Wt.-Lbs.	Cab
25 DI	8900.00	6590.00	7030.00	7240.00	Simpson	2	102D	8F2R	23	3450	No
35 DI	11100.00	8210.00	8770.00	9030.00	Simpson	3	144D	8F2R	30	3700	No
45 DI	12200.00	9030.00	9640.00	9930.00	Simpson	3	152D	8F2R	41	3900	No
45 DI 4WD	18600.00	13760.00	14690.00	15130.00	Simpson	3	152D	8F2R	41	4700	No

1999

Model	Approx. Retail Price New	Fair	Good	Premium	Engine Make	No. Cyls.	Displ. Cu.-In.	No. Speeds	P.T.O. H.P.	Approx. Shipping Wt.-Lbs.	Cab
25 DI	9375.00	7780.00	8160.00	8410.00	Simpson	2	102D	8F2R	23	3450	No
25 DI	9375.00	7780.00	8160.00	8410.00	Simpson	2	102D	8F2R	23	3450	No
35 DI	11750.00	9750.00	10220.00	10530.00	Simpson	3	144D	8F2R	30	3700	No
35 DI	11750.00	9750.00	10220.00	10530.00	Simpson	3	144D	8F2R	30	3700	No
45 DI	12900.00	10710.00	11220.00	11560.00	Simpson	3	152D	8F2R	41	3900	No
45 DI	12900.00	10710.00	11220.00	11560.00	Simpson	3	152D	8F2R	41	3900	No
45 DI 4WD	17900.00	14860.00	15570.00	16040.00	Simpson	3	152D	8F2R	41	4700	No
45 DI 4WD	17900.00	14860.00	15570.00	16040.00	Simpson	3	152D	8F2R	41	4700	No

Versatile

1971

Model	Approx. Retail Price New	Fair	Good	Premium	Engine Make	No. Cyls.	Displ. Cu.-In.	No. Speeds	P.T.O. H.P.	Approx. Shipping Wt.-Lbs.	Cab
118	13720.00	5350.00	6450.00	7290.00	Cummins	V6	352D	9F-3R		12650	No
145	16980.00	6620.00	7980.00	9020.00	Cummins	V8	470D	9F-3R		14560	No

1972

Model	Approx. Retail Price New	Fair	Good	Premium	Engine Make	No. Cyls.	Displ. Cu.-In.	No. Speeds	P.T.O. H.P.	Approx. Shipping Wt.-Lbs.	Cab
700	19800.00	6930.00	8710.00	9760.00	Cummins	V8	555D	12F-4R		17200	No
900	25900.00	9070.00	11400.00	12770.00	Cummins	V8	903D	12F-4R		18500	No

1973

Model	Approx. Retail Price New	Fair	Good	Premium	Engine Make	No. Cyls.	Displ. Cu.-In.	No. Speeds	P.T.O. H.P.	Approx. Shipping Wt.-Lbs.	Cab
300	16804.00	6050.00	7560.00	8390.00	Cummins	V6	378D	Infinite		12700	No
700	21216.00	7640.00	9550.00	10600.00	Cummins	V8	555D	12F-4R		18100	No
800	23970.00	8630.00	10790.00	11980.00	Cummins	6	855D	12F-4R		18980	No
850	26418.00	9510.00	11890.00	13200.00	Cummins	6T	855D	12F-4R		19140	No
900	28152.00	10140.00	12670.00	14060.00	Cummins	V8	903D	12F-4R		18590	No

1974

Model	Approx. Retail Price New	Fair	Good	Premium	Engine Make	No. Cyls.	Displ. Cu.-In.	No. Speeds	P.T.O. H.P.	Approx. Shipping Wt.-Lbs.	Cab
700	28975.00	10720.00	13330.00	14800.00	Cummins	V8	555D	12F-4R		18100	C,H,A
800	34250.00	12670.00	15760.00	17490.00	Cummins	6	855D	12F-4R		18980	C,H,A

Versatile (Cont.)

Model	Approx. Retail Price New	Estimated Average Value Less Repairs Fair	Good	Premium	Engine Make	No. Cyls.	Displ. Cu.-In.	No. Speeds	P.T.O. H.P.	Approx. Shipping Wt.-Lbs.	Cab
1974 (Cont.)											
850	37260.00	13790.00	17140.00	19030.00	Cummins	6T	855D	12F-4R		19140	C,H,A
900	38690.00	14320.00	17800.00	19760.00	Cummins	V8	903D	12F-4R		18590	C,H,A
1975											
700	32162.00	12220.00	15120.00	16780.00	Cummins	V8	555D	12F-4R		18100	C,H,A
800	38018.00	14450.00	17870.00	19840.00	Cummins	6	855D	12F-4R		18980	C,H,A
850	41359.00	15720.00	19440.00	21580.00	Cummins	6T	855D	12F-4R		19140	C,H,A
900	42946.00	16320.00	20190.00	22410.00	Cummins	V8	903D	12F-4R		18590	C,H,A
1976											
700 II	36700.00	14310.00	17620.00	19380.00	Cummins	V8	555D	12F-4R		18650	C,H,A
750 II	42090.00	16420.00	20200.00	22220.00	Cummins	6	855D	12F-4R		19750	C,H,A
800 II	43482.00	16960.00	20870.00	22960.00	Cummins	6	855D	12F-4R		19830	C,H,A
850 II	47422.00	18500.00	22760.00	25040.00	Cummins	6T	855D	12F-4R		20850	C,H,A
900 II	48829.00	19040.00	23440.00	25780.00	Cummins	V8	903D	12F-4R		20250	C,H,A
1977											
700 II	37774.00	15110.00	18510.00	20360.00	Cummins	V8	555D	12F-4R		18650	C,H,A
750 II	43321.00	17330.00	21230.00	23350.00	Cummins	6	855D	12F-4R		19750	C,H,A
800 II	44756.00	17900.00	21930.00	24120.00	Cummins	6	855D	12F-4R		19830	C,H,A
825 II	46040.00	18420.00	22560.00	24820.00	Cummins	6T	855D	12F-4R		19870	C,H,A
850 II	48811.00	19520.00	23920.00	26310.00	Cummins	6T	855D	12F-4R		20850	C,H,A
900 II	50259.00	20100.00	24630.00	27090.00	Cummins	V8	903D	12F-4R		20250	C,H,A
950 II	54030.00	21610.00	26480.00	29130.00	Cummins	V8T	903D	12F-4R		21000	C,H,A
1978											
500	34738.00	15990.00	19500.00	21450.00	Cummins	V8	504D	15F-5R	160.00	15000	C,H,A
835	44980.00	18450.00	22500.00	24750.00	Cummins	6T	855D	12F-4R	195.00	19750	C,H,A
855	47221.00	20180.00	24610.00	27070.00	Cummins	6T	855D	12F-4R	212.00	19830	C,H,A
875	48354.00	20650.00	25180.00	27700.00	Cummins	6T	855D	12F-4R	233.00	20850	C,H,A
935	53791.00	22870.00	27900.00	30690.00	Cummins	V8T	903D	12F-4R	280.00	20850	C,H,A
950 II	54261.00	23890.00	29130.00	32040.00	Cummins	V8T	903D	12F-4R	295.00	21000	C,H,A
1979											
500	45468.00	19100.00	23190.00	25280.00	Cummins	V8	504D	15F-5R	160.00	15000	C,H,A
835	54888.00	23050.00	27990.00	30510.00	Cummins	6T	855D	12F-4R	198.00	19750	C,H,A
855	59902.00	25160.00	30550.00	33300.00	Cummins	6T	855D	12F-4R	212.00	19830	C,H,A
875	61341.00	25760.00	31280.00	34100.00	Cummins	6T	855D	12F-4R	248.07	20850	C,H,A
935	66642.00	27990.00	33990.00	37050.00	Cummins	V8T	903D	12F-4R	282.00	19775	C,H,A
950	67224.00	28230.00	34280.00	37370.00	Cummins	V8T	903D	12F-4R	300.00	20610	C,H,A
1980											
555	58571.00	9240.00	12710.00	14240.00	Cummins	V8T	555D	15F-5R	182.25	16800	C,H,A
835	64230.00	22480.00	28260.00	30800.00	Cummins	6T	855D	12F-4R	198.00	18100	C,H,A
855	71205.00	24920.00	31330.00	34150.00	Cummins	6T	855D	12F-4R	212.00	18100	C,H,A
875	72979.00	25540.00	32110.00	35000.00	Cummins	6T	855D	12F-4R	247.16	18380	C,H,A
895	76713.00	26850.00	33750.00	36790.00	Cummins	6TA	855D	12F-4R		18250	C,H,A
935	80628.00	28220.00	35480.00	38670.00	Cummins	V8T	903D	12F-4R	282.00	18045	C,H,A
950	81331.00	28470.00	35790.00	39010.00	Cummins	V8T	903D	12F-4R	300.00	18045	C,H,A
1981											
555	64877.00	11000.00	14960.00	16760.00	Cummins	V8T	555D	15F-5R	182.25	16800	C,H,A
835	70931.00	25540.00	31920.00	34790.00	Cummins	6T	855D	12F-4R	198.23	18100	C,H,A
855	78688.00	28330.00	35410.00	38600.00	Cummins	6T	855D	12F-4R	212.00	18380	C,H,A
875	80569.00	29010.00	36260.00	39520.00	Cummins	6T	855D	12F-4R	247.16	18380	C,H,A
895	84683.00	30490.00	38110.00	41540.00	Cummins	6TA	855D	12F-4R		18250	C,H,A
935	88995.00	30960.00	38700.00	42180.00	Cummins	V8T	903D	12F-4R	282.00	18045	C,H,A
950	89769.00	31320.00	39150.00	42670.00	Cummins	V8T	903D	12F-4R	300.00	18045	C,H,A
1982											
555	72170.00	13520.00	18200.00	20380.00	Cummins	V8T	555D	15F-5R	182.25	16800	C,H,A
835	78904.00	29190.00	36300.00	39200.00	Cummins	6T	855D	12F-4R	198.23	18100	C,H,A
855	87533.00	30340.00	37720.00	40740.00	Cummins	6T	855D	12F-4R	212.00	18380	C,H,A
875	89626.00	31080.00	38640.00	41730.00	Cummins	6T	855D	12F-4R	247.16	18380	C,H,A
895	94202.00	31820.00	39560.00	42730.00	Cummins	6TA	855D	12F-4R		18250	C,H,A
935	98998.00	32560.00	40480.00	43720.00	Cummins	V8T	903D	12F-4R	282.00	18045	C,H,A
950	99860.00	32930.00	40940.00	44220.00	Cummins	V8T	903D	12F-4R	300.00	18045	C,H,A
1983											
160	38000.00	19380.00	22420.00	24210.00	Waukesha	4	220D	Infinite	70.00	8050	C,H,A
555	77251.00	14180.00	18900.00	21170.00	Cummins	V8T	555D	15F-5R	182.25	16800	C,H,A
555 w/3 Pt. Hitch	81960.00	15360.00	20480.00	22940.00	Cummins	V8T	555D	15F-5R	182.25	17300	C,H,A
835	93692.00	29640.00	36660.00	39590.00	Cummins	6T	855D	12F-4R		18100	C,H,A
835 w/3 Pt. & PTO	109947.00	30780.00	38070.00	41120.00	Cummins	6T	855D	12F-4R	198.23	20200	C,H,A
835 w/3 Pt. Hitch	101282.00	31160.00	38540.00	41620.00	Cummins	6T	855D	12F-4R		18900	C,H,A
875	106243.00	31920.00	39480.00	42640.00	Cummins	6T	855D	12F-4R		18380	C,H,A
875 w/3 Pt. & PTO	122498.00	33060.00	40890.00	44160.00	Cummins	6TA	855D	12F-4R	247.16	20380	C,H,A
875 w/3 Pt. Hitch	113833.00	32300.00	39950.00	43150.00	Cummins	6T	855D	12F-4R		19180	C,H,A
895	115528.00	34200.00	42300.00	45680.00	Cummins	6TA	855D	12F-4R		19000	C,H,A
895 w/3 Pt. Hitch	123118.00	35340.00	43710.00	47210.00	Cummins	6TA	855D	12F-4R		19800	C,H,A
925	117000.00	33060.00	40890.00	44160.00	Cummins	6TA	855D	12F-2R		20160	C,H,A
945	122498.00	34960.00	43240.00	46700.00	Cummins	6TA	855D	12F-4R		20060	C,H,A
945 w/3 Pt. Hitch	130088.00	37240.00	46060.00	49750.00	Cummins	6TA	855D	12F-4R		20860	C,H,A
955	143041.00	39140.00	48410.00	52280.00	Cummins	6TA	855D	12F-4R		21000	C,H,A

Versatile (Cont.)

Model	Approx. Retail Price New	Estimated Average Value Less Repairs Fair	Good	Premium	Engine Make	No. Cyls.	Displ. Cu.-In.	No. Speeds	P.T.O. H.P.	Approx. Shipping Wt.-Lbs.	Cab
1983 (Cont.)											
955 w/3 Pt. Hitch	150631.00	43700.00	54050.00	58370.00	Cummins	6TA	855D	12F-4R		21800	C,H,A
975	130735.00	41800.00	51700.00	55840.00	Cummins	6TA	855D	12F-4R		22000	C,H,A
975 w/3 Pt. Hitch	138325.00	43700.00	54050.00	58370.00	Cummins	6TA	855D	12F-4R		22800	C,H,A
1150	163452.00	36450.00	48600.00	54430.00	Cummins	6TA	1150D	8F-2R		33000	C,H,A
1150 PS	191449.00	37800.00	50400.00	56450.00	Cummins	6TA	1150D	12F-2R		33000	C,H,A
PS - Power Shift											
1984											
256	38000.00	19760.00	22800.00	24620.00	Cummins	4T	239D	Infinite	85.08	8850	C,H,A
555	77255.00	15740.00	20790.00	23290.00	Cummins	V8T	555D	15F-5R	182.25	16800	C,H,A
555 w/3 Pt. Hitch	81960.00	16490.00	21790.00	24410.00	Cummins	V8T	555D	15F-5R	182.25	17300	C,H,A
835	93692.00	32640.00	40180.00	43390.00	Cummins	6T	855D	12F-4R		18100	C,H,A
835 w/3 Pt. & PTO	109950.00	33740.00	41520.00	44840.00	Cummins	6T	855D	12F-4R	198.23	20200	C,H,A
835 w/3 Pt. Hitch	101282.00	34400.00	42340.00	45730.00	Cummins	6T	855D	12F-4R		18900	C,H,A
875	106243.00	35300.00	43440.00	46920.00	Cummins	6T	855D	12F-4R		18380	C,H,A
875 w/3 Pt. & PTO	122498.00	36080.00	44400.00	47950.00	Cummins	6T	855D	12F-4R	247.16	20380	C,H,A
875 w/3 Pt. Hitch	113833.00	35410.00	43580.00	47070.00	Cummins	6T	855D	12F-4R		19180	C,H,A
895	115530.00	37050.00	45600.00	49250.00	Cummins	6TA	855D	12F-4R		19000	C,H,A
895 w/3 Pt. Hitch	123120.00	38220.00	47040.00	50800.00	Cummins	6TA	855D	12F-4R		19800	C,H,A
925	117000.00	33930.00	41760.00	45100.00	Cummins	6TA	855D	12F-2R		20160	C,H,A
945	122500.00	39000.00	48000.00	51840.00	Cummins	6TA	855D	12F-4R		20060	C,H,A
945 w/3 Pt. Hitch	130090.00	40170.00	49440.00	53400.00	Cummins	6TA	855D	12F-4R		20860	C,H,A
955	143045.00	44070.00	54240.00	58580.00	Cummins	6TA	855D	12F-4R		21000	C,H,A
955 w/3 Pt. Hitch	150635.00	44850.00	55200.00	59620.00	Cummins	6TA	855D	12F-4R		21800	C,H,A
975	130735.00	42900.00	52800.00	57020.00	Cummins	6TA	855D	12F-4R		22000	C,H,A
975 w/3 Pt. Hitch	138325.00	44460.00	54720.00	59100.00	Cummins	6TA	855D	12F-4R		22800	C,H,A
1150	163455.00	37800.00	49950.00	55940.00	Cummins	6TA	1150D	8F-2R		33000	C,H,A
1150 PS	191450.00	39480.00	52170.00	58430.00	Cummins	6TA	1150D	12F-2R		33000	C,H,A
PS - Power Shift.											
1985											
256	38000.00	20140.00	23180.00	25030.00	Cummins	4T	239D	Infinite	85.08	8850	C,H,A
276	42000.00	22260.00	25620.00	27670.00	Cummins	4TA	239D	Infinite	100.22	8900	C,H,A
836	78130.00	30000.00	36750.00	39320.00	Cummins	6T	611D	12F-4R	180.00	21000	C,H,A
836	85700.00	30280.00	37090.00	39690.00	Cummins	6T	611D	15F-3R	197.18	21000	C,H,A
836PS	91400.00	32400.00	39690.00	42470.00	Cummins	6T	611D	12F-3R	185.62	21000	C,H,A
856	94190.00	33600.00	41160.00	44040.00	Cummins	6TA	611D	12F-4R	200.00	21000	C,H,A
856PS	103940.00	35200.00	43120.00	46140.00	Cummins	6TA	611D	12F-3R	209.28	21000	C,H,A
876	100830.00	34400.00	42140.00	45090.00	Cummins	6TA	611D	12F-4R		21000	C,H,A
876PS	110280.00	36000.00	44100.00	47190.00	Cummins	6TA	611D	12F-3R		21000	C,H,A
936	109300.00	38000.00	46550.00	49810.00	Cummins	6TA	855D	12F-4R		22000	C,H,A
936PS	122650.00	39600.00	48510.00	51910.00	Cummins	6TA	855D	12F-2R		22000	C,H,A
956	114750.00	37600.00	46060.00	49280.00	Cummins	6TA	855D	12F-4R		22000	C,H,A
956PS	126850.00	39600.00	48510.00	51910.00	Cummins	6TA	855D	12F-2R		22000	C,H,A
976	119700.00	35600.00	43610.00	46660.00	Cummins	6TA	855D	12F-4R		22000	C,H,A
976PS	132790.00	40800.00	49980.00	53480.00	Cummins	6TA	855D	12F-2R		22000	C,H,A
1150	163455.00	42000.00	53200.00	59050.00	Cummins	6TA	1150D	8F-2R		33000	C,H,A
1150 PS	191450.00	43500.00	55100.00	61160.00	Cummins	6TA	1150D	12F-2R		33000	C,H,A
PS - Power Shift.											
1986											
256 w/3 Pt. & PTO	38888.00	21000.00	24110.00	26040.00	Cummins	4T	239D	Infinite	85.08	8850	C,H,A
276	42000.00	22680.00	26040.00	28120.00	Cummins	4TA	239D	Infinite	100.22	8900	C,H,A
756	51775.00	25370.00	30030.00	32430.00	Cummins	6	855D	12F-4R	168.00		C,H,A
756	55347.00	26120.00	30910.00	33380.00	Cummins	6	855D	15F-3R	168.00		C,H,A
756 PS	59767.00	27440.00	32480.00	35080.00	Cummins	6	855D	12F-3R	168.00		C,H,A
836	78130.00	29930.00	36500.00	39060.00	Cummins	6T	611D	12F-4R	180.00	21000	C,H,A
836	85700.00	31040.00	37850.00	40500.00	Cummins	6T	611D	15F-3R	197.18	21000	C,H,A
836PS	91400.00	33210.00	40500.00	43340.00	Cummins	6T	611D	12F-3R	185.62	21000	C,H,A
856	94190.00	34440.00	42000.00	44940.00	Cummins	6TA	611D	12F-4R	200.00	21000	C,H,A
856PS	103940.00	36080.00	44000.00	47080.00	Cummins	6TA	611D	12F-3R	209.28	21000	C,H,A
876	100830.00	36900.00	45000.00	48150.00	Cummins	6TA	611D	12F-4R		21000	C,H,A
876PS	110280.00	38950.00	47500.00	50830.00	Cummins	6TA	611D	12F-3R		21000	C,H,A
936	109300.00	40590.00	49500.00	52970.00	Cummins	6TA	855D	12F-4R		22000	C,H,A
936PS	122650.00	41820.00	51000.00	54570.00	Cummins	6TA	855D	12F-2R		22000	C,H,A
956	114750.00	38540.00	47000.00	50290.00	Cummins	6TA	855D	12F-4R		22000	C,H,A
956PS	126850.00	43460.00	53000.00	56710.00	Cummins	6TA	855D	12F-2R		22000	C,H,A
976	119700.00	40590.00	49500.00	52970.00	Cummins	6TA	855D	12F-4R		22000	C,H,A
976PS	132790.00	41820.00	51000.00	54570.00	Cummins	6TA	855D	12F-2R		22000	C,H,A
1150	163455.00	42560.00	51870.00	57580.00	Cummins	6TA	1150D	8F-2R		33000	C,H,A
1150 PS	191450.00	48000.00	58500.00	64940.00	Cummins	6TA	1150D	12F-2R		33000	C,H,A
PS - Power Shift.											
1987											
256 w/3 Pt. & PTO	41900.00	23600.00	27030.00	29190.00	Cummins	4T	239D	Infinite	85.14	9000	C,H,A
276	45100.00	24810.00	28410.00	30680.00	Cummins	4T	239D	Infinite	100.45	9000	C,H,A
836	70000.00	28560.00	34680.00	37110.00	Cummins	6T	611D	15F-5R	192.54	21000	C,H,A
856	85800.00	35700.00	43350.00	46390.00	Cummins	6T	611D	12F-4R	209.28	21000	C,H,A
876	95200.00	36960.00	44880.00	48020.00	Cummins	6T	611D	12F-4R		21000	C,H,A
936	105000.00	39900.00	48450.00	51840.00	Cummins	6T	855D	12F-4R		22000	C,H,A
956	107300.00	40740.00	49470.00	52930.00	Cummins	6T	855D	12F-4R		22000	C,H,A
976	115300.00	42000.00	51000.00	54570.00	Cummins	6TA	855D	12F-4R		22000	C,H,A
1156	151400.00	44680.00	52560.00	57820.00	Cummins	6TA	1150D	8F-2R		33000	C,H,A

See NEW HOLLAND/VERSATILE for later models.

Model	Approx. Retail Price New	Estimated Average Value Less Repairs Fair	Good	Premium	Engine Make	No. Cyls.	Displ. Cu.-In.	No. Speeds	P.T.O. H.P.	Approx. Shipping Wt.-Lbs.	Cab
White											
			1975								
2-105	20424.00	6130.00	7970.00	8850.00	Perkins	6T	354D	18F-6R	105.61	11635	C,H,A
2-105 4WD	25220.00	7570.00	9840.00	10920.00	Perkins	6T	354D	18F-6R	105.00	13135	C,H,A
2-150	25571.00	7670.00	9970.00	11070.00	White	6	585D	18F-6R	147.49	15500	C,H,A
2-85	18136.00	5440.00	7070.00	7850.00	Perkins	6	354D	18F-6R	85.54	11350	C,H,A
2-85 4WD	22952.00	6890.00	8950.00	9940.00	Perkins	6	354D	18F-6R	85.00	12850	C,H,A
4-150 4WD	29950.00	5320.00	7840.00	8780.00	Cat.	V8	636D	18F-6R	151.87	14500	C,H
4-180 4WD	36990.00	6270.00	9240.00	10350.00	Cat.	V8	636D	12F-4R	181.07	17900	C,H
			1976								
2-105	22673.00	7030.00	9070.00	10070.00	Perkins	6T	354D	18F-6R	105.61	11635	C,H,A
2-105 4WD	28022.00	8690.00	11210.00	12440.00	Perkins	6T	354D	18F-6R	105.00	12850	C,H,A
2-135	26806.00	8310.00	10720.00	11900.00	White	6T	478D	18F-6R	137.64	13960	C,H,A
2-135 4WD	30810.00	9550.00	12320.00	13680.00	White	6T	478D	18F-6R	137.00	14900	C,H,A
2-150	28412.00	8810.00	11370.00	12620.00	White	6	585D	18F-6R	147.49	15500	C,H,A
2-155	28922.00	8970.00	11570.00	12840.00	White	6T	478D	18F-6R	157.43	13500	C,H,A
2-50	9580.00	3740.00	4600.00	5060.00	Fiat	3	158D	8F-2R	47.00	3800	No
2-50	9957.00	3880.00	4780.00	5260.00	Fiat	3	158D	12F-3R	47.02	4004	No
2-50 4WD	13380.00	5220.00	6420.00	7060.00	Fiat	3	158D	8F-2R	47.00	4440	No
2-50 4WD	13757.00	5370.00	6600.00	7260.00	Fiat	3	158D	12F-3R	47.00	4604	No
2-60	11375.00	4440.00	5460.00	6010.00	Fiat	4	211D	8F-2R	63.00	4360	No
2-60	11725.00	4570.00	5630.00	6190.00	Fiat	4	211D	12F-3R	63.22	4566	No
2-60 4WD	14730.00	5750.00	7070.00	7780.00	Fiat	4	211D	8F-2R	63.00	4694	No
2-60 4WD	15080.00	5880.00	7240.00	7960.00	Fiat	4	211D	12F-3R	63.00	4900	No
2-70	12965.00	4020.00	5190.00	5760.00	Waukesha	6	265G	18F-6R		7023	No
2-70	14421.00	4470.00	5770.00	6410.00	Waukesha	6	283D	18F-6R	70.71	7315	No
2-70 4WD	18646.00	5780.00	7460.00	8280.00	Waukesha	6	265G	18F-6R		8733	No
2-70 4WD	19760.00	6130.00	7900.00	8770.00	Waukesha	6	283D	18F-6R		8850	No
2-85	20152.00	6250.00	8060.00	8950.00	Perkins	6	354D	18F-6R	85.54	11350	C,H,A
2-85 4WD	25502.00	7910.00	10200.00	11320.00	Perkins	6	354D	18F-6R	85.00	12500	C,H,A
4-150 4WD	34340.00	6600.00	9570.00	10720.00	Cat.	V8	636D	18F-6R	151.87	14500	C,H
4-180 4WD	40970.00	7600.00	11020.00	12340.00	Cat.	V8	636D	12F-4R	181.07	17900	C,H
			1977								
2-105	23866.00	7640.00	9790.00	10870.00	Perkins	6T	354D	18F-6R	10561	11635	C,H,A
2-105 4WD	29497.00	8960.00	11480.00	12740.00	Perkins	6T	354D	18F-6R	105.00	12850	C,H,A
2-135	28217.00	8640.00	11070.00	12290.00	White	6T	478D	18F-6R	137.64	13960	C,H,A
2-155	30444.00	9280.00	11890.00	13200.00	White	6T	478D	18F-6R	157.43	13500	C,H,A
2-180	33300.00	6720.00	9600.00	10750.00	Cat.	V8	636D	18F-6R	181.89	16000	C,H,A
2-50	10225.00	4090.00	5010.00	5510.00	Fiat	3	158D	8F-2R	47.00	3800	No
2-50	10602.00	4240.00	5200.00	5720.00	Fiat	3	158D	12F-3R	47.02	4004	No
2-50 4WD	13679.00	5470.00	6700.00	7370.00	Fiat	3	158D	8F-2R	47.00	4440	No
2-50 4WD	14056.00	5620.00	6890.00	7580.00	Fiat	3	158D	12F-3R	47.00	4604	No
2-60	12260.00	4900.00	6010.00	6610.00	Fiat	4	211D	8F-2R	63.00	4360	No
2-60	12581.00	5030.00	6170.00	6790.00	Fiat	4	211D	12F-3R	63.22	4566	No
2-60 4WD	15615.00	6250.00	7650.00	8420.00	Fiat	4	211D	8F-2R	63.00	4694	No
2-60 4WD	15936.00	6370.00	7810.00	8590.00	Fiat	4	211D	12F-3R	63.00	4900	No
2-70	13647.00	4370.00	5600.00	6220.00	Waukesha	6	265G	18F-6R		7023	No
2-70	15180.00	4860.00	6220.00	6900.00	Waukesha	6	283D	18F-6R	70.71	7315	No
2-70 4WD	19627.00	6280.00	8050.00	8940.00	Waukesha	6	265G	18F-6R		8733	No
2-70 4WD	20800.00	6660.00	8530.00	9470.00	Waukesha	6	283D	18F-6R	70.00	8850	No
2-85	21213.00	6790.00	8700.00	9660.00	Perkins	6	354D	18F-6R	85.54	11350	C,H,A
2-85 4WD	26844.00	8590.00	11010.00	12220.00	Perkins	6	354D	18F-6R	85.00	12500	C,H,A
4-150 4WD	36868.00	6930.00	9900.00	11090.00	Cat.	V8	636D	18F-6R	151.87	14500	C,H,A
4-180 4WD	44124.00	8190.00	11700.00	13100.00	Cat.	V8	636D	12F-4R	181.07	17900	C,H,A
			1978								
2-105	25059.00	8270.00	10530.00	11580.00	Perkins	6T	354D	18F-6R	105.61	11635	C,H,A
2-105 4WD	30972.00	10220.00	13010.00	14310.00	Perkins	6T	354D	18F-6R	105.00	12850	C,H,A
2-135	29628.00	9780.00	12440.00	13680.00	White	6T	478D	18F-6R	137.64	13960	C,H,A
2-135 4WD	35128.00	11220.00	14280.00	15710.00	White	6T	478D	18F-6R	137.00	14900	C,H,A
2-155	31966.00	10550.00	13430.00	14770.00	White	6T	478D	18F-6R	157.43	13500	C,H,A
2-155 4WD	37466.00	11550.00	14700.00	16170.00	White	6T	478D	18F-6R	157.00	15200	C,H,A
2-180	39800.00	8140.00	11470.00	12850.00	Cat.	V8	636D	18F-6R	181.89	16000	C,H,A
2-180 4WD	45300.00	9240.00	13020.00	14580.00	Cat.	V8	636D	18F-6R	181.00	17500	C,H,A
2-50	10736.00	4400.00	5370.00	5910.00	Fiat	3	158D	8F-2R	47.00	3800	No
2-50	11132.00	4560.00	5570.00	6130.00	Fiat	3	158D	12F-3R	47.02	4004	No
2-50 4WD	14363.00	5890.00	7180.00	7900.00	Fiat	3	158D	8F-2R	47.00	4440	No
2-50 4WD	14759.00	6050.00	7380.00	8120.00	Fiat	3	158D	12F-3R	47.00	4604	No
2-60	12873.00	5280.00	6440.00	7080.00	Fiat	4	211D	8F-2R	63.00	4360	No
2-60	13210.00	5420.00	6610.00	7270.00	Fiat	4	211D	12F-3R	63.22	4566	No
2-60 4WD	16396.00	6720.00	8200.00	9020.00	Fiat	4	211D	8F-2R	63.00	4694	No
2-60 4WD	16733.00	6860.00	8370.00	9210.00	Fiat	4	211D	12F-3R	63.00	4900	No
2-70	14329.00	4730.00	6020.00	6620.00	Waukesha	6	265G	18F-6R		7023	No
2-70	15939.00	5260.00	6690.00	7360.00	Waukesha	6	283D	18F-6R	70.71	7315	No
2-70 4WD	20608.00	6800.00	8660.00	9530.00	Waukesha	6	265G	18F-6R		8733	No
2-70 4WD	21840.00	7210.00	9170.00	10090.00	Waukesha	6	283D	18F-6R	70.00	8850	No
2-85	22274.00	7350.00	9360.00	10300.00	Perkins	6	354D	18F-6R	85.54	11350	C,H,A
2-85 4WD	28186.00	9300.00	11840.00	13020.00	Perkins	6	354D	18F-6R	85.00	12500	C,H,A
4-150 4WD	38711.00	7700.00	10850.00	12150.00	Cat.	V8	636D	18F-6R	151.87	14500	C,H,A
4-180 4WD	46330.00	8800.00	12400.00	13890.00	Cat.	V8	636D	12F-4R	181.07	17900	C,H,A
4-210 4WD	58816.00	10560.00	14880.00	16670.00	Cat.	V8	636D	18F-6R	182.44	22320	C,H,A

Model	Approx. Retail Price New	Estimated Average Value Less Repairs Fair	Good	Premium	Engine Make	No. Cyls.	Displ. Cu.-In.	No. Speeds	P.T.O. H.P.	Approx. Shipping Wt.-Lbs.	Cab
White (Cont.)											
			1979								
2-105	26312.00	8950.00	11310.00	12330.00	Perkins	6T	354D	18F-6R	105.61	11635	C,H,A
2-105 4WD	32521.00	11060.00	13980.00	15240.00	Perkins	6T	354D	18F-6R	105.00	12850	C,H,A
2-135	31109.00	10580.00	13380.00	14580.00	White	6T	478D	18F-6R	137.64	13960	C,H,A
2-135 4WD	36884.00	11900.00	15050.00	16410.00	White	6T	478D	18F-6R	137.00	14900	C,H,A
2-155	33564.00	11410.00	14430.00	15730.00	White	6T	478D	18F-6R	157.43	13500	C,H,A
2-155 4WD	39339.00	12580.00	15910.00	17340.00	White	6T	478D	18F-6R	157.00	15200	C,H,A
2-180	41790.00	9200.00	12800.00	14340.00	Cat.	V8	636D	18F-6R	181.89	16000	C,H,A
2-180 4WD	47565.00	10350.00	14400.00	16130.00	Cat.	V8	636D	18F-6R	181.00	17500	C,H,A
2-30	6400.00	2690.00	3260.00	3550.00	Isuzu	3	91D	8F-2R	28.33	2624	No
2-30 4WD	7500.00	3150.00	3830.00	4180.00	Isuzu	3	91D	8F-2R	28.00	3400	No
2-35	7700.00	3230.00	3930.00	4280.00	Isuzu	3	108D	8F-2R	32.84	2756	No
2-50	11273.00	4740.00	5750.00	6270.00	Fiat	3	158D	8F-2R	47.00	3800	No
2-50	11689.00	4910.00	5960.00	6500.00	Fiat	3	158D	12F-3R	47.02	4004	No
2-50 4WD	15081.00	6330.00	7690.00	8380.00	Fiat	3	158D	8F-2R	47.00	4440	No
2-50 4WD	15497.00	6510.00	7900.00	8610.00	Fiat	3	158D	12F-3R	47.00	4604	No
2-60	13517.00	5680.00	6890.00	7510.00	Fiat	4	211D	8F-2R	63.00	4360	No
2-60	13871.00	5830.00	7070.00	7710.00	Fiat	4	211D	12F-3R	63.22	4456	No
2-60 4WD	17216.00	7230.00	8780.00	9570.00	Fiat	4	211D	8F-2R	63.00	4694	No
2-60 4WD	17570.00	7380.00	8960.00	9770.00	Fiat	4	211D	12F-3R	63.00	4900	No
2-70	15045.00	5120.00	6470.00	7050.00	Waukesha	6	265G	18F-6R		7023	No
2-70	16736.00	5690.00	7200.00	7850.00	Waukesha	6	283D	18F-6R	70.71	7315	No
2-70 4WD	21638.00	7360.00	9300.00	10140.00	Waukesha	6	265G	18F-6R		8733	No
2-70 4WD	22932.00	7800.00	9860.00	10750.00	Waukesha	6	283D	18F-6R	70.00	8850	No
2-85	23388.00	7950.00	10060.00	10970.00	Perkins	6	354D	18F-6R	85.54	11350	C,H,A
2-85 4WD	29595.00	10060.00	12730.00	13880.00	Perkins	6	354D	18F-6R	85.00	12500	C,H,A
4-175 4WD	45947.00	10350.00	14400.00	16130.00	Cat.	V8	636D	18F-6R	151.69	16600	C,H,A
4-210 4WD	60016.00	11500.00	16000.00	17920.00	Cat.	V8	636D	18F-6R	182.44	22320	C,H,A
			1980								
2-105	26345.00	9220.00	11590.00	12630.00	Perkins	6T	354D	6F-2R	105.00	11320	C,H,A
2-105	27628.00	9670.00	12160.00	13250.00	Perkins	6T	354D	18F-6R	105.61	11635	C,H,A
2-105 4WD	32862.00	11500.00	14460.00	15760.00	Perkins	6T	354D	6F-2R	105.00	12535	C,H,A
2-105 4WD	34147.00	11950.00	15030.00	16380.00	Perkins	6T	354D	18F-6R	105.00	12850	C,H,A
2-135	30680.00	10740.00	13500.00	14720.00	White	6T	478D	6F-2R	137.00	13645	C,H,A
2-135	32664.00	11430.00	14370.00	15660.00	White	6T	478D	18F-6R	137.64	13960	C,H,A
2-135 4WD	36744.00	12860.00	16170.00	17630.00	White	6T	478D	6F-2R	137.00	14885	C,H,A
2-135 4WD	38728.00	12950.00	16280.00	17750.00	White	6T	478D	18F-6R	137.00	14900	C,H,A
2-155	33258.00	11640.00	14630.00	15950.00	White	6T	478D	6F-2R	157.00	13185	C,H,A
2-155	35242.00	12340.00	15510.00	16910.00	White	6T	478D	18F-6R	157.43	13500	C,H,A
2-155 4WD	39321.00	13300.00	16720.00	18230.00	White	6T	478D	6F-2R	157.00	14885	C,H,A
2-155 4WD	41306.00	13720.00	17250.00	18800.00	White	6T	478D	18F-6R	157.00	15200	C,H,A
2-180	41895.00	9600.00	13200.00	14780.00	Cat.	V8	636D	6F-2R	181.00	15685	C,H,A
2-180	43880.00	9840.00	13530.00	15150.00	Cat.	V8	636D	18F-6R	181.89	16000	C,H,A
2-180 4WD	45675.00	10320.00	14190.00	15890.00	Cat.	V8	636D	6F-2R	181.00	17185	C,H,A
2-180 4WD	49943.00	11040.00	15180.00	17000.00	Cat.	V8	636D	18F-6R	181.00	17500	C,H,A
2-30	7600.00	3270.00	3950.00	4270.00	Isuzu	3	91D	8F-2R	28.33	2624	No
2-30 4WD	8408.00	3620.00	4370.00	4720.00	Isuzu	3	91D	8F-2R	28.00	3400	No
2-35	8550.00	3680.00	4450.00	4810.00	Isuzu	3	108D	8F-2R	32.84	2756	No
2-45	9500.00	4090.00	4940.00	5340.00	Isuzu	4	169D	20F-4R	43.00	5015	No
2-45 4WD	10800.00	4640.00	5620.00	6070.00	Isuzu	4	169D	20F-4R	43.73	5795	No
2-50	12400.00	5330.00	6450.00	6970.00	Fiat	3	158D	8F-2R	47.00	3800	No
2-50	12858.00	5530.00	6690.00	7230.00	Fiat	3	158D	12F-3R	47.02	4004	No
2-50 4WD	16589.00	7130.00	8630.00	9320.00	Fiat	3	158D	8F-2R	47.00	4440	No
2-50 4WD	17047.00	7330.00	8860.00	9570.00	Fiat	3	158D	12F-3R	47.00	4604	No
2-60	14869.00	6390.00	7730.00	8350.00	Fiat	4	211D	8F-2R	63.00	4360	No
2-60	15258.00	6560.00	7930.00	8560.00	Fiat	4	211D	12F-3R	63.22	4456	No
2-60 4WD	18938.00	8140.00	9850.00	10640.00	Fiat	4	211D	8F-2R	63.00	4694	No
2-60 4WD	19327.00	8310.00	10050.00	10850.00	Fiat	4	211D	12F-3R	63.00	4900	No
2-62	13900.00	5980.00	7230.00	7810.00	Isuzu	4	219D	20F-4R	61.00	5269	No
2-62 4WD	18000.00	7740.00	9360.00	10110.00	Isuzu	4	219D	20F-4R	61.46	6065	No
2-70	15797.00	5530.00	6950.00	7580.00	Waukesha	6	265G	18F-6R		7023	No
2-70	17573.00	6150.00	7730.00	8430.00	Waukesha	6	283D	18F-6R	70.71	7315	No
2-70 4WD	22720.00	7950.00	10000.00	10900.00	Waukesha	6	265G	18F-6R		8733	No
2-70 4WD	24079.00	8430.00	10600.00	11550.00	Waukesha	6	283D	18F-6R	70.00	8850	No
2-85	24557.00	8600.00	10810.00	11780.00	Perkins	6	354D	18F-6R	85.54	11350	C,H,A
2-85 4WD	31075.00	10880.00	13670.00	14900.00	Perkins	6	354D	18F-6R	85.00	12500	C,H,A
4-175 4WD	48365.00	11280.00	15510.00	17370.00	Cat.	V8	636D	18F-6R	151.69	16600	C,H,A
4-210 4WD	63175.00	12720.00	17490.00	19590.00	Cat.	V8	636D	18F-6R	182.44	22320	C,H,A
			1981								
2-105	30391.00	10940.00	13680.00	14910.00	Perkins	6T	354D	18F-6R	105.61	11635	C,H,A
2-105 4WD	37562.00	12960.00	16200.00	17660.00	Perkins	6T	354D	18F-6R	105.00	12850	C,H,A
2-135	35930.00	12600.00	15750.00	17170.00	White	6T	478D	18F-6R	137.64	13960	C,H,A
2-135 4WD	42601.00	14400.00	18000.00	19620.00	White	6T	478D	18F-6R	137.00	14900	C,H,A
2-155	42290.00	14760.00	18450.00	20110.00	White	6T	478D	18F-6R	157.43	13500	C,H,A
2-155 4WD	49567.00	16920.00	21150.00	23050.00	White	6T	478D	18F-6R	157.00	15200	C,H,A
2-180	52656.00	12500.00	17000.00	19040.00	Cat.	V8	636D	18F-6R	181.89	16000	C,H,A
2-180 4WD	59932.00	13750.00	18700.00	20940.00	Cat.	V8	636D	18F-6R	181.00	17500	C,H,A
2-30	8000.00	3520.00	4240.00	4580.00	Isuzu	3	91D	8F-2R	28.33	2624	No
2-30 4WD	8850.00	3890.00	4690.00	5070.00	Isuzu	3	91D	8F-2R	28.00	3400	No
2-35	9000.00	3960.00	4770.00	5150.00	Isuzu	3	108D	8F-2R	32.84	2756	No
2-45	10946.00	4820.00	5800.00	6260.00	Isuzu	4	169D	20F-4R	43.00	5015	No
2-45 4WD	15975.00	7030.00	8470.00	9150.00	Isuzu	4	169D	20F-4R	43.73	5795	No
2-50	14880.00	6550.00	7890.00	8520.00	Fiat	3	158D	8F-2R	47.00	3800	No

White (Cont.)

1981 (Cont.)

Model	Approx. Retail Price New	Fair	Good	Premium	Engine Make	No. Cyls.	Displ. Cu.-In.	No. Speeds	P.T.O. H.P.	Approx. Shipping Wt.-Lbs.	Cab
2-50	15430.00	6790.00	8180.00	8830.00	Fiat	3	158D	12F-3R	47.02	4004	No
2-50 4WD	19906.00	8760.00	10550.00	11390.00	Fiat	3	158D	8F-2R	47.00	4440	No
2-50 4WD	20456.00	9000.00	10840.00	11710.00	Fiat	3	158D	12F-3R	47.00	4604	No
2-60	17843.00	7850.00	9460.00	10220.00	Fiat	4	211D	8F-2R	63.00	4360	No
2-60	18310.00	8060.00	9700.00	10480.00	Fiat	4	211D	12F-3R	63.22	4456	No
2-60 4WD	22726.00	10000.00	12050.00	13010.00	Fiat	4	211D	8F-2R	63.00	4694	No
2-60 4WD	23192.00	10200.00	12290.00	13270.00	Fiat	4	211D	12F-3R	63.00	4900	No
2-62	16919.00	7440.00	8970.00	9690.00	Isuzu	4	219D	20F-4R	61.00	5269	No
2-62 4WD	21950.00	9660.00	11630.00	12560.00	Isuzu	4	219D	20F-4R	61.63	6065	No
2-70	20500.00	7380.00	9230.00	10060.00	White	6	283D	18F-6R	70.71	7315	No
2-70 4WD	25000.00	9000.00	11250.00	12260.00	White	6	283D	18F-6R	70.00	8850	No
2-85	25468.00	9170.00	11460.00	12490.00	Perkins	6	354D	18F-6R	85.54	11350	C,H,A
2-85 4WD	37290.00	13420.00	16780.00	18290.00	Perkins	6	354D	18F-6R	85.00	12500	C,H,A
4-175 4WD	50910.00	12000.00	16320.00	18280.00	Cat.	V8	636D	18F-6R	151.69	16600	C,H,A
4-210 4WD	66500.00	14000.00	19040.00	21330.00	Cat.	V8	636D	18F-6R	182.44	22320	C,H,A

1982

Model	Approx. Retail Price New	Fair	Good	Premium	Engine Make	No. Cyls.	Displ. Cu.-In.	No. Speeds	P.T.O. H.P.	Approx. Shipping Wt.-Lbs.	Cab
2-105	36360.00	13450.00	16730.00	18070.00	Perkins	6T	354D	18F-6R	105.61	11635	C,H,A
2-105 4WD	44322.00	15540.00	19320.00	20870.00	Perkins	6T	354D	18F-6R	105.00	12850	C,H,A
2-110	40900.00	14430.00	17940.00	19380.00	Perkins	6T	354D	18F-6R	110.52	11685	C,H,A
2-110 4WD	49200.00	17390.00	21620.00	23350.00	Perkins	6T	354D	18F-6R	110.52	12900	C,H,A
2-135	41739.00	14800.00	18400.00	19870.00	White	6T	478D	18F-6R	137.64	13960	C,H,A
2-135 4WD	50313.00	17760.00	22080.00	23850.00	White	6T	478D	18F-6R	137.00	14900	C,H,A
2-135 Series 3	47465.00	16650.00	20700.00	22360.00	White	6T	478D	18F-6R	137.64	14000	C,H,A
2-135 Series 3 4WD	56600.00	19610.00	24380.00	26330.00	White	6T	478D	18F-6R	137.00	14950	C,H,A
2-155	48820.00	16650.00	20700.00	22360.00	White	6T	478D	18F-6R	157.43	14250	C,H,A
2-155 4WD	57394.00	19610.00	24380.00	26330.00	White	6T	478D	18F-6R	157.00	15200	C,H,A
2-155 Series 3	52500.00	18500.00	23000.00	24840.00	White	6T	478D	18F-6R	157.43	15000	C,H,A
2-155 Series 3 4WD	61460.00	20720.00	25760.00	27820.00	White	6T	478D	18F-6R	157.00	15950	C,H,A
2-180	55030.00	13520.00	18200.00	20380.00	Cat.	V8	636D	18F-6R	181.89	16000	C,H,A
2-180 4WD	63383.00	15340.00	20650.00	23130.00	Cat.	V8	636D	18F-6R	181.00	17500	C,H,A
2-180 Series 3	59365.00	14300.00	19250.00	21560.00	Cat.	V8	636D	18F-6R	181.89	16100	C,H,A
2-180 Series 3 4WD	68000.00	16380.00	22050.00	24700.00	Cat.	V8	636D	18F-6R	181.00	17500	C,H,A
2-30	9095.00	4090.00	4910.00	5300.00	Isuzu	3	91D	8F-2R	28.33	2624	No
2-30 4WD	10808.00	4860.00	5840.00	6310.00	Isuzu	3	91D	8F-2R	28.00	3400	No
2-35	9555.00	4300.00	5160.00	5570.00	Isuzu	3	108D	8F-2R	32.84	2756	No
2-45	14369.00	6470.00	7760.00	8380.00	Isuzu	4	169D	20F-4R	43.00	5015	No
2-45 4WD	19398.00	8730.00	10480.00	11320.00	Isuzu	4	169D	20F-4R	43.73	5795	No
2-55	16380.00	7370.00	8850.00	9560.00	Isuzu	4	199D	16F-4R	53.32	5072	No
2-55 4WD	21210.00	9550.00	11450.00	12370.00	Isuzu	4	199D	16F-4R	53.32	5875	No
2-62	17438.00	7850.00	9420.00	10170.00	Isuzu	4	219D	20F-4R	61.00	5269	No
2-62 4WD	22669.00	10200.00	12240.00	13220.00	Isuzu	4	219D	20F-4R	61.46	6065	No
2-65	18572.00	8360.00	10030.00	10830.00	Isuzu	4	235D	16F-4R	62.50	5314	No
2-65 4WD	23637.00	10640.00	12760.00	13780.00	Isuzu	4	235D	16F-4R	62.50	5814	No
2-70	23807.00	8810.00	10950.00	11830.00	White	6	283D	18F-6R	70.71	7315	No
2-70 4WD	29500.00	10920.00	13570.00	14660.00	White	6	283D	18F-6R	70.00	8850	No
2-75	21919.00	8110.00	10080.00	10890.00	Isuzu	6	329D	16F-4R	75.39	6107	No
2-75 4WD	27399.00	10140.00	12600.00	13610.00	Isuzu	6	329D	16F-4R	75.39	7642	No
2-85	30857.00	11420.00	14190.00	15330.00	Perkins	6	354D	18F-6R	85.54	11350	C,H,A
2-85 4WD	38819.00	14360.00	17860.00	19290.00	Perkins	6	354D	18F-6R	85.00	12500	C,H,A
2-88	35900.00	13280.00	16510.00	17830.00	Perkins	6	354D	18F-6R	86.78	11685	C,H,A
2-88 4WD	45000.00	16650.00	20700.00	22360.00	Perkins	6	354D	18F-6R	86.78	12835	C,H,A
4-175 4WD	53589.00	13930.00	18760.00	21010.00	Cat.	V8	636D	18F-6R	151.69	16600	C,H,A
4-210 4WD	70040.00	15340.00	20650.00	23130.00	Cat.	V8	636D	18F-6R	182.44	22320	C,H,A
4-225 4WD	75479.00	16640.00	22400.00	25090.00	Cat.	V8T	636D	18F-6R	195.65	23000	C,H,A
4-270 4WD	80000.00	17940.00	24150.00	27050.00	Cat.	6T	638D	16F-4R	239.25	26000	C,H,A

1983

Model	Approx. Retail Price New	Fair	Good	Premium	Engine Make	No. Cyls.	Displ. Cu.-In.	No. Speeds	P.T.O. H.P.	Approx. Shipping Wt.-Lbs.	Cab
2-105	37087.00	14090.00	17430.00	18820.00	Perkins	6T	354D	18F-6R	105.61	11635	C,H,A
2-105 4WD	45208.00	17180.00	21250.00	22950.00	Perkins	6T	354D	18F-6R	105.00	12850	C,H,A
2-110	41718.00	15850.00	19610.00	21180.00	Perkins	6T	354D	18F-6R	110.52	11685	C,H,A
2-110 4WD	50184.00	18240.00	22560.00	24370.00	Perkins	6T	354D	18F-6R	110.52	12900	C,H,A
2-135 Series 3	47465.00	17480.00	21620.00	23350.00	White	6T	478D	18F-6R	137.64	13960	C,H,A
2-135 Series 3 4WD	56600.00	20330.00	25150.00	27160.00	White	6T	478D	18F-6R	137.00	14900	C,H,A
2-155 Series 3	52500.00	19000.00	23500.00	25380.00	White	6T	478D	18F-6R	157.43	15000	C,H,A
2-155 Series 3 4WD	61460.00	22040.00	27260.00	29440.00	White	6T	478D	18F-6R	157.00	15950	C,H,A
2-180 Series 3	59365.00	15260.00	20340.00	22780.00	Cat.	V8	636D	18F-6R	181.89	16100	C,H,A
2-180 Series 3 4WD	68000.00	17280.00	23040.00	25810.00	Cat.	V8	636D	18F-6R	181.00	17500	C,H,A
2-30	9277.00	4270.00	5100.00	5510.00	Isuzu	3	91D	8F-2R	28.33	2624	No
2-30 4WD	11024.00	5070.00	6060.00	6550.00	Isuzu	3	91D	8F-2R	28.00	3400	No
2-35	9746.00	4480.00	5360.00	5790.00	Isuzu	3	108D	8F-2R	32.84	2756	No
2-45	14656.00	6740.00	8060.00	8710.00	Isuzu	4	169D	20F-4R	43.00	5015	No
2-45 4WD	19772.00	9100.00	10880.00	11750.00	Isuzu	4	169D	20F-4R	43.73	5795	No
2-55	16708.00	7690.00	9190.00	9930.00	Isuzu	4	199D	16F-4R	53.32	5072	No
2-55 4WD	21634.00	9950.00	11900.00	12850.00	Isuzu	4	199D	16F-4R	53.32	5875	No
2-62	17787.00	8180.00	9780.00	10560.00	Isuzu	4	219D	20F-4R	61.00	5269	No
2-62 4WD	23122.00	10640.00	12720.00	13740.00	Isuzu	4	219D	20F-4R	61.46	6065	No
2-65	18943.00	8710.00	10420.00	11250.00	Isuzu	4	235D	16F-4R	62.50	5314	No
2-65 4WD	24110.00	11090.00	13260.00	14320.00	Isuzu	4	235D	16F-4R	62.50	5814	No
2-70	24283.00	9230.00	11410.00	12320.00	White	6	283D	18F-6R	70.71	7315	No
2-70 4WD	30090.00	11430.00	14140.00	15270.00	White	6	283D	18F-6R	70.00	8850	No
2-75	22357.00	8500.00	10510.00	11350.00	Isuzu	6	329D	16F-4R	75.39	6107	No
2-75 4WD	27947.00	10620.00	13140.00	14190.00	Isuzu	6	329D	16F-4R	75.39	7642	No
2-85	31474.00	11960.00	14790.00	15970.00	Perkins	6	354D	18F-6R	85.54	11350	C,H,A

White (Cont.)

1983 (Cont.)

Model	Approx. Retail Price New	Estimated Average Value Less Repairs: Fair	Good	Premium	Engine: Make	No. Cyls.	Displ. Cu.-In.	No. Speeds	P.T.O. H.P.	Approx. Shipping Wt.-Lbs.	Cab
2-85 4WD	39595.00	15050.00	18610.00	20100.00	Perkins	6	354D	18F-6R	85.00	12500	C,H,A
2-88	36618.00	13640.00	16870.00	18220.00	Perkins	6	354D	18F-6R	86.78	11685	C,H,A
2-88 4WD	45900.00	17100.00	21150.00	22840.00	Perkins	6	354D	18F-6R	86.78	12835	C,H,A
4-175 4WD	60126.00	15120.00	20160.00	22580.00	Cat.	V8	636D	18F-6R	151.72	16600	C,H,A
4-225 4WD	76010.00	17280.00	23040.00	25810.00	Cat.	V8T	636D	18F-6R	195.65	23000	C,H,A
4-270 4WD	84960.00	19980.00	26640.00	29840.00	Cat.	6T	638D	16F-4R	239.25	26000	C,H,A
4-270 4WD w/3 Pt.	89410.00	21330.00	28440.00	31850.00	Cat.	6T	638D	16F-4R	239.25	26800	C,H,A

1984

Model	Approx. Retail Price New	Fair	Good	Premium	Make	No. Cyls.	Displ. Cu.-In.	No. Speeds	P.T.O. H.P.	Approx. Shipping Wt.-Lbs.	Cab
2-110	41925.00	15600.00	19200.00	20740.00	Perkins	6T	354D	18F-6R	110.52	11685	C,H,A
2-110 4WD	50430.00	18720.00	23040.00	24880.00	Perkins	6T	354D	18F-6R	110.52	12900	C,H,A
2-135 Series 3	49365.00	18330.00	22560.00	24370.00	White	6T	478D	18F-6R	137.64	13960	C,H,A
2-135 Series 3 4WD	58865.00	21840.00	26880.00	29030.00	White	6T	478D	18F-6R	137.00	14900	C,H,A
2-155 Series 3	54600.00	20280.00	24960.00	26960.00	White	6T	478D	18F-6R	157.43	15000	C,H,A
2-155 Series 3 4WD	63915.00	23400.00	28800.00	31100.00	White	6T	478D	18F-6R	157.00	15950	C,H,A
2-180 Series 3	61740.00	16240.00	21460.00	24040.00	Cat.	V8	636D	18F-6R	181.89	16100	C,H,A
2-180 Series 3 4WD	70720.00	18480.00	24420.00	27350.00	Cat.	V8	636D	18F-6R	181.00	17500	C,H,A
2-30	9280.00	4360.00	5200.00	5620.00	Isuzu	3	91D	8F-2R	28.33	2624	No
2-30 4WD	11025.00	5180.00	6170.00	6660.00	Isuzu	3	91D	8F-2R	28.00	3400	No
2-35	9750.00	4580.00	5460.00	5900.00	Isuzu	3	108D	8F-2R	32.84	2756	No
2-55	16935.00	7960.00	9480.00	10240.00	Isuzu	4	199D	16F-4R	53.32	5072	No
2-55 4WD	21635.00	10170.00	12120.00	13090.00	Isuzu	4	199D	16F-4R	53.32	5875	No
2-65	19395.00	9120.00	10860.00	11730.00	Isuzu	4	235D	16F-4R	62.50	5314	No
2-65 4WD	24110.00	11330.00	13500.00	14580.00	Isuzu	4	235D	16F-4R	62.50	5814	No
2-75	23160.00	9030.00	11120.00	12010.00	Isuzu	6	329D	16F-4R	75.39	6293	No
2-75 4WD	29105.00	11350.00	13970.00	15090.00	Isuzu	6	329D	16F-4R	75.39	6778	No
2-88	36620.00	14000.00	17230.00	18610.00	Perkins	6	354D	18F-6R	86.78	11685	C,H,A
2-88 4WD	45900.00	17550.00	21600.00	23330.00	Perkins	6	354D	18F-6R	86.78	12835	C,H,A
4-175 4WD	60130.00	15960.00	21090.00	23620.00	Cat.	V8	636D	18F-6R	151.72	16600	C,H,A
4-225 4WD	78500.00	17920.00	23680.00	26520.00	Cat.	V8T	636D	18F-6R	195.65	23000	C,H,A
4-270 4WD	85200.00	20720.00	27380.00	30670.00	Cat.	6T	638D	16F-4R	239.25	26000	C,H,A
4-270 4WD w/3 Pt.	91465.00	22120.00	29230.00	32740.00	Cat.	6T	638D	16F-4R	239.25	26800	C,H,A

1985

Model	Approx. Retail Price New	Fair	Good	Premium	Make	No. Cyls.	Displ. Cu.-In.	No. Speeds	P.T.O. H.P.	Approx. Shipping Wt.-Lbs.	Cab
2-110	42975.00	17190.00	21060.00	22530.00	Perkins	6T	354D	18F-6R	110.52	11685	C,H,A
2-110 4WD	52000.00	20000.00	24500.00	26220.00	Perkins	6T	354D	18F-6R	110.52	12900	C,H,A
2-135 Series 3	51450.00	20580.00	25210.00	26980.00	White	6T	478D	18F-6R	137.64	13960	C,H,A
2-135 Series 3 4WD	61280.00	23600.00	28910.00	30930.00	White	6T	478D	18F-6R	137.64	14900	C,H,A
2-155 Series 3	57025.00	22000.00	26950.00	28840.00	White	6T	478D	18F-6R	157.43	15000	C,H,A
2-155 Series 3 4WD	66710.00	24400.00	29890.00	31980.00	White	6T	478D	18F-6R	157.43	15950	C,H,A
2-180 Series 3	64200.00	17700.00	22420.00	24890.00	Cat.	V8	636D	18F-6R	181.89	16100	C,H,A
2-180 Series 3 4WD	73550.00	20100.00	25460.00	28260.00	Cat.	V8	636D	18F-6R	181.89	17500	C,H,A
2-32	9280.00	4450.00	5290.00	5710.00	Isuzu	4	91D	18F-6R	30.00	2915	No
2-32 4WD	11490.00	5520.00	6550.00	7070.00	Isuzu	4	91D	18F-6R	30.00	3135	No
2-55	17485.00	8390.00	9970.00	10770.00	Isuzu	4	199D	16F-4R	53.32	5072	No
2-55 4WD	21965.00	10540.00	12520.00	13520.00	Isuzu	4	199D	16F-4R	53.32	5875	No
2-65	19945.00	9570.00	11370.00	12280.00	Isuzu	4	235D	16F-4R	62.50	5314	No
2-65 4WD	24190.00	11610.00	13790.00	14890.00	Isuzu	4	235D	16F-4R	62.50	5814	No
2-75	23710.00	11380.00	13520.00	14600.00	Isuzu	6	329D	16F-4R	75.39	6293	No
2-75 4WD	29655.00	14230.00	16900.00	18250.00	Isuzu	6	329D	16F-4R	75.39	6778	No
2-88	36620.00	14360.00	17590.00	18820.00	Perkins	6	354D	18F-6R	86.78	11685	C,H,A
2-88 4WD	45900.00	18000.00	22050.00	23590.00	Perkins	6	354D	18F-6R	86.78	12835	C,H,A
4-225 4WD	78500.00	19500.00	24700.00	27420.00	Cat.	V8T	636D	18F-6R	195.65	23000	C,H,A
4-270 4WD	87495.00	22500.00	28500.00	31640.00	Cat.	6T	638D	16F-4R	239.25	26000	C,H,A

1986

Model	Approx. Retail Price New	Fair	Good	Premium	Make	No. Cyls.	Displ. Cu.-In.	No. Speeds	P.T.O. H.P.	Approx. Shipping Wt.-Lbs.	Cab
2-110	42975.00	17620.00	21490.00	22990.00	Perkins	6T	354D	18F-6R	110.52	11685	C,H,A
2-110 4WD	52000.00	21320.00	26000.00	27820.00	Perkins	6T	354D	18F-6R	110.52	12900	C,H,A
2-135 Series 3	51450.00	21100.00	25730.00	27530.00	White	6T	478D	18F-6R	137.64	13550	C,H,A
2-135 Series 3 4WD	61280.00	25130.00	30640.00	32790.00	White	6T	478D	18F-6R	137.64	14900	C,H,A
2-155 Series 3	57025.00	23380.00	28510.00	30510.00	White	6T	478D	18F-6R	157.43	14300	C,H,A
2-155 Series 3 4WD	66710.00	27350.00	33360.00	35700.00	White	6T	478D	18F-6R	157.43	15950	C,H,A
2-180 Series 3	64200.00	26320.00	32100.00	34350.00	Cat.	V8	636D	18F-6R	181.89	16100	C,H,A
2-180 Series 3 4WD	73550.00	30160.00	36780.00	39360.00	Cat.	V8	636D	18F-6R	181.89	17500	C,H,A
2-32	9776.00	4790.00	5670.00	6120.00	Isuzu	4	91D	18F-6R	28.00	2915	No
2-32 4WD	11490.00	5630.00	6660.00	7190.00	Isuzu	4	91D	18F-6R	28.00	3135	No
2-55	17485.00	8570.00	10140.00	10950.00	Isuzu	4	199D	16F-4R	53.32	5072	No
2-55 4WD	21965.00	10760.00	12740.00	13760.00	Isuzu	4	199D	16F-4R	53.32	5557	No
2-65	19945.00	9770.00	11570.00	12500.00	Isuzu	4	235D	16F-4R	62.50	5314	No
2-65 4WD	24190.00	11850.00	14030.00	15150.00	Isuzu	4	235D	16F-4R	62.50	5799	No
2-75	23710.00	9720.00	11860.00	12690.00	Isuzu	6	329D	16F-4R	75.39	6108	No
2-75 4WD	29655.00	12160.00	14830.00	15870.00	Isuzu	6	329D	16F-4R	75.39	6593	No
2-88	35900.00	14720.00	17950.00	19210.00	Perkins	6	354D	18F-6R	86.78	11350	C,H,A
2-88 4WD	45000.00	18450.00	22500.00	24080.00	Perkins	6	354D	18F-6R	86.78	12835	C,H,A
4-225 4WD	78500.00	20800.00	25350.00	28140.00	Cat.	V8T	636D	18F-6R	195.65	23000	C,H,A
4-270 4WD	91800.00	24000.00	29250.00	32470.00	Cat.	6T	638D	16F-4R	239.25	26000	C,H,A

1987

Model	Approx. Retail Price New	Fair	Good	Premium	Make	No. Cyls.	Displ. Cu.-In.	No. Speeds	P.T.O. H.P.	Approx. Shipping Wt.-Lbs.	Cab
2-110	42975.00	17220.00	20910.00	22370.00	Perkins	6T	354D	18F-6R	110.52	11685	C,H,A
2-110 4WD	52000.00	21210.00	25760.00	27560.00	Perkins	6T	354D	18F-6R	110.52	12900	C,H,A
2-135 Series 3	51450.00	21000.00	25500.00	27290.00	White	6T	478D	18F-6R	137.64	13550	C,H,A
2-135 Series 3 4WD	61280.00	23940.00	29070.00	31110.00	White	6T	478D	18F-6R	137.64	14900	C,H,A
2-155 Series 3	57025.00	22680.00	27540.00	29470.00	White	6T	478D	18F-6R	157.43	11250	C,H,A
2-155 Series 3 4WD	66710.00	26460.00	32130.00	34380.00	White	6T	478D	18F-6R	157.43	15950	C,H,A

Model	Approx. Retail Price New	Estimated Average Value Less Repairs Fair	Good	Premium	Engine Make	No. Cyls.	Displ. Cu.-In.	No. Speeds	P.T.O. H.P.	Approx. Shipping Wt.-Lbs.	Cab
White (Cont.)											
			1987 (Cont.)								
2-32	9776.00	**4890.00**	**5770.00**	**6230.00**	Isuzu	4	91D	18F-6R	30.00	2915	No
2-32 4WD	11486.00	**5740.00**	**6780.00**	**7320.00**	Isuzu	4	91D	18F-6R	30.00	3135	No
2-55	18530.00	**9270.00**	**10930.00**	**11800.00**	Isuzu	4	199D	16F-4R	53.32	5257	No
2-55 4WD	23285.00	**11640.00**	**13740.00**	**14840.00**	Isuzu	4	199D	16F-4R	53.32	5807	No
2-65	21135.00	**10570.00**	**12470.00**	**13470.00**	Isuzu	4	253D	16F-4R	62.50	5499	No
2-65 4WD	25640.00	**12820.00**	**15130.00**	**16340.00**	Isuzu	4	253D	16F-4R	62.50	5998	No
2-75	25130.00	**12570.00**	**14830.00**	**16020.00**	Isuzu	6	329D	16F-4R	75.39	6293	No
2-75 4WD	31430.00	**15720.00**	**18540.00**	**20020.00**	Isuzu	6	329D	16F-4R	75.39	6778	No
2-88	35900.00	**15080.00**	**18310.00**	**19590.00**	Perkins	6	354D	18F-6R	86.78	11685	C,H,A
2-88 4WD	45000.00	**18900.00**	**22950.00**	**24560.00**	Perkins	6	354D	18F-6R	86.78	12835	C,H,A
4-225 4WD	78500.00	**22100.00**	**26000.00**	**28600.00**	Cat.	V8T	636D	18F-6R	195.65	24140	C,H,A
4-270 4WD	91800.00	**26520.00**	**31200.00**	**34320.00**	Cat.	V8TA	636D	16F-4R	239.25	30650	C,H,A
Field Boss 16	6300.00	**3150.00**	**3720.00**	**4020.00**	Mitsubishi	3	52D	6F-2R			No
Field Boss 16 4WD	6950.00	**3480.00**	**4100.00**	**4430.00**	Mitsubishi	3	52D	6F-2R			No
Field Boss 21	7250.00	**3630.00**	**4280.00**	**4620.00**	Isuzu	3	71D	12F-4R			No
Field Boss 21 4WD	8100.00	**4050.00**	**4780.00**	**5160.00**	Isuzu	3	71D	12F-4R			No
Field Boss 31	8950.00	**4480.00**	**5280.00**	**5700.00**	Isuzu	3	91D	12F-4R			No
Field Boss 31 4WD	10150.00	**5080.00**	**5990.00**	**6470.00**	Isuzu	3	91D	12F-4R			No
Field Boss 37	10950.00	**5480.00**	**6460.00**	**6980.00**	Isuzu	4	111D	18F-6R			No
Field Boss 37 4WD	12730.00	**6370.00**	**7510.00**	**8110.00**	Isuzu	4	111D	18F-6R			No
Field Boss 43	14700.00	**7350.00**	**8670.00**	**9360.00**	Isuzu	4	145D	12F-4R			No
Field Boss 43 4WD	17900.00	**8950.00**	**10560.00**	**11410.00**	Isuzu	4	145D	12F-4R			No
185 4WD	74600.00	**25360.00**	**29840.00**	**32820.00**	Cummins	6TA	505D	18F-6R	187.55		C,H,A
			1988								
2-55	18290.00	**9330.00**	**10970.00**	**11740.00**	Isuzu	4	199D	16F-4R	53.32		No
2-55 4WD	23006.00	**11730.00**	**13800.00**	**14770.00**	Isuzu	4	199D	16F-4R	53.32		No
2-65	20861.00	**10640.00**	**12520.00**	**13400.00**	Isuzu	4	253D	16F-4R	62.50		No
2-65 4WD	25334.00	**12920.00**	**15200.00**	**16260.00**	Isuzu	4	253D	16F-4R	62.50		No
2-65HC 4WD Mudder	26964.00	**13750.00**	**16180.00**	**17310.00**	Isuzu	4	253D	16F-4R			No
2-75	24805.00	**12650.00**	**14880.00**	**15920.00**	Isuzu	6	329D	16F-4R	75.39		No
2-75 4WD	31054.00	**15840.00**	**18630.00**	**19930.00**	Isuzu	6	329D	16F-4R	75.39		No
4-225 4WD	75560.00	**23400.00**	**27300.00**	**30030.00**	Cat.	V8T	636D	18F-6R	195.65		C,H,A
4-270 4WD	88403.00	**28080.00**	**32760.00**	**36040.00**	Cat.	V8TA	636D	16F-4R	239.25		C,H,A
16 Hydro 4WD	9298.00	**4740.00**	**5580.00**	**5970.00**	Mitsubishi	3	52D	Variable			No
Field Boss 16	7298.00	**3720.00**	**4380.00**	**4690.00**	Mitsubishi	3	52D	6F-2R			No
Field Boss 16 4WD	8198.00	**4180.00**	**4920.00**	**5260.00**	Mitsubishi	3	52D	6F-2R			No
Field Boss 16 Hydro	8098.00	**4130.00**	**4860.00**	**5200.00**	Mitsubishi	3	52D	Variable			No
Field Boss 21	8398.00	**4280.00**	**5040.00**	**5390.00**	Iseki	3	71D	12F-4R			No
Field Boss 21 4WD	9398.00	**4790.00**	**5640.00**	**6040.00**	Iseki	3	71D	12F-4R			No
Field Boss 31	10598.00	**5410.00**	**6360.00**	**6810.00**	Iseki	3	91D	12F-4R			No
Field Boss 31 4WD	11998.00	**6120.00**	**7200.00**	**7700.00**	Iseki	3	91D	12F-4R			No
Field Boss 37	11998.00	**6120.00**	**7200.00**	**7700.00**	Isuzu	4	111D	10F-6R			No
Field Boss 37 4WD	13998.00	**7140.00**	**8400.00**	**8990.00**	Isuzu	4	111D	10F-6R			No
Field Boss 43	15698.00	**8010.00**	**9420.00**	**10080.00**	Isuzu	4	145D	12F-4R			No
Field Boss 43 4WD	19298.00	**9840.00**	**11580.00**	**12390.00**	Isuzu	4	145D	12F-4R			No
100	35541.00	**15280.00**	**18480.00**	**19590.00**	Cummins	6	359D	18F-6R	94.36		C,H,A
100 4WD	42026.00	**18070.00**	**21850.00**	**23160.00**	Cummins	6	359D	18F-6R			C,H,A
120	39865.00	**17140.00**	**20730.00**	**21970.00**	Cummins	6T	359D	18F-6R	119.13		C,H,A
120 4WD	46961.00	**19350.00**	**23400.00**	**24800.00**	Cummins	6T	359D	18F-6R			C,H,A
140	43606.00	**18060.00**	**21840.00**	**23150.00**	Cummins	6T	359D	18F-6R	138.53		C,H,A
140 4WD	51874.00	**21500.00**	**26000.00**	**27560.00**	Cummins	6T	359D	18F-6R			C,H,A
160	49898.00	**20640.00**	**24960.00**	**26460.00**	Cummins	6T	505D	18F-6R	162.47		C,H,A
160 4WD	58014.00	**24080.00**	**29120.00**	**30870.00**	Cummins	6T	505D	18F-6R	162.47		C,H,A
185	55463.00	**23220.00**	**28080.00**	**29770.00**	Cummins	6T	505D	18F-6R	187.55		C,H,A
185 4WD	63410.00	**25800.00**	**31200.00**	**33070.00**	Cummins	6T	505D	18F-6R	187.55		C,H,A
			1989								
2-55	18290.00	**9510.00**	**11160.00**	**11940.00**	Isuzu	4	199D	16F-4R	53.32		No
2-55 4WD	23006.00	**11960.00**	**14030.00**	**15010.00**	Isuzu	4	199D	16F-4R	53.32		No
2-75 4WD	31054.00	**16150.00**	**18940.00**	**20270.00**	Isuzu	6	329D	16F-4R	75.39		No
16 Hydro 4WD	9298.00	**4840.00**	**5670.00**	**6070.00**	Mitsubishi	3	52D	Variable			No
Field Boss 16	7298.00	**3800.00**	**4450.00**	**4760.00**	Mitsubishi	3	52D	6F-2R			No
Field Boss 16 4WD	8198.00	**4260.00**	**5000.00**	**5350.00**	Mitsubishi	3	52D	6F-2R			No
Field Boss 16 Hydro	8098.00	**4210.00**	**4940.00**	**5290.00**	Mitsubishi	3	52D	Variable			No
Field Boss 21	9068.00	**4720.00**	**5530.00**	**5920.00**	Iseki	3	71D	12F-4R			No
Field Boss 21 4WD	10157.00	**5280.00**	**6200.00**	**6630.00**	Iseki	3	71D	12F-4R			No
Field Boss 31	11448.00	**5950.00**	**6980.00**	**7470.00**	Iseki	3	91D	12F-4R			No
Field Boss 31 4WD	12997.00	**6760.00**	**7930.00**	**8490.00**	Iseki	3	91D	12F-4R			No
Field Boss 37	13052.00	**6790.00**	**7960.00**	**8520.00**	Isuzu	4	111D	10F-6R			No
Field Boss 37 4WD	15241.00	**7930.00**	**9300.00**	**9950.00**	Isuzu	4	111D	10F-6R			No
Field Boss 43	15698.00	**8160.00**	**9580.00**	**10250.00**	Isuzu	4	145D	12F-4R			No
Field Boss 43 4WD	19298.00	**10040.00**	**11770.00**	**12590.00**	Isuzu	4	145D	12F-4R			No
100	37796.00	**16630.00**	**20030.00**	**21230.00**	Cummins	6	359D	18F-6R	94.36		C,H,A
100 4WD	44938.00	**19770.00**	**23820.00**	**25250.00**	Cummins	6	359D	18F-6R			C,H,A
120	42780.00	**18820.00**	**22670.00**	**24030.00**	Cummins	6T	359D	18F-6R	119.13		C,H,A
120 4WD	50642.00	**21120.00**	**25440.00**	**26970.00**	Cummins	6T	359D	18F-6R			C,H,A
140	46895.00	**19800.00**	**23850.00**	**25280.00**	Cummins	6T	359D	18F-6R	138.53		C,H,A
140 4WD	56012.00	**23760.00**	**28620.00**	**30340.00**	Cummins	6T	359D	18F-6R			C,H,A
160	52831.00	**22000.00**	**26500.00**	**28090.00**	Cummins	6T	505D	18F-6R	162.47		C,H,A
160 4WD	61702.00	**25520.00**	**30740.00**	**32580.00**	Cummins	6T	505D	18F-6R	162.47		C,H,A
185	58439.00	**24820.00**	**29890.00**	**31680.00**	Cummins	6T	505D	18F-6R	187.55		C,H,A
185 4WD	67045.00	**28340.00**	**34130.00**	**36180.00**	Cummins	6T	505D	18F-6R	187.55		C,H,A

Model	Approx. Retail Price New	Estimated Average Value Less Repairs Fair	Good	Premium	Engine Make	No. Cyls.	Displ. Cu.-In.	No. Speeds	P.T.O. H.P.	Approx. Shipping Wt.-Lbs.	Cab
White (Cont.)											
				1990							
4-225 Field Boss	75560.00	**27600.00**	**31740.00**	**34910.00**	Cat.	6T	639D	18F-6R			C,H,A
4-270 Field Boss	88403.00	**31200.00**	**35880.00**	**39470.00**	Cat.	6TA	639D	16F-4R			C,H,A
60	18741.00	**9930.00**	**11620.00**	**12430.00**	Cummins	4	239D	6F-2R		6940	No
60 4WD	24431.00	**12950.00**	**15150.00**	**16210.00**	Cummins	4	239D	6F-2R		7440	No
60 PS	20741.00	**10990.00**	**12860.00**	**13760.00**	Cummins	4	239D	18F-6R			No
60 PS 4WD	26431.00	**14010.00**	**16390.00**	**17540.00**	Cummins	4	239D	18F-6R			No
80	22029.00	**11680.00**	**13660.00**	**14620.00**	Cummins	4	239D	6F-2R		7150	No
80 4WD	28029.00	**14860.00**	**17380.00**	**18600.00**	Cummins	4	239D	6F-2R		7650	No
80 PS	24029.00	**12740.00**	**14900.00**	**15940.00**	Cummins	4	239D	18F-6R			No
80 PS 4WD	30029.00	**15920.00**	**18620.00**	**19920.00**	Cummins	4	239D	18F-6R			No
100	39999.00	**18000.00**	**21600.00**	**22900.00**	Cummins	6	359D	18F-6R			C,H,A
100 4WD	46999.00	**21150.00**	**25380.00**	**26900.00**	Cummins	6	359D	18F-6R			C,H,A
120	44999.00	**20250.00**	**24300.00**	**25760.00**	Cummins	6	359D	18F-6R	119.13		C,H,A
120 4WD	52999.00	**23850.00**	**28620.00**	**30340.00**	Cummins	6T	359D	18F-6R			C,H,A
Workhorse 125	49145.00	**21600.00**	**25920.00**	**27480.00**	Cummins	6T	359D	18F-6R			C,H,A
Workhorse 125 4WD	57345.00	**24750.00**	**29700.00**	**31480.00**	Cummins	6T	359D	18F-6R			C,H,A
140	48999.00	**21150.00**	**25380.00**	**26900.00**	Cummins	6T	359D	18F-6R	138.53		C,H,A
140 4WD	57999.00	**24750.00**	**29700.00**	**31480.00**	Cummins	6T	359D	18F-6R			C,H,A
160	54999.00	**23850.00**	**28620.00**	**30340.00**	Cummins	6T	505D	18F-6R	162.47		C,H,A
160 4WD	63999.00	**27230.00**	**32670.00**	**34630.00**	Cummins	6T	505D	18F-6R	162.47		C,H,A
Workhorse 170	58915.00	**25200.00**	**30240.00**	**32050.00**	Cummins	6T	505D	18F-6R			C,H,A
Workhorse 170 4WD	68245.00	**28800.00**	**34560.00**	**36630.00**	Cummins	6T	505D	18F-6R			C,H,A
185	60999.00	**25520.00**	**30620.00**	**32460.00**	Cummins	6TA	505D	18F-6R	187.55		C,H,A
185 4WD	69999.00	**30150.00**	**36180.00**	**38350.00**	Cummins	6TA	505D	18F-6R	187.55		C,H,A
Workhorse 195	65765.00	**28080.00**	**33700.00**	**35720.00**	Cummins	6TA	505D	18F-6R			C,H,A
Workhorse 195 4WD	76995.00	**31500.00**	**37800.00**	**40070.00**	Cummins	6TA	505D	18F-6R			C,H,A
				1991							
60	20990.00	**11340.00**	**13220.00**	**14010.00**	Cummins	4	239D	6F-2R		6940	No
60 4WD	26680.00	**14410.00**	**16810.00**	**17820.00**	Cummins	4	239D	6F-2R		7440	No
60 4WD w/Cab	33585.00	**18140.00**	**21160.00**	**22430.00**	Cummins	4	239D	6F-2R	61.07		C,H,A
60 PS	23010.00	**12430.00**	**14500.00**	**15370.00**	Cummins	4	239D	18F-6R	61.07	8855	No
60 PS 4WD	28700.00	**15500.00**	**18080.00**	**19170.00**	Cummins	4	239D	18F-6R	61.07	8855	No
60 PS 4WD w/Cab	35605.00	**19230.00**	**22430.00**	**23780.00**	Cummins	4	239D	18F-6R	61.07		C,H,A
60 PS w/Cab	29915.00	**16150.00**	**18850.00**	**19980.00**	Cummins	4	239D	18F-6R	61.07		C,H,A
60 w/Cab	27895.00	**15060.00**	**17570.00**	**18620.00**	Cummins	4	239D	6F-2R	61.07		C,H,A
80	24672.00	**13320.00**	**15540.00**	**16470.00**	Cummins	4	239D	6F-2R		7150	No
80 4WD	30672.00	**16560.00**	**19320.00**	**20480.00**	Cummins	4	239D	6F-2R	81.48	7650	No
80 4WD w/Cab	37577.00	**20290.00**	**23670.00**	**25090.00**	Cummins	4	239D	6F-2R	81.48		C,H,A
80 PS	26692.00	**14410.00**	**16820.00**	**17830.00**	Cummins	4	239D	18F-6R	81.48		No
80 PS 4WD	32692.00	**17650.00**	**20600.00**	**21840.00**	Cummins	4	239D	18F-6R	81.48	11340	No
80 PS w/Cab	33597.00	**18140.00**	**21170.00**	**22440.00**	Cummins	4	239D	18F-3R	81.48		C,H,A
80 w/Cab	31577.00	**17050.00**	**19890.00**	**21080.00**	Cummins	4	239D	6F-2R	81.48		C,H,A
100	39999.00	**18400.00**	**22000.00**	**23320.00**	Cummins	6	359D	18F-6R			C,H,A
100 4WD	46999.00	**21620.00**	**25850.00**	**27400.00**	Cummins	6	359D	18F-6R			C,H,A
120	44999.00	**20700.00**	**24750.00**	**26240.00**	Cummins	6	359D	18F-6R	119.13		C,H,A
120 4WD	52999.00	**24380.00**	**29150.00**	**30900.00**	Cummins	6T	359D	18F-6R			C,H,A
Workhorse 125	49145.00	**22080.00**	**26400.00**	**27980.00**	Cummins	6T	359D	18F-6R		12250	C,H,A
Workhorse 125 4WD	57345.00	**25300.00**	**30250.00**	**32070.00**	Cummins	6T	359D	18F-6R			C,H,A
140	48999.00	**21620.00**	**25850.00**	**27400.00**	Cummins	6T	359D	18F-6R	138.53		C,H,A
140 4WD	57999.00	**25580.00**	**30580.00**	**32420.00**	Cummins	6T	359D	18F-6R			C,H,A
Workhorse 145	52495.00	**23460.00**	**28050.00**	**29730.00**	Cummins	6TA	359D	18F-6R			C,H,A
Workhorse 145 4WD	63110.00	**27600.00**	**33000.00**	**34980.00**	Cummins	6TA	359D	18F-6R			C,H,A
160	54999.00	**23920.00**	**28600.00**	**30320.00**	Cummins	6T	505D	18F-6R	162.47		C,H,A
160 4WD	63999.00	**27880.00**	**33330.00**	**35330.00**	Cummins	6T	505D	18F-6R	162.47		C,H,A
Workhorse 170	58915.00	**25900.00**	**30970.00**	**32830.00**	Cummins	6T	505D	18F-6R			C,H,A
Workhorse 170 4WD	68245.00	**29670.00**	**35480.00**	**37610.00**	Cummins	6T	505D	18F-6R			C,H,A
185	60999.00	**26680.00**	**31900.00**	**33810.00**	Cummins	6TA	505D	18F-6R	187.55		C,H,A
185 4WD	69999.00	**30270.00**	**36190.00**	**38360.00**	Cummins	6TA	505D	18F-6R	187.55		C,H,A
Workhorse 195	65765.00	**28520.00**	**34100.00**	**36150.00**	Cummins	6TA	505D	18F-6R			C,H,A
Workhorse 195 4WD	76995.00	**31280.00**	**37400.00**	**39640.00**	Cummins	6TA	505D	18F-6R			C,H,A
				1992							
60	20990.00	**11750.00**	**13430.00**	**14240.00**	Cummins	4	239D	6F-2R		6940	No
60 4WD	26680.00	**14940.00**	**17080.00**	**18110.00**	Cummins	4	239D	6F-2R		7440	No
60 4WD w/Cab	33585.00	**18810.00**	**21490.00**	**22780.00**	Cummins	4	239D	6F-2R	61.07		C,H,A
60 PS	23010.00	**12890.00**	**14730.00**	**15610.00**	Cummins	4	239D	18F-6R	61.07	8855	No
60 PS 4WD	28700.00	**16070.00**	**18370.00**	**19470.00**	Cummins	4	239D	18F-6R	61.07	8855	No
60 PS 4WD w/Cab	35605.00	**19940.00**	**22790.00**	**24160.00**	Cummins	4	239D	18F-6R	61.07		C,H,A
60 PS w/Cab	29915.00	**16750.00**	**19150.00**	**20300.00**	Cummins	4	239D	18F-6R	61.07		C,H,A
60 w/Cab	27895.00	**15620.00**	**17850.00**	**18920.00**	Cummins	4	239D	6F-2R	61.07		C,H,A
80	24672.00	**13820.00**	**15790.00**	**16740.00**	Cummins	4	239D	6F-2R		7150	No
80 4WD	30672.00	**17180.00**	**19630.00**	**20810.00**	Cummins	4	239D	6F-2R	81.48	7650	No
80 4WD w/Cab	37577.00	**21040.00**	**24050.00**	**25490.00**	Cummins	4	239D	6F-2R	81.48		C,H,A
80 PS	26692.00	**14950.00**	**17080.00**	**18110.00**	Cummins	4	239D	18F-6R	81.48		No
80 PS 4WD	32692.00	**18310.00**	**20920.00**	**22180.00**	Cummins	4	239D	18F-6R	81.48	11340	No
80 PS w/Cab	33597.00	**18810.00**	**21500.00**	**22790.00**	Cummins	4	239D	18F-3R	81.48		C,H,A
80 w/Cab	31577.00	**17680.00**	**20210.00**	**21420.00**	Cummins	4	239D	6F-2R	81.48		C,H,A
100	40399.00	**19390.00**	**22620.00**	**23750.00**	Cummins	6	359D	18F-6R			C,H,A
100 4WD	47469.00	**22790.00**	**26580.00**	**27910.00**	Cummins	6	359D	18F-6R			C,H,A
Workhorse 125	51110.00	**24000.00**	**28000.00**	**29400.00**	Cummins	6T	359D	18F-6R		12250	C,H,A
Workhorse 125 4WD	59640.00	**27840.00**	**32480.00**	**34100.00**	Cummins	6T	359D	18F-6R			C,H,A
Workhorse 145	54595.00	**25440.00**	**29680.00**	**31160.00**	Cummins	6TA	359D	18F-6R			C,H,A
Workhorse 145 4WD	65635.00	**29760.00**	**34720.00**	**36460.00**	Cummins	6TA	359D	18F-6R			C,H,A

White (Cont.)

Model	Approx. Retail Price New	Estimated Average Value Less Repairs Fair	Good	Premium	Engine Make	No. Cyls.	Displ. Cu.-In.	No. Speeds	P.T.O. H.P.	Approx. Shipping Wt.-Lbs.	Cab
			1992 (Cont.)								
Workhorse 170	61270.00	**28320.00**	**33040.00**	**34690.00**	Cummins	6T	505D	18F-6R			C,H,A
Workhorse 170 4WD	70975.00	**31680.00**	**36960.00**	**38810.00**	Cummins	6T	505D	18F-6R			C,H,A
Workhorse 195	68395.00	**31200.00**	**36400.00**	**38220.00**	Cummins	6TA	505D	18F-6R			C,H,A
Workhorse 195 4WD	80075.00	**35520.00**	**41440.00**	**43510.00**	Cummins	6TA	505D	18F-6R			C,H,A
			1993								
60	21200.00	**12300.00**	**13780.00**	**14610.00**	Cummins	4	239D	6F-2R	61.0	6940	No
60 4WD	26950.00	**15630.00**	**17520.00**	**18570.00**	Cummins	4	239D	6F-2R	61.0	7440	No
60 4WD w/Cab	33925.00	**19680.00**	**22050.00**	**23370.00**	Cummins	4	239D	6F-2R	61.0		C,H,A
60 PS 4WD	28990.00	**16810.00**	**18840.00**	**19970.00**	Cummins	4	239D	18F-6R	61.0	8855	No
60 PS 4WD w/Cab	35965.00	**20860.00**	**23380.00**	**24780.00**	Cummins	4	239D	18F-6R	61.0		C,H,A
60 PS w/Cab	23240.00	**13480.00**	**15110.00**	**16020.00**	Cummins	4	239D	18F-6R	61.0	8855	No
60 PS w/Cab	30215.00	**17530.00**	**19640.00**	**20820.00**	Cummins	4	239D	18F-6R	61.0		C,H,A
60 w/Cab	28175.00	**16340.00**	**18310.00**	**19410.00**	Cummins	4	239D	6F-2R	61.0		C,H,A
80	24920.00	**14450.00**	**16200.00**	**17170.00**	Cummins	4	239D	6F-2R	81.48	7150	No
80 4WD	30980.00	**17970.00**	**20140.00**	**21350.00**	Cummins	4	239D	6F-2R	81.48	7650	No
80 4WD w/Cab	37955.00	**22010.00**	**24670.00**	**26150.00**	Cummins	4	239D	6F-2R	81.48		C,H,A
80 PS	26960.00	**15640.00**	**17520.00**	**18570.00**	Cummins	4	239D	18F-6R	81.48		No
80 PS 4WD	33020.00	**19150.00**	**21460.00**	**22750.00**	Cummins	4	239D	18F-6R	81.48	11340	No
80 PS w/Cab	33935.00	**19680.00**	**22060.00**	**23380.00**	Cummins	4	239D	18F-3R	81.48		C,H,A
80 w/Cab	31895.00	**18500.00**	**20730.00**	**21970.00**	Cummins	4	239D	6F-2R	81.48		C,H,A
100	40800.00	**20400.00**	**23660.00**	**24840.00**	Cummins	6	359D	18F-6R			C,H,A
100 4WD	47945.00	**23970.00**	**27810.00**	**29200.00**	Cummins	6	359D	18F-6R			C,H,A
Workhorse 125	53145.00	**26570.00**	**30820.00**	**32360.00**	Cummins	6T	359D	18F-6R		12250	C,H,A
Workhorse 125 4WD	62025.00	**30000.00**	**34800.00**	**36540.00**	Cummins	6T	359D	18F-6R			C,H,A
Workhorse 145	56780.00	**27500.00**	**31900.00**	**33500.00**	Cummins	6TA	359D	18F-6R			C,H,A
Workhorse 145 4WD	68260.00	**32000.00**	**37120.00**	**38980.00**	Cummins	6TA	359D	18F-6R			C,H,A
Workhorse 170	63720.00	**31000.00**	**35960.00**	**37760.00**	Cummins	6T	505D	18F-6R			C,H,A
Workhorse 170 4WD	73815.00	**35000.00**	**40600.00**	**42630.00**	Cummins	6T	505D	18F-6R			C,H,A
Workhorse 195 4WD	83280.00	**38500.00**	**44660.00**	**46890.00**	Cummins	6TA	505D	18F-6R			C,H,A
6065	23768.00	**13790.00**	**15450.00**	**16380.00**	SLH	4	244D	16F-16R	62.77	5379	No
6065 4WD	29081.00	**16870.00**	**18900.00**	**20030.00**	SLH	4	244D	16F-16R	62.77	6096	No
6065 4WD w/Cab	38670.00	**22430.00**	**25140.00**	**26650.00**	SLH	4	244D	16F-16R	62.77	6768	C,H,A
6065 w/Cab	33163.00	**19240.00**	**21560.00**	**22850.00**	SLH	4	244D	12F-12R	62.77	6305	C,H,A
6085	30147.00	**17490.00**	**19600.00**	**20780.00**	SLH	4T	244D	12F-12R	80.15	6173	No
6085 4WD	36655.00	**21260.00**	**23830.00**	**25260.00**	SLH	4T	244D	12F-12R	80.15	6779	No
6085 4WD	36848.00	**21370.00**	**23950.00**	**25390.00**	SLH	4T	244D	16F-16R	80.15	6779	No
6085 4WD w/Cab	43862.00	**25440.00**	**28510.00**	**30220.00**	SLH	4T	244D	12F-12R	80.15	7385	C,H,A
6085 4WD w/Cab	44057.00	**25550.00**	**28640.00**	**30360.00**	SLH	4T	244D	16F-16R	80.15	7385	C,H,A
6085 w/Cab	37355.00	**21670.00**	**24280.00**	**25740.00**	SLH	4T	244D	12F-12R	80.15	6724	C,H,A
6085 w/Cab	37549.00	**21780.00**	**24410.00**	**25880.00**	SLH	4T	244D	16F-16R	80.15	6724	C,H,A
6105	48710.00	**24360.00**	**28250.00**	**29660.00**	SLH	6	366D	36F-36R	106.34	10013	C,H,A
6105 4WD	55986.00	**27990.00**	**32470.00**	**34090.00**	SLH	6	366D	36F-36R	106.34	10759	C,H,A
Workhorse 6125	67828.00	**33000.00**	**38280.00**	**40190.00**	Cummins	6T	359D	18F-9R	124.0	14950	C,H,A
Workhorse 6125 4WD	80050.00	**38000.00**	**44080.00**	**46280.00**	Cummins	6T	359D	18F-9R	124.0	16150	C,H,A
Workhorse 6145	71938.00	**34750.00**	**40310.00**	**42330.00**	Cummins	6TA	359D	18F-9R	142.0	14950	C,H,A
Workhorse 6145 4WD	83412.00	**40000.00**	**46400.00**	**48720.00**	Cummins	6TA	359D	18F-9R	142.0	16150	C,H,A
Workhorse 6175	82610.00	**39500.00**	**45820.00**	**48110.00**	Cummins	6T	504D	18F-9R	175.0	16300	C,H,A
Workhorse 6175 4WD	93957.00	**44500.00**	**51620.00**	**54200.00**	Cummins	6T	504D	18F-9R	175.0	17850	C,H,A
Workhorse 6195 4WD	103164.00	**49000.00**	**56840.00**	**59680.00**	Cummins	6TA	504D	18F-9R	200.0	17950	C,H,A
			1994								
Workhorse 125	55953.00	**29660.00**	**33570.00**	**35250.00**	Cummins	6T	359D	18F-6R	121.9	12250	C,H,A
Workhorse 125 4WD	65000.00	**33390.00**	**37800.00**	**39690.00**	Cummins	6T	359D	18F-6R	121.9	13500	C,H,A
Workhorse 145	59635.00	**30740.00**	**34800.00**	**36540.00**	Cummins	6TA	359D	18F-6R	140.3	12250	C,H,A
Workhorse 145 4WD	71233.00	**35510.00**	**40200.00**	**42210.00**	Cummins	6TA	359D	18F-6R	140.3	13800	C,H,A
Workhorse 170	66728.00	**34450.00**	**39000.00**	**40950.00**	Cummins	6T	504D	18F-6R	165.9	13300	C,H,A
Workhorse 170 4WD	77100.00	**39220.00**	**44400.00**	**46620.00**	Cummins	6T	504D	18F-6R	165.9	15400	C,H,A
Workhorse 195 4WD	86835.00	**42930.00**	**48600.00**	**51030.00**	Cummins	6TA	504D	18F-6R	192.4	15545	C,H,A
6065	23768.00	**14500.00**	**15930.00**	**16730.00**	SLH	4	244D	16F-16R	62.77	5379	No
6065 4WD	29081.00	**17740.00**	**19480.00**	**20450.00**	SLH	4	244D	16F-16R	62.77	6096	No
6065 4WD w/Cab	38670.00	**23590.00**	**25910.00**	**27210.00**	SLH	4	244D	16F-16R	62.77	6768	C,H,A
6085	30147.00	**18390.00**	**20200.00**	**21210.00**	SLH	4T	244D	12F-12R	80.15	6173	No
6085 4WD	36848.00	**22480.00**	**24690.00**	**25930.00**	SLH	4T	244D	16F-16R	80.15	6779	No
6085 4WD w/Cab	44057.00	**26880.00**	**29520.00**	**31000.00**	SLH	4T	244D	16F-16R	80.15	7385	C,H,A
6085 w/Cab	37549.00	**22910.00**	**25160.00**	**26420.00**	SLH	4T	244D	16F-16R	80.15	6724	C,H,A
6090 HC	38644.00	**21010.00**	**23080.00**	**24230.00**	SLH	4T	244D	20F-20R	80.15	7831	No
6105	48710.00	**25820.00**	**29230.00**	**30690.00**	SLH	6	366D	36F-36R	106.34	10013	C,H,A
6105 4WD	55986.00	**29670.00**	**33590.00**	**35270.00**	SLH	6	366D	36F-36R	106.34	10759	C,H,A
Workhorse 6124	63521.00	**32860.00**	**37200.00**	**39060.00**	Cummins	6T	359D	32F-32R	124.0	14200	C,H,A
Workhorse 6124 4WD	74169.00	**38160.00**	**43200.00**	**45360.00**	Cummins	6T	359D	32F-32R	124.0	15300	C,H,A
Workhorse 6125	67828.00	**34450.00**	**39000.00**	**40950.00**	Cummins	6T	359D	18F-9R	124.0	14950	C,H,A
Workhorse 6125 4WD	80050.00	**40810.00**	**46200.00**	**48510.00**	Cummins	6T	359D	18F-9R	124.0	16150	C,H,A
Workhorse 6144	67440.00	**34450.00**	**39000.00**	**40950.00**	Cummins	6TA	359D	32F-32R	142.0	14200	C,H,A
Workhorse 6144 4WD	80133.00	**41370.00**	**46830.00**	**49170.00**	Cummins	6TA	359D	32F-32R	142.0	15300	C,H,A
Workhorse 6145	71938.00	**37100.00**	**42000.00**	**44100.00**	Cummins	6TA	359D	18F-9R	142.0	14950	C,H,A
Workhorse 6145 4WD	83412.00	**42610.00**	**48240.00**	**50650.00**	Cummins	6TA	359D	18F-9R	142.0	16150	C,H,A
Workhorse 6175	82610.00	**42080.00**	**47640.00**	**50020.00**	Cummins	6T	504D	18F-9R	175.0	16300	C,H,A
Workhorse 6175 4WD	93957.00	**47700.00**	**54000.00**	**56700.00**	Cummins	6T	504D	18F-9R	175.0	17850	C,H,A
Workhorse 6195 4WD	103164.00	**51940.00**	**58800.00**	**61740.00**	Cummins	6TA	504D	18F-9R	200.0	17950	C,H,A
Workhorse 6215 4WD	112813.00	**55650.00**	**63000.00**	**66150.00**	Cummins	6TA	504D	18F-9R	215.0	17250	C,H,A

White (Cont.)

Model	Approx. Retail Price New	Estimated Average Value Less Repairs Fair	Good	Premium	Engine Make	No. Cyls.	Displ. Cu.-In.	No. Speeds	P.T.O. H.P.	Approx. Shipping Wt.-Lbs.	Cab
			1995								
6065	24600.00	**15740.00**	**17220.00**	**18080.00**	SLH	4	244D	16F-16R	62.77	5379	No
6065 4WD	30099.00	**19260.00**	**21070.00**	**22120.00**	SLH	4	244D	16F-16R	62.77	6096	No
6065 4WD w/Cab	40023.00	**25620.00**	**28020.00**	**29420.00**	SLH	4	244D	16F-16R	62.77	6768	C,H,A
6085	31202.00	**19970.00**	**21840.00**	**22930.00**	SLH	4T	244D	12F-12R	80.15	6173	No
6085 4WD	38138.00	**24410.00**	**26700.00**	**28040.00**	SLH	4T	244D	16F-16R	80.15	6779	No
6085 4WD w/Cab	45599.00	**29180.00**	**31920.00**	**33520.00**	SLH	4T	244D	16F-16R	80.15	7385	C,H,A
6085 w/Cab	38863.00	**24870.00**	**27200.00**	**28560.00**	SLH	4T	244D	16F-16R	80.15	6724	C,H,A
6090 HC	34441.00	**22040.00**	**24110.00**	**25320.00**	SLH	4T	244D	20F-20R	80.15	7831	No
6090 HC 4WD	39997.00	**25600.00**	**28000.00**	**29400.00**	SLH	4T	244D	20F-20R	80.15	7831	No
6105	50415.00	**28230.00**	**31760.00**	**33030.00**	SLH	6	366D	36F-36R	106.34	10013	C,H,A
6105 4WD	57946.00	**32450.00**	**36510.00**	**37970.00**	SLH	6	366D	36F-36R	106.34	10759	C,H,A
Workhorse 6124	66096.00	**37010.00**	**41640.00**	**43310.00**	Cummins	6T	359D	32F-32R	124.0	14200	C,H,A
Workhorse 6124 4WD	75920.00	**42520.00**	**47830.00**	**49740.00**	Cummins	6T	359D	32F-32R	124.0	15300	C,H,A
Workhorse 6125	70576.00	**39520.00**	**44460.00**	**46240.00**	Cummins	6T	359D	18F-9R	124.0	14950	C,H,A
Workhorse 6125 4WD	82706.00	**44800.00**	**50400.00**	**52420.00**	Cummins	6T	359D	18F-9R	124.0	16150	C,H,A
Workhorse 6144	70176.00	**39300.00**	**44210.00**	**45980.00**	Cummins	6TA	359D	32F-32R	142.0	14200	C,H,A
Workhorse 6144 4WD	79750.00	**43120.00**	**48510.00**	**50450.00**	Cummins	6TA	359D	32F-32R	142.0	15300	C,H,A
Workhorse 6145	75526.00	**41440.00**	**46620.00**	**48490.00**	Cummins	6TA	359D	18F-9R	142.0	14950	C,H,A
Workhorse 6145 4WD	86596.00	**47040.00**	**52920.00**	**55040.00**	Cummins	6TA	359D	18F-9R	142.0	16150	C,H,A
Workhorse 6175	84775.00	**45920.00**	**51660.00**	**53730.00**	Cummins	6T	504D	18F-9R	175.0	16300	C,H,A
Workhorse 6175 4WD	96266.00	**52080.00**	**58590.00**	**60930.00**	Cummins	6T	504D	18F-9R	175.0	17850	C,H,A
Workhorse 6195 4WD	105706.00	**56000.00**	**63000.00**	**65520.00**	Cummins	6TA	504D	18F-9R	200.0	17950	C,H,A
Workhorse 6215 4WD	112964.00	**60480.00**	**68040.00**	**70760.00**	Cummins	6TA	504D	18F-9R	215.0	17200	C,H,A
			1996								
6045	19510.00	**13070.00**	**14240.00**	**14810.00**	SLH	3	183D		45.0		No
6045 4WD	25320.00	**16960.00**	**18480.00**	**19220.00**	SLH	3	183D		45.0		No
6065	25705.00	**17220.00**	**18770.00**	**19520.00**	SLH	4	244D	16F-16R	62.77	5379	No
6065 4WD	31455.00	**21080.00**	**22960.00**	**23880.00**	SLH	4	244D	16F-16R	62.77	6096	No
6065 4WD w/Cab	41825.00	**28020.00**	**30530.00**	**31750.00**	SLH	4	244D	16F-16R	62.77	6768	C,H,A
6065 w/Cab	36065.00	**24160.00**	**26330.00**	**27380.00**	SLH	4	244D	16F-16R	62.77		C,H,A
6085	32815.00	**21990.00**	**23960.00**	**24920.00**	SLH	4T	244D	16F-16R	80.15	6173	No
6085 4WD	39855.00	**26700.00**	**29090.00**	**30250.00**	SLH	4T	244D	16F-16R	80.15	6779	No
6085 4WD w/Cab	47650.00	**31930.00**	**34790.00**	**36180.00**	SLH	4T	244D	16F-16R	80.15	7385	C,H,A
6085 w/Cab	40610.00	**27210.00**	**29650.00**	**30840.00**	SLH	4T	244D	16F-16R	80.15	6724	C,H,A
6090 HC	36290.00	**24310.00**	**26490.00**	**27550.00**	SLH	4T	244D	20F-20R	80.15		No
6090 HC 4WD	42097.00	**28210.00**	**30730.00**	**31960.00**	SLH	4T	244D	20F-20R	80.15	7831	No
6105	51000.00	**31110.00**	**34170.00**	**35540.00**	SLH	6	366D	24F-12R	106.34	10013	C,H,A
6105 4WD	57310.00	**34960.00**	**38400.00**	**39940.00**	SLH	6	366D	24F-12R	106.34	10759	C,H,A
6105 Auto 4WD	61565.00	**37560.00**	**41250.00**	**42900.00**	SLH	6	366D	36F-36R	106.34		C,H,A
Workhorse 6124	69355.00	**41480.00**	**45560.00**	**47380.00**	Cummins	6T	359D	32F-32R	124.94	14200	C,H,A
Workhorse 6124 4WD	79440.00	**46970.00**	**51590.00**	**53650.00**	Cummins	6T	359D	32F-32R	124.94	15300	C,H,A
Workhorse 6125	74605.00	**43920.00**	**48240.00**	**50170.00**	Cummins	6T	359D	18F-9R	124.94	14950	C,H,A
Workhorse 6125 4WD	87155.00	**51850.00**	**56950.00**	**59230.00**	Cummins	6T	359D	18F-9R	124.94	16150	C,H,A
Workhorse 6144	73540.00	**43310.00**	**47570.00**	**49470.00**	Cummins	6TA	359D	32F-32R	142.56	14200	C,H,A
Workhorse 6144 4WD	83365.00	**48800.00**	**53600.00**	**55740.00**	Cummins	6TA	359D	32F-32R	142.56	15300	C,H,A
Workhorse 6145	79725.00	**47280.00**	**51930.00**	**54010.00**	Cummins	6TA	359D	18F-9R	142.56	14950	C,H,A
Workhorse 6145 4WD	91185.00	**53680.00**	**58960.00**	**61320.00**	Cummins	6TA	359D	18F-9R	142.56	16150	C,H,A
Workhorse 6175	89375.00	**52460.00**	**57620.00**	**59930.00**	Cummins	6T	504D	18F-9R	175.47	16300	C,H,A
Workhorse 6175 4WD	101635.00	**59780.00**	**65660.00**	**68290.00**	Cummins	6T	504D	18F-9R	175.47	17850	C,H,A
Workhorse 6195 4WD	111450.00	**64050.00**	**70350.00**	**73160.00**	Cummins	6TA	504D	18F-9R	200.46	17950	C,H,A
Workhorse 6215 4WD	119460.00	**67100.00**	**73700.00**	**76650.00**	Cummins	6TA	504D	18F-9R	215.0	17200	C,H,A
			1997								
6045	20750.00	**14940.00**	**15980.00**	**16620.00**	SLH	3	183D		45.0		No
6045 4WD	26765.00	**19270.00**	**20610.00**	**21430.00**	SLH	3	183D		45.0		No
6065	27215.00	**19600.00**	**20960.00**	**21800.00**	SLH	4	244D	16F-16R	62.77	5379	No
6065 4WD	33165.00	**23880.00**	**25540.00**	**26560.00**	SLH	4	244D	16F-16R	62.77	6096	No
6065 4WD w/Cab	43290.00	**31170.00**	**33330.00**	**34660.00**	SLH	4	244D	16F-16R	62.77	6768	C,H,A
6065 w/Cab	37325.00	**26870.00**	**28740.00**	**29890.00**	SLH	4	244D	16F-16R	62.77		C,H,A
6085	33965.00	**24460.00**	**26150.00**	**27200.00**	SLH	4T	244D	16F-16R	80.15	6173	No
6085 4WD	41250.00	**29700.00**	**31760.00**	**33030.00**	SLH	4T	244D	16F-16R	80.15	6779	No
6085 4WD w/Cab	49320.00	**35510.00**	**37980.00**	**39500.00**	SLH	4T	244D	16F-16R	80.15	7385	C,H,A
6085 w/Cab	42030.00	**30260.00**	**32360.00**	**33650.00**	SLH	4T	244D	16F-16R	80.15	6724	C,H,A
6090	36710.00	**26430.00**	**28270.00**	**29400.00**	SLH	4T	244D	19F-19R	80.15		No
6090 4WD	41915.00	**30180.00**	**32280.00**	**33570.00**	SLH	4T	244D	19F-19R	80.15	7831	No
6105	52785.00	**38010.00**	**40640.00**	**42270.00**	SLH	6	366D	24F-12R	106.34	10013	C,H,A
6105 4WD	59315.00	**42710.00**	**45670.00**	**47500.00**	SLH	6	366D	24F-12R	106.34	10759	C,H,A
Workhorse 6124	69836.00	**45560.00**	**49640.00**	**51630.00**	Cummins	6T	359D	32F-32R	124.94	14200	C,H,A
Workhorse 6124 4WD	80222.00	**52260.00**	**56940.00**	**59220.00**	Cummins	6T	359D	32F-32R	124.94	15300	C,H,A
Workhorse 6125	76281.00	**49580.00**	**54020.00**	**56180.00**	Cummins	6T	359D	18F-9R	124.94	14950	C,H,A
Workhorse 6125 4WD	88167.00	**57620.00**	**62780.00**	**65290.00**	Cummins	6T	359D	18F-9R	124.94	16150	C,H,A
Workhorse 6144	74146.00	**48240.00**	**52560.00**	**54660.00**	Cummins	6TA	359D	32F-32R	142.56	14200	C,H,A
Workhorse 6144 4WD	84262.00	**54940.00**	**59860.00**	**62250.00**	Cummins	6TA	359D	32F-32R	142.56	15300	C,H,A
Workhorse 6145	81654.00	**52930.00**	**57670.00**	**59980.00**	Cummins	6TA	359D	18F-9R	142.56	14950	C,H,A
Workhorse 6145 4WD	93435.00	**60300.00**	**65700.00**	**68330.00**	Cummins	6TA	359D	18F-9R	142.56	16150	C,H,A
Workhorse 6175	91594.00	**59300.00**	**64610.00**	**67190.00**	Cummins	6T	504D	18F-9R	175.47	16300	C,H,A
Workhorse 6175 4WD	104200.00	**67000.00**	**73000.00**	**75920.00**	Cummins	6T	504D	18F-9R	175.47	17850	C,H,A
Workhorse 6195 4WD	113898.00	**71690.00**	**78110.00**	**81230.00**	Cummins	6TA	504D	18F-9R	200.46	17950	C,H,A
Workhorse 6215 4WD	121673.00	**77050.00**	**83950.00**	**87310.00**	Cummins	6TA	504D	18F-9R	215.0	17200	C,H,A
			1998								
6045	21375.00	**16670.00**	**17530.00**	**18060.00**	SLH	3	183D		45.0		No
6045 4WD	27570.00	**21510.00**	**22610.00**	**23290.00**	SLH	3	183D		45.0		No

White (Cont.)

1998 (Cont.)

Model	Approx. Retail Price New	Estimated Average Value Less Repairs: Fair	Good	Premium	Engine: Make	No. Cyls.	Displ. Cu.-In.	No. Speeds	P.T.O. H.P.	Approx. Shipping Wt.-Lbs.	Cab
6065	27825.00	**21700.00**	**22820.00**	**23510.00**	SLH	4	244D	12F-12R	62.77	5379	No
6065 4WD	33960.00	**26490.00**	**27850.00**	**28690.00**	SLH	4	244D	12F-12R	62.77	6096	No
6065 4WD w/Cab	44370.00	**34610.00**	**36380.00**	**37470.00**	SLH	4	244D	12F-12R	62.77	6768	C,H,A
6065 w/Cab	38240.00	**29830.00**	**31360.00**	**32300.00**	SLH	4	244D	12F-12R	62.77	6305	C,H,A
6085	33965.00	**26490.00**	**27850.00**	**28690.00**	SLH	4T	244D	16F-16R	80.15	6173	No
6085 4WD	41250.00	**32180.00**	**33830.00**	**34850.00**	SLH	4T	244D	16F-16R	80.15	6779	No
6085 4WD w/Cab	49320.00	**38470.00**	**40440.00**	**41650.00**	SLH	4T	244D	16F-16R	80.15	7385	C,H,A
6085 w/Cab	42030.00	**32780.00**	**34470.00**	**35500.00**	SLH	4T	244D	16F-16R	80.15	6724	C,H,A
6090 HC	38715.00	**30200.00**	**31750.00**	**32700.00**	SLH	4T	244D	19F-19R	80.15		No
6090 HC 4WD	45900.00	**35800.00**	**37640.00**	**38770.00**	SLH	4T	244D	19F-19R	80.15	7831	No
6105	52785.00	**39060.00**	**41700.00**	**42950.00**	SLH	6	366D	24F-12R	106.34	10013	C,H,A
6105 4WD	59315.00	**43890.00**	**46860.00**	**48270.00**	SLH	6	366D	24F-12R	106.34	10759	C,H,A
Workhorse 6124	71436.00	**51800.00**	**55300.00**	**56960.00**	Cummins	6T	359D	32F-32R	124.94	14200	C,H,A
Workhorse 6124 4WD	81825.00	**59500.00**	**63520.00**	**65430.00**	Cummins	6T	359D	32F-32R	124.94	15300	C,H,A
Workhorse 6125	76841.00	**55800.00**	**59570.00**	**61360.00**	Cummins	6T	359D	18F-9R	124.94	14950	C,H,A
Workhorse 6125 4WD	88445.00	**63940.00**	**68260.00**	**70310.00**	Cummins	6T	359D	18F-9R	124.94	16150	C,H,A
Workhorse 6144	75746.00	**54540.00**	**58220.00**	**59970.00**	Cummins	6TA	359D	32F-32R	142.56	14200	C,H,A
Workhorse 6144 4WD	85862.00	**61640.00**	**65810.00**	**67780.00**	Cummins	6TA	359D	32F-32R	142.56	15300	C,H,A
Workhorse 6145	82116.00	**59200.00**	**63200.00**	**65100.00**	Cummins	6TA	359D	18F-9R	142.56	14950	C,H,A
Workhorse 6145 4WD	93917.00	**67930.00**	**72520.00**	**74700.00**	Cummins	6TA	359D	18F-9R	142.56	16150	C,H,A
Workhorse 6175	93194.00	**67480.00**	**72040.00**	**74200.00**	Cummins	6T	504D	18F-9R	175.47	16300	C,H,A
Workhorse 6175 4WD	104682.00	**75250.00**	**80330.00**	**82740.00**	Cummins	6T	504D	18F-9R	175.47	17850	C,H,A
Workhorse 6195 4WD	114795.00	**81400.00**	**86900.00**	**89510.00**	Cummins	6TA	504D	18F-9R	200.46	17950	C,H,A
Workhorse 6215 4WD	123042.00	**88060.00**	**94010.00**	**96830.00**	Cummins	6TA	504D	18F-9R	215.0	17200	C,H,A
6410	32275.00	**23880.00**	**25500.00**	**26270.00**	Cummins	4T	239D	12F-4R	70.0		No
6410 4WD	38555.00	**28530.00**	**30460.00**	**31370.00**	Cummins	4T	239D	12F-4R	70.0		No
6410 4WD w/cab	46060.00	**32560.00**	**34760.00**	**35800.00**	Cummins	4T	239D	12F-4R	70.0		C,H,A
6410 w/cab	39780.00	**29440.00**	**31430.00**	**32370.00**	Cummins	4T	239D	12F-4R	70.0		C,H,A
6510	35165.00	**26020.00**	**27780.00**	**28610.00**	Cummins	4T	239D	12F-4R	85.0		No
6510 4WD	42850.00	**31710.00**	**33850.00**	**34870.00**	Cummins	4T	239D	12F-4R	85.0		No
6510 4WD w/cab	50750.00	**35520.00**	**37920.00**	**39060.00**	Cummins	4T	239D	12F-4R	85.0		C,H,A
6510 w/cab	43065.00	**31870.00**	**34020.00**	**35040.00**	Cummins	4T	239D	12F-4R	85.0		C,H,A
6710	43000.00	**31820.00**	**33970.00**	**34990.00**	Cummins	6T	359D	32F-32R	95.0		No
6710 4WD	50237.00	**37180.00**	**39690.00**	**40880.00**	Cummins	6T	359D	32F-32R	95.0		No
6710 4WD w/cab	62385.00	**44400.00**	**47400.00**	**48820.00**	Cummins	6T	359D	32F-32R	95.0		C,H,A
6710 w/cab	54832.00	**40580.00**	**43320.00**	**44620.00**	Cummins	6T	359D	32F-32R	95.0		C,H,A
6810	51375.00	**38020.00**	**40590.00**	**41810.00**	Cummins	6T	359D	32F-32R	110.0		No
6810 4WD	60575.00	**44830.00**	**47850.00**	**49290.00**	Cummins	6T	359D	32F-32R	110.0		No
6810 4WD w/cab	73068.00	**51800.00**	**55300.00**	**56960.00**	Cummins	6T	359D	32F-32R	110.0		C,H,A
6810 w/cab	63210.00	**46780.00**	**49940.00**	**51440.00**	Cummins	6T	359D	32F-32R	110.0		C,H,A
Fieldmaster 8310	73130.00	**52650.00**	**56310.00**	**58000.00**	Cummins	6T	359D	32F-32R	125.0		C,H,A
Fieldmaster 8310 4WD	84310.00	**57600.00**	**61600.00**	**63450.00**	Cummins	6T	359D	32F-32R	125.0		C,H,A
Fieldmaster 8410	78680.00	**56650.00**	**60580.00**	**62400.00**	Cummins	6TA	359D	32F-32R	145.0		C,H,A
Fieldmaster 8410 4WD	90950.00	**61200.00**	**65450.00**	**67410.00**	Cummins	6TA	359D	32F-32R	145.0		C,H,A

1999

Model	Approx. Retail Price New	Estimated Average Value Less Repairs: Fair	Good	Premium	Engine: Make	No. Cyls.	Displ. Cu.-In.	No. Speeds	P.T.O. H.P.	Approx. Shipping Wt.-Lbs.	Cab
6045	22015.00	**18490.00**	**19370.00**	**19760.00**	SLH	3	183D	12F-12R	45.0		No
6045 4WD	28395.00	**23850.00**	**24990.00**	**25490.00**	SLH	3	183D	12F-12R	45.0		No
6065	28660.00	**24070.00**	**25220.00**	**25720.00**	SLH	4	244D	12F-12R	62.77	5379	No
6065 4WD	34980.00	**29380.00**	**30780.00**	**31400.00**	SLH	4	244D	12F-12R	62.77	6096	No
6065 4WD w/Cab	45700.00	**38390.00**	**40220.00**	**41020.00**	SLH	4	244D	12F-12R	62.77	6768	C,H,A
6065 w/Cab	39385.00	**33080.00**	**34660.00**	**35350.00**	SLH	4	244D	12F-12R	62.77	6305	C,H,A
6085	33965.00	**28530.00**	**29890.00**	**30490.00**	SLH	4T	244D	16F-16R	80.15	6173	No
6085 4WD	41250.00	**34650.00**	**36300.00**	**37030.00**	SLH	4T	244D	16F-16R	80.15	6779	No
6085 4WD w/Cab	49320.00	**41430.00**	**43400.00**	**44270.00**	SLH	4T	244D	16F-16R	80.15	7385	C,H,A
6085 w/Cab	42030.00	**35310.00**	**36990.00**	**37730.00**	SLH	4T	244D	16F-16R	80.15	6724	C,H,A
6090 HC	40900.00	**34360.00**	**35990.00**	**36710.00**	SLH	4T	244D	19F-19R	80.15		No
6090 HC 4WD	47270.00	**39710.00**	**41600.00**	**42430.00**	SLH	4T	244D	19F-19R	80.15	7831	No
6105	54910.00	**45580.00**	**47770.00**	**49200.00**	SLH	6	366D	24F-12R	106.34	10013	C,H,A
6105 4WD	61440.00	**51000.00**	**53450.00**	**55050.00**	SLH	6	366D	24F-12R	106.34	10759	C,H,A
Workhorse 6124	71440.00	**58100.00**	**60900.00**	**62730.00**	Cummins	6T	359D	32F-32R	124.94	14200	C,H,A
Workhorse 6124 4WD	81825.00	**65570.00**	**68730.00**	**70790.00**	Cummins	6T	359D	32F-32R	124.94	15300	C,H,A
Workhorse 6125	76845.00	**61750.00**	**64730.00**	**66670.00**	Cummins	6T	359D	18F-9R	124.94	14950	C,H,A
Workhorse 6125 4WD	88390.00	**71380.00**	**74820.00**	**77070.00**	Cummins	6T	359D	18F-9R	124.94	16150	C,H,A
Workhorse 6144	75750.00	**61420.00**	**64380.00**	**66310.00**	Cummins	6TA	359D	32F-32R	142.56	14200	C,H,A
Workhorse 6144 4WD	85865.00	**69140.00**	**72470.00**	**74640.00**	Cummins	6TA	359D	32F-32R	142.56	15300	C,H,A
Workhorse 6145	82120.00	**66480.00**	**69690.00**	**71780.00**	Cummins	6TA	359D	18F-9R	142.56	14950	C,H,A
Workhorse 6145 4WD	92540.00	**74700.00**	**78300.00**	**80650.00**	Cummins	6TA	359D	18F-9R	142.56	16150	C,H,A
Workhorse 6175	92060.00	**74120.00**	**77690.00**	**80020.00**	Cummins	6T	504D	18F-9R	175.47	16300	C,H,A
Workhorse 6175 4WD	103305.00	**84080.00**	**88130.00**	**90770.00**	Cummins	6T	504D	18F-9R	175.47	17850	C,H,A
Workhorse 6195 4WD	115270.00	**93960.00**	**98480.00**	**101430.00**	Cummins	6TA	504D	18F-9R	200.46	17950	C,H,A
Workhorse 6215 4WD	123045.00	**99600.00**	**104400.00**	**107530.00**	Cummins	6TA	504D	18F-9R	215.0	17200	C,H,A
6410	34250.00	**28430.00**	**29800.00**	**30690.00**	Cummins	4T	239D	12F-4R	70.0		No
6410 4WD	40780.00	**33850.00**	**35480.00**	**36540.00**	Cummins	4T	239D	12F-4R	70.0		No
6410 4WD w/cab	48625.00	**40360.00**	**42300.00**	**43570.00**	Cummins	4T	239D	12F-4R	70.0		C,H,A
6410 w/cab	42095.00	**34940.00**	**36620.00**	**37720.00**	Cummins	4T	239D	12F-4R	70.0		C,H,A
6510	36775.00	**30520.00**	**31990.00**	**32950.00**	Cummins	4T	239D	12F-4R	85.0		No
6510 4WD	44710.00	**37110.00**	**38900.00**	**40070.00**	Cummins	4T	239D	12F-4R	85.0		No
6510 4WD w/cab	52965.00	**43960.00**	**46080.00**	**47460.00**	Cummins	4T	239D	12F-4R	85.0		C,H,A
6510 w/cab	45030.00	**37380.00**	**39180.00**	**40360.00**	Cummins	4T	239D	12F-4R	85.0		C,H,A
6710	44935.00	**37300.00**	**39090.00**	**40260.00**	Cummins	6T	359D	32F-32R	95.0		No
6710 4WD	52535.00	**43600.00**	**45710.00**	**47080.00**	Cummins	6T	359D	32F-32R	95.0		No
6710 4WD w/cab	65190.00	**54110.00**	**56720.00**	**58420.00**	Cummins	6T	359D	32F-32R	95.0		C,H,A
6710 w/cab	57300.00	**47560.00**	**49850.00**	**51350.00**	Cummins	6T	359D	32F-32R	95.0		C,H,A

White (Cont.)

1999 (Cont.)

Model	Approx. Retail Price New	Estimated Average Value Less Repairs Fair	Good	Premium	Engine Make	No. Cyls.	Displ. Cu.-In.	No. Speeds	P.T.O. H.P.	Approx. Shipping Wt.-Lbs.	Cab
6810	51900.00	43080.00	45150.00	46510.00	Cummins	6T	359D	32F-32R	110.0		No
6810 4WD	63910.00	53050.00	55600.00	57270.00	Cummins	6T	359D	32F-32R	110.0		No
6810 4WD w/cab	76565.00	63550.00	66610.00	68610.00	Cummins	6T	359D	32F-32R	110.0		C,H,A
6810 w/cab	63735.00	52900.00	55450.00	57110.00	Cummins	6T	359D	32F-32R	110.0		C,H,A
Fieldmaster 8310	75000.00	61500.00	64500.00	65790.00	Cummins	6T	359D	32F-32R	125.0		C,H,A
Fieldmaster 8310 PS	80210.00	65770.00	68980.00	70360.00	Cummins	6T	359D	18F-6R	125.0		C,H,A
Fieldmaster 8310 4WD	86540.00	70960.00	74420.00	75910.00	Cummins	6T	359D	32F-32R	125.0		C,H,A
Fieldmaster 8310 4WD PS	91750.00	75240.00	78910.00	80490.00	Cummins	6T	359D	18F-6R	125.0		C,H,A
Fieldmaster 8410	79515.00	65200.00	68380.00	69750.00	Cummins	6TA	359D	32F-32R	145.0		C,H,A
Fieldmaster 8410 PS	86020.00	70540.00	73980.00	75460.00	Cummins	6TA	359D	18F-6R	145.0		C,H,A
Fieldmaster 8410 4WD	90620.00	74310.00	77930.00	79490.00	Cummins	6TA	359D	32F-32R	145.0		C,H,A
Fieldmaster 8410 4WD PS	97125.00	79640.00	83530.00	85200.00	Cummins	6TA	359D	18F-6R	145.0		C,H,A
Fieldmaster 8510 PS	104955.00	86060.00	90260.00	92070.00	Cummins	6T	505D	18F-6R	160.0		C,H,A
Fieldmaster 8610 PS	113500.00	93070.00	97610.00	99560.00	Cummins	6TA	505D	18F-6R	180.0		C,H,A
Fieldmaster 8710 PS	123025.00	100880.00	105800.00	107920.00	Cummins	6TA	505D	18F-6R	200.0		C,H,A
Fieldmaster 8810 PS	137180.00	112490.00	117980.00	120340.00	Cummins	6TA	505D	18F-6R	225.0		C,H,A

Yanmar

1977

Model	Approx. Retail Price New	Fair	Good	Premium	Make	No. Cyls.	Displ. Cu.-In.	No. Speeds	P.T.O. H.P.	Approx. Shipping Wt.-Lbs.	Cab
YM 135	3514.00	1410.00	1720.00	1890.00	Yanmar	2	38D	6F-2R		995	No
YM 135 D	3863.00	1550.00	1890.00	2080.00	Yanmar	2	38D	6F-2R		1090	No
YM 155	3725.00	1490.00	1830.00	2010.00	Yanmar	2	40D	6F-2R		1060	No
YM 155 D	4123.00	1650.00	2020.00	2220.00	Yanmar	2	40D	6F-2R		1145	No
YM 240	4837.00	1940.00	2370.00	2610.00	Yanmar	2	70D	8F-2R	19.76	1700	No

1978

Model	Approx. Retail Price New	Fair	Good	Premium	Make	No. Cyls.	Displ. Cu.-In.	No. Speeds	P.T.O. H.P.	Approx. Shipping Wt.-Lbs.	Cab
YM 135	3589.00	1470.00	1800.00	1980.00	Yanmar	2	38D	6F-2R		995	No
YM 135 D	3938.00	1620.00	1970.00	2170.00	Yanmar	2	38D	6F-2R		1090	No
YM 155	3875.00	1590.00	1940.00	2130.00	Yanmar	2	40D	6F-2R		1060	No
YM 155 D	4273.00	1750.00	2140.00	2350.00	Yanmar	2	40D	6F-2R		1145	No
YM 195	4569.00	1870.00	2290.00	2520.00	Yanmar	2	61D	6F-2R		1655	No
YM 240	5007.00	2050.00	2500.00	2750.00	Yanmar	2	70D	8F-2R	19.76	1700	No
YM 240 D	5733.00	2350.00	2870.00	3160.00	Yanmar	2	70D	8F-2R	19.76	1950	No
YM 330	7753.00	3020.00	3680.00	4050.00	Yanmar	3	91D	8F-2R		2550	No
YM 330 D	9025.00	3540.00	4310.00	4740.00	Yanmar	3	91D	8F-2R		2890	No

1979

Model	Approx. Retail Price New	Fair	Good	Premium	Make	No. Cyls.	Displ. Cu.-In.	No. Speeds	P.T.O. H.P.	Approx. Shipping Wt.-Lbs.	Cab
YM 135	3669.00	1540.00	1870.00	2040.00	Yanmar	2	38D	6F-2R		995	No
YM 135 D	4052.00	1700.00	2070.00	2260.00	Yanmar	2	38D	6F-2R		1090	No
YM 155	4065.00	1710.00	2070.00	2260.00	Yanmar	2	40D	6F-2R		1060	No
YM 155 D	4389.00	1840.00	2240.00	2440.00	Yanmar	2	40D	6F-2R		1145	No
YM 195	4868.00	2050.00	2480.00	2700.00	Yanmar	2	61D	6F-2R		1655	No
YM 195 D	5487.00	2310.00	2800.00	3050.00	Yanmar	2	61D	6F-2R		1805	No
YM 240	5201.00	2180.00	2650.00	2890.00	Yanmar	2	70D	8F-2R	19.76	1700	No
YM 240 D	5972.00	2510.00	3050.00	3330.00	Yanmar	2	70D	8F-2R	19.76	1950	No
YM 330	7680.00	3140.00	3820.00	4160.00	Yanmar	3	91D	8F-2R		2550	No
YM 330 D	8865.00	3680.00	4470.00	4870.00	Yanmar	3	91D	8F-2R		2890	No

1980

Model	Approx. Retail Price New	Fair	Good	Premium	Make	No. Cyls.	Displ. Cu.-In.	No. Speeds	P.T.O. H.P.	Approx. Shipping Wt.-Lbs.	Cab
YM 135	3760.00	1620.00	1960.00	2120.00	Yanmar	2	38D	6F-2R		995	No
YM 135 D	4151.00	1790.00	2160.00	2330.00	Yanmar	2	38D	6F-2R		1090	No
YM 155	4166.00	1790.00	2170.00	2340.00	Yanmar	2	40D	6F-2R		1060	No
YM 155 D	4498.00	1930.00	2340.00	2530.00	Yanmar	2	40D	6F-2R		1145	No
YM 186	5184.00	2230.00	2700.00	2920.00	Yanmar	3	54D	9F-3R		1411	No
YM 186 D	5770.00	2480.00	3000.00	3240.00	Yanmar	3	54D	9F-3R		1539	No
YM 195	4982.00	2140.00	2590.00	2800.00	Yanmar	2	61D	6F-2R		1655	No
YM 195 D	5617.00	2420.00	2920.00	3150.00	Yanmar	2	61D	6F-2R		1830	No
YM 240	5321.00	2290.00	2770.00	2990.00	Yanmar	2	70D	8F-2R	19.76	1700	No
YM 240 D	6111.00	2630.00	3180.00	3430.00	Yanmar	2	70D	8F-2R	19.76	1950	No
YM 330	8210.00	3230.00	3910.00	4220.00	Yanmar	3	91D	8F-2R		2550	No
YM 330 D	9425.00	3800.00	4590.00	4960.00	Yanmar	3	91D	8F-2R		2890	No
YM 336	8476.00	3650.00	4410.00	4760.00	Yanmar	3	91D	12F-4R	26.98	2854	No
YM 336 D	9788.00	4210.00	5090.00	5500.00	Yanmar	3	91D	12F-4R	26.98	3091	No

1981

Model	Approx. Retail Price New	Fair	Good	Premium	Make	No. Cyls.	Displ. Cu.-In.	No. Speeds	P.T.O. H.P.	Approx. Shipping Wt.-Lbs.	Cab
YM 135	4250.00	1870.00	2250.00	2430.00	Yanmar	2	38D	6F-2R		995	No
YM 135 D	4650.00	2050.00	2470.00	2670.00	Yanmar	2	38D	6F-2R		1090	No
YM 155	4750.00	2090.00	2520.00	2720.00	Yanmar	2	40D	6F-2R		1060	No
YM 155 D	5200.00	2290.00	2760.00	2980.00	Yanmar	2	40D	6F-2R		1145	No
YM 165	4900.00	2160.00	2600.00	2810.00	Yanmar	2	40D	6F-2R		1011	No
YM 165 D	5400.00	2380.00	2860.00	3090.00	Yanmar	2	40D	6F-2R		1216	No
YM 186	6000.00	2640.00	3180.00	3430.00	Yanmar	3	54D	9F-3R		1345	No
YM 186 D	6400.00	2820.00	3390.00	3660.00	Yanmar	3	54D	9F-3R		1435	No
YM 226	6990.00	3080.00	3710.00	4010.00	Yanmar	3	69D	9F-3R	19.42	1874	No
YM 226 D	7790.00	3430.00	4130.00	4460.00	Yanmar	3	69D	9F-3R	19.42	1962	No
YM 240	6200.00	2730.00	3290.00	3550.00	Yanmar	2	70D	8F-2R	19.76	1700	No
YM 240 D	7100.00	3120.00	3760.00	4060.00	Yanmar	2	70D	8F-2R	19.76	1950	No
YM 276	7900.00	3480.00	4190.00	4530.00	Yanmar	3	86D	12F-4R	23.00	2205	No
YM 276 D	8990.00	3960.00	4770.00	5150.00	Yanmar	3	86D	12F-4R	23.00	2282	No
YM 330	7570.00	3330.00	4010.00	4330.00	Yanmar	3	91D	8F-2R		2550	No
YM 330 D	8900.00	3920.00	4720.00	5100.00	Yanmar	3	91D	8F-2R		2890	No
YM 336	9300.00	3960.00	4770.00	5150.00	Yanmar	3	91D	12F-4R	26.98	2854	No

Yanmar (Cont.)

Model	Approx. Retail Price New	Estimated Average Value Less Repairs Fair	Good	Premium	Engine Make	No. Cyls.	Displ. Cu.-In.	No. Speeds	P.T.O. H.P.	Approx. Shipping Wt.-Lbs.	Cab
1981 (Cont.)											
YM 336 D	10500.00	4620.00	5570.00	6020.00	Yanmar	3	91D	12F-4R	26.98	3091	No
1982											
YM 165	5495.00	2470.00	2970.00	3210.00	Yanmar	2	40D	6F-2R		1011	No
YM 165 D	6995.00	3150.00	3780.00	4080.00	Yanmar	2	40D	6F-2R		1216	No
YM 186	6395.00	2880.00	3450.00	3730.00	Yanmar	3	54D	9F-3R		1345	No
YM 186 D	6995.00	3150.00	3780.00	4080.00	Yanmar	3	54D	9F-3R		1435	No
YM 220	6300.00	2840.00	3400.00	3670.00	Yanmar	3	69D	8F-2R		1874	No
YM 220 D	7130.00	3210.00	3850.00	4160.00	Yanmar	3	69D	8F-2R		2026	No
YM 226	7195.00	3240.00	3890.00	4200.00	Yanmar	3	69D	9F-3R	19.42	1874	No
YM 226 D	7790.00	3510.00	4210.00	4550.00	Yanmar	3	69D	9F-3R	19.42	1962	No
YM 276	8140.00	3660.00	4400.00	4750.00	Yanmar	3	86D	12F-4R	23.00	2205	No
YM 276 D	9240.00	4160.00	4990.00	5390.00	Yanmar	3	86D	12F-4R	23.00	2282	No
YM 336	9795.00	4070.00	4890.00	5280.00	Yanmar	3	91D	12F-4R	26.98	2854	No
YM 336 D	11195.00	4770.00	5720.00	6180.00	Yanmar	3	91D	12F-4R	26.98	3091	No
1983											
YM 165	5605.00	2580.00	3080.00	3330.00	Yanmar	2	40D	6F-2R		1011	No
YM 165D 4WD	7135.00	3280.00	3920.00	4230.00	Yanmar	2	40D	6F-2R		1216	No
YM 180	5995.00	2760.00	3300.00	3560.00	Yanmar	3	54D	8F-2R		1523	No
YM 180 D 4WD	6595.00	3030.00	3630.00	3920.00	Yanmar	3	54D	8F-2R		1650	No
YM 186 D 4WD PS	7135.00	3280.00	3920.00	4230.00	Yanmar	3	54D	9F-3R		1435	No
YM 186 PS	6523.00	3000.00	3590.00	3880.00	Yanmar	3	54D	9F-3R		1345	No
YM 220	6426.00	2960.00	3530.00	3810.00	Yanmar	3	69D	8F-2R		1874	No
YM 220 D 4WD	7273.00	3350.00	4000.00	4320.00	Yanmar	3	69D	8F-2R		2026	No
YM 226 D 4WD PS	7946.00	3660.00	4370.00	4720.00	Yanmar	3	69D	9F-3R	19.42	1962	No
YM 226 PS	7339.00	3380.00	4040.00	4360.00	Yanmar	3	69D	9F-3R	19.42	1874	No
YM 276 D 4WD PS	9425.00	4340.00	5180.00	5590.00	Yanmar	3	86D	12F-4R	23.00	2282	No
YM 276 PS	8303.00	3820.00	4570.00	4940.00	Yanmar	3	86D	12F-4R	23.00	2205	No
YM 336 D 4WD PS	11419.00	4970.00	5940.00	6420.00	Yanmar	3	91D	12F-4R	26.98	3091	No
YM 336 PS	9991.00	4230.00	5060.00	5470.00	Yanmar	3	91D	12F-4R	26.98	2854	No
1984											
YM 122	4260.00	2000.00	2390.00	2580.00	Yanmar	1	33D	6F-3R	12*	829	No
YM 140-2	5879.00	2760.00	3290.00	3550.00	Yanmar	2	39D	6F-3R	14*	1406	No
YM 140-4 4WD	6339.00	2980.00	3550.00	3830.00	Yanmar	2	39D	6F-3R	14*	1406	No
YM 146	4990.00	2350.00	2790.00	3010.00	Yanmar	2	39D	6F-3R	14*	844	No
YM 147-2 PS	6282.00	2950.00	3520.00	3800.00	Yanmar	2	39D	6F-2R	14*	1421	No
YM 147-4 PS 4WD	6786.00	3190.00	3800.00	4100.00	Yanmar	2	39D	6F-2R	14*	1522	No
YM 165-2	5810.00	2730.00	3250.00	3510.00	Yanmar	2	40D	6F-2R	16*	1011	No
YM 165D 4WD	6310.00	2970.00	3530.00	3810.00	Yanmar	2	40D	6F-2R	16*	1216	No
YM 180-2	6545.00	3080.00	3670.00	3960.00	Yanmar	3	54D	8F-2R	18*	1673	No
YM 180-4 4WD	7205.00	3390.00	4040.00	4360.00	Yanmar	3	54D	8F-2R	18*	1793	No
YM 186-2 PS	6750.00	3170.00	3780.00	4080.00	Yanmar	3	54D	9F-3R	18*	1412	No
YM 186-4 PS 4WD	7350.00	3460.00	4120.00	4450.00	Yanmar	3	54D	9F-3R	18*	1538	No
YM 220-2	7170.00	3370.00	4020.00	4340.00	Yanmar	3	69D	8F-2R	22*	2019	No
YM 220-4 4WD	7970.00	3750.00	4460.00	4820.00	Yanmar	3	69D	8F-2R	22*	2178	No
YM 226-2 PS	7851.00	3690.00	4400.00	4750.00	Yanmar	3	69D	9F-3R	19.42	2022	No
YM 226-4 PS 4WD	8651.00	4070.00	4850.00	5240.00	Yanmar	3	69D	9F-3R	19.42	2178	No
YM 276-2 PS	9062.00	3980.00	4740.00	5120.00	Yanmar	3	86D	12F-4R	23.00	2361	No
YM 276-4 PS 4WD	10210.00	4510.00	5380.00	5810.00	Yanmar	3	86D	12F-4R	23.00	2393	No
YM 336-2 PS	10765.00	4420.00	5260.00	5680.00	Yanmar	3	91D	12F-4R	26.98	3039	No
YM 336-4 PS 4WD	12165.00	5170.00	6160.00	6650.00	Yanmar	3	91D	12F-4R	26.98	3267	No
* Bare engine HP											
1985											
YM 122	4260.00	2050.00	2430.00	2620.00	Yanmar	1	33D	6F-3R	12*	829	No
YM 140-2	5879.00	2820.00	3350.00	3620.00	Yanmar	2	39D	6F-3R	14*	1406	No
YM 140-4 4WD	6339.00	3040.00	3610.00	3900.00	Yanmar	2	39D	6F-3R	14*	1406	No
YM 146	4990.00	2400.00	2840.00	3070.00	Yanmar	2	39D	6F-3R	14*	844	No
YM 147-2 PS	6282.00	3020.00	3580.00	3870.00	Yanmar	2	39D	6F-2R	14*	1421	No
YM 147-4 PS 4WD	6786.00	3260.00	3870.00	4180.00	Yanmar	2	39D	6F-2R	14*	1522	No
YM 165-2	5810.00	2790.00	3310.00	3580.00	Yanmar	2	40D	6F-2R	16*	1011	No
YM 165D 4WD	6310.00	3030.00	3600.00	3890.00	Yanmar	2	40D	6F-2R	16*	1216	No
YM 180-2	6545.00	3140.00	3730.00	4030.00	Yanmar	3	54D	8F-2R	18*	1673	No
YM 180-4 4WD	7205.00	3460.00	4110.00	4440.00	Yanmar	3	54D	8F-2R	18*	1793	No
YM 186-2 PS	6750.00	3240.00	3850.00	4160.00	Yanmar	3	54D	9F-3R	18*	1412	No
YM 186-4 PS 4WD	7350.00	3530.00	4190.00	4530.00	Yanmar	3	54D	9F-3R	18*	1538	No
YM 220-2	7170.00	3440.00	4090.00	4420.00	Yanmar	3	69D	8F-2R	22*	2019	No
YM 220-4 4WD	7970.00	3830.00	4540.00	4900.00	Yanmar	3	69D	8F-2R	22*	2178	No
YM 226-2 PS	7851.00	3770.00	4480.00	4840.00	Yanmar	3	69D	9F-3R	19.42	2022	No
YM 226-4 PS 4WD	8651.00	4150.00	4930.00	5320.00	Yanmar	3	69D	9F-3R	19.42	2178	No
YM 276-2 PS	9062.00	4250.00	5050.00	5450.00	Yanmar	3	86D	12F-4R	23.00	2361	No
YM 276-4 PS 4WD	10210.00	4700.00	5590.00	6040.00	Yanmar	3	86D	12F-4R	23.00	2393	No
YM 336-2 PS	10765.00	4630.00	5500.00	5940.00	Yanmar	3	91D	12F-4R	26.98	3039	No
YM 336-4 PS 4WD	12165.00	5380.00	6380.00	6890.00	Yanmar	3	91D	12F-4R	26.98	3267	No
* Bare engine HP, PS - Power Shift											
1986											
YM 122	4260.00	2090.00	2470.00	2670.00	Yanmar	1	33D	6F-3R	12*	829	No
YM 140-2	5879.00	2880.00	3410.00	3680.00	Yanmar	2	39D	6F-3R	14*	1406	No
YM 140-4 4WD	6339.00	3110.00	3680.00	3970.00	Yanmar	2	39D	6F-3R	14*	1406	No
YM 146	4990.00	2450.00	2890.00	3120.00	Yanmar	2	39D	6F-3R	14*	844	No
YM 147-2 PS	6282.00	3080.00	3640.00	3930.00	Yanmar	2	39D	6F-2R	14*	1421	No

Yanmar (Cont.)

1986 (Cont.)

Model	Approx. Retail Price New	Fair	Good	Premium	Make	No. Cyls.	Displ. Cu.-In.	No. Speeds	P.T.O. H.P.	Approx. Shipping Wt.-Lbs.	Cab
YM 147-4 PS 4WD	6786.00	3330.00	3940.00	4260.00	Yanmar	2	39D	6F-2R	14*	1522	No
YM 165-2	5810.00	2850.00	3370.00	3640.00	Yanmar	2	40D	6F-2R	16*	1011	No
YM 165D 4WD	6310.00	3090.00	3660.00	3950.00	Yanmar	2	40D	6F-2R	16*	1216	No
YM 169	7100.00	3480.00	4120.00	4450.00	Yanmar	3	54D	6F-2R		1190	No
YM 169 D 4WD	7900.00	3870.00	4580.00	4950.00	Yanmar	3	54D	6F-2R		1279	No
YM 180-2	6545.00	3210.00	3800.00	4100.00	Yanmar	3	54D	8F-2R	18*	1673	No
YM 180-4 4WD	7205.00	3530.00	4180.00	4510.00	Yanmar	3	54D	8F-2R	18*	1793	No
YM 186-2 PS	6750.00	3310.00	3920.00	4230.00	Yanmar	3	54D	9F-3R	18*	1412	No
YM 186-4 PS 4WD	7350.00	3600.00	4260.00	4600.00	Yanmar	3	54D	9F-3R	18*	1538	No
YM 187	7600.00	3720.00	4410.00	4760.00	Yanmar	3	54D	9F-3R	18*	1523	No
YM 220-2	7170.00	3510.00	4160.00	4490.00	Yanmar	3	69D	8F-2R	22*	2019	No
YM 220-4 4WD	7970.00	3910.00	4620.00	4990.00	Yanmar	3	69D	8F-2R	22*	2178	No
YM 226-2 PS	7851.00	3850.00	4550.00	4910.00	Yanmar	3	69D	9F-3R	19.42	2022	No
YM 226-4 PS 4WD	8651.00	4240.00	5020.00	5420.00	Yanmar	3	69D	9F-3R	19.42	2178	No
YM 276-2 PS	9062.00	4440.00	5260.00	5680.00	Yanmar	3	86D	12F-4R	23.00	2361	No
YM 276-4 PS 4WD	10210.00	4900.00	5800.00	6260.00	Yanmar	3	86D	12F-4R	23.00	2393	No
YM 336-2 PS	10765.00	4830.00	5710.00	6170.00	Yanmar	3	91D	12F-4R	26.98	3039	No
YM 336-4 PS 4WD	12165.00	5680.00	6730.00	7270.00	Yanmar	3	91D	12F-4R	26.98	3267	No

* Bare engine HP, PS - Power Shift

1987

Model	Approx. Retail Price New	Fair	Good	Premium	Make	No. Cyls.	Displ. Cu.-In.	No. Speeds	P.T.O. H.P.	Approx. Shipping Wt.-Lbs.	Cab
YM 122	4260.00	2130.00	2510.00	2710.00	Yanmar	1	33D	6F-3R	12*	829	No
YM 140-2	5879.00	2940.00	3470.00	3750.00	Yanmar	2	39D	6F-3R	14*	1406	No
YM 140-4 4WD	6339.00	3170.00	3740.00	4040.00	Yanmar	2	39D	6F-3R	14*	1406	No
YM 146	4990.00	2500.00	2940.00	3180.00	Yanmar	2	39D	6F-3R	14*	844	No
YM 147-2 PS	6282.00	3140.00	3710.00	4010.00	Yanmar	2	39D	6F-2R	14*	1421	No
YM 147-4 PS 4WD	6786.00	3390.00	4000.00	4320.00	Yanmar	2	39D	6F-2R	14*	1522	No
YM 165-2	5810.00	2910.00	3430.00	3700.00	Yanmar	2	40D	6F-2R	16*	1011	No
YM 165D 4WD	6310.00	3160.00	3720.00	4020.00	Yanmar	2	40D	6F-2R	16*	1216	No
YM 169	7100.00	3550.00	4190.00	4530.00	Yanmar	3	54D	6F-2R		1190	No
YM 169 D 4WD	7900.00	3950.00	4660.00	5030.00	Yanmar	3	54D	6F-2R		1279	No
YM 180-2	6545.00	3270.00	3860.00	4170.00	Yanmar	3	54D	8F-2R	18*	1673	No
YM 180-4 4WD	7205.00	3600.00	4250.00	4590.00	Yanmar	3	54D	8F-2R	18*	1793	No
YM 186-2 PS	6750.00	3380.00	3980.00	4300.00	Yanmar	3	54D	9F-3R	18*	1412	No
YM 186-4 PS 4WD	7350.00	3680.00	4340.00	4690.00	Yanmar	3	54D	9F-3R	18*	1538	No
YM 187	7600.00	3800.00	4480.00	4840.00	Yanmar	3	54D	9F-3R	18*	1523	No
YM 220-2	7170.00	3590.00	4230.00	4570.00	Yanmar	3	69D	8F-2R	22*	2019	No
YM 220-4 4WD	7970.00	3990.00	4700.00	5080.00	Yanmar	3	69D	8F-2R	22*	2178	No
YM 226-2 PS	7851.00	3930.00	4630.00	5000.00	Yanmar	3	69D	9F-3R	19.42	2022	No
YM 226-4 PS 4WD	8651.00	4330.00	5100.00	5510.00	Yanmar	3	69D	9F-3R	19.42	2178	No
YM 276-2 PS	9062.00	4580.00	5410.00	5840.00	Yanmar	3	86D	12F-4R	23.00	2361	No
YM 276-4 PS 4WD	10210.00	5080.00	5990.00	6470.00	Yanmar	3	86D	12F-4R	23.00	2393	No
YM 336-2 PS	10765.00	5050.00	5960.00	6440.00	Yanmar	3	91D	12F-4R	26.98	3039	No
YM 336-4 PS 4WD	12165.00	5850.00	6900.00	7450.00	Yanmar	3	91D	12F-4R	26.98	3267	No

* Bare engine HP, PS - Power Shift

1988

Model	Approx. Retail Price New	Fair	Good	Premium	Make	No. Cyls.	Displ. Cu.-In.	No. Speeds	P.T.O. H.P.	Approx. Shipping Wt.-Lbs.	Cab
YM 122	4260.00	2170.00	2560.00	2740.00	Yanmar	1	33D	6F-3R	12*	829	No
YM 140-2	5879.00	3000.00	3530.00	3780.00	Yanmar	2	39D	6F-3R	14*	1406	No
YM 140-4 4WD	6339.00	3230.00	3800.00	4070.00	Yanmar	2	39D	6F-3R	14*	1406	No
YM 146	4990.00	2550.00	2990.00	3200.00	Yanmar	2	39D	6F-3R	14*	844	No
YM 147-2 PS	6282.00	3200.00	3770.00	4030.00	Yanmar	2	39D	6F-2R	14*	1421	No
YM 147-4 PS 4WD	6786.00	3460.00	4070.00	4360.00	Yanmar	2	39D	6F-2R	14*	1522	No
YM 165-2	5810.00	2960.00	3490.00	3730.00	Yanmar	2	40D	6F-2R	16*	1011	No
YM 165D 4WD	6310.00	3220.00	3790.00	4060.00	Yanmar	2	40D	6F-2R	16*	1216	No
YM 169	7100.00	3620.00	4260.00	4560.00	Yanmar	3	54D	6F-2R		1190	No
YM 169 D 4WD	7900.00	4030.00	4740.00	5070.00	Yanmar	3	54D	6F-2R		1279	No
YM 180-2	6545.00	3340.00	3930.00	4210.00	Yanmar	3	54D	8F-2R	18*	1673	No
YM 180-4 4WD	7205.00	3680.00	4320.00	4620.00	Yanmar	3	54D	8F-2R	18*	1793	No
YM 186-2 PS	6750.00	3440.00	4050.00	4330.00	Yanmar	3	54D	9F-3R	18*	1412	No
YM 186-4 PS 4WD	7350.00	3750.00	4410.00	4720.00	Yanmar	3	54D	9F-3R	18*	1538	No
YM 187	7600.00	3880.00	4560.00	4880.00	Yanmar	3	54D	9F-3R	18*	1523	No
YM 220-2	7170.00	3660.00	4300.00	4600.00	Yanmar	3	69D	8F-2R	22*	2019	No
YM 220-4 4WD	7970.00	4070.00	4780.00	5120.00	Yanmar	3	69D	8F-2R	22*	2178	No
YM 226-2 PS	7851.00	4000.00	4710.00	5040.00	Yanmar	3	69D	9F-3R	19.42	2022	No
YM 226-4 PS 4WD	8651.00	4410.00	5190.00	5550.00	Yanmar	3	69D	9F-3R	19.42	2178	No
YM 276-2 PS	9062.00	4740.00	5580.00	5970.00	Yanmar	3	86D	12F-4R	23.00	2361	No
YM 276-4 PS 4WD	10210.00	5260.00	6190.00	6620.00	Yanmar	3	86D	12F-4R	23.00	2393	No
YM 336-2 PS	10765.00	5490.00	6460.00	6910.00	Yanmar	3	91D	12F-4R	26.98	3039	No
YM 336-4 PS 4WD	12165.00	6200.00	7300.00	7810.00	Yanmar	3	91D	12F-4R	26.98	3267	No

* Bare engine HP, PS - Power Shift

1989

Model	Approx. Retail Price New	Fair	Good	Premium	Make	No. Cyls.	Displ. Cu.-In.	No. Speeds	P.T.O. H.P.	Approx. Shipping Wt.-Lbs.	Cab
YM 122	4295.00	2230.00	2620.00	2800.00	Yanmar	1	33D	6F-3R	12*	829	No
YM 140-2	6450.00	3350.00	3940.00	4220.00	Yanmar	2	39D	6F-3R	14*	1406	No
YM 140-4 4WD	6950.00	3610.00	4240.00	4540.00	Yanmar	2	39D	6F-3R	14*	1406	No
YM 146	5250.00	2730.00	3200.00	3420.00	Yanmar	2	39D	6F-3R	14*	844	No
YM 147-2 PS	6895.00	3590.00	4210.00	4510.00	Yanmar	2	39D	6F-2R	14*	1421	No
YM 147-4 PS 4WD	7450.00	3870.00	4550.00	4870.00	Yanmar	2	39D	6F-2R	14*	1522	No
YM 169	8300.00	4320.00	5060.00	5410.00	Yanmar	3	54D	6F-2R		1190	No
YM 169 D 4WD	9100.00	4730.00	5550.00	5940.00	Yanmar	3	54D	6F-2R		1279	No
YM 180-2	7450.00	3870.00	4550.00	4870.00	Yanmar	3	54D	8F-2R	18*	1673	No
YM 180-4 4WD	8150.00	4240.00	4970.00	5320.00	Yanmar	3	54D	8F-2R	18*	1793	No
YM 187	7695.00	4000.00	4690.00	5020.00	Yanmar	3	54D	9F-3R	18*	1523	No

Yanmar (Cont.)

1989 (Cont.)

Model	Approx. Retail Price New	Estimated Average Value Less Repairs Fair	Good	Premium	Engine Make	No. Cyls.	Displ. Cu.-In.	No. Speeds	P.T.O. H.P.	Approx. Shipping Wt.-Lbs.	Cab
YM 220-2	8250.00	**4290.00**	**5030.00**	**5380.00**	Yanmar	3	69D	8F-2R	22*	2019	No
YM 220-4 4WD	9195.00	**4780.00**	**5610.00**	**6000.00**	Yanmar	3	69D	8F-2R	22*	2178	No
YM 226-2 PS	8995.00	**4680.00**	**5490.00**	**5870.00**	Yanmar	3	69D	9F-3R	19.42	2022	No
YM 226-4 PS 4WD	9945.00	**5170.00**	**6070.00**	**6500.00**	Yanmar	3	69D	9F-3R	19.42	2178	No
YM 276-2 PS	10295.00	**4940.00**	**5800.00**	**6210.00**	Yanmar	3	86D	12F-4R	23.00	2361	No
YM 276-4 PS 4WD	11495.00	**5460.00**	**6400.00**	**6850.00**	Yanmar	3	86D	12F-4R	23.00	2393	No
YM 336-2 PS	12350.00	**5720.00**	**6710.00**	**7180.00**	Yanmar	3	91D	12F-4R	26.98	3039	No
YM 336-4 PS 4WD	13895.00	**6450.00**	**7560.00**	**8090.00**	Yanmar	3	91D	12F-4R	26.98	3267	No

* Bare engine HP, PS - Power Shift

Zetor

1986

Model	Approx. Retail Price New	Fair	Good	Premium	Make	No. Cyls.	Displ. Cu.-In.	No. Speeds	P.T.O. H.P.	Approx. Shipping Wt.-Lbs.	Cab
5211	9265.00	**3800.00**	**4630.00**	**4950.00**	Zetor	3	165D	10F-2R	42.51	6000	No
5211 w/Cab	11265.00	**4620.00**	**5630.00**	**6020.00**	Zetor	3	165D	10F-2R	42.51	6000	C,H
5245	11130.00	**4560.00**	**5570.00**	**5960.00**	Zetor	3	165D	10F-2R	42.51	6000	No
5245 w/Cab	13130.00	**5380.00**	**6570.00**	**7030.00**	Zetor	3	165D	10F-2R	42.51	6000	C,H
6211	11175.00	**4580.00**	**5590.00**	**5980.00**	Zetor	4	211D	10F-2R	53.09	6350	No
6211 w/Cab	13375.00	**5480.00**	**6690.00**	**7160.00**	Zetor	4	211D	10F-2R	53.09	6350	C,H
6245 4WD	13305.00	**5460.00**	**6650.00**	**7120.00**	Zetor	4	211D	10F-2R	53.09	7400	No
6245 4WD w/Cab	15505.00	**6360.00**	**7750.00**	**8290.00**	Zetor	4	211D	10F-2R	53.09	7400	C,H
7211	12320.00	**5050.00**	**6160.00**	**6590.00**	Zetor	4	220D	10F-2R	58.28	6400	No
7211 w/Cab	14580.00	**5740.00**	**7000.00**	**7490.00**	Zetor	4	220D	10F-2R	58.28	6400	C,H
7245 4WD	14720.00	**6040.00**	**7360.00**	**7880.00**	Zetor	4	220D	10F-2R	58.28	7400	No
7245 4WD w/Cab	16990.00	**6270.00**	**7650.00**	**8190.00**	Zetor	4	220D	10F-2R	58.28	7400	C,H
8111	15800.00	**4740.00**	**5770.00**	**6410.00**	Zetor	4	278D	16F-8R	70.8	8700	No
8111 w/Cab	17800.00	**5380.00**	**6550.00**	**7270.00**	Zetor	4	278D	16F-8R	70.8	8700	C,H
8145 4WD	19800.00	**6020.00**	**7330.00**	**8140.00**	Zetor	4	278D	16F-8R	70.8	9400	No
8145 4WD w/Cab	21800.00	**6400.00**	**7800.00**	**8660.00**	Zetor	4	278D	16F-8R	70.8	9400	C,H
10111	19120.00	**5790.00**	**7060.00**	**7840.00**	Zetor	4	278D	16F-8R	100.	8770	No
10111 w/Cab	21120.00	**6110.00**	**7450.00**	**8270.00**	Zetor	4	278D	16F-8R	100.	8770	C,H
10145 4WD	23400.00	**6530.00**	**7960.00**	**8840.00**	Zetor	4	278D	16F-8R	100.	9500	No
10145 4WD w/Cab	25400.00	**7360.00**	**8970.00**	**9960.00**	Zetor	4	278D	16F-8R	100.	9500	C,H
12111	21020.00	**6140.00**	**7490.00**	**8310.00**	Zetor	6	417D	16F-8R	108.	9900	No
12111 w/Cab	23020.00	**6780.00**	**8270.00**	**9180.00**	Zetor	6	417D	16F-8R	108.	9900	C,H
12145 4WD	25490.00	**7490.00**	**9130.00**	**10130.00**	Zetor	6	417D	16F-8R	108.	9900	No
12145 4WD w/Cab	27490.00	**8000.00**	**9750.00**	**10820.00**	Zetor	6	417D	16F-8R	108.	9900	C,H
16145 4WD	29900.00	**8740.00**	**10650.00**	**11820.00**	Zetor	6	417D	12F-6R	140.	11200	No
16145 4WD w/Cab	31900.00	**9380.00**	**11430.00**	**12690.00**	Zetor	6	417D	12F-6R	140.	11200	C,H

1987

Model	Approx. Retail Price New	Fair	Good	Premium	Make	No. Cyls.	Displ. Cu.-In.	No. Speeds	P.T.O. H.P.	Approx. Shipping Wt.-Lbs.	Cab
5211	9265.00	**3890.00**	**4730.00**	**5060.00**	Zetor	3	165D	10F-2R	43.	5550	No
5211 w/Cab	11265.00	**4730.00**	**5750.00**	**6150.00**	Zetor	3	165D	10F-2R	43.	5550	C,H
5245 4WD	11130.00	**4680.00**	**5680.00**	**6080.00**	Zetor	3	165D	10F-2R	43.	6280	No
5245 4WD w/Cab	13130.00	**5520.00**	**6700.00**	**7170.00**	Zetor	3	165D	10F-2R	43.	6280	C,H
6211	11175.00	**4690.00**	**5700.00**	**6100.00**	Zetor	4	211D	10F-2R	53.09	5850	No
6211 w/Cab	13375.00	**5620.00**	**6820.00**	**7300.00**	Zetor	4	211D	10F-2R	53.09	5850	C,H
6245 4WD	13305.00	**5590.00**	**6790.00**	**7270.00**	Zetor	4	211D	10F-2R	53.09	6950	No
6245 4WD w/Cab	15505.00	**6510.00**	**7910.00**	**8460.00**	Zetor	4	211D	10F-2R	53.09	6950	C,H
7211	12320.00	**5170.00**	**6280.00**	**6720.00**	Zetor	4	220D	10F-2R	58.	6200	No
7211 w/Cab	14580.00	**6120.00**	**7440.00**	**7960.00**	Zetor	4	220D	10F-2R	58.	6200	C,H
7245 4WD	14720.00	**6180.00**	**7510.00**	**8040.00**	Zetor	4	220D	10F-2R	58.	7250	No
7245 4WD w/Cab	16990.00	**7140.00**	**8670.00**	**9280.00**	Zetor	4	220D	10F-2R	58.	7250	C,H
8111	15800.00	**5370.00**	**6320.00**	**6950.00**	Zetor	4	278D	16F-8R	72.	8350	No
8111 w/Cab	17800.00	**6050.00**	**7120.00**	**7830.00**	Zetor	4	278D	16F-8R	72.	8350	C,H
8145 4WD	19800.00	**6390.00**	**7520.00**	**8270.00**	Zetor	4	278D	16F-8R	72.	9600	No
8145 4WD w/Cab	21800.00	**6970.00**	**8200.00**	**9020.00**	Zetor	4	278D	16F-8R	72.	9600	No
10111	19120.00	**5780.00**	**6800.00**	**7480.00**	Zetor	4T	278D	16F-8R	88.	8650	No
10111 w/Cab	21120.00	**6490.00**	**7640.00**	**8400.00**	Zetor	4T	278D	16F-8R	88.	8650	C,H
10145 4WD	23400.00	**7280.00**	**8560.00**	**9420.00**	Zetor	4T	278D	16F-8R	88.	10400	No
10145 4WD w/Cab	25400.00	**7960.00**	**9360.00**	**10300.00**	Zetor	4T	278D	16F-8R	88.	10400	C,H
12111	21020.00	**6460.00**	**7600.00**	**8360.00**	Zetor	6	417D	16F-8R	108.	9700	No
12111 w/Cab	23020.00	**7210.00**	**8480.00**	**9330.00**	Zetor	6	417D	16F-8R	108.	9700	C,H
12145 4WD	25490.00	**7960.00**	**9360.00**	**10300.00**	Zetor	6	417D	16F-8R	108.	10400	No
12145 4WD w/Cab	27490.00	**8500.00**	**10000.00**	**11000.00**	Zetor	6	417D	16F-8R	108.	10400	C,H
16145 4WD w/Cab	31900.00	**9520.00**	**11200.00**	**12320.00**	Zetor	6T	417D	12F-6R	140.	11300	C,H

1988

Model	Approx. Retail Price New	Fair	Good	Premium	Make	No. Cyls.	Displ. Cu.-In.	No. Speeds	P.T.O. H.P.	Approx. Shipping Wt.-Lbs.	Cab
5211	9495.00	**4080.00**	**4940.00**	**5240.00**	Zetor	3	165D	10F-2R	43.	5550	No
5211 w/Cab	11265.00	**4840.00**	**5860.00**	**6210.00**	Zetor	3	165D	10F-2R	43.	5550	C,H
5245 4WD	11360.00	**4890.00**	**5910.00**	**6270.00**	Zetor	3	165D	10F-2R	43.	6280	No
5245 4WD w/Cab	13130.00	**5650.00**	**6830.00**	**7240.00**	Zetor	3	165D	10F-2R	43.	6280	C,H
6211	11295.00	**4860.00**	**5870.00**	**6220.00**	Zetor	4	211D	10F-2R	53.09	5850	No
6211 w/Cab	13375.00	**5750.00**	**6960.00**	**7380.00**	Zetor	4	211D	10F-2R	53.09	5850	C,H
6245 4WD	13500.00	**5810.00**	**7020.00**	**7440.00**	Zetor	4	211D	10F-2R	53.09	6950	No
6245 4WD w/Cab	15500.00	**6670.00**	**8060.00**	**8540.00**	Zetor	4	211D	10F-2R	53.09	6950	C,H
7211	13220.00	**5690.00**	**6870.00**	**7280.00**	Zetor	4	220D	10F-2R	58.	6200	No
7211 w/Cab	14960.00	**6430.00**	**7780.00**	**8250.00**	Zetor	4	220D	10F-2R	58.	6200	C,H
7245 4WD	15620.00	**6720.00**	**8120.00**	**8610.00**	Zetor	4	220D	10F-2R	58.	7250	No
7245 4WD w/Cab	17890.00	**7690.00**	**9300.00**	**9860.00**	Zetor	4	220D	10F-2R	58.	7250	C,H
8111	15800.00	**6790.00**	**8220.00**	**8710.00**	Zetor	4	278D	16F-8R	72.	8350	No
8111 w/Cab	17800.00	**6410.00**	**7480.00**	**8230.00**	Zetor	4	278D	16F-8R	72.	8350	C,H
8145 4WD	19800.00	**6770.00**	**7900.00**	**8690.00**	Zetor	4	278D	16F-8R	72.	9600	No

Zetor (Cont.)

Model	Approx. Retail Price New	Estimated Average Value Less Repairs Fair	Good	Premium	Engine Make	No. Cyls.	Displ. Cu.-In.	No. Speeds	P.T.O. H.P.	Approx. Shipping Wt.-Lbs.	Cab
1988 (Cont.)											
8145 4WD w/Cab	21800.00	7380.00	8610.00	9470.00	Zetor	4	278D	16F-8R	72.	9600	No
10111	19120.00	6120.00	7140.00	7850.00	Zetor	4T	278D	16F-8R	88.	8650	No
10111 w/Cab	21120.00	6840.00	7980.00	8780.00	Zetor	4T	278D	16F-8R	88.	8650	C,H
10145 4WD	23400.00	7700.00	8990.00	9890.00	Zetor	4T	278D	16F-8R	88.	10400	No
10145 4WD w/Cab	25900.00	8460.00	9870.00	10860.00	Zetor	4T	278D	16F-8R	88.	10400	C,H
12111	21020.00	7090.00	8270.00	9100.00	Zetor	6	417D	16F-8R	108.	9700	No
12111 w/Cab	23020.00	7560.00	8820.00	9700.00	Zetor	6	417D	16F-8R	108.	9700	C,H
12145 4WD	25490.00	8280.00	9660.00	10630.00	Zetor	6	417D	16F-8R	108.	10400	No
12145 4WD w/Cab	27690.00	9000.00	10500.00	11550.00	Zetor	6	417D	16F-8R	108.	10400	C,H
16145 4WD w/Cab	31900.00	10080.00	11760.00	12940.00	Zetor	6T	417D	12F-6R	140.	11300	C,H
1989											
5211	9665.00	4250.00	5120.00	5430.00	Zetor	3	165D	10F-2R	42.51	5370	No
5211 w/Cab	11265.00	4960.00	5970.00	6330.00	Zetor	3	165D	10F-2R	42.51	6030	C,H
5245 4WD	11530.00	5070.00	6110.00	6480.00	Zetor	3	165D	10F-2R	42.51	6175	No
5245 4WD w/Cab	13130.00	5780.00	6960.00	7380.00	Zetor	3	165D	10F-2R	42.51	6835	C,H
6211	11575.00	5090.00	6140.00	6510.00	Zetor	4	211D	10F-2R	53.09	5810	No
6211 w/Cab	13375.00	5890.00	7090.00	7520.00	Zetor	4	211D	10F-2R	53.09	6470	C,H
6245 4WD	13700.00	6030.00	7260.00	7700.00	Zetor	4	211D	10F-2R	53.09	6810	No
6245 4WD w/Cab	15500.00	6420.00	7740.00	8200.00	Zetor	4	211D	10F-2R	53.09	7470	C,H
7711	14050.00	5900.00	7100.00	7530.00	Zetor	4	239D	10F-2R	65.74	6020	No
7711 T w/Cab	18520.00	7170.00	8640.00	9160.00	Zetor	4T	239D	10F-2R	75.	6700	C,H
7711 w/Cab	15850.00	6600.00	7950.00	8430.00	Zetor	4	239D	10F-2R	65.74	6680	C,H
7745 4WD	17350.00	7260.00	8750.00	9280.00	Zetor	4	239D	10F-2R	65.74	7230	No
7745 4WD w/Cab	19190.00	7920.00	9540.00	10110.00	Zetor	4	239D	10F-2R	65.74	7890	C,H
7745 T w/Cab	21860.00	8580.00	10340.00	10960.00	Zetor	4T	239D	10F-2R	75.	7910	C,H
8111	15800.00	6600.00	7950.00	8430.00	Zetor	4	278D	16F-8R	70.	8140	No
8111 w/Cab	17800.00	7350.00	8850.00	9380.00	Zetor	4	278D	16F-8R	70.	8840	C,H
8145 4WD	19800.00	7920.00	9540.00	10110.00	Zetor	4	278D	16F-8R	70.	8910	No
8145 4WD w/Cab	22800.00	8800.00	10600.00	11240.00	Zetor	4	278D	16F-8R	70.	9610	C,H
10111	19120.00	6500.00	7520.00	8270.00	Zetor	4T	278D	16F-8R	87.	8230	No
10111 w/Cab	21120.00	7600.00	8800.00	9680.00	Zetor	4T	278D	16F-8R	87.	8930	C,H
10145 4WD	23400.00	8130.00	9420.00	10360.00	Zetor	4T	278D	16F-8R	87.	9400	No
10145 4WD w/Cab	26400.00	8890.00	10300.00	11330.00	Zetor	4T	278D	16F-8R	87.	9700	C,H
12111	21020.00	7410.00	8580.00	9440.00	Zetor	6	417D	16F-8R	101.	9330	No
12111 w/Cab	23020.00	8060.00	9330.00	10260.00	Zetor	6	417D	16F-8R	101.	10030	C,H
12145 4WD	25490.00	8740.00	10120.00	11130.00	Zetor	6	417D	16F-8R	101.	10060	No
12145 4WD w/Cab	28490.00	9690.00	11220.00	12340.00	Zetor	6	417D	16F-8R	101.	10760	C,H
16145 4WD w/Cab	32900.00	10940.00	12670.00	13940.00	Zetor	6T	417D	12F-6R	136.	11310	C,H
1990											
5211.0	10575.00	4760.00	5710.00	6050.00	Zetor	3	165D	10F-2R	42.51	5550	No
5211.0 w/Cab	12300.00	5540.00	6640.00	7040.00	Zetor	3	165D	10F-2R	42.51		C,H
5211.0L Low Profile	9835.00	4430.00	5310.00	5630.00	Zetor	3	165D	10F-2R	42.51	5100	No
5245.0 4WD	12595.00	5670.00	6800.00	7210.00	Zetor	3	165D	10F-2R	42.51	6500	No
5245.0 4WD w/Cab	14320.00	6440.00	7730.00	8190.00	Zetor	3	165D	10F-2R	42.51		C,H
6211.0	12465.00	5610.00	6730.00	7130.00	Zetor	4	211D	10F-2R	53.09	5850	No
6211.0 w/Cab	14425.00	6490.00	7790.00	8260.00	Zetor	4	211D	10F-2R	53.09		C,H
6245.0 4WD	14765.00	6640.00	7970.00	8450.00	Zetor	4	211D	10F-2R	53.09	6950	No
6245.0 4WD w/Cab	16725.00	7530.00	9030.00	9570.00	Zetor	4	211D	10F-2R	53.09		C,H
7711.0	14685.00	6610.00	7930.00	8410.00	Zetor	4	239D	10F-2R	65.74	6250	No
7711.0 w/Cab	16465.00	7410.00	8890.00	9420.00	Zetor	4	239D	10F-2R	65.74		C,H
7745.0 4WD	18135.00	8160.00	9790.00	10380.00	Zetor	4	239D	10F-2R	65.74	7250	No
7745.0 4WD w/Cab	19915.00	8960.00	10750.00	11400.00	Zetor	4	239D	10F-2R	65.74		C,H
8111.0	15800.00	7110.00	8530.00	9040.00	Zetor	4	278D	16F-8R	70.8	8350	No
8111.0 w/Cab	19450.00	7780.00	8950.00	9850.00	Zetor	4	278D	16F-8R	70.8		C,H
8145 4WD	19800.00	7920.00	9110.00	10020.00	Zetor	4	278D	16F-8R	70.6	9600	No
8145 4WD w/Cab	24960.00	8880.00	10210.00	11230.00	Zetor	4	278D	16F-8R	70.6	9600	C,H
10111.0	19120.00	7000.00	8050.00	8860.00	Zetor	4	278D	16F-8R	87.1	8650	No
10111.0 w/Cab	23150.00	8000.00	9200.00	10120.00	Zetor	4	278D	16F-8R	87.1		C,H
10145.0 4WD	23400.00	8560.00	9840.00	10820.00	Zetor	4	278D	16F-8R	88.	9600	No
10145.0 4WD w/Cab	28550.00	9400.00	10810.00	11890.00	Zetor	4	278D	16F-8R	88.		C,H
12111.0	21020.00	8000.00	9200.00	10120.00	Zetor	6	417D	16F-8R	101.	9700	No
12111.0 w/Cab	25430.00	8960.00	10300.00	11330.00	Zetor	6	417D	16F-8R	101.		C,H
12145.0 4WD	25490.00	9200.00	10580.00	11640.00	Zetor	6	417D	16F-8R	102.3	10350	No
12145.0 4WD w/Cab	31090.00	10800.00	12420.00	13660.00	Zetor	6	417D	16F-8R	102.3		C,H
16145.1 w/Cab	35935.00	12000.00	13800.00	15180.00	Zetor	6	417D	12F-6R	135.9	11300	C,H
1991											
5211.0	11325.00	5210.00	6230.00	6600.00	Zetor	3	165D	10F-2R	42.51	5550	No
5211.0 w/Cab	13185.00	6070.00	7250.00	7690.00	Zetor	3	165D	10F-2R	42.51		C,H
5245.0	13500.00	6210.00	7430.00	7880.00	Zetor	3	165D	10F-2R	42.51	6500	No
5245.0 w/Cab	15400.00	7080.00	8470.00	8980.00	Zetor	3	165D	10F-2R	42.51		C,H
6211.0	13350.00	6140.00	7340.00	7780.00	Zetor	4	211D	10F-2R	53.09	5850	No
6211.0 w/Cab	15450.00	6620.00	7920.00	8400.00	Zetor	4	211D	10F-2R	53.09		C,H
6245.0	15810.00	7270.00	8700.00	9220.00	Zetor	4	211D	10F-2R	53.09	6950	No
6245.0 w/Cab	17885.00	7590.00	9080.00	9630.00	Zetor	4	211D	10F-2R	53.09		C,H
7711.0	15730.00	6900.00	8250.00	8750.00	Zetor	4	239D	10F-2R	65.74	6250	No
7711.0 w/Cab	17745.00	7820.00	9350.00	9910.00	Zetor	4	239D	10F-2R	65.74		C,H
7745.0	19425.00	8740.00	10450.00	11080.00	Zetor	4	239D	10F-2R	65.74	7250	No
7745.0 w/Cab	21485.00	9200.00	11000.00	11660.00	Zetor	4	239D	10F-2R	65.74		C,H
8211.0	19920.00	8280.00	9900.00	10490.00	Zetor	4	278D	16F-8R	70.8	10200	No
8211.0 w/Cab	23060.00	9660.00	11550.00	12240.00	Zetor	4	278D	16F-8R	70.8		C,H
8245.0	24675.00	10350.00	12380.00	13120.00	Zetor	4	278D	16F-8R	70.8	11250	No

Model	Approx. Retail Price New	Estimated Average Value Less Repairs Fair	Good	Premium	Engine Make	No. Cyls.	Displ. Cu.-In.	No. Speeds	P.T.O. H.P.	Approx. Shipping Wt.-Lbs.	Cab
Zetor (Cont.)											
			1991 (Cont.)								
8245.0 w/Cab	29600.00	11680.00	13970.00	14810.00	Zetor	4	278D	16F-8R	70.8		C,H
10211.0	23875.00	9030.00	10320.00	11250.00	Zetor	4	278D	16F-8R	87.4	10200	No
10211.0 w/Cab	27300.00	10290.00	11760.00	12820.00	Zetor	4	278D	16F-8R	87.4		C,H
10245.0	28935.00	10880.00	12430.00	13550.00	Zetor	4	278D	16F-8R	87.4	11250	No
10245.0 w/Cab	33825.00	11970.00	13680.00	14910.00	Zetor	4	278D	16F-8R	87.4		C,H
12211.0	26125.00	10120.00	11570.00	12610.00	Zetor	6	417D	16F-8R	102.5	11400	No
12211.0 w/Cab	30135.00	10920.00	12480.00	13600.00	Zetor	6	417D	16F-8R	102.5		C,H
12245.0	31935.00	11760.00	13440.00	14650.00	Zetor	6	417D	16F-8R	102.5	12100	No
12245.0 w/Cab	36910.00	12980.00	14830.00	16170.00	Zetor	6	417D	16F-8R	102.5		C,H
16245 w/Cab	42630.00	14910.00	17040.00	18570.00	Zetor	6	417D	12F-6R	135.8	13970	C,H
			1992								
5211.0	11325.00	5440.00	6340.00	6660.00	Zetor	3	165D	10F-2R	42.51	5550	No
5211.0 w/Cab	13185.00	6330.00	7380.00	7750.00	Zetor	3	165D	10F-2R	42.51		C,H
5245.0	13500.00	6480.00	7560.00	7940.00	Zetor	3	165D	10F-2R	42.51	6500	No
5245.0 w/Cab	15400.00	7390.00	8620.00	9050.00	Zetor	3	165D	10F-2R	42.51		C,H
6211.0	13350.00	6410.00	7480.00	7850.00	Zetor	4	211D	10F-2R	53.09	5850	No
6211.0 w/Cab	15450.00	6910.00	8060.00	8460.00	Zetor	4	211D	10F-2R	53.09		C,H
6245.0	15810.00	7590.00	8850.00	9290.00	Zetor	4	211D	10F-2R	53.09	6950	No
6245.0 w/Cab	17885.00	7920.00	9240.00	9700.00	Zetor	4	211D	10F-2R	53.09		C,H
7711.0	15730.00	7200.00	8400.00	8820.00	Zetor	4	239D	10F-2R	65.74	6250	No
7711.0 w/Cab	17745.00	8160.00	9520.00	10000.00	Zetor	4	239D	10F-2R	65.74		C,H
7745.0	19425.00	9120.00	10640.00	11170.00	Zetor	4	239D	10F-2R	65.74	7250	No
7745.0 w/Cab	21485.00	9600.00	11200.00	11760.00	Zetor	4	239D	10F-2R	65.74		C,H
8211.0	19920.00	8640.00	10080.00	10580.00	Zetor	4	278D	16F-8R	70.8	10200	No
8211.0 w/Cab	23060.00	10080.00	11760.00	12350.00	Zetor	4	278D	16F-8R	70.8		C,H
8245.0	24675.00	10800.00	12600.00	13230.00	Zetor	4	278D	16F-8R	70.8	11250	No
8245.0 w/Cab	29600.00	12960.00	15120.00	15880.00	Zetor	4	278D	16F-8R	70.8		C,H
10211.0	23875.00	9460.00	10970.00	11850.00	Zetor	4	278D	16F-8R	87.4	10200	No
10211.0 w/Cab	27300.00	10780.00	12500.00	13500.00	Zetor	4	278D	16F-8R	87.4		C,H
10245.0	28935.00	11400.00	13210.00	14270.00	Zetor	4	278D	16F-8R	87.4	11250	No
10245.0 w/Cab	33825.00	12540.00	14540.00	15700.00	Zetor	4	278D	16F-8R	87.4		C,H
12211.0	26125.00	10600.00	12290.00	13270.00	Zetor	6	417D	16F-8R	102.5	11400	No
12211.0 w/Cab	30135.00	11440.00	13260.00	14320.00	Zetor	6	417D	16F-8R	102.5		C,H
12245.0	31935.00	12320.00	14280.00	15420.00	Zetor	6	417D	16F-8R	102.5	12100	No
12245.0 w/Cab	36910.00	13600.00	15760.00	17020.00	Zetor	6	417D	16F-8R	102.5		C,H
16245 w/Cab	42630.00	16060.00	18620.00	20110.00	Zetor	6	417D	12F-6R	135.8	13970	C,H
			1994								
2520 Zebra	8370.00	5360.00	5860.00	6150.00	Zetor	2	95D	10F-2R	25		No
3320.0	14115.00	7480.00	8470.00	8890.00	Zetor	3	165D	10F-2R	42.5		No
3320.2 w/Cab	16255.00	8620.00	9750.00	10240.00	Zetor	3	165D	10F-2R	42.5		C,H
3340.0 4WD	16820.00	8920.00	10090.00	10600.00	Zetor	3	165D	10F-2R	42.5		No
3340.2 4WD	19485.00	10330.00	11690.00	12280.00	Zetor	3	165D	10F-2R	42.5		C,H
3520 Zebra	9500.00	5040.00	5700.00	5990.00	Zetor	3	143D	10F-2R	35		No
4320.0	16280.00	8630.00	9770.00	10260.00	Zetor	4	211D	10F-2R	53.1		No
4320.2 w/Cab	18785.00	9960.00	11270.00	11830.00	Zetor	4	211D	10F-2R	53.1		C,H
4340.0 4WD	19435.00	10300.00	11660.00	12240.00	Zetor	4	211D	10F-2R	53.1		No
4340.2 4WD w/Cab	22525.00	11660.00	13200.00	13860.00	Zetor	4	211D	10F-2R	53.1		C,H
5213.0	15100.00	8000.00	9060.00	9510.00	Zetor	3	165D	10F-2R	42.5		No
5213.2 w/Cab	17720.00	9390.00	10630.00	11160.00	Zetor	3	165D	10F-2R	42.5		C,H
5243.0 4WD	17380.00	9210.00	10430.00	10950.00	Zetor	3	165D	10F-2R	42.5		No
5243.2 4WD w/Cab	21000.00	10870.00	12300.00	12920.00	Zetor	3	165D	10F-2R	42.5		C,H
6320.0	18207.00	9650.00	10920.00	11470.00	Zetor	4	239D	10F-2R	65.7		No
6320.2 w/Cab	20421.00	10820.00	12250.00	12860.00	Zetor	4	239D	10F-2R	65.7		C,H
6340.0 4WD	22882.00	12130.00	13730.00	14420.00	Zetor	4	239D	10F-2R	65.7		No
6340.2 4WD w/Cab	25587.00	13560.00	15350.00	16120.00	Zetor	4	239D	10F-2R	65.7		C,H
8520.1 w/Cab	28645.00	14310.00	16200.00	17010.00	Zetor	4	254D	18F-6R	85.7		C,H
8540.1 4WD w/Cab	33270.00	15900.00	18000.00	18900.00	Zetor	4	254D	18F-6R	85.7		C,H
9520.1 w/Cab	30920.00	13720.00	15960.00	16920.00	Zetor	4T	254D	18F-6R	75.8		C,H
9540.1 4WD w/Cab	35395.00	15680.00	18240.00	19330.00	Zetor	4T	254D	18F-6R	75.8		C,H
			1995								
2040 Zebra	8500.00	5610.00	6210.00	6520.00	Zetor	2	70D	6F-3R	20		No
2520 Zebra	8570.00	5660.00	6260.00	6570.00	Zetor	2	95D	10F-2R	25		No
3320.0	14235.00	7970.00	8970.00	9330.00	Zetor	3	165D	10F-2R	42.5		No
3320.2 w/Cab	16555.00	9270.00	10430.00	10850.00	Zetor	3	165D	10F-2R	42.5		C,H
3340.0 4WD	17620.00	9870.00	11100.00	11540.00	Zetor	3	165D	10F-2R	42.5		No
3340.2 4WD	20085.00	11250.00	12650.00	13160.00	Zetor	3	165D	10F-2R	42.5		C,H
3520 Zebra	9500.00	5320.00	5990.00	6230.00	Zetor	3	143D	10F-2R	35		No
4320.0	16880.00	9450.00	10630.00	11060.00	Zetor	4	211D	10F-2R	53.1		No
4320.2 w/Cab	19585.00	10970.00	12340.00	12830.00	Zetor	4	211D	10F-2R	53.1		C,H
4340.0 4WD	20235.00	11330.00	12750.00	13260.00	Zetor	4	211D	10F-2R	53.1		No
4340.2 4WD w/Cab	23105.00	12940.00	14560.00	15140.00	Zetor	4	211D	10F-2R	53.1		C,H
5213.0	15445.00	8650.00	9730.00	10120.00	Zetor	3	165D	10F-2R	42.5		No
5213.2 w/Cab	18420.00	10320.00	11610.00	12070.00	Zetor	3	165D	10F-2R	42.5		C,H
5243.0 4WD	18080.00	10130.00	11390.00	11850.00	Zetor	3	165D	10F-2R	42.5		No
5243.2 4WD w/Cab	21220.00	11880.00	13370.00	13910.00	Zetor	3	165D	10F-2R	42.5		C,H
6320.0	18807.00	10530.00	11850.00	12320.00	Zetor	4	239D	10F-2R	65.7		No
6320.2 w/Cab	21221.00	11880.00	13370.00	13910.00	Zetor	4	239D	10F-2R	65.7		C,H
6340.0 4WD	23682.00	13260.00	14920.00	15520.00	Zetor	4	239D	10F-2R	65.7		No
6340.2 4WD w/Cab	26187.00	14670.00	16500.00	17160.00	Zetor	4	239D	10F-2R	65.7		C,H
8211.0	22025.00	12330.00	13880.00	14440.00	Zetor	4	278D	16F-8R	70.8		No
8211.1 w/Cab	25495.00	14280.00	16060.00	16700.00	Zetor	4	278D	16F-8R	70.8		C,H

Zetor (Cont.)

1995 (Cont.)

Model	Approx. Retail Price New	Estimated Average Value Less Repairs Fair	Good	Premium	Engine Make	No. Cyls.	Displ. Cu.-In.	No. Speeds	P.T.O. H.P.	Approx. Shipping Wt.-Lbs.	Cab
8245.0 4WD	27280.00	15280.00	17190.00	17880.00	Zetor	4	278D	16F-8R	70.8		No
8245.1 4WD w/Cab	32725.00	16520.00	18590.00	19330.00	Zetor	4	278D	16F-8R	70.8		C,H
8520.1 w/Cab	29345.00	15120.00	17010.00	17690.00	Zetor	4	254D	18F-6R	85.7		C,H
8540.1 4WD w/Cab	33770.00	16800.00	18900.00	19660.00	Zetor	4	254D	18F-6R	85.7		C,H
9520.1 w/Cab	31820.00	14840.00	17080.00	17930.00	Zetor	4T	254D	18F-6R	75.8		C,H
9540.1 4WD w/Cab	36095.00	17490.00	20130.00	21140.00	Zetor	4T	254D	18F-6R	75.8		C,H
10211.0	26395.00	12720.00	14640.00	15370.00	Zetor	4T	278D	16F-8R	87.4		No
10211.1 w/Cab	30180.00	14520.00	16710.00	17550.00	Zetor	4T	278D	16F-8R	87.4		C,H
10245.0 4WD	31990.00	15110.00	17390.00	18260.00	Zetor	4T	278D	16F-8R	87.4		No
10245.1 4WD w/Cab	37395.00	17600.00	20250.00	21260.00	Zetor	4T	278D	16F-8R	87.4		C,H
12211.0	28880.00	13520.00	15560.00	16340.00	Zetor	6	417D	16F-8R	102.5		No
12211.1 w/Cab	33315.00	15370.00	17690.00	18580.00	Zetor	6	417D	16F-8R	102.5		C,H
12245.0 4WD	34755.00	16220.00	18670.00	19600.00	Zetor	6	417D	16F-8R	102.5		No
12245.1 4WD w/Cab	40805.00	18290.00	21050.00	22100.00	Zetor	6	417D	16F-8R	102.5		C,H

1996

Model	Approx. Retail Price New	Fair	Good	Premium	Make	No. Cyls.	Displ. Cu.-In.	No. Speeds	P.T.O. H.P.	Approx. Shipping Wt.-Lbs.	Cab
2522.0 Zebra	9000.00	5490.00	6030.00	6270.00	Zetor	2	95D	10F-2R	25	3500	No
3320.0	14960.00	9130.00	10020.00	10420.00	Zetor	3	165D	10F-2R	42.5	5370	No
3320.2 w/Cab	17400.00	10610.00	11660.00	12130.00	Zetor	3	165D	10F-2R	42.5	6030	C,H
3340.0 4WD	18516.00	11300.00	12410.00	12910.00	Zetor	3	165D	10F-2R	42.5	6170	No
3340.2 4WD w/Cab	21108.00	12880.00	14140.00	14710.00	Zetor	3	165D	10F-2R	42.5	6830	C,H
3522.0 Zebra	11845.00	7230.00	7940.00	8260.00	Zetor	3	143D	10F-2R	35	3800	No
4320.0	17913.00	10930.00	12000.00	12480.00	Zetor	4	211D	10F-2R	53.1	5810	No
4320.2 w/Cab	20877.00	12740.00	13990.00	14550.00	Zetor	4	211D	10F-2R	53.1	6470	C,H
4340.0 4WD	21472.00	13100.00	14390.00	14970.00	Zetor	4	211D	10F-2R	53.1	6810	No
4340.2 4WD w/Cab	24632.00	15030.00	16500.00	17160.00	Zetor	4	211D	10F-2R	53.1	7470	C,H
4522.0 Zebra	14035.00	8560.00	9400.00	9780.00	Zetor	3	153D	8F-2R	45	4600	No
5213.0	15445.00	9420.00	10350.00	10760.00	Zetor	3	165D	10F-2R	42.5	4320	No
5213.2 w/Cab	18420.00	11240.00	12340.00	12830.00	Zetor	3	165D	10F-2R	42.5	4770	C,H
5243.0 4WD	18080.00	11030.00	12110.00	12590.00	Zetor	3	165D	10F-2R	42.5	4700	No
5243.2 4WD w/Cab	21220.00	12940.00	14220.00	14790.00	Zetor	3	165D	10F-2R	42.5	5150	C,H
6320.0	19995.00	12200.00	13400.00	13940.00	Zetor	4	239D	10F-2R	65.7	5990	No
6320.2 w/Cab	22623.00	13800.00	15160.00	15770.00	Zetor	4	239D	10F-2R	65.7	6650	C,H
6340.0 4WD	25128.00	15330.00	16840.00	17510.00	Zetor	4	239D	10F-2R	65.7	7040	No
6340.2 4WD	27917.00	17030.00	18700.00	19450.00	Zetor	4	239D	10F-2R	65.7	7710	C,H
7320.0	22435.00	13690.00	15030.00	15630.00	Zetor	4T	239D	10F-2R	75		No
7320.2 w/Cab	25115.00	15320.00	16830.00	17500.00	Zetor	4T	239D	10F-2R	75		C,H
7320.2 w/Cab	27065.00	16510.00	18130.00	18860.00	Zetor	4T	239D	10F-2R	75		C,H,A
7340.0	27608.00	16840.00	18500.00	19240.00	Zetor	4T	239D	10F-2R	75		No
7340.2 w/Cab	30409.00	17690.00	19430.00	20210.00	Zetor	4T	239D	10F-2R	75		C,H
7340.2 w/Cab	32360.00	18910.00	20770.00	21600.00	Zetor	4T	239D	10F-2R	75		C,H,A
9620.1 w/Cab	33922.00	19180.00	21450.00	22520.00	Zetor	4T	254D	18F-6R	75.8	8570	C,H
9640.1 4WD w/Cab	38481.00	21540.00	24090.00	25300.00	Zetor	4T	254D	18F-6R	75.8	9420	C,H
10540.1 w/Cab	44581.00	23900.00	26730.00	28070.00	Zetor	4T	254D	18F-6R	92	9920	C,H
10540.1 w/Cab	46530.00	25080.00	28050.00	29450.00	Zetor	4T	254D	18F-6R	92	9920	C,H,A

1997

Model	Approx. Retail Price New	Fair	Good	Premium	Make	No. Cyls.	Displ. Cu.-In.	No. Speeds	P.T.O. H.P.	Approx. Shipping Wt.-Lbs.	Cab
2522.0 Zebra	9000.00	6030.00	6570.00	6830.00	Zetor	2	95D	10F-2R	25	3500	No
3320.0	14960.00	10020.00	10920.00	11360.00	Zetor	3	165D	10F-2R	42.5	5370	No
3320.2 w/Cab	17400.00	11660.00	12700.00	13210.00	Zetor	3	165D	10F-2R	42.5	6030	C,H
3340.0 4WD	18516.00	12410.00	13520.00	14060.00	Zetor	3	165D	10F-2R	42.5	6170	No
3340.2 4WD w/Cab	21108.00	14140.00	15410.00	16030.00	Zetor	3	165D	10F-2R	42.5	6830	C,H
3522.0 Zebra	11845.00	7940.00	8650.00	9000.00	Zetor	3	143D	10F-2R	35	3800	No
4320.0	17913.00	12000.00	13080.00	13600.00	Zetor	4	211D	10F-2R	53.1	5810	No
4320.2 w/Cab	20877.00	13990.00	15240.00	15850.00	Zetor	4	211D	10F-2R	53.1	6470	C,H
4340.0 4WD	21472.00	14390.00	15680.00	16310.00	Zetor	4	211D	10F-2R	53.1	6810	No
4340.2 4WD w/Cab	24632.00	16500.00	17980.00	18700.00	Zetor	4	211D	10F-2R	53.1	7470	C,H
4522.0 Zebra	14035.00	9400.00	10250.00	10660.00	Zetor	3	153D	8F-2R	45	4600	No
5213.0	15445.00	10350.00	11280.00	11730.00	Zetor	3	165D	10F-2R	42.5	4320	No
5213.2 w/Cab	18420.00	12340.00	13450.00	13990.00	Zetor	3	165D	10F-2R	42.5	4770	C,H
5243.0 4WD	18080.00	12110.00	13200.00	13730.00	Zetor	3	165D	10F-2R	42.5	4700	No
5243.2 4WD w/Cab	21220.00	14220.00	15490.00	16110.00	Zetor	3	165D	10F-2R	42.5	5150	C,H
6320.0	19995.00	13400.00	14600.00	15180.00	Zetor	4	239D	10F-2R	65.7	5990	No
6320.2 w/Cab	22623.00	15160.00	16520.00	17180.00	Zetor	4	239D	10F-2R	65.7	6650	C,H
6340.0 4WD	25128.00	16080.00	17520.00	18220.00	Zetor	4	239D	10F-2R	65.7	7040	No
6340.2 4WD w/Cab	27917.00	17420.00	18980.00	19740.00	Zetor	4	239D	10F-2R	65.7	7710	C,H
7320.0	22435.00	14070.00	15330.00	15940.00	Zetor	4T	239D	10F-2R	7		No
7320.2 w/Cab	25115.00	15410.00	16790.00	17460.00	Zetor	4T	239D	10F-2R	75		C,H
7320.2 w/Cab	27065.00	16750.00	18250.00	18980.00	Zetor	4T	239D	10F-2R	75		C,H,A
7340.0	27608.00	17420.00	18980.00	19740.00	Zetor	4T	239D	10F-2R	75		No
7340.2 w/Cab	30409.00	18760.00	20440.00	21260.00	Zetor	4T	239D	10F-2R	75		C,H
7340.2 w/Cab	32360.00	20100.00	21900.00	22780.00	Zetor	4T	239D	10F-2R	75		C,H,A
9620.1 w/Cab	33922.00	20800.00	22720.00	23630.00	Zetor	4T	254D	18F-6R	75.8	8570	C,H
9640.1 4WD w/Cab	38481.00	23080.00	25210.00	26220.00	Zetor	4T	254D	18F-6R	75.8	9420	C,H
10540.1 w/Cab	44581.00	26000.00	28400.00	29540.00	Zetor	4T	254D	18F-6R	92	9920	C,H
10540.1 w/Cab	46530.00	27300.00	29820.00	31010.00	Zetor	4T	254D	18F-6R	92	9920	C,H,A

1998

Model	Approx. Retail Price New	Fair	Good	Premium	Make	No. Cyls.	Displ. Cu.-In.	No. Speeds	P.T.O. H.P.	Approx. Shipping Wt.-Lbs.	Cab
3320.0	15320.00	11340.00	12100.00	12460.00	Zetor	3	165D	10F-2R	43.0	5370	No
3320.2 w/Cab	17820.00	13190.00	14080.00	14500.00	Zetor	3	165D	10F-2R	43.0	6030	C,H
3340.0 4WD	18960.00	14030.00	14980.00	15430.00	Zetor	3	165D	10F-2R	43.0	6170	No
3340.2 4WD w/Cab	21620.00	16000.00	17080.00	17590.00	Zetor	3	165D	10F-2R	43.0	6830	C,H
4320.0	18480.00	13680.00	14600.00	15040.00	Zetor	4	211D	10F-2R	54.0	5810	No
4320.2 w/Cab	21380.00	15820.00	16890.00	17400.00	Zetor	4	211D	10F-2R	54.0	6470	C,H

Model	Approx. Retail Price New	Estimated Average Value Less Repairs Fair	Good	Premium	Engine Make	No. Cyls.	Displ. Cu.-In.	No. Speeds	P.T.O. H.P.	Approx. Shipping Wt.-Lbs.	Cab
Zetor (Cont.)											
			1998 (Cont.)								
4340.0 4WD	21990.00	**16270.00**	**17370.00**	**17890.00**	Zetor	4	211D	10F-2R	54.0	6810	No
4340.2 4WD w/Cab	25100.00	**18570.00**	**19830.00**	**20430.00**	Zetor	4	211D	10F-2R	54.0	7470	C,H
5320.0	19340.00	**14310.00**	**15280.00**	**15740.00**	Zetor	4	220D	10F-2R	58.0		No
5320.2 w/Cab	22300.00	**16500.00**	**17620.00**	**18150.00**	Zetor	4	220D	10F-2R	58.0		C,H
5340.0 4WD	23900.00	**17690.00**	**18880.00**	**19450.00**	Zetor	4	220D	10F-2R	58.0		No
5340.2 4WD w/Cab	26980.00	**19970.00**	**21310.00**	**21950.00**	Zetor	4	220D	10F-2R	58.0		C,H
6320.0	20630.00	**15270.00**	**16300.00**	**16790.00**	Zetor	4	239D	10F-2R	66.0	5990	No
6320.2 w/Cab	23510.00	**17400.00**	**18570.00**	**19130.00**	Zetor	4	239D	10F-2R	66.0	6650	C,H
6340.0 4WD	25995.00	**19240.00**	**20540.00**	**21160.00**	Zetor	4	239D	10F-2R	66.0	7040	No
6340.2 4WD w/Cab	29095.00	**21530.00**	**22990.00**	**23680.00**	Zetor	4	239D	10F-2R	66.0	7710	C,H
7320.0	22990.00	**17010.00**	**18160.00**	**18710.00**	Zetor	4T	239D	10F-2R	75.		No
7320.2 w/Cab	25845.00	**19130.00**	**20420.00**	**21030.00**	Zetor	4T	239D	10F-2R	75.		C,H
7340.0 4WD	28275.00	**20130.00**	**21490.00**	**22140.00**	Zetor	4T	239D	10F-2R	75.		No
7340.2 4WD w/Cab	31170.00	**22200.00**	**23700.00**	**24410.00**	Zetor	4T	239D	10F-2R	75.		C,H
9620.1 w/Cab	34740.00	**23760.00**	**25410.00**	**26170.00**	Zetor	4T	254D	18F-6R	86.0	8570	C,H
9640.1 4WD w/Cab	39420.00	**26930.00**	**28800.00**	**29660.00**	Zetor	4T	254D	18F-6R	86.0	9420	C,H
10540.1 w/Cab	45650.00	**29880.00**	**31960.00**	**32920.00**	Zetor	4TI	254D	18F-6R	92.	9920	C,H
			1999								
3320.0	15320.00	**12720.00**	**13330.00**	**13730.00**	Zetor	3	165D	10F-2R	43.0	5370	No
3320.2 w/Cab	17820.00	**14790.00**	**15500.00**	**15970.00**	Zetor	3	165D	10F-2R	43.0	6030	C,H
3340.0 4WD	18960.00	**15740.00**	**16500.00**	**17000.00**	Zetor	3	165D	10F-2R	43.0	6170	No
3340.2 4WD w/Cab	21620.00	**17950.00**	**18810.00**	**19370.00**	Zetor	3	165D	10F-2R	43.0	6830	C,H
4320.0	18480.00	**15340.00**	**16080.00**	**16560.00**	Zetor	4	239D	10F-2R	56.0	5810	No
4320.2 w/Cab	21380.00	**17750.00**	**18600.00**	**19160.00**	Zetor	4	239D	10F-2R	56.0	6470	C,H
4321.1 w/Cab	22860.00	**18970.00**	**19890.00**	**20490.00**	Zetor	4	239D	10F-2R	56.0	6620	C,H
4340.0 4WD	21990.00	**18250.00**	**19130.00**	**19700.00**	Zetor	4	239D	10F-2R	56.0	6810	No
4340.2 4WD w/Cab	25100.00	**20830.00**	**21840.00**	**22500.00**	Zetor	4	239D	10F-2R	56.0	7470	C,H
4341.1 4WD w/Cab	26860.00	**22290.00**	**23370.00**	**24070.00**	Zetor	4	239D	10F-2R	56.0	7570	C,H
6320.0	20630.00	**17120.00**	**17950.00**	**18490.00**	Zetor	4	239D	10F-2R	66.0	5990	No
6320.2 w/Cab	23510.00	**19510.00**	**20450.00**	**21060.00**	Zetor	4	239D	10F-2R	66.0	6650	C,H
6321.1 w/Cab	25160.00	**20880.00**	**21890.00**	**22550.00**	Zetor	4	239D	10F-2R	62.0	6830	C,H
6340.0 4WD	25995.00	**21580.00**	**22620.00**	**23300.00**	Zetor	4	239D	10F-2R	66.0	7040	No
6340.2 4WD w/Cab	29095.00	**24150.00**	**25310.00**	**26070.00**	Zetor	4	239D	10F-2R	66.0	7710	C,H
6341.1 4WD w/Cab	31130.00	**25840.00**	**27080.00**	**27890.00**	Zetor	4	239D	10F-2R	66.0	7800	C,H
7320.0	22990.00	**19080.00**	**20000.00**	**20600.00**	Zetor	4T	239D	10F-2R	75.		No
7320.2 w/Cab	25845.00	**21450.00**	**22490.00**	**23170.00**	Zetor	4T	239D	10F-2R	75.		C,H
7321.1 w/Cab	28200.00	**22410.00**	**23490.00**	**24200.00**	Zetor	4T	239D	10F-2R	75.	6950	C,H
7340.0 4WD	28275.00	**22830.00**	**23930.00**	**24650.00**	Zetor	4T	239D	10F-2R	75.		No
7340.2 4WD w/Cab	31170.00	**24900.00**	**26100.00**	**26880.00**	Zetor	4T	239D	10F-2R	75.		C,H
7341.1 4WD w/Cab	33980.00	**27310.00**	**28620.00**	**29480.00**	Zetor	4T	239D	10F-2R	75.	7960	C,H
8620.0	29400.00	**22960.00**	**24080.00**	**24560.00**	Zetor	4T	254D	18F-6R	82.0	7890	No
8620.1 w/Cab	31990.00	**25420.00**	**26660.00**	**27190.00**	Zetor	4T	254D	18F-6R	82.0	8550	C,H
8640.0 4WD	34000.00	**27060.00**	**28380.00**	**28950.00**	Zetor	4T	254D	18F-6R	82.0	8740	No
8640.1 4WD w/cab	36600.00	**29520.00**	**30960.00**	**31580.00**	Zetor	4T	254D	18F-6R	82.0	9400	C,H
9620.1 w/Cab	34740.00	**27880.00**	**29240.00**	**29830.00**	Zetor	4T	254D	18F-6R	86.0	8570	C,H
9640.1 4WD w/Cab	39420.00	**31490.00**	**33020.00**	**33680.00**	Zetor	4T	254D	18F-6R	86.0	9420	C,H
10540.1 w/Cab	45650.00	**34850.00**	**36550.00**	**37280.00**	Zetor	4TI	254D	18F-6R	92.	9920	C,H

Equipment Serial Numbers with Location

Contents

ADVANCE-RUMELY OIL PULL

Model B (25-45)
1910 ... 1
1911 ... 2101
1912 ... 2270

Model E (30-60)
1910 ... 101
1911 ... 237
1912 ... 747
1913 ... 1679
1915 ... 1819
1916 ... 2019
1917 ... 2997
1918 ... 8725
1919 ... 11500
1920 ... 12252
1921 ... 12352
1922 ... 12404
1923 ... 12454

Model F (18-35)
1911 ... 5001
1912 ... 5681
1913 ... 6739
1914 ... 7500
1916 ... 7857
1917 ... 8085
1918 ... 8903

Model G (20-40)
1918 ... 10425
1919 ... 10751
1919 ... G741
1920 ... G949
1921 ... G1728
1922 ... G2242
1923 ... G2690
1924 ... G3559

Model H (16-30)
1917 ... 8627
1918 ... 9178
1919 ... 10711
1919 ... H3751
1920 ... H4393
1921 ... H7240
1922 ... H7396
1923 ... H8646
1924 ... H9046

Model K (12-20)
1918 ... 12000
1919 ... 12101
1920 ... 13657
1921 ... 17640
1922 ... 18649
1923 ... 19269
1924 ... 20511

Model L (15-25)
1924 ... 1
1925 ... 11
1926 ... 1607
1927 ... 4214

Model M (20-35)
1924 ... 1
1925 ... 2
1926 ... 1014
1927 ... 3085

Model R (25-45)
1924 ... 1
1925 ... 2
1926 ... 139
1927 ... 648

Model S (30-60)
1924 ... 1
1925 ... 5
1926 ... 35
1927 ... 235
1928 ... 435

Model W (20-30)
1928 ... 1
1929 ... 2129
1930 ... 3734

Model X (25-40)
1928 ... 1
1929 ... 1546
1930 ... 2260

Model Y (30-50)
1929 ... 1

Model Z (40-60)
1929 ... 1

ALLIS-CHALMERS

Model 15-25
1921 ... 20001
1922 ... 20335
1923 ... 20498
1924 ... 20906
1925 ... 20996
1926 ... 21371
1927 ... 21682

Model 170
Front of torque housing on left side.
1968 ... 2721
1969 ... 5374
1970 ... 6369
1971 ... 6988
1972 ... 7797
1973 ... 8821

Model 175
Front of torque housing on left side.
1970 ... 1001
1971 ... 1477
1972 ... 1624
1973 ... 1740
1974 ... 2153
1975 ... 3255
1976 ... 3754
1977 ... 4809
1978 ... 5670
1979 ... 6321
1980 ... 6999

Model 18-30 & 20-35
1919 ... 5006
1920 ... 5161
1921 ... 6015
1923 ... 6161
1924 ... 6397
1925 ... 6755
1926 ... 7369
1927 ... 8070
1928 ... 9870
1929 ... 16762

Model 180
Front of torque housing on left side.
1968 ... 2682
1969 ... 6094
1970 ... 9235
1971 ... 10561
1972 ... 11729
1973 ... 12447

Model 185
Front of torque housing on left side.
1970 ... 1001
1971 ... 1952
1972 ... 2935
1973 ... 3763
1974 ... 4961
1975 ... 6542
1976 ... 8292
1977 ... 10003
1978 ... 11631
1979 ... 13160
1980 ... 14672
1981 ... 15648

Model 190 & 190XT
Front of torque housing on left side.
1964 ... 1001
1965 ... 2485
1966 ... 8219
1967 ... 13273
1968 ... 19262
1969 ... 23234
1970 ... 25901
1971 ... 29136
1972 ... 31118
1973 ... 33101

Model 200
Front of torque housing on left side.
1972 ... 1001
1973 ... 3344
1974 ... 6294
1975 ... 9250

Model 210
Front of torque housing on left side.
1970 ... 1001
1971 ... 1107
1972 ... 2082
1973 ... 2469

Model 220
Front of torque housing on left side.
1970 ... 1938
1971 ... 2451
1972 ... 2626
1973 ... 2860

Model 4W220
Top surface of left side frame.
1982 ... 1001
1983 ... 1081
1984 ... 1145

Model 4W305
Top surface of left side frame.
1982 ... 1001
1983 ... 1112
1984 ... 1176
1985 ... 1338

Model 5015
Plate above gearshift lever.
1982 ... 1001
1983 ... 1727
1984 ... 3277
1985 ... 4236

Model 5020
Plate on console under steering wheel.
1978 ... 2220
1979 ... 3091
1980 ... 4115
1981 ... 5790
1982 ... 7034
1983 ... 8388
1984 ... 8734
1985 ... 9217

Model 5030
Plate on console under steering wheel.
1979 ... 2005
1980 ... 2255
1981 ... 2976
1982 ... 3520
1983 ... 4066
1984 ... 4214
1985 ... 4359

Model 5040
Plate on console under steering wheel.
1976 ... 408455
1977 ... 410364
1978 ... 462148
1979 ... 473000
1980 ... 474000

Model 5045
Plate on console under steering wheel.
1981 ... 988500

Model 5050
Plate on console under steering wheel.
1977 ... 573461
1978 ... 579632
1979 ... 584000
1980 ... 591000
1981 ... 596014
1982 ... 597730
1983 ... 599191

Model 6060
Right side of engine adapter housing.
1980 ... 1001
1981 ... 1297
1982 ... 2463
1983 ... 3894
1984 ... 4572

Model 6070
Right side of engine adapter housing.
1985 ... 1609

Model 6080
Right side of engine adapter housing.
1980 ... 1001
1981 ... 1152
1982 ... 3002
1983 ... 4567
1984 ... 5780
1985 ... 6853

Model 6140
Plate on left side of clutch housing.
1982 ... 1001
1983 ... 1726
1984 ... 1851
1985 ... 2711

Model 7000
Right side of differential housing.
1975 ... 1001
1976 ... 1641
1977 ... 5037
1978 ... 6373
1979 ... 8963

Model 7010
Above PTO guard.
1980 ... 1925
1981 ... 2806

Model 7020
Above PTO guard.
1978 ... 1317
1979 ... 2732
1980 ... 3842
1981 ... 4710

Model 7030
Above PTO guard.
1973 ... 1001
1974 ... 2596

Model 7040
Above PTO guard.
1975 ... 1303
1976 ... 4089
1977 ... 6839

Model 7045
Above PTO guard.
1978 ... 1234
1979 ... 2152
1980 ... 3399
1981 ... 4225

Model 7050
Above PTO guard.
1973 ... 1001
1974 ... 1688

Model 7060
Above PTO guard.
1974 ... 1001
1975 ... 1299
1976 ... 2741
1977 ... 4580
1978 ... 6001
1979 ... 6789
1980 ... 7693
1981 ... 8442

Model 7080
Above PTO guard.
1975 ... 1007
1976 ... 1572
1977 ... 2051
1978 ... 3001
1979 ... 3268
1980 ... 3648
1981 ... 3954

Model 7580
Left rear side of front frame.
1976 ... 1001
1977 ... 1287
1978 ... 1605
1979 ... 2218
1980 ... 2486
1981 ... 2717

Model 8010
Above PTO guard.
1982 ... 1020
1983 ... 1712
1984 ... 2266
1985 ... 2609

Model 8030
Above PTO guard.
1982 ... 1001
1983 ... 2093
1984 ... 2701
1985 ... 3146

Model 8050
Above PTO guard.
1982 ... 1016
1983 ... 1924
1984 ... 2596
1985 ... 3187

Model 8070
Above PTO guard.
1982 ... 1001
1983 ... 1430
1984 ... 2090
1985 ... 2903

Model 8550
Left side of front frame.
1978 ... 1083
1979 ... 1342
1980 ... 1553
1981 ... 1723

Model A
Top of transmission case.
1936 ... 25701
1937 ... 25726
1938 ... 26305
1939 ... 26614
1940 ... 26782
1941 ... 26896
1942 ... 26915

Model B
Top of transmission rear of shift lever.
1938 ... 101
1939 ... 11800
1940 ... 33394
1941 ... 49721
1942 ... 56782
1943 ... 64501
1944 ... 65502
1945 ... 70210
1946 ... 72301
1947 ... 73370
1948 ... 80056
1949 ... 92295
1950 ... 102393
1951 ... 114258
1952 ... 118674
1953 ... 122310
1954 ... 124202
1955 ... 124711
1956 ... 126497
1957 ... 127186

ALLIS-CHALMERS (Cont.)

Model C
Top of transmission rear of shift lever.

1940	1
1941	112
1942	12389
1943	18782
1944	23908
1945	30695
1946	36378
1947	39168
1948	51515
1949	68281

Model CA
Top of transmission rear of shift lever.

1950	14
1951	305
1952	10395
1953	22181
1954	31424
1955	32907
1956	37203
1957	38618

Model D-10
Front of torque housing on left side.

1959	1001
1960	1950
1961	2801
1962	4511
1963	6801
1964	7675
1965	8204
1966	9486
1967	9795

Model D-12
Front of torque housing on left side.

1959	1001
1960	1950
1961	2801
1962	3638
1963	5501
1964	6012
1965	9192
1966	9508
1967	9830

Model D-14
Front of torque housing on left side.

1957	1001
1958	9400
1959	14900
1960	21800

Model D-15
Front of torque housing on left side.

1960	1001
1961	1900
1962	6470
1963	13001
1964	16928
1965	19681
1966	21375
1967	23734

Model D-17
Front of torque housing on left side.

1957	1001
1958	4300
1959	16500
1960	28200
1961	33100
1962	38070
1963	65001
1964	70611
1965	77090
1966	80533
1967	86061

Model D-19
Front of torque housing on left side.

1961	1001
1962	1250
1963	12001

Model D-21
Front of torque housing on left side.

1963	1001
1964	1417
1965	2079
1966	2408
1967	2863
1968	3777
1969	4498

Model G
Top of transmission rear of shift lever.

1948	6
1949	10961
1950	23180
1951	24006
1952	25269
1953	26497
1954	28036
1955	29036

Model RC
Top of transmission case.

1939	4
1940	4392
1941	5417

Model U
Rear of differential housing.

1929	1
1930	1751
1931	3676
1932	5525
1933	7405
1934	8896
1935	10596
1936	12086
1937	13576
1938	14855
1939	15587
1940	16078
1941	16722
1942	17137
1943	17470
1944	17801
1945	18022
1946	18325
1947	20774
1948	21022
1949	22128
1950	23029
1951	22548

Model UC
Rear of differential housing.

1930	1
1931	336
1932	826
1933	1268
1934	1750
1935	2230
1936	2712
1937	3194
1938	3757
1939	4547
1940	4770
1941	4972

Model WC
Rear differential housing, just above operator platform.

1934	10158
1935	22815
1936	35475
1937	48133
1938	60790
1939	75216
1940	91534
1941	103517
1942	114534
1943	123171
1944	127642
1945	134624
1946	148091
1947	152845
1948	170174

Model WD
Top of left differential brake housing.

1948	7
1949	9280
1950	35471
1951	72356
1952	105216
1953	131273

Model WD-45
Top of left differential brake housing.

1953	146607
1954	160386
1955	190933
1956	217992
1957	230295

Model WF
Rear differential housing, just above operator platform.

1938	389
1939	1336
1940	1892
1941	2300
1942	2704
1943	None
1944	3004
1945	3195
1946	3510
1947	3748
1948	4111
1949	5500
1950	7318
1951	8316

B.F. AVERY

A
Right side of gear case.

1945	4A786
1946	7A305
1947	9A867
1948	13A247
1949	17A456
1950	19A366

BF
Right side of gear case.

1950	R500
1951	R1839
1952	R4460

BFH
Right side of gear case.

1953	58000001

BFS
Right side of gear case.

1953	57600001

BFW
Right side of gear case.

1953	R6538

BG
Right side of gear case.

1953	57900001
1954	57900601
1955	57900769
1956	57900938

V
Right side of gear case.

1946	1V5
1947	1V144
1948	2V577
1949	4V490
1950	5V501
1951	6V207
1952	6V422

BIG BUD

All Models

1987	87000
1988	88000
1989	89000
1990	90000

Model 450

1991	91501

Model 500

1991	91601

Model 700

1991	91701

CASE

Model 10-18

1918	13285
1919	22223
1920	32841
1921	42256
1922	43943

Model 10-20

1915	2842
1916	3691
1917	7492
1918	13285

Model 1030
Plate fastened to instrument panel.

1966	8279001
1967	8306501
1968	8332101
1969	8356251

Model 1031 & 1032
Plate fastened to instrument panel.

1966	8279001
1967	8306501
1968	8322101
1969	8356251

Model 1090 & 1170
Plate fastened to instrument panel.

1970	8650001
1971	8674001

Model 1190
Plate fastened to clutch housing.

1980	11030101
1981	11031792
1982	11033166
1983	11035592

Model 1194
Plate fastened to clutch housing.

1983	11038050

Model 12-20

1921	42256
1922	43943
1923	45281
1924	48227
1925	48402
1926	55919
1927	62409

Model 12-25

1914	2496
1915	2842
1916	3691
1917	7492
1918	13285

Model 1200TK
Plate fastened to clutch housing.

1966	9802101
1967	9806101
1968	9808000
1969	9808276

Model 1270 & 1370
Plate fastened to instrument panel.

1972	8693001
1973	8712001
1974	8736601
1975	8770001
1976	8797501
1977	8809950
1978	8830001

Model 1290
Plate fastened to clutch housing.

1980	11050101
1981	11050444
1982	11053999
1983	11055483

Model 1294
Plate fastened to clutch housing.

1983	11058050

Model 1390
Plate fastened to clutch housing.

1980	11120101
1981	11122928
1982	11126132
1983	11130040

Model 1394
Plate fastened to clutch housing.

1983	11131000

Model 1470TK
Plate fastened to instrument panel.

1969	9810000
1970	9811301
1971	8674001
1972	8691801

Model 1490
Plate fastened to clutch housing.

1980	11180101
1981	11182782
1982	11185693
1983	11188540

Model 1494
Plate fastened to clutch housing.

1983	11192050

Model 15-27

1919	22223
1920	42435
1921	42835
1922	42852
1923	43435
1924	48413

CASE (Cont.)

Model 1570
Plate fastened to instrument panel.
1976 8797501
1977 8809950
1978 8830001

Model 1594
Plate fastened to clutch housing.
1983 11219050

Model 1690
Plate fastened to clutch housing.
1980 11120101
1981 11121841
1982 11213684
1983 11214373

Model 18-32
1925 51678
1926 55919
1927 62409

Model 1896
1984 9931800

Model 20-40
1912 100
1913 691
1914 2496
1915 2842
1916 3691
1917 7492
1918 13285
1919 22223

Model 200B & 210B
Plate fastened to instrument panel.
1958 6095001
1959 6120001

Model 2090, 2290, 2390 & 2590
Plate fastened to instrument panel.
1978 8835443
1979 8840001
1980 9901001
1981 9910025
1982 9918830
1983 9924700

Model 22-40
1919 22223
1920 32841
1921 42256
1922 43943
1923 45281
1924 48413
1925 51678

Model 2470
Left side of instrument panel.
1971 8674001
1972 8693001
1973 8712001
1974 8762001
1975 8767001
1976 8792901
1977 8825069
1978 8827601

Model 2670 & 2870
Left side of instrument panel.
1974 8762001
1975 8767001
1976 8792901
1977 8825069
1978 8827601

Model 30-60
1912 100
1913 691
1914 2496
1915 2842
1916 3691

Model 300 & 320
Plate fastened to instrument panel.
1956 6050301
1957 6075001

Model 300B, 310B & 320B
Plate fastened to instrument panel.
1958 6095001
1959 6120001

Model 40-72
1921 42256
1922 43943
1923 45281

Model 40-80
1915 2842

Model 400
Plate fastened to instrument panel.
1955 8060001
1956 8080001
1957 8100001

Model 400B, 500B & 600B
Plate fastened to instrument panel.
1958 6095001
1959 6120001

Model 420B
Plate fastened to instrument panel.
1958 6095001
1959 6120001
1960 3012275

Model 430 & 530
Plate fastened to instrument panel.
1960 6144001
1961 6162601
1962 8190001
1963 8208001
1964 8229001
1965 8253501
1966 8279001
1967 8306501
1968 8332101
1969 8356251

Model 440, 540, 740, 840 & 940
Plate fastened to instrument panel.
1960 8160001
1961 8168801
1962 8190001
1963 8208001
1964 8229001
1965 8253501
1966 8279001
1967 8306501
1968 8332101
1969 8356251

Model 4490, 4690, 4890
Plate fastened to instrument panel.
1979 8854307
1980 8855925
1981 8859025
1982 8861530
1983 8863700

Model 470, 570 & 770
Plate fastened to instrument panel.
1970 8650001
1971 8674001
1972 8693001
1973 8712001

Model 500
Plate fastened to instrument panel.
1953 5622406
1954 8035001
1955 8060001
1956 8080001
1957 8100001

Model 600
Plate fastened to instrument panel.
1957 8100001

Model 630
Plate fastened to instrument panel.
1960 6144001
1961 6162601
1962 8190001
1963 8208001

Model 700, 800 & 900
Plate fastened to instrument panel.
1957 8100001
1958 8120001
1959 8140001

Model 730, 830 & 930
Plate fastened to instrument panel.
1960 8160001
1961 8168801
1962 8190001
1963 8208001
1964 8229001
1965 8253501
1966 8279001
1967 8306501
1968 8332101
1969 8356251

Model 870
Plate fastened to instrument panel.
1970 8650001
1971 8670001
1972 8693001
1973 8712001
1974 8736601
1975 8770001

Model 9-18
1912 100
1913 891
1914 2496
1915 2842
1916 3691
1917 7492
1918 13285

Model 970 & 1070
Plate fastened to instrument panel.
1970 8650001
1971 8674001
1972 8693001
1973 8712001
1974 8736601
1975 8770001
1976 8797501
1977 8809950
1978 8830001

Model A, AE, AI
1928 69004
1929 69803

Model C, D, LA, R, S, V
Tractor serial number located on instrument panel name plate.
1929 300201
1930 300301
1931 300401
1932 300501
1933 300601
1934 300701
1935 300801
1936 300901
1937 301001
1938 4200001
1939 4300001
1940 4400001
1941 4500001
1942 4600001
1943 4700001
1944 4800001
1945 4900001
1946 5000001
1947 5100001
1948 5200001
1949 5300001
1950 5400001
1951 5500001
1952 5600001
1953 5700001
1954 5800001
1955 5900001
1956 6000001

Model K
Plate fastened to instrument panel.
1928 69004
1929 69803

Model L & LI
Plate fastened to instrument panel.
1929 303201
1930 303301
1931 303401
1932 303501
1933 303601
1934 303701
1935 303801
1936 303901
1937 304001
1938 4200001
1939 4300001
1940 4400001

Model S
Plate fastened to instrument panel.
1953 5700001
1954 8035001

Model T & TE
1928 69004
1929 69803

Model VA
Plate fastened to instrument panel.
1953 5750001
1954 6011001
1955 6038001

CASE-INTERNATIONAL

Model 1194
Plate fastened to clutch housing.
1984 11038494
1985 11480001

Model 1294
Plate fastened to clutch housing.
1984 11058714
1985 11490001

Model 1394
Plate fastened to clutch housing.
1984 11136920
1985 11500001
1986 11504636
1987 11506453
1988 11508682
1989 11510950
1990 11513200

Model 1494
Plate fastened to clutch housing.
1984 11192813
1985 11515001
1986 11519378
1987 11520410
1988 11521062
1989 11521443
1990 11521823

Model 1594
Plate fastened to clutch housing.
1984 11219214
1985 11525120
1986 11526518
1987 11527297
1988 11528442
1989 11529076
1990 11529706

Model 1896
Inside cab, above rear window.
1985 9938112
1986 9941619
1987 9946868
1988 9948517
1989 17895512
1990 17896472

Model 2094
Inside cab, above rear window.
1984 9931800

Model 2096
Inside cab, above door.
1985 9938100
1986 9941586
1987 9945448
1988 9948517
1990 17898686

Model 2294
Plate inside cab or on right side of front frame.
1984 9931808
1985 9938113
1986 9941577
1987 9945448
1988 9949350

Model 234
Right front frame.
1985 09405
1986 10454

Model 235
Right front frame.
1986 17626500
1987 17627429
1988 .... CCJ0001501
1989 .... CCJ0002370
1990 .... CCJ0031120
1991 .... CCJ0059570
1992 .... CCJ0087720

Model 2394
Plate inside cab or on right side of front frame.
1984 9931802
1985 9939020
1986 9941573
1987 9945454
1988 9948517

Model 244
Right front frame.
1985 09805
1986 11180

Model 245
Right front frame.
1986 17636500
1987 17637275
1988 .... CCJ0009001
1989 .... CCJ0009993
1990 .... CCJ0010844
1991 .... CCJ0011694
1992 .... CCJ0012495

Model 254
Right front frame.
1985 09450
1986 11465

Model 255
Right front frame.
1986 17646500
1987 17647065
1988 .... CCJ0018001
1989 .... CCJ0018787
1990 .... CCJ0019378
1991 .... CCJ0019968
1992 .... CCJ0020558

CASE-INTERNATIONAL (Cont.)

Model 2594
Plate inside cab or on right side of front frame.
1984 9931803
1985 9938951
1986 9941789
1987 9945455
1988 9948517

Model 265
Right front frame.
1987 17666500
1988 ..... CCJ0025001
1989 ..... CCJ0025194
1990 ..... CCJ0059281
1991 ..... CCJ0089368
1992 ..... CCJ0119455

Model 275
Right front frame.
1986 17656500
1987 17656510
1988 ..... CCJ0028001
1989 ..... CCJ0028615
1990 ..... CCJ0029301
1991 ..... CCJ0029992
1992 ..... CCJ0030672

Model 284
Right front frame.
1985 4031
1986 4371
1987 4716

Model 3294
Plate inside cab or on right side of front frame.
1984.......... 9932190
1985.......... 9938125

Model 3394
Plate inside cab or on right side of front frame.
1985.......... 9938100
1986.......... 9941574
1987.......... 9945459
1988.......... 9948518

Model 3594
Plate inside cab or on right side of front frame.
1985.......... 9938100
1986.......... 9941578
1987.......... 9945452
1988.......... 9948518

Model 385
Right front bolster.
1985............ 15000
1986............ 18000
1987........ E0018806
1988........ E0019454
1989........ E0020881
1990........ E0022231
1991........ E0023570

Model 4494
Plate inside cab.
1984.......... 8865000
1985.......... 8866200
1986 8866971
1987 8867559
1987 8867560
1988 8868521

Model 4694
Plate inside cab.
1984 8865001
1985 8866204
1985 8866200
1986 8866973
1986 8866971
1987 8867559
1988 8868521

Model 485
Right front bolster.
1985 15000
1986 18000
1987 .... E0019057
1988 .... E0021250
1989 .... E0023490
1990 .... E0024938
1991 .... E0026386

Model 4894
Plate inside cab.
1984 8865013
1985 8866200
1985 8866205
1986 8866972
1986 8866971
1987 8867559
1988 8868521

Model 4994
Plate inside cab.
1984.......... 8865008
1985.......... 8866200
1986.......... 8866971
1987.......... 8867745
1987.......... 8867559
1988.......... 8868521

Model 5120, 5130 & 5140
Plate inside cab.
1989....... JJF1000001
1990....... JJF1000650
1991....... JJF1006114
1992....... JJF1015072
1993....... JJF1023187

Model 585
Right front bolster.
1985............ 15000
1986............ 18000
1987......... E0019201
1988......... E0022268
1989......... E0024954
1990......... E0027087

Model 685
Right front bolster.
19856........... 15000
1986............ 18000
1987......... E0019558
1988......... E0023107
1989......... E0026391
1990......... E0029371

Model 7110, 7120, 7130, 7140 & 7150
Plate inside cab.
1988...... JJA0001501
1989...... JJA0009957
1990...... JJA0020439
1991...... JJA0030160
1992...... JJA0039300
1993...... JJA0046350

Model 885
Right front bolster.
1985............ 15000
1986............ 18000
1987........ E0019138
1988........ E0022668
1989........ E0027254
1990........ E0030427

Model 9110, 9130, 9150, 9170, 9180 & 9190
1986......... 17900150
1987......... 17900550
1988...... JCB0001501
1989...... JCB0002500
1990...... JCB0004600

Model 9210, 9230, 9240, 9250, 9260 & 9270
1990...... JCB0004600
1991...... JCB0026501
1992...... JCB0028400
1993...... JCB0030500
1994...... JEE0031773
1995...... JEE0032808

COCKSHUTT

Note: For Cockshutt serial numbers on tractors built in 1962 and later, refer to appropriate model number listing under Oliver.

Model 20
Left side of main frame.
1952 101
1953 1657
1954 2568
1955 10001
1956 20001
1957 30001
1958 40001

Model 30
Left side of main frame.
1946 101
1947 442
1948 6705
1949 17371
1950 26161
1951 28505
1952 32389
1953............ 35580
1954............ 35974
1955............ 40001
1956............ 50001
1957............ 60001

Model 35
Left side of main frame.
1956............. 1001
1957............ 10001

Model 40
Left side of main frame.
1950.............. 194
1951............. 4101
1952............. 6901
1953............ 10501
1954............ 11401
1955............ 20001
1956............ 30001
1957 40001
1958 50001

Model 40D4 and Golden Eagle
Left side of main frame.
1954 27001
1955 30001
1956 40028
1957 50001

Model 50
Left side of main frame.
1953 101
1954 1801
1955 10001
1956 20001
1957 30001

Model 540
Right side of main frame.
1958.......... AM1001
1959.......... AN5001
1960............. None
1961.......... AP1001
1962.......... AR1001

Model 550
Right side of main frame.
1958.......... BM1001
1959.......... BM5001
1960.......... BO1001
1961.......... BP1001

Model 560
Right side of main frame.
1958.......... CM1001
1959.......... CN5001
1960.......... CO7001
1961.......... CP1001

Model 570
Right side of main frame.
1958.......... DM1001
1959.......... DN5001
1960.......... DO7001

Model 570 Super
Right side of main frame.
1961.......... DP1001
1962.......... DR1001

Model Golden Arrow
Left side of main frame.
1956............ 16001

DAVID BROWN/CASE

Model 1200
Plate on side of clutch housing.
1967 700001
1968 704433
1969 707958
1970 712203
1971 716091

Model 1210
Plate on side of clutch housing.
1971 720001
1972 720053
1973 722305
1974 724659
1975 728080
1976 11150001
1977 11154968
1978 11159654
1979 11163305
1980 11166342

Model 1212
Plate on side of clutch housing.
1971 1000001
1972 1000240
1973.......... 1001182
1974.......... 1002487
1975.......... 1005238

Model 1410
Plate on side of clutch housing.
1976......... 11200001
1977......... 11201692
1978......... 11203836
1979......... 11205159
1980......... 11206160

Model 1412
Plate on side of clutch housing.
1975.......... 1050004

Model 770
Right side of front frame.
1965........... 580001
1966........... 582513
1967........... 588673
1968........... 588579
1969........... 590646
1970........... 592237

Model 780
Right side of front frame.
1967 600001
1968 600879
1969 602853
1970 606109
1971 609665

Model 880
Right side of front frame.
1961 350001
1962 351038
1963 354478
1964 358954
1965 522384
1966 531022
1967 539410
1968 546000
1969 551553
1970 557013
1971 560766
1972 620336
1973 624731
1974 630611
1975 634830

Model 885
Right side of front frame.
1971........... 620001
1972........... 620336
1973........... 624731
1974........... 630611
1975........... 634830
1976......... 11000001
1977......... 11005148
1978......... 11011088
1979......... 11015095
1980......... 11019389

Model 990
Right side of front frame.
1961........... 440001
1962........... 441323
1963........... 450376
1964........... 460538
1965........... 472273
1966........... 483768
1967........... 496283
1968........... 504690
1969........... 808150
1970........... 818301
1971........... 850001
1972........... 850600
1973........... 854403
1974........... 859367
1975........... 863900
1976......... 11070001
1977......... 11080236
1978......... 11089141
1979......... 11096828
1980......... 11104577

Model 995
Right side of front frame.
1971........... 920001
1972........... 921383
1973........... 925158
1974........... 928575
1975........... 931772
1976......... 11070001
1977......... 11080236
1978......... 11089141
1979......... 11096828
1980......... 11104577

Model 996
Right side of front frame.
1972........... 980001
1973........... 981776
1974........... 984145
1975........... 986272
1976......... 11070001

Model 5215
1987 1001

Model 5220
1985 1001
1986 1001
1987 1919
1988 2170
1989 2341

Model 5230
1986 1001
1987 1657
1988 1885
1989 2000

Model 6035
1986 7866-1338

Model 6150
1989 4600286

Model 6240
Left side of clutch housing.
1985 7722-0001
1986 7722-0489
1987 7722-1247
1988 7722-1746
1989 7722-3129
1990 7722-3400

Model 6240 4WD
Left side of clutch housing.
1986 7726-0201
1987 7726-0573
1988 7726-0711
1989 7726-3122

Model 6240A
Left side of clutch housing.
1985 7726-0001
1986 7726-0201
1987 7726-0573
1988 7726-0711
1989 7726-3122

Model 6250
Left side of clutch housing.
1985 7730-0001
1986 7730-0801
1987 7730-1694
1988 7730-1972
1989 7730-3067
1990 7722-3400

Model 6250 4WD
Left side of clutch housing.
1986 7734-0439
1987 7734-0874
1988 7734-1028
1989 7734-3104
1990 7734-3217

Model 6250A
Left side of clutch housing.
1985 7734-0001
1986 7734-0439
1987 7734-0874
1988 7734-1028
1989 7734-3104
1990 7734-3217

Model 6250VA
Left side of clutch housing.
1988 7773-0308
1989 7773-0334

Model 6260
Left side of clutch housing.
1985 7738-0001
1986 7738-0694
1987 7738-1342
1988 7738-1499
1989 7738-3141

Model 6260 4WD
1987 7742-1159
1988 7742-1315
1989 7742-3140

Model 6260 4WD Cab
Left side of clutch housing.
1986 7744-1192
1987 7744-2206
1988 7744-3102
1989 7744-3353
1990 7744-3672

Model 6260 4WD ROPS
Left side of clutch housing.
1986 7742-0542

Model 6260 Cab
Left side of clutch housing.
1986 7740-0584
1987 7740-1226
1988 7740-3048
1989 7740-3160

Model 6260 ROPS
Left side of clutch housing.
1986 7738-0694
1987 7738-1342
1988 7738-1499

Model 6260A
Left side of clutch housing.
1985 7742-0001
1986 7742-0542
1987 7742-1159
1988 7742-1315
1989 7742-3140

Model 6260C
Left side of clutch housing.
1985 7740-0001
1986 7740-0584
1987 7740-1226
1988 7740-3048
1989 7740-3106

Model 6260CA
Left side of clutch housing.
1985 7744-0001
1986 7744-1192
1987 7744-2206
1988 7744-3102
1989 7744-3353
1990 7744-3672

Model 6260F
Left side of clutch housing.
1988 7774-0300
1989 7774-0378
1990 7774-0378

Model 6260FA
Left side of clutch housing.
1988 7775-0306
1989 7775-0403
1990 7775-0489
1991 7775-0489

Model 6260L
Left side of clutch housing.
1988 7774-0302
1989 . . . . None
1990 7780-0024

Model 6260LA
Left side of clutch housing.
1988 7775-0309
1989 7781-0082
1990 7787-0099

Model 6265
Left side of clutch housing.
1985 7746-0001
1986 7746-0566
1987 7746-1128
1988 7746-1317
1989 7746-3109

Model 6265 4WD Cab
Left side of clutch housing.
1986 7752-0784
1987 7752-1352

Model 6265 4WD ROPS
Left side of clutch housing.
1986 7750-0463
1987 7750-1116

Model 6265 Cab
Left side of clutch housing.
1986 7748-0599
1987 7748-1042

Model 6265 ROPS
Left side of clutch housing.
1986 7746-0566
1987 7746-1128

Model 6265A
Left side of clutch housing.
1985 7750-0001
1986 7750-0463
1987 7750-1116
1988 7750-1437
1989 7750-3189

Model 6265C
Left side of clutch housing.
1985 7748-0001
1986 7748-0599
1987 7748-1042
1988 7748-3025
1989 7748-3097

Model 6265CA
Left side of clutch housing.
1985 7760-0001
1986 7752-0784
1987 7752-1352
1988 7752-1648
1989 7752-3067

Model 6275
Left side of clutch housing.
1985 7754-0001
1986 7754-0329
1987 7754-0635
1988 7754-3001
1989 7754-3133

Model 6275 4WD Cab
Left side of clutch housing.
1986 7760-1138
1987 7760-2063

Model 6275 4WD ROPS
Left side of clutch housing.
1986 7758-0229
1987 7758-0527

Model 6275 Cab
Left side of clutch housing.
1986 7756-0575
1987 7756-1004

Model 6275 ROPS
Left side of clutch housing.
1986 7754-0329
1987 7754-0635

Model 6275A
Left side of clutch housing.
1985 7758-0001
1986 7758-0229
1987 7758-0527
1988 7758-3011
1989 7758-3155

Model 6275C
Left side of clutch housing.
1985 7756-0001
1986 7756-0575
1987 7756-1004
1988 7756-3000
1989 7756-3184

Model 6275CA
Left side of clutch housing.
1985 7760-0001
1986 7760-1138
1987 7760-2063
1988 7760-2620
1989 7760-3743

Model 6275F
Left side of clutch housing.
1988 7778-0301

Model 6275FA
Left side of clutch housing.
1988 7779-0301
1989 7779-0387
1990 7779-0475

Model 6275L
Left side of clutch housing.
1988 7778-0300
1989 7782-0005
1990 7782-0008

Model 6275LA
Left side of clutch housing.
1988 7779-0300
1989 7783-0086
1990 7783-0149

Model 6365A
1990 7767-0102

Model 6365CA
1990 7768-2057

Model 6375C
1990 7634-0124

Model 6375CA
1990 7635-1606

Model 7085
1985 7434-0408
1986 7434-3030
1987 7434-3242
1988 7434-3459
1989 7434-6199
1990 7434-6464

Model 7085 4WD Cab
1986 7435-3031

Model 7085 4WD ROPS
1986 7435-3065
1987 7435-3815

Model 7085 Cab
1986 7434-3006
1987 7434-3225

Model 7085 ROPS
1986 7434-3030
1987 7434-3242

Model 7085A
1985 7435-1438
1986 7435-3065
1987 7435-3815
1988 7435-4784
1989 7435-6577
1990 7435-7417

Model 7085C
1986 7434-3006
1987 7434-3225

Model 7085CA
1986 7434-3031
1987 7435-3815

Model 7110
1985 7438-0203
1986 . . . . None
1987 7438-3134
1988 7438-3259
1989 7438-6028
1990 7438-6096

Model 7110 4WD
1987 7439-3500

Model 7110A
1985 7439-1274
1986 . . . . None
1987 7439-3500
1988 7439-4324
1989 7439-6544
1990 7439-7402

Model 7120
1985 7440-0086
1986 . . . . None
1987 7440-3094
1988 7440-3216
1989 7440-6018
1990 7440-6047

Model 7120 4WD
1987 7741-3228

Model 7120A
1985 7441-0646
1986 . . . . None
1987 7441-3228
1988 7441-3893
1989 7441-6317
1990 7441-6758

Model 7145
1987 7642-3005
1988 7642-6000

Model 7145 4WD
1987 7643-3090

Model 7145A
1985 7643-0049
1986 . . . . None
1987 7643-3090
1988 7643-3382

Model 9130
1991 9130-1001

Model 9150
1989 . . . . 9150F-1005
1990 . . . . 9150F-1365

Model 9150A
1989 . . . . 9150T-1070
1990 . . . . 9150T-1289

Model 9170
1989 . . . . 9170F-1020
1990 . . . . 9170F-1243

Model 9170A
1989 . . . . 9170T-1005
1990 . . . . 9170T-1283

Model 9190A
1989 . . . . 9190F-1004
1990 . . . . 9190F-1308

DEUTZ-FAHR

Model 3.50 CA
1985 .... 7740/0001

Model D3607
1985 7866-0001

Model D4507
Plate on right side of hood.
1980 .... 7548/1862
1981 .... 7548/2317
1982 .... 7548/3047
1983 .... 7548/3779
1984 .... 7548/5422
1985 .... 7548/7055

Model D4507A
1981 .... 7868/1797
1982 .... 7868/1856
1983 .... 7868/1995
1984 .... 7868/2141

Model D5207
Plate on right side of hood.
1981 .... 7557/8675
1982 .... 7557/9668
1983 .... 7558/0255
1984 .... 7558/0258

Model D5207A
1981 .... 7554/3448
1982 .... 7554/3606
1983 .... 7554/3805
1984 .... 7554/4153

Model D6207
Plate on right side of hood.
1980 .... 7761/1710
1981 .... 7761/2522
1982 .... 7761/4015

Model D6207A
1980 .... 7562/5268
1981 .... 7562/5661
1982 .... 7562/6376

Model D6507
Plate on right side of hood.
1983 .... 7716/0005
1984 .... 7716/0635

Model D6507A
1983 .... 7717/0003
1984 .... 7717/0429

Model D6507C
1983 .... 7741/0334
1984 .... 7741/0875

Model D6507CA
1983 .... 7743/0534
1984 .... 7743/0840

Model D6807
Plate on right side of hood.
1980 .... 7569/8469
1981 .... 7570/0529
1982 .... 7770/1798

Model D6807A
1980 .... 7566/3880
1981 .... 7566/4189
1982 .... 7566/4577

Model D7007
Plate on right side of hood.
1982 .... 7718/0003
1983 .... 7718/0091
1984 .... 7718/1539

Model D7007A
1983 .... 7719/0179
1984 .... 7719/0250

Model D7007C
1983 .... 7749/0039
1984 .... 7749/0155

Model D7007CA
1983 .... 7751/0035
1984 .... 7751/0100

Model D7807
1982 .... 7594/0859
1983 .... 7594/1038
1984 .... 7594/1378

Model D7807A
1982 .... 7596/0867
1983 .... 7596/0962
1984 .... 7596/1074

Model D7807C
1983 .... 7757/0795
1984 .... 7757/1280

Model DX110
Right side of front axle support.
1979 .... 7620/0186
1980 .... 7620/0867

Model DX110A
1979 .... 7621/0002
1980 .... 7621/1933

Model DX120
Right side of front axle support.
1980 .... 7626/0001
1981 .... 7626/0076
1982 .... 7826/0004
1983 .... 7826/0292

Model DX120A
1980 .... 7627/0001
1981 .... 7627/0222
1982 .... 7827/0037
1983 .... 7827/0742

Model DX130
Right side of front axle support.
1980 .... 7632/0001
1981 .... 7632/0070
1982 .... 7832/0008
1983 .... 7832/0130

Model DX130A
1980 .... 7633/0001
1981 .... 7633/0123
1982 .... 7833/0029
1983 .... 7833/0367

Model DX140
Right side of front axle support.
1979 .... 7622/0009
1980 .... 7622/0168

Model DX140A
1979 .... 7623/0245
1980 .... 7623/0885

Model DX160
Right side of front axle support.
1979 .... 7624/0002
1980 .... 7624/0352
1981 .... 7624/0569
1982 .... 7824/0011
1983 .... 7824/0145

Model DX160A
1979 .... 7625/0006
1980 .... 7625/0514
1981 .... 7625/1215
1982 .... 7825/0004
1983 .... 7825/0429
1984 .... 7443/0089

Model DX3.10
1985 .... 7722/0001

Model DX3.10A
1985 .... 7726/0001

Model DX3.30
1985 .... 7730/0001

Model DX3.30A
1985 .... 7734/0001

Model DX3.50
1985 .... 7738/0001

Model DX3.50A
1985 .... 7742/0001

Model DX3.50C
1985 .... 7740/0001

Model DX3.70
1985 .... 7746/0001

Model DX3.70A
1985 .... 7750/0001

Model DX3.70C
1985 .... 7748/0001

Model DX3.70CA
1985 .... 7752/0001

Model DX3.90
1985 .... 7754/0001

Model DX3.90A
1985 .... 7758/0001

Model DX3.90C
1985 .... 7756/0001

Model DX3.90CA
1985 .... 7760/0001

Model DX4.70
Plate riveted to hood on right side and cut into housing under hood on right side.
1983 .... 7434/0001
1984 .... 7434/0126
1985 .... 7434/0408
1986 .... 7434/0640

Model DX4.70A
1984 .... 7435/0311
1985 .... 7435/1438
1986 .... 7435/2625

Model DX6.30
Plate riveted to hood on right side and cut into housing under hood on right side.
1984 .... 7438/0026
1985 .... 7438/0203

Model DX6.30A
1984 .... 7439/0245
1985 .... 7439/1274

Model DX6.50
Plate riveted to hood on right side and cut into housing under hood on right side.
1984 .... 7440/0001
1985 .... 7440/0086

Model DX6.50A
1984 .... 7441/0100
1985 .... 7441/0646

Model DX7.10
Plate riveted to hood on right side and cut into housing under hood on right side.
1984 .... 7642/0001

Model DX7.10A
1984 .... 7643/0001
1985 .... 7643/0049
1986 .... 7643/0718

Model DX8.30A
1985 .... 7479/001

Model DX90
Right side of front axle support.
1979 .... 7618/0433
1980 .... 7618/1371
1981 .... 7618/2028
1982 .... 7818/0004
1983 .... 7818/0843

Model DX90A
1979 .... 7619/0426
1980 .... 7619/1635
1981 .... 7619/2566
1982 .... 7819/0058
1983 .... 7819/0304

FERGUSON

Model F40
1956 400001
1957 405671

Model TE20
Plate on instrument panel.
1948 20800
1949 77770
1950 116551
1951 167923

Model TO20
Plate on instrument panel.
1948 1
1949 1801
1950 14660
1951 39163

Model TO30
Plate on instrument panel.
1951 60001
1952 .... TO72680
1953 .... TO108645
1954 .... TO125958

Model TO35
Plate on instrument panel.
1954 .... TO140001
1955 .... TO140006
1956 .... TO167157
1957 .... TO171741

FORD

All 1965 and later Series 2000 (3 Cyl.) through TW35
1965 .... C100001
1966 .... C124200
1967 .... C161300
1968 .... C190200
1969 .... C226000
1970 .... C257600
1971 .... C292100
1972 .... C327200
1973 .... C367300
1974 .... C405200
1975 .... C450700
1976 .... C490300
1977 .... C527300
1978 .... C560500
1979 .... C595800
1980 .... C635700
1981 .... C660700
1982 .... C682000
1983 .... C694500
1984 .... C707400
1985 .... C732600
1986 .... C750422
1987 .... C763228
1988 .... C777683

Fordson Dexta
Left side of hand-clutch housing.
1958 00144
1959 22588
1960 46216
1961 ..... 09A-312001M

Fordson Major
Left side of flywheel housing or right side of engine block.
1953 1247381
1954 1276857
1955 1322525
1956 1371418
1957 1412409
1958 1458381

Fordson Power Major
Left side of flywheel housing or right side of engine block.
1958 1481091
1959 1494448
1960 1538056
1961 1583906

Fordson Super Dexta
1961 ..... 08A-300001M
1962 ..... 09B-070000A
1963 ..... 09C-731454A
1964 ..... 09D-900000A

Fordson Super Major
1961 1583906
1962 ..... 08B-740000-A
1963 .... 08C-781370-A

Model 1000
Left side of clutch housing.
1973 .... U100001
1974 .... U100821
1975 .... U102021
1976 .... U102771
1977 .... U105013
1978 .... U108449

Model 1100
Left side rail above front axle.
1979 .... U125001
1980 .... U127591
1981 .... U129066
1982 .... U130665
1983 .... U131359

Model 1110
Left side of transmission housing.
1983 .... UB00001
1984 .... UB00785
1985 .... UB01622
1986 .... UB02107

Model 1200
Left side rail above front axle.
1980 .... U200001
1981 .... U201258
1982 .... U202107
1983 .... U202737

Model 1210
Left side of transmission housing.
1983 .... UC00001
1984 .... UC01851
1985 .... UC03937
1986 .... UC07232

Model 1300
Left side of transmission housing.
1979 .... U300001
1980 .... U302697
1981 .... U303446
1982 .... None
1983 .... U304962

Model 1310
Left side of transmission housing.
1983 .... UE00001
1984 .... UE01019
1985 .... UE02438
1986 .... UE04444

Model 1500
Left side of transmission housing.
1979 .... U500001
1980 .... U503026
1981 .... U504437
1982 .... U505813
1983 .... U506674

FORD (Cont.)

Model 1510
Left side of transmission housing.
- 1983 .... UH00001
- 1984 .... UH01280
- 1985 .... UH02828
- 1986 .... UH04797

Model 1600
Left side of clutch housing.
- 1976 .... U103361
- 1977 .... U105013
- 1978 .... U108449
- 1979 .... U113129

Model 1700
Left side of transmission housing.
- 1979 .... U700001
- 1980 .... U704803
- 1981 .... U709687
- 1982 .... U712953
- 1983 .... U715471

Model 1710
Left side of transmission housing.
- 1983 .... UL00001
- 1984 .... UL03489
- 1985 .... UL07985
- 1986 .... UL13798

Model 1710 Offset
- 1985 .... N00001
- 1986 .... N00201

Model 1900
Left side of transmission housing.
- 1979 .... U900001
- 1980 .... U903187
- 1981 .... U905826
- 1982 .... U908557
- 1983 .... U911488

Model 1910
Left side of transmission housing.
- 1983 .... UP0001
- 1984 .... UP01089
- 1985 .... UP04638
- 1986 .... UP08193

Model 2110
Left side of transmission housing.
- 1983 .... UV00010
- 1984 .... UV00734
- 1985 .... UV02153
- 1986 .... UV03580
- 1987 .... UV04673

Model 2810, 2910, 3910, 4610, 5610, 6610, 7610, 7710 & 8210
Right front cover of transmission and on I.D. plate affixed to inside of engine compartment.
- 1982 .... C681910
- 1983 .... C695880
- 1984 .... C713459
- 1985 .... C737800
- 1986 .... BA80100
- 1986 .... C754100
- 1987 .... BB06622
- 1987 .... C768000

Model 2N
Left side of engine block.
- 1942 99047
- 1943 105375
- 1944 126538
- 1945 169982
- 1946 198731
- 1947 258504

Model 8N
Left side of engine block.
- 1947 1
- 1948 37908
- 1949 141370
- 1950 245637
- 1951 343593
- 1952 442035

Model 9N
Left side of engine block.
- 1939 1
- 1940 10234
- 1941 45976
- 1942 88888

Model FW20
- 1977 100001
- 1978 100070
- 1979 100117
- 1980 100135
- 1981 100145

Model FW30
- 1977 200001
- 1978 200106
- 1979 200191
- 1980 200264
- 1981 200303

Model FW40
- 1977 300001
- 1978 300077
- 1979 300121

Model FW60
- 1977 400001
- 1978 400087
- 1979 400143
- 1980 400202
- 1981 400223

Model NAA
Left side of transmission or right side of engine.
- 1952 1
- 1953 2380
- 1954 77475

Model TW-5, TW-15, TW-25, TW-35
Identification plate located above right front corner of radiator, accessible by removing right front grille panel.
- 1984 .... C713459
- 1985 .... C737800
- 1986 .... A916000
- 1986 .... A915854
- 1987 .... A917560

Series 2000 (4-Cyl.); 4000 (4-Cyl.) & 6000
Upper right corner of transmission or inside of right hood panel.
- 1962 1001
- 1963 11948
- 1964 38931

Series 600, 700, 800 & 900
Top left front corner of transmission case.
- 1954 1
- 1955 10615
- 1956 77271
- 1957 116368

Series 601, 701, 801 & 901
Top left corner of transmission case.
- 1957 1001
- 1958 11977
- 1959 58312
- 1960 105943
- 1961 131427
- 1962 155531

FORD NEW HOLLAND

Model 1120
Left side of transmission housing.
- 1987 .... UB21002
- 1988 .... UB21281
- 1989 .... UB21919
- 1990 .... UB22142
- 1991 .... UB22329
- 1992 .... UB22439
- 1993 .... UB22527

Model 1215
- 1993 .... UA20001
- 1994 .... UA20463
- 1995 .... UA21150
- 1996 .... UA21632

Model 1220
Left side of transmission housing.
- 1987 .... UC21006
- 1988 .... UC21707
- 1989 .... UC23199
- 1990 .... UC24279
- 1991 .... UC25359
- 1992 .... UC26052
- 1993 .... UC26585
- 1994 .... UC27015
- 1995 .... UC27524
- 1996 .... UC27839
- 1997 .... UC28245

Model 1320
Left side of transmission housing.
- 1987 .... UE21001
- 1988 .... UE22001
- 1989 .... UE23391
- 1990 .... UE24517
- 1991 .... UE25495
- 1992 .... UE26189
- 1993 .... UE26960
- 1994 .... UE27441
- 1995 .... UE28084
- 1996 .... UE28490
- 1997 .... UE28925

Model 1520
Left side of transmission housing.
- 1987 .... UH21001
- 1988 .... UH22102
- 1989 .... UH23801
- 1990 .... UH25507
- 1991 .... UH26935
- 1992 .... UH28254
- 1993 .... UH29228
- 1994 .... UH30030
- 1995 .... UH31125
- 1996 .... UH31815

Model 1620
- 1992 .... UJ20136
- 1993 .... UJ20911
- 1994 .... UJ21591
- 1995 .... UJ22718
- 1996 .... UJ23587

Model 1710 Offset
- 1988 .... UN00474

Model 1715
- 1993 .... UK20307
- 1994 .... UK22180
- 1995 .... UK25017

Model 1720
Left side of transmission housing.
- 1987 .... UL21001
- 1988 .... UL22701
- 1989 .... UL26556
- 1990 .... UL28601
- 1991 .... UL30784
- 1992 .... UL32230
- 1993 .... UL33920
- 1994 .... UL35013
- 1995 .... UL36435
- 1996 .... UL37607

Model 1920
Left side of transmission housing.
- 1987 .... UP21001
- 1988 .... UP21710
- 1989 .... UP24896
- 1990 .... UP27229
- 1991 .... UP29354
- 1992 .... UP30817
- 1993 .... UP32448
- 1994 .... UP34038
- 1995 .... UP35988
- 1996 .... UP37672

Model 2120
Left side of transmission housing.
- 1988 .... UV21003
- 1989 .... UV22274
- 1990 .... UV23599
- 1991 .... UV24295
- 1992 .... UV25141
- 1993 .... UV25891
- 1994 .... UV26738
- 1995 .... UV27935
- 1996 .... UV28911
- 1997 .... UV29898

Model 2810, 2910, 3910
Right front cover of transmission and on I.D. plate affixed to inside of engine compartment.
- 1988 .... C777683
- 1988 .... BB31777
- 1989 .... BB84620
- 1990 .... BC26239
- 1991 .... BC68791

Model 3230
- 1990 .... BC26239
- 1991 .... BC68791
- 1992 .... BD07628
- 1993 .... BD32445
- 1994 .... BD60322

Model 3415
- 1993 .... UX20001
- 1994 .... UX20799
- 1995 .... UX21715
- 1996 .... UX22323

Model 3430
- 1990 .... BC26239
- 1991 .... BC68791
- 1992 .... BD03778
- 1993 .... BD36144
- 1994 .... BD66161
- 1995 .... BD77434
- 1996 .... 018613B

Model 3930
- 1990 .... BC26239
- 1991 .... BC68791
- 1992 .... BD05932
- 1993 .... BD36207
- 1994 .... BD63909
- 1995 .... BD93327
- 1996 .... 011128B

Model 4030N
Right front cover of transmission and on I.D. plate affixed to inside of engine compartment.
- 1993 .... F005600
- 1994 .... F022000
- 1995 .... F046874
- 1996 .... F066554

Model 4230N
Right front cover of transmission and on I.D. plate affixed to inside of engine compartment.
- 1992 .... F622650
- 1993 .... F656580
- 1994 .... F021000
- 1995 .... F042000
- 1996 .... F072739

Model 4430N
Right front cover of transmission and on I.D. plate affixed to inside of engine compartment.
- 1992 .... F622950
- 1993 .... F659700
- 1994 .... F021000
- 1995 .... F042000
- 1996 .... F070920

Model 4610, 5610, 6610
Right front cover of transmission and on I.D. plate affixed to inside of engine compartment.
- 1988 .... BB31777
- 1989 .... BB80620
- 1990 .... BC26239

Model 4630
Right front cover of transmission and on I.D. plate affixed to inside of engine compartment.
- 1990 .... BC26239
- 1991 .... BC68791
- 1992 .... BD05270
- 1993 .... BD36800
- 1994 .... BD64162
- 1995 .... BD93484
- 1996 .... 015251B

Model 5030
- 1992 .... 2A01-2M31
- 1993 .... 3A01-3M31
- 1994 .... 4A01-4M31
- 1995 .... 5A01-5M31

Model 5640
Behind weight carrier or on right hand lift up hood.
- 1992 .... BD02865
- 1993 .... BD35935
- 1994 .... BD65544
- 1995 .... BD98440
- 1996 .... 018936B

Model 6640
Behind weight carrier or on right hand lift up hood.
- 1993 .... BD35935
- 1994 .... BD65544
- 1995 .... BD98440
- 1996 .... 014792B

Model 7610, 7710, 7810, 8210
Right front cover of transmission and on I.D. plate affixed to inside of engine compartment.
- 1988 .... BB31777
- 1989 .... BB80260
- 1990 .... BC26239
- 1991 .... BC68791

Model 7740, 7840
Behind weight carrier or on right hand lift up hood.
- 1993 .... BD35935
- 1994 .... BD65544
- 1995 .... BD98440
- 1996 .... 019149B

Model 8240, 8340
Behind weight carrier or on right hand lift up hood.
- 1993 .... BD35935
- 1994 .... BD65544
- 1995 .... BD98440
- 1996 .... 018936B

FORD NEW HOLLAND (Cont.)

Model 8530, 8630, 8730, 8830
1990 .... A925439
1991 .... A928924
1992 .... A930626
1993 .... A931957

Model 9030
Lower L/H corner of cab (cab forward configuration).
1992 .... D487501
1993 .... D932000
1994 .... D200000
1995 .... D201023
1996 .... D201894

Model 9280
Lower L/H rear cab cross member.
1995 .... D101694

Model 9480
Lower L/H rear cab cross member.
1995 .... D101696

Model 9680
Lower L/H rear cab cross member.
1995 .... D101800

Model 9880
Lower L/H rear cab cross member.
1995 .... D101879

Model TW5, TW15, TW25, TW35
Plate mounted on right front corner of front frame.
1988 .... A919400
1988 .... A919438
1989 .... A922535
1990 .... A925099

INTERNATIONAL HARVESTER

Farmall Regular
1924 501
1925 701
1926 1539
1927 5969
1928 15471
1929 40370
1930 75691
1931 117784
1932 131872

Model 10-20 Gear Drive (KC) Regular Tread
1923 501
1924 7641
1925 18869
1926 37728
1927 62824
1928 89470
1929 119823
1930 159111
1931 191486
1932 201213
1933 204239
1934 206179
1935 207275
1936 210235
1937 212425
1938 214886

Model 10-20 Gear Drive (NC & NT) Narrow Tread
1926 501
1927 649
1928 832
1929 1155
1930 1543
1931 1750
1932 1833
1933 1912
1934 1952

Model 184
1977 43802
1978 46163
1979 48030
1980 49873

Model 234
Right side of front fender rail and right side of transmission housing.
1982 8010
1983 8110
1984 8383
1985 8646

Model 244
Right side of front axle bracket and right side of transmission housing.
1982 8002
1983 8460
1984 9089
1985 9716

Model 254
Right side of front axle bracket and right side of transmission housing.
1982 8000
1983 8386
1984 8811
1985 9236

Model 3088
Right side of rear frame in front of axle.
1981 501
1982 507
1983 937
1984 1421
1985 1853

Model 3288
1981 501
1982 1063
1983 1286
1984 1464
1985 1651

Model 3388
Right side of rear frame in front of axle.
1978 8801
1979 8816
1980 10037
1981 10714

Model 3488
Right side of rear frame in front of axle.
1981 501
1982 715
1983 723
1984 829

Model 3588
Right side of rear frame in front of axle.
1978 8801
1979 8844
1980 11797
1981 13561

Model 3688
Right side of rear frame in front of axle.
1981 501
1982 1743
1983 2482
1984 2695
1985 3068

Model 482, 582, 682, 782 & 982
1980-1981665001-700000

Model 5088
Right side of transmission housing or right side of control center or ROPS.
1981 501
1982 3551
1983 6015
1984 7307
1985 8623

Model 5288
Right side of transmission housing or right side of control center or ROPS.
1981 501
1982 2292
1983 4086
1984 5054
1985 6334

Model 5488
Right side of transmission housing or right side of control center or ROPS.
1981 501
1982 523
1983 2416
1984 3112
1985 4390

Model 6388
Right side of frame or right side of control center or ROPS.
1981 8801
1982 8962
1983 9060
1984 9241
1985 9361

Model 6588
Right side of frame or right side of control center or ROPS.
1981 8801
1982 8966
1983 9164
1984 9361
1985 9526

Model 6788
Right side of frame or right side of control center or ROPS.
1981 8801
1982 8810
1983 8840
1984 8871
1985 8946

Model A, AV, & B
Left side of seat support.
1939 501
1940 6744
1941 41500
1942 80739
1943 .... None
1944 96390
1945 113218
1946 146700
1947 182964

Model C
Left side of seat support.
1948 501
1949 22624
1950 47010
1951 71880

Model Cub
Right side of steering gear housing.
1947 501
1948 11348
1949 57831
1950 99536
1951 121454
1952 144455
1953 162284
1954 179412
1955 186441
1956 193658
1957 198231
1958 204389
1959 211441
1960 214974
1961 217382
1962 220038
1963 221383
1964 223453
1965 225110
1966 227209
1967 229225
1968 231005
1969 232981
1970 234868
1971 236827
1972 238560
1973 240581
1974 242786
1975 245651
1976 248618
1977 250832
1978 252109
1979 253156

Model Cub 154 Lo-Boy
Right side of steering gear housing.
1968 3273
1969 3505
1970 15502
1971 20332
1972 23343
1973 27538
1974 31766

Model Cub 185 Lo-Boy
Right side of steering gear housing.
1974 37001
1975 37316
1976 42241

Model Cub Lo-Boy
Right side of steering gear housing.
1955 501
1956 2555
1957 3929
1958 5582
1959 10567
1960 12371
1961 13904
1962 15506
1963 16440
1964 17928
1965 19406
1966 21176
1967 23115
1968 24481

Model F-100
Left side of clutch housing.
1954 501
1955 1720
1956 12895

Model F-1026
Left side of hydrostatic drive housing.
1970 7501
1971 9707

Model F-1066
Left side of clutch housing.
1971 7101
1972 12677
1973 24205
1974 34949
1975 46855
1976 56672

Model F-12
1932 501
1933 526
1934 4881
1935 17411
1936 48660
1937 81837
1938 117518

Model F-1206
Right side of clutch housing.
1965 7501
1966 8626
1967 12731

Model F-1256
Right side of clutch housing.
1967 7501
1968 8849
1969 13140

Model F-130 & I-130
Left side of clutch housing.
1956 501
1957 1120
1958 8363

Model F-14
1938 124000
1939 139607

Model F-140 & I-140
Left side of clutch housing.
1958 501
1959 2011
1960 8082
1961 11168
1962 16637
1963 21181
1964 25387
1965 28408
1966 31285
1967 34818
1968 37352
1969 39906
1970 42300
1971 44424
1972 46605
1973 48507
1974 50720
1975 54723
1976 57773
1977 60839
1978 63111
1979 64544

Model F-1456
Right side of clutch housing.
1969 10001
1970 10405
1971 14149

Model F-1466
Left side of clutch housing.
1971 7101
1972 10408
1973 15533
1974 19746
1975 25404
1976 29516

Model F-1468
Left side of clutch housing.
1971 7201
1972 7239
1973 9109
1974 9670

Model F-1566
Left side of clutch housing.
1974 7101
1975 7837
1976 12589

Model F-1568
Left side of clutch housing.
1974 7201
1975 7821
1976 7975

Model F-20

1932	501
1933	1251
1934	3001
1935	6382
1936	32716
1937	68749
1938	105597
1939	130865
1940	135700

Model F-200
Right side of clutch housing.

1954	501
1955	1032
1956	10904

Model F-230
Right side of clutch housing.

1956	501
1957	815
1958	6827

Model F-240
Right side of clutch housing.

1958	501
1959	1777
1960	3415
1961	3989

Model F-30

1931	501
1932	1184
1933	4305
1934	5526
1935	7032
1936	10407
1937	18684
1938	27186
1939	29007

Model F-300
Right side of clutch housing.

1954	501
1955	1779
1956	23224

Model F-350
Right side of clutch housing.

1956	501
1957	1004
1958	14175

Model F-400
Left side of clutch housing.

1954	501
1955	2588
1956	29065

Model F-404
Right side of clutch housing.

1961	501
1962	826
1963	1936
1964	2259
1965	2568
1966	2790
1967	2980

Model F-450
Left side of clutch housing.

1956	501
1957	1734
1958	21871

Model F-460
Right side of clutch housing.

1958	501
1959	4765
1960	16902
1961	22622
1962	28029
1963	31552

Model F-504
Right side of clutch housing.

1961	501
1962	810
1963	7000
1964	7732
1965	10696
1966	13596
1967	15113
1968	16115

Model F-544
Right side of clutch housing.

1968	10250
1969	12541
1970	13585
1971	14507
1972	15262
1973	15738

Model F-560
Right side of clutch housing.

1958	501
1959	7341
1960	26914
1961	36125
1962	47798
1963	60278

Model F-656
Right side of clutch housing.

1965	8501
1966	15505
1967	24372
1968	32007
1969	38861
1970	42518
1971	45497
1972	47951

Model F-666 & I-666
Right side of clutch housing.

1972	7500
1973	8200
1974	11585
1975	13131
1976	15739

Model F-706
Right side of clutch housing.

1963	501
1964	7073
1965	21162
1966	30288
1967	38521

Model F-756
Right side of clutch housing.

1967	7501
1968	9940
1969	14125
1970	17832
1971	18374

Model F-766
Left side of clutch housing.

1971	7101
1972	7416
1973	9611
1974	12378
1975	14630
1976	16840

Model F-806
Right side of clutch housing.

1963	501
1964	4709
1965	15946
1966	24038
1967	34943

Model F-826
Right side of hydrostatic drive housing.

1969	7501
1970	8153
1971	16352

Model F-856
Right side of clutch housing.

1967	7501
1968	9854
1969	19554
1970	28693
1971	32420

Model F-966
Left side of clutch housing.

1971	7101
1972	11815
1973	17794
1974	22526
1975	28119
1976	31772

Model H & HV
Left side of clutch housing.

1939	501
1940	10653
1941	52387
1942	93237
1943	122091
1944	150251
1945	186123
1946	214820
1947	241143
1948	268991
1949	300876
1950	327975
1951	351923
1952	375861
1953	390500

Model Hydro 100
Left side of hydrostatic drive housing.

1973	7501
1974	7727
1975	10915
1976	12434

Model Hydro 186
Right side of rear frame in front of axle.

1976	8601
1977	8813
1978	9806
1979	10626
1980	11465
1981	12279

Model Hydro 70
Right side of hydrostatic drive housing.

1973	7501
1974	7570
1975	8681
1976	10094

Model Hydro 84
Right rear corner of front bolster.

1978	501
1979	787
1980	1481
1981	5564
1982	6014
1983	8069

Model Hydro 86
Right side of hydrostatic drive housing.

1976	7501
1977	7608
1978	8171
1979	8661
1980	9114

Model I-100
Left side of clutch housing.

1954	501
1955	504
1956	575

Model I-1026
Left side of hydrostatic drive housing.

1970	7501
1971	7550

Model I-1086
Right side of rear frame in front of axle.

1976	8601
1977	14725
1978	25672
1979	34731
1980	42186
1981	51671

Model I-1206
Right side of clutch housing.

1965	7501
1966	7772
1967	8492

Model I-1256
Right side of clutch housing.

1967	7501
1968	7703
1969	8444

Model I-1456
Right side of clutch housing.

1969	1001
1970	10025
1971	10249

Model I-1486
Right side of rear frame in front of axle.

1976	8601
1977	9798
1978	14851
1979	18774
1980	23162
1981	27426

Model I-1586
Right side of rear frame in front of axle.

1976	8601
1977	10652
1978	14506
1979	16347
1980	18451
1981	21501

Model I-240
Right side of clutch housing.

1958	501
1959	4835
1960	8628
1961	10079
1962	10727

Model I-254
Right side of front axle bracket and right side of transmission housing.

1982	8001
1983	8386
1984	8811
1985	9236

Model I-274
Right side of transmission housing.

1981	8306
1982	8948
1983	9556

Model I-284
Right side of transmission housing.

1976	8005
1977	8125
1978	10705
1979	12425
1980	13207
1981	13419

Model I-284 Diesel 2WD
Right side of transmission housing.

1980	670
1981	2146
1982	2999
1983	3378

Model I-284 Diesel 4WD
Right side of transmission housing.

1980	1211
1981	2267
1982	3035

Model I-300 U
Right side of clutch housing.

1955	501
1956	20219

Model I-330 U
Right side of clutch housing.

1957	501
1958	1488

Model I-340
Right side of clutch housing.

1958	501
1959	2467
1960	5741
1961	8736
1962	11141
1963	12032

Model I-350
Right side of clutch housing.

1956	501
1957	1963
1958	15049

Model I-364
Right side of clutch housing.

1976	4283
1977	5763

Model I-384
Right side of clutch housing.

1978	501
1979	1581
1980	3818

Model I-404
Right side of clutch housing.

1961	501
1962	1045
1963	4205
1964	6452
1965	8292
1966	9548
1967	10534
1968	11032

Model I-4100
Left side of clutch housing.

1966	8001
1967	8723
1968	8986

Model I-4156
Left side of clutch housing.

1969	9219
1970	9365

Model I-4166
Left side of clutch housing.

1972	10001
1973	10769
1974	11255
1975	11684
1976	12200

Model I-4186
Left side of front frame.

1976	18610
1977	18697
1978	19301

Model I-424
Right side of clutch housing.

1964	501
1965	1402
1966	7841
1967	13627

Model I-4366
Left side on top step.

1973	7501
1974	7780
1975	8616
1976	10227

Model I-4386
Left side on top step.

1976	501
1977	707
1978	1430
1979	2033
1980	2206
1981	2798

Model I-444
Right side of clutch housing.
1967 ... 501
1968 ... 1190
1969 ... 5270
1970 ... 9010
1971 ... 12357

Model I-454
Left side of clutch housing.
1970 ... 501
1971 ... 508
1972 ... 4908
1973 ... 8064

Model I-4568
1975 ... 8001
1976 ... 8368

Model I-4586
Left side on top step.
1976 ... 501
1977 ... 815
1978 ... 1340
1979 ... 1945
1980 ... 2501
1981 ... 2853

Model I-460
Right side of clutch housing.
1958 ... 501
1959 ... 2711
1960 ... 6883
1961 ... 9420
1962 ... 11619
1963 ... 11898

Model I-4786
Left side on top step.
1978 ... 501
1979 ... 689
1980 ... 2501
1981 ... 2556

Model I-504
Right side of clutch housing.
1962 ... 501
1963 ... 3376
1964 ... 6797
1965 ... 10996
1966 ... 14695
1967 ... 17992
1968 ... 20392

Model I-544
Right side of clutch housing.
1968 ... 10250
1969 ... 12699
1970 ... 14589
1971 ... 16018
1972 ... 16838
1973 ... 17341

Model I-560
Right side of clutch housing.
1958 ... 501
1959 ... 1210
1960 ... 3103
1961 ... 4032
1962 ... 4944
1963 ... 5598

Model I-574
Left side of transmission housing.
1970 ... 504
1971 ... 650
1972 ... 3329
1973 ... 7074
1974 ... 102961
1975 ... 107880
1976 ... 111783
1977 ... 114195
1978 ... 117065

Model I-584
Right side of front axle support.
1978 ... 501
1979 ... 2130
1980 ... 3871
1981 ... 5766
1982 ... 8001
1983 ... 8416

Model I-6 & ID-6
Left side of clutch housing.
1940 ... 501
1941 ... 1225
1942 ... 3718
1943 ... 5057
1944 ... 6371
1945 ... 9518
1946 ... 14198
1947 ... 17317
1948 ... 24021
1949 ... 28868
1950 ... 35472
1951 ... 38518
1952 ... 44318
1953 ... 45274

Model I-600
Plate on fuel tank support.
1956 ... 501

Model I-606
Right side of clutch housing.
1962 ... 501
1963 ... 1702
1964 ... 3214
1965 ... 5041
1966 ... 6960
1967 ... 7922

Model I-650
Plate on fuel tank support.
1956 ... 501
1957 ... 688
1958 ... 11659

Model I-656
Right side of clutch housing.
1966 ... 7501
1967 ... 7842
1968 ... 9929
1969 ... 11802
1970 ... 13353
1971 ... 14194
1972 ... 14952
1973 ... 15746

Model I-660
Right side of clutch housing.
1959 ... 501
1960 ... 3398
1961 ... 4259
1962 ... 5883
1963 ... 6995

Model I-664
Right side of clutch housing.
1972 ... 2501
1973 ... 3512

Model I-674
Left side of transmission housing.
1973 ... 100001
1974 ... 101862
1975 ... 103172
1976 ... 105946
1977 ... 107555

Model I-684
Right side of front axle support.
1978 ... 501
1979 ... 1687
1980 ... 3533
1981 ... 6037
1982 ... 8001
1983 ... 8512

Model I-686
Right side of clutch housing.
1976 ... 7500
1977 ... 7729
1978 ... 9899
1979 ... 11417
1980 ... 12923

Model I-706 & 2706
Right side of clutch housing.
1963 ... 501
1964 ... 1251
1965 ... 3478
1966 ... 4789
1967 ... 5316

Model I-756
Right side of clutch housing.
1967 ... 7501
1968 ... 7672
1969 ... 8164
1970 ... 8424
1971 ... 8427

Model I-784
Right side of front axle support.
1978 ... 501
1979 ... 1442
1980 ... 2752
1981 ... 5906
1982 ... 8001
1983 ... 8219

Model I-786
Right side of rear frame.
1980 ... 8601
1981 ... 8936

Model I-806
Right side of clutch housing.
1963 ... 501
1964 ... 1403
1965 ... 3758
1966 ... 5917
1967 ... 7409

Model I-826
Right side of hydrostatic drive housing.
1969 ... 7501
1970 ... 7518
1971 ... 7719

Model I-856
Right side of clutch housing.
1967 ... 7501
1968 ... 7904
1969 ... 9016
1970 ... 9544
1971 ... 9653

Model I-884
Right side of front axle support.
1979 ... 501
1980 ... 710
1981 ... 5575
1982 ... 6738
1983 ... 8238

Model I-886
Right side of rear frame.
1976 ... 8601
1977 ... 10010
1978 ... 12455
1979 ... 14414
1980 ... 15985
1981 ... 17406

Model I-9, ID-9
Fuel tank support.
1940 ... 501
1941 ... 578
1942 ... 2993
1943 ... 3651
1944 ... 5394
1945 ... 11459
1946 ... 17289
1947 ... 22714
1948 ... 29207
1949 ... 36159
1950 ... 45551
1951 ... 51739
1952 ... 59407
1953 ... 64014

Model I-986
Right side of rear frame in front of axle.
1976 ... 8601
1977 ... 11145
1978 ... 15624
1979 ... 19288
1980 ... 22696
1981 ... 25220

Model I-W400
Left side of clutch housing.
1955 ... 510
1956 ... 2187

Model I-W450
Left side of clutch housing.
1956 ... 501
1957 ... 568
1958 ... 1661

Model M, MV, MD & MDV
Left side of clutch housing.
1939 ... 501
1940 ... 7240
1941 ... 25371
1942 ... 50988
1943 ... 60011
1944 ... 67424
1945 ... 88085
1946 ... 105564
1947 ... 122823
1948 ... 151708
1949 ... 180414
1950 ... 213579
1951 ... 247518
1952 ... 290923

Model O-4, OS-4
Left side of clutch housing.
1940 ... 501
1941 ... 943
1942 ... 4056
1943 ... 5693
1944 ... 7593
1945 ... 11171
1946 ... 13934
1947 ... 16022
1948 ... 18880
1949 ... 21912
1950 ... 24470
1951 ... 28167
1952 ... 31214
1953 ... 33067

Model O-6, OS-6, ODS-6
Left side of clutch housing.
1940 ... 501
1941 ... 1225
1942 ... 3718
1943 ... 5057
1944 ... 6313
1945 ... 9396
1946 ... 14153
1947 ... 17792
1948 ... 22981
1949 ... 28704
1950 ... 33698
1951 ... 38518
1952 ... 44318
1953 ... 45274

Model Super A
Left side of seat support.
1947 ... 250001
1948 ... 250082
1949 ... 268196
1950 ... 281269
1951 ... 300126
1952 ... 324470
1953 ... 336880
1954 ... 353348

Model Super C
Left side of seat support.
1951 ... 100001
1952 ... 131157
1953 ... 159130
1954 ... 187788

Model Super H
Left side of seat support.
1953 ... 501
1954 ... 22202

Model Super M, MD, MDV, MTA & MV
Left side of clutch housing.
1952 ... F501
1952 ... L500001
1953 ... F12516
1953 ... L501906
1954 ... F51977

Model Super W-6, W6-TA & WD-6
Left side of clutch housing.
1952 ... 501
1953 ... 2908
1954 ... 8997

Model Super WD-9 & WDR-9
Fuel tank support.
1953 ... 501
1954 ... 1935
1955 ... 5238
1956 ... 6866

Model SW-4
Left side of clutch housing.
1953 ... 501
1954 ... 2668

Model W-12
1934 ... 503
1935 ... 1356
1936 ... 2031
1937 ... 2768
1938 ... 3799

Model W-14
Fuel tank support.
1938 ... 4134
1939 ... 4610

Model W-4
Left side of clutch housing.
1940 ... 501
1941 ... 943
1942 ... 4056
1943 ... 5693
1944 ... 7593
1945 ... 11171
1946 ... 13934
1947 ... 16022
1948 ... 18880
1949 ... 21912
1950 ... 24470
1951 ... 28167
1952 ... 31214
1953 ... 33067

INTERNATIONAL HARVESTER (Cont.)

Model W-40 & WD-40
Left side of clutch housing.

1935 501
1936 1441
1937 5120
1938 7665
1939 9756
1940 10323

Model W-9, WD-9, WDR-9 & WR-9
Fuel tank support.

1940 501
1941 578
1942 2993
1943 3651
1944 5394
1945 11459
1946 17289
1947 22714
1948 29207
1949 36159
1950 45551
1951 51739
1952 59407
1953 64014

Model W30
Left side of clutch housing.

1932 501
1933 522
1934 548
1935 3182
1936 9723
1937 15095
1938 23834
1939 29922
1940 32482

Model WR-9-S
Fuel tank support.

1953 501
1954 550
1955 722
1956 744

JOHN DEERE

Model 1010
Plate on right side of engine block.

1960 10001
1961 13692
1962 23630
1963 32188
1964 43900
1965 53722

Model 1020
Right side of transmission case.

1965 14501
1966 14682
1967 42715
1968 65184
1969 82409
1970 102039
1971 117500
1972 134700
1973 157109

Model 1050
Rear of transmission case below PTO.

1980 1000
1981 5280
1982 6572
1983 9001
1984 11006
1985 14001
1986 17001
1987 19501
1988 21479

Model 1070

1989 001001
1990 002265
1991 100001
1992 115001
1993 120001
1994 130001
1995 140001
1996 150001
1997 160001
1998 170001

Model 1250
Rear of transmission case below PTO.

1982 1000
1983 1258
1984 3001
1985 4001
1986 5001
1987 5501
1988 5785
1989 6501

Model 1450
Rear of transmission case below PTO.

1984 1020
1985 2201
1986 3001
1987 3501
1988 3530
1989 3558

Model 1520
Right side of transmission case.

1968 76112
1969 82405
1970 102061
1971 117500
1972 134700
1973 157109

Model 1530

1974 .... 176601T
1974 .... 108811L
1975 .... 145500L

Model 1650
Rear of transmission case below PTO.

1984 1021
1985 2401
1986 3001
1987 3501
1988 3579

Model 2010
Plate on right side of engine block.

1960 10001
1961 10991
1962 21807
1963 31250
1964 44036
1965 58186

Model 2020
Right side of transmission case.

1965 14502
1966 14680
1967 42721
1968 65176
1969 82404
1970 102032
1971 117500

Model 2030
Right side of transmission case.

1972 .... 134700T
1973 .... 157109T
1974 .... 187301T
1974 .... 140000L
1975 .... 213350T
1975 .... 145500L

Model 2040
Right side of frame.

1976 179963
1977 221555
1978 266057
1979 304165
1980 350000
1981 392026
1982 419145

Model 2150
Right side of frame.

1983 433467
1984 505001
1985 532000
1986 562001
1987 587950
1988 592001

Model 2155
Right side of frame.

1987 600000
1988 624800
1989 654344
1990 686146
1991 717916
1992 746510

Model 2240
Right side of frame.

1976 179298
1977 221716
1978 266267
1979 305307
1980 350000
1981 392292
1982 418608

Model 2255 Orchard
Right side of frame.

1983 468228
1984 505001
1985 532000
1986 562001
1987 587950
1988 592001

Model 2350
Right side of frame.

1983 433474
1984 505001
1985 532000
1986 562001
1987 587950
1988 592001

Model 2355
Right side of frame.

1987 600000
1988 624800
1989 654344
1990 685855
1991 717916
1992 746510
1993 775104
1994 803700

Model 2355N
Right side of frame.

1987 601693
1988 524800
1989 654344
1990 685855
1991 717916
1992 746510
1993 775104
1994 803700

Model 2440
Right side of frame.

1976 235210
1977 258106
1978 280789
1979 305501
1980 341000
1981 362173
1982 376746

Model 2510
Differential housing on rear of tractor.

1966 1000
1967 8958
1968 14291

Model 2520
Differential housing on rear of tractor.

1969 17000
1970 19416
1971 22000
1972 22911
1973 23865

Model 2550
Right side of frame.

1983 433480
1984 505001
1985 532000
1986 562001
1987 587950
1988 592001

Model 2555
Right side of frame.

1987 600000
1988 624800
1989 654344
1990 685748
1991 717916
1992 746510
1993 775104
1994 803700

Model 2630
Below right-hand side of grille screen.

1974 188601
1975 213360

Model 2640
Right side of frame.

1976 235313
1977 258106
1978 280789
1979 305505
1980 341000
1981 362175
1982 376744

Model 2750
Right side of frame.

1983 433494
1984 505001
1985 532000
1986 562001
1987 587950
1988 592001

Model 2755
Right side of frame.

1987 600000
1988 624800
1989 654344
1990 685854
1991 717916
1992 746510
1993 775104
1994 803700

Model 2840
Right side of frame.

1977 214909
1978 264711
1979 304654

Model 2855N

1987 601693
1988 624800
1989 654344
1990 685908
1991 717916
1992 746510

Model 2940
Right side of frame.

1980 350000
1981 390496
1982 418953

Model 2950
Right side of frame.

1983 433508
1984 505001
1985 532000
1986 562001
1987 587950
1988 592001

Model 2955
Right side of frame.

1987 600000
1988 624800
1989 654344
1990 685843
1991 717916
1992 746510

Model 3010
Differential housing on rear of tractor.

1961 1000
1962 19801
1963 32400

Model 3020
Differential housing on rear of tractor.

1964 50000
1965 68000
1966 84000
1967 97286
1968 112933
1969 123000
1970 129897
1971 150000
1972 154197

Model 3055

1991 717916
1992 736426
1993 746510

Model 3150

1985 532000
1986 562001
1987 587950

Model 3155

1987 618645
1988 624591
1989 654344
1990 685845
1991 717916
1992 746510

Model 320
Left side center frame near clutch bell housing.

1956 320001
1957 321220
1958 325127

Model 3255

1991 717916
1992 736426
1993 755536

Model 330
Left side center frame near clutch bell housing.

1958 330001
1959 330171
1960 330935

Model 40 Hi Crop
Left side center frame near clutch bell housing.

1954 60001
1955 60060

Model 40 Special
Left side center frame near clutch bell housing.

1955 60001

Model 40 Standard
Left side center frame near clutch bell housing.

1953 60001
1954 67359
1955 69474

Model 40 Tricycle
Left side center frame near clutch bell housing.

1953 60001
1954 72167
1955 75131

Model 40 Two Row Utility
Left side center frame near clutch bell housing.

1955 60001

Model 40 Utility
Left side center frame near clutch bell housing.
1953 60001
1954 60202
1955 63140

Model 4000
Differential housing on rear of tractor.
1969 211422
1970 222143
1971 250000
1972 260791

Model 4010
Differential housing on rear of tractor.
1961 1000
1962 20201
1963 38200

Model 4020
Differential housing on rear of tractor.
1964 65000
1965 91000
1966 119000
1967 145660
1968 173982
1969 201000
1970 222160
1971 250000
1972 260791

Model 4030
Differential housing on rear of tractor.
1973 1000
1974 6700
1975 10153
1976 13022
1977 15417

Model 4040
Differential housing on rear of tractor.
1978 1000
1979 14820
1979 3199
1980 6033
1980 29539
1981 42665
1981 8707
1982 11727
1982 56346

Model 4050
Differential housing on rear of tractor.
1983 1000
1984 3501
1985 5001
1986 6501
1987 007001
1988 007501
1989 009501

Model 4055
Differential housing on rear of tractor.
1989 1001
1990 2501
1991 5001
1992 10001

Model 4100 Gear
1998 .. LV4100G110031

Model 4100 HST
1998 .. LV4100H110134

Model 420
Left side center frame near clutch bell housing.
1956 80001
1957 107813
1958 127782

Model 4230
1973 1000
1974 13000
1975 22074
1976 28957
1977 35588

Model 4240
Differential housing on rear of tractor.
1978 1000
1979 7434
1980 14394
1981 20186
1982 25670

Model 4250
Differential housing on rear of tractor.
1983 1000
1984 6001
1985 9001
1986 11001
1987 012501
1988 013501
1989 020001

Model 4255
Differential housing on rear of tractor.
1989 1001
1990 3001
1991 5501
1992 10001

Model 430
Left side center frame near clutch bell housing.
1958 140001
1959 142671
1960 158632

Model 4320
Differential housing on rear of tractor.
1971 6000
1972 17031

Model 435
Left side center frame near clutch bell housing.
1959 435001
1960 437655

Model 4430
Differential housing on rear of tractor.
1973 1000
1974 17500
1975 33050
1976 47222
1977 62960

Model 4440
Differential housing on rear of tractor.
1978 1000
1979 14820
1980 29539
1981 42665
1982 56346

Model 4450
Differential housing on rear of tractor.
1983 1000
1984 11001
1985 18001
1986 22001
1987 024001
1988 026001
1989 031001

Model 4455
Differential housing on rear of tractor.
1989 1001
1990 5001
1991 10001
1992 20001

Model 4520
Differential housing on rear of tractor.
1969 1000
1970 7038

Model 4555
Differential housing on rear of tractor.
1989 1001
1990 3001
1991 6001
1992 9001

Model 4560
1992 1001
1993 3221
1994 4501

Model 4620
Differential housing on rear of tractor.
1971 10000
1972 13692

Model 4630
Differential housing on rear of tractor.
1973 1000
1974 7022
1975 11717
1976 18392
1977 25794

Model 4640
Differential housing on rear of tractor.
1978 1000
1979 7422
1980 13860
1981 19459
1982 25729

Model 4650
Differential housing on rear of tractor.
1983 1000
1984 7001
1985 10001
1986 12501
1987 014001
1988 015501
1989 017501

Model 4755
Differential housing on rear of tractor.
1989 1001
1990 3001
1991 6501

Model 4760
1992 1001
1993 4535
1994 7901

Model 4840
Differential housing on rear of tractor.
1978 1000
1979 4233
1980 7539
1981 11042
1982 14933

Model 4850
Differential housing on rear of tractor.
1983 1000
1984 5001
1985 8001
1986 10001
1987 011001
1988 012001
1989 014501

Model 4955
Differential housing on rear of tractor.
1989 1001
1990 3501
1991 7001
1992 1001
1992 10501

Model 4960
1992 1001

Model 50
Right side of tractor on main case in distributor or magneto area.
1952 5000001
1953 5001254
1954 5016041
1955 5021977
1956 5030600

Model 5010
1963 1000
1964 4500
1965 8000

Model 5020
1966 12000
1967 15650
1968 20399
1969 24038
1970 26624
1971 30000
1972 30608

Model 520
Adjacent to crankcase dipstick outlet.
1956 5200000
1957 5202982
1958 5209029

Model 5200
1992 110000
1993 220000
1994 221268
1995 420141
1996 520001
1997 620000

Model 530
Adjacent to crankcase dipstick outlet.
1958 5300000
1959 5301671
1960 5307749

Model 5300
Plate on right side of engine block.
1992 120000
1993 230000
1994 231671
1995 430180
1996 530001
1997 630000

Model 60
Right side of tractor on main case in distributor or magneto area.
1952 6000001
1953 6027694
1954 6027995
1955 6042500
1956 6057650

Model 6030
Differential housing on rear of tractor.
1972 33000
1973 33550
1974 34586
1975 35400
1976 36014
1977 36577

Model 620
Adjacent to crankcase dipstick outlet.
1956 6200000
1957 6203778
1958 6215049

Model 6200
1993 100000
1994 117686
1995 135565
1996 153587

Model 630
1958 6300000
1959 6302749
1960 6314381

Model 6300, 6400
Plate on right side of engine block.
1993 100000
1994 117697
1995 135565
1996 153567
1997 177240

Model 650
Rear of transmission case below PTO.
1981 1000
1982 3539
1983 6250
1984 10543
1985 15001
1986 19001
1987 22501
1988 24298

Model 6500
Plate on right side of engine block.
1996 153587

Model 655
Plate located below rear PTO shaft.
1986 .... M0360001
1987 .... M0420001
1988 .... M0475001
1989 .... M0615001

Model 670
1989 1001
1990 2889
1991 100001
1992 110001
1993 120001
1994 130001
1995 140001
1996 150001
1997 160001

Model 70
Right side of tractor on main case in distributor or magneto area.
1953 7000001
1954 7005692
1955 7017501
1956 7034950

Model 7020
Differential housing on rear of tractor.
1971 1000
1972 2006
1973 2700
1974 3156
1975 3579

Model 720
Adjacent to crankcase dipstick outlet.
1956 7200000
1957 7203420
1958 7217368

Model 7200
Plate on right side of engine block.
1994 1001
1995 2595
1996 4001

Model 7210
1997 1001
1998 10001

Model 730
Adjacent to crankcase dipstick outlet.
1958 7300000
1959 7303761
1960 7322075

Model 7400
Plate on right side of engine block.
1994 1001
1995 2995
1996 6001

Model 7410
1997 1001
1998 10001

Model 750
Rear of transmission case below PTO.
1981 1000
1982 3448
1983 5613
1984 8457
1985 13001
1986 18501
1987 22601
1988 26450

Model 7520
Differential housing on rear of tractor.
1972 1000
1973 1600
1974 3054
1975 4945

Model 755
Plate located below rear PTO shaft.

1986	M0360001
1987	M0420001
1988	M0475001
1989	M0600001
1990	M010001
1991	M0100001
1992	LV100700
1993	LV130000
1994	LV165001
1995	LVA165180
1996	LVE190001
1997	LVE200001

Model 7600
Plate on right side of engine block.

1993	1457
1994	4601
1995	6195
1996	15001

Model 7610

1997	1001
1998	10001

Model 770

1989	1001
1990	4111
1991	100001
1992	115001
1993	120001
1994	130001
1995	140001
1996	150001
1997	160001
1998	170001

Model 7700
Plate on right side of engine block.

1993	1502
1994	4601
1995	7701
1996	10001

Model 7710

1997	1001
1998	10001

Model 7800
Plate on right side of engine block.

1993	2329
1994	5701
1995	10495
1996	15001

Model 7810
Plate on right side of engine block.

1997	1001
1998	10001

Model 80
Right side of tractor on main case in distributor or magneto area.

1955	8000001
1956	8000775

Model 8010

1961	1000

Model 8020

1964	1000

Model 8100
Right side of transmission case.

1995	1001
1996	3001
1997	10001
1998	20001

Model 820 (Three-Cyl.)
Below right-hand side grille screen.

1968	10000
1969	23100
1970	36000
1971	54000
1972	71850
1973	90200
1974	109507
1975	145500

Model 820 (Two-Cyl.)
Adjacent to crankcase dipstick outlet.

1956	8200000
1957	8200565
1958	8203850

Model 8200
Plate on right side of engine block.

1995	1001
1996	4001
1997	10001
1998	20001

Model 830 (Two-Cyl.)
Adjacent to crankcase dipstick outlet.

1958	8300000
1959	8300727
1960	8305301

Model 8300
Plate on right side of engine block.

1995	1001
1996	5001
1997	10001
1998	20001

Model 840 (Two-Cyl.)

1958	8400000
1959	8400033
1960	8400619

Model 8400
Plate on right side of engine block.

1995	1001
1996	6001
1997	10001
1998	20001

Model 8430
Differential housing on rear of tractor.

1975	1000
1976	1690
1977	3962
1978	5323

Model 8440
Differential housing on rear of tractor.

1979	1000
1980	2266
1981	3758
1982	5235

Model 8450
Differential housing on rear of tractor.

1982	1000
1983	2000
1984	3501
1985	5001
1986	5501
1987	006001
1988	006501

Model 850
Rear of transmission case below PTO.

1978	1024
1979	3859
1980	7389
1981	11338
1982	12481
1983	14183
1984	16006
1985	18001
1986	22001
1987	25501
1988	28337

Model 855
Plate located below rear PTO shaft.

1986	M0360001
1987	M0420001
1988	M0475001
1989	M0615001
1990	M010001
1991	M0100001
1992	LV100700
1993	LV130000
1994	LV165001
1995	LVB170123
1996	LVE190001
1997	LVE200001
1998	LVE300001

Model 8560

1989	1001
1990	1501
1991	2001
1992	2331
1993	3325

Model 8570
Plate on right side of engine block.

1993	1001
1994	1551
1995	2591
1996	3001

Model 8630
Differential housing on rear of tractor.

1975	1000
1976	2382
1977	5222
1978	7626

Model 8640
Differential housing on rear of tractor.

1979	1500
1980	3198
1981	5704
1982	7960

Model 8650
Differential housing on rear of tractor.

1982	1500
1983	3000
1984	5001
1985	7001
1986	8001
1987	008501
1988	009001

Model 870

1989	1001
1990	1625
1991	100001
1992	110001
1993	120001
1994	130001
1995	140001
1996	150001
1997	160001
1998	170001

Model 8760

1989	1001
1990	2001
1991	3501
1992	4322
1993	5756

Model 8770
Plate on right side of engine block.

1993	1001
1994	1771
1995	2791
1996	4001

Model 8850
Differential housing on rear of tractor.

1982	2000
1983	4000
1984	5101
1985	6001
1986	6501
1987	007001
1988	007501

Model 8870
Plate on right side of engine block.

1993	1001
1994	1881
1995	2891
1996	5001

Model 8960

1989	1001
1990	1501
1991	2501
1992	2937

Model 8970
Plate on right side of engine block.

1993	1001
1994	1991
1995	2991
1996	6001

Model 9100, 9200

1997	1001
1998	10001

Model 9300, 9400

1997	1001
1998	10001

Model 950
Rear of transmission case below PTO.

1978	1024
1979	5229
1980	10453
1981	14893
1982	16204
1983	18204
1984	20007
1985	23001
1986	26001
1987	28501
1988	30082

Model 955
Plate located below rear PTO shaft.

1990	M010001
1991	M0100001
1992	LV100700
1993	LV130000
1994	LV165001
1995	LVC175130
1996	LVE190001
1997	LVE200001
1998	LVE300001

Model 970

1989	001001
1990	001338
1991	100001
1992	110001
1993	120001
1994	130001
1995	140001
1996	150001
1997	160001
1998	170001

Model A Styled
Right side of tractor on main case in distributor or magneto area.

1939	477000
1940	488852
1941	500849
1942	514127
1943	523133
1944	528778
1945	548352
1946	558817
1947	578516
1948	594433
1949	620843
1950	646530
1951	667390
1952	689880

Model A Unstyled
Right side of tractor on main case in distributor or magneto area.

1934	410000
1935	412866
1936	424025
1937	442151
1938	466787

Model AO Styled
Right side of tractor on main case in distributor or magneto area.

1937	AO-1000
1938	AO-1539
1939	AO-1725
1940	AO-1801

Model AO, AR Unstyled
Right side of tractor on main case in distributor or magneto area.

1936	250000
1937	253521
1938	255416
1939	257004
1940	258045
1941	260000
1942	261558
1943	262243
1944	263223
1945	264738
1946	265870
1947	267082
1948	268877
1949	270646

Model AR Styled
Right side of tractor on main case in distributor or magneto area.

1949	272000
1950	272985
1951	276078
1952	279772
1953	282551

Model B Styled
Right side of tractor on main case in distributor or magneto area.

1939	60000
1940	81600
1941	98711
1942	126345
1943	143420
1944	152862
1945	173179
1946	183673
1947	199744
1948	215055
1949	237346
1950	258205
1951	276557
1952	299175

Model B Unstyled
Right side of tractor on main case in distributor or magneto area.

1935	1000
1936	12012
1937	27389
1938	46175

Model BR, BO
Right side of tractor on main case in distributor or magneto area.

1936	325000
1937	326655
1938	328111
1939	329000
1940	330633
1941	332039
1942	332427
1943	332780
1944	333156
1945	334219
1946	335641
1947	336746

Model D Styled
Rear of transmission housing.

1939	143800
1940	146566
1941	149500
1942	152840
1943	155005
1944	155426
1945	159888
1946	162598
1947	167250
1948	174879
1949	183516
1950	188420
1951	189701
1952	191180
1953	191439

JOHN DEERE (Cont.)

Model D Unstyled
Rear of transmission housing.

1924	30401
1925	31280
1926	35309
1927	43410
1928	54554
1929	71561
1930	95367
1931	109944
1932	115477
1935	119100
1936	125430
1937	130700
1938	138413

Model G Styled
Right side of tractor on main case in distributor or magneto area.

1943	13000
1944	13748
1945	13905
1946	16694
1947	20527
1948	28127
1949	34587
1950	40761
1951	47194
1952	56510
1953	63489

Model G Unstyled
Right side of tractor on main case in distributor or magneto area.

1938	1000
1939	7734
1940	9321
1941	10489
1942	12059
1943	12941

Model GP (Standard)
Right side of tractor on main case in distributor or magneto area.

1928	200211
1929	202566
1930	216139
1931	224321
1932	228666
1933	229051
1934	229216
1935	230515

Model GP (Wide)
Right side of tractor on main frame in distributor or magneto area.

1929	400000
1930	400936
1931	402040
1932	404810
1933	405110

Model GPO
Right side of tractor on main frame in distributor or magneto area.

1931	15000
1932	15226
1933	15387
1934	15412
1935	15589

Model H
Right side of tractor on main case in flywheel area.

1939	1000
1940	10780
1941	23654
1942	40995
1943	44755
1944	47796
1945	48392
1946	55956
1947	60107

Model L Styled
Rear of differential housing.

1938	625000
1939	626265
1940	630160
1941	634841
1942	640000
1943	640738
1944	641038
1945	641538
1946	641958

Model L Unstyled
Rear of differential housing.

1937	621000
1938	621079

Model LA
Rear of differential housing.

1941	1001
1942	5361
1943	6029
1944	6159
1945	9732
1946	11529

Model M
Instrument panel under ignition switch.

1947	10001
1948	13734
1949	25604
1950	35659
1951	43525
1952	50580

Model MT

1949	10001
1950	18544
1951	26203
1952	35845

Model R
Right side of tractor on main case in distributor or magneto area.

1949	1000
1950	3451
1951	5505
1952	10725
1953	15720
1954	19485

Waterloo Boy L & LA

1914	1000

Waterloo Boy N

1917	10000
1918	10221
1919	13461
1920	18924
1921	27026
1922	27812
1923	28119
1924	29520

Waterloo Boy R

1915	1026
1916	1401
1917	3556
1918	6982
1919	9056

KIOTI

Model LB1714
Forward of the clutch pedal on the transmission housing.

1988	400001
1989	500001
1990	600001
1991	700001
1992	800001
1993	900001

Model LB1914
Forward of the clutch pedal on the transmission housing.

1990	600001
1991	700001
1992	800001
1993	900001

Model LB2202
Forward of the clutch pedal on the transmission housing.

1987	300001
1988	400001
1989	500001
1990	600001
1991	700001
1992	800001
1993	900001

Model LB2204
Forward of the clutch pedal on the transmission housing.

1986	200001
1987	300001
1988	400001
1989	500001
1990	600001
1991	700001
1992	800001
1993	900001

Model LB2214
Forward of the clutch pedal on the transmission housing.

1990	600001
1991	700001
1992	800001
1993	900001

Model LB2614
Forward of the clutch pedal on the transmission housing.

1990	600001
1991	700001
1992	800001
1993	900001

KUBOTA

Model B4200DT

1987	10003
1988	10619
1989	30014
1990	44409
1991	58806
1992	73203

Model B5100DT
Left side of clutch housing.

1976	10001
1977	11031
1978	14661
1979	16477
1980	17255
1981	18360
1982	50001
1983	50880
1984	51639
1985	52249
1986	52554

Model B5100E
Left side of clutch housing.

1977	10001
1978	10196
1979	12014
1980	12788
1981	13524
1982	14568
1983	15959
1984	16847
1985	17321
1986	17795

Model B5200DT

1983	10003
1984	11800
1985	30003
1986	48216
1987	66409
1988	74602
1989	82795
1990	90488
1991	97681
1992	104372

Model B6100D
Left side of clutch housing.

1976	10001
1977	13181
1978	18781
1979	25699
1980	30108
1981	32873
1982	50001
1983	51152
1984	51844
1985	52075

Model B6100E
Left side of clutch housing.

1976	10001
1977	10051
1978	10801
1979	12987
1980	15287
1981	16911
1982	17923
1983	18815
1984	18823

Model B6100HSD

1980	10001
1981	30001
1982	50001
1983	51127
1984	52253
1985	52853
1986	53456

Model B6100HSE

1981	10001
1982	10886
1983	11140
1984	11396
1985	11650
1986	11904

Model B6100HST
Left side of clutch housing.

1980-1981	10002
1982	50001
1983	51127
1984	52253
1985	52853
1986	53456

Model B6100HST-E
Left side of clutch housing.

1981	10002
1982	10886
1983	11140
1984	11396
1985	11650
1986	11904

Model B6200DGP

1983	50001
1984	50972
1985	51943
1986	52916
1987	53886
1988	54856

Model B6200E

1983	10001
1984	11022
1985	20183
1986	29344
1987	38505
1988	49666

Model B6200EGP

1983	10001
1984	11022
1985	20183
1986	29344
1987	38505
1988	49666

Model B6200HSD

1983	50001
1984	50972
1985	51943
1986	52916
1987	53886
1988	54856

Model B7100D
Left side of clutch housing.

1976	10001
1977	13931
1978	36646
1979	54221
1980	64448
1981	70678
1982	74217
1983	76009
1984	77309
1985	78435

Model B7100DT

1976	10001
1977	13931
1978	36646
1979	54221
1980	64448
1981	70678
1982	74217
1983	76009
1984	77309
1985	78435

Model B7100HST-D
Left side of clutch housing.

1980	10001
1981	10890
1982	50001
1983	51993
1984	53662
1985	54897
1986	56132

Model B7100HST-E
Left side of clutch housing.

1980	10001
1981	11035
1982	11501
1983	12008
1984	12669
1985	12958
1986	13246

Model B7200DT

1983	50001
1984	51740
1985	61210

KUBOTA (Cont.)

Model B7200EGP
1983 10001
1984 10908

Model B7200HSD
1984 50001
1985 50867

Model B7200HSE
1984 10001
1985 10619

Model B8200DT
1981 10001
1982 50001
1983 51644
1984 53823
1985 56002
1986 58081
1987 60056

Model B8200E
1981 10001
1982 10483
1983 11070
1984 12025
1985 20329
1986 28631
1987 36432

Model L185
Left side of clutch housing.
1976 10001
1977 10606
1978 12446
1979 12506
1980 12842
1981 13177
1982 13511

Model L185-2
Left side of clutch housing.
1977 5001
1978 51640
1979 53700
1980 55139
1981 56061
1982 56491
1983 56691

Model L185DT-2
Left side of clutch housing.
1977 50001
1978 50651
1979 51656
1980 53004
1981 55139
1982 70001
1983 70062
1984 70102
1985 70142

Model L185F
1976 10001
1977 10606
1978 12446
1979 12506
1980 12842
1981 13177
1982 13511

Model L245
Left side of clutch housing.
1976 10001
1977 10436
1978 13666
1979 13769
1980 13872
1981 13972
1982 14072

Model L245-2
Left side of clutch housing.
1977 50001
1978 51001
1979 51440
1980 52878
1981 54028
1982 54932
1983 55728

Model L245DT
Left side of clutch housing.
1976 10001
1977 10666
1978 12081
1979 12330
1980 12579
1981 12828
1982 13053
1983 71195
1984 71854
1985 72602

Model L245DT-2
Left side of clutch housing.
1977 50001
1978 51736
1979 56509
1980 59597
1981 62167
1982 70001
1983 71195

Model L285
Left side of clutch housing.
1975 10001
1976 10151
1977 12701
1978 20301
1979 27901
1980 35401
1981 42001
1982 48101

Model L285DT
Left side of clutch housing.
1977 10001
1978 10013
1979 11758
1980 13503
1981 15243
1982 16943

Model L285HF
Left side of clutch housing.
1977 10001
1978 10013
1979 11758
1980 13503
1981 15243
1982 16943

Model L295DT
Left side of clutch housing.
1977 10001
1978 10431
1979 12531
1980 14631
1981 15681
1982 16731

Model L295F
Left side of clutch housing.
1977 10001
1978 10321
1979 10641
1980 10961
1981 11116
1982 11271

Model L305DT
Left side of clutch housing.
1980 10001
1981 10565
1982 50001
1983 50602
1984 50645
1985 50735
1986 50825

Model L305F
Left side of clutch housing.
1980 10001
1981 10327
1982 10521
1983 10715
1984 10940
1985 11176
1986 11412

Model L345DT
Left side of clutch housing.
1979 10001
1980 11121
1981 11914
1982 50001
1983 50602
1984 50645
1985 50735
1986 50841

Model L345F
Left side of clutch housing.
1978 10001
1979 10418
1980 10958
1981 11365
1982 12354
1983 50001
1984 50436
1985 50491
1986 50566

Model M4000
Left side of clutch housing.
1976 10061
1977 10361
1978 11071
1979 10124
1980 10164
1981 11204
1982 11244
1983 11284

Model M4030DT
1985 50001

Model M4030F
1985 10001

Model M4050DT
1981 50002
1981 50002
1982 50004
1982 50004
1983 50297
1983 50297
1984 50500
1984 50500
1985 50648
1985 50648
1986 50798
1987 50948
1988 51088

Model M4050F
Left side of clutch housing.
1981 10001
1982 10004
1983 10547
1984 10792
1985 11192
1986 11592
1987 11992
1988 12392

Model M4500DC
1980 10001
1981 10253
1982 10264
1983 10276
1984 10282
1985 10384
1986 10486

Model M4500DT
1978 10001
1979 10316
1980 11025
1981 11588
1982 12604
1983 12483
1984 50803

Model M4500F
1978 10001
1979 10011
1980 10147
1981 10596
1982 10699
1983 10802
1984 10902
1985 11002
1986 11102

Model M4950DT
Left side of frame.
1980 10001
1981 10006
1982 50001
1983 50053
1984 51001
1985 51289
1986 51577
1987 51867
1988 52157
1989 52447
1990 52723
1991 53013
1992 53293

Model M4950F
Left side of frame.
1980 10001
1981 10041
1982 10095
1983 10136
1984 11001
1985 11167
1986 11333
1987 11501
1988 11671
1989 11841
1990 12011
1991 12181
1992 12351

Model M5030DT
1985 50001

Model M5030F
1985 50001

Model M5500DT
Left side of clutch housing.
1979 10001
1980 10452
1981 10596
1982 10733
1983 10804
1984 50108
1985 50176
1986 50241

Model M5500F
Left side of clutch housing.
1980 10001
1981 10164
1982 10222
1983 50002
1984 50192
1985 50176
1986 53136

Model M5950DT
Left side of frame.
1980 10001
1981 10006
1982 50001
1983 50002
1984 51001
1985 51239
1986 51239
1987 51477
1988 51711
1989 51951

Model M5950F
Left side of frame.
1980 10001
1981 10005
1982 10045
1983 10085
1984 11001
1985 11092

Model M6030DT
1985 50001

Model M6030F
1985 10001

Model M6950DT
Left side of frame.
1983 10001
1984 10004
1985 50001
1986 50002
1987 50639
1988 50693

Model M6950F
Left side of frame.
1983 10001
1984 10004
1985 10012
1986 10039
1987 10159

Model M7030DT
1985 50001

Model M7030F
1985 10001

Model M7500C
Left side of clutch housing.
1979 10001
1980 10026
1981 10294
1982 10577

Model M7500DT
Left side of clutch housing.
1978 10001
1979 10401
1980 10436
1981 10761
1982 11490
1983 11744
1984 50056
1985 60011
1986 69966

Model M7950DT
Left side of frame.
1983 10001
1984 10009
1985 50001
1986 50103
1987 51847

Model M7950F
Left side of frame.
1983 10001
1984 10004
1985 10011
1986 10080
1987 10130
1988 10196

Model M8030DT
1985 50001

Model M8030F
1985 10001

Model M8950DT
1985 50001
1986 50007
1987 50425

LANDINI

Model DT5830
1985 22201001
1986 22202733
1987 22203556

Model DT6530F
1985 23201001
1986 23201344
1987 . . . . 232A01754

Model DT6830
1985 22101001
1986 22103628
1987 22104826

Model DT7830
1985 22001001
1986 22001221
1987 22001596

Model DT8550
1985 22500001
1986 22500960
1987 22501218

LANDINI (Cont.)

Model DT8830
1985 22300001
1986 22801652
1987 22302505

Model R5830
1985 12201001
1986 12201921
1987 12202407

Model R6530F
1985 13200001
1986 13200653
1987 132A00912

Model R6830
1985 12101001
1986 12101780
1987 12102301

Model R7830
1985 12000001
1986 12000709
1987 12000911

Model R8530F
1985 14100001
1986 14100021
1987 141B00055

Model R8550
1985 12500001
1986 12500300
1987 12500343

Model R8830
1985 12300001
1986 12300531
1987 12300858

MASSEY FERGUSON

Model MF1010-2
Steering cover below dash.
1982 00101
1983 00613
1984 10901
1985 11727
1986 12471
1987 13902
1988 14433
1989 None
1990 14549
1991 14826
1992 14937

Model MF1010-4
Steering cover below dash.
1982 40101
1983 40607
1984 40809
1985 41491
1986 42317
1987 43683
1988 44498
1989 44696
1990 44886
1991 45166
1992 45362

Model MF1010H-2
Steering cover below dash.
1987 13953
1988 14455
1989 14549
1990 14600
1991 14836
1992 15158

Model MF1010H-4
Steering cover below dash.
1987 43640
1988 44370
1989 44696
1990 44907
1991 45175
1992 45545

Model MF1020-2
Steering cover below dash.
1983 00101
1984 00411
1985 00809
1986 01548
1987 02394
1988 02707
1989 02768
1990 02913
1991 03153
1992 03262

Model MF1020-4
Steering cover below dash.
1983 40101
1984 40395
1985 40549
1986 41002
1987 41787
1988 42273
1989 42532
1990 42963
1991 43276
1992 43647

Model MF1020H-2
Steering cover below dash.
1987 02319
1988 02707
1989 02768
1990 02933
1991 03146
1992 03381

Model MF1020H-4
Steering cover below dash.
1987 41709
1988 42343
1989 42641
1990 43016
1991 43264
1992 43694

Model MF1030-2
Left side of clutch housing.
1984 00101
1985 00820
1986 01501
1987 02542
1988 03139
1989 03285
1990 03308
1991 03686
1992 03917

Model MF1030-4
Left side of clutch housing.
1984 40101
1985 40600
1986 41245
1987 42167
1988 42594
1989 42953
1990 43251
1991 43492
1992 44024

Model MF1035-2
Left side of clutch housing.
1986 00100
1987 00315
1988 None
1989 00540
1990 00585
1991 00729
1992 00872

Model MF1035-4
Left side of clutch housing.
1986 40100
1987 40377
1988 40691
1989 40936
1990 41058
1991 41223
1992 41388

Model MF1040-2
Left side of clutch housing.
1984 00101
1985 00155
1986 00552

Model MF1040-4
Left side of clutch housing.
1984 40101
1985 40351
1986 40562
1987 40773

Model MF1045-2
Left side of clutch housing.
1986 00100
1987 00234
1988 None
1989 None
1990 00334
1991 00367
1992 00399

Model MF1045-4
Left side of clutch housing.
1986 40100
1987 40275
1988 40566
1989 40757
1990 41144
1991 41531
1992 41916

Model MF1080
1967 9B10001
1968 9B14693
1969 9B18673
1970 9B23486
1971 9B28238
1972 9B31959

Model MF1085
Left side ahead of instrument panel.
1972 9B36563
1973 9B36841
1974 9B42685
1975 9B50494
1976 9B58735
1977 9B66276
1978 9B74241
1979 9B76058

Model MF1100
Right side forward of transmission.
1965 650000174
1966 650001997
1967 650005482
1967 late 9B10001
1968 9B14693
1969 9B18673
1970 9B23486
1971 9B28238
1972 9B31959

Model MF1105
Left side ahead of instrument panel.
1972 9B36563
1973 9B36851
1974 9B42685
1975 9B50494
1976 9B58735
1977 9B66276
1978 9B74241
1979 9B76058

Model MF1130
Right side forward of transmission.
1965 651500022
1966 651500082
1967 651501613
1967 late 9B10001
1968 9B14693
1969 9B18673
1970 9B23486
1971 9B28238
1972 9B31959

Model MF1135
Left side ahead of instrument panel.
1972 9B36563
1973 9B36841
1974 9B42685
1975 9B50494
1976 9B58735
1977 9B66276
1978 9B74241
1979 9B76058

Model MF1150
Right side forward of transmission.
1967 9B10001
1968 9B14693
1969 9B18673
1970 9B23486
1971 9B28238
1972 9B31959

Model MF1155
Left side ahead of instrument panel.
1972 9B36563
1973 9B36851
1974 9B42685
1975 9B50494
1976 9B58735
1977 9B66276
1978 9B74241
1979 9B76058

Model MF1160
1992 A70101
1993 B70101
1994 C00101
1995 D00101
1996 E00101
1997 F00101

Model MF1180
1992 A80101
1993 B80101
1994 C00101
1995 D00101
1996 E00101
1997 F00101

Model MF1190
1992 A90101
1993 B90101
1994 C00101
1995 D00101
1996 E00101
1997 F00101

Model MF135
Steering column below instrument panel.
1964 641000003
1965 641004422
1966 641016741
1967 641024446
1967 late 9A1000
1968 9A39836
1969 9A63148
1970 9A87325
1971 9A107597
1972 9A128141
1973 9A152025
1974 9A179544
1975 9A207681

Model MF150
Steering column below instrument panel.
1964 642000003
1965 642000859
1966 642003946
1967 642005474
1967 late 9A1000
1968 9A39836
1969 9A63158
1970 9A87325
1971 9A107597
1972 9A128141
1973 9A152025
1974 9A179544
1975 9A207681

Model MF1500
Left of instrument panel.
1971 9C1000
1972 9C1912
1973 9C2462
1974 9C3025

Model MF1505
Left of instrument panel.
1974 9C3601
1975 9C4227
1976 9C6086
1977 9C7858

Model MF154-2S
Lower right side of instrument console.
1986 13300288
1987 133A00489
1988 133C00645
1989 133C00791

Model MF154-4
Front of instrument console and left rear of center housing casting.
1980 2226706
1981 2227212
1982 2229282
1983 2229927
1984 2210485

Model MF154-4S
Front of instrument console and left rear of center housing casting.
1986 23300755
1987 233A01012
1988 233C01304
1989 233C01511

Model MF165
Steering column below instrument panel.
1964 643000003
1965 643000481
1966 643007763
1967 643014673
1967 late 9A1000
1968 9A39836
1969 9A63158
1970 9A87325
1971 9A107597
1972 9A128141
1973 9A152025
1974 9A179544
1975 9A207681

Model MF174-2S
Front of instrument console and left rear of center housing casting.
1986 13200653
1987 132A00912
1988 132C01178
1989 132C01413

Model MF174-4S
Front of instrument console and left rear of center housing casting.
1986 23201344
1987 232A01754
1988 232C02271
1989 232C02679

Model MF175
Steering column below instrument panel.
1964 644000001
1965 644001494
1966 644003041
1967 9A1000
1968 9A39836
1969 9A63158
1970 9A87325
1971 9A107597
1972 9A128141
1973 9A152025
1974 9A179544
1975 9A207681

Model MF180
Steering column below instrument panel.
1965 645000007
1966 645002423
1967 645004713
1967 late....... 9A1000
1968 .... 9A39836
1969 .... 9A63158
1970 .... 9A87325
1971 .... 9A107597
1972 .... 9A128141
1973 .... 9A152025
1974 .... 9A179544
1975 .... 9A207681

Model MF1800
Top of cab plenum chamber.
1971 .... 9C1000
1972 .... 9C1912
1973 .... 9C2462
1974 .... 9C3025

Model MF1805
Left of instrument panel.
1974 .... 9C3601
1975 .... 9C4227
1976 .... 9C6086
1977 .... 9C7858
1978 .... 9C8810

Model MF184-4
Front of instrument console and left rear of center housing casting.
1976 22000001
1977 22000930
1978 22001860
1979 22002789
1980 22003890
1981 22046000

Model MF194-2F
Lower right side of instrument console.
1986 14000014
1987 .... 140D00024
1988 .... 140D00037
1989 .... 140D00062

Model MF194-4F
Lower right side of instrument console.
1986 24000129
1987 .... 240D00382
1988 .... 240D00925
1989 .... 240D01456

Model MF205
Steering column below instrument panel.
1978 00101
1979 00315
1980 00683
1981 01512
1982 01966
1983 02159
1984 02337

Model MF205-4
Steering column below instrument panel.
1979 00101
1980 00677
1981 00916
1982 01390
1983 01440
1984 01516

Model MF210
Steering column below instrument panel.
1978 00101
1979 00961
1980 01711
1981 02700
1982 03892
1983 04231
1984 04902

Model MF210-4
Steering column below instrument panel.
1979 00101
1980 00711
1981 00764
1982 01595
1983 01915
1984 02209

Model MF220
Steering column below instrument panel.
1978 00101
1979 00300
1980 00552
1981 00750
1982 01339
1983 01458
1984 01708

Model MF220-4
Steering column below instrument panel.
1979 00101
1980 00520
1981 00868
1982 01673
1983 01981
1984 02163

Model MF230
Steering column below instrument panel.
1974 .... 9A202190
1975 .... 9A207681
1976 .... 9A232539
1977 .... 9A254045
1978 .... 9A276935
1979 .... 9A296946
1980 .... 9A326169
1981 .... 9A339343
1982 .... 9A350584
1983 .... 9A354679

Model MF231
Lower right side of instrument console.
1989 .... P17001
1990 .... Q01001
1990 .... R01001
1991 .... S01001
1992 .... A01001
1993 .... B01001
1994 .... C01002
1995 .... D01001
1996 .... E01001
1997 .... F01001

Model MF235
Lower left side of instrument console.
1972 .... 9A128141
1973 .... 9A152025
1974 .... 9A179544
1975 .... 9A207681
1976 .... 9A232539

Model MF240
Lower right side of instrument console.
1983 524172
1984 552016
1985 557882
1986 562369
1987 .... V01001
1988 .... N01001
1989 .... P01001
1990 .... R01001
1991 .... S01001
1992 .... A01001
1993 .... B01001
1994 .... C01001
1995 .... D01001
1996 .... E01001
1997 .... F01001

Model MF245
Steering column below instrument panel.
1974 .... 9A202190
1975 .... 9A207681
1976 .... 9A232539
1977 .... 9A254045
1978 .... 9A276935
1979 .... 9A296946
1980 .... 9A326169
1981 .... 9A339343
1982 .... 9A350584
1983 .... 9A354679

Model MF250
Lower right side of instrument console.
1983 621838
1984 624021
1985 627250
1986 629926
1987 632601

Model MF253
Lower right side of instrument console.
1988 .... N01001
1989 .... P01001
1990 .... R01001
1991 .... S01001
1992 .... A01001
1993 .... B01001
1994 .... C01001
1995 .... D01001
1996 .... E01001
1997 .... F01001

Model MF254-4
1982 2229282
1983 2229927
1984 22210485
1985 .... 222M01750
1986 22202733
1987 22203556
1988 22204689

Model MF255, MF265
Steering column below instrument panel.
1974 .... 9A202190
1975 .... 9A207681
1976 .... 9A232539
1977 .... 9A254045
1978 .... 9A276935
1979 .... 9A296946
1980 .... 9A326169
1981 .... 9A339343
1982 .... 9A350584
1983 .... 9A354679

Model MF261
Steering column below instrument panel.
1992 .... A22001
1993 .... B01001
1994 .... C01001
1995 .... D01001
1996 .... E01001
1997 .... F01001

Model MF2640
Right side ahead of instrument panel.
1982 .... S276213
1983 .... B160217
1983 .... K181026

Model MF2675, MF2705, MF2745, MF2775 & MF2805
Left side of instrument console.
1976 .... 9R000001
1977 .... 9R000048
1978 .... 9R000602
1979 .... 9R002782
1980 .... 9R007282
1981 .... 9R010307
1982 .... 9R013230
1983 .... 9R013525

Model MF270
Lower right side of instrument console.
1983 286152
1984 287179
1985 288016
1986 288425
1987 288835

Model MF274-4
1982 22111297
1983 22112162
1984 22112828
1985 .... 221N02384
1986 22103628
1987 22104826
1988 22106115

Model MF275
Steering column below instrument panel.
1974 .... 9A202190
1975 .... 9A207681
1976 .... 9A232539
1977 .... 9A254015
1978 .... 9A276935
1979 .... 9A296946
1980 .... 9A326169
1981 .... 9A339343
1982 .... 9A350584
1983 .... 9A354679

Model MF283
1988 00102
1989 01202
1990 .... R01001
1991 02052
1992 .... A01001
1993 .... B01001
1994 .... C01001
1995 .... D01001
1996 .... E01001
1997 .... F01001

Model MF285
Steering column below instrument panel.
1974 .... 9A202190
1975 .... 9A207681
1976 .... 9A232539
1977 .... 9A254045
1978 .... 9A276935
1979 .... 9A296946
1980 .... 9A326169
1981 .... 9A339343
1982 .... 9A350584
1983 .... 9A344679

Model MF290
Lower right side of instrument console.
1983 286453
1984 289947
1985 393422
1986 723909
1987 454396
1988 454983

Model MF294-4
Lower right side of instrument console.
1982 2235938
1983 2236290
1984 2236511
1985 .... 223D00915
1986 22301652
1987 22302505
1988 23303121

Model MF298
Lower right side of instrument console.
1983 702586
1984 703062
1985 703760
1986 704095

Model MF3050
On implement control panel right side of operator.
1986 .... U031001
1987 .... V001001
1988 .... N001001
1989 .... P001001
1990 .... R001001
1991 .... S001001
1992 .... A001001

Model MF3060, MF3070, MF3090
On implement control panel right side of operator.
1986 .... U031001
1987 .... V001001
1988 .... N001001
1989 .... P001001
1990 .... R001001
1991 .... S001001
1992 .... A001001

Model MF3120, MF3140
On implement control panel right side of operator.
1990 .... R001001
1991 .... S001001
1992 .... A001001

Model MF35
1960 203202
1961 211072
1962 223896
1963 237276
1964 247605

Model MF3505
Right side ahead of instrument panel.
1983 .... K241203
1984 .... T101201
1985 .... L101201
1986 .... U031201
1987 .... V001201

Model MF3525
Right side ahead of instrument panel.
1983 .... K241213
1984 .... T101201
1985 .... L101201
1986 .... U031201
1987 .... V001201
1988 .... N001001

Model MF3545
Right side ahead of instrument panel.
1983 .... K242206
1984 .... T101201
1985 .... L101201
1986 .... U031201
1987 .... V001201
1988 .... N001001

Model MF360
Lower right side of steering cover.
1986 .... U01001
1987 .... V01001
1988 .... N01001
1989 .... P01001
1990 .... R01001
1991 .... S01001
1992 .... A01001
1993 .... B01001

Model MF362
Lower right side of steering cover.
1990 .... R01001
1991 .... S01001
1992 .... A01001
1993 .... B01001
1995 .... C01001
1996 .... D01001
1997 .... E01001

Model MF3630, MF3650
On implement control panel right side of operator.
1987 .... V001001
1988 .... N001001
1989 .... P001001
1990 .... R001001
1991 .... S001001
1992 .... A001001

Model MF364S, 374S, 384S, 394S
Lower right side of instrument console.
1989 .... P01001
1990 .... R01001
1991 .... S01001
1992 .... A01001
1993 .... B01001

Model MF3660
On implement control panel right side of operator.
1990 .... R001001
1991 .... S001001
1992 .... A001001

Model MF3680
On implement control panel right side of operator.
1988 .... N293001
1989 .... P001001
1990 .... R001001
1991 .... S001001
1992 .... A001001

MASSEY FERGUSON (Cont.)

Model MF375
Lower right side of steering cover.

1987	V01001
1988	N01001
1989	P01001
1990	R01001
1991	S01001
1992	A01001
1993	B01001
1994	C01001
1995	D01001
1996	E01001
1997	F01001

Model MF383
Lower right side of steering cover.

1987	V01001
1988	N01001
1989	P01001
1990	R01001
1991	S01001
1992	A01001
1993	B01001
1994	C01001
1995	D01001
1996	E01001
1997	F01001

Model MF390
Lower right side of steering cover.

1987	V01001
1988	N01001
1989	P01001
1990	R01001
1991	S01001
1992	A01001
1993	B01001
1994	C01001
1995	D01001
1996	E01001
1997	F01001

Model MF390T
Lower right side of steering cover.

1989	P01001
1990	R01001
1991	S01001
1992	A01001
1993	B01001
1994	C01001
1995	D01001
1996	E01001
1997	F01001

Model MF396
Lower right side of steering cover.

1992	A01001
1993	B01001
1994	C01001
1995	D01001
1996	E01001
1997	F01001

Model MF398
Lower right side of steering cover.

1987	V01001
1988	N01001
1989	P01001
1990	R01001
1991	S01001
1992	A01001
1993	B01001
1994	C01001
1995	D01001
1996	E01001
1997	F01001

Model MF399
Lower right side of steering cover.

1987	V01001
1988	N01001
1989	P01001
1990	R01001
1991	S01001
1992	A01001
1993	B01001
1994	C01001
1995	D01001
1996	E01001
1997	F01001

Model MF4800, MF4840, MF4880 & MF4900
Right rear of cab.

1978	9D001001
1979	9D001008
1980	9D002102
1981	9F002752
1982	9D003515
1983	9D003897
1984	9D004196
1985	9D004446
1986	9D004826
1987	9D005476
1988	9D006241

Model MF50
Plate on instrument panel.

1957	510764
1958	515708
1959	522693
1960	528163
1961	528419
1962	530416
1963	533851
1964	536063

Model MF65
Right side of instrument panel.

1958	650001
1959	661164
1960	671379
1961	680210
1962	685370
1963	693040
1964	701057

Model MF670
Left of clutch pedal on plate on side of instrument panel shroud.

1983	K183027
1983	B207021
1984	T101001
1985	L101001
1986	U031001

Model MF690
Left of clutch pedal on plate on side of instrument panel shroud.

1983	B197022
1983	K181026
1984	T101001
1985	L101001
1986	U031001
1987	V034001

Model MF698
Left of clutch pedal on plate on side of instrument panel shroud.

1983	B201031
1983	K186009
1984	T101001
1985	L101001
1986	U031001

Model MF699
Left of clutch pedal on plate on side of instrument panel shroud.

1984	T101001
1985	L101001
1986	U031001
1987	V034001

Model MF85
Right side of battery box.

1958	800001
1959	800048
1960	804355
1961	807750
1962	808564
1963	1001
1964	1353
1965	1775
1966	1995

Model MF88
Right side of battery box.

1959	880001
1960	881453
1961	882229
1962	882496

Model MF90
Right side of battery box.

1962	810000
1963	813170
1964	816113
1965	819342
1966	0001
1967	0305
1968	0501
1969	0840
1970	1101
1971	1632

Model MF90WR

1962	885000
1963	835870
1964	886829
1965	888238

Model MF97

1962	25200001
1963	25200506
1964	25202005
1965	25203504

MASSEY HARRIS

Model 101 Jr.
Rear left side of frame forward of transmission case.

1939	375001
1940	377928
1941	379500
1942	379815
1943	379855
1944	380641
1945	382569
1946	384288

Model 101 Sr. Row Crop
Rear left side of frame forward of transmisssion case.

1938	255001
1939	256085
1940	257281
1941	258769
1942	259762
1943	260430
1944	260796
1945	263020
1945	270001
1946	270145

Model 101 Sr. Standard
Rear left side of frame forward of transmission case.

1938	355001
1939	355603
1940	356792
1941	358188
1942	358869
1943	358975
1944	359458
1945	360927
1946	362520

Model 102 Jr. Row Crop
Rear left side of frame forward of transmission case.

1939	387001
1940	387031
1941	387127
1942	387419
1943	387601
1944	387844
1945	388240
1946	388995

Model 102 Jr. Standard
Rear left side of frame forward of transmission case.

1939	385001
1940	385204
1941	385450
1942	386099
1943	386662
1944	390001
1945	390994
1946	391913

Model 102 Sr.
Rear left side of frame forward of transmission case.

1941	365001
1942	365202
1943	366062
1944	366183
1945	367535

Model 20 Row Crop

1946	1001
1947	1580
1948	3584

Model 20 Standard

1947	1001
1948	2230

Model 201
Rear left side of frame forward of transmission case.

1940	91201
1941	91704

Model 202
Left side of main frame.

1941	95001
1942	95224
1943	95444
1944	95654

Model 203
Left side of main frame.

1940	95001
1941	95002
1942	95182
1943	95202
1944	95223
1945	95259
1946	95295
1947	95338

Model 20K Row Crop

1947	1001
1948	1354

Model 20K Standard

1947	1001
1948	2230

Model 21 Colt
Rear left side of frame forward of transmission case.

1952	1001
1953	1417
1954	2629
1955	4256
1956	5886
1957	7511

Model 22 Row Crop
Rear left side of frame forward of transmission case.

1948	1001
1949	2096
1950	4580
1951	7624
1952	10145
1953	20046
1954	20585
1955	28705

Model 22 Standard
Rear left side of frame forward of transmission case.

1948	1001
1949	1542
1950	3208
1951	4533
1952	5717
1953	20046
1954	20585
1955	24375

Model 22K Row Crop
Rear left side of frame forward of transmission case.

1948	1001
1949	1154
1950	1488
1951	1570
1952	1748
1953	20001
1954	20585
1955	28705

Model 22K Standard
Rear left side of frame forward of transmission case.

1948	1001
1949	1317
1950	1488
1951	1570
1952	1748
1953	20001
1954	20585
1955	28705

Model 23 Mustang
Rear left side of frame forward of transmission case.

1952	1001
1953	1666
1954	4346
1955	4553
1956	4773

Model 30 Row Crop
Rear left side of frame forward of transmission case.

1946	1001
1947	1002
1948	3386
1949	6825
1950	9345
1951	13816
1952	17934
1952	30001
1953	30596

Model 30 Standard
Rear left side of frame forward of transmission case.

1946	1001
1947	1002
1948	2120
1949	3194
1950	5368
1951	7491
1952	8696
1952	30001
1953	30596

Model 30K Row Crop
Rear left side of frame forward of transmission case.

1947	1001
1948	1225
1949	2010
1950	2393
1951	2719
1952	30001
1953	30596

Model 30K Standard
Rear left side of frame forward of transmission case.

1947	1001
1948	1894
1949	3251
1950	3531
1951	3861
1952	30001
1953	30596

MASSEY HARRIS (Cont.)

Model 33
Rear left side of frame forward of transmission case.

1952	1001
1953	2055
1954	6617
1955	9782

Model 333
Rear left side of frame forward of transmission case.

1956	20001
1957	22649
1958	22950

Model 44 Row Crop
Rear left side of frame forward of transmission case.

1947	1002
1948	2048
1949	5312
1950	13828
1951	21815
1952	31275
1953	43700
1954	51364
1955	58067

Model 44 Special
Rear left side of frame forward of transmission case.

1946	1001
1947	1141
1948	1871
1949	4528
1950	9581
1951	13726
1952	40001
1952	17059
1953	50001
1954	51364
1955	58067

Model 44 Standard
Rear left side of frame forward of transmission case.

1946	1001
1947	1141
1948	1871
1949	4528
1950	9581
1951	13726
1952	17059
1953	43700
1954	51364
1955	58067

Model 44-6 Row Crop
Rear left side of frame forward of transmission case.

1947	1002
1948	2983
1949	4755
1950	5255
1951	5509

Model 44-6 Standard
Rear left side of frame forward of transmission case.

1947	1001
1948	2001
1949	2601
1950	2730

Model 444
Rear left side of frame forward of transmission case.

1956	70001
1957	73989
1958	22950

Model 44D Row Crop
Rear left side of frame forward of transmission case.

1949	1001
1950	1004
1951	2483
1952	4704
1953	43700
1954	51364
1955	58067

Model 44D Standard
Rear left side of frame forward of transmission case.

1948	1001
1949	1023
1950	2180
1951	3989
1952	5639
1953	43700
1954	51364
1955	58067

Model 44K Row Crop
Rear left side of frame forward of transmission case.

1947	1001
1948	1079
1949	1856
1950	2599
1951	3329
1952	4001
1953	43700
1954	51364
1955	58067

Model 44K Standard
Rear left side of frame forward of transmission case.

1947	1001
1948	1441
1949	3598
1950	4827
1951	6019
1952	6787
1953	43700
1954	51364
1955	58067

Model 55
Rear left side of frame forward of transmission case.

1946	1001
1947	1116
1948	2132
1949	3581
1950	5468
1951	6399
1952	10001
1953	13017
1954	15299
1955	17059

Model 555
Rear left side of frame forward of transmission case.

1955	20001
1956	20133
1957	21133
1958	22950

Model 55D
Rear left side of frame forward of transmission case.

1949	1001
1950	1022
1951	2058
1952	2822
1953	13017
1954	15299
1955	17059

Model 55K
Rear left side of frame forward of transmission case.

1946	1001
1947	1013
1948	1554
1949	3033
1950	4078
1951	4808
1952	5503
1953	13017
1954	15299
1955	17059

Model 81 Row Crop
Rear left side of frame forward of transmission case.

1941	400001
1942	403168
1943	403211
1944	403354
1945	403364
1946	403464
1947	403564
1948	404664

Model 81 Standard
Rear left side of frame forward of transmission case.

1941	425001
1942	425678
1943	425717
1944	425757
1945	425780
1946	426803

Model 82 Row Crop
Rear left side of frame forward of transmission case.

1941	420001
1942	420055
1943	420128
1944	420201
1945	420274
1946	420307

Model 82 Standard
Rear left side of frame forward of transmission case.

1941	435001
1942	435279
1943	435452
1944	435455
1945	435458
1946	435738

Model MH11 Pony
Right side of front frame.

1947	PGA1001
1948	PGA1382
1949	PGA5501
1950	PGA10817
1951	PGA13591
1952	PGA17994
1953	20571
1954	23149
1955	25727
1956	28305
1957	30883

Model MH16 Pacer

1954	50001
1955	51613
1956	53212
1957	54724

Model MH50

1955	500001
1956	500473

MINNEAPOLIS-MOLINE

Model 1050 LP
Side of transmission case.

1969	43000001
1970	43000041
1971	43000061
1972	43000106

Model 335 Universal
Side of transmission case.

1957	11600001
1958	11600302
1959	11600307

Model 335 Utility
Side of transmission case.

1956	10400001
1957	10400102
1958	10402088
1959	10402337
1960	10402440
1961	10402490

Model 445 Diesel Utility
Side of transmission case.

1959	15400001
1960	15400018

Model 445 Universal
Side of transmission case.

1956	10100001
1957	10102855
1958	10104126
1959	10104805

Model 445 Utility
Side of transmission case.

1956	10200001
1957	10201446
1958	10202102
1959	10202243

Model 5 Star Diesel Standard
Side of transmission case.

1958	14500001
1959	14500166
1960	14500189

Model 5 Star Diesel Universal
Side of transmission case.

1957	14400001
1958	14400204
1959	14400786
1960	14401296

Model 5 Star Standard
Side of transmission case.

1958	11200001
1959	11200212
1960	11800022

Model 5 Star Universal
Side of transmission case.

1957	11000001
1958	11001058
1959	11002068
1960	11700060
1961	18900041

Model A4T-1600 Diesel

1970	45600001
1971	45600188
1972	45600701

Model A4T-1600 LP

1970	45700001
1971	45700127
1972	45700198

Model BF
Right frame rail.

1950	R500
1951	R1839
1952	R4460
1953	57900001
1954	57900601
1955	57900769
1956	57900938
1957	57901106

Model BFD

1953	57700001
Last Number	57700358

Model BFH

1953	58000001
Last Number	58000150

Model BFS

1953	57600001
Last Number	57600047

Model BFW

1953	6538
Last Number	R7571

Model BG
Right frame rail.

1950	500
1951	1839
1952	4460
1953	6538
1953	57900001
1954	57900601
1955	57900769
1956	57900938

Model G1000 Diesel Row Crop
Side of transmission case.

1965	30600001
1966	30600501
1967	30601126
1968	30601286

Model G1000 Row Crop
Side of transmission case.

1965	30500001
1966	30500451
1967	30500927
1968	30501042

Model G1000 Vista
Side of transmission case.

1967	34500011

Model G1000 Vista D
Side of transmission case.

1968	34600016
1969	34600736
1970	34601186

Model G1000 Vista LP
Side of transmission case.

1967	34500011
1968	34500291
1969	34500391
1970	34500791

Model G1000 Wheatland
Side of transmission case.

1966	32600001
1967	32600516
1968	32600651
1969	None
1970	32600653

Model G1000 Wheatland D
Side of transmission case.

1966	32700001
1967	32700734
1968	32701451
1969	None
1970	32701775

Model G1050 Diesel
Side of transmission case.

1969	43100001
1970	43100286
1971	43100416

Model G1050LP
Side of transmission case.

1969	43000001
1970	43000041
1971	43000061
1972	43000106

Model G1350 Diesel
Side of transmission case.

1970	43300001
1971	43300043
1972	43300254

Model G1350 LP
Side of transmission case.

1971	43200045
1972	43200098

Model G1350 Row Crop LP
Side of transmission case.

1969	43200001
1970	43200023

Model G1355
Side of transmission case.
- 1972 ... 236442
- 1973 ... 237875
- 1974 ... 245258

Model G704
Side of transmission case.
- 1962 ... 23400001

Model G704 Diesel
Side of transmission case.
- 1962 ... 23500001

Model G705
Side of transmission case.
- 1962 ... 23800001
- 1963 ... 23800079
- 1964 ... 23800591
- 1965 ... 23801093

Model G705 Diesel
Side of transmission case.
- 1962 ... 23900001
- 1963 ... 23900051
- 1964 ... 23900899
- 1965 ... 23901869

Model G706
Side of transmission case.
- 1962 ... 24000001
- 1963 ... 24000073
- 1964 ... 24000306
- 1965 ... 24000351

Model G706 Diesel
Side of transmission case.
- 1962 ... 24100001
- 1963 ... 24100107
- 1964 ... 24100550
- 1965 ... 24100796

Model G707
Side of transmission case.
- 1965 ... 31200001

Model G707 Diesel
Side of transmission case.
- 1965 ... 31300001

Model G708
Side of transmission case.
- 1965 ... 31400001

Model G708 Diesel
Side of transmission case.
- 1965 ... 31500001

Model G900
Side of transmission case.
- 1967 ... 33000001
- 1968 ... 33000111
- 1969 ... 33000548

Model G900 Diesel
Side of transmission case.
- 1967 ... 33100001
- 1968 ... 33100317
- 1969 ... 33101377

Model G900 LP
Side of transmission case.
- 1969 ... 36300001

Model G950 Diesel
Side of transmission case.
- 1969 ... 43600001
- 1970 ... 43600211
- 1971 ... 43600416
- 1972 ... 43600830

Model G950 LP
Side of transmission case.
- 1969 ... 43500001
- 1970 ... 43500061
- 1971 ... 43500086

Model G955
Side of transmission case.
- 1973 ... 239825
- 1974 ... 244559

Model GB
Side of transmission case.
- 1955 ... 08900001
- 1956 ... 08901501
- 1957 ... 08902602
- 1958 ... 08903402
- 1959 ... 08904252

Model GBD
Side of transmission case.
- 1955 ... 09000001
- 1956 ... 09000851
- 1957 ... 09001526
- 1958 ... 09002146
- 1959 ... 09002656

Model GT
Side of transmission.
- 1938 ... 160001
- 1939 ... 160077
- 1940 ... 160580
- 1941 ... 160879

Model GTA
Side of transmission case.
- 1942 ... 162001
- 1943 ... 162301
- 1944 ... 162303
- 1945 ... 162660
- 1946 ... 162870
- 1947 ... 163220

Model GTB
Side of transmission case.
- 1947 ... 164001
- 1948 ... 0164800001
- 1949 ... 0164900001
- 1950 ... 016500001
- 1951 ... 01601864
- 1952 ... 01603397
- 1953 ... 01604890
- 1954 ... 01605973

Model GTBD
Side of transmission case.
- 1953 ... 06800001
- 1954 ... 06800002

Model GTC
Side of transmission case.
- 1951 ... 04700001
- 1952 ... 04700019
- 1953 ... 04700677

Model GVI
Side of transmission case.
- 1959 ... 16000002
- 1960 ... 16000877
- 1961 ... 16001676
- 1962 ... 16002033

Model GVI Diesel
Side of transmission case.
- 1959 ... 16200001
- 1960 ... 16200806
- 1961 ... 16201891
- 1962 ... 16202961

Model Jet Star
Side of transmission case.
- 1959 ... 16500001
- 1960 ... 16500285
- 1961 ... 16500835
- 1962 ... 16501702

Model Jet Star 2
Side of transmission case.
- 1963 ... 25800001

Model Jet Star 2 Diesel
Side of transmission case.
- 1963 ... 25700001

Model Jet Star 3
Side of transmission case.
- 1964 ... 28300001
- 1965 ... 28301001
- 1966 ... 28300002
- 1967 ... 28302895
- 1968 ... 28304156
- 1969 ... 28304801
- 1970 ... 28305086

Model Jet Star 3 Diesel
Side of transmission case.
- 1964 ... 28400001
- 1965 ... 28400051
- 1966 ... 28400201
- 1967 ... 28400386
- 1968 ... 28400464
- 1969 ... 28400527
- 1970 ... 28400602

Model Jet Star Diesel
Side of transmission case.
- 1960 ... 17500011
- 1961 ... 17500061
- 1962 ... 17500136

Model M5
Side of transmission case.
- 1960 ... 17100001
- 1961 ... 17101536
- 1962 ... 17103496
- 1963 ... 17104708

Model M5 Diesel
Side of transmission case.
- 1960 ... 17200001
- 1961 ... 17201041
- 1962 ... 17202000
- 1963 ... 17202507

Model M504
Side of transmission case.
- 1962 ... 24300001

Model M504 Diesel
Side of transmission case.
- 1962 ... 24200001
- 1963 ... 24200021

Model M602
Side of transmission case.
- 1963 ... 26600001
- 1964 ... 26601276

Model M602 Diesel
Side of transmission case.
- 1963 ... 26700001
- 1964 ... 26700743

Model M604
Side of transmission case.
- 1963 ... 26800001
- 1964 ... 26800051

Model M604 Diesel
Side of transmission case.
- 1963 ... 26900001
- 1964 ... 26900051

Model M670
Side of transmission case.
- 1964 ... 29900001
- 1965 ... 29900007
- 1966 ... 29901892
- 1967 ... 29903580
- 1968 ... 29904455
- 1969 ... 29904595
- 1970 ... 29905005

Model M670 Diesel
Side of transmission case.
- 1964 ... 30000001
- 1965 ... 30000005
- 1966 ... 30000820
- 1967 ... 30001635
- 1968 ... 30002310
- 1969 ... 30002570
- 1970 ... 30002861

Model RT
Side of transmission case.
- 1939 ... 400001
- 1940 ... 402201
- 1941 ... 405576
- 1942 ... 407951
- 1943 ... 408826
- 1944 ... 409358
- 1945 ... 410748
- 1946 ... 413755
- 1947 ... 416545
- 1948 ... 0014800001
- 1948 ... 0044800001
- 1948 ... 0034800001
- 1949 ... 0024900001
- 1949 ... 0034900001
- 1949 ... 0044900001
- 1949 ... 0014900001

Model RTE
Side of transmission case.
- 1948 ... 044800001
- 1949 ... 044900001
- 1950 ... 0045000001
- 1951 ... 00400205
- 1952 ... 00400282
- 1953 ... 00400283
- Last Number ... 00400287

Model RTN
Side of transmission case.
- 1948 ... 0034800001
- 1949 ... 0034900001
- 1950 ... 0035000001
- 1951 ... 00300094
- Last Number ... 00300173

Model RTS
Side of transmission case.
- 1949 ... 0024900001
- 1950 ... 0025000001
- 1951 ... 00200301
- 1952 ... 00200402
- 1953 ... 00200552
- Last Number ... 00200701

Model RTU
Side of transmission case.
- 1948 ... 0014800001
- 1949 ... 0014900001
- 1950 ... 0015000001
- 1951 ... 00102156
- 1952 ... 00103973
- 1953 ... N/A
- 1954 ... 00104824
- Last Number ... 00104831

Model U & UT
Side of transmission case.
- 1938 ... 310026
- 1939 ... 310626
- 1940 ... 312451
- 1941 ... 314893
- 1942 ... 316501
- 1943 ... 317702
- 1944 ... 318163
- 1945 ... 321102
- 1946 ... 325231
- 1947 ... 329752
- 1948 ... 337418
- Last Number ... 339682

Model U302
Side of transmission case.
- 1964 ... 27600001
- 1965 ... 27601001
- 1966 ... 27601301
- 1967 ... 27602301
- 1968 ... 27602360
- 1969 ... 27602760
- 1970 ... 27602860

Model U302 Diesel
Side of transmission case.
- 1967 ... 27700001
- 1968 ... 27700101
- 1969 ... 27700151
- 1970 ... 27700165

Model UB Special
Side of transmission case.
- 1955 ... 09700001
- Last Number ... 09701475

Model UBD Special
Side of transmission case.
- 1955 ... 09800001
- 1956 ... 09800301
- 1957 ... 09800465
- Last Number ... 09800521

Model UBE
Side of transmission case.
- 1953 ... 05900001
- 1954 ... 05900897
- 1955 ... 05901069
- Last Number ... 05901421

Model UBED
Side of transmission case.
- 1954 ... 07000001
- 1955 ... 07000232
- Last Number ... 07000362

Model UBG
Side of transmission case.
- 1953 ... 05900001

Model UBN
Side of transmission case.
- 1953 ... 06000001
- 1954 ... 06000203
- 1955 ... 06000208
- Last Number ... 06000241

Model UBND
Side of transmission case.
- 1953 ... 06000001
- 1954 ... 06000203

Model UBU
Side of transmission case.
- 1953 ... 05800001
- 1954 ... 05802913
- 1955 ... 05804003
- Last Number ... 05805077

Model UBUD
Side of transmission case.
- 1954 ... 07800001
- 1955 ... 07800747
- Last Number ... 07801041

Model UDS & UTSD
Side of transmission case.
- 1952 ... 05000001
- 1953 ... 05000010
- 1954 ... 05000019
- 1955 ... 05000955
- 1956 ... 05002105

Model UDU
Side of transmission case.
- 1952 ... 04900001
- 1953 ... 04900002
- Last Number ... 04900030

Model UTC
Side of transmission case.
- 1948 ... 0154800001
- 1949 ... 0154900001
- 1950 ... 0155000001
- 1951 ... 01500101
- 1952 ... 01500181
- 1953 ... 01500201
- 1954 ... 10500266
- 1954 ... 08800001
- 1955 ... 08800061
- Last Number ... 08800110

Model UTE
Side of transmission case.
- 1951 ... 04300001
- 1952 ... 04300112
- 1953 ... 04300262
- Last Number ... 04300265

Model UTN
Side of transmission case.
- 1950 ... 0385000001
- 1951 ... 03800102
- 1952 ... 03800205
- Last Number ... 03800354

Model UTS
Side of transmission case.
- 1948 ... 0124800001
- 1949 ... 0124900001
- 1950 ... 0125000001
- 1951 ... 01203851
- 1952 ... 01207139
- 1953 ... 01210571
- 1954 ... 01213220
- 1955 ... 01213326
- 1956 ... 01214126
- 1957 ... 01215101

Model UTSD-M
Side of transmission case.
- 1955 ... 05001155
- 1956 ... 10600001
- 1957 ... 10800246
- 1958 ... 10800391

Model UTU
Side of transmission case.
- 1948 ... 0114800001
- 1949 ... 0114900001
- 1950 ... 0115000001
- 1951 ... 01105384
- 1952 ... 01110118
- 1953 ... 01113449
- 1954 ... 01113450
- 1955 ... 01113454

Model V
Side of transmission case.
- 1947 ... 1V144
- 1948 ... 2V577
- 1949 ... 4V490
- 1950 ... 5V501
- 1951 ... 6V207
- 1952 ... 6V422
- Last Number ... 7V271

MINNEAPOLIS-MOLINE (Cont.)

Model ZAE
Side of transmission case.
1949 0094900001
1950 0095000001
1951 00900374
1952 00900577
1953 00900998
1954 06300001
1955 06300076
1956 06300307
Last Number. . 00901122

Model ZAN
Side of transmission case.
1949 0084900001
1950 0085000001
1951 00800239
1952 00800443
1953 00800619
Last Number . . 00800620

Model ZAS
Side of transmission case.
1949 0074900001
1950 0075000001
1951 00700481
1952 00701286
1953 00701911
Last Number . . 00702610

Model ZAU
Side of transmission case.
1949 0064900001
1950 0065000001
1951 00605436
1952 00609940
Last Number . . 00614658

Model ZBE
Side of transmission case.
1953 06300001
1954 06300076
1955 06300307
Last Number . . 06300501

Model ZBN
Side of transmission case.
1954 06400001
1955 06400073
Last Number . . 06400106

Model ZBU
Side of transmission case.
1953 06200001
1954 06200958
1955 06202480
Last Number . . 06203059

Model ZM
Side of transmission case.
1953 07600001
1954 07600018

Model ZTN & ZTU
Side of transmission case.
1936 560001
1937 560038
1938 562975
1939 565407
1940 567155
1941 568755
1942 570822
1943 571422
1944 572968
1945 575713
1946 576814
1947 578014
1948. 581815
Last Number 585817

Model ZTS
Side of transmission case.
1937. 610001
1938. 610036
1939. 610389
1940. 610685
1941. 611088
1942. 611343
1943. 611447
1944. 611966
1945. 612486
1946. 612886
1947. 613086
Last Number 613490

OLIVER

Model 1250
1965 705376
1966 712833
1967 728661
1968 739527
1969 742526

Model 1250-A
1969 305985
1970 312957
1971 317338

Model 1255
1969 309381
1970 312957
1971 317000

Model 1265
1970 302402
1971 302458
1972 304497
1973 307221
1974 341369
1975 317900

Model 1350
1966 28302844
1967 28303141
1968 28304546

Model 1355
1969 503287
1970 512698
1971 524000

Model 1365
1971 706251
1972 706277
1973 714614
1974 725451
1975 729125

Model 1370
1973 714614
1974 725451
1975 729125

Model 1450
1967 132382
1968 147482
1969 155479

Model 1465
1973 827183
1974 827287
1975 827580

Model 1470
1973 827183
1974 827287
1975 827580

Model 1550
Rear side of instrument panel support.
1965 157841
1966 168919
1967 184488
1968 196301
1969 213243

Model 1555
Rear side of instrument panel support.
1969 218128
1970 221295
1971 236883
1971 223072
1972 232089
1974 244937
1975 256165

Model 1600A
Rear side of instrument panel support.
1962 124420
1963 127044

Model 1600B
Rear side of instrument panel support.
1963 137710
1964 140723

Model 1650
Rear side of instrument panel support.
1964 149836
1965 153855
1966 167668
1967 183923
1968 201091
1969 212733

Model 1655
Rear side of instrument panel support.
1969 218025
1970 222600
1971 222761
1972 231772
1973 236586
1974 244735
1975 257700

Model 1750
Rear side of instrument panel support.
1964 140893
1965 149835
1966 181062
1967 185301
1968 200217
1969 214936

Model 1755
Rear side of instrument panel support.
1970 221603
1971 226445
1972 231415
1973 238136
1974 245667
1975 257515

Model 18-27
1930 100001
1931 102649
1932 103319
1933 103618
1934 104039
1935 104851
1936 1073112
1937 108574

Model 18-28 99
1930 800001
1931 800460
1932 800964
1933. 800985
1934. 801051
1935. 801241
1936. 801990
1937. 802938

Model 1800A
Rear side of instrument panel support.
1960. 90525
1961. 111025
1962. 118344

Model 1800B
Rear side of instrument panel support.
1962. 124397
1963. 129286

Model 1800C
Rear side of instrument panel support.
1964. 140893

Model 1850
Rear side of instrument panel support.
1964. 150421
1965. 153421
1966. 168127
1967. 183382
1968. 200360
1969. 212673

Model 1855
Rear side of instrument panel support.
1969. 220640
1970. 221099
1971. 223507
1972. 231366
1973. 236585
1974. 247436
1975. 255727

Model 1900A
Rear side of instrument panel support.
1960. 90532
1961. 111028
1962. 118356

Model 1900B
Rear side of instrument panel support.
1962. 124396
1963. 128422

Model 1900C
Rear side of instrument panel support.
1963. 138440
1964. 141168

Model 1950
Rear side of instrument panel support.
1964. 150492
1965. 153016
1966. 168190
1967. 189009
1968. 200541
1969. 213355
1970. 223073
1971 225820
1972 233007
1973 237150
1974 244625

Model 1950T
Rear side of instrument panel support.
1967 188974
1968 201931
1969 213376

Model 1955
Rear side of instrument panel support.
1967 188974
1968 200084
1969 211194
1970 222304
1971 226458
1972 232958
1973 239032
1974 247871

Model 2050
Rear side of instrument panel support.
1968 204444
1969 212560

Model 2150
Rear side of instrument panel support.
1968 204480
1969 212554

Model 2255
Rear side of instrument panel support.
1972 235598
1973 237210
1974 244825
1975 258472
1976 266683

Model 28-44
1930 500001
1931 503600
1932 506185
1933 506212
1934 506255
1935 506401
1936 507176
1937 508016

Model 440
Left side of input shaft seal.
1960 87725
1962 121833
1963 122543

Model 550
Left side of center frame.
1953 51831
1954 51924
1955 51951
1956 52035
1957 56268
1958 60501
1959 72632
1960 84416
1961 111868
1962 117541
1963. 127365
1964. 140620
1965. 162265
1966. 171923
1967. 186165
1968. 206095
1969. 213340
1970. 222833
1971. 226965
1972. 232918
1973. 238237
1974. 248375
1975. 259255

Model 60 RC
Left front of engine.
1940. 600001
1941. 600071
1942. 606304
1943. 607395
1944. 608526
1945. 612047
1946. 615628
1947. 616707
1948. 620257

Model 60 Standard
Left front of engine.
1942. 410001
1943. 410501
1944. 410511
1945. 410617
1946. 410911
1947. 411311
1948. 411961

Model 66
Front right side of rear main frame and transmission.
1953. 3503990
1954. 4500309

Model 66 RC
Front right side of rear main frame and transmission.
1949. 420001
1950. 423101
1951. 426649
1952. 429771

Model 66 Standard
Front right side of rear main frame and transmission.
1949. 470004
1950. 471051
1951. 472792
1952. 474233
1953. 3510050
1954. 4500309

Model 660
Rear panel assembly.
1959. 73132
1960. 84554
1961. 111213
1962. 117873
1963. 127356
1964. 141160

OLIVER (Cont.)

Model 70 RC
Left front of engine.

1939	223255
1940	231116
1941	236356
1942	241391
1943	243640
1944	244711
1945	250180
1946	252780
1947	258140
1948	262840

Model 70 Standard
Left front of engine.

1937	300634
1938	302084
1939	303465
1940	305362
1941	306594
1942	307580
1943	308188
1944	308484
1945	310418
1946	311116
1947	312699
1948	314221

Model 77
Rear hood support panel below instrument panel.

1953	3500001
1954	4501667

Model 77 RC
Front right side of rear main frame and transmission.

1948	320001
1949	320241
1950	327901
1951	337243
1952	347904

Model 77 Standard
Front right side of rear main frame and transmission.

1948	320001
1949	269697
1950	271267
1951	272466
1952	273376

Model 770
Rear panel assembly.

1958	60504
1959	71001
1960	84554
1961	111472
1962	117600
1963	127319
1964	141901
1965	153255
1966	171515
1967	183649

Model 80 RC
Right rear of engine.

1937	109152
1938	109162
1939	109783
1940	110221
1941	110615
1942	110945
1943	111319
1944	111391
1945	111929
1946	112879
1947	114144
1948	114944

Model 80 Standard
Right rear of engine.

1937	803929
1938	803991
1939	805377
1940	806880
1941	808125
1942	809051
1943	809991
1944	810470
1945	811991
1946	813067
1947	814565
1948	815216

Model 88
Rear hood support panel below instrument panel.

1953	3500977
1954	4500076

Model 88 RC
Front right side of rear main frame and transmission.

1947	120001
1948	120353
1949	123301
1950	128653
1951	132863
1952	138184

Model 88 Standard
Front right side of rear main frame and transmission.

1947	820001
1948	820136
1949	821086
1950	824241
1951	825811
1952	826917

Model 880
Rear panel assembly.

1958	60505
1959	71640
1960	84555
1961	111262
1962	117640
1963	128911

Model 90 & 99
Right rear of engine.

1937	508918
1938	508935
1939	509617
1940	510008
1941	510564
1942	510977
1943	511296
1944	511474
1945	512044
1946	512821
1947	513106
1948	513856
1949	514856
1950	516276
1951	516891
1952	517951
1953	518300
1954	519245
1955	519516
1956	520354
1957	520868

Model 950, 990 & 995
Left side of clutch dust cover.

1958	53001
1959	71245
1960	84487
1961	110064

Model Super 44

1957	1002
1958	1551
1959	7121

Model Super 55

1954	6001
1955	11887
1956	35001
1957	43916
1958	56501

Model Super 66
Rear hood support panel below instrument panel.

1954	7085
1955	14099
1956	39371
1957	45846
1958	57858

Model Super 77
Rear hood support panel below instrument panel.

1954	8303
1955	10001
1956	38500
1957	44167
1958	56917

Model Super 88
Rear hood support panel below instrument panel.

1954	6503
1955	10075
1956	36774
1957	43901
1958	56580

Model Super 99
Right side on clutch compartment below fuel tank or right of engine block.

1954	519245
1955	519516
1956	520354
1957	521300
1958	521496

STEIGER

Bearcat III PT-225

1977	141-00001
1978	141-00157
1979	141-00336
1980	141-00537
1981	141-00651
1982	141-01501
1983	141-02501

Bearcat III ST-225

1980	109-00001
1981	109-00170
1982	109-01501
1983	109-02501

Bearcat IV CM-225

1983	109-03001
1984	109-03201
1985	109-05001

Bearcat IV KM-225

1983	112-03001
1984	112-03201
1985	112-05001

Cougar III PTA-280 (Cat)

1981	155-00001
1982	155-01501
1983	155-02501

Cougar III PTA-280 (Cummins)

1981	154-00001
1982	154-01501
1983	154-02501

Cougar III ST-250

1976	104-00001
1977	104-00266
1978	104-00381
1979	104-00501
1980	104-00751
1981	104-01001
1982	104-01501
1983	104-02501

Cougar III ST-280 (Cat)

1981	111-00001
1982	111-01501
1983	111-02501

Cougar III ST-280 (Cummins)

1981	110-00001
1982	110-01501
1983	110-02501

Cougar IV CM-250

1983	104-03001
1984	104-03201
1985	104-05001

Cougar IV CM-280

1983	111-03201
1984	111-03201
1985	111-05001

Cougar IV CS-280

1983	155-02501
1984	155-03001
1985	155-05001

Cougar IV KM-280

1983	110-03001
1984	110-03201
1985	110-05001

Cougar IV KS-280

1983	154-02501
1984	154-03001
1985	154-05001

Model CR-1225

1985	C01-05001
1986	C05-05001
1987	C09-05001

Model CR-1280

1985	C03-05001
1986	C07-05001
1987	C11-05001

Model KR-1225

1985	C02-05001
1986	C06-05001
1987	C10-05001

Model KR-1280

1985	C04-05001
1986	C08-05001
1987	C12-05001

Panther CP-1325

1982	P03-00001
1983	P03-02501
1984	P03-03001
1985	P03-05001
1986	P03-07001
1987	P03-09001

Panther CP-1360

1982	P07-00001
1983	P07-02501
1984	P07-03001
1985	P07-05001
1986	P07-07001
1987	P07-09001

Panther CP-1400

1982	P09-00001
1983	P09-02501
1984	P09-03001
1985	P09-05001
1986	P09-07001
1987	P09-09001

Panther III PTA-310

1980	152-00001
1981	152-00070
1982	152-01501
1983	152-02501

Panther III PTA-325

1979	150-00001
1980	150-00036
1981	150-00273
1982	150-01501
1983	150-02501

Panther III ST-310

1976	107-00001
1977	107-00314
1978	107-00463
1979	107-00612
1980	107-00887
1981	107-01079
1982	107-01501
1983	107-02501

Panther III ST-325

1976	123-00001
1977	123-00123
1978	123-00370
1979	123-00627
1980	123-00887
1981	123-01124
1982	123-01501
1983	123-02501

Panther IV CM-325

1983	123-03001
1984	123-03201
1985	123-05001

Panther IV CM-360

1983	115-03001
1984	115-03201
1985	115-05001

Panther IV CS-325

1984	150-03001
1985	150-05001

Panther IV CS-360

1984	156-03001
1985	156-05001

Panther IV KM-325

1983	117-03001
1984	117-03201
1985	117-05001

Panther IV KM-360

1983	116-03001
1984	116-03201
1985	116-05001

Panther IV KS-325

1983	152-02501
1984	152-03001
1985	152-05001

Panther IV KS-360

1984	157-03001
1985	157-05001

Panther IV SM-325

1983	119-03201
1984	119-04001
1985	119-05001

Panther KP-1325

1982	P04-00001
1983	P03-02501
1984	P04-03001
1985	P04-05001
1986	P04-07001
1987	P04-09001

Panther KP-1360

1982	P08-00001
1983	P08-02501
1984	P08-03001
1985	P08-05001
1986	P08-07001
1987	P08-09001

Panther KP-1400

1982	P10-00001
1983	P10-02501
1984	P10-03001
1985	P10-05001
1986	P10-07001
1987	P10-09001

Tiger III ST-450

1979	129-00001
1980	129-00007
1981	129-00010
1982	129-01501
1983	129-02501

Tiger III ST-470

1977	130-00001
1978	130-00047
1979	130-00097
1980	130-00174
1981	130-00209
1982	130-01501
1983	130-02501

Tiger IV KP-525

1983	131-03001
1984	131-03201
1985	131-05001

VERSATILE

Model 1150
On cab door post.
1981 81201001
1982 82201101
1983 83204101
1984 84204351
1985 85237075

Model 1156
On cab door post.
1986 86270100
1987 87300708
1988 88331116
1989 .... 89D430159
1990 .... 90D450001
1991 .... 91D475128
1992 .... 92D500001

Model 256
On steering console.
1984 205101
1985 253500

Model 276
On steering console.
1985 27685253500
1986 27686273100
1988 332100
1989 432100
1990 453100
1991 470100

Model 836
On cab door post.
1985 83685250500
1986 83686270100

Model 846
On cab door post.
1987 330335
1988 330791
1989 430159
1990 450298
1991 475001
1992 500001

Model 856
On cab door post.
1985 83685250500
1986 85686270100

Model 876
On cab door post.
1985 87685250500
1986 87686270100

1988 330100
1989 430159
1990 .... 90D450167
1991 .... 91D475041
1992 .... 92D500001

Model 9030
1990 332147
1991 470100
1992 608053

Model 936 & 946
On cab door post.
1985 93685250500
1986 93686270100
1988 330170
1989 330616
1990 430159

1991 432147

Model 956
On cab door post.
1985 95685250500
1986 95686270100
1987 95686310155
1988 95686314210

Model 976
On cab door post.
1985 97685250500
1986 97686270100
1988 330140
1989 430100
1990 450100
1991 .... 91D475198
1992 .... 92D500001

WHITE

Model 100
1987 Dec. 401236
1988 401361
1989 402661

Model 120
1987 Oct. 401121
1988 401304
1989 402521

Model 125 Workhorse
1990 404066
1991 404601
1993 500001

Model 140
1987 Nov. 401151
1988 401326
1989 402736

Model 145 Workhorse
1991 404826
1992 501001

Model 160
1987 Sept. 401096
1988 401569
1989 403540
1990 404825
1991 501001

Model 170 Workhorse
1989 404001
1990 404766
1991 404826
1992 510001

Model 185
1987 400881
1988 401579
1989 402761

Model 195 Workhorse
1989 404166
1990 404496
1991 404826
1992 511001

Model 2-105
Left rear side of main frame.
1975 255538
1976 265928
1977 273760
1978 282102
1979 287197
1980 294109
1981 296878
1982 300779
1983 304280

Model 2-110
Left side of main frame above step.
1982 300783
1983 301998
1984 302334
1985 303552
1986 400231
1987 400763
1988 405242
1989 410251

Model 2-135
Left side of instrument panel support and on left side of frame above step.
1976 272663
1977 273629
1978 282825
1979 288201
1980 294330
1981 296611
1982 300380
1983 302159
1984 302715

Model 2-135 Series 3
Left side of instrument panel support and on left side of frame above step.
1982 301116
1983 302159
1984 302715
1986 400167
1987 400831
1988 418875

Model 2-150
Left rear side of main frame.
1975 257899
1976 266783

Model 2-155
Left side of instrument panel support and on left side of frame above step.
1976 272595
1977 276055
1978 282280
1979 287812
1980 296160
1981 297134
1982 300259

Model 2-155 Series 3
Left side of instrument panel support and on left side of frame above step.
1982 300928
1984 302791
1986 400718
1987 407889
1988 415671

Model 2-180
Left side of instrument panel support and on left side of frame above step.
1977 281993
1978 282088
1979 289447
1980 294655
1981 296571
1982 300159
1983 303389

Model 2-180 Series 3
Left side of instrument panel support and on left side of frame above step.
1982 301922
1983 301966
1984 302951
1985 351451
1986 400082
1987 403850
1988 407618

Model 2-30
Left front of frame.
1979 100337
1980 100712
1981 100925
1982 101275
1983 101412
1984 101428

Model 2-30 4WD
Left front of frame.
1979 001417
1980 001941
1981 003812
1982 004701
1983 006331
1984 006471

Model 2-32
Left front of frame.
1984 6100071
1985 00007
1986 100245
1987 100419
1988 100665

Model 2-32 4WD
Left front of frame.
1984 61000175
1985 00210
1986 00245
1987 00280
1988 00326

Model 2-35
Left front of frame.
1979 004001
1980 004465
1981 004697
1982 005062
1983 005570
1984 005396
1985 006226
1986 006651
1987 007076

Model 2-45
On left side of frame.
1980 ..... T5000E00001
1981 ..... T5000E00548
1982 ..... T6000E00887
1983 ..... T6000E01270

Model 2-45 4WD
On left side of frame.
1980 ... T5000EF000001
1981 .... T5000EF00405
1982 .... T5000EF00631
1983 .... T5000EF00861

Model 2-50
Instrument panel.
1976 516625
1977 518782
1978 521635
1979 525268
1980 525726
1981 526121

Model 2-55
Plate on left side of frame and stamped on front frame at left corner of radiator grille.
1982 .. T6000EN00097M
1983 00329

1984 00377
1985 00569
1986 00587
1987 00596
1988 00606

Model 2-55 4WD
Plate on left side of frame and stamped on front frame at left corner of radiator grille.
1982 .. T6000ENF00173
1983 00411
1984 00464
1985 00678
1986 00706
1987 00733
1988 01321

Model 2-60
Instrument panel.
1976 780725
1977 790273
1978 946285
1979 959280
1980 986532
1981 1001039

Model 2-62
On left side of frame.
1980 .... T6500E000001
1981 ..... T6500E01143
1982 ..... T6500E02057
1983 ..... T6500E02399

Model 2-62 4WD
On left side of frame.
1980 ... T6500EF000001
1981 .... T6500EF00974
1982 .... T6500EF01362
1983 .... T6500EF01848

Model 2-65 2WD
Plate on left side of frame and stamped on front frame at left corner of radiator grille.
1982 .. T7000EN00099M
1983 00288
1984 00341
1985 00547
1986 00672
1987 01021
1988 01296

Model 2-65 4WD
Plate on left side of frame and stamped on front frame at left corner of radiator grille.
1982 . T7000ENF001131
1983 00308
1984 00595
1985 00897
1986 00950
1987 01040
1988 001056

Model 2-70
Rear panel support.
1976 266173
1977 274543
1978 283917
1979 287528
1980 293819
1981 296246

1982 299887
1983 300464

Model 2-75 2WD
Plate on left side of frame and stamped on front frame at left corner of radiator grille.
1982 .... T9000EN00177
1983 00242
1984 00295
1985 00508
1986 00555
1987 00711
1988 00894
1989 01076

Model 2-75 4WD
Plate on left side of frame and stamped on front frame at left corner of radiator grille.
1982 ... T9000ENF00247
1983 00305
1984 00501
1985 00728
1986 00782
1987 00892
1988 00980

Model 2-85
Left rear side of main frame.
1975 263341
1976 268142
1977 274287
1978 282339
1979 287469
1980 294063
1981 297751
1982 300092
1983 302199

Model 2-88
1982 301457
1984 302464
1985 400001
1986 400433
1987 400734
1988 400866
1989 401299

Model 4-150
Left side of center frame.
1974 246001
1975 246871
1976 262244
1977 275051
1978 275570

Model 4-175
1979 292187
1980 295808
1981 297293
1982 299886
1983 302150
1984 304196

Model 4-180
Left side of center frame.
1975 256587
1976 262524
1977 268112
1978 275502

Model 4-180 III

1982 301922
1983 301966
1984 302951
1985 351451
1986 400082
1987 403850
1988 407618

Model 4-210

Left side of center frame.

1978 275572
1979 275944
1980 295391
1981 296471
1982 300694
1983 300780

Model 4-225

Left side of center frame.

1983 302234
1984 302620
1985 351450
1986........... 400347
1987........... 400901
1988........... 444355
1989........... 493250
1990........... 536701

Model 4-270

Left side of center frame.

1983........... 302274
1984........... 302655
1985........... 303086
1986........... 400639
1987........... 401411
1988........... 401411
1989........... 404226
1990........... 407041

Model 60

Left front of frame.

1989........... 402965
1990........... 404422
1991........... 405028
1992........... 405654

Model 80

1989 402596
1990 404266
1991 405048
1992 405674

Model FB16 2WD

Left front of frame.

1986 002314
1987 002393

Model FB16 4WD

Left front of frame.

1986 014422
1987 014660
1988 016528

Model FB185

Left side of instrument panel support and on left side of frame above step.

1986 400659
1987 400881
1988 401579
1989........... 402761

Model FB21 2WD

Left front of frame.

1986............ 00595
1987............ 00677
1988............ 00967

Model FB21 4WD

Left front of frame.

1986............ 02879
1987............ 03079
1988............ 04003

Model FB31 2WD

Left front of frame.

1986............ 00126
1987............ 00174
1988............ 00276

Model FB31 4WD

Left front of frame.

1986............ 00028
1987............ 00149
1988............ 00568

Model FB37 2WD

Left front of frame.

1986............ 00083
1987............ 00121
1988............ 00221

Model FB37 4WD

Left front of frame.

1986............ 00679
1987............ 00713
1988............ 01025

Model FB43 2WD

Left front of frame.

1986............ 00060
1987............ 00068

Model FB43 4WD

Left front of frame.

1986............ 00322
1987............ 00329

Manfacturers' Addresses

AGCO ALLIS
AGCO Corp
4205 River Green Pkwy
Duluth GA 30136
770-813-9200
FT

AGCO WHITE
AGCO Corp
4205 River Green Pkwy
Duluth GA 30136
770-813-9200
FT

BELARUS
Belarus Machinery of USA Inc
PO Box 23608
Milwaukee WI 53223
414-355-2000 FAX 414-355-6903
FT

CASE-INTERNATIONAL
Case Corporation
700 State St
Racine WI 53404
414-636-6011
FT

CUB CADET BY MTD
MTD Products Inc
PO Box 368023
Cleveland OH 44136-9723
330-225-2600 FAX 330-225-9133
LGT WM RT ST ET FT

HURLIMANN
Amatex Inc
7075 West Parkland Court
Milwaukee WI 53223
888-988-4453 FAX 414-355-8370
FT

IMT, TAFE
Robison & Grissom Tractor Co Inc
Hwy 348 W Rt 2 Box 36
Guntown MS 38849
601-869-1028 FAX 601-869-1030
FT

JOHN DEERE
Deere & Company
1 John Deere Place
Moline IL 61265
309-765-8000 FAX 309-765-9980
FT

KIOTI
Kioti Tractor Division
4608 Lely Rd
Wilson NC 27893
919-291-6111 FAX 919-291-9161
FT

KUBOTA
Kubota Tractor Corp
3401 Del Amo Blvd
Torrance CA 90509
310-370-3370 FAX 310-370-2370
FT LGT RT WM

LANDINI
AGCO Corp
4205 River Green Pkwy
Duluth GA 30136
770-813-9200
FT

LONG
Long Mfg NC Inc
111 Fairview St
Tarboro NC 27886
919-823-4151 FAX 919-823-4151
FT

MASSEY FERGUSON
AGCO Corp
4205 River Green Pkwy
Duluth GA 30136
770-813-9200
FT

NEW HOLLAND/FORD
New Holland North America
500 Diller Ave #306
New Holland PA 17557-0903
717-355-1261
WM LGT RT ST FT

ZETOR
Zetor Tractors America Jawa Ltd
7301 Allentown Blvd
Harrisburg PA 17112
717-540-5618 FAX 717-540-5863
FT

I&T SHOP SERVICE MANUALS

I&T Shop Service Manuals provide information for most models of American wheel-type farm tractors. Easy-to-follow procedures and illustrations make these manuals a valuable source for complete tractor maintenance and repair information. Also available...I&T Collections. Each collection contains an assortment of I&T Shop Service Manuals covering models from one manufacturer. I&T Shop Service Manuals are available from the same store that provided you with the *2000 Used Tractor Price Guide*.

Allis-Chalmers
- Models B, C, CA, G, RC, WC, WD, WD45, WD45 Diesel, WF **AC-11**
- Models 6060, 6070, 6080 . . . **AC-35**
- Models 8010, 8030, 8050, 8070. **AC-36**

Allis-Chalmers Collections
- Models D-10, D-10 Series III, D-12, D-12 Series III; Models D-14, D-15, D-15 Series II, D-17, D-17 Series III, D-17 Series IV; Model 160; Models 170, 175. . . . . **AC-201**
- Models D-21, D-21 Series II, Two-Ten, Two-Twenty; Models D-19, D-19 Diesel; Models 7010, 7020, 7030, 7040, 7045, 7050, 7060, 7080; Models 180, 185, 190, 190XT, 200, 7000 . . . . **AC-202**

B.F. Avery
- Models A, R, V. **MM-201**

Case/International
- Models 1190, 1290, 1390, 1490, 1690, 1194, 1294, 1394, 1494, 1594 . . . . **C-36**
- Models 2090, 2094, 2290, 2294, 2390, 2394, 2590, 2594 . . . . **C-37**
- Models 1896, 2096 . . . . **C-38**
- Models 385, 485, 585, 685, 885 . . . . **C-39**
- Magnum Models 7110, 7120, 7130, 7140 . . . . **C-40**
- Maxxum Models 5120, 5130, 5140 . . . . **C-41**
- Models 235, 245, 255, 265, 275 . . . . **C-42**

Case & David Brown Collections
- Series C, D, L, LA, R, S, V, VA, VAC; Series 200B, 300, 300B, 350, 400B, 500B, 600B; Series 400, 700B, 800B **C-201**
- Series 500, 600, 900B; Series 730, 830, 930, 1030; Series 430, 470, 530, 570, 630 . . . . **C-202**
- Series 770, 870, 970, 1070, 1090, 1170, 1175; Models 885, 995, 1210, 1212, 1410, 1412; Models 770, 780, 880 (After Serial No. 52100), 990 (After Serial No. 467870), 1200, 3800, 4600; Models 1270, 1370, 1570. . . . . **C-203**

Deutz-Allis
- Models 6240, 6250, 6260, 6265, 6275. . . . . **D-1**

Ferguson
- Models TE20, TO20, TO30. . . . . **FE-2**
- Models TO35, F40. . . . . **MF-14**

Ford New Holland
- Series 2N, 8N, 9N **FO-4**
- Model NAA (Golden Jubilee). **FO-19**
- Series 501, 600, 601, 700, 701, 800, 801, 900, 901, 1801, 2000 (4-Cyl.), 4000 (4-Cyl.). . **FO-20**
- Series 2000 (3-Cyl.), 3000 (3-Cyl.), 4000 (3-Cyl.) Covers Models Prior To 1975. . . . . . . **FO-31**
- Models 2310, 2600, 2610, 3600, 3610, 4100 (After 1974), 4110, 4600, 4610 (Prior To 1984), 4600SU, 4610SU (Prior To 1984) **FO-41**
- Series 5000, 5600, 5610, 6600, 6610, 6700, 6710, 7000, 7600, 7610, 7700, 7710 . . . . **FO-42**
- Models 2810, 2910, 3910 . . . . **FO-43**
- Models 1100, 1110, 1200, 1210, 1300, 1310, 1500, 1510, 1700, 1710, 1900, 1910, 2110. . . . . **FO-44**
- Models TW-5, TW-15, TW-25, TW-35 . . . . **FO-45**
- Models 1120, 1220, 1320, 1520, 1720, 1920, 2120 . . . . **FO-46**
- Models 3230, 3430, 3930, 4630, 4830 . . . . **FO-47**
- Models 5640, 6640, 7740, 7840, 8240, 8340 . . . **FO-48**

Ford/Fordson Collection
- Models Fordson Dexta, Fordson Super Dexta, 2000 Super Dexta, New Performance Super Dexta; Models Fordson Major Diesel (FMD), Fordson Power Major (FPM), Fordson Super Major (FSM), New Performance Fordson Super Major (New FSM), 5000 Super Major; Series 6000, Commander 6000; Series 1000, 1600; Series 8000, 8600, 8700, 9000, 9600, 9700, TW-10, TW-20, TW-30 . . . . **FO-201**

John Deere
- Series A (Serial No. 499000 and up), Series B (Serial No. 96000 and up), G (Serial No. 13000 and up), H; Models D (Serial No. 143800 and up), M, MT **JD-4**
- Models 50, 60, 70. . . . . **JD-10**
- Series 520, 530, 620, 630, 720, 730 . . . . **JD-16**
- Series 1010, 2010 . . . . **JD-21**
- Series 1020, 1520, 1530, 2020, 2030. . . . . **JD-37**
- Series 850, 950, 1050. . . . . **JD-47**
- Series 4030, 4230, 4430, 4630 . . . . **JD-50**
- Models 1250, 1450, 1650 . . . . **JD-55**
- Models 2840, 2940, 2950 . . . . **JD-56**
- Models 4050, 4250, 4450, 4650, 4850 . . . . **JD-57**
- Models 2150, 2155, 2255, 2350, 2355, 2355N, 2550, 2555. . . . . **JD-58**
- Models 2750, 2755, 2855, 2955. . . . . **JD-59**
- Models 4055, 4255, 4455, 4555, 4755, 4955 . . . **JD-60**
- Models 655, 755, 756, 855, 856, 955 . . . . **JD-61**
- Models 670, 770, 870, 970, 1070. . . . . **JD-62**

John Deere Collections
- Models 720 Diesel, 730 Diesel; Series 40, 320, 330, 420, 430, 440; Models 80, 820, 830 (Two Cylinder Diesel Models); Series 820, 830 (3 Cylinder Models); Models 435D, 440ID (Diesel Models) **JD-201**
- Model 2040; Models 2510, 2520; Models 2240, 2440, 2630, 2640; Model 2840; Models 4040, 4240, 4440, 4640, 4840 . . . . **JD-202**
- Model 6030; Models 3020, 4000, 4020, 4320, 4520, 4620; Models 3010, 4010, 5010, 5020 . . **JD-203**

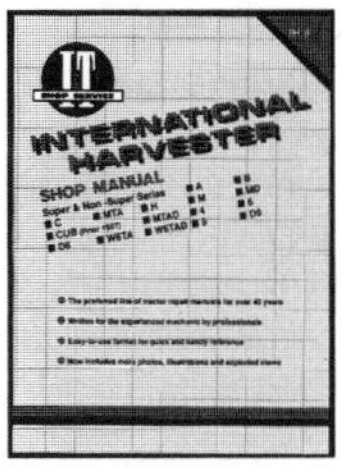

International Harvester
- Super/Non-Super Series A, B, C, MTA, H, M, MD, Cub (Prior to 1957), MTAD, 4, 6, D6, W6TA, W6TAD, 9, D9........ **IH-8**
- Models 300, 300 Utility, 350, 350 Utility, 350D, 350D Utility, 400, 400D, W400, W400D, 450, 450D, W450, W450D **IH-10**
- Models 460, 560, 606, 660, 2606 .... **IH-25**
- Models 706, 756, 806, 856, 1206, 1256, 1456, 2706, 2756, 2806, 2856, 21206, 21256, 21456 .... **IH-32**
- Models Int'l Cub 154 Lo-Boy, Int'l Cub 184 Lo-Boy, Int'l Cub 185 Lo-Boy, Farmall Cub, Int'l Cub, Int'l Cub Lo-Boy **IH-50**
- Models 3088, 3288, 3488 Hydro, 3688......... **IH-54**
- Models 234, 234 Hydro, 244, 254............. **IH-55**
- Models 5088, 5288, 5488 .... **IH-56**

International Harvester Collections
- Models 100, 130, 140, 200, 230, 240, 404, 2404; Models 330, 340, 504, 2504; Models B-275, B-414, 354, 364, 384, 424, 444, 2424, 2444 ... **IH-201**
- Models 544, 656, 666, 686, Hydro 70, Hydro 86; Models Hydro 100, Hydro 186, 1466, 1468, 1486, 1566, 1568, 1586; Models 684, 784, 884, Hydro 84 .... **IH-202**
- Models 766, 826, 966, 1026, 1066; Models 454, 464, 484, 574, 584, 674; Models 786, 886, 986, 1086 .... **IH-203**

Massey-Ferguson
- Models TE20, TO20, TO30 ... **FE-2**
- Models TO35, TO35 Diesel, F40, MH50, MHF202, MF35, MF35 Diesel, MF50, MF202, MF204 .... **MF-14**
- Models MF135, MF150, MF165 .... **MF-27**
- Model MF285.............. **MF-36**
- Models MF670, MF690, MF698................................. **MF-41**
- Models MF230, MF235, MF240, MF245, MF250................................. **MF-42**
- Models MF255, MF265, MF270, MF275, MF290................................. **MF-43**
- Models MF362, MF365, MF375, MF383, MF390, MF390T, MF398.................. **MF-45**
- Models MF340, MF350, MF355, MF360, MF399................................. **MF-46**
- Models MF1010 (Standard, Hydro), 1020 (Standard, Hydro)......................... **MF-47**

Massey-Ferguson Collections
- Model MF65; Models MF85, MF88, MF Super 90, MF Super 90WR; Models MF1100, MF1130; Model MF1150; Models MF1105, MF1135, MF1155; Models MF1080, MF1085 .... **MF-201**
- Models MF175, MF180; Models MF205, MF210, MF220; Models MF2675, MF2705; Models MF2745, MF2775, MF2805 .... **MF-202**

Minneapolis-Moline Collection
- Models GTA, GTB; Series R, U, ZA, ZT; Models BF, BG, V, Avery Models A, R, V; Series GB, UB, ZB; Models 335, 445, Jet Star, Jet Star Two, Jet Star Three, 4 Star, 4 Star Super, U-302; Models UB Special, UTS Special, 5 Star, M5, M504, M602, M604, M670, M670 Super; Models G-VI, G-705, G-706, G-707, G-708, G-900, G-950, G-1000, G-1000 Vista, G-1050, G-1350, MF Models MF-95 (After Serial No. 17300000), MF97......... **MM-201**

Oliver & Cockshutt
- Series Oliver 2050, 2150, Cockshutt 2050, 2150........ **O-22**

Oliver & Cockshutt Collections
- Models 99 (6 Cyl.) 4-Speed, Super 99 (6 Cyl.) 6-Speed, Super 99 GM (3-Cyl.) 6-Speed, Super and Non-Super Models 66, 77, 88, 660, 770, 880; Series 99 GMTC, 950, 990, 995; Series Super 55, 550...................... **O-201**
- Series 1750, 1800, 1850, 1900, 1950, 1950-T; Series 1550, 1555, 1600, 1650, 1655; Minneapolis-Moline Models G-550, G-750; Series 1755, 1855, 1955; Minneapolis-Moline Models G-850, G-940; Oliver Model 2255; Minneapolis-Moline Models G-955, G-1355.... **O-202**

White Collection
- Models 2-70, 2-85, 2-105, 2-150; Models 2-135, 2-155; Models 2-30, 2-35; Models 2-45, 2-62; Models 2-55, 2-65, 2-75.... **W-201**

IMPORT MANUFACTURERS

Kubota Collection
- Models L175, L210, L225, L225DT, L260, Models B5100D, B5100E, B6100D, B6100E, B6100HST-D, B6100HST-E, B7100D, B7100HST-D, B7100HST-E, Models L185, L235, L245, L275, L285, L295, L305, L345, L355......................... **K-201**

Mitsubishi
- Models MT160, MT160D, MT180, MT180D, MT180H, MT180HD, MT210, MT210D, MT250, MT250D, MT300, MT300D **M-1**

Yanmar
- Models YM135, YM135D, YM155, YM155D, YM195, YM195D, YM240, YM240D, YM330, YM330D **YM-1**

ENGINE SERVICE MANUALS

Small Diesel Engine Service Manual
This manual provides detailed service and repair information on more than 200 different models of small air-cooled and liquid-cooled diesel engines with up to 160 cubic inches (2600cc) displacement. 288 pgs/3rd edition/1991©

Catalog Number......................... **SDS-3**

Large Diesel Engine Service Manual
Servicing, maintaining and repairing industrial engines which have 150 to 500 cubic inch (2.5-8.2L) displacement is made possible with this comprehensive manual. 192 pgs/1st edition/1983©

Catalog Number......................... **LDS-1**

Large Air-Cooled Engine Service Manual, 1988 and Prior Volume 1
This manual offers valuable repair information for the engines that power pumps, farm equipment, skid steer

loaders, construction equipment and more. Covering models produced through 1988, this service manual includes maintenance and repair information for one-, two- and four-cylinder air-cooled gasoline engines with 15 cubic inch (245cc) displacement and over. 344 pgs/4th edition/1989©
Catalog Number **LES1-4**

Large Air-Cooled Engine Service Manual, Through 1992 Volume 2
This volume includes service information for one-, two- and four-cylinder large air-cooled engines with 15 cubic inch (245cc) displacement and over. Covers engines produced from 1989 through 1992. 384 pgs/1st edition/1993©
Catalog Number **LES2-1**

Small Air-Cooled Engine Service Manual
This manual is a popular source for comprehensive maintenance and repair information for small air-cooled engines. Coverage includes over 30 different manufacturers, more than 500 basic model types and hundreds of variations of small engines with under 15 cubic inch (245cc) displacement (2- and 4-stroke). 492 pgs/17th edition/1992©
Catalog Number **SES-17**

Small Air-Cooled Engine Service Manual Volume 2
This manual offers detailed maintenance and repair information for small air-cooled engines produced during 1990 and later. Covering over 15 manufacturers, *Small Air-Cooled Engine Service Manual, Volume 2* includes information on more than 130 model types and variations of side valve and overhead valve engines with under 15 cubic inch (245cc) displacement (2- and 4-stroke). 328 pgs/1st edition/1994©
Catalog Number **SES2-1**

Small AC Generator Service Manual
This thorough service manual provides maintenance, overhaul and troubleshooting information on electrical power plants under 8 kw and driven by air-cooled engines. Coverage includes stationary and portable generators weighing approximately 300 pounds or less. 405 pgs/3rd edition/1991©
Catalog Number **GSM-3**

OUTDOOR POWER EQUIPMENT SERVICE MANUALS

Yard & Garden Tractor Service Manual Single-Cylinder Models
A valuable resource providing detailed service information necessary to properly maintain and repair yard and garden tractors powered by single-cylinder engines. 624 pgs/1st edition/1992©
Catalog Number **YGT1-1**

Yard & Garden Tractor Service Manual Multi-Cylinder Models
Covering the latest models and improvements in tractors with multi-cylinder air-cooled and liquid-cooled engines, this popular manual provides complete maintenance and repair information for more than 20 different manufacturers of tractors and engines. 452 pgs/1st edition/1991©
Catalog Number **YGT2-1**

Riding Lawn Mower Service Manual
This service manual covers most riding lawn mower models available. With hundreds of models and over 30 popular manufacturers, this manual provides basic information on safety interlock systems, cutting blades and more. 528 pgs/4th edition/1993©
Catalog Number **RLMS-4**

Walk-Behind Lawn Mower Service Manual
This manual provides information on engine operating priciples, problems and remedies, a troubleshooting chart, routine maintenance and service procedures for walk-behind lawn mowers. 280 pgs/4th edition/1991©
Catalog Number **WLMS-5**

Chain Saw Service Manual
This service manual provides detailed tear down, repair, reassembly, maintenance and adjustment procedures. This manual also includes sections covering the saw chain, guide bar, sprockets, clutch and carburetor troubleshooting and service. Covers 29 different manufacturers and more than 700 chain saw models. 564 pgs/9th edition/1993©
Catalog Number **CSS-10**

Rotary Tiller Service Manual
This manual offers comprehensive repair information for rotary tillers, plus individual engine sections provide service information for the specific engines used to power rotary tillers. Coverage includes 40 different manufacturers of rotary tillers and engines. 280 pgs/3rd edition/1989©
Catalog Number **RTS-3**

All-Terrain Vehicle Maintenance Manual Volume 1
This comprehensive manual provides ATV specifications and maintenance data for 3- and 4-wheel models produced from 1974 to 1987. Coverage includes maintenance intervals, adjustments and tune-up procedures for 56 polular models of ATVs. 432 pgs/2nd edition/1988©
Catalog Number **ATV1-2**

All-Terrain Vehicle Maintenance Manual Volume 2
This maintenance manual provides complete specifications, maintenance data, adjustments and tune-up procedures for 4-wheel ATVs produced from 1988 to 1992. Covers 5 different manufacturers and 47 models of ATVs. 424 pgs/1st edition/1993©
Catalog Number **ATV2-1**